business
essentials

business

essentials

TENTH EDITION

Global Edition

Ronald J. Ebert

Ricky W. Griffin

PEARSON

Boston   Columbus   Indianapolis   New York   San Francisco   Upper Saddle River
Amsterdam   Cape Town   Dubai   London   Madrid   Milan   Munich   Paris   Montréal   Toronto
Delhi   Mexico City   São Paulo   Sydney   Hong Kong   Seoul   Singapore   Taipei   Tokyo

Editor in Chief: Stephanie Wall
Program Management Lead: Ashley Santora
Program Manager: Claudia Fernandes
Development Editor: Deepa Chungi
Editorial Assistant: Kaylee Rotella
Head of Learning Asset Acquisition, Global Edition: Laura Dent
Senior Acquisitions Editor, Global Edition: Steven Jackson
Project Editor, Global Edition: Laura Thompson
Director of Marketing: Maggie Moylan
Senior Marketing Manager: Erin Gardner
International Marketing Manager: Kristin Schneider
Project Management Lead: Judy Leale
Senior Project Manager: Jacqueline A. Martin

Senior Manufacturing Controller, Global Edition: Trudy Kimber
Procurement Specialist: Michelle Klein
Creative Director: Jayne Conte
Cover Designer: Karen Noferi
Text Designer: LCI Design
VP, Director of Digital Strategy & Assessment: Paul Gentile
Digital Editor: Brian Surette
Digital Development Manager: Robin Lazrus
Digital Project Manager: Alana Coles
MyLab Product Manager: Joan Waxman
Digital Production Project Manager: Lisa Rinaldi
Full-Service Project Management and Composition: Integra
Cover image: Foto-Ruhrgebiet/Shutterstock

Credits and acknowledgments borrowed from other sources and reproduced, with permission, in this textbook appear on the appropriate page within the text.

Pearson Education Limited
Edinburgh Gate
Harlow
Essex CM20 2JE
England

and Associated Companies throughout the world

Visit us on the World Wide Web at:
www.pearson.com/uk

© Pearson Education Limited 2015

The right of Ronald J. Ebert and Ricky W. Griffin to be identified as authors of this work has been asserted by them in accordance with the Copyright, Designs and Patents Act 1988.

Authorised adaptation from the United States edition, entitled Business Essentials, Tenth Edition, ISBN 978-0-13-345442-0 by Ronald J. Ebert and Ricky W. Griffin, published by Pearson Education © 2015.

ISBN-13: 978-1-292-01690-0
ISBN-10: 1-292-01690-6

British Library Cataloguing-in-Publication Data
A catalogue record for this book is available from the British Library

10 9 8 7 6 5 4 3 2
15

Typeset in 10/12 Palatino by Integra
Printed and bound by Courier/Kendallville in United States of America

PEARSON

To Emery—Unmasking her disguise as a storybook princess,
the enchanting lady bewitches all whose lives she touches.
—R. J. E.

For Griffin—The newest light in my universe.
—R. W. G.

brief contents

Part 1: The Contemporary Business World

1 The U.S. Business Environment 28
2 Understanding Business Ethics and Social Responsibility 60
3 Entrepreneurship, New Ventures, and Business Ownership 96
4 Understanding the Global Context of Business 130

Part 2: The Business of Managing

5 Managing the Business 164
6 Organizing the Business 198
7 Operations Management and Quality for Producing Goods and Services 228

Part 3: People in Organizations

8 Employee Behavior and Motivation 268
9 Leadership and Decision Making 302
10 Human Resource Management and Labor Relations 334

Part 4: Principles of Marketing: Building Relationships with Customers for Competitive Advantage

11 Marketing Processes and Consumer Behavior 372
12 Developing and Pricing Products 410
13 Distributing and Promoting Products 442

Part 5: Managing Information for Better Business Decisions

14 Information Technology (IT) for Business 476
15 The Role of Accountants and Accounting Information 510

Part 6: The Financial System and Issues in Financial Management

16 Understanding Money and the Role of Banking 548
17 Managing Business Finances 584

Appendices

Appendix I: Risk Management 623
Appendix II: The Legal Context of Business 627
Appendix III: Managing Your Personal Finances 633
Appendix IV: Unions and Labor Management 645

Glossary 661
Index 681

contents

Letter from the Authors **17**

About the Authors **18**

Special Thanks to Our Super
   Reviewers **19**

Preface **20**

Part 1: The Contemporary Business
   World

1 The U.S. Business Environment **28**

Chapter Opening Case: What Goes Up...Can Go
   Even Higher! **31**

The Concept of Business and the Concept of Profit **32**

The External Environments of Business **33**

   Domestic Business Environment **33**

   Global Business Environment **34**

   Technological Environment **34**

   Political-Legal Environment **35**

   Sociocultural Environment **35**

   Economic Environment **36**

   managing in turbulent times: What Goes
      Around... **36**

Economic Systems **37**

   Factors of Production **37**

   Types of Economic Systems **38**

   finding a better way: Blending Capitalism and Social
      Responsibility at Mercy Corps **41**

The Economics of Market Systems **41**

   Demand and Supply in a Market Economy **41**

   Private Enterprise and Competition in a Market
      Economy **44**

   entrepreneurship and new ventures: Business ...
      and Pleasure **46**

Economic Indicators **46**

   Economic Growth, Aggregate Output, and Standard
      of Living **47**

   Economic Stability **51**

   Managing the U.S. Economy **52**

   summary of learning objectives • key terms • questions
   & exercises • building a business: continuing team
   exercise • building your business skills • exercising
   your ethics • team exercise • cases • end notes

2 Understanding Business
Ethics and Social
Responsibility **60**

Chapter Opening Case: Is Fair Trade
   Really Fair? **63**

Ethics in the Workplace **64**

   Individual Ethics **65**

   Ambiguity, the Law, and the Real World **65**

   Individual Values and Codes **65**

   Business and Managerial Ethics **65**

   managing in turbulent times: Just When They
      Need It Most **66**

   Assessing Ethical Behavior **67**

   Company Practices and Business Ethics **68**

Social Responsibility **71**

   The Stakeholder Model of Responsibility **71**

   entrepreneurship and new ventures:
      The Electronic Equivalent of Paper
      Shredding **72**

   Contemporary Social Consciousness **73**

Areas of Social Responsibility **74**

   Responsibility toward the Environment **74**

   finding a better way: Zero Waste **75**

   Responsibility toward Customers **76**

   Responsibility toward Employees **78**

   Responsibility toward Investors **79**

**Implementing Social Responsibility
Programs** **80**

   Approaches to Social Responsibility **80**

   Social Responsibility and the Small
      Business **81**

**The Government and Social
Responsibility** **82**

   How Governments Influence Organizations **83**

   How Organizations Influence Government **84**

Managing Social Responsibility **84**

   Formal Organizational Dimensions **85**

   Informal Organizational Dimensions **85**

   Evaluating Social Responsibility **86**

   summary of learning objectives • key terms •
   questions & exercises • building a business:
   continuing team exercises • building your
   business skills • exercising your ethics • team
   exercises • cases • end notes

3 **Entrepreneurship, New Ventures, and Business Ownership** **96**

Chapter Opening Case: Launching a Business in the Gym   99

What is a "Small" Business   100
The Importance of Small Business in the U.S. Economy   101
Popular Areas of Small Business Enterprise   102
finding a better way: The Rise of Services   104
managing in turbulent times: The Wide World of Risk   105

Entrepreneurship   105
Entrepreneurship Goals   105
Entrepreneurial Characteristics   106

Starting and Operating a New Business   106
Understanding Distinctive Competencies   107
Crafting a Business Plan   108
Starting the Small Business   108
Financing the Small Business   110

Trends, Successes, and Failures in New Ventures   111
Trends in Small Business Start-Ups   111
Reasons for Failure   113
Reasons for Success   113
entrepreneurship and new ventures: Harvard Dropout Turned Billionaire   114

Noncorporate Business Ownership   114
Sole Proprietorships   114
Partnerships   115
Cooperatives   117

Corporations   117
The Corporate Entity   117
Types of Corporations   118
Managing a Corporation   120
Special Issues in Corporate Ownership   120
summary of learning objectives • key terms • questions & exercises • building a business: continuing team exercises • building your business skills • exercising your ethics • team exercise • cases • end notes

4 **Understanding the Global Context of Business** **130**

Chapter Opening Case: The Embargo Grinds On   133

The Contemporary Global Economy   134
The Major World Marketplaces   136
finding a better way: Too Much of a Good Thing? China's Success Creates More Jobs in Mexico   137
Trade Agreements and Alliances   138

International Trade   140
Balance of Trade   140
Balance of Payments   142
Exchange Rates   143
Forms of Competitive Advantage   144
entrepreneurship and new ventures: Rolling in the Worldwide Dough   144

International Business Management   145
Going International   145
Levels of International Involvement   147
International Organization Structures   148
managing in turbulent times: The Ups and Downs of Globalization   148

Understanding the Cultural Environment   149
Values, Symbols, Beliefs, and Language   150
Employee Behavior across Cultures   150

Barriers to International Trade   152
Economic Differences   152
Legal and Political Differences   153
summary of learning objectives • Key terms • questions & exercises • building a business: continuing team exercise • building your business skills • exercising your ethics • team exercise • cases • crafting a business plan • end notes

Part 2: The Business of Managing

5 **Managing the Business** **164**

Chapter Opening Case: Google Keeps Growing   167

The Management Process   168
Basic Management Functions   168
The Science and the Art of Management   171
Becoming a Manager   171

Types of Managers   173
Levels of Management   173
Areas of Management   174

Management Roles and Skills   175
Managerial Roles   175
Basic Management Skills   177
Management Skills for the Twenty-First Century   178

Strategic Management: Setting Goals and Formulating Strategy   179
Setting Business Goals   180
entrepreneurship and new ventures: ButterflEYE   180
Types of Strategy   182

finding a better way: A New Model for Going Green 183

Formulating Strategy 183

A Hierarchy of Plans 185

managing in turbulent times: Challenging Times for Gulf Airlines 186

Contingency Planning and Crisis Management 186

Contingency Planning 187

Crisis Management 187

Management and the Corporate Culture 188

Building and Communicating Culture 188

Changing Culture 189

summary of learning objectives • key terms • questions & exercises • building a business: continuing team exercise • building your business skills • exercising your ethics • team exercise • cases • end notes

6 Organizing the Business 198

Chapter Opening Case: Organizing for Success at South African Airways 201

What Is Organizational Structure? 202

Organization Charts 203

Determinants of Organizational Structure 203

The Building Blocks of Organizational Structure 204

Specialization 204

Specialization and Growth 205

finding a better way: Blending the Old with the New 206

Departmentalization 206

Establishing the Decision-Making Hierarchy 208

Distributing Authority: Centralization and Decentralization 208

managing in turbulent times: The Complexities of Offshoring 209

The Delegation Process 211

Three Forms of Authority 212

Basic Forms of Organizational Structure 213

Functional Structure 213

Divisional Structure 213

Matrix Structure 214

entrepreneurship and new ventures: Making the Grade 215

International Structure 215

Organizational Design for the Twenty-first Century 216

Informal Organization 218

Informal Groups 218

Organizational Grapevine 219

Intrapreneuring 219

summary of learning objectives • key terms • questions & exercises • building a business: continuing team exercise • building your business skills • follow-up questions • exercising your ethics • team exercise • cases • end notes

7 Operations Management and Quality for Producing Goods and Services 228

Chapter Opening Case: Ryanair Customer Satisfaction—but Who to Believe? 231

What Does *Operations* Mean Today? 232

Growth in the Services and Goods Sectors 233

Creating Value through Operations 234

Differences between Service and Goods Manufacturing Operations 235

Operations Processes 236

Business Strategy as the Driver of Operations 238

The Many Faces of Production Operations 238

Operations Planning 240

Capacity Planning 240

entrepreneurship and new ventures: A Better Path to Planning Meals (and Better Eating, Too) 241

Location Planning 241

finding a better way: "Going Green" Yields a Better Way to Spin Clean 242

Layout Planning 242

Quality Planning 244

Methods Planning 245

Operations Scheduling 246

The Master Operations Schedule 246

Detailed Schedules 247

Staff Schedules and Computer-Based Scheduling 247

Project Scheduling 248

Operations Control 249

Materials Management 249

Quality Control 251

Quality Improvement and Total Quality Management 251

The Quality-Productivity Connection 252

Managing for Quality 252

managing in turbulent times: Quick Footed Egyptian Businesses 253

Tools for Total Quality Management 254

Adding Value through Supply Chains 256

The Supply Chain Strategy 256

Outsourcing and Global Supply Chains 257

summary of learning objectives • key terms • questions & exercises • building a business: continuing team exercise • building your business skills • exercising your ethics • team exercise • cases • crafting a business plan • end notes

Part 3: People in Organizations

8 Employee Behavior and Motivation 268

Chapter Opening Case: Chicken or Egg? 271

Forms of Employee Behavior 272
Performance Behaviors 273
Organizational Citizenship 273
Counterproductive Behaviors 274
managing in turbulent times: The Law of Well-Being 274

Individual Differences among Employees 275
Personality at Work 275
Attitudes at Work 278

Matching People and Jobs 280
Psychological Contracts 280
The Person-Job Fit 282

Basic Motivation Concepts and Theories 282
Classical Theory 282
Early Behavioral Theory 282
entrepreneurship and new ventures: Motivation at Bigfoot 286
Contemporary Motivation Theory 287

Strategies and Techniques for Enhancing Motivation 289
Reinforcement/Behavior Modification 289
Using Goals to Motivate Behavior 289
finding a better way: Carrot or Stick? 290
Participative Management and Empowerment 291
Team Structures 291
Job Enrichment and Job Redesign 291
Modified Work Schedules and Alternative Workplaces 292
summary of learning objectives • key terms • questions & exercises • building a business: continuing team exercise • building your business skills • exercising your ethics • team exercise • cases • end notes

9 Leadership and Decision Making 302

Chapter Opening Case: Middle Eastern Business Leadership 305

The Nature of Leadership 306
Leadership and Management 306
Leadership and Power 307

Early Approaches to Leadership 308
Trait Approaches to Leadership 308
Behavioral Approaches to Leadership 309

The Situational Approach to Leadership 310

Leadership through the Eyes of the Followers 311
Transformational Leadership 311
Charismatic Leadership 312
managing in turbulent times: Leading during Tough Times 313

Special Issues in Leadership 313
Leadership Substitutes 313
Leadership Neutralizers 314

The Changing Nature of Leadership 314
Leaders as Coaches 315
Gender and Leadership 315
Cross-Cultural Leadership 315
finding a better way: Creating Board Diversity 316

Emerging Issues in Leadership 317
Strategic Leadership 317
Ethical Leadership 317
Virtual Leadership 317

Leadership, Management, and Decision Making 318
The Nature of Decision Making 318
entrepreneurship and new ventures: A Bad Decision at Wesabe 320
Rational Decision Making 320
Behavioral Aspects of Decision Making 323
summary of learning objectives • key terms • questions & exercises • building a business: continuing team exercise • building your business skills • exercising your ethics • team exercise • cases • end notes

10 Human Resource Management and Labor Relations 334

Chapter Opening Case: A Unique Partnership Drives Wegmans 337

The Foundations of Human Resource Management 338
The Strategic Importance of HRM 338
HR Planning 339

The Legal Context of HRM 341
Equal Employment Opportunity 341
Compensation and Benefits 342
Labor Relations 343
Health and Safety 343
Other Legal Issues 343

Staffing the Organization 344
Recruiting HR 344
Selecting HR 345
finding a better way: Dock Strike in Hong Kong 346

Compensation and Benefits 348
Wages and Salaries 348
Incentive Programs 348

Benefits Programs   349

entrepreneurship and new ventures: Whole Benefits?   350

Developing the Workforce   351

Training and Development   351

Performance Appraisal   352

New Challenges in the Changing Workplace   354

Managing Workforce Diversity   354

Managing Knowledge Workers   354

Contingent and Temporary Workers   355

managing in turbulent times: Temp or Perm?   356

Dealing with Organized Labor   357

Unionism Today   357

Collective Bargaining   358

summary of learning objectives • key terms • questions & exercises • building a business: continuing team exercise • building your business skills • exercising your ethics • team exercise • cases • crafting a business plan • end notes

Part 4: Principles of Marketing: Building Relationships with Customers for Competitive Advantage

11 Marketing Processes and Consumer Behavior   372

Chapter Opening Case: Starbucks Brews a New Marketing Mix   375

What Is Marketing?   376

Delivering Value   376

Goods, Services, and Ideas   378

Relationship Marketing and Customer Relationship Management   378

The Marketing Environment   379

managing in turbulent times: Feeling the Pressure for "Green"   381

Developing the Marketing Plan   382

Marketing Strategy: Planning the Marketing Mix   383

Marketing Strategy: Target Marketing and Market Segmentation   386

Identifying Market Segments   387

Geographic Segmentation   387

Demographic Segmentation   387

Geo-Demographic Segmentation   387

Psychographic Segmentation   388

Behavioral Segmentation   388

Marketing Research   388

The Research Process   389

Research Methods   390

Understanding Consumer Behavior   391

Influences on Consumer Behavior   391

The Consumer Buying Process   392

finding a better way: The Truth about Your Online Customer Service   393

Organizational Marketing and Buying Behavior   394

Business Marketing   394

B2B Buying Behavior   394

Social Media and Marketing   395

The International Marketing Mix   396

Small Business and the Marketing Mix   397

entrepreneurship and new ventures: Social Networking for Jobs in Good Times and in Bad   398

Small-Business Products   398

Small-Business Pricing   399

Small-Business Distribution   399

Small-Business Promotion   399

summary of learning objectives • key terms • questions & exercises • building a business: continuing team exercise • building your business skills • exercising your ethics • team exercise • cases • end notes

12 Developing and Pricing Products   410

Chapter Opening Case: iTunes Is It   413

What Is A Product?   414

The Value Package   414

Classifying Goods and Services   415

The Product Mix   416

Developing New Products   417

The New Product Development Process   417

entrepreneurship and new ventures: This Business Is *App*solutely Booming   418

Product Mortality Rates   419

The Seven-Step Development Process   420

Variations in the Process for Services   420

Product Life Cycle   421

Stages in the PLC   421

Extending Product Life: An Alternative to New Products   423

Identifying Products   423

Determining Prices   425

Pricing to Meet Business Objectives   426

finding a better way: Fixed Prices in UAE   426

Price-Setting Tools   427

Pricing Strategies and Tactics   429

Pricing Strategies   429

managing in turbulent times: How Recessionary Times Became a Stimulus for Innovative Pricing and Promotion   431

Pricing Tactics   431

International Pricing   432

summary of learning objectives • key terms • questions & exercises • building a business: continuing team exercise • building your business skills • exercising your ethics • team exercise • cases • end notes

13 Distributing and Promoting Products   442

Chapter Opening Case: With Its Worldly View, Netflix Wants an Entire Globe of Streamers   445

The Distribution Mix   446

Intermediaries and Distribution Channels   446

Distribution Strategies   448

Channel Conflict and Channel Leadership   449

Wholesaling   449

Merchant Wholesalers   449

Agents and Brokers   450

The Advent of the E-Intermediary   450

Retailing   451

Types of Brick-and-Mortar Retail Outlets   451

finding a better way: Bye-Bye Cash Registers, Hello Tablets!   452

Nonstore Retailing   452

Online Retailing   453

Physical Distribution   454

Warehousing Operations   455

Transportation Operations   455

entrepreneurship and new ventures: Running in Two Speeds at Once: Paperless and Paper   456

Distribution through Supply Chains as a Marketing Strategy   457

The Importance of Promotion   457

Promotional Objectives   457

Promotional Strategies   458

The Promotional Mix   458

Advertising Promotions   459

Personal Selling   460

Personal Selling Situations   460

Personal Selling Tasks   461

managing in turbulent times: Direct Mail Marketing: Back from a "Slow Death"?   462

The Personal Selling Process   463

Sales Promotions   464

Direct (or Interactive) Marketing   464

Publicity and Public Relations   465

summary of learning objectives • key terms • questions & exercises • building a business: continuing team exercise • building your business skills • exercising your ethics • team exercise • cases • crafting a business plan • end notes

Part 5: Managing Information for Better Business Decisions

14 Information Technology (IT) for Business   476

Chapter Opening Case: Online Pirates Feast on Economic Downturn   479

Information Technology Impacts: A Driver of Changes for Business   480

Creating Portable Offices: Providing Remote Access to Instant Information   480

Enabling Better Service by Coordinating Remote Deliveries   481

Creating Leaner, More Efficient Organizations   481

Enabling Increased Collaboration   482

Enabling Global Exchange   482

Improving Management Processes   482

Providing Flexibility for Customization   483

Providing New Business Opportunities   483

Improving the World and Our Lives   484

IT Building Blocks: Business Resources   485

The Internet and Other Communication Resources   486

Networks: System Architecture   487

Hardware and Software   490

Information Systems: Harnessing the Competitive Power of IT   491

managing in turbulent times: When Cash Gets Scarce, Businesses Switch to Internet Bartering   491

Leveraging Information Resources: Data Warehousing and Data Mining   492

entrepreneurship and new ventures: Speaking Loud and Clear: A New Voice Technology   493

Types of Information Systems   494

IT Risks and Threats   496

Hackers   496

Identity Theft   497

Intellectual Property Theft   497

Computer Viruses, Worms, and Trojan Horses   497

Spyware   497

Spam   498

IT Protection Measures 498

Preventing Unauthorized Access: Firewalls 498

Preventing Identity Theft 498

Preventing Infectious Intrusions: Anti-Virus
Software 499

Protecting Electronic Communications: Encryption
Software 499

Avoiding Spam and Spyware 499

finding a better way: The Pentagon's New Career
Track: Cyberwarfare 500

Ethical Concerns in IT 500

summary of learning objectives • key terms • questions
& exercises • building a business: continuing team
exercise • building your business skills • exercising
your ethics • team exercise • cases • end notes

**15 The Role of Accountants and
Accounting Information 510**

Chapter Opening Case: Frenkel's Forensics 513

**What Is Accounting, and Who Uses Accounting
Information? 514**

Who Are Accountants and What Do They Do? 515

Financial versus Managerial Accounting 515

Certified Public Accountants 515

Private Accountants and Management
Accountants 518

Forensic Accountants 518

Federal Restrictions on CPA Services and Financial
Reporting: Sarbox 519

The Accounting Equation 520

Assets and Liabilities 521

Owners' Equity 521

Financial Statements 521

Balance Sheets 522

Income Statements 523

Statements of Cash Flows 525

The Budget: An Internal Financial Statement 526

Reporting Standards and Practices 526

Revenue Recognition and Activity Timing 527

Full Disclosure 527

Analyzing Financial Statements 527

managing in turbulent times: The "Fairness"
Dilemma: What's an Asset's Real Value? 528

Solvency Ratios: Borrower's Ability to Repay Debt 529

Profitability Ratios: Earnings Power for Owners 529

entrepreneurship and new ventures: How Will
Twitter Turn Tweets into Treasure? 530

Activity Ratios: How Efficiently Is the Firm Using Its
Resources? 530

finding a better way: Ageing Asia 531

**Bringing Ethics into the Accounting
Equation 531**

Why Accounting Ethics? 532

Internationalizing Accounting 533

International Accounting Standards Board 533

finding a better way: Accounting Practices for the
Small Business 534

Why One Set of Global Practices? 535

summary of learning objectives • key terms • questions
& exercises • building a business: continuing team
exercise • building your business skills • exercising
your ethics • team exercise • cases • crafting a
business plan • end notes

Part 6: The Financial System
and Issues in Financial
Management

**16 Understanding Money and the
Role of Banking 548**

Chapter Opening Case: A Tale of Two Worlds in
Banking 551

What Is Money? 552

The Characteristics of Money 552

The Functions of Money 553

M-1: The Spendable Money Supply 553

M-2: M-1 Plus the Convertible Money Supply 554

Credit Cards and Debit Cards: Plastic Money? 556

The U.S. Financial System 556

Financial Institutions 556

The Growth of Financial Services 558

managing in turbulent times: Getting Serious with
Credit Standards 559

**Financial Institutions Create Money and Are
Regulated 560**

Regulation of the Banking System 561

The Federal Reserve System 562

The Structure of the Fed 562

The Functions of the Fed 563

The Tools of the Fed 563

The Changing Money and Banking System 564

finding a better way: In Search of a Much-Needed
Economic "Fix," the Fed Finds a Better Way 565

Government Intervention for Stabilizing the U.S.
Financial System 565

Anticrime and Antiterrorism Regulations 566

The Impact of Electronic Technologies 567

entrepreneurship and new ventures: Cultivating a Social Side for Community Banking 568

International Banking and Finance 569

Currency Values and Exchange Rates 570

The International Payments Process 571

International Bank Structure 571

summary of learning objectives • key terms • questions & exercises • building a business: continuing team exercise • building your business skills • exercising your ethics • team exercise • cases • end notes

17 Managing Business Finances 584

Chapter Opening Case: Investing in Green 587

Maximizing Capital Growth 588

The Time Value of Money and Compound Growth 588

Common Stock Investments 589

Investing to Fulfill Financial Objectives 591

Reasons for Investing 591

Most Mutual Funds Don't Match the Market 591

Exchange-Traded Funds 592

The Business of Trading Securities 592

Primary and Secondary Securities Markets 593

Stock Exchanges 593

Nonexchange Trading: Electronic Communication Networks 595

Individual Investor Trading 595

Tracking the Market Using Stock Indexes 596

entrepreneurship and new ventures: An Entrepreneurship of Evil 598

The Risk–Return Relationship 599

Investment Dividends (or Interest), Appreciation, and Total Return 599

Fantasy Stock Markets 600

Managing Risk with Diversification and Asset Allocation 601

Finding a Better Way: Mass Communications with IT Puts Stock Trading within Easy Reach 602

Financing the Business Firm 603

Secured Loans for Equipment 603

Working Capital and Unsecured Loans from Banks 603

Angel Investors and Venture Capital 604

Sale of Corporate Bonds 605

Managing in Turbulent Times: Weakening South African Housing Market? 606

Becoming a Public Corporation 607

Going Public Means Selling off Part of the Company 608

Stock Valuation 608

Market Capitalization 609

Choosing Equity versus Debt Capital 609

Regulating Securities Markets 611

The Securities and Exchange Commission 611

Regulations against Insider Trading 612

summary of learning objectives • key terms • questions & exercises • building a business: continuing team exercise • building your business skills • exercising your ethics • team exercise • cases • crafting a business plan • end notes

Appendices

Appendix I: Risk Management 623

Coping with Risk 623

Insurance as Risk Management 624

Appendix II: The Legal Context of Business 627

The U.S. Legal and Judicial Systems 627

Types of Law 627

The U.S. Judicial System 628

Business Law 629

Contract Law 629

Tort Law 629

Property Law 630

Agency Law 631

Commercial Law 631

Bankruptcy Law 631

The International Framework of Business Law 632

Appendix III: Managing Your Personal Finances 633

Building Your Financial Plan 633

Assessing Your Current Financial Condition 634

Develop Your Financial Goals 635

Making Better Use of the Time Value of Money 636

Planning for the Golden Years 636

Time Value as a Financial-Planning Tool 637

Conserving Money by Controlling It 637

Credit Cards: Keys to Satisfaction or Financial Handcuffs? 638

Save Your Money: Lower Interest Rates and Faster Payments 638

Financial Commitments of Home Ownership 639

How Much House Can You Afford? 639

Cashing out from Tax Avoidance (Legally) 640

The IRA Tax Break 641

Protecting Your Net Worth 642

Why Buy Life Insurance? 643

What Does Life Insurance Do? 643

How Much Should I Buy? 643

Why Consider Term Insurance? 643

How Much Does It Cost? 643

Appendix IV: Unions and Labor Management 645

Why Do Workers Unionize? 645

The Evolution of Unionism in the United States 645

Early Unions 646

The Emergence of the Major Unions 646

Unionism Today 648

Trends in Union Membership 648

Trends in Union-Management Relations 649

Trends in Bargaining Perspectives 650

The Future of Unions 650

Contemporary Union Structure 651

Locals 651

Laws Governing Labor-Management Relations 652

The Major Labor Laws 652

How Unions Are Organized and Certified 654

Collective Bargaining 655

Reaching Agreement on Contract Terms 656

Contract Issues 656

When Bargaining Fails 657

Administering a Labor Agreement 659

end notes

Glossary **661**
Index **681**

Businesses today face constant change—change in their competitive landscape, change in their workforce, change in governmental regulation, change in economic conditions, change in technology, change in … well, you get the idea. As we began to plan this revision, we, too, recognized the need for change. Changing demands from instructors, changing needs and preferences of students, and changing views on what material to cover in this course and how to cover it have all affected how we planned and revised the book.

A new editorial team was assembled to guide and shape the creation and development of the book. Along with suggestions from many loyal users, the business world itself provided us with dozens of new examples, new challenges, new successes and failures, and new perspectives on what they must do to remain competitive. And a new dedication to relevance guided our work from beginning to end. For example, we know that some business students will go to work for big companies. Others will work for small firms. Some will start their own business. Still others may join a family business. Nonbusiness students, too, as interested citizens, are curious about its whys and hows of businesses. So, we accepted the challenge of striving to make the book as relevant as possible to all students, regardless of their personal and career goals and objectives.

We also carefully reviewed the existing book line by line, eliminating extraneous material and adding new material. Examples were updated or replaced with newer ones. We worked extra hard to make our writing as clear and as crisp as possible. More recent business practices and issues are included throughout the text. We've also engaged the student by opening each chapter with the question "What's in It for Me?" We then answer that question by identifying the key elements in the chapter that are most central to the student's future relationships to business—be it as employee, manager, consumer, investor, or interested citizen. And because so much work in modern organizations is performed by teams, we included the special team ethics exercise at the end of each chapter and retained the companion individual ethics exercises that have been so popular in previous editions.

We are proud of what we have accomplished and believe that we have taken this book to a higher level of excellence. Its content is stronger, its learning framework is better, its design is more accessible, and its support materials are the best in the market. We hope that you enjoy reading and learning from this book and its supporting resources as much as we enjoyed creating them. And who knows? Perhaps one day we can tell your story of business success to future students.

Ron Ebert
Ricky Griffin

about the authors

Ronald J. Ebert is Emeritus Professor at the University of Missouri–Columbia where he lectures in the Management Department and serves as advisor to students and student organizations. Professor Ebert draws on more than 30 years of teaching experience at such schools as Sinclair College, University of Washington, University of Missouri, Lucian Blaga University of Sibiu (Romania), and Consortium International University (Italy). His consulting alliances have included such firms as Mobay Corporation, Kraft Foods, Oscar Mayer, Atlas Powder, and John Deere. He has designed and conducted management development programs for such diverse clients as the American Public Power Association, the U.S. Savings and Loan League, and the Central Missouri Manufacturing Training Consortium.

His experience as a practitioner has fostered an advocacy for integrating concepts with best business practices in business education. The five business books he has coauthored have been translated into Spanish, Chinese (Simplified), Chinese (Traditional), Malaysian, Bahasa Indonesian, and Romanian languages.

Professor Ebert has served as the Editor of the *Journal of Operations Management*. He is a Past-President and Fellow of the Decision Sciences Institute. He has served as consultant and external evaluator for *Quantitative Reasoning for Business Studies*, an introduction-to-business project sponsored by the National Science Foundation.

Ricky Griffin received his Ph.D. in management from the University of Houston. After spending three years on the faculty at the University of Missouri–Columbia, he moved to Texas A&M University. During his career at Texas A&M he has taught undergraduate and graduate courses in management, organizational behavior, human resource management, and international business.

Professor Griffin's research interests include workplace aggression and violence, organizational security, workplace culture, and leadership. His work has been published in such journals as *Academy of Management Review*, *Academy of Management Journal*, *Administrative Science Quarterly*, and *Journal of Management*. He served as Associate Editor and then as Editor of *Journal of Management*.

In addition, Professor Griffin has also authored or coauthored several leading textbooks and coedited three scholarly books. His books are used in more than 500 colleges and universities in the United States and abroad and have been translated into Spanish, Russian, Polish, and Chinese.

He has served the Academy of Management as Chair of the Organizational Behavior Division and as Program Chair of the Research Methods Division. He has served as President of the Southwest Division of the Academy of Management and on the Board of Directors of the Southern Management Association. Professor Griffin is a Fellow of both the Academy of Management and the Southern Management Association. He has also won several awards for research and has been supported by more than $400,000 in federal research funding.

Professor Griffin has served as Director of the Center for Human Resource Management and Head of the Department of Management at Texas A&M University. He has also served as Executive Associate Dean and Interim Dean at the Mays Business School. He currently serves as Head of the Department of Management.

We would like to personally thank our panel of super reviewers for their deep involvement with this edition of the book.

 Chi Archibong, North Carolina A&T State University

 Todd Jamison, Chadron State College

George Bernard, Seminole State College of Florida

 Pierre Laguerre, Bergen County Community College

 Kevin Bradford, Somerset Community College

 Pam McElligott, St. Louis Community College – Meramec

 Glen Chapuis, Saint Charles Community College

 Steve Nichols, Metropolitan Community College

John Despagna, Nassau Community College

 Jo Ann Rawley, Reading Area Community College

 Tracy Fulce, Oakton Community College

Storm Russo, Valencia College – East Campus

Heidi Fuller, American River College

Michael Schaefer, Blinn College

Linda Hoffman, Ivy Tech – Fort Wayne

 Sarah Shepler, Ivy Tech – Terre Haute

19

preface

New to This Edition

- Six kinds of chapter-ending involvement activities—to reinforce and practice the use of chapter concepts—are back by popular demand (see detailed descriptions that follow).

- Hundreds of new real-life business examples added throughout the text, as requested by reviewers and users.

- Seven brand-new chapter-opening cases cover key concepts in Chapter 2, Understanding Business Ethics and Social Responsibility; Chapter 3, Entrepreneurship, New Ventures, and Business Ownership; Chapter 4, The Global Context of Business; Chapter 6, Organizing the Business; Chapter 8, Employee Behavior and Motivation; Chapter 10, Human Resource Management and Labor Relations; and Chapter 13, Distributing and Promoting Products. These openers cover everything from fair trade and embargoes to the rise of Netflix and the reorganization of South African Airways to labor relations at Wegmen's. Accessible and relatable topics introduce each chapter, drawing the reader into the content and how it is used in the business world.

- Chapter 1 includes an updated version of the opening case dealing with supply-and-demand and several new or updated examples.

- We have added new coverage of social responsibility and the small business, the government and social responsibility, and managing social responsibility in Chapter 2. The chapter also has several new examples, that focus on Diamond Nuts and Hewlett-Packard's accounting errors which we use to illustrate key points.

- Chapter 3 features new coverage of distinctive competencies and sources of financing for small businesses. All statistics in this chapter have been updated, there are several new examples, and we feature expanded coverage of service businesses.

- We have added significant new coverage of the role of culture in international business in Chapter 4. This chapter also includes several new examples, such as ones that navigate relaxed laws in Asia and the Cayman Islands, and updated statistics.

- Chapter 5 includes new coverage of the science and art of management and key managerial roles and skills.

- In Chapter 6, we have added new coverage of functional departmentalization and the organizational grapevine, plus, several new examples that center on companies such as United Airlines and Steinway.

- The substantial revisions in Chapter 7 emphasize operations for organizations that are service providers. New operations examples reinforce the prominence of service industries such as tourism, consulting, transportation, and hospitality in today's economy.

- Chapter 8 has been expanded to include new coverage of personality traits at work, how individual attitudes are formed, cognitive dissonance, and other important individual needs.

- We added additional material on leadership and power, situational approaches to leadership, and the nature of decision making to Chapter 9. This chapter also has several new examples, including one about how the Internet company, Wasabe, failed as a result of bad business decisions.

- Chapter 10 now includes new or expanded coverage of the strategic importance of human resource management, the legal context of human resource management, compensation and benefits, and developing the workforce. The chapter has also been reorganized and includes several new examples, such as one about how top software companies compete for programmers.

- After hearing the needs of and feedback from instructors, we expanded coverage of marketing topics to three chapters: Chapter 11, Marketing Processes and Consumer Behavior, includes an example of the cruise industry's use of pre-trip social networking among passengers; Chapter 12, Developing and Pricing Products, includes a new case on Singaporean pricing policies; and Chapter 13, Distributing and Promoting Products, contains new discussions on personal selling situations and personal selling processes.

- New examples in Chapter 14 discuss the abilities of service industries to customize products such as pet care and clothing designs. We also updated the popular presentation on ethical issues arising with information technology with recent examples.

- A new "Finding a Better way" box provides guidelines on accounting practices for the small business in Chapter 15.

- Discussion of sources for financing the small business was added into Chapter 17. Key points include the value of establishing bank credit, along with presentation of a business plan for gaining longer-term sources of funding.

- The new Appendix on Labor Relations is an expansion of material covered in Chapter 10, providing a better understanding of how and why workers organize into labor unions, how unions and businesses relate to each other, and how the collective bargaining process works.

In-Chapter Features

"What's in It for Me?"
Each chapter opens with a section called "What's in It for Me?" In this section, we answer that question by identifying the key elements in the chapter that are most central to your future careers in business, be it as an employee, manager, investor, or as an outside consumer or interested citizen—making it clear why each chapter really matters.

Two-Part Chapter Case Vignettes
We've updated or completely replaced the chapter-opening cases, keeping them fresh, relevant, and up to date. Covering companies from Netflix to South African Airways and iTunes and Starbucks to Google, these chapter case vignettes pique your interest at the beginning of the chapter and reinforce concepts you've learned throughout the chapter by adding a new case wrap-up using discussion questions at the end of the chapter. The questions require students to apply chapter content to issues in the chapter-opening case.

"Entrepreneurship and New Ventures"
If your plan is to work for a large corporation, start your own business, or anything in between, you need to be both entrepreneurial and *intrapreneurial*. These updated, popular boxed features touch on entrepreneurs who have really made a difference, some in large firms, others in smaller start-up companies. New "Entrepreneurship and New Ventures" boxes include lessons from Facebook

founder, Mark Zuckerburg, employee motivation tactics at Bigfoot, misleading health benefit offerings from Whole Foods, and the duality of online greeting cards at Paperless Post.

"Managing in Turbulent Times"

Whatever your role with any business, as employee, customer, or investor, you need to see the challenges and consequences firms encounter during economic downturns. Experiences from real companies reveal both disappointments and unexpected new opportunities arising from the 2008 recession and the uncertainties of a prolonged economic recovery. New lessons come from companies such as McDonald's and their offshoring hurdles and the U.S. Post Office and the return of "snail mail."

"Finding a Better Way"

Although businesses face challenges for survival, they also find new opportunities for displacing existing business practices with more efficient ones that improve the organization's stature and competitive success in today's changing markets. This new boxed feature reveals examples of organizations that are "Finding a Better Way" to meet these business challenges and describes how they are doing it.

We cover a wide array of topics in this new section, including:

- DuPont's "zero-waste" facilities and their contagious socially responsible nature

- The manufacturing shift from China back to Mexico

- The success of the UK's Natural Disaster Rapid Response Unit

- The replacement of cash registers with tablets, and

- The recent rise in cyber warfare

End-of-Chapter Features

We've also brought back several end-of-chapter features that, along with new features, are designed to help you review and apply chapter concepts and build skills.

Summary of Learning Objectives

Offers a quick guide for you to review the major topics covered in each chapter.

Key Terms

With page references to help reinforce chapter concepts.

Questions and Exercises

Include a set of questions for review, questions for analysis, and application exercises that test the students' understanding of the chapter topics.

Building a Business: Continuing Team Exercise

Is designed for student teams to develop business plans cumulatively from the ground up, chapter-by-chapter, throughout the course. Each chapter-ending assignment directs teams into discussions and applications of that chapter's contents as they apply to their team's business plan.

Building Your Business Skills

Activities allow you to apply your knowledge and critical-thinking skills to an extended problem drawn from a wide range of realistic business experiences.

Exercising Your Ethics

Exercises ask you to examine an ethical dilemma and think critically about how you would approach and resolve it.

Team Exercises

Present the students with a business situation and provide action steps that guide students through the team activities.

Cases

Challenge the student to *apply* the chapter content by responding to a set of questions about the practical business situation presented in the chapter-opening case as well as an additional case.

Crafting a Business Plan

At the end of each part, there is a **Crafting a Business Plan** exercise, guiding students through the steps of creating a business plan related to the topics covered in those chapters.

What's in It for *You*?

If you're like many other students, you may be starting this semester with some questions about why you're here. Whether you're taking this course at a two-year college, at a four-year university, or at a technical school, in a traditional classroom setting or online, you may be wondering just what you're supposed to get from this course and how it will benefit you. In short, you may be wondering, "What's in it for me?"

Regardless of what it may be called at your school, this is a survey course designed to introduce you to the many exciting and challenging facets of business, both in the United States and elsewhere. The course fits the needs of a wide variety of students. You may be taking this course as the first step toward earning a degree in business, you may be thinking about business and want to know more about it, or you may know you want to study business but are unsure of the area you want to pursue. Maybe you plan to major in another field but want some basic business background and are taking this course as an elective. Or you may be here because, frankly, this course is required or is a prerequisite to another course.

For those of you with little work experience, you may be uncertain as to what the business world is all about. If you have a lot of work experience, you may even be a bit skeptical about what you can actually learn about business from an introductory course. One of our biggest challenges as authors is to write a book that meets the needs of such a diverse student population, especially when we acknowledge the legitimacy of your right to ask "What's in it for me?" We also want to do our best to ensure that you find the course challenging, interesting, and useful.

The world today is populated with a breathtaking array of businesses and business opportunities. Big and small businesses, established and new businesses, broad-based and niche businesses, successful and unsuccessful businesses, global and domestic businesses—throughout this book we'll discuss how they get started and how they work, why they grow and why some fail, and how they affect you. Regardless of where your future takes you, we hope that you look back on this course as one of your first steps.

Going forward, we also urge you to consider that what you get out of this course—what's in it for you—is shaped by at least three factors. One factor is this book and the various learning aids that accompany it. Another factor is your instructor. He or she is a dedicated professional who wants to help you grow and develop intellectually and academically.

The third factor? You. Learning is an active process that requires you to be a major participant. Simply memorizing the key terms and concepts in this book may help you achieve an acceptable course grade; but true learning requires that you read, study, discuss, question, review, experience, and evaluate as you go along. Although tests and homework may be a "necessary evil," we believe we will have done our part if you finish this course with new knowledge and increased enthusiasm for the world of business. We know your instructor will do his or her best to facilitate your learning. The rest, then, is up to you. We wish you success.

To help lay the foundation for meeting these challenges, let's look at the various hats that you may wear, both now and in the future.

Wearing the Hats

There's an old adage that refers to people wearing different "hats." In general, this is based on the idea that any given person usually has different roles to play in different settings. For example, your roles may include student, child, spouse, employee, friend, or parent. You could think of each of these roles as needing a different hat—when you play the role of a student, for example, you wear one hat, but when you leave campus and go to your part-time job, you put on a different hat. From the perspective of studying and interfacing with the world of *business*, there are at least four distinct hats that you might wear:

- *The Employee Hat.* One business hat is as an employee working for a business. Many people wear this hat during the early stages of their career. To wear the hat successfully, you will need to understand your place in the organization—your job duties and responsibilities, how to get along with others, how to work with your boss, what your organization is all about, and so on. You'll begin to see how to best wear this hat as you learn more about organizing business enterprises in Chapter 6 and how organizations manage their human resources in Chapter 10, as well as in several other places in this book.

- *The Employer or Boss Hat.* Another business hat that many people wear is as an employer or boss. Whether you start your own business or get promoted within someone else's business, one day people will be working for you. You'll still need to know your job duties and responsibilities. But you'll now also need to understand how to manage other people—how to motivate and reward them, how to lead them, how to deal with conflict among them, and the legal parameters that may affect how you treat them. Chapters 3, 5, 8, and 9 provide a lot of information about how you can best wear this hat, although the role of employer runs throughout the entire book.

- *The Consumer Hat.* Even if you don't work for a business, you will still wear the hat of a consumer. Whenever you fill your car with Shell gasoline, bid for something on eBay, buy clothes at Urban Outfitters, or download a song from iTunes, you're consuming products or services created by business. To wear this hat effectively, you need to understand how to assess the value of what you're buying, your rights as a consumer, and so on. We discuss how you can best wear this hat in Chapters 4, 7, 11, 12, and 13.

- *The Investor Hat.* The final business hat many people wear is that of an investor. You may buy your own business or work for a company that allows you to buy its own stock. You may also invest in other companies through the purchase of stocks or shares of a mutual fund. For you to invest wisely, you must understand some basics, such as financial markets, business earnings, and the basic costs of investment. Chapters 4, 15, 16, 17, and an appendix will help you learn how to best wear this hat.

Many people wear more than one of these hats at the same time. Regardless of how many hats you wear or when you may be putting them on, it should be clear that you have in the past, do now, and will in the future interface with many businesses in different ways. Knowing how to best wear all these hats is what this book is all about.

Supplements

At the Instructor Resource Center, www.pearsonglobaleditions.com/ebert, instructors can access a variety of print, digital, and presentation resources available with this text in downloadable format. Registration is simple and gives you immediate access to new titles and new editions. As a registered faculty member, you can download resource files and receive immediate access to and instructions for installing course management content on your campus server. In case you ever need assistance, our dedicated technical support team is ready to help with the media supplements that accompany this text. Visit http://247.pearsoned.com for answers to frequently asked questions and toll-free user support phone numbers.

The following supplements are available for download to adopting instructors:

- Instructor's Resource Manual
- Test Bank
- TestGen® Computerized Test Bank
- PowerPoint Presentation

CourseSmart eTextbook—CourseSmart eTextbooks were developed for students looking to save on required or recommended textbooks. Students simply select their eText by title or author and purchase immediate access to the content for the duration of the course using any major credit card. With a CourseSmart eText, students can search for specific keywords or page numbers, take notes online, print out reading assignments that incorporate lecture notes, and bookmark important passages for later review. For more information or to purchase a CourseSmart eTextbook, visit www.coursesmart.com. This product may not be available in all markets. For more details, please visit www.coursesmart.co.uk or contact your local Pearson representative.

Acknowledgements

Pearson Education wishes to acknowledge and thank the following people for their work on the Global Edition:

Contributors:
Jon and Diane Sutherland

Reviewers:
Anushia Chelvarayan, Multimedia University, Malaysia
Marko Korac, Hogeschool Rotterdam, Netherlands
Ayman Metwally, Arab Academy for Science, Technology, and Maritime
    Transport, Egypt
Amy Yu Lai Peng, Macao Polytechnic Institute, Macao
Larry Lei I Sun, Macao Polytechnic Institute, Macao

business
essentials

chapter 1

The U.S. Business Environment

S PRICES

High

The best way to make money is to make products

that consumers want or need. While

this sounds simple,

only   a   few   strike   gold.

AFTER READING THIS CHAPTER, YOU SHOULD BE ABLE TO:

OBJECTIVE 1 **Define** the nature of U.S. business and identify its main goals and functions.

OBJECTIVE 2 **Describe** the external environments of business and discuss how these environments affect the success or failure of any organization.

OBJECTIVE 3 **Describe** the different types of global economic systems according to the means by which they control the factors of production.

OBJECTIVE 4 **Show** how markets, demand, and supply affect resource distribution in the United States, identify the elements of private enterprise, and explain the various degrees of competition in the U.S. economic system.

OBJECTIVE 5 **Explain** the importance of the economic environment to business and identify the factors used to evaluate the performance of an economic system.

MyBizLab®

⭐ Improve Your Grade!

Visit **pearsonglobaleditions.com/mybizlab** for simulations, tutorials, and end-of-chapter problems.

Over 10 million students improved their results using the Pearson MyLabs.

What Goes Up . . . Can Go Even Higher!

What did you pay for the last bottle of water or cup of coffee you bought? If you paid, say $1.50, you likely paid the same price the last time you bought one and will the next time as well. Although the price may eventually go up, increases generally happen only occasionally and then remain the same for a while. Now, how much did you pay for a gallon of gasoline the last time you filled your tank? How did that price compare to the time before? How about the time before that? Chances are, each time you fill up the price is a little different—sometimes a few cents more, sometimes a few cents less. But sometimes the prices jump—or drop—substantially more than just a few cents. Indeed, over the past few years the average price for a gallon of regular gasoline in the United States has ranged from a high of $4.10 in 2008 to a low of $3.22 in 2012.

Why have gasoline prices gone up and down so dramatically and why do prices change from one day to the next? In general, gas prices fluctuate as a result of four forces: supply, demand, global trends, and uncertainty. In the past, gas prices generally increased only when the supply was reduced. But the circumstances underlying the increases from 2004 to 2012 were much more complex. First, global supplies of gasoline have been increasing at a rate that has more than offset the steady decline in U.S. domestic production of gasoline since 1972. As a result, the United States has been relying more on foreign producers and is, therefore, subject to whatever prices those producers want to charge. Second, demand for gasoline in the United States has continued to rise as a result of a growing population, the continued popularity of large gas-guzzling vehicles, and a strong demand for other petroleum-based products.

Another major piece of the puzzle has been a surging global economy that, until recently, caused a higher demand for oil and gasoline. China, in particular, has become a major consumer of petroleum, passing Japan in 2005 to trail only the United States in total consumption. The global recession that started in 2008, however, reduced demand in most industrialized countries. The recession, in fact, probably played a role in the dip in prices in 2009 just as the gradual recovery that started in 2010 has helped spur higher prices once again. Political turmoil in the Middle East from 2011 to 2014 also played a major role.

The price fluctuations have also led to a wide array of related consequences. Automobile manufacturers stepped up their commitment to making more

Andres Rodriguez/fotolia

what's in it for me?

The forces that have caused jumps in gas prices reflect both the opportunities and challenges you'll find in today's business world. All businesses are subject to the influences of economic forces. But these same economic forces also provide astute managers and entrepreneurs with opportunities for profits and growth. By understanding these economic forces and how they interact, you'll be better able to (1) appreciate how managers must contend with the challenges and opportunities resulting from economic forces from the standpoint of an employee and a manager or business owner, and (2) understand why prices fluctuate from the perspective of a consumer. You should have a deeper appreciation of the environment in which managers work and a better understanding why the prices you pay for goods and services go up and down.

In this chapter, we'll first introduce the concepts of profit and loss and then describe the external environments of businesses. As we will see, the domestic business environment, the global business environment, and the technological, political-legal, sociocultural, and economic environments are all important. Next we'll look at some basic elements of economic systems and describe the economics of market systems. We'll also introduce and discuss several indicators that are used to gauge the vitality of our domestic economic system.

fuel-efficient cars even as automobile sales plummeted during the recent recession. Refiners posted record profits (indeed, some critics charged that the energy companies were guilty of price gouging). And even local police officers were kept busy combating a surge in gasoline theft, yet another indication that gas was becoming an increasingly valuable commodity!

And while surging oil and gas prices occupied the thoughts of consumers in 2014, government officials began to worry about the bigger picture. The surging global demand for gasoline has been forcing experts to face a stark reality—the global supply of petroleum will soon peak and then slowly begin to decline. Although no one can pinpoint when this will happen, virtually all the experts agree that it will happen well before the middle of this century.

So then what? The laws of supply and demand will continue to work, but in perhaps different ways. First, just because the supply of oil will decline doesn't mean that it will disappear immediately. Although there may be gradual reductions in supply, oil and gas will remain available for at least another century—but at prices that may make those of today seem like a bargain. New technology may also allow businesses to extract petroleum from locations that are not currently accessible, such as from the deepest areas under the oceans.

Second, and more significantly, there will be market incentives for businesses everywhere to figure out how to replace today's dependence on oil and gas with fuel-free alternatives. For instance, automobile manufacturers are already seeing increased demand for their hybrid products, which are cars and trucks that use a combination of gasoline and electrical power. Hence, firms that can produce alternative sources of energy will spring up, and those who find viable answers will prosper; companies that can figure out how to replace today's plastic products with new products that don't rely on petroleum will also find willing buyers.[1] (After studying the content in this chapter you should be able to answer the set of discussion questions found at the end of the chapter.)

The Concept of Business and the Concept of Profit

OBJECTIVE 1
Define
the nature of U.S. business and identify its main goals and functions.

Business *organization that provides goods or services to earn profits*

Profits *difference between a business's revenues and its expenses*

What do you think of when you hear the word *business*? Does it conjure up images of large, successful corporations, such as Apple and Google? Or of once-great but now struggling companies like Kmart, Kodak, and Yahoo!? Are you reminded of smaller firms, such as your local supermarket or favorite restaurant? Or do you think of even smaller family-owned operations, such as your neighborhood pizzeria or the florist down the street?

All these organizations are **businesses,** organizations that provide goods or services that are then sold to earn profits. Indeed, the prospect of earning **profits,** the difference between a business's revenues and its expenses, is what encourages people to open and expand businesses. After all, profits are the rewards owners get for risking their money and time. The right to pursue profits distinguishes a business from those organizations—such as most universities, hospitals, and government agencies—that run in much the same way but that generally don't seek profits.[2]

Consumer Choice and Demand In a capitalistic system, such as that in the United States, businesses exist to earn profits for owners; within certain broad constraints an owner is free to set up a new business, grow that business, sell it, or even shut it down. But consumers also have freedom of choice. In choosing how to pursue profits, businesses must take into account what consumers want or need. No matter how efficient a business is, it won't survive if there is no demand for its goods or services. Neither a snowblower shop in Florida nor a beach umbrella store in Alaska is likely to do well.

Opportunity and Enterprise If enterprising businesspeople can spot a promising opportunity and then develop a good plan for capitalizing on it, they can succeed. For example, although large retailers such as Circuit City and Linens-N-Things closed their doors in 2009, other firms profited from these closings by handling the inventory liquidations of those failed retailers. The opportunity always involves goods or services that consumers need or want—especially if no one else is supplying them or if existing businesses are doing so inefficiently or incompletely.

The Benefits of Business So what are the benefits of businesses? Businesses produce most of the goods and services we consume, and they employ most working people. They create most new innovations and provide a vast range of opportunities for new businesses, which serve as their suppliers. A healthy business climate also contributes to the quality of life and standard of living of people in a society. Business profits enhance the personal incomes of millions of owners and stockholders, and business taxes help to support governments at all levels. Many businesses support charities and provide community leadership. However, some businesses also harm the environment, and their decision makers sometimes resort to unacceptable practices for their own personal benefit.

In this chapter, we begin our introduction to business by examining the environment in which businesses operate. Understanding the environment provides a foundation for our subsequent discussions dealing with economic forces that play a major role in the success and failure of businesses everywhere.

The External Environments of Business

OBJECTIVE 2
Describe
the external environments of business and discuss how these environments affect the success or failure of any organization.

All businesses, regardless of their size, location, or mission, operate within a larger external environment. This **external environment** consists of everything outside an organization's boundaries that might affect it. (Businesses also have an *internal environment*, more commonly called *corporate culture*; we discuss this in Chapter 5.) Not surprisingly, the external environment plays a major role in determining the success or failure of any organization. Managers must, therefore, have a complete and accurate understanding of their environment and then strive to operate and compete within it. Businesses can also influence their environments.

Figure 1.1 shows the major dimensions and elements of the external environment as it affects businesses today. As you can see, these include the *domestic business environment*, the *global business environment*, the *technological environment*, the *political-legal environment*, the *sociocultural environment*, and the *economic environment*.

External Environment *everything outside an organization's boundaries that might affect it*

Domestic Business Environment

The **domestic business environment** refers to the environment in which a firm conducts its operations and derives its revenues. In general, businesses seek to be close to their customers, to establish strong relationships with their suppliers, and to distinguish themselves from their competitors. Take Urban Outfitters, for example. The firm initially located its stores near urban college campuses; it now also locates stores in other, often more upscale, areas as well. The company also has a strong network of suppliers and is itself a wholesale supplier to other retailers through its Free People division. And it has established a clear identity for itself within the domestic business environment that enables it to compete effectively with such competitors as Aeropostale and dELiA*s.

Domestic Business Environment *the environment in which a firm conducts its operations and derives its revenues*

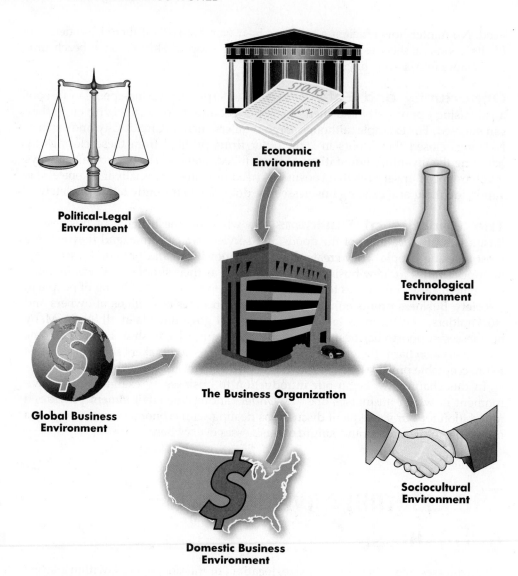

FIGURE 1.1 Dimensions of the External Environment

Global Business Environment

Global Business Environment
the international forces that affect a business

The **global business environment** refers to the international forces that affect a business. Factors affecting the global environment at a general level include international trade agreements, international economic conditions, political unrest, and so forth. For example, as political protests spread through much of the Middle East from 2011 through 2013, oil prices began to surge and companies with operations in the region took emergency measures to protect their employees. At a more immediate level, any given business is likely to be affected by international market opportunities, suppliers, cultures, competitors, and currency values. For instance, Urban Outfitters currently has stores in the United States, Canada, Belgium, Denmark, Germany, Ireland, Scotland, and Sweden and ships to customers in 133 countries. But as it has expanded into other parts of the world, it has to contend with different languages, more diverse cultures, different forms of technology, different currencies, and many other factors. Complicating things further, many of its suppliers are foreign companies.

Technological Environment

Technological Environment *all the ways by which firms create value for their constituents*

The **technological environment** generally includes all the ways by which firms create value for their constituents. Technology includes human knowledge, work methods, physical equipment, electronics and telecommunications, and various processing systems that are used to perform business activities. For instance, Urban Outfitters

Urban Outfitters is affected by the external environment in many different ways. The domestic business environment, global business environment, technological environment, political-legal environment, sociocultural environment, and economic environment all interact to provide Urban Outfitters with both opportunities and challenges.

LE Robshaw/Alamy

relies on a sophisticated information system that tracks sales and inventory levels to be highly responsive to its customers. The firm also enjoys considerable success with its e-commerce websites. Urban Outfitters has developed a strong market presence in Japan, for example, even though it has no traditional brick-and-mortar retail outlets in that country.

Political-Legal Environment

The **political-legal environment** reflects the relationship between business and government, usually in the form of government regulation of business. This environment is important for several reasons. First, the legal system defines in part what an organization can and can't do. For instance, Urban Outfitters is subject to a variety of political and legal forces, including product identification laws, employee hiring restrictions, and local zoning requirements. Likewise, various government agencies regulate important areas, such as advertising practices, safety and health considerations, and acceptable standards of business conduct. Pro- or anti-business sentiment in government and political stability are also important considerations, especially for international firms. For instance, shortly after President Barack Obama first took office, a number of new regulations were imposed on businesses. For instance, the president signed legislation that imposes new restrictions on lobbying and on political action committees (these regulations are discussed in Chapter 2).

Political-Legal Environment *the relationship between business and government*

Sociocultural Environment

The **sociocultural environment** includes the customs, mores, values, and demographic characteristics of the society in which an organization functions. Sociocultural processes also determine the goods and services, as well as the standards of business conduct, that a society is likely to value and accept. For example, a few years ago, Urban Outfitters introduced a Monopoly-like game called Ghettopoly. The company

Sociocultural Environment *the customs, mores, values, and demographic characteristics of the society in which an organization functions*

received a lot of unfavorable publicity about the game, based on critics' charges that it made light of poverty and other social problems. In response, Urban Outfitters pulled it from shelves and discontinued its sale. But the firm continues to push the limits. For instance, in recent years Urban Outfitters has been criticized for selling t-shirts with a pocket patch resembling the yellow stars Jews were forced to wear during the Nazi regime in Germany, for clothing items with a color option listed as Obama Black, and for a holiday catalog with numerous items containing potentially offensive words and images.[3]

Economic Environment

Economic Environment *relevant conditions that exist in the economic system in which a company operates*

The **economic environment** refers to relevant conditions that exist in the economic system in which a company operates. For example, if an economy is doing well enough that most people have jobs, a growing company may find it necessary to pay higher wages and offer more benefits to attract workers from other companies. But if many people in an economy are looking for jobs, as was the case during the 2008 recession, a firm may be able to pay less and offer fewer benefits. Like many retailers, Urban Outfitters experienced some financial pressures during the recession but reports that its revenues and profits are now increasing again. The rest of this chapter is devoted to the economic environment; the other environments of business are covered throughout the rest of the book.

managing in turbulent times

What Goes Around...

It seems like just yesterday. In 2005 the global economy was booming. In the United States, for example, business profits were soaring, jobs were plentiful, and home ownership was at an all-time high. The stock market reached unprecedented highs, pension plans were burgeoning, and new business opportunities were plentiful.

Fast-forward just five short years to 2010, and things looked a lot different. Business profits were down, hundreds of thousands of jobs were lost and unemployment claims soared, and mortgage foreclosures were the order of the day. The stock market plummeted, pension plans went broke, and it seemed like no one wanted to start a new business (and even those who did had a hard time getting financing).

What happened in this short period of time? Economists call it the *business cycle*. Historically, our economy has followed long periods of growth and prosperity with periods of cutbacks and retreats. And that's what started in 2008. During extended periods of prosperity, people sometimes start to act as though good times will last forever. They continue to bid up stock prices, for instance, far beyond rational value. They also take on too much debt, save too little money, and spend beyond their means. Businesses, too, start taking more risks, carrying larger inventories, expanding too quickly, and hiring too many people. But things have a way of correcting themselves, and that's what happened when our economy went into recession beginning in 2008.

So what does the future hold? Well, although no one has a real crystal ball, most experts agree that the bad times will run their course and things will start looking up again. Indeed, by

justasc/Shutterstock

mid-2011 the stock market was inching back up, continued to slowly recover throughout 2012, and hit an all-time high in early 2013. The housing market continues to improve, and unemployment is gradually declining, with many businesses cautiously hiring again. It may take awhile longer for growth to really take off again, but one day profits will again start to surge, businesses will embark on ambitious hiring plans, the stock market will continue to soar, and business opportunities will again be plentiful. Until then, though, managers have to focus on following core business principles and do their best to steer their organizations through today's turbulence. And they should try to remember, of course, that even when the good times are rolling again there will be another correction somewhere down the road.

Economic Systems

A U.S. business operates differently from a business in France or the People's Republic of China, and businesses in these countries differ from those in Japan or Brazil. A key factor in these differences is the economic system of a firm's *home country*, the nation in which it does most of its business. An **economic system** is a nation's system for allocating its resources among its citizens, both individuals and organizations.

Economic System *a nation's system for allocating its resources among its citizens*

Factors of Production

A basic difference between economic systems is the way in which a system manages its **factors of production,** the resources that a country's businesses use to produce goods and services. Economists have long focused on four factors of production: *labor, capital, entrepreneurs*, and *physical resources*. In addition to these traditional four factors, economists include *information resources* as well. Note that the concept of factors of production can also be applied to the resources that an individual organization *manages* to produce tangible goods and intangible services.

Factors of Production *resources used in the production of goods and services—labor, capital, entrepreneurs, physical resources, and information resources*

Labor People who work for businesses provide labor. **Labor,** sometimes called **human resources,** includes the physical and intellectual contributions people make while engaged in economic production. Starbucks, for example, employs more than 160,000 people.[4] The firm's workforce includes the baristas who prepare coffees for customers, store managers, regional managers, coffee tasters, quality control experts, coffee buyers, marketing experts, financial specialists, and other specialized workers and managers.

Labor (Human Resources) *physical and mental capabilities of people as they contribute to economic production*

Capital Obtaining and using labor and other resources requires **capital,** the financial resources needed to operate a business. You need capital to start a new business and then to keep it running and growing. For example, when Howard Schultz decided to buy the fledgling Starbucks coffee outfit back in 1987, he used personal savings and a loan to finance his acquisition. As Starbucks grew, he came to rely more on Starbucks' profits. Eventually, the firm sold stock to other investors to raise even more money. Starbucks continues to rely on a blend of current earnings and both short- and long-term debt to finance its operations and fuel its growth. Moreover, even when the firm decided to close several hundred coffee shops a few years ago, it employed capital to pay off leases and provide severance pay to employees who lost their jobs.

Capital *funds needed to create and operate a business enterprise*

Entrepreneurs An **entrepreneur** is a person who accepts the risks and opportunities entailed in creating and operating a new business. Three individuals founded Starbucks back in 1971 and planned to emphasize wholesale distribution of fresh coffee beans. However, they lacked either the interest or the vision to see the retail potential for coffee. But Schultz was willing to accept the risks associated with retail growth and, after buying the company, he capitalized on the market opportunities for rapid growth. Had his original venture failed, Schultz would have lost most of his savings. Most economic systems encourage entrepreneurs, both to start new businesses and to make the decisions that allow them to create new jobs and make more profits for their owners.

Entrepreneur *individual who accepts the risks and opportunities involved in creating and operating a new business venture*

Physical Resources **Physical resources** are the tangible things that organizations use to conduct their business. They include natural resources and raw materials, offices, storage and production facilities, parts and supplies, computers and peripherals, and a variety of other equipment. For example, Starbucks relies on coffee beans and other food products, the equipment it uses to make its coffee drinks, paper products for packaging, as well as office equipment and storage facilities for running its business at the corporate level.

Physical Resources *tangible items that organizations use in the conduct of their businesses*

Starbucks uses various factors of production, including (a) labor, such as this Starbucks barista; (b) entrepreneurs, such as CEO Howard Schultz; and (c) physical resources, including coffee beans.

Information Resources *data and other information used by businesses*

Information Resources The production of tangible goods once dominated most economic systems. Today, **information resources,** data and other information used by businesses, play a major role. Information resources that businesses rely on include market forecasts, the specialized knowledge of people, and economic data. In turn, much of what businesses do with the information results either in the creation of new information or the repackaging of existing information for new users. For example, Starbucks uses various economic statistics to decide where to open new outlets. It also uses sophisticated forecasting models to predict the future prices of coffee beans. And consumer taste tests help the firm decide when to introduce new products.

Types of Economic Systems

Different types of economic systems view these factors of production differently. In some systems, for example (and in theory), the ownership of both the factors of production and businesses themselves is private. That is, ownership is held by entrepreneurs, individual investors, and other businesses. As discussed next, these are market economies. In other systems, though (and also in theory), the factors of production and all businesses are owned or controlled by the government. These are called *planned economies*. Note that we described these kinds of systems as being "in theory." Why? Because in reality, most systems fall between these extremes.

Economic systems also differ in the ways decisions are made about production and allocation. A **planned economy** relies on a centralized government to control all or most factors of production and to make all or most production and allocation

Planned Economy *economy that relies on a centralized government to control all or most factors of production and to make all or most production and allocation decisions*

decisions. In a **market economy,** individual producers and consumers control production and allocation by creating combinations of supply and demand. Let's look at each of these types of economic systems as well as mixed market economies in more detail.

Planned Economies   There are two basic forms of planned economies: *communism* (discussed here) and *socialism* (discussed later as a form of mixed market economy). As envisioned by nineteenth-century German economist Karl Marx, **communism** is a system in which the government owns and operates all factors of production. Under such a system, the government would assign people to jobs; it would also own all business and control business decisions—what to make, how much to charge, and so forth. Marx proposed that individuals would contribute according to their abilities and receive benefits according to their needs. He also expected government ownership of production factors to be temporary; once society had matured, government would wither away, and workers would take direct ownership of the factors of production.

The former Soviet Union and many Eastern European countries embraced communism until the end of the twentieth century. In the early 1990s, however, one country after another renounced communism as both an economic and a political system. Today, North Korea, Vietnam, and the People's Republic of China are among the few nations with openly communist systems. Even in these countries, however, planned economic systems are making room for features of the free enterprise system.

Market Economies   A **market** is a mechanism for exchange between the buyers and sellers of a particular good or service. (Like *capital*, the term *market* can have multiple meanings.) Market economies rely on capitalism and free enterprise to create an environment in which producers and consumers are free to sell and buy what they choose (within certain limits). As a result, items produced and prices paid are largely determined by supply and demand. The underlying premise of a market economy is to create shared value—in theory, at least, effective businesses benefit because they earn profits on what they sell, and customers also benefit by getting what they want for the best price available.[5]

To understand how a market economy works, consider what happens when you go to a fruit market to buy apples. One vendor is selling apples for $1 per pound, another is charging $1.50. Both vendors are free to charge what they want, and you are free to buy what you choose. If both vendors' apples are of the same quality, you will buy the cheaper ones. If the $1.50 apples are fresher and healthier-looking, you may buy them instead. In short, both buyers and sellers enjoy freedom of choice. That is, the vendors are free to charge whatever price they choose for their apples and the customer is free to decide whether to buy the $1 apples, the $1.50 apples, someone else's apples, or no apples at all.

Taken to a more general level of discussion, individuals in a market system are free to not only buy what they want but also to work where they want and to invest, save, or spend their money in whatever manner they choose. Likewise, businesses are free to decide what products to make, where to sell them, and what prices to charge. This process contrasts markedly with that of a planned economy, in which individuals may be told where they can and cannot work, companies may be told what they can and cannot make, and consumers may have little or no choice in what they purchase or how much they pay. The political basis of market processes is called **capitalism,** which allows the private ownership of the factors of production and encourages entrepreneurship by offering profits as an incentive. The economic basis of market processes is the operation of demand and supply, which we discuss in the next section.

Mixed Market Economies   In reality, there are really no "pure" planned or "pure" market economies. Most countries rely on some form of **mixed market economy** that features characteristics of both planned and market economies. Even a market economy that strives to be as free and open as possible, such as the U.S. economy, restricts certain activities. Some products can't be sold legally, others can be sold only to people of a certain age, advertising must be truthful, and so forth.

Market Economy *economy in which individuals control production and allocation decisions through supply and demand*

Communism *political system in which the government owns and operates all factors of production*

Market *mechanism for exchange between buyers and sellers of a particular good or service*

Capitalism *system that sanctions the private ownership of the factors of production and encourages entrepreneurship by offering profits as an incentive*

Mixed Market Economy *economic system featuring characteristics of both planned and market economies*

Many formerly planned economies have moved toward a more mixed economic model. For example, the People's Republic of China has used a planned economic model for decades but is now moving more toward a mixed market economy. Hong Kong, meanwhile, has been using the mixed market model for years. These signs on a busy Hong Kong street, for instance, are promoting a variety of goods and services provided by merchants along the street.

Geoff A Howard/Alamy

And the People's Republic of China, the world's most important planned economy, is increasingly allowing certain forms of private ownership and entrepreneurship (although with government oversight).

When a government is making a change from a planned economy to a market economy, it usually begins to adopt market mechanisms through **privatization,** the process of converting government enterprises into privately owned companies. In Poland, for example, the national airline was sold to a group of private investors. In recent years, this practice has spread to many other countries as well. For example, the postal system in many countries is government-owned and government-managed. The Netherlands, however, privatized its TNT Post Group N.V., and it is already among the world's most efficient post-office operations. Canada has also privatized its air traffic control system. In each case, the new enterprise reduced its payroll, boosted efficiency and productivity, and quickly became profitable. More recently the government of Iran has privatized numerous oil refineries and petrochemical plants that were previously state owned (although they have not revealed their productivity data).

In the partially planned system called **socialism,** the government owns and operates selected major industries. In such mixed market economies, the government may control banking, transportation, or industries producing basic goods such as oil and steel. Smaller businesses, such as clothing stores and restaurants, are privately owned. Many Western European countries, including England and France, allow free market operations in most economic areas but keep government control of others, such as health care. And when the U.S. government took an ownership stake in General Motors and Chrysler as part of the recession-driven bailout in 2009, many critics of President Obama called the decision an act of socialism.

Privatization *process of converting government enterprises into privately owned companies*

Socialism *planned economic system in which the government owns and operates only selected major sources of production*

finding a better way

Blending Capitalism and Social Responsibility at Mercy Corps

Mercy Corps, a nongovernmental, nonprofit organization that provides humanitarian aid and development assistance around the world, is one of the top *social business enterprises (SBEs)* in the United States. What's an SBE? It's a business formed to pursue social objectives in such areas as health, education, poverty, or the environment. Legally speaking, an SBE is a *non-loss/non-dividend company*: It strives for sustainability in its operations, and investors don't take profits; earnings are used to expand the organization and enhance its efforts to achieve its goals. The idea originated with Muhammad Yunus, a Bangladeshi economist and banker who's also responsible for the concept of *microcredit*, the principle of making small loans (called *microloans*) to entrepreneurs who can't meet the minimum qualifications for credit from traditional sources.

Today, microcredit is actually one form of *microfinance*—providing a broad range of financial services to the same type of underserved borrower. Mercy Corps has long been active in providing immediate response assistance in times of crisis, such as the aftermath of the 2010 earthquake that killed 230,000 people in Haiti. Since the mid-1990s, however, Mercy Corps has concentrated more of its resources on sustainable financial assistance as a means of producing lasting change. "Traditional ways of doing things," says CEO Neal Keny-Guyer, "haven't produced the kind of progress we all hoped for. So we're trying to come up with new approaches that are fully transformational." In 2008, for example, Mercy Corps launched Bank Andara in Indonesia to provide financial services and products to reliable microfinance institutions (MFIs), which, in turn, make direct microloans to entrepreneurs and small businesses.

Keny-Guyer likens his organization's financial focus to that of *venture capitalists*, investors who specialize in companies with significant growth potential (see Chapter 3). "You could say we're social VCs," he says, and he hopes to exercise financial strength in the public sphere in much the same way that VCs exercise it in

Marco Secchi/Alamy

the private sector—"by bringing economic opportunity, through financial services, to low-income businesspeople." In the business world, explains Keny-Guyer, "the infrastructure is aligned to support innovation and entrepreneurship," but "in the public sphere, we haven't had the financial infrastructure to support innovation."

He's convinced, however, that things are changing in the world of SBEs and that "new paradigms for creating social value are emerging." Bank Andara, for example, along with other initiatives in microfinancial outreach, put Mercy Corps on what Keny-Guyer calls "the edge of…prudent risk." It's an important step in SBE strategy, he insists, because undeveloped economies don't need more well-funded retail institutions. What's needed is to develop MFI as a real industry that's integrated with the commercial banks, so there will be a seamless web of financial institutions that serve everyone, from the poorest borrower to the richest, with a full range of products and services. That's the real home run.[6]

The Economics of Market Systems

OBJECTIVE 4
Show

how markets, demand, and supply affect resource distribution in the United States, identify the elements of private enterprise, and explain the various degrees of competition in the U.S. economic system.

Understanding the complex nature of the U.S. economic system is essential to understanding the environment in which U.S. businesses operate. In this section, we describe the workings of the U.S. market economy. Specifically, we examine the nature of *demand and supply*, *private enterprise*, and *degrees of competition*. We will then discuss private enterprise and forms of competition.

Demand and Supply in a Market Economy

A market economy consists of many different markets that function within that economy. As a consumer, for instance, the choices you have and the prices you pay for gas, food, clothing, and entertainment are all governed by different sets of market forces. Businesses also have many different choices about buying and selling their products. Dell Computer, for instance, can purchase keyboards from literally hundreds of different manufacturers. In addition to deciding where to buy supplies, its managers also have to decide what inventory levels should be, at what prices they should sell their goods, and how they will distribute these goods. Similarly, online retailers can decide to use FedEx, UPS, or the U.S. postal service to deliver products bought by customers. Literally billions of exchanges take place every day between businesses and individuals; between businesses; and among individuals, businesses, and governments. Moreover, exchanges conducted in one area often affect exchanges elsewhere. For instance, the high cost of gas may also lead to prices going up for other products, ranging from food to clothing to delivery services. Why? Because each of these businesses relies heavily on gas to transport products.

The Laws of Demand and Supply On all economic levels, decisions about what to buy and what to sell are determined primarily by the forces of demand and supply.[7] **Demand** is the willingness and ability of buyers to purchase a product (a good or a service). **Supply** is the willingness and ability of producers to offer a good or service for sale. Generally speaking, demand and supply follow basic laws:

- The **law of demand:** Buyers will purchase (demand) *more* of a product as its price *drops* and *less* of a product as its price *increases*.

- The **law of supply:** Producers will offer (supply) *more* of a product for sale as its price *rises* and *less* of a product as its price *drops*.

THE DEMAND AND SUPPLY SCHEDULE To appreciate these laws in action, consider the market for pizza in your town (or neighborhood). If everyone is willing to pay $25 for a pizza (a relatively high price), the town's only pizzeria will produce a large supply. But if everyone is willing to pay only $5 (a relatively low price), it will make fewer pizzas. Through careful analysis, we can determine how many pizzas will be sold at different prices. These results, called a **demand and supply schedule,** are obtained from marketing research, historical data, and other studies of the market. Properly applied, they reveal the relationships among different levels of demand and supply at different price levels.

DEMAND AND SUPPLY CURVES The demand and supply schedule can be used to construct demand and supply curves for pizza in your town. A **demand curve** shows how many products—in this case, pizzas—will be demanded (bought) at different prices. A **supply curve** shows how many pizzas will be supplied (baked or offered for sale) at different prices.

Figure 1.2 shows demand and supply curves for pizzas. As you can see, demand increases as price decreases; supply increases as price increases. When demand and supply curves are plotted on the same graph, the point at which they intersect is the **market price** (also called the **equilibrium price**), the price at which the quantity of goods demanded and the quantity of goods supplied are equal. In Figure 1.2, the equilibrium price for pizzas in our example is $10. At this point, the quantity of pizzas demanded and the quantity of pizzas supplied are the same: 1,000 pizzas per week.

SURPLUSES AND SHORTAGES What if the pizzeria decides to make some other number of pizzas? For example, what would happen if the owner tried to increase profits by making *more* pizzas to sell? Or what if the owner wanted to lower overhead, cut back on store hours, and *reduce* the number of pizzas offered for sale? In either case, the result would be an inefficient use of resources and lower profits. For instance, if the pizzeria supplies 1,200 pizzas and tries to sell them for $10 each, 200 pizzas will not be bought. Our demand schedule shows that only 1,000 pizzas will

Demand *the willingness and ability of buyers to purchase a good or service*

Supply *the willingness and ability of producers to offer a good or service for sale*

Law of Demand *principle that buyers will purchase (demand) more of a product as its price drops and less as its price increases*

Law of Supply *principle that producers will offer (supply) more of a product for sale as its price rises and less as its price drops*

Demand and Supply Schedule *assessment of the relationships among different levels of demand and supply at different price levels*

Demand Curve *graph showing how many units of a product will be demanded (bought) at different prices*

Supply Curve *graph showing how many units of a product will be supplied (offered for sale) at different prices*

Market Price (equilibrium price) *profit-maximizing price at which the quantity of goods demanded and the quantity of goods supplied are equal*

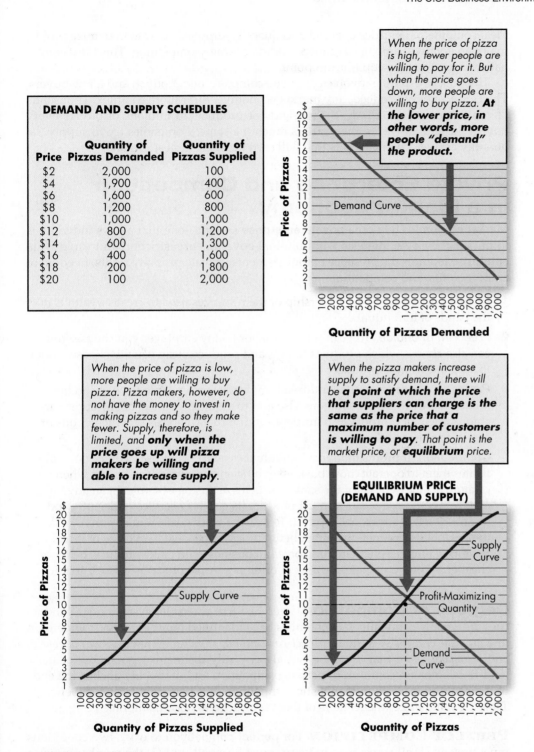

FIGURE 1.2 Demand and Supply

be demanded at this price. The pizzeria will therefore have a **surplus,** a situation in which the quantity supplied exceeds the quantity demanded. It will lose the money that it spent making those extra 200 pizzas.

Conversely, if the pizzeria supplies only 800 pizzas, a **shortage** will result, meaning the quantity demanded will be greater than the quantity supplied. The pizzeria will "lose" the extra profit that it could have made by producing 200 more pizzas. Even though consumers may pay more for pizzas because of the shortage, the pizzeria will still earn lower total profits than if it had made 1,000 pizzas. It will also risk angering customers who cannot buy pizzas and encourage other entrepreneurs to set up competing pizzerias to satisfy unmet demand. Businesses should seek the

Surplus *situation in which quantity supplied exceeds quantity demanded*

Shortage *situation in which quantity demanded exceeds quantity supplied*

ideal combination of price charged and quantity supplied so as to maximize profits, maintain goodwill among customers, and discourage competition. This ideal combination is found at the equilibrium point.

This simple example involves only one company, one product, and a few buyers. The U.S. economy—indeed, any market economy—is far more complex. Thousands of companies sell hundreds of thousands of products to millions of buyers every day. In the end, however, the result is much the same: Companies try to supply the quantity and selection of goods that will earn them the largest profits.

Private Enterprise and Competition in a Market Economy

Private Enterprise *economic system that allows individuals to pursue their own interests without undue governmental restriction*

Market economies rely on a **private enterprise** system—one that allows individuals to pursue their own interests with minimal government restriction. In turn, private enterprise requires the presence of four elements: private property rights, freedom of choice, profits, and competition.

1 *Private property rights.* Ownership of the resources used to create wealth is in the hands of individuals.

2 *Freedom of choice.* You can sell your labor to any employer you choose. You can also choose which products to buy, and producers can usually choose whom to hire and what to produce.

3 *Profits.* The lure of profits (and freedom) leads some people to abandon the security of working for someone else and to assume the risks of entrepreneurship. Anticipated profits also influence individuals' choices of which goods or services to produce.

Competition *vying among businesses for the same resources or customers*

4 *Competition.* If profits motivate individuals to start businesses, competition motivates them to operate those businesses efficiently. **Competition** occurs when two or more businesses vie for the same resources or customers. To gain an advantage over competitors, a business must produce its goods or services efficiently and be able to sell at a reasonable profit. To achieve these goals, it must convince customers that its products are either better or less expensive than those of its competitors. Competition, therefore, forces all businesses to make products better or cheaper. A company that produces inferior, expensive products is likely to fail.

Degrees of Competition Even in a free enterprise system, not all industries are equally competitive. Economists have identified four degrees of competition in a private enterprise system: *perfect competition, monopolistic competition, oligopoly,* and *monopoly*. Note that these are not always truly distinct categories but actually tend to fall along a continuum; perfect competition and monopoly anchor the ends of the continuum, with monopolistic competition and oligopoly falling in between. Table 1.1 summarizes the features of these four degrees of competition.

Perfect Competition *market or industry characterized by numerous small firms producing an identical product*

PERFECT COMPETITION For **perfect competition** to exist, two conditions must prevail: (1) all firms in an industry must be small, and (2) the number of firms in the industry must be large. Under these conditions, no single firm is powerful enough to influence the price of its product. Prices are, therefore, determined by such market forces as supply and demand.

In addition, these two conditions also reflect four principles:

1 The products of each firm are so similar that buyers view them as identical to those of other firms.

2 Both buyers and sellers know the prices that others are paying and receiving in the marketplace.

3 Because each firm is small, it is easy for firms to enter or leave the market.

4 Going prices are set exclusively by supply and demand and accepted by both sellers and buyers.

table 1.1 Degrees of Competition

Characteristic	Perfect Competition	Monopolistic Competition	Oligopoly	Monopoly
Example	Local farmer	Stationery store	Steel industry	Public utility
Number of competitors	Many	Many, but fewer than in perfect competition	Few	None
Ease of entry into industry	Relatively easy	Fairly easy	Difficult	Regulated by government
Similarity of goods or services offered by competing firms	Identical	Similar	Can be similar or different	No directly competing goods or services
Level of control over price by individual firms	None	Some	Some	Considerable

U.S. agriculture is a good example of perfect competition. The wheat produced on one farm is the same as that from another. Both producers and buyers are aware of prevailing market prices. It is relatively easy to start producing wheat and relatively easy to stop when it's no longer profitable.

MONOPOLISTIC COMPETITION In **monopolistic competition,** there are numerous sellers trying to make their products at least seem to be different from those of competitors. Although there are many sellers involved in monopolistic competition, there tend to be fewer than in pure competition. Differentiating strategies include brand names (Tide versus Cheer versus in-store house brands), design or styling (Diesel versus Lucky versus True Religion jeans), and advertising (Coke versus Pepsi versus Dr. Pepper). For example, in an effort to attract health-conscious consumers, Kraft Foods promotes such differentiated products as low-fat Cool Whip, low-calorie Jell-O, and sugar-free Kool-Aid.

Monopolistically competitive businesses may be large or small, but they can still enter or leave the market easily. For example, many small clothing stores compete successfully with large apparel retailers, such as Abercrombie & Fitch, Banana Republic, and J. Crew. A good case in point is bebe stores. The small clothing chain controls its own manufacturing facilities and can respond just as quickly as firms such as the Gap to changes in fashion tastes. Likewise, many single-store clothing businesses in college towns compete by developing their own T-shirt and cap designs with copyrighted slogans and logos.

Product differentiation also gives sellers some control over prices. For instance, even though Target shirts may have similar styling and other features, Ralph Lauren Polo shirts can be priced with little regard for lower Target prices. But the large number of buyers relative to sellers applies potential limits to prices; although Polo might be able to sell shirts for $20 more than a comparable Target shirt, it could not sell as many shirts if they were priced at $200 more.

OLIGOPOLY When an industry has only a handful of sellers, an **oligopoly** exists. As a general rule, these sellers are quite large. The entry of new competitors is hard because large capital investment is needed. Thus, oligopolistic industries (the automobile, airline, and steel industries) tend to stay that way. Only two companies make large commercial aircraft: Boeing (a U.S. company) and Airbus (a European consortium). Furthermore, as the trend toward globalization continues, most experts believe that oligopolies will become increasingly prevalent.

Oligopolists have more control over their strategies than do monopolistically competitive firms, but the actions of one firm can significantly affect the sales of every other firm in the industry. For example, when one firm cuts prices or offers incentives to increase sales, the others usually protect sales by doing the same.

Monopolistic Competition *market or industry characterized by numerous buyers and relatively numerous sellers trying to differentiate their products from those of competitors*

Oligopoly *market or industry characterized by a handful of (generally large) sellers with the power to influence the prices of their products*

entrepreneurship and new ventures

Business...and Pleasure

Americans are multitaskers. We sip lattes while driving, we walk the dog while checking stock quotes, and we pay our bills online while watching TV; it is no surprise that this trend has taken on bigger dimensions. In many sectors, business and entertainment are no longer considered two separate entities. Entertainment used to be defined as amusement parks, miniature golf, baseball games, and movies. Business was business: work, dine, shop, etc. But now, in a recessionary market economy, industries feel even more pressure to mix business with entertainment. The brightly colored play structures in McDonald's and the first mall roller coaster paved the way for this upsurge of integration that is now almost impossible to avoid.

Apple and Starbucks have a partnership that allows customers to preview Apple iTunes songs while waiting in line for their coffee. The customers also have the option to buy or download music onto their iPod touch, iPhone, PC, or Mac. JetBlue has partnered with XM Radio to offer passengers a sample of satellite radio, United Airlines broadcasts DirecTV satellite television on some of its flights, and several other airlines provide Internet access. Select Walmart stores host live broadcasts of concerts

Ian Shaw/Alamy

enticing shoppers to linger just a little longer. This growing trend is not likely to change anytime soon. But businesses should be wary of new business cycles created in the entertainment realm. Entertainment-driven corporations are always at a high risk of deflation when the economy falters. Those businesses that rely on partnerships with these high-risk firms may not be as grounded as they seem.

Likewise, when one firm raises prices, others generally follow suit. Therefore, the prices of comparable products are usually similar. When an airline announces new fare discounts, others adopt the same strategy almost immediately. Just as quickly, when discounts end for one airline, they usually end for everyone else.

Monopoly *market or industry in which there is only one producer that can therefore set the prices of its products*

MONOPOLY A **monopoly** exists when an industry or market has only one producer (or else is so dominated by one producer that other firms cannot compete with it). A sole supplier enjoys complete control over the prices of its products. Its only constraint is a decrease in consumer demand as a result of increased prices. In the United States, laws, such as the Sherman Antitrust Act (1890) and the Clayton Act (1914), forbid many monopolies and regulate prices charged by **natural monopolies,** industries in which one company can most efficiently supply all needed goods or services. Many electric companies are natural monopolies because they can supply all the power needed in a local area. Duplicate facilities—such as two power plants and two sets of power lines—would be wasteful.

Natural Monopoly *industry in which one company can most efficiently supply all needed goods or services*

OBJECTIVE 5
Explain
the importance of the economic environment to business and identify the factors used to evaluate the performance of an economic system.

Economic Indicators

Because economic forces are so volatile and can be affected by so many things, the performance of a country's economic system varies over time. Sometimes it gains strength and brings new prosperity to its members (this describes the U.S. economy during the early years of the twenty-first century); other times it weakens and damages their fortunes (as was the case during 2009–2010). Clearly, then, knowing how an economy is performing is useful for both business owners and investors alike.

Most experts look to various **economic indicators**—statistics that show whether an economic system is strengthening, weakening, or remaining stable—to help assess the performance of an economy.

Economic Indicator *a statistic that helps assess the performance of an economy*

Economic Growth, Aggregate Output, and Standard of Living

At one time, about half the U.S. population was involved in producing the food that we needed. Today, less than 1.6 percent of the U.S. population works in agriculture, and this number is expected to decrease slightly over the next decade.[8] But agricultural efficiency has improved because the industry has devised better ways of producing products with more efficient technology. We can say that agricultural productivity has increased because we have been able to increase total output in the agricultural sector.

We can apply the same concepts to a nation's economic system, although the computations are more complex. Fundamentally, how do we know whether an economic system is growing or not? Experts call the pattern of short-term ups and downs (or, better, expansions and contractions) in an economy the **business cycle.** The primary measure of growth in the business cycle is **aggregate output,** the total quantity of goods and services produced by an economic system during a given period.[9]

Business Cycle *short-term pattern of economic expansions and contractions*

Aggregate Output *the total quantity of goods and services produced by an economic system during a given period*

To put it simply, an increase in aggregate output is growth (or economic growth). When output grows more quickly than the population, two things usually follow:

- Output per capita—the quantity of goods and services per person—goes up.

- The system provides more of the goods and services that people want.

When these two things occur, people living in an economic system benefit from a higher **standard of living,** which refers to the total quantity and quality of goods and services that they can purchase with the currency used in their economic system. To know how much your standard of living is improving, you need to know how much your nation's economic system is growing (see Table 1.2).[10] For instance, although the U.S. economy reflects overall growth in most years, in 2009 the economy actually shrank by 2.6 percent due to the recession.

Standard of Living *the total quantity and quality of goods and services people can purchase with the currency used in their economic system*

Gross Domestic Product   **Gross domestic product (GDP)** refers to the total value of all goods and services produced within a given period by a national economy through domestic factors of production. GDP is a measure of aggregate output. Generally speaking, if GDP is going up, aggregate output is going up; if aggregate output is going up, the nation is experiencing *economic growth*.

Gross Domestic Product (GDP) *total value of all goods and services produced within a given period by a national economy through domestic factors of production*

Sometimes, economists also use the term **gross national product (GNP),** which refers to the total value of all goods and services produced by a national economy within a given period regardless of where the factors of production are located. What, precisely, is the difference between GDP and GNP? Consider a General Motors automobile plant in Brazil. The profits earned by the factory are included in U.S. GNP—but not in GDP—because its output is not produced domestically (that is, in the United States). Conversely, those profits are included in Brazil's GDP—but not GNP—because they are produced domestically (that is, in Brazil). Calculations quickly become complex because of different factors of production. The labor, for example, will be mostly Brazilian but the capital mostly American. Thus, wages paid to Brazilian workers are part of Brazil's GNP even though profits are not.

Gross National Product (GNP) *total value of all goods and services produced by a national economy within a given period regardless of where the factors of production are located*

REAL GROWTH RATE GDP and GNP usually differ by less than 1 percent, but economists argue that GDP is a more accurate indicator of domestic economic performance because it focuses only on domestic factors of production. With that in mind, let's look at the middle column in Table 1.2. Here we find that the real growth rate of U.S. GDP—the growth rate of GDP *adjusted for inflation and changes in the value of the country's currency*—was 1.8 percent in 2011. But what does this number actually mean? Remember that *growth depends on output increasing at a faster rate than population.*

table 1.2 U.S. GDP and GDP per Capita

2011 GDP ($ Trillion)	2011 GDP: Real Growth Rate (%)	2011 GDP per Capita: Purchasing Power Parity
$15.08	1.8%	$48,300

GDP, gross domestic product

The U.S. population is growing at a rate of 0.92 percent per year.[11] The *real growth rate* of the U.S. economic system, therefore, has for the past few years been only modest.

GDP Per Capita *gross domestic product divided by total population*

GDP PER CAPITA The number in the third column of Table 1.2 is a reflection of the standard of living: **GDP per capita** means GDP per person. We get this figure by dividing total GDP ($15.08 trillion) by total population, which happens to be a bit over about 312 million.[12] In a given period (usually calculated on an annual basis), the United States produces goods and services equal in value to $48,300 for every person in the country. Figure 1.3 shows both GDP and GDP per capita in the United States between 1950 and 2011. GDP per capita is a better measure than GDP itself of the economic well-being of the average person.

Real GDP *GDP adjusted to account for changes in currency values and price changes*

REAL GDP **Real GDP** means that GDP has been adjusted to account for changes in currency values and price changes. To understand why adjustments are necessary, assume that pizza is the only product in a hypothetical economy. In 2010, a pizza cost $10; in 2011, a pizza cost $11. In both years, exactly 1,000 pizzas were produced. In 2010, the local GDP was $10,000 ($10 × 1,000); in 2011, the local GDP was $11,000

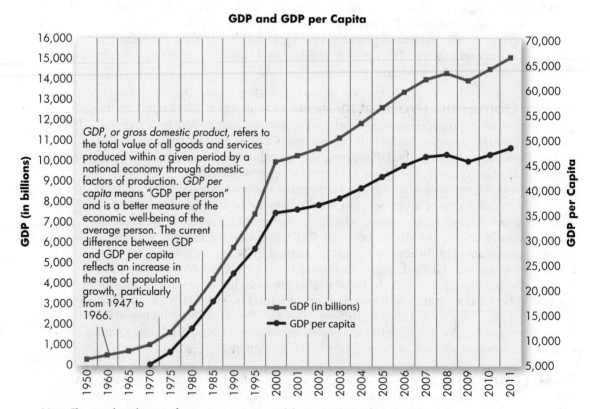

FIGURE 1.3 GDP and GDP per Capita

Sources: http://www.bea.gov/iTable/index_nipa.cfm and http://www.census.gov/popest/data/historical/index.html

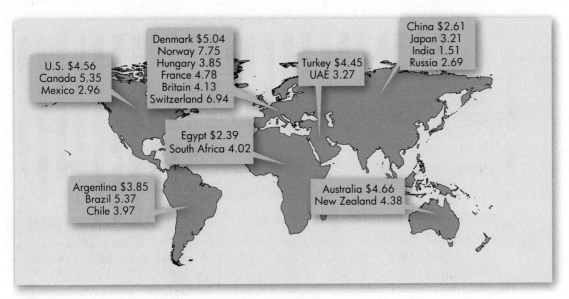

FIGURE 1.4 Price of a Big Mac in U.S. Currency in July 2013

($11 × 1,000). Has the economy grown? No. Because 1,000 pizzas were produced in both years, *aggregate output* remained the same. The point is to not be misled into believing that an economy is doing better than it is. If it is not adjusted, local GDP for 2011 is **nominal GDP**—GDP measured in current dollars or with all components valued at current prices.[13]

Nominal GDP *GDP measured in current dollars or with all components valued at current prices*

PURCHASING POWER PARITY In the example, *current prices* would be 2011 prices. On the other hand, we calculate real GDP when we adjust GDP to account for changes in *currency values and price changes*. When we make this adjustment, we account for both GDP and **purchasing power parity,** the principle that exchange rates are set so that the prices of similar products in different countries are about the same. Purchasing power parity gives us a much better idea of *what people can actually buy with the financial resources allocated to them by their respective economic systems*. In other words, it gives us a better sense of standards of living across the globe. Figure 1.4 illustrates a popular approach to see how purchasing power parity works in relation to a Big Mac. For instance, the figure pegs the price of a Big Mac in the United States at $4.20. Based on currency exchange rates, a Big Mac would cost $6.81 in Switzerland and $6.79 in Norway. But the same burger would cost only $2.34 in Malaysia and $2.12 in Hong Kong.

Purchasing Power Parity *the principle that exchange rates are set so that the prices of similar products in different countries are about the same*

Productivity

A major factor in the growth of an economic system is **productivity,** which is a measure of economic growth that compares how much a system produces with the resources needed to produce it. Let's say that it takes 1 U.S. worker and 1 U.S. dollar to make 10 soccer balls in an 8-hour workday. Let's also say that it takes 1.2 Saudi workers and the equivalent of 1.5 dollars in riyals, the currency of Saudi Arabia, to make 10 soccer balls in the same 8-hour workday. We can say that the U.S. soccer-ball industry is more productive than the Saudi soccer-ball industry. The two factors of production in this extremely simple case are labor and capital.

Productivity *a measure of economic growth that compares how much a system produces with the resources needed to produce it*

If more products are being produced with fewer factors of production, the prices of these products will likely go down. As a consumer, therefore, you would need less of your currency to purchase the same quantity of these products. In short, your standard of living—at least with regard to these products—has improved. If your entire economic system increases its productivity, then your overall standard of living improves. In fact, standard of living improves *only* through increases in productivity.[14] Real growth in GDP reflects growth in productivity.

Productivity in the United States is generally increasing, and as a result, so are GDP and GDP per capita in most years (excluding the 2008 recession). Ultimately,

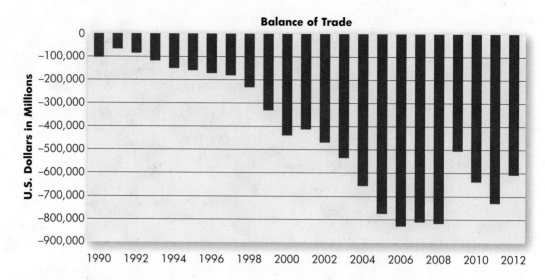

FIGURE 1.5 Balance of Trade
Source: http://www.census.gov/foreign-trade/balance/c0004.html#2008

increases in these measures of growth mean an improvement in the standard of living. However, things don't always proceed so smoothly. Several factors can inhibit the growth of an economic system, including *balance of trade* and the *national debt*.

Balance of Trade *the economic value of all the products that a country exports minus the economic value of all the products it imports*

BALANCE OF TRADE A country's **balance of trade** is the economic value of all the products that it exports minus the economic value of its imported products. The principle here is quite simple:

- A *positive* balance of trade results when a country exports (sells to other countries) more than it imports (buys from other countries).

- A *negative* balance of trade results when a country imports more than it exports.

A negative balance of trade is commonly called a *trade deficit*. In 2012, the U.S. trade deficit was about $600 billion. The United States is a *debtor nation* rather than a *creditor nation*. Recent trends in the U.S. balance of trade are shown in Figure 1.5.

Trade deficit affects economic growth because the amount of money spent on foreign products has not been paid in full. Therefore, it is, in effect, borrowed money, and borrowed money costs more in the form of interest. The money that flows out of the country to pay off the deficit can't be used to invest in productive enterprises, either at home or overseas.

National Debt *the amount of money the government owes its creditors*

NATIONAL DEBT Its **national debt** is the amount of money that the government owes its creditors. As of this writing, the U.S. national debt is more than $58.1 trillion. You can find out the national debt on any given day by going to any one of several Internet sources, including the U.S. National Debt Clock at www.brillig.com/debt_clock.

How does the national debt affect economic growth? Although taxes are the most obvious way the government raises money, it also sells *bonds*—securities through which it promises to pay buyers certain amounts of money by specified future dates. (In a sense, a bond is an IOU with interest.)[15] These bonds are attractive investments because they are extremely safe: The U.S. government is not going to default on them (that is, fail to make payments when due). Even so, they must also offer a decent return on the buyer's investment, and they do this by paying interest at a competitive rate. By selling bonds, therefore, the U.S. government competes with every other potential borrower for the available supply of loanable money. The more money the government borrows, the less money is available for the private borrowing and investment that increase productivity.

Economic Stability

Stability is a condition in which the amount of money available in an economic system and the quantity of goods and services produced in it are growing at about the same rate. A chief goal of an economic system, stability can be threatened by certain factors.

Inflation **Inflation** occurs when an economic system experiences widespread price increases. Instability results when the amount of money injected into an economy exceeds the increase in actual output, so people have more money to spend but the same quantity of products available to buy. As supply and demand principles tell us, as people compete with one another to buy available products, prices go up. These high prices will eventually bring the amount of money in the economy back down. However, these processes are imperfect—the additional money will not be distributed proportionately to all people, and price increases often continue beyond what is really necessary. As a result, purchasing power for many people declines.

Keeping in mind that our definition of inflation is the occurrence of widespread price increases throughout an economic system, it stands to reason that we can measure inflation by measuring price increases. Price indexes such as the **consumer price index (CPI)** measure the prices of typical products purchased by consumers living in urban areas.[16] The CPI is expressed as a percentage of prices as compared to a base period. The current base period used to measure inflation is 1982–1984, which is set at 100 (indicating a percentage). For comparison purposes, the CPI index was 172.2 in 2000, 195.3 in 2005, 218.1 in 2010, and 224.9 in 2011. So, prices in 2011 were more than double the level in the 1982–1984 base period.

Although we tend to view inflation as bad, in most ways it is better than *deflation*, which happens when there are widespread price cuts. Whereas inflation creates instability, it also generally indicates the overall economy is growing (just in an erratic manner). But deflation generally means the overall economy is shrinking, a more serious problem by most measures.

Unemployment Finally, we need to consider the effect of unemployment on economic stability. **Unemployment** is the level of joblessness among people actively seeking work in an economic system. When unemployment is low, there is a shortage of labor available for businesses to hire. As businesses compete with one another for the available supply of labor, they raise the wages they are willing to pay. Then, because higher labor costs eat into profit margins, they raise the prices of their products. Although consumers have more money to inject into the economy, this increase is soon undone by higher prices, so purchasing power declines.

There are at least two related problems:

- If wage rates get too high, businesses will respond by hiring fewer workers and unemployment will go up.

- Businesses could raise prices to counter increased labor costs, but they won't be able to sell as many of their products at higher prices. Because of reduced sales, they will cut back on hiring and, once again, unemployment will go up.

What if the government tries to correct this situation by injecting more money into the economic system—say by cutting taxes or spending more money? Prices in general may go up because of increased consumer demand. Again, purchasing power declines and inflation may set in.[17] During the recession of 2008 and its aftermath, millions of workers lost their jobs as businesses such as Circuit City closed their doors, and others, such as General Motors and Kodak, cut thousands of jobs in an effort to stem losses. Indeed, in early 2010 unemployment in the United States reached a 25-year high of 10.2 percent. By November 2011, as the economy was gradually pulling out of recession, unemployment had dropped to around 8.7 percent, and by November of 2012, official unemployment was 7.7 percent.[18]

RECESSIONS AND DEPRESSIONS Unemployment is sometimes a symptom of a system-wide disorder in the economy. During a downturn in the business

Stability *condition in which the amount of money available in an economic system and the quantity of goods and services produced in it are growing at about the same rate*

Inflation *occurs when widespread price increases occur throughout an economic system*

consumer price index (CPI) *a measure of the prices of typical products purchased by consumers living in urban areas*

Unemployment *the level of joblessness among people actively seeking work in an economic system*

cycle, people in different sectors may lose their jobs at the same time. As a result, overall income and spending may drop. Feeling the pinch of reduced revenues, businesses may cut spending on the factors of production—including labor. Yet more people will be put out of work, and unemployment will only increase further. Unemployment that results from this vicious cycle is called *cyclical unemployment*.

If we look at the relationship between unemployment and economic stability, we are reminded that when prices get high enough, consumer demand for goods and services goes down. We are also reminded that when demand for products goes down, producers cut back on hiring and, not surprisingly, eventually start producing less. Consequently, aggregate output decreases. When we go through a period during which aggregate output declines, we have a recession. During a *recession*, producers need fewer employees—less labor—to produce products. Unemployment, therefore, goes up.

Recession *a period during which aggregate output, as measured by GDP, declines*

To determine whether an economy is going through a recession, we start by measuring aggregate output. Recall that this is the function of real GDP, which we find by making necessary adjustments to the total value of all goods and services produced within a given period by a national economy through domestic factors of production. A **recession** is more precisely defined as a period during which aggregate output, as measured by real GDP, declines. As noted previously, most economists agree that the U.S. economy went into recession in 2008; most also predicted that we were gradually emerging from recession in early 2011. A prolonged and deep recession is a **depression.** The last major depression in the United States started in 1929 and lasted more than 10 years. Most economists believe that the 2008–2011 recession, although the worst in decades, was not really a depression.

Depression *a prolonged and deep recession*

Managing the U.S. Economy

Fiscal Policies *policies used by a government regarding how it collects and spends revenue*

The government acts to manage the U.S. economic system through two sets of policies: fiscal and monetary. It manages the collection and spending of its revenues through **fiscal policies.** Tax rates, for example, can play an important role in fiscal policies helping to manage the economy. One key element of President Obama's presidential platform was an overhaul of the U.S. tax system. Among other things, he proposed cutting taxes for the middle class while simultaneously raising taxes for both higher-income people and businesses.

Monetary Policies *policies used by a government to control the size of its money supply*

Monetary policies focus on controlling the size of the nation's money supply. Working primarily through the Federal Reserve System (the nation's central bank, often referred to simply as "the Fed"), the government can influence the ability and willingness of banks throughout the country to lend money. For example, to help offset the 2008 recession, the government injected more money into the economy through various stimulus packages. On the one hand, officials hoped that these funds would stimulate business growth and the creation of new jobs. On the other hand, though, some experts feared that increasing the money supply might also lead to inflation.

Stabilization Policy *government economic policy intended to smooth out fluctuations in output and unemployment and to stabilize prices*

Taken together, fiscal policy and monetary policy make up **stabilization policy,** government economic policy in which the goal is to smooth out fluctuations in output and unemployment and to stabilize prices. In effect, the economic recession that started in 2008 was a significant departure from stabilization as business valuations dropped and jobs were eliminated. The various government interventions, such as financial bailouts, represented strategies to restore economic stability.

summary of learning objectives

OBJECTIVE 1

Define the nature of U.S. business and identify its main goals and functions. (pp. 32–33)

A *business* is an organization that sells goods or services to earn profits. The prospect of earning *profits*, the difference between a business's revenues and expenses, encourages people to open and expand businesses. Businesses produce most of the goods and services that Americans consume and employ most working people. A healthy business environment supports innovation and contributes to the quality of life and standard of living of people in a society.

OBJECTIVE 2

Describe the external environments of business and discuss how these environments affect the success or failure of any organization. (pp. 33–36)

The *external environment* of business refers to everything outside its boundaries that might affect it. Both the *domestic* and the *global business environment* affect virtually all businesses. The domestic business environment is the environment in which a business conducts its operations and derives its revenues. The global business environment also refers to the international forces that affect a business such as international trade agreements, economic conditions, and political unrest.

The *technological, political-legal, sociocultural,* and *economic environments* are also important. The technological environment includes all of the ways by which firms create value for their constituents. Technology includes human knowledge, work methods, physical equipment, electronics, and telecommunications and various processing systems that are used to perform business functions. The political-legal environment reflects the relationship between business and government, usually in the form of government regulation of business. The sociocultural environment includes the customs, mores, values, and demographic characteristics of the society in which an organization functions. Sociocultural processes also determine the goods and services that a society is likely to value and accept. The economic environment refers to the relevant conditions that exist in the economic system in which an organization functions.

OBJECTIVE 3

Describe the different types of global economic systems according to the means by which they control the factors of production. (pp. 37–41)

Economic systems differ in the ways in which they manage the five *factors of production* (1) *labor,* or *human resources,* (2) *capital,* (3) *entrepreneurship,* (4) *physical resources,* and (5) *information resources.* Labor, or human resources, includes the physical and intellectual contributions people make while engaged in business. Capital includes all financial resources needed to operate a business. Entrepreneurs are an essential factor of production. They are the people who accept the risks and opportunities associated with creating and operating business. Virtually every business will rely on physical resources, the tangible things organizations use to conduct their business. Physical resources include raw materials, storage and production facilities, computers, and equipment. Finally, information resources are essential to the success of a business enterprise. Information resources include data and other information used by business.

Economic systems can be differentiated based on the way that they allocate the factors of production. A *planned economy* relies on a centralized government to control factors of production and make decisions. Under *communism,* the government owns and operates all sources of production. In a *market economy,* individuals—producers and consumers—control production and allocation decisions through supply and demand. A *market* is a mechanism for exchange between the buyers and sellers of a particular product or service. Sellers can charge what they want, and customers can buy what they choose. The political basis of market processes is *capitalism*, which fosters private ownership of the factors of production and encourages entrepreneurship by offering profits as an incentive. Most countries rely on some form of *mixed market economy*—a system featuring characteristics of both planned and market economies. *Socialism* may be considered a planned economy or a mixed economy, with government ownership of selected industries but considerable private ownership, especially among small businesses.

OBJECTIVE 4

Show how markets, demand, and supply affect resource distribution in the United States, identify the elements of private enterprise, and explain the various degrees of competition in the U.S. economic system. (pp. 41–46)

Decisions about what to buy and what to sell are determined by the forces of demand and supply. *Demand* is the willingness and ability of buyers to purchase a product or service. *Supply* is the willingness and ability of producers to offer a product or service for sale. A *demand and supply schedule* reveals the relationships among different levels of demand and supply at different price levels. The point at which the demand and supply curves intersect is called the market or equilibrium price. If a seller attempts to sell above the market price, he will have a surplus where the quantity supplied exceeds the demand at that price. Conversely, a shortage occurs when a product is sold below the equilibrium price and demand outstrips supply.

Market economies reflect the operation of a *private enterprise system*, a system that allows individuals to pursue their own interests without government restriction. Private enterprise requires the presence of four elements: (1) private property rights, (2) freedom of choice, (3) profits, and (4) competition. Economists have identified four degrees of competition in a private enterprise system: (1) *perfect competition*, (2) *monopolistic competition*, (3) *oligopoly*, and (4) *monopoly*. Perfect competition exists when all firms in an industry are small, there are many of them, and no single firm is powerful enough to influence prices. In monopolistic competition numerous sellers try to differentiate their product from that of the other firms. An oligopoly exists when an industry has only a few sellers. It is usually quite difficult to enter the market in an oligopoly and the firms tend to be large. A monopoly exists when there is only one seller in a market. A firm operating in a monopoly has complete control over the price of its products.

OBJECTIVE 5

Explain the importance of the economic environment to business and identify the factors used to evaluate the performance of an economic system. (pp. 46–52)

Economic indicators are statistics that show whether an economic system is strengthening, weakening, or remaining stable. The overall health of the economic environment—the economic system in which they operate—affects organizations. The two key goals of the U.S. system are *economic growth* and *economic stability*. Growth is assessed by *aggregate output, the total quantity of goods and services produced by an economic system*. Although gains in productivity can create growth, the *balance of trade* and the *national debt can inhibit growth*. While growth is an important goal, some countries may pursue economic stability. *Economic stability* means that the amount of money available in an economic system and the quantity of goods and services produced in it are growing at about the same rate. There are two key threats to stability: *inflation* and *unemployment*. The government manages the economy through two sets of policies: *fiscal policies* (such as tax increases) and *monetary policies* that focus on controlling the size of the nation's money supply.

key terms

aggregate output (p. 47)
balance of trade (p. 50)
business (p. 32)
business cycle (p. 47)
capital (p. 37)
capitalism (p. 39)
communism (p. 39)
competition (p. 44)
consumer price index (CPI) (p. 51)
demand (p. 42)
demand and supply schedule (p. 42)
demand curve (p. 42)
depression (p. 52)
domestic business environment (p. 33)
economic environment (p. 36)
economic indicators (p. 47)
economic system (p. 37)
entrepreneur (p. 37)
external environment (p. 33)
factors of production (p. 37)
fiscal policies (p. 52)

global business environment (p. 34)
GDP per capita (p. 48)
gross domestic product (GDP) (p. 47)
gross national product (GNP) (p. 47)
inflation (p. 51)
information resources (p. 38)
labor (human resources) (p. 37)
law of demand (p. 42)
law of supply (p. 42)
market (p. 39)
market economy (p. 39)
market price (equilibrium price) (p. 42)
mixed market economy (p. 39)
monetary policies (p. 52)
monopolistic competition (p. 45)
monopoly (p. 46)
national debt (p. 50)
natural monopoly (p. 46)
nominal GDP (p. 49)
oligopoly (p. 45)
perfect competition (p. 44)

physical resources (p. 37)
planned economy (p. 38)
political-legal environment (p. 35)
private enterprise (p. 44)
privatization (p. 40)
productivity (p. 49)
profits (p. 32)
purchasing power parity (p. 49)
real GDP (p. 48)
recession (p. 52)
shortage (p. 43)
socialism (p. 40)
sociocultural environment (p. 35)
stability (p. 51)
stabilization policy (p. 52)
standard of living (p. 47)
supply (p. 42)
supply curve (p. 42)
surplus (p. 43)
technological environment (p. 34)
unemployment (p. 51)

MyBizLab

Go to **pearsonglobaleditions.com/mybizlab** to complete the problems marked with this icon ✪.

questions & exercises

QUESTIONS FOR REVIEW

✪ 1-1. What are the benefits of businesses? Can a business negatively affect society?

1-2. What are the factors of production? Is one factor more important than the others? If so, which one? Why?

1-3. What is a demand curve? A supply curve? At what point to they intersect?

✪ 1-4. Why is inflation both good and bad? How does the government try to control it?

QUESTIONS FOR ANALYSIS

✪ 1-5. Identify and describe at least three trends in the external environment that affect college enrollment. Explain how each trend affects colleges and universities.

1-6. Give an example of a situation in which a surplus of a product led to decreased prices. Similarly, give an example of a situation in which a shortage led to increased prices. What eventually happened in each case? Why?

1-7. Explain how current economic indicators, such as inflation and unemployment, affect you personally. Explain how they may affect you as a manager.

1-8. At first glance, it might seem as though the goals of economic growth and stability are inconsistent with one another. How can you reconcile this apparent inconsistency?

APPLICATION EXERCISES

1-9. Visit a local shopping mall or shopping area. List each store that you see and determine what degree of competition it faces in its immediate environment. For example, if there is only one store in the mall that sells shoes, that store represents a "local" monopoly. Note those businesses with direct competitors (two jewelry stores) and show how they compete with one another.

1-10. Interview a business owner or senior manager. Ask this individual to describe for you the following things: (1) how demand and supply affect the business, (2) what essential factors of production are most central to the firm's operations, and (3) how fluctuations in economic indicators affect his or her business.

building a business: continuing team exercise

Build a team of three to five classmates. You will be working with this team throughout the semester to make decisions about the launch of a new product.

Assignment

Meet with your team members and develop specific responses to the following:

1-11. Have each member of the team work individually to identify at least three trends in the external environment that will create business opportunities. Come together as a group and create a master list of trends.

1-12. Which trend do you think creates the greatest opportunity for success? Why?

1-13. Identify a product, either a good or a service, which will take advantage of this opportunity. Although you will refine this throughout the semester, write a four to six sentence description of your product and how it will spark buyer interest.

1-14. Who is your competition for this product, either direct competition or substitute products?

building your business skills

PAYING THE PRICE OF DOING E-BUSINESS

Goal

To help you understand how the economic environment affects a product's price.

Background Information

Assume that you are the owner of a local gym and fitness studio. You've worked hard to build a loyal customer base and your facility is top-notch, with the latest equipment and a variety of classes for customers at all fitness levels. Within your area, there are three other gyms, each charging the same price—$40 per month for individuals, $60 per month for a couple, and $75 per month for families. However, you've become concerned because one of your competitors has just announced that they will be reducing membership costs by $10 per month for each of the three categories of memberships. Rumor has it that another facility plans to follow suit in the near future. You can't afford to get into a price war because you are just barely marking a profit at your current price structure.

Method

STEP 1

Divide into groups of four or five people. Each group should develop a general strategy for responding to competitors' price changes. Be sure to consider the following factors:

- How demand for your product is affected by price changes
- The number of competitors selling the same or a similar product

- The methods you can use—other than price—to attract new customers and retain current customers

STEP 2

Develop specific pricing strategies based on each of the following situations:

- A month after dropping prices by $5 per month, one of your competitors returns to your current pricing.
- Two of your competitors drop their prices even further, reducing membership costs by $8 per month. As a result, your business falls off by 25 percent.
- One of the competitors has announced that it will keep its prices low, but it will charge members $2 per session for high demand classes such as Pilates.
- Each of the competitors that lowers the prices makes an adjustment, with reduced rates for families and couples, but they plan to return to $40 per month for single members.
- All four providers (including you) have reduced their monthly fees. One goes out of business, and you know that another is in poor financial health.

FOLLOW-UP QUESTIONS

1-15. Discuss the role that various inducements other than price might play in affecting demand and supply in this market.

1-16. Is it always in a company's best interest to feature the lowest prices?

1-17. Eventually, what form of competition is likely to characterize this market?

exercising your ethics

PRESCRIBING A DOSE OF COMPETITIVE MEDICINE

The Situation

You are a businessperson in a small town, where you run one of two local pharmacies. The population and economic base are fairly stable. Each pharmacy controls about 50 percent of the market. Each is reasonably profitable, generating solid if unspectacular revenues.

The Dilemma

You have just been approached by the owner of the other pharmacy. He has indicated an interest either in buying your pharmacy or in selling his to you. He argues that neither of you can substantially increase your profits and complains that if one pharmacy raises its prices, customers will simply go to the other one. He tells you outright that if you sell to him, he plans to raise prices by 10 percent. He believes that the local market will have to accept the increase for two reasons: (1) The town is too small to attract national competitors, such as Walgreens or CVS, and (2) local customers can't go elsewhere to shop because the nearest town with a pharmacy is 40 miles away.

QUESTIONS TO ADDRESS

1-18. What are the roles of supply and demand in this scenario?

1-19. What are the underlying ethical issues?

1-20. What would you do if you were actually faced with this situation?

team exercise

MAKING THE RIGHT DECISION

The Situation

Pioneer County has recently received a proposal from an international mining company. The company has a number of facilities within the United States and the central location of Pioneer County suggests that it might be the ideal location for a processing facility. Rocks and minerals from existing operations in neighboring counties and estates would be transported to this new facility for processing.

The Dilemma

Pioneer County has a current population of 50,000 residents and has been economically depressed for more than two decades. In the 1950s, a large textile operation was established in the county seat, providing hundreds of jobs from employment in the textile factory. New homes were built and new stores, from grocery stores to clothing stores, to restaurants and dry cleaners, opened up. However, in 1991, the textile company closed the factory and moved all production overseas to save on labor costs. As a result, unemployment has been high and housing values have plummeted. Many stores have closed and county residents often must travel out of the county for jobs and to buy necessities.

The proposed processing facility will bring jobs during construction and operation. It is estimated that there will be 400 new jobs during the one-year construction period. When the plant becomes operational, the company has promised that there will be at least 300 full-time jobs with excellent benefits. Although some managers may be transferred in from other locations, most of these jobs would be filled by current residents of Pioneer County.

Virtually everyone in the county has an opinion on the proposed processing facility, but there is a lot of disagreement. Many residents enjoy the quiet nature of Pioneer County and are concerned about large trucks rolling through the streets of the county once the facility becomes operational. On the other hand, local store owners, many of whom are just barely making a profit, look forward to the economic boom and support

the proposed facility. The county government is considering a number of options:

1-21. Approve the construction of the proposed processing facility based on the potential positive economic impact.

1-22. Reject the proposal and seek out other types of business opportunities.

1-23. Accept the proposal for the processing facility, but place conditions on its size, location, and operations.

Team Activity

Assemble a group of four students and assign each group member to one of the following roles:

- Pioneer County Councilman
- Mining company executive
- Local storeowner
- Environmental activist

ACTION STEPS

1-24. Before hearing any of your group's comments on this situation, and from the perspective of your assigned role, which of the three options do you think is the best choice? Write down the reasons for your position.

1-25. Before hearing any of your group's comments on this situation, and from the perspective of your assigned role, what are the underlying issues, if any, in this situation? Write down the issues.

1-26. Gather your group together and reveal, in turn, each member's comments on the best choice of the three options. Next, reveal the issues listed by each member.

1-27. Appoint someone to record main points of agreement and disagreement within the group. How do you explain the results? What accounts for any disagreement?

1-28. What does your group conclude is the most appropriate action that should be taken by the county in this situation?

1-29. Develop a group response to the following question: Can your team identify other solutions that might help satisfy both extreme views?

cases

What Goes Up...Can Go Even Higher!

Continued from page 32

At the beginning of this chapter you read about how a variety of forces affect retail gasoline prices. Using the information presented in this chapter you should now be able to answer these questions.

QUESTIONS FOR DISCUSSION

1-30. What were the basic factors of production in the petroleum industry? What do you think the factors of production might be in the future?

1-31. Explain how the concepts of the demand and supply of petroleum combine to determine market prices.

1-32. What are the economic indicators most directly affected by energy prices?

1-33. Does the global energy situation increase or decrease your confidence in a capitalistic system based on private enterprise?

1-34. Should there be more government intervention in the exploration for and pricing of petroleum products? Why or why not?

Taking a Bite Out of Internet Radio

For more than a decade, Apple has been recognized as one of the most innovative companies in the world. In 2003, Apple revolutionized the music industry with the launch of the iTunes music store. While there is lots of competition in the digital music market, Apple still controls about 65% of the market. In 2007, Apple unveiled the iPhone—integrating smart phone technology with their popular iPod interface. However, in recent years, competition from competitors like Samsung has cut into Apple's market dominance. Samsung controlled only 4.3% of the smart phone market at the beginning of 2010, but controlled 21.1% by the end of 2012.

In June 2013, Apple announced its intention to roll out the iTunes Radio service in the fall of the same year. Streaming radio is the fastest growing form of music listening. According to the Recording Industry Association of America, while overall music sales were down in 2012, digital music sales were up by 14%. iTunes Radio has more than 200 stations and the ability, like competitor Pandora, for users to create custom stations to fit their personal musical tastes. The service also integrates with the Siri mobile assistant, allowing users to ask Siri "Who plays this song?", an option similar to something currently available through Shazam. There is a free ad-supported option for the service, as well as a yearly ad-free option for $24.99.[19]

However, Apple has no shortage of competition in this venture, and they were late to enter the market. Market leader Pandora offers a free ad-supported version and a subscription service for $36 per year. Additionally, Pandora is available for Android, BlackBerry, and Window's Phone, as well as the iPhone. Pandora is not the only competition. Spotify has more than 20 million licensed songs in its library and Xbox Music has over 30 million choices. Apple's service, in comparison, is built on a library of 26 million songs and builds on the customer loyalty associated with the iTunes Store.[20]

Industry analysts, however, are unsure about Apple's venture into Internet radio. Ken Volkman, chief technical officer at SRV Network concludes "They have a large and loyal customer base established and the capability to be competitive with advertising revenue rates, both providing great incentive for music publishers." Not everyone is convinced. Rocco Pendola, from the finance site The Street, told CNN "iTunes Radio is a Pandora knockoff. It absolutely will not come close to Pandora in terms of functionality and user experience. It can't possibly do that. Pandora is a 13-year old company…Apple is just doing what everyone else has done—copying it."[21]

While the future of iTunes Radio is uncertain, it is clear that the future of Internet radio is bright. Will Apple surge past its competitors or fade into the background? Only time will tell.

QUESTIONS FOR DISCUSSION

1-35. Identify the external environments of business that will affect the success or failure of Apple's iTunes Radio.

1-36. What factors will influence the demand for iTunes Radio?

1-37. In terms of degrees of competition, how would you describe the market for Internet radio? Do you think that this will change in the next five years? If so, how?

1-38. To customize your listening experience, Internet radio services collect data on your listening habits. Are you comfortable with this use of "big data"? Why or why not?

1-39. Do you think that Apple will be successful in this new venture? Do you think that it was a wise decision for them to enter the already crowded market?

MyBizLab

Go to **pearsonglobaleditions.com/mybizlab** *for the following Assisted-graded writing questions:*

1-40. Competition is one of the four elements necessary for private enterprises to exist. Consider all of the degrees of competition and how they may impact the operations of a private enterprise. Select one of the degrees of competition. Write an essay (a) describing under which conditions the degree of competition exists, (b) provide examples of the degree of competition, and (c) describe how the efficiency of this degree of competition's operations may differ from other degrees of competition.

1-41. Stakeholders in businesses often look to economic indicators to determine the health of the economy. These indicators affect the way these stakeholders react to the current economic environment. Choose two economic indicators. Explain how each indicator is important to measuring the health of an economic system. Which of these do you think is more important to private enterprises versus public enterprises? Global enterprises versus domestic enterprises? Owners versus investors? Support your decision.

1-42. Mybizlab Only—comprehensive writing assignment for this chapter.

end notes

1. "If Unrest Spreads, Gas May Hit $5," *USA Today*, February 22, 2011, p. 1A; "Why the World Is One Storm Away from Energy Crisis," *Wall Street Journal*, September 24, 2005, A1, A2; "Higher and Higher—Again: Gasoline Prices Set a Record," *USA Today*, May 25, 2004, p. B1; "Who Wins and Loses When Gas Prices Skyrocket?" *Time*, May 8, 2006, p. 28; "Gas Prices Climbing Despite Hefty Supply," *USA Today*, February 2, 2011, pp. B1, B2; "Fear and Loathing in the Oil Markets," *Time*, March 14, 2011, p. 22; "Low Gas Prices of 2012 on Verge of Evaporating," *USA Today*, January 7, 2013, p. 3A.

2. See Paul Heyne, Peter J. Boetke, and David L. Prychitko, *The Economic Way of Thinking*, 12th ed. (Upper Saddle River, NJ: Pearson, 2010), 171–176.

3. See "Urban Outfitters Swears by Naughty Holiday Catalog," *USA Today*, December 12, 2012, p. 1B.

4. *Hoover's Handbook of American Business* 2013 (Austin: Hoover's, 2013), pp. 790–791.

5. Michael Porter and Mark Kramer, "Creating Shared Value," *Harvard Business Review*, January–February 2011, pp. 62–77.

6. Bija Gutoff, Steve Hamm, "Social Entrepreneurs Turn Business Sense to Good," *BusinessWeek*, November 25, 2011, at www.businessweek.com, accessed on March 22, 2013; "Neal Keny-Guyer—Social Entrepreneurship at Mercy Corps," *Global Envision*, December 11, 2010, at www.mercycorps.org, accessed on March 22, 2013; Richard Read, "Mercy Corps Teams Up with Bank, Telecom in New Haiti Program," *Oregon Live*, September 21, 2010, at http://blog.oregonlive.com, accessed on March 22, 2013.

7. See Karl E. Case and Ray C. Fair, *Principles of Economics*, 10th ed., updated (Upper Saddle River, NJ: Prentice Hall, 2011), 103–105.

8. http://quickfacts.census.gov/qfd/states/00000.html (February 15, 2010).

9. Case and Fair, *Principles of Economics*, 432–433.

10. https://www.cia.gov/library/publications/the-world-fact-book/geos/us.html, accessed on March 15, 2013.

11. http://www.census.gov/popest/data/historical/2010s/vintage_2011/index.html, accessed on March 15, 2013.

12. http://www.census.gov/popest/data/historical/2010s/vintage_2011/index.html, accessed on March 15, 2013.

13. See Olivier Blanchard, *Macroeconomics*, 6th ed. (Upper Saddle River, NJ: Pearson, 2013), 24–26.

14. See Jay Heizer and Barry Render, *Operations Management*, 11th ed. (Upper Saddle River, NJ: Prentice Hall, 2013), 14.

15. Paul Heyne, Peter J. Boetke, and David L. Prychitko, *The Economic Way of Thinking*, 12th ed. (Upper Saddle River, NJ: Pearson, 2010), 491–493.

16. Ronald M. Ayers and Robert A. Collinge, *Economics: Explore and Apply*, (Upper Saddle River, NJ: Prentice Hall, 2004), 163–167.

17. See Heyne, Boetke, and Prychitko, *The Economic Way of Thinking*, 403–409, 503–504.

18. http://www.bls.gov/news.release/pdf/empsit.pdf, accessed on March 15, 2013.

19. Blair, Nancy. "Apple's iTunes Radio Service: 3 Things to Know." *USA Today*. N.p., 11 June 2013. Web. 13 June 2013.

20. Gross, Doug. "Apple Arrives (Late?) to Music Streaming with iTunes Radio." *CNN.com*. Cable News Network, 11 June 2013. Web. 13 June 2013.

21. Peoples, Glenn. "Leading from the Front." *Billboard* May 2013: n. pag. *EBSCO Business Source Premier*. Web. 13 June 2013.

chapter 2 | Understanding Business Ethics and Social Responsibility

How do companies that care about society

balance social welfare with

profits? Do we

punish those that don't?

AFTER READING THIS CHAPTER, YOU SHOULD BE ABLE TO:

OBJECTIVE 1   **Explain** how individuals develop their personal codes of ethics and why ethics are important in the workplace.

OBJECTIVE 2   **Distinguish** social responsibility from ethics, identify organizational stakeholders, and characterize social consciousness today.

OBJECTIVE 3   **Show** how the concept of social responsibility applies both to environmental issues and to a firm's relationships with customers, employees, and investors.

OBJECTIVE 4   **Identify** four general approaches to social responsibility and note the role of social responsibility in small business.

OBJECTIVE 5   **Explain** the role of government in social responsibility in terms of how governments and businesses influence each other.

OBJECTIVE 6   **Discuss** how businesses manage social responsibility in terms of both formal and informal dimensions and how organizations can evaluate their social responsibility.

MyBizLab®

⭐ Improve Your Grade!

Visit **pearsonglobaleditions.com/mybizlab** for simulations, tutorials, and end-of-chapter problems.

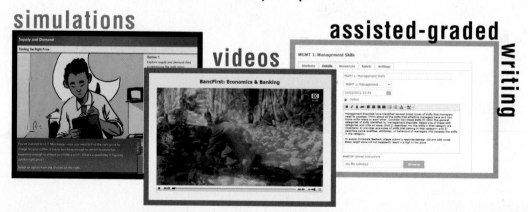

simulations   videos   assisted-graded writing

Over 10 million students improved their results using the Pearson MyLabs.

Is Fair Trade
Really Fair?

Do you know where chocolate comes from? It comes from cocoa, which is produced by roasting and grinding the almond-sized beans that grow on cacao trees. More than 40 percent of the world's supply of cacao beans comes from small farms scattered throughout the West African nation of Ivory Coast, which may ship as much as 47,000 tons per month to the United States. According to reports issued at the end of the 1990s by the United Nations Children's Fund and the U.S. State Department, much of the labor involved in Ivory Coast cocoa production is performed by children, chiefly boys ranging in age from 12 to 16. Most of them have been tricked or sold into forced labor by destitute parents unable to feed them.

How did enslaving children become "business as usual" in the Ivory Coast cocoa industry? One third of the country's economy is based on cocoa exports, and the Ivory Coast is heavily dependent on world market prices for cocoa. Unfortunately, cocoa is an extremely unstable commodity—global prices fluctuate significantly. Because of this instability, profitability depends on prices over which farmers have no control. This problem is compounded by unpredictable natural conditions, such as drought, over which they also have no control. To improve their chances of making a profit, cocoa farmers look for ways to cut costs, and the use of slave labor is the most effective money-saving measure.

This is where the idea of "fair trade" comes in. *Fair trade* refers to programs designed to ensure that export-dependent farmers in developing countries receive fair prices for their crops. Several such programs are sponsored by Fairtrade Labeling Organizations (FLO) International, a global nonprofit network of fair-trade groups headquartered in Germany. FLO partners with cooperatives representing cocoa producers in Africa and Latin America to establish certain standards, not only for the producers' products but for their operations and socially relevant policies (such as enforcing antichild labor laws and providing education and healthcare services). In return, FLO guarantees producers a "Fairtrade Minimum Price" for their products. Since 2007, FLO has guaranteed cocoa farmers a price of $1,750 per ton. If the market price falls below that level, FLO ensures farmers that they will make up the difference. If the market price tops $1,750, FLO pays producers a premium of $150 per ton.

Where does the money come from? The cost is borne by the importers, manufacturers, and distributors who buy and sell cocoa from FLO-certified producers. These companies are in turn monitored by

Rob Byron/fotolia

what's in it for me?

Suppose you were the owner of a convenience store that carries the same candy lines sold everywhere—Snicker's, Hershey, and so forth—and three new candy distributors want you to start selling their products as well. You know that one distributor's candy is made by standard methods in which ingredients are bought for the lowest price possible and all profits go to the manufacturer. Another distributor is promoting a line of candy labeled "fair trade," costs a dollar more per candy bar, and the supplier of the cacao bean gets a about a quarter of that dollar. The third distributor's products cost two dollars more than the first item but you know the grower of the cacao bean would get half of the extra—a dollar more. Because of the price differences you know that you can sell more of the first distributor's candy, a little less of the second distributor's candy, and even less of the third distributor's candy. Which product would you choose to sell in your store?

Business practices today are under more scrutiny than ever before. Business owners and managers are often torn between doing what makes sense for the bottom line (such as increasing profit) versus doing what makes sense for general social welfare. By understanding the material in this chapter, you'll be better able to assess ethical and socially responsible issues facing you as an employee and as a boss or business owner and understand the ethical and socially responsible actions of businesses you deal with as a consumer and as an investor.

In this chapter, we'll look at ethics and social responsibility—what they mean and how they apply to environmental issues and to a firm's relationships with customers, employees, and investors. Along the way, we look at general approaches to social responsibility, the steps businesses must take to implement social responsibility programs, how issues of social responsibility and ethics affect small businesses, and how businesses attempt to manage social responsibility programs. But first, we begin this chapter by discussing ethics in the workplace—individual, business, and managerial.

a network of FLO-owned organizations called TransFair, which ensures that FLO criteria are met and that FLO-certified producers receive the fair prices guaranteed by FLO.

What incentive encourages importers, manufacturers, and distributors not only to adopt FLO-TransFair standards but to bear the costs of subsidizing overseas producers? They get the right to promote their chocolate products not only as "fair trade" but, often, as "organic" products as well—both of which categories typically command premium retail prices. In fact, organic fair-trade chocolate products are priced in the same range as luxury chocolates, but consumers appear to be willing to pay the relatively high asking prices—not only for organic products but for all kinds of chocolate products bearing the "Fair Trade Certified™" label. TransFair U.S. chief executive Paul Rice explains that when consumers know they're supporting programs to empower farmers in developing countries, sellers and resellers can charge "dramatically higher prices, often two to three times higher." Consumers, he says, "put their money where their mouth is and pay a little more."

A 3.5-ounce candy bar labeled "organic fair trade" may sell for $3.49, compared to about $1.50 for one that's not. Why so much? Because the fair-trade candy bar, says TransFair U.S. spokesperson Nicole Chettero, still occupies a niche market. She predicts, however, that, "as the demand and volume of Fair Trade–certified products increase, the market will work itself out.... [R]etailers will naturally start to drop prices to remain competitive." Ultimately, she concludes, "there is no reason why fair-trade [products] should cost astronomically more than traditional products."

Some critics of fair-trade practices and prices agree in principle but contend that consumers don't need to be paying such excessive prices even under *current* market conditions. They point out that, according to TransFair's own data, cocoa farmers get only 3 cents of the $3.49 that a socially conscious consumer pays for a Fair Trade–certified candy bar. "Farmers often receive very little," reports consumer researcher Lawrence Solomon. "Often fair trade is sold at a premium," he charges, "but the entire premium goes to the middlemen."

Critics like Solomon suggest that sellers of fair-trade products are taking advantage of consumers who are socially but not particularly price conscious. They point out that if sellers priced that $3.49 candy bar at $2.49, farmers would still be entitled to 3 cents. The price, they allege, is inflated to $3.49 simply because there's a small segment of the market willing pay it (while farmers still get only 3 cents). Fair-trade programs, advises English economist Tim Harford, "make a promise that the producers will get a good deal. They do not promise that the consumer will get a good deal. That's up to you as a savvy shopper."[1] (After studying the content in this chapter you should be able to answer the set of discussion questions found at the end of the chapter.)

OBJECTIVE 1
Explain
how individuals develop their personal codes of ethics and why ethics are important in the workplace.

Ethics beliefs about what is right and wrong or good and bad in actions that affect others

Ethics in the Workplace

Just what is ethical behavior? **Ethics** are beliefs about what's right and wrong or good and bad. An individual's values and morals, plus the social context in which his or her behavior occurs, determine whether behavior is regarded as ethical or unethical. In other words, **ethical behavior** is behavior that conforms to individual beliefs and social norms about what's right and good. **Unethical behavior** is behavior that conforms to individual beliefs and social norms about what is defined as wrong and bad. **Business ethics** is a term often used to refer to ethical or unethical behaviors by employees and managers in the context of their jobs.

Individual Ethics

Because ethics are based on both individual beliefs and social concepts, they vary from person to person, from situation to situation, and from culture to culture. Social standards are broad enough to support differences in beliefs. Without violating general standards, people may develop personal codes of ethics reflecting a wide range of attitudes and beliefs.

Thus, ethical and unethical behaviors are determined partly by the individual and partly by the culture. For instance, virtually everyone would agree that if you see someone drop $20, it would be ethical to return it to the owner. But there'll be less agreement if you find $20 and don't know who dropped it. Should you turn it in to the lost-and-found department? Or, because the rightful owner isn't likely to claim it, can you just keep it?

Ethical Behavior *behavior conforming to generally accepted social norms concerning beneficial and harmful actions*

Unethical Behavior *behavior that does not conform to generally accepted social norms concerning beneficial and harmful actions*

Business Ethics *ethical or unethical behaviors by employees in the context of their jobs*

Ambiguity, the Law, and the Real World

Societies generally adopt formal laws that reflect prevailing ethical standards or social norms. For example, because most people regard theft as unethical, we have laws against such behavior and ways of punishing those who steal. We try to make unambiguous laws, but interpreting and applying them can still lead to ethical ambiguities. Real-world situations can often be interpreted in different ways, and it isn't always easy to apply statutory standards to real-life behavior. For instance, during the aftermath of Hurricane Katrina, desperate survivors in New Orleans looted grocery stores for food. Although few people criticized this behavior, such actions were against the law.

Unfortunately, the epidemic of scandals that dominated business news over the past decade shows how willing people can be to take advantage of potentially ambiguous situations—and even create them. For example, Tyco sold itself to the smaller ADT Ltd. Because its new parent company was based in the tax haven of Bermuda, Tyco no longer had to pay U.S. taxes on its non-U.S. income. Tyco's subsidiaries in such tax-friendly nations soon doubled, and the company slashed its annual U.S. tax bill by $600 million. "Tyco," complained a U.S. congressman, "has raised tax avoidance to an art," but one tax expert replied that Tyco's schemes "are very consistent with the [U.S.] tax code."[2] Even in the face of blistering criticism and the indictment of its former CEO, Tyco retains its offshore ownership structure.[3]

Individual Values and Codes

How should we deal with business behavior that we regard as unethical, especially when it's legally ambiguous? No doubt we have to start with the individuals in a business, its managers, employees, and other legal representatives. Each person's personal code of ethics is determined by a combination of factors. We start to form ethical standards as children in response to our perceptions of the behavior of parents and other adults. Soon, we enter school, where we're influenced by peers, and as we grow into adulthood, experience shapes our lives and contributes to our ethical beliefs and our behavior. We also develop values and morals that contribute to ethical standards. If you put financial gain at the top of your priority list, you may develop a code of ethics that supports the pursuit of material comfort. If you set family and friends as a priority, you'll no doubt adopt different standards.

Business and Managerial Ethics

Managerial ethics are the standards of behavior that guide individual managers in their work.[4] Although your ethics can affect your work in any number of ways, it's helpful to classify them in terms of three broad categories.

Managerial Ethics *standards of behavior that guide individual managers in their work*

Behavior toward Employees
This category covers such matters as hiring and firing, wages and working conditions, and privacy and respect. Ethical and legal guidelines suggest that hiring and firing decisions should be based solely

managing in turbulent times

Just When They Need It Most

In many ways, it's a pretty bitter irony. Volunteer organizations and charitable enterprises, such as the American Red Cross, the Salvation Army, and the United Way, do much good in our society. When emergency strikes, the Red Cross is usually first on the scene. The Salvation Army provides much-needed relief for people without means. And the United Way supports a wide array of charities and social programs.

All three of these organizations depend on contributions from people and businesses to provide the services people often need. The Red Cross calls on the assistance of more than a million volunteers each year. The Salvation Army volunteers, for example, ring holiday bells outside retailers and collect spare change in red kettles. And the United Way helps organize giving campaigns within business and government organizations.

But when the economy takes a downturn, as it did from 2008 through 2010, charitable giving almost always goes down. Most individuals and businesses find that they have less discretionary income and have to reduce their spending, and giving to help others is one area that gets cut back. Indeed, the Red Cross, Salvation Army, and United Way all reported a drop in income in all three years of the recession. As the economy began to recover in 2011, income for these organizations increased by a small amount and again in 2012. However, it is still well below the prerecession levels of 2006 and 2007.

Ironically, it's in these difficult and turbulent times that more people than ever need just the kind of assistance these

Dorothy Alexander/Alamy

organizations provide. When people lose their jobs, when their savings disappear, when they can't make their mortgage payment, or when second jobs during holiday periods are reduced, many people need to be able to turn to the Salvation Army to help feed their children.

Fortunately, the leadership at these organizations generally anticipates difficult times and has plans in place that allow them to dip into reserves and cut back on their own expenses as necessary. As a result of these efforts, at least for the time being, they have been able to provide the same basic levels of support as in past years. Hopefully, as economic conditions continue to improve they can begin to once again think about expanding services and providing more support to those who need it most.

on a person's ability to perform a job. A manager who discriminates against African Americans or women in hiring exhibits both unethical and illegal behavior. But what about the manager who hires a friend or relative when someone else might be more qualified? Although such decisions may not be illegal, they may be objectionable on ethical grounds.

Wages and working conditions, although regulated by law, are also areas for controversy. A manager may pay a worker less than he deserves because the manager knows that the employee can't afford to quit or risk his job by complaining. While it is hard to judge whether some cases are clearly ethical or unethical, others are fairly clear-cut. Consider the behavior of Enron management toward company employees. Enron management encouraged employees to invest retirement funds in company stock and then, when financial problems began to surface, refused to permit them to sell the stock (even though top officials were allowed to sell). Ultimately, the firm's demise cost thousands of employees to lose their jobs and much of their pensions.

Behavior toward the Organization Ethical issues also arise from employee behavior toward employers, especially in such areas as conflict of interest, confidentiality, and honesty. A *conflict of interest* occurs when an activity may benefit the individual to the detriment of his or her employer. Most companies have policies that forbid buyers from accepting gifts from suppliers because such gifts might be construed as a bribe or an attempt to induce favoritism. Businesses in highly competitive industries—software and fashion apparel, for example—have safe-guards against designers selling company secrets to competitors.

Relatively common problems in the general area of honesty include stealing supplies, padding expense accounts, and using a business phone to make personal, long-distance calls. Most employees are honest, but many organizations remain vigilant. Again, Enron is a good example of employees' unethical behavior toward an organization; top managers not only misused corporate assets, but they often also committed the company to risky ventures to further their own personal interests.

Behavior toward Other Economic Agents Ethics also comes into play in the relationship of a business and its employees with so-called *primary agents of interest*, mainly customers, competitors, stockholders, suppliers, dealers, and unions. In dealing with such agents, there is room for ethical ambiguity in just about every activity—advertising, financial disclosure, ordering and purchasing, bargaining and negotiation, and other business relationships. Bernard Madoff's investment scams cost hundreds of his clients their life savings. He led them to believe their money was safe and that they were earning large returns when in fact their money was being hidden and used to support his own extravagant lifestyle. He used funds from new clients to pay returns to older clients. Madoff's scheme showed a blatant disregard for his investors.

From a more controversial perspective, businesses in the pharmaceutical industry are often criticized because of the rising prices of drugs. Critics argue that pharmaceutical companies reap huge profits at the expense of the average consumer. In its defense, the pharmaceutical industry argues that prices must be set high to cover the costs of research and development programs to develop new drugs. The solution to such problems seems obvious: find the right balance between reasonable pricing and price gouging (responding to increased demand with overly steep price increases). But like so many questions involving ethics, there are significant differences of opinion about the proper balance.

Another problem is global variations in business practices. In many countries, bribes are a normal part of doing business. U.S. law, however, forbids bribes, even if rivals from other countries are paying them. A U.S. power-generating company recently lost a $320 million contract in the Middle East because it refused to pay bribes that a Japanese firm used to get the job. Walmart's Mexico subsidiary has been charged with paying $24 million in bribes to local officials to sidestep regulations and obtain construction permits for new stores.[5] Although these bribes are illegal in Mexico, local experts note that it is also common practice. We'll discuss some of the ways in which social, cultural, and legal differences among nations affect international business in Chapter 4.

Assessing Ethical Behavior

What distinguishes ethical from unethical behavior is often subjective and subject to differences of opinion. So how can we decide whether a particular action or decision is ethical? The following three steps set a simplified course for applying ethical judgments to situations that may arise during the course of business activities:

1 Gather the relevant factual information.

2 Analyze the facts to determine the most appropriate moral values.

3 Make an ethical judgment based on the rightness or wrongness of the proposed activity or policy.

Unfortunately, the process doesn't always work as smoothly as these three steps suggest. What if the facts aren't clear-cut? What if there are no agreed-on moral values? Nevertheless, you must make the judgment and decide how to go forward. Experts point out that judgments and decisions made in a moral and ethical manner lead to increased trust among all parties concerned. And trust is indispensable in any business transaction.

To fully assess the ethics of specific behavior, we need a more complex perspective. Consider a common dilemma faced by managers with expense accounts. Companies routinely provide managers with accounts to cover work-related expenses, hotel bills, meals, and rental cars, or taxis when they're traveling on company business or entertaining clients for business purposes. They expect employees to claim only work-related expenses.

If a manager takes a client to dinner and spends $100, submitting a $100 reimbursement receipt for that dinner is accurate and appropriate. But suppose that this manager has a $100 dinner the next night with a good friend for purely social purposes. Submitting that receipt for reimbursement would be unethical, but some managers rationalize that it's okay to submit a receipt for dinner with a friend when they are on a business trip. Perhaps they'll tell themselves that they're underpaid and just "recovering" income due to them.

Ethical *norms* also come into play in a case like this. Consider four such norms and the issues they entail:[6]

1 *Utility.* Does a particular act optimize the benefits to those who are affected by it? (That is, do all relevant parties receive "fair" benefits?)

2 *Rights.* Does it respect the rights of all individuals involved?

3 *Justice.* Is it consistent with what's fair?

4 *Caring.* Is it consistent with people's responsibilities to each other?

Figure 2.1 incorporates the consideration of these ethical norms into a model of ethical judgment making.

Now let's return to our case of the inflated expense account. Although the utility norm acknowledges that the manager benefits from a padded account, others, such as coworkers and owners, don't. Most experts would also agree that the act doesn't respect the rights of others (such as investors, who have to foot the bill). Moreover, it's clearly unfair and compromises the manager's responsibilities to other stakeholders by violating their trust. This particular act, then, appears to be clearly unethical.

Figure 2.1, however, also provides mechanisms for dealing with unique circumstances. Suppose, for example, that our manager loses the receipt for the legitimate dinner but retains the receipt for the social dinner. Some people will now argue that it's okay to submit the illegitimate receipt because the manager is only doing so to get proper reimbursement. Others, however, will reply that submitting the alternative receipt is wrong under any circumstances. We won't pretend to arbitrate the case, and we will simply make the following point: changes in most situations can make ethical issues either more or less clear-cut.

Company Practices and Business Ethics

As unethical and even illegal activities by both managers and employees plague more companies, many firms have taken additional steps to encourage ethical behavior in the workplace. Many set up codes of conduct and develop clear ethical positions on how the firm and its employees will conduct business. An increasingly controversial area regarding business ethics and company practices involves the privacy of e-mail and other communication that takes place inside an organization. For instance, some companies monitor the Web searches conducted by their employees; the appearance of certain key words may trigger a closer review of how an employee is using the company's computer network. Although some companies argue they do this for business reasons, some employees claim that it violates their privacy.

Perhaps the single most effective step that a company can take is to demonstrate top management support of ethical standards. This policy contributes to a corporate culture that values ethical standards and announces that the firm is as concerned with good citizenship as with profits. For example, when United Technologies (UT), a Connecticut-based industrial conglomerate, published its 21-page code of ethics, it also named a vice president for business practices to ensure that UT conducted business ethically and responsibly. By formulating a detailed code of ethics and

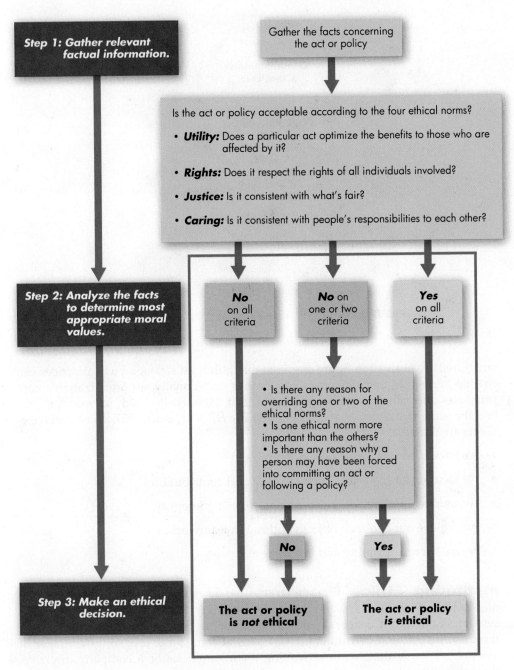

FIGURE 2.1 Model of Ethical Judgment Making

employing a senior official to enforce it, the firm sent a signal that it expects ethical conduct from its employees.

Two of the most common approaches to formalizing top management commitment to ethical business practices are *adopting written codes* and *instituting ethics programs*.

Adopting Written Codes Many companies, like UT, have written codes that formally announce their intent to do business in an ethical manner. The number of such companies has risen dramatically in the last three decades, and today almost all major corporations have written codes of ethics. Even Enron had a code of ethics, but managers must follow the code if it's going to work. On one occasion, Enron's board of directors voted to set aside the code to complete a deal that would violate it; after the deal was completed, they then voted to reinstate it!

Figure 2.2 illustrates the role that corporate ethics and values should play in corporate policy. You can use it to see how a good ethics statement might be

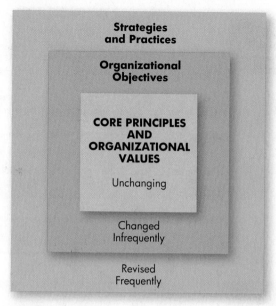

FIGURE 2.2 Core Principles and Organizational Values

structured. Basically, the figure suggests that although strategies and practices can change frequently and objectives can change occasionally, an organization's core principles and values should remain steadfast. Hewlett-Packard, for example, has had the same written code of ethics, called *The HP Way*, since 1957. Its essential elements are these:

- We have trust and respect for individuals.

- We focus on a high level of achievement and contribution.

- We conduct our business with uncompromising integrity.

- We achieve our common objectives through teamwork.

- We encourage flexibility and innovation.

Instituting Ethics Programs   Many examples suggest that companies can learn ethical responses through experience. For instance, in a classic case several years ago, a corporate saboteur poisoned Tylenol capsules, resulting in the deaths of several consumers. Employees at Johnson & Johnson, the maker of Tylenol, all knew that, without waiting for instructions or a company directive, they should get to retailers' shelves and pull the product as quickly as possible. They reported that they knew pulling the medicine immediately was what the company would want them to do. But can business ethics be taught, either in the workplace or in schools? Not surprisingly, business schools have become important players in the debate about ethics education. Most analysts agree that even though business schools must address the issue of ethics in the workplace, companies must take the chief responsibility for educating employees. In fact, more and more firms are doing so.

For example, both ExxonMobil and Boeing have major ethics programs. All managers must go through periodic ethics training to remind them of the importance of ethical decision making and to update them on the most current laws and regulations that might be particularly relevant to their firms. Interestingly, some of the more popular ethics training programs today are taught by former executives who have spent time in prison for their own ethical transgressions.[7] Others, such as Texas Instruments, have ethical hotlines, numbers that an employee can call, either to discuss the ethics of a particular problem or situation or to report unethical behavior or activities by others.

Social Responsibility

Ethics affect individual behavior in the workplace. **Social responsibility** is a related concept that addresses the overall way in which a business attempts to balance its commitments to relevant groups and individuals in its social environment. These groups and individuals are often called **organizational stakeholders**, who are groups, individuals, and organizations that are directly affected by the practices of an organization and, therefore, have a stake in its performance. Major corporate stakeholders are identified in Figure 2.3.

The Stakeholder Model of Responsibility

Most companies that strive to be responsible to their stakeholders concentrate first and foremost on five main groups: (1) *customers*, (2) *employees*, (3) *investors*, (4) *suppliers*, and (5) the *local communities* where they do business. They may then select other stakeholders that are particularly relevant or important to the organization and try to address their needs and expectations as well.

Customers Businesses that are responsible to their customers strive to treat them fairly and honestly. They also seek to charge fair prices, honor warranties, meet delivery commitments, and stand behind the quality of the products they sell. L.L. Bean, Lands' End, Dell Computer, and Johnson & Johnson are among those companies with excellent reputations in this area. In recent years, many small banks have increased their profits by offering much stronger customer service than the large national banks (such as Wells Fargo and Bank of America). For instance, some offer their customers free coffee and childcare while they're in the bank conducting

OBJECTIVE 2
Distinguish

social responsibility from ethics, identify organizational stakeholders, and characterize social consciousness today.

Social Responsibility *the attempt of a business to balance its commitments to groups and individuals in its environment, including customers, other businesses, employees, investors, and local communities*

Organizational Stakeholders *those groups, individuals, and organizations that are directly affected by the practices of an organization and who therefore have a stake in its performance*

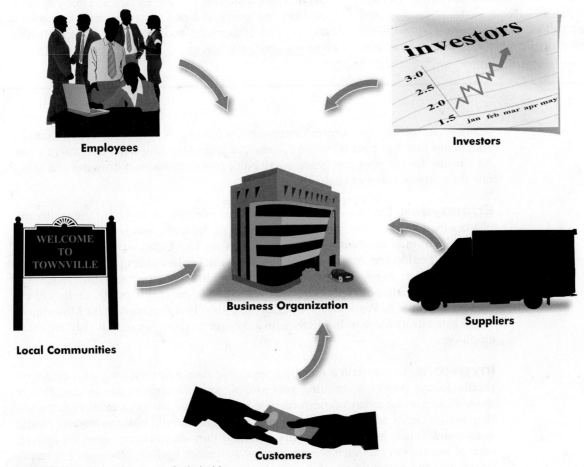

Employees

Investors

Local Communities

Business Organization

Suppliers

Customers

FIGURE 2.3 Major Corporate Stakeholders

entrepreneurship and new ventures

The Electronic Equivalent of Paper Shredding

In virtually every major corporate scandal of the last few years, the best-laid plans of managerial miscreants have come unraveled, at least in part, when supposedly private e-mail surfaced as a key piece of evidence. At Citigroup, for example, analyst Jack Grubman changed stock recommendations in exchange for favors from CEO Sandy Weill and then sent an e-mail to confirm the arrangement. Investigators found that David Duncan, Arthur Andersen's head Enron auditor, had attempted to delete incriminating e-mails shortly after the start of the Justice Department's investigation. After Tim Newington, an analyst for Credit Suisse First Boston, refused to give in to pressure to change a client's credit rating, an e-mail circulated on the problem of Newington's troublesome integrity: "Bigger issue," warned an upper manager, "is what to do about Newington in general. I'm not sure he's salvageable at this point."

Many corporations are nervous about the potential liability that employee e-mail may incur, but some entrepreneurs detect an opportunity in this same concern. A few software-development houses are busily designing programs to meet the needs of cautious corporate customers.

One such software house is Omniva Policy Systems. E-mail senders using Omniva's e-mail software can send encrypted messages and specify an expiration date after which encrypted e-mail messages can no longer be decrypted—the electronic equivalent of paper shredding. In addition, Omniva software can

also prevent resending or printing, and users cannot unilaterally delete their own e-mail on their own initiative. In the event of a lawsuit or investigation, administrators can hit a "red button" that prevents all deletions.

"Our goal," says Omniva CEO Kumar Sreekanti, "is to keep the honest people honest.... We help organizations comply with regulations automatically so they don't have to rely on people to do it." Removing responsibility (and temptation) has become an increasingly popular strategy among executives who, like those at Metropolitan Life, the CIA, Eli Lilly, and many other organizations, are looking to e-mail-security systems to help them avoid the kind of exposure encountered by Citigroup, Arthur Andersen, and Credit Suisse.

---

business. According to Gordon Goetzmann, a leading financial services executive, "Big banks just don't get it" when it comes to understanding what customers want. As a result, for the past few years, small bank profits have been growing at a faster rate than profits at larger chain banks.

Employees Businesses that are socially responsible in their dealings with employees treat workers fairly, make them a part of the team, and respect their dignity and basic human needs. Organizations, such as The Container Store, Starbucks, Microsoft, FedEx, and American Express, have established strong reputations in this area. In addition, many of the same firms also go to great lengths to find, hire, train, and promote qualified minorities. Each year, *Fortune* magazine publishes lists of the "Best Companies to Work for in America" and the "Best Companies for Minorities." These lists attract more individuals who are eager to work for such highly regarded employers.

Investors To maintain a socially responsible stance toward investors, managers should follow proper accounting procedures, provide appropriate information to shareholders about financial performance, and manage the organization to protect shareholder rights and investments. These managers should be accurate and candid in assessing future growth and profitability, and they should avoid even the appearance of impropriety in such sensitive areas as insider trading, stock-price manipulation, and the withholding of financial data. Indeed, many of today's accounting scandals have stemmed from similarly questionable practices. For example, Diamond Foods, distributor of nuts and popcorn snacks, has had to restate its earnings twice in the last two years after announcing it had improperly accounted for $80 million in payments to almond growers.[8] Similarly, Hewlett-Packard has been dealing with an accounting scandal involving how it handled various transactions when it bought a British software developer for $11.1 billion.[9]

Suppliers   Businesses and managers should also manage their relations with suppliers with care. For example, it might be easy for a large corporation to take advantage of suppliers by imposing unrealistic delivery schedules and reducing profit margins by constantly pushing for lower prices. Many firms now recognize the importance of mutually beneficial partnership arrangements with suppliers. Thus, they keep them informed about future plans, negotiate delivery schedules and prices that are acceptable to both firms, and so forth. Toyota and Amazon.com are among the firms acknowledged to have excellent relationships with their suppliers.

Local and International Communities   Most businesses try to be socially responsible to their local communities. They may contribute to local programs, such as Little League baseball, get actively involved in charitable programs, such as the United Way, and strive to simply be good corporate citizens by minimizing their negative impact on communities. Target, for example, donates a percentage of sales to the local communities where it does business. The company says it gives over $3.4 million each week to neighborhoods, programs, and schools across the country.[10]

The stakeholder model can also provide some helpful insights into the conduct of managers in international business. In particular, to the extent that an organization acknowledges its commitments to its stakeholders, it should also recognize that it has multiple sets of stakeholders in each country where it does business. Daimler, for example, has investors not only in Germany but also in the United States, Japan, and other countries where its shares are publicly traded. It also has suppliers, employees, and customers in multiple countries; its actions affect many different communities in dozens of different countries. Similarly, international businesses must also address their responsibilities in areas, such as wages, working conditions, and environmental protection, across different countries that have varying laws and norms regulating such responsibilities. ExxonMobil, for instance, has helped build hospitals and expand schools in the west African nation of Angola, where it has established a growing oil business. The firm also supports a local anti-malaria program in the area.

Contemporary Social Consciousness

Social consciousness and views toward social responsibility continue to evolve. The business practices of such entrepreneurs as John D. Rockefeller, J. P. Morgan, and Cornelius Vanderbilt raised concerns about abuses of power and led to the nation's first laws regulating basic business practices. In the 1930s, many people blamed the Great Depression on a climate of business greed and lack of restraint. Out of this economic turmoil emerged new laws that dictated an expanded role for business in protecting and enhancing the general welfare of society. Hence, the concept of *accountability* was formalized. The new laws and regulations contributed to a sense of laissez-faire feelings about business during the growing economic prosperity of the late 1940s and 1950s.

In the 1960s and 1970s, however, business was again characterized as a negative social force. Some critics even charged that defense contractors had helped to promote the Vietnam War to spur their own profits. Eventually, increased social activism prompted increased government regulation in a variety of areas. Health warnings were placed on cigarettes, for instance, and stricter environmental protection laws were enacted.

During the 1980s and 1990s, the general economic prosperity most sectors of the economy enjoyed led to another period of laissez-faire attitudes toward business. Although the occasional scandal or major business failure occurred, for the most part people seemed to view business as a positive force in society and one that was generally able to police itself through self-control and free-market forces. Many businesses continue to operate in enlightened and socially responsible ways. For example, retailers such as Sears and Target have policies against selling handguns and other weapons. GameStop refuses to sell mature-rated games to minors and Anheuser-Busch promotes the concept of responsible drinking in some of its advertising.

Firms in numerous other industries have also integrated socially conscious thinking into their production plans and marketing efforts. The production of environmentally safe products has become a potential boom area, and many companies introduce products designed to be environmentally friendly. Electrolux, a Swedish appliance maker, has developed a line of water-efficient washing machines, a solar-powered lawn mower, and ozone-free refrigerators. Ford and General Motors (GM) are both aggressively studying and testing ways to develop and market low-pollution vehicles fueled by electricity, hydrogen, and other alternative energy sources. Panera has a few locations where down-and-out customers pay only what they say they can afford. And Nordstrom recently opened a test store where all profits will go to charity.[11]

OBJECTIVE 3
Show
how the concept of social responsibility applies both to environmental issues and to a firm's relationships with customers, employees, and investors.

Areas of Social Responsibility

When defining its sense of social responsibility, a firm typically confronts four areas of concern: responsibilities toward the *environment*, its *customers*, its *employees*, and its *investors*.

Responsibility toward the Environment

The topic of global warming has become a major issue for business and government alike. However, although most experts agree that the earth is warming, the causes, magnitude, and possible solutions are all subject to widespread debate. It appears that climate change is occurring at a relatively mild pace, and we are experiencing few day-to-day changes in the weather. We are, however, increasing the likelihood of having troublesome weather around the globe—droughts, hurricanes, winter sieges, and so forth.[12] The charges leveled against greenhouse emissions are disputed, but as one researcher puts it, "The only way to prove them for sure is to hang around 10, 20, or 30 more years, when the evidence would be overwhelming. But in the meantime, we're conducting a global experiment. And we're all in the test tube." The movie *The Day After Tomorrow* portrayed one possible scenario of rapid climate changes wrought by environmental damage and 2011's *Contagion* and 2013's *World War Z* illustrated the possible effects of a global pandemic.

Controlling *pollution*, the injection of harmful substances into the environment, is a significant challenge for contemporary business. Although noise pollution is now attracting increased concern, air, water, and land pollution remain the greatest problems in need of solutions from governments and businesses alike. In the following sections, we focus on the nature of the problems in these areas and on some of the current efforts to address them.

Air Pollution Air pollution results when several factors combine to lower air quality. Carbon monoxide emitted by cars contributes to air pollution, as do smoke and other chemicals produced by manufacturing plants. Air quality is usually worst in certain geographic locations, such as the Denver area and the Los Angeles basin, where pollutants tend to get trapped in the atmosphere. For this reason, the air around Mexico City is generally considered to be the most polluted in the entire world.

Legislation has gone a long way toward controlling air pollution. Under new laws, many companies must now install special devices to limit the pollutants they expel into the air, but such efforts are costly. Air pollution is compounded by such

finding a better way

Zero Waste

DuPont was once a major generator of trash, routinely dumping thousands of tons of waste materials in landfills each year. But a few years ago, the firm announced its intentions to dramatically reduce the waste it was sending to landfills, with a goal of achieving total recycling wherever possible. To initiate this effort, the firm first set a standard for each of its business units and facilities. Next, it developed procedures for monitoring progress toward those standards.

Take DuPont's Building Innovations unit, for example, which makes products such as kitchen countertops and Tyvek building wrap. In 2008 the business was sending 81 million pounds of waste to landfills each year. But by January 2013, it was not sending anything to landfills! Among the new practices leading to this milestone are:

rob245/Fotolia

- Composting cafeteria waste and using it in landscaping;

- Repairing shipping pallets to extend their use life, and shredding those not repairable for use as animal bedding;

- Recycling countertop waste into landscape stone.

There is even a new term that has been coined to reflect this accomplishment: *zero-landfill status*. DuPont isn't alone, of course. GM recently reported that 81 of its North American manufacturing plants have achieved zero-landfill status. Moreover, GM also says that it recycles 92 percent of all wasted generated by its facilities worldwide. Honda reports that 10 of its 14 North American factories have achieved zero-landfill status. And

Toyota claims that its North American operations are at "near" zero-landfill status.

Outside of the auto industry, Boeing says that a renovated Chinook helicopter plant is at zero-landfill status. And PepsiCo's Frito-Lay facilities are, in the words of the company, approaching zero-landfill status at some of its facilities. For now, though, there are still a few roadblocks and challenges faced by businesses trying to improve their environmental footprint through control procedures. For one thing, some waste products are simply difficult to recycle. For example, DuPont noted that reducing waste by 80 percent was surprisingly easy, but that last 20 percent posed real challenges. There is also no independent resource for verifying zero-landfill status. Regardless, though, critics agree that even if a firm takes small liberties in reporting waste reductions they are still making progress.[13]

problems as acid rain, which occurs when sulfur is pumped into the atmosphere, mixes with natural moisture, and falls to the ground as rain. Much of the damage to forests and streams in the eastern United States and Canada has been attributed to acid rain originating in sulfur from manufacturing and power plants in the midwestern United States. The North American Free Trade Agreement (NAFTA) also includes provisions that call for increased controls on air pollution, especially targeting areas that affect more than one member nation.

Water Pollution Water becomes polluted primarily from chemical and waste dumping. For years, businesses and cities dumped waste into rivers, streams, and lakes with little regard for the consequences. Cleveland's Cuyahoga River was once so polluted that it literally burst into flames one hot summer day.

Thanks to new legislation and increased awareness, water quality in many areas of the United States is improving. The Cuyahoga River is now home to fish and is even used for recreation. Laws in New York and Florida forbidding dumping of phosphates (an ingredient found in many detergents) have helped to make Lake Erie and other major waters safe again for fishing and swimming. Both the Passaic River in New Jersey and the Hudson River in New York are much cleaner now than they were just a few years ago as a result of these new laws.

Land Pollution Two key issues characterize land pollution. The first is how to restore the quality of land that has already been damaged. Land and water damaged by toxic waste, for example, must be cleaned up for the simple reason that people still need to use them. The second problem is the prevention of future contamination. New forms of solid-waste disposal constitute one response to these problems. Combustible wastes can be separated and used as fuels in industrial boilers, and decomposition can be accelerated by exposing waste matter to certain microorganisms.

TOXIC WASTE DISPOSAL An especially controversial problem in land pollution is toxic waste disposal. Toxic wastes are dangerous chemical or radioactive by-products of manufacturing processes. U.S. manufacturers produce between 40 and 60 million tons of such material each year. As a rule, toxic waste must be stored; it cannot be destroyed or processed into harmless material. Few people, however, want toxic waste storage sites in their backyards. A few years ago, American Airlines pled guilty—and became the first major airline to gain a criminal record—to a felony charge that it had mishandled some hazardous materials packed as cargo in passenger airplanes. Although fully acknowledging the firm's guilt, Anne McNamara, American's general counsel, argued that "this is an incredibly complicated area with many layers of regulation. It's very easy to inadvertently step over the line."

RECYCLING Recycling is another controversial area in land pollution. Recycling, the reconversion of waste materials into useful products, has become an issue not only for municipal and state governments but also for many companies engaged in high-waste activities. Certain products, such as aluminum cans and glass, can be efficiently recycled, whereas others are more troublesome. For example, brightly colored plastics, such as some detergent and juice bottles, must be recycled separately from clear plastics, such as milk jugs. Most plastic bottle caps, meanwhile, contain a vinyl lining that can spoil a normal recycling batch. Nevertheless, many local communities actively support various recycling programs, including curbside pickup of aluminum, plastics, glass, and pulp paper. Unfortunately, consumer awareness and interest in this area—and the policy priorities of businesses—are more acute at some times than at others.

Responsibility toward Customers

A company that does not act responsibly toward its customers will ultimately lose their trust and business. To encourage responsibility, the Federal Trade Commission (FTC) regulates advertising and pricing practices, and the Food and Drug Administration (FDA) enforces labeling guidelines for food products. These government regulating bodies can impose penalties against violators, who may also face civil litigation. For example, in 2006, the FTC fined the social networking site Xanga $1 million for allowing children under the age of 13 to create accounts in clear violation of the Children's Online Privacy Protection Act.[14] Table 2.1 summarizes the central elements of so-called "green marketing," the marketing of environmentally friendly goods.

Consumerism *form of social activism dedicated to protecting the rights of consumers in their dealings with businesses*

Consumer Rights Current interest in business responsibility toward customers can be traced to the rise of **consumerism**, social activism dedicated to protecting the rights of consumers in their dealings with businesses. The first formal declaration of consumer rights protection came in the early 1960s, when President John F. Kennedy identified four basic consumer rights. Since then, general agreement on two additional rights has emerged; these rights are described in Figure 2.4. The Consumer Bill of Rights is backed by numerous federal and state laws.

Merck provides an instructive example of what can happen to a firm that violates one or more of these consumer rights. For several years the firm aggressively marketed the painkiller Vioxx, which it was forced to recall in 2004 after clinical trials linked it to an increased risk of heart attacks and strokes. After the recall was announced, it was revealed that Merck had known about these risks as early as 2000 and downplayed them so that they could continue selling it. In 2007, Merck agreed to pay $4.85 billion to individuals or families of those who were injured or died as a result of taking the drug.[15]

table 2.1 The Elements of Green Marketing

- **Production Processes** Businesses, such as Ford Motors and General Electric, modify their production processes to limit the consumption of valuable resources such as fossil fuels by increasing energy efficiency and reducing their output of waste and pollution by cutting greenhouse gas emissions.
- **Product Modification** Products can be modified to use more environmentally friendly materials, a practice S. C. Johnson encourages with its Greenlist of raw materials classified according to their impact on health and the environment. Committed to only using the safest materials on this list, S. C. Johnson eliminated 1.8 million pounds of volatile organic compounds from its glass cleaner Windex.[16]
- **Carbon Offsets** Some companies are committed to replenishing, repairing, or restoring those parts of the environment that are damaged by their operations, especially those that produce carbon dioxide (CO_2). In 2007, Volkswagen began a program of planting trees in the so-called VW Forest in the lower Mississippi alluvial valley to offset the CO_2 emissions of every car they sell.[17]
- **Packaging Reduction** Reducing and reusing materials used in packaging products is another important strategy of green marketing, which Starbucks has pioneered. In 2004 the FDA gave the coffee retailer the first-ever approval to use recycled materials in its food and beverage packaging. Starbucks estimates that using cups composed of 10 percent recycled fibers reduces its packaging waste by more than 5 million pounds per year.[18]
- **Sustainability** Using renewable resources and managing limited resources responsibly and efficiently are important goals for any business pursuing a green policy. For example, Whole Foods Market is committed to buying food from farmers who use sustainable agriculture practices that protect the environment and agricultural resources, such as land and water.

Unfair Pricing Interfering with competition can take the form of illegal pricing practices. **Collusion** occurs when two or more firms collaborate on such wrongful acts as price fixing. In 2007, the European airlines Virgin and Lufthansa admitted to colluding with rivals to raise the prices of fuel surcharges on passenger flights as

Collusion *illegal agreement between two or more companies to commit a wrongful act*

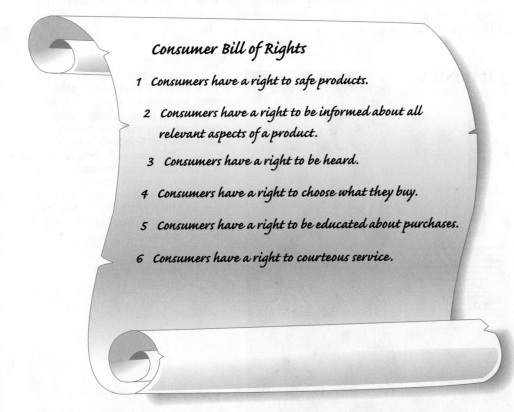

Consumer Bill of Rights

1 Consumers have a right to safe products.

2 Consumers have a right to be informed about all relevant aspects of a product.

3 Consumers have a right to be heard.

4 Consumers have a right to choose what they buy.

5 Consumers have a right to be educated about purchases.

6 Consumers have a right to courteous service.

FIGURE 2.4 Consumer Bill of Rights

much as 12 times the regular price between August 2004 and January 2006. British Airways and Korean Air Lines were heavily fined, but in exchange for turning them in, Virgin and Lufthansa were not penalized.[19] More recently the Justice Department has charged Apple with price fixing and collusion related to its pricing of e-books.

Firms can also come under attack for *price gouging*, responding to increased demand with overly steep (and often unwarranted) price increases. For example, during threats of severe weather, people often stock up on bottled water and batteries. Unfortunately, some retailers take advantage of this pattern by marking up the prices of these items. Reports were widespread of gasoline retailers doubling or even tripling prices immediately after the events of September 11, 2001, and following the U.S. invasion of Iraq in 2003. Similar problems arose after hurricanes Katrina and Rita damaged oil refineries along the Gulf Coast in late 2005 and still again after the BP drilling accident in 2010.

Ethics in Advertising In recent years, increased attention has been given to ethics in advertising and product information. Controversy arose when *Newsweek* magazine reported that Sony had literally created a movie critic who happened to be particularly fond of movies released by Sony's Columbia Pictures. When advertising its newest theatrical releases, the studio had been routinely using glowing quotes from a fictitious critic. After the story broke, Sony hastily stopped the practice and apologized.

Another issue concerns advertising that some consumers consider morally objectionable—for products such as underwear, condoms, alcohol, tobacco products, and firearms. Laws regulate some of this advertising (for instance, tobacco cannot be promoted in television commercials but can be featured in print ads in magazines), and many advertisers use common sense and discretion in their promotions. But some companies, such as Calvin Klein and Victoria's Secret, have come under fire for being overly explicit in their advertising.

Responsibility toward Employees

In Chapter 10, we will show how a number of human resource management activities are essential to a smoothly functioning business. These activities, recruiting, hiring, training, promoting, and compensating, are also the basis for social responsibility toward employees.

This magazine ad for cigarettes is legal in India but not in the United States. Indeed, advertising standards vary in many different ways. In some cases differences stem from sociocultural factors. Ads and billboards in Europe, for example, occasionally include nudity and may be quite provocative while ads in some Asian countries are very conservative. Legal restrictions also affect advertising for products such as tobacco (as shown here), alcohol, and similar products.

Jeff Morgan/Alamy

Legal and Social Commitments By law, businesses cannot practice a wide variety of forms of discrimination against people in any facet of the employment relationship. For example, a company cannot refuse to hire someone because of ethnicity or pay someone a lower salary than someone else on the basis of gender. A company that provides its employees with equal opportunities without regard to race, sex, or other irrelevant factors is meeting both its legal and its social responsibilities. Firms that ignore these responsibilities risk losing good employees and leave themselves open to lawsuits.

Most would also agree that an organization should strive to ensure that the workplace is physically and socially safe. Companies with a heightened awareness of social responsibility also recognize an obligation to provide opportunities to balance work and life pressures and preferences, help employees maintain job skills, and when terminations or layoffs are necessary, treat them with respect and compassion.

ETHICAL COMMITMENTS: THE SPECIAL CASE OF WHISTLE-BLOWERS Respecting employees as people also means respecting their behavior as ethical individuals. Ideally, an employee who discovers that a business has been engaging in illegal, unethical, or socially irresponsible practices should be able to report the problem to higher-level management and feel confident that managers will stop the questionable practices. However, if no one in the organization will take action, the employee may inform a regulatory agency or the media and become what is known as a **whistle-blower**, an employee who discovers and tries to put an end to a company's unethical, illegal, or socially irresponsible actions by publicizing them.[20]

Whistle-Blower *employee who detects and tries to put an end to a company's unethical, illegal, or socially irresponsible actions by publicizing them*

Unfortunately, whistle-blowers may be demoted, fired, or, if they remain in their jobs, treated with mistrust, resentment, or hostility by coworkers. One recent study suggests that about half of all whistle-blowers eventually get fired, and about half of those who get fired subsequently lose their homes or families.[21] The law offers some recourse to employees who take action. The current whistle-blower law stems from the False Claims Act of 1863, which was designed to prevent contractors from selling defective supplies to the Union Army during the Civil War. With 1986 revisions to the law, the government can recover triple damages from fraudulent contractors. If the Justice Department does not intervene, a whistle-blower can proceed with a civil suit. In that case, the whistle-blower receives 25 to 30 percent of any money recovered.[22] Unfortunately, however, the prospect of large cash awards has generated a spate of false or questionable accusations.[23] In the wake of the Madoff investment scams, news broke that a Boston fraud investigator had been trying to convince the Securities and Exchange Commission (SEC) for years that Madoff was engaging in illegal and unethical practices. His warnings, though, had been ignored. This embarrassing revelation led to the SEC's recent announcement that it was reviewing all of its procedures regarding whistle-blowing and a pledge from the SEC chairman that new procedures would be put into place to safeguard against future problems.

Responsibility toward Investors

Managers can abuse their responsibilities to investors in several ways. As a rule, irresponsible behavior toward shareholders means abuse of a firm's financial resources so that shareholder owners do not receive their due earnings or dividends. Companies can also act irresponsibly toward shareholder owners by misrepresenting company resources.

Improper Financial Management Blatant financial mismanagement, such as paying excessive salaries to senior managers, sending them on extravagant "retreats" to exotic resorts, and providing frivolous perks, may be unethical but not necessarily illegal. In such situations, creditors and stockholders have few options for recourse. Forcing a management changeover is a difficult process that can drive down stock prices—a penalty that shareholders are usually unwilling to impose on themselves.

INSIDER TRADING **Insider trading** is using confidential information to gain from the purchase or sale of stocks. Suppose, for example, that a small firm's stock is currently

Insider Trading *illegal practice of using special knowledge about a firm for profit or gain*

trading at $50 a share. If a larger firm is going to buy the smaller one, it might have to pay as much as $75 a share for a controlling interest. Individuals aware of the impending acquisition before it is publicly announced, such as managers of the two firms or the financial institution making the arrangements, could gain by buying the stock at $50 in anticipation of selling it for $75 after the proposed acquisition is announced.

Informed executives can also avoid financial loss by selling stock that's about to drop in value. Legally, stock can only be sold on the basis of public information available to all investors. Potential violations of this regulation were at the heart of the 2002 Martha Stewart scandal. Sam Waksal, president of ImClone, learned that the company's stock was going to drop in value and hastily tried to sell his own stock. He also allegedly tipped off close friend Stewart, who subsequently sold her stock as well. Stewart, who argued that she never received Waksal's call and sold her stock only because she wanted to use the funds elsewhere, eventually pled guilty to other charges (lying to investigators) and served time in prison. Waksal, meanwhile, received a much stiffer sentence because his own attempts to dump his stock were well documented.

MISREPRESENTATION OF FINANCES In maintaining and reporting its financial status, every corporation must conform to generally accepted accounting principles (GAAP; see Chapter 14). Unethical managers might project profits in excess of what they actually expect to earn, hide losses or expenses to boost paper profits, or slant financial reports to make the firm seem stronger than is really the case. In 2002, the U.S. Congress passed the *Sarbanes-Oxley Act*, which requires an organization's chief financial officer to personally guarantee the accuracy of all financial reporting (see Chapter 14).

Implementing Social Responsibility Programs

OBJECTIVE 4
Identify
four general approaches to social responsibility and note the role of social responsibility in small business.

Opinions differ dramatically concerning social responsibility as a business goal. Although some oppose any business activity that threatens profits, others argue that social responsibility must take precedence. Some skeptics fear that businesses will gain too much control over the ways social projects are addressed by society as a whole or that they lack the expertise needed to address social issues. Still, many believe that corporations should help improve the lives of citizens because they are citizens themselves, often control vast resources, and may contribute to the problems that social programs address.

Approaches to Social Responsibility

Given these differences of opinion, it is little wonder that corporations have adopted a variety of approaches to social responsibility. As Figure 2.5 illustrates, the four stances that an organization can take concerning its obligations to society fall along a continuum ranging from the lowest to the highest degree of socially responsible practices.

Obstructionist Stance approach to social responsibility that involves doing as little as possible and may involve attempts to deny or cover up violations

Obstructionist Stance The few organizations that take an **obstructionist stance** to social responsibility usually do as little as possible to solve social or

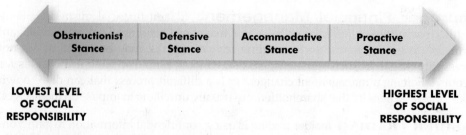

FIGURE 2.5 Spectrum of Approaches to Corporate Social Responsibility

environmental problems, have little regard for ethical conduct, and will go to great lengths to deny or cover up wrongdoing. For example, IBP, a leading meat-processing firm, has a long record of breaking environmental protection, labor, and food processing laws and then trying to cover up its offenses. Similarly, in 2009 a Georgia peanut processing plant owned by Peanut Corporation of America shipped products contaminated with salmonella. The firm's top manager allegedly knew that the products had failed safety tests but shipped them anyway to avoid losing money.

Defensive Stance Organizations that take a **defensive stance** will do everything that is legally required, including admitting to mistakes and taking corrective actions, but nothing more. Defensive stance managers insist that their job is to generate profits and might, for example, install pollution-control equipment dictated by law but not higher-quality equipment to further limit pollution. Tobacco companies generally take this position in their marketing efforts. In the United States, they are legally required to include product warnings and to limit advertising to prescribed media. Domestically, they follow these rules to the letter of the law, but in many Asian and African countries, which don't have these rules, cigarettes are heavily promoted, contain higher levels of tar and nicotine, and carry few or no health warning labels.

Defensive Stance approach to social responsibility by which a company meets only minimum legal requirements in its commitments to groups and individuals in its social environment

Accommodative Stance A firm that adopts an **accommodative stance** meets and, in certain cases, exceeds its legal and ethical requirements. Such firms will agree to participate in social programs if solicitors convince them that given programs are worthy of their support. Both Shell and IBM, for example, will match contributions made by their employees to selected charitable causes.

Accommodative Stance approach to social responsibility by which a company, if specifically asked to do so, exceeds legal minimums in its commitments to groups and individuals in its social environment

Proactive Stance Firms with the highest degree of social responsibility exhibit the **proactive stance**; they take to heart the arguments in favor of social responsibility, view themselves as citizens in a society, indicate sincere commitment to improve the general social welfare, and surpass the accommodative stance by proactively seeking opportunities to contribute. The most common—and direct—way to implement this stance is to set up a foundation for providing direct financial support for various social programs. Table 2.2, using the most recent data, lists the top 25 corporate foundations.

Proactive Stance approach to social responsibility by which a company actively seeks opportunities to contribute to the well-being of groups and individuals in its social environment

An excellent example of a proactive stance is the McDonald's Corporation's Ronald McDonald House program. These houses, located close to major medical centers, can be used for minimal cost by families while their sick children are receiving medical treatment nearby. However, these categories are not sharply distinct; organizations do not always fit neatly into one category or another. The Ronald McDonald House program has been widely applauded, but McDonald's has also been accused of misleading consumers about the nutritional value of its food products.

Social Responsibility and the Small Business

As the owner of a garden supply store, how would you respond to a building inspector's suggestion that a cash payment will speed your application for a building permit? As the manager of a liquor store, would you call the police, refuse to sell, or sell to a customer whose identification card looks forged? As the owner of a small laboratory, would you call the state board of health to make sure that it has licensed the company with whom you want to contract to dispose of medical waste? Who will really be harmed if a small firm pads its income statement to help it get a much-needed bank loan?

Many of the examples in this chapter illustrate big business responses to ethical and social responsibility issues, but small businesses must answer many of the same questions. Differences between the two types of businesses are primarily differences of scale.

At the same time, the ethical issues are largely questions of *individual* ethics. What about questions of social responsibility? Can a small business, for example, afford a social agenda? Should it sponsor Little League baseball teams, make donations to the United Way, and buy light bulbs from the Lion's Club? Do joining the chamber of commerce and supporting the Better Business Bureau cost too much?

table 2.2 Top 25 Corporate Foundations

Rank	Name/(state)	Total Giving ($)	As of Fiscal Year End Date
1	Sanofi-aventis Patient Assistance Foundation (NJ)	392,778,999	12/31/2010
2	Novartis Patient Assistance Foundation, Inc. (NJ)	239,531,453	12/31/2010
3	The Bank of America Charitable Foundation, Inc. (NC)	197,954,354	12/31/2010
4	The Wal-Mart Foundation, Inc. (AR)	164,588,396	1/31/2011
5	The JPMorgan Chase Foundation (NY)	133,757,626	12/31/2010
6	GE Foundation (CT)	112,221,740	12/31/2010
7	Wells Fargo Foundation (CA)	107,542,374	12/31/2011
8	ExxonMobil Foundation (TX)	72,154,563	12/31/2010
9	Citi Foundation (NY)	63,573,500	12/31/2010
10	Verizon Foundation (NJ)	59,365,756	12/31/2010
11	The Coca-Cola Foundation, Inc. (GA)	56,569,252	12/31/2010
12	The PNC Foundation (PA)	54,221,909	12/31/2011
13	Johnson & Johnson Family of Companies Foundation (NJ)	49,556,298	12/31/2009
14	Intel Foundation (OR)	48,108,474	12/31/2010
15	The Merck Company Foundation (NJ)	47,673,821	12/31/2010
16	MetLife Foundation (NY)	39,800,039	12/31/2010
17	The UPS Foundation (GA)	39,497,732	12/31/2010
18	Illinois Tool Works Foundation (IL)	36,176,325	12/31/2011
19	Caterpillar Foundation (IL)	35,807,264	12/31/2010
20	Lucasfilm Foundation (CA)	35,418,825	12/31/2010
21	Eli Lilly and Company Foundation (IN)	31,946,050	12/31/2010
22	BP Foundation, Inc. (TX)	31,248,005	12/31/2010
23	Abbott Fund (IL)	29,545,990	12/31/2011
24	The Bristol-Myers Squibb Foundation, Inc. (NY)	28,850,815	12/31/2011
25	Nationwide Insurance Foundation (OH)	28,260,551	12/31/2010

Source: 50 Largest Corporate Foundations by Total Giving, 2012 © 2013 The Foundation Center. Used by permission.

Clearly, ethics and social responsibility are decisions faced by all managers in all organizations, regardless of rank or size. One key to business success is to decide in advance how to respond to the issues that underlie all questions of ethical and social responsibility.

The Government and Social Responsibility

OBJECTIVE 5
Explain
the role of government in social responsibility in terms of how governments and businesses influence each other.

An especially important element of social responsibility is the relationship between business and government. In planned economies, for example, the government heavily regulates business activities, ostensibly to ensure that business supports some overarching set of social ideals. And even in market economies, there is still considerable government control of business, much of it directed at making sure that business interests do not damage social interests. Alternatively, businesses also attempt to influence the government by attempting to offset or reverse government restrictions. Businesses and the government use several methods in their attempts to influence each other.

How Governments Influence Organizations

The government (national, state, or local) attempts to shape social responsibility practices through both direct and indirect channels. Direct influence most frequently is manifested through *regulation*, whereas indirect influence can take a number of forms, most notably taxation policies.[24]

Direct Regulation   The government most often directly influences organizations through **regulation**, the establishment of laws and rules that dictate what organizations can and cannot do. This regulation usually evolves from social beliefs about how businesses should conduct themselves. To implement legislation, the government generally creates special agencies to monitor and control certain aspects of business activity. For example, the Environmental Protection Agency handles environmental issues; the FTC and the FDA focus on consumer-related concerns; the Equal Employee Opportunity Commission, the National Labor Relations Board, and the Department of Labor help protect employees; and the SEC handles investor-related issues. These agencies have the power to levy fines or bring charges against organizations that violate regulations.

> **Regulation** *the establishment of laws and rules that dictate what organizations can and cannot do*

Another approach that governments can use to regulate business practices is through legislation. For instance, the U.S. Foreign Corrupt Practices Act provides for financial sanctions against businesses or business officials who engage in bribery. They recently investigated Siemens AG, a large German engineering firm, for practices that included routine bribery of foreign officials to win infrastructure construction projects. All told, the firm was alleged to have spent more than $1 billion in bribing officials in at least 10 different countries. Siemens recently agreed to pay the U.S. government a fine of $800 million; German officials, meanwhile, are continuing to investigate both criminal and civil misconduct at the firm. (The U.S. government had the authority to fine Siemens because the German firm has a class of stock listed on the New York Stock Exchange and was thus subject to the Foreign Corrupt Practices Act.)[25] Similarly, another German firm, Daimler AG, has been charged with bribery in 22 countries, helping the company earn more than $50 million in profit. The company was alleged to have given millions of dollars in bribes to foreign officials to win contracts supplying their governments with vehicles. Charges include conspiracy and falsifying records. Daimler agreed to pay $185 million in its settlement.[26]

Indirect Regulation   Other forms of regulation are indirect. For example, the government can indirectly influence the social responsibility of organizations through its tax codes. In effect, the government can influence how organizations spend their social responsibility dollars by providing greater or lesser tax incentives. For instance, suppose that the government wanted organizations to spend more on training the chronic unemployed, people who lack most basic job skills and who routinely have trouble finding jobs. Congress could then pass laws that provided tax incentives to companies that opened new training facilities, and as a result of the tax break, more businesses would probably do so. Of course, some critics argue that regulation is already excessive. They maintain that a free market system would eventually accomplish the same goals as regulation, with lower costs to both organizations and the government.

How Organizations Influence Government

Just as governments can influence businesses, so too can businesses influence the government. Businesses have four main methods of addressing governmental pressures for more social responsibility: (1) personal contacts, (2) lobbying, (3) political action committees, and (4) favors. (During the early days of President Barrack Obama's administration, he implemented several measures designed to restrict or regulate business influence on the government, especially through lobbying.[27])

Personal Contacts Because many corporate executives and political leaders travel in the same social circles, personal contacts and networks offer one method of influence. A business executive may be able to contact a politician directly and present his or her case regarding a piece of legislation being considered.

Lobbying the use of persons or groups to formally represent an organization or group of organizations before political bodies

Lobbying **Lobbying**, or the use of persons or groups to formally represent an organization or group of organizations before political bodies, is also an effective way to influence the government. The National Rifle Association (NRA), for example, has a staff of lobbyists in Washington with a substantial annual budget. These lobbyists work to represent the NRA's position on gun control and to potentially influence members of Congress when they vote on legislation that affects the firearms industry and the rights of gun owners. As noted previously, President Obama has taken numerous steps to control or limit lobbying. For instance, any discussion between a lobbyist and a member of Congress that goes beyond general conversation has to be written in the form of a letter and posted online.

Political Action Committees (PACs) special organizations created to solicit money and then distribute it to political candidates

Political Action Committees Companies themselves cannot legally make direct donations to political campaigns, so they influence the government through *political action committees*. **Political action committees (PACs)** are special organizations created to solicit money and then distribute it to political candidates. Employees of a firm may be encouraged to make donations to a particular PAC because managers know that it will support candidates with political views similar to their own. PACs, in turn, make the contributions themselves, usually to a broad slate of state and national candidates. For example, FedEx's PAC is called FedExpac. FedExpac makes regular contributions to the campaign funds of political candidates who are most likely to work in the firm's best interests. As with lobbying, President Obama has implemented measures to limit the influence of PACs.

Favors Finally, organizations sometimes rely on favors and other influence tactics to gain support. Although these favors may be legal, they are still subject to criticism. A few years back, for example, two influential members of a House committee attending a fund-raising function in Miami were needed in Washington to finish work on a piece of legislation that FedEx wanted passed. The law being drafted would allow the company and its competitors to give their employees standby seats on airlines as a tax-free benefit. As a favor, FedEx provided one of its corporate jets to fly the committee members back to Washington. FedEx was eventually reimbursed for its expenses, so its assistance was not illegal, but some people argue that such actions are dangerous because of how they might be perceived.

OBJECTIVE 6
Discuss
how businesses manage social responsibility in terms of both formal and informal dimensions and how organizations can evaluate their social responsibility.

Managing Social Responsibility

The demands for social responsibility placed on contemporary organizations by an increasingly sophisticated and educated public are stronger than ever. As we have seen, there are pitfalls for managers who fail to adhere to high ethical standards and for companies that try to circumvent their legal obligations. Organizations need to fashion an approach to social responsibility in the same way that they develop any other business strategy. In other words, they should view social responsibility as a major challenge that requires careful planning, decision making, consideration, and evaluation. They may accomplish this through both formal and informal dimensions of managing social responsibility.

Formal Organizational Dimensions

Some dimensions of managing social responsibility involve a formal and planned activity on the part of the organization. Indeed, some businesses are approaching social responsibility from a strategic perspective.[28] Formal organizational dimensions that can help manage social responsibility are (1) legal compliance, (2) ethical compliance, and (3) philanthropic giving.

Legal Compliance   **Legal compliance** is the extent to which the organization conforms to local, state, federal, and international laws. The task of managing legal compliance is generally assigned to the appropriate functional managers. For example, the organization's top human resource executive is responsible for ensuring compliance with regulations concerning hiring, pay, and workplace safety and health. Likewise, the top financial executive generally oversees compliance with securities and banking regulations. The organization's legal department provides general oversight and answering queries from managers about the appropriate interpretation of laws and regulations. Unfortunately, though, legal compliance may not be enough; in some cases, for instance, perfectly legal accounting practices have still resulted in deception and other problems.[29]

Legal Compliance *the extent to which the organization conforms to local, state, federal, and international laws*

Ethical Compliance   **Ethical compliance** is the extent to which the members of the organization follow basic ethical (and legal) standards of behavior. We noted previously that organizations have increased their efforts in this area by providing training in ethics and developing guidelines and codes of conduct. These activities serve as vehicles for enhancing ethical compliance. Many organizations also establish formal ethics committees. These committees might review proposals for new projects, help evaluate new hiring strategies, or assess a new environmental protection plan. They might also serve as a peer review panel to evaluate alleged ethical misconduct by an employee.[30]

Ethical Compliance *the extent to which the members of the organization follow basic ethical (and legal) standards of behavior*

Philanthropic Giving   Finally, **philanthropic giving** is the awarding of funds or gifts to charities or other worthy causes. Target Corporation routinely gives 5 percent of its taxable income to charity and social programs. Omaha Steaks gives more than $100,000 per year to support the arts.[31] Giving across national boundaries is also becoming more common. For example, Alcoa gave $112,000 to a small town in Brazil to build a sewage treatment plant. And Japanese firms such as Sony and Mitsubishi make contributions to a number of social programs in the United States. However, in the current climate of cutbacks, many corporations have also had to limit their charitable gifts over the past several years as they continue to trim their own budgets.[32] And many firms that continue to make contributions are increasingly targeting them to programs or areas where the firm will get something in return. For example, firms today are more likely to give money to job training programs than to the arts. The logic is that they get more direct payoff from the former type of contribution—in this instance, a better-trained workforce from which to hire new employees.[33] And indeed, corporate donations to arts programs declined 5 percent between 2003 and 2012.[34]

Philanthropic Giving *the awarding of funds or gifts to charities or other worthy causes*

Informal Organizational Dimensions

In addition to these formal dimensions for managing social responsibility, there are also informal ones. Organization leadership and culture and how the organization responds to whistle-blowers all help shape and define people's perceptions of the organization's stance on social responsibility.

Organization Leadership and Culture Leadership practices and organizational culture can go a long way toward defining the social responsibility stance an organization and its members will adopt.[35] Ethical leadership often sets the tone for the entire organization. For example, for years Johnson & Johnson executives provided a consistent message to employees that customers, employees, communities where the company did business, and shareholders were all important—and primarily in that order. Thus, when packages of poisoned Tylenol showed up on store shelves several years ago, Johnson & Johnson employees did not need to wait for orders from headquarters to know what to do; they immediately pulled all the packages from shelves before any other customers could buy them without considering how this act would affect the shareholders.[36]

Whistle-Blowing As we noted previously, whistle-blowing is the disclosure by an employee of illegal or unethical conduct on the part of others within the organization.[37] How an organization responds to this practice often illustrates its stance on social responsibility. Whistle-blowers may have to proceed through a number of channels to be heard, and they may even get fired for their efforts.[38] Many organizations, however, welcome their contributions. A person who observes questionable behavior typically first reports the incident to his or her boss. If nothing is done, the whistle-blower may then inform higher-level managers or an ethics committee, if one exists. Eventually, the person may have to go to a regulatory agency or even the media to be heard. For example, Charles W. Robinson, Jr., worked as a director of a SmithKline lab in San Antonio. One day he noticed a suspicious billing pattern that the firm was using to collect lab fees from Medicare; the bills were considerably higher than the firm's normal charges for the same tests. He pointed out the problem to higher-level managers, but they ignored his concerns. He subsequently took his findings to the U.S. government, which sued SmithKline and eventually reached a settlement of $325 million.[39]

More recently, David Magee, a former employee of Mississippi's Stennis Space Center, reported to superiors and federal agents that government employees conspired with Lockheed Martin and Science Applications International Corporation to ensure they would win the contract to work on the Naval Oceanographic Office Major Shared Resource Center, violating the False Claims Act. Allegedly, the defendants shared secret information about the bidding process, ensuring a successful bid. For filing the suit, Magee will receive $560,000 of the $2 million settlement against Lockheed.[40] Harry Markopolos, a portfolio manager at Rampart Investments, spent nine years trying to convince the SEC that Madoff's money-management firm was falsifying the results it was reporting to investors. Only when the U.S. economy went into recession in 2008 did the truth about Madoff come out.[41] In response, the SEC announced plans to overhaul its whistle-blowing system.[42]

Evaluating Social Responsibility

To make sure their efforts are producing the desired benefits, any business that is serious about social responsibility must apply the concept of control to social responsibility. Many organizations now require all employees to read their guidelines or code of ethics and then sign a statement agreeing to abide by it. A business should also evaluate how it responds to instances of questionable legal or ethical conduct. Does it follow up immediately? Does it punish those involved? Or does it use delay and cover-up tactics? Answers to these questions can help an organization form a picture of its approach to social responsibility.

More formally, an organization may sometimes actually evaluate the effectiveness of its social responsibility efforts. For example, when BP Amoco established a job training program in Chicago, it allocated additional funds to evaluate how well the program was meeting its goals. Additionally, some businesses occasionally conduct an **corporate social audit**, a formal and thorough analysis of the effectiveness of a firm's social performance. A task force of high-level managers from within the firm usually conducts the audit. It requires that the organization clearly define all of its social goals, analyze the resources it devotes to each goal, determine how well it is achieving the various goals, and make recommendations about which areas need additional attention. Recent estimates suggest that around 80 percent of the world's 250 largest firms now issue annual reports summarizing their efforts in the areas of environmental and social responsibility.

Corporate Social Audit *systematic analysis of a firm's success in using funds earmarked for meeting its social responsibility goals*

summary of learning objectives

OBJECTIVE 1

Explain how individuals develop their personal codes of ethics and why ethics are important in the workplace. (pp. 64–70)

Ethics are beliefs about what's right and wrong or good and bad. *Ethical behavior* conforms to individual beliefs and social norms about what's right and good, and *unethical behavior* is behavior that individual beliefs and social norms define as wrong and bad. Though ethical behavior and the law are often the same, there can also be ambiguity. *Managerial ethics* are standards of behavior that guide managers. There are three broad categories of ways in which managerial ethics can affect people's work: (1) *behavior toward employees*, (2) *behavior toward the organization*, and (3) *behavior toward other economic agents*.

One model for applying ethical judgments to business situations recommends the following three steps: (1) Gather relevant factual information, (2) analyze the facts to determine the most appropriate moral values, and (3) make an ethical judgment based on the rightness or wrongness of the proposed activity or policy. Perhaps the single most effective step that a company can take is to *demonstrate top management support*. In addition to promoting attitudes of honesty and openness, firms can also take specific steps to formalize their commitment: (1) *adopting written codes* and (2) *instituting ethics programs*.

OBJECTIVE 2

Distinguish social responsibility from ethics, identify organizational stakeholders, and characterize social consciousness today. (pp. 71–74)

Ethics affect individual behavior. *Social responsibility* is a related concept that refers to the way a firm attempts to balance its commitments to organizational stakeholders—those groups, individuals, and organizations that are directly affected by the practices of an organization and, therefore, have a stake in its performance. Many companies concentrate on five main groups: (1) *customers*, (2) *employees*, (3) *investors*, (4) *suppliers*, and (5) *local communities*.

Attitudes toward social responsibility have changed. The late nineteenth century, though characterized by the entrepreneurial spirit and the laissez-faire philosophy, also featured labor strife and predatory business practices. Concern about unbridled business activity was soon translated into laws regulating business practices. Out of the economic turmoil of the 1930s, when greed was blamed for business failures and the loss of jobs, came new laws protecting and enhancing social well-being. During the 1960s and 1970s, activism prompted increased government regulation in many areas of business. The economic prosperity of the 1980s and 1990s marked a return to the laissez-faire philosophy, but the recent epidemic of corporate scandals threatens to revive the 1930s call for more regulation and oversight.

OBJECTIVE 3

Show how the concept of social responsibility applies both to environmental issues and to a firm's relationships with customers, employees, and investors. (pp. 74–80)

A firm confronts four primary areas of concern when addressing social responsibility. These are:

- responsibility toward the environment (including issues associated with climate change and air, water, and land pollution);
- responsibility toward customers (largely stemming from issues about consumer rights, unfair pricing, ethics in advertising, and green marketing);
- responsibility toward employees (including legal and social commitments and the special case of the whistle-blower); and
- responsibility toward investors (including concerns about improper financial management, insider trading, and misrepresentation of finances).

OBJECTIVE 4

Identify four general approaches to social responsibility and note the role of social responsibility in small business. (pp. 80–82)

A business can take one of four stances concerning its social obligations to society: (1) *obstructionist stance*, (2) *defensive stance*, (3) *accommodative stance*, or (4) *proactive stance*. The few organizations that take an *obstructionist stance* to social responsibility usually do as little as possible to solve social or environmental problems, have little regard for ethical conduct, and will go to great lengths to deny or cover up wrongdoing. Organizations that take a *defensive stance* will do everything that is legally required, including admitting to mistakes and taking corrective actions, but nothing more. A firm that adopts an *accommodative stance* meets and, in certain cases exceeds, its legal and ethical requirements. Firms with the highest degree of social responsibility exhibit the *proactive stance*; they take to heart the arguments in favor of social responsibility, view themselves as citizens in a society, indicate sincere commitment to improve the general social welfare, and surpass the accommodative stance by proactively seeking opportunities to contribute.

For small business owners and managers, ethical issues are questions of individual ethics. But in questions of social responsibility, they must ask themselves if they can afford a social agenda. They should also realize that managers in *all* organizations face issues of ethics and social responsibility.

OBJECTIVE 5

Explain the role of government in social responsibility in terms of how governments and businesses influence each other. (pp. 82–84)

An especially important element of social responsibility is the relationship between business and government. The government (national, state, or local) attempts to shape social responsibility practices through direct and indirect channels. The government most often directly influences organizations through *regulation*, or the establishment of rules that dictate what organizations can and cannot do. To implement these rules and regulations, the government often creates special agencies to monitor and control certain aspects of business activity. Governments may also use legislation to forbid unethical practices such as bribery. Other forms of regulation are indirect, such as using tax codes that may encourage or discourage certain business decisions.

Businesses have four main methods of addressing governmental pressures for more social responsibility. Personal contacts and networks offer one method of influence. *Lobbying*, or the use of persons or groups to formally represent an organization or group of organizations before political bodies, is another. Companies themselves cannot legally make direct donations to political campaigns, so they influence the government through *political action committees (PACs)*, special organizations created to solicit money and then distribute it to political candidates. Finally, organizations sometimes rely on favors and other influence tactics to gain support.

OBJECTIVE 6

Discuss how businesses manage social responsibility in terms of both formal and informal dimensions and how organizations can evaluate their social responsibility. (pp. 84–87)

Organizations need to fashion an approach to social responsibility in the same way that they develop any other business strategy. Formal organizational dimensions that can help manage social responsibility are legal compliance, ethical compliance, and philanthropic giving. *Legal compliance* is the extent to which the organization conforms to local, state, federal, and international laws, and *ethical compliance* is the extent to which the members of the organization follow basic ethical (and legal) standards of behavior. Finally, *philanthropic giving* is the awarding of funds or gifts to charities or other worthy causes.

Informal methods of managing social responsibility include an organization's thoughts on leadership and culture and how organizations respond to whistle-blowers. Leadership practices and organization culture can go a long way toward defining the social responsibility stance an organization and its members will adopt. Ethical leadership often sets the tone for the entire organization. A key issue in social responsibility is how the organization handles whistle-blowers. Whistle-blowing is the disclosure by an employee of illegal or unethical conduct on the part of others within the organization. Although some organizations welcome the contributions of whistle-blowers, it is not uncommon for managers to ignore concerns.

To ascertain whether their efforts are producing the desired benefits, a business should evaluate how it responds to instances of questionable legal or ethical conduct. More formally, an organization may sometimes actually evaluate the effectiveness of its social responsibility efforts. A *corporate social audit* is a formal and thorough analysis of the effectiveness of a firm's social performance.

key terms

accommodative stance (p. 81)
business ethics (p. 64)
collusion (p. 77)
consumerism (p. 76)
corporate social audit (p. 87)
defensive stance (p. 81)
ethical behavior (p. 64)
ethical compliance (p. 85)

ethics (p. 64)
insider trading (p. 79)
legal compliance (p. 85)
lobbying (p. 84)
managerial ethics (p. 65)
obstructionist stance (p. 80)
organizational stakeholders (p. 71)
philanthropic giving (p. 85)

political action committees
    (PACs) (p. 84)
proactive stance (p. 81)
regulation (p. 83)
social responsibility (p. 71)
unethical behavior (p. 64)
whistle-blower (p. 79)

MyBizLab

Go to **pearsonglobaleditions.com/mybizlab** to complete the problems marked with this icon ✪.

questions & exercises

QUESTIONS FOR REVIEW

✪ **2-1.** What factors determine an individual's ethics? For you, which factor has been most significant?

2-2. Who are the major stakeholders that a business should consider?

2-3. What are the major areas of social responsibility with which businesses should be concerned?

2-4. What are the four basic approaches to social responsibility?

2-5. How does government shape the social responsibility of organizations?

QUESTIONS FOR ANALYSIS

✪ **2-6.** What kind of wrongdoing would most likely prompt you to be a whistle-blower? What kind of wrongdoing would be least likely? Why?

✪ **2-7.** In your opinion, which area of social responsibility is most important? Why? Are there areas other than those noted in the chapter that you consider important?

2-8. The Foreign Corrupt Practices Act makes it illegal for U.S. firms to bribe government officials in other countries. What challenges could this create for a company doing business abroad?

APPLICATION EXERCISES

2-9. Describe your personal code of ethics. Be sure to include what you think is right and wrong, as well as your ethical framework for making decisions.

2-10. Using newspapers, magazines, and other business references, identify at least three companies that take a defensive stance to social responsibility, three that take an accommodative stance, and three that take a proactive stance. For each company, highlight the actions that support your conclusion.

building a business: continuing team exercises

Assignment

Meet with you team members and discuss your new business venture within the context of this chapter. Develop specific responses to the following:

2-11. Discuss whether or not your venture should have a formal statement of company practices and business ethics or simply rely on your own individual ethical standards. What are the pros and cons of each approach?

2-12. Who are the primary stakeholders in your new venture? Rank them in order of their relative importance.

2-13. What approach to social responsibility will you take in your new venture? Why?

2-14. Does it make sense for a new business to develop a formal social responsibility program? Why or why not?

building your business skills

TO LIE OR NOT TO LIE: THAT IS THE QUESTION

Goal

To encourage you to apply general concepts of business ethics to specific situations.

Background Information

It seems workplace lying has become business as usual. According to one survey, one-quarter of working adults in the United States said that they had been asked to do something illegal or unethical on the job; 4 in 10 did what they were told. Another survey of more than 2,000 secretaries showed that many employees face ethical dilemmas in their day-to-day work.

Method

STEP 1

Working with a small group of other students, discuss ways in which you would respond to the following ethical dilemmas. When there is a difference of opinion among group members, try to determine the specific factors that influence different responses.

- Would you lie about your supervisor's whereabouts to someone on the phone? Would it depend on what the supervisor was doing?
- Would you lie about who was responsible for a business decision that cost your company thousands of dollars to protect your own or your supervisor's job?
- Would you inflate sales and revenue data on official company accounting statements to increase stock value? Would you do so if your boss ordered it?
- Would you say that you witnessed a signature when you did not if you were acting in the role of a notary?

- Would you keep silent if you knew that the official minutes of a corporate meeting had been changed? Would the nature of the change matter?
- Would you destroy or remove information that could hurt your company if it fell into the wrong hands?

STEP 2

Research the commitment to business ethics at Johnson & Johnson (www.jnj.com) and Texas Instruments (www.ti.com/corp/docs/ethics/home.htm) by checking out their respective websites. As a group, discuss ways in which these statements are likely to affect the specific behaviors mentioned in Step 1.

STEP 3

Working with group members, draft a corporate code of ethics that would discourage the specific behaviors mentioned in Step 1. Limit your code to a single printed page, but make it sufficiently broad to cover different ethical dilemmas.

FOLLOW-UP QUESTIONS

2-15. What personal, social, and cultural factors do you think contribute to lying in the workplace?

2-16. Do you agree or disagree with the statement "The term *business ethics* is an oxymoron." Support your answer with examples from your own work experience or that of someone you know.

2-17. If you were your company's director of human resources, how would you make your code of ethics a "living document"?

2-18. If you were faced with any of the ethical dilemmas described in Step 1, how would you handle them? How far would you go to maintain your personal ethical standards?

exercising your ethics

THE CASE OF ORPHAN DRUGS

The Situation

You are an executive at a major U.S. pharmaceutical firm. A team of your employees has been conducting research into new drugs for acid reflux, a common ailment. The researchers were surprised to discover that one of the investigational pharmaceuticals was effective at treating a rare neurological disorder, although it was completely ineffective at treating acid reflux. The research team is elated with their discovery and would like the company to move forward with clinical trials, FDA approval, and commercialization.

The Dilemma

You are the financial manager for the pharmaceutical company and the CEO is asking for your recommendation about moving ahead with clinical trials of this new drug. There are many things to consider. On one hand, advocacy groups have made you aware of the great suffering of children afflicted with this rare neurological disorder. They even organized a rally encouraging your company to move toward making the drug commercially available. Doing so could create a lot of great press for the company and could ease the suffering of those afflicted with the disorder.

However, despite all the arguments for moving ahead with clinical trials, you are concerned that there is little potential for profit with this new drug. Clinical trials are required for FDA approval and are extremely expensive. The costs associated with trials, FDA approval, and production of the drug are much greater than the potential revenues from sales. Although your company's mission is to produce drugs that make people's lives better, you also have a responsibility to stockholders to be as profitable as possible. From the perspective of maximizing profits, it just doesn't make sense to go ahead with this drug.

The CEO is pressing you for a recommendation and you are torn. You must recommend moving ahead with clinical trials with the goal of commercialization or refocusing the company's efforts on new drugs that could generate profits.

QUESTIONS TO ADDRESS

2-19. Putting yourself in the shoes of the financial manager, which course of action would you recommend?

2-20. Are the short-term consequences of your decision different from the long-term consequences? Describe the short- and long-term impacts.

2-21. How could the government encourage companies to commercialize "orphan" drugs that treat or cure rare conditions but are not economically desirable? If you were a member of Congress, would you support government intervention in this situation?

team exercises

ON THE VERGE OF COLLAPSE

The Situation

Managers often find it necessary to find the right balance among the interests of different stakeholders. For instance, paying employees the lowest possible wages can enhance profits, but paying a living wage might better serve the interests of workers. As more businesses outsource production to other countries, these trade-offs become even more complicated.

The Dilemma

In April 2013, the eight-story Rana Plaza collapsed in Bangladesh. The building was home to five garment factories that produced apparel for a variety of U.S. and foreign retailers. More than 1,000 people died in the building collapse and more than 2,500 were rescued, many with extremely severe injuries. U.S. companies found it desirable to work with manufacturers in Bangladesh, where wage rates are low.

However, with the horror of the building collapse, consumer groups are encouraging people to boycott companies with production in Bangladesh. You are the Vice-President of Operations for Luxury Brands, a high-end manufacturer of mens' and womens' apparel. For the past five years, your company has worked closely with several manufacturers in Bangladesh. These partnerships have allowed your company to generate substantial profits. However, your company's risk manager is concerned about continuing to do business in Bangladesh given the negative press about unsafe working conditions and extremely low wages.

Team Activity

Assemble a group of four students and assign each group member to one of the following roles:

- Vice-President of Operations for Luxury Brands
- Owner of factory in Bangladesh
- An employee from the factory in Bangladesh
- Consumer advocacy group leader

ACTION STEPS

2-22. Before hearing any of your group's comments on this situation, and from the perspective of your assigned role, what do you think that Luxury Brands should do? Write down the reasons for your position.

2-23. Before hearing any of your group's comments on this situation, and from the perspective of your assigned role, what are the underlying ethical issues in this situation? Write down the issues.

2-24. Gather your group together and reveal, in turn, each member's comments on their choices. Next, reveal the ethical issues listed by each member.

2-25. Appoint someone to record main points of agreement and disagreement within the group. How do you explain the results? What accounts for any disagreement?

2-26. From an ethical standpoint, what does your group conclude is the most appropriate choice for the company in this situation?

cases

Is Fair Trade Really Fair?

Continued from page 64

At the beginning of this chapter you read about fair-trade practices, especially as they apply to the market for cacao beans.

Using the information presented in this chapter you should now be able to respond to these questions.

QUESTIONS FOR DISCUSSION

2-27. What are the trade-offs in the fair-trade process? Do you think fair trade promotes fair trade-offs? Why or why not?

2-28. Do you pay attention to fair-trade products in your own purchasing behavior? For what kinds of products might you be willing to pay a premium price to help those who produce the ingredients?

2-29. Under what circumstances could unethical parties abuse the fair-trade concept?

2-30. Under what circumstances might fair trade actually cause harm? to whom? At what point would fair-trade trade-offs no longer be acceptable?

Stepping Up

Ten thousand consumers in a range of countries around the world were canvassed for the 2013 Cone Communications Disaster Relief Trend Tracker survey. Some 87 percent of global consumers expressed the opinion that businesses should respond in the event of a natural disaster. Interestingly, 67 percent of the respondents believed that corporations were better able to respond than charities or governments.

In the UK, the Charity Commission published a guide to disaster relief appeals in the summer of 2012. They were of the opinion that the best way to help in the event of a disaster was to work through existing charities that already had the necessary infrastructure to deal with the situation. The key was always to ensure that any monies donated were being used where intended.

In March 2012, the UK Department For International Development (DFID), launched the Natural Disaster Rapid Response Unit. The group consisted of 32 UK based charities and businesses. The members of the unit, within 72 hours of the disaster occurring, would be given access to the necessary funding to respond. Alongside key charities were businesses including the water purification specialists, Lifesaver Systems and ToughStuff, who supply solar power systems.

Lifesaver Systems, based in Essex, provide the Lifesaver C2. The company was able to deploy 1,500 of the units across Malaysia by September 2013. The units have been given to isolated communities and have managed to provide clean water to 1 million people in the country. The initiative have helped to eradicate cholera and norovirus outbreaks.

The UK charity Oxfam and global retailer Marks and Spencer launched the 'Shwopping' initiative in April 2012, which encouraged to donate unwanted clothing. In the first year, 3.8 million garments were donated, worth US$3.68 million for Oxfam. Consumers are incentivized to donate by receiving a discount voucher that can be redeemed in-store.

The initiative is the latest in a long-standing partnership between the charity and the retailer. Collectively, they have raised some US$15.2 million. The Shwopping scheme raised sufficient funds in the first year to fund Oxfam's entire operations in Nepal, estimated to benefit around 200,000 people.

The relationship represents a win-win outcome for the retailer. Working through a charity, they can maintain their profile as a donator, whilst generating sales and support from their consumers.[43]

QUESTIONS FOR DISCUSSION

2-31. Why might it be the case that corporations are perhaps better suited to provide direct aid in the event of natural disasters? Why might it be counter-productive to work via charities?

2-32. Do you think that social responsibility is good for business? What would motivate a profit-seeking company like appliance manufacturer Whirlpool to incur the expense running initiatives like Shwopping?

2-33. How would you characterize Marks & Spencer's approach to social responsibility? Be sure to support your conclusion.

2-34. Do you think that domestic businesses have a greater responsibility to support rebuilding in their own countries or overseas? Defend your answer.

2-35. What is the appropriate role of government in the event of a natural disaster?

MyBizLab

Go to **pearsonglobaleditions.com/mybizlab** *for the following Assisted-graded writing questions:*

2-36. Competition is one of the four elements necessary for private enterprises to exist. Consider all of the degrees of competition and how they may impact the operations of a private enterprise. Select one of the degrees of competition. Write an essay (a) describing under which conditions the degree of competition exists, (b) provide examples of the degree of competition, and (c) describe how the efficiency of this degree of competition's operations may differ from other degrees of competition.

2-37. Stakeholders to businesses often look to economic indicators to determine the health of the economy. These indicators affect the way these stakeholders react to the current economic environment. Choose two economic indicators. Explain how each indicator is important to measuring the health of an economic system. Which of these do you think is more important to private enterprises versus public enterprises? Global enterprises versus domestic enterprises? Owners versus investors? Support your decision.

2-38. Mybizlab Only—comprehensive writing assignment for this chapter.

end notes

1 Rodney North, "V-Day's Dark Side," *Equal Exchange*, February 2010, at www.equalexchange.com, accessed on March 30, 2013; "Cocoa's Bitter Child Labour Ties," *BBC News*, March 30, 2013, at http://newsvote.bbc.co, accessed on March 30, 2013; Bill Baue, "Abolishing Child Labor on West African Cocoa Farms," *Social Funds*, April 24, 2008, at www.socialfunds.com, accessed on March 30, 2013; Fairtrade International, "Our Vision," "Aims of Fairtrade Standards," "Cocoa," 2010, at www.fairtrade.net, accessed on March 30, 2013; TransFair USA, "What Is Fair Trade?" "Cocoa," 2010, at www.transfairusa.org, accessed on March 30, 2013; Leslie, Josephs, "Selling Candy with a Conscience," *Wall Street Journal*, December 24, 2010, at http://online.wsj.com, accessed on March 30, 2013; Jennifer Alsever, "Fair Prices for Farmers: Simple Idea, Complex Reality," *New York Times*, March 19, 2006, at www.nytimes.com, accessed on March 30, 2013.

2 William G. Symonds, Geri Smith, "The Tax Games Tyco Played," *BusinessWeek* (July 1, 2002), 40–41.

3 "Tyco Votes to Stay Offshore," *BBC News* (March 6, 2003), p. 18.

4 This section follows the logic of Gerald F. Cavanaugh, *American Business Values: A Global Perspective*, 5th ed. (Upper Saddle River, NJ: Prentice Hall, 2006), Chapter 3.

5 "Walmart's Discounted Ethics," *Time*, May 7, 2012, p. 19.

6 Manuel G. Velasquez, *Business Ethics: Concepts and Cases*, 6th ed. (Upper Saddle River, NJ: Prentice Hall, 2006), Chapter 2. See also John R. Boatright, *Ethics and the Conduct of Business*, 4th ed. (Upper Saddle River, NJ: Prentice Hall, 2003), 34–35, 57–59.

7 Jeffrey S. Harrison, R. Edward Freeman, "Stakeholders, Social Responsibility, and Performance: Empirical Evidence and Theoretical Perspectives," *Academy of Management Journal*, 1999, vol. 42, no. 5, 479–485. See also David P. Baron, *Business and Its Environment*, 5th ed. (Upper Saddle River, NJ: Prentice Hall, 2006), Chapter 18.

8 "Diamond Foods Restating Profits After an Audit," *Bloomberg Businessweek*, February 13–February 19, 2012, p. 28.

9 See "Whitman Dinged for HP Write-Down," *USA Today*, November 21, 2012, p. 7B.

10 http://target.com/target_group/community_giving/index.jhtml, accessed March 30, 2013.

11 "Be Kind and They Will come," *USA Today*, March 26, 2013, pp. 1A, 2A.

12 For a recent summary of these questions see "Can Geoengineering Put the Freeze on Global Warming?" *USA Today*, February 25, 2011, pp. 1B, 2B.

13 "Companies Air for Zero Success in Waste Recycling," *USA Today*, January 30, 2013, p. 3B; "Ford to Accelerate Waste Reduction Effort," greenbiz.com/news, accessed on March 4, 2013; "Waste Reduction," gm.com/vision/waste_reduction, accessed on March 5, 2013.

14 Bob Sullivan, "FTC Fines Xanga for Violating Kids' Privacy," (September 7, 2006), at http://www.msnbc.msn.com/id/14718350.

15 Alex Berenson, "Merck Agrees to Pay $4.85 Billion in Vioxx Claims," *New York Times* (November 9, 2007), at http://www.nytimes.com/2007/11/09/business/09cnd-merck.html?ref=business; Rita Rubin, "How Did Vioxx Debacle Happen?" *USA Today*, (October 12, 2004), at http://www.usatoday.com/news/health/2004-10-12-vioxx-cover_x.htm.

16 http://money.cnn.com/galleries/2007/fortune/0703/gallery.green_giants.fortune/7.html, accessed May 30, 2008; http://www.scjohnson.com/environment/growing_1.asp, accessed May 30, 2008.

17 http://www.nytimes.com/2008/01/09/business/09offsets.html?_r=1&ex=1357707600&en=05dc8be5247f9737&ei=5088&partner=rssnyt&emc=rss&oref=slogin, accessed May 30, 2008.

18 http://www.starbucks.com/csrnewsletter/winter06/csrEnvironment.asp, accessed May 30, 2008.

19 "British Airways and Korean Air Lines Fined in Fuel Collusion," *New York Times* (August 2, 2007), at http://www.nytimes.com/2007/08/02/business/worldbusiness/02air.html?scp=2&sq=british+airways+price+fixing&st=nyt.

20 Jerald Greenberg and Robert A. Baron, *Behavior in Organizations: Understanding and Managing the Human Side of Work*, 8th ed. (Upper Saddle River, NJ: Prentice Hall, 2003), 410–413.

21 Cora Daniels, "It's a Living Hell," *Fortune* (April 15, 2002), 367–368.

22 Henry R. Cheeseman, *Business Law: Legal, E-Commerce, Ethical, and International Environments*, 5th ed. (Upper Saddle River, NJ: Prentice Hall, 2004), 128–129.

23 http://www.usdoj.gov/usao/iln/pr/chicago/2008/pr0318_01.pdf, accessed May 30, 2008; Jacob Goldstein, "CVS to Pay $37.5 Million to Settle Pill Switching Case," *Wall Street Journal* (March 18, 2008), at http://blogs.wsj.com/health/2008/03/18/cvs-to-pay-375-million-to-settle-pill-switching-case.

24 Nina Easton and Telis Demos, "The Business Guide to Congress," *Fortune*, May 11, 2012, pp. 72–75.

25 "Siemens to Pay Huge Fine in Bribery Inquiry," *Wall Street Journal*, December 15, 2011, pp. B1, B5.

26 "Daimler Pleads Guilty to Bribing Foreign Governments," *Business Pundit*, April 5, 2010; "Daimler Charged with Bribing Government Officials," *Motor Trend*, March 23, 2010, pp. 58–59.

27 Nina Easton and Telis Demos, "The Business Guide to Congress," *Fortune*, May 11, 2012, pp. 72–75.

28 Peter A. Heslin and Jenna Ochoa, "Understanding and Developing Strategic Corporate Social Responsibility," *Organizational Dynamics*, 2008, Vol. 37, No. 2, pp. 125–144.

29 "Legal—But Lousy," *Fortune*, September 2, 2009, p. 192.

30 Lynn Sharp Paine, "Managing for Organizational Integrity," *Harvard Business Review*, March–April 2004, pp. 106–115.

31 "To Give, or Not to Give," *Time*, May 11, 2012, p. 10.

32 "Battling 'Donor Dropsy,'" *Wall Street Journal*, July 19, 2010, pp. B1, B4.

33 "A New Way of Giving," *Time*, July 24, 2010, pp. 48–51. See also Michael Porter and Mark Kramwe, "The Competitive Advantage of Corporate Philanthropy," *Harvard Business Review*, December 2009, pp. 57–66.

34 "To Give, or Not to Give," *Time*, May 11, 2012, p. 10.

35 David M. Messick and Max H. Bazerman, "Ethical Leadership and the Psychology of Decision Making," *Sloan Management Review*, Winter 1996, pp. 9–22; see also Muel Kaptein, "Developing and Testing a Measure

for the Ethical Culture of Organizations," *Journal of Organizational Behavior*, 2008, Vol. 29, pp. 923–947.

[36] "Ethics in Action: Getting It Right," *Selections*, Fall 2012, pp. 24–27.

[37] For a thorough review of the literature on whistle-blowing, see Janet P. Near and Marcia P. Miceli, "Whistle-Blowing: Myth and Reality," *Journal of Management*, 1996, Vol. 22, No. 3, pp. 507–526. See also Michael Gundlach, Scott Douglas, and Mark Martinko, "The Decision to Blow the Whistle: A Social Information Processing Framework," *Academy of Management Review*, 2003, Vol. 28, No.1, pp. 107–123.

[38] For instance, see "The Complex Goals and Unseen Costs of Whistle-Blowing," *Wall Street Journal*, November 25, 2012, pp. A1, A10.

[39] "A Whistle-Blower Rocks an Industry," *BusinessWeek*, June 24, 2002, pp. 126–130.

[40] "Lockheed to Pay $2 Million to Settle Lawsuit," *Washington Post*, January 25, 2011, p. B1; "Feds Intervening in Mississippi Bid-Rigging Lawsuit at Stennis Space Center," *Associated Press Wire Story*, July 3, 2009, ap.com, accessed on September 5, 2009.

[41] "He Blew a Whistle for 9 Years," *USA Today*, February 13, 2010, pp. 1B, 2B.

[42] "SEC Announces a Whistle-Blower Overhaul Plan," *USA Today*, March 6, 2011, p. 1B.

[43] *Consumers Now Expect Companies to Step Up During Disaster Relief Efforts*, Jennifer Elks, http://www.sustainablebrands .com/news_and_views/communications/consumers-now-expect-companies-step-during-disaster-relief-efforts (accessed 14/10/2013) *Disaster appeal guidance discourages launching new charities, Niki May Young*, http://www .civilsociety.co.uk/governance/news/content/13169/ disaster_appeal_guidance_advises_not_to_set_up_ new_charities (accessed 14/10/2013) http://www .lifesaversystems.com/documents/PRESS_RELEASE_ DSEI_2013_VC3b.pdf(accessed 14/10/2013)http://www .oxfam.org.uk/donate/donate-goods/mands-and-oxfam-shwopping (accessed 15/10/2013)

What makes entrepreneurs tick? What drives

them to thrive where others fail?

The lessons they offer

pave the road to business victory.

AFTER READING THIS CHAPTER, YOU SHOULD BE ABLE TO:

OBJECTIVE 1 **Define** *small business*, discuss its importance to the U.S. economy, and explain popular areas of small business.

OBJECTIVE 2 **Explain** entrepreneurship and describe some key characteristics of entrepreneurial personalities and activities.

OBJECTIVE 3 **Describe** distinctive competence, the business plan, and the start-up decisions made by small businesses and identify sources of financial aid available to such enterprises.

OBJECTIVE 4 **Discuss** the trends in small business start-ups and identify the main reasons for success and failure among small businesses.

OBJECTIVE 5 **Explain** sole proprietorships, partnerships, and cooperatives and discuss the advantages and disadvantages of each.

OBJECTIVE 6 **Describe** corporations, discuss their advantages and disadvantages, and identify different kinds of corporations; explain the basic issues involved in managing a corporation and discuss special issues related to corporate ownership.

MyBizLab®

✪ Improve Your Grade!

Visit **pearsonglobaleditions.com/mybizlab** for simulations, tutorials, and end-of-chapter problems.

simulations

videos

assisted-graded

writing

Over 10 million students improved their results using the Pearson MyLabs.

Launching a Business in the Gym

Several years ago Reed Hastings, a California entrepreneur between start-up ventures, incurred a $40 late fee at Blockbuster. "It was six weeks late," he admits. "I had misplaced the cassette [and] I didn't want to tell my wife....I was embarrassed about it." The next day he dropped off the VHS cassette and paid the late fee on his way to the gym. As it turns out, his itinerary for the day was quite opportune: In the middle of his workout, he recalls, "I realized [the gym] had a much better business model. You could pay $30 or $40 a month and work out as little or as much as you wanted."

Thus, the idea for Netflix was born. But Hastings knew he needed to start slowly. So, when Netflix was launched in 1997, its only innovations involved the convenience of ordering movies over the Internet and receiving and returning them by mail; Netflix merely rented movies for $4 apiece plus $2 for postage (and, yes, it charged late fees). Basically, the customer base consisted of people who wanted to watch movies without having to leave the house. But Hastings and co-founder Marc Randolph quickly decided to test a subscription-based model, unlimited rentals by mail for a flat fee and, perhaps most importantly, no due dates (and thus no late fees). Current customers were first offered the opportunity to shift from their pay-per-rental plans to subscription plans on a free-trial basis and then given the chance to renew the subscription plan on a paid basis. "We knew it wouldn't be terrible," says Hastings, "but we didn't know if it would be great." In the first month, however, 80 percent of Netflix users who'd tried the no-cost subscription plan had renewed on a paid basis.

"Having unlimited due dates and no late fees," said Hastings back in 2003, "has worked in a powerful way and now seems obvious, but at that time, we had no idea if customers would even build and use an online queue." The "queue," as any Netflix user will tell you, is the list of movies that the customer wants to watch. Netflix maintains your queue, follows your online directions in keeping it up to date, and automatically sends you the next movie you want each time you send one back.

The essence of queuing—and of the Netflix business model—is clearly convenience. Although the ability to enhance customer convenience, even when combined with cost savings, often gives a company a competitive advantage in its industry, it doesn't always have the industry-wide effect that it's had in the case of Netflix. Not only did the Netflix subscriber model improve

what's in it for me?

A recent Gallup poll suggests that almost half of the young people in the United States today are interested in entrepreneurship.[1] Even if you are not among that number, you will still be called on to interact with small businesses and entrepreneurs as a customer, as an investor, or as a client. You may also be trying to sell products or services to small businesses and entrepreneurs. One key to understanding entrepreneurship is to understand entrepreneurs themselves and what it takes for them to succeed. Reed Hastings displays many of the characteristics key to entrepreneurial success. Netflix also highlights some of the problems inherent in converting a great business idea into a profitable enterprise. If you ever aspire to start and run your own businesses you can learn valuable lessons from the experiences of Hastings and his management team. As an investor, you should also be better prepared to assess the market potential for new and up-and-coming businesses. This chapter will discuss these and additional issues important for starting and owning a business, including the business plan, reasons for success and failure, and the advantages and disadvantages of different kinds of ownership. First, we'll start by defining a small business and identifying its importance in the U.S. economy.

the service provided by the industry in an unexpected way, but ultimately it also weakened the competitive positions of companies already doing business in the industry—notably, Blockbuster. In late 2012, the onetime industry leader's market capitalization, which had peaked at $5 billion in 2002, was languishing at $35 million. At the same time, Netflix's market cap stood at nearly $10 billion and would reach nearly $15 billion by early 2013.

How had Hastings' upstart company managed to put itself in such an enviable position? For one thing, it got off to a fast start. In 1997, when DVDs were just being test-marketed in the United States, Hastings and Randolph decided that the new medium would eventually overtake videocassettes as the format of choice for both the home-movie industry and the home-movie renter. They were right, of course. By 2002, one in four U.S. households owned a DVD player, but the number today is close to 9 in 10. (In any case, it would have cost about $4 to mail a videocassette both ways, compared to the $0.78 that it costs to ship a DVD disc back and forth.)

More importantly, as the first company to rent movies by mail, Netflix was the first to establish a rental-by-mail customer base. At first, says Hastings, "people thought the idea was crazy. But it was precisely because it was a contrarian idea that [it] enabled us to get ahead of our competitors." As Netflix has continued to expand and nurture its subscriber base, it's also generated both brand recognition and brand loyalty. "Netflix has customer loyalty. It's a passion brand," explains Hastings, who hastens to add that keeping customers happy is crucial "because the more someone uses Netflix, the more likely they are to stay with us."

Today Netflix continues to be at the forefront of innovation and has established a strong position in the emerging video-on-demand market. In 2013, the company obtained exclusive rights to distribute the original series *The House of Cards* and the fourth season of *Arrested Development*. Never one to stand still, Hastings continues to look for the "next big thing."[2] (After studying this chapter you should be able to answer the set of discussion questions found at the end of the chapter.)

OBJECTIVE 1
Define

small business, discuss its importance to the U.S. economy, and explain popular areas of small business.

Small Business Administration (SBA) *government agency charged with assisting small businesses*

Small Business *independently owned business that has relatively little influence in its market*

What is a "Small" Business

The term *small business* defies easy definition. Locally owned and operated restaurants, dry cleaners, and hair salons are obviously small businesses, and giant corporations, such as Dell, Starbucks, Apple, and Netflix, are clearly big businesses. Between these two extremes, though, fall thousands of companies that cannot be easily categorized.

The U.S. Department of Commerce considers a business "small" if it has fewer than 500 employees. The U.S. **Small Business Administration (SBA),** a government agency that assists small businesses, regards some companies with as many as 1,500 employees as small, but only if the business has relatively low annual revenues. Because strict numerical terms sometimes lead to contradictory classifications, we will consider a **small business** to be one that is independent (that is, not part of a larger business) and that has relatively little influence in its market. A small neighborhood grocer would be small, assuming it is not part of a chain and that the prices it pays to wholesalers and that it can charge its customers are largely set by market forces. Dell Computer was a small business when founded by Michael Dell in 1984, but today it's one of the world's largest computer companies and is not small in any sense of the term. Hence, it can negotiate from a position of strength with its suppliers and can set its prices with less consideration for what other computer firms are charging.

The Importance of Small Business in the U.S. Economy

As Figure 3.1 shows, most U.S. businesses employ fewer than 100 people, and most U.S. workers are employed by small business. Moreover, this same pattern exists across most free market economies.

Figure 3.1(a) shows that 89.29 percent of all businesses employ 20 or fewer people. Another 8.88 percent employ between 20 and 99 people, and 1.52 percent employ between 100 and 499. Only about .16 of 1 percent employ 1,000 or more people. Figure 3.1(b) also shows that 17.74 percent of all workers are employed by firms with fewer than 20 people, and 17.11 percent are employed by firms with between 20 and 99 people. Another 14.52 percent are employed by firms with between 100 and 499 people. So, around half of all workers are employed by firms with 500 or less employees and the other half work for larger organizations. We can measure the contribution of small business in terms of its impact on key aspects of the U.S. economic system, including *job creation*, *innovation*, and their *contributions to big business*.

Job Creation Small businesses—especially in certain industries—are an important source of new (and often well paid) jobs. In recent years, small businesses have accounted for around 40 percent of all new jobs in high technology sectors of the economy.[3] Jobs are created by companies of all sizes, all of which hire and lay off workers. Although small firms often hire at a faster rate, they also tend to cut jobs at a higher rate. They are generally the first to hire in times of economic recovery, and big firms are generally the last to lay off workers during downswings.

However, relative job growth among businesses of different sizes is not easy to determine. For one thing, when a successful small business starts adding employees

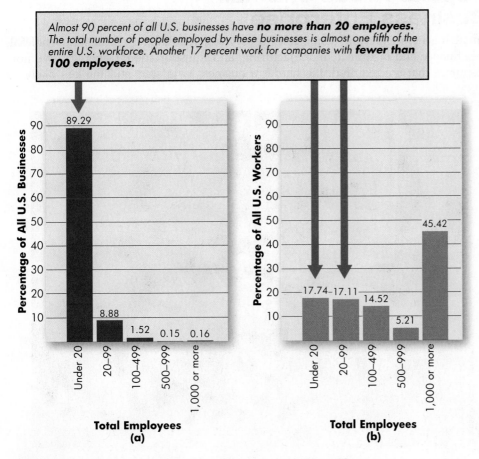

Almost 90 percent of all U.S. businesses have **no more than 20 employees.** The total number of people employed by these businesses is almost one fifth of the entire U.S. workforce. Another 17 percent work for companies with **fewer than 100 employees.**

FIGURE 3.1 The Pervasiveness of Small Business in the United States
Source: Data from www.census.gov/

at a rapid clip, it may quickly cease being small. For example, Dell Computer had 1 employee in 1984 (Dell himself). But the payroll grew to 100 employees in 1986; 2,000 in 1992; more than 39,000 in 2004; 94,300 in 2010; and 103,300 in 2013. Although there was no precise point at which Dell turned from "small" into "large," some of the jobs it created could be counted in the small business sector and some in the large.

Innovation   History reminds us that major innovations are as likely to come from small businesses (or individuals) as from big ones. Small firms and individuals invented the PC, the stainless steel razor blade, the photocopier, the jet engine, Facebook, Amazon, and eBay. Innovations are not always new products, though. Dell didn't invent the PC; he developed an innovative way to build it (buy finished components and then assemble them) and an innovative way to sell it (directly to consumers, first by telephone and now via the Internet). Today, small businesses produce 13 times as many patents per employee as large patenting firms.[4]

Contributions to Big Business   Most of the products made by big businesses are sold to consumers by small ones. For example, most dealerships that sell Fords, Toyotas, and Volvos are independently operated. Even as more shoppers turn to the Internet, smaller businesses still play critical roles. For instance, most larger online retailers actually outsource the creation of their websites and the distribution of their products to other firms, many of them small or regional companies. Smaller businesses also provide data storage services for larger businesses. Moreover, small businesses provide big ones with many of their services and raw materials. Microsoft, for instance, relies on hundreds of small firms for most of its routine code writing functions.

Popular Areas of Small Business Enterprise

Small businesses play a major role in services, retailing, construction, wholesaling, finance and insurance, manufacturing, and transportation. Generally, the more resources that are required, the harder a business is to start and the less likely an

New businesses often emerge in response to emerging opportunities. For instance, an increase in the number of working families with pets has created an opportunity for professional dog walkers. Most dog walkers, in turn, are individual entrepreneurs.

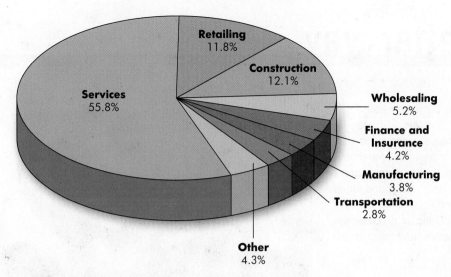

FIGURE 3.2 Small Business by Industry
Source: www.census.gov/econ/susb/

industry is dominated by small firms. Remember, too, that *small* is a relative term. The criteria (number of employees and total annual sales) differ among industries and are often meaningful only when compared with truly large businesses. Figure 3.2 shows the distribution of all U.S. businesses employing fewer than 20 people across industry groups.

Services
About 55.8 percent of businesses with fewer than 20 employees are involved in the service industry, which ranges from marriage counseling to computer software, from management consulting to professional dog walking. Partly because they require few resources (and hence don't cost as much to start), service providers are the fastest-growing segment of small business.

Retailing
Retailers, which sell products made by other firms directly to consumers, account for about 11.8 percent of small businesses. Usually, people who start small retail businesses favor specialty shops, such as big men's clothing or gourmet coffees that let the owners focus limited resources on narrow or small market segments.

Construction
About 12.1 percent of all U.S. businesses are involved in construction. Because many construction jobs are small local projects, such as a homeowner adding a garage or remodeling a room, local contractors are often best suited to handle them.

Wholesaling
Small business owners often do well in wholesaling, which accounts for about 5.2 percent of businesses with fewer than 20 employees. Wholesalers buy products in bulk from manufacturers or other producers and store them in quantities and locations convenient for selling them to retailers.

Finance and Insurance
Financial and insurance firms account for about 4.2 percent of small businesses. Most of these businesses, such as local State Farm Insurance offices, are affiliates of or agents for larger national firms. Small locally owned banks are also common in smaller communities and rural areas.

Manufacturing
More than any other industry, manufacturing lends itself to big business, but it still accounts for about 3.8 percent of firms with fewer than 20 employees. Indeed, small manufacturers sometimes outperform big ones in such innovation-driven industries as electronics, equipment and machine parts, and computer software.

finding a better way

The Rise of Services

Manufacturing is a form of business that combines and transforms resources into tangible outcomes that are then sold to others. Goodyear is a manufacturer because it combines rubber and chemical compounds and uses blending equipment and molding machines to create tires. Broyhill is a manufacturer because it buys wood and metal components, pads, and fabric and then combines them into furniture. And Apple is a manufacturer because it uses electronic, metal, plastic, and composite components to build smartphones, computers, and other digital products.

Manufacturing was once the dominant technology in the United States. During the 1970s, though, manufacturing entered a long period of decline, primarily because of foreign competition. U.S. firms had grown lax and sluggish, and new foreign competitors came onto the scene with better equipment and much higher levels of efficiency. For example, steel companies in Asia were able to produce high-quality steel for much lower prices than large U.S. steel companies such as Bethlehem Steel and U.S. Steel. Faced with a battle for survival, some companies disappeared, but many others underwent a long and difficult period of change by eliminating waste and transforming themselves into leaner and more efficient and responsive entities. They reduced their workforces dramatically, closed antiquated or unnecessary plants, and modernized their remaining plants. Over the last decade or so, however, their efforts have started to pay dividends because U.S. manufacturing has regained a competitive position in many different industries. Although low wages continue to center a great deal of global manufacturing in Asia, once-strong manufacturers are once again thriving in the United States.

During the decline of the manufacturing sector, a tremendous growth in the service sector, often fueled by visionary entrepreneurs, kept the overall U.S. economy from declining at the same rate. A service organization is one that transforms resources into an intangible output and creates time or place utility for its customers. For example, Netflix provides video rentals through mail order and online delivery options. Facebook offers its members a venue for networking and interacting with others. And your local

Gemenacom/Shutterstock

hairdresser cuts your hair. In 1947, the service sector was responsible for less than half of the U.S. gross national product (GNP). By 1975, however, this figure reached 65 percent, and by 2006 had surpassed 75 percent. The service sector has been responsible for almost 90 percent of all new jobs created in the United States since 1990. Moreover, employment in service occupations is expected to grow 26.8 percent between 2010 and 2020.

Managers have come to see that many of the tools, techniques, and methods that are used in a factory are also useful to a service firm. For example, managers of automobile plants and hair salons each have to decide how to design their facility, identify the best location for it, determine optimal capacity, make decisions about inventory storage, set procedures for purchasing raw materials, and set standards for productivity and quality. At the same time, though, service-based firms must hire and train employees based on a different skill set than is required by most manufacturers. For instance, consumers seldom come into contact with the Toyota employee who installs the seats in their car, so that person can be hired based on technical skills. But Toyota must also recruit people for sales and customer service jobs who not only know how to do a job but who can also effectively interface with a variety of consumers.[5]

Transportation About 2.8 percent of small companies are in transportation and related businesses, including many taxi and limousine companies, charter airplane services, and tour operators.

Other The remaining 4.3 percent or so of small businesses are in other industries, such as small research and development laboratories and independent media companies—start-up web channels, small town newspapers, and radio broadcasters.

managing in turbulent times

The Wide World of Risk

One reason why globalization has become such a factor in everyday business life is the expanded reach and power of multinational companies. Many large corporations have actually become engines for innovation as well as growth, adapting to new markets and new economic circumstances. In a highly interconnected world, however, it's often hard to figure out the complex ownership and organizational structures of many global corporations. Sometimes, for example, their branding strategies and management structures lead people to think that they're local companies when, in fact, the real source of corporate power may lie thousands of miles away on another continent. For example, there are more than 200 hundred Aldi supermarkets in the United States, but Aldi itself is a German firm. One thing's for sure, if you're going to be dealing with a company overseas, you'd better have a good idea of where and how decisions are made, and who has the real power to make them.

Remember, too, that different cultures have different attitudes when it comes to entrepreneurship. In some countries and cultures, like that of the United States, there's a lively entrepreneurial spirit. Businesspeople are open to taking risks, and if they fail, they tend to pick themselves up and move on to something else. In some Asian countries, the entrepreneurial spirit is often

Nmedia/Fotolia

tempered by the need for consensus and getting everyone on board. This approach requires a lot of patience and the ability to compromise. Knowing the cultural forces that shape both a business organization and people's attitudes toward risk, success, and failure is an elementary but important component of international business.

Entrepreneurship

OBJECTIVE 2
Explain
entrepreneurship and describe some key characteristics of entrepreneurial personalities and activities.

We noted previously that Dell Computer started as a one-person operation and grew into a giant corporation. Dell's growth was spurred by the imagination and skill of Michael Dell, the entrepreneur who founded the company. **Entrepreneurs** are people, like Dell, who assume the risk of business ownership.[6] **Entrepreneurship** is the process of seeking business opportunities under conditions of risk. However, not all entrepreneurs have the same goals.

Entrepreneur *businessperson who accepts both the risks and the opportunities involved in creating and operating a new business venture*

Entrepreneurship Goals

People may decide to pursue entrepreneurship for a variety of different reasons. Many entrepreneurs seek to launch a new business with the goal of independence—independence from working for someone else coupled with some reasonable degree of financial security. Such entrepreneurs want to achieve a safe and secure financial future for themselves and their families but do not aspire to grow their business beyond their capacity to run it. Consider Jack Matz, a former corporate executive in Houston who lost his job when his firm merged with another. Rather than look for another management position, Matz opened a photocopying business near a local university. His goal is to earn enough money to lead a comfortable life until he retires in 10 years. The term *small business* is most closely associated with these kinds of enterprises.

Other entrepreneurs, however, launch new businesses with the goal of growth and expansion—that is, to transform their venture into a large business. This was

Entrepreneurship *the process of seeking businesses opportunities under conditions of risk*

Dell's vision when he started his business; likewise, when Howard Schultz took over Starbucks, he too had plans to grow and develop the fledgling coffee company into a much larger enterprise. Terms such as *new ventures* and *start-ups* are often used to refer to these kinds of businesses.

In still other cases, the goals of an entrepreneur may not always be clear in the early stages of business development. For instance, one entrepreneur might launch a business with little or no expectation that it will have huge growth potential but then find that it can grow dramatically. Mark Zuckerberg, for example, had no idea that his Facebook firm would grow to its present size. Another entrepreneur might start out with ambitious growth plans but find that expected opportunities cannot be realized; perhaps there really is no large market or another firm establishes dominance over that market first.

Entrepreneurial Characteristics

Regardless of their goals, many successful entrepreneurs share certain characteristics. Among these characteristics are resourcefulness and a concern for good, often personal, customer relations. Most of them also have a strong desire to be their own bosses. Many express a need to "gain control over my life" or "build for the family" and believe that building successful businesses will help them do it. They can also deal with uncertainty and risk.

Yesterday's entrepreneur was often stereotyped as "the boss"—self-reliant, male, and able to make quick, firm decisions. Today's entrepreneur is seen more often as an open-minded leader who relies on networks, business plans, and consensus. Past and present entrepreneurs also have different views on such topics as how to succeed, how to automate business, and when to rely on experience in the trade or on basic business acumen.[7]

Consider Yoshiko Shinohara, who had lost her father by the age of 8, was divorced by the age of 28, and never received a college education. At the age of 70, she is president of Tempstaff, a Japanese temp agency that she started out of her one-room apartment more than 30 years ago. Fueled by Japan's need for temps during a period of stagnation in the 1990s and Shinohara's ambition, Tempstaff is now a $2.3 billion company with a high-rise headquarters in Tokyo.[8]

Among other things, Shinohara's story illustrates what is almost always a key element in entrepreneurship: risk. Interestingly, most successful entrepreneurs seldom see what they do as risky. Whereas others may focus on possibilities for failure and balk at gambling everything on a new venture, most entrepreneurs are so passionate about their ideas and plans that they see little or no likelihood of failure. For example, when Shinohara started Tempstaff, few Japanese businesses understood or had even heard of the temporary worker concept. But Shinohara felt that she "had nothing to lose anyway" and preferred taking that risk to ending up "serving tea or just being a clerical assistant."[9]

Starting and Operating a New Business

OBJECTIVE 3
Describe
the business plan and the start-up decisions made by small businesses and identify sources of financial aid available to such enterprises.

The Internet has changed the rules for starting and operating a small business. Setting up is easier and faster than ever, there are more potential opportunities than at any other time, and the ability to gather and assess information is at an all-time high. Today, for example, many one person retailers do most of their business—both buying and selling—on Internet auction sites, such as eBay.

Even so, would be entrepreneurs must make the right start-up decisions. For instance, they need to have a clear vision of why their business will succeed. They must also decide how to get into business—should they buy an existing business or build from the ground up? They must know when to seek expert advice and where to find sources of financing. If, for example, a new firm needs financial backing from investors or a line of credit from vendors or distributors, the entrepreneur must have in place a comprehensive, well-crafted business plan. Creating a business plan begins with understanding the potential firm's distinctive competences.

Understanding Distinctive Competencies

An organization's distinctive competencies are the aspects of business that the firm performs better than its competitors. The distinctive competencies of small business usually fall into three areas: (1) the ability to identify new niches in established markets, (2) the ability to identify new markets, and (3) the ability to move quickly to take advantage of new opportunities.

Identifying Niches in Established Markets
An **established market** is one in which many firms compete according to relatively well-defined criteria. For example, the video rental market was well-established when Hastings decided to launch Netflix. Blockbuster was the dominant firm, but many independent video rental firms were also prospering. Retail outlets kept an inventory of video products available for rent. Customers drove or walked to the stores, paid a fee, and took the video home. They kept it for a defined period of time and then returned it to the store (with a late fee, if they kept it too long). A **niche** is simply a segment of a market that is not currently being exploited. In general, small entrepreneurial businesses are better at discovering these niches than are larger organizations. Large organizations usually have so many resources committed to older, established business practices that they may be unaware of new opportunities. Entrepreneurs can see these opportunities and move quickly to take advantage of them. Hastings' decision to rent by mail allowed Netflix to exploit a niche.

More recently, Dave Gilboa and Neil Blumenthal founded Warby Parker, a business that sells prescription eyewear through the mail. The entrepreneurs realized that most consumers disliked the experience of going to an optical shop to try on glasses and then were irritated at the price of those glasses. So, Warby Parker offers lower-priced glasses with hip designs and a money-back guarantee. Astute marketing then allowed them to get a quick start with their niche business, selling more than 50,000 pairs of glasses and generating profits after only a single year of operation.[10]

Identifying New Markets
Successful entrepreneurs also excel at discovering whole new markets. Discovery can happen in at least two ways. First, an entrepreneur can transfer a product or service that is well established in one geographic market to a second market. This is what Marcel Bich did with ballpoint pens, which occupied a well-established market in Europe before Bich introduced them to this country more than 50 years ago. Bich's company, Société Bic, eventually came to dominate the U.S. market.

Second, entrepreneurs can sometimes create entire industries. Entrepreneurial inventions of the dry paper copying process and the semiconductor have created vast new industries. Not only have the first companies into these markets been successful (Xerox and National Semiconductor, respectively), but their entrepreneurial activity has spawned the development of hundreds of other companies and hundreds of thousands of jobs. Again, because entrepreneurs are not encumbered with a history of doing business in a particular way, they are usually better at discovering new markets than are larger, more mature organizations.

First-Mover Advantages
A **first-mover advantage** is any advantage that comes to a firm because it exploits an opportunity before any other firm does. Sometimes large firms discover niches within existing markets or new markets at just about the same time small entrepreneurial firms do, but are not able to move as quickly as small companies to take advantage of these opportunities. Many of the "app" developers for smartphones are exploiting first-mover advantage.

Established Market *one in which many firms compete according to relatively well-defined criteria*

Niche *a segment of a market that is not currently being exploited*

First-Mover Advantage *any advantage that comes to a firm because it exploits an opportunity before any other firm does*

There are numerous reasons for the difference. For example, many large organizations make decisions slowly because each of their many layers of hierarchy has to approve an action before it can be implemented. Also, large organizations may sometimes put a great deal of their assets at risk when they take advantage of new opportunities. Every time Boeing decides to build a new model of a commercial jet, it is making a decision that could literally bankrupt the company if it does not turn out well. The size of the risk may make large organizations cautious. The dollar value of the assets at risk in a small organization, in contrast, is quite small. Managers may be willing to "bet the company" when the value of the company is only $100,000. They might be unwilling to "bet the company" when the value of the company is $1 billion.

Crafting a Business Plan

Business Plan *document in which the entrepreneur summarizes his or her business strategy for the proposed new venture and how that strategy will be implemented*

After the would-be entrepreneur has defined a potential distinctive competence and made the decision to proceed, the next step is formulating a **business plan** in which the entrepreneur describes his or her business strategy for the new venture and demonstrates how it will be implemented.[11] A real benefit of a business plan is the fact that in the act of preparing it, the would-be entrepreneur is forced to develop the business idea on paper and firm up his or her thinking about how to launch it before investing time and money in it. The idea of the business plan isn't new. What is new is the use of specialized business plans, mostly because creditors and investors demand them as tools for deciding whether to finance or invest.

Setting Goals and Objectives   A business plan describes the match between the entrepreneur's abilities and experiences and the requirements for producing or marketing a particular product. It also defines strategies for production and marketing, legal elements and organization, and accounting and finance. In particular, a business plan should answer three questions: (1) What are the entrepreneur's goals and objectives? (2) What strategies will be used to obtain them? (3) How will these strategies be implemented?

Sales Forecasting   Although a key element of any business plan is sales forecasts, plans must carefully build an argument for likely business success based on sound logic and research. Entrepreneurs, for example, can't forecast sales revenues without first researching markets. Simply asserting that the new venture will sell 100,000 units per month is not credible; the entrepreneur must demonstrate an understanding of the current market, of the strengths and weaknesses of existing firms, and of the means by which the new venture will compete. Without the sales forecast, no one can estimate the required size of a plant, store, or office or decide how much inventory to carry and how many employees to hire.

Financial Planning   Financial planning refers to the entrepreneur's plan for turning all other activities into dollars. It generally includes a cash budget, an income statement, balance sheets, and a breakeven chart. The cash budget shows how much money you need before you open for business and how much you need to keep the business going before it starts earning a profit.

Starting the Small Business

An old Chinese proverb says that a journey of a thousand miles begins with a single step. This is also true of a new business. The first step is the individual's commitment to becoming a business owner. In preparing a business plan, the entrepreneur must choose the industry and market in which he or she plans to compete. This choice means assessing not only industry conditions and trends but also one's own abilities and interests. Like big business managers, small business owners must understand the nature of the enterprises in which they are engaged.

Buying an Existing Business After an entrepreneur has forecast sales and completed the financial planning, then he or she must decide whether to buy an existing business or start from scratch. Many experts recommend the first approach because, quite simply, the odds are better: If it's successful, an existing business has already proven its ability to attract customers and generate profit. It has also established relationships with lenders, suppliers, and other stakeholders. Moreover, an existing track record gives potential buyers a much clearer picture of what to expect than any estimate of a start-up's prospects.

Ray Kroc bought McDonald's as an existing business, added entrepreneurial vision and business insight, and produced a multinational giant. Both Southwest Airlines and Starbucks were small but struggling operations when entrepreneurs took over and grew them into large businesses. About 35 percent of all new businesses that were started in the past decade were bought from someone else.

Franchising Most McDonald's, Subway, 7 Eleven, RE/Max, Ramada, and Dunkin' Donuts outlets are franchises operating under licenses issued by parent companies to local owners. A **franchise** agreement involves two parties, a *franchisee* (the local owner) and a *franchiser* (the parent company).[12]

Franchise *arrangement in which a buyer (franchisee) purchases the right to sell the good or service of the seller (franchiser)*

Franchisees benefit from the parent corporation's experience and expertise, and the franchiser may even supply financing. It may pick the store location, negotiate the lease, design the store, and purchase equipment. It may train the first set of employees and managers and issue standard policies and procedures. Once the business is open, the franchiser may offer savings by allowing the franchisee to purchase from a central location. Marketing strategy (especially advertising) may also be handled by the franchiser. In short, franchisees receive—that is, invest in—not only their own ready-made businesses but also expert help in running them.

Franchises have advantages for both sellers and buyers. Franchises can grow rapidly by using the investment money provided by franchisees. The franchisee gets to own a business and has access to big business management skills. The franchisee does not have to build a business step by step, and because each franchise outlet is probably a carbon copy of every other outlet, failure is less likely. Recent statistics show that franchising is on the upswing, having increased by more than 20 percent during the past decade.

Perhaps the most significant disadvantage in owning a franchise is the start-up cost. Franchise prices vary widely. The fee for a Fantastic Sam's hair salon is $30,000; however, the franchisee must also invest additional funds in building and outfitting the salon. A McDonald's franchise has an initial fee of $45,000 but again requires the additional funds to construct and outfit a restaurant; the costs generally run the total outlay to around $1 million. And professional sports teams (which are also franchises) can cost several hundred million dollars. Franchisees may also be obligated to contribute a percentage of sales to parent corporations. From the perspective of the parent company, some firms choose not to franchise to retain more control over quality and earn more profits for themselves. Starbucks, for instance, does not franchise its coffee shops. (Starbucks does have licensing agreements where other firms operate Starbucks kiosks and other niche outlets; it does not, though, franchise individual free-standing coffee shops to individuals.)

Starting from Scratch Despite the odds, some people seek the satisfaction that comes from planting an idea and growing it into a healthy business. There are also practical reasons to start from scratch. A new business doesn't suffer the ill effects of a prior owner's errors, and the start-up owner is free to choose lenders, equipment, inventories, locations, suppliers, and workers. Of all new businesses begun in the past decade, about 64 percent were started from scratch. Dell Computer, Walmart, Microsoft, and Twitter are among today's most successful businesses that were started from scratch by an entrepreneur.

But as we have already noted, the risks of starting a business from scratch are greater than those of buying an existing firm. New business founders can only make projections about their prospects. Success or failure depends on identifying a genuine opportunity, such as a product for which many customers will pay well but which is currently unavailable. To find openings, entrepreneurs must study markets and answer the following questions:

- Who and where are my customers?
- How much will those customers pay for my product?
- How much of my product can I expect to sell?
- Who are my competitors?
- Why will customers buy my product rather than the product of my competitors?

Financing the Small Business

Although the choice of how to start a business is obviously important, it's meaningless unless you can get the money to finance your ideas. Among the more common sources for funding are family and friends, personal savings, lending institutions, investors, and governmental agencies. Lending institutions are more likely to help finance the purchase of an existing business because the risks are better understood. Individuals starting new businesses will probably have to rely on personal resources. One of the many causes of the 2008–2011 recession was a sharp reduction in the availability of credit, including funds to help start new businesses. This credit crunch, in turn, limited both new start-up funding and funding for existing businesses wanting to make new investments.

According to the National Federation of Independent Business, personal resources, not loans, are the most important sources of money. Including money borrowed from friends and relatives, personal resources account for more than two thirds of all money invested in new small businesses, and one half of that is used to purchase existing businesses. Getting money from banks, independent investors, and government loans requires extra effort. At a minimum, banks and private investors will want to review business plans, and government loans have strict eligibility guidelines.

Venture Capital Company *group of small investors who invest money in companies with rapid growth potential*

Venture capital companies are groups of small investors seeking to make profits on companies with rapid growth potential. Most of these firms do not lend money. They invest it, supplying capital in return for partial ownership (like stocks, discussed later in this chapter). They may also demand representation on boards of directors. In some cases, managers need approval from the venture capital company before making major decisions. In most cases, venture capitalists do not provide money to start a new business; instead, once a business has been successfully launched and its growth potential established, they provide the funds to fuel expansion. Of all venture capital currently committed in the United States, about 30 percent comes from true venture capital firms. Steve Case, founder of AOL, operates a successful venture capital company. He looks to invest in new start-ups that have a great business idea, a passionate entrepreneur, and a solid and well-crafted business plan.[13]

Small Business Investment Company (SBIC) *government regulated investment company that borrows money from the SBA to invest in or lend to a small business*

Small business investment companies (SBICs) also invest in companies with potential for rapid growth. They are federally licensed to borrow money from the SBA and to invest it in or lend it to small businesses, and they are themselves investments for their shareholders. Past beneficiaries of SBIC capital include Apple Computer, Intel, and FedEx. The government also sponsors *minority enterprise small business investment companies (MESBICs)*. As the name suggests, MESBICs target minority owned businesses.

SBA Financial Programs Since its founding in 1953, the SBA has sponsored financing programs for small businesses that meet standards in size and independence. Eligible firms must be unable to get private financing at reasonable terms. The most common form of SBA financing, its *7(a) loans programs*, allows small businesses to borrow from commercial lenders and guarantees to repay a maximum of 75 percent. The SBA's *special purpose loans* target businesses with specific needs, such as meeting international demands or implementing pollution control measures. For loans under $35,000, the SBA offers the *micro loan program*.

The *Certified Development Company (504) program* offers fixed interest rates on loans from nonprofit community based lenders to boost local economies.[14]

The SBA also helps entrepreneurs improve their management skills. The Service Corps of Retired Executives (SCORE) is made up of retired executives who volunteer to help entrepreneurs start new businesses. The **Small Business Development Center (SBDC)** program consolidates information from various disciplines and institutions for use by new and existing small businesses.

Small Business Development Center (SBDC) *SBA program designed to consolidate information from various disciplines and make it available to small businesses*

Other Sources of Financing Some entrepreneurs find financing from overseas investors. James Buck developed a new implantable heart device to treat certain heart conditions but could not find adequate funding to start his business. He ended up looking to investors in Asia and obtained $5 million from the government of Malaysia.[15]

The Internet has also opened doors to new financing options. For instance, Kabbage.com is an online company that provides cash advances to small business.[16]

Trends, Successes, and Failures in New Ventures

OBJECTIVE 4
Discuss
the trends in small business start-ups and identify the main reasons for success and failure among small businesses.

For every Sam Walton, Mark Zuckerberg, Mary Kay Ash, or Bill Gates—entrepreneurs who transformed small businesses into big ones—there are many entrepreneurs who fail. Each year there are generally between 610,000 and 835,000 new businesses launched in the United States. On the other hand, there are also between 605,000 and 805,000 failures each year as well.[17] In 2010, for instance, 668,861 new firms started operations and another 690,504 closed down. In this section, we look first at a few key trends in small business start-ups. Then we examine some of the reasons for success and failure in small business undertakings.

Trends in Small Business Start-Ups

As noted previously, thousands of new businesses are started in the United States every year. Several factors account for this trend, and in this section, we focus on five of them.

Emergence of E-commerce The most significant recent trend is the rapid emergence of e-commerce. Because the Internet provides fundamentally new ways of doing business, savvy entrepreneurs have created and expanded new businesses faster and easier than ever before. Such leading-edge firms as Google, Amazon.com, and eBay owe their existence to the Internet. Figure 3.3 underscores this point by summarizing the growth in e-commerce from 2003 through 2010.

Crossovers from Big Business More businesses are being started by people who have opted to leave big corporations and put their experience to work for themselves. In some cases, they see great new ideas that they want to develop. Others get burned out in the corporate world. Some have lost their jobs, only to discover that working for themselves was a better idea anyway. John Chambers spent several years working at IBM and Wang Laboratories/GLOBAL before he decided to try his hand at entrepreneurship. After resigning from Wang in 1991, he signed on to help Cisco, then a small and struggling firm. Under his leadership and entrepreneurial guidance, Cisco has become one of the largest and most important technology companies in the world.

Opportunities for Minorities and Women More small businesses are also being started by minorities and women.[18] The number of businesses owned by African Americans increased by 60 percent during the most recent five-year period for which data are available and now totals about 2 million. The number of

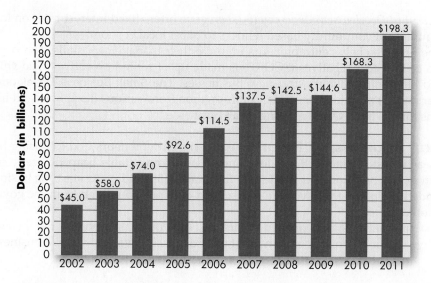

FIGURE 3.3 Growth of Online Retail Spending
Source: http://www.census.gov/retail/

Hispanic-owned businesses has grown 44 percent and now totals about 2.25 million. Ownership among Asians has increased 41 percent and among Pacific Islanders 35 percent.[19]

Almost 8 million businesses are now owned by women, and they generate a combined $200 trillion in revenue a year and employ about 13 million workers.[20] Figure 3.4 shows some of the reasons women cite for starting their own businesses.

Global Opportunities
Many entrepreneurs are also finding new opportunities in foreign markets. Doug Mellinger is founder and CEO of PRT Group, a software development company. One of Mellinger's biggest problems was finding trained programmers. There aren't enough U.S.-based programmers to go around, and foreign-born programmers face strict immigration quotas. So Mellinger set up shop on Barbados, a Caribbean island where the government helps him attract foreign programmers and does everything it can to make things easier. Today, PRT has customers and suppliers from dozens of nations.

Better Survival Rates
More people are encouraged to test their skills as entrepreneurs because the small business failure rate has declined. During the 1960s and 1970s, less than half of all new start-ups survived more than 18 months; only one in five lasted 10 years. Now, however, 44 percent can expect to survive for at least four years.[21]

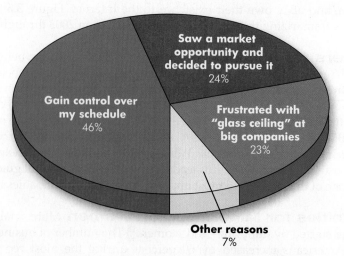

FIGURE 3.4 Reasons Women Give for Starting Businesses

Reasons for Failure

Unfortunately, more than half of all new businesses will not enjoy long-term success. Why do some succeed and others fail? Although no set pattern has been established, four general factors contribute to failure:

1 *Managerial incompetence or inexperience.* Some entrepreneurs put too much faith in common sense, overestimate their own managerial skills, or believe that hard work alone ensures success. If managers don't know how to make basic business decisions or don't understand basic management principles, they aren't likely to succeed in the long run.

2 *Neglect.* Some entrepreneurs try to launch ventures in their spare time, and others devote only limited time to new businesses. But starting a small business demands an overwhelming time commitment. If you aren't willing to put in the time and effort that a business requires, you aren't likely to survive.

3 *Weak control systems.* Effective control systems keep a business on track and alert managers to potential trouble. If your control systems don't signal impending problems, you may be in serious trouble before you spot more obvious difficulties. For instance, some businesses fail because they do a poor job of managing their credit collection policies. Anxious to grow, they may be too liberal in extending credit to their customers and then end up not being able to collect all the money that is owed to them.

4 *Insufficient capital.* Some entrepreneurs are overly optimistic about how soon they'll start earning profits. In most cases, it takes months or even years. Amazon.com didn't earn a profit for 10 years but obviously still required capital to pay employees and to cover other expenses. Experts say you need enough capital to operate at least six months without earning a profit; some recommend enough to last a year.[22]

Reasons for Success

Four basic factors are also typically cited to explain small business success:

1 *Hard work, drive, and dedication.* Small business owners must be committed to succeeding and willing to spend the time and effort to make it happen. Gladys Edmunds, a single mother in Pittsburgh, wanted to open a travel agency but did not have enough money to get started. So, she washed laundry, made chicken dinners to sell to cab drivers, and sold fire extinguishers door to door to earn start-up money. Now Edmunds Travel Consultants employs eight people and earns about $6 million a year.

2 *Market demand for the products or services being provided.* Careful analysis of market conditions can help small business owners assess the probable reception of their products. Attempts to expand restaurants specializing in baked potatoes, muffins, and gelato often struggle, but hamburger and pizza chains continue to expand.

3 *Managerial competence.* Successful owners may acquire competence through training or experience or by drawing on the expertise of others. Few, however, succeed alone or straight out of college. Most spend time in successful companies or partner with others to bring expertise to a new business.

4 *Luck.* After Alan McKim started Clean Harbors, an environmental cleanup firm in New England, he struggled to keep his business afloat. Then the U.S. government committed $1.6 billion to toxic waste cleanup—McKim's specialty. He landed several large government contracts and put his business on solid financial footing. Had the government fund not been created at just the right time, McKim might well have failed. Similarly, Netflix might not have succeeded if it had not started just as customers were shifting away from video cassettes to DVDs.

entrepreneurship and new ventures

Harvard Dropout Turned Billionaire

Do you Facebook? An estimated 175 million people in the United States do, and almost half are college students. The immensely popular social networking website was started by Harvard sophomore Mark Zuckerberg in February 2004 as a way for his classmates to network. The site proved to be so popular that he quickly opened it up to other schools. By November 2004, the site boasted 1 million users. A mere 18 months later, membership had ballooned to 7 million members at 2,100 colleges and 22,000 high schools. When it began accepting non-students in October 2006, membership doubled from 12 million to 24 million in just 8 months. Today, Facebook.com is one of the most visited sites on the Internet, running neck and neck with Google among U.S. college students. The total number of worldwide Facebook users exceeds 1 billion, with more than half of them visiting Facebook daily.

Although Facebook began as a noncommercial enterprise, it wasn't long before Zuckerberg realized that if he had more cash he could convert it into a business. PayPal cofounder Peter Thiel invested $500,000 in 2004, and substantial investments of additional venture capital followed. The new company lost $3.6 million in fiscal 2005, but with projected revenues of $150 million in 2007, Microsoft paid $240 million for a 1.6 percent stake in the company, pushing its valuation to $15 billion. When Facebook started trading its stock in 2012, Zuckerberg became a billionaire.

But interestingly, from a pure business standpoint, Facebook has a problem that is not widely known—it's actually finding it hard to make a profit. Approximately 85 percent of the company's total revenue comes from advertising (about $210 million in 2011), with another $35 million to $50 million coming from sales of virtual gifts, little icons that pop up in certain Facebook

programs and that users can exchange for about $1. In 2009, Facebook sold about $3 million worth of virtual gifts every month, but revenues for the year—about $260 million—fell short of the company's $300 million projection. It was time to get serious about profit.

If we look even more closely at these numbers, we notice an interesting phenomenon: user rates and revenues aren't going in the same direction. Since its inception, Facebook has had a problem with monetization—how to make a profit. It's a problem that Facebook shares with MySpace, which still commands a substantial share of the income from social networking. The solution, of course, is ad revenue; user fees are negligible, and even $3 million a month in virtual gift sales won't begin to cover server costs. When they first appeared on the Internet scene, social networks seemed like turbocharged revenue generators, but both Facebook and MySpace have found that selling spots on Web pages dedicated to personal profiles and group interchanges isn't as easy as it seemed.[23]

OBJECTIVE 5

Explain
sole proprietorships, partnerships, and cooperatives and discuss the advantages and disadvantages of each.

Noncorporate Business Ownership

Whether they intend to launch a small local business or a new venture projected to grow rapidly, all entrepreneurs must decide which form of legal ownership best suits their goals: *sole proprietorship*, *partnership*, or *corporation*. Because this choice affects a host of managerial and financial issues, few decisions are more critical. Entrepreneurs must consider their own preferences, their immediate and long-range needs, and the advantages and disadvantages of each form. Table 3.1 compares the most important differences among the three major ownership forms.

Sole Proprietorships

Sole Proprietorship *business owned and usually operated by one person who is responsible for all of its debts*

The **sole proprietorship** is owned and usually operated by one person. About 74 percent of all U.S. businesses are sole proprietorships; however, they account for only about 4 percent of total business revenues. Though usually small, they may be as large as steel mills or department stores.

table 3.1 Comparative Summary: Three Forms of Business Ownership

Business Form	Liability	Continuity	Management	Sources of Investment
Proprietorship	Personal, unlimited	Ends with death or decision of owner	Personal, unrestricted	Personal
General Partnership	Personal, unlimited	Ends with death or decision of any partner	Unrestricted or depends on partnership agreement	Personal by partner(s)
Corporation	Capital invested	As stated in charter, perpetual or for specified period of years	Under control of board of directors, which is selected by stockholders	Purchase of stock

Advantages of Sole Proprietorships Freedom may be the most important benefit of sole proprietorships. Because they own their businesses, sole proprietors answer to no one but themselves. Sole proprietorships are also easy to form. Sometimes, you can go into business simply by putting a sign on the door. The simplicity of legal setup procedures makes this form appealing to self-starters and independent spirits, as do low start-up costs.

Another attractive feature is the tax benefits extended to businesses that are likely to suffer losses in their early stages. Tax laws permit owners to treat sales revenues and operating expenses as part of their personal finances, paying taxes based on their personal tax rate. They can cut taxes by deducting business losses from income earned from personal sources other than the business.

Disadvantages of Sole Proprietorships A major drawback is **unlimited liability;** a sole proprietor is personally liable for all debts incurred by the business. If the company fails to generate enough cash, bills must be paid out of the owner's pocket. Another disadvantage is lack of continuity; a sole proprietorship legally dissolves when the owner dies. Although the business can be reorganized by a successor, executors or heirs must otherwise sell its assets.

Unlimited Liability *legal principle holding owners responsible for paying off all debts of a business*

Finally, a sole proprietorship depends on the resources of one person whose managerial and financial limitations may constrain the business. Sole proprietors often find it hard to borrow money to start-up or expand. Many bankers fear that they won't be able to recover loans if owners become disabled or insolvent.

Partnerships

The most common type of partnership, the **general partnership,** is similar to a sole proprietorship but is owned by more than one person. Partners may invest equal or unequal sums of money. In most cases, partners share the profits equally or in proportion to their investment. In certain cases, though, the distribution of profits may be based on other things. A locally prominent athlete, for instance, may lend her or his name to the partnership and earn profits without actually investing funds. And sometimes one partner invests all of the funds needed for the business but plays no role in its management; this person is usually called a *silent partner*. Another partner might invest nothing but provide all the labor. In this case, the financial investor likely owns the entire business, and the labor partner owns nothing. But over time, and as specified in a contract, the labor partner gradually gains an ownership stake in the business (usually called *sweat equity*).

General Partnership *business with two or more owners who share in both the operation of the firm and the financial responsibility for its debts*

Advantages of Partnerships The most striking advantage of general partnerships is the ability to grow by adding new talent and money. Because banks prefer to make loans to enterprises that are not dependent on single individuals, partnerships find it easier to borrow money when compared to sole proprietorships. They can also invite new partners to join by investing money.

Like a sole proprietorship, a partnership can be organized by meeting only a few legal requirements. Even so, all partnerships must begin with an agreement of some kind. In all but two states, the Revised Uniform Limited Partnership Act requires the filing of specific information about the business and its partners. Partners may also agree to bind themselves in ways not specified by law. In any case, an agreement should answer questions such as the following:

- Who invested what sums?

- Who will receive what share of the profits?

- Who does what, and who reports to whom?

- How may the partnership be dissolved? In the event of dissolution, how will assets be distributed?

- How will surviving partners be protected from claims made by a deceased partner's heirs?

The partnership agreement is strictly a private document. No laws require partners to file agreements with any government agency. Nor are partnerships regarded as legal entities. In the eyes of the law, a partnership is just two or more people working together. Because partnerships have no independent legal standing, the Internal Revenue Service (IRS) taxes partners as individuals.

Disadvantages of Partnerships For general partnerships as for sole proprietorships, unlimited liability is the greatest drawback. Each partner may be liable for all debts incurred by the partnership. If any partner incurs a business debt, all partners may be liable, even if some of them did not know about or agree to the new debt.

Partnerships also share with sole proprietorships the potential lack of continuity. When one partner dies or leaves, the original partnership dissolves, even if one or more of the other partners want it to continue. But dissolution need not mean a loss of sales revenues. Survivors may form a new partnership to retain the old firm's business.

A related disadvantage is difficulty in transferring ownership. No partner may sell out without the consent of the others. A partner who wants to retire or to transfer interest to a son or daughter must have the other partners' consent.

Limited Partnership *type of partnership consisting of limited partners and a general (or managing) partner*

Limited Partner *partner who does not share in a firm's management and is liable for its debts only to the limits of said partner's investment*

General (or Active) Partner *partner who actively manages a firm and who has unlimited liability for its debts*

Master Limited Partnership *form of ownership that sells shares to investors who receive profits and that pays taxes on income from profits*

Alternatives to General Partnerships Because of these disadvantages, general partnerships are among the least popular forms of business. Roughly 3.5 million U.S. partnerships generate only 15 percent of total sales revenues. To resolve some of the problems inherent in general partnerships, especially unlimited liability, some partners have tried alternative agreements. The **limited partnership** allows for **limited partners** who invest money but are liable for debts only to the extent of their investments. They cannot, however, take active roles in business operations. A limited partnership must have at least one **general (or active) partner,** mostly for liability purposes. This is usually the person who runs the business and is responsible for its survival and growth.

Under a **master limited partnership,** an organization sells shares (partnership interests) to investors on public markets such as the New York Stock Exchange. Investors are paid back from profits. The master partner retains at least 50 percent ownership and runs the business, and minority partners have no management voice. (The master partner differs from a general partner, who has no such ownership restriction.) The master partner must regularly provide minority partners with detailed operating and financial reports.

Cooperatives

Sometimes, groups of sole proprietorships or partnerships agree to work together for their common benefit by forming cooperatives. **Cooperatives** combine the freedom of sole proprietorships with the financial power of corporations. They give members greater production power, greater marketing power, or both. On the other hand, they are limited to serving the specific needs of their members. Although cooperatives make up only a minor segment of the U.S. economy, their role is still important in agriculture. Ocean Spray, the Florida Citrus Growers, Riceland, and Cabot Cheese are among the best-known cooperatives.

Cooperative *form of ownership in which a group of sole proprietorships or partnerships agree to work together for common benefits*

Corporations

There are about 5.8 million corporations in the United States. As you can see from Figure 3.5, they account for about 17 percent of all U.S. businesses but generate about 81 percent of all sales revenues.[24] Almost all large businesses use this form, and corporations dominate global business. As we will see, corporations need not be large; many small businesses also elect to operate as corporations.

According to the most recent data, Walmart, the world's largest corporation, posted annual revenue of over $446 billion, with total profits of more than $15 billion. Even "smaller" large corporations post huge sales figures. The New York Times Company, though five hundredth in size among U.S. corporations, posted a net loss of $38.7 million on annual sales of $2.32 billion. Given the size and influence of this form of ownership, we devote a great deal of attention to various aspects of corporations.

The Corporate Entity

When you think of corporations, you probably think of giant operations such as General Motors and IBM. The very word *corporation* inspires images of size and power. In reality, however, your corner newsstand has as much right to incorporate as

OBJECTIVE 6
Describe
corporations, discuss their advantages and disadvantages, and identify different kinds of corporations; explain the basic issues involved in managing a corporation and discuss special issues related to corporate ownership.

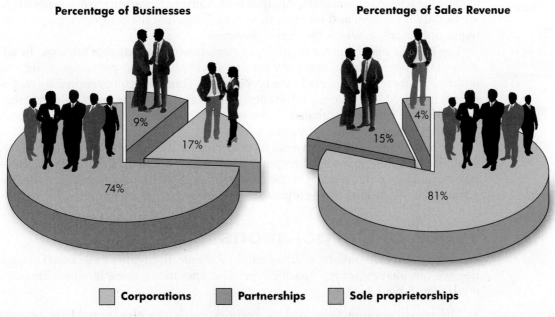

FIGURE 3.5 Proportions of U.S. Firms in Terms of Organization Type and Sales Revenue
Sources: http://www.census.gov/compendia/statab/2012/tables/12s0744.pdf, http://www.irs.gov/pub/irssoi/08coccr.pdf, http://www.irs.gov/pub/irssoi/08pareturnsnap.pdf, http://www.irs.gov/pub/irssoi/10sumbulsolprop.pdf

Corporation *business that is legally considered an entity separate from its owners and is liable for its own debts; owners' liability extends to the limits of their investments*

a giant automaker. Moreover, the newsstand and GM would share the characteristics of all **corporations:** legal status as separate entities, property rights and obligations, and indefinite life spans.

In 1819, the U.S. Supreme Court defined a corporation as "an artificial being, invisible, intangible, and existing only in contemplation of the law." The court defined the corporation as a legal person. Corporations may, therefore, perform the following activities:

- Sue and be sued

- Buy, hold, and sell property

- Make and sell products

- Commit crimes and be tried and punished for them

Limited Liability *legal principle holding investors liable for a firm's debts only to the limits of their personal investments in it*

Advantages of Incorporation
The biggest advantage of corporations is **limited liability;** investor liability is limited to personal investment (through stock ownership, covered later) in the corporation. In the event of failure, the courts may seize and sell a corporation's assets but cannot touch the investors' personal possessions. If, for example, you invest $1,000 in stock in a corporation that ends up failing, you may lose your $1,000, but no more. In other words, your liability is limited to the $1,000 you invested.

Another advantage is continuity. Because it has a legal life independent of founders and owners, a corporation can, at least in theory, continue forever. Shares of stock may be sold or passed on to heirs, and most corporations also benefit from the continuity provided by professional management. Finally, corporations have advantages in raising money. By selling stock, they expand the number of investors and the amount of available funds. Continuity and legal status tend to make lenders more willing to grant loans.

Tender Offer *offer to buy shares made by a prospective buyer directly to a target corporation's shareholders, who then make individual decisions about whether to sell*

Double Taxation *situation in which taxes may be payable both by a corporation on its profits and by shareholders on dividend incomes*

Disadvantages of Incorporation
Although a chief attraction is ease of transferring ownership, this same feature can create complications. For example, using a legal process called a **tender offer,** an offer to buy shares made by a prospective buyer directly to a corporation's shareholders, a corporation can be taken over against the will of its managers. Another disadvantage is start-up cost. Corporations are heavily regulated, and incorporation entails meeting the complex legal requirements of the state in which the firm is chartered.

The biggest disadvantage of incorporation, however, is **double taxation.** In addition to income taxes on company profits, stockholders also pay taxes on income returned by their investments in the corporation. Thus, the profits earned by corporations are taxed twice—once at the corporate level and then again at the ownership level. Because profits are treated as owners' personal income, sole proprietorships and partnerships are taxed only once.

The advantages and disadvantages of corporate ownership have inspired laws establishing different kinds of corporations. Most are intended to help businesses take advantage of the benefits of the corporate model without assuming all the disadvantages. We discuss these corporate forms next.

Types of Corporations

We can classify corporations as either *public* or *private.* But within these broad categories, we can identify several specific types of corporations, some of which are summarized in Table 3.2.

Closely Held (or Private) Corporation *corporation whose stock is held by only a few people and is not available for sale to the general public*

- The most common form of U.S. corporation is the **closely held (or private) corporation.** Stock is held by only a few people and is not available for sale to the public. The controlling group of stockholders may be a family, a management group, or even the firm's employees. Most smaller corporations fit this profile.

table 3.2 Types of Corporations

Type	Distinguishing Features	Examples
Closely Held	Stock held by only a few people Subject to corporate taxation	Blue Cross/Blue Shield MasterCard Primestar
Publicly Held	Stock widely held among many investors Subject to corporate taxation	Apple Starbucks Texas Instruments
Subchapter S	Organized much like a closely held corporation Subject to additional regulation Subject to partnership taxation	Minglewood Associates Entech Pest Systems Frontier Bank
Limited Liability	Organized much like a publicly held corporation Subject to additional regulation Subject to partnership taxation	Pacific Northwest Associates Global Ground Support Ritz Carlton
Professional	Subject to partnership taxation Limited business liability Unlimited professional liability	Norman Hui, DDS & Associates B & H Engineering Anderson, McCoy & Oria
Multinational	Spans national boundaries Subject to regulation in multiple countries	Toyota Nestlé General Electric

- When shares are publicly issued, the firm becomes a **publicly held** (or **public**) **corporation.** Stock is widely held and available for sale to the public. Many large businesses are of this type.

- The **S corporation** (more fully called the *Subchapter S corporation*) is a hybrid of a closely held corporation and a partnership. It is organized and operates like a corporation, but it is treated like a partnership for tax purposes. To qualify, firms must meet stringent legal conditions. For instance, stockholders must be individual U.S. citizens.

- Another hybrid is the **limited liability corporation (LLC).** Owners are taxed like partners, each paying personal taxes only. However, they also enjoy the benefits of limited liability accorded to publicly held corporations. LLCs have grown in popularity in recent years, partially because of IRS rulings that allow corporations, partnerships, and foreign investors to be partial owners.

- **Professional corporations** are most likely composed of doctors, lawyers, accountants, or other professionals. Although the corporate structure protects from unlimited financial liability, members are not immune from unlimited liability. Professional negligence by a member can entail personal liability on the individual's part.

- As the term implies, the **multinational (or transnational) corporation** spans national boundaries. Stock may be traded on the exchanges of several countries, and managers are likely to be of different nationalities.

Publicly Held (or Public) Corporation *corporation whose stock is widely held and available for sale to the general public*

S Corporation *hybrid of a closely held corporation and a partnership, organized and operated like a corporation but treated as a partnership for tax purposes*

Limited Liability Corporation (LLC) *hybrid of a publicly held corporation and a partnership in which owners are taxed as partners but enjoy the benefits of limited liability*

Professional Corporation *form of ownership allowing professionals to take advantage of corporate benefits while granting them limited business liability and unlimited professional liability*

Multinational (or Transnational) Corporation *form of corporation spanning national boundaries*

Managing a Corporation

Creating any type of corporation can be complicated because of the various legal conditions that must be met. In addition, once the corporate entity comes into existence, it must be managed by people who understand the principles of **corporate governance,** the roles of shareholders, directors, and other managers in corporate decision making and accountability. In this section, we discuss the principles of *stock ownership* and *stockholders' rights* and describe the role of *boards of directors*. We then examine some special issues related to corporate ownership.

Corporate governance is established by the firm's bylaws and usually involves three distinct bodies. **Stockholders (or shareholders)** are the owners of a corporation, investors who buy ownership shares in the form of stock. The *board of directors* is a group elected by stockholders to oversee corporate management. Corporate *officers* are top managers hired by the board to run the corporation on a day-to-day basis.

Corporate Governance *roles of shareholders, directors, and other managers in corporate decision making and accountability*

Stockholder (or Shareholder) *owner of shares of stock in a corporation*

Stock Ownership and Stockholders' Rights

Corporations sell shares, called *stock*, to investors who then become stockholders, or shareholders. Profits are distributed among stockholders in the form of *dividends*, and corporate managers serve at stockholders' discretion. In a closely held corporation, only a few people own stock. Shares of publicly held corporations are widely held.

Boards of Directors

Board of Directors *governing body of a corporation that reports to its shareholders and delegates power to run its day-to-day operations while remaining responsible for sustaining its assets*

The governing body of a corporation is its **board of directors.** Boards communicate with stockholders and other stakeholders through such channels as an annual report, a summary of a firm's financial health. They also set policy on dividends, major spending, and executive compensation. They are legally responsible and accountable for corporate actions and are increasingly being held personally liable for them.

Officers

Although board members oversee operations, most do not participate in day-to-day management. Rather, they hire a team of managers to run the firm. This team, called **officers,** is usually headed by the firm's **chief executive officer (CEO),** who is responsible for overall performance. Other officers typically include a *president*, who is responsible for internal management, and *vice-presidents*, who oversee various functional areas such as marketing and operations.

Officers *top management team of a corporation*

chief executive officer (CEO) *top manager who is responsible for the overall performance of a corporation*

Special Issues in Corporate Ownership

In recent years, several issues have grown in importance in the area of corporate ownership, including *joint ventures and strategic alliances, employee stock ownership plans,* and *institutional ownership*. Other important issues in contemporary corporate ownership involve *mergers, acquisitions, divestitures,* and *spin offs*.

Joint Ventures and Strategic Alliances

Strategic Alliance *strategy in which two or more organizations collaborate on a project for mutual gain*

Joint Venture *strategic alliance in which the collaboration involves joint ownership of the new venture*

In a **strategic alliance,** two or more organizations collaborate on a project for mutual gain. When partners share ownership of what is essentially a new enterprise, it is called a **joint venture.** The number of strategic alliances has increased rapidly in recent years on both domestic and international fronts. For example, General Motors and Ford recently announced a new strategic alliance to jointly develop 10-speed transmissions for automobiles.[25] Ford also has joint ventures with Volkswagen (in South America) and Mazda (in Japan).

Employee Stock Ownership Plans

Employee Stock Ownership Plan (ESOP) *arrangement in which a corporation holds its own stock in trust for its employees, who gradually receive ownership of the stock and control its voting rights*

An **employee stock ownership plan (ESOP)** allows employees to own a significant share of the corporation through trusts established on their behalf. Current estimates count about 11,500 ESOPs in the United States. The growth rate in new ESOPs has slowed a bit in recent years, but they still are an important part of corporate ownership patterns in the United States.

Institutional Ownership Most individual investors don't own enough stock to exert influence on corporate managers. In recent years, however, more stock has been purchased by **institutional investors.** Because they control enormous resources, these investors—especially mutual and pension funds—can buy huge blocks of stock. The national teachers' retirement system (TIAA CREF) has assets of more than $400 billion, much of it invested in stocks. Institutional investors own almost 55 percent of all the stock issued in the United States.

Mergers, Acquisitions, Divestitures, and Spin Offs Another important set of issues includes mergers, acquisitions, divestitures, and spin offs. Mergers and acquisitions involve the legal joining of two or more corporations. A divestiture occurs when a corporation sells a business operation to another corporation; with a spin off, it creates a new operation.

MERGERS AND ACQUISITIONS (M&As) A **merger** occurs when two firms combine to create a new company. For example, United Airlines and Continental recently merged to create one of the world's largest airlines. The new airline bears the United name but retains the equipment design of Continental. Continental's CEO assumed control of the new company. The firm took more than two years to integrate their respective operations into a unified new firm. Even more recently, American Airlines and US Airlines announced that they, too, were merging.

In an **acquisition,** one firm buys another outright. Many deals that are loosely called mergers are really acquisitions. Why? Because one of the two firms will usually control the newly combined ownership. In general, when the two firms are roughly the same size, the combination is usually called a merger even if one firm is taking control of the other. When the acquiring firm is substantially larger than the acquired firm, the deal is really an acquisition. So-called M&As are an important form of corporate strategy. They let firms increase product lines, expand operations, go international, and create new enterprises. Halliburton Corporation recently acquired Boots and Coots, an oilfield firefighting business.

DIVESTITURES AND SPIN OFFS Sometimes, a corporation decides to sell a part of its existing business operations or set it up as a new and independent corporation. There may be several reasons for such a step. A firm might decide, for example, that it should focus more specifically on its core businesses, and thus it will sell off unrelated or underperforming businesses. Such a sale is called a **divestiture.** When a firm sells part of itself to raise capital, the strategy is known as a **spin off.** A spin off may also mean that a firm deems a business unit more valuable as a separate company. The Limited, for example, spun off three of its subsidiaries, Victoria's Secret, Bath & Body Works, and White Barn Candle Co., to create a new firm, Intimate Brands, which it then offered through an Initial Public Offering (IPO). The Limited retained 84 percent ownership of Intimate Brands while getting an infusion of new capital.

Institutional Investor *large investor, such as a mutual fund or a pension fund, that purchases large blocks of corporate stock*

Merger *the union of two corporations to form a new corporation*

Acquisition *the purchase of one company by another*

Divestiture *strategy whereby a firm sells one or more of its business units*

Spin Off *strategy of setting up one or more corporate units as new, independent corporations*

summary of learning objectives

OBJECTIVE 1

Define *small business*, **discuss its importance to the U.S. economy, and explain popular areas of small business.** (pp. 100–105)

A *small business* is independently owned and managed and has relatively little influence in its market. Most U.S. businesses are small businesses and employ less than 20 people. Small businesses are vitally important to the economy because of (1) *job creation*, (2) *innovation*, and (3) *contributions to big business*. The most common types of small businesses are firms engaged in (1) *services*, (2) *retailing*, and (3) *construction*. Services comprise the largest sector, in part because most service businesses require relatively little capital to start. In contrast, there are relatively fewer small businesses who manufacture products because the start-up costs are often high.

OBJECTIVE 2

Explain entrepreneurship and describe some key characteristics of entrepreneurial personalities and activities. (pp. 105–106)

Entrepreneurs are people who assume the risk of business ownership. Some entrepreneurs have a goal of independence and financial security, and others want to launch a new venture that can be grown into a large business. Most successful entrepreneurs are resourceful and concerned for customer relations. They have a strong desire to be their own bosses and can handle ambiguity and surprises. Today's entrepreneur is often an open-minded leader who relies on networks, business plans, and consensus and is just as likely to be female as male. Finally, although successful entrepreneurs understand the role of risk, they do not necessarily regard what they do as being risky.

OBJECTIVE 3

Describe the business plan and the start-up decisions made by small businesses and identify sources of financial aid available to such enterprises. (pp. 106–111)

A new business must first understand its potential distinctive competence, such as the ability to identify a niche (or unmet need) in an established market. Another distinctive competence is the ability to serve a new unexploited market. Still another is the ability to move quickly to take advantage of new opportunities, often called "first-mover advantage."

After identifying a potential distinctive competence, the next step in entrepreneurship is developing a business plan. A *business plan* summarizes business strategy for the new venture and shows how it will be implemented. The key elements of a business plan are setting goals and objectives, sales forecasting, and financial planning. Business plans are increasingly important because creditors and investors demand them as tools for deciding whether to finance or invest.

Entrepreneurs must also decide whether to buy an existing business, operate a franchise, or start from scratch. Entrepreneurs who choose to buy an existing business have better chances for success compared to those who start from scratch because of existing relationships with vendors and customers. Franchises provide considerable support in setup and operation, but franchise costs can be high and severely cut into profits. Starting a business from scratch can be the most risky, yet rewarding, way to start a new business.

To start a new business, it is essential to have money to finance the operation. Common funding sources include personal funds, family and friends, savings, lenders, investors, and governmental agencies. Lending institutions are more likely to finance an existing business than a new business because the risks are better understood. *Venture capital companies* are groups of small investors seeking to make profits on companies with rapid growth potential.

Most of these firms do not lend money but rather invest it, supplying capital in return for partial ownership. New businesses may also seek funding from small business investment companies (SBICs) as well as through Small Business Administration (SBA) programs.

OBJECTIVE 4

Discuss the trends in small business start-ups and identify the main reasons for success and failure among small businesses. (pp. 111–114)

Five trends have helped facilitate the growth in new businesses started in the United States every year. These trends are: (1) *the emergence of e-commerce*; (2) *crossovers from big business*; (3) *increased opportunities for minorities and women*; (4) *new opportunities in global enterprise*; and (5) *improved rates of survival among small businesses*.

However, more than half of all small businesses fail. Four basic factors that contribute to most small business failure: (1) *managerial incompetence or inexperience*; (2) *neglect*; (3) *weak control systems*; and (4) *insufficient capital*. Likewise, four basic factors explain most small business success: (1) *hard work, drive, and dedication*; (2) *market demand for the products or services being provided*; (3) *managerial competence*; and (4) *luck*.

OBJECTIVE 5

Explain sole proprietorships, partnerships, and cooperatives and discuss the advantages and disadvantages of each. (pp. 114–117)

A *sole proprietorship* is a business that is owned by one person. The most significant advantage to organizing as a sole proprietorship is the freedom to make decisions. In addition, it is relatively easy to form and operate a sole proprietorship. There are tax benefits for new businesses that are likely to suffer losses in early stages because these losses can offset income from another business or job on the tax return of a sole proprietor. A major drawback is *unlimited liability*, which is the legal concept that makes the owners of a sole proprietorship personally responsible for all its debts. Another disadvantage is that a sole proprietorship lacks continuity; when the owner dies or leaves the business, it does not continue to exist. Finally, a sole proprietorship depends on the resources of a single individual.

A *general partnership* is a sole proprietorship multiplied by the number of partner owners. The biggest advantage is its ability to grow by adding new talent and money. Partners report their share of the partnership's income and it is taxed on their individual tax return. Like a sole proprietorship, *unlimited liability* is a drawback. Partnerships may lack continuity and transferring ownership may be hard. No partner may sell out without the consent of the others. There are also special forms of partnerships, most notably limited partnerships and master limited partnerships.

Cooperatives combine the freedom of sole proprietorships with the financial power of corporations. A cooperative is a group of sole proprietorships or partnerships working together to gain greater production or marketing power.

OBJECTIVE 6

Describe corporations, discuss their advantages and disadvantages, and identify different kinds of corporations; explain the basic issues involved in managing a corporation and discuss special issues related to corporate ownership. (pp. 117–121)

All *corporations* share certain characteristics: legal status as separate entities, property rights and obligations, and indefinite life spans. They may sue and be sued; buy, hold, and sell property; make and sell products; and commit crimes and be tried and punished for them. The biggest advantage of incorporation is *limited liability*: investor liability is limited to one's personal investments in the corporation. Another advantage is continuity; a corporation can last indefinitely and does not end with the death or withdrawal of an owner. Finally, corporations have advantages in raising money. By selling stock, they expand the number of investors and the amount of available funds. Continuity and the ability to sell stock tend to make lenders more willing to grant loans.

One disadvantage is that a corporation can be taken over against the will of its managers. Another disadvantage is start-up cost. Corporations are heavily regulated and must meet complex legal requirements in the states in which they're chartered. The greatest potential drawback to incorporation is *double taxation* of profits. They are taxed first at the level of the corporation and then taxed as dividends when distributed to the stockholders. Corporations may be either private or public. In a private, or closely held, corporation, there are only a small number of owners and shares of stock are not available to the general public. Public corporations are able to sell their stock on the stock exchanges and have the ability to raise large amounts of capital. Special forms of ownership, such as S corporations, LLCs, and professional corporations, combine limited liability of a corporation with tax treatment of partnerships.

Corporations sell shares, called *stock*, to investors who then become *stockholders* (or shareholders) and the real owners. Profits are distributed among stockholders in the form of *dividends*, and managers serve at their discretion. The governing body of a corporation is its *board of directors*. Most board members do not participate in day-to-day management but rather hire a team of managers. This team, called *officers*, is usually headed by a *chief executive officer (CEO)* who is responsible for overall performance.

Several issues have grown in importance in the area of corporate ownership. In a *strategic alliance*, two or more organizations collaborate on a project for mutual gain. When partners share ownership of a new enterprise, the arrangement is called a *joint venture*. An *employee stock ownership plan (ESOP)* allows employees to own a significant share of the corporation through trusts established on their behalf. More stock is now being purchased by *institutional investors*. A *merger* occurs when two firms combine to create a new company, and in an *acquisition*, one firm buys another outright. A *divestiture* occurs when a corporation sells a part of its existing business operations or sets it up as a new and independent corporation. When a firm sells part of itself to raise capital, the strategy is known as a *spin off*.

key terms

acquisition (p. 121)
board of directors (p. 120)
business plan (p. 108)
chief executive officer (CEO) (p. 120)
closely held (or private) corporation (p. 118)
cooperative (p. 117)
corporate governance (p. 120)
corporation (p. 118)
divestiture (p. 121)
double taxation (p. 118)
employee stock ownership plan (ESOP) (p. 120)
entrepreneur (p. 105)
entrepreneurship (p. 105)
established market (p. 107)
first-mover advantage (p. 107)

franchise (p. 109)
general (or active) partner (p. 116)
general partnership (p. 115)
institutional investor (p. 121)
joint venture (p. 120)
limited liability (p. 118)
limited liability corporation (LLC) (p. 119)
limited partner (p. 116)
limited partnership (p. 116)
master limited partnership (p. 116)
merger (p. 121)
multinational (or transnational) corporation (p. 119)
niche (p. 107)
officers (p. 120)
professional corporation (p. 119)

publicly held (or public) corporation (p. 119)
S corporation (p. 119)
small business (p. 100)
Small Business Administration (SBA) (p. 100)
Small Business Development Center (SBDC) (p. 111)
small business investment company (SBIC) (p. 110)
sole proprietorship (p. 114)
spin off (p. 121)
stockholder (or shareholder) (p. 120)
strategic alliance (p. 120)
tender offer (p. 118)
unlimited liability (p. 115)
venture capital company (p. 110)

Go to **pearsonglobaleditions.com/mybizlab** to complete the problems marked with this icon ✪.

questions & exercises

QUESTIONS FOR REVIEW

⭐ **3-1.** Why are small businesses important to the U.S. economy?

3-2. Which industries are easiest for a small business to enter? Which are hardest? Why?

3-3. What are the primary reasons for new business failure and success?

3-4. What are the basic forms of noncorporate business ownership? What are the key advantages and disadvantages of each?

QUESTIONS FOR ANALYSIS

⭐ **3-5.** After considering the characteristics of entrepreneurs, do you think that you would be a good candidate to start your own business? Why or why not?

3-6. If you were going to open a new business, what type would it be? Why?

⭐ **3-7.** Would you prefer to buy an existing business or start from scratch? Why?

3-8. Why might a closely held corporation choose to remain private? Why might it choose to be publicly traded?

APPLICATION EXERCISES

3-9. Interview the owner/manager of a sole proprietorship or a general partnership. What characteristics of that business form led the owner to choose it? Does he or she ever contemplate changing the form of the business?

3-10. Although more than half of all small businesses don't survive five years, franchises have a much better track record. However, it can be difficult to buy a franchise. Research a popular food industry franchise, such as Panera Bread, Sonic, California Tortilla, or Subway, and detail the requirements for net worth and liquid cash for the franchisee as well as up-front and annual fees.

building a business: continuing team exercises

Assignment

Meet with your team members and discuss your new business venture within the context of this chapter. Develop specific responses to the following:

3-11. To what extent do each of you really want to be an entrepreneur?

3-12. For the specific business you are starting (in this exercise), does it make more sense to start from scratch, to buy an existing business, or to buy a franchise? Why?

3-13. How will you most likely finance your new venture?

3-14. What factors will most likely contribute to your success? What factors might cause your business to fail? Is there a way to minimize of eliminate these risk factors?

3-15. What form of ownership will your group use? What are the advantages and disadvantages of this approach?

building your business skills

A TASTY IDEA

Goal

To encourage you to identify options for financing a new business.

Background Information

Suppose that you and three friends from college would like to open a new restaurant. Collectively, you have almost 20 years of experience in the restaurant industry and, with lots of new houses in the area, you think that there's an opportunity to make a lot of money if you can offer interesting food at good prices. You've even identified a great location, but you realize that it's going to take a lot of money to get this business off the ground. As recent college graduates, you don't have a lot of money, so you're looking for the best source of funding. Realistically, you realize that you're going to need at least $100,000 to sustain operations until your business starts to return a profit.

Method

STEP 1

Individually or in a group of two or three students, brainstorm a list of options for financing. You'll want to do a little online research to find out more about some of the loan programs identified in the text.

STEP 2

For each of the funding options, develop a list of pros and cons. Be sure to consider all the implications of each form of financing, considering interest rates, repayment options, and eligibility requirements.

FOLLOW-UP QUESTIONS

3-16. Before getting financing, what will be expected of you and your business partners?

3-17. Which source of financing would be best for you and your partners? Why?

3-18. What form of business ownership would be most appropriate for your new restaurant and why?

exercising your ethics

BREAKING UP IS HARD TO DO

The Situation

Connie and Mark began a 25-year friendship after finishing college and discovering their mutual interest in owning a business. Established as a general partnership, their home furnishings center is a successful business sustained for 20 years by a share and share-alike relationship. Start-up cash, daily responsibilities, and profits have all been shared equally. The partners both work four days each week except when busy seasons require both of them to be in the store. Shared goals and compatible personalities have led to a solid give-and-taken relationship that helps them overcome business problems while maintaining a happy interpersonal relationship.

The division of work is a natural match and successful combination because of the partners' different but complementary interests. Mark buys the merchandise and maintains up-to-date contacts with suppliers; he also handles personnel matters (hiring and training employees). Connie manages the inventory, buys shipping supplies, keeps the books, and manages the finances. Mark does more selling, with Connie helping out only during busy seasons. Both partners share in decisions about advertising and promotions.

The Dilemma

Things began changing two years ago, when Connie became less interested in the business and got more involved in other activities. Whereas Mark's enthusiasm remained high, Connie's time was increasingly consumed by travel, recreation, and community service activities. At first, she reduced her work commitment from four to three days a week. Then she indicated that she wanted to cut back further, to just two days. "In that case," Mark replied, "we'll have to make some changes."

Mark insisted that profit sharing be adjusted to reflect his larger role in running the business. He proposed that Connie's monthly salary be cut in half (from $4,000 to $2,000). Connie agreed. He recommended that the $2,000 savings be shifted to his salary because of his increased workload, but this time Connie balked, arguing that Mark's current $4,000 salary already compensated him for his contributions. She proposed to split the difference, with Mark getting a $1,000 increase and the other $1,000 going into the firm's cash account. Mark said no and insisted on a full $2,000 raise. To avoid a complete falling out, Connie finally gave in, even though she thought it unfair for Mark's salary to jump from $4,000 per month to $6,000. At that point, she made a promise to herself: "To even things out, I'll find a way to get at least $1,000 worth of inventory for personal use each month."

QUESTIONS TO ADDRESS

3-19. Identify the ethical issues, if any, regarding Mark's and Connie's respective positions on Mark's proposed $2,000 salary increase.

3-20. What kind of salary adjustments do you think would be fair in this situation? Explain why.

3-21. There is another way for Mark and Connie to solve their differences: Because the terms of participation have changed, it might make sense to dissolve the existing partnership. What do you recommend in this regard?

team exercise

PUBLIC OR PRIVATE? THAT IS THE QUESTION

The Situation

The Thomas Corporation is a well-financed, private corporation with a solid and growing product line, little debt, and a stable workforce. However, in the past few months, there has been a growing rift among the board of directors that has created considerable differences of opinion as to the future directions of the firm.

The Dilemma

Some board members believe the firm should "go public" with a stock offering. Because each board member owns a large block of corporate stock, each would make a considerable amount of money if the company went public. One board member put it this way, "We've all worked hard to make the company a success and I think that it's time that we see the fruits of our labor." Other board members see the opportunity to bring in more cash and expand into international markets.

On the other side, some board members want to maintain the status quo as a private corporation. The biggest advantage of this approach is that the firm maintains its current ability to remain autonomous in its operations. Most of the board members have been with the company from the beginning. They enjoy the family friendly environment and are afraid that new investors will want to make changes.

Team Activity

Assemble a group of four students and assign each group member to one of the following roles:

- An employee at the Thomas Corporation
- A customer of the Thomas Corporation
- A board member who is the current company president
- A board member seeking cash

ACTION STEPS

3-22. Before hearing any of your group's comments on this situation, and from the perspective of your assigned role, which option do you think is best? Write down the reasons for your position.

3-23. Allow each member of the group to share their perspective on the decision as well as their reasons.

3-24. As a group, develop a list of the advantages and disadvantages of going public.

3-25. Develop a recommendation for the board of directors of Thomas Corporation based on your discussions.

3-26. Gather your group together and reveal, in turn, each member's comments on the situation.

cases

Launching a Business in the Gym

Continued from page 100

At the beginning of this chapter you read about how the idea for Netflix came about and how the company chose their business model. Using the information presented in this chapter you should now be able to answer the following questions:

QUESTIONS FOR DISCUSSION

3-27. What are some of the primary reasons that Netflix has been successful?

3-28. Netflix is a corporation. Why do you think the firm uses this form of ownership?

3-29. What threats might derail Netflix's success? What steps might the firm take today in order to thwart those threats?

3-30. Suppose Reed Hastings asked you for advice on how to make Netflix better. What would you tell him?

Ice Cream Headache

If you have ever visited a Cold Stone Creamery, you are familiar with the seemingly endless list of ice creams and toppings, as well as prepared cakes and other confections. You may not be aware, however, that Cold Stone is a franchise sold by Kahala Corporation, whose other brands include Blimpie's sandwich shops and Samurai Sam's Teriyaki Grills.[26] Cold Stone has approximately 1,500 locations in 17 countries. In case you are considering opening your own Cold Stone, you might be interested in the conditions of ownership. Those who wish to purchase a Cold Stone franchise must show that they are financially sound, with at least $125,000 of cash available and a $250,000 net worth. The up-front franchise fee is $42,000 and the franchise is good for a ten-year term. Cold Stone provides plenty of assistance in selecting a location and opening a store, but startup costs are estimated to be over $250,000. The company estimates that the average time to open a location is four to twelve months, which presents a real challenge for a new franchise owner. Once in operation, franchisees will pay a royalty fee of 6% of gross sales and an advertising fee of 3% of gross sales.[27]

Cold Stone's parent organization provides support in site selection, lease terms, and equipment selection. They provide 11 days of training at the company's headquarters and three additional days of training at the franchisee's location. Once the business is up and running, they provide continued support through newsletters and annual meetings, cooperative advertising arrangements, and a toll-free hotline. In 2013, Entreprenuer.com ranked Cold Stone Creamery #53 in its list of Top 500 franchise opportunities.[28]

Revenues for Cold Stone franchises have declined in recent years. In 2005, the typical location earned approximately $400,000 in revenues, but this number dipped to $352,000 in 2011. Tough economic times cut into discretionary spending, hurting the ice cream business. In 2012, a group of Cold Stone Creamery franchise owners threatened to file suit against the company, alleging that the company was not delivering on promised marketing campaigns. Additionally, there was an on-going dispute over revenue and interest from unused gift cards. Tension between franchisors and franchisees are becoming increasingly common. Eric Stites, managing director of *Franchise Business Review,* reflects "When franchises aren't making money, that's when you see them form associations and sue the franchiser." Franchises in the food industry seem to have been hurt especially hard. Although the initial investment is often close to $450,000, annual profits average only $88,382. Although a bowl of ice cream will brighten almost anyone's day, a Cold Stone Franchise may not be a sure thing.[29]

QUESTIONS FOR DISCUSSION

3-31. What would be the advantages of buying a Cold Stone Creamery franchise as opposed to starting a business from scratch?

3-32. What are the disadvantages of buying a Cold Stone Creamery franchise?

3-33. While franchise owners must have at least $125,000 of cash available, average startup costs are more than double this amount. What are the most likely sources of funding for a franchise?

3-34. How would you research a franchise purchase before making the decision to invest?

3-35. Do you think that you would be interested in owning a Cold Stone Creamery franchise? Why or why not?

MyBizLab

Go to **pearsonglobaleditions.com/mybizlab** *for the following Assisted-graded writing questions:*

3-36. Research suggests that there are certain characteristics common across most entrepreneurs. Pick three and explain why they are important for an entrepreneurial mind-set. Compare and contrast how some might be more important than others given different situations. Are there situations where these characteristics might hinder successful entrepreneurship? Explain your answers.

3-37. One group of special issues regarding contemporary corporate ownerships involves whether a corporation should acquire another business, sell an existing business, or create a new business within the corporation. Consider mergers, acquisitions, divestitures, and spin-offs in the international market. How would these issues affect manager/employee relationships? How would these issues be handled globally? Would the implementation of one of these issues change corporate strategy? How?

3-38. Mybizlab Only—comprehensive writing assignment for this chapter.

end notes

[1] "Oh, To Be Young, and An Entrepreneur," *USA Today*, February 8, 2013, p. 8B.

[2] "How Netflix Got Started," *CNNMoney.com*, January 28, 2009, at http://money.cnn.com, accessed on October 25, 2011; Reed Hastings, "How I Did It: Reed Hastings, Netflix," *Inc.com*, December 1, 2005, at www.inc.com, accessed on October 25, 2011; Craig Tomashoff, "You Are What You Queue," *New York Times*, March 2, 2003, at www.nytimes.com, accessed on October 25, 2011; Sally Aaron, "Netflix Script Spells Disruption," *Harvard Business School Working Knowledge*, March 22, 2004, at http://hbswk.hbs.edu, accessed on October 25, 2011; Beth Snyder Bulik, "How Netflix Stays Ahead of Shifting Consumer Behavior," *Advertising Age*, February 22, 2010, at http://adage.com, accessed on October 25, 2011; John M. Caddell, "Frontiers of Innovation—Netflix Demolishes Its Own Business Model," *PennLive.com*, February 11, 2009, at http://blog.pennlive.com, accessed on June 21, 2010; Larry Dignan, "Netflix's Saga: The Dark Side of Creative Destruction," *BSNews.com*, October 25, 2011, at www.cbsnews.com, accessed on October 25, 2011; "Netflix Subscriber Loss Triggers Panic Selling," *CBSNews.com*, October 24, 2011, at www.cbsnews.com, accessed on October 25, 2011; Andrew Goldman, "Reed Hastings Knows He Messed Up," *New York Times*, October 20, 2011, at www.nytimes.com, accessed on October 25, 2011.

[3] See http://www.sba.gov.

[4] See http://www.sba.gov/aboutsba.

[5] *Employment Projections: 2010–2020 Summary*, U.S. Bureau of Labor Statistics, April 3, 2013.

[6] John Byrne, "The 12 Greatest Entrepreneurs of Our time," *Fortune*, April 9, 2012, pp. 68–86.

[7] "A New Generation Re Writes the Rules," *Wall Street Journal* (May 22, 2002), R4; See also Mark Henricks, "Up to the Challenge," *Entrepreneur* (February 2006), 64–67.

[8] "Special Report—Stars of Asia," *BusinessWeek* (July 12, 2004), p. 18.

[9] "Special Report—Stars of Asia," p. 18.

[10] "A Startup's New Prescription for Eyewear," *Business Week*, July 4–10, 2011, pp. 49–51.

[11] See Thomas Zimmerer and Norman Scarborough, *Essentials of Entrepreneurship and Small Business Management*, 5th ed. (Upper Saddle River, NJ: Prentice Hall, 2008).

[12] James Combs, David Ketchen, Christopher Shook, and Jeremy Short, "Antecedents and Consequences of Franchising: Past Accomplishments and Future Challenges, *Journal of Management*, January 2011, pp. 99–126.

[13] "Case Looks for Passion in Start-Ups," *USA Today*, March 26, 2013, p. 3B.

[14] http://www.census.gov/ces/dataproducts/bds/data_firm.html.

[15] "To Fund a Startup, Go to Kuala Lumpur," *Bloomberg Businessweek*, February 25–March 3, 2012.

[16] "Small Businesses Go Alternative for Loans," *USA Today*, November 14, 2012, p. 1B.

[17] http://www.census.gov/ces/dataproducts/bds/data_firm.html.

[18] U.S. Census Bureau, "1997 Economic Census Surveys of Minority and Women Owned Business Enterprises," at http://www.census.gov/csd/mwb.

[19] Peter Hoy, "Minority and Women Owned Businesses Skyrocket," *Inc.* (May 1, 2006), pp. 20–24.

[20] Zimmerer and Scarborough, *Essentials of Entrepreneurship and Small Business Management*, 20.

[21] See U.S. Small Business Administration, "Frequently Asked Questions," at http://app1.sba.gov/faqs/faqIndexAll.cfm?areaid=24, accessed on February 20, 2011.

[22] Zimmerer and Scarborough, *Essentials of Entrepreneurship and Small Business Management*.

[23] David Kushner, "The Web's Hottest Site: Facebook.com," *Rolling Stone*, April 7, 2006, pp. 5–7; Brad Stone, "Microsoft Buys Stake in Facebook," *New York Times*, October 25, 2007, p. B1; Michael Arrington, "Social Networking: Will Facebook Overtake MySpace in the U.S. in 2009?" *Tech Crunch*, January 13, 2009, p. 4; "MySpace Might Have Friends, But It Wants Ad Money," *New York Times*, June 16, 2008, p. 9; C. T. Moore, "The Future of Facebook Revenues," *ReveNews*, February 15, 2009, pp. 4–6; http://mashable.com/2012/05/16/facebook ipo timeline/, accessed on April 2, 2013.

[24] Ibid.

[25] "GM, ford Team to Develop 10-Speed Transmissions," *USA Today*, April 16, 2013, p. 2B.

[26] "Benefits of Franchising." *Cold Stone Creamery*. Kahala Franchising, LLC, n.d. Web. 13 June 2013.

[27] "Cold Stone Creamery Franchise Information." *Entrepreneur.com*. Entrepreneur Media, Inc, n.d. Web. 13 June 2013.

[28] "Facts on Ownership." *Cold Stone Creamery*. Kahala Franchising, LLC, n.d. Web. 13 June 2013.

[29] Needleman, Sarah E. "Tough Times for Franchising." *Wall Street Journal*. Dow Jones Company, Inc., 9 Feb. 2012. Web. 13 June 2013.

Understanding the Global Context of Business

chapter 4

No matter where in the world a firm is,

management drives its success.

International

businesses create unique management

challenges in

markets scattered

around the globe.

AFTER READING THIS CHAPTER, YOU SHOULD BE ABLE TO:

OBJECTIVE 1 **Discuss** the rise of international business and describe the major world marketplaces, trade agreements, and alliances.

OBJECTIVE 2 **Explain** how differences in import-export balances, exchange rates, and foreign competition determine the ways in which countries and businesses respond to the international environment.

OBJECTIVE 3 **Discuss** the factors involved in deciding to do business internationally and in selecting the appropriate levels of international involvement and international organizational structure.

OBJECTIVE 4 **Explain** the role and importance of the cultural environment in international business.

OBJECTIVE 5 **Describe** some of the ways in which economic, legal, and political differences among nations affect international business.

MyBizLab®

⭐ Improve Your Grade!

Visit **pearsonglobaleditions.com/mybizlab** for simulations, tutorials, and end-of-chapter problems.

Over 10 million students improved their results using the Pearson MyLabs.

The Embargo
Grinds On

Because of their love of certain types of coffee, some Americans coffee enthusiasts only buy coffee that's labeled "Cuban." As it turns out, though, such brands as Nescafé Café con Leche and Pilon Café Cubano aren't actually made from Cuban coffee beans: Because of a U.S. embargo against Cuban products, the so-called "Cuban coffee" available in this country comes from beans grown in such countries as Nicaragua, Mexico, or Guatemala, basically, anywhere but Cuba. Indeed, Americans cannot legally buy any products from Cuba—coffee, cigars, alcohol, or anything else.

But consider the Canadian firm, Merchants of Green Coffee. According to its website its mission is to deliver the best-tasting coffee experience to discerning consumers through a supply chain with integrity and a unique commitment to quality. The company buys only the finest beans from small growers in Africa, Latin America, and Cuba, and stocks premium products like Cuba Turquino. This premium coffee is made from beans grown under shade-tree canopies at elevations above 3,000 feet. As the name indicates, Cuba Turquino is made from Cuban coffee beans, and for that reason, again, U.S. coffee connoisseurs can't buy it.

Now, coffee beans from other Latin American nations are also of high quality, and they're often certified organic. They're just not *Cuban* coffee beans, and to some people in the coffee business, it's the principle that matters. Paul Katzeff, founder of Thanksgiving Coffee Co., a California producer of specialty coffees, regards the U.S. embargo as impractical (on the grounds that it hasn't achieved its goals) and immoral (on the grounds that it punishes the Cuban people rather than their government). These two reasons are why his company has been marketing a line of beans called "End the Embargo Coffee" for more than a decade. The coffee actually comes from Nicaragua, but the packaging, emblazoned with the image of Cuban revolutionary Che Guevara, gets the point across. Katzeff hastens to point out that he's not going violate U.S. law, but in addition to selling distinctive, high-quality coffee, he is interested in raising U.S. consumer awareness of how the embargo affects them. For the past eight years, Thanksgiving has also donated 15 cents from every package sold to the U.S. Cuba Sister Cities Association, a nonprofit that works to establish relationships between similar-sized cities in the two countries.

The U.S. embargo, which was first imposed in 1962 in response to the revolutionary communist government's appropriation of U.S. land holdings in the country, prevents "U.S. persons" and entities "owned or controlled" by "U.S. persons" from engaging in any transactions in which Cuba has an "interest of any nature

what's in it for me?

Do you think it's fair that consumers in a so-called "free market" such as the United States cannot buy Cuban coffee, but people in Canada can? Obviously, it's a complicated issue, and both sides in the debate have solid arguments in their favor. As we will see in this chapter, global forces—business as well as political—affect each and every one of us on a daily basis. And as you begin your business career, regardless of whether you see yourself living abroad, working for a big company, or starting your own business, the global economy will affect you in a variety of ways. Exchange rates for different currencies and global markets for buying and selling are all of major importance

Minerva Studio/fotolia

to everyone, regardless of their role or perspective. As a result, this chapter will better enable you to (1) understand how global forces affect you as a customer, (2) understand how globalization affects you as an employee, and (3) assess how global opportunities and challenges can affect you as a business owner and as an investor. You will also gain insights into how wages and working conditions in different regions are linked to what we buy and the prices we pay.

This chapter explores the global context of business. We begin with an exploration of the major world marketplaces and trade agreements that affect international business. Next, we examine several factors that help determine how countries and businesses respond to international opportunities and challenges. We then direct our attention to some of the decisions managers must make if they intend to compete in international markets. Finally, we conclude with a discussion of some of the social, cultural, economic, legal, and political factors that affect international business.

whatsoever, direct or indirect." Cuba, therefore, has no access to the U.S. market, does without U.S. imports, and amasses substantial debts to other trading partners. But observers also point out that if the embargo was dropped the effects might not be as dramatic as some people think. Why? Basically because the embargo doesn't really have much effect on Cuba or its people.

Cubans now buy ice cream and soft drinks from Swiss-based Nestlé, soap and shampoo from Anglo-Dutch Unilever, and cigarettes from Brazil's Souza Cruz. The fact that the United States is the world's largest market for rum did not deter French-owned Pernod-Ricard from building a new distillery in Cuba, and Britain's Imperial Tobacco expects to double sales when Americans can once again purchase premium hand-rolled Cuban cigars. Most of the directors of Canada's Sherritt International are barred from the United States by provisions of the embargo, but they apparently regard the ban as a small price to pay for future returns on a $1.5-billion investment in Cuba's nickel and oil and gas industries. Cuba has also lifted restrictions on many products once unavailable to Cuban consumers, such as computers, DVDs, and mobile phones, and sales of all these products will be a boon to Telecom Italia, which holds a 27 percent stake in the country's state-owned telecom operations.

Katzeff is thinking the same thing that a lot of U.S. businesspeople are undoubtedly thinking—when the embargo is dropped there will be new business opportunities. As he sees it, Cuban coffee has a promising post-embargo future: Its potential is enormous because of the quality of the coffee beans. And although Katzeff's geopolitics may rankle some people, his business sense seems sound. At present, of course, he can't actually do business with Cuban coffee growers, but he has figured out a way to lay the groundwork. He has already established working relationships with coffee cooperatives, groups of individual growers who pool their crops to enter the export market and secure higher prices, in Latin America and Africa. His longer-term goal is to invest the same capital and acquired know-how in relationships with Cuban growers.

The director of Thanksgiving's Cuba project, Nick Hoskins, has also already developed contacts in Cuba's coffee-growing regions, and Katzeff hopes to establish a *twinning agreement*, an exchange of people-to-people programs, with cooperatives in the coffee-growing province of Santiago de Cuba. In the meantime, though, Thanksgiving is willing to settle for a public relations program of transactions— monetary and otherwise—with U.S. coffee drinkers.[1] (After studying this chapter you should be able to respond to the set of discussion questions found at the end of the chapter.)

OBJECTIVE 1
Discuss
the rise of international business and describe the major world marketplaces, trade agreements, and alliances.

Globalization *process by which the world economy is becoming a single interdependent system*

Import *product made or grown abroad but sold domestically*

The Contemporary Global Economy

The total volume of world trade is immense—more than $18.2 trillion in merchandise trade each year. Foreign investment in the United States exceeds $150 billion, and U.S. investment abroad is more than $300 billion. As more firms engage in international business, the world economy is fast becoming an interdependent system though a process called **globalization.**

We often take for granted the diversity of products we can buy as a result of international trade. Your television, your shoes, and even your morning coffee or juice are probably **imports,** products made or grown abroad and sold domestically in the United States. At the same time, the success of many U.S. firms depends on

exports, products made or grown here, such as machinery, electronic equipment, and grains, and shipped for sale abroad.

Firms such as McDonald's, Microsoft, Apple, and Starbucks have found international markets to be a fruitful area for growth. But firms sometime stumble when they try to expand abroad. Home Depot has closed most of the stores it opened in China, for example, because labor costs are so low there few homeowners are interested in "do-it-yourself" projects. Similarly, Best Buy also closed its stores in China because consumers there tend to buy their electronics goods at lower prices from local or online merchants.[2]

And the impact of globalization doesn't stop with firms looking to open locations abroad or having to close locations that fail. Small firms with no international operations (such as an independent coffee shop) may still buy from international suppliers, and even individual contractors or self-employed people can be affected by fluctuations in exchange rates.

Indeed, international trade is becoming increasingly important to most nations and their businesses. Many countries that once followed strict policies to protect domestic business now encourage trade just as aggressively. They are opening borders to foreign business, offering incentives for domestic businesses to expand internationally, and making it easier for foreign firms to partner with local firms. Likewise, as more industries and markets become global, so, too, are the firms that compete in them.

Several forces have combined to spark and sustain globalization. For one thing, governments and businesses are more aware of the benefits of globalization to businesses and shareholders. These benefits include the potential for higher standards of living and improved business profitability. New technologies have made international travel, communication, and commerce faster and cheaper than ever before. Finally, there are competitive pressures; sometimes a firm must expand into foreign markets simply to keep up with competitors.

Globalization is not without its detractors. Some critics charge that globalization allows businesses to exploit workers in less-developed countries and bypass domestic environmental and tax regulations. For example, businesses pay workers in Vietnam and Indonesia lower wages than their counterparts in the United States. Factories in China are not subject to the same environmental protection laws as are firms in Europe. And businesses that headquarter their corporate offices in the Cayman Islands pay lower taxes. They also charge that globalization leads to the

Export *product made or grown domestically but shipped and sold abroad*

Some globalization protestors, like this man, fear that multinational companies will wipe out small domestic businesses like family farms.

loss of cultural heritages and often benefits the rich more than the poor. For instance, as the English language becomes increasingly widespread throughout the world, some local languages are simply disappearing. Similarly, local residents in Africa receive relatively little economic benefits when oil or precious minerals are discovered on their land; prosperous investors buy the rights from landowners, who often don't realize the value of these resources. As a result, many international gatherings of global economic leaders are marked by protests and demonstrations.

The Major World Marketplaces

Managers involved with international businesses need to have a solid understanding of the global economy, including the major world marketplaces. This section examines some fundamental economic distinctions between countries based on wealth and then looks at some of the world's major international marketplaces.

Distinctions Based on Wealth The World Bank, an agency of the United Nations, uses per-capita income, average income per person, to make distinctions among countries. Its current classification method consists of four different categories of countries:[3]

1 *High-income countries.* Those with annual per-capita income greater than $11,115
2 *Upper-middle-income countries.* Those with annual per-capita income of $11,115 or less but more than $3,595
3 *Lower-middle-income countries.* Those with annual per-capita income of $3,595 or lower but more than $905
4 *Low-income countries* (often called *developing countries*). Those with annual per-capita income of $905 or less

Geographic Clusters The world economy revolves around three major marketplaces: North America, Europe, and Pacific Asia. In general, these clusters include relatively more of the upper-middle and high-income nations but relatively few low- and lower-middle-income countries.

NORTH AMERICA As the world's largest marketplace and most stable economy, the United States dominates the North American market. Canada also plays a major role in the international economy, and the United States and Canada are each other's largest trading partners.

Mexico has become a major manufacturing center, especially along the U.S. border, where cheap labor and low transportation costs have encouraged many firms from the United States and other countries to build factories. However, Mexico's role as a low-cost manufacturing center is in flux. Just a few years ago many experts believed that the emergence of China as a low-cost manufacturing center would lead companies to begin to shift their production from Mexico to China.[4] (The escalating drug-related violence along the northern Mexican border is also contributing to this shift.) But a recent reversal of this trend is discussed in the boxed insert *Finding a Better Way*.

EUROPE Europe is often regarded as two regions—Western and Eastern. Western Europe, dominated by Germany, the United Kingdom, and France, has long been a mature but fragmented marketplace. The transformation of this region via the European Union (discussed later in this chapter) into an integrated economic system has further increased its importance. E-commerce and technology have also become increasingly important in this region. There has been a surge in Internet start-ups in southeastern England, the Netherlands, and the Scandinavian countries; Ireland is now one of the world's largest exporters of software; Strasbourg, France, is a major center for biotech start-ups; Barcelona, Spain, has many flourishing software and Internet companies; and the Frankfurt region of Germany is dotted with software and biotech start-ups.

finding a better way

Too Much of a Good Thing? China's Success Creates More Jobs in Mexico

In today's competitive global economy, businesses strive for every possible advantage. Many manufacturers, for example, locate their factories in countries in which there is an ample supply of low-cost skilled labor. During the 1980s and 1990s, the place to be was Mexico. Hundreds of factories were built just across the U.S.–Mexican border, and workers streamed to the region from other parts of Mexico for stable and well-paying jobs. But in the late 1990s the world started to shift.

Mexican prosperity, fueled in part by its role as a center of manufacturing, led to increases in the cost-of-living followed quickly by wage increases so workers could keep up. At about this same time, China began to emerge as an attractive manufacturing alternative. For instance, in 2012, wages in China were only one-sixth of the wages in Mexico. And there was certainly no shortage of workers eager to take steady jobs in factories making products for other countries. China's boom was Mexico's bust, as one company after another reduced or eliminated manufacturing there and moved to Asia.

But in recent years, things have started to tilt back in Mexico's favor. Why? As China's economy has flourished, its labor costs have crept higher and higher so it's less of a bargain than it used to be. Whereas Mexican wages were six times higher than wages in China 10 years ago, today they are only about 40 percent higher. When manufacturers factor in shipping costs (which have increased because of fuel prices), producing in Mexico may cost about the same as China. And time differences between the United States and China

vario images GmbH & Co.KG/Alamy

sometimes make it difficult to schedule video conferences and telephone calls. Several companies have also been burned by China's lack of protection for industrial and intellectual property.

Robert Moser is president of Casabella, a New York firm that makes a line of cleaning products and kitchen gadgets. Moser had all of the firm's manufacturing centered in Mexico in the 1990s but moved it to China in 2002. Now, however, Casabella is in the process of moving its manufacturing work from China back to Mexico, for all of the reasons noted previously. Los Angeles-based Manufacturing Marvel produces toys in both China and Mexico but is considering moving everything to Mexico in the next year or so. A company official indicates that counterfeiting of its products in China has been on the upswing, and that is playing a big role in its decision.[5]

Eastern Europe, once primarily communist, has also gained in importance, both as a marketplace and as a producer. Such multinational corporations as Daewoo, Nestlé, General Motors, and ABB Asea Brown Boveri have all set up operations in Poland. Ford, General Motors, Suzuki, and Volkswagen have all built new factories in Hungary. On the other hand, governmental instability has hampered development in parts of Russia, Bulgaria, Albania, Romania, and other countries.

PACIFIC ASIA Pacific Asia is generally agreed to consist of Japan, China, Thailand, Malaysia, Singapore, Indonesia, South Korea, Taiwan, the Philippines, and Australia. Fueled by strong entries in the automobile, electronics, and banking industries, the economies of these countries grew rapidly in the 1970s and 1980s. After a currency crisis in the late 1990s that slowed growth in virtually every country of the region, Pacific Asia showed clear signs of revitalization until the global recession in 2009. As the global economy begins to regain its momentum, Pacific Asia is expected to again be on the forefront. This is especially true of Japan, which, led by firms such as Toyota, Toshiba, and Nippon Steel, dominates the region. South Korea (home to firms Samsung and Hyundai, among others), Taiwan (owner of Chinese Petroleum and the manufacturing home of many foreign firms), and Hong Kong (a major financial center) are also successful players in the international economy.

China, the world's most densely populated country, has emerged as an important market and now boasts the world's third-largest economy, behind only the European Union and the United States.[6] Although its per-capita income remains low, the sheer number of potential consumers makes it an important market. India, though not part of Pacific Asia, is also rapidly emerging as one of the globe's most important economies.

As in North America and Europe, technology promises to play an increasingly important role in the future of this region. In some parts of Asia, however, poorly developed electronic infrastructures, slower adoption of computers and information technology, and a higher percentage of lower-income consumers hamper the emergence of technology firms.

Trade Agreements and Alliances

Various legal agreements have sparked international trade and shaped the global business environment. Virtually every nation has formal trade treaties with other nations. A *treaty* is a legal agreement that specifies areas in which nations will cooperate with one another. Among the most significant treaties is the *North American Free Trade Agreement*. The *European Union*, the *Association of Southeast Asian Nations*, and the *World Trade Organization*, all governed by treaties, are also instrumental in promoting international business activity.

North American Free Trade Agreement (NAFTA) *agreement to gradually eliminate tariffs and other trade barriers among the United States, Canada, and Mexico*

North American Free Trade Agreement
The **North American Free Trade Agreement (NAFTA)** removes most tariffs and other trade barriers among the United States, Canada, and Mexico and includes agreements on environmental issues and labor abuses.

Most observers agree that NAFTA is achieving its basic purpose—to create a more active North American market. It has created several hundred thousand new jobs, although this number is smaller than NAFTA proponents had hoped. One thing is clear, though; the flood of U.S. jobs lost to Mexico predicted by NAFTA critics, especially labor unions, has not occurred.

European Union (EU) *agreement among major European nations to eliminate or make uniform most trade barriers affecting group members*

The European Union
The **European Union (EU)** includes most European nations, as shown in Figure 4.1. These nations have eliminated most quotas and set uniform tariff levels on products imported and exported within their group. In 1992, virtually all internal trade barriers went down, making the EU the largest free marketplace in the world. The adoption of a common currency, the euro, by most member nations further solidified the EU's position in the world economy.

Association of Southeast Asian Nations (ASEAN) *organization for economic, political, social, and cultural cooperation among Southeast Asian nations*

The Association of Southeast Asian Nations
The **Association of Southeast Asian Nations (ASEAN)** was founded in 1967 as an organization for economic, political, social, and cultural cooperation. In 1995, Vietnam became the group's first Communist member. Figure 4.2 shows a map of the ASEAN countries. Because of its relative size, the ASEAN does not have the same global economic significance as NAFTA and the EU.

General Agreement on Tariffs and Trade (GATT) *international trade agreement to encourage the multilateral reduction or elimination of trade barriers*

World Trade Organization (WTO) *organization through which member nations negotiate trading agreements and resolve disputes about trade policies and practices*

The World Trade Organization
The **General Agreement on Tariffs and Trade (GATT)** was signed in 1947. Its purpose was to reduce or eliminate trade barriers, such as tariffs and quotas. It did so by encouraging nations to protect domestic industries within agreed-on limits and to engage in multilateral negotiations. The GATT proved to be relatively successful. So, to further promote globalization, most of the world's countries joined to create the **World Trade Organization (WTO),** which began on January 1, 1995. (The GATT is the actual treaty that governs the WTO.) The 152-member countries are required to open markets to international trade, and the WTO is empowered to pursue three goals:[7]

1 Promote trade by encouraging members to adopt fair-trade practices.

2 Reduce trade barriers by promoting multilateral negotiations.

3 Establish fair procedures for resolving disputes among members.

FIGURE 4.1 The Nations of the European Union
Source: http://europa.eu/abc/maps/index_en.htm, accessed April 5, 2013.

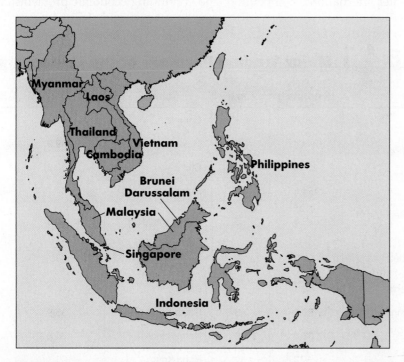

FIGURE 4.2 The Nations of the Association of Southeast Asian Nations (ASEAN)

OBJECTIVE 2
Explain
how differences in import-export
balances, exchange rates, and
foreign competition determine
the ways in which countries
and businesses respond to the
international environment.

International Trade

The global economy is essentially defined by international trade. International trade occurs when an exchange takes place across national boundaries. Although international trade has many advantages, it can also pose problems if a country's imports and exports don't maintain an acceptable balance. Table 4.1 lists the United States' major trading partners. The left of the table shows the 10 largest markets for exports from the United States, and the right of the table shows the 10 largest markets that import to the United States. Note that many countries are on both lists (China and Canada, for instance). However, the United States also does business with many more countries. For instance, in 2012, the United States exported $5.1 billion to Egypt, $2.4 billion to Kuwait, $3.0 billion to Poland, and $132.9 million to Zambia; imports from those same countries were $2.8 billion, $12.2 billion, $4.2 billion, and $62 million, respectively. In deciding whether an overall balance exists between imports and exports, economists use two measures: *balance of trade* and *balance of payments*.

Balance of Trade

Balance of Trade *economic value of all products a country exports minus the economic value of all products it imports*

A country's **balance of trade** is the total economic value of all the products that it exports minus the economic value of all the products that it imports. A *positive balance of trade* results when a country exports (sells to other countries) more than it imports (buys from other countries). A *negative balance of trade* results when a country imports more than it exports.

Relatively small trade imbalances are common and are unimportant. Large imbalances, however, are another matter. The biggest concern about trade balances involves the flow of currency. When U.S. consumers and businesses buy foreign products, dollars flow from the United States to other countries; when U.S. businesses are selling to foreign consumers and businesses, dollars flow back into the United States. A large negative balance of trade means that many dollars are controlled by interests outside the United States.

Trade Deficit *situation in which a country's imports exceed its exports, creating a negative balance of trade*

Trade Surplus *situation in which a country's exports exceed its imports, creating a positive balance of trade*

A **trade deficit** occurs when a country's imports exceed its exports, when it has a negative balance of trade. When exports exceed imports, the nation enjoys a **trade surplus.** Several factors, such as general economic conditions and the effect of trade agreements, influence trade deficits and surpluses. For example, higher domestic costs, greater international competition, and continuing economic problems among

table 4.1 Major Trading Partners of the United States

Country	Imports ($ billions)	Rank	Country	Exports ($ billions)	Rank
China	390.8	1	Canada	270.1	1
Canada	298.4	2	Mexico	199.9	2
Mexico	257.3	3	China	100.2	3
Japan	134.6	4	Japan	64	4
Federal Republic of Germany	99.3	5	United Kingdom	50.8	5
Korea, South	54.3	6	Federal Republic of Germany	45	6
Saudi Arabia	52	7	Brazil	40.2	7
United Kingdom	50.6	8	South Korea	38.9	8
France	38.3	9	Netherlands	36.8	9
India	37.7	10	Hong Kong	33.1	10

some of its regional trading partners have slowed the tremendous growth in exports that Japan once enjoyed. But rising prosperity in China and India has led to strong increases in both exports from and imports to those countries.

Figures 4.3 and 4.4 highlight two series of events: (1) recent trends in U.S. exports and imports and (2) the resulting trade deficit. As Figure 4.3 shows, both U.S. imports and U.S. exports have, with minor variations, increased over the past eight years—a trend that's projected to continue.

Trade deficits between 2000 and 2011 are shown in Figure 4.4. There was a deficit in each of these years because more money flowed out to pay for foreign imports than flowed in to pay for U.S. exports. For example, in 2008, the United States exported

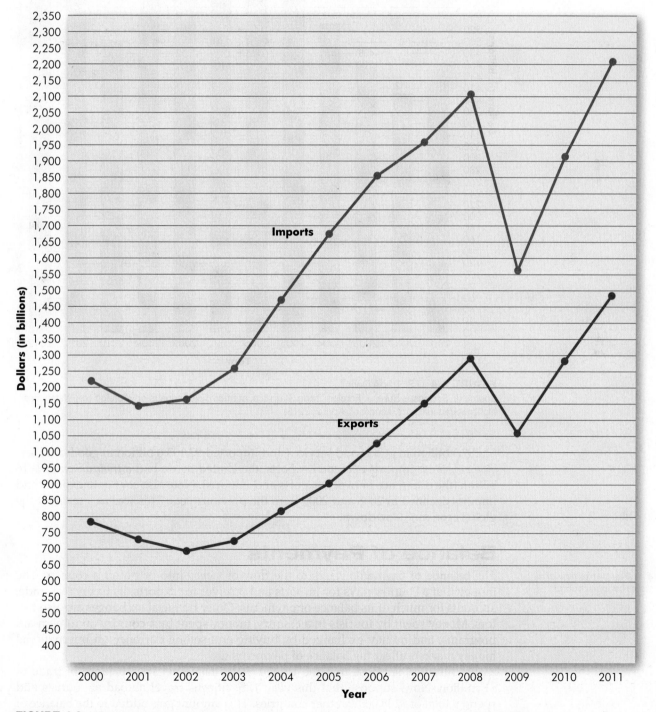

FIGURE 4.3 U.S. Imports and Exports
Source: U.S. Census Bureau: Foreign Trade Statistics, at http://www.census.gov/foreign-trade/statistics/highlights/annual.html, accessed April 2, 2013.

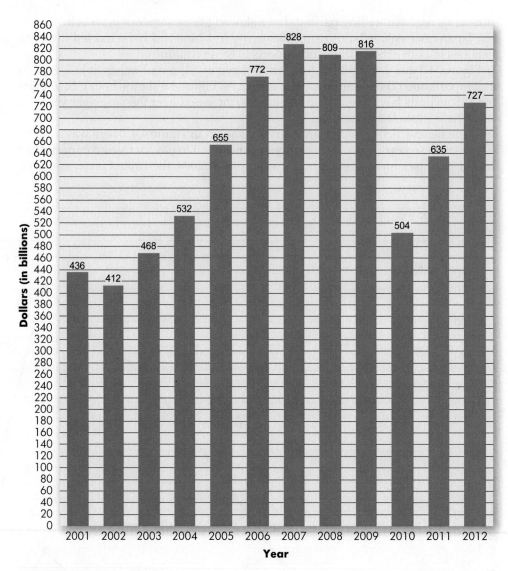

FIGURE 4.4 U.S. Trade Deficit
Source: U.S. Census Bureau: Foreign Trade Statistics, at http://www.census.gov/foreign-trade/statistics/ highlights/annual.html, accessed April 2, 2013.

$1,287.4 billion in goods and services and imported $2,103.6 billion in goods and services. Because imports exceeded exports, the United States had a *trade deficit* of $816 billion (the difference between exports and imports). Note also that both exports and imports declined in 2008 and 2009 from the previous year. This was as a result of the global economic slowdown.

Balance of Payments

Balance of Payments *flow of all money into or out of a country*

The **balance of payments** refers to the flow of *money* into or out of a country. The money that a country pays for imports and receives for exports, its balance of trade, accounts for much of its balance of payments. Other financial exchanges are also factors. Money spent by tourists in a country, money spent by a country on foreign-aid programs, and money exchanged by buying and selling currency on international money markets affect the balance of payments.

For instance, suppose that the United States has a negative balance of trade of $1 million. Now, suppose that this year, U.S. citizens travel abroad as tourists and spend a total of $200,000 in other countries. This amount gets added to the balance of trade to form the balance of payments, which is now a negative $1.2 million dollars. Now, further suppose that tourists from other countries come to the United States and spend the equivalent of $300,000 while they are here. This has the effect of reducing the negative balance of payments to $900,000. Then, further suppose that the United States then sends $600,000 in aid to help the victims of a tsunami-ravaged country in Asia. Because this represents additional dollars leaving the United States, the balance of payments is now a negative $1.5 million. For many years, the United States enjoyed a positive balance of payments. Recently, however, the overall balance has become negative.

Exchange Rates

The balance of imports and exports between two countries is affected by the rate of exchange between their currencies. An **exchange rate** is the rate at which the currency of one nation can be exchanged for that of another. Suppose, for example, that the exchange rate between the U.S. dollar and the British pound was $2 to £1. This means that it costs £1 to "buy" $2 or $1 to "buy" £0.5. Stated differently, £1 and $2 have the same purchasing power, or £1 = $2.

At the end of World War II, the major nations of the world agreed to set *fixed exchange rates*. The value of any country's currency relative to that of another would remain constant. The goal was to allow the global economy to stabilize. Today, however, *floating exchange rates* are the norm, and the value of one country's currency relative to that of another varies with market conditions. For example, when many British citizens want to spend pounds to buy U.S. dollars (or goods), the value of the dollar relative to the pound increases. Demand for the dollar is high, and a currency is strong when demand for it is high. It's also strong when there's high demand for the goods manufactured with that currency. On a daily basis, exchange rates fluctuate very little. Significant variations usually occur over longer time spans. Highly regulated economic systems such as China are among the few that still use fixed exchange rates. The Chinese government regulates the flow of currency—its own as well as all others—into and out of China and determines the precise rate of exchange within its borders.

Exchange-rate fluctuation can have an important impact on balance of trade. Suppose you want to buy some English tea for £10 per box. At an exchange rate of $2 to £1, a box will cost you $20 (£10 × 2 = 20). But what if the pound is weaker? At an exchange rate of, say, $1.25 to £1, the same box would cost you only $12.50 (£10 × 1.25 = 12.50). If the dollar is strong in relation to the pound, the prices of all U.S.-made products will rise in England, and the prices of all English-made products will fall in the United States. The English would buy fewer U.S. products, and Americans would be prompted to spend more on English-made products. The result would probably be a U.S. trade deficit with England.

One of the most significant developments in foreign exchange has been the introduction of the **euro,** the common currency of the EU. The euro was officially introduced in 2002 and has replaced other currencies, such as the German Deutsche Mark and the French franc. In the years since its debut, the euro has become one of the world's most important currencies. When it was first introduced, the euro's value was pegged as being equivalent to the dollar: €1 = $1. But because the dollar has been relatively weak in recent years, its value has eroded relative to that of the euro. In April 2013, for example, $1 was worth only about €0.76.

Companies with international operations must watch exchange-rate fluctuations closely because changes affect overseas demand for their products and can be a major factor in competition. In general, when the value of a country's currency rises—becomes stronger—companies based there find it harder to export products to foreign markets and easier for foreign companies to enter local markets. It also makes it more cost-efficient for domestic companies to move operations to lower-cost foreign sites. When the value of a currency declines—becomes weaker—the opposite occurs. As the value of a country's currency falls, its balance of trade usually improves because domestic companies should experience a boost in exports. There should also be less reason for foreign companies to ship products into the domestic market and less reason to establish operations in other countries.

Exchange Rate *rate at which the currency of one nation can be exchanged for the currency of another nation*

Euro *a common currency shared among most of the members of the EU (excluding Denmark, Sweden, and the United Kingdom)*

Forms of Competitive Advantage

Before we discuss the fundamental issues involved in international business management, we must consider one last factor: forms of *competitive advantage*. Because no country can produce everything that it needs, countries tend to export what they can produce better or less expensively than other countries and use the proceeds to import what they can't produce as effectively. This principle doesn't fully explain why nations export and import what they do. Such decisions hinge partly on the advantages that a particular country enjoys regarding its abilities to create or sell certain products and resources.[8] Economists traditionally focused on absolute and comparative advantage to explain international trade. But because this approach focuses narrowly on such factors as natural resources and labor costs, a more contemporary view of national competitive advantage has emerged.

Absolute Advantage *the ability to produce something more efficiently than any other country can*

Absolute Advantage

An **absolute advantage** exists when a country can produce something that is cheaper or of higher quality than any other country. Saudi oil, Brazilian coffee beans, and Canadian timber come close (because these countries have such abundant supplies of these resources), but examples of true absolute advantage are rare. For example, many experts say that the vineyards of France produce the world's finest wines. But the burgeoning wine business in California demonstrates that producers there can also make good wine—wines that rival those from France but come in more varieties and at lower prices.

Comparative Advantage *the ability to produce some products more efficiently than others*

Comparative Advantage

A country has a **comparative advantage** in goods that it can produce more efficiently or better than other nations. If businesses in a given country can make computers more efficiently than they can make automobiles, then that nation has a comparative advantage in computer manufacturing.

entrepreneurship and new ventures

Rolling in the Worldwide Dough

Is any business more confined to a local market than a bakery? Breads and pastries get stale quickly, and even the largest operations, such as those that make buns for McDonald's, only move products over short distances. But a bakery in Paris has refused to accept geographic limitations and sells its famous bread in global markets.

When Lionel Poilâne took over the family business more than 30 years ago, he was determined to return bread making to its roots. Poilâne built clay ovens based on sixteenth-century plans and technology, trained his bread makers in ancient techniques, and began selling old-style dark bread with a thick, chewy, fire-tinged flavor. It quickly became a favorite in Parisian bistros, and demand soared.

To help meet demand, Poilâne built two more bakeries in Paris; today they sell more than 17,000 loaves of bread a day. Poilâne also opened a bakery in London, but his efforts to expand to Japan were stymied; local ordinances prohibited wood-burning ovens, and Poilâne refused to compromise. During the negotiation process, however, he came to realize that he didn't really even *want* to build new bakeries all over the world.

Instead, he turned to modern technology to expand his old-fashioned business. The key was the big FedEx hub at

Brenda Carson/Shutterstock

Paris Roissy Charles de Gaulle Airport near Poilâne's largest Paris bakery. After launching a website to promote his venture, Poilâne started taking international orders. New orders are packaged as the bread cools and then picked up by FedEx. A quick warm-up in the customer's oven gives it the same taste as it had when it came out of Poilâne's oven. Today, a loaf of bread baked in Paris in the morning can easily be reheated for tomorrow night's dinner in more than 25 countries.[9]

In general, both absolute and comparative advantages translate into competitive advantage. Brazil, for instance, can produce and market coffee beans knowing full well that there are few other countries with the right mix of climate, terrain, and altitude to enter the coffee bean market. The United States has comparative advantages in the computer industry (because of technological sophistication) and in farming (because of large amounts of fertile land and a temperate climate). South Korea has a comparative advantage in electronics manufacturing because of efficient operations and cheap labor. As a result of each country's comparative advantage, U.S. firms export computers and grain to South Korea and import DVD players from South Korea. South Korea can produce food, and the United States can build DVD players, but each nation imports certain products because the other holds a comparative advantage in the relevant industry.

National Competitive Advantage   In recent years, a theory of national competitive advantage has become a widely accepted model of why nations engage in international trade.[10] **National competitive advantage** derives from four conditions:

National Competitive Advantage *international competitive advantage stemming from a combination of factor conditions, demand conditions, related and supporting industries, and firm strategies, structures, and rivalries*

1 *Factor conditions* are the factors of production we discussed in Chapter 1—*labor, capital, entrepreneurs, physical resources*, and *information resources*.
2 *Demand conditions* reflect a large domestic consumer base that promotes strong demand for innovative products.
3 *Related and supporting industries* include strong local or regional suppliers or industrial customers.
4 *Strategies, structures, and rivalries* refer to firms and industries that stress cost reduction, product quality, higher productivity, and innovative products.

When all attributes of national competitive advantage exist, a nation is likely to be heavily involved in international business. Japan, for instance, has an abundance of natural resources and strong domestic demand for automobiles. Its carmakers have well-oiled supplier networks, and domestic firms have competed intensely with one another for decades. These circumstances explain why Japanese car companies such as Toyota and Honda are successful in foreign markets.

International Business Management

OBJECTIVE 3
Discuss
the factors involved in deciding to do business internationally and in selecting the appropriate levels of international involvement and international organizational structure.

Regardless of where a firm is located, its success depends largely on how well it's managed. International business is so challenging because basic management tasks—planning, organizing, directing, and controlling—are much more difficult when a firm operates in markets scattered around the globe.

Managing means making decisions. In this section, we examine the three basic decisions that a company must make when considering globalization. The first decision is whether to go international at all. Once that decision has been made, managers must decide on the level of international involvement and on the organizational structure that will best meet the firm's global needs.

Going International

As the world economy becomes globalized, more firms are conducting international operations. U.S. firms are aggressively expanding abroad, and foreign companies such as BP and Nestlé continue to expand into foreign markets as well, including the U.S. market. This route, however, isn't appropriate for every company. If you buy and sell fresh fish, you'll find it more profitable to confine your activities to limited geographic areas because storage and transport costs may be too high to make international operations worthwhile. As Figure 4.5 shows, several factors affect the decision to go international.

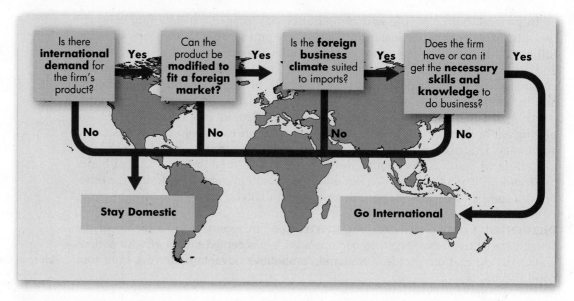

FIGURE 4.5 Going International

Gauging International Demand In considering international expansion, a company must consider whether there is a demand for its products abroad. Products that are successful in one country may be useless in another. Even when there is demand, advertising may still need to be adjusted. For example, bicycles are largely used for recreation in the United States but are seen as basic transportation in China. Hence, a bicycle maker would need to have different advertising strategies in each of these two countries. Market research or the prior market entry of competitors may indicate whether there's an international demand for a firm's products.

Adapting to Customer Needs If its product is in demand, a firm must decide whether and how to adapt it to meet the special demands of foreign customers. For example, to satisfy local tastes, McDonald's sells wine in France, beer in Germany, and provides some vegetarian sandwiches in India. Likewise, consumer electronics companies have to be aware that different countries use different kinds of electric sockets and different levels of electric power. Therefore, regardless of demand, customer needs must still be considered.

Outsourcing and Offshoring **Outsourcing,** the practice of paying suppliers and distributors to perform certain business processes or to provide needed materials or services, has become a popular option for going international. It has become so popular because (1) it helps firms focus on their core activities and avoid getting sidetracked on secondary activities, and (2) it reduces costs by locating certain business functions in areas where relevant costs are low.[11]

The practice of outsourcing to foreign countries is more specifically referred to as **offshoring.** Many companies today contract their manufacturing to low-cost factories in Asia. Similarly, many service call centers today are outsourced to businesses located in India. The Oscar-winning movie *Slumdog Millionaire* featured a young Indian man who worked for an international call center in Mumbai. In real life, Dell Computer, Chase Bank Credit Card Services, and several home mortgage support businesses have established call centers in India and have enjoyed considerable success. On the other hand, though, the network of FTD florists opened a call center in India but subsequently closed it. As it turns out, many people who call to order flowers need more personal assistance—advice on type of flowers, colors of arrangements, and so forth—than can be provided by someone on the other side of the world.

Outsourcing *the practice of paying suppliers and distributors to perform certain business processes or to provide needed materials or services*

Offshoring *the practice of outsourcing to foreign countries*

Levels of International Involvement

After deciding to go international, a firm must determine the level of its involvement. Several levels are possible: a firm may act as an exporter or importer, organize as an international firm, or (like most of the world's largest industrial firms) operate as a multinational firm.

Exporters and Importers   An **exporter** makes products in one country to distribute and sell in others. An **importer** buys products in foreign markets and brings them home for resale. Both conduct most of their business in their home nations. Both entail the lowest level of involvement in international operations, and both are good ways to learn the fine points of global business. Many large firms entered international business as exporters. IBM and Coke, among others, exported to Europe for several years before setting up production sites there.

Exporter *firm that distributes and sells products to one or more foreign countries*

Importer *firm that buys products in foreign markets and then imports them for resale in its home country*

International Firms   As exporters and importers gain experience and grow, many move to the next level of involvement. **International firms** conduct a good deal of their business abroad and may even maintain overseas manufacturing facilities. An international firm may be large, but it's still basically a domestic company with international operations. Hershey, for instance, buys ingredients for its chocolates from several foreign suppliers, but makes all of its products in the United States. Moreover, although it sells its products in approximately 50 other countries, it generates most of its revenues from its domestic market.[12]

International Firm *firm that conducts a significant portion of its business in foreign countries*

Multinational Firms   Most **multinational firms,** firms that design, produce, and market products in many nations, such as ExxonMobil, Nestlé, IBM, and Ford, don't think of themselves as having domestic and international divisions. Headquarters locations are almost irrelevant, and planning and decision making are geared to international markets. The world's largest multinationals in 2011 based on sales, profits, and employees are shown in Table 4.2.

We can't underestimate the economic impact of multinational firms. Consider just the impact of the 500 largest multinationals: In 2012, these 500 firms generated

Multinational Firm *firm that designs, produces, and markets products in many nations*

table 4.2 The World's Largest Non-U.S. Companies by Sales, Profits, and Number of Employees (2011)

Company	Sales ($ million)	Profits ($ million)	Employees (in millions)
Royal Dutch Shell	378,152		
BP	308,928		
Sinopec	273,422		
China National Petroleum	240,192		
State Grid	226,294		
Nestle		32,843	
OAO Gazprom		31,895	
Industrial & Commercial Bank of China		24,398	
Royal Dutch Shell		20,127	
PETROBRAS		19,184	
Chinese National Petroleum			1.7
State Grid			1.6
National Health Service (England)			1.4
Indian Railways			1.4
China Post Group			0.9

Source: http://money.cnn.com/magazines/fortune/global500/2011/full_list/ and http://www.businessinsider.com/the-10-biggest-employers-in-the-world-2011-9?op=1, accessed on April 5, 2013.

$24.9 trillion in revenues and $1.6 trillion in owner profits.[13] They employed tens of millions of people, bought materials and equipment from literally thousands of other firms, and paid billions in taxes. Moreover, their products affected the lives of hundreds of millions of consumers, competitors, investors, and even protestors.

International Organization Structures

Different levels of international involvement entail different kinds of organizational structure. A structure that would help coordinate an exporter's activities would be inadequate for those of a multinational. In this section, we consider the spectrum of organizational strategies, including *independent agents*, *licensing arrangements*, *branch offices*, *strategic alliances*, and *foreign direct investment*.

Independent Agent *foreign individual or organization that agrees to represent an exporter's interests*

Independent Agents   An **independent agent** is a foreign individual or organization that represents an exporter in foreign markets. Independent agents often act as sales representatives: They sell the exporter's products, collect payment, and make sure that customers are satisfied. They often represent several firms at once and usually don't specialize in a particular product or market. Peter So operates an import-export office in Hong Kong. He and his staff of three handle imports from about 15 foreign companies into Hong Kong and about 10 Hong Kong firms that export products abroad.

managing in turbulent times

The Ups and Downs of Globalization

International business has been around for thousands of years. For example, as far back as 2000 B.C.E., tribes in northern Africa took dates and clothing to Babylonia and Assyria in the Middle East and traded them for spices and olive oil. By 500 B.C.E., Chinese merchants were actively exporting silk and jade to India and Europe, and trade routes were being established between many countries in Europe, Asia, and Africa.

But even as recently as 100 years ago, international trade was only a small part of the global economy. The effects of any given country's economy had a minimal effect on the rest of the world. It wasn't until the Great Depression that swept the world in 1929 that experts realized how interdependent the global economy had become.

Globalization brings with it both advantages and disadvantages. On the plus side, globalization has increased the standard of living of billions of people and has helped to create enormous wealth in many different parts of the globe. On the other hand, there are many people who have not shared in the benefits of globalization, and some critics believe that globalization has both hurt less-developed countries and destroyed or damaged the unique cultures that exist in different parts of the world.

Globalization has also led to such a high degree of interdependence that no major country's economy is immune from what happens in the rest of the world. The recession of 2008–2011 demonstrated this fact once again: As the economy of the United States ground to a halt, so did the economies of virtually all major European and Asian countries. Global stock trading,

mffoto/Shutterstock

real-time information available on the Internet, and worldwide financial networks combined to paralyze just about every major business in the world.

Managers seeking to reverse the tide and get their businesses going again had to juggle more factors than ever before. Domestic forces such as consumer demand, interest rates, and production costs all had to be considered. But so, too, did international business conditions. And many businesses, such as Circuit City and Chrysler, struggled mightily only to fail. But those with managers and leaders who really understood the global economy did in fact regain their footing. And as global economic conditions improve, so too does the outlook for these businesses.

Licensing Arrangements Companies seeking more involvement may opt for licensing arrangements. A **licensing arrangement** is a contract under which one firm allows another to use its brand name, operating procedures, or proprietary technology. Firms give foreign individuals or companies exclusive rights (called *licensing agreements*) to manufacture or market their products in that market. In return, the exporter receives a fee plus ongoing payments (royalties) that are calculated as a percentage of the license holder's sales. Franchising is a popular form of licensing. For example, McDonald's, Pizza Hut, and Hertz franchise around the world.

Licensing Arrangement *arrangement in which firms choose foreign individuals or organizations to manufacture or market their products in another country*

Branch Offices Instead of developing relationships with foreign agents or licensing companies, a firm may send its own managers to overseas **branch offices,** where the firm has more direct control than it does over agents or license holders. Branch offices also furnish a more visible public presence in foreign countries, and foreign customers tend to feel more secure when there's a local branch office. Halliburton, a Houston-based oil field supply and services company, recently opened a branch office in Dubai to more effectively establish relationships with customers in the Middle East.

Branch Office *foreign office set up by an international or multinational firm*

Strategic Alliances In a **strategic alliance**, a company finds a partner in the country in which it wants to do business. Each party agrees to invest resources and capital into a new business or to cooperate in some mutually beneficial way. This new business, the alliance, is owned by the partners, who divide its profits. Such alliances are sometimes called *joint ventures*, but the term *strategic alliance* has arisen because such partnerships are playing increasingly important roles in the strategies of major companies. Ford and Russian automaker Sollers recently launched a new joint venture; Sollers will manufacture Ford products in Russia and the two partners will then work together on marketing them.[14] In many countries, such as Mexico, India, and China, laws make alliances virtually the only way to do international business. Mexico, for example, requires that all foreign firms investing there have local partners.

Strategic Alliance *arrangement (also called* joint venture*) in which a company finds a foreign partner to contribute approximately half of the resources needed to establish and operate a new business in the partner's country*

In addition to easing the way into new markets, alliances give firms greater control over foreign activities than agents and licensees. Alliances also allow firms to benefit from the knowledge and expertise of foreign partners. Microsoft, for example, relies heavily on alliances as it expands into international markets. This approach has helped the firm learn the intricacies of doing business in China and India, two of the hardest emerging markets to crack.

Foreign Direct Investment **Foreign direct investment (FDI)** involves buying or establishing tangible assets in another country. Dell Computer, for example, has built assembly plants in Europe and China. Volkswagen has built a factory in Brazil, and Disney has built theme parks in France and Hong Kong. Each of these activities represents FDI by a firm in another country.

Foreign Direct Investment (FDI) *arrangement in which a firm buys or establishes tangible assets in another country*

Understanding the Cultural Environment

OBJECTIVE 4
Describe
some of the ways in which social, cultural, economic, legal, and political differences among nations affect international business.

A major factor in the success—or failure—of international business activity is having a deep understanding of the cultural environment and how it affects business. Disney's Hong Kong theme park struggled after it first opened, in large part because Disney made the mistake of minimizing all elements of Chinese culture in the park—essentially, making it a generic miniature reproduction of the original Disneyland in California. Disney also confused potential visitors with ads showing a father, mother, and two children walking hand-in-hand toward the theme park, overlooking China's laws that restrict many families to a single child. Only after a refurbishment to make the park more Chinese and a revised ad campaign did attendance begin to improve.[15] A country's culture includes all the values, symbols, beliefs, and language that guide behavior.

Values, Symbols, Beliefs, and Language

Cultural values and beliefs are often unspoken; they may even be taken for granted by those who live in a particular country. Cultural factors do not necessarily cause problems for managers when the cultures of two countries are similar. Difficulties can arise, however, when there is little overlap between the home culture of a manager and the culture of the country in which business is to be conducted. For example, most U.S. managers find the culture and traditions of England relatively familiar. The people of both countries speak the same language and share strong historical roots, and there is a history of strong commerce between the two countries. When U.S. managers begin operations in Japan or the People's Republic of China, however, most of those commonalities disappear.

In Japanese, the word *hai* (pronounced "hi") means "yes." In conversation, however, this word is used much like people in the United States use "uh-huh"; it moves a conversation along or shows the person with whom you are talking that you are paying attention. So when does *hai* mean "yes" and when does it mean "uh-huh"? This turns out to be a relatively difficult question to answer. If a U.S. manager asks a Japanese manager if he agrees to some trade arrangement, the Japanese manager is likely to say, "Hai"—but this may mean "Yes, I agree," "Yes, I understand," or "Yes, I am listening." Many U.S. managers become frustrated in negotiations with the Japanese because they believe that the Japanese continue to raise issues that have already been settled (because the Japanese managers said "Yes"). What many of these managers fail to recognize is that "yes" does not always mean "yes" in Japan.

Cultural differences between countries can have a direct impact on business practice. For example, the religion of Islam teaches that people should not make a living by exploiting the misfortune of others; as a result, charging interest payments is seen as immoral. This means that in Saudi Arabia there are few businesses that provide auto towing services to take stalled cars to a garage for repair (because that would be capitalizing on misfortune), and in the Sudan banks cannot pay or charge interest. Given these cultural and religious constraints, those two businesses—automobile towing and banking—do not seem to hold great promise for international managers in those particular countries!

Some cultural differences between countries can be even more subtle and yet have a major impact on business activities. For example, in the United States, most managers clearly agree about the value of time. Most U.S. managers schedule their activities tightly and then try to adhere to their schedules. Other cultures do not put such a premium on time. In the Middle East, managers do not like to set appointments, and they rarely keep appointments set too far into the future. U.S. managers interacting with managers from the Middle East might misinterpret the late arrival of a potential business partner as a negotiation ploy or an insult, when it is rather a simple reflection of different views of time and its value.[16]

Language itself can be an important factor. Beyond the obvious and clear barriers posed by people who speak different languages, subtle differences in meaning can also play a major role. For example, Imperial Oil of Canada markets gasoline under the brand name Esso. When the firm tried to sell its gasoline in Japan, it learned that *esso* means "stalled car" in Japanese. Likewise, when Chevrolet first introduced a U.S. model called the Nova in Latin America, General Motors executives could not understand why the car sold poorly. They eventually learned, though, that, in Spanish, *no va* means "it doesn't go." The color green is used extensively in Muslim countries, but it signifies death in some other countries. The color associated with femininity in the United States is pink, but in many other countries, yellow is the most feminine color.

Employee Behavior across Cultures

Managers in international business also have to understand that there are differences in what motivates people in different cultures. Although it's impossible to predict exactly how people from different cultures will react in the workplace, some insights have been developed from research on individual behaviors and attitudes

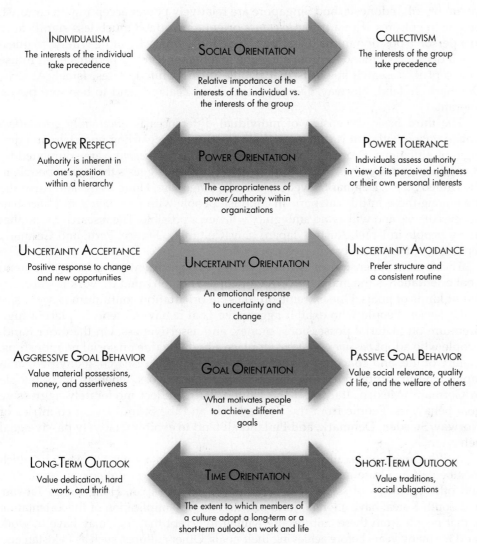

FIGURE 4.6 Hofstede's Five Dimensions of National Culture

across different cultures. This research, conducted by Geert Hofstede, identifies five important dimensions along which people seem to differ across cultures. These dimensions are illustrated in Figure 4.6.

The first dimension is social orientation. **Social orientation** is a person's beliefs about the relative importance of the individual versus groups to which that person belongs. The two extremes of social orientation are individualism and collectivism. *Individualism* is the cultural belief that the person comes first. Research suggested that people in the United States, the United Kingdom, Australia, Canada, New Zealand, and the Netherlands tend to be relatively individualistic. *Collectivism* is the belief that the group comes first. Research has found that people from Mexico, Greece, Hong Kong, Taiwan, Peru, Singapore, Colombia, and Pakistan tend to be relatively collectivistic in their values. In countries with higher levels of individualism, many workers may prefer reward systems that link pay with the performance of individual employees. In a more collectivistic culture, such a reward system may in fact be counterproductive.

A second important dimension is **power orientation,** the beliefs that people in a culture hold about the appropriateness of power and authority differences in hierarchies such as business organizations. Some cultures are characterized by *power respect*. This means that people tend to accept the power and authority of their superiors simply on the basis of their position in the hierarchy and to respect their right to hold that power. Research has found that people in France, Spain, Mexico,

Social Orientation *a person's beliefs about the relative importance of the individual versus groups to which that person belongs*

Power Orientation *the beliefs that people in a culture hold about the appropriateness of power and authority differences in hierarchies such as business organizations*

Japan, Brazil, Indonesia, and Singapore are relatively power accepting. In contrast, people in cultures with a *power tolerance* orientation attach much less significance to a person's position in the hierarchy. These individuals are more willing to question a decision or mandate from someone at a higher level or perhaps even refuse to accept it. Research suggests that people in the United States, Israel, Austria, Denmark, Ireland, Norway, Germany, and New Zealand tend to be more power tolerant.

The third basic dimension of individual differences is *uncertainty orientation.* **Uncertainty orientation** is the feeling individuals have regarding uncertain and ambiguous situations. People in cultures with *uncertainty acceptance* are stimulated by change and thrive on new opportunities. The research suggests that many people in the United States, Denmark, Sweden, Canada, Singapore, Hong Kong, and Australia are among those in this category. In contrast, people with *uncertainty avoidance* tendencies dislike and will avoid ambiguity whenever possible. The research found that many people in Israel, Austria, Japan, Italy, Columbia, France, Peru, and Germany tend to avoid uncertainty whenever possible.

The fourth dimension of cultural values is goal orientation. In this context, **goal orientation** is the manner in which people are motivated to work toward different kinds of goals. One extreme on the goal orientation continuum is *aggressive goal behavior.* People who exhibit aggressive goal behaviors tend to place a high premium on material possessions, money, and assertiveness. On the other hand, people who adopt *passive goal behavior* place a higher value on social relationships, quality of life, and concern for others. According to the research, many people in Japan tend to exhibit relatively aggressive goal behaviors, whereas many people in Germany, Mexico, Italy, and the United States reflect moderately aggressive goal behaviors. People from the Netherlands and the Scandinavian countries of Norway, Sweden, Denmark, and Finland all tend to exhibit relatively passive goal behaviors.

A fifth dimension is called **time orientation.** Time orientation is the extent to which members of a culture adopt a long-term versus a short-term outlook on work, life, and other elements of society. Some cultures, such as Japan, Hong Kong, Taiwan, and South Korea, have a longer-term orientation. One implication of this orientation is that people from these cultures are willing to accept that they may have to work hard for many years before achieving their goals. Other cultures, such as Pakistan and West Africa, are more likely to have a short-term orientation. As a result, people from these cultures may prefer jobs that provide more immediate rewards. Research suggests that people in the United States and Germany tend to have an intermediate time orientation.[17]

Uncertainty Orientation *the feeling individuals have regarding uncertain and ambiguous situations*

Goal Orientation *the manner in which people are motivated to work toward different kinds of goals*

Time Orientation *the extent to which members of a culture adopt a long-term versus a short-term outlook on work, life, and other elements of society*

OBJECTIVE 5
Describe
some of the ways in which economic, legal, and political differences among nations affect international business.

Barriers to International Trade

Whether a business is truly multinational or sells to only a few foreign markets, several factors will affect its international operations. Success in foreign markets will largely depend on the ways it responds to *social and cultural forces* (as described previously) *and economic, legal,* and *political barriers* to international trade.

Economic Differences

Although cultural differences are often subtle, economic differences can be fairly pronounced. As we discussed in Chapter 1, in dealing with mixed market economies like those of France and Sweden, firms must know when—and to what extent—the government is involved in a given industry. The French government, for instance, is heavily involved in all aspects of airplane design and manufacturing. The impact of economic differences can be even greater in planned economies such as those of China and Vietnam, where the government owns and operates many factors of production.

Legal and Political Differences

Governments can affect international business in many ways. They can set conditions for doing business within their borders and even prohibit doing business altogether. They can control the flow of capital and use tax legislation to discourage or encourage activity in a given industry. They can even confiscate the property of foreign-owned companies. In this section, we discuss some of the more common legal and political issues in international business: *quotas, tariffs*, and *subsidies; local content laws;* and *business practice laws.*

Quotas, Tariffs, and Subsidies

Even free market economies, such as the United States, have some quotas or tariffs, both of which affect prices and quantities of foreign-made products. A **quota** restricts the number of products of a certain type that can be imported and, by reducing supply, raises the prices of those imports. That's why Belgian ice-cream makers can't ship more than 922,315 kilograms to the United States each year, and Canada can ship no more than 14.7 billion board feet of softwood timber per year. Quotas are often determined by treaties. Better terms are often given to friendly trading partners, and quotas are typically adjusted to protect domestic producers.

> **Quota** *restriction on the number of products of a certain type that can be imported into a country*

The ultimate quota is an **embargo,** a government order forbidding exportation or importation of a particular product—or even all products—from a specific country. Many nations control bacteria and disease by banning certain agricultural products. Because the United States has embargoes against Cuba (as discussed in our opening case) and Libya, U.S. firms can't invest in these countries, and their products can't legally be sold in U.S. markets.

> **Embargo** *government order banning exportation or importation of a particular product or all products from a particular country*

Tariffs are taxes on imported products. They raise the prices of imports by making consumers pay not only for the products but also for tariff fees. Tariffs take two forms: revenue and protectionist. Revenue tariffs are imposed to raise money for governments, but most tariffs, called protectionist tariffs, are meant to discourage particular imports. Did you know that firms that import ironing-board covers into the United States pay a 7-percent tariff on the price of the product? Firms that import women's athletic shoes pay a flat rate of $0.90 per pair plus 20 percent of the product price. Such figures are determined through a complicated process designed to put foreign and domestic firms on competitive footing (that is, to make the foreign goods about the same cost as the domestic goods).

> **Tariff** *tax levied on imported products*

Quotas and tariffs are imposed for numerous reasons. The U.S. government aids domestic automakers by restricting the number of Japanese cars imported into this country. Because of national security concerns, we limit the export of technology (for example, computer and nuclear technology to China). The United States isn't the only country that uses tariffs and quotas. To protect domestic firms, Italy imposes high tariffs on electronic goods. As a result, DVD players are prohibitively expensive there.

A **subsidy** is a government payment to help a domestic business compete with foreign firms. They're actually indirect tariffs that lower the prices of domestic goods rather than raise the prices of foreign goods. For example, many European governments subsidize farmers to help them compete against U.S. grain imports.

> **Subsidy** *government payment to help a domestic business compete with foreign firms*

The Protectionism Debate

In the United States, **protectionism,** the practice of protecting domestic business at the expense of free market competition, is controversial. Supporters argue that tariffs and quotas protect domestic firms and jobs as well as shelter new industries until they're able to compete internationally. They contend that we need such measures to counter steps taken by other nations. During the recent London Olympics critics were outraged when it was discovered that Ralph Lauren, provider of official U.S. team uniforms, had outsourced the production of those uniforms to firms in China. These critics charged that the jobs of making the uniforms should have gone to U.S. workers. On the other hand, Ralph Lauren pointed out that it the uniforms would have cost a lot more if they had been made in the United States. Other advocates justify protectionism in the name of

> **Protectionism** *practice of protecting domestic business against foreign competition*

national security. A nation, they argue, must be able to produce efficiently the goods needed for survival in case of war.

Critics cite protectionism as a source of friction between nations. They also charge that it drives up prices by reducing competition. They maintain that although jobs in some industries would be lost as a result of free trade, jobs in other industries (for example, electronics and automobiles) would be created if all nations abandoned protectionist tactics.

Protectionism sometimes takes on almost comic proportions. Neither Europe nor the United States grows bananas, but both European and U.S. firms buy and sell bananas in foreign markets. Problems arose when the EU put a quota on bananas imported from Latin America, a market dominated by two U.S. firms, Chiquita and Dole, to help firms based in current and former European colonies in the Caribbean. To retaliate, the United States imposed a 100-percent tariff on certain luxury products imported from Europe, including Louis Vuitton handbags, Scottish cashmere sweaters, and Parma ham.

Local Content Laws

Local Content Law *law requiring that products sold in a particular country be at least partly made there*

Many countries, including the United States, have **local content laws,** requirements that products sold in a country be at least partly made there. Firms seeking to do business in a country must either invest there directly or take on a domestic partner. In this way, some of the profits from doing business in a foreign country stay there rather than flow out to another nation. In some cases, the partnership arrangement is optional but wise. In Mexico, for instance, Radio Shack de México is a joint venture owned by Tandy Corporation (49 percent) and Mexico's Grupo Gigante (51 percent). This allows the retailer to promote a strong Mexican identity; it also makes it easier to address certain import regulations that are easier for Mexican than for U.S. firms. Both China and India currently require that when a foreign firm enters into a joint venture with a local firm, the local partner must have the controlling ownership stake.

Business Practice Laws

Business Practice Law *law or regulation governing business practices in given countries*

Many businesses entering new markets encounter problems in complying with stringent regulations and bureaucratic obstacles. Such practices are affected by the **business practice laws** by which host countries govern business practices within their jurisdictions. As part of its entry strategy in Germany several years ago, Walmart had to buy existing retailers rather than open brand-new stores because, at the time, the German government was not issuing new licenses to sell food products. Walmart also was not allowed to follow its normal practice of refunding price differences on items sold for less by other stores because the practice is illegal in Germany. In addition, Walmart had to comply with business-hour restrictions: Stores can't open before 7:00 A.M., must close by 8:00 P.M. on weeknights and 4:00 P.M. on Saturday, and must remain closed on Sunday. After a few years, Walmart eventually decided its meager profits in Germany didn't warrant the effort it required to generate them and closed all of its stores there.

Cartel *association of producers whose purpose is to control supply and prices*

Sometimes, a legal—even an accepted—practice in one country is illegal in another. In some South American countries, for example, it is sometimes legal to bribe business and government officials. The existence of **cartels,** associations of producers that control supply and prices, gives tremendous power to some nations, such as those belonging to the Organization of Petroleum Exporting Countries (OPEC). U.S. law forbids both bribery and cartels.

Dumping *practice of selling a product abroad for less than the cost of production*

Finally, many (but not all) countries forbid **dumping,** selling a product abroad for less than the cost of production at home. U.S. antidumping legislation sets two conditions for determining whether dumping is being practiced:

1 Products are being priced at "less than fair value."
2 The result unfairly harms domestic industry.

Just a few years ago, the United States charged Japan and Brazil with dumping steel at prices 70 percent below normal value. To protect local manufacturers, the U.S. government imposed a significant tariff on steel imported from those countries.

summary of learning objectives

OBJECTIVE 1

Discuss the rise of international business and describe the major world marketplaces, trade agreements, and alliances. (pp. 134–139)

Importing and exporting products from one country to another greatly increases the variety of products available to consumers and businesses. Several forces have combined to spark and sustain globalization. Governments and businesses have become aware of the potential for higher standards of living and increased profits. New technologies make international travel, communication, and commerce faster and less expensive. Additionally, some companies expand into foreign markets just to keep up with their competitors.

North America, Europe, and Pacific Asia represent three geographic clusters that are the major marketplaces for international business activity. These major marketplaces include relatively more of the upper-middle and high-income nations but relatively few low and low-middle income countries.

Trade treaties are legal agreements that specify how countries will work together to support international trade. The most significant treaties are (1) the *North American Free Trade Agreement (NAFTA)*; (2) the *European Union (EU)*; (3) the Association of Southeast *Asian Nations (ASEAN)*; and (4) the *General Agreement on Tariffs and Trade (GATT)*.

OBJECTIVE 2

Explain how differences in import-export balances, exchange rates, and foreign competition determine the ways in which countries and businesses respond to the international environment. (pp. 140–145)

Economists use two measures to assess the balance between imports and exports. A nation's *balance of trade* is the total economic value of all products that it exports minus the total economic value of all products that it imports. When a country's imports exceed its exports, it has a *negative balance of trade* and it suffers a *trade deficit*. A *positive balance of trade* occurs when exports exceed imports, resulting in a *trade surplus*.

The *balance of payments* refers to the flow of money into or out of a country. Payments for imports and exports, money spent by tourists, funding from foreign-aid programs, and proceeds from currency transactions all contribute to the balance of payments.

Exchange rates, the rate at which one nation's currency can be exchanged for that of another, are a major influence on international trade. Most countries use *floating exchange rates,* in which the value of one currency relative to that of another varies with market conditions.

Countries *export* what they can produce better or less expensively than other countries and use the proceeds to *import* what they can't produce as effectively. Economists once focused on two forms of advantage to explain international trade: *absolute advantage* and *comparative advantage*. Today, the theory of *national competitive advantage* is a widely accepted model of why nations engage in international trade. According to this theory, comparative advantage derives from four conditions: (1) factor of production conditions, (2) demand conditions; (3) related and supporting industries; and (4) strategies, structures, and rivalries.

OBJECTIVE 3

Discuss the factors involved in deciding to do business internationally and in selecting the appropriate levels of international involvement and international organizational structure. (pp. 145–149)

Several factors enter into the decision to go international. A company wishing to sell products in foreign markets should consider the following questions: (1) Is there a *demand* for its products abroad? (2) If so, must it *adapt* those products for international consumption? Companies may also go international through outsourcing and offshoring.

After deciding to go international, a firm must decide on its level of involvement. Several levels are possible: (1) *exporters and importers*; (2) *international firms*; and (3) *multinational firms*. Different levels of involvement require different kinds of organizational structure. The spectrum of international organizational strategies includes the following: (1) *independent agents*; (2) *licensing arrangements*; (3) *branch offices*; (4) *strategic alliances* (or *joint ventures*); and (5) *foreign direct investment (FDI)*. Independent agents are foreign individuals or organizations that represent an exporter in foreign markets. Another option, licensing arrangements, represents a contract under which one firm allows another to use its brand name, operating procedures, or proprietary technology. Companies may also consider establishing a branch office by sending managers overseas to set up a physical presence. A strategic alliance occurs when a company seeking international expansion finds a partner in the country in which it wishes to do business. Finally, FDI is the practice of buying or establishing tangible assets in another country.

OBJECTIVE 4

Describe some of the ways in which social, cultural, economic, legal, and political differences among nations affect international business. (pp. 149–152)

A country's culture includes all the values, symbols, beliefs, and language that guide behavior. Cultural values and beliefs are often unspoken; they may even be taken for granted by those who live in a particular country. Cultural factors do not necessarily cause problems for managers when the cultures of two countries are similar. Difficulties can arise, however, when there is little overlap between the home culture of a manager and the culture of the country in which business is to be conducted. Cultural differences between countries can have a direct impact on business practice. Some cultural differences between countries, such as the meaning of time, can be even more subtle and yet have a major impact on business activities. Language itself can be an important factor. Beyond the obvious and clear barriers posed by people who speak different languages, subtle differences in meaning can also play a major role.

Managers in international business also have to understand that there are differences in what motivates people in different cultures. Social orientation is a person's beliefs about the relative importance of the individual versus groups to which that person belongs. A second important dimension is power orientation, the beliefs that people in a culture hold about the appropriateness of power and authority differences in hierarchies, such as business organizations. Uncertainty orientation is the feeling individuals have regarding uncertain and ambiguous situations. Goal orientation is the manner in which people are motivated to work toward different kinds of goals. Time orientation is the extent to which members of a culture adopt a long-term versus a short-term outlook on work, life, and other elements of society.

OBJECTIVE 5

Describe some of the ways in which economic, legal, and political differences among nations affect international business. (pp. 152–154)

Economic differences among nations can be fairly pronounced and can affect businesses in a variety of ways. Common legal and political issues in international business include *quotas*, *tariffs*, *subsidies*, *local content laws*, and *business practice laws*. Quotas restrict the number of certain products that can be imported into a country, and a tariff is a tax that a country imposes on imported products. Subsidies are government payments to domestic companies to help them better compete with international companies. Another legal strategy to support a nation's businesses is implementing local content laws that require that products sold in a country be at least partially made there. Business practice laws control business activities within their jurisdiction and create obstacles for businesses trying to enter new markets.

The term *protectionism* describes the practice of protecting domestic businesses at the expense of free market competition. Although some economists argue that legal strategies such as quotas, tariffs, and subsidies are necessary to protect domestic firms, others argue that protectionism ultimately hurts consumers as a result of higher prices.

A final obstacle to international business is that business practices that are legal in one country may not be legal in another. Bribery, the formation of cartels, and dumping are forbidden in the United States, but legal in other countries, challenging U.S. companies trying to enter some foreign markets.

Key terms

absolute advantage (p. 144)
Association of Southeast Asian Nations (ASEAN) (p. 138)
balance of payments (p. 142)
balance of trade (p. 140)
branch office (p. 149)
business practice law (p. 154)
cartel (p. 154)
comparative advantage (p. 144)
dumping (p. 154)
embargo (p. 153)
euro (p. 143)
European Union (EU) (p. 138)
exchange rate (p. 143)
export (p. 135)
exporter (p. 147)

foreign direct investment (FDI) (p. 149)
General Agreement on Tariffs and Trade (GATT) (p. 138)
goal orientation (p. 152)
globalization (p. 134)
import (p. 134)
importer (p. 147)
independent agent (p. 148)
international firm (p. 147)
licensing arrangement (p. 149)
local content law (p. 154)
multinational firm (p. 147)
national competitive advantage (p. 145)
North American Free Trade Agreement (NAFTA) (p. 138)

offshoring (p. 146)
outsourcing (p. 146)
power orientation (p. 151)
protectionism (p. 153)
quota (p. 153)
social orientation (p. 151)
strategic alliances (p. 149)
subsidy (p. 153)
tariff (p. 153)
time orientation (p. 152)
trade deficit (p. 140)
trade surplus (p. 140)
uncertainty orientation (p. 152)
World Trade Organization (WTO) (p. 138)

MyBizLab

Go to **pearsonglobaleditions.com/mybizlab** to complete the problems marked with this icon ✪.

questions & exercises

QUESTIONS FOR REVIEW

✪ **4-1.** What are the advantages and disadvantages of globalization?

4-2. What are the three possible levels of involvement in international business? Give examples of each.

4-3. What are the elements of national competitive advantage?

4-4. Describe the five international organizational structures.

QUESTIONS FOR ANALYSIS

4-5. List all the major items in your bedroom, including furnishings, and identify the country in which each item was made. Develop a hypothesis about why each product was made in the United States or abroad.

4-6. Describe the United States in terms of the five cultural orientations.

✪ **4-7.** Do you support protectionist tariffs for the United States? If so, in what instances and for what reasons? If not, why?

✪ **4-8.** Do you think that a firm operating internationally is better advised to adopt a single standard of ethical conduct or to adapt to local conditions? Under what kinds of conditions might each approach be preferable?

APPLICATION EXERCISES

4-9. The World Bank uses per-capita income to make distinctions among countries. Use Web or database research to identify at least three countries in the following categories for last year: high-income countries, upper-middle-income countries, lower-middle-income countries, and lower-income countries. Additionally, identify the source of the data that you used to draw these conclusions.

4-10. China is one of the fastest-growing markets in the world. Use Web or database research to uncover how to best describe China according to the five cultural dimensions. Cite the source for your information.

building a business: continuing team exercise

Assignment

Meet with your team members and discuss your new business venture within the context of this chapter. Develop specific responses to the following:

4-11. In what ways, if any, are exchange rates likely to affect your business?

4-12. Are you likely to acquire any of your materials, products, or services from abroad? Why or why not?

4-13. Are there likely to be any export opportunities for your products or services? Why or why not?

4-14. To what extent, if any, will your new venture be affected by social and cultural differences, economic differences, and/or legal and political differences across cultures?

building your business skills

FINDING YOUR PLACE

Goal

To encourage you to apply global business strategies to a small-business situation.

Background Information

Some people might say that Yolanda Lang is a bit too confident. Others might say that she needs confidence—and more—to succeed in the business she's chosen. But one thing is certain: Lang is determined to grow INDE, her handbag design company, into a global enterprise. At only 28 years of age, she has time on her side—if she makes the right business moves now.

These days, Lang spends most of her time in Milan, Italy. Backed by $50,000 of her parents' personal savings, she is trying to compete with Gucci, Fendi, and other high-end handbag makers. Her target market is U.S. women willing to spend $200 on a purse. Ironically, Lang was forced to set up shop in Italy because of the snobbishness of these customers, who buy high-end bags only if they're European made. "Strangely enough," she muses, "I need to be in Europe to sell in America."

To succeed, she must first find ways to keep production costs down—a tough task for a woman in a male-dominated business culture. Her fluent Italian is an advantage, but she's often forced to turn down inappropriate dinner invitations. She also has to figure out how to get her 22-bag collection into stores worldwide. Retailers are showing her bags in Italy and Japan, but she's had little luck in the United States. "I intend to be a global company," says Lang. The question is how to succeed first as a small business.

Method

STEP 1

Join together with three or four other students to discuss the steps that Lang has taken so far to break into the U.S. retail market. These steps include:

- Buying a mailing list of 5,000 shoppers from high-end department store Neiman Marcus and selling directly to these customers.

- Linking with a manufacturer's representative to sell her line in major U.S. cities while she herself concentrates on Europe.

STEP 2

Based on what you learned in this chapter, suggest other strategies that might help Lang grow her business. Working with group members, consider whether the following options would help or hurt Lang's business. Explain why a strategy is likely to work or likely to fail.

- Lang could relocate to the United States and sell abroad through an independent agent.
- Lang could relocate to the United States and set up a branch office in Italy.
- Lang could find a partner in Italy and form a strategic alliance that would allow her to build her business on both continents.

FOLLOW-UP QUESTIONS

4-15. What are the most promising steps that Lang can take to grow her business? What are the least promising?

4-16. Lang thinks that her trouble breaking into the U.S. retail market stems from the fact that her company is unknown. How would this circumstance affect the strategies suggested in Steps 1 and 2?

4-17. When Lang deals with Italian manufacturers, she is a young woman in a man's world. Often she must convince men that her purpose is business and nothing else. How should Lang handle personal invitations that get in the way of business? How can she say no while still maintaining business relationships? Why is it often difficult for U.S. women to do business in male-dominated cultures?

4-18. The U.S. consulate has given Lang little business help because her products are made in Italy. Do you think the consulate's treatment of a U.S. businessperson is fair or unfair? Explain your answer.

4-19. Do you think Lang's relocation to Italy will pay off? Why or why not?

4-20. With Lang's goals of creating a global company, can INDE continue to be a one-person operation?

exercising your ethics

PAYING HEED TO FOREIGN PRACTICES

The Situation

Assume that you're an up-and-coming manager at a medium-sized manufacturing company. Your company is one of only a few companies making certain components for radiant floor heating systems. The primary advantage of these systems is that they are energy efficient and can result in significantly lower heating costs. Although radiant floor heating is just catching on the United States, there is a lot of potential in foreign markets where energy is expensive. You've been assigned to head up your company's new operations in a Latin American country. Because at least two of your competitors are also trying to enter this same market, your boss wants you to move as quickly as possible. You also sense that your success in this assignment will likely determine your future with the company.

You would like to build a production facility and have just completed meetings with local government officials. However, you're pessimistic about your ability to get things moving quickly. You've learned, for example, that it will take 10 months to get a building permit for a needed facility. Moreover, once the building's up, it will take another 6 months to get utilities.

Finally, the phone company says that it may take up to two years to install the phone lines that you need for high-speed Internet access.

The Dilemma

Various officials have indicated that time frames could be considerably shortened if you were willing to pay special "fees." You realize that these fees are bribes, and you're well aware that the practice of paying such fees is both unethical and illegal in the United States. In this foreign country, however, it's not illegal and not even considered unethical. Moreover, if you don't pay and one of your competitors does, you'll be at a major competitive disadvantage. In any case, your boss isn't likely to understand the long lead times necessary to get the operation running. Fortunately, you have access to a source of funds that you could spend without the knowledge of anyone in the home office.

QUESTIONS TO ADDRESS

4-21. What are the key ethical issues in this situation?

4-22. What do you think most managers would do in this situation?

4-23. What would you do?

team exercise

WEIGHING THE TRADE-OFFS

The Situation

Able Systems is a software company specializing in technology solutions for the food industry, including supermarkets and restaurants. All of your customers are located in the United States and operate nearly 24 hours a day. You provide excellent phone support for customers who have an issue, but your expenses are increasing and you're looking for ways to contain costs.

The Dilemma

Able Systems has tried to stem escalating support phone support costs by limiting the number of specialists working on each shift, but long wait times have angered customers. Because of the technical and problem-solving skills needed to provide remote support, hiring less-qualified employees is just not an option. You're looking at your competitors and you've noticed that many have offshored their operations—hiring employees in other countries to provide support. Because of a large number of English speakers and an adequate supply of applicants with the education needed for a support position, you are considering setting up a phone support center in Jamaica.

This solution is not without concerns. If you offshore your support operation, you will have to lay off most of the U.S. support employees. You're willing to provide outplacement services to make sure that they can find new jobs, but you're still concerned about the impact of layoffs on your remaining employees. A group of programmers who caught wind of this proposal have begun to wonder if their jobs are next.

Additionally, local elected officials are concerned about the impact of layoffs on the local economy. Your boss is pressuring you for a recommendation and you're weighing the pros and cons of both options.

Team Activity

Assemble a group of four students and assign each group member to one of the following roles:

- CEO of the Able Systems
- Programmer at Able Systems
- Liaison from a technical college in Jamaica who has graduates looking for jobs in their country
- Local government official

ACTION STEPS

4-24. Before hearing any of your group's comments on this situation, and from the perspective of your assigned role, do you think that phone support should be offshored to Jamaica? Write down the reasons for your position.

4-25. Gather your group together and reveal, in turn, each member's comments on whether phone support should be offshored.

4-26. Appoint someone to record main points of agreement and disagreement within the group.

4-27. Considering the interests of all stakeholders, what is the best option in this situation?

4-28. Develop a group response to the following question: Can your team identify other solutions to this dilemma?

cases

The Embargo Grinds On

Continued from page 134

At the beginning of this chapter you read about the effects of embargos, especially as they apply to the coffee bean market. Using the information presented in this chapter you should now be able to respond to these questions.

QUESTIONS FOR DISCUSSION

4-29. In your opinion, is Thanksgiving Coffee's Paul Katzeff doing the right thing in working against the U.S. embargo? Explain your opinion. If your answer is yes, can you think of any additional steps that Katzeff might take?

4-30. How have changes in the *structure of the global economy* affected the U.S. embargo, which has been in effect for around 50 years? More specifically, how can U.S. companies deal with changing *environmental challenges—economic, political and legal*, and *cultural*—in their relations not only with Cuba but also with other countries in Latin America?

4-31. How might U.S. businesses best prepare themselves for a possible elimination of the embargo?

Not My Cup of Tea

China is a country famous for tea. Over thousands of years, tea has been the beverage of choice in China. This, however, did not deter Starbucks from entering one of the fastest growing consumer markets in the world. The first Starbucks opened in Taipei, Taiwan in 1998 and the first mainland store was opened in Beijing in 1999. Since that time, Starbucks has opened hundreds of stores and they hope to have over 1,500 locations by 2015.

Starbucks analyzed the Chinese market and found that their brand was valued not only for their food and beverage offerings, but for the atmosphere of Starbucks stores. Chinese consumers enjoyed the opportunity to meet with friends and business partners in a comfortable location and appreciated the upbeat music and chic interiors. While kiosks have become popular in the U.S., some Chinese Starbucks locations are as large as 3,800 square feet.

Starbucks has customized its product offerings, introducing the Green Tea Frappuccino ® Blended Crème beverage in 2002 and Starbucks bottled Frappuccino ® coffee drinks into Chinese markets in 2007. Not all Chinese consumers are fans of Starbucks coffee. Cheng Xiaochen, an English teacher who likes to meet students at Starbucks exclaims "It's a good place to meet people, but the coffee is so bitter it tastes like Chinese medicine." Responding to Mr. Cheng and others like him, the company offers mint hot chocolate and red bean frappuccinos. Food offerings have also been customized to the Chinese market, with Hainan chicken sandwiches and rice wraps.[18]

Starbucks acknowledges that employees are at the center of its success and make a considerable investment in training, developing, and retaining these employees. However, Starbucks faced a challenge in an achievement-oriented Chinese culture, where parents aspire for their children to take jobs in traditionally successful fields such as financial services and banking. In response, Starbucks launched a family forum in 2012, which provided stories from managers who have worked their way up the career ladder with Starbucks.

Starbucks has worked to extend every component of its corporate culture into its Chinese expansion. The company has a long established tradition of community commitment, and they have brought this to China. Through a five million dollar grant to the Starbucks China Education Project, the company aims to help students and teachers in rural china, increase access to clean drinking water, and provide relief from the 2008 Sichaun earthquake.[19] Starbucks has demonstrated that a long-term commitment and sensitivity to international market conditions are the keys to success.[20]

QUESTIONS FOR DISCUSSION

4-32. What motivates companies like Starbucks to expand into international markets with little perceived interest for their product?

4-33. How has Starbucks adapted to Chinese culture?

4-34. Are you concerned that Starbucks expansion into China threatens their traditional culture? Why or why not?

4-35. China has a collectivist culture. How do you believe that this will affect managers in a Starbucks store?

4-36. If China wished to slow Starbucks' expansion, what legal barriers would be most helpful? How would these barriers affect Chinese consumers and businesses?

crafting a business plan

PART 1: THE CONTEMPORARY BUSINESS ENVIRONMENT

Goal of the Exercise

In Chapter 3 we discussed how the starting point for virtually every new business is a *business plan*. Business plans describe the business strategy for any new business and demonstrate how that strategy will be implemented. One benefit of a business plan is that in preparing it, would-be entrepreneurs must develop their idea on paper and firm up their thinking about how to launch their business before investing time and money in it. In this exercise, you'll get started on creating your own business plan.

Exercise Background: Part 1 of the Business Plan

The starting point for any business plan is coming up with a "great idea." This might be a business that you've already considered setting up. If you don't have ideas for a business already, look around. What are some businesses that you come into contact with on a regular basis? Restaurants, childcare services, and specialty stores are a few examples you might consider. You may also wish to create a business that is connected with a talent or interest you have, such as crafts, cooking, or car repair. It's important that you create a company from "scratch" rather than use a company that already exists. You'll learn more if you use your own ideas.

Once you have your business idea, your next step is to create an "identity" for your business. This includes determining a name for your business and an idea of what your business will do. It also includes identifying the type of ownership your business will take, topics we discussed in Chapter 3. The first part of the plan also briefly looks at who your ideal customers are as well as how your business will stand out from the crowd. Part 1 of the plan also looks at how the business will interact with the community and demonstrate social responsibility, topics we discussed in Chapter 2. Finally, almost all business plans today include a perspective on the impact of global business.

Your Assignment

STEP 1

To complete this assignment, you first need to download the *Business Plan Student Template* file from the book's Companion website at www.pearsonhighered.com/ebert. This is a Microsoft Word file you can use to complete your business plan. For this assignment, you will fill in "Part 1" of the plan.

STEP 1

Once you have the *Business Plan Student Template* file, you can begin to answer the following questions in "Part 1: The Contemporary Business Environment."

4-37. What is the name of your business?
Hint: When you think of the name of your business, make sure that it captures the spirit of the business you're creating.

4-38. What will your business do?
Hint: Imagine that you are explaining your idea to a family member or a friend. Keep your description to 30 words or less.

4-39. What form of business ownership (sole proprietorship, partnership, or corporation) will your business take? Why did you choose this form?
Hint: For more information on types of business ownership, refer to the discussion in Chapter 3.

4-40. Briefly describe your ideal customer. What are they like in terms of age, income level, and so on?
Hint: You don't have to give too much detail in this part of the plan; you'll provide more details about customers and marketing in later parts of the plan.

4-41. Why will customers choose to buy from your business instead of your competition?
Hint: In this section, describe what will be unique about your business. For example, is the product special or will you offer the product at a lower price?

4-42. All businesses have to deal with ethical issues. One way to address these issues is to create a code of ethics. List three core principles your business will follow.
Hint: To help you consider the ethical issues that your business might face, refer to the discussion in Chapter 2.

4-43. A business shows social responsibility by respecting all of its stakeholders. What steps will you take to create a socially responsible business?
Hint: Refer to the discussion of social responsibility in Chapter 2. What steps can you take to be a "good citizen" in the community? Consider also how you may need to be socially responsible toward your customers and, if applicable, investors, employees, and suppliers.

4-44. Will you sell your product in another country? If so, what countries and why? What challenges will you face?
Hint: To help you consider issues of global business, refer to Chapter 4. Consider how you will expand internationally (i.e., independent agent, licensing, etc.). Do you expect global competition for your product? What advantages will foreign competitors have?
Note: Once you have answered the questions, save your Word document. You'll be answering additional questions in later chapters.

MyBizLab

Go to **pearsonglobaleditions.com/mybizlab** *for the following Assisted-graded writing questions:*

4-45. Some countries have a higher national competitive advantage than others. Based on the four conditions described to create national competitive advantage, what are some national competitive advantage opportunities in the United States? In China? In India? Provide examples of businesses utilizing these advantages. How can each of these countries benefit from the national competitive advantage of the other?

4-46. E-commerce is one business area where international business is becoming a key issue. Pretend you are retailer who accepts orders online and ships the products through the mail. You have done your research and determined that there is significant demand internationally. Develop a strategy for expanding your business internationally. What factors might affect this strategy? How would your strategy change if you shipped perishable goods? How would your strategy change if you shipped hazardous goods?

4-47. Mybizlab Only—comprehensive writing assignment for this chapter.

end notes

1 Merchants of Green Coffee, "About the Merchants," at www.merchantsofgreencoffee.com, accessed on April 5, 2013,; "Cuban Organic Shade-Grown Coffee from Merchants of Green Coffee," *TreeHugger.com*, May, 19, 2005, at www.treehugger.com, accessed on April 5, 2013; Thanksgiving Coffee Co., "End the Embargo on Cuba," at www.endtheembargo.com, accessed on April 5, 2013; Larry Luxner, "Coffee with a Cause," *Tea & Coffee Trade Journal*, at www.teaandcoffee.net, accessed on April 5, 2013; Carol J. Williams, "Some Cuban Exiles Hope Obama Can Help," *Los Angeles Times*, November 10, 2008, at http://articles.latimes.com, accessed on April 5, 2013; Doug Palmer, "Business Urges Obama to Loosen Cuba Embargo," December 4, 2008, *Reuters*, at www.reuters.com, accessed on April 5, 2013; "Cuba Embargo Benefits European, Canadian Firms," *Reuters*, March 20, 2008, at www.reuters.com, accessed on April 5, 2013; Paul Katzeff, "Cooperatives," Thanksgiving Coffee Co., at www.thanksgivingcoffee.com, accessed on April 5, 2013.

2 "Best Buy, Home Depot Find China Market a Tough Sell," *USA Today*, February 23, 2011, p. 5B.

3 Ricky W. Griffin and Michael W. Pustay, *International Business: A Managerial Perspective,* 8th ed. (Upper Saddle River, NJ: Prentice Hall, 2015).

4 Thomas Friedman, *The World Is Flat* (New York: Farrar, Straus, and Giroux, 2005).

5 Ricky W. Griffin and Michael W. Pustay, *International Business: A Managerial Perspective,* 8th ed. (Upper Saddle River, NJ: Prentice Hall, 2015). "Some Manufacturers Say 'Adios' to China," *USA Today*, March 19, 2013, p. 7B.

6 "World," *Time*, February 28, 2011, p. 15.

7 World Trade Organization, at http://www.wto.org/English/thewto_e/whatis_e/tif_e/org6_e.htm, accessed on February 27, 2011.

8 Griffin and Pustay, *International Business: A Managerial Perspective*; see also Steven Husted and Michael Melvin, *International Economics*, 5th ed. (Boston: Addison Wesley Longman, 2001), 54–61; and Karl E. Case and Ray C. Fair,

Principles of Economics, 8th ed. (Upper Saddle River, NJ: Prentice Hall, 2007), 700–708.

[9] Ron Lieber, "Give Us This Day Our Global Bread," *Fast Company*, March 2001, 164–167; Poilâne: "Our History," at http://www.poilane.fr/pages/en/company_univers_histoire.php, accessed on April 5, 2013; "Les Boulangeries-Pâtisseries de Paris: Poilâne," (June 14, 2006), at http://louisrecettes.blogspot.com/2006/06/les-boulangeries-ptisseries-de-paris.html, accessed on April 5, 2013.

[10] Michael Porter, *The Competitive Advantage of Nations* (Boston: Addison-Wesley Longman, 2001), 54–61; see also Case and Fair, *Principles of Economics*, 669–677.

[11] Lee J. Krajewski, Manoj Malhotra, and Larry P. Ritzman, *Operations Management: Processes and Value Chains*, 8th ed. (Upper Saddle River, NJ: Prentice Hall, 2007), 401–403.

[12] *Hoover's Handbook of American Business 2011* (Austin, Texas: Hoover's Business Press, 20116), 432–433.

[13] http://money.cnn.com/magazines/fortune/global500/2012/full_list/index.html, accessed on April 5, 2013.

[14] "Ford, Russian Automaker Make Deal," *USA Today*, February 21, 2011, p. 1B.

[15] "Main Street, H.K.—Disney Localizes Mickey to Boost Its Hong Kong Theme Park," *Wall Street Journal*, January 23, 2008, pp. B1, B2.

[16] "What if There Weren't Any Clocks to Watch?" *Newsweek*, June 30, 1997, p. 14.

[17] Geert Hofstede, *Culture's Consequences: International Differences in Work-Related Values* (Beverly Hills, CA: Sage, 1980); Geert Hofstede, "The Business of International Business Is Culture," *International Business Review*, 1994, Vol. 3, No. 1, pp. 1–14.

[18] Burkitt, Laurie. "Starbucks Plays to Local Chinese Tastes." *Wall Street Journal*. Dow Jones Company, Inc., 26 Nov. 2012. Web. 13 June 2013.

[19] "Greater China." *Starbucks.com*. Starbucks Corporation, n.d. Web. 13 June 2013.

[20] Wang, Helen H. "Five Things Starbucks Did to Get China Right." *Forbes*. Forbes.com, LLC, 10 Aug. 2012. Web. 13 June 2013.

Managing the Business

chapter 5

Eric Carr/Alamy

Science and statistics don't hold all the answers;

managers must rely on their gut—on

the   basis   of

intuition,   experience,   instinct,   and

personal insight.

AFTER READING THIS CHAPTER, YOU SHOULD BE ABLE TO:

OBJECTIVE 1   **Describe** the nature of management and identify the four basic functions that constitute the management process.

OBJECTIVE 2   **Identify** different types of managers likely to be found in an organization by level and area.

OBJECTIVE 3   **Describe** the basic roles and skills required of managers.

OBJECTIVE 4   **Explain** the importance of strategic management and effective goal setting in organizational success.

OBJECTIVE 5   **Discuss** contingency planning and crisis management in today's business world.

OBJECTIVE 6   **Describe** the development and explain the importance of corporate culture.

MyBizLab®

⭐ Improve Your Grade!

Visit **pearsonglobaleditions.com/mybizlab** for simulations, tutorials, and end-of-chapter problems.

Over 10 million students improved their results using the Pearson MyLabs.

Google Keeps
Growing

Sergey Brin and Larry Page met at Stanford University in 1995, when both were graduate students in computer science. At the time, Page was working on a software-development project designed to create an index of websites

by scouring sites for key words and other linkages. Brin joined him on the project, and when they were satisfied that they'd developed something with commercial value, they tried to license the technology to other search companies. As luck would have it, they couldn't find a buyer and settled instead for procuring enough investment capital to keep refining and testing their product.

In 2000, Brin and Page ran across the description of a business model based on the concept of selling advertising in the form of sponsored links and search-specific ads. They adapted it to their own concept and went into business for themselves, eventually building Google into the world's largest search engine. Google generally processes more than 11,300 million searches a month by a user base of 380 million people in 181 different countries and using 146 languages. Following an initial public offering (IPO) in 2004, the company's market capitalization rose steadily; it stood at more than $243.65 billion by 2012, when Google controlled 66.7 percent of the U.S. search market (compared to Yahoo!'s 12.1 percent and Microsoft's 16.3 percent). Google, however, is much more than a mere search engine. Services include searches for news, shopping, local businesses, interactive maps, and discussion groups, as well as blogs, web-based e-mail and voice mail, and a digital photo-management system. You can access the results of any Google search from the Google website, from your own user's toolbar, from your Windows taskbar, and from wireless devices such as smartphones and tablets. Google estimates that 15 percent of searches conducted each day are new—never having been searched before.

How did two young computer scientists build this astoundingly successful company, and where will they take it in the future? Brin and Page remain in the forefront of Google's search for technological innovations. They believe in the power of mathematics and have developed unique algorithms for just about every form of activity in the firm. One of the most successful is an algorithm for auctioning advertising placements that ensures the highest possible prices.

Brin and Page have also been remarkably successful in attracting talented and creative employees and providing them with a work environment and culture that foster the kind of productivity and innovation for which they were hired.

what's in it for me?

Sergey Brin and Larry Page are clearly effective managers, and they understand what it takes to build a business and then keep it at the forefront of its industry. A **manager** is someone whose primary responsibility is to carry out the management process. In particular, a manager is someone who plans and makes decisions, organizes, leads, and controls human, financial, physical, and information resources. Today's managers face a variety of interesting and challenging situations. The average executive works more than 60 hours a week, has enormous demands placed on his or her time, and faces increased complexities posed by globalization, domestic competition, government regulation, shareholder pressure, and Internet-related uncertainties. The job is complicated even more by rapid changes (such as therecession of 2008–2011 and the recovery that really began to take hold in 2013), unexpected disruptions, exciting new opportunities, and both minor and major crises. The manager's job is unpredictable and fraught with challenges, but it is also filled with opportunities to make a difference. Good managers can propel an organization into unprecedented realms of success, whereas poor managers can devastate even the strongest of organizations.[2] After reading this chapter, you'll be better positioned to carry out various management responsibilities yourself. And from the perspective of a consumer or investor, you'll be able to more effectively assess and appreciate the quality of management in various companies.

In this chapter, we explore the importance of strategic management and effective goal setting to organizational success. We also examine the functions that constitute the management process and identify different types of managers likely to be found in an organization by level and area. Along the way, we look at basic management skills and roles and explain the importance of corporate culture.

Finally, although the founders avoid formal strategic planning, they've managed to diversify extensively through acquisitions and key alliances. Typically, Google absorbs an acquired firm and then improves on its technology, thereby adding variety to its own online offerings. Recent acquisitions include YouTube, a leader in online video sharing, Postini, a leader in communications-security products, and Double Click, a leader in online advertising services. Strategic alliances include those with foreign online service providers that offer Google searches on their sites.

For the immediate future, at least, Google plans on following its basic proven recipe for success, competing head to head with financial-service providers for stock information and with iTunes for music and videos. Also committed to the in-house development of new features and services, Google spent $2.8 billion on research and development (R&D) in 2012 (up from $1.2 billion in 2006) and another $1 billion to acquire new information technology (IT) assets. Innovations in the works include an automated universal language translator for translating documents in any language into any other language and personalized home pages that will allow users to design automatic searches and display the results in personal "newspapers."

Nobody knows for sure what else is on the drawing board. In fact, outsiders—notably potential investors—often criticize Google for being a "black box" when they want a few more details on Google's long-range strategy. "We don't talk about our strategy," explains Page, "….because it's strategic. I would rather have people think we're confused than let our competitors know what we're going to do." [1] (After studying this chapter you should be able to answer a set of discussion questions found at the end of this chapter.)

OBJECTIVE 1
Describe
the nature of management and identify the four basic functions that constitute the management process.

The Management Process

All corporations depend on effective management. Whether they run a multibillion-dollar business such as Google or a small local fashion boutique, managers perform many of the same functions and have many of the same responsibilities. These include analyzing their competitive environments and planning, organizing, directing, and controlling day-to-day operations of their business. Ultimately, they are also responsible for the performance and effectiveness of the teams, divisions, or companies that they head.

Although our focus is on managers in business settings, remember that the principles of management apply to all kinds of organizations. Managers work in charities, churches, social organizations, educational institutions, and government agencies. The prime minister of Canada, curators at the Museum of Modern Art, the dean of your college, and the chief administrator of your local hospital are all managers. Remember, too, that managers bring to small organizations much the same kinds of skills—the ability to make decisions and respond to a variety of challenges—that they bring to large ones. Regardless of the nature and size of an organization, managers are among its most important resources.

Basic Management Functions

Management *process of planning, organizing, leading, and controlling an organization's resources to achieve its goals*

Management itself is the process of planning, organizing, leading, and controlling an organization's financial, physical, human, and information resources to achieve its goals. Managers oversee the use of all these resources in their respective firms. All aspects of a manager's job are interrelated. Any given manager is likely to be

Kenneth Chenault (CEO of American Express), Indra Nooyi (Chairman and CEO of PepsiCo), and Jeffrey Smisek (President and CEO of United Airlines) are all senior managers responsible for overseeing the planning, organizing, leading, and control functions in their businesses.

engaged in each of these activities during the course of any given day. Consider the management process at Google. Brin and Page must first create goals and plans that articulate what they want the company to accomplish. Then they rely on effective organization to help make those goals and plans reality. Brin and Page also pay close attention to the people who work for the company, and they keep a close eye on how well the company is performing. Each of these activities represents one of the four basic managerial functions—(1) setting goals is part of planning, (2) setting up the organization is part of organizing, (3) managing people is part of leading, and (4) monitoring performance is part of controlling.

Planning Determining what the organization needs to do and how best to get it done requires *planning*. **Planning** has three main components. It begins when managers determine the firm's goals. Next, they develop a comprehensive *strategy* for achieving those goals. After a strategy is developed, they design *tactical and operational plans* for implementing the strategy. We discuss these three components in more detail later in this chapter. When Alan Mulally took over the ailing Ford Motor Company a few years ago, he walked into a business that had low cash reserves, an unpopular product line, a confusing strategy, and a culture that was so resistant to change that one insider said it was "calcified." His first agenda was to set performance goals for all of Ford's top executives and clarify the strategic direction that would guide Ford in the future. He also worked to ensure that strategic, tactical and operational planning were all integrated and consistent with one another.[3] Planning is covered in more detail later in this chapter.

Planning *management process of determining what an organization needs to do and how best to get it done*

Organizing Managers must also organize people and resources. For example, some businesses prepare charts that diagram the various jobs within the company and how those jobs relate to one another. These *organization charts* help everyone understand roles and reporting relationships, key parts of the **organizing** function. Some businesses go so far as to post their organization chart on an office wall. But in most larger businesses, roles and reporting relationships, although important, may be too complex to draw as a simple box-and-line diagram. After Mulally clarified Ford's strategy, he then overhauled the company's bureaucratic structure to facilitate coordination across divisions and promote faster decision making. We explore organizing in more detail in Chapter 6.

Organizing *management process of determining how best to arrange an organization's resources and activities into a coherent structure*

Leading Managers have the power to give orders and demand results. Leading, however, involves more complex activities. When **leading,** a manager works to guide and motivate employees to meet the firm's objectives. Legendary management

Leading *management process of guiding and motivating employees to meet an organization's objectives*

figures such as Walt Disney, Sam Walton (of Walmart), and Herb Kelleher (of Southwest Airlines) had the capacity to unite their employees in a clear and targeted manner and motivate them to work in the best interests of their employer. Their employees respected them, trusted them, and believed that by working together, both the firm and themselves as individuals would benefit. Mulally has taken several steps to change the leadership culture that existed at Ford. The firm had previously used a directive, top-down approach to management. But Mulally decentralized many activities so as to put the responsibility for making decisions in the hands of those best qualified to make them. He also clarified channels of communication and revamped the incentive system used for senior managers. Leading involves a number of different processes and activities, which are discussed in Chapter 9.

Controlling *management process of monitoring an organization's performance to ensure that it is meeting its goals*

Controlling

Controlling is the process of monitoring a firm's performance to make sure that it is meeting its goals. All CEOs must pay close attention to costs and performance. Managers at United Airlines, for example, focus almost relentlessly on numerous indicators of performance that they can constantly measure and adjust. Everything from on-time arrivals to baggage-handling errors to the number of empty seats on an airplane to surveys of employee and customer satisfaction are regularly and routinely monitored. If on-time arrivals start to slip, managers focus on the problem and get it fixed. If customers complain too much about the food, catering managers figure out how to improve. As a result, no single element of the firm's performance can slip too far before it's noticed and fixed. At Ford, Mulally installed a more rigorous financial reporting system so that he could better assess how various parts of the far-flung Ford empire were performing and get information he needed to make strategic decisions faster and easier than was the case when he first took over.

Figure 5.1 illustrates the control process that begins when management establishes standards, often for financial performance. If, for example, a company sets a goal of increasing its sales by 20 percent over the next 10 years, an appropriate standard to assess progress toward the 20-percent goal might be an increase of about 2 percent a year.

Managers then measure actual performance each year against standards. If the two amounts agree, the organization continues along its present course. If they vary significantly, however, one or the other needs adjustment. If sales have increased 2.1

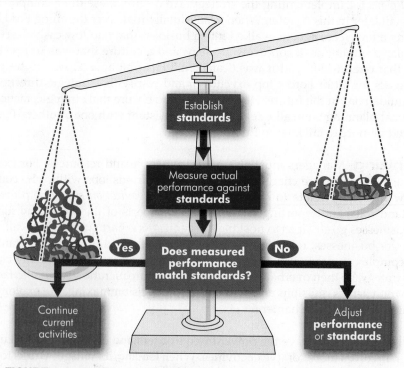

FIGURE 5.1 The Control Process

percent by the end of the first year, things are probably fine. If sales have dropped 1 percent, some revision in plans may be needed. For example, managers can decide to lower the original goal or spend more money on advertising.

Control can also show where performance is running better than expected and can serve as a basis for providing rewards or reducing costs. For example, when Chevrolet introduced the Super Sport Roadster (a classic, late-1940s pickup-style vehicle with a two-seat roadster design), the firm thought it had a major hit on its hands. But poor sales led to Chevrolet's decision to suspend production of the vehicle. On the other hand, Apple's iPad has been so successful that the firm has not been forced to discount or offer incentives for people to buy the device.

The Science and the Art of Management

Given the complexity inherent in the manager's job, one may ask whether management is more of a science or an art. In fact, effective management is a blend of both science and art. And successful executives recognize the importance of combining both the science and the art of management as they practice their craft.[4]

The Science of Management Many management problems and issues can be approached in ways that are rational, logical, objective, and systematic. Managers can gather data, facts, and objective information. They can use quantitative models and decision-making techniques to arrive at "correct" decisions. They need to take such a scientific approach to solving problems whenever possible, especially when they are dealing with relatively routine and straightforward issues. When Starbucks considers entering a new market, its managers look closely at a wide variety of objective details as they formulate their plans. Technical, diagnostic, and decision-making skills (which we will discuss later in the chapter) are especially important when approaching a management task or problem from a scientific perspective.

The Art of Management Even though managers may try to be scientific as often as possible, they must frequently make decisions and solve problems on the basis of intuition, experience, instinct, and personal insights. Relying heavily on conceptual, communication, interpersonal, and time-management skills, for example, a manager may have to decide among multiple courses of action that look equally attractive. And even "objective facts" may prove to be wrong. When Starbucks was planning its first store in New York City, market research clearly showed that New Yorkers preferred drip coffee to more exotic espresso-style coffees. After first installing more drip coffee makers and fewer espresso makers than in their other stores, managers had to backtrack when New Yorkers lined up, clamoring for espresso. Starbucks now introduces a standard menu and layout in all its stores, regardless of presumed market differences, and then makes necessary adjustments later. Thus, managers must blend an element of intuition and personal insight with hard data and objective facts.[5]

Becoming a Manager

How does one acquire the skills necessary to blend the science and art of management and become a successful manager? Although there are as many variations as there are managers, the most common path involves a combination of education and experience.[6]

The Role of Education Many of you reading this book right now are doing so because you are enrolled in a management course at a college or university. You are already acquiring management skills in an educational setting. When you complete the course (and this book), you will have a foundation for developing your management skills in more advanced courses. A college degree has become almost a requirement for career advancement in business, and virtually all CEOs in the United States have a college degree. MBA degrees are also common among

Education plays a vital role in becoming a manager. Prospective managers usually complete at least one degree in business, taking courses in finance, marketing, accounting, management, and other areas.

Marco Cristofori/Alamy

successful executives today. More and more foreign universities, especially in Europe, are also beginning to offer academic programs in management.

Even after obtaining a degree, most prospective managers have not seen the end of their management education. Many middle and top managers periodically return to campus to participate in executive or management development programs, ranging in duration from a few days to several weeks. First-line managers also take advantage of extension and continuing education programs offered by institutions of higher education or through online media. A recent innovation in extended management education is the executive MBA program offered by many top business schools, in which middle and top managers with several years of experience complete an accelerated program of study on weekends.[7] Finally, many large companies have in-house training programs for furthering managers' education. Indeed, some firms have even created what are essentially corporate universities to provide the specialized education they feel is required for their managers for them to remain successful.[8] McDonald's and Shell Oil are among the leaders in in-house courses. Alongside formal education routes, there is also a distinct trend toward online educational development for managers.[9]

The primary advantage of education as a source of management skills is that, as a student, a person can follow a well-developed program of study, becoming familiar with current research and thinking on management. Many college students can devote full-time energy and attention to learning. On the negative side, management education is often general, meeting the needs of a wide variety of students; specific know-how may be hard to obtain. Further, although many aspects of the manager's job can be discussed in a book; it is hard to appreciate and understand them until you have experienced them.

The Role of Experience This book will help provide you with a solid foundation for enhancing your management skills. Even if you were to memorize every word in every management book ever written, however, you could not then step into a top management position and immediately be effective. Why not? Management skills must also be learned through experience. Most managers advanced to their present positions from other jobs. Only by experiencing the day-to-day pressures a manager faces and by meeting a variety of managerial challenges can an individual develop insights into the real nature and character of managerial work.

For this reason, most large companies, and many smaller ones as well, have developed management training programs for their prospective managers. People are hired from college campuses, from other organizations, or from the ranks of the organization's first-line managers and operating employees. These people are systematically assigned to a variety of jobs. Over time, the individual is exposed to most, if not all, of the major aspects of the organization. In this way the manager learns by experience. The training programs at some companies, such as Procter & Gamble, General Mills, and Shell Oil, are so good that other companies try to hire people who have graduated from them.[10] Even without formal training programs, managers can achieve success as they profit from varied experiences. For example, Kelleher was a practicing attorney before he took over at Southwest Airlines and led it to become one of the most successful and admired businesses in the United States. Of course, natural ability, drive, and self-motivation also play roles in acquiring experience and developing management skills.

Most effective managers learn their skills through a combination of education and experience. Some type of college degree, even if it is not in business administration, usually provides a foundation for a management career. The individual then gets his or her first job and subsequently progresses through a variety of management situations. During the manager's rise in the organization, occasional education "updates," such as management development programs, may supplement on-the-job experience. And, increasingly, managers need to acquire international expertise as part of their personal development. As with general managerial skills, international expertise can be acquired through a combination of education and experience.[11]

Types of Managers

OBJECTIVE 2
Identify
different types of managers likely to be found in an organization by level and area.

Although all managers plan, organize, lead, and control, not all managers have the same degree of responsibility for these activities. It is helpful to classify managers according to levels and areas of responsibility.

Levels of Management

The three basic levels of management are *top*, *middle*, and *first-line* management. As summarized in Table 5.1, most firms have more middle managers than top managers and more first-line managers than middle managers. Both the power of managers and the complexity of their duties increase as they move up the ladder.

Top Managers Like Brin, Page, and Mulally, the fairly small number of executives who get the chance to guide the fortunes of most companies are top managers. Common titles for top managers include *president*, *vice-president*, *treasurer*, *chief executive officer* (CEO), and *chief financial* officer (CFO). **Top managers** are responsible for the overall performance and effectiveness of the firm. They set general policies, formulate strategies, approve all significant decisions, and represent the company in dealings with other firms and with government bodies. Indra Nooyi, Chairperson and CEO of PepsiCo, is a top manager.

Top Manager *manager responsible for a firm's overall performance and effectiveness*

Middle Managers Just below the ranks of top managers is another group of managers who also occupy positions of considerable autonomy and importance and who are called middle managers. Titles such as *plant manager*, *operations manager*, and *division manager* designate middle-management slots. In general, **middle managers** are responsible for implementing the strategies and working toward the goals set by top managers.[12] For example, if top management decides to introduce a new product in 12 months or to cut costs by 5 percent in the next quarter, middle managers are primarily responsible for determining how to meet these goals. The manager of an American Express service center or a regional sales manager of Frito-Lay snack products (a division of PepsiCo) will likely be a middle manager.

Middle Manager *manager responsible for implementing the strategies and working toward the goals set by top managers*

table 5.1 The Three Levels of Management

Level	Examples	Responsibilities
Top managers	President, vice-president, treasurer, CEO, chief financial officer (CFO)	• Responsible for the overall performance and effectiveness of the firm • Set general policies, formulate strategies, and approve all significant decisions • Represent the company in dealings with other firms and with government bodies
Middle managers	Plant manager, operations manager, division manager, regional sales manager	• Responsible for implementing the strategies and working toward the goals set by top managers
First-line managers	Supervisor, office manager, project manager, group leader, sales manager	• Responsible for supervising the work of employees who report to them • Ensure employees understand and are properly trained in company policies and procedures

First-Line Manager *manager responsible for supervising the work of employees*

First-Line Managers Those who hold such titles as *supervisor*, *office manager*, *project manager*, and *group leader* are **first-line managers.** Although they spend most of their time working with and supervising the employees who report to them, first-line managers' activities are not limited to that arena. At a building site, for example, the project manager not only ensures that workers are carrying out construction as specified by the architect, but also interacts extensively with materials suppliers, community officials, and middle- and upper-level managers at the home office. The supervisor of delivery drivers for Frito-Lay products in Kansas City would be considered to be a first-line manager.

Areas of Management

In any large company, top, middle, and first-line managers work in a variety of areas, including human resources, operations, marketing, information, and finance. For the most part, these areas correspond to the types of basic management skills described later in this chapter and to the wide range of business principles and activities discussed in the rest of this book.

Human Resource Managers Most companies have *human resource managers* who hire and train employees, evaluate performance, and determine compensation. At large firms, separate departments deal with recruiting and hiring, wage and salary levels, and labor relations. A smaller firm may have a single department—or a single person—responsible for all human resource activities. (We discuss some key issues in human resource management in Chapter 10.)

Operations Managers As we will see in Chapter 7, the term *operations* refers to the systems by which a firm produces goods and services. Among other duties, *operations managers* are responsible for production, inventory, and quality control. Manufacturing companies such as Texas Instruments, Ford, and Caterpillar have a strong need for operations managers at many levels. Such firms typically have a *vice-president for operations* (top manager), *plant managers* (middle managers), and *production supervisors* (first-line managers). In recent years, sound operations management practices have become increasingly important to a variety of service organizations.

Marketing Managers As we will see in Chapter 11, marketing encompasses the development, pricing, promotion, and distribution of goods and services.

Marketing managers are responsible for getting products from producers to consumers. Marketing is especially important for firms that manufacture consumer products, such as Nike, Coca-Cola, and Apple. Such firms often have large numbers of marketing managers at several levels. For example, a large consumer products firm is likely to have a *vice-president for marketing* (top manager), several *regional marketing managers* (middle managers), and several *district sales managers* (first-line managers).

Information Managers Occupying a fairly new managerial position in many firms, *information managers* design and implement systems to gather, organize, and distribute information. Huge increases in both the sheer volume of information and the ability to manage it have led to the emergence of this important function. Although still relatively few in number, the ranks of information managers are growing at all levels. Some firms have a top-management position for a *chief information officer (CIO)*. Middle managers help design information systems for divisions or plants. Computer systems managers within smaller businesses are usually first-line managers. We'll discuss information management in more detail in Chapter 13.

Financial Managers Nearly every company has *financial managers* to plan and oversee its accounting functions and financial resources. Levels of financial management may include *CFO* or *vice-president for finance* (top), a *division controller* (middle), and an *accounting supervisor* (first-line manager). Some financial institutions, such as NationsBank and Prudential, have even made effective financial management the company's reason for being. We'll discuss financial management in more detail in Chapters 14 and 15.

Other Managers Some firms also employ other specialized managers. Many companies, for example, have public relations managers. Chemical and pharmaceutical companies such as Monsanto and Merck have research and development managers. The range of possibilities is wide, and the areas of management are limited only by the needs and imagination of the firm.

Management Roles and Skills

OBJECTIVE 3
Describe
the basic skills required of managers.

Regardless of their levels or areas within an organization, all managers must play certain roles and exhibit certain skills if they are to be successful. The concept of a role, in this sense, is similar to the role an actor plays in a theatrical production. A person does certain things, meets certain needs, and has certain responsibilities in the organization. In the sections that follow, we first highlight the basic roles managers play and then discuss the skills they need to be effective.

Managerial Roles

Research offers a number of interesting insights into the nature of managerial roles.[13] Based on detailed observations of what executives do, it appears that many of their activities fall into 10 different roles. These roles, summarized in Table 5.2, fall into three basic categories: interpersonal, informational, and decisional.

Interpersonal Roles There are three **interpersonal roles** inherent in the manager's job. First, the manager is often expected to serve as a *figurehead*—taking visitors to dinner, attending ribbon-cutting ceremonies, and the like. These activities are typically more ceremonial and symbolic than substantive. The manager is also expected to serve as a *leader*—hiring, training, and motivating employees. A manager who formally or informally shows subordinates how to do things and how to perform under pressure is leading. Finally, managers can have a *liaison* role. This role often involves serving as a coordinator or link among people, groups, or organizations. For example, companies in the computer industry may use liaisons to keep

Interpersonal Roles *A category of managerial roles including figurehead, leader, and liaison.*

table 5.2 Basic Managerial Roles

Category	Role	Sample Activities
Interpersonal	Figurehead	Attending ribbon-cutting ceremony for new plant
	Leader	Encouraging employees to improve productivity
	Liaison	Coordinating activities of two project groups
Informational	Monitor	Scanning industry reports to stay abreast of developments
	Disseminator	Sending memos outlining new organizational initiatives
	Spokesperson	Making a speech to discuss growth plans
Decisional	Entrepreneur	Developing new ideas for innovation
	Disturbance handler	Resolving conflict between two subordinates
	Resource allocator	Reviewing and revising budget requests
	Negotiator	Reaching agreement with a key supplier or labor union

other companies informed about their plans. This enables Microsoft, for example, to create software for interfacing with new Hewlett-Packard printers at the same time those printers are being developed. And, at the same time, managers at Hewlett-Packard can incorporate new Microsoft features into the printers they introduce.

Informational Roles The three **informational roles** flow naturally from the interpersonal roles just discussed. The process of carrying out the interpersonal roles places the manager at a strategic point to gather and disseminate information. The first informational role is that of *monitor*, one who actively seeks information that may be of value. The manager questions subordinates, is receptive to unsolicited information, and attempts to be as well informed as possible. The manager is also a *disseminator* of information, transmitting relevant information back to others in the workplace. When the roles of monitor and disseminator are viewed together, the manager emerges as a vital link in the organization's chain of communication. The third informational role focuses on external communication. The *spokesperson* formally relays information to people outside the unit or outside the organization. For example, a plant manager at Union Carbide may transmit information to top-level managers so that they will be better informed about the plant's activities. The manager may also represent the organization before a chamber of commerce or consumer group. Although the roles of spokesperson and figurehead are similar, there is one basic difference between them. When a manager acts as a figurehead, the manager's presence as a symbol of the organization is what is of interest. In the spokesperson role, however, the manager carries information and communicates it to others in a formal sense.

Decisional Roles The manager's informational roles typically lead to the **decisional roles.** The information acquired by the manager as a result of performing the informational roles has a major bearing on important decisions that he or she makes. There are four decisional roles. First, the manager has the role of *entrepreneur*, the voluntary initiator of change. A manager at 3M Company developed the idea for the Post-it note pad but had to "sell" it to other skeptical managers inside the company. A second decisional role is initiated not by the manager but by some other individual or group. The manager responds to her role as *disturbance handler* by handling such problems as strikes, copyright infringements, or problems in public relations or corporate image.

The third decisional role is that of *resource allocator*. As resource allocator, the manager decides how resources are distributed and with whom he or she will work

Informational Roles *A category of managerial roles including monitor, disseminator, and spokesperson.*

Decisional Roles *a category of managerial roles including entrepreneur, disturbance handler, resource allocator, and negotiator*

Managers play a variety of important roles. One key interpersonal role is that of figurehead. These managers, for example, are cutting a ribbon symbolizing the opening of a new business.

most closely. For example, a manager typically allocates the funds in the unit's operating budget among the unit's members and projects. A fourth decisional role is that of *negotiator*. In this role the manager enters into negotiations with other groups or organizations as a representative of the company. For example, managers may negotiate a union contract, an agreement with a consultant, or a long-term relationship with a supplier. Negotiations may also be internal to the organization. The manager may, for instance, mediate a dispute between two subordinates or negotiate with another department for additional support.

Basic Management Skills

In addition to fulfilling numerous roles, managers also need a number of specific skills if they are to succeed. The most fundamental management skills are *technical, interpersonal, conceptual, diagnostic, communication, decision-making,* and *time-management* skills.[14]

Technical Skills　The skills needed to perform specialized tasks are called **technical skills.** A programmer's ability to write code, an animator's ability to draw, and an accountant's ability to audit a company's records are all examples of technical skills. People develop technical skills through a combination of education and experience. Technical skills are especially important for first-line managers. Many of these managers spend considerable time helping employees solve work-related problems, training them in more efficient procedures, and monitoring performance.

Technical Skills *skills needed to perform specialized tasks*

Human Relations Skills　Effective managers also generally have good **human relations skills,** skills that enable them to understand and get along with other people. A manager with poor human relations skills may have trouble getting along with subordinates, cause valuable employees to quit or transfer, and contribute to poor morale. Although human relations skills are important at all levels, they are probably most important for middle managers, who must often act as bridges between top managers, first-line managers, and managers from other areas of the organization. Managers should possess good communication skills. Many managers have found that being able both to understand others and to get others to understand them can go a long way toward maintaining good relations in an organization.

Human Relations Skills *skills in understanding and getting along with people*

Conceptual Skills　**Conceptual skills** refer to a person's ability to think in the abstract, to diagnose and analyze different situations, and to see beyond the present situation. Conceptual skills help managers recognize new market opportunities

Conceptual Skills *abilities to think in the abstract, diagnose and analyze different situations, and see beyond the present situation*

and threats. They can also help managers analyze the probable outcomes of their decisions. The need for conceptual skills differs at various management levels. Top managers depend most on conceptual skills, first-line managers least. Although the purposes and everyday needs of various jobs differ, conceptual skills are needed in almost any job-related activity. In many ways, conceptual skills may be the most important ingredient in the success of executives in e-commerce businesses. For example, the ability to foresee how a particular business application will be affected by or can be translated to the Internet is clearly conceptual in nature.

Decision-Making Skills *skills in defining problems and selecting the best courses of action*

Decision-Making Skills
Decision-making skills include the ability to effectively define a problem and to select the best course of action. These skills involve gathering facts, identifying solutions, evaluating alternatives, and implementing the chosen alternative. Periodically following up and evaluating the effectiveness of the choice are also part of the decision-making process. These skills allow some managers to identify effective strategies for their firm, such as Michael Dell's commitment to direct marketing as the firm's primary distribution model. But poor decision-making skills can also lead to failure and ruin. Indeed, poor decision making played a major role in the downfall of such U.S. business stalwarts as Montgomery Ward, Studebaker, Circuit City, and Enron. We'll discuss decision making more fully in Chapter 9.

Time Management Skills *skills associated with the productive use of time*

Time Management Skills
Time management skills are the productive use that managers make of their time. Suppose, for example, that a CEO is paid $2 million in base salary (this is not an especially large CEO salary, by the way!). Assuming that she works 50 hours a week and takes two weeks' vacation, our CEO earns $800 an hour—a little more than $13 per minute. Any amount of time that she wastes clearly represents a large cost to the firm and its stockholders. Most middle and lower-level managers receive much smaller salaries than this, of course, but their time is still valuable, and poor use of it still translates into costs and wasted productivity.

To manage time effectively, managers must address four leading causes of wasted time:

1 *Paperwork.* Some managers spend too much time deciding what to do with letters and reports. Most documents of this sort are routine and can be handled quickly. Managers must learn to recognize those documents that require more attention.

2 *Telephone calls.* Experts estimate that managers get interrupted by the telephone every five minutes. To manage this time more effectively, they suggest having an assistant screen all calls and setting aside a certain block of time each day to return the important ones. Unfortunately, the explosive use of cell phones seems to be making this problem even worse for many managers.

3 *Meetings.* Many managers spend as much as four hours a day in meetings. To help keep this time productive, the person handling the meeting should specify a clear agenda, start on time, keep everyone focused on the agenda, and end on time.

4 *E-mail.* Increasingly, managers are relying heavily on e-mail and other forms of digital communication. Time is wasted when managers have to sort through spam and a variety of electronic folders, in-boxes, and archives.

Management Skills for the Twenty-First Century

Although the skills discussed in this chapter have long been important parts of every successful manager's career, new skill requirements continue to emerge. Today, most experts point to the growing importance of skills involving *global management* and *technology*.

Global Management Skills Tomorrow's managers must equip themselves with the special tools, techniques, and skills needed to compete in a global environment. They will need to understand foreign markets, cultural differences, and the motives and practices of foreign rivals. They also need to understand how to collaborate with others around the world on a real-time basis.

On a more practical level, businesses will need more managers who are capable of understanding international operations. In the past, most U.S. businesses hired local managers to run their operations in the various countries in which they operated. More recently, however, the trend has been to transfer U.S. managers to foreign locations. This practice helps firms transfer their corporate cultures to foreign operations. In addition, foreign assignments help managers become better prepared for international competition as they advance within the organization. The top management teams of large corporations today are also likely to include directors from other countries.

Management and Technology Skills Another significant issue facing tomorrow's managers is technology, especially as it relates to communication. Managers have always had to deal with information. In today's world, however, the amount of information has reached staggering proportions. In the United States alone, people exchange hundreds of millions of e-mail messages every day. New forms of technology have added to a manager's ability to process information while simultaneously, making it even more important to organize and interpret an ever-increasing wealth of input.

Technology has also begun to change the way the interaction of managers shapes corporate structures. Elaborate networks control the flow of a firm's lifeblood—information. This information no longer flows strictly up and down through hierarchies. It now flows to everyone simultaneously. As a result, decisions are made quicker, and more people are directly involved. With e-mail, videoconferencing, and other forms of communication, neither time nor distance—nor such corporate boundaries as departments and divisions—can prevent people from working more closely together. More than ever, bureaucracies are breaking down, and planning, decision making, and other activities are beginning to benefit from group building and teamwork. We discuss the effects technology has on business in more detail in Chapter 13.

Strategic Management: Setting Goals and Formulating Strategy

OBJECTIVE 4
Explain
the importance of strategic management and effective goal setting in organizational success.

As we noted previously, planning is a critical part of the manager's job. Managers today are increasingly being called on to think and act strategically. **Strategic management** is the process of helping an organization maintain an effective alignment with its environment. For instance, if a firm's business environment is heading toward fiercer competition, the business may need to start cutting its costs and developing more products and services before the competition really starts to heat up. Likewise, if an industry is globalizing, a firm's managers may need to start entering new markets and developing international partnerships during the early stages of globalization rather than waiting for its full effects.

Strategic Management *process of helping an organization maintain an effective alignment with its environment*

The starting point in effective strategic management is setting **goals,** objectives that a business hopes and plans to achieve. Every business needs goals. Remember, however, that deciding what it intends to do is only the first step for an organization. Managers must also make decisions about what actions will and will not achieve company goals. Decisions cannot be made on a problem-by-problem basis or merely to meet needs as they arise. In most companies, a broad program underlies those decisions. That program is called a **strategy,** which is a broad set of organizational plans for implementing the decisions made for achieving organizational goals. Let's begin by examining business goals more closely.

Goal *objective that a business hopes and plans to achieve*

Strategy *broad set of organizational plans for implementing the decisions made for achieving organizational goals*

Setting Business Goals

Goals are performance targets, the means by which organizations and their managers measure success or failure at every level. At AmEx, however, Kenneth Chenault is focusing more on revenue growth and the firm's stock price. Indra Nooyi's goals at Pepsi include keeping abreast of changing consumer tastes and leveraging the firm's current products into new markets. And Jeffrey Smisek's goals at United Airlines are to continue the smooth integration of Continental and United into the world's largest airline.

Purposes of Goal Setting An organization functions systematically when it sets goals and plans accordingly. An organization commits its resources on all levels to achieve its goals. Specifically, we can identify four main purposes in organizational goal setting:

1 *Goal setting provides direction and guidance for managers at all levels.* If managers know precisely where the company is headed, there is less potential for error in the different units of the company. Starbucks, for example, has a goal of increasing capital spending by 10 percent, with all additional expenditures devoted to opening new stores. This goal clearly informs everyone in the firm that expansion into new territories is a high priority for the firm.

2 *Goal setting helps firms allocate resources.* Areas that are expected to grow will get first priority. The company allocates more resources to new projects with large sales potential than it allocates to mature products with established but

entrepreneurship and new ventures

ButterflEYE

Hind Hobeika was a swimmer in the American University of Beirut team. She had always wondered why the success of swimming practices were determined by measurement of heart rates at the end of swim. Commonly used measuring equipment included watches and belts, both of which slowed down the swimming and broke the rhythm.

Thinking laterally, she designed the prototype of the ButterflEYE goggles. Using the temporal artery to read the pulse, the device signals a green light if the swimmer is on target, a yellow light if the swimmer needs to increase speed and a red light if the swimmer needs to slow down.

Although the prototype was bulky, it clearly had promise. Hobieka won third place in the *Star of Science* reality TV show based in Qatar. This gave her access to US$100,000 in development funds.

Hobieka used her mechanical engineering background to help her to waterproof the circuit. This meant choosing the correct materials and developing the right aerodynamic design. She taught herself the necessary electronics for the digital part of the design process.

Straight after the competition, she was contacted by several investors keen to help her develop and market the goggles.

She chose Berytech, a business and development center located on the outskirts of Beirut. The deal incorporated the US$100,000 seed capital funds she needed. The development

yanlev/Fotolia

of the goggles is on course to ensure that they will be launched December 2013.

The goggles, now marketed under the name Instabeat, have come a long way in just two years. The device can now be mounted into any pair of swimming goggles and provides real-time feedback and can be synced to mobile apps or computers. It will measure the heartbeat, calories used, laps, and flip turns, all invaluable data for the serious swimmer. The product will launch with a retail price of US$149.[15]

stagnant sales potential. Thus, Starbucks is primarily emphasizing new store expansion, and its e-commerce initiatives are currently given a lower priority. "Our management team," says CEO Howard Schultz, "is 100 percent focused on growing our core business without distraction…from any other initiative."

3 *Goal setting helps to define corporate culture.* For years, the goal at General Electric has been to push each of its divisions to first or second in its industry. The result is a competitive (and often stressful) environment and a corporate culture that rewards success and has little tolerance for failure. At the same time, however, GE's appliance business, medical technology, aircraft engine unit, and financial services business are each among the best in their respective industries. Eventually, the firm's CEO set an even higher companywide standard: to make the firm the most valuable one in the world.

4 *Goal setting helps managers assess performance.* If a unit sets a goal of increasing sales by 10 percent in a given year, managers in that unit who attain or exceed the goal can be rewarded. Units failing to reach the goal will also be compensated accordingly. GE has a long-standing reputation for evaluating managerial performance, richly rewarding those who excel—and getting rid of those who do not. Each year, the lower 10 percent of GE's managerial force are informed that either they make dramatic improvements in performance or consider alternative directions for their careers.

Kinds of Goals
Goals differ from company to company, depending on the firm's purpose and mission. Every enterprise has a purpose, or a reason for being. Businesses seek profits, universities seek to discover and transmit new knowledge, and government agencies seek to set and enforce public policy. Many enterprises also have missions and **mission statements,** statements of how they will achieve their purposes in the environments in which they conduct their businesses.

Mission Statement organization's statement of how it will achieve its purpose in the environment in which it conducts its business

A company's mission is usually easy to identify, at least at a basic level. Starbucks sums up its mission succinctly: the firm intends to "establish Starbucks as the premier purveyor of the finest coffee in the world while maintaining our uncompromising principles while we grow." But businesses sometimes have to rethink their strategies and mission as the competitive environment changes. A few years ago, for example, Starbucks announced that Internet marketing and sales were going to become core business initiatives. Managers subsequently realized, however, that this initiative did not fit the firm as well as they first thought. As a result, they scaled back this effort and made a clear recommitment to their existing retail business. The demands of change force many companies to rethink their missions and revise their statements of what they are and what they do.

In addition to its mission, every firm also has *long-term, intermediate,* and *short-term goals:*

- **Long-term goals** relate to extended periods of time, typically five years or more. For example, AmEx might set a long-term goal of doubling the number of participating merchants during the next 10 years. Nikon might adopt a long-term goal of increasing its share of the digital camera market by 10 percent during the next eight years.

Long-Term Goal goal set for an extended time, typically five years or more into the future

- **Intermediate goals** are set for a period of one to five years. Companies usually set intermediate goals in several areas. For example, the marketing department's goal might be to increase sales by 3 percent in two years. The production department might want to reduce expenses by 6 percent in four years. Human resources might seek to cut turnover by 10 percent in two years. Finance might aim for a 3-percent increase in return on investment in three years.

Intermediate Goal goal set for a period of one to five years into the future

- **Short-term goals** are set for perhaps one year and are developed for several different areas. Increasing sales by 2 percent this year, cutting costs by 1 percent next quarter, and reducing turnover by 4 percent over the next six months are examples of short-term goals.

Short-Term Goal goal set for the near future

After a firm has set its goals, it then focuses attention on strategies to accomplish them.

Types of Strategy

As shown in Figure 5.2, the three types of strategy that are usually considered by a company are *corporate strategy*, *business (or competitive) strategy*, and *functional strategy*.

Corporate Strategy *strategy for determining the firm's overall attitude toward growth and the way it will manage its businesses or product lines*

Corporate Strategy
The purpose of **corporate strategy** is to determine what business or businesses a company will own and operate. Some corporations own and operate only a single business. The makers of WD-40, for example, concentrate solely on that brand. Other corporations own and operate many businesses. A company may decide to *grow* by increasing its activities or investment or to *retrench* by reducing them.

Sometimes a corporation buys and operates multiple businesses in compatible industries as part of its corporate strategy. For example, the restaurant chains operated by YUM! (KFC, Pizza Hut, and Taco Bell) are clearly related to one another. This strategy is called *related diversification*. However, if the businesses are not similar, the strategy is called *unrelated diversification*. Samsung, which owns electronics, construction, chemicals, catering, and hotel businesses is following this approach. Under Kenneth Chenault, AmEx corporate strategy calls for strengthening operations through a principle of growth called *e-partnering*, buying shares of small companies that can provide technology that AmEx itself does not have.

Business (or Competitive) Strategy *strategy, at the business-unit or product-line level, focusing on improving a firm's competitive position*

Business (or Competitive) Strategy
When a corporation owns and operates multiple businesses, it must develop strategies for each one. **Business (or competitive) strategy,** then, takes place at the level of the business unit or product line and focuses on improving the company's competitive position. For example, at this level, AmEx makes decisions about how best to compete in an industry that includes Visa, MasterCard, and other credit card companies. In this respect, the company has committed heavily to expanding its product offerings and serving customers through new technology. Pepsi, meanwhile, has one strategy for its soft drink business as it competes with Coca-Cola and a different strategy for its sports drink business and yet another strategy for its New Age beverage company. It has still other strategies for its snack foods businesses.

Functional Strategy *strategy by which managers in specific areas decide how best to achieve corporate goals through productivity*

Functional Strategy
At the level of **functional strategy,** managers in specific areas such as marketing, finance, and operations decide how best to achieve corporate goals by performing their functional activities most effectively. At AmEx, for example, each business unit has considerable autonomy in deciding how to use the single website at which the company has located its entire range of services. Pepsi,

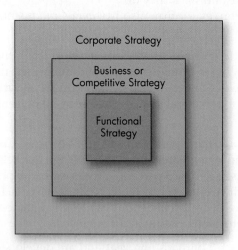

FIGURE 5.2 Hierarchy of Strategy
Source: Based on Thomas L. Wheelen and J. David Hunger, *Strategic Management and Business Policy*, 8th ed. (Upper Saddle River, NJ: Prentice Hall, 2002), 14.

finding a better way

A New Model for Going Green

Darin Budwig, a registered nurse in Glendale, California, wanted to do the "green" thing by going solar. Price, however, was a problem: "I wanted to do the right thing for the environment," says Budwig, "but I really had to ask whether it was worth taking on $30,000 in debt." According to Lyndon Rive, CEO of SolarCity, a provider of solar-energy systems located in Foster City, California, the average cost is actually closer to $20,000, but he understands Budwig's reservations. "Even those who really want to make an environmental change," admits Rive, "can't part with $20,000....The solution is just too costly for them."

That's why Rive revamped his strategy to make solar panels affordable for a much broader range of environmentally conscious consumers. He realized that he could put solar panels on people's roofs in much the same way that automakers put more expensive vehicles in their garages: by leasing them rather than selling them outright. Instead of borrowing $20,000, Budwig only had to put $1,000 down and agree to lease a SolarCity system for 15 years. At a cost of $73 a month, Budwig figured to save about $95 a month and recoup his $1,000 in less than a year. Too good to be true? "We hear that a lot," says Rive. "But we do save you money, and it doesn't cost you a cent to go solar." With leasing, he adds, "we can essentially make it so that everybody can now afford clean power." By introducing leasing, Rive also changed the control model being used by SolarCity to focus more on cash flow rather than revenue.

At the same time, however, Rive understands that price isn't the only consideration for potential customers like Budwig. "Widespread adoption," he admits, "will come if you can take away the complexity and hassle of installing solar." SolarCity thus made things easier for Budwig by lining up building permits, financing, and tax breaks. The company also streamlined costs by using innovative computer automation to custom-design Budwig's installation, which was based on satellite images of his rooftop. SolarCity even compiled utility-rate data to estimate Budwig's return on his solar investment. Again, Rive's new approach reflects a change to a more service-oriented strategy.

ZUMA Press, Inc./Alamy

The company recently added another automated service to its innovative product line. With the acquisition of Building Solutions, a firm specializing in software-controlled home energy audits, SolarCity entered the market for home-efficiency upgrades. Company auditors now come into a house armed with duct blowers, infrared cameras, and combustion analyzers to check for leaks and test heaters. The data are then analyzed to determine what can be done at what cost and to calculate the homeowner's best return on his or her upgrade investment. Chief Operations Officer Peter Rive (Lyndon's older brother) is especially optimistic about the company's ability to combine panel-installation services with such services as energy audits and building-envelope sealing (sealing leaks in walls, doors, and windows). "As of right now," he points out, "there aren't residential energy-efficiency providers with any serious scale. We're going to be able to bring serious economies of scale" to bear on the costs to both the provider and the customer. Both Rive brothers relied on several management skills, especially conceptual and technical skills, to add these services.

Like Budwig, Google engineer Michael Flaster leased a SolarCity system for his home in Menlo Park, California. He saves $100 a month on his energy bill and expects to save more than $16,000 over the 15 years of his lease. His employers at Google, a longtime supporter of clean-energy innovations, were impressed and recently announced a $280 million fund to help SolarCity finance solar installations across the country.[16]

---

meanwhile, develops functional strategies for marketing its beverage and snack foods products and operations strategies for distributing them. The real challenges—and opportunities—lie in successfully creating these strategies. Therefore, we now turn our attention to the basic steps in strategy formulation.

Formulating Strategy

Planning is often concerned with the nuts and bolts of setting goals, choosing tactics, and establishing schedules. In contrast, *strategy* tends to have a wider scope. By definition, it is a broad concept that describes an organization's intentions. Further,

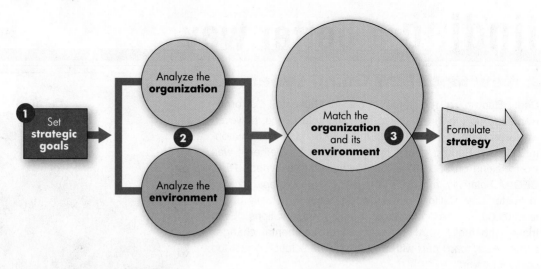

FIGURE 5.3 Strategy Formulation
Source: Adapted from Stephen P. Robbins and Mary Coulter, *Management*, 12th ed. (Upper Saddle River, NJ: Prentice Hall, 2014), 242.

a strategy outlines how the business intends to meet its goals and includes the organization's responsiveness to new challenges and new needs. Because a well-formulated strategy is so vital to a business's success, most top managers devote substantial attention and creativity to this process. **Strategy formulation** involves the three basic steps summarized in Figure 5.3 and discussed next.

Step 1: *Setting Strategic Goals* **Strategic goals** are derived directly from a firm's mission statement. For example, Martin Winterkorn, CEO of Volkswagen, has clear strategic goals for the European carmaker. When he took over several years ago, Volkswagen was only marginally profitable, was regarded as an also-ran in the industry, and was thinking about pulling out of the U.S. market altogether because its sales were so poor. Over the next few years, however, Winterkorn totally revamped the firm, acquired Audi, Skoda, Scania, and Porsche, and is now making big profits. Volkswagen is also now a much more formidable force in the global automobile industry.

Step 2: *Analyzing the Organization and the Environment: SWOT Analysis* After strategic goals have been established, managers usually attempt to assess both their organization and its environment. A common framework for this assessment is called a **SWOT analysis.** This process involves assessing organizational strengths and weaknesses (the **S** and **W**) and environmental opportunities and threats (the **O** and **T**). In formulating strategy, managers attempt to capitalize on organizational strengths and take advantage of environmental opportunities. During this same process, they may seek ways to overcome or offset organizational weaknesses and avoid or counter environmental threats. Scanning the business environment for threats and opportunities is often called **environmental analysis.** Changing consumer tastes and hostile takeover offers are threats, as are new government regulations that will limit a firm's opportunities. Even more important threats come from new products and new competitors. For example, online music services such as iTunes are a major threat to manufacturers of CDs and CD players. Likewise, the emergence of digital photography has dramatically weakened companies tied to print photography. Opportunities, meanwhile, are areas in which the firm can potentially expand, grow, or take advantage of existing strengths. For example, when Pepsi managers recognized the growing market potential for bottled water, they moved quickly to launch their Aquafina brand and to position it for rapid growth.

Strategy Formulation *creation of a broad program for defining and meeting an organization's goals*

Strategic Goal *goal derived directly from a firm's mission statement*

SWOT Analysis *identification and analysis of organizational strengths and weaknesses and environmental opportunities and threats as part of strategy formulation*

Environmental Analysis *process of scanning the business environment for threats and opportunities*

In addition to analyzing external factors by performing an environmental analysis, managers must also examine internal factors. The purpose of such an **organizational analysis** is to better understand a company's strengths and weaknesses. Strengths might include surplus cash, a dedicated workforce, an ample supply of managerial talent, technical expertise, or little competition. For example, Pepsi's strength in beverage distribution through its network of soft drink distributors was successfully extended to distribution of bottled water. A cash shortage, aging factories, a heavily unionized workforce, and a poor public image can all be important weaknesses.

Organizational Analysis *process of analyzing a firm's strengths and weaknesses*

Step 3: *Matching the Organization and Its Environment* The final step in strategy formulation is matching environmental threats and opportunities against corporate strengths and weaknesses. This matching process is at the heart of strategy formulation. That is, a firm should attempt to leverage its strengths so as to capitalize on opportunities and counteract threats; it should also attempt to shield its weaknesses, or at least not allow them to derail other activities. For instance, knowing how to distribute consumer products (a strength) allows Pepsi to add new businesses and extend existing ones that use the same distribution models. But a firm that lacked a strong understanding of consumer product distribution would be foolish to add new products whose success relied heavily on efficient distribution.

Understanding strengths and weaknesses may also determine whether a firm typically takes risks or behaves more conservatively. Either approach can be successful. Blue Bell, for example, is one of the most profitable ice cream makers in the world, even though it sells its products in only about a dozen states. Based in Brenham, Texas, Blue Bell controls more than 50 percent of the market in each state where it does business. The firm, however, has resisted the temptation to expand too quickly. Its success is based on product freshness and frequent deliveries, strengths that may suffer if the company grows too large.

A Hierarchy of Plans

The final step in formulating strategy is translating the strategy into more operational language. This process generally involves the creation of actual plans. Plans can be viewed on three levels: *strategic, tactical,* and *operational.* Managerial responsibilities are defined at each level. The levels constitute a hierarchy because implementing plans is practical only when there is a logical flow from one level to the next.

- **Strategic plans** reflect decisions about resource allocations, company priorities, and the steps needed to meet strategic goals. They are usually created by the firm's top management team but, as noted previously, often rely on input from others in the organization. So, the fundamental outcome of the strategic planning process is the creation of a strategic plan. General Electric's decision that viable businesses must rank first or second within their respective markets is a matter of strategic planning.

Strategic Plan *plan reflecting decisions about resource allocations, company priorities, and steps needed to meet strategic goals*

- **Tactical plans** are shorter-term plans for implementing specific aspects of the company's strategic plans. That is, after a strategic plan has been created, managers then develop shorter-term plans to guide decisions so they are consistent with the strategic plan. They typically involve upper and middle management. Dell's effort to extend its distribution expertise into the markets for televisions and other home electronics is an example of tactical planning.

Tactical Plan *generally short-term plan concerned with implementing specific aspects of a company's strategic plans*

- **Operational plans,** which are developed by mid-level and lower-level managers, set short-term targets for daily, weekly, or monthly performance. Starbucks, for instance, has operational plans dealing with how its stores must buy, store, and brew coffee.

Operational Plan *plan setting short-term targets for daily, weekly, or monthly performance*

managing in turbulent times

Challenging Times for Gulf Airlines

Without doubt, Qatar Airways, Etihad (Abu Dhabi), and Emirates (Dubai) have seen rapid growth over the past few years. They have quickly built a tremendous reputation for quality of service and have competed successfully against more established airlines and won. After several years of unparalleled success, the Gulf-based airlines now face difficult times. The global price of oil has skyrocketed, and uncertainty in the region has had a marked impact on business. According to the International Air Transport Association, the outlook for airlines worldwide is bleak, as they predict a fall of nearly 50 percent in profits in 2011–2012 compared to the previous year.

It will be a test of the airline industry in the Gulf to see just how they respond to difficult times and whether all the companies will survive. There have and probably will be more casualties. With fuel prices now representing around 40 percent of the costs of airlines, it would seem that those with the lowest margins would be the first to fail. This was certainly the view of airlines such as Emirates, but according to Air Arabia, the Middle East's largest budget airline, this could not be further from the truth.

The CEO of Air Arabia, Adel Ali, suggested the fact that their business is, essentially, regional. The difficulties in some Middle East countries have encouraged people to travel all the more, and on certain routes there has actually been increased demand. Oman Air has had to double the wages of some of its employees in order to settle strike action, but the airline is struggling with the problem of passing on increased fuel charges to its customers.

The Kuwaiti-based carrier Wataniya was the first casualty in March 2011. They announced that they had ceased all operations, but this did not come as a great shock, as they were already in grave trouble. In December 2010, they slashed their fleet and their network to service just six cities instead of twelve.

When the airline collapsed in March 2011, the stark figures were revealed. The airline had lost some $50.8 million in the year to December 2010. Losses in the previous year had been considerably larger. At the same time, the Kuwaiti budget carrier Jazeera Airways, although recognizing the challenging business environment, has reacted by reducing its capacity and as

Jose Gill/Fotolia

a result, the losses it posted for 2010 were under a third of the losses in the previous year. In October 2011, Jazeera Airways posted its third-quarter results. They showed a 36 percent year on year growth and the fact that they had turned a net profit of $22.2 million. The airline had served some 338,000 passengers in the third quarter. It was a remarkable turnaround, having posted considerable losses for the corresponding period in 2010. The results, however, were not quite as they seemed, as they included the operations of their leasing company Sahaab.

New entrants to the market, such as FlyDubai, have taken the low-cost airline model and adapted it to the environment. Unlike Europe and many other parts of the world, the Middle East does not tend to have secondary airports that give the low-cost airlines the opportunity to operate out of these cheaper airports. Against this is the fact that the airports in the Middle East operate around the clock. FlyDubai has also looked for alternatives to the traditional direct selling of flights on the Internet. On some routes, as much as 40 percent of the ticket sales come via travel agents.

It is expected that there may well be more failures of airlines in the Middle East, but analysts believe that as the airlines reconfigure themselves during these difficult times, it will be a question of consolidation and slow growth rather than a case of spectacular successes and failures. Without doubt, the situation in the Middle East will be a true test of the solidity of the airlines' business models.[17]

OBJECTIVE 5
Discuss
contingency planning and crisis management in today's business world.

Contingency Planning and Crisis Management

Because business environments are often difficult to predict and because the unexpected can create major problems, most managers recognize that even the best-laid plans sometimes simply do not work out. For instance, when Walt Disney announced plans to launch a cruise line replete with familiar Disney characters and themes, managers also began aggressively developing and marketing packages linking cruises with visits to Disney World in Florida. The inaugural sailing was sold out more than a year in advance, and the first year was booked solid six months before the ship was launched. Three months before the first sailing, however, the shipyard constructing Disney's first ship (the *Disney Magic*) notified the company that it was behind schedule and that delivery would be several weeks late. When similar problems befall other cruise lines, they can offer to rebook passengers on alternative itineraries. But because Disney had no other ship, it had no choice but to refund the money it had collected as prebooking deposits for its first 15 cruises.

The 20,000 displaced customers were offered big discounts if they rebooked on a later cruise. Many of them, however, could not rearrange their schedules and requested full refunds. Moreover, quite a few blamed Disney for the problem and expressed outrage at what they saw as poor planning by the entertainment giant. Fortunately for Disney, however, the *Disney Magic* was eventually launched and has now become popular and profitable. Because managers know such things can happen, they often develop alternative plans in case things go awry. Two common methods of dealing with the unknown and unforeseen are *contingency planning* and *crisis management*.

Contingency Planning

Contingency planning seeks to identify in advance important aspects of a business or its market that might change. It also identifies the ways in which a company will respond to changes. Suppose, for example, that a company develops a plan to create a new division. It expects sales to increase at an annual rate of 10 percent for the next five years, and it develops a marketing strategy for maintaining that level. But suppose that sales have increased by only 5 percent by the end of the first year. Does the firm (1) abandon the venture, (2) invest more in advertising, or (3) wait to see what happens in the second year? Whichever choice the firm makes, its efforts will be more efficient if managers decide in advance what to do in case sales fall below planned levels.

Contingency Planning *identifying aspects of a business or its environment that might entail changes in strategy*

Contingency planning helps them do exactly that. Disney learned from its mistake with its first ship; when the second ship was launched a year later, managers allowed for an extra two weeks between when the ship was supposed to be ready for sailing and its first scheduled cruise.

Crisis Management

A crisis is an unexpected emergency requiring immediate response. **Crisis management** involves an organization's methods for dealing with emergencies. Seeing the consequences of poor crisis management after California wildfires in 2010, the impact of Hurricane Sandy in 2012, and the Carnival cruise ship debacle in 2013 many firms today are working to create new and better crisis management plans and procedures.

Crisis Management *organization's methods for dealing with emergencies*

For example, both Reliant Energy and Duke Energy rely on computer trading centers where trading managers actively buy and sell energy-related commodities. If a terrorist attack or natural disaster were to strike their trading centers, they would essentially be out of business. Consequently, Reliant and Duke have created secondary trading centers at other locations. In the event of a shutdown at their main trading centers, these firms can quickly transfer virtually all their core trading activities to their secondary centers within 30 minutes or less.[18] Still, however many firms do not have comprehensive crisis management strategies. For example, as concerns grew about the outbreak of H1N1 (swine) flu in 2009 and some officials warned of a possible pandemic, a survey found that only about 57 percent of U.S. businesses had plans in place to deal with a flu pandemic.

Management and the Corporate Culture

OBJECTIVE 6
Describe
the development and explain the importance of corporate culture.

Corporate Culture *the shared experiences, stories, beliefs, and norms that characterize an organization*

Every organization—big or small, more successful or less successful—has an unmistakable "feel" to it. Just as every individual has a unique personality, every company has a unique identity or a **corporate culture,** the shared experiences, stories, beliefs, and norms that characterize an organization. This culture helps define the work and business climate that exists in an organization.

A strong corporate culture serves several purposes. For one thing, it directs employees' efforts and helps everyone work toward the same goals. Some cultures, for example, stress financial success to the extreme, whereas others focus more on quality of life. In addition, corporate culture helps newcomers learn accepted behaviors. If financial success is the key to a culture, newcomers quickly learn that they are expected to work long, hard hours, and that the "winner" is the one who brings in the most revenue. But if quality of life is more fundamental, newcomers learn that it's more acceptable to spend less time at work and that balancing work and nonwork is encouraged.

Building and Communicating Culture

Where does a business's culture come from? In some cases, it emanates from the days of an organization's founder. Firms such as Walt Disney, Hewlett-Packard, Walmart, and J. C. Penney, for example, still bear the imprint of their founders. In other cases, an organization's culture is forged over a long period of time by a constant and focused business strategy. Pepsi, for example, has an achievement-oriented culture tied to its long-standing goal of catching its biggest competitor, Coca-Cola. Similarly, Google has a sort of "work hard, play hard" culture stemming from its constant emphasis on innovation and growth coupled with lavish benefits and high pay.

Corporate culture influences management philosophy, style, and behavior. Managers, therefore, must carefully consider the kind of culture they want for their organizations and then work to nourish that culture by communicating with everyone who works there.

To use a firm's culture to its advantage, managers must accomplish several tasks, all of which hinge on effective communication. First, managers themselves must have a clear understanding of the culture. Second, they must transmit the culture

Sam Walton honed his craft as a retailer at Walton's five and dime. He then used his experience to create a unique corporate culture when he founded Walmart.

to others in the organization. Thus, training and orientation for newcomers in an organization often includes information about the firm's culture. A clear and meaningful statement of the organization's mission is also a valuable communication tool. Finally, managers can maintain the culture by rewarding and promoting those who understand it and work toward maintaining it.

Changing Culture

Organizations must sometimes change their cultures. In such cases, they must also communicate the nature of the change to both employees and customers. According to the CEOs of several companies that have undergone radical change in the last decade or so, the process usually goes through three stages:

1 *At the highest level, analysis of the company's environment highlights extensive change as the most effective response to its problems.* This period is typically characterized by conflict and resistance.

2 *Top management begins to formulate a vision of a new company.* Whatever that vision, it must include renewed focus on the activities of competitors and the needs of customers.

3 *The firm sets up new systems for appraising and compensating employees who enforce the firm's new values.* The purpose is to give the new culture solid shape from within the firm.

Continental and United Airlines recently merged into a single, much larger airline. Top managers then developed a plan for creating one new unified corporate culture drawing from the best of the cultures at the two individual airlines. The entire process took more than three years.[19]

summary of learning objectives

OBJECTIVE 1

Describe the nature of management and identify the four basic functions that constitute the management process.
(pp. 168–173)

Management is the process of planning, organizing, leading, and controlling of a firm's resources to achieve its goals. *Planning* is determining what the organization needs to do and how best to get it done. The process of arranging resources and activities into a coherent structure is called *organizing*. When *leading*, a manager guides and motivates employees to meet the firm's objectives. *Controlling* is the process of monitoring performance to make sure that a firm is meeting its goals.

Effective management is a blend of both science and art. Many management problems and issues can be approached in ways that are rational, logical, objective, and systematic. Managers can gather data, facts, and objective information and use quantitative models and decision-making techniques to arrive at "correct" decisions. But even though managers may try to be scientific as often as possible, they must frequently make decisions and solve problems on the basis of intuition, experience, instinct, and personal insights.

The most common path to becoming a successful manager involves a combination of education and experience. A college degree has become almost a requirement for career advancement in business, and virtually all CEOs in the United States have a college degree. Management skills must also be learned through experience. Most managers advanced to their present positions from other jobs. Only by experiencing the day-to-day pressures a manager faces and by meeting a variety of managerial challenges can an individual develop insights into the real nature and character of managerial work.

OBJECTIVE 2

Identify different types of managers likely to be found in an organization by level and area. (pp. 173–175)

There are three levels of management: top, middle, and first-line. The few executives who are responsible for the overall performance of large companies are *top managers*. Just below top managers are *middle managers*, including plant, operations, and division managers, who implement strategies, policies, and decisions made by top managers. Supervisors and office managers are the *first-line managers* who work with and supervise the employees who report to them.

In any large company, most managers work in one of five areas. *Human resource managers* hire and train employees, evaluate performance, and determine compensation. *Operations managers* are responsible for production, inventory, and quality control. *Marketing managers* are responsible for getting products from producers to consumers. *Information managers* design and implement systems to gather, organize, and distribute information. Finally, *financial managers*, including the chief financial officer (top), division controllers (middle), and accounting supervisors (first-line), oversee accounting functions and financial resources.

OBJECTIVE 3

Describe the basic skills required of managers. (pp. 175–179)

Most managerial activities fall into 10 different roles. These roles fall into three basic categories: interpersonal, informational, and decisional. There are three interpersonal roles inherent in the manager's job: *figurehead*; *leader*; and *liaison*. The three informational roles are *monitor*; *disseminator*; and *spokesperson*. The four decisional roles are: *entrepreneur*; *disturbance handler*; *resource allocator*; and *negotiator*.

Effective managers must develop a number of important skills. Traditionally, five managerial skills have been identified: technical skills, human relations skills, conceptual skills, decision-making skills, and time management skills. *Technical skills* are skills needed to perform specialized tasks, including a programmer's ability to write code or an animator's ability to draw. *Human relations skills* are skills in understanding and getting along with other people. *Conceptual skills* refer to the ability to think abstractly, diagnose and analyze different situations, and see beyond the present. *Decision-making skills* include the ability to define a problem and select the best course of action. *Time management skills* refer to the productive use of time, including managing e-mail, telephone calls, meetings, and e-mail. In the twenty-first century, several new skills have become increasingly important to managers. *Global management skills* include understanding foreign markets, cultural differences, and the motives and practices of foreign rivals. *Technology management skills* include the ability to process, organize, and interpret an ever-increasing amount of information.

OBJECTIVE 4

Explain the importance of strategic management and effective goal setting in organizational success. (pp. 179–186)

Strategic management is the process of helping an organization maintain an effective alignment with its environment. It starts with setting *goals*, objectives that a business hopes (and plans) to achieve. Goal setting is vitally important to the organization for several reasons. Goal setting provides direction and guidance for managers at all levels. Goal setting also helps firms to allocate resources and define corporate culture. Finally, goal setting is essential to managers who wish to assess performance. Most companies will create mission statements and long-term, intermediate, and short-term goals.

Strategy refers to a broad set of organizational plans for achieving organizational goals. The three types of strategy that are usually considered by a company are *corporate strategy*, *business* (or *competitive*) *strategy*, and *functional strategy*. Formulating strategy involves setting strategic goals, analyzing the organization and its environment, and then matching the organization to its environment. Most organizations have a hierarchy of strategic, tactical, and operational plans.

OBJECTIVE 5

Discuss contingency planning and crisis management in today's business world. (pp. 186–187)

Companies often develop alternative plans in case things go awry. There are two common methods of dealing with the unforeseen, *contingency planning* and *crisis management*. Contingency planning is planning for change: It seeks to identify in advance important aspects of a business or its market that might change. It also identifies the ways in which a company will respond to changes. Crisis management involves an organization's methods for dealing with emergencies.

OBJECTIVE 6

Describe the development and explain the importance of corporate culture. (pp. 188–189)

Every company has a unique identity called *corporate culture*: its shared experiences, stories, beliefs, and norms. It helps define the work and business climate of an organization. A strong corporate culture directs efforts and helps everyone work toward the same goals. Corporate culture can also help new employees learn acceptable behaviors. Managers must carefully consider the kind of culture they want for their organizations and then work to nourish that culture by communicating with everyone who works there. If an organization must change its culture, it must communicate the nature of the change to both employees and customers.

key terms

business (or competitive) strategy (p. 182)
conceptual skills (p. 177)
contingency planning (p. 187)
controlling (p. 170)
corporate culture (p. 188)
corporate strategy (p. 182)
crisis management (p. 187)
decision-making skills (p. 178)
decisional roles (p. 176)
environmental analysis (p. 184)
first-line manager (p. 174)
functional strategy (p. 182)

goal (p. 179)
human relations skills (p. 177)
informational roles (p. 176)
intermediate goal (p. 181)
interpersonal roles (p. 175)
leading (p. 169)
long-term goal (p. 181)
management (p. 168)
manager (p. 167)
middle manager (p. 173)
mission statement (p. 181)
operational plan (p. 185)
organizational analysis (p. 185)

organizing (p. 169)
planning (p. 169)
short-term goal (p. 181)
strategic goal (p. 184)
strategic management (p. 179)
strategic plan (p. 185)
strategy (p. 179)
strategy formulation (p. 184)
SWOT analysis (p. 184)
tactical plan (p. 185)
technical skills (p. 177)
time management skills (p. 178)
top manager (p. 173)

MyBizLab

Go to **pearsonglobaleditions.com/mybizlab** to complete the problems marked with this icon ✪.

questions & exercises

QUESTIONS FOR REVIEW

5-1. Describe the roles of top, middle, and first-line managers.

5-2. What are the four main purposes of setting goals in an organization?

5-3. Identify and explain the three basic steps in strategy formulation.

✪ **5-4.** What is corporate culture? How is it formed? How is it sustained?

QUESTIONS FOR ANALYSIS

5-5. Relate the five basic management skills (technical, human relations, conceptual, decision-making, and time management) to the four activities in the management process (planning, organizing, leading, and controlling). For example, which skills are most important in leading?

✪ **5-6.** Identify managers by level and area at your school, college, or university.

✪ **5-7.** What specific types of contingency plans would a company need to develop in an area where hurricanes are common?

5-8. What differences might you expect to find in the corporate cultures of a 100-year-old manufacturing firm based in the Northeast and a 1-year-old e-commerce firm based in Silicon Valley?

APPLICATION EXERCISES

5-9. Interview a manager at any level of a local company. Inquire about the manager's education and work experience. Which management skills are most important for this manager's job?

5-10. Compare and contrast the corporate cultures of two companies that do business in your community. Give examples of the culture of each company.

building a business: continuing team exercise

Assignment

Meet with your team members and discuss your new business venture within the context of this chapter. Develop specific responses to the following:

5-11. What areas of management will be most important in your business? Will these change over time?

5-12. What basic management skills will be most important to your business? Will these change over time?

5-13. What are the specific business goals of your new venture?

5-14. For your venture, is there a difference between your corporate and business strategies?

5-15. Does your management team (that is, your team) need to develop any contingency plans? Why or why not?

5-16. What sort of corporate culture do you want to create for your venture? What steps will you take to do so?

building your business skills

SPEAKING WITH POWER

Goal

To encourage you to appreciate effective speaking as a critical human relations skill.

Background Information

A manager's ability to understand and get along with supervisors, peers, and subordinates is a critical human relations skill. At the heart of this skill, says Harvard University Professor of Education Sarah McGinty, is the ability to speak with power and control. McGinty defines "powerful speech" in terms of the following characteristics:

- The ability to speak at length and in complete sentences
- The ability to set a conversational agenda
- The ability to deter interruptions
- The ability to argue openly and to express strong opinions about ideas, not people
- The ability to make statements that offer solutions rather than pose questions
- The ability to express humor

Taken together, says McGinty, "all this creates a sense of confidence in listeners."

Method

STEP 1

Working alone, compare your own personal speaking style with McGinty's description of powerful speech by taping yourself as you speak during a meeting with classmates or during a phone conversation. (Tape both sides of the conversation only if the person to whom you are speaking gives permission.) Listen for the following problems:

- Unfinished sentences
- An absence of solutions

- Too many disclaimers ("I'm not sure I have enough information to say this, but…")
- The habit of seeking support from others instead of making definitive statements of personal conviction (saying, "I recommend consolidating the medical and fitness functions," instead of, "As Emily stated in her report, I recommend consolidating the medical and fitness functions")
- Language fillers (saying, "you know," "like," and "um" when you are unsure of your facts or uneasy about expressing your opinion)

STEP 2

Join with three or four other classmates to evaluate each other's speaking styles. Finally,

FOLLOW-UP QUESTIONS

5-17. How do you think the power content of speech affects a manager's ability to communicate? Evaluate some of the ways in which effects may differ among supervisors, peers, and subordinates.

5-18. How do you evaluate yourself and group members in terms of powerful and powerless speech? List the strengths and weaknesses of the group.

5-19. Do you agree or disagree with McGinty that business success depends on gaining insight into your own language habits? Explain your answer.

5-20. In our age of computers and e-mail, why do you think personal presentation continues to be important in management?

5-21. McGinty believes that power language differs from company to company and that it is linked to the corporate culture. Do you agree, or do you believe that people express themselves in similar ways no matter where they are?

exercising your ethics

TIME FOR THE AX?

The Situation

You are the sales manager for a well-established medical equipment company. You've been with the company a long time and, generally, you really enjoy your job. The company's new president is interested in proving herself and has set a goal of 10-percent sales growth per year. Each sales representative has a quota that they are expected to meet. Those who exceed their quota will receive a bonus, and those who fall short of their quota will be fired or placed on probation.

The Dilemma

Your sales staff have worked really hard over the past year to meet their new quotas. Six of the eight representatives met their quotas and received bonuses. However, two others have fallen

below. Jane fell 2 percent short of her quota and you're not surprised. She's not hard working and often leaves work early to play golf. Bill, on the other hand, has been with the company a long time and is widely respected for his work ethic. However, he's struggling to care for his sick mother and fell 7 percent below his quota. You know that control is an important part of being a manager, but you're unsure what to do. The company president has asked to meet with you tomorrow to discuss the situation.

QUESTIONS TO ADDRESS

5-22. What are the ethical issues in this situation?

5-23. What do you think most managers would do in this situation?

5-24. What would you do?

team exercise

DREAMS CAN COME TRUE

The Situation

Arturo Juarez has years of experience in the travel industry as a manager at a high-end hotel as well as sales director at a large travel agency. He is ready to start his own business, Dream Vacations, offering travel planning services for individuals and families. His company will research destinations, hotels, and activities and help their customers to make travel memories by providing top-notch service and creative solutions. To achieve this goal, Arturo is working to develop contracts with resorts in the Caribbean, South America, and the Mediterranean to get better pricing for his customers. He hopes that his business will grow at least 10 percent per year over the first five years through advertising and referrals. Initially, Arturo plans to operate out of office space in Atlanta, but his goal is to have offices in South Carolina, Alabama, and Tennessee within two years.

Team Activity

Arturo has asked for a team of students to provide him with assistance getting his company going. Form a group of three to five students to provide guidance to Arturo.

ACTION STEPS

5-25. Working with your group, develop a mission statement for Dream Vacations. Why is developing a mission statement important?

5-26. Considering Dream Vacation's mission statement and the information provided in the case, what are the company's long-term goals? How should Arturo measure these goals?

5-27. What intermediate goals will help Dream Vacations meet their long-term goals and realize their mission? What types of corrective action should Arturo take if the company fails to meet these goals?

5-28. Identify Dream Vacation's short-term goals. Are short-term goals more or less important than long-term goals?

cases

Want to Know the Future? Just Google It...

Continued from page 168

At the beginning of this chapter you read about how Google's founders manage their employees and plan for the future. Using the information presented in this chapter you should now be able to answer the following questions:

QUESTIONS FOR DISCUSSION

5-29. Describe examples of each of the management functions illustrated in this case.

5-30. Which management skills seem to be most exemplified in Sergey Brin and Larry Page?

5-31. What role have goals and strategy played in the success of Google?

5-32. How would you describe the corporate culture at Google?

When Old is New and New is Old

Late in 2011, J.C. Penney made a dramatic move, ousting CEO Myron Ullman and bringing in Ron Johnson. Johnson was perceived as a change agent who could reinvent the company as a new, hip place to shop, just as he had transformed the Apple Store from a run-of-the-mill mall store to an entertainment destination.[20] His vision was clear, stating "In the U.S., the department store has a chance to regain its status as the leader in style, the leader in excitement. It will be a period of true innovation for this company." Johnson proposed offering new product and interesting product lines, such as Martha Stewart and Joe Fresh, to lure in high-end customers. He also envisioned J.C. Penney as a destination, where shoppers would look forward to spending time browsing the store, similar to the excitement one often finds in an Apple Store.

Unfortunately for J.C. Penney, Johnson's new vision was a near complete failure. Penney's loyal customer base was unhappy with the new store and pricing strategies. The company failed to attract new customers and sales fell by 25% in one year. Even the major shareholder who championed Johnson's recruitment, Bill Ackman, realized that the company had made a new fatal error, lamenting "One of the biggest mistakes was perhaps too much change too quickly without adequate testing on what the impact would be." Notre Dame marketing Professor Carol Phillips points out that the company failed to understand the buyer with its new value pricing, no sale strategy. "JCP's CEO Ron Johnson was… clueless about what makes shopping fun for women. It's the thrill of the hunt, not the buying." The new strategy was a mismatch with the company's existing managers, product lines, pricing strategies, and customer base. Sadly, the company moved too quickly without carefully analyzing the steps needed to implement the new vision. According to Virgin America CEO David Cush, "Don't destroy your old revenue model before you have proved your new revenue model. That's the box that JCPenney has put themselves in." [21]

In April 2013, J.C. Penney's board reinstated former CEO Ullman, whose number one priority was reconnecting with the company's former customer base. Matthew Boss, an analyst at JPMorgan Chase, reports "He talked about having the right product, but more importantly having the price and the value perception, something that he believes was lost over the past year." This means returning to the company's prior pricing strategy of marking up prices, then offering heavy discounts and abundant coupons and other promotional offers. Ullman plans to begin a slow process of analyzing the company's environment and adjusting the company's strategy to increase sales and profitability. [22]

QUESTIONS FOR DISCUSSION

5-33. As CEO, both Ullman and Johnson were involved in each of the four management functions. Briefly describe the types of decisions that the CEO of J.C. Penney must make as they relate to each of the four functions.

5-34. The text describes a variety of skills that are essential to management. Which two skills do you think will be most important for CEO Mike Ullman, the reinstated CEO?

5-35. Do you think that Ron Johnson changed the mission of J.C. Penney or just implemented new strategies? Be sure to support your conclusion.

5-36. What do you think were Ron Johnson's biggest mistakes?

5-37. Do you think that Ullman will be successful in rescuing J.C. Penney or is it too late?

MyBizLab

Go to **pearsonglobaleditions.com/mybizlab** *for the following Assisted-graded writing questions:*

5-38. Every business, whether big or small, needs a strategy to successfully operate under. Strategies across industries, organizations, and even departments often differ. Pretend you are a candy bar manufacturing company. How would your corporate strategy, business strategy, and functional strategies differ? How would these change if your company acquired a peanut company? A gum company? A cracker company? How would these change if you found out there was a better manufacturing method for candy bars?

5-39. Managers can be found at nearly every level of an organization. As a manager moves up the corporate ladder, their responsibilities increase. If you were a manager in the manufacturing industry, how might your responsibilities differ if you were a top manager, middle manage, and first-line manager? Would your responsibilities differ in each of these positions if you were in a different industry? What management skills would be more important for each level of management?

5-40. Mybizlab Only—comprehensive writing assignment for this chapter.

end notes

1 Google, "Corporate Information," April 11, 2013, at http://www.google.com; "The Secret to Google's Success," *BusinessWeek*, March 6, 2008, http://www.businessweek.com; "In Search of the Real Google," *Time*, February 20, 2007, http://www.time.com; http://www.google.com/competition/howgooglesearchworks.html.

2 See "The Best (& Worst) Managers of the Year," *BusinessWeek*, January 22, 2013, pp. 50–72.

3 "Ford's Savior?" *BusinessWeek*, March 16, 2009, pp. 31–34.

4 Gary Hamel and C. K. Prahalad, "Competing for the Future," *Harvard Business Review*, July–August 1994, pp. 122–128; see also Joseph M. Hall and M. Eric Johnson, "When Should a Process Be Art, Not Science?" *Harvard Business Review*," March 2009, pp. 58–65.

5 James Waldroop and Timothy Butler, "The Executive as Coach," *Harvard Business Review*, November–December 1996, pp. 111–117.

6 See Steven J. Armstrong and Anis Mahmud, "Experiential Learning and the Acquisition of Managerial Tacit Knowledge," *Academy of Management Learning & Education*, 2008, Vol. 7, No. 2, pp. 189–208.

7 "The Executive MBA Your Way," *BusinessWeek*, October 18, 1999, pp. 88–92.

8 "Despite Cutbacks, Firms Invest in Developing Leaders," *Wall Street Journal*, February 9, 2009, p. B4.

9 "Turning B-School into E-School," *BusinessWeek*, October 18, 1999, p. 94.

10 See "Reunion at P&G University," *Wall Street Journal*, June 7, 2000, pp. B1, B4, for a discussion of Procter & Gamble's training programs.

11 For an interesting discussion of these issues, see Rakesh Khurana, "The Curse of the Superstar CEO," *Harvard Business Review*, September 2002, pp. 60–70.

12 Anneloes Raes, Mrielle Heijltjes, Ursula Glunk, and Robert Row, "The Interface of the Top Management Team and Middle Managers: A Process Model," *Academy of Management Review*, January 2011, pp. 102–126.

13 Henry Mintzberg, *The Nature of Managerial Work* (Englewood Cliffs, NJ: 1973).

14 See Robert L. Katz, "The Skills of an Effective Administrator," *Harvard Business Review*, September–October 1974, pp. 90–102, for a classic discussion of several of these skills. For a recent perspective, see J. Brian Atwater, Vijay R. Kannan, and Alan A. Stephens, "Cultivating Systemic Thinking in the Next Generation of Business Leaders," *Academy of Management Learning & Education*, 2008, Vol. 7, No. 1, pp. 9–25.

15 http://www.instabeat.me/index.php (accessed 15/10/2013)

[16] Pete Engardio and Adam Aston, "The Next Energy Innovators," *BusinessWeek*, July 16, 2009, at www.businessweek.com, accessed on April 10, 2013; "Solar Power for Less Than Your Cable Bill," *Environmental Forum*, April 24, 2008, at http://blogs.reuters.com, accessed on April 10, 2013; Julie Schmidt, "SolarCity Aims to Make Solar Power More Affordable," *USA Today*, November 10, 2009, at www.usatoday.com, accessed on April 10, 2013; Eric Wesoff, "SolarCity Adds Energy Efficiency to Solar Finance, Design and Monitoring," *Greentech Media*, October 14, 2010, at www.greentechmedia.com, accessed on April 10, 2013; David A. Hill, "Solar City Takes Aim at Home Energy Audit Market," *Colorado Energy News*, May 14, 2010, at http://coloradoenergynews.com, accessed on April 10, 2013; Rick Needham, "Helping Homeowners Harness the Sun," *The Official Google Blog*, June 14, 2011, at http://googleblog.blogspot.com, accessed on April 10, 2013.

[17] Flight Global, http://www.flightglobal.com/news/articles/kuwaits-wataniya-airways-ceases-operations-354453/; *The Economist*, http://www.economist.com/blogs/gulliver/2011/03/jet_fuel_prices; *Financial Times*, "Gulf's budget carriers aim high," http://cachef.ft.com/cms/s/0/e7788770-9a63-11df-87fd-00144feab49a.html#axzz1cSphEBQR.

[18] Del Jones, "Next Time," *USA Today* (October 4, 2005), 1B, 2B.

[19] "Marriage at 30,000 Feet," *Bloomberg Businessweek*, February 6–February 12, 2012, pp. 36–40.

[20] Clifford, Stephanie. "J.C. Penney's New Plan Is to Reuse Its Old Plans." *The New York Times*. N.p., 16 May 2013. Web. 17 June 2013.

[21] Denning, Steve. "J.C.Penney: Was Ron Johnson's Strategy Wrong?" *Forbes*. Forbes Magazine, 09 Apr. 2013. Web. 17 June 2013.

[22] "Saving JC Penney: New CEO Ullman Plans Coupons, Discounts." *CNBC.com*. N.p., 10 Apr. 2013. Web. 17 June 2013.

The secret to success lies with the people behind the products. The relationship between **managers and** employees can make or break **any company.**

AFTER READING THIS CHAPTER, YOU SHOULD BE ABLE TO:

OBJECTIVE 1   **Discuss** the factors that influence firm's organizational structure.

OBJECTIVE 2   **Explain** specialization and departmentalization as two of the building blocks of organizational structure.

OBJECTIVE 3   **Describe** centralization and decentralization, delegation, and authority as the key ingredients in establishing the decision-making hierarchy.

OBJECTIVE 4   **Explain** the differences among functional, divisional, matrix, and international organizational structures and describe the most popular new forms of organizational design.

OBJECTIVE 5   **Describe** the informal organization and discuss intrapreneuring.

MyBizLab®

⭐ Improve Your Grade!

Visit **pearsonglobaleditions.com/mybizlab** for simulations, tutorials, and end-of-chapter problems.

Over 10 million students improved their results using the Pearson MyLabs.

Organizing for Success at South African Airways

South African Airways (SAA) will celebrate its 80th anniversary in 2014. It is one of the oldest airlines in the world and has won plaudits from numerous magazines and international organizations.

The airline has one of the most advanced aircraft fleets in the world. Its over-riding vision is to become the first African airline with a truly global reach. In order to achieve this, the airline places a great emphasis on safety, customer-focus, accountability, and integrity. Yet all of this is dependent on one thing: the ability to value its own people.

The airline has an international network that connects South Africa with every continent across the globe. SAA connects with 21 locations across Africa. It continues to refresh, improve, and expand its fleet. The airline is also instrumental in providing technical support for other African carriers.

In September 2013, after several years of government funding support, the airline announced that it would merge with regional operator SA Express and the low cost carrier Mango. This move is seen as a necessary step to ensure that SAA's business model was changed and that it could once again become self-funded.

For many years, deregulation and increased competition had eroded SAA's ability to fund its own operations without government support. The merger, designed to allow SAA to use their assets more efficiently, would also allow them to use their available capital in a better way. The new alliance would allow SAA to retain its position as a premium carrier. The role of SA Express would be that of a "feeder airline" and Mango would offer customers a lower cost alternative.

This model has worked successfully in Kenya and Ethiopia. In both countries, coordination between airlines has produced greater efficiency and savings in terms of fleet purchase, use of airports, and the right to operate on particular routes. The South African move is not seen as a short term fix, rather a medium to long-term solution.

Interestingly, the merger will mean that three organizational structures will have to be dovetailed together to make a coherent entity. SAA had already begun a deep and fundamental restructuring process in 2007. It aimed to simplify the organization. In addition to this, SAA recognized the need to have the right size of management at various levels. A key part of the restructuring process was also to re-skill the workforce and provide incentives to employees and management.

Radu Razvan/fotolia

what's in it for me?

All managers need the assistance of others to succeed and so must trust the members of their team to do their jobs and carry out their responsibilities. The team members themselves need the support of their boss and a clear understanding of their role in the organization. The working relationship between managers and their subordinates is one of the most critical elements comprising an organization. As you will see in this chapter, managing the basic frameworks that organizations use to get their work done, *structure*, is a fundamental part of the management process.

Imagine asking a child to build a castle with a set of building blocks. She selects a few small blocks and other larger ones. She uses some square ones, some round ones, and some triangular ones. When she finishes, she has her own castle, unlike any other. Another child, presented with the same task, constructs a different castle. He selects different blocks, for example, and combines them in different ways. The children's activities, choosing certain combinations of blocks and then putting them together in unique ways, are in many ways analogous to the manager's job of organizing. Managers at similar companies competing in the same industries may create structures that are nearly identical to one another, completely different from one another, or somewhere in between.

Organizing is deciding how best to group organizational elements. Just as children select different kinds of building blocks, managers can choose a variety of structural possibilities. And just as the children can assemble the blocks in any number of ways, so, too, can managers put the organization together in many different ways. Understanding the nature of these building blocks and the different ways in which they can be configured can have a powerful impact on a firm's competitiveness.

By understanding the material in this chapter, you'll also be prepared to understand your "place" in the organization that employs you. Similarly, as a boss or owner, you'll be better equipped to create the optimal structure for your own organization. This chapter examines factors that influence a firm's organizational structure. We discuss the building blocks of organizational structure as well as the differences between decision making in different types of organizations. Along the way, we look at a variety of organizational structures and describe the most popular new forms of organizational design.

When this initial restructuring plan was devised (in the financial year 2006/2007), many of the assumptions were based on the price of oil. Oil prices, and subsequently fuel prices, determine the profitability and competitiveness of airlines, and at this point, the targets were based on the fact that oil was trading at US$50–60 a barrel. By the time that the restructuring had begun in 2007, oil was trading at more than twice that price. Clearly, this put tremendous pressure on the margins.

SAA's response was to ground aircraft and focus on profitable routes. This was a short-term fix and not a long-term solution. Cost-cutting measures were implemented and determined efforts were made to streamline the organization and management of the business. As another result of cost cutting, the estimated restructuring costs was slashed to a third of the original estimated costs.

In 2005, SAA had suffered a ruinous labor dispute. The estimated cost of the strikes over pay increases had cost SAA at least 50 percent of its daily turnover. At the end of the dispute, SAA had to radically change its whole approach to labor relations. It recognized that it needed to build and sustain relationships with its workforce. This would encompass shared goals, knowledge and, above all, mutual respect.

This was the backdrop which had prompted the restructuring process. The new organization structure would have to incorporate ongoing communication (meaning that it had to be timely and frequent). At the same time, employees would need to feel that they had a stake and say in the decision making of SAA.

The airline industry represents a series of situations that require excellent planning, coordination, and cooperation. Teamwork across the organization is necessary to ensure that aircraft are turned around quickly. Flight departure times are very constrained and demand cooperation in order to be fulfilled.

Latest developments for SAA, the merger of Mango and SA Express, seem to suggest that this will be the trend for African airlines over the next two decades. As a legacy airline (an established operator with existing routes, prior to the deregulation of the market), SAA has begun to seek international alliances. They have already partnered with the Australian airline Qantas and the Middle Eastern operator, Emirates. It is estimated that the African airline fleet will need to double by 2030 in order to keep up with increasing demand.

SAA will need to continue to streamline and reorganize in order to respond not only to the increased competition, but the opportunities that alliances will offer. Links to China, India, and Latin America could be very lucrative. First, however, and reflected in the merger with Mango and SA Express, is to capture the dominant share of the domestic market.

It would seem that SAA will follow the model of SA Express, which had already flattened its organizational structure and positively encouraged employee stakeholders to take a more active role in decision making. Responsive, team orientated, and lean were the key elements of the independent SA Express organizational structure.[1] (After studying this chapter you should be able to answer the set of questions found at the end of the chapter.)

OBJECTIVE 1

Discuss
the factors that influence a firm's organizational structure.

Organizational Structure *specification of the jobs to be done within an organization and the ways in which they relate to one another*

What Is Organizational Structure?

One key decision that business owners and managers must address is how best to structure their organization. Stated differently, they must decide on an appropriate organizational structure. We can define **organizational structure** as the specification of the jobs to be done within an organization and the ways in which those jobs relate to one another.[2] Perhaps the easiest way to understand structure is in terms of an *organization chart*.

Organization Charts

Most small businesses prepare an **organization chart** to clarify structure and to show employees where they fit into a firm's operations. Figure 6.1 is an organization chart for Contemporary Landscape Services, a small but thriving business in a small Texas community. Each box in the chart represents a job. The solid lines define the *chain of command*. The **chain of command**, in turn, refers to *reporting relationships* within the company. In theory, such reporting relationships follow a "chain" from the highest level in the organization to the lowest. For example, the retail shop, nursery, and landscape operations managers all report to the owner and president. Within the landscape operation is one manager for residential accounts and another for commercial accounts. Similarly, there are other managers in the retail shop and the nursery.

The organization charts of large firms are far more complex and include individuals at many more levels than those shown in Figure 6.1. Size prevents many large firms from even having charts that include all their managers. Typically, they create one organization chart showing overall corporate structure, separate charts for each division, and even more charts for individual departments or units.

Recall our definition of organizational structure: the specification of the jobs to be done within an organization and the ways in which those jobs relate to one another. The boxes in the organization chart represent the jobs, and the lines connecting the boxes show how the jobs are related. As we will see, however, even though organizational structure can be broken down into a series of boxes and lines, virtually no two organizations will have the same structure. What works for Texas Instruments will not work for Google, Southwest Airlines, Shell Oil, Amazon.com, or the U.S. Department of Justice. Likewise, the structure of the American Red Cross will probably not work for Urban Outfitters, Union Carbide, Starbucks, or the University of Minnesota.

Organization Chart *diagram depicting a company's structure and showing employees where they fit into its operations*

Chain of Command *reporting relationships within a company*

Determinants of Organizational Structure

How is an organization's structure determined? Ideally, managers carefully assess a variety of important factors as they plan for and then create an organizational structure that will allow their organization to function efficiently.

Many factors play a part in determining an organization's optimal structure. Chief among them are the organization's *mission* and *strategy*. A dynamic and rapidly growing business, for example, needs an organizational structure that allows it to be flexible, to respond to changes in its environment and strategy, and to grow. A stable organization with only modest growth goals and a more conservative strategy will most likely function best with a different organizational structure.

Size of the company and aspects of the organization's environment also affect organizational structure. As we saw in Chapter 5, organizing is a key part of the

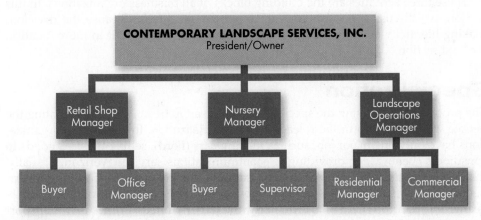

FIGURE 6.1 The Organization Chart

management process. As such, it must be conducted with an equal awareness of both a firm's external and internal environments. A large services provider or manufacturer operating in a strongly competitive environment, such as Delta Airlines or Hewlett-Packard, requires a different organizational structure than a local barbershop or clothing boutique. Even after an organizational structure has been created, it is rarely free from tinkering—or even outright re-creation. Most organizations change their structures on an almost continuing basis.

Since it was first incorporated in 1903, Ford Motor Company has undergone literally dozens of major structural changes, hundreds of moderate changes, and thousands of minor changes. In the last 20 years alone, Ford has initiated several major structural changes. In 1994, for instance, the firm announced a major restructuring plan called Ford 2000, which was intended to integrate all of Ford's vast international operations into a single, unified structure by the year 2000.

By 1998, however, midway through implementation of the grand plan, top Ford executives announced major modifications, indicating that (1) additional changes would be made, (2) some previously planned changes would not be made, and (3) some recently realigned operations would be changed again. In early 1999, managers announced another set of changes intended to eliminate corporate bureaucracy, speed decision making, and improve communication and working relationships among people at different levels of the organization. Early in 2001, Ford announced yet more sweeping changes intended to boost the firm's flagging bottom line and stem a decline in product quality. More significant changes followed in both 2003 and 2004, and in 2006, the firm announced several plant closings, resulting in even more changes. Not surprisingly, yet another major reorganization was announced in 2010 as the firm sought to deal with a global recession and a major slump in automobile sales.[3] And in 2011 the firm announced even more restructuring to gain more international market share.[4]

The Building Blocks of Organizational Structure

The first step in developing the structure of any business, large or small, involves three activities:

1 *Specialization.* Determining who will do what
2 *Departmentalization.* Determining how people performing certain tasks can best be grouped together
3 *Establishment of a Decision-Making Hierarchy.* Deciding who will be empowered to make which decisions and who will have authority over others

These three activities are the building blocks of all business organizations. In this section, we discuss specialization and departmentalization. Because the decision-making hierarchy actually includes several elements, we cover it in more detail in the next section.

Specialization

Job Specialization *the process of identifying the specific jobs that need to be done and designating the people who will perform them*

The process of identifying the specific jobs that need to be done and designating the people who will perform them leads to **job specialization**. In a sense, all organizations have only one major job, such as making cars (Ford), selling finished goods to consumers (Lenova), or providing telecommunications services (Verizon). Usually, that job is more complex in nature. For example, the job of Nucor Steel is converting scrap steel (such as wrecked automobiles) into finished steel products (such as beams and reinforcement bars). Similarly, the job of United Airlines is to transport passengers and their luggage from one airport to another.

To perform this one overall job, managers actually break it down, or specialize it, into several smaller jobs. Thus, some workers transport the scrap steel to the company's mills. Others operate shredding equipment before turning raw materials over to the workers who then melt them into liquid form. Other specialists oversee the flow of the liquid into molding equipment, where it is transformed into new products. Finally, other workers are responsible for moving finished products to a holding area before they are shipped out to customers. At United, some specialists schedule flights, others book passengers, others fly the planes, and still others deal with passenger luggage and other cargo. When the overall job of the organization is broken down like this, workers can develop real expertise in their jobs, and employees can better coordinate their work with that done by others.

Specialization and Growth

In a small organization, the owner may perform every job. As the firm grows, however, so does the need to specialize jobs so that others can perform them. To see how specialization can evolve in an organization, consider the case of the Walt Disney Company. When Walt Disney first opened his animation studio, he and his brother Roy did everything. For example, when they created their first animated feature, *Steamboat Willy*, they wrote the story, drew the pictures, transferred the pictures to film, provided the voices, and went out and sold the cartoon to theater operators.

Today, however, a Disney animated feature is made possible only through the efforts of thousands of people. The job of one animator may be to create the face of a single character throughout an entire feature. Another artist may be charged with coloring background images in certain scenes. People other than artists are responsible for the subsequent operations that turn individual computer-generated images into a moving picture or for the marketing of the finished product.

Job specialization is a natural part of organizational growth. It also has certain advantages. For example, specialized jobs are learned more easily and can be performed more efficiently than nonspecialized jobs, and it is also easier to replace people who leave an organization if they have highly specialized jobs. However, jobs at lower levels of the organization are especially susceptible to overspecialization. If such jobs become too narrowly defined, employees may become bored and careless, derive less satisfaction from their jobs, and lose sight of their roles in the organization.

When Walt Disney was just starting out, he did most of the work on his animated features all by himself. But today's features like Disney's 2013 hit *Monsters University* require the work of hundreds of people.

finding a better way

Blending the Old with the New

In 1883, the great composer and piano virtuoso Franz Liszt wrote Heinrich Steinway, founder of Steinway & Sons, to praise the Steinway grand piano. In particular, Liszt had good things to say about the tonal effect of the piano's *scale*, the arrangement of its strings. Thirty years earlier, Henry Steinway Jr., had patented a technique for scaling called *overstringing*: Instead of running them parallel to the piano's treble strings, he taught his workers to fan the bass strings above and diagonally to create a second tier of strings. As a result, he was able to improve the instrument's tone by using longer strings with superior vibratory quality.

Another feature developed by Steinway and his employees in the mid-nineteenth century made it possible to use strings that were also bigger—and thus louder. If you look under a piano, you'll see a cast-iron plate. This component was once made of wood fortified by metal braces, but Steinway had made the cast-iron plate a regular feature by the 1840s. The metal plate, of course, is much stronger and allowed the piano maker to apply much greater tension to the strings; in turn, the ability to increase string tension made it possible to tune the piano to more exacting standards of pitch.

Steinway was the first piano maker to combine the cast-iron plate with the technique of overstringing, and little has changed in the construction of a grand piano since these and a few other facets of traditional technology were first introduced. In effect, just as the job of a Disney animator has changed as the firm and its technology have changed, so too have the jobs at Steinway. Indeed, Steinway's workers still perform specialized jobs, but the jobs have also changed dramatically over the years. Take, for example, the soundboard, which you'll see if you open up a grand piano and look inside. A solid wooden "diaphragm" located between the strings and the metal plate, the *soundboard* is a marvel of deceptively simple design that vibrates to amplify the sound of the strings while withstanding the 1,000 pounds of pressure that they place on it. Because they're constructed by hand, no two soundboards are exactly the same size. Nor is any one piano *case*, the curved lateral surface that runs around the whole instrument, the same size as any other. The important thing is that the case is fitted—and fitted *precisely*—to a soundboard.

Because the soundboard is measured first and the case then fitted to it, there's only one case for each soundboard. To ensure a satisfactory fit between case and soundboard, the case must

Ulrich Perrey/Newscom

be *frazed*, sawed and planed to specification. Performed by hand, this task took 14 hours, but today it's done in 1 1/2 hours by a *computer numerically controlled* (CNC) milling machine, a system in which a computerized storage medium issues programmed commands to a variety of specialized tools. Steinway workers, then, must be masters of their craft to perform effectively.

Granted, CNC technology is fairly new at Steinway—the million-dollar milling machine and several other pieces of CNC technology were introduced only in the last 10 years or so. Most of Steinway's CNC tools are highly specialized, and the company custom-built many of them. Obviously, such technology leads to a lot of labor savings, but Steinway officials are adamant about the role of technology in maintaining rather than supplanting Steinway tradition: Some people, says Director of Quality Robert Berger, "think that Steinway is automating to save on labor costs or improve productivity. But these investments are all about quality. We're making a few specific technology investments in areas where we can improve the quality of our product."[5]

Departmentalization

After jobs are specialized, they must be grouped into logical units, which is the process of **departmentalization**. Departmentalized companies benefit from this division of activities; control and coordination are narrowed and made easier, and top managers can see more easily how various units are performing.

Departmentalization allows the firm to treat each department as a **profit center**, a separate company unit responsible for its own costs and profits. Thus, Sears can

Departmentalization *process of grouping jobs into logical units*

Profit Center *separate company unit responsible for its own costs and profits*

calculate the profits it generates from men's clothing, appliances, home furnishings, and every other department within a given store separately. Managers can then use this information in making decisions about advertising and promotional events, space allocation, budgeting, and so forth.

Managers do not departmentalize jobs randomly. They group them logically, according to some common thread or purpose. In general, departmentalization may occur along *functional, product, process, customer,* or *geographic* lines (or any combination of these).

Functional Departmentalization Many service and manufacturing companies, especially smaller ones just getting started, use **functional departmentalization** to create departments according to a group's functions or activities. Most new firms, for instance, use functional departmentalization. Such firms typically have production, marketing and sales, human resources, and accounting and finance departments. Departments may be further subdivided. For example, the marketing department might be divided into separate groups for market research, advertising, and sales promotions.

Functional Departmentalization
dividing an organization according to groups' functions or activities

Product Departmentalization Both manufacturers and service providers often opt for **product departmentalization**, dividing an organization according to the specific product or service being created. This becomes especially true when a firm grows and starts to offer multiple products or services. Kraft Foods uses this approach to divide departments. For example, the Oscar Mayer division focuses on hot dogs and lunch meats, the Kraft Cheese division focuses on cheese products, and the Maxwell House and Post division focus on coffee and breakfast cereal, respectively.[6] Because each division represents a defined group of products or services, managers at Kraft Foods are able—in theory—to focus on *specific* product lines in a clear and defined way.

Product Departmentalization
dividing an organization according to specific products or services being created

Process Departmentalization Other manufacturers favor **process departmentalization**, in which the organization is divided according to production processes used to create a good or service. This principle is logical for Vlasic, which has three separate departments to transform cucumbers into either fresh-packed pickles, pickles cured in brine, or relishes. Cucumbers destined to become fresh-packed pickles must be packed into jars immediately, covered with a solution of water and vinegar, and prepared for sale. Those slated to be brined pickles must be aged in brine solution before packing. Relish cucumbers must be minced and combined with a host of other ingredients. Each process requires different equipment and worker skills, and different departments were created for each. Some service providers also use this approach as well. For instance, an insurance company might use one department to receive claims, another to review coverage, and another to issue payments.

Process Departmentalization
dividing an organization according to production processes used to create a good or service

Customer Departmentalization Retail stores actually derive their generic name, department stores, from the manner in which they are structured—a men's department, a women's department, a luggage department, a lawn and garden department, and so on. Each department targets a specific customer category (men, women, people who want to buy luggage, people who want to buy a lawn mower) by using **customer departmentalization** to create departments that offer products, and meet the needs of, identifiable customer groups. Thus, a customer shopping for a baby's playpen at Sears can bypass lawn and garden supplies and head straight for children's furniture. In general, the store is more efficient, and customers get better service because salespeople tend to specialize and gain expertise in their departments. Another illustration of customer departmentalization is reflected in most banks. A customer wanting a consumer loan goes to the retail banking office, whereas a small business owner goes to the commercial banking office and a farmer goes to the agricultural loan department.

Customer Departmentalization
dividing an organization to offer products and meet needs for identifiable customer groups

Geographic Departmentalization **Geographic departmentalization** divides firms according to the areas of the country or the world that they serve.

Geographic Departmentalization
dividing an organization according to the areas of the country or the world served by a business

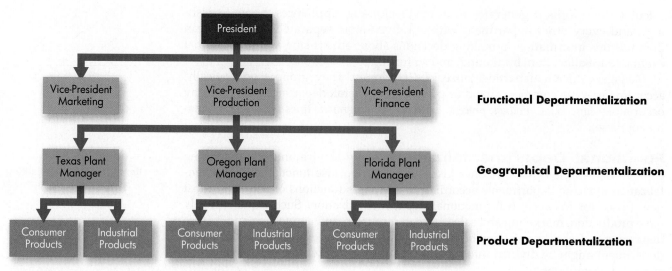

FIGURE 6.2 Multiple Forms of Departmentalization

Levi Strauss, for instance, has one division for North and South America; one for Europe, the Middle East, and North Africa; and one for the Asia Pacific region.[7] Within the United States, geographic departmentalization is common among utilities. For example, Southern Company organizes its power subsidiaries into four geographic departments—Alabama, Georgia, Gulf, and Mississippi Power.[8]

Multiple Forms of Departmentalization Because different forms of departmentalization have different advantages, as firms grow in size they tend to adopt different types of departmentalization for various levels. The company illustrated in Figure 6.2 uses functional departmentalization at the top level. At the middle level, production is divided along geographic lines. At a lower level, marketing is departmentalized by product group. Larger firms are certain to use all of these different forms of departmentalization in various areas.

Establishing the Decision-Making Hierarchy

OBJECTIVE 3
Describe
centralization and decentralization, delegation, and authority as the key ingredients in establishing the decision-making hierarchy.

The third major building block of organizational structure is the establishment of a decision-making hierarchy. This is usually done by formalizing reporting relationships. When the focus is on the reporting relationships among individual managers and the people who report to them, it is most commonly referred to as delegation. However, when the focus is on the overall organization, it becomes a question of decentralization versus *centralization*.

Distributing Authority: Centralization and Decentralization

Some managers make the conscious decision to retain as much decision-making authority as possible at the higher levels of the organizational structure; others decide to push authority as far down the hierarchy as possible. Although we can think of these two extremes as anchoring a continuum, most companies fall somewhere between the middle of such a continuum and one end point or the other.

Centralized Organization
organization in which most decision-making authority is held by upper-level management

Centralized Organizations
In a **centralized organization**, most decision-making authority is held by upper-level managers.[9] McDonald's practices centralization as a way to maintain standardization. All restaurants must follow precise

managing in turbulent times

The Complexities of Offshoring

From computer programmers in the Philippines and molecular biologists in Russia to customer-service agents in India, the practice of *offshoring* (or *outsourcing*) is bringing workers from around the world into the workforces of U.S. corporations in a broad range of industries. When U.S. firms "offshore," they're hiring foreign firms and foreign personnel to perform their business functions. In so doing, they're not only increasing the diversity of their workforces but altering the processes by which they conduct organizational business.

"In theory," says business journalist Pete Engardio, offshoring is making it "possible to buy, off the shelf, practically any function you need to run a company." In part, that's why the offshoring processes at some firms are almost dizzying in their complexity. At Penske Truck Leasing, for instance, drivers submit their paper logs for data entry to a facility in Mexico, which forwards them to Hyderabad, India, where they're analyzed and the results reported to Penske management back in the United States. How does a company's data-processing function come to consist of such far-flung operations? As in most other decisions, companies choose operational partners according to the value-creation capabilities that they bring to the overall process.

Ideally, of course, offshoring should benefit the contractor as well as the contracting firm. Take, for example, the case of Wisconsin-based PCMC, which designs and makes paper packaging. PCMC had a problem with its engineering function; although it had a large base of potential customers, it often lost them because its engineering group was too small to create new designs fast enough to keep pace with customer needs. Nor could the company afford to expand its engineering department. To solve the problem, PCMC entered into an offshoring contract with an Indian company that agreed to provide a 160-member staff to support PCMC's engineering function. The result? Not only 160 new jobs in India but also more orders and more jobs in Wisconsin as well.

Obviously, offshoring arrangements don't always work out as well as the one established by PCMC and its Indian partner. Problems can arise, for example, when the process requires

Jim West/Alamy

significant interaction between foreign contract personnel and people in the contracting firm's home country—not only its employees but also its customers. For one thing, language and culture differences can make communication difficult, especially when it's conducted by e-mail or phone.

McDonald's experimented with using a call center in India to process customer orders at drive-through locations in the California. When customers placed their orders at drive-through order stands, the person to whom they were speaking was actually in India. The order taker was supposed to enter the order online and transmit it to the McDonald's order filler for fulfillment. However, the error rate increased dramatically because of the order takers lack of understanding of such special orders as "extra mustard, no mayonnaise" and so forth. After just a few weeks McDonald's abandoned the experiment.

The decision made sense; typically, it costs six times as much to replace a customer as to keep one. Fortunately, the company had a plan B, "homeshoring" or hiring in-country contract workers. Homeshoring employees are more expensive than overseas contractors, but they're less expensive than full-time on-site employees. They connect with U.S. customers, and they also alleviate the concerns that some U.S. consumers have about their private data being shipped overseas.[10]

---

steps in buying products and making and packaging menu items. Most advertising is handled at the corporate level, and any local advertising must be approved by a regional manager. Restaurants even have to follow prescribed schedules for facilities' maintenance and upgrades such as floor polishing and parking lot cleaning. Centralized authority is most commonly found in companies that face relatively stable and predictable environments and is also typical of small businesses.

Decentralized Organizations   As a company gets larger and more decisions must be made, the company tends to adopt **decentralized organization**, in which much decision-making authority is delegated to levels of management at various points below the top. Decentralization is typical in firms that have

Decentralized Organization
organization in which a great deal of decision-making authority is delegated to levels of management at points below the top

complex and dynamic environmental conditions. It is also common in businesses that specialize in customer services. Decentralization makes a company more responsive by allowing managers increased discretion to make quick decisions in their areas of responsibility. For example, Urban Outfitters practices relative decentralization in that it allows individual store managers considerable discretion over merchandising and product displays. Whole Foods Market takes things even further in its decentralization. Stores are broken up into small teams, which are responsible for making decisions on issues such as voting on which new staff members to hire and which products to carry based on local preferences. This practice taps into the idea that the people who will be most affected by decisions should be the ones making them.[11]

Tall and Flat Organizations Decentralized firms tend to have relatively fewer layers of management, resulting in a **flat organizational structure** like that of the hypothetical law firm shown in Figure 6.3(a). Centralized firms typically require multiple layers of management and thus **tall organizational structures**, as in the U.S. Army example in Figure 6.3(b). Because information, whether upward or downward bound, must pass through so many organizational layers, tall structures are prone to delays in information flow.

As organizations grow in size, it is both normal and necessary that they become at least somewhat taller. For instance, a small firm with only an owner-manager and a few employees is likely to have two layers, the owner-manager and the employees who report to that person. As the firm grows, more layers will be needed. A manager

Flat Organizational Structure *characteristic of decentralized companies with relatively few layers of management*

Tall Organizational Structure *characteristic of centralized companies with multiple layers of management*

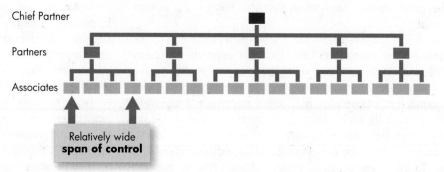

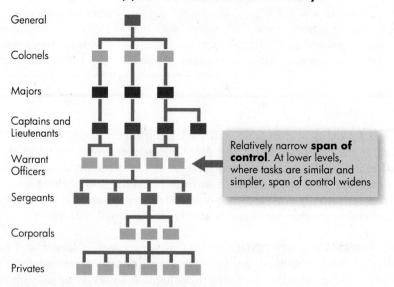

FIGURE 6.3 Organizational Structures and Span of Control

must ensure that he or she has only the number of layers his or her firm needs. Too few layers can create chaos and inefficiency, whereas too many layers can create rigidity and bureaucracy.

Span of Control As you can see in Figure 6.3, the distribution of authority in an organization also affects the number of people who work for any individual manager. In a flat organizational structure, the number of people directly managed by one supervisor, the manager's **span of control**, is usually wide. In tall organizations, span of control tends to be narrower. Employees' abilities and the supervisor's managerial skills influence how wide or narrow the span of control should be, as do the similarity and simplicity of tasks and the extent to which they are interrelated.

> **Span of Control** *number of people supervised by one manager*

If lower-level managers are given more decision-making authority, their supervisors will have less work to do and may then be able to take on a widened span of control. Similarly, when several employees perform either the same simple task or a group of interrelated tasks, a wide span of control is possible and often desirable. For instance, because of the routine and interdependent nature of jobs on an assembly line, one supervisor may well control the entire line.

In contrast, when jobs are more diversified or prone to change, a narrow span of control is preferable. Consider how Electronic Arts develops video games. Design, art, audio, and software development teams have specialized jobs whose products must come together in the end to create a coherent game. Although related, the complexities involved with and the advanced skills required by each job mean that one supervisor can oversee only a small number of employees.

The Delegation Process

Delegation is the process through which a manager allocates work to subordinates. In general, the delegation process involves:

> **Delegation** *process through which a manager allocates work to subordinates*
>
> **Responsibility** *duty to perform an assigned task*
>
> **Authority** *power to make the decisions necessary to complete a task*
>
> **Accountability** *obligation employees have to their manager for the successful completion of an assigned task*

1 Assigning **responsibility**, the duty to perform an assigned task

2 Granting **authority**, or the power to make the decisions necessary to complete the task

3 Creating **accountability**, the obligation employees have for the successful completion of the task

For the delegation process to work smoothly, responsibility and authority must be equivalent. Table 6.1 lists some common obstacles that hinder the delegation process, along with strategies for overcoming them.

table 6.1 Learning to Delegate Effectively

I'm afraid to delegate because...	Solution
My team doesn't know how to get the job done.	If members of your team are exhibiting opportunities for improved performance, offer them the training necessary for them to become more effective at their jobs.
I like controlling as many things as possible.	Recognize that trying to accomplish everything yourself while your team does nothing only sets you up for burnout and failure. As you begin to relinquish control, you will come to trust your team more as you watch your team members succeed.
I don't want anyone on my team outperforming me.	High-performing team members are a reflection of your success as a manager. Encourage them to excel, praise them for it, and share the success of your team with the rest of the organization.
I don't know how to delegate tasks effectively.	Consider taking a management training course or reading some books on the topic of delegating effectively.

Three Forms of Authority

As individuals are delegated responsibility and authority, a complex web of interactions develops in the form of *line, staff*, and *committee and team* authorities.

Line Authority The type of authority that flows up and down the chain of command is **line authority**. Most companies rely heavily on **line departments** linked directly to the production and sales of specific products. For example, in the division of Clark Equipment that produces forklifts and small earthmovers, line departments include purchasing, materials handling, fabrication, painting, and assembly (all of which are directly linked to production) along with sales and distribution (both of which are directly linked to sales).

As the doers and producers, each line department is essential to an organization's ability to sell and deliver finished goods. A bad decision by the manager in one department can hold up production for an entire plant. For example, the painting department manager at Clark Equipment changes a paint application on a batch of forklifts, which then show signs of peeling paint. The batch will have to be repainted (and perhaps partially reassembled) before the machines can be shipped.

Line Authority *organizational structure in which authority flows in a direct chain of command from the top of the company to the bottom*

Line Department *department directly linked to the production and sales of a specific product*

Staff Authority Some companies also rely on **staff authority**, which is based on special expertise and usually involves advising line managers in areas such as law, accounting, and human resources. A corporate attorney, for example, may advise the marketing department as it prepares a new contract with the firm's advertising agency, but will not typically make decisions that affect how the marketing department does its job. **Staff members** help line departments make decisions but do not usually have the authority to make final decisions.

Typically, the separation between line authority and staff responsibility is clearly delineated and is usually indicated in organization charts by solid lines (line authority) and dotted lines (staff responsibility), as shown in Figure 6.4. It may help to understand this separation by remembering that whereas *staff members* generally provide services to management, *line managers* are directly involved in producing the firm's products.

Staff Authority *authority based on expertise that usually involves counseling and advising line managers*

Staff Members *advisers and counselors who help line departments in making decisions but who do not have the authority to make final decisions*

Committee and Team Authority Recently, more organizations have started to grant *committee and team authority* to groups that play central roles in daily operations. A committee, for example, may consist of top managers from several major areas. If the work of the committee is especially important and if the committee members will be working together for an extended time, the organization may grant it **committee and team authority**, special authority as a decision-making body beyond the individual authority possessed by each of its members.

Committee and Team Authority *authority granted to committees or teams involved in a firm's daily operations*

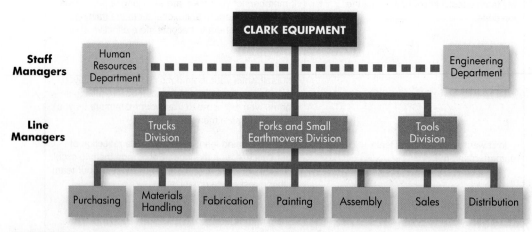

FIGURE 6.4 Line and Staff Organization

At the operating level, many firms today use **work teams** that are empowered to plan, organize, and perform their work with minimal supervision and often with special authority as well. Most U.S. companies today use teams in at least some areas; some make widespread use of teams throughout every area of their operations.

> **Work Team** *groups of operating employees who are empowered to plan and organize their own work and to perform that work with a minimum of supervision*

Basic Forms of Organizational Structure

OBJECTIVE 4

Explain

the differences among functional, divisional, matrix, and international organizational structures and describe the most popular new forms of organizational design.

Organizations can structure themselves in an almost infinite number of ways; according to specialization, for example, or departmentalization, or the decision-making hierarchy. Nevertheless, it is possible to identify four basic forms of organizational structure that reflect the general trends followed by most firms: (1) *functional*, (2) *divisional*, (3) *matrix*, and (4) *international*.

Functional Structure

Under a **functional structure**, relationships between group functions and activities determine authority. Functional structure is used by most small to medium-sized firms, which are usually structured around basic business functions: a marketing department, an operations department, and a finance department. The benefits of this approach include specialization within functional areas and smoother coordination among them.

In large firms, coordination across functional departments becomes more complicated. Functional structure also fosters centralization (which can be desirable but is usually counter to the goals of larger businesses) and makes accountability more difficult. As organizations grow, they tend to shed this form and move toward one of the other three structures. Figure 6.5 illustrates a functional structure.

> **Functional Structure** *organization structure in which authority is determined by the relationships between group functions and activities*

Divisional Structure

A **divisional structure** relies on product departmentalization. Organizations using this approach are typically structured around several product-based **divisions** that resemble separate businesses in that they produce and market their own products. The head of each division may be a corporate vice-president or, if the organization is large enough, a divisional president. In addition, each division usually has its own identity and operates as a relatively autonomous business under the larger corporate umbrella. Figure 6.6 illustrates a divisional structure.

> **Divisional Structure** *organizational structure in which corporate divisions operate as autonomous businesses under the larger corporate umbrella*
>
> **Division** *department that resembles a separate business in that it produces and markets its own products*

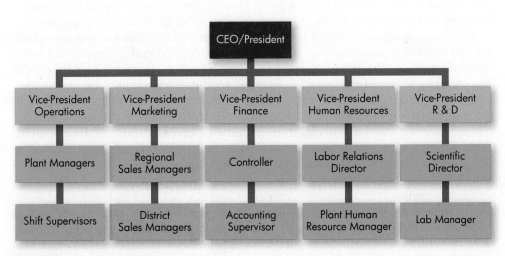

FIGURE 6.5 Functional Structure

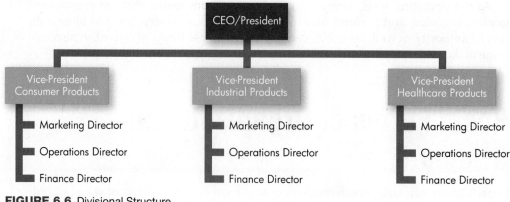

FIGURE 6.6 Divisional Structure

Johnson & Johnson, one of the most recognizable names in healthcare products, organizes its company into three major divisions: consumer healthcare products, medical devices and diagnostics, and pharmaceuticals. Each major division is then broken down further. The consumer healthcare products division relies on product departmentalization to separate baby care, skin and hair care, topical health care, oral health care, women's health, over-the-counter medicines, and nutritionals. These divisions reflect the diversity of the company, which can protect it during downturns, such as the one in 2008–2011, which showed the slowest pharmaceutical growth in four decades. Because they are divided, the other divisions are protected from this blight and can carry the company through it.

Consider that Johnson & Johnson's over-the-counter pain management medicines are essentially competition for their pain management pharmaceuticals. Divisions can maintain healthy competition among themselves by sponsoring separate advertising campaigns, fostering different corporate identities, and so forth. They can also share certain corporate-level resources (such as market research data). However, if too much control is delegated to divisional managers, corporate managers may lose touch with daily operations. Also, competition between divisions can become disruptive, and efforts in one division may duplicate those of another.[12]

Matrix Structure

Matrix Structure *organizational structure created by superimposing one form of structure onto another*

Sometimes a **matrix structure**, a combination of two separate structures, works better than either simpler structure alone. This structure gets its matrix-like appearance, when shown in a diagram, by using one underlying "permanent" organizational structure (say, the divisional structure flowing up-and-down in the diagram), and then superimposing a different organizing framework on top of it (e.g., the functional form flowing side-to-side in the diagram). This highly flexible and readily adaptable structure was pioneered by NASA for use in developing specific space programs.

Suppose a company using a functional structure wants to develop a new product as a one-time special project. A team might be created and given responsibility for that product. The project team may draw members from existing functional departments, such as finance and marketing, so that all viewpoints are represented as the new product is being developed; the marketing member may provide ongoing information about product packaging and pricing issues, for instance, and the finance member may have useful information about when funds will be available.

In some companies, the matrix organization is a temporary measure installed to complete a specific project and affecting only one part of the firm. In these firms, the end of the project usually means the end of the matrix—either a breakup of the team or a restructuring to fit it into the company's existing line-and-staff structure. Ford, for example, uses a matrix organization to design new models, such as the newest Mustang. A design team composed of people with engineering, marketing, operations, and finance expertise was created to design the new car. After its work was done, the team members moved back to their permanent functional jobs.[13]

entrepreneurship and new ventures

Making the Grade

In 1965, undistinguished Yale undergrad Fred Smith wrote a paper describing how automated technology necessitated quicker, more reliable transportation. According to legend, the paper received a poor grade. But Smith himself debunks this myth. "It's become a well-known story because everybody likes to flout authority. But to be honest, I don't really remember what grade I got."

Whatever the grade, the idea was a winner. After serving in Vietnam, Smith invested his own money to start the air transport business Federal Express. Now called FedEx, the firm was revolutionary in pioneering the hub-and-spoke system and using bar codes, handheld PDAs, and package tracking to compete with the monopolistic U.S. Postal Service.

When rival UPS entered the airfreight segment in 2000, FedEx acquired several key players in the ground transportation industry. "The economics of airplanes are such that we couldn't just keep taking prices down," Smith says. "We finally realized that if we wanted to grow, we had to get into surface transportation." FedEx's new fleet capitalized on the brand's reputation for speed and reliability: "People say 'FedEx this' when they mean 'Get it someplace fast,'" says investor Timothy M. Ghriskey. "No one says 'UPS this.'"

Although standardization is important, FedEx's commitment to decentralization breeds innovation. Managers are

Sorge/Alamy

encouraged and rewarded for questioning, challenging, and developing new ideas, which are always given serious consideration. Developments have included teaming up with Motorola and Microsoft to create a proprietary pocket-size PC, sending package information to cell phones, and creating software products for small business logistics. "Engage in constant change," is a mantra for CEO Smith, and he adds, "Companies that don't take risks—some of which are going to work and some of which aren't—are going to end up getting punched up by the marketplace."[14]

In other settings, the matrix organization is a semipermanent fixture. Figure 6.7 shows how Martha Stewart Living Omnimedia has created a permanent matrix organization for its lifestyle business. As you can see, the company is organized broadly into media and merchandising groups, each of which has specific product and product groups. For instance, there is an Internet group housed within the media group. Layered on top of this structure are teams of lifestyle experts led by area specialists organized into groups, such as cooking, entertainment, weddings, crafts, and so forth. Although each group targets specific customer needs, they all work, as necessary, across all product groups. An area specialist in weddings, for example, might contribute to an article on wedding planning for an Omnimedia magazine, contribute a story idea for an Omnimedia cable television program, and supply content for an Omnimedia site. This same individual might also help select fabrics suitable for wedding gowns that are to be retailed.

International Structure

Several different **international organizational structures** have emerged in response to the need to manufacture, purchase, and sell in global markets.

For example, when Walmart opened its first store outside the United States in 1992, it set up a special projects team. In the mid-1990s, the firm created a small international department to handle overseas expansion. By 1999 international sales and expansion had become such a major part of operations that a separate international division headed up by a senior vice-president was created. By 2002, international operations had become so important that the international division was further divided into geographic areas, such as Mexico and Europe. And as the firm expands into more foreign markets, such as Russia and India, new units are created to oversee those operations.[15]

International Organizational Structures *approaches to organizational structure developed in response to the need to manufacture, purchase, and sell in global markets*

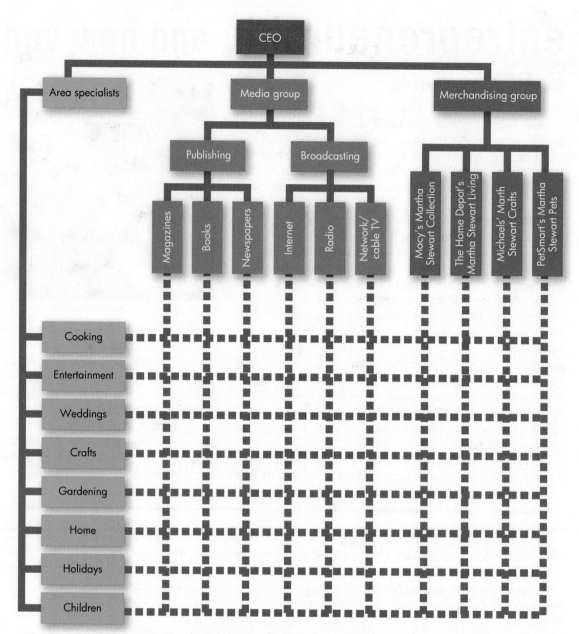

FIGURE 6.7 Matrix Organization of Martha Stewart Living Omnimedia

Some companies adopt a truly global structure in which they acquire resources (including capital), produce goods and services, engage in research and development, and sell products in whatever local market is appropriate, without consideration of national boundaries. Until a few years ago, General Electric (GE) kept its international business operations as separate divisions, as illustrated in Figure 6.8. Now, however, the company functions as one integrated global organization. GE businesses around the world connect and interact with each other constantly, and managers freely move back and forth among them. This integration is also reflected in GE's executive team, which includes executives from Spain, Japan, Scotland, Ireland, and Italy.[16]

Organizational Design for the Twenty-first Century

As the world grows increasingly complex and fast-paced, organizations also continue to seek new forms of organization that permit them to compete effectively. Among the most popular of these new forms are the *team organization*, the *virtual organization*, and the *learning organization*.

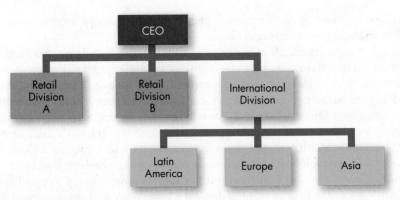

FIGURE 6.8 International Division Structure

Team Organization *Team organization* relies almost exclusively on project-type teams, with little or no underlying functional hierarchy. People float from project to project as dictated by their skills and the demands of those projects. As the term suggests, team authority is the underlying foundation of organizations that adopt this organizational structure.

Virtual Organization Closely related to the team organization is the *virtual organization.* A virtual organization has little or no formal structure. Typically, it has only a handful of permanent employees, a small staff, and a modest administrative facility. As the needs of the organization change, its managers bring in temporary workers, lease facilities, and outsource basic support services to meet the demands of each unique situation. As the situation changes, the temporary workforce changes in parallel, with some people leaving the organization and others entering. Facilities and the subcontracted services also change. In other words, the virtual organization exists only in response to its own needs.[17] This structure would be applicable to research or consulting firms that hire consultants based on the specific content knowledge required by each unique project. As the projects change, so too does the composition of the organization. Figure 6.9 illustrates a hypothetical virtual organization.

Learning Organization The so-called *learning organization* works to integrate continuous improvement with continuous employee learning and development. Specifically, a learning organization works to facilitate the lifelong learning and

FIGURE 6.9 The Virtual Organization

personal development of all of its employees while continually transforming itself to respond to changing demands and needs.

Although managers might approach the concept of a learning organization from a variety of perspectives, the most frequent goals are superior quality, continuous improvement, and performance measurement. The idea is that the most consistent and logical strategy for achieving continuous improvement is to constantly upgrade employee talent, skill, and knowledge. For example, if each employee in an organization learns one new thing each day and can translate that knowledge into work-related practice, continuous improvement will logically follow. Indeed, organizations that wholeheartedly embrace this approach believe that only through constant employee learning can continuous improvement really occur. Shell Oil's Shell Learning Center boasts state-of-the-art classrooms and instructional technology, lodging facilities, a restaurant, and recreational amenities. Line managers rotate through the center to fulfill teaching assignments, and Shell employees routinely attend training programs, seminars, and related activities.

OBJECTIVE 5
Describe
the informal organization and discuss intrapreneuring.

Informal Organization *network, unrelated to the firm's formal authority structure, of everyday social interactions among company employees*

Informal Organization

The structure of a company, however, is by no means limited to the *formal organization* as represented by the organization chart and the formal assignment of authority. Frequently, the **informal organization**, everyday social interactions among employees that transcend formal jobs and job interrelationships, effectively alters a company's formal structure.[18] This level of organization is sometimes just as powerful—if not more powerful—than the formal structure. When Hewlett-Packard fired its CEO, Carly Fiorina, a few years ago, much of the discussion that led to her firing took place outside formal structural arrangements in the organization. Members of the board of directors, for example, held secret meetings and reached confidential agreements among themselves before Fiorina's future with the company was addressed in a formal manner.[19]

On the negative side, the informal organization can reinforce office politics that put the interests of individuals ahead of those of the firm and can disseminate distorted or inaccurate information. For example, if the informal organization is highlighting false information about impending layoffs, valuable employees may act quickly (and unnecessarily) to seek other employment.

Informal Groups

Informal groups are simply groups of people who decide to interact among themselves. They may be people who work together in a formal sense or who just get together for lunch, during breaks, or after work. They may talk about business, the boss, or nonwork-related topics such as families, movies, or sports. Their impact on the organization may be positive (if they work together to support the organization), negative (if they work together in ways that run counter to the organization's interests), or irrelevant (if what they do is unrelated to the organization).

Informal groups can be a powerful force that managers cannot ignore.[20] One writer described how a group of employees at a furniture factory subverted their boss's efforts to increase production. They tacitly agreed to produce a reasonable amount of work but not to work too hard. One man kept a stockpile of completed work hidden as a backup in case he got too far behind. In another example, auto workers described how they left out gaskets and seals and put soft-drink bottles inside doors to cause customer complaints.[21] Of course, informal groups can also be a positive force, as when people work together to help out a colleague who has suffered a personal tragedy. For example, several instances of this behavior were reported in the wake of the devastating tornadoes that swept through Alabama and Missouri in 2011 and after hurricane Sandy devastated parts of the northeast in 2012.

In recent years the Internet has served as a platform for the emergence of more and different kinds of informal or interest groups. As one example, Yahoo! includes a wide array of interest groups that bring together people with common interests. And increasingly, workers who lose their jobs as a result of layoffs are banding together electronically to offer moral support to one another and to facilitate networking as they all look for new jobs.[22] Indeed, social media plays a major role in informal groups today.

Organizational Grapevine

The **grapevine** is an informal communication network that can permeate an entire organization. Grapevines are found in all organizations except the smallest, but they do not always follow the same patterns as, nor do they necessarily coincide with, formal channels of authority and communication. Research has identified two kinds of grapevines.[23] One such grapevine, the gossip chain, occurs when one person spreads the message to many other people. Each one, in turn, may either keep the information confidential or pass it on to others. The gossip chain is likely to carry personal information. The other common grapevine is the cluster chain, in which one person passes the information to a selected few individuals. Some of the receivers pass the information to a few other individuals; the rest keep it to themselves.

Grapevine *informal communication network that runs through an organization*

There is some disagreement about how accurate the information carried by the grapevine is, but research is increasingly finding it to be fairly accurate, especially when the information is based on fact rather than speculation. One study found that the grapevine may be between 75 percent and 95 percent accurate.[24] That same study also found that informal communication is increasing in many organizations for several basic reasons. One contributing factor is the recent increase in merger, acquisition, and takeover activity. Because such activity can greatly affect the people within an organization, it follows that they may spend more time talking about it.[25] The second contributing factor is that as more and more corporations move facilities from inner cities to suburbs, employees tend to talk less and less to others outside the organization and more and more to one another. Yet another contributing factor is simply the widespread availability of information technology that makes it easier than ever before for people to communicate quickly and easily. Much like in informal groups, social media plays a growing role in the grapevine.

More recently, another study looked at the effects of the recent recession and large-scale job losses on informal communication. More than half of the survey participants reported a sharp increase in gossip and rumors in their organizations. The same survey also reported an increase in the amount of eavesdropping in the most businesses.[26] Further, in another recent survey, 32 percent of people claimed to use their work e-mail inappropriately and 48 percent admitted gossiping with other employees through their e-mail.[27]

Attempts to eliminate the grapevine are fruitless, but fortunately the manager does have some control over it. By maintaining open channels of communication and responding vigorously to inaccurate information, the manager can minimize the damage the grapevine can do. The grapevine can actually be an asset. By learning who the key people in the grapevine are, for example, the manager can partially control the information they receive and use the grapevine to sound out employee reactions to new ideas, such as a change in human resource policies or benefit packages. The manager can also get valuable information from the grapevine and use it to improve decision making.[28]

Intrapreneuring

Good managers recognize that the informal organization exists whether they want it or not and can use it not only to reinforce the formal organization, but also to harness its energy to improve productivity.

Many firms, including Rubbermaid, Dreamworks, 3M, and Xerox, support **intrapreneuring**, creating and maintaining the innovation and flexibility of a small-business environment within a large, bureaucratic structure. Historically, most innovations have

Intrapreneuring *process of creating and maintaining the innovation and flexibility of a small-business environment within the confines of a large organization*

come from individuals in small businesses. As businesses increase in size, however, innovation and creativity tend to become casualties in the battle for more sales and profits. In some large companies, new ideas are even discouraged, and champions of innovation have been stalled in midcareer. At Lockheed Martin, the Advanced Development Programs (ADP) encourages intrapreneurship in the tradition of Skunk Works, a legendary team developed in 1943 as engineer Kelly Johnson's response to Lockheed's need for a powerful jet fighter. Johnson's innovative organization approach broke all the rules, and not only did it work, but it also taught Lockheed the value of encouraging that kind of thinking.[29]

There are three intrapreneurial roles in large organizations.[30] To successfully use intrapreneurship to encourage creativity and innovation, the organization must find one or more individuals to perform these roles. The *inventor* is the person who actually conceives of and develops the new idea, product, or service by means of the creative process. Because the inventor may lack the expertise or motivation to oversee the transformation of the product or service from an idea into a marketable entity, however, a second role comes into play. A *product champion* is usually a middle manager who learns about the project and becomes committed to it. He or she helps overcome organizational resistance and convinces others to take the innovation seriously. The product champion may have only limited understanding of the technological aspects of the innovation. Nevertheless, product champions are skilled at knowing how the organization works, whose support is needed to push the project forward, and where to go to secure the resources necessary for successful development. A *sponsor* is a top-level manager who approves of and supports a project. This person may fight for the budget needed to develop an idea, overcome arguments against a project, and use organizational politics to ensure the project's survival. With a sponsor in place, the inventor's idea has a much better chance of being successfully developed.

summary of learning objectives

OBJECTIVE 1

Discuss the factors that influence a firm's organizational structure. (pp. 202–204)

Each organization must develop an appropriate *organizational structure*—the specification of the jobs to be done and the ways in which those jobs relate to one another. Most organizations change structures almost continuously. Firms prepare *organization charts* to clarify structure and to show employees where they fit into a firm's operations. Each box represents a job, and solid lines define the *chain of command*, or *reporting relationships*. The charts of large firms are complex and include individuals at many levels. Because size prevents them from charting every manager, they may create single organization charts for overall corporate structure and separate charts for divisions. An organization's structure is determined by a variety of factors, including the organization's mission and strategy, size, environment, and history. Structure is not static but is changed and modified frequently.

OBJECTIVE 2

Explain specialization and departmentalization as two of the building blocks of organizational structure. (pp. 204–208)

The process of identifying specific jobs and designating people to perform them leads to *job specialization*. After they're specialized, jobs are grouped into logical units—the process of *departmentalization*. Departmentalization follows one (or any combination) of five forms:

1. *functional departmentalization* based on functions or activities
2. *product departmentalization* based on products or services offered
3. *process departmentalization* based on production processes used to create goods and services
4. *customer departmentalization* based on customer types or customer groups
5. *geographic departmentalization* based on geographic areas

Larger companies may take advantage of different types of departmentalization for various levels.

OBJECTIVE 3

Describe centralization and decentralization, delegation, and authority as the key ingredients in establishing the decision-making hierarchy. (pp. 208–213)

After jobs have been specialized and departmentalized, firms establish decision-making hierarchies. One major issue addressed through the creation of the decision-making hierarchy involves whether the firm will be relatively *centralized* or relatively *decentralized.* In a centralized organization, decision-making authority is retained at the top levels of the organization. Centralized authority systems typically require multiple layers of management and thus *tall organizational structures.* Conversely, in a decentralized organization, most decision-making authority is delegated to lower levels of management. A related concept is *span of control*, which refers to the number of people who report to a manager. Tall, centralized organizations tend to have a narrow span of control, whereas flat, centralized organizations tend to have wider spans of control.

Decentralized firms tend to have relatively fewer layers of management, resulting in a *flat organizational structure. Delegation* is the process through which a manager allocates work to subordinates. In general, the delegation process involves three steps:

1. the assignment of *responsibility*
2. the granting of *authority,*
3. the creation of *accountability.*

As individuals are delegated responsibility and authority in a firm, a complex web of interactions develops.

These interactions may take one of three forms of authority: line, staff, or committee and team. Line authority follows the chain of command, and staff authority relies on expertise in areas such as law, accounting, and human resources.

OBJECTIVE 4

Explain the differences among functional, divisional, matrix, and international organizational structures and describe the most popular new forms of organizational design. (pp. 213–218)

Most firms rely on one of four basic forms of organizational structure: (1) *functional*, (2) *divisional*, (3) *matrix*, or (4) *international*. A functional structure is based on organizational functions, such as marketing, finance, or operations. A divisional structure, in contrast, groups activities in terms of distinct product or service groups. A matrix structure, a combination of two structures, imposes one type of structure on top of another. Several different international organizational structures have emerged in response to the need to manufacture, purchase, and sell in global markets. A company may start with a small international department that may grow into an international division. As global competition becomes more complex, companies may experiment with ways to respond. Some adopt truly global structures, acquiring resources and producing and selling products in local markets without consideration of national boundaries.

Organizations also continue to seek new forms of organization that permit them to compete effectively. The most popular new forms include

1. *team organizations*, which rely almost exclusively on project-type teams with little or no underlying functional hierarchy.
2. *virtual organizations*, which have little or no formal structure and just a handful of employees.
3. *learning organizations*, which work to integrate continuous improvement with ongoing employee learning and development.

OBJECTIVE 5

Describe the informal organization and discuss intrapreneuring. (pp. 218–220)

The *formal organization* is the part that can be represented in chart form. The *informal organization*, everyday social interactions among employees that transcend formal jobs and job interrelationships, may alter formal structure. There are two important elements in most informal organizations. *Informal groups* consist of people who decide to interact among themselves. Their impact on a firm may be positive, negative, or irrelevant. The *grapevine* is an informal communication network that can run through an entire organization. Because it can be harnessed to improve productivity, some organizations encourage the informal organization. Many firms also support *intrapreneuring*—creating and maintaining the innovation and flexibility of a small business within the confines of a large, bureaucratic structure. In large organizations, intrapreneurship requires the participation of individuals who will serve roles as inventors, product champions, and sponsors.

key terms

accountability (p. 211)
authority (p. 211)
centralized organization (p. 208)
chain of command (p. 203)
committee and team
    authority (p. 212)
customer departmentalization (p. 207)
decentralized organization (p. 209)
delegation (p. 211)
departmentalization (p. 206)
division (p. 213)
divisional structure (p. 213)

flat organizational structure (p. 210)
functional departmentalization (p. 207)
functional structure (p. 213)
geographic departmentalization (p. 207)
grapevine (p. 219)
informal organization (p. 218)
international organizational structures
    (p. 215)
intrapreneuring (p. 219)
job specialization (p. 204)
line authority (p. 212)
line department (p. 212)

matrix structure (p. 214)
organization chart (p. 203)
organizational structure (p. 202)
process departmentalization (p. 207)
product departmentalization (p. 207)
profit center (p. 206)
responsibility (p. 211)
span of control (p. 211)
staff authority (p. 212)
staff members (p. 212)
tall organizational structure (p. 210)
work team (p. 213)

MyBizLab

Go to **pearsonglobaleditions.com/mybizlab** to complete the problems marked with this icon ⊛.

questions & exercises

QUESTIONS FOR REVIEW

6-1. Describe the five basic forms of departmentalization.

6-2. What are the advantages and disadvantages of a centralized organizational structure?

6-3. What is the difference between responsibility and authority?

⊛ **6-4.** Why do some managers have difficulties in delegating authority? Of these reasons, which do you think would be the most significant issue for you?

⊛ **6-5.** Why is a company's informal organization important?

QUESTIONS FOR ANALYSIS

6-6. Draw up an organization chart for your college or university.

6-7. Describe a hypothetical organizational structure for a small printing firm. Describe changes that might be necessary as the business grows.

⊛ **6-8.** Do you think that you would want to work in a matrix organization, such as Martha Stewart Living Omnimedia, where you were assigned simultaneously to multiple units or groups? Why or why not?

APPLICATION EXERCISES

6-9. Interview the manager of a local service business, such as a fast-food restaurant. What types of tasks does this manager typically delegate? Is the appropriate authority also delegated in each case?

6-10. Select a company where you would like to work one day. Using online research, determine if the company has a functional, divisional, matrix, international, team, virtual, or learning organization. Explain how you arrived at this conclusion. Do you believe that their organizational structure is consistent with the organization's mission?

building a business: continuing team exercise

Assignment

Meet with your team members and discuss your new business venture within the context of this chapter. Develop specific responses to the following:

6-11. Thinking ahead one year, how many employees do you expect that you will have in your business? How did you come to this conclusion?

6-12. Draw a sample organization chart for your business in one year. Although you won't know the names of all your employees, your organization chart should include job titles.

6-13. Will decision-making in your business be centralized or decentralized? Be sure to support your conclusion.

6-14. How do you think that your organizational structure will change over time? Will it be the same in 10 years?

building your business skills

GETTING WITH THE PROGRAM

Goal

To encourage you to understand the relationship between organizational structure and a company's ability to attract and keep valued employees.

Background Information

You are the founder of a small but growing high-tech company that develops new computer software. With your current workload and new contracts in the pipeline, your business is thriving, except for one problem: You cannot find computer programmers for product development. Worse yet, current staff members are being lured away by other high-tech firms. After suffering a particularly discouraging personnel raid in which competitors captured three of your most valued employees, you schedule a meeting with your director of human resources to plan organizational changes designed to encourage worker loyalty. You already pay top dollar, but the continuing exodus tells you that programmers are looking for something more.

Method

Working with three or four classmates, identify some ways in which specific organizational changes might improve the working environment and encourage employee loyalty. As you analyze the following factors, ask yourself the obvious question: If I were a programmer, what organizational changes would encourage me to stay?

- *Level of job specialization.* With many programmers describing their jobs as tedious because of the focus on detail in a narrow work area, what changes, if any, would you make in job specialization? Right now, for instance, few of your programmers have any say in product design.
- *Decision-making hierarchy.* What decision-making authority would encourage people to stay? Is expanding employee authority likely to work better in a centralized or decentralized organization?
- *Team authority.* Can team empowerment make a difference? Taking the point of view of the worker, describe the ideal team.
- *Intrapreneuring.* What can your company do to encourage and reward innovation?

follow-up questions

6-15. With the average computer programmer earning nearly $70,000, and with all competitive firms paying top dollar, why might organizational issues be critical in determining employee loyalty?

6-16. If you were a programmer, what organizational factors would make a difference to you? Why?

6-17. As the company founder, how willing would you be to make major organizational changes in light of the shortage of qualified programmers?

exercising your ethics

I HEARD IT THROUGH THE GRAPEVINE

The Situation

Assume that you are a divisional manager at a large high-tech company. The company has just lost a large contract, and the human resources direction has just advised company executives that they must cut the workforce by 10 percent within three months to preserve their financial position. You are distressed at the prospect of losing long-time employees, especially those nearing retirement or with young families.

The Dilemma

As you ponder the situation, another regional member has brought up a potential solution that will spare you from actually laying off employees. "The grapevine has worked against us in the past, so let's make it work for us this time. If we leak word that the company is planning to cut pay by 15 percent for most of the workforce as a result of the loss of this contract, people will get scared. They'll start looking for jobs or reevaluating retirement and they layoff will take care of itself. Once we've reach the desired level of resignations, we will reassure the remaining employees that their jobs are secure."

QUESTION TO ADDRESS

6-18. What are the ethical issues in this situation?

6-19. What do you think most people would do in this situation?

6-20. What would you do in this situation?

team exercise

TO POACH, OR NOT TO POACH...

The Situation

Platinum Resorts is a chain of all-inclusive luxury resorts, with locations in Playa Del Carmen, Mexico; Negril, Jamaica; Freeport, Bahamas; and Key West, Florida. Some customers return to the same location year after year, and others enjoy trying out different locations in the group. However, sales are down and customer complaints are up. Resort managers are pointing fingers and insisting that the middle managers at each location (front desk, food service, housekeeping, and maintenance) are not upholding company standards. Currently, the company has adopted a divisional structure, with a vice-president for each of the four resorts.

The Decision

Frustrated by inconsistent service and weak sales, Platinum Resorts has enlisted the services of a consultant. After visiting each of the resorts and speaking with employees and guests, the consultant is recommending that the company move from its current divisional structure to a matrix organization. The consultant explains that a matrix organization is used by many innovative organizations, such as NASA, to achieve functional and divisional control. Although some managers think that this is a great idea, others are concerned that their authority and control may be undermined by this new organizational structure. Platinum Resorts knows that something has to change, but you are unsure if this is the right solution.

Team Activity

Assemble a group of four students and assign each group member to one of the following roles:
- President of Platinum Resorts
- Sales manager for the Playa Del Carmen, Mexico resort
- Housekeeper at the Key West, Florida resort
- Guest at the Negril, Jamaica resort

ACTION STEPS

6-21. Without consulting other members of the team, and from the perspective of your assigned role, do you think that Platinum Resorts should adopt a matrix structure?

6-22. Assemble your group and have each member present the potential pros and cons of organizing as a matrix organization.

6-23. As a group, develop an organizational chart for the company in its current divisional structure and the proposed matrix structure.

6-24. Develop a list of alternatives to converting to a matrix structure.

6-25. Considering all perspectives, what is the best decision of Platinum Resorts?

cases

Organizing for Success at South African Airways

Continued from page 202

In April 2013, SAA received a South African government approved new CEO. Monwabisi Kalawe was the third person to take up the position since September 2012. At that point, Chairwoman Cheryl Carolus and her entire board had walked out, including the CEO Siza Mzimela. Any talk of a coherent reorganization of SAA hung in the balance.

QUESTIONS FOR DISCUSSION

6-26. Identify as many examples related to organization structure as possible in this case.

6-27. In what ways does its structure help and hurt South African Airways?

6-28. If South African Airways wanted to change its structure, what structure would you suggest?

6-29. What aspects, if any, of virtual and learning organization structure do you see at South African Airways?

Heard it Through the Grapevine

When you think of the word "gossip," it's most likely that the term has negative connotations. Take it one step farther, into the workplace, and you almost certainly have concerns. However, there is considerable research to support the claim that gossip, or the grapevine, is an important part of organizational culture. According to Professor Kathleen Reardon of the USC Marshall School of Business, "We learn who we are through what people say to us and about us."[31] Managing the office grapevine and your role in this informal communication can be tricky.

Several guidelines can help you understand when to participate in gossip as a sender or receiver. First, you should understand the benefits of gossip. Gossip, or the office grapevine, may be the first place that you hear important information, such as a new job opening up or a major contract that the company is about to sign. However, as you pass along information, you must remember that what you say will reflect upon you. If you share negative information about a coworker, it is very likely that others may come to distrust you. In addition, you should carefully consider the people with whom you share gossip and information, making sure that they will keep confidential information private. Your supervisor may be particularly uncomfortable if you develop a reputation as a gossip, as your comments may be perceived as threatening. Finally, be very careful about the medium that you choose to share information. An email is never private and should not be used for any communication that you would not want shared publicly.[32]

As a manager, you may have a slightly different perspective on gossip or the office grapevine. You may be concerned that gossip limits your ability to control how information is shared and may limit your power. Holly Green, in an article in *Fortune* magazine, shares several suggestions about managing the office grapevine.[33] A vigorous grapevine is often the sign of boredom. Rather than having employees spend hours a week gossiping about others, find other outlets for their creative abilities. You should also realize that grapevines grow most quickly when information is scarce. Employees turn to the grapevine when they believe that they are not getting enough information from formal channels of communication. Therefore, to control rampant gossip, a manager should work towards intentionally sharing as much information as possible. Managers should also keep their ear to the grapevine, as it may convey important information, such as manageable concerns of employees. Managed correctly, the grapevine can be a powerful tool for employees and managers.

QUESTIONS FOR DISCUSSION

6-30. Thinking about your office or college, what types of information is conveyed through the grapevine? How often is the information accurate?

6-31. Does a flat organization encourage or discourage office gossip? What leads you to this conclusion?

6-32. Do you think that the grapevine would be more or less active in a matrix organization? Why?

6-33. Many companies encourage their employees to form social relationships outside of work to build a sense of camaraderie. How would these informal groups feed or limit the grapevine?

6-34. Consider the following situation: You are the HR manager at a medium sized business and the company's executives have decided that they must cut the workforce by 5%. You don't want to layoff anyone, so you "leak" information to a few people in the company that layoffs are imminent, hoping that this might motivate some employees to find jobs elsewhere. If people end up leaving on their own, you will not have to implement layoffs. Do you think that this is an ethical use of the grapevine? Why or why not?

MyBizLab

Go to **pearsonglobaleditions.com/mybizlab** *for the following Assisted-graded writing questions:*

6-35. Each organization's structure is unique, but most structures can be grouped into four basic forms. There are advantages and disadvantages to each form of organization structure. Which of the four basic forms of organizational structure would you rather work in? Write an essay: (a) Explaining your choice, including the advantages and disadvantages of that form of organizational structure, and (b) Describing under what conditions that structure might work best.

6-36. Many new organization types have emerged in the 21st Century. Among these are team organizations, virtual organizations, and learning organizations. What challenges are imposed by the implementation of each of these organizational designs? How does each type affect manager/employee relationships? What impact would each type of organization have on strategy?

6-37. Mybizlab Only—comprehensive writing assignment for this chapter.

end notes

1 http://www.flysaa.com/mg/en/home.action (accessed 15/10/2013); http://www.staralliance.com/en/about/airlines/south-africa_airlines/ (accessed 15/10/2013)

2 See Royston Greenwood and Danny Miller, "Tackling Design Anew: Getting Back to the Heart of Organizational Theory," *Academy of Management Perspectives*, November 2010, pp. 78–88.

3 Joann S. Lublin, "Place vs. Product: It's Tough to Choose a Management Model," *Wall Street Journal*, June 27, 2001, A1, A4; Joann Muller, "Ford: Why It's Worse Than You Think," *BusinessWeek*, June 25, 2001, pp. 58–59; *Hoover's Handbook of American Business 2013*, (Austin, Texas: Hoover's Business Press, 2013), pp. 140–142.

4 "How Mulally Helped Turn Ford Around," *USA Today*, July 18, 2011, p. 2B; http://corporate.ford.com/microsites/sustainability-report-2011-12/blueprint-strategy.

5 Steinway & Sons, "Steinway History: Leadership Through Craftsmanship and Innovation," 2012, at www.steinway.com, accessed on April 11, 2013; Steinway & Sons, "Online Factory Tour," 2012, at http://archive.steinway.com, accessed on April 11, 2013; Victor Verney, "88 Keys: The Making of a Steinway Piano," *All About Jazz*, June 18, 2012, at www.allaboutjazz.com, accessed on April 11, 2013; WGBH (Boston), "*Note by Note*: The Making of Steinway L1037," 2010, at www.wgbh.org, accessed on April 11, 2013; M. Eric Johnson, Joseph Hall, and David Pyke, "Technology and Quality at Steinway & Sons," Tuck School of Business at Dartmouth, May 13, 2005, at http://mba.tuck.dartmouth.edu, accessed on April 11, 2013.

6 AllBusiness.com, "Kraft Foods North America Announces New Management Structure," September 28, 2000 (March 5, 2011), at http://www.allbusiness.com/food-beverage/food-beverage-overview/6505848-1.html.

7   See Levi Strauss & Co., at http://www.levistrauss.com/ Company/WorldwideRegions.aspx.

8   "Blowing Up Pepsi," *BusinessWeek*, April 27, 2009, pp. 32–36; *Hoover's Handbook of American Business 2013* (Austin, Texas: Hoover's Business Press, 2013), pp. 638–639.

9   Michael E. Raynor and Joseph L. Bower, "Lead From the Center," *Harvard Business Review*, May 2001, 93–102.

10   Michelle Conlin, "Call Centers in the Rec Room," *BusinessWeek*, January 23, 2006, at www.businessweek.com, accessed on April 11, 2013; Pete Engardio, "The Future of Outsourcing," *BusinessWeek*, January 30, 2006, at www.businessweek.com, accessed on April 11, 2013; Manjeet Kripalani with Brian Grow, "Offshoring: Spreading the Gospel," *BusinessWeek*, March 6, 2006, at www.businessweek.com, accessed on April 11, 2013.

11   Gary Hamel, "What Google, Whole Foods Do Best," *Fortune*, September 27, 2007, p. 59.

12   *Hoover's Handbook of American Business 2013* (Austin, Texas: Hoover's Business Press, 2013), pp. 58–60; Brian Dumaine, "How I Delivered the Goods," *Fortune Small Business*, October 2002, pp. 78–81; Charles Haddad, "FedEx: Gaining on the Ground," *BusinessWeek*, December 16, 2002, pp. 126–128; Claudia H. Deutsch, "FedEx Has Hit the Ground Running, but Will Its Legs Tire?" *New York Times*, October 13, 2002, p. BU7; http://www.Forbes.com/finance (February 16, 2006); PBS.org, "Who Made America" (June 19, 2008), at http://www.pbs.org/wgbh/theymadeamerica/whomade/fsmith_hi.html.

13   phx.corporate-ir.net/phoenix.zhtml?c=96022&p=irol-newsArticle&ID=1489110&highlight=.

14   John Simons, "Prognosis Looks Good for J&J," *Fortune*, November 16, 2007, pp. 70–71; Johnson & Johnson, "Company Structure" (June 19, 2008), at http://www.jnj.com/connect/about-jnj/company-structure/.

15   "Wal-Mart Acquires Interspar," *Management Ventures* (July 20, 2001), at http://www.mvi-insights.com/Index.aspx; Kerry Capell et al., "Wal-Mart's Not-So-Secret British Weapon," *BusinessWeek Online* (July 20, 2001), at http://www.businessweek.com/2000/00_04/b3665095.htm; Brent Schlender, "Wal-Mart's $288 Billion Meeting," *Fortune*, April 18, 2005, pp. 90–106; see http://walmartstores.com.

16   Thomas A. Stewart, "See Jack. See Jack Run," *Fortune*, September 27, 1999, pp. 124–271; Jerry Useem, "America's Most Admired Companies," *Fortune*, March 7, 2005, pp. 67–82; See GE.com, "Executive Leaders," at http://www.ge.com/company/leadership/executives.html.

17   Leslie P. Willcocks and Robert Plant, "Getting from Bricks to Clicks," *Sloan Management Review*, Spring 2001, pp. 50–60.

18   "The Office Chart That Really Counts," *BusinessWeek*, February 27, 2006, pp. 48–49.

19   Carol Loomis, "How the HP Board KO'd Carly," *Fortune*, March 7, 2005, pp. 99–102.

20   Rob Cross, Nitin Nohria, and Andrew Parker, "Six Myths about Informal Networks—And How to Overcome Them," *Sloan Management Review*, Spring 2002, pp. 67–77.

21   Robert Schrank, *Ten Thousand Working Days* (Cambridge, MA: MIT Press, 1978); Bill Watson, "Counter Planning on the Shop Floor," in Peter Frost, Vance Mitchell, and Walter Nord (eds.), *Organizational Reality*, 2nd ed. (Glenview, IL: Scott, Foresman, 1982), pp. 286–294.

22   "After Layoffs, More Workers Band Together," *Wall Street Journal*, February 26, 2002, p. B1.

23   Keith Davis, "Management Communication and the Grapevine," *Harvard Business Review*, September–October 1953, pp. 43–49.

24   "Spread the Word: Gossip Is Good," *Wall Street Journal*, October 4, 1988, p. B1.

25   See David M. Schweiger and Angelo S. DeNisi, "Communication with Employees Following a Merger: A Longitudinal Field Experiment," *Academy of Management Journal*, March 1991, pp. 110–135.

26   "Job Fears Make Offices All Fears," *Wall Street Journal*, January 20, 2009, p. B7.

27   Institute of Leadership and Management, "32% of People Making Inappropriate Use of Work Emails," April 20, 2011; accessed on April 12, 2013.

28   Nancy B. Kurland and Lisa Hope Pelled, "Passing the Word: Toward a Model of Gossip and Power in the Workplace," *Academy of Management Review*, 2000, Vol. 25, No. 2, pp. 428–438.

29   Lockheed Martin, "Skunk Works" (June 19, 2008), at http://www.lockheedmartin.com/aeronautics/skunkworks/index.html.

30   See Gifford Pinchot III, *Intrapreneuring* (New York: Harper & Row, 1985).

31   Gallo, Amy. "Go Ahead and Gossip." *Harvard Business Review*. N.p., 21 Mar. 2013. Web. 19 June 2013.

32   Spiers, Carole. "Managing Office Gossip." Gulfnews.com. Al Nisr Publishing LLC, 7 Jan. 2013. Web. 19 June 2013

33   Green, Holly. "How to Prune Your Organizational Grapevine." Forbes. *Forbes Magazine*, 22 May 2012. Web. 19 June 2013.

There isn't a "perfect" way to produce a product or service; just be flexible. An open

mind and the

willingness to try new things drive efficient

operations.

AFTER READING THIS CHAPTER, YOU SHOULD BE ABLE TO:

OBJECTIVE 1 **Explain** the meaning of the term *production* or *operations* and describe the three kinds of utility that operations processes provide for adding customer value.

OBJECTIVE 2 **Identify** the characteristics that distinguish *service operations* from *goods production*.

OBJECTIVE 3 **Explain** how companies with different business strategies are best served by having different operations capabilities.

OBJECTIVE 4 **Identify** the major factors that are considered in operations planning.

OBJECTIVE 5 **Discuss** the information contained in four kinds of operations schedules—the master operations schedule, detailed schedule, staff schedule, and project schedule.

OBJECTIVE 6 **Discuss** the two key activities required for operations control.

OBJECTIVE 7 **Identify** the activities and underlying objectives involved in total quality management.

OBJECTIVE 8 **Explain** how a supply chain strategy differs from traditional strategies for coordinating operations among firms.

MyBizLab®

✪ Improve Your Grade!

Visit **pearsonglobaleditions.com/mybizlab** for simulations, tutorials, and end-of-chapter problems.

simulations

videos

assisted-graded writing

Over 10 million students improved their results using the Pearson MyLabs.

Ryanair Customer Satisfaction— but Who to Believe?

Ryanair is a Dublin-based, low-cost airline. It was founded in 1985 when it offered a single route from Waterford to London. The company went public in 1997 and used the revenue to finance a rapid expansion program to make it a pan-European airline. Since then, it has continued to grow and is now one of Europe's largest carriers.

Ryanair is the epitome of low-cost airlines, often at the forefront of pushing the concept of no-frills to the absolute limit. Recent aircraft feature non-reclining seats, no seat-back pockets, and life jackets stored overhead. These changes were made to reduce the turnaround time.

Ryanair has had its fair share of customer complaints. Indeed, it has been described as having an appalling customer service policy. In 2007, *The Economist* described the company as being somewhat off-hand with a reputation for being nasty and rude. In response to European Union Regulation 261/2004, which requires airlines to pay for meals and accommodation to customers who have experienced cancelled or delayed flights, the airline's reaction was innovative. Beginning April 2011, all tickets would carry a surcharge to cover the airline's potential costs of providing this support. In 2004, in response to the demand that wheelchairs should be provided for all flights, Ryanair had added a similar surcharge to cover costs. Despite criticism, Ryanair does not allow customers to contact them via e-mail; customer services can only be contacted via a premium-rate telephone number.

Ryanair continues to grow; their own website suggests that customer satisfaction is extremely high, while independent surveys rate the airline as the worst European operation in terms of food, comfort, and pre-flight arrangements.

In October 2011, Ryanair released the latest of the customer service statistics covering September. Of their 45,000 flights over the course of the month, 92 percent of them arrived on time; this was up 9 percent from September 2010. At the same time, the airline announced that they received only one complaint per 1,000 passengers and had only mislaid one bag per 1,000 passengers. The airline was also keen to state that 99 percent of all complaints were handled within seven days. Ryanair would also claim that customers were continuing to switch to their airline from competitors and that majority of customers satisfied with the level of customer service.

If Ryanair is content with its own customer satisfaction surveys, then there seems to be a mismatch in terms of other

what's in it for me?

If, like the thousands of airline customers disrupted by inconvenience and mistreatment, you've ever been disappointed in a good or service that you bought, you'll find it easy to relate to the topics in this chapter. We'll explore the numerous ways companies align their operations processes with their business plans, and discuss how these decisions contribute to a firm's ability to create a high-quality product. Gaining an appreciation for the many steps it takes to bring high-quality goods and services to market will help make you a smarter consumer and more effective employee. And if you're a manager, understanding that production activities are pliable and should be reoriented to better support new business strategies will help you redefine your company and its marketplace over time.

assessments of their operations. In a survey carried out by the consumer group Which? in 2008, the airline received an overall customer satisfaction score of only 47 percent. Ryanair was criticized by customers for the helpfulness of cabin staff, cleanliness, and the way it dealt with delays. Food (which is an additional charge to passengers) was given a poor rating. The efficiency of the check-in staff, online check-in, policy on baggage, and seating was criticized.

According to research carried out for the UK-based price comparison website Go Compare, Ryanair was the clear winner of the worst airline category in a customer satisfaction survey on airlines. It scored half as many votes as its nearest rival EasyJet.

Ryanair's Head of Communications Stephen McNamara pointed out that price and punctuality are the two key considerations rather than quality. They embrace negative press stories and see them as an opportunity to achieve publicity. He was also keen to point out that, according to Ryanair's own customer surveys, over one-half of their passengers fly with them four or more times a year.[1]

OBJECTIVE 1
Explain

the meaning of the term *production* or *operations* and describe the three kinds of utility that operations processes provide for adding customer value.

Service Operations (Service Production) *activities producing intangible and tangible products, such as entertainment, transportation, and education*

Goods Operations (Goods Production) *activities producing tangible products, such as radios, newspapers, buses, and textbooks*

Operations (Production) *activities involved in making products—goods and services—for customers*

What Does *Operations* Mean Today?

Although you're not always aware of it, as a customer you are constantly involved in business activities that provide goods and services to customers. You wake up to the sound of your favorite radio station, and on your bus ride to work or school, you are texting on a cell phone. Your instructors, the bus driver, the messaging provider, and the morning radio announcer all work in **service operations** (or **service production**). They provide intangible and tangible service products, such as entertainment, transportation, education, and communications services. Firms that make only tangible products—radios, cell phones, buses, textbooks—are engaged in activities for **goods operations** (or **goods production**).

The term **operations** (or **production**) refers to all the activities involved in making products—goods and services—for customers. In modern societies, much of what we need or want, from health care to fast food, is produced by service operations. As a rule, managers in the service sector give more consideration to the human element in operations (as opposed to the equipment or technology involved), because success or

General Electric (GE) can be classified as both a goods producer (e.g., of the GE Wind Turbine) and a service provider (e.g., commercial finance).

failure depends often on provider-customer contact. As we saw with airlines in the opening story, employees who deal directly with customers affect customer feelings about the service. As we will see, a key difference between goods and services operations is the customer's involvement in the latter.

Although companies are typically classified as either goods producers or service providers, the distinction is often blurred. Consider General Electric (GE). When you think of GE, you most likely think of appliances and jet engines. However, GE is not just a goods producer. According to its annual report, GE's "growth engines"—its most vibrant business activities—are service operations, including insurance and real estate, consumer and commercial finance, investment, transportation services, and healthcare information, which account for more than 70 percent of the company's revenues.[2]

Growth in the Services and Goods Sectors

Historically, agriculture was the dominant sector in the early years of the United States. Thereafter, manufacturing grew, becoming the economic backbone from the nineteenth century into the mid-twentieth century. Services then began a rapid climb in economic importance in terms of both number of employees and percentage of gross domestic product (GDP)—the value of all goods and services produced by the economy, excluding foreign income. The outsourcing of U.S. manufacturing to other countries became a major concern in recent decades, so that by the year 2000, employment in the goods-producing sector (mining, construction, and manufacturing) was only about 20 percent of private sector employment versus 80 percent in services. Still, as recently as 2004 the United States remained the world's leader in manufactured exports, followed by Germany and Japan.

Of course, both goods and service industries are important, but as you can see from Figure 7.1, employment has risen significantly in the service sector and has leveled off at just 11 to 12 percent in goods-producing industries for years 2003 through 2012. Much of this growth comes from e-commerce, business services, health care, amusement and recreation, and education.

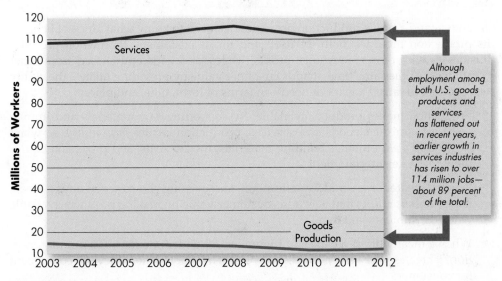

FIGURE 7.1 Employment in Goods and Services Sectors
Source: http://data.bls.gov/timeseries/CES0700000001?data_tool=XGtable, accessed March 3, 2013.

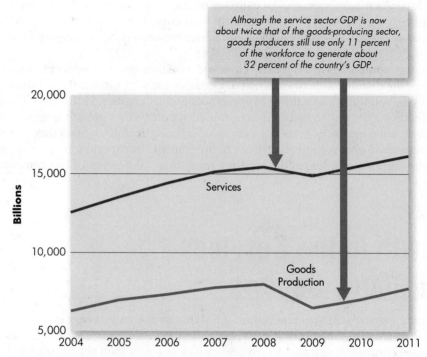

> Although the service sector GDP is now about twice that of the goods-producing sector, goods producers still use only 11 percent of the workforce to generate about 32 percent of the country's GDP.

FIGURE 7.2 GDP from Goods and Services
Source: http://www.bea.gov/iTable/iTable.cfm?ReqID=5&step=1#reqid=5&step=4&is uri=1&402=15&403=1, accessed March 3, 2013.

By 2011, the service sector's growth generated about 68 percent of private-sector national income. As Figure 7.2 shows, the service sector's greater percentage of GDP has hovered above 65 percent in recent years. At the same time, the smaller 11 percent of the workforce in goods-producing jobs produced 32 percent of national income.

Globally, U.S. manufacturing faces intense competition from other nations. A recent international survey of industrial executives ranks China as the most competitive manufacturing country, followed by Germany (second), the United States (third), Canada (seventh), and Japan (tenth)[3].

OBJECTIVE 2
Identify
the characteristics that distinguish *service operations* from *goods production.*

Utility *product's ability to satisfy a human want or need*

Creating Value through Operations

To understand a firm's production processes, we need to know what kinds of benefits its production provides, both for itself and for its customers. Production provides businesses with economic results: profits, wages, and goods purchased from other companies. At the same time, it adds customer value by providing **utility**—the ability of a product to satisfy a want or need—in terms of form, time, and place:

- Production makes products available: By converting raw materials and human skills into finished goods and services, production creates *form utility*, as when Regal Cinemas combines building materials, theater seats, and projection equipment to create entertainment.

- When a theater offers midday, afternoon, and evening shows seven days a week, it creates *time utility*; that is, it adds customer value by making products available when consumers want them.

- When a theater offers a choice of 15 movies, all under one roof, at a popular location, it creates *place utility*: It makes products available where they are convenient for consumers.

Creating a product that customers value is no accident; it results from organized effort. **Operations (production) management** is the systematic direction and control

Operations (Production) Management *systematic direction and control of the activities that transform resources into finished products that create value for and provide benefits to customers*

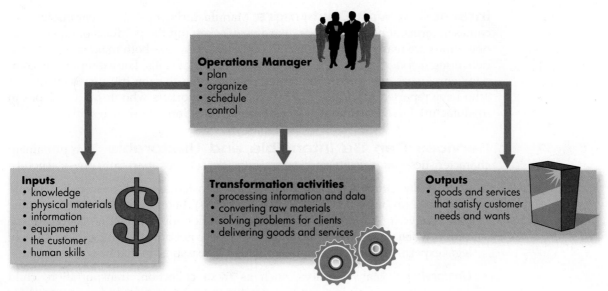

FIGURE 7.3 The Resource Transformation Process

of the activities that transform resources into finished services and goods that create value for and provide benefits to customers. In overseeing production, **operations (production) managers** are responsible for ensuring that operations activities create what customers want and need.

As Figure 7.3 shows, operations managers draw up plans to transform resources into products. First, they bring together basic resources: knowledge, physical materials, information, equipment, the customer, and human skills. Then, they put them to effective use in a facility where the service is provided or the physical good is produced. As demand for a product increases, operations managers schedule and control work to produce the required amount. Finally, they control costs, quality levels, inventory, and facilities and equipment. In some businesses, often in small startup firms such as sole proprietorships, the operations manager is one person. Typically, however, different employees work together to complete these different responsibilities.

Some operations managers work in service "factories," such as FedEx package-sorting depots, whereas others work in factories making cell phones; still others work in offices, restaurants, hospitals, and stores. Farmers are operations managers who create utility by transforming soil, seeds, fuel, and other inputs into soybeans, milk, and other outputs. They may hire crews of workers to plant and harvest, opt instead for automated machinery, or prefer some combination of workers and machinery. These types of decisions affect costs and determine the kinds of buildings and equipment farmers include in their operations and the quality and quantity of the goods they produce.

Differences between Service and Goods Manufacturing Operations

Both service and manufacturing operations transform raw materials into finished products. In service operations, however, the raw materials, or inputs, are not things like glass or steel. These service inputs are people who have either unsatisfied needs or possessions needing care or alteration. In service operations, finished products or outputs are people with needs met and possessions serviced.

There are several obvious differences between service and manufacturing operations. Four aspects of service operations can make service production more complicated than simple goods production: (1) interacting with customers, (2) the intangible and unstorable nature of some services, (3) the customer's presence in the process, and (4) service quality considerations.

Operations (Production) Managers
managers responsible for ensuring that operations activities create value and provide benefits to customers

Interacting with Customers Manufacturing operations emphasize outcomes in terms of physical goods, like a new jacket. But the products of most *service* operations are really combinations of goods and services—both making a pizza *and* delivering (serving) it. Service workers need different skills. For example, gas company employees may need strong interpersonal skills to calm frightened customers who have reported gas leaks. In contrast, factory workers who install gas pipes in manufactured homes without any customer contact don't need such skills.

Services Can Be Intangible and Unstorable Two prominent characteristics—*intangibility* and *unstorability*—set services apart from physical goods:

- *Intangibility.* Often, services can't be touched, tasted, smelled, or seen, but they're still there. An important satisfier for customers, therefore, is the *intangible* value they receive in the form of pleasure, gratification, or a feeling of safety. For example, when you hire an attorney, you purchase not only the intangible quality of legal expertise but also the equally intangible reassurance that help is at hand.

- *Unstorability.* Many services, such as trash collection, transportation, child care, and house cleaning, can't be produced ahead of time and then stored for high-demand periods. If a service isn't used when available, it's usually wasted. Services, then, are typically characterized by a high degree of *unstorability*.

Customers' Presence in the Operations Process Because service operations transform customers or their possessions, the customer is often present in the operations process. To get a haircut, for example, most of us have to go to the barbershop or hair salon. As participants in the operations process, customers can affect it. As a customer, you expect the salon to be conveniently located (place utility), to be open for business at convenient times (time utility), to provide safe and comfortable facilities, and to offer high-quality grooming (form utility) at reasonable prices (value for money spent). Accordingly, the manager sets hours of operation, available services, and an appropriate number of employees to meet her customer requirements. But what happens if a customer, scheduled to receive a haircut, also asks for additional services, such as highlights or a shave when he or she arrives? In this case, the service provider must quickly adjust the service activities to provide customer satisfaction. High customer contact has the potential to affect the process significantly. The manufacturers who produce the salon's scissors, on the other hand, don't have to worry if a customer makes a last-minute change in demands.

Intangibles Count for Service Quality Consumers use different measures to judge services and goods because services include intangibles, not just physical objects. Most service managers know that quality of work and quality of service are not necessarily the same thing. Your car, for example, may have been flawlessly repaired (quality of work), but you'll probably be unhappy with the service if you're forced to pick it up a day later than promised (quality of service).

Operations Processes

To better understand the diverse kinds of production in various firms and industries, it is helpful to classify production according to differences in operations processes. An **operations process** is a set of methods and technologies used to produce a good or a service. Banks, for example, use two processes—document shredding and data encryption—to protect confidential information. Automakers use precision painting methods (equipment and materials) to produce a glittering paint finish.

We can classify goods production into broad groupings, by asking whether its operations process has a "make-to-order" or a "make-to-stock" emphasis. We can classify services according to the extent of customer contact required.

Operations Process *set of methods and technologies used to produce a good or a service*

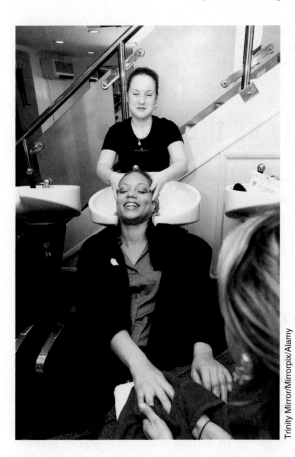

Because service operations transform customers or their possessions, the customer is often present in the operations process.

Trinity Mirror/Mirrorpix/Alamy

Goods Production Processes: Make-to-Order versus Make-to-Stock Processes

Clothing, such as evening gowns, is available either off-the-shelf in department stores or custom-made at a designer or tailor shop. The designer or tailor's **make-to-order operations** respond to one-of-a-kind gown requirements, including unique patterns, materials, sizes, and shapes, depending on customers' characteristics. **Make-to-stock operations**, in contrast, produce standard gowns in large quantities to be stocked on store shelves or in displays for mass consumption. The production processes are quite different for the two settings, including procedures for designing gowns; planning for materials purchases; equipment and work methods for cutting, sewing, and assembling gowns; and employee skills for production.

Make-To-Order Operations *activities for one-of-a-kind or custom-made production*

Make-To-Stock Operations *activities for producing standardized products for mass consumption*

Service Production Processes: Extent of Customer Contact

In classifying services, we may ask whether we can provide a service without the customers' being present in the production system. In answering this question, we classify services according to *extent of customer contact.*

LOW-CONTACT SYSTEMS Consider the postal delivery operations at your local U.S. post office. Postal employees gather mail, sort it, and send it on its delivery journey to addressees. This operation is a **low-contact system:** Customers are not in contact with the post office while the service is performed. They receive the service—mail sent and mail received—without setting foot in the processing center. Gas and electric companies, auto repair shops, and lawn-care services are other examples of low-contact systems.

Low-Contact System *level of customer contact in which the customer need not be part of the system to receive the service*

HIGH-CONTACT SYSTEMS Think about your local public transit system. The service is transportation; when you purchase transportation, you board a bus or train. For example, the Bay Area Rapid Transit (BART) system, which connects San Francisco with outlying suburbs is, like all public transit systems, a **high-contact system:** To receive the service, the customer must be part of the system. Thus, managers must worry about the cleanliness of trains, safety of

High-Contact System *level of customer contact in which the customer is part of the system during service delivery*

passengers, and the usability of its ticket kiosks. By contrast, a firm that ships coal is less concerned with the appearance of its trains since no paying passengers are riding on them. A coal-shipping firm is a low-contact system.

Business Strategy as the Driver of Operations

OBJECTIVE 3

Explain

how companies with different business strategies are best served by having different operations capabilities.

There is no one standard way for doing production, either for services or for goods. Rather, it is a flexible activity that can be molded into many shapes to give quite different operations capabilities for different purposes. How, then, do companies go about selecting the kind of production that is best for them? They aim to adopt the kind of production that achieves the firm's larger business strategy in the most efficient way possible.

The Many Faces of Production Operations

Consider the four firms listed in Table 7.1. Two are in goods production (Toyota and 3M), and the other two (Save-a-Lot and FedEx) are in services. These successful companies have contrasting business strategies and, as we shall see, they have chosen different operations capabilities. Each company has identified a business strategy that it uses for attracting customers in its industry. More than 40 years ago, Toyota chose *quality* as the strategy for competing in selling autos. Save-A-Lot grocery stores, in contrast to others in the grocery industry, offer customers *lower prices*. The *flexibility* strategy at 3M emphasizes new product development in an ever-changing line of products for home and office. FedEx captures the overnight delivery market by emphasizing delivery *dependability*.

Business Strategy Determines Operations Capabilities

Successful firms design their operations to support the company's business strategy.[4] In other words, managers adjust production operations to support the firms' target markets. Because our four firms use different business strategies, we should expect to see differences in their operations, too. The top-priority **operations capability (production capability)**—the special ability that production does especially well to outperform the competition—is listed for each firm in Table 7.2, along with key operations characteristics for implementing that capability. Each company's operations

Operations Capability (Production Capability) *special ability that production does especially well to outperform the competition*

table 7.1 Business Strategies that Win Customers for Four Companies

Company	Strategy for Attracting Customers	What the Company Does to Implement Its Strategy
Toyota	Quality	Cars perform reliably, have an appealing fit and finish, and consistently meet or exceed customer expectations at a competitive price
Save-A-Lot	Low price	Foods and everyday items offered at savings up to 40 percent less than conventional food chains
3M	Flexibility	Innovation, with more than 55,000 products in a constantly changing line of convenience items for home and office
FedEx	Dependability	Every delivery is fast and on time, as promised

table 7.2 Operations Capabilities and Characteristics for Four Companies

Operations Capability	Key Operations Characteristics
Quality (Toyota)	• High-quality standards for materials suppliers • Just-in-time materials flow for lean manufacturing • Specialized, automated equipment for consistent product buildup • Operations personnel are experts on continuous improvement of product, work methods, and materials
Low Cost (Save-A-Lot)	• Avoids excessive overhead and costly inventory (no floral departments, sushi bars, or banks that drive up costs) • Limited assortment of products, staples, in one size only for low-cost restocking, lower inventories, and less paperwork • Many locations; small stores—less than half the size of conventional grocery stores—for low construction and maintenance costs • Reduces labor and shelving costs by receiving and selling merchandise out of custom shipping cartons
Flexibility (3M)	• Maintains some excess (expensive) production capacity available for fast startup on new products • Adaptable equipment and facilities for production changeovers from old to new products • Hires operations personnel who thrive on change • Many medium- to small-sized manufacturing facilities in diverse locations, which enhances creativity
Dependability (FedEx)	• Customer automation: uses electronic and online communications tools with customers to shorten shipping time • Wireless information system for package scanning by courier, updating of package movement, and package tracking by customer • Maintains a company air force, global weather forecasting center, and ground transportation for pickup and delivery, with backup vehicles for emergencies • The 25 automated regional distribution hubs process 3.5 million packages per day for next-day deliveries

capability matches up with its business strategy so that the firm's activities—from top to bottom—are focused in a particular direction.

For example, because Toyota's top priority focuses on quality, its operations, the resource inputs for production, the transformation activities, and the outputs from production, are devoted first and foremost to that characteristic. Its car designs and production processes emphasize appearance, reliable performance, and desirable features at a reasonable price. All production processes, equipment, and training are designed to build better cars. The entire culture supports a quality emphasis among employees, suppliers, and dealerships. Had Toyota instead chosen to compete as the low-price car in the industry, as some successful car companies do, then a cost-minimization focus would have been appropriate, giving Toyota's operations an altogether different form. Toyota's operations support its chosen business strategy, and did it successfully until quality problems arose in 2008. Soon thereafter, the commitment to quality intensified. By 2012, Toyota had regained its position as the world's top-selling auto maker. Before the 2008 downfall, the company had more than 35 consecutive years of increasing sales for which quality was the foundation for greatness.

Expanding into Additional Capabilities Finally, it should be noted that excellent firms learn, over time, how to achieve more than just one competence. The firms in Table 7.1 eventually became excellent in several capabilities. Aside from dependability, FedEx is also noted for world-class service quality and cost containment. Regarding quality, FedEx was honored in the "2012 Customer Service Hall of Fame," ranking 7th for service quality among 150 companies in *MSN Money*'s annual survey. To reduce costs, the company eliminates jobs that become unnecessary with advances in technology, sells off its older inefficient airplanes, and reduces the number of flights by re-routing its air and ground fleets.

OBJECTIVE 4
Identify
the major factors that are considered in operations planning.

Operations Planning

Let's turn now to a discussion of production activities and resources that are considered in every business organization. Like all good managers, we start with planning. Managers from many departments contribute to decisions about operations. As Figure 7.4 shows, however, no matter how many decision makers are involved, the process is a logical sequence of decisions.

The business plan and forecasts developed by top managers provide guidance for long-term operations plans. Covering a two- to five-year period, the operations plan anticipates the number of plants or service facilities and the amount of labor, equipment, transportation, and storage needed to meet future demand for new and existing products. The planning activities fall into five categories: *capacity*, *location*, *layout*, *quality*, and *methods planning*.

Capacity Planning

Capacity *amount of a product that a company can produce under normal conditions*

The amount of a product that a company can produce under normal conditions is its **capacity.** A firm's capacity depends on how many people it employs and the number and size of its facilities. A supermarket's capacity for customer checkouts, for instance, depends on its number of checkout stations. A typical store has excess capacity—more cash registers than it needs—on an average day, but on Saturday morning or during the three days before Thanksgiving, they'll all be running at full capacity.

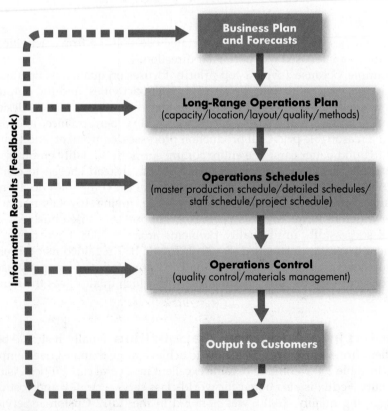

FIGURE 7.4 Operations Planning and Control

entrepreneurship and new ventures

A Better Path to Planning Meals (and Better Eating, Too)

Want to eat better at home, while saving time and money, too? Folks in Bradenton, Florida, are doing exactly that, using Erika Vitiene's online meal-planning venture, *Grocery Dash*. Vitiene has used her personal shopping experience, together with carefully developed meal-planning steps, to design the *grocerydash. com* website where subscribers get help for their at-home dinner planning.

Vitiene's motivation is to save over-burdened moms the time and money ordinarily spent on planning meals and meal preparation. Every family's meal planner, eventually, feels the challenge of finding new and different dishes, instead of serving "the same old thing, week after week." Although new meal ideas provide greater variety, they also require more time searching for and using different recipes, and buying new ingredients at the right price.[5]

Although the website doesn't use formal terms such as "methods improvement" and "process flowchart," its contents reflect Erika's intuitive understanding of the sequence of steps for improving the meal-planning process: It identifies the meal planner (the user who will gain better meal planning), the planner's objectives (good meals at lower cost and time savings), and provides information resources such as ready-made menus, lists of ingredients, and local produce and grocery sales. Menus for seven dinners are displayed weekly, along with their recipes, lists of ingredients, and an aisle-by-aisle shopping list, all arranged around the price specials at local grocery stores.

Grant Jefferis/Newscom

Subscribers can download additional free resources, printable grocery lists, a freezer guide showing how long food will keep (and a list of foods that do not freeze well), and a pantry checklist for an up-to-date inventory of foods on hand at home.[6]

Erika used her system a long time, and proved its effectiveness to herself—saving 25 to 50 percent on her grocery bill—before presenting it online. Although originally intended for moms, and with a subscription price at $4.95 per month, *grocerydash.com* can also become a valued resource to singles, students, and others whose busy schedules and tight budgets can benefit from nutritious ready-planned meals at lower cost, instead of just fast foods.[7]

Long-range capacity planning considers both current and future requirements. If capacity is too small for demand, the company must turn away customers, a situation that cuts into profits and alienates both customers and salespeople. If capacity greatly exceeds demand, the firm is wasting money by maintaining facilities that are too large, keeping excess machinery online, or employing too many workers.

The stakes are high in capacity decisions: While expanding fast enough to meet future demand and to protect market share from competitors, managers must also consider the costs of expanding. When markets are growing, greater capacity is desirable. In troubled times, however, existing capacity may be too large and too expensive to maintain, requiring a reduction in size.

Location Planning

Because location affects production costs and flexibility, sound location planning is crucial for factories, offices, and stores. Depending on its site, a company may be able to produce low-cost products, or it may find itself at a cost disadvantage relative to its competitors.

Consider the reasons why Slovakia has become known as "Detroit East." With the worldwide slowdown in car sales, Slovakia's auto production is suffering. Still, during the 2012 Euro-zone economic crisis it produced more cars per capita—including Volkswagen SUVs, Peugeot Citroens, and Kias—than most other Euro-zone countries. Its auto factories are well-positioned to resume high-volume

finding a better way

"Going Green" Yields a Better Way to Spin Clean

To open her start-up self-service "green laundry," entrepreneur Deborah Dower found plenty of empty commercial space available in the sagging 2010 economy. Business slowdowns forced other firms in the Sacramento, California, area to abandon excess capacity, making space available at below-market prices. The location and cost were well-suited for Dower's new Paradise Laundry start-up, with a business strategy of offering a refreshing change, an eco-friendly and affordable laundry. With its motto, "Wash Green—Save Green," Paradise attracted a favorable public response, and together with her willingness to take a financial risk, Dower expanded capacity by opening a second Paradise Laundry. Paradise Laundry quickly gained the desired reputation—"The Cleanest and Greenest Laundries in Sacramento." As popularity increased, Dower opened a third store in 2012. This newest facility is "topless," using only front-loading (no top-loading) machines to save water. Dower notes that, "An older top-loading washer can use up to 42 gallons of water to wash one load, which is more than twice as much water of a high-efficiency (HE) front-load washer."

The necessity for water conservation is a growing concern for California cities. With increasing demand for water resources, the need for new costly infrastructure (replacing underground water pipes and sewers) is growing. Accordingly, water users face higher water and sewer rates, so finding ways to use the resource more efficiently reduces users' operating costs. Paradise's front-loading washers reduce those costs, thereby maintaining better affordability for its customers. The laundry's

ZUMA Press, Inc./Alamy

conservation practices resulted in using 40 percent less water even though the laundry's wash capacity rose by 150 percent. For these environment-friendly efforts, the Sacramento Board of Supervisors publicly honored Dower and Paradise in 2012.

Along with its green initiatives, Paradise Laundries take pride in cleanliness—"The Cleanest..." in the area. First, they have brand-new washers and dryers to avoid mildew that can accumulate in older equipment. Second, they are the only laundry in the area that uses a professional janitorial service to clean and sanitize all the surfaces in the facilities daily. Finally, they use a monthly pest control service to keep out annoying creepy critters. By emphasizing "clean," "affordable," and "green" Dower is looking forward to an even brighter future for Paradise Laundries, and for the environment.[8]

production as the worldwide economy improves. The central European country is an ideal place to produce cars. It has a good railroad system and nearby access to the Danube River, meaning economical transportation for incoming materials and outgoing cars once auto factories are in operation. The area also has skilled, hard-working laborers, and wages lower than those of surrounding countries.[9]

In contrast to manufacturing, consumer services concentrate on being located near customers. Thus, fast-food restaurants, such as Taco Bell and McDonald's, are located near areas with high traffic, such as college campuses, hospital cafeterias, and shopping malls. At retail giant Walmart, managers of the company's huge distribution centers regard Walmart outlets as their customers. To ensure that truckloads of merchandise flow quickly to stores, distribution centers are located near the hundreds of Walmart stores that they supply, not near the companies that supply them.

Layout Planning

Layout is the physical location or floor plan for service centers, machinery, equipment, customers, and supplies. It determines whether a company can respond efficiently to demand for more and different products or whether it finds itself unable to match competitors' speed and convenience. Among the many layout possibilities, three well-known alternatives—*(1) process layouts (or custom-products layouts)*, *(2) product layouts (or same-steps layouts)*, and *(3) fixed-position layouts*—are presented here to illustrate how different layouts serve different purposes for operations.

Process Layouts In a **process layout** (also called **custom-product layout**), which is well suited to *make-to-order shops* (or *job shops*) specializing in custom work, equipment and people are grouped according to function. FedEx Office stores (formerly Kinko's Copy Centers), for example, use custom-products layouts to accommodate a variety of custom jobs. Specific activities or processes, such as photocopying, faxing, computing, binding, and laminating, are performed in separate, specialized areas of the store. Walk-in customers—local individuals and small-business clients—move from area-to-area using the self-service they need.

> **Process Layout (Custom-Product Layout)** *physical arrangement of production activities that groups equipment and people according to function*

The main advantage of process layouts is flexibility—at any time, the shop can process individual customer orders, each requiring different kinds of work. Depending on its work requirements, a client being served or a job being processed may flow through three activity areas, another through just one area, and still others through four or more work zones. Figure 7.5 shows the process layout of a service provider—a medical clinic. The path taken through the facility reflects the unique treatments for one patient's visit. Goods producers such as machine shops, woodworking and print shops, dry cleaning stores, as well as health clinics and physical fitness studios, are among the many facilities using custom-products layouts.

Product Layouts A **product layout** (also called a **same-steps layout** or **assembly line layout**) is set up to provide one type of service or make one type of product in a fixed sequence of production steps. All units go through the same set of steps. It is efficient for large-volume make-to-stock operations that mass-produce many units of a product quickly: A partially finished product moves step by step through the plant on conveyor belts or other equipment, often in a straight line, as it passes through each stage until the product is completed. Automobile, food-processing, and television-assembly plants use same-steps layouts, as do mail-processing facilities, such as UPS or FedEx.

> **Product Layout (Same-Steps Layout)** *physical arrangement of production steps designed to make one type of product in a fixed sequence of activities according to its production requirements*
>
> **Assembly Line Layout** *a same-steps layout in which a product moves step by step through a plant on conveyor belts or other equipment until it is completed*

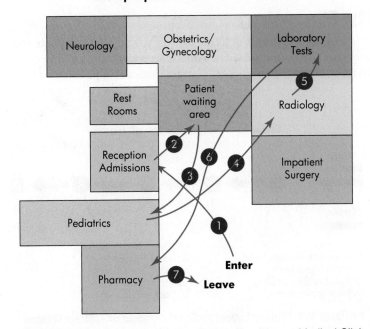

Example patient flow for one customer

FIGURE 7.5 Process Layout for a Service Provider—a Medical Clinic

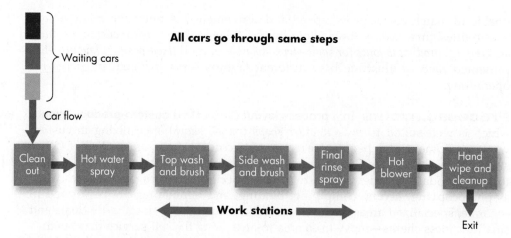

FIGURE 7.6 Product Layout for a Service—Automated Car Wash

Figure 7.6 shows a product layout at a service provider—an automatic car wash. Figure 7.7 is a goods-producer assembling parts needed to make storm windows.

Same-steps layouts are efficient because the work skill is built into the equipment, allowing unskilled labor to perform simple tasks. But they are often inflexible, especially where they use specialized equipment that's hard to rearrange for new applications.

Fixed-Position Layout *labor, equipment, materials, and other resources are brought to the geographic location where all production work is done*

Fixed Position Layouts
A **fixed-position layout** is necessary when, because of size, shape, or any other reason, managers cannot move the service to another production facility. In fixed-position layouts the product or client remains at one location; equipment, materials and human skills are moved to that location, as needed, to perform the service or to build the product. While recovering at home from a knee replacement, for example, physical rehabilitation specialists come to the patient's home for rehab services. When home plumbing goes bad or the roof leaks, repair services are brought to that home—at its fixed position—where the services are performed. Such layouts are used for building huge ships that can't be moved, for constructing buildings, and for agricultural operations—plowing, fertilizing, and harvesting—at farm sites.

Quality Planning

Quality *combination of "characteristics of a product or service that bear on its ability to satisfy stated or implied needs"*

Every operations plan includes activities for ensuring that products meet the firm's and customers' quality standards. The American Society for Quality defines **quality** as a subjective term, the combination of "characteristics of a product or service that bear

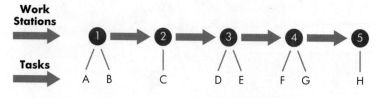

FIGURE 7.7 Product Layout for Goods Production—Storm Window Assembly

on its ability to satisfy stated or implied needs."[10] Such characteristics may include a reasonable price and dependability in delivering the benefits it promises.

Planning for quality begins when products are being designed. As we will see later, product design is a marketing responsibility, but it involves operations managers, too. Early in the process, goals are established for both performance and consistency. **Performance** refers to how well the product does what it is supposed to do. For loyal buyers of Godiva premium chocolates, performance includes such sensory delights as aroma, flavor, color, and texture. "Truly fine chocolates," observes master chocolatier Thierry Muret, "are always fresh, contain high-quality ingredients like cocoa beans and butter…and feature unusual textures and natural flavors." The recipe was designed to provide these features. Superior performance helps Godiva remain one of the world's top brands.[11]

In addition to performance, quality also includes **consistency**, the sameness of product quality from unit to unit. Business travelers using Courtyard by Marriott, for example, enjoy high consistency with each overnight stay, which is one reason Courtyard by Marriott is among the best-selling brands in the lodging industry. Courtyard by Marriot achieved this status by maintaining the same features at all of Marriott's 900 Courtyard hotels in 37 countries. Designed for business travelers, most guest rooms include a Courtyard Suite with high-speed Internet access, meeting space, and access to an exercise room, restaurant and lounge, swimming pool, and 24-hour access to food. The layout of the suites is identical at many locations, the rooms are always clean, and check-in/checkout procedures are identical so that lodgers know what to expect with each overnight stay. This consistency is achieved by monitoring for uniformity of materials and supplies, encouraging conscientious work, training employees, and maintaining equipment.

In addition to product design, quality planning includes employees deciding what constitutes a high-quality product—for both goods and services—and determining how to measure these quality characteristics.

Performance *dimension of quality that refers to how well a product does what it is supposed to do*

Consistency *dimension of quality that refers to sameness of product quality from unit to unit*

Methods Planning

In designing operations systems, managers must identify each production step and the specific methods for performing it. They can then reduce waste and inefficiency by examining procedures on a step-by-step basis by using an approach called *methods improvement*.

Improving Process Flows
Improvements for operations begin by documenting current production practices. A detailed description, often using a diagram called a *process flowchart*, is helpful in organizing and recording information. The flowchart identifies the sequence of production activities, movements of materials, and work performed at each stage of the process. It can then be analyzed to isolate wasteful activities, sources of delay, and other inefficiencies in both goods and services operations. The final step is implementing improvements.

Improving Customer Service
Consider, for example, the traditional checkout method at hotels. The process flowchart in Figure 7.8 shows five stages of customer activities. Hotel checkout can be time consuming for customers standing in line to pay. They become impatient and annoyed, especially during popular checkout times when lines are long. Other hotel tasks are disrupted, too, as managers are forced to reassign employees to the front desk to assist with surging checkout lines. Hotel managers developed an improved checkout method that avoids wasting time in line for customers and reduces interruptions of other staff duties as well. It saves time by eliminating steps 1, 2, 3A, and 5. On the morning of departure customers find a copy of charges delivered under their room door. Or, they can scan their bills on television in the privacy of their rooms any time before departure. If the bill is correct, no further checkout is required, and the hotel submits the charges against the credit card that the customer submitted during check-in.

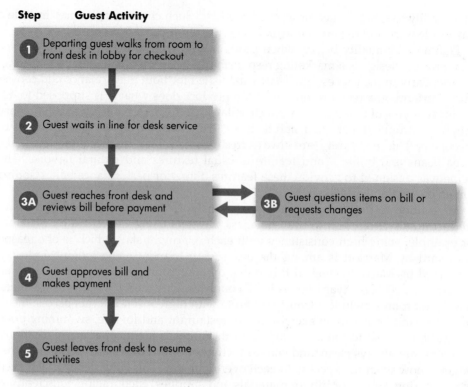

FIGURE 7.8 Flowchart of Traditional Guest Checkout

OBJECTIVE 5
Discuss

the information contained in four kinds of operations schedules—the master operations schedule, detailed schedule, staff schedule, and project schedule.

Operations Scheduling

Continuing with the flow of activities in Figure 7.4, once managers and their teams have determined the operations plans, they then develop timetables for implementing the plans. This aspect of operations, called *operations scheduling*, identifies times when specific activities will occur.

In this section we consider four general kinds of schedules. (1) The *master schedule* is "the game plan" for deciding the volume of upcoming activities for months ahead. (2) *Detailed schedules* show day-to-day activities that will occur in production. (3) *Staff schedules* identify who and how many employees will be working, and when. (4) Finally, *project schedules* provide coordination for completing large-scale projects.

The Master Operations Schedule

Master Operations Schedule
schedule showing which products will be produced, and when, in upcoming time periods

Scheduling of operation occurs at different levels. First, a top-level **master operations schedule** shows which services or products will be produced and when, in upcoming time periods. Logan Aluminum, for example, makes coils of aluminum that it supplies to customer companies that use it to make beverage cans. Logan's master schedule, with a format like the partial schedule shown in Figure 7.9, covers production for 60 weeks in which more than 300,000 tons will be produced. For various types of coils

Coil # (Product)	8/4/14	8/11/14	8/18/14	...	11/3/14	11/10/14
TC016	1,500	2,500			2,100	600
TC032	900		2,700		3,000	
TR020	300		2,600			1,600

FIGURE 7.9 Example of Partial Master Operations Schedule

KEY RESOURCES	Quarter/Year							
	1/2014	2/2014	3/2014	4/2014	1/2015	2/2015	3/2015	4/2015
Number of Stores	17	17	18	19	20	20	21	22
Staffing Level (no. of Employees)	1,360	1,360	1,530	1,615	1,700	1,700	1,653	1,827
Fresh Vegetables (tons)	204	204	192	228	240	240	230	260
Canned Goods (case loads)	73,950	77,350	80,100	80,100	83,000	84,500	88,600	90,200
Fresh Meats Etc.	–	–	–	–	–	–	–	–
–								
–								
–								

FIGURE 7.10 Food Retailer's Partial Operations Schedule

(products), the master schedule specifies how many tons will be produced each week, helping managers determine the kinds of materials, equipment, and other resources that will be needed for each upcoming week.

The master schedule for a service provider, such as a regional food retailer, may begin with the planned number of retail stores to be operating in each quarter of the coming two years. Then, key resources needed in each quarter to provide customer services for all stores are identified (estimated). Figure 7.10 shows an example of such a partial master schedule. It provides information for planning on how many people the company will have to hire and train, planning for purchases of food products and the financing needed for those purchases, and planning for construction requirements of new stores.

Detailed Schedules

Although the master production schedule is the backbone for overall scheduling, additional information comes from **detailed schedules**, schedules showing daily work assignments with start and stop times for assigned jobs at each work station. Logan's production personnel need to know the locations of all coils in the plant and their various stages of completion. Managers must assign start and stop times, and employees need scheduled work assignments daily, not just weekly. Detailed short-term schedules allow managers to use customer orders and information about equipment status to update sizes and the variety of coils to be made each day.

Detailed Schedule *schedule showing daily work assignments with start and stop times for assigned jobs*

Staff Schedules and Computer-Based Scheduling

Scheduling is useful for employee staffing in service companies, too, including restaurants, hotels, and transportation and landscaping companies. **Staff schedules**, in general, specify assigned working times in upcoming days—perhaps for as many

Staff Schedule *assigned working times in upcoming days for each employee on each work shift*

as 30 days or more—for each employee on each work shift. Staff schedules consider employees' needs and the company's efficiency and costs, including the ebbs and flows of demand for production.

Computer-based scheduling, using tools such as the *ABS Visual Staff Scheduler® PRO* (VSS Pro) software, can easily handle multishift activities for many employees—both part-time and full-time. It accommodates vacation times, holiday adjustments, and daily adjustments in staffing for unplanned absences and changes in production schedules.

Project Scheduling

Special projects, such as new business construction or redesigning a product, require close coordination and precise timing among many activities. In these cases, project management is facilitated by project scheduling tools, including Gantt charts and PERT.

The Gantt Graphical Method   Named after its developer, Henry Gantt, a **Gantt chart** breaks down large projects into steps to be performed and specifies the time required to perform each one. The project manager lists all activities needed to complete the work, estimates the time required for each step, records the progress on the chart, and checks the progress against the time scale on the chart to keep the project moving on schedule. If work is ahead of schedule, some employees may be shifted to another project. If it's behind schedule, workers may be added or completion delayed.

Figure 7.11 shows a Gantt chart for the renovation of a college classroom. It shows progress to date and schedules for remaining work and that some steps can be performed at the same time (e.g., step D can be performed during the same time as steps C and E), but others cannot (e.g., step A must be completed before any of the others can begin). Step E is behind schedule; it should have been completed before the current date.

Project Scheduling with PERT Charts   The *Program Evaluation and Review Technique (PERT)* provides even more information for controlling the progress of large projects. Along with times required to perform the activities, the layout of the **PERT chart** uses arrows to show the necessary *sequence* among activities, from

Gantt Chart *production schedule that breaks down large projects into steps to be performed and specifies the time required to perform each step*

PERT Chart *production schedule specifying the sequence of activities, time requirements, and critical path for performing the steps in a project*

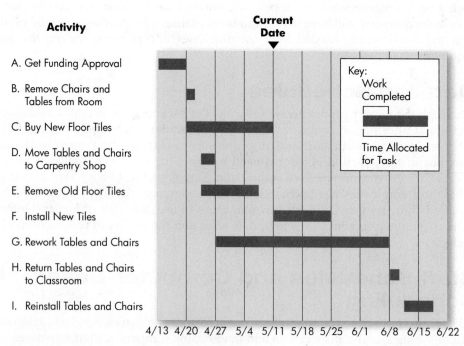

FIGURE 7.11 Gantt Chart

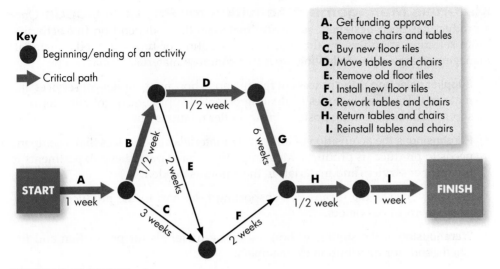

Key

● Beginning/ending of an activity

➤ Critical path

A. Get funding approval
B. Remove chairs and tables
C. Buy new floor tiles
D. Move tables and chairs
E. Remove old floor tiles
F. Install new floor tiles
G. Rework tables and chairs
H. Return tables and chairs
I. Reinstall tables and chairs

FIGURE 7.12 PERT Chart

start to finish, for completing the project. It also identifies the *critical path*, the most time-consuming set of activities, for completing the project.

Figure 7.12 shows a PERT chart for renovating the college classroom. The project's nine activities and the times required to complete them are identified. Each activity is represented by an arrow. The arrows are positioned to show the required sequence for performing the activities. For example, chairs and tables can't be returned to the classroom (H) until after they've been reworked (G) and after new floor tiles are installed (F). Accordingly, the diagram shows arrows for G and F coming before activity H. Similarly, funding approval (A) has to occur before anything else can get started.

The critical path is informative because it reveals the most time-consuming path for project completion, and for most projects, speed of completion is vital. The critical path for classroom renovation consists of activities A, B, D, G, H, and I, requiring 9.5 weeks. It's critical because a delay in completing any of those activities will cause corresponding lateness beyond the planned completion time (9.5 weeks after startup). Project managers will watch those activities and, if potential delays arise, take special action—by reassigning workers and equipment—to speed up late activities and stay on schedule.

Operations Control

OBJECTIVE 6
Discuss
the two key activities required for operations control.

Once long-range plans have been put into action and schedules have been drawn up, **operations control** requires managers to monitor performance by comparing results with detailed plans and schedules. If employees do not meet schedules or quality standards, managers can take corrective action. **Follow-up**, checking to ensure that production decisions are being implemented, is a key and ongoing facet of operations.

Operations control includes *materials management* and *quality control*. Both activities ensure that schedules are met and products delivered, both in quantity and in quality.

Operations Control *process of monitoring production performance by comparing results with plans and taking corrective action when needed*

Follow-Up *operations control activity for ensuring that production decisions are being implemented*

Materials Management

Most of us have difficulty keeping track of personal items now and then—clothes, books, cell phones, and so on. Imagine keeping track of thousands, or even millions, of things at any one time. That's the challenge in **materials management**, the process by which managers plan, organize, and control the flow of materials from sources of supply through distribution of finished goods. For manufacturing firms, typical materials costs make up 50 to 75 percent of total product costs.

Materials Management *process of planning, organizing, and controlling the flow of materials from sources of supply through distribution of finished goods*

Supplier Selection *process of finding and choosing suppliers from whom to buy*

Purchasing *acquisition of the materials and services that a firm needs to produce its products*

Transportation *activities in transporting resources to the producer and finished goods to customers*

Warehousing *storage of incoming materials for production and finished goods for distribution to customers*

Inventory Control *process of receiving, storing, handling, and counting of all raw materials, partly finished goods, and finished goods*

Lean Production System *production system designed for smooth production flows that avoid inefficiencies, eliminate unnecessary inventories, and continuously improve production processes*

Just-in-Time (JIT) Production *type of lean production system that brings together all materials at the precise time they are required at each production stage*

Materials Management Activities for Physical Goods Once a product has been designed, successful materials flows depend on five activities. From selecting suppliers on through the distribution of finished goods, materials managers engage in the following areas that compose materials management:

- **Supplier selection** is the process of finding and choosing suppliers of services and materials. This step includes evaluating potential suppliers, negotiating terms of service, and maintaining positive buyer–seller relationships.

- **Purchasing** is the acquisition of all the raw materials and services that a company needs to produce its products. Most large firms have purchasing departments to buy proper services and materials in the amounts needed.

- **Transportation** is the means of transporting resources to the producer and finished goods to customers.

- **Warehousing** is the storage of both incoming materials for production and finished goods for distribution to customers.

- **Inventory control** includes the receiving, storing, handling, and counting of all raw materials, partly finished goods, and finished goods. It ensures that enough materials inventories are available to meet production schedules, while at the same time avoiding expensive excess inventories.

Lean Production Systems
Managers must take timing into consideration when managing materials, as well. Pioneered by Toyota, **lean production systems** are designed for smooth production flows that avoid inefficiencies, eliminate unnecessary inventories, and continuously improve production processes. **Just-in-time (JIT) production**, a type of lean system, brings together all needed materials at the precise moment they are required for each production stage, not before, thus creating fast and efficient responses to customer orders. All resources flow continuously—from arrival as raw materials to final assembly and shipment of finished products.

JIT production reduces the number of goods in process (goods not yet finished) to practically nothing. It minimizes inventory costs, reduces storage space requirements for inventories, and saves money by replacing stop-and-go production with smooth movement. Once smooth flow is the norm, disruptions are more visible and employees can resolve them more quickly. Finding and eliminating disruptions by the continuous improvement of production is a major objective of JIT production.

Inventory Management is Crucial for Producing Services
For many service firms, too, the materials stakes are high. UPS delivers 20 million packages every day and promises that all of them will arrive on schedule. It keeps this promise by tracking the locations, schedules, and on-time performance of 600 aircraft and 100,000 vehicles. However, the most important "inventory" used for many high-contact services is not physical goods but exists in the form of information about service product offerings, clients, their interests, needs, activities, and even their plans for interactions with other clients.

Consider, as an example, the *inventories of information* at Collette Vacations where the *management of information* is a vital activity. Collette offers three product lines, Classic Touring, Explorations (for smaller groups), and Family Vacations, that collectively offer more than 150 escorted tours on seven continents including more than 50 countries. Each tour (the product), designed by a professional tour planner, includes a complete itinerary, duration, advanced arrangements for accommodations, and pricing. Vacationers select from among land tours, river cruises, and rail journeys that include sightseeing, meals, entertainment, and accommodations to experience new places, people history, and culture.

As a tour begins, one of the company's more than 100 Professional Tour Managers interacts face-to-face with clients as friend and guide for the entire duration, often 8-to-14 days, while handling all day-to-day details—confirming meals availabilities,

Quality control means taking action to ensure that operations produce products that meet specific quality standards.

ensuring hotel room accommodations, arranging local transportation, helping with sight-seeing selections, providing knowledge of local culture, assisting each tourist with any questions or problems, and handling emergencies.

As you can see, these many activities create vast amounts of information—the *inventory of information*—that must be accurate and accessible for success with current tours and clients, and for all the thousands of clients booked on hundreds of future tours. It is also vital for contacting many thousands of potential customers with advance information about tours that will be offered a year or two in the future.[12]

Quality Control

Quality control is taking action to ensure that operations produce goods or services that meet specific quality standards. Consider, for example, service operations in which customer satisfaction depends largely on the employees who provide the service. By monitoring services, managers and other employees can detect mistakes and make corrections. First, however, managers or other personnel must establish specific standards and measurements. At a bank, for example, quality control for teller services might require supervisors to observe employees periodically and evaluate their work according to a checklist. Managers would either review the results with employees and either confirm proper performance or indicate changes for bringing performance up to standards.

The high quality of customer-employee interactions is no accident in firms that monitor customer encounters and provide training for employee skills development. Many managers realize that without employees trained in customer-relationship skills, quality suffers, and businesses, such as airlines—as we saw in our opening story—and hotels, can lose customers to better-prepared competitors.

Quality Control *action of ensuring that operations produce products that meet specific quality standards*

Quality Improvement and Total Quality Management

OBJECTIVE 7
Identify
the activities and underlying objectives involved in total quality management.

It is not enough to *control* quality by inspecting products and monitoring service operations as they occur, as when a supervisor listens in on a catalog sales service representative's customer calls. Businesses must also consider *building* quality into goods and services in the first place. Hospitals, such as St. Luke's Hospital of

Kansas City, for example, use employee teams to design quality-assured treatment programs and patient-care procedures. Learning from past problems of staff and patients, teams continuously redesign treatments, work methods, and procedures to eliminate the sources of quality problems, rather than allowing existing conditions to continue. That is, they insist that every job be done correctly without error ("do it right the first time"), rather than relying on inspection to catch mistakes and make corrections after they occur. To compete on a global scale, U.S. companies continue to emphasize a quality orientation. All employees, not just managers, participate in quality efforts, and firms have embraced new methods to measure progress and to identify areas for improvement. In many organizations, quality improvement has become a way of life.

The Quality-Productivity Connection

It's no secret that *quality* and *productivity* are watchwords in today's competitive environment. Companies are not only measuring productivity and insisting on improvements; they also are requiring that quality brings greater satisfaction to customers, improves sales, and boosts profits.

Productivity *the amount of output produced compared with the amount of resources used to produce that output*

Productivity is a measure of economic performance: It compares how much we produce with the resources we use to produce it. The formula is fairly simple. The more services and goods we can produce while using fewer resources, the more productivity grows and the more everyone—the economy, businesses, and workers—benefits. At the national level, the most common measure is called *labor productivity*, because it uses the amount of labor worked as the resource to compare against the benefits, the country's GDP, resulting from using that resource:

$$\text{Labor productivity of a country} = \frac{\text{GDP for the year}}{\text{Total number of labor hours worked for the year}}$$

This equation illustrates the general idea of productivity. We prefer the focus on labor, rather than on other resources (such as capital or energy), because most countries keep accurate records on employment and hours worked. Thus, national labor productivity can be used for measuring year-to-year changes and to compare productivities with other countries. For 2011, for example, U.S. labor productivity was $60.59 of output per hour worked by the nation's labor force. By comparison, Norway was first at $81.47, Ireland second at $66.74, Belgium fourth with $60.17, and the Republic of Korea at $27.14 was lowest among the 20 measured countries.[13]

However, focusing on just the amount of output is a mistake because productivity refers to both the *quantity and quality* of what we produce. When resources are used more efficiently, the quantity of output is certainly greater. But experience has shown businesses that unless the resulting products are of satisfactory quality, consumers will reject them. And when consumers don't buy what is produced, GDP suffers and productivity falls. Producing quality, then, means creating fitness for use—offering features that customers want.

Managing for Quality

Total Quality Management (TQM) *all activities involved in getting high-quality goods and services into the marketplace*

Total quality management (TQM) includes all the activities necessary for getting high-quality goods and services into the marketplace. TQM begins with leadership and a desire for continuously improving both processes and products. It must consider all aspects of a business, including customers, suppliers, and employees. To marshal the interests of all these stakeholders, TQM first evaluates the costs of poor quality. TQM then identifies the sources causing unsatisfactory quality, assigns responsibility for corrections, and ensures that those who are responsible take steps for improving quality.

The Cost of Poor Quality As seen prominently in the popular press, Toyota recalled more than 10 million cars in 2009–2010, costing the world's then-number-one automaker billions of dollars and a severe blemish to its high-quality image. Problems

managing in turbulent times

Quick Footed Egyptian Businesses

Many of Egypt's smaller businesses are struggling in an environment of unrest. With a paralyzed governmental system, and banks and overseas investors unwilling to help, businesses in many sectors are finding it difficult to keep afloat.

Added to this, there are security issues, power interruptions, and difficulty in ensuring reliable sources of fuel. Petroleum demand is high but, lacking dollars, the government cannot easily pay for importation. Labor disputes and unrest are widespread, adding to the problems.

Yet there is still domestic demand, particularly in the food sector. Growth and demand is also high in construction, where the race is on to build homes for the rapidly growing population.

For Egypt's businesses, the situation, although uncertain, has its opportunities. The government has all but ceased its policing of its strict zoning regulations. This has led to an increase in illegal construction. Extra floors are being added to existing urban dwellings and land earmarked for agriculture has been transformed into housing. The tile maker and sanitary ware manufacturer Lecico Egypt is one of the many businesses benefiting from the boom. They are selling more products at higher prices than ever. Their revenue is up 15 percent and their net profit up 28 percent.

Egyptian banks used to ask for letters of guarantee and advanced payment of up to 40 percent if a business was buying products on credit. Now, there is virtually no credit available. Any buying has to be financed by sales. Some businesses have found new markets abroad in order to generate cash to fund purchases to service the domestic demand. What little funds banks have are being used up by increasing government demands for money. This is another key factor in the availability of funds for

Vitas/Fotolia

businesses. It is typical for a bank to charge an interest rate of at least 18 percent on a loan.

This all means that many Egyptian businesses have to pay in advance with cash for their supplies. At the same time, foreign currency is more difficult to obtain in order to pay overseas suppliers. To prevent pressure on the Egyptian currency, the government has increased controls. Even if the business has the necessary funds, they are only allowed to withdraw a maximum of US$30,000 a day. This in itself is problematic, as the overseas supplier may have to accept being paid in installments over a period of time.

If a business has funds, there are huge opportunities. With many competitors, with less access to overseas currency effectively suspending operations, those with partnerships with overseas businesses can profit. Aller Aqua, a fish food manufacturer with a Danish partner, has been able increase capacity by 300 percent and build a new factory.[14]

ranging from sticking gas pedals to stalling engines and malfunctioning fuel pumps were dangerous and costly not only to Toyota, but also to many consumers.

As with goods producers, service providers and customers suffer financial distress from poor-quality service products. The banking industry is a current example. As a backbone of the U.S. financial system, banks and their customers are still suffering because of bad financial products, most notably home mortgage loans. Lenders during "good times" began relaxing (or even ignoring altogether) traditional lending standards for determining whether borrowers were creditworthy. Lenders in some cases intentionally overstated property values so customers could borrow more money than the property justified. Borrowers were sometimes encouraged to overstate (falsify) their incomes and were not required to present evidence of income or even employment. Some borrowers, unaware of the terms of their loan agreements, were surprised after an initial time lapse when a much higher interest rate (and monthly payment) suddenly kicked in. Unable to meet their payments, borrowers had to abandon their homes. Meanwhile, banks were left holding foreclosed properties, unpaid (defaulted) loans, and no cash. With shortages of bank funds threatening to shut down the entire financial system, the entire nation felt the widespread costs of poor quality—loss of equity by homeowners from foreclosures, a weakened economy, high unemployment, loss of retirement funds in peoples' savings accounts.

Quality Ownership: Taking Responsibility for Quality To ensure high-quality goods and services, many firms assign responsibility for some aspects of TQM to specific departments or positions. These specialists and experts may be called in to assist with quality-related problems in any department, and they keep everyone informed about the latest developments in quality-related equipment and methods. They also monitor quality-control activities to identify areas for improvement.

Quality Ownership *principle of total quality management that holds that quality belongs to each person who creates it while performing a job*

The backbone of TQM, however, and its biggest challenge, is motivating all employees and the company's suppliers to achieve quality goals. Leaders of the quality movement use various methods and resources to foster a quality focus, such as training, verbal encouragement, teamwork, and tying compensation to work quality. When those efforts succeed, employees and suppliers will ultimately accept **quality ownership**, the idea that quality belongs to each person who creates it while performing a job.

With TQM, everyone—purchasers, engineers, janitors, marketers, machinists, suppliers, and others—must focus on quality. At Saint Luke's Hospital of Kansas City, for example, every employee receives the hospital's "balanced scorecard" showing whether the hospital is meeting its goals: fast patient recovery for specific illnesses, 94 percent or better patient-satisfaction rating, every room cleaned when a patient is gone to X-ray, and the hospital's return on investment being good enough to get a good bond rating in the financial markets. Quarterly scores show the achievement level reached for each goal. Every employee can recite where the hospital is excelling and where it needs improvement. In recognition of its employees' dedication to quality performance, Saint Luke's received the Malcolm Baldrige National Quality Award, the prestigious U.S. award for excellence in quality, and is a three-time winner of the Missouri Quality Award.[15]

Tools for Total Quality Management

Hundreds of tools have proven useful for quality improvement, ranging from statistical analysis of product data, to satisfaction surveys of customers, to **competitive product analysis**, a process by which a company analyzes a competitor's products to identify desirable improvements. Using competitive analysis, for example, Toshiba might take apart a Xerox copier and test each component. The results would help managers decide which Toshiba product features are satisfactory, which features should be upgraded, and which operations processes need improvement.

Competitive Product Analysis *process by which a company analyzes a competitor's products to identify desirable improvements*

In this section, we survey five of the most commonly used tools for TQM: (1) *value-added analysis*, (2) *quality improvement teams*, (3) *getting closer to the customer*, (4) *the ISO series*, and (5) *business process reengineering*.

Value-Added Analysis **Value-added analysis** refers to the evaluation of all work activities, materials flows, and paperwork to determine the value that they add for customers. It often reveals wasteful or unnecessary activities that can be eliminated without jeopardizing customer service. The basic tenet is so important that Tootsie Roll Industries, the venerable candy company, employs it as a corporate principle: "We run a trim operation and continually strive to eliminate waste, minimize cost, and implement performance improvements."[16]

Value-Added Analysis *process of evaluating all work activities, materials flows, and paperwork to determine the value that they add for customers*

Quality Improvement Teams Companies throughout the world have adopted **quality improvement teams**, which are patterned after the successful Japanese concept of *quality circles*, collaborative groups of employees from various work areas who meet regularly to define, analyze, and solve common production problems. The teams' goal is to improve both their own work methods and the products they make. Quality improvement teams organize their own work, select leaders, and address problems in the workplace. For years, Motorola has sponsored

Quality Improvement Team *total quality management tool in which collaborative groups of employees from various work areas work together to improve quality by solving common shared production problems*

companywide team competitions to emphasize the value of the team approach, to recognize outstanding team performance, and to reaffirm the team's role in the company's continuous-improvement culture.

Getting Closer to the Customer Successful businesses take steps to know what their customers want in the products they consume. On the other hand, struggling companies have often lost sight of customers as the driving force behind all business activity. Such companies waste resources by designing products that customers do not want. Sometimes, they ignore customer reactions to existing products, an example of which is the outpouring of complaints about airline services that go unanswered (see this chapter's opening case). Or companies fail to keep up with changing customer preferences. BlackBerry mobile devices, for example, fell behind competing products because they did not offer customers the features that Samsung, Motorola, and Apple provided.

Successful firms take steps to know what their customers want in the products they consume. Caterpillar's (CAT) financial services department, for example, received the Malcolm Baldrige National Quality Award for high ratings by its customers (that is, dealers and buyers of Caterpillar equipment). Buying and financing equipment from Cat Financial became easier as CAT moved its services increasingly online. Customers now have 24/7 access to information on how much they owe on equipment costing anywhere from $30,000 to $2 million, and they can make payments around the clock, too. In the past, the 60,000 customers had to phone a Cat representative, who was often unavailable, resulting in delays and wasted time. The improved online system is testimony to Cat Financial's dedication in knowing what customers want, and then providing it.[17]

IDENTIFYING CUSTOMERS—INTERNAL AND EXTERNAL
Improvement projects are undertaken for both external and internal customers. Internal suppliers and internal customers exist wherever one employee or activity relies on others. For example, marketing managers rely on internal accounting information—costs for materials, supplies, and wages—to plan marketing activities for coming months. The marketing manager is a customer of the firm's accountants, the information user relies on the information supplier. Accountants in a TQM environment recognize this supplier–customer connection and take steps to improve information for marketing.

The ISO Series Perhaps you've driven past companies proudly displaying large banners announcing, "This Facility Is ISO Certified." The ISO (pronounced ICE-oh) label is a mark of quality achievement that is respected throughout the world and, in some countries, it's a requirement for doing business.

ISO 9000 **ISO 9000** is a certification program attesting that a factory, a laboratory, or an office has met the rigorous quality management requirements set by the International Organization for Standardization (ISO). Today, more than 160 countries have adopted ISO 9000 as a national standard. Nearly 1 million certificates have been issued to organizations worldwide meeting the ISO standards.

ISO 9000 *program certifying that a factory, laboratory, or office has met the quality management standards set by the International Organization for Standardization*

The standards of *ISO 9000* allow firms to show that they follow documented procedures for testing products, training workers, keeping records, and fixing defects. It allows international companies to determine (or be assured of) quality of product (or the business) when shipping for, from, and to suppliers across borders. To become certified, companies must document the procedures followed by workers during every stage of production. The purpose is to ensure that a company's processes can create products exactly the same today as it did yesterday and as it will tomorrow.

ISO 14000 The **ISO 14000** program certifies improvements in environmental performance by requiring a firm to develop an *environmental management system*: a plan documenting how the company has acted to improve its performance in using resources (such as raw materials) and in managing pollution. A company must not only identify hazardous wastes that it expects to create, but it must also stipulate plans for treatment and disposal.

ISO 14000 *certification program attesting to the fact that a factory, laboratory, or office has improved its environmental performance*

Business Process Reengineering Every business consists of processes, activities that it performs regularly and routinely in conducting business, such as receiving and storing materials from suppliers, billing patients for medical treatment, filing insurance claims for auto accidents, and filling customer orders from Internet sales. Any business process can increase customer satisfaction by performing it well. By the same token, any business process can disappoint customers when it's poorly managed.

Business Process Reengineering *rethinking and radical redesign of business processes to improve performance, quality, and productivity*

Business process reengineering focuses on improving a business process—rethinking each of its steps by starting from scratch. *Reengineering* is the fundamental rethinking and radical redesign of business processes to achieve dramatic improvements as measured by cost, quality, service, and speed. The discussion of CAT's changeover to an online system for customers is an example. CAT reengineered the whole payments and financing process by improving equipment, retraining employees, and connecting customers to CAT's databases. As the example illustrates, redesign is guided by a desire to improve operations and thereby provide higher-value services for customers.

OBJECTIVE 8
Explain

how a supply chain strategy differs from traditional strategies for coordinating operations among firms.

supply chain (value chain) *flow of information, materials, and services that starts with raw-materials suppliers and continues adding value through other stages in the network of firms until the product reaches the end customer*

Adding Value through Supply Chains

The term *supply chain* refers to the group of companies and stream of activities that work together to create a product. A **supply chain** (or **value chain**) for any product is the flow of information, materials, and services that starts with raw-materials suppliers and continues adding value through other stages in the network of firms until the product reaches the end customer.

Figure 7.13 shows the chain of activities for supplying baked goods to consumers. Each stage adds value for the final customer. This bakery example begins with raw materials (grain harvested from the farm). It also includes storage and transportation activities, factory operations for baking and wrapping, and distribution to retailers. Each stage depends on the others for success in getting freshly baked goods to consumers. However, a failure by any link can spell disaster for the entire chain.

The Supply Chain Strategy

Traditional strategies assume that companies are managed as individual firms rather than as members of a coordinated supply system. Supply chain strategy is based on the idea that members of the chain will gain competitive advantage by working as a coordinated unit. Although each company looks out for its own interests, it works closely with suppliers and customers throughout the chain. Everyone focuses on the entire chain of relationships rather than on just the next stage in the chain.

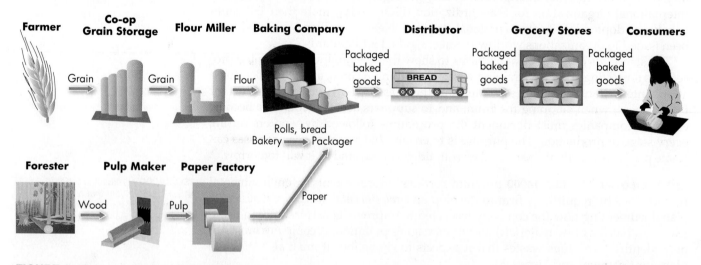

FIGURE 7.13 Supply Chain for Baked Goods

A traditionally managed bakery, for example, would focus simply on getting production inputs from flour millers and paper suppliers, and then on supplying baked goods to distributors. Unfortunately, this approach limits the chain's performance and doesn't allow for possible improvements when activities are more carefully coordinated. Proper management and better coordination among supply chain activities can provide fresher baked goods at lower prices.

Supply Chain Management Supply chain management (SCM) looks at the chain as a whole to improve the overall flow through a system composed of companies working together. Because customers ultimately get better value, supply chain management gains competitive advantage for each of the chain's members.

An innovative supply chain strategy was the heart of Michael Dell's vision when he established Dell Inc. Dell's concept improves performance by sharing information among chain members. Dell's long-term production plans and up-to-the-minute sales data are available to suppliers via the Internet. The process starts when customer orders are automatically translated into updated production schedules in the factory. These schedules are used not only by operations managers at Dell but also by such parts suppliers as Sony, which adjust their own production and shipping activities to better meet Dell's production needs. In turn, parts suppliers' updated schedules are transmitted to their materials suppliers, and so on up the chain. As Dell's requirements change, suppliers up and down the chain synchronize their schedules to produce only the right materials and parts. As a result, Dell's prices are low and turnaround time for shipping PCs to customers is reduced to a matter of hours instead of days.

> **Supply Chain Management (SCM)** *principle of looking at the supply chain as a whole to improve the overall flow through the system*

Reengineering Supply Chains for Better Results Process improvements and reengineering often are applied in supply chains to lower costs, speed up service, and coordinate flows of information and material. Because the smoother flow of accurate information along the chain reduces unwanted inventories and transportation, avoids delays, and cuts supply times, materials move faster to business customers and individual consumers. SCM offers faster deliveries and lower costs than customers could get if each member acted only according to its own operations requirements.

Outsourcing and Global Supply Chains

Outsourcing is the strategy of paying suppliers and distributors to perform certain business processes or to provide needed materials or services. The decision to outsource expands supply chains. The movement of manufacturing and service operations from the United States to countries such as China, Mexico, and India has reduced U.S. employment in traditional jobs. It has also created new operations jobs for SCM. Maytag, for example, had to develop its own internal global operations expertise before it could decide to open a new refrigerator factory in Mexico, import refrigerators from South Korea's Daewoo, and get laundry appliances from South Korea's Samsung Electronics. In departing from a long-standing practice of domestic production, Maytag adopted new supply chain skills for evaluating prospective outsourcing partners.

> **Outsourcing** *replacing internal processes by paying suppliers and distributors to perform business processes or to provide needed materials or services*

Skills for coordinating Maytag's domestic activities with those of its cross-border partners didn't end with the initial decision to get appliances from Mexico and Korea. Maytag personnel in their Newton, Iowa, headquarters have near-constant interaction with their partners on a host of continuing new operations issues. Product redesigns are transferred from the United States and used at remote manufacturing sites. Arrangements for cross-border materials flows require compliance with each country's commerce regulations. Production and global transportation scheduling are coordinated with U.S. market demand so that outsourced products arrive in the right amounts and on time without tarnishing Maytag's reputation for high quality. Although manufacturing operations are located remotely, they are closely integrated with the firm's home-base activities. That tightness of integration demands on-site operations expertise on both sides of the outsourcing equation. Global communication technologies are essential. The result for outsourcers is a greater need of operations skills for integration among dispersed facilities.

summary of learning objectives

OBJECTIVE 1

Explain the meaning of the term *production* or *operations* and describe the three kinds of utility that operations processes provide for adding customer value. (pp. 232–234)

Operations (or *production*) refers to all the activities involved in making products—goods and services—for customers. In modern societies, much of what we need or want is produced by service operations, where success or failure depends on provider-customer contact. Many companies, such as General Electric, provide both goods and services. Employment has risen significantly in the service sector over the past 10 years. However, the 11 percent of the U.S. workforce employed in producing goods generate 32 percent of national income.

Production or operations adds customer value by providing *utility*—the ability of a product to satisfy a want or need—in terms of form, time, and place: (1) *Form utility*: By turning raw materials and human skills into finished goods and services, production adds customer value by making products available. (2) *Time utility*: Production provides customer value by making products available when customers want them. (3) *Place utility*: Production adds customer value by making products available where they are convenient for customers.

Operations management is the systematic direction and control of the activities that transform resources into finished goods and services that create value for and provide benefits to customers. Through their operations processes—using resources that include knowledge, physical materials, information, equipment, the customer, and human skills—firms provide benefits for themselves and for their customers.

OBJECTIVE 2

Identify the characteristics that distinguish service operations from goods production. (pp. 234–238)

Although the creation of both goods and services involves resources, transformations, and finished products, service operations differ from goods manufacturing in several important ways. In service production, the raw materials are not things such as glass or steel, but rather people who choose among sellers because they have unsatisfied needs or possessions in need of care or alteration. Therefore, whereas services are typically performed, goods are physically produced. In addition, services are largely *intangible* and more *unstorable* than most physical goods. It is difficult, as an example, to store a supply (an inventory) of childcare services. If the services are not consumed when available, they are lost forever.

Service businesses, therefore, focus explicitly on the intangibility and unstorable nature of their products. Because services are intangible, for instance, providers work to ensure that customers receive value in the form of pleasure, satisfaction, or a feeling of safety. Often they also focus on both the transformation process and the final product (such as, making the loan interview a pleasant experience as well as providing the loan itself). As part of the transformation process, service providers typically focus on *customer-provider contact*. This requires service workers who, because they interact with customers, possess different skills than workers producing physical goods.

An *operations process* is a set of methods and technologies used to produce a good or service. Goods production can be classified as *make-to-order* or *make-to-stock*. Make-to-order operations respond to specific customer specifications, and make-to-stock operations produce standardized goods for mass consumption.

Service operations can be classified according to the extent of customer contact. In a *low-contact system*, customers have a limited presence as the service is performed. Low-contact systems include mail and package delivery, auto repair, lawn care services, and gas and electric providers. On the other hand, in a *high-contact system*, the customer is present as the service is delivered. Examples of high-contact systems include airlines and hair salons.

OBJECTIVE 3

Explain how companies with different business strategies are best served by having different operations capabilities. (pp. 238–240)

Production is a flexible activity that can be molded into many shapes to give different operations capabilities (production capabilities) for different purposes. Its design is best driven from above by the firm's larger business strategy. When firms adopt different strategies for winning customers in specific target markets, they should also adjust their *operations capabilities*—what production must do especially well—to match the chosen strategy. That is, different target markets have different desires or expectations for the products—services and goods—that they seek. Accordingly, operations managers must clarify and understand their target market's most-preferred product characteristic, from among the following: Do they want low-cost products? Highest quality products? Dependability of product performance? A wide variety of offerings rather than just a few? To meet any chosen strategy, then, they adopt an operations capability that is geared toward meeting the target customers' needs. The operations capability that is appropriate for a low-cost strategy, for example, is different than the kind of competence that is best for a dependability strategy. Accordingly, the operations characteristics, such as number and size of production facilities, employee skills, kinds of equipment, and its operations activities will be different, resulting in different operations capabilities to better support their different purposes.

OBJECTIVE 4

Identify the major factors that are considered in operations planning. (pp. 240–246)

Operations planning includes five major considerations: (1) *Capacity planning* considers current and future capacity requirements for meeting anticipated customer demand. The amount of a product that a company can produce under normal conditions is its *capacity*, and it depends on how many people it employs and the number and sizes of its facilities. (2) *Location planning* is crucial because a firm's location affects costs of production, ease of transportation, access to skilled workers, and convenient accessibility for customers. (3) *Layout planning* determines the physical location of service teams, machinery, equipment, and facilities and affects how efficiently a company can respond to customer demand. A *process (custom-products) layout* is effective for make-to-order production specializing in custom designed services or goods. A *product (same-steps) layout*, such as an assembly line, is often used for large-volume, make-to-stock production of services or goods. A *fixed-position layout* is necessary when, because of size, shape, or any other reason the service to be provided cannot be moved to another facility. Instead, the product or client remains at one location; equipment, materials and human skills are moved to that location, as needed, to perform the service or to build the product. (4) *Quality planning* begins when products are being designed and extends into production operations for ensuring that the desired performance and consistency are built into products. Quality is defined as the combination of "characteristics of a product or service that bear on its ability to satisfy stated or implied needs." Quality planning involves setting goals for both *performance* and *consistency*. (5) *Methods planning* considers each production step and the specific methods for performing it for producing services and goods. The purpose is to reduce waste and inefficiency by methods improvement procedures.

OBJECTIVE 5

Discuss the information contained in four kinds of operations schedules—the master operations schedule, detailed schedule, staff schedule, and project schedule. (pp. 246–249)

Operations scheduling identifies times when specific operations activities will occur. The *master schedule*, the top-level schedule for upcoming production, shows how many of which products (services or goods) will be produced in each time period, in weeks or months ahead, to meet upcoming customer demand. Thereafter, the schedule shows how many units of each major resource—materials, employees, equipment—will be required. By identifying these future resource requirements, managers can develop plans for acquiring the resources on time for upcoming time periods.

Detailed schedules take a shorter-range perspective by specifying daily work assignments with start and stop times for assigned jobs at each workstation. Detailed schedules allow managers and other employees to make last-minute adjustments so that resources are available and matched to meet immediate customer service requirements.

Staff schedules identify who and how many employees will be working and their assigned working times on each work shift for the upcoming month or months. Staff scheduling considers the needs of employees as well as the company's goals of maximizing efficiency and controlling costs.

Finally, *project schedules* provide information for completing large-scale projects using project scheduling tools, such as Gantt and *PERT charts. A Gantt chart* breaks down special large projects into the sequence of steps to be performed and specifies the time required to perform each. Gantt charts help managers to assess if work is ahead or behind schedule so that adjustments can be made. PERT charts show the necessary sequence among activities, and identify the critical path—the most time-consuming set of activities for completing the project.

OBJECTIVE 6

Discuss the two key activities required for operations control. (pp. 249–251)

Materials management and quality control are two key activities of operations control. Once plans and schedules have been drawn up, operations control requires managers to monitor performance by comparing results against those plans and schedules. If schedules or quality standards are not met, managers take corrective action. Follow-up—checking to ensure that decisions are being implemented—is an essential facet of operations control. Materials management—including supplier selection, purchasing, transportation, warehousing, and inventory control—facilitates the flow of materials. Materials management is the process by which managers plan, organize, and control the flow of materials and services from sources of supply through distribution of finished products to customers. For producing and delivering physical goods, it may use lean production systems, such as just-in-time-operations, for smooth production flows that avoid inefficiencies, comply with schedules, eliminate unnecessary inventories, and continuously improve production processes. For high-contact services, such as tourism and vacation services, inventory exists in the form of information about service offerings, facilities arrangements, clients, client interests, activities schedules, and plans for interactions among and with clients. Quality control means taking action to ensure that operations produce goods and services that meet specific quality standards. By monitoring products and services, managers and other employees can detect mistakes, identify potential quality failures, and make corrections to avoid poor quality. Both materials management and quality control are essential to ensure that schedules are met and products delivered, both in quality and quantity.

OBJECTIVE 7

Identify the activities and underlying objectives involved in total quality management. (pp. 251–256)

Successful companies focus on productivity, which measures both the quantity and quality of the products produced or delivered. Productivity compares the level of production with the amount of resources used to produce it. *Total quality management (TQM)* is a customer-driven culture for offering products with characteristics that customers want. It includes all the activities necessary for getting customer-satisfying goods and services into the marketplace and, internally, getting every job to give better service to internal customers (other departments) within the organization. TQM begins with leadership and a desire for continuously improving both processes and products. It considers all aspects of a business, including customers, suppliers, and employees. The TQM culture fosters an attitude of *quality ownership* among employees and suppliers, the idea that quality belongs to each person who creates it while performing a job, so that quality improvement becomes a continuous way of life. It identifies the *costs of poor quality*, including all forms of financial distress resulting from poor-quality products, and uses cost-of-poor-quality information as a guide for process improvement to prevent such costs in the future.

Numerous quality-improvement tools can then be used to gain those improvements and reduce those costs. Some process improvement tools of TQM include competitive product analysis, value-added analysis, the use of quality improvement teams, business process reengineering, and "getting closer to the customer" to gain valid information of what customers really want, so that improved products more closely meet customer desires.

ISO 9000 is a certification program attesting that a factory, laboratory, or office has met the rigorous quality management requirements set by the International Organization for Standardization. Similarly, *ISO 14000* certifies improvements in environmental performance. Finally, business process reengineering focuses on the radical redesign of business processes to achieve improvements in cost, quality, service, and speed.

OBJECTIVE 8

Explain how a supply chain strategy differs from traditional strategies for coordinating operations among firms. (pp. 256–257)

The supply chain strategy is based on the idea that members of the *supply chain*, the stream of all activities and companies that add value in creating a product, will gain competitive advantage by working together as a coordinated unit. The supply chain for any product, be it a service or a physical good, is the flow of information, materials, and services that starts with raw-materials suppliers and continues adding value through other stages in the network of firms until the product reaches the end customer. In contrast, traditional strategies assume that companies are managed as individual firms, each acting in its own interest. By managing the chain as a whole—using *supply chain management*—companies can more closely coordinate activities throughout the chain. Because accurate information is shared between companies along the chain, they can reduce unwanted materials and transportation, avoid delays in deliveries to cut supply times, quickly add service centers to meet upsurges in demand, and move materials faster through the chain. By sharing information across all stages in the chain, overall costs and inventories can be reduced, quality can be improved, and overall flow through the system improves, thus providing customers higher value from faster deliveries and lower costs.

Outsourcing, the strategy of paying suppliers and distributors to perform certain business processes or to provide needed materials or services, expands supply chains. The prevalence of outsourcing has created new operations jobs in supply chain management.

key terms

assembly line layout (p. 243)
business process reengineering (p. 256)
capacity (p. 240)
competitive product analysis (p. 254)
consistency (p. 245)
detailed schedule (p. 247)
fixed-position layout (p. 244)
follow-up (p. 249)
Gantt chart (p. 248)
goods operations (goods production) (p. 232)
high-contact system (p. 237)
inventory control (p. 250)
ISO 9000 (p. 255)
ISO 14000 (p. 255)
just-in-time (JIT) production (p. 250)
lean production system (p. 250)
low-contact system (p. 237)

make-to-order operations (p. 237)
make-to-stock operations (p. 237)
master operations schedule (p. 246)
materials management (p. 249)
operations capability (production capability) (p. 238)
operations control (p. 249)
operations process (p. 236)
operations (production) (p. 232)
operations (production) management (p. 234)
operations (production) managers (p. 235)
outsourcing (p. 257)
process layout (custom-product layout) (p. 243)
product layout (same-steps layout) (p. 243)
productivity (p. 252)
performance (p. 245)

PERT chart (p. 248)
purchasing (p. 250)
quality (p. 244)
quality control (p. 251)
quality improvement team (p. 254)
quality ownership (p. 254)
service operations (service production) (p. 232)
staff schedule (p. 247)
supplier selection (p. 250)
supply chain management (SCM) (p. 257)
supply chain (value chain) (p. 256)
total quality management (TQM) (p. 252)
transportation (p. 250)
utility (p. 234)
value-added analysis (p. 254)
warehousing (p. 250)

Go to **pearsonglobaleditions.com/mybizlab** to complete the problems marked with this icon ✪.

questions & exercises

QUESTIONS FOR REVIEW

7-1. Describe the three forms of utility created through production.

7-2. What are the major differences between goods-production operations and service operations?

⭐ **7-3.** What are the major differences between high-contact and low-contact service systems?

7-4. What are the five major categories of operations planning?

QUESTIONS FOR ANALYSIS

⭐ **7-5.** Although we typically use these terms with goods production, is your college a make-to-order or make-to-stock operation? Be sure to support your conclusion.

7-6. What type of business strategy is used at Disney theme parks? What specific operations activities are most important?

7-7. Develop a list of internal customers and internal suppliers for some business that you use frequently (or where you work), such as a cafeteria, a dormitory or hotel, or a movie theater. Identify areas for potential quality improvement in these internal customer–supplier activity relationships.

⭐ **7-8.** If you were a member of a quality improvement team at your college, what would be five specific high-impact recommendations that you would support?

APPLICATION EXERCISES

7-9. Think of an everyday activity, either personal or professional, that you would like to streamline for faster performance or more convenience. It could be something like gassing up your car, going to work or school, enrolling in classes at school, or any other activity that involves several stages with which you are familiar. Describe how you would use methods planning as described in the chapter to improve the activity. Draw a process flowchart that shows the stages in the activity you chose, and then tell how you would use it.

7-10. Interview the manager of a local service business, such as a restaurant or hair salon. Identify the major decisions involved in planning that business's service operations.

building a business: continuing team exercise

Assignment

Meet with your team members to consider your new business venture and how it relates to the operations management and quality topics in this chapter. Develop specific responses to the following:

7-11. In what ways is your business connected with service operations? Identify the ways it is connected with goods production. Which of these, service operations or goods production, is more important to your business? Why?

7-12. The product(s) your business offers to its customers will depend, as part of the business strategy, on your target market (a chosen segment of customers you have, or will, identify). Explain what must be done to ensure that your operations capabilities are consistent with your business strategy.

7-13. Discuss how your team is going to identify the key operations characteristics that best provide support for accomplishing your business strategy. Based on the discussion, what are the key characteristics that seem to be most prominent at this stage of development of your business?

7-14. Analyze the planned production activities for your business to determine the operations processes for which total quality management will be important.

7-15. In what ways, if any, will supply chains be of concern for your business? Explain.

building your business skills

THE ONE-ON-ONE ENTREPRENEUR

Goal

To encourage you to apply the concept of customization to an entrepreneurial idea.

Background Information

You are an entrepreneur who wants to start your own service business. You are intrigued with the idea of creating some kind of customized one-on-one service that would appeal to baby boomers, who often like to be pampered, and working women, who have little time to get things done.

Method

STEP 1

Get together with three or four other students to brainstorm ideas for services that would appeal to busy working people. Here are just a few:

- A concierge service in office buildings that would handle such personal and business services as arranging children's birthday parties and booking guest speakers for business luncheons.
- A personal-image consultation service aimed at helping clients improve appearance, etiquette, and presentation style.
- A mobile pet-care network through which vets and groomers make house calls.

STEP 2

Choose one of these ideas or one that your team thinks of. Then write a memo explaining why you think your idea will succeed. Research may be necessary as you target any of the following:

- A specific demographic group or groups (Who are your customers, and why would they buy your service?)
- Features that make your service attractive to this group
- The social factors in your local community that would contribute to success

FOLLOW-UP QUESTIONS

7-16. Why is the customization of and easy access to personal services so desirable?

7-17. As services are personalized, do you think quality will become more or less important? Why?

7-18. Why does the trend toward personalized, one-on-one service present unique opportunities for entrepreneurs?

7-19. In a personal one-on-one business, how important are the human relations skills of those delivering the service? Can you make an argument that they are more important than the service itself?

exercising your ethics

PROMISES, PROMISES

The Situation

Unfortunately, false promises are not uncommon when managers feel pressure to pump up profits. Many operations managers no doubt recall times when excited marketing managers asked for unrealistic commitments from production to get a new customer contract. This exercise will introduce you to some ethical considerations pertaining to such promises and commitments.

The Dilemma

You are an operations manager for a factory that makes replacement car mufflers and tailpipes. Your products are distributed throughout the country to muffler-repair shops that install them on used vehicles. After several years of modest but steady growth, your company recently suffered a downturn and shut down 5 percent of the factory's production capacity. Two supervisors and 70 production workers were laid off.

After returning from lunch, you get a phone call from the general manager of King Kong Mufflers, one of the nation's top three muffler-repair chains, who says the following:

I suppose you know that we're about to sign a contract for your firm to supply us with replacement parts in large volumes,

beginning two months from now. Your sales manager assures me that you can reliably meet my needs, and I just want to confirm that promise with you before I sign the contract.

This is the first you've heard about this contract. While your potential customer is talking, you realize that meeting his needs will require a 20-percent increase in your current production capacity. Two months, however, isn't enough time to add more equipment, acquire tools, hire and train workers, and contract for supplies. An increase this large might even require a bigger building (which would take considerably more than two months to arrange). On the other hand, you also know how much your firm needs the business. Your thoughts are interrupted when the caller says, "So what's your production situation insofar as meeting our needs?" The caller waits in silence while you gather your thoughts.

QUESTIONS TO ADDRESS

7-20. What are the underlying ethical issues in this situation?

7-21. From an ethical standpoint, what is an appropriate response to the customer's question? What steps should you take in responding to it? Explain.

7-22. What would you say on the phone at this time to this customer?

team exercise

CALCULATING THE COST OF CONSCIENCE

The Situation

Product quality and cost affect every firm's reputation and profitability, as well as the satisfaction of customers. As director of quality for a major appliance manufacturer, Ruth was reporting to the executive committee on the results of a program for correcting problems with a newly redesigned compressor (the motor that cools the refrigerator) that the company had recently begun using in its refrigerators. Following several customer complaints, the quality lab had determined that some of the new compressor units ran more loudly than expected, although it still effectively cooled the units.

The Decision

Faced with this information, Ruth has been asked to recommend a strategy for the company. One corrective option was simply waiting until customers complained and responding to each complaint if and when it occurred. Fixing noisy units could be expensive, but the company wishes to maintain its high-quality image.

Ruth, however, decided that this approach was inconsistent with the company's policy of being the high-quality leader in the industry. Insisting on a proactive, "pro-quality" approach, Ruth suggests a program for contacting all customers who had purchased refrigerators containing the new compressor. Unfortunately, the "quality-and-customers-first" policy will be expensive. Service representatives nationwide will have to phone every customer, make appointments for home visits, and replace original compressors with a newer model. Because replacement time is only 30 minutes, customers will hardly be inconvenienced, and food will stay refrigerated without interruption.

Others have even suggested that the company require consumers to pay a part of the cost of repairing the noisy compressor because the compressors still meet all expectations with respect to cooling, and this is the primary function of the refrigerator. Advocates of this position argue that the new compressors will extend the life of the refrigerator and customers will benefit.

Team Activity

Assemble a group of four students and assign each group member to one of the following roles:

- Ruth, director of quality
- Ruth's boss, the Vice-President for Operations
- a customer
- a company investor

ACTION STEPS

7-23. Before hearing any of your group's comments on this situation, and from the perspective of your assigned role, how should the company deal with the noisy compressors? List the reasons for your position.
7-24. Have each member of your team reveal their recommendation and reasons from the perspective of their assigned role.
7-25. Which is the best of the three options in the short-term? What about in the long-term?
7-26. How could the company have avoided this situation?

cases

Ryanair Customer Satisfaction— but Who to Believe?

Continued from page 232

At the beginning of this chapter you read about the experiences of airline passengers and their reactions, both negative and positive, to the quality of services received. Using the information presented in this chapter you should now be able to answer these questions.

7-27. How would you define *quality* and how is quality measured in this industry? Are some measurements more useful than others? Explain.
7-28. Some *service activities*, such as delayed departures, are not under total control by airlines, but are affected by outside factors. Among all service activities that affect quality for customers, identify three or more that are totally controlled by airlines, and three or more that airlines cannot totally control. Should both sets of activities be included in the airlines' quality ratings? Explain.

QUESTIONS FOR DISCUSSION

7-29. How would you define quality, and how is quality measured in this industry? Are some measurements more useful than others? Explain.
7-30. Some service activities, such as delayed departures, are not under total control by airlines, but are also affected by outside factors. Among all service activities that affect quality for customers, identify three or more that are totally controlled by airlines, and three or more that airlines cannot totally control. Should both sets of activities be included in the airlines' quality ratings? Explain.
7-31. Describe how process flowcharts may be helpful for methods improvement in airline service operations. What kinds of information would you hope to gain from the flowcharts?
7-32. Identify a major airline that has received poor quality ratings. Who are its customers, and what are the basic causes that led to declining quality?
7-33. U.S. airplane passengers must choose between two controversial security screening procedures: full-body image detection or probing pat-downs. How might these procedures affect customers' perceptions of airlines' services? What actions would you recommend be considered by airlines to overcome negative perceptions?

Telecommuting Boosts Quality and Productivity… Or Does It?

Early in 2013, Yahoo! CEO Marissa Mayer made the controversial decision to ban employees from working exclusively at home. Her action seems to run in the face of a years-long trend in the opposite direction by her company and other businesses across many industries. The question, then, that faces many organizations (and employees) is the following: Is telecommuting really beneficial? And if so, who reaps those benefits? Certainly today's information technologies provide telecommuting possibilities on a larger scale than ever before. Yahoo, like many other firms, has an internal Virtual Private Network, into which thousands of employees can log in at remote locations for conducting company business. Mayer's decision suggests that disadvantages outweigh advantages for her company at the present time.[18]

Included among the key questions at Yahoo and other companies is the following: "What happens with employee productivity and quality?" More and more U.S. employees are working remotely than ever before, and the trend is increasing. In 2010, for example, some 13.4 million were working at home one day or more per week. Previously, in 1997, that number was just 9.2 million. Because those numbers are growing, the future stakes for businesses and employees will depend even more on decisions about home-based versus office-based employment.[19]

Advocates for telecommuting cite its benefits. A Stanford study indicates a 13-percent productivity increase for call center employees working at home. It also cites greater work satisfaction and less employee turnover. Other studies report home-based employees work up to seven hours longer in their workweek than do those working at the office, have greater productivity, and less absenteeism. At-home employees note that they don't get distracted by co-workers, they avoid unnecessary commute time, take breaks when they prefer, and have a better quality of life, among other benefits.[20]

Critics, in contrast, note telecommuting's downside. Some people simply don't like to work alone. Others are not as productive working alone because better ideas and problem solutions are more forthcoming through face-to-face interactions and being physically nearby for work-related discussions. Also cited are advantages of separating home and workplace, avoiding the many distractions at home, and claims that telecommuting is widely abused. Employers report that having at least some scheduled on-site work time, even if not full-time, provides better performance including problem solutions for customer service.

Mayer concluded that Yahoo's quality and productivity were at unacceptable levels because of too many employees working exclusively at home. She is reported to favor working at the office, citing benefits of gaining information and ideas from meeting new people, from spontaneous conversations in the hallways, and quick accessibility to other face-to-face interactions for solving problems. "Speed and quality are often sacrificed when we work from home." Accordingly, Mayer suspected that Yahoo's telecommuting may be less productive than it should be. Rather than relying on mere suspicions, she wanted some factual basis, preferable backed up by data. So, she turned to Yahoo's Virtual Private Network and looked at the data files showing frequencies of employees' log-ins. She concluded that they were not checking in enough, thus indicating too much inactivity and too little productivity.[21]

Does face-to-face contact among employees really affect quality and productivity? A study of workers in call-center teams at Bank of America found that, yes, it does matter. Productivity was found to be greatest for workers in close-knit teams where workers mingled more frequently, rather than when working alone. Collaboration and spontaneous information sharing seemed to enhance productivity. But what about in other jobs where workers face different kinds of tasks, some more complex and others much simpler? Does either the office setting or the telecommuting setting, in general, always provide more promise for better productivity and quality? The answer is more likely to be situational rather than "one size fits all."[22]

QUESTIONS FOR DISCUSSION

7-32. How would you define *quality* for Yahoo's situation in this case? Explain why.

7-33. To figure out if Yahoo's telecommuting is less productive than it should have been Mayer looked at the log of Yahoo's Virtual Private Network to see how frequently employees checked in. What do you think of this as a measure of productivity and quality? What other measure(s) would you suggest instead of the one she used?

7-34. Go to the Internet (or other sources) and look at the kinds of jobs available at Yahoo. From these, identify two job descriptions that you recommend as appropriate for telecommuting. Identify two others that are appropriate for office-based employment. Explain the reasons for your recommendations.

7-35. Consider businesses such as hotels, television broadcasting, or others that provide services products to consumers. Suppose you want to improve the quality of such a service (choose one or two services). To do so, suppose you are considering allowing telecommuting by some employees, but requiring others to be office-based employees. Identify two kinds of work suitable for telecommuting, and two kinds for office-only jobs. Explain your reasoning.

7-36. In general, how would you measure a service-provider's quality and productivity? Recommend specific measures that will enable you to track changes in quality and productivity with the passage of time.

crafting a business plan

PART 2: THE BUSINESS OF MANAGING

Goal of the Exercise

In Part 1 of the business plan project, you formulated a basic identity for your business. Part 2 of the business plan project asks you to think about the goals of your business, some internal and external factors affecting the business, as well as the organizational structure of the business.

Exercise Background: Part 2 of the Business Plan

As you learned in Chapter 5, every business sets goals. In this part of the plan, you'll define some of the goals for your business.

Part 2 of the business plan also asks you to perform a basic SWOT analysis for your business. As you'll recall from Chapter 5, a SWOT analysis looks at the business's *strengths, weaknesses, opportunities*, and *threats*. The strengths and weaknesses are internal factors—things that the business can control. The opportunities and threats are generally external factors that affect the business:

Sociocultural forces	Will changes in population or culture help your business or hurt it?
Economic forces	Will changes in the economy help your business or hurt it?
Technological forces	Will changes in technology help your business or hurt it?
Competitive forces	Does your business face much competition or very little?
Political-legal forces	Will changes in laws help your business or hurt it?

Each of these forces will affect different businesses in different ways, and some of these may not apply to your business at all.

Part 2 of the business plan also asks you to determine how the business is to be run. Part of this will require you to create an organizational chart to get you thinking about the different tasks needed for a successful business. You'll also examine various factors relating to operating your business.

Your Assignment

STEP 1

Open the saved *Business Plan* file you began working on in Part 1. You will continue to work from the same file you started working on in Part 1.

STEP 2

For the purposes of this assignment, you will answer the questions in "Part 2: The Business of Managing:"

7-37. Provide a brief mission statement for your business.
Hint: Refer to the discussion of mission statements in Chapter 5. Be sure to include the name of your business, how you will stand out from your competition, and why a customer will buy from you.

7-38. Consider the goals for your business. What are three of your business goals for the first year? What are two intermediate to long-term goals?
Hint: Refer to the discussion of goal setting in Chapter 5. Be as specific and realistic as possible with the goals you set. For example, if you plan on selling a service, how many customers do you want by the end of the first year, and how much do you want each customer to spend?

7-39. Perform a basic SWOT analysis for your business, listing its main strengths, weaknesses, opportunities, and threats.
Hint: We explained previously what factors you should consider in your basic SWOT analysis. Look around at your world, talk to classmates, or talk to your instructor for other ideas in performing your SWOT analysis.

7-40. Who will manage the business? *Hint*: Refer to the discussion of managers in Chapter 5. Think about how many *levels* of management as well as what *kinds* of managers your business needs.

7-41. Show how the "team" fits together by creating a simple organizational chart for your business. Your chart should indicate who will work for each manager as well as each person's job title.
Hint: As you create your organizational chart, consider the different tasks involved in the business. Whom will each person report to? Refer to the discussion of organizational structure in Chapter 6 for information to get you started.

7-42. Create a floor plan of the business. What does it look like when you walk through the door?
Hint: When sketching your floor plan, consider where equipment, supplies, and furniture will be located.

7-43. Explain what types of raw materials and supplies you will need to run your business. How will you produce your good or service? What equipment do you need? What hours will you operate?
Hint: Refer to the discussion of operations in this chapter for information to get you started.

7-44. What steps will you take to ensure that the quality of the product or service stays at a high level? Who will be responsible for maintaining quality standards?
Hint: Refer to the discussion of quality improvement and TQM in this chapter for information to get you started. *Note*: Once you have answered the questions, save your Word document. You'll be answering additional questions in later chapters.

MyBizLab

Go to **pearsonglobaleditions.com/mybizlab** *for the following Assisted-graded writing questions:*

7-45. Operations (production) management exists in both services-producing companies and physical-goods producing businesses. Think about the meaning of the term "operations (or production)," and what it is like in services and in goods-producing companies. (a) Describe the meaning of the term *production* or *operations* management. (b) Describe how operations in services-producing companies are similar to those in goods-producing companies. (c) In what important ways are operations different for goods-producing operations versus services-producers? Give examples of how and why operations activities are different in the two settings.

7-46. Successful business leaders say that any business's success depends on the matchup (or compatibility) between its operations capabilities and its overall business strategy. That is, major competitive weaknesses exist when operations capabilities are not consistent with or conflict with company strategy. In contrast, successful companies ensure that operations are designed to support overall strategy. Compare and contrast two companies that have chosen different strategies for attracting customers, as follows: (a) Describe the differences in their strategies. (b) Identify and describe key operations capabilities and characteristics for each company. (c) Explain for each company how its operations characteristics either support its strategy, or how those characteristics do not support its overall strategy.

7-47. Mybizlab Only—comprehensive writing assignment for this chapter.

end notes

1 *The Economist,* "Snarling all the way to the bank." August 23, 2007; RTE Ryanair introducing €2 passenger levy, http://www.rte.ie/news/2011/0330/ryanair.html; Ryanair, http://www.ryanair.com/en/news/ryanair-no-1customer-servicestats-september-2011.

2 General Electric Company, *Annual Report for Year Ended Dec. 31, 2011, FORM 10-K,* (U.S. Securities and Exchange Commission, February 24, 2012).

3 2013 Global Manufacturing Competitiveness Index, Delottte Touche Tohmatsu Limited, at http://www.deloitte.com/assets/Dcom-Global/Local%20Assets/Documents/Manufacturing/dttl_2013%20Global%20Manufacturing%20Competitiveness%20Index_11_15_12.pdf, accessed on March 1, 2013.

4 Alex Hill and Terry Hill, *Manufacturing Operations Strategy,* 3rd edition (Basingstoke, UK: Palgrave Macmillan, 2009); James A. Fitzsimmons, Mona J. Fitzsimmons, *Service Management: Operations Strategy, Information Technology,* 6th edition (Boston: Irwin McGraw-Hill, 2008), 46–48.

5 Grace Gagliano, "Turning Meal Planning into a Business," *BRADENTON.COM,* August 19, 2010, at http://www.bradenton.com/2010/08/19/2515525/turning-meal-planning-into-a-business.html#ixzz0x3CL8WIj; http://www.grocerydash.com.

6 Star-Ledger Wire Services, "Moms Combine Tech with Frugality to Save Money, Time at Supermarket," *NJ.com,* August 24, 2010 at http://www.nj.com/business/index.ssf/2010/08/moms_combine_tech_with_frugali.html; http://www.grocerydash.com.

7 http://www.grocerydash.com.

8 The Sacramento Bee, "Paradise Found," September 1, 2010 *Columbia Daily Tribune,* 6B; "Paradise Laundry Goes 'Topless' in New Store," *ACO American Coin-Op,* September 5, 2012, at https://www.americancoinop.com/articles/paradise-laundry-goes-'topless'-new-store; *Paradise Laundries* at http://www.paradiselaundries.com.

9 Martin Santa, "Slowing Car Production Prompts Slovak Industrial Output Decline," *Reuters.com,* February 8, 2013, at http://www.reuters.com/article/2013/02/08/slovakia-economy-idUSL5N0B85G120130208; Jack Ewing, "The Auto Slump Hits Slovakia," *SPIEGEL ONLINE,* June 19, 2009 at http://www.spiegel.de/international/business/0,1518,druck-631388,00.html; Gail Edmondson, Willam Boston, Andrea Zammert, "Detroit East," *BusinessWeek,* July 25, 2005, at http://www.businessweek.com/print/magazine/content/05_30/b3944003.htm?chan=gl/.

10 American Society for Quality, "ASQ Glossary of Terms," at asq.org/glossary/q.html, accessed on February 25, 2013.

11 "How We Make Chocolate," at http://www.godiva.com/experience-godiva/HowWeMakeChocolate_RichArticle,default,pg.html, accessed on February 25, 2013.

12 "About Collette" and "Ways to Tour," *Collette Vacations* at www.collettevacations.com, accessed July 24, 2013.

13 "International Comparisons of GDP per Capita and per Hour, 1960-2011," *U.S. Bureau of Labor Statistics,* at http://www.bls.gov/ilc/intl_gdp_capita_gdp_hour.htm#table03, accessed on March 3, 2013.

14 *Some Egypt businesses thrive in crush of economic downturn,* Shaimaa Fayed and Patrick Werr, Chicago Tribune/Reuters, August 11 2013 (http://articles.chicagotribune.com/2013-08-11/business/sns-rt-us-egypt-business-20130811_1_businesses-6-percent-economy) accessed 13/11/2013 *Aller Aqua Group builds new factory in Egypt* (http://www.panoramaacuicola.com/noticias/2013/03/19/aller_aqua_group_builds_new_factory_in_egypt.html) accessed 13/11/2013.

15 "Missouri Quality Award: Fifth Win for Saint Luke's, Second Time as a Health System," November 2010, at https://www.saintlukeshealthsystem.org/article/missouri-quality-award; Del Jones, "Baldrige Award Honors Record 7 Quality Winners," *USA Today,* November 26, 2003, 6B.

16 Tootsie Roll Industries, Inc., *Annual Report 2009* (Chicago: 2010), p. 1.

17 Del Jones, "Baldrige Award Honors Record 7 Quality Winners," *USA Today,* November 26, 2003, 6B.

18 Nicholas Carlson, "How Marissa Mayer Figured Out Work-At-Home Yahoos Were Slacking Off," *Business Insider,* March 2, 2013 at http://www.businessinsider.com/how-marissa-mayer-figured-out-work-at-home-yahoos-were-slacking-off-2013-3.

19 Neil Shah, "More Americans Working Remotely," *Wall Street Journal,* March 3, 2013, A3.

20 Leanne Italie, "Yahoo Ban Turns Spotlight on Telecommuting," *Fort Worth Star Telegram,* March 9, 2013 at http://www.star-telegram.com/2013/03/09/4671879/yahoo-ban-turns-spotlight-on-telecommuting.html.

21 "Yahoo CEO Marissa Mayer Demands Telecommuters Report to Office," *Huff Post Business,* February 23, 2013 at http://www.huffingtonpost.com/2013/02/23/yahoo-working-remote_n_2750698.html.

22 Rachel Emma Silverman, "Tracking Sensors Invade the Workplace," *Wall Street Journal,* March 7, 2013, B1–B2.

chapter 8 | **Employee Behavior and Motivation**

Rido/Fotolia

Keeping employees involved and invested is the

key to a company's bottom line. When

employees stop

caring, everyone suffers.

AFTER READING THIS CHAPTER, YOU SHOULD BE ABLE TO:

OBJECTIVE 1   **Identify** and discuss the basic forms of behaviors that employees exhibit in organizations.

OBJECTIVE 2   **Describe** the nature and importance of individual differences among employees.

OBJECTIVE 3   **Explain** the meaning and importance of psychological contracts and the person-job fit in the workplace.

OBJECTIVE 4   **Identify** and summarize the most important models and concepts of employee motivation.

OBJECTIVE 5   **Describe** some of the strategies and techniques used by organizations to improve employee motivation.

MyBizLab®

⭐ Improve Your Grade!

Visit **pearsonglobaleditions.com/mybizlab** for simulations, tutorials, and end-of-chapter problems.

Over 10 million students improved their results using the Pearson MyLabs.

Chicken or Egg?

Sara Caputo is the founder and owner of Radiant Organizing, a training and coaching firm located in Santa Barbara, California. As a productivity consultant, her work includes both one-on-one sessions with clients and speaking engagements on how to get things done in the workplace. One day, she recalls, as she was in the middle of a presentation at a professional conference, "I just felt myself really loving what I do…This got me thinking," she says. "What comes first—happiness in your work or productivity in your work? Are we *more productive* in our jobs and at work because we enjoy what we do and [because] that in itself is a motivator? Or are we *happier* in our jobs and at work because we're productive?"

At first, Caputo admits, she was willing to accept the likelihood that her question came down to "sort of a chicken/egg dilemma." On further reflection, however, she decided that happiness probably comes first. "At one point in your life," she reasons, "you had a calling to do what you're doing right now. Then time goes by, and what gets in the way? All the 'other stuff.' At the end of the day, if you're not happy doing what you do on a daily basis, you'll have a hard time sustaining your productivity because you'll just be getting things done for the sake of getting things done."

Although Caputo's workplace experience may be somewhat happier than the average person's, her bottom-line perspective on the cause-and-effect relationship between happiness and productivity is pretty much in line with most thinking on the subject. Another productivity consultant, for example, advises that "if you want to get more done at work…you should start by liking what you do… [T]he productivity gurus out there," warns Alexander Kjerulf, founder and CHO (Chief Happiness Officer) of Spoing!, a Danish consulting firm, "will tell you that it's all about having the right system. You need to prioritize your tasks. You must keep detailed logs of how you spend your time, [and] to-do lists are of course essential. You must learn to structure your calendar, and much, much more…[But] no system, no tool or methodology in the world can beat the productivity boost you get from really, really enjoying your work."

"Happiness at work," says Kjerulf, "is the #1 productivity booster," and he cites a number of reasons why: happy people work better with others, fix problems rather than complain about them, and make better decisions; they're optimistic and "way more motivated," and they have more energy and get sick less often.

Kjerulf admits that there's still a "question of causation"—the chicken-or-egg issue of which

what's in it for me?

Think about human behavior as a jigsaw puzzle. Puzzles consist of various pieces that fit together in precise ways. And of course, no two puzzles are exactly alike. They have different numbers of pieces, the pieces are of different sizes and shapes, and they fit together in different ways. The same can be said of human behavior and its determinants. Each of us is a whole picture, like a fully assembled jigsaw puzzle, but the puzzle pieces that define us and the way those pieces fit together are unique. Every person in an organization is fundamentally different from everyone else. To be successful, managers must recognize that these differences exist and attempt to understand them.

They also need to understand why people work. People obviously work for a wide variety of different reasons. Some people want money, some want a challenge, and some want power. What people in an organization want from work and how they think they can achieve it plays an instrumental role in determining their motivation to work. As we see in this chapter, motivation is vital to all organizations. Indeed, the difference between highly effective organizations and less effective ones often lies in the motivations of their members.

Successful managers usually have at least a fundamental understanding of what accounts for employee behavior and motivation in organizations. Thus, managers need to understand the nature of individual motivation, especially as it applies to work situations. By understanding the basic elements of this chapter, you'll be better able to (1) understand your own feelings toward your work from the perspective of an employee and (2) understand the feelings of others toward their work from the perspective of a boss or owner. To start developing your understanding, let's begin by describing the different forms of behaviors that employees exhibit at work. We'll then examine many of the ways that people differ from one another. Later in the chapter, we'll look at some important models and concepts of employee motivation, as well as some strategies and techniques used by organizations to improve employee motivation.

came first, happiness or productivity. "The link," he concludes, "goes both ways," but "the link is strongest from happiness to productivity, which means that if you want to be more productive, the very best thing you can do is focus on being happy with what you do."

Not everyone, however, sees the happiness-productivity link from the same perspective. For Paul Larson, a veteran of operations management in a variety of industries, the "legend that happy workers are productive employees has been a part of our organizational thinking for so long that many just take for granted that it has to be true." Larson, founder and president of The Myrddin Group, a Texas-based consultancy specializing in organizational design and development, agrees that "productive workers do seem to be happier." But that, he suggests, is "where the confusion is coming from…[P]roductivity leads to satisfaction and happiness," he argues, "not the other way around. People who do a good job tend to feel intrinsically good about it." To boost productivity, Larson advises, companies should train and support managers "in their efforts to keep the troops fully engaged. It's that engagement that provides the venues for achievement and recognition."

Charles Kerns, a behavioral psychologist at Pepperdine University's Graziado School of Business and Management, agrees with Larson that engagement is the best goal for a manager who wants "to influence the happiness level of his or her employees." He's not quite so sure, however, that enhancing either personal or organizational productivity hinges on solving the chicken/egg dilemma. "Job satisfaction researchers," he points out, "have had a long-standing debate as to whether employees are happy first and performers second, or performers first and happy second," and he doesn't think that the matter is going to be resolved any time soon. For practical purposes, he suggests, "both happiness and job performance need to be addressed."

This is where *engagement* comes in. On the one hand, according to Kerns, managers should probably resign themselves to the fact that improving engagement is about the best they can hope for. On the other hand, improving an employee's engagement with his or her work is no small achievement. Engagement can be measured by the extent to which an individual has *more happy or positive experiences than negative ones*, and the key to increasing positive experiences, says Kerns, is engaging an employee's strengths: "An employee's level of engagement…and subsequent happiness," he contends, "is likely boosted when he or she has the opportunity to do what he or she does best at work: Utilizing one's strengths is a positive experience." With engagement as a starting point, Kerns thinks that the happiness-productivity equation can be formulated in more practical terms: Happiness, he explains, "comes from work experiences that yield positive emotions [and] positive thoughts," and "people who approach tasks with positivity [are] more productive."[1] (After studying the content of this chapter you should be able to answer the set of discussion questions found at the end of the chapter.)

OBJECTIVE 1
Identify
and discuss the basic forms of behaviors that employees exhibit in organizations.

Employee Behavior *the pattern of actions by the members of an organization that directly or indirectly influences the organization's effectiveness*

Forms of Employee Behavior

Employee behavior is the pattern of actions by the members of an organization that directly or indirectly influences the organization's effectiveness. Some employee behaviors, called *performance behaviors*, directly contribute to productivity and performance. Other behaviors, referred to as *organizational citizenship*, provide positive benefits to the organization but in more indirect ways. *Counterproductive behaviors* detract from performance and actually cost the organization. Let's look at each of these types of behavior in a bit more detail.

Performance Behaviors

Performance behaviors are the total set of work-related behaviors that the organization expects employees to display. Essentially, these are the behaviors directly targeted at performing a job. For some jobs, performance behaviors can be narrowly defined and easily measured. For example, an assembly-line worker who sits by a moving conveyor and attaches parts to a product as it passes by has relatively few performance behaviors. He or she is expected to remain at the workstation for a predetermined number of hours and correctly attach the parts. Such performance can often be assessed quantitatively by counting the percentage of parts correctly attached.

For many other jobs, however, performance behaviors are more diverse and difficult to assess. For example, consider the case of a research-and-development scientist at Merck Pharmaceuticals. The scientist works in a lab trying to find new scientific breakthroughs that have commercial potential. The scientist must apply knowledge and experience gained from previous research. Intuition and creativity are also important. But even with all the scientist's abilities and effort, a desired breakthrough may take months or even years to accomplish.

Performance Behaviors *the total set of work-related behaviors that the organization expects employees to display*

Organizational Citizenship

Employees can also engage in positive behaviors that do not directly contribute to the bottom line. Such behaviors are often called **organizational citizenship**.[2] Organizational citizenship refers to the behavior of individuals who make a positive overall contribution to the organization. Consider, for example, an employee who does work that is highly acceptable in terms of both quantity and quality. However, she refuses to work overtime, won't help newcomers learn the ropes, and is generally unwilling to make any contribution beyond the strict performance requirements of her job. This person may be seen as a good performer, but she is not likely to be seen as a good organizational citizen. Another employee may exhibit a comparable level of performance, but she always works late when the boss asks her to, she takes time to help newcomers learn their way around, and she is perceived as being helpful and committed to the organization's success. She is likely to be seen as a better organizational citizen.

A number of factors, including individual, social, and organizational variables, play roles in promoting or minimizing organizational citizenship behaviors. For example, the personality, attitudes, and needs of the individual may cause some people to be more helpful than others. Similarly, the individual's work group may encourage or discourage such behaviors. And the organization itself, especially its corporate culture, may or may not promote, recognize, and reward these types of behaviors.

Organizational Citizenship *positive behaviors that do not directly contribute to the bottom line*

Organizational citizenship is the behavior of individuals who make a positive contribution to the organization above-and-beyond strict job performance. This manager, for example, is helping her colleagues better understand important organizational processes and customer expectations.

Counterproductive Behaviors

Counterproductive Behaviors *behaviors that detract from organizational performance*

Absenteeism *when an employee does not show up for work*

Still other work-related behaviors are counterproductive. **Counterproductive behaviors** are those that detract from, rather than contribute to, organizational performance. **Absenteeism** occurs when an employee does not show up for work. Some absenteeism has a legitimate cause, such as illness, jury duty, or death or illness in the family. Other times, the employee may report a feigned legitimate cause that's actually just an excuse to stay home. When an employee is absent, legitimately or not, his or her work does not get done at all, a substitute must be hired to do it, or others in the organization must pick up the slack, In any event, though, absenteeism results in direct costs to a business.

Turnover *annual percentage of an organization's workforce that leaves and must be replaced*

Turnover occurs when people quit their jobs. An organization usually incurs costs in replacing workers who have quit, lost productivity while seeking a replacement,

managing in turbulent times

Law of Well-being

The words "moral harassment" are used in the Belgian Law of Well-being (2007). This term is used to describe a wide range of abusive conduct, particularly in the workplace.

Moral harassment is seen, in Belgium, as being conduct that hurts people, endangers stable employment, or damages the social environment. Under the terms of the law, the conduct does not have to take place over a period of time, nor does it have to be repeated.

The law allows for workers to use an internal procedure to complain. Employees have to be given access to an advisor or counselor on a confidential basis. If the conduct involved a third party (not a company employee), then the company is bound to provide the worker with psychological support. In the event of the internal procedures failing, then a labor court is used to settle the complaint.

According to the Werkbaarheidsmonitor, a report produced by the Socio-Economic Council of Flanders, younger workers tended to suffer from more physical violence in the workplace when compared older workers. The latest figures suggest that over a period of 12 months, around 5.5 percent of workers had faced some kind of physical violence in the workplace.

The same data revealed that 14.4 percent of Belgian workers faced bullying in the workplace. This suggests that bullying is more prevalent in Belgium compared to the European Union averages. A second Belgian study put this figure at 13 percent for those who suffered from bullying from time to time, compared to 2 percent that suffered from it on a regular basis.

Since the introduction of the Law of Well-being, the procedures designed to protect employees have become clear and standardized in Belgium. In the first instance, an employee that feels that they have suffered psychosocial violence at work can turn to their manager. At the same time, they can seek the aid of the safety advisor or occupational physician. The choices lay with the employee at this early stage in the procedure. They can refer the matter to the regional

Laurent Hamels/Fotolia

committee of the inspectorate for well-being at work or begin court proceedings in serious cases.

If the employer wants to take action or when the employee wants to reconcile with the offender, the internal procedure is usually sufficient to deal with the situation. If the business does not have a designated safety advisor, then the regional committee of the inspectorate for well-being is called in. They will investigate the situation and control the procedures.

If the case goes to an industrial tribunal, there are a number of potential outcomes. The employee can ask the judge to order the offender to stop their actions or face sanctions. The employer can be ordered to take necessary measures or the employer and the offender can be required to pay compensation.

As a final resort, criminal procedures can take place through the correctional court. The court can sanction the offender and/or the employer, although this stage is usually only reached if the offender has not complied with an order to stop their actions.[3]

training someone new, and so on. Turnover results from a number of factors, including aspects of the job, the organization, the individual, the labor market, and family influences. In general, a poor person-job fit (which we'll discuss later in the chapter) is also a likely cause of turnover. There are some employees whose turnover doesn't hurt the business, but when productive employees leave an organization, it does reflect counterproductive behavior.

Other forms of counterproductive behavior may be even more costly for an organization. *Theft and sabotage*, for example, result in direct financial costs for an organization. *Sexual and racial harassment* also cost an organization, both indirectly (by lowering morale, producing fear, and driving off valuable employees) and directly (through financial liability if the organization responds inappropriately). *Workplace aggression and violence* are also a growing concern in some organizations.

Individual Differences among Employees

OBJECTIVE 2
Describe
the nature and importance of individual differences among employees.

What causes some employees to be more productive than others, to be better citizens than others, or to be more counterproductive than others? As we already noted, every individual is unique. **Individual differences** are personal attributes that vary from one person to another. Individual differences may be physical, psychological, and emotional. The individual differences that characterize a specific person make that person unique. As we see in the sections that follow, basic categories of individual differences include *personality* and *attitudes*.[4]

Individual Differences *personal attributes that vary from one person to another*

Personality at Work

Personality is the relatively stable set of psychological attributes that distinguish one person from another. In recent years, researchers have identified five fundamental traits that are especially relevant to organizations. These are commonly called the *"big five" personality traits. Emotional intelligence*, although not part of the "big five," also plays a large role in employee personality.

Personality *the relatively stable set of psychological attributes that distinguish one person from another*

The "Big Five" Personality Traits The **"big five" personality traits** are shown in Figure 8.1 and can be summarized as follows.

"Big Five" personality traits *five fundamental personality traits especially relevant to organizations*

- *Agreeableness* is a person's ability to get along with others. A person with a *high* level of agreeableness is gentle, cooperative, forgiving, understanding, and good-natured in their dealings with others. A person with a *low* level of agreeableness is often irritable, short-tempered, uncooperative, and generally antagonistic toward other people. Highly agreeable people are better at developing good working relationships with coworkers, whereas less agreeable people are not likely to have particularly good working relationships.

- *Conscientiousness* in this context refers to the individual's persistence, dependability, and orderliness. *Highly conscientious* people tend to focus on relatively few tasks at one time; as a result, they are likely to be organized, systematic, careful, thorough, responsible, and self-disciplined. *Less conscientious* people tend to pursue a wider array of tasks; as a result, they are often more disorganized and irresponsible, as well as less thorough and self-disciplined. Highly conscientious people tend to be relatively higher performers in a variety of different jobs.

- *Emotionality* refers to the degree to which people tend to be positive or negative in their outlook and behaviors toward others. People with *positive* emotionality are relatively poised, calm, resilient, and secure; people with negative emotionality are more excitable, insecure, reactive, and subject to mood swings. People

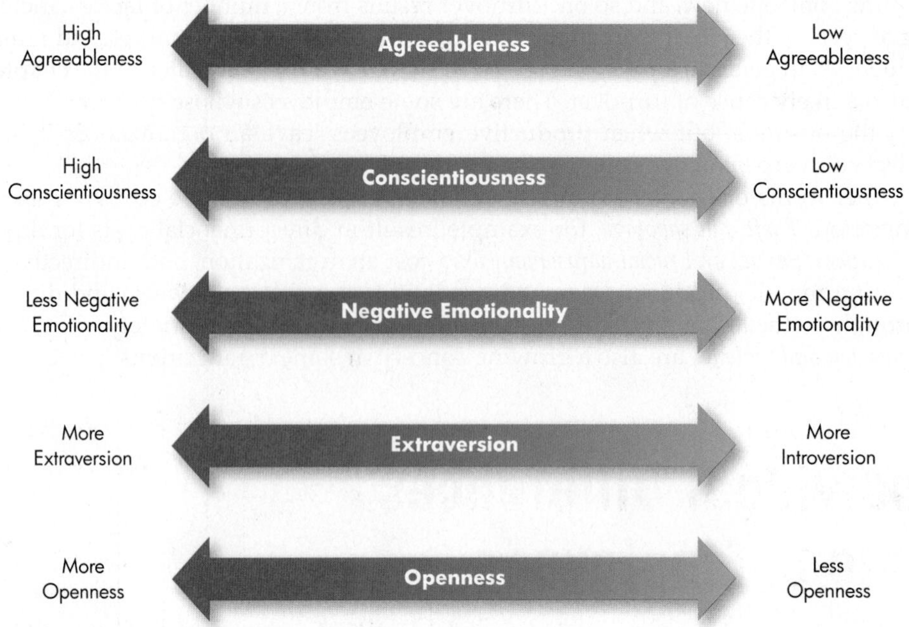

FIGURE 8.1 The "Big Five" Personality Traits

with positive emotionality might be expected to better handle job stress, pressure, and tension. Their stability might also lead them to be seen as being more reliable than their less-stable counterparts.

- *Extraversion* refers to a person's comfort level with relationships. *Extroverts* are sociable, talkative, assertive, and open to establishing new relationships. *Introverts* are much less sociable, talkative, and assertive, and more reluctant to begin new relationships. Extroverts tend to be higher overall job performers than introverts and are more likely to be attracted to jobs based on personal relationships, such as sales and marketing positions.

- *Openness* reflects how open or rigid a person is in terms of his or her beliefs. People with *high* levels of openness are curious and willing to listen to new ideas and to change their own ideas, beliefs, and attitudes in response to new information. People with *low* levels of openness tend to be less receptive to new ideas and less willing to change their minds. People with more openness are often better performers because of their flexibility and the likelihood that they will be better accepted by others in the organization.

The "big five" framework continues to attract the attention of both researchers and managers. The potential value of this framework is that it encompasses an integrated set of traits that appear to be valid predictors of certain behaviors in certain situations. Thus, managers who can both understand the framework and assess these traits in their employees are in a good position to understand how and why they behave as they do.

The Myers-Briggs Framework Another interesting approach to understanding personalities in organizations is the Myers-Briggs framework. This framework, based on the classical work of Carl Jung, differentiates people in terms of four general dimensions. These are defined as follows.

- *Extraversion (E) Versus Introversion (I).* Extraverts get their energy from being around other people, whereas introverts are worn out by others and need solitude to recharge their energy.

- *Sensing (S) Versus Intuition (N).* The sensing type prefers concrete things, whereas intuitives prefer abstract concepts.

- *Thinking (T) Versus Feeling (F).* Thinking individuals base their decisions more on logic and reason, whereas feeling individuals base their decisions more on feelings and emotions.

- *Judging (J) Versus Perceiving (P).* People who are the judging type enjoy completion or being finished, whereas perceiving types enjoy the process and open-ended situations.

To use this framework, people complete a questionnaire designed to measure their personality on each dimension. Higher or lower scores in each of the dimensions are used to classify people into one of 16 different personality categories.

The **Myers-Briggs Type Indicator (MBTI)** is a popular questionnaire that some organizations use to assess personality types. It is among the most popular selection instruments used today, with as many as 2 million people taking it each year. Research suggests that the MBTI is a useful method for determining communication styles and interaction preferences. In terms of personality attributes, however, questions exist about both the validity and the stability of the MBTI.

Myers-Briggs Type Indicator (MBTI) *a popular questionnaire that some organizations use to assess personality types*

Emotional Intelligence   The concept of emotional intelligence has been identified in recent years and also provides some interesting insights into personality. **Emotional intelligence,** or **emotional quotient (EQ),** refers to the extent to which people are self-aware, can manage their emotions, can motivate themselves, express empathy for others, and possess social skills.[5] These various dimensions can be described as follows:

- *Self-awareness* refers to a person's capacity for being aware of how they are feeling. In general, more self-awareness allows people to more effectively guide their own lives and behaviors.

- *Managing emotions* refers to a person's capacities to balance anxiety, fear, and anger so that they do not overly interfere with getting things accomplished.

- *Motivating oneself* is a person's ability to remain optimistic and to continue striving in the face of setbacks, barriers, and failure.

- *Empathy* is a person's ability to understand how others are feeling even without being explicitly told.

- *Social skills* help people get along with others and establish positive relationships.

Emotional Intelligence (Emotional Quotient, Eq) *the extent to which people are self-aware, can manage their emotions, can motivate themselves, express empathy for others, and possess social skills*

Preliminary research suggests that people with high EQs may perform better than others, especially in jobs that require a high degree of interpersonal interaction (such as a public relations specialist) or that involve influencing or directing the work of others (such as a project manager). Moreover, EQ appears to be something that isn't biologically based but which can be developed.

Other Personality Traits at Work   Besides these complex models of personality, several other specific personality traits are also likely to influence behavior in organizations. Among the most important are locus of control, self-efficacy, authoritarianism, Machiavellianism, self-esteem, and risk propensity.

Locus of control is the extent to which people believe that their behavior has a real effect on what happens to them.[6] Some people, for example, believe that if they work hard they will succeed. They may also believe that people who fail do so because they lack ability or motivation. People who believe that individuals are in control of their lives are said to have an internal locus of control. Other people think that fate, chance, luck, or other people's behavior determines what happens to them. For example, an employee who fails to get a promotion may attribute that failure to a politically motivated boss or just bad luck, rather than to his or her own lack of skills or poor performance record. People who think that forces beyond their control dictate what happens to them are said to have an external locus of control.

Locus of Control *the extent to which people believe that their behavior has a real effect on what happens to them*

Self-efficacy is a related but subtly different personality characteristic. A person's **self-efficacy** is that person's belief about his or her capabilities to perform a task. People with high self-efficacy believe that they can perform well on a specific task,

Self-Efficacy *a person's belief about his or her capabilities to perform a task*

Authoritarianism *the extent to which a person believes that power and status differences are appropriate within hierarchical social systems such as organizations*

whereas people with low self-efficacy tend to doubt their ability to perform a specific task. Coupled with the individual's personality, self-assessments of ability contribute to self-efficacy. Some people simply have more self-confidence than others. This belief in their ability to perform a task effectively results in their being more self-assured and better able to focus their attention on performance.[7]

Another important personality characteristic is **authoritarianism,** the extent to which a person believes that power and status differences are appropriate within hierarchical social systems such as organizations.[8] For example, a person who is highly authoritarian may accept directives or orders from someone with more authority purely because the other person is "the boss." On the other hand, a person who is not highly authoritarian, although he or she may still carry out reasonable directives from the boss, is more likely to question things, express disagreement with the boss, and even refuse to carry out orders if they are for some reason objectionable. A highly authoritarian manager may be relatively autocratic and demanding, and highly authoritarian subordinates are more likely to accept this behavior from their leader. On the other hand, a less authoritarian manager may allow subordinates a bigger role in making decisions, and less authoritarian subordinates might respond more positively to this behavior.

Machiavellianism *used to describe behavior directed at gaining power and controlling the behavior of others*

Machiavellianism is another important personality trait. This concept is named after Niccolo Machiavelli, a sixteenth-century author. In his book *The Prince*, Machiavelli explained how the nobility could more easily gain and use power. The term *Machiavellianism* is now used to describe behavior directed at gaining power and controlling the behavior of others. Research suggests that the degree of Machiavellianism varies from person to person. More Machiavellian individuals tend to be rational and nonemotional, may be willing to lie to attain their personal goals, put little emphasis on loyalty and friendship, and enjoy manipulating others' behavior. Less Machiavellian individuals are more emotional, less willing to lie to succeed, value loyalty and friendship highly, and get little personal pleasure from manipulating others.

Self-Esteem *the extent to which a person believes that he or she is a worthwhile and deserving individual*

Self-esteem is the extent to which a person believes that he or she is a worthwhile and deserving individual. A person with high self-esteem is more likely to seek higher-status jobs, be more confident in his or her ability to achieve higher levels of performance, and derive greater intrinsic satisfaction from his or her accomplishments. In contrast, a person with less self-esteem may be more content to remain in a lower-level job, be less confident of his or her ability, and focus more on extrinsic rewards (extrinsic rewards are tangible and observable rewards such as a paycheck, job promotion, and so forth). Among the major personality dimensions, self-esteem is the one that has been most widely studied in other countries. Although more research is clearly needed, the published evidence suggests that self-esteem as a personality trait does indeed exist in a variety of countries and that its role in organizations is reasonably important across different cultures.

Risk Propensity *the degree to which a person is willing to take chances and make risky decisions*

Risk propensity is the degree to which a person is willing to take chances and make risky decisions. A manager with a high risk propensity, for example, might experiment with new ideas and gamble on new products. Such a manager might also lead the organization in new and different directions. This manager might be a catalyst for innovation or, if the risky decisions prove to be bad ones, might jeopardize the continued well-being of the organization. A manager with low risk propensity might lead an organization to stagnation and excessive conservatism or might help the organization successfully weather turbulent and unpredictable times by maintaining stability and calm. Thus, the potential consequences of a manager's risk propensity depend heavily on the organization's environment.

Attitudes at Work

Attitudes *a person's beliefs and feelings about specific ideas, situations, or people*

People's attitudes also affect their behavior in organizations. **Attitudes** reflect our beliefs and feelings about specific ideas, situations, or other people. Attitudes are important because they are the mechanism through which we express our feelings. An employee's comment that he feels underpaid reflects his feelings about his pay. Similarly, when a manager says that she likes the new advertising campaign, she is expressing her feelings about the organization's marketing efforts.

How Attitudes Are Formed Attitudes are formed by a variety of forces, including our personal values, our experiences, and our personalities. For example, if we value honesty and integrity, we may form especially favorable attitudes toward a manager whom we believe to be honest and moral. Similarly, if we have had negative and unpleasant experiences with a particular coworker, we may form an unfavorable attitude toward that person. Any of the "big five" or individual personality traits may also influence our attitudes. Understanding the basic structure of an attitude helps us see how attitudes are formed and can be changed.

Attitude Structure Attitudes are usually viewed as stable dispositions to behave toward objects in a certain way. For any number of reasons, a person might decide that he or she does not like a particular political figure or a certain restaurant (a disposition). We would expect that person to express consistently negative opinions of the candidate or restaurant and to maintain the consistent, predictable intention of not voting for the political candidate or not eating at the restaurant. In this view, attitudes contain three components: (1) cognition, (2) affect, and (3) intention.

Cognition is the knowledge a person presumes to have about something. You may believe you like a class because the textbook is excellent, the class meets at your favorite time, the instructor is outstanding, and the workload is light. This "knowledge" may be true, partially true, or totally false. For example, you may intend to vote for a particular candidate because you think you know where the candidate stands on several issues. In reality, depending on the candidate's honesty and your understanding of his or her statements, the candidate's thinking on the issues may be exactly the same as yours, partly the same, or totally different. Cognitions are based on perceptions of truth and reality, and, as we note later, perceptions agree with reality to varying degrees.

A person's **affect** is his or her feelings toward something. In many ways, affect is similar to emotion; it is something over which we have little or no conscious control. For example, most people react to words such as *love, hate, sex,* and *war* in a manner that reflects their feelings about what those words convey. Similarly, you may like one of your classes, dislike another, and be indifferent toward a third. If the class you dislike is an elective, you may not be particularly concerned about your participation or final grade. But if it is the first course in your chosen major, your affective reaction may cause you considerable anxiety.

Intention guides a person's behavior. If you like your instructor, you may intend to take another class from him or her next semester. Intentions are not always translated into actual behavior, however. If the instructor's course next semester is scheduled for 8 A.M., you may decide that another instructor is just as good. Some attitudes, and their corresponding intentions, are much more central and significant to an individual than others. You may intend to do one thing (take a particular class) but later alter your intentions because of a more significant and central attitude (fondness for sleeping late).

Cognitive Dissonance When two sets of cognitions or perceptions are contradictory or incongruent, a person experiences a level of conflict and anxiety called **cognitive dissonance.** Cognitive dissonance also occurs when people behave in a fashion that is inconsistent with their attitudes. For example, a person may realize that smoking and overeating are dangerous yet continue to do both. Because the attitudes and behaviors are inconsistent with each other, the person probably will experience a certain amount of tension and discomfort and may try to reduce these feelings by changing the attitude, altering the behavior, or perceptually distorting the circumstances. For example, the dissonance associated with overeating might be resolved by continually deciding to go on a diet "next week." Cognitive dissonance affects people in a variety of ways. We frequently encounter situations in which our attitudes conflict with each other or with our behaviors. Dissonance reduction is the way we deal with these feelings of discomfort and tension. In organizational settings, people contemplating leaving the organization may wonder why they continue to stay and work hard. As a result of this dissonance, they may conclude that the company is not so bad after all, that they have no immediate options elsewhere, or that they will leave "soon."

Cognition *the knowledge a person presumes to have about something*

Affect *a person's feelings toward something*

Intention *part of an attitude that guides a person's behavior*

Cognitive Dissonance *when two sets of cognitions or perceptions are contradictory or incongruent*

Key Work-Related Attitudes People in an organization form attitudes about many different things. Employees are likely to have attitudes about their salary, their promotion possibilities, their boss, employee benefits, and so on. Especially important attitudes are *job satisfaction* and *organizational commitment*.

Job Satisfaction *degree of enjoyment that people derive from performing their jobs*

- **Job satisfaction** reflects the extent to which people have positive attitudes toward their jobs. (Some people use the word *morale* instead of job satisfaction.) A satisfied employee tends to be absent less often, to be a good organizational citizen, and to stay with the organization. Dissatisfied employees may be absent more often, may experience stress that disrupts coworkers, and may be continually looking for another job. Contrary to what a lot of managers believe, however, high levels of job satisfaction do not necessarily lead to higher levels of productivity.

Organizational Commitment *an individual's identification with the organization and its mission*

- **Organizational commitment,** sometimes called *job commitment*, reflects an individual's identification with the organization and its mission. A highly committed person will probably see himself or herself as a true member of the firm (for example, referring to the organization in personal terms, such as "we make high-quality products"), overlook minor sources of dissatisfaction, and see himself or herself remaining a member of the organization. A less committed person is more likely to see himself as an outsider (e.g., referring to the organization in less personal terms, such as "they don't pay their employees very well"), to express more dissatisfaction about things, and to not see himself or herself as a long-term member of the organization.

There are a few critical things managers can do to promote satisfaction and commitment. For one thing, if the organization treats its employees fairly and provides reasonable rewards and job security, its employees are more likely to be satisfied and committed. Allowing employees to have a say in how things are done can also promote these attitudes. Designing jobs so that they are stimulating can enhance both satisfaction and commitment. Another key element is understanding and respecting what experts call *psychological contracts*, which we will discuss in the next section.

OBJECTIVE 3
Explain
the meaning and importance of psychological contracts and the person-job fit in the workplace.

Matching People and Jobs

Given the array of individual differences that exists across people and the many different forms of employee behaviors that can occur in organizations, it stands to reason that managers would like to have a good match between people and the jobs they are performing. Two key methods for helping to understand how this match can be better understood are *psychological contracts* and the *person-job fit*.

Psychological Contracts

Psychological Contract *set of expectations held by an employee concerning what he or she will contribute to an organization (referred to as* contributions) *and what the organization will in return provide the employee (referred to as* inducements)

A **psychological contract** is the overall set of expectations held by employees and the organization regarding what employees will contribute to the organization and what the organization will provide in return. Unlike a business contract, a psychological contract is not written on paper, nor are all of its terms explicitly negotiated.[9]

Figure 8.2 illustrates the essential nature of a psychological contract. The individual makes a variety of *contributions* to the organization, such as effort, ability, loyalty, skills, and time. These contributions satisfy their obligation under the contract. For example, Jill Henderson, a branch manager for Merrill Lynch, uses her knowledge of financial markets and investment opportunities to help her clients make profitable investments. Her MBA in finance, coupled with hard work and motivation, have led her to become one of the firm's most promising young managers. The firm believed she had these attributes when it hired her and expected that she would do well.

In return for these contributions, the organization provides *inducements* to the individual. These inducements satisfy the organization's contract obligation. Some inducements, such as pay and career opportunities, are tangible rewards. Others,

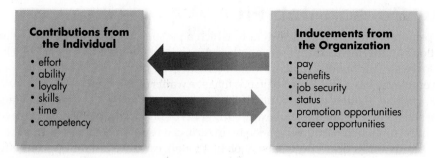

Contributions from the Individual	**Inducements from the Organization**
• effort • ability • loyalty • skills • time • competency	• pay • benefits • job security • status • promotion opportunities • career opportunities

FIGURE 8.2 The Psychological Contract

such as job security and status, are more intangible. Henderson started at Merrill Lynch at a competitive salary and has received a salary increase each of the six years she has been with the firm. She has also been promoted twice and expects another promotion in the near future.

In this instance, both Henderson and Merrill Lynch apparently perceive that the psychological contract is fair and equitable. Both will be satisfied with the relationship and will do what they can to continue it. Henderson is likely to continue to work hard and effectively, and Merrill Lynch is likely to continue to increase her salary and give her promotions. In other situations, however, things might not work out as well. If either party sees an inequity in the contract, that party may initiate a change. The employee might ask for a pay raise or promotion, put forth less effort, or look for a better job elsewhere. The organization can also initiate change by training the worker to improve his or her skills, transferring him or her to another job, or firing him or her.

All organizations face the basic challenge of managing psychological contracts. They want value from their employees, and they need to give employees the right inducements. For instance, underpaid employees may perform poorly or leave for better jobs elsewhere. Similarly, an employee may even occasionally start to steal from the company as a way to balance the psychological contract.

Recent trends in downsizing and cutbacks have complicated the process of managing psychological contracts. For example, many organizations used to offer at least reasonable assurances of job permanence as a fundamental inducement to employees. Now, however, job permanence is less likely so alternative inducements may be needed. Among the new forms of inducements, some companies are providing additional training opportunities and increased flexibility in working schedules.

Sergey Smirnov/Alamy

Person-job fit is an important consideration when hiring people to perform specific jobs. For instance, some people might thrive working in extreme weather conditions, performing risky jobs, or traveling most of the time. Other people, in contrast, would balk at any of these opportunities and instead only want to work under mild weather conditions, performing low risk tasks, or never traveling. Consider, for example, the job of cleaning external windows on high-rise buildings like the person shown here. Some people can handle jobs like this easily while others might be terrified!

The Person-Job Fit

Person-Job Fit *the extent to which a person's contributions and the organization's inducements match one another*

The **person-job fit** refers to the extent to which a person's contributions and the organization's inducements match one another. A good person-job fit is one in which the employee's contributions match the inducements the organization offers. In theory, each employee has a specific set of needs that she wants fulfilled and a set of job-related behaviors and abilities to contribute. If the organization can take perfect advantage of those behaviors and abilities and exactly fulfill his or her needs, it will have achieved a perfect person-job fit. Good person-job fit, in turn, can result in higher performance and more positive attitudes. A poor person-job fit, though, can have just the opposite effects.

Basic Motivation Concepts and Theories

OBJECTIVE 4
Identify
and summarize the most important models and concepts of employee motivation.

Motivation *the set of forces that cause people to behave in certain ways*

Broadly defined, **motivation** is the set of forces that cause people to behave in certain ways. One worker may be motivated to work hard to produce as much as possible, whereas another may be motivated to do just enough to survive. Managers must understand these differences in behavior and the reasons for them.

Over the years, a steady progression of theories and studies has attempted to address these issues. In this section, we survey the major studies and theories of employee motivation. In particular, we focus on three approaches to human relations in the workplace that reflect a basic chronology of thinking in the area: (1) *classical theory* and *scientific management*, (2) *early behavioral theory*, and (3) *contemporary motivational theories*.

Classical Theory

Classical Theory of Motivation *theory holding that workers are motivated solely by money*

According to the **classical theory of motivation,** workers are motivated solely by money. In his 1911 book, *The Principles of Scientific Management*, industrial engineer Frederick Taylor proposed a way for both companies and workers to benefit from this widely accepted view of life in the workplace. If workers are motivated by money, Taylor reasoned, paying them more should prompt them to produce more. Meanwhile, the firm that analyzed jobs and found better ways to perform them would be able to produce goods more cheaply, make higher profits, and pay and motivate workers better than its competitors.

Taylor's approach is known as *scientific management*. His ideas captured the imagination of many managers in the early twentieth century. Soon, manufacturing plants across the United States were hiring experts to perform time-and-motion studies: Industrial engineering techniques were applied to each facet of a job to determine how to perform it most efficiently. These studies were the first scientific attempts to break down jobs into easily repeated components and to devise more efficient tools and machines for performing them.[10]

Early Behavioral Theory

In 1925, a group of Harvard researchers began a study at the Hawthorne Works of Western Electric outside Chicago. With an eye to increasing productivity, they wanted to examine the relationship between changes in the physical environment and worker output.

The results of the experiment were unexpected, even confusing. For example, increased lighting levels improved productivity. For some reason, however, so did lower lighting levels. Moreover, against all expectations, increased pay failed to increase productivity. Gradually, the researchers pieced together the puzzle. The explanation lay in the workers' response to the attention they were receiving. The researchers concluded that productivity rose in response to almost any management action that workers interpreted as special attention. This finding, known today as the **Hawthorne effect,** had a major influence on human relations theory, although in many cases it amounted simply to convincing managers that they should pay more attention to employees.

Hawthorne Effect *tendency for productivity to increase when workers believe they are receiving special attention from management*

Treating employees with respect and recognizing that they are valuable members of the organization can go a long way toward motivating employees to perform at their highest levels.

Ariel Skelley/Blend Images/Alamy

Following the Hawthorne studies, managers and researchers alike focused more attention on the importance of good human relations in motivating employee performance. Stressing the factors that cause, focus, and sustain workers' behavior, most motivation theorists became concerned with the ways in which management thinks about and treats employees. The major motivation theories include the *human resources model*, the *hierarchy of needs model*, and *two-factor theory*.

Human Resources Model: Theories X and Y In one important book, behavioral scientist Douglas McGregor concluded that managers had radically different beliefs about how best to use the human resources employed by a firm. He classified these beliefs into sets of assumptions that he labeled "Theory X" and "Theory Y." The basic differences between these two theories are shown in Table 8.1.

Managers who subscribe to **Theory X** tend to believe that people are naturally lazy and uncooperative and must be either punished or rewarded to be made productive. Managers who are inclined to accept Theory Y tend to believe that people are naturally energetic, growth-oriented, self-motivated, and interested in being productive.

McGregor argued that **Theory Y** managers are more likely to have satisfied and motivated employees. Theory X and Y distinctions are somewhat simplistic and offer little concrete basis for action. Their value lies primarily in their ability to highlight and classify the behavior of managers in light of their attitudes toward employees.

Theory X *theory of motivation holding that people are naturally lazy and uncooperative*

Theory Y *theory of motivation holding that people are naturally energetic, growth-oriented, self-motivated, and interested in being productive*

Maslow's Hierarchy of Needs Model Psychologist Abraham Maslow's **hierarchy of human needs model** proposed that people have several different needs that they attempt to satisfy in their work. Maslow classified these needs into five basic types and suggested that they be arranged in the hierarchy of importance, as shown in Figure 8.3. According to Maslow, needs are hierarchical because lower-level needs must be met before a person will try to satisfy higher-level needs.

Hierarchy of Human Needs Model *theory of motivation describing five levels of human needs and arguing that basic needs must be fulfilled before people work to satisfy higher-level needs*

table 8.1 Theory X and Theory Y

Theory X	Theory Y
People are lazy.	People are energetic.
People lack ambition and dislike responsibility.	People are ambitious and seek responsibility.
People are self-centered.	People can be self-less.
People resist change.	People want to contribute to business growth and change.
People are gullible and not bright.	People are intelligent.

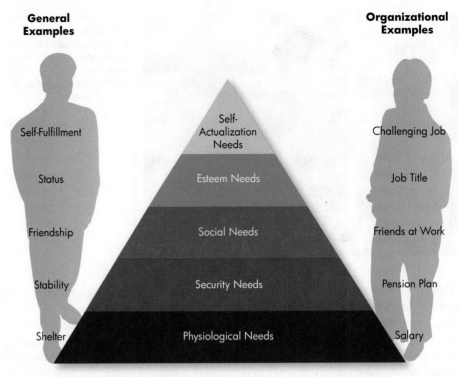

FIGURE 8.3 Maslow's Hierarchy of Human Needs
Source: Maslow, Abraham H.; Frager, Robert D.; Fadiman, James, *Motivation and Personality*, 3rd Ed., © 1987. Adapted and Electronically reproduced by permission of Pearson Education, Inc., Upper Saddle River, NJ.

Once a set of needs has been satisfied, it ceases to motivate behavior. For example, if you feel secure in your job (that is, your security needs have been met), additional opportunities to achieve even more security, such as being assigned to a long-term project, will probably be less important to you than the chance to fulfill social or esteem needs, such as working with a mentor or becoming the member of an advisory board.

If, however, a lower-level need suddenly becomes unfulfilled, most people immediately refocus on that lower level. Suppose, for example, you are seeking to meet your self-esteem needs by working as a divisional manager at a major company. If you learn that your division and, consequently, your job may be eliminated, you might well find the promise of job security at a new firm as motivating as a promotion once would have been at your old company.

Two-Factor Theory After studying a group of accountants and engineers, psychologist Frederick Herzberg concluded that job satisfaction and dissatisfaction depend on two factors: *hygiene factors*, such as working conditions, and *motivation factors*, such as recognition for a job well done.

According to Herzberg's **two-factor theory,** hygiene factors affect motivation and satisfaction only if they are absent or fail to meet expectations. For example, workers will be dissatisfied if they believe they have poor working conditions. If working conditions are improved, however, they will not necessarily become satisfied; they will simply not be dissatisfied. If workers receive no recognition for successful work, they may be neither dissatisfied nor satisfied. If recognition is provided, they will likely become more satisfied.

Figure 8.4 illustrates the two-factor theory. Note that motivation factors lie along a continuum from satisfaction to no satisfaction. Hygiene factors, in contrast, are likely to produce feelings that lie on a continuum from dissatisfaction to no dissatisfaction. Whereas motivation factors are directly related to the work that employees actually perform, hygiene factors refer to the environment in which they work.

This theory suggests that managers should follow a two-step approach to enhancing motivation. First, they must ensure that hygiene factors, such as working conditions or clearly stated policies, are acceptable. This practice will result in an

Two-Factor Theory *theory of motivation holding that job satisfaction depends on two factors, hygiene and motivation*

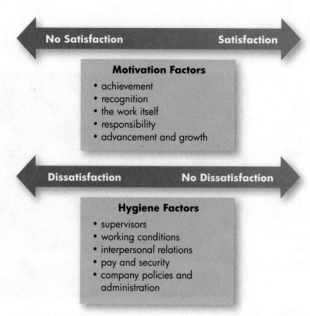

FIGURE 8.4 Two-Factor Theory of Motivation

absence of dissatisfaction. Then they must offer motivation factors, such as recognition or added responsibility, as a way to improve satisfaction and motivation.

Other Important Needs   Each theory discussed so far describes interrelated sets of important individual needs within specific frameworks. McClelland's acquired needs theory hypothesized three other needs, the needs for achievement, affiliation, and power. Most people, however, are more familiar with the three needs as stand-along concepts rather than the original theory itself.

The **need for achievement** arises from an individual's desire to accomplish a goal or task as effectively as possible.[11] Individuals who have a high need for achievement tend to set moderately difficult goals and to make moderately risky decisions. High-need achievers also want immediate, specific feedback on their performance. They want to know how well they did something as quickly after finishing it as possible. For this reason, high-need achievers frequently take jobs in sales, where they get almost immediate feedback from customers, and avoid jobs in areas such as research and development, where tangible progress is slower and feedback comes at longer intervals. Preoccupation with work is another characteristic of high-need achievers. They think about it on their way to the workplace, during lunch, and at home. They find it difficult to put their work aside, and they become frustrated when they must stop working on a partly completed project. Finally, high-need achievers tend to assume personal responsibility for getting things done. They often volunteer for extra duties and find it difficult to delegate part of a job to someone else. Accordingly, they derive a feeling of accomplishment when they have done more work than their peers without the assistance of others.

Many individuals also experience the **need for affiliation**—the need for human companionship.[12] Researchers recognize several ways that people with a high need for affiliation differ from those with a lower need. Individuals with a high need tend to want reassurance and approval from others and usually are genuinely concerned about others' feelings. They are likely to act and think as they believe others want them to, especially those with whom they strongly identify and desire friendship. As we might expect, people with a strong need for affiliation most often work in jobs with a lot of interpersonal contact, such as sales and teaching positions.

A third major individual need is the **need for power**—the desire to control one's environment, including financial, material, informational, and human resources.[13] People vary greatly along this dimension. Some individuals spend much time and energy seeking power; others avoid power if at all possible. People with a high need for power can be successful managers if three conditions are met. First, they must

Need for Achievement *an individual's desire to accomplish a goal or task as effectively as possible*

Need for Affiliation *an individual's desire for human companionship*

Need for Power *the desire to control one's environment, including financial, material, informational, and human resources*

entrepreneurship and new ventures

Motivation at Bigfoot

Bigfoot Entertainment, distributor of such diverse films as *Midnight Movie* (a horror flick) and *3 Needles* (about the worldwide AIDS crisis), was founded by a German serial entrepreneur named Michael Gleissner. Gleissner is in some ways a model for the sort of creative people that Bigfoot likes to back. He was certainly the model for the hero of *Hui Lu*, a 2007 Bigfoot film that Gleissner wrote and directed about a highly successful young entrepreneur who sells his company but finds himself pushed to the edge despite his millions. "What was I going to do," Gleissner replied when asked about his unusual career move, "buy more boats, buy more houses? I discovered there's a creative side in me." Indeed, Gleissner is motivated by a variety of different things.

Gleissner was an e-commerce pioneer in Germany, where he founded Telebook, Germany's number-one online bookstore, and WWW-Service GmbH, the country's first, and one of its most successful, web-hosting companies. In 1998, he sold Telebook to Amazon.com, where he served two years as a vice-president before cashing in and, moving to Asia as a base for a new round of entrepreneurial activities in 2001. When he bought Bigfoot, it was an e-mail management firm, but Gleissner quickly re-created it as an international entertainment company whose main business, according to its mission statement, is producing and financing "innovative entertainment content, including independent feature films, television series, and reality shows." As head of Bigfoot, Gleissner served as executive producer on *Midnight Movie* and *3 Needles*, as well as on *Irreversi*, his second effort at writing and directing, and on *Shanghai Kiss*, in which he also tried his hand at acting.

Bigfoot maintains offices in Los Angeles and a small production facility in Venice, California, but the centerpiece of its operations is Bigfoot Studios, which opened in 2004 on the island of Mactan, in Cebu, home to the second-largest city in the Philippines. The state-of-the-art facility features six large soundstages, fully equipped editing suites and sound-mixing studios, and the latest in high-tech cameras and other equipment. Gleissner's goal is to turn Cebu into a destination of choice for filmmakers who want to cut costs by shooting and finishing movies outside the United States, and when Bigfoot Entertainment finds a film suitable for financing and development, the deal usually requires the director to do some production work at the Cebu facility. By the time the studio opened, the Philippines were already an attractive location for animators looking for cheap post-production help, but the pool of talent available for work on live-action films was quite limited.

Clinton Wallace/ZUMAPRESS/Newscom

Gleissner's solution? He founded the International Academy of Film and Television (IAFT), not only to staff Bigfoot Studios but also to train what executive director Keith Sensing calls "the next generation of global filmmakers." IAFT, says Sensing, looks for creative people who "have a desire for adventure" and "an education that will set them apart from people who have a strictly Hollywood background."

IAFT enrollment is currently 60 percent international and 40 percent Filipino, but "all of our students," says Sensing, "have the opportunity to participate in real projects going on at Bigfoot Studios…Many IAFT graduates," he adds, "have gone on to write, produce, and direct their own films" and often follow in Bigfoot's steps by finding distribution for their independent features on the international festival circuit. Three recent graduates landed jobs on Gleissner's most recent project, a thriller set in the Philippines revolving around a female diver. Gleissner not only co-wrote and directed *Deep Gold* but drew on his experience as an underwater photographer to shoot key scenes in Bigfoot's specially designed 170,000-gallon Underwater Studio.

To bolster its ability to get its films into theaters (most of the company's features have gone straight to DVD or sold to cable TV), Bigfoot has also become the largest shareholder in Carmike Cinemas, the fourth-largest theater chain in the United States. It also purchased the historic Majestic Crest theater in Los Angeles. The acquisition, says Andrews, goes hand in hand with Bigfoot's purchase of Ascendant: "We wanted a great theater to showcase our films—not only ones we produce but ones we plan to acquire. Everyone knows the Crest," she adds. "It gives us a lot of prestige."[14]

seek power for the betterment of the organization rather than for their own interests. Second, they must have a fairly low need for affiliation because fulfilling a personal need for power may well alienate others in the workplace. Third, they need plenty of self-control to curb their desire for power when it threatens to interfere with effective organizational or interpersonal relationships.[15]

Contemporary Motivation Theory

Recently, other more complex models of employee behavior and motivation have been developed.[16] Two of the more interesting and useful ones are *expectancy theory* and *equity theory*.

Expectancy Theory

Expectancy theory suggests that people are motivated to work toward rewards that they want and that they believe they have a reasonable chance—or expectancy—of obtaining. A reward that seems out of reach is likely to be undesirable even if it is intrinsically positive. Figure 8.5 illustrates expectancy theory in terms of issues that are likely to be considered by an individual employee.

Consider the case of an assistant department manager who learns that her firm needs to replace a retiring division manager three levels above her in the organization. Even though she wants the job, she does not apply because she doubts she will be selected. In this case, she considers the performance-reward issue: She believes that her performance will not get her the position. She also learns that the firm is looking for a production manager on the night shift. She thinks she could get this job but does not apply because she does not want to work nights (the rewards—personal goals issue). Finally, she learns of an opening one level higher—department manager—in her own division. She may well apply for this job because she both wants it and thinks that she has a good chance of getting it. In this case, her consideration of all the issues has led to an expectancy that she can reach a goal.

Expectancy theory helps explain why some people do not work as hard as they can when their salaries are based purely on seniority. Paying employees the same whether they work hard or just hard enough to get by removes the financial incentive for them to work harder. In other words, they ask themselves, "If I work harder, will I get a pay raise?" (the performance–reward issue) and conclude that the answer is "no". Similarly, if hard work will result in one or more undesirable outcomes, such as a transfer to another location or a promotion to a job that requires unpleasant travel (the rewards–personal goal issue), employees will not be motivated to work hard.

Expectancy Theory *theory of motivation holding that people are motivated to work toward rewards that they want and that they believe they have a reasonable chance of obtaining*

Equity Theory

Equity theory focuses on social comparisons, people evaluating their treatment by the organization relative to the treatment of others. This approach holds that people begin by analyzing inputs (what they contribute to their jobs in terms of time, effort, education, experience) relative to outputs (what they receive in return—salary, benefits, recognition, security). This comparison is similar to the psychological contract. As viewed by equity theory, the result is a ratio of contribution to return. When they compare their own ratios with those of other employees, they ask whether their ratios are equal to, greater than, or less than those of the people with whom they are comparing themselves. Depending on their assessments, they experience feelings of equity or inequity. Figure 8.6 illustrates the three possible results of such an assessment.

For example, suppose a new college graduate gets a starting job at a large manufacturing firm. His starting salary is $45,000 a year, he gets an inexpensive company car, and he shares an assistant with another new employee. If he later learns that another new employee has received the same salary, car, and staff arrangement, he

Equity Theory *theory of motivation holding that people evaluate their treatment by the organization relative to the treatment of others*

FIGURE 8.5 Expectancy Theory Model

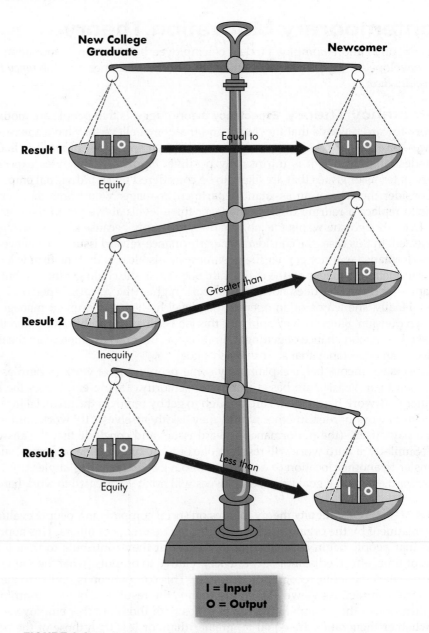

FIGURE 8.6 Equity Theory: Possible Assessments

will feel equitably treated (result 1 in Figure 8.6). If the other newcomer, however, has received $70,000, a more expensive company car, and her own personal assistant, he may feel inequitably treated (result 2 in Figure 8.6).

Note, however, that for an individual to feel equitably treated, the two ratios do not have to be identical, only equitable. Assume, for instance, that our new employee has a bachelor's degree and two years of work experience. Perhaps he learns subsequently that the other new employee has an advanced degree and 10 years of experience. After first feeling inequity, the new employee may conclude that the person with whom he compared himself is actually contributing more to the organization. That employee is equitably entitled, therefore, to receive more in return (result 3 in Figure 8.6).

When people feel they are being inequitably treated, they may do various constructive and some not so constructive things to restore fairness. For example, they may speak to their boss about the perceived inequity. Or (less constructively) they may demand a raise, reduce their efforts, work shorter hours, or just complain to their coworkers. They may also rationalize ("management succumbed to pressure to promote a woman/Asian American"), find different people with whom to compare themselves, or leave their jobs.

Strategies and Techniques for Enhancing Motivation

OBJECTIVE 5
Describe
some of the strategies and techniques used by organizations to improve employee motivation.

Understanding what motivates workers is only one part of the manager's job. The other part is applying that knowledge. Experts have suggested—and many companies have implemented—a range of programs designed to make jobs more interesting and rewarding, to make the work environment more pleasant, and to motivate employees to work harder.

Reinforcement/Behavior Modification

Some companies try to control—and even alter or modify—workers' behavior through systematic rewards and punishments for specific behaviors. Such companies first try to define the specific behaviors that they want their employees to exhibit (working hard, being courteous to customers, stressing quality) and the specific behaviors they want to eliminate (wasting time, being rude to customers, ignoring quality). Then they try to shape employee behavior by linking *positive reinforcement* with desired behaviors and punishment with undesired behaviors.

Positive reinforcement is used when a company or manager provides a reward when employees exhibit desired behaviors, such as working hard, helping others, and so forth. When rewards are tied directly to performance, they serve as positive reinforcement. For example, paying large cash bonuses to salespeople who exceed quotas prompts them to work even harder during the next selling period. John Deere has adopted a reward system based on positive reinforcement. The firm gives pay increases when its workers complete college courses and demonstrate mastery of new job skills.

Positive Reinforcement *reward that follows desired behaviors*

Punishment is designed to change behavior by presenting people with unpleasant consequences if they exhibit undesired behaviors. Employees who are repeatedly late for work, for example, may be suspended or have their pay docked. Similarly, when the National Football League or Major League Baseball fines or suspends players found guilty of substance abuse, the organization is seeking to change players' behavior.

Punishment *unpleasant consequences of an undesirable behavior*

Social learning occurs when people observe the behaviors of others, recognize their consequences, and alter their own behavior as a result. A person can learn to do a new job by observing others or by watching videotapes. Or an employee may learn to avoid being late by seeing the boss chew out fellow workers. Social learning theory, then, suggests that individual behavior is determined by a person's cognitions and social environment. More specifically, people are presumed to learn behaviors and attitudes at least partly in response to what others expect of them.

Social Learning *learning that occurs when people observe the behaviors of others, recognize their consequences, and alter their own behavior as a result*

Using Goals to Motivate Behavior

Performance goals are also commonly used to direct and motivate behavior. The most frequent method for setting performance goals is called **management by objectives (MBO)**, which is a system of collaborative goal setting that extends from the top of an organization to the bottom. MBO involves managers and subordinates in setting goals and evaluating progress. After the program is started, the organization specifies its overall goals and plans. Managers then collaborate with each of their subordinates to set individual goals that will best contribute to the organization's goals. Managers meet periodically to review progress toward individual goals, and then, usually on an annual basis, they evaluate goal achievement and use the results as a basis for starting the cycle over again.

Management By Objectives (MBO) *set of procedures involving both managers and subordinates in setting goals and evaluating progress*

According to many experts, motivational impact is the biggest advantage of MBO. When employees sit down with managers to set upcoming goals, they learn more about companywide objectives, feel that they are an important part of a team, and see how they can improve companywide performance by reaching their own goals. If an MBO system is used properly, employees should leave meetings not only with an understanding of the value of their contributions but also with fair rewards for their performances. They should also accept and be committed to the moderately difficult and specific goals they have helped set for themselves.[17]

finding a better way

Carrot or Stick?

Assume that you are the general manager of a supermarket, and you've just finished a department-by-department year-end review of your managers' performances. Every department—meats, dairy, seafood, deli, bakery, and so forth—has performed up to or beyond expectations. All except one; produce fell 12 percent short of upper management's forecast. You decide to reward all your managers with healthy bonuses, except for your produce manager. In other words, you plan to use *punishment* to motivate your produce manager and *positive reinforcement* to motivate all of your other managers. You congratulate yourself for having reached a fair and logical decision.

According to Daniel Kahneman, a psychologist who won the Nobel Prize in economics for his work on behavioral and decision-making models, your decision is actually probably not fair (at least not altogether), and it's certainly not logical—at least not when the reality of the situation is taken into consideration. Here's how Kahneman sees the logic you apparently used in your two-pronged decision-making model:

> Manager's department performs well → You reward manager → Department expected to continue to perform well in the future

> Manager's department performs poorly → You punish manager → Department expected to perform better in the future

But Kahneman argues that your logic may be flawed. The key to his criticism is called *regression to the mean*, the principle that, *from one performance measurement to the next, the change in performance will be toward the overall average level of performance*. To see how this works, let's examine a different kind of example. Say that you're an avid runner and that you run a mile along the same route every morning. On average, it takes you 7 minutes to run your mile. Of course, you seldom run the mile in *exactly* 7 minutes, but across many different days, your times average out to be 7 minutes. Now assume its Monday and you run the mile in 6 minutes and 10 seconds—a great time and well below your average. On Tuesday, your time will probably be longer—back in the direction of 7 minutes. Technically, regression to the mean is a *law*, and not a *rule*: You could run an even faster time on Tuesday, but *most of the time*, if you run faster than your average, one day you will run slower the second day and, similarly, if you run slower than your average one day you will likely run faster the next day.

Why does regression to the mean occur? Because usually—and probably—a complex combination of factors determines any outcome. And because this combination is complex, it's not likely that the same combination will repeat itself the next time you measure the outcome. Factors that influence your running speed, for example, might include how much sleep you got and what you ate for dinner the night before, temperature and other

Tyler Olson/Shutterstock

weather conditions, your motivation on a particular day, and so forth.

Which brings us back to your produce manager: *It's not likely that his managerial performance was the sole (or even necessarily the primary) factor in his department's poor performance.* Other factors might include variations in competition, economic and market conditions, and decisions made by other managers—all of which are largely random and which will undoubtedly be different from one performance measurement to the next.

Now that you understand a little about the reality of regression to the mean, compare your decision-making model to a model that reflects reality:

> Manager's department performs above average in one period → Department probably does not perform as well the next period

> Manager's department performs below average in one period → Department probably performs better in next period

Your reinforcement decision will *probably* have little or nothing to do with next year's outcome in any of your store's departments. And you've *probably* been unfair to your produce manager.

Kahneman isn't inclined to be overly critical of your mistaken belief that you've made a logical, fair, and effective decision: "It's very difficult for people to detect their own errors," he admits. "You're too busy making a mistake to detect it at the same time." He does, however, reserve the right to be pessimistic: "The failure to recognize the import of regression," he warns,

> can have pernicious consequences…We normally reinforce others when their behavior is good and punish them when their behavior is bad. By regression alone [however], they are most likely to improve after being punished and most likely to deteriorate after being rewarded. Consequently, we are exposed to a lifetime schedule in which we are most often rewarded for punishing others and punished for rewarding [them].[18]

Participative Management and Empowerment

In **participative management and empowerment,** employees are given a voice in how they do their jobs and in how the company is managed; they become empowered to take greater responsibility for their own performance. Not surprisingly, participation and empowerment often makes employees feel more committed to organizational goals they have helped to shape.

Participation and empowerment can be used in large firms or small firms, both with managers and operating employees. For example, managers at General Electric who once needed higher-level approval for any expenditure more than $5,000 now have the autonomy to make their own expense decisions up to as much as $50,000. At Adam Hat Company, a small firm that makes men's dress, military, and cowboy hats, workers who previously had to report all product defects to supervisors now have the freedom to correct problems themselves or even return products to the workers who are responsible for them. Sports gear company And1 also practices empowerment by allowing its designers considerable latitude in testing new ideas. For instance, a designer can make a few prototypes of a new product, distribute them to kids on a neighborhood basketball court, and then get their feedback.

Although some employees thrive in participative programs, such programs are not for everyone. People may be frustrated by responsibilities they are not equipped to handle. Moreover, participative programs may actually result in dissatisfied employees if workers see the invitation to participate as more symbolic than substantive. One key, say most experts, is to invite participation only to the extent that employees want to have input and only if participation will have real value for an organization.

Participative Management and Empowerment *method of increasing job satisfaction by giving employees a voice in the management of their jobs and the company*

Team Structures

We have already noted the increased use of teams in organizations. Yet another benefit that some companies get from using teams is increased motivation and enhanced job satisfaction among those employees working in teams. Although teams are often less effective in traditional and rigidly structured bureaucratic organizations, they often help smaller, more flexible organizations make decisions more quickly and effectively, enhance companywide communication, and encourage organizational members to feel more like a part of an organization. In turn, these attitudes usually lead to higher levels of both employee motivation and job satisfaction.[19]

But managers should remember that teams are not for everyone. Levi Strauss, for example, encountered major problems when it tried to use teams. Individual workers previously performed repetitive, highly specialized tasks, such as sewing zippers into jeans, and were paid according to the number of jobs they completed each day. In an attempt to boost productivity, company management reorganized everyone into teams of 10 to 35 workers and assigned tasks to the entire group. Each team member's pay was determined by the team's level of productivity. In practice, however, faster workers became resentful of slower workers because they reduced the group's total output. Slower workers, meanwhile, resented the pressure put on them by faster-working coworkers. As a result, motivation, satisfaction, and morale all dropped, and Levi Strauss eventually abandoned the teamwork plan altogether.

Job Enrichment and Job Redesign

Whereas goal setting and MBO programs and empowerment can work in a variety of settings, *job enrichment* and *job redesign* programs are generally used to increase satisfaction in jobs significantly lacking in motivating factors.

Job Enrichment Programs **Job enrichment** is designed to add one or more motivating factors to job activities. For example, *job rotation* programs expand growth opportunities by rotating employees through various positions in the same firm. Workers gain not only new skills but also broader overviews of their work and their organization. Other programs focus on increasing responsibility or recognition.

Job Enrichment *method of increasing job satisfaction by adding one or more motivating factors to job activities*

At United Airlines, for example, flight attendants now have more control over their own scheduling. The jobs of flight service managers were enriched when they were given more responsibility and authority for assigning tasks to flight crew members.

Job Redesign *method of increasing job satisfaction by designing a more satisfactory fit between workers and their jobs*

Job Redesign Programs **Job redesign** acknowledges that different people want different things from their jobs. By restructuring work to achieve a more satisfactory fit between workers and their jobs, job redesign can motivate individuals with strong needs for career growth or achievement. Job redesign is usually implemented in one of three ways: through *combining tasks, forming natural work groups*, or *establishing client relationships*.

COMBINING TASKS The job of combining tasks involves enlarging jobs and increasing their variety to make employees feel that their work is more meaningful. In turn, employees become more motivated. For example, the job done by a programmer who maintains computer systems might be redesigned to include some system design and system development work. While developing additional skills, the programmer also gets involved in the overall system development.

FORMING NATURAL WORK GROUPS People who do different jobs on the same projects are candidates for natural work groups. These groups are formed to help employees see the place and importance of their jobs in the total structure of the firm. They are valuable to management because the people working on a project are usually the most knowledgeable about it and the most capable problem solvers.

ESTABLISHING CLIENT RELATIONSHIPS Establishing client relationships means letting employees interact with customers. This approach increases job variety. It gives workers both a greater sense of control and more feedback about performance than they get when their jobs are not highly interactive. For example, software writers at Microsoft watch test users work with programs and discuss problems with them directly rather than receive feedback from third-party researchers.

Modified Work Schedules and Alternative Workplaces

As another way of increasing job satisfaction, many companies are experimenting with *modified work schedules*, different approaches to working hours and the workweek. The two most common forms of modified scheduling are *work-share programs* and *flextime programs*, including alternative workplace strategies.[20] Alternative workplaces are also becoming more and more common.

Work Sharing (Job Sharing) *method of increasing job satisfaction by allowing two or more people to share a single full-time job*

Work-Share Programs At Steelcase, the country's largest maker of office furnishings, two talented women in the marketing division both wanted to work only part-time. The solution: they now share a single full-time job. With each working 2.5 days a week, both got their wish and the job gets done—and done well. The practice, known as **work sharing** (or **job sharing**), has "brought sanity back to our lives," according to at least one Steelcase employee.

Job sharing usually benefits both employees and employers. Employees, for instance, tend to appreciate the organization's attention to their personal needs. At the same time, the company can reduce turnover and save on the cost of benefits. On the negative side, job-share employees generally receive fewer benefits than their full-time counterparts and may be the first to be laid off when cutbacks are necessary.

Flextime Programs *method of increasing job satisfaction by allowing workers to adjust work schedules on a daily or weekly basis*

Flextime Programs and Alternative Workplace Strategies

Flextime programs allow people to choose their working hours by adjusting a standard work schedule on a daily or weekly basis. There are limits to flextime. The Steelcase program, for instance, requires all employees to work certain core hours. This practice allows everyone to reach coworkers at a specified time of day. Employees can then decide whether to make up the rest of the standard eight-hour day by coming in and leaving early (by working 6:00 A.M. to 2:00 P.M. or 7:00 A.M. to 3:00 P.M.) or late (9:00 A.M. to 5:00 P.M. or 10:00 A.M. to 6:00 P.M.).

In one variation, companies may also allow employees to choose four, five, or six days on which to work each week. Some, for instance, may choose Monday through Thursday, others Tuesday through Friday. By working 10 hours in four workdays, employees still complete 40-hour weeks.

Alternative Workplaces   A rapidly growing number of U.S. workers do a significant portion of their work via **telecommuting,** performing some or all of a job away from standard office settings. Working from a home office outfitted with a PC, high-speed Internet, and a company intranet connection, telecommuters can keep abreast of everything going on at the office. In 2010, around 24 percent of all U.S. workers spent at least part of their working hours telecommuting. This trend is on the rise: In 2005, 44 percent of U.S. companies offered some telecommuting options, up from 32 percent in 2001.[21] And in 2010 almost 80 percent of white collar and other professional workers in the United States performed at least some of their work from a location other than their office.

Telecommuting *form of flextime that allows people to perform some or all of a job away from standard office settings*

Advantages and Disadvantages of Modified Schedules and Alternative Workplaces   Flextime gives employees more freedom in their professional and personal lives. It allows workers to plan around the work schedules of spouses and the school schedules of young children. Studies show that the increased sense of freedom and control reduces stress and improves individual productivity.

Companies also benefit in other ways. In urban areas, for example, such programs can reduce traffic congestion and similar problems that contribute to stress and lost work time. Furthermore, employers benefit from higher levels of commitment and job satisfaction. John Hancock Insurance, Shell Oil, and Metropolitan Life are among the major U.S. corporations that have successfully adopted some form of flextime.

Conversely, flextime sometimes complicates coordination because people are working different schedules. In addition, if workers are paid by the hour, flextime may make it difficult for employers to keep accurate records of when employees are actually working.

As for telecommuting, it may not be for everyone. For instance, some people may be attracted to telecommuting because they envision not having to shave or put on make up and relish the idea of spending the day in their pajamas. But not everyone has the necessary self-discipline to work from home without supervision and others come to miss the social interaction of the workplace. One study has shown that even though telecommuters may be producing results, those with strong advancement ambitions may miss networking and rubbing elbows with management on a day-to-day basis.

Another obstacle to establishing a telecommuting program is convincing management that it can be beneficial for all involved. Telecommuters may have to fight the perception from both bosses and coworkers that if they are not being supervised, they are not working. Managers, admits one experienced consultant, "usually have to be dragged kicking and screaming into this. They always ask 'How can I tell if someone is working when I can't see them?'" By the same token, he adds, "that's based on the erroneous assumption that if you can see them, they are working." Most experts agree that re-education and constant communication are requirements of a successful telecommuting arrangement. Both managers and employees must determine expectations in advance.

As we have illustrated in this chapter, employee behavior and motivation are important concepts for managers to understand. They are also complex processes that require careful consideration by managers. For example, a clumsy attempt to motivate employees to work harder without fully considering all factors can actually have just the opposite effect. But managers who do take the time to understand the people with whom they work can better appreciate their efforts. Another important factor that affects employee behavior is *leadership*, the subject of our next chapter.

summary of learning objectives

OBJECTIVE 1

Identify and discuss the basic forms of behaviors that employees exhibit in organizations. (pp. 272–275)

Employee behavior is the pattern of actions by the members of an organization that directly or indirectly influences the organization's effectiveness. *Performance behaviors* are the total set of work-related behaviors that the organization expects employees to display. They directly contribute to productivity and performance. *Organizational citizenship*, on the other hand, refers to the behavior of individuals who make a positive overall contribution to the organization, although not directly contributing to the bottom line. A number of factors, including individual and organizational variables, play roles in promoting or minimizing organizational citizenship behaviors. *Counterproductive behaviors* are those that detract from, rather than contribute to, organizational performance. Counterproductive behaviors include absenteeism, turnover, theft and sabotage, sexual and racial harassment, and workplace aggression and violence.

OBJECTIVE 2

Describe the nature and importance of individual differences among employees. (pp. 275–280)

Individual differences are personal attributes that vary from one person to another, such as personality and attitudes. *Personality* is the relatively stable set of psychological attributes that distinguish one person from another. The *"big five" personality traits* are *agreeableness, conscientiousness, emotionality, extraversion,* and *openness*. *Agreeableness* is a person's ability to get along with others. *Conscientiousness*, another of the "big five" traits, refers to the individual's persistence, dependableness, and orderliness. *Emotionality* refers to the degree to which people tend to be positive or negative in their outlook and behaviors toward others. *Extraversion* refers to a person's comfort level with relationships. Extraverts are sociable, talkative, assertive, and open to new relationships and tend to be higher performers. Finally, *openness* is how open or rigid a person is in terms of his or her beliefs. People with a high level of openness are curious and willing to listen to new ideas and are, therefore, often higher performers. The potential value of this framework is that it encompasses an integrated set of traits that appear to be valid predictors of certain behaviors in certain situations. Thus, managers who can both understand the framework and assess these traits in their employees are in a good position to understand how and why they behave as they do.

The Myers-Briggs framework differentiates people in terms of four general dimensions: sensing, intuiting, judging, and perceiving. Higher and lower positions in each of the dimensions are used to classify people into one of 16 different personality categories. Research suggests that the Myers-Briggs Type Indicator is a useful method for determining communication styles and interaction preferences.

Emotional intelligence, or *emotional quotient (EQ)*, refers to the extent to which people are self-aware, can manage their emotions, can motivate themselves, express empathy for others, and possess social skills. Preliminary research suggests that people with high EQs perform better than others. Just as important, it appears that emotional intelligence is not biologically based but can be learned.

Other important personality traits are locus of control, self-efficacy, authoritarianism, Machiavellianism, self-esteem, and risk propensity. *Locus of control* is the extent to which people believe that their behavior has a real effect on what happens to them. People with an internal locus of control believe that they will succeed if they work hard, whereas those with an external locus of control believe that fate, chance, luck, or the behavior of others determines their own success. A similar concept is *self-efficacy*. A person's self-efficacy is their belief about their ability to perform a task. *Authoritarianism* is the extent to which a person believes that power and status differences are acceptable within an organization. A person who is highly authoritarian is more likely to accept direction and orders from a supervisor. *Machiavellianism* is a personality trait related to an individual's desire to gain power and control the behavior of others. *Self-esteem* is a personality trait that refers to the extent to which a person believes that he or she is worthwhile and deserving. Individuals with high self-esteem are more likely to seek higher-status jobs and are more confident in their performance. Finally, *risk propensity* refers to the degree to which a person is willing to take chances and make risky decisions. This characteristic can be a major influence on a manager's decision making behavior.

Attitudes reflect our beliefs and feelings about specific ideas, situations, or other people. Attitudes are important because they are the mechanism through which we express our feelings. Attitudes are formed by a variety of forces, including our personal values, our experiences, and our personalities. Attitudes are usually viewed as stable dispositions to behave toward objects in a certain way and contain three components: cognition, affect, and intention. *Cognition* is the knowledge a person presumes to have about something. A person's *affect* is his or her feelings toward something, and *intention* guides a person's behavior. When two sets of cognitions or perceptions are contradictory or incongruent, a person experiences a level of conflict and anxiety called *cognitive dissonance*. Especially important work-related attitudes are *job satisfaction* and *organizational commitment*. Job satisfaction, also known as morale, is the extent to which people have positive attitudes toward their jobs. Organizational commitment, in contrast, reflects an individual's identification with the organization and its mission.

OBJECTIVE 3

Explain the meaning and importance of psychological contracts and the person-job fit in the workplace. (pp. 280–282)

A *psychological contract* is the overall set of expectations held by employees and the organization regarding what employees will contribute to the organization and what the organization will provide in return. An individual makes a variety of contributions to the organization, such as effort, ability, loyalty, skills, and time. In return, the organization provides inducements such as pay, career opportunities, job security, and status. All organizations must manage psychological contracts, providing the right inducements to retain employees.

A good *person-job fit* is achieved when the employee's contributions match the inducements the organization offers. Having a good match between people and their jobs can help enhance performance, job satisfaction, and motivation.

OBJECTIVE 4

Identify and summarize the most important models and concepts of employee motivation. (pp. 282–288)

Motivation is the set of forces that cause people to behave in certain ways. Early approaches to motivation assumed that workers are motivated solely by money. Managers employed this theory through *scientific management* by paying workers for productivity and finding more efficient ways of getting things done. However, the results of a study at Western Electric revealed that worker productivity improves in response to special attention, a phenomenon known as the *Hawthorne effect*.

As a result, researchers focused more on the effect of human relations on employee performance. Abraham Maslow's *hierarchy of human needs* model holds that people at work try to satisfy one or more of five different needs: physiological, security, social, esteem, and self-actualization. According to this theory, people are motivated by their lowest level of unsatisfied need.

Frederick Herzberg's *two-factor theory* argues that satisfaction and dissatisfaction depend on *hygiene factors*, such as working conditions, and *motivation factors*, such as recognition for a job well done. Herzberg suggests that the absence of hygiene factors causes dissatisfaction, but the presence of these same factors does not cause motivation. Employees are motivated by the presence of one or more motivation factors.

McClelland's acquired needs theory hypothesized that workers may have three types of needs: the needs for achievement, affiliation, and power. These needs are shaped over time and influence behavior. Those with high achievement needs are motivated by challenging tasks, whereas those with high affiliation needs desire to develop personal connections with other workers. Employees with high power needs have a desire to control their environment.

Douglas McGregor proposed the human resources model. He described two types of managers. Theory X managers believe that workers are naturally lazy and unmotivated and Theory Y managers believe that people are naturally self-motivated and interested in being productive.

Expectancy theory suggests that people are motivated to work toward rewards that they have a reasonable expectancy of obtaining. *Equity theory* focuses on social comparisons—people evaluating their treatment by the organization relative to the treatment of others.

OBJECTIVE 5

Describe some of the strategies and techniques used by organizations to improve employee motivation. (pp. 289–293)

There are several major strategies and techniques often used to make jobs more interesting and rewarding. *Positive reinforcement* is used when a company or manager provides a reward when employees exhibit desired behaviors whereas *punishment* is designed to change behavior by presenting employees with unpleasant consequences if they exhibit undesired behaviors. *Social learning* occurs when people observe the behaviors of others and recognize their consequences, altering their own behavior as a result.

Management by objectives (MBO) is a system of collaborative goal setting that extends from the top of an organization to the bottom. Managers periodically meet with subordinates to review progress toward goals, increasing satisfaction and commitment. In *participative management and empowerment*, employees are given a voice in how they do their jobs and in how the company is managed. Participative management tends to increase employee commitment to organizational goals.

Using *teams* is another strategy to increase motivation. Job enrichment and job redesign are generally used to increase satisfaction in jobs significantly lacking motivating factors. *Job enrichment* adds motivating factors to job activities. *Job redesign* is a method of increasing job satisfaction by designing a more satisfactory fit between workers and their jobs through combining tasks, forming natural workgroups, or establishing client relationships. Some companies also use *modified work schedules*—different approaches to working hours and the workweek. Common options include *work sharing (job sharing)*, *flextime programs*, and *telecommuting*.

key terms

absenteeism (p. 274)
affect (p. 279)
attitudes (p. 278)
authoritarianism (p. 278)
"big five" personality traits (p. 275)
classical theory of motivation (p. 282)
cognition (p. 279)
cognitive dissonance (p. 279)
counterproductive behavior (p. 274)
emotional intelligence (emotional quotient, EQ) (p. 277)
employee behavior (p. 272)
equity theory (p. 287)
expectancy theory (p. 287)
flextime programs (p. 292)
Hawthorne effect (p. 282)
hierarchy of human needs model (p. 283)

individual differences (p. 275)
intention (p. 279)
job enrichment (p. 291)
job redesign (p. 292)
job satisfaction (p. 280)
locus of control (p. 277)
Machiavellianism (p. 278)
management by objectives (MBO) (p. 289)
motivation (p. 282)
Myers-Briggs Type Indicator (MBTI) (p. 277)
need for achievement (p. 285)
need for affiliation (p. 285)
need for power (p. 285)
organizational citizenship (p. 273)
organizational commitment (p. 280)
participative management and empowerment (p. 291)

performance behaviors (p. 273)
personality (p. 275)
person-job fit (p. 282)
positive reinforcement (p. 289)
psychological contract (p. 280)
punishment (p. 289)
risk propensity (p. 278)
self-efficacy (p. 277)
self-esteem (p. 278)
social learning (p. 289)
telecommuting (p. 293)
Theory X (p. 283)
Theory Y (p. 283)
turnover (p. 274)
two-factor theory (p. 284)
work sharing (or job sharing) (p. 292)

Go to **pearsonglobaleditions.com/mybizlab** to complete the problems marked with this icon ★.

questions & exercises

QUESTIONS FOR REVIEW

8-1. Describe the "big five" personality traits and how they contribute to employee performance.

8-2. What are the three components of attitudes? Be sure to describe each.

8-3. Compare and contrast the hierarchy of human needs with the two-factor theory of motivation.

✪ 8-4. How can participative management programs enhance employee satisfaction and motivation?

QUESTIONS FOR ANALYSIS

✪ 8-5. Describe the psychological contract you currently have or have had in the past with an employer. If you have never worked, describe the psychological contract that you have with the instructor in this class.

✪ 8-6. Do you think that most people are relatively satisfied or dissatisfied with their work? What factors do you think most contribute to satisfaction or dissatisfaction?

8-7. Some evidence suggests that recent college graduates show high levels of job satisfaction. Levels then drop dramatically as they reach their late twenties, only to increase gradually once they get older. What might account for this pattern?

8-8. What would you tell a low-skill worker performing a simple and routine job who wants more challenge and enjoyment from work?

APPLICATION EXERCISES

8-9. Assume you are about to start your own business. What might you do from the beginning to ensure that your employees will be satisfied and motivated?

8-10. Interview your employer or an administrator at your college. Ask the manager what they believe motivates their employees. Identify one or more theories of motivation that seems consistent with this manager's approach.

building a business: continuing team exercise

Assignment

Meet with you team members and discuss your new business venture within the context of this chapter. Develop specific responses to the following:

8-11. Thinking about your new business venture, what performance behaviors will you expect from your employees? What counterproductive behaviors would be most detrimental to your business?

8-12. If you were able to measure the emotional intelligence of prospective employees, which dimension or dimensions will be most important to you?

8-13. There are many theories of motivation. If you believe that Maslow's needs hierarchy best explains motivation in the workplace, how will you motivate your employees to work hard?

8-14. Another popular theory of motivation is Herzberg's two-factor theory. How could you apply this theory to your new business venture?

8-15. In your new company, will employees be able to work from home or work flexible hours? Why or why not?

building your business skills

TOO MUCH OF A GOOD THING

Goal

To encourage you to apply different motivational theories to a workplace problem involving poor productivity.

Background Information

For years, working for George Uhe, a small chemicals broker in Paramus, New Jersey, made employees feel as if they were members of a big family. Unfortunately, this family was going broke because too few "members" were working hard enough to make money for it. Employees were happy, comfortable, complacent—and lazy.

With sales dropping in the pharmaceutical and specialty-chemicals division, Uhe brought in management consultants to analyze the situation and to make recommendations. The

outsiders quickly identified a motivational problem affecting the sales force: Sales representatives were paid a handsome salary and received automatic, year-end bonuses regardless of performance. They were also treated to bagels every Friday and regular group birthday lunches that cost as much as $200. Employees felt satisfied but had little incentive to work hard. Eager to return to profitability, Uhe's owners waited to hear the consultants' recommendations.

Method

STEP 1

In groups of four, step into the role of Uhe's management consultants. Start by analyzing your client's workforce-motivation problems from the following perspectives (our questions focus on key motivational issues):

- *Job satisfaction and morale.* As part of a 77-year-old, family-owned business, Uhe employees were happy and loyal, in part because they were treated so well. Can high morale have a downside? How can it breed stagnation, and what can managers do to prevent stagnation from taking hold?
- *Theory X versus Theory Y.* Although the behavior of these workers seems to make a case for Theory X, why is it difficult to draw this conclusion about a company that focuses more on satisfaction than on sales and profits?
- *Two-factor theory.* Analyze the various ways in which improving such motivational factors as recognition, added responsibility, advancement, and growth might reduce the importance of hygiene factors, including pay and security.
- *Expectancy theory.* Analyze the effect on productivity of redesigning the company's sales force compensation structure—namely, by paying lower base salaries while offering greater earnings potential through a sales-based incentive system. Why would linking performance with increased pay that is achievable through hard work

motivate employees? Why would the threat of a job loss also motivate greater effort?

STEP 2

Write a short report based on your analysis making recommendations to Uhe's owners. The goal of your report is to change the working environment in ways that will motivate greater effort and generate greater productivity.

FOLLOW-UP QUESTIONS

8-16. What is your group's most important recommendation? Why do you think it is likely to succeed?

8-17. Changing the corporate culture to make it less paternalistic may reduce employees' sense of belonging to a family. If you were an employee, would you consider a greater focus on profits to be an improvement or a problem? How would it affect your motivation and productivity?

8-18. What steps would you take to improve the attitude and productivity of longtime employees who resist change?

exercising your ethics

TOO MUCH OF A GOOD THING

The Situation

Longines Corporation is a financial services company located in a large urban area. Because of omnipresent traffic issues, Longines has implemented a number of strategies. They have implemented alternative work schedules, such as a four-day work week and flextime, to help employees avoid the heaviest traffic times. Additionally, many employees are able to telecommute and work from home.

Longines' CEO realizes that the company's biggest asset is its loyal and talented workforce. They have had a low level of turnover because of excellent working conditions and a collaborative work environment. Despite the popularity of flextime, four-day work weeks, and telecommuting, the CEO and board are becoming concerned that these popular programs are actually hurting the company. The CEO has announced that these programs will be discontinued in three months and employees are upset.

The Dilemma

You are the human resource manager for Longines and the CEO has come to you for advice. She understands that her decision is unpopular, but she believes that it is the right one. In recent

years, it has become increasingly difficult to organize meetings with employees working from home and on alternate work schedules. The CEO believes that this has impaired the ability of Longines to respond to changes in the market and to solve complex problems. She is asking you to take a strong stance in support of this new plan and has suggested that your continued employment depends on your support. However, despite the CEO's concerns, you believe that these alternative work schedules and telecommuting options are actually positive elements. You've had personal experience with this, as you have been able to manage your work and home life because your wife is able to telecommute for her job four days per week. A number of trusted employees have come to you and suggested that this change is a fundamental change in their relationship with the company. After years of hard work, options are being taken away. You feel as if you are being pulled in two directions and you are unsure about exactly how to proceed.

QUESTIONS TO ADDRESS

8-19. What are the ethical issues in this case?

8-20. What do you think most managers would do in this situation?

8-21. What would you do?

team exercise

TAKING ONE FOR THE TEAM

The Situation

You are a skilled technician who has worked for a major electronics firm for the past 10 years. You love your job—it is interesting, stimulating, and enjoyable, and you are well paid for what you do. The plant where you work is one of five manufacturing

centers your firm operates in a major metropolitan area. The firm is currently developing a new prototype for one of its next-generation products. To ensure that all perspectives are reflected, the company has identified a set of technicians from each plant who will work together as a team for the next two months. If the team is successful, there could be significant opportunities for advancement within the company for the team members.

The Decision

You have just met with your new teammates and have been elected as the team leader. However, it looks like your job may be difficult. The technicians from two of the manufacturing centers have heard rumors that your company is planning to close at least three of the centers and move production to a lower-cost factory in another country. These individuals are upset. Moreover, they have made it clear that they (1) do not intend to put forth much extra effort on this project and (2) they are all looking for new jobs. On the other hand, you have not heard anything to support these rumors and you, as well as several others, are quite happy with your jobs.

Team Activity

8-22. Working alone, write a brief summary of how you would handle this situation. For instance, would you seek more information or just go about your work? Would you start looking for another job, would you try to form a subgroup just with those technicians who share your views, or would you try to work with everyone?

8-23. Form a small group with some of your classmates. Develop a list of alternatives after listening to each group member's perspective

8-24. Formulate a group recommendation for the best course of action.

cases

Chicken or Egg?

Continued form page 272

At the beginning of this chapter you read about the relationship between employee happiness and productivity. Using the information presented in this chapter you should now be able to answer these questions.

QUESTIONS FOR DISCUSSION

8-25. How do you think happiness and productivity relate to one another?

8-26. Which do you think is more important, motivation or engagement?

8-27. What factors motivate you personally?

8-28. Suppose you have an employee who seems unhappy and is not performing well. Until recently, though, this person was always happy and was a top performer. What would you do?

8-29. How important would the opportunity to telecommute be to you in accepting a job offer? Why?

Searching for a Great Place to Work

In 1995, Larry Page met Sergey Brin when he visited Stanford University as a prospective graduate student in computer science. Although they did not initially hit it off, a year later they were collaborating on a new search engine called BackRub. By 1998, they had investors and incorporated Google, the new name of their search engine and the name of their new business venture. From the beginning, Page and Brin realized that happy, motivated employees were at the center of successful organizations. Karen May, current Vice-President of People Development at Google shares their vision, "Imagine a world where most organizations were the best place to work. Imagine what we could be getting done on the planet if this were true."[22]

Google has grown quickly, from a two-person operation to a company with more than 37,000 employees in 40 countries. Google has become famous for its over-the-top perks, such as on-site bowling alleys and pool tables, free haircuts during work hours, and Lego rooms. However, unlike other companies, Google is analytical about the perks it offers, using complex metrics to evaluate which are most valued by employees.[23] Google is also a pay leader, offering salaries well above the market average.

Google executives believe that it is essential that people love what they do at work. Every employee has the opportunity to spend at least 20 percent of their work time on a project of their choice using Google's extensive resources. For example, Chade-Meng Tan, an engineer at Google, has been working on a project to achieve world peace in his lifetime. Although this goal is likely unattainable, Tan has been encouraged to develop his energy to the project. He has developed a course on mindfulness for Google employees and has written on the topic, all while working to create Google's mobile search engine.

Prasad Setty, Vice-President of People Analytics and Compensation, is a strong supporter of Google's flexible work hours policy. Employees are given a great amount of freedom to decide when to work or when to go the gym, play volleyball, or get a free massage. "One of the tenets we strongly believe in is if you give people freedom, they will amaze you." However, for this autonomy to work, Google has a highly selective and deliberate hiring process directed at employing people that are ambitious and achievement-oriented.[24]

Finally, Google employees are given a voice in company decision making. The company selects feedback on compensation as well as the types of bikes available to ride around the campus. Every Friday, Brin and Page hold employee forums to respond to commonly asked questions. Employees are also given access to detailed company information that is often a closely guarded secret. Google's revolutionary approach to the workplace has paid off—the company's stock has increased in value by 650 percent in less than seven years—a statistic that is all the more impressive since the Dow Jones has increased only 44 percent in the same period of time.

QUESTIONS FOR DISCUSSION

8-30. Page and Brin were young when they started Google. Do you think that they identified most with Theory X or Theory Y? Why?

8-31. Describe how Maslow's needs hierarchy could be applied to Google's approach to employee motivation.

8-32. Use Herzberg's two-factor theory to explain how Google motivates employees.

8-33. Google is obviously a great place to work, but it's probably not right for everyone. What types of people are best and least suited for work at Google?

8-34. Google has a fantastic package of compensation and benefits. To retain employees, will they have to continually add new perks? How could they avoid this?

MyBizLab

Go to **pearsonglobaleditions.com/mybizlab** *for the following Assisted-graded writing questions:*

8-35. Although each individual's personality is unique, many personality traits can be summarized in five encompassing traits. Which of the "Big Five" personality traits are better for first-line, middle, and top managers? Support your answer. What if a manager becomes an ex-patriot; does this change your answer? If so, how? Support your answer. How might the "Big Five" personality traits affect employee attitudes at work? (For example, do you think people with a positive emotionality would experience more job satisfaction or organizational commitment than a person with a negative emotionality?)

8-36. Due to rapid growth and changing demographics in the workplace, companies have been discovering innovative ways for employees to perform their work in their own time in the form of modified work schedules. Given the variety of modified work schedules discussed in the text, do any seem more desirable to you or would you rather have a normal work schedule? Explain your choice. The text describes advantages of these modified schedules on the employee and the community. Can you describe advantages that the company would receive? What advantages could be received in a global company?

8-37. Mybizlab Only—comprehensive writing assignment for this chapter.

end notes

1 "Do Happy Workers Mean Higher Profits?" *USA Today*, February 20, 2013, p. 1B; Sara Caputo, "Which Comes First: Happiness or Productivity?" *Toolbox for HR*, April 15, 2009, at http://hr.toolbox.com, accessed on April 13, 2013; Alexander Kjerulf, "Top 10 Reasons Why Happiness at Work Is the Ultimate Productivity Booster," *PositiveSharing.com*, March 27, 2007, at http://positivesharing.com, accessed on April 13, 2013; Paul Larson, "Employee Motivation in the Workplace," *Suite101.com*, May 4, 2009, at http://paul-larson.suite101.com, accessed on April 13, 2013; Charles Kerns, "Putting Performance and Happiness Together in the Workplace," *Graziado Business Report*, 2008, vol. 11, at http://gbr.pepperdine.edu, accessed on April 13, 2013.

2 Dennis W. Organ, Philip M. Podsakoff, and Nathan P. Podsakoff, "Expanding the Criterion Domain to Include Organizational Citizenship Behavior: Implications for Employee Selection," in Sheldon Zedeck, (Ed.), *Handbook of Industrial and Organizational Psychology* (American Psychological Association: Washington, D.C., 2010).

3 FPS Employment, Labour and Social Dialogue (http://www.employment.belgium.be) accessed 13/11/2013 *Workplace Bullying: A Global Health and Safety Issue* Ellen Pinkos Cobb, The Isosceles Group (http://ilera2012.wharton.upenn.edu/refereedpapers/cobbellen.pdf) accessed 13/11/2013.

4 Oleksandr S. Chernyshenko, Stephen Stark, and Fritz Drasgow, "Individual Differences: Their Measurement and Validity," in Sheldon Zedeck, (Ed.), *Handbook of Industrial and Organizational Psychology* (American Psychological Association: Washington, D.C., 2010).

5 See Daniel Goleman, *Emotional Intelligence: Why It Can Matter More Than IQ* (New York: Bantam Books, 1995); see also Kenneth Law, Chi-Sum Wong, and Lynda Song, "The Construct and Criterion Validity of Emotional Intelligence and Its Potential Utility for Management Studies," *Journal of Applied Psychology*, 2004, vol 89, no. 3, 483–596.

6 J. B. Rotter, "Generalized Expectancies for Internal vs. External Control of Reinforcement," *Psychological Monographs*, 1966, vol. 80, pp. 1–28; Bert De Brabander and Christopher Boone, "Sex Differences in Perceived Locus of Control," *Journal of Social Psychology*, 1990, vol. 130, pp. 271–276.

7 See Jeffrey Vancouver, Kristen More, and Ryan Yoder, "Self-Efficacy and Resource Allocation: Support for a Nonmonotic, Discontinuous Model," *Journal of Applied Psychology*, 2008, vol. 93, no. 1, pp. 35–47.

8 T. W. Adorno, E. Frenkel-Brunswick, D. J. Levinson, and R. N. Sanford, *The Authoritarian Personality* (New York: Harper & Row, 1950).

9 Denise M. Rousseau, "The Individual-Organization Relationship: The Psychological Contract," in Sheldon Zedeck, (Ed.), *Handbook of Industrial and Organizational Psychology* (American Psychological Association: Washington, D.C., 2010).

10 See Daniel Wren, *The History of Management Thought*, 5th ed. (New York: John Wiley & Sons), 2004.

11 David McClelland, *The Achieving Society* (Princeton, NJ: Nostrand, 1961). See also David C. McClelland, *Human Motivation* (Cambridge, UK: Cambridge University Press, 1988).

12 Stanley Schachter, *The Psychology of Affiliation* (Palo Alto: Stanford University Press, 1959).

13 David McClelland and David H. Burnham, "Power Is the Great Motivator," *Harvard Business Review*, March–April 1976, pp. 100–110.

14 Kellen Merrill, "The Big Imprint in the Film Industry," *inmag.com*, 2010, at www.inmag.com, accessed on March 9, 2011; Stephanie N. Mehta, "Hollywood, South Pacific-Style," *CNNMoney.com*, June 8, 2006, at http://money.cnn.com, accessed on April 13, 2013, see http://money.cnn.com/magazines/fortune/fortune_archive/2006/06/12/8379271/; http://www.bigfootfilms.com/about-us/; Marlene Rodriguez, "Bigfoot Entertainment's International Academy of Film and Television in Mactan

Island, Cebu," *NEDA Knowledge Emporium*, November 5, 2007, at www.neda.gov.ph, accessed on April 13, 2013; Josh Elmets with Rebecca Pahle, "International Academy of Film and TV Flourishes in the Philippines," *MovieMaker*, January 29, 2010, at www.moviemaker.com, accessed on April 13, 2013 see http://www.moviemaker.com/articles-moviemaking/keith-sensing-international-academy-of-film-and-television-20100121/; Jonathan Landreth, "Bigfoot Entertainment Expands, Launches Distribution Company," *Hollywood Reporter*, November 2, 2010, at www.hollywoodreporter.com, accessed on April 13, 2013; Richard Verrier, "Indie Filmmaker Bigfoot Has an Insider Track to Theater," *Los Angeles Times*, October 6, 2010, at http://articles.latimes.com, accessed on April 13, 2013. See http://articles.latimes.com/2010/oct/06/business/la-fi-ct-crest-20101006.

[15] Pinder, *Work Motivation in Organizational Behavior*, 2nd ed. (Upper Saddle River, NJ: Prentice-Hall, 2008); McClelland and Burnham, "Power Is the Great Motivator."

[16] Lyman Porter, Gregory Bigley, and Richard Steers, *Motivation and Work Behavior*, 8th ed. (New York: McGraw-Hill), 2008.

[17] Gary P. Latham, "The Importance of Understanding and Changing Employee Outcome Expectancies for Gaining Commitment to an Organizational Goal," *Personnel Psychology*, 2001, vol. 54, 707–720.

[18] Bryan Burke, "Fighter Pilots and Firing Coaches," *Advanced NFL Stats*, February 19, 2009, at www.advancednflstats.com, accessed on April 12, 2013; David Hall, "Daniel Kahneman Interview," *New Zealand Listener*, January 21, 2012, at www.listener.co.nz, accessed on April 12, 2013; Steve Miller, "We're Not Very Good Statisticians," *Information Management*, March 26, 2012, at www.information-management.com, accessed on April 12, 2013; Galen Strawson, "*Thinking, Fast and Slow* by Daniel Kahneman—Review," *The Guardian*, December 13, 2011, at www.guardian.co.uk, accessed on April 12, 2013; *Judgment under Uncertainty: Heuristics and Biases*, ed. Daniel Kahneman, Paul Slovic, and Amos Tversky (Cambridge, UK: Cambridge University Press, 1982), at http://books.google.com, accessed on April, 21, 2013, page 68.

[19] Adam M. Grant, Yitzhak Fried, and Tina Juillerat, "Work Matters: Job Design in Classic and Contemporary Perspectives," in Sheldon Zedeck, (Ed.), *Handbook of Industrial and Organizational Psychology* (American Psychological Association: Washington, D.C., 2010).

[20] Stephanie Armour, "Working 9-to-5 No Longer," *USA Today*, December 6, 2004, 1B, 2B.

[21] http://www.bls.gov/news.release/archives/atus_06222011.pdf

[22] Crowley, Mark C. "Not A Happy Accident: How Google Deliberately Designs Workplace Satisfaction | Fast Company | Business Innovation." *Fast Company*. March 23, 2013, at http://www.fastcompany.com/3007268/where-are-they-now/not-happy-accident-how-google-deliberately-designs-workplace-satisfaction, accessed on June 18, 2013.

[23] "How We Hire—Google Jobs." How We Hire—Google Jobs, at http://www.google.com/about/jobs/lifeatgoogle/hiringprocess/, accessed on June 18, 2013.

[24] "Benefits—Google Jobs." Benefits—Google Jobs, at http://www.google.com/about/jobs/lifeatgoogle/benefits/, accessed on June 18, 2013.

chapter 9

Leadership and Decision Making

© Rade Lukovic/Fotolia

The secret to success is management AND organization.

By combining these two forces,

companies can

plan change while staying on task.

AFTER READING THIS CHAPTER, YOU SHOULD BE ABLE TO:

OBJECTIVE 1   **Define** *leadership* and distinguish it from management.

OBJECTIVE 2   **Summarize** early approaches to the study of leadership.

OBJECTIVE 3   **Discuss** the concept of situational approaches to leadership.

OBJECTIVE 4   **Describe** transformational and charismatic perspectives on leadership.

OBJECTIVE 5   **Identify** and discuss leadership substitutes and neutralizers.

OBJECTIVE 6   **Discuss** leaders as coaches and examine gender and cross-cultural issues in leadership.

OBJECTIVE 7   **Describe** strategic leadership, ethical leadership, and virtual leadership.

OBJECTIVE 8   **Relate** leadership to decision making and discuss both rational and behavioral perspectives on decision making.

MyBizLab®

⭐ Improve Your Grade!

Visit **pearsonglobaleditions.com/mybizlab** for simulations, tutorials, and end-of-chapter problems.

simulations

videos

assisted-graded writing

Over 10 million students improved their results using the Pearson MyLabs.

Middle Eastern
Business
Leadership

Nasser Al-Jaidah is the Director of Oil and Gas Ventures for Qatar Petroleum. He is a strong believer in the notion that a great leader is measured by the ability to communicate, motivate, and listen. In 2009, in the role

of CEO of Qatar Petroleum International, Al-Jaidah announced the company's plans to build two petrochemical plants in Asia with a combined budget of $9.8 billion. The project was due for completion by 2015. Qatar Petroleum International is a unit of the emirate's state-run oil company and would partner Cnooc Ltd. and a Chinese partner to build a $5.8 billion plant in Hainan Province. At the same time, the second project, based in Vietnam, would cost a further $4 billion. Both of the plants would handle Qatar's liquefied petroleum gas to make chemicals.

Typically, Al-Jaidah had a straightforward approach when he announced the projects in Tokyo stating that they served a dual purpose. In other words, Qatar would have direct access to both of these important and growing markets while at the same time ensuring a market for Qatar's liquefied petroleum gas. This announcement was just part of Qatar's mission to find new markets for their liquefied petroleum gas, which was due to double in terms of production to 12 million metric tons by 2010.

Al-Jaidah has committed Qatar to some huge projects including a $25 billion metro and train project, a $4 billion bridge to link Qatar to Bahrain, an airport in Doha ($10 billion), and another $7 billion project on a new deepwater port. This was in addition to some $20 billion already committed to improving the road networks. For the 2022 World Cup alone, Qatar pledged $4 billion on building and renovating 12 stadia.

In detailing these new projects, Al-Jaidah indicated the kind of leadership skills and requirements that would be needed to manage all of these challenges. Logistics, administrative efficiency, planning and coordination, and financial awareness were all key elements. He was also conscious of potential debt and of the importance of budget.

The work of Saddi, Sabbugh, and Shediac suggests that three leadership qualities will be needed in the upcoming generations.

1. To retain a farsighted vision that recognizes the need to build sustainable enterprises.
2. To be pragmatic and adapt ideas from abroad
3. To have the ability to work to ensure that the region establishes itself as a global force.

Research suggests that Al-Jaidah, and more broadly Qatar, have already embraced these leadership needs.

what's in it for me?

Is your boss a manager? A leader? What does she or he do to inspire you to work harder? Do you aspire to be a manager or a leader? When you have a leadership position, what will you do to inspire your employees to work harder? Do you think management and leadership are the same thing? These are some of the issues we'll explore in this chapter. In Chapter 8 we described the primary determinants of employee behavior and noted that managers can influence the behavior and enhance the motivation of employees. Now it's time to examine in detail how leaders actually go about influencing employee behavior and motivating employee performance. We will place these strategies and tactics in the context of various approaches to leadership through the years, including the situational perspective accepted today. Understanding these concepts will help you function more effectively as a leader and

chunumunu/fotolia

give you more insight into how your manager or boss strives to motivate you through his or her own leadership.

We start this chapter by taking a look at the nature of leadership. We then describe early approaches to leadership, as well as the situational perspective accepted today. Next, we examine leadership through the eyes of followers as well as alternatives to leadership. The changing nature of leadership and emerging issues in leadership are discussed next. Finally, we describe the important related concept of decision making.

Farsighted vision is seen as the way in which the Middle East region can fulfill its destiny. While economic growth is important, infrastructure and institutions are being embedded in order to ensure that future generations can benefit.

Being pragmatic means looking for the very best business and management ideas and processes and applying them in a meaningful way in the Middle East. This means carefully restructuring and modifying the ideas. In fact, as far as Middle Eastern leadership is concerned, the modification of ideas is as important a skill as having identified them as being valuable in the first place.

Countries like Qatar, and through leaders such as Al-Jaidah, recognize that sweeping change is important, while ensuring that the culture of the country is not undermined. This goes back to what Al-Jaidah stated as the three qualities of great leaders: communication, motivation, and listening. It is about building trust and being persistent, and recognizing that different groups within society have varying outlooks on the outcome of projects and ideas. This means looking at everything very carefully and never seeking to make a unilateral or quick decision. It is imperative that, as Al-Jaidah states, all stakeholders have an opportunity to contribute and are included at every stage.[1]

OBJECTIVE 1
Define
leadership and distinguish it from management.

Leadership *the processes and behaviors used by someone, such as a manager, to motivate, inspire, and influence the behaviors of others*

The Nature of Leadership

Because *leadership* is a term that is often used in everyday conversation, you might assume that it has a common and accepted meaning. It is also, however, a word that is often misused. We define **leadership** as the processes and behaviors used by someone, such as a manager, to motivate, inspire, and influence the behaviors of others.

Leadership and Management

One of the biggest errors people make is assuming that leadership and management mean the same thing when they are really different concepts. A person can be a manager, a leader, both, or neither.[2] Some of the basic distinctions between the two are summarized in Figure 9.1. As illustrated in the circle on the left, management focuses primarily on the activities of planning, organizing, leading, and controlling. Leadership, in contrast, is much more closely related to activities such as agenda setting, aligning, inspiring, and monitoring. As also illustrated in the figure, management and leadership may occasionally overlap but each is also a discrete and separate set of activities. Hence, a person may be a manager (but not a leader), a leader (but not a manager), or both a manager and a leader.

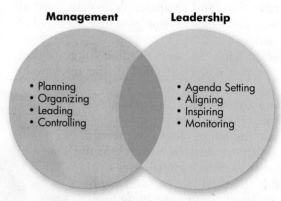

FIGURE 9.1 Distinctions between Management and Leadership

Consider the various roles of managers and leaders in a hospital setting. The chief of staff (chief physician) of a large hospital, though clearly a manager by virtue of his position, may not be respected or trusted by others and may have to rely solely on the authority vested in the position to get people to do things. On the other hand, a nurse in the emergency department with no formal authority may be quite effective at taking charge of a chaotic situation and directing others in dealing with specific patient problems. The chief of staff is a manager but not really a leader, whereas the nurse is a leader but not really a manager.

Finally, the head of pediatrics, supervising a staff of 20 other doctors, nurses, and attendants, may also enjoy the staff's complete respect, confidence, and trust. They readily take her advice and follow directives without question, and often go far beyond what is necessary to help carry out the unit's mission. Thus, the head of pediatrics is both a manager (by virtue of the position she occupies) and a leader (by virtue of the respect she commands from others and their willingness to follow her direction).

Organizations need both management and leadership if they are to be effective. Management in conjunction with leadership can help achieve planned orderly change, and leadership in conjunction with management can keep the organization properly aligned with its environment.

Leadership and Power

To fully understand leadership, it is also necessary to understand *power*. **Power** is the ability to affect the behavior of others. Of course, one can have power without actually using it. For example, a football coach has the power to bench a player who is not performing up to par. The coach seldom has to use this power because players recognize that the power exists and work hard to keep their starting positions. In organizational settings, there are usually five kinds of power: legitimate, reward, coercive, referent, and expert power.[3]

Power *the ability to affect the behavior of others*

Legitimate power is power granted through the organizational hierarchy; it is the power defined by the organization to be accorded to people occupying a particular position. A manager can assign tasks to a subordinate, and a subordinate who refuses to do them can be reprimanded or even fired. Such outcomes stem from the manager's legitimate power as defined and vested in her or him by the organization. Legitimate power, then, is authority. All managers have legitimate power over their subordinates. The mere possession of legitimate power, however, does not by itself make someone a leader. Some subordinates follow only orders that are strictly within the letter of organizational rules and policies. If asked to do something not in their job descriptions, they refuse or do a poor job. The manager of such employees is exercising authority but not leadership.

Legitimate Power *power granted through the organizational hierarchy*

Reward power is the power to give or withhold rewards. Rewards that a manager may control include salary increases, bonuses, promotion recommendations, praise, recognition, and interesting job assignments. In general, the greater the number of rewards a manager controls and the more important the rewards are to subordinates, the greater is the manager's reward power. If the subordinate values only the formal organizational rewards provided by the manager, then the manager is not a leader. If the subordinate also wants and appreciates the manager's informal rewards, such as praise, gratitude, and recognition, however, then the manager is also exercising leadership.

Reward Power *the power to give or withhold rewards*

Coercive power is the power to force compliance by means of psychological, emotional, or physical threat. In the past, physical coercion in organizations was relatively common. In most organizations today, however, coercion is limited to verbal reprimands, written reprimands, disciplinary layoffs, fines, demotion, and termination. Some managers occasionally go so far as to use verbal abuse, humiliation, and psychological coercion in an attempt to manipulate subordinates. (Of course, most people would agree that these are not appropriate managerial behaviors.) James Dutt, a "legendary" former CEO of a major company, once told a subordinate that if his wife and family got in the way of his working a 24-hour

Coercive Power *the power to force compliance by means of psychological, emotional, or physical threat*

day seven days a week, he should get rid of them.[4] More recently, Charlie Ergen, founder and CEO of Dish Network, has a reputation for yelling at employees, belittling managers in front of their peers, and imposing harsh penalties on those who disagree with him.[5] The more punitive the elements under a manager's control and the more important they are to subordinates, the more coercive power the manager possesses. On the other hand, the more a manager uses coercive power, the more likely he is to provoke resentment and hostility and the less likely he is to be seen as a leader.[6]

Referent Power *power based on identification, imitation, loyalty, or charisma*

Compared with legitimate, reward, and coercive power, which are relatively concrete and grounded in objective facets of organizational life, **referent power** is abstract. It is based on identification, imitation, loyalty, or charisma. Followers may react favorably because they identify in some way with a leader, who may be like them in personality, background, or attitudes. In other situations, followers might choose to imitate a leader with referent power by wearing the same kind of clothes, working the same hours, or espousing the same management philosophy. Referent power may also take the form of charisma, an intangible attribute of the leader that inspires loyalty and enthusiasm. Thus, a manager might have referent power, but it is more likely to be associated with leadership.

Expert Power *power derived from information or expertise*

Expert power is derived from information or expertise. A manager who knows how to interact with an eccentric but important customer, a scientist who is capable of achieving an important technical breakthrough that no other company has dreamed of, and an administrative assistant who knows how to unravel bureaucratic red tape all have expert power over anyone who needs that information. The more important the information and the fewer the people who have access to it, the greater is the degree of expert power possessed by any one individual. In general, people who are both leaders and managers tend to have a lot of expert power.

OBJECTIVE 2
Summarize

early approaches to the study of leadership.

Early Approaches to Leadership

Although leaders and leadership have profoundly influenced history, careful scientific study of them began only about a century ago. Early studies focused on the *traits*, or personal characteristics, of leaders. Later research shifted to examine actual leader *behaviors*.

Trait Approaches to Leadership

Trait Approach to Leadership *focused on identifying the essential traits that distinguished leaders*

Early researchers believed that notable leaders had some unique set of qualities or traits that distinguished them from their peers and endured throughout history. This **trait approach to leadership** led researchers to focus on identifying the essential leadership traits, including intelligence, dominance, self-confidence, energy, activity (versus passivity), and knowledge about the job. Unfortunately, the list of potential leadership traits quickly became so long that it lost any practical value. In addition, the results of many studies were inconsistent. For example, one argument stated that the most effective leaders were tall, like Abraham Lincoln. But critics were quick to point out that neither Napoleon Bonaparte nor Adolf Hitler was tall, but both were effective leaders in their own way.

Although the trait approach was all but abandoned several decades ago, in recent years, it has resurfaced. For example, some researchers have again started to focus on a limited set of traits. These traits include emotional intelligence, mental intelligence, drive, motivation, honesty and integrity, self-confidence, knowledge of the business, and charisma. Some people even believe that biological factors, such as appearance or height, may play a role in leadership. However, it is too early to know whether these traits really do relate to leadership.

Bettmann/CORBIS

MPVHistory/Alamy

GL Archive/Alamy

Dinodia Photo/AGE Fotostock

When asked to identify important leaders, people often mention influential historical figures such as Winston Churchill, Abraham Lincoln, Martin Luther King, Jr., and Mother Teresa.

Behavioral Approaches to Leadership

In the late 1940s, most researchers began to shift away from the trait approach and to look at leadership as a set of actual behaviors. The goal of the **behavioral approach to leadership** was to determine what *behaviors* were employed by effective leaders. These researchers assumed that the behaviors of effective leaders differed somehow from the behaviors of less effective leaders, and that the behaviors of effective leaders would be the same across all situations.

This research led to the identification of two basic forms of leader behavior. Although different researchers applied different names, the basic leader behaviors identified during this period were

- **Task-focused leader behavior:** Task-focused leader behavior occurs when a leader focuses on how tasks should be performed to meet certain goals and to achieve certain performance standards.

- **Employee-focused leader behavior:** Employee-focused leader behavior occurs when a leader focuses on the satisfaction, motivation, and well-being of his or her employees.

During this period, people believed that leaders should always try to engage in a healthy dose of both behaviors, one to increase performance and the other to increase job satisfaction and motivation. Experts also began to realize that they could train managers to engage in these behaviors in a systematic manner. But they also discovered that there were other leader behaviors that needed to be considered, and that there were circumstances in which different combinations of leader behavior might be more effective than other combinations.

For instance, suppose a new manager takes over a work site that is plagued by low productivity and whose workers, although perhaps satisfied, are not motivated to work hard. The leader should most likely focus on task-focused behaviors to improve lagging productivity. But now suppose the situation is different—productivity is high, but workers are stressed out about their jobs and have low levels of job satisfaction. In this instance, the manager should most likely concentrate on employee-focused behaviors to help improve job satisfaction. This line of thinking led to the creation of *situational theories.*

Behavioral Approach to Leadership *focused on determining what behaviors are employed by leaders*

Task-Focused Leader Behavior *leader behavior focusing on how tasks should be performed to meet certain goals and to achieve certain performance standards*

Employee-Focused Leader Behavior *leader behavior focusing on satisfaction, motivation, and well-being of employees*

The Situational Approach to Leadership

OBJECTIVE 3
Discuss
the concept of situational
approaches to leadership.

Situational Approach to Leadership
*assumes that appropriate leader behav-
ior varies from one situation to another*

The **situational approach to leadership** assumes that appropriate leader behavior varies from one situation to another, as shown in Figure 9.2. The trait and behavioral approaches to leadership were both universal in nature; they attempted to prescribe leader behaviors that would lead to a set of universal set of outcomes and consequences. For instance, proponents of these universal perspectives might argue that tall and intelligent people or people who are always employee-focused will always be good leaders. In reality, though, research has found this to simply be untrue. So, the situational approach to leadership attempts to identify various forms of leader behavior that result in contingent outcomes and consequences. By contingent, we mean that they depend on elements of the situation and characteristics of both the leader and followers.

Consider, for example, how Jeff Smisek, CEO of United Airlines, has to vary his leadership style when he is interacting with different kinds of people. When he is dealing with investors he has to convey an impression of confidence about the company's financial picture. When he interacts with union officials he needs to take a firm stand on cost control combined with collaboration. Smisek often speaks to leaders at other airlines and has to balance their mutual interests against United's own competitive situation. And when dealing with customers he has to be charming and respectful.

Leadership characteristics include the manager's value system, confidence in subordinates, personal inclinations, feelings of security, and actual behaviors. Subordinate characteristics include the subordinates' need for independence, readiness to assume responsibility, tolerance for ambiguity, interest in the problem, understanding of goals, knowledge, experience, and expectations. Situational characteristics that affect decision making include the type of organization, group effectiveness, the problem itself, and time pressures. Three important situational approaches to leadership are (1) the *path-goal theory*, (2) the *decision tree approach*, and (3) the *leader-member exchange model*.

Path–Goal Theory *theory of leadership that is a direct extension of the
expectancy theory of motivation*

The **path–goal theory** of leadership is a direct extension of the expectancy theory of motivation discussed in Chapter 8.[7] Recall that the primary components of expectancy theory include the likelihood of attaining various outcomes and the value associated with those outcomes. The path–goal theory of leadership suggests that the primary

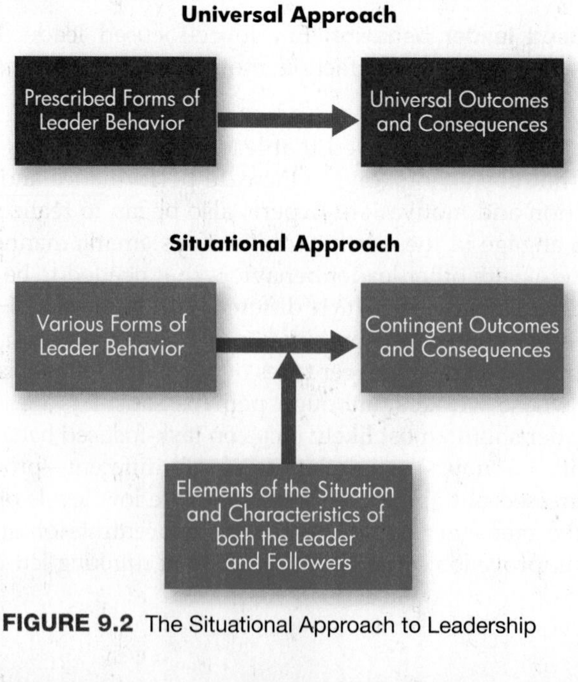

FIGURE 9.2 The Situational Approach to Leadership

functions of a leader are to make valued or desired rewards available in the workplace and to clarify for the subordinate the kinds of behavior that will lead to goal accomplishment and valued rewards. The leader should clarify the paths to goal attainment.

Path–goal theory identifies four kinds of behaviors that leaders can use, depending on the situation. *Directive leader behavior* lets subordinates know what is expected of them, gives guidance and direction, and schedules work. *Supportive leader behavior* is being friendly and approachable, showing concern for subordinates' welfare, and treating members as equals. *Participative leader behavior* includes consulting with subordinates, soliciting suggestions, and allowing participation in decision making. *Achievement-oriented leader behavior* sets challenging goals, expects subordinates to perform at high levels, encourages subordinates, and shows confidence in subordinates' abilities.

Another major contemporary approach to leadership is the **decision tree approach.** Like the path–goal theory, this approach attempts to prescribe a leadership style appropriate to a given situation. It also assumes that the same leader may display different leadership styles. But the decision tree approach concerns itself with only a single aspect of leader behavior: subordinate participation in decision making. The decision tree approach assumes that the degree to which subordinates should be encouraged to participate in decision making depends on the characteristics of the situation. In other words, no one decision-making process is best for all situations. After evaluating a variety of problem attributes (characteristics of the problem or decision), the leader determines an appropriate decision style that specifies the amount of subordinate participation.

Decision Tree Approach *approach to leadership that provides decision rules for deciding how much participation to allow*

The **leader–member exchange (LMX) model** stresses the importance of variable relationships between supervisors and each of their subordinates.[8] Each superior–subordinate pair represents a "vertical dyad." The model differs from previous approaches in that it focuses on the differential relationship leaders often establish with different subordinates. This model suggests that supervisors establish a special relationship with a small number of trusted subordinates, referred to as "the in-group." The in-group usually receives special duties requiring responsibility and autonomy; they may also receive special privileges. Subordinates who are not a part of this group are called "the out-group," and they receive less of the supervisor's time and attention. However, the key element of this theory is the concept of individual vertical dyads and how leaders have different relationships with each of their subordinates.

Leader–Member Exchange (LMX) Model *approach to leadership that stresses the importance of variable relationships between supervisors and each of their subordinates*

Leadership through the Eyes of Followers

OBJECTIVE 4
Describe
transformational and charismatic perspectives on leadership.

Another recent perspective that has been adopted by some leadership experts focuses on how leaders are seen through the eyes of their followers. The two primary approaches to leadership through the eyes of followers are *transformational leadership* and *charismatic leadership*. Barrack Obama's successful bid for the U.S. presidency was fueled in part by many people's perceptions that he was both a transformational and charismatic leader. Indeed, during both of his campaigns, he frequently talked about the need to transform the way the United States addressed issues such as health care, education, and foreign policy. And his personal charisma undoubtedly attracted support from many people as well.

Transformational Leadership

Transformational leadership focuses on the importance of leading for change (as opposed to leading during a period of stability). According to this view, much of what a leader does involves carrying out what might be thought of as basic management "transactions," such as assigning work, evaluating performance, and making decisions. Occasionally, however, the leader has to engage in transformational leadership to initiate and manage major change, such as managing a merger, creating a new work team, or redefining the organization's culture.

Transformational Leadership *the set of abilities that allows a leader to recognize the need for change, to create a vision to guide that change, and to execute the change effectively*

Transactional Leadership *comparable to management, it involves routine, regimented activities*

Thus, **transformational leadership** is the set of abilities that allows a leader to recognize the need for change, to create a vision to guide that change, and to execute the change effectively. Some experts believe that change is such a vital organizational function that even successful firms need to change regularly to avoid becoming complacent and stagnant. In contrast, **transactional leadership** is essentially the same as management in that it involves routine, regimented activities. Only a leader with tremendous influence can hope to perform both functions successfully. Some experts believe that change is such a vital organizational function that even successful firms need to change regularly to avoid becoming complacent and stagnant; accordingly, leadership for change is extremely important.

Some leaders are able to adopt either transformational or transactional perspectives, depending on their circumstances. For instance, Rupert Murdoch, CEO of News Corp., has a long history of transforming the media properties he acquires to expand their reach and turn a profit. Early in his career Murdoch relaunched *The Sun*, a British daily newspaper, as a tabloid notorious for its sensationalistic focus on sex. On the other hand, he has generally avoided retooling another of his British acquisitions, the well-regarded *Times*. When he purchased the struggling *Wall Street Journal* in 2007, he pledged to remain a hands-off manager. But in the following months the paper's signature coverage of U.S. business news decreased to make room for increased coverage of politics and foreign events, and it remains to be seen how Murdoch will balance transformational and transactional leadership at the *Journal*.[9]

Charismatic Leadership

Charismatic Leadership *type of influence based on the leader's personal charisma*

Charismatic leadership is a type of influence based on the leader's charisma, a form of interpersonal attraction that inspires support and acceptance. Charismatic leaders are likely to have a lot of confidence in their beliefs and ideals and a strong need to influence people. They also tend to communicate high expectations about follower performance and to express confidence in their followers. Many of the most influential leaders in history have been extremely charismatic, including entrepreneurs Mary Kay Ash, Steve Jobs, and Ted Turner; civil rights leader Martin Luther King, Jr.; and Pope John Paul II. Unfortunately, charisma can also empower leaders in other directions. Adolf Hitler, for instance, had strong charismatic qualities.

Most experts today acknowledge three crucial elements of charismatic leadership:[10]

1 Charismatic leaders envision likely future trends and patterns, set high expectations for themselves and for others, and behave in ways that meet or exceed those expectations.

2 Charismatic leaders energize others by demonstrating personal excitement, personal confidence, and consistent patterns of success.

3 Charismatic leaders enable others by supporting them, empathizing with them, and expressing confidence in them.

Charismatic leadership ideas are quite popular among managers today and are the subject of numerous books and articles.[11] Unfortunately, few studies have specifically attempted to test the meaning and impact of charismatic leadership. Lingering ethical concerns about charismatic leadership also trouble some people. They stem from the fact that some charismatic leaders inspire such blind faith in their followers that they may engage in inappropriate, unethical, or even illegal behaviors just because the leader instructed them to do so. This tendency likely played a role in the unwinding of both Enron and Arthur Andersen because people followed orders from their charismatic bosses to hide information, shred documents, and mislead investigators.

Taking over a leadership role from someone with substantial personal charisma is also a challenge. For instance, the immediate successors to successful and charismatic athletic coaches such as Vince Lombardi (Green Bay Packers) and Phil Jackson (Chicago Bulls) each failed to measure up to their predecessors' legacies and were subsequently fired.

managing in turbulent times

Leading during Tough Times

How does one go about leading in a recession? What adjustments do you have to make when money is scarce, markets are volatile, and morale needs boosting? Dennis Carey, vice chairman of Korn Ferry International, an executive-search firm, suggests that top managers should start by acknowledging that leading in extreme circumstances means calling into question everything they do under normal circumstances. "You can't rely on a peacetime general to fight a war," he reminds fellow executives. "The wartime CEO prepares for the worst so that his or her company can take market share away from players who haven't." Hire away your competitors' best people, advises Carey, and keep *them* from grabbing *yours*. Or buy up their assets while they can be had at bargain prices.

Jack Hayhow, consultant and founder of Opus Training and ReallyEasyHR, adds that leaders need to make sure that their employees know why they're making changes during hard times. State the facts: there is a recession going on. Stop obsessing about the things you can't control and concentrate on what you have control over.

Motivating your staff is another critical component when managing people during any challenging time. Although challenging, this is not impossible. Tap into everyone's strengths and then begin to pair that with tasks. With this, you maximize the employee's talent. Also vital is never underestimating the power of choice. When your employees have choices, even small ones, this leads to empowerment and joy in the task.

Ex-Starbucks CEO Jim Donald, who's now CEO of Extended Stay Hotels, advises that communication is the key during any crisis. It is imperative that you communicate with everyone from the entry-level recently hired all the way up to the top executives. Your message must reach all your employees. Kip Tindell, who's been CEO of the Container Store since its founding in 1978, agrees. That's why his managers "run around like chickens relentlessly trying to communicate everything to every single employee at all times." He admits that, practically speaking, it's an impossible task, but he's also convinced that the effort is

Jeff Greenberg "0 people images"/Alamy

more important than ever in times of crisis. He also contends that his company is in a better position to ride out the economic storm "because we're so dedicated to the notion that communication and leadership are the same thing." At the very least, he says, "we're fortunate to be minus the paranoia that goes with employees who feel they don't know what's going on."[12]

Special Issues in Leadership

OBJECTIVE 5
Identify
and discuss leadership substitutes and neutralizers.

Another interesting perspective on leadership focuses on *alternatives* to leadership. In some cases, certain factors may actually *substitute* for leadership, making actual leadership unnecessary or irrelevant. In other cases, factors may exist that *neutralize* or negate the influence of a leader even when that individual is attempting to exercise leadership.

Leadership Substitutes

Leadership substitutes are individual, task, and organizational characteristics that tend to outweigh the need for a leader to initiate or direct employee performance. In other words, if certain factors are present, the employee will perform his or her job capably, without the direction of a leader. Table 9.1 identifies several basic leadership substitutes.

Leadership Substitutes *individual, task, and organizational characteristics that tend to outweigh the need for a leader to initiate or direct employee performance*

table 9.1 Leadership Substitutes and Neutralizers

Individual factors	• Individual professionalism • Individual ability, knowledge, and motivation • Individual experience and training • Indifference to rewards
Job factors	• Structured/automated • Highly controlled • Intrinsically satisfying • Embedded feedback
Organization factors	• Explicit plans and goals • Rigid rules and procedures • Rigid reward system not tied to performance • Physical distance between supervisor and subordinate
Group factors	• Group performance norms • High level of group cohesiveness • Group interdependence

Consider, for example, what happens when an ambulance with a critically injured victim screeches to the door of a hospital emergency department. Do the emergency department employees stand around waiting for someone to take control and instruct them on what to do? The answer is no; they are highly trained and well-prepared professionals who know how to respond and work together as a team without someone playing the role of leader. When a U.S. Airways flight crashed into the Hudson River in 2009, all members of the flight crew knew exactly what to do, without waiting for orders. As a result of their effective and prompt actions, a disaster was averted, and all passengers on the plane were quickly rescued.

Leadership Neutralizers

In other situations, even if a leader is present and attempts to engage in various leadership behaviors, those behaviors may be rendered ineffective—or neutralized—by various factors that can be called **leadership neutralizers.** Suppose, for example, that a relatively new and inexperienced leader is assigned to a work group composed of experienced employees with long-standing performance norms and a high level of group cohesiveness. The norms and cohesiveness of the group may be so strong that there is nothing the new leader can do to change things.

In addition to group factors, elements of the job itself may also limit a leader's ability to "make a difference." Consider, for example, employees working on a moving assembly line. Employees may only be able to work at the pace of the moving line, so performance quantity and quality are constrained by the speed of the line and simplicity of each individual task.

Finally, organizational factors can also neutralize at least some forms of leader behavior. Suppose a new leader is accustomed to using merit pay increases as a way to motivate people. But in his or her new job, pay increases are dictated by union contracts and are based primarily on employee seniority and cost of living. The leader's previous approach to motivating people would be neutralized, and new approaches would have to be identified.

Leadership Neutralizers *factors that may render leader behaviors ineffective*

OBJECTIVE 6
Discuss
leaders as coaches and examine gender and cross-cultural issues in leadership.

The Changing Nature of Leadership

Various alternatives to leadership aside, many settings still call for at least some degree of leadership, although the nature of that leadership continues to evolve. Among the recent changes in leadership that managers should recognize are the increasing role of *leaders as coaches* as well as *gender and cross-cultural patterns* of leader behavior.

Leaders as Coaches

We noted in Chapter 6 that many organizations today are using teams. Many other organizations are attempting to become less hierarchical by eliminating the old-fashioned command-and-control mentality often inherent in bureaucratic organizations and motivating and empowering individuals to work independently. In each case, the role of leaders is also changing. Whereas leaders were once expected to control situations, direct work, supervise people, closely monitor performance, make decisions, and structure activities, many leaders today are being asked to change how they manage people. Perhaps the best description of this new role is for the leader to become a *coach* instead of an *overseer*.[13]

From the standpoint of a business leader, a coaching perspective would call for the leader to help select and train team members and other new employees, to provide some general direction, and to help the team get the information and other resources it needs. Coaches from different teams may play important roles in linking the activities and functions of their respective teams. Some leaders may function as *mentors*, helping less experienced employees learn the ropes and better preparing them to advance within the organization; they may also help resolve conflicts among team members and mediate other disputes that arise. But beyond these activities, the leader keeps a low profile and lets the group get its work done with little or no direct oversight, just as during a game an athletic coach trusts his or her players to execute the plays successfully.

Jeff Bezos, founder and CEO of Amazon.com often plays the role of coach. He likes to focus on long-term, strategic issues and leave the daily management of Amazon.com to senior managers. But their decisions must also be consistent with his vision for the firm. As a result, he works with them on a regular basis to help them develop their decision-making skills and to equip them with the information they need to help lead the firm in the directions he has set.

Gender and Leadership

Another factor that is clearly altering the face of leadership is the growing number of women advancing to higher levels in organizations. Given that most leadership theories and research studies have focused on male leaders, developing a better understanding of how women lead is clearly an important next step. Some early observers, for instance, predicted that (consistent with prevailing stereotypes) female leaders would be relatively warm, supportive, and nurturing as compared to their male counterparts. But research suggests that female leaders are not necessarily more nurturing or supportive than male leaders. Likewise, male leaders are not systematically harsher, more controlling, or more task focused than female leaders.

The one difference that has arisen in some cases is that women may be slightly more democratic in making decisions, whereas men have a tendency to be more autocratic.[14] However, much more work needs to be done to better understand the dynamics of gender and leadership. In the meantime, high-profile and successful female leaders, such as Indra Nooyi (CEO of PepsiCo), Andrea Jung (CEO of Avon Products) and Angela Merkel (chancellor of Germany), continue to demonstrate the effectiveness with which women can be exceptional leaders.

Cross-Cultural Leadership

Another changing perspective on leadership relates to cross-cultural issues. In this context, *culture* is used as a broad concept to encompass both international differences and diversity-based differences within one culture. For instance, Japan is generally characterized by *collectivism* (group before individual), whereas the United States is based more on *individualism* (individual before group). So when a Japanese firm sends an executive to head up the firm's operation in the United States, that person will likely find it necessary to recognize the importance of individual contributions and rewards and the differences in individual and group roles that exist in Japanese and U.S. businesses.

For instance, Ghosn knows that cultural differences cause his European managers to expect him to lead in certain ways, whereas his Japanese managers expect him to lead in slightly different ways. More specifically, in Europe, leaders must often be aggressive, and meetings are often characterized by loud verbal exchanges and arguments. In Japan, though, more emphasis is put on consensus building and polite exchanges of dialogue.

Similarly, cross-cultural factors also play a growing role in organizations as their workforces become more diverse. As African Americans, Asian Americans, Hispanics, and members of other ethnic groups achieve leadership positions, it may be necessary to reassess how applicable current theories and models of leadership are when applied to an increasingly diverse pool of leaders.

finding a better way

Creating Board Diversity

"It's been proven again and again," says Carl Brooks, CEO of the Executive Leadership Council, a network of senior African American executives, "that companies with board members who reflect gender and ethnic diversity also tend to have better returns on equity and sales." According to Marc H. Morial, CEO of the National Urban League, which promotes economic empowerment for African Americans, a minority presence on corporate boards is also necessary to protect the interests of minority consumers and other stakeholders. Specifically, Morial argues that African Americans need more representation on corporate boards so that business decisions are made affecting African American communities can be made in a more informed manner.

Kablonk!/Golden Pixels LLC/Alamy

Unfortunately, Morial goes on to point out that African Americans still represent only a small percentage of board-level corporate leadership in the United States. Citing a recent study by the Executive Leadership Council, Morial points out that the number of African Americans on *Fortune 500* boards has actually *declined* in recent years. Even though African Americans comprise 13 percent of the U.S. population, representation on corporate boards stands at "a meager 7 percent."

The same trend was confirmed with the release of the U.S. Senate Democratic Hispanic Task Force report on minority and women representation on *Fortune 500* boards and executive teams (CEOs plus their direct reports). Here are some of the survey's findings:

- Women comprise 18 percent of all board members and just under 20 percent of executive team members (roughly 1 in 5). Those figures, of course, are far below the 50-percent proportion of women in the population.

- Minorities comprise 14.5 percent of all directors— about 1 out of every 7—and an even smaller percentage of executive-team members. That's less than half of their 35-percent proportion of the population.

- Although African Americans boast the highest minority representation on boards—8.8 percent—that's equivalent to only 69 percent of their total proportion of the population. Representation on executive teams is only 4.2 percent.

- Hispanics fared worse than any other minority. Although they represent 15 percent of the U.S. population, they comprise only 3.3 percent of board members and 3 percent of executive-team members.

The report, says task force chair Robert Menendez (the lone Hispanic member of the U.S. Senate),

clearly confirms what we had suspected all along—that American corporations need to do better when it comes to having the board rooms on Wall Street reflect the reality on Main Street. We need to change the dynamic and make it commonplace for minorities to be part of the American corporate structure. It is not just about doing what's right, but it's a good business decision that will benefit both corporations and the communities they're tapping into and making investments in.[15]

Emerging Issues in Leadership

Finally, there are also three emerging issues in leadership that warrant discussion. These issues are *strategic leadership, ethical leadership*, and *virtual leadership*.

Strategic Leadership

Strategic leadership is a new concept that explicitly relates leadership to the role of top management. **Strategic leadership** is a leader's ability to understand the complexities of both the organization and its environment and to lead change in the organization so as to enhance its competitiveness. Howard Schutz, CEO of Starbucks, is recognized as a strong strategic leader. Not content to continue functioning as "simply" a coffee retailer, Schutz is always on the lookout for new opportunities and how Starbucks can effectively exploit those opportunities.

To be effective as a strategic leader, a manager needs to have a thorough and complete understanding of the organization—its history, its culture, its strengths, and its weaknesses. In addition, the leader needs a firm grasp of the organization's external environment. This understanding needs to include current business and economic conditions and circumstances as well as significant trends and issues on the horizon. The strategic leader also needs to recognize the firm's current strategic advantages and shortcomings.

Strategic Leadership *leader's ability to understand the complexities of both the organization and its environment and to lead change in the organization so as to enhance its competitiveness*

Ethical Leadership

Most people have long assumed that business leaders are ethical people. But in the wake of corporate scandals at firms such as Enron, Boeing, and AIG, faith in business leaders has been shaken. Perhaps now more than ever, high standards of ethical conduct are being held up as a prerequisite for effective leadership. More specifically, business leaders are being called on to maintain high ethical standards for their own conduct, to unfailingly exhibit ethical behavior, and to hold others in their organizations to the same standards—in short, to practice **ethical leadership.**

The behaviors of top leaders are being scrutinized more than ever, and those responsible for hiring new leaders for a business are looking more closely at the backgrounds of those being considered. And the emerging pressures for stronger corporate governance models are likely to further increase the commitment to select only those individuals with high ethical standards for leadership positions in business and to hold them more accountable than in the past for both their actions and the consequences of those actions.

Ethical Leadership *leader behaviors that reflect high ethical standards*

Virtual Leadership

Finally, **virtual leadership** is also emerging as an important issue for organizations. In previous times, leaders and their employees worked together in the same physical location and engaged in face-to-face interactions on a regular basis. But in today's world, both leaders and their employees may work in locations that are far from one another. Such arrangements might include people telecommuting from a home office one or two days a week to people actually living and working far from company headquarters.

Increasingly, then, communication between leaders and their subordinates happens largely by telephone and e-mail. One implication may be that leaders in these situations must work harder at creating and maintaining relationships with their employees that go beyond words on a computer screen. Although nonverbal communication, such as smiles and handshakes, may not be possible online, managers can instead make a point of adding a few personal words in an e-mail (whenever appropriate) to convey appreciation, reinforcement, or constructive feedback.

Virtual Leadership *leadership in settings where leaders and followers interact electronically rather than in face-to-face settings*

Leadership, Management, and Decision Making

OBJECTIVE 8
Relate
leadership to decision making
and discuss both rational and
behavioral perspectives on
decision making.

We noted previously the differences and similarities between managing and leading. *Decision making* is another important related concept. Indeed, decision making is a fundamental component of both leadership and management—managers and leaders must frequently make decisions.

The Nature of Decision Making

Decision Making *choosing one alternative from among several options*

Decision making can refer to either a specific act or a general process. **Decision making** is the act of choosing one alternative from among a set of alternatives. The decision-making process, however, is much more than this. One step of the process, for example, is that the person making the decision must both recognize that a decision is necessary and identify the set of feasible alternatives before selecting one. Hence, the **decision-making process** includes recognizing and defining the nature of a decision situation, identifying alternatives, choosing the "best" alternative, and putting it into practice.[16]

Decision-Making Process *recognizing and defining the nature of a decision situation, identifying alternatives, choosing the "best" alternative, and putting it into practice*

The word *best* implies effectiveness. Effective decision making requires that the decision maker understand the situation driving the decision. Most people would consider an effective decision to be one that optimizes some set of factors, such as profits, sales, employee welfare, and market share. In some situations, though, an effective decision may be one that minimizes losses, expenses, or employee turnover. It may even mean selecting the best method for going out of business, laying off employees, or terminating a strategic alliance.

We should also note that managers make decisions about both problems and opportunities. For example, making decisions about how to cut costs by 10 percent reflects a problem—an undesirable situation that requires a solution. But decisions are also necessary in situations of opportunity. Learning that the firm is earning higher-than-projected profits, for example, requires a subsequent decision. Should the extra funds be used to increase shareholder dividends, reinvest in current operations, or expand into new markets? Of course, it may take a long time before a manager can know if the right decision was made.

Programmed Decision *decision that is relatively structured or recurs with some frequency (or both)*

Types of Decisions Managers must make many different types of decisions. In general, however, most decisions fall into one of two categories: *programmed* and *nonprogrammed*.[17] A **programmed decision** is one that is relatively structured or recurs with some frequency (or both). Starbucks uses programmed decisions to purchase new supplies of coffee beans, cups, and napkins, and Starbucks employees are trained in exact procedures for brewing coffee. Likewise, the College Station Ford dealer made a decision that he will sponsor a youth soccer team each year. Thus, when the soccer club president calls, the dealer already knows what he will do. Many decisions regarding basic operating systems and procedures and standard organizational transactions are of this variety and can therefore be programmed.[18]

Nonprogrammed Decision *decision that is relatively unstructured and that occurs with low frequency*

Nonprogrammed decisions, on the other hand, are relatively unstructured and occur much less often. Disney's decision to buy the *Stars Wars* properties was a nonprogrammed decision. Managers faced with such decisions must treat each one as unique, investing enormous amounts of time, energy, and resources into exploring the situation from all perspectives. Intuition and experience are major factors in nonprogrammed decisions. Most of the decisions made by top managers involving strategy (including mergers, acquisitions, and takeovers) and organization design are nonprogrammed. Nonprogrammed decisions also include those concerning new facilities, new products, labor contracts, and legal issues.

Decision-Making Conditions Just as there are different kinds of decisions, there are also different conditions in which decisions must be made. Managers sometimes have an almost perfect understanding of conditions surrounding a decision, but at other times they have few clues about those conditions. In general the circumstances that exist for the decision maker are conditions of certainty, risk, or uncertainty.[19]

CERTAINTY When the decision maker knows with reasonable certainty what the alternatives are and what conditions are associated with each alternative, a **state of certainty** exists. Suppose, for example, that managers at Singapore Airlines make a decision to buy five new jumbo jets. Their next decision is from whom to buy them. Because there are only two companies in the world that make jumbo jets, Boeing and Airbus, Singapore Airlines knows its options exactly. Each has proven products and will guarantee prices and delivery dates. The airline thus knows the alternative conditions associated with each. There is little ambiguity and relatively little chance of making a bad decision.

Few organizational decisions, however, are made under conditions of true certainty. The complexity and turbulence of the contemporary business world make such situations rare. Even the airplane purchase decision we just considered has less certainty than it appears. The aircraft companies may not be able to really guarantee delivery dates, so they may write cost-increase or inflation clauses into contracts. Thus, the airline may be only partially certain of the conditions surrounding each alternative.

RISK A more common decision-making condition is a state of risk. Under a **state of risk,** the availability of each alternative and its potential payoffs and costs are all associated with probability estimates.[20] Suppose, for example, that a labor contract negotiator for a company receives a "final" offer from the union right before a strike deadline. The negotiator has two alternatives: to accept or to reject the offer. The risk centers on whether the union representatives are bluffing. If the company negotiator accepts the offer, he or she avoids a strike but commits to a relatively costly labor contract. If he or she rejects the contract, he or she may get a more favorable contract if the union is bluffing, but he or she may provoke a strike if it is not.

On the basis of past experience, relevant information, the advice of others, and her own judgment, he or she may conclude that there is about a 75 percent chance that union representatives are bluffing and about a 25 percent chance that they will back up their threats. Thus, he or she can base a calculated decision on the two alternatives (accept or reject the contract demands) and the probable consequences of each. When making decisions under a state of risk, managers must reasonably estimate the probabilities associated with each alternative. For example, if the union negotiators are committed to a strike if their demands are not met, and the company negotiator rejects their demands because he or she guesses they will not strike, the miscalculation will prove costly. Decision making under conditions of risk is accompanied by moderate ambiguity and chances of a bad decision.

UNCERTAINTY Most of the major decision making in contemporary organizations is done under a **state of uncertainty.** The decision maker does not know all the alternatives, the risks associated with each, or the likely consequences of each alternative. This uncertainty stems from the complexity and dynamism of contemporary organizations and their environments. The emergence of the Internet as a significant force in today's competitive environment has served to increase both revenue potential and uncertainty for most managers.

To make effective decisions in these circumstances, managers must acquire as much relevant information as possible and approach the situation from a logical and rational perspective. Intuition, judgment, and experience always play major roles in the decision-making process under conditions of uncertainty. Even so, uncertainty is the most ambiguous condition for managers and the one most prone to error.[21] Lorraine Brennan O'Neil is the founder and CEO of 10 Minute Manicure, a quick service salon located in airports. The company found quick success and experienced rapid growth from its start in 2006, but the economic downturn required O'Neil to rethink her plans in an attempt to stay afloat through a rocky and unknown future. Knowing that the company no longer had the time to wait and monitor new stores' success, she opted to focus solely on existing stores with profits, shutting down

State of Certainty *when the decision maker knows with reasonable certainty what the alternatives are and what conditions are associated with each alternative*

State of Risk *when the availability of each alternative and its potential payoffs and costs are all associated with probability estimates*

State of Uncertainty *when the decision maker does not know all the alternatives, the risks associated with each, or the likely consequences of each alternative*

entrepreneurship and new ventures

A Bad Decision at Wesabe

As far as U.S. small business was concerned, the first quarter of 2010 could have been worse. There was a net loss of only 96,000 companies with fewer than 100 employees. As a matter of fact, the first quarter of 2009 *was* worse—a *lot* worse: By the end of the quarter, there were 400,000 fewer small businesses than there had been at the beginning.

One of the companies that shut down in 2010 was Wesabe, which had launched in 2006 as an online site to help people manage their money and make better financial decisions. It was one of the first companies to enter the financial sector of what's often referred to as *Web 2.0*, the world of web applications that allow users to interact and collaborate on content that they create themselves. The idea was to let customers access data from several financial institutions and then compare their own money management practices to those of online peers.

Wesabe actually got off to a reasonably good start. Within the first year, founders Marc Hedlund and Jason Knight secured venture capital totaling $4.7 million and attracted 150,000 members. The first signs of trouble appeared in the second year, just after a competitor called Mint.com came online. Nine months after its launch, Mint.com boasted $17 million in venture capital and 300,000 users. In 2009, Intuit, a creator of financial and tax-preparation software, purchased Mint.com for $170 million. Wesabe held on until mid-2010, when Hedlund and Knight announced that the company could no longer handle users' highly sensitive data "with shoestring operations and security staff."

So what went wrong? Naturally, there's no single reason for Wesabe's failure, but both Hedlund, who blogged a postmortem shortly after the shutdown, and independent observers point to one crucial business decision as a key factor. In the early stages of the startup process, Hedlund and Knight rejected a partnership with a firm called Yodlee, which had already developed a system for accessing transaction data from banks. But because the Yodlee process worked with users' passwords, Wesabe considered it too great a security risk and proceeded to work on its own process, which, though more secure, was also more cumbersome.

"Everyone—I mean 90-percent-plus of everybody," says Hedlund, "told me that they would never in a million years use a startup website that asked them for their bank passwords." When Mint came online in 2007, it was using Yodlee technology, password-access included, and Hedlund acknowledges that he'd made a mistake by relying on his own informal market research: "We should have known," he admits, "that somebody would go with Yodlee, and we should have aimed at [Yodlee] as what we needed to achieve." By 2008, Wesabe, too, was accepting users' passwords to simplify the process of pulling bank data into its system. "We just didn't build it nearly fast enough," says Hedlund of Wesabe's own data-access system. "That one mistake—not using or replacing Yodlee before Mint had a chance to launch on Yodlee—was probably enough to kill Wesabe alone."[22]

those with losses. Aside from this, she restructured her business plan, seeking nontraditional locations, reducing corporate overhead, cutting products, and developing an online product line as a second source of income.[23]

Rational Decision Making

Managers and leaders should strive to be rational in making decisions. Figure 9.3 shows the steps in the rational decision-making process.

Recognizing and Defining the Decision Situation

The first step in rational decision making is recognizing that a decision is necessary; there must be some stimulus or spark to initiate the process. The stimulus for a decision may be either positive or negative. Managers who must decide how to invest surplus funds, for example, face a positive decision situation. A negative financial stimulus could involve having to trim budgets because of cost overruns.

Inherent in making such a decision is the need to define precisely what the problem is. Consider the situation currently being faced in the international air travel industry. Because of the growth of international travel related to business, education,

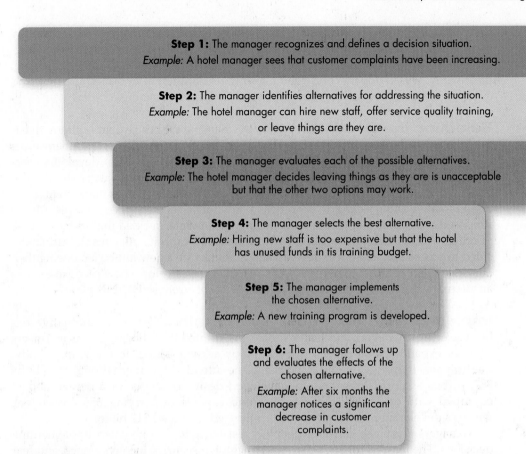

Step 1: The manager recognizes and defines a decision situation.
Example: A hotel manager sees that customer complaints have been increasing.

Step 2: The manager identifies alternatives for addressing the situation.
Example: The hotel manager can hire new staff, offer service quality training, or leave things are they are.

Step 3: The manager evaluates each of the possible alternatives.
Example: The hotel manager decides leaving things as they are is unacceptable but that the other two options may work.

Step 4: The manager selects the best alternative.
Example: Hiring new staff is too expensive but that the hotel has unused funds in tis training budget.

Step 5: The manager implements the chosen alternative.
Example: A new training program is developed.

Step 6: The manager follows up and evaluates the effects of the chosen alternative.
Example: After six months the manager notices a significant decrease in customer complaints.

FIGURE 9.3 Steps in the Rational Decision-Making Process
Source: Based on Griffin, *Management* 8e. © 2005 South-Western, a part of Cengage Learning, Inc. Reproduced by permission. www.cengage.com/permissions. Courtesy of Ronald Ebert.

and tourism, global carriers need to increase their capacity. Because most major international airports are already operating at or near capacity, adding a significant number of new flights to existing schedules is not feasible. As a result, the most logical alternative is to increase capacity on existing flights. Thus, Boeing and Airbus, the world's only manufacturers of large commercial aircraft, recognized an important opportunity and defined their decision situations as how best to respond to the need for increased global travel capacity.[24]

Identifying Alternatives Once the decision situation has been recognized and defined, the second step is to identify alternative courses of effective action. Developing both obvious, standard alternatives and creative, innovative alternatives is useful. In general, the more important the decision, the more attention is directed to developing alternatives. Although managers should seek creative solutions, they must also recognize that various constraints often limit their alternatives. Common constraints include legal restrictions, moral and ethical norms, and constraints imposed by the power and authority of the manager, available technology, economic considerations, and unofficial social norms. After assessing the question of how to increase international airline capacity, Boeing and Airbus identified three different alternatives: They could independently develop new large planes, they could collaborate in a joint venture to create a single new large plane, or they could modify their largest existing planes to increase their capacity.

Evaluating Alternatives The third step in the decision-making process is evaluating each of the alternatives. Some alternatives may not be feasible because of legal or financial barriers. Limited human, material, and information resources may make other alternatives impractical. Managers must thoroughly evaluate all the alternatives to increase the chances that the alternative finally chosen will be successful. For example, Airbus felt it would be at a disadvantage if it tried simply to enlarge its existing planes because the Boeing 747 was at the time already the largest aircraft being made and could readily be expanded to remain the largest. Boeing, meanwhile, was seriously concerned about the risk inherent in building a new and even larger plane, even if it shared the risk with Airbus as a joint venture.

Selecting the Best Alternative Choosing the best available alternative is the real crux of decision making. Even though many situations do not lend themselves to objective, mathematical analysis, managers and leaders can often develop subjective estimates and weights for choosing an alternative. Decision makers should also remember that finding multiple acceptable alternatives may be possible; selecting just one alternative and rejecting all the others might not be necessary. For example, Airbus proposed a joint venture with Boeing. Boeing, meanwhile, decided that its best course of action was to modify its existing 747 to increase its capacity. As a result, Airbus decided to proceed on its own to develop and manufacture a new jumbo jet. Boeing then decided that in addition to modifying its 747, it would develop a new plane to offer as an alternative, albeit one not as large as the 747 or the proposed Airbus plane.

Implementing the Chosen Alternative After an alternative has been selected, managers and leaders must put it into effect. Boeing set its engineers to work expanding the capacity of its 747 by adding 30 feet to the plane's body; the firm also began developing another plane intended for international travel, the 787. Airbus engineers, meanwhile, developed design concepts for a new jumbo jet equipped with escalators and elevators and capable of carrying 655 passengers. Airbus's development costs alone were estimated to exceed $12 billion.

Managers must also consider people's resistance to change when implementing decisions. The reasons for such resistance include insecurity, inconvenience, and fear of the unknown. Managers should anticipate potential resistance at various stages of the implementation process. However, even when all alternatives have been evaluated as precisely as possible and the consequences of each alternative have been weighed, unanticipated consequences are still likely. Employees may resist or protest change; they may even quit rather than agree to it. Other factors, such as unexpected cost increases, a less-than-perfect fit with existing organizational subsystems, or unpredicted effects on cash flow or operating expenses, could develop after implementation has begun. Both Boeing and Airbus were plagued by production delays that pushed back delivery of their respective aircrafts by years and could end up costing each company billions of dollars. Airbus got its plane to market first (it began flying in late 2007), but profits have been pushed far into the future because the global recession caused many airlines to cancel or delay orders for several years.

Following up and Evaluating the Results The final step in the decision-making process requires that managers and leaders evaluate the effectiveness of their decision. They should make sure that the chosen alternative has served its original purpose. If an implemented alternative appears not to be working, they can respond in several ways. Another previously identified alternative (the original second or third choice, for instance) could be adopted. Or they might recognize that the situation was not correctly defined to begin with and start the process all over again. Finally, managers and leaders might decide that the original alternative is in fact appropriate but either has not yet had time to work or should be implemented in a different way.

At this point, both Boeing and Airbus are nearing the crucial period when they will learn whether they made good decisions. Airbus's A380 made its first commercial flight in 2007, though delays continue to push back its production schedule. The plane has also been hampered by technical problems. Meanwhile, Boeing's 787 faced numerous delays, and widespread use of the plane continues to be delayed by technical issues.[25] The expanded 747 was launched on schedule, however, and was in service in 2011. Most airlines have been willing to wait patiently for the 787s, which are designed to be much more fuel efficient than other international airplanes. Given the dramatic surge in fuel costs in recent years, a fuel-efficient option like the 787 could be an enormous success. Indeed, Airbus has begun developing its own fuel-efficient jet, the A350.[26]

Behavioral Aspects of Decision Making

If all decision situations were approached as logically as described in the previous section, more decisions would prove successful. Yet decisions are often made with little consideration for logic and rationality. Some experts have estimated that U.S. companies use rational decision-making techniques less than 20 percent of the time. Of course, even when organizations try to be logical, they sometimes fail. For example, when Starbucks opened its first coffee shops in New York, it relied on scientific marketing research, taste tests, and rational deliberation in making a decision to emphasize drip over espresso coffee. However, that decision proved wrong because it became clear that New Yorkers strongly preferred the same espresso-style coffees that were Starbucks mainstays in the West. Hence, the firm had to reconfigure its stores hastily to meet customer preferences.

On the other hand, sometimes a decision made with little regard for logic can still turn out to be correct.[27] Important ingredients in how these forces work are behavioral aspects of decision making. These include *political forces, intuition, escalation of commitment*, and *risk propensity*.

Political Forces in Decision Making Political forces contribute to the behavioral nature of decision making. One major element of politics, *coalitions*, is especially relevant to decision making. A **coalition** is an informal alliance of individuals or groups formed to achieve a common goal. This common goal is often a preferred decision alternative. For example, coalitions of stockholders frequently band together to force a board of directors to make a certain decision.

Coalition *an informal alliance of individuals or groups formed to achieve a common goal*

The New York Yankees once contacted three major sneaker manufacturers, Nike, Reebok, and Adidas, and informed them that they were looking to make a sponsorship deal. While Nike and Reebok were carefully and rationally assessing the possibilities, managers at Adidas quickly realized that a partnership with the Yankees made a lot of sense for them. They responded quickly to the idea and ended up hammering out a contract while the competitors were still analyzing details.[28]

When these coalitions enter the political arena and attempt to persuade lawmakers to make decisions favorable to their interests, they are called *lobbyists*. Lobbyists may also donate money to help elect a candidate who is more likely to pursue their agendas. A recurring theme in U.S. politics is the damaging influence these special interest groups have on politicians, who may feel unduly obligated to favor campaign donors when making decisions.

Intuition **Intuition** is an innate belief about something, often without conscious consideration. Managers sometimes decide to do something because it "feels right" or they have a hunch. This feeling is usually not arbitrary, however. Rather, it is based on years of experience and practice in making decisions in similar situations. Such an inner sense may help managers make an occasional decision without going through a full-blown rational sequence of steps.

Intuition *an innate belief about something, often without conscious consideration*

That said, all managers, but most especially inexperienced ones, should be careful not to rely too heavily on intuition. If rationality and logic are continually flouted for "what feels right," the odds are that disaster will strike one day.

Escalation of Commitment Another important behavioral process that influences decision making is **escalation of commitment** to a chosen course of action. In particular, decision makers sometimes make decisions and then become so committed to the course of action suggested by that decision that they stay with it, even when it appears to have been wrong.[29] For example, when people buy stock in a company, they sometimes refuse to sell it even after repeated drops in price. They choose a course of action, buying the stock in anticipation of making a profit, and then stay

Escalation of Commitment *condition in which a decision maker becomes so committed to a course of action that she or he stays with it even when it appears to have been wrong*

with it even in the face of increasing losses. Moreover, after the value drops they may rationalize that they can't sell at such a low price because they will lose money.

Risk Propensity and Decision Making The behavioral element of **risk propensity** is the extent to which a decision maker is willing to gamble when making a decision. Some managers are cautious about every decision they make. They try to adhere to the rational model and are extremely conservative in what they do. Such managers are more likely to avoid mistakes, and they infrequently make decisions that lead to big losses. Others are extremely aggressive in making decisions and willing to take risks.[30] They rely heavily on intuition, reach decisions quickly, and often risk big investments on their decisions. As in gambling, these managers are more likely than their conservative counterparts to achieve big successes with their decisions; they are also more likely to incur greater losses.[31] The organization's culture is a prime ingredient in fostering different levels of risk propensity.

Risk Propensity *extent to which a decision maker is willing to gamble when making a decision*

summary of learning objectives

OBJECTIVE 1

Define leadership and distinguish it from management.

(pp. 306–308)

Leadership refers to the processes and behaviors used by someone to motivate, inspire, and influence the behaviors of others. Although leadership and management are often related, they are not the same thing. Leadership involves such things as developing a vision, communicating that vision, and directing change. Management, meanwhile, focuses more on outlining procedures, monitoring results, and working toward outcomes.

Power is the ability to affect the behavior of others. In organizational settings, there are usually five kinds of power: (1) legitimate, (2) reward, (3) coercive, (4) referent, and (5) expert power. *Legitimate power* is power granted through the organizational hierarchy; it is the power defined by the organization to be accorded to people occupying a particular position. *Reward power* is the power to give or withhold rewards. *Coercive power* is the power to force compliance by means of psychological, emotional, or physical threat. *Referent power* is based on identification, imitation, loyalty, or charisma. *Expert power* is derived from information or expertise.

OBJECTIVE 2

Summarize early approaches to the study of leadership.

(pp. 308–309)

The *trait approach to leadership* focused on identifying the traits of successful leaders. The earliest researchers believed that important leadership traits included intelligence, dominance, self-confidence, energy, activity (versus passivity), and knowledge about the job. However, this research did not produce conclusive results. More recent researchers have started to focus on traits such as emotional and mental intelligence, drive, motivation, honesty and integrity, self-confidence, knowledge of the business, and charisma.

The *behavioral approach* to leadership sought to determine what behaviors were employed by effective leaders. Research identified two basic and common leader behaviors: *task-focused* and *employee-focused* leader behaviors. It is thought that leaders should engage in both behaviors to increase performance and motivation.

OBJECTIVE 3

Discuss the concept of situational approaches to leadership.

(pp. 310–311)

The *situational approach to leadership* proposes that there is no single best approach to leadership. Instead, situational factors influence the approach to leadership that is most effective. This approach was proposed as a continuum of leadership behavior, ranging from having the leader make decisions alone to having employees make decisions with minimal guidance from the leader. Each point on the continuum is influenced by *characteristics of the leader, his or her subordinates*, and the *situation*.

The path–goal theory of leadership is a direct extension of the expectancy theory of motivation. It suggests that the primary functions of a leader are to make valued or desired rewards available in the workplace and to clarify for the subordinate the kinds of behavior that will lead to goal accomplishment and valued rewards. The leader should clarify the paths to goal attainment. Path–goal theory identifies four kinds of behaviors that leaders can use, depending on the situation: (1) *directive leader behavior,* (2) *supportive leader behavior,* (3) *participative leader behavior,* and (4) *achievement-oriented leader behavior.*

The decision tree approach attempts to prescribe a leadership style appropriate to a given situation. The decision tree approach assumes that the degree to which subordinates should be encouraged to participate in decision making depends on the characteristics of the situation. After evaluating a variety of problem attributes (characteristics of the problem or decision), the leader determines an appropriate decision style that specifies the amount of subordinate participation.

The *leader-member exchange (LMX) model of leadership* stresses the importance of variable relationships between supervisors and each of their subordinates. Each superior–subordinate pair represents a "vertical dyad." The model differs from previous approaches in that it focuses on the differential relationship leaders often establish with different subordinates.

OBJECTIVE 4

Describe transformational and charismatic perspectives on leadership. (pp. 311–313)

Transformational leadership (as distinguished from *transactional leadership*) focuses on the set of abilities that allows a leader to recognize the need for change, to create a vision to guide that change, and to execute the change effectively. *Charismatic leadership* is influence based on the leader's personal charisma. The basic concept of charisma suggests that charismatic leaders are likely to have self-confidence, confidence in their beliefs and ideals, and a need to influence people. They also tend to communicate high expectations about follower performance and to express confidence in their followers.

OBJECTIVE 5

Identify and discuss leadership substitutes and neutralizers. (pp. 313–314)

Leadership substitutes are individual, task, and organizational factors that tend to outweigh the need for a leader to initiate or direct employee performance. In other words, if certain factors are present, the employee will perform his or her job without the direction of a leader. Examples of leadership substitutes include individual professionalism, highly structured jobs, explicit plans and goals, and group performance norms. Even if a leader attempts to engage in leadership behaviors, *leadership neutralizers* may render the leader's efforts ineffective. Such neutralizers include group cohesiveness as well as elements of the job itself.

OBJECTIVE 6

Discuss leaders as coaches and examine gender and cross-cultural issues in leadership. (pp. 314–316)

Many organizations expect their leaders to play the role of *coach*—to select team members, provide direction, train and develop, but otherwise allow the group to function autonomously. Some leaders may function as mentors, helping less experienced employees learn the ropes and better preparing them to advance in an organization.

Another factor that is altering the face of leadership is the number of women advancing to higher levels. Although there appear to be few differences between men and women leaders, the growing number of women leaders suggests a need for more study. There does appear to be evidence that women are more democratic in decision making and have the potential to be excellent leaders, as evidenced by a number of high-profile, successful women leaders.

Another changing perspective on leadership relates to cross-cultural issues. In this context, *culture* encompasses international differences and diversity-based differences within one culture. For example, the level of collectivism or individualism can affect a manager's leadership style.

OBJECTIVE 7

Describe strategic leadership, ethical leadership, and virtual leadership. (p. 317)

Strategic leadership is the leader's ability to lead change in the organization so as to enhance its competitiveness. To be effective as a strategic leader, a manager needs to have a thorough and complete understanding of the organization's history, culture, strengths, and weaknesses. Business leaders are also being called on to practice *ethical leadership*—that is, to maintain high ethical standards for their own conduct, and to hold others in their organizations to the same standards. As more leaders and employees work in different settings, a better understanding of *virtual leadership* is also becoming more important.

OBJECTIVE 8

Relate leadership to decision making and discuss both rational and behavioral perspectives on decision making.
(pp. 318–324)

Decision making—choosing one alternative from among several options—is a critical management and leadership skill. Decision making can refer to either a specific act or a general process. Most decisions fall into one of two categories: programmed and nonprogrammed. A programmed decision is one that is relatively structured or recurs with some frequency (or both). Nonprogrammed decisions are relatively unstructured and occur much less often. There are three different conditions in which decisions must be made. These are conditions of certainty, risk, or uncertainty. When the decision maker knows what the alternatives are and the likely outcomes, a *state of certainty* exists. Under a *state of risk*, the availability of each alternative and its payoffs and costs are not clear. Finally, in a st*ate of uncertainty*, the decision maker does not know all the alternatives, risks, or consequences.

The *rational perspective* prescribes a logical process for making decisions. It involves six steps (1) recognizing and defining the decision situation, (2) identifying alternatives, (3) evaluating alternatives, (4) selecting the best alternative, (5) implementing the chosen alternative, and (6) following up and evaluating the results. The *behavioral perspective* acknowledges that things such as *political forces, intuition, escalation of commitment*, and *risk propensity* are also important aspects of decision making.

key terms

behavioral approach to leadership (p. 309)
charismatic leadership (p. 312)
coalition (p. 323)
coercive power (p. 307)
decision making (p. 318)
decision-making process (p. 318)
decision tree approach (p. 311)
employee-focused leader behavior (p. 309)
escalation of commitment (p. 323)
ethical leadership (p. 317)
expert power (p. 308)
intuition (p. 323)

leader-member exchange (LMX) model (p. 311)
leadership (p. 306)
leadership neutralizers (p. 314)
leadership substitutes (p. 313)
legitimate power (p. 307)
nonprogrammed decision (p. 318)
path-goal theory (p. 310)
power (p. 307)
programmed decision (p. 318)
referent power (p. 308)
reward power (p. 307)

risk propensity (p. 324)
situational approach to leadership (p. 310)
state of certainty (p. 319)
state of risk (p. 319)
state of uncertainty (p. 319)
strategic leadership (p. 317)
task-focused leader behavior (p. 309)
trait approach to leadership (p. 308)
transactional leadership (p. 312)
transformational leadership (p. 312)
virtual leadership (p. 317)

MyBizLab

Go to **pearsonglobaleditions.com/mybizlab** to complete the problems marked with this icon ✪.

questions & exercises

QUESTIONS FOR REVIEW

✪ 9-1. What are the basic differences between management and leadership?

9-2. Summarize the basic premises underlying the trait approach to leadership.

9-3. What are leadership substitutes and neutralizers?

9-4. List and briefly explain the steps in rational decision making.

QUESTIONS FOR ANALYSIS

✪ 9-5. Describe the five types of power. Which type or types does your current supervisor exercise?

9-6. When is task-focused leader behavior most important? When is it more important for a leader to exhibit employee-focused behavior?

9-7. The impact of virtual leadership is likely to grow in the future. As a potential "follower" in a virtual leadership situation, what issues would be of most concern to you? What would the issues be from the perspective of the "leader" role in such a situation?

⭐ 9-8. Identify a leader that you believe exhibits charismatic leadership and explain the behaviors that support this conclusion.

APPLICATION EXERCISES

9-9. Overwhelmingly, the CEOs of the largest companies in the United States are white males, but women and minorities are making inroads. Identify a leader who is a member of a minority group and describe the challenges that he or she faced and overcame.

9-10. In 2012, Marrisa Mayer was appointed president and CEO of Yahoo!. In her tenure with Yahoo!, she has made a number of bold decisions, not all of which were popular. Research Mayer's career, especially at Yahoo! What type of leader is Mayer? How would you describe her leadership style? Do you think she is effective?

building a business: continuing team exercise

Assignment

Meet with your team members to consider your new business venture and how it relates to the leadership topics in this chapter. Develop specific responses to the following:

9-11. How will you select a leader for your organization? What traits or characteristics will be most important to you when selecting a leader?

9-12. Which types of power will be most important to the leader of your business venture?

9-13. What leadership substitutes could support your business venture as you get started?

9-14. Are there any leadership neutralizers that could derail your new effort?

9-15. As your business venture gets off the ground, you will have to make many important decisions. Will you rely more heavily on rational decision making or intuition? Why?

building your business skills

LEARNING TO LEAD

Goal

To encourage you to appreciate your own strengths and weaknesses as they relate to critical leadership skills.

Background Information

Although not all experts agree, most believe that businesses can teach their managers to become more effective leaders. Indeed, most large businesses devote considerable resources to identifying those managers with the most leadership potential and providing training and development opportunities for those managers to enhance and refine their leadership skills. One major U.S. energy company, for instance, has identified the following traits, characteristics, and skills as reflecting how it sees leadership:

- Personal integrity
- Decision-making skills
- Interpersonal skills
- Communication skills
- Strategic thinking skills
- Global awareness skills
- Financial management skills

Method

STEP 1

Working alone or with classmates (as directed by your instructor), develop or describe indicators and measures a business could use to assess each of these traits, characteristics, and skills in managers so as to most effectively select those with the strongest potential for leadership. That is, describe how you would go about selecting managers for special leadership training and development.

STEP 1

Working alone or with classmates (again, as directed by your instructor), develop or describe the techniques and methods that might potentially serve to best enhance the traits, characteristics, and skills noted previously. That is, having chosen those managers with the strongest potential for growth as leaders, describe how you would go about teaching and developing those individuals so as to enhance their leadership potential and capability.

FOLLOW-UP QUESTIONS

9-16. Comment on the traits, characteristics, and skills used by the energy company. Do you agree or disagree that these would differentiate between those who might be described as both managers and leaders versus those best described simply as managers? Are there others you might include?

9-17. How simple or easy would you expect it to be to select managers for leadership and development at this company?

9-18. Do you believe that leadership can be taught? What are the assumptions underlying your answer?

9-19. If you personally were selected for a program such as this, what would you expect to encounter during the training and development? What would you expect to be different after the training and development were complete?

exercising your ethics

EXERCISING CHARISMA

The Situation

You are the chief financial officer (CFO) for Advanced Nutriceuticals, a leading manufacturer of nutritional supplements in the United States. The company's CEO, Jeff Johnson, is passionate about health and the value of nutritional supplements. Jeff has a compelling story—he is a survivor of Stage 4 skin cancer, an outcome he attributes to the use of nutritional supplements. He is featured widely in company advertising and is admired by most of the company's employees.

Unlike prescription medications, nutritional supplements are not subject to U.S. Food and Drug Administration regulation and the company does not have a lot of well-supported research to support the efficacy of its products. Additionally, there has been considerable competition from manufacturers outside the United States, who can produce the same products at a much lower cost. The company has spent a year developing a long-term strategy that involves increasing production and expansion into international markets.

The Dilemma

As the CFO, you have been asked to develop a budget for the next three years. The company has plans to expand their operations and you have projected that there will be a need for a large amount of capital. You have presented your budget to the CEO and board of directors and have discussed various options for raising capital, such as the sale of bonds and a public offering of additional stock. After analyzing each of the alternatives that you have presented, Jeff has come back with a new option: he wants to move all of the employee's retirement funds to stock in Advanced Nutriceuticals and encourage every employee to show "company spirit" by investing as much as possible. Jeff is convinced that he can sell this to the employees based on his charm and charisma. However, you're concerned that this is a risky move for employees. If the company is not successful, they will be out of a job and a retirement fund. On the other hand, you risk losing your job if you don't support the CEO's plan.

QUE STIONS TO ADDRESS

9-20. What are the ethical issues in this situation?

9-21. What do you think most managers would do in this situation?

9-22. What would you do?

team exercise

FORCING THE HAND

The Situation

Commonwealth Services is a commercial cleaning service, with customers across the state of Virginia. Your company provides cleaning services for office buildings and other commercial customers.

The Decision

Commonwealth is a lean operation, with a flat organizational structure and a small number of managers. The recession took its toll on the company and employees have not had a raise in years. To make matters worse, your employees don't find that cleaning is particularly rewarding work. Customers expect a consistently high level of service and dependability, but you're finding it hard to motivate employees. To expand your customer base, Commonwealth has decided to expand their services and will now offer clean-up services for foreclosed properties being prepared for sale. These properties are often in a great state of disarray and the work can be particularly unappealing. Employees are not excited about these new customers and are not supportive of the change. The company has asked you to come in as a consultant and conduct leadership workshops for the management team. Your job is to develop a set of concrete recommendations about how to lead employees through this change in strategy.

Team Activity

Assemble a group of four students and assign each group member to one of the following approaches to leadership:

- leader-member exchange (LMX) model
- path-goal theory
- task-focused leader
- employee-focused leader

ACTION STEPS

9-23. Working individually, develop a leadership strategy based in your assigned approach to leadership. What will be most important to your success? How will you communicate with employees and motivate them?

9-24. Assemble your group and share your assignment perspectives.

9-25. As a group, develop a list of advantages and disadvantages of each approach.

9-26. Select the most appropriate leadership style and develop a justification for your decision.

cases

Middle Eastern Business Leadership

Continued from page 306

At the beginning of this chapter you read about the role of business leaders in the Middle East. Using the information presented in this chapter you should now be able to respond to these questions.

QUESTIONS FOR DISCUSSION

9-27. What does this case illustrate about the nature of leadership?

9-28. In what ways has information technology changed the work of leaders?

9-29. How do you think the work of leaders will change in the future?

The Man Behind the Genius

There is no doubt that Steve Jobs, co-founder of Apple, was a one-of-a-kind leader. In many ways, Jobs was defined by his passion for innovation and willingness to take risks. As the leader of a company that created the iMac, iPhone, iPod, iPhone, and iPad, Jobs demonstrated that he could see beyond the present and motivate his employees by sharing his vision clearly and compellingly. According to Apple's current CEO, "Even though he was running a large company, he kept making bold moves that I don't think that anyone else would have done."[32]

The challenge, however, for Jobs and Apple was this same vision and passion. A visionary leader's strength is their ability to mobilize their employees to work towards a goal at super-human speed. Yet, when the vision is flawed, the employees demonstrate the same commitment and moving quickly, and even dangerously, in the wrong direction.[33] Often, these visionary leaders effectively screen out negative chatter, but this is not always positive, particularly when employees discover a fatal flaw.

Jobs had a unique managerial style. According to Joe Nocera of *The New York Times*, he "violated every rule of management. He was not a consensus builder but a dictator who listed mainly to his own intuition. He was a maniacal micromanager. He had an astonishing aesthetic sense, which businesspeople almost always lack.... He never mellowed, never let up on Apple employees, never stopped relying on his singular instincts in making decisions about how Apple products should look and how they should work."[34]

Although inspiring thousands of employees and millions of customers, Jobs could be brutal when dealing with employees who failed to successfully implement his vision. Despite many successes, Apple had its failures. One of the most notable was the MobileMe e-mail system. Jobs was so disappointed by flaws in the system that he fired the employee leading the MobileMe effort in front of a crowd of employees.

Jobs' passion was at the core of his being. When Jobs had a liver transplant in 2009, he found himself in the hospital with an oxygen mask. He pulled off the mask and told the pulmonologist that he was unwilling to suffer through the poor design, though barely able to speak. Ultimately, Jobs succumbed to pancreatic cancer in 2011, but he left an indelible mark on the world.

QUESTIONS FOR DISCUSSION

9-30. Do you think that Steve Jobs was a charismatic leader? What leads you to this conclusion?

9-31. Jobs enjoyed almost cult-like loyalty among his employees. Why do you think that people clamored to work for Apple under Jobs' leadership?

9-32. What challenges face employees working for a leader such as Jobs?

9-33. Describe Jobs with respect to intuition, escalation of commitment, and risk propensity.

9-34. Do you think that you would have enjoyed working for Apple during Jobs' leadership? Why or why not?

MyBizLab

Go to **pearsonglobaleditions.com/mybizlab** *for the following Assisted-graded writing questions:*

9-35. Many followers prefer to have transformational or charismatic leaders. Do you think that a transformational focus and charisma guarantees for success? Does being a transformational or charismatic leader indicate successful management? Are there situations where charisma can mislead followers about a leader's ability? Support your answers.

9-36. Due to the rapidly changing nature of the current workplace, there are three emerging trends in leadership: strategic, ethical, and virtual leaders. Write an essay explaining the importance of each of these types of leaders. Explain how each of these leadership trends affects the manager/employee relationship. How might these trends be impact global companies?

9-37. Mybizlab Only—comprehensive writing assignment for this chapter.

end notes

1 Saddi, Sabbugh, and Shediac, "Measures of Leadership," *Strategy and Business,* (59) Summer 2010; Bloomberg, "Qatar to Build $9.8 Billion Plants in China, Vietnam," November 18, 2009 at http://www.bloomberg.com/apps/news?pid=newsarchive&sid=apYDH34yCCwE.

2 See John Kotter, "What Leaders Really Do," *Harvard Business Review,* December 2001, 85–94.

3 John R. P. French and Bertram Raven, "The Bases of Social Power," in Dorwin Cartwright (ed.), *Studies in Social Power* (Ann Arbor, MI: University of Michigan Press, 1959), pp. 150–167.

4 Hugh D. Menzies, "The Ten Toughest Bosses," *Fortune,* April 21, 1980, pp. 62–73.

5 "Management Secrets from the Meanest Company in America," *Bloomberg BusinessWeek,* January 2, 2013, pp. 46–51.

6 "Bad Bosses Can Be Bad for Your Health," USA Today, August 8, 2012, p. 5B; Bennett J. Tepper, "Abusive Supervision in Work Organizations: Review, Synthesis, and Research Agenda," *Journal of Management,* 2007, Vol. 33, No. 3, pp. 261–289.

7 Martin G. Evans, "The Effects of Supervisory Behavior on the Path-Goal Relationship," *Organizational Behavior and Human Performance,* May 1970, pp. 277–298; Robert J. House and Terence R. Mitchell, "Path-Goal Theory of Leadership," *Journal of Contemporary Business,* Autumn 1974, pp. 81–98. See also Gary Yukl, *Leadership in Organizations* 8th ed. (Upper Saddle River: Prentice-Hall, 2013).

8 George Graen and J. F. Cashman, "A Role-Making Model of Leadership in Formal Organizations: A Developmental Approach," in J. G. Hunt and L. L. Larson (eds.), *Leadership Frontiers* (Kent, OH: Kent State University Press, 1975), pp. 143–165; Fred Dansereau, George Graen, and W. J. Haga, "A Vertical Dyad Linkage Approach to Leadership Within Formal Organizations: A Longitudinal Investigation of the Role-Making Process," *Organizational Behavior and Human Performance,* 1975, Vol. 15, pp. 46–78.

9 David Gunzareth, "Murdoch, Rupert K.," The Museum of Broadcast Communications (May 27, 2008), at http://www.museum.tv/archives/etv/M/htmlM/murdochrupe/murdochrupe.htm; Johnnie L. Roberts, "Murdoch, Ink.," *Newsweek,* April 28, 2008 (May 27, 2008), at http://www.newsweek.com/id/132852; BBC News, "Murdoch: I Decide Sun's Politics," November 24, 2007 (May 27, 2008), at http://news.bbc.co.uk/2/hi/uk_news/7110532.stm; Mark Jurkowitz, "How Different Is Murdoch's New *Wall Street Journal?*" April 23, 2008 (May 27, 2008), at http://journalism.org/node/10769; Richard Siklos and Andrew Ross Sorkin, "Murdoch on Owning the *Wall Street Journal,*" *The New York Times,* May 4, 2007 (May 27, 2008), at http://www.nytimes.com/2007/05/04/business/media/04murdoch.html?pagewanted=print.

10 Ronald Ebert; David A. Waldman and Francis J. Yammarino, "CEO Charismatic Leadership: Levels-of-Management and Levels-of-Analysis Effects," *Academy of Management Review,* 1999, vol. 24, no. 2, pp. 266–285.

11 Jane Howell and Boas Shamir, "The Role of Followers in the Charismatic Leadership Process: Relationships and Their Consequences," *Academy of Management Review,* January 2005, pp. 96–112.

12 "In Tough Times, Bosses Need to Get Out and Talk to Employees," *USA Today,* August 8, 2012, p. 1B; Emily Thornton, "Managing through a Crisis: The New Rules," *Bloomberg Businessweek,* January 8, 2009, at www.businessweek.com, accessed on April 14, 2013; Anthony Portuesi, "Leading in a Recession: An Interview with Jack Hayhow," *Driven Leaders,* February 24, 2009, at http://drivenleaders.com, accessed on April 14, 2013; Jim Donald, "Guest Post: Former Starbucks CEO's Tips for Tough Times," *CNNMoney,* April 1, 2009, at http://postcards.blogs.fortune.cnn.com, accessed on April 14, 2013; Ellen Davis, "Retail Execs Offer Insights on Leadership in Tough Economic Times," *Retail's BIG Blog,* January 15, 2009, at http://blog.nrf.com, accessed on April 14, 2013.

13 J. Richard Hackman and Ruth Wageman, "A Theory of Team Coaching," *Academy of Management Review,* April 2005, pp. 269–287.

14 "How Women Lead," *Newsweek,* October 24, 2005, pp/ 46–70.

15 "African Americans Lost Ground on Fortune 500 Boards," *Savoy,* August 2009, at http://savoynetwork.com, accessed on April 14, 2013; Marc H. Morial, "National Urban League Trains African Americans for Corporate Boards," *Philadelphia Tribune,* April 14, 2011, at www.phillytrib.com, accessed on April 14, 2013; "Results of Menendez's Major Fortune 500 Diversity Survey: Representation of Women and Minorities on Corporate Boards Still Lags Far Behind National Population," August 4, 2010, Senator Robert Menendez's website (press release), at www.menendez.senate.gov, accessed on July 23, 2012.

16 For a review of decision making, see E. Frank Harrison, *The Managerial Decision Making Process,* 5th ed. (Boston: Houghton Mifflin, 1999). See also Elke U. Weber and Eric J. Johnson, "Mindful Judgment and Decision Making," in Susan T. Fiske, Daniel L. Schacter, and Robert Sternberg (eds.), *Annual Review of Psychology 2009* (Palo Alto, CA: Annual Reviews, 2009), pp. 53–86; Gerd Gigerenzer and Wolfgang Gaissmaier, "Heuristic Decision Making," in Susan T. Fiske, Daniel L. Schacter, and Shelley Taylor (eds.), *Annual Review of Psychology 2011* (Palo Alto, CA: Annual Reviews, 2011), pp. 451–482.

17 George P. Huber, *Managerial Decision Making* (Glenview, IL: Scott, Foresman, 1980).

18 For an example, see Paul D. Collins, Lori V. Ryan, and Sharon F. Matusik, "Programmable Automation and the Locus of Decision-Making Power," *Journal of Management,* 1999, Vol. 25, pp. 29–53.

19 Huber, *Managerial Decision Making.* See also David W. Miller and Martin K. Starr, *The Structure of Human Decisions*

(Englewood Cliffs, NJ: Prentice-Hall, 1976); Alvar Elbing, *Behavioral Decisions in Organizations*, 2nd ed. (Glenview, IL: Scott, Foresman, 1978).

20 Rene M. Stulz, "Six Ways Companies Mismanage Risk," *Harvard Business Review*, March 2009, pp. 86–94.

21 Gerard P. Hodgkinson, Nicola J. Bown, A. John Maule, Keith W. Glaister, and Alan D. Pearman, "Breaking the Frame: An Analysis of Strategic Cognition and Decision Making under Uncertainty," *Strategic Management Journal*, 1999, Vol. 20, pp. 977–985.

22 Eilene Zimmerman, "How Six Companies Failed to Survive 2010," *New York Times*, January 5, 2011, at www.nytimes.com, accessed on April 14, 2013; Anthony Ha, "Personal Finance Startup Wesabe to Shut Down," *VentureBeat*, June 30, 2010, at http://venturebeat.com, accessed on April 14, 2013, see http://venturebeat.com/2010/06/30/wesabe-shutdown/; Marc Hedlund, "Why Wesabe Lost to Mint," *Marc Hedlund's Blog*, October 1, 2010, at http://blog.precipice.org, accessed on April 14, 2013; "Some Lessons Learned from the Rise and Fall of Wesabe," *Credit Union Journal*, December 16, 2010, at www.cunatechnologycouncil.org, accessed on April 14, 2013. See http://www.cunatechnologycouncil.org/news/4001.html.

23 "Using Intuition in Your Business Plan," *Forbes*, September 20, 2010, pp. 34–36.

24 Jerry Useem, "Boeing vs. Boeing," *Fortune*, October 2, 2000, pp. 148–160; "Airbus Prepares to 'Bet the Company' As It Builds a Huge New Jet," *Wall Street Journal*, November 3, 1999, pp. A1, A10.

25 "Dreamliner Reliability in Doubt After Failures," *USA Today*, January 9, 2013, pp. 1A, 5A.

26 "Accommodating the A380," *Wall Street Journal*, November 29, 2005, B1; "Boeing Roars Ahead," *BusinessWeek*, November 7, 2005, pp. 44–45; "Boeing's New Tailwind," *Newsweek*, December 5, 2005, p. 45; Judith Crown, "Even More Boeing 787 Delays?" *BusinessWeek*, April 4, 2008 (May 27, 2008), at http://www.businessweek.com/bwdaily/dnflash/content/apr2008/db2008043_948354.htm?campaign_id=rss_daily; Aaron Karp, *ATW Daily*

News, April 9, 2008 (May 27, 2008), at http://www.
atwonline.com/news/story.html?storyID=12338;
"Airbus: New Delays for A380 Deliveries," CNNMoney.
com, May 13, 2008 (May 27, 2008), at http://money.
cnn.com/2008/05/13/news/international/airbus_
delay.ap/index.htm?postversion=2008051304; "Airbus
A380 Delays Not Disclosed for Months," MSNBC.com,
May 29, 2007 (May 27, 2008), at http://www.msnbc.
msn.com/id/18918869/.

[27] "Making Decisions in Real Time," *Fortune*, June 26, 2000,
332–334; see also Malcolm Gladwell, *Blink* (New York:
Little, Brown, 2005).

[28] Charles P. Wallace, "Adidas—Back in the Game," *Fortune*,
August 18, 1997, pp. 176–182.

[29] Barry M. Staw and Jerry Ross, "Good Money After Bad,"
Psychology Today, February 1988, pp. 30–33; D. Ramona
Bobocel and John Meyer, "Escalating Commitment to a
Failing Course of Action: Separating the Roles of Choice
and Justification," *Journal of Applied Psychology*, vol. 79,
1994, pp. 360–363.

[30] Gerry McNamara and Philip Bromiley, "Risk and Return
in Organizational Decision Making," *Academy of
Management Journal*, vol. 42, 1999, pp. 330–339.

[31] See Brian O'Reilly, "What It Takes to Start a Startup," *Fortune*,
June 7, 1999, pp. 135–140, for an example.

[32] Caulfield, Brian. "Steve Jobs Bio: Neither Insane Nor Great."
Forbes. Forbes Magazine, October 26, 2011, at http://
www.forbes.com/sites/briancaulfield/2011/10/26/
steve-jobs-bio-neither-insane-nor-great/, accessed on
June 28 2013.

[33] Sherman, Erik. "The Problem with Charismatic Leaders."
Inc.com. May 6, 2013, at http://www.inc.com/erik-
sherman/the-problem-with-charismatic-leaders.html,
accessed on June 28, 2013.

[34] Allen, Frederick E. "Steve Jobs Broke Every Leadership
Rule. Don't Try It Yourself." *Forbes. Forbes Magazine*,
August 27, 2011, at http://www.forbes.com/sites/
frederickallen/2011/08/27/steve-jobs-broke-every-
leadership-rule-dont-try-that-yourself/, accessed on
June 28, 2013.

chapter 10

Human Resource Management and Labor Relations

Strong human resource management is a business'

lifeblood. Putting people first is the

best   strategy

a   firm   can   have.

AFTER READING THIS CHAPTER, YOU SHOULD BE ABLE TO:

OBJECTIVE 1 **Define** *human resource management*, discuss its strategic significance, and explain how managers plan for their organization's human resource needs.

OBJECTIVE 2 **Discuss** the legal context of human resource management and identify contemporary legal issues.

OBJECTIVE 3 **Identify** the steps in staffing a company and discuss ways in which organizations recruit and select new employees.

OBJECTIVE 4 **Describe** the main components of a compensation and benefits system.

OBJECTIVE 5 **Describe** how managers develop the workforce in their organization through training and performance appraisal.

OBJECTIVE 6 **Discuss** workforce diversity, the management of knowledge workers, and the use of a contingent workforce as important changes in the contemporary workplace.

OBJECTIVE 7 **Explain** why workers organize into labor unions and describe the collective bargaining process.

A Unique Partnership
Drives Wegmans

If you're looking for the best Parmesan cheese for your chicken parmigiana recipe, you might try Wegmans, especially if you happen to live in the vicinity of Pittsford, New York. Cheese department manager Carol Kent will be happy to recommend the best brand because her job calls for knowing cheese as well as managing some 20 subordinates. Kent is a knowledgeable employee, and Wegmans sees that as a key asset. Specifically, Wegmans believes that its employees are more knowledgeable than are the employees of its competitors.

Wegmans Food Markets, a family-owned East Coast chain with nearly 80 outlets in six states, prides itself on its commitment to customers, and it shows. It ranks at the top of the latest *Consumer Reports* survey of the best national and regional grocery stores. But commitment to customers is only half of Wegmans' overall strategy, which calls for reaching its customers through its employees. "How do we differentiate ourselves?" asks Wegman, who then proceeds to answer his own question: "If we can sell products that require knowledge in terms of how you use them, that's our strategy. Anything that requires knowledge and service gives us a reason to be." That's the logic behind one of Kent's recent assignments—one which she understandably regards as a perk. Wegmans sent her to Italy to conduct a personal study of Italian cheese. "We sat with the families" that make the cheeses, she recalls, "broke bread with them. It helped me understand that we're not just selling a piece of cheese. We're selling a tradition, a quality."

Kent and the employees in her department also enjoy the best benefits package in the industry, including fully paid health insurance. And that includes part-timers, who make up about two-thirds of the company's workforce of more than 37,000. In part, the strategy of extending benefits to this large segment of the labor force is intended to make sure that stores have enough good workers for crucial peak periods, but there's no denying that the costs of employee-friendly policies can mount up. At 15 to 17 percent of sales, for example, Wegmans' labor costs are well above the 12 percent figure for most supermarkets. But according to one company HR executive, holding down labor costs isn't necessarily a strategic priority: "We would have stopped offering free health insurance [to part-timers] a long time ago," she admits, "if we tried to justify the costs."

Besides, employee turnover at Wegmans is about 6 percent—a mere fraction of an industry average that hovers around 19 percent (and can approach 100 percent for part-timers). And this is an industry in which total turnover costs have

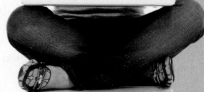

Kurhan/fotolia

what's in it for me?

Do you—or will you in the future—work for someone else as an employee? Do you—or will you in the future—own a business and have employees who work for you? In either case, human resource management is a critical activity for you to understand. Effectively managing human resources is the lifeblood of organizations. A firm that takes this activity seriously and approaches it from a strategic perspective has a much better chance for success than does a firm that simply goes through the motions. By understanding the material in this chapter, you'll be better able to understand (1) the importance of properly managing human resources in a unit or business you own or supervise and (2) why and how your employer provides the working arrangements that most directly affect you.

We start this chapter by explaining how managers plan for their organization's human resource needs. We'll also discuss ways in which organizations select, develop, and appraise employee performance and examine the main components of a compensation system. Along the way, we'll look at some key legal issues involved in hiring, compensating, and managing workers in today's workplace and discuss workforce diversity. Finally, we'll explain why workers organize into labor unions and describe the collective bargaining process. Let's get started with some basic concepts of human resource management.

been known to outstrip total annual profits by 40 percent. Wegmans employees tend to be knowledgeable because about 20 percent of them have been with the company for at least years, and many have logged at least a quarter century. Says one 19-year-old college student who works at an upstate-New York Wegmans while pursuing a career as a high school history teacher, "I love this place. If teaching doesn't work out, I would so totally work at Wegmans." Edward McLaughlin, who directs the Food Industry Management Program at Cornell University, understands this sort of attitude: "When you're a 16-year-old kid, the last thing you want to do is wear a geeky shirt and work for a supermarket," but at Wegmans, he explains, "it's a badge of honor. You're not a geeky cashier. You're part of the social fabric."

Wegmans recently placed third in *Fortune* magazine's annual list of "100 Best Companies to Work For"—good for 15 consecutive years on the list and seven straight top-seven finishes. "It says that we're doing something right," says a company spokesperson, "and that there's no better way to take care of our customers than to be a great place for our employees to work." In addition to its healthcare package, Wegmans has been cited for such perks as fitness center discounts, compressed work weeks, telecommuting, and domestic-partner benefits (which extend to same-sex partners).

Finally, under the company's Employee Scholarship Program, full-time workers can receive up to $2,200 a year for four years and part-timers up to $1,500. Since its inception in 1984, the program has handed out $76 million in scholarships to more than 23,500 employees. Like most Wegman policies, this one combines employee outreach with long-term corporate strategy: "This program has made a real difference in the lives of many young people," says president Colleen Wegman, who adds that it's also "one of the reasons we've been able to attract the best and the brightest to work at Wegmans."

Granted, Wegmans, which has remained in family hands since its founding in 1915, has an advantage in being as generous with its resources as its family of top executives wants to be. It doesn't have to do everything with quarterly profits in mind, and the firm likes to point out that taking care of its employees is a long-standing priority. Profit sharing and fully funded medical coverage were introduced in 1950 by Robert Wegman, son and nephew of brothers Walter and John, who opened the firm's original flagship store in Rochester, New York, in 1930. Why did Robert Wegman make such generous gestures to his employees way back then? "Because," he says simply, "I was no different from them."[1]

The Foundations of Human Resource Management

OBJECTIVE 1
Define
human resource management
and explain how managers plan for their organization's human resource needs.

Human Resource Management (HRM) *set of organizational activities directed at attracting, developing, and maintaining an effective workforce*

Human resource management (HRM) is the set of organizational activities directed at attracting, developing, and maintaining an effective workforce.

The Strategic Importance of HRM

Human resources (HR) are critical for effective organizational functioning. HRM (or "personnel," as it is sometimes called) was once relegated to second-class status in many organizations, but its importance has grown dramatically in the last two decades. Its new importance stems from increased legal complexities, the recognition that HR are a valuable means for improving productivity, and the awareness of the costs associated with poor HRM.[2] For example, Microsoft recently announced that it was laying off 5,000 people in downsized areas of its business. At the same time, though, the firm began developing strategies for hiring highly talented people for jobs related to Internet search, an important growth area for the company.[3] This careful and systematic approach, reducing HR in areas where they are no longer needed and adding new HR to key growth areas, reflects a strategic approach to HRM.

Indeed, managers now realize that the effectiveness of their HR function has a substantial impact on the bottom-line performance of the firm. Poor HR planning can result in spurts of hiring followed by layoffs, which are costly in terms of unemployment compensation payments, training expenses, and morale. Haphazard compensation systems do not attract, keep, and motivate good employees, and outmoded recruitment practices can expose the firm to expensive and embarrassing discrimination lawsuits. Consequently, the chief HR executive of most large businesses is a vice-president directly accountable to the CEO, and many firms are developing strategic HR plans and integrating those plans with other strategic planning activities.[4]

Even organizations with as few as 200 employees usually have a HR manager and a HR department charged with overseeing these activities. Responsibility for HR activities, however, is shared between the HR department and line managers. The HR department may recruit and initially screen candidates, but the final selection is usually made by managers in the department where the new employee will work. Similarly, although the HR department may establish performance appraisal policies and procedures, the actual evaluation and coaching of employees is done by their immediate superiors.

The growing awareness of the strategic significance of HRM has even led to new terminology to reflect a firm's commitment to people. **Human capital** reflects the organization's investment in attracting, retaining, and motivating an effective workforce. Hence, just as the phrase financial capital is an indicator of a firm's financial resources and reserves, so, too, does *human capital* serve as a tangible indicator of the value of the people who comprise an organization.[5]

Human Capital *reflects the organization's investment in attracting, retaining, and motivating an effective workforce*

HR Planning

As you can see in Figure 10.1, the starting point in attracting qualified HR is planning. Specifically, HR planning involves job analysis and forecasting the demand for, and supply of, labor.

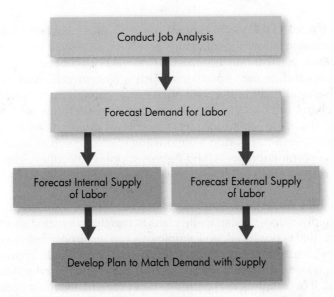

FIGURE 10.1 The HR Planning Process

Job Analysis *systematic analysis of jobs within an organization*

Job Description *description of the duties and responsibilities of a job, its working conditions, and the tools, materials, equipment, and information used to perform it*

Job Specification *description of the skills, abilities, and other credentials and qualifications required by a job*

Job Analysis

Job analysis is a systematic analysis of jobs within an organization; most firms have trained experts who handle these analyses. A job analysis results in two things:

- The **job description** lists the duties and responsibilities of a job; its working conditions; and the tools, materials, equipment, and information used to perform it.

- The **job specification** lists the skills, abilities, and other credentials and qualifications needed to perform the job effectively.

Job analysis information is used in many HRM activities. For instance, knowing about job content and job requirements is necessary to develop appropriate selection methods, create job-relevant performance appraisal systems, and set equitable compensation rates.

Forecasting HR Demand and Supply

After managers comprehend the jobs to be performed within an organization, they can start planning for the organization's future HR needs. The manager starts by assessing trends in past HR usage, future organizational plans, and general economic trends.

Forecasting the supply of labor is really two tasks:

1. Forecasting *internal supply*, the number and type of employees who will be in the firm at some future date.

2. Forecasting *external supply*, the number and type of people who will be available for hiring from the labor market at large.

Replacement Chart *list of each management position, who occupies it, how long that person will likely stay in the job, and who is qualified as a replacement*

REPLACEMENT CHARTS At higher levels of an organization, managers plan for specific people and positions. The technique most commonly used is the **replacement chart**, which lists each important managerial position, who occupies it, how long that person will probably stay in it before moving on, and who is now qualified or soon will be qualified to move into it. (In most firms today, this information is computerized.) This technique allows ample time to plan developmental experiences for people identified as potential successors for critical managerial jobs. Halliburton, for instance, has a detailed replacement system that the firm calls its Executive Succession System (ESS). When a manager has his or her performance reviewed each year, notations are placed in the system about the person's readiness for promotion, potential positions for promotion, and what development activities are needed to prepare the individual for promotion. Other managers throughout the firm can access the system whenever they have vacant positions available.

Employee Information System (Skills Inventory) *computerized system containing information on each employee's education, skills, work experiences, and career aspirations*

SKILLS INVENTORIES To facilitate both planning and identifying people for transfer or promotion, some organizations also have **employee information systems (skills inventories)** that contain information on each employee's education, skills, work experience, and career aspirations. Such a system can quickly locate every employee who is qualified to fill a position. Again, although these systems were once handled with charts and files they are almost always in electronic form today.

Forecasting the external supply of labor is a different problem altogether. Planners must rely on information from outside sources, such as state employment commissions, government reports, and figures supplied by colleges on the numbers of students in major fields.

Matching HR Supply and Demand

After comparing future demand and internal supply, managers can make plans to manage predicted shortfalls or overstaffing. If a shortfall is predicted, new employees can be hired, present employees can be retrained and transferred into understaffed areas, individuals approaching retirement can be convinced to stay on, or labor-saving or productivity-enhancing systems can be installed. If overstaffing is expected to be a problem, the main options are transferring the extra employees, not replacing individuals who quit, encouraging early retirement, and laying off workers. During the 2008 recession, many firms found it necessary to reduce the size of their workforces through layoffs. Others accomplished the same thing by reducing the number of hours their employees worked.

The Legal Context of HRM

A number of laws regulate various aspects of employee–employer relations, especially in the areas of equal employment opportunity, compensation and benefits, labor relations, and occupational safety and health. Several major ones are summarized in Table 10.1.

Equal Employment Opportunity

Title VII of the Civil Rights Act of 1964 forbids discrimination in all areas of the employment relationship, such as hiring, opportunities for advancement, compensation increases, lay-offs, and terminations against members of certain protected classes based on factors such as race, color, gender, religious beliefs, or national origin. The intent of Title VII is to ensure that employment decisions are made on the basis of an individual's qualifications rather than on the basis of personal biases. The law has reduced direct forms of discrimination (refusing to promote African Americans into management, failing to hire men as flight attendants, refusing to hire women as

OBJECTIVE 2
Discuss
the legal context of human resource management and identify contemporary legal issues.

Title VII of the Civil Rights Act of 1964 *forbids discrimination in all areas of the employment relationship*

table 10.1

Equal Employment Opportunity

Title VII of the Civil Rights Act of 1964 (as amended by the Equal Employment Opportunity Act of 1972). Forbids discrimination in all areas of the employment relationship.

Age Discrimination in Employment Act. Outlaws discrimination against people older than 40 years.

Various executive orders, especially Executive Order 11246 in 1965. Requires employers with government contracts to engage in affirmative action.

Pregnancy Discrimination Act. Specifically outlaws discrimination on the basis of pregnancy.

Vietnam Era Veterans Readjustment Assistance Act. Extends affirmative action mandate to military veterans who served during the Vietnam War.

Americans with Disabilities Act. Specifically outlaws discrimination against disabled persons.

Civil Rights Act of 1991. Makes it easier for employees to sue an organization for discrimination but limits punitive damage awards if they win.

Compensation and Benefits

Fair Labor Standards Act. Establishes minimum wage and mandated overtime pay for work in excess of 40 hours per week.

Equal Pay Act of 1963. Requires that men and women be paid the same amount for doing the same job.

Employee Retirement Income Security Act (ERISA) of 1974. Regulates how organizations manage their pension funds.

Family and Medical Leave Act (FMLA) of 1993. Requires employers to provide up to 12 weeks of unpaid leave for family and medical emergencies.

Labor Relations

National Labor Relations Act. Spells out procedures by which employees can establish labor unions and requires organizations to bargain collectively with legally formed unions; also known as the *Wagner Act.*

Labor-Management Relations Act. Limits union power and specifies management rights during a union-organizing campaign; also known as the *Taft-Hartley Act.*

Health and Safety

Occupational Safety and Health Act (OSHA) of 1970. Mandates the provision of safe working conditions.

construction workers) as well as indirect forms of discrimination (using employment tests that Caucasians pass at a higher rate than African Americans do). Note, however, that managers are free to base employment decisions on such job-related factors as qualifications, performance, seniority, and so forth. For example, an organization can certainly hire a male job applicant instead of a female applicant if he is more qualified (i.e., has more education and/or experience related to the job). However, he cannot be hired simply because of his gender.

Employment requirements such as test scores and other qualifications are legally defined as having an **adverse impact** on minorities and women when such individuals meet or pass the requirement at a rate less than 80 percent of the rate of majority group members. Criteria that have an adverse impact on protected groups can be used only when there is solid evidence that they effectively identify individuals who are better able than others to do the job. The **Equal Employment Opportunity Commission (EEOC)** is charged with enforcing Title VII as well as several other employment-related laws.

The **Age Discrimination in Employment Act**, passed in 1967, amended in 1978 and 1986, is an attempt to prevent organizations from discriminating against older workers. In its current form, it outlaws discrimination against people older than 40 years. Both the Age Discrimination in Employment Act and Title VII require passive nondiscrimination, or **equal employment opportunity**. Employers are not required to seek out and hire minorities, but they must treat all who apply fairly.

Several executive orders, however, require that employers holding government contracts engage in **affirmative action**, intentionally seeking and hiring employees from groups that are underrepresented in the organization. These organizations must have a written **affirmative action plan** that spells out employment goals for underused groups and how those goals will be met. These employers are also required to act affirmatively in hiring Vietnam-era veterans (as a result of the Vietnam Era Veterans Readjustment Assistance Act) and qualified handicapped individuals. Finally, the Pregnancy Discrimination Act forbids discrimination against women who are pregnant.

In 1990 Congress passed the **Americans with Disabilities Act**, which forbids discrimination on the basis of disabilities and requires employers to provide reasonable accommodations for disabled employees.

More recently, the **Civil Rights Act of 1991** amended the original Civil Rights Act as well as other related laws by both making it easier to bring discrimination lawsuits (which partially explains the aforementioned backlog of cases) while simultaneously limiting the amount of punitive damages that can be awarded in those lawsuits.

Compensation and Benefits

Laws also regulate compensation and benefits. The **Fair Labor Standards Act**, passed in 1938 and amended frequently since then, sets a minimum wage and requires the payment of overtime rates for work in excess of 40 hours per week. Salaried professional, executive, and administrative employees are exempt from the minimum hourly wage and overtime provisions. The **Equal Pay Act of 1963** requires that men and women be paid the same amount for doing the same job. Attempts to circumvent the law by having different job titles and pay rates for men and women who perform the same work are also illegal. Basing an employee's pay on seniority or performance is legal, however, even if it means that a man and woman are paid different amounts for doing the same job.

The provision of benefits is also regulated in some ways by state and federal laws. Certain benefits are mandatory, such as workers' compensation insurance for employees who are injured on the job. Employers who provide a pension plan for their employees are regulated by the **Employee Retirement Income Security Act (ERISA) of 1974**. The purpose of this act is to help ensure the financial security of pension funds by regulating how they can be invested. The **Family and Medical Leave Act (FMLA) of 1993** requires employers to provide up to 12 weeks of unpaid leave for family and medical emergencies.

Adverse Impact *when minorities and women meet or pass the requirement for a job at a rate less than 80 percent of the rate of majority group members*

Equal Employment Opportunity Commission (EEOC) *federal agency enforcing several discrimination-related laws*

Age Discrimination in Employment Act *outlaws discrimination against people older than 40 years*

Equal Employment Opportunity *legally mandated nondiscrimination in employment on the basis of race, creed, sex, or national origin*

Affirmative Action *intentionally seeking and hiring employees from groups that are underrepresented in the organization*

Affirmative Action Plan *written statement of how the organization intends to actively recruit, hire, and develop members of relevant protected classes*

Americans With Disabilities Act *forbids discrimination on the basis of disabilities and requires employers to provide reasonable accommodations for disabled employees*

Civil Rights Act of 1991 *amended the original Civil Rights Act*

Fair Labor Standards Act *sets a minimum wage and requires the payment of overtime rates for work in excess of 40 hours per week*

Equal Pay Act of 1963 *requires that men and women be paid the same amount for doing the same job*

Employee Retirement Income Security Act (ERISA) of 1974 *ensures the financial security of pension funds by regulating how they can be invested*

Family and Medical Leave Act (FMLA) of 1993 *requires employers to provide up to 12 weeks of unpaid leave for family and medical emergencies*

In the last few years some large employers, most notably Walmart, have come under fire because they do not provide health care for all of their employees. In response to this, the state of Maryland passed a law, informally called the "Walmart bill," that requires employers with more than 10,000 workers to spend at least 8 percent of their payrolls on health care or else pay a comparable amount into a general fund for uninsured workers. Walmart appealed this rule and the case is still pending; meanwhile, several other states are considering the passage of similar laws.[6]

Labor Relations

Union activities and management's behavior toward unions constitute another heavily regulated area. The **National Labor Relations Act** (also known as the) **Wagner Act**, passed in 1935, sets up a procedure for employees to vote on whether to have a union. If they vote for a union, management is required to bargain collectively with the union. The **National Labor Relations Board (NLRB)** was established by the Wagner Act to enforce its provisions. Following a series of severe strikes in 1946, the **Labor-Management Relations Act** (also known as the **Taft-Hartley Act)** was passed in 1947 to limit union power. The law increases management's rights during an organizing campaign. The Taft-Hartley Act also contains the National Emergency Strike provision, which allows the president of the United States to prevent or end a strike that endangers national security. Taken together, these laws balance union and management power. Employees can be represented by a legally created and managed union, but the business can make nonemployee-related business decisions without interference.

National Labor Relations Act *(also known as the Wagner Act) sets up a procedure for employees to vote on whether to have a union*

National Labor Relations Board (NLRB) *established by the Wagner Act to enforce its provisions*

Labor-Management Relations Act *(also known as the Taft-Hartley Act) passed to limit union power*

Health and Safety

The **Occupational Safety and Health Act (OSHA) of 1970** directly mandates the provision of safe working conditions. It requires that employers (1) provide a place of employment that is free from hazards that may cause death or serious physical harm and (2) obey the safety and health standards established by the Department of Labor. Safety standards are intended to prevent accidents, whereas occupational health standards are concerned with preventing occupational disease. For example, standards limit the concentration of cotton dust in the air because this contaminant has been associated with lung disease in textile workers. The standards are enforced by OSHA inspections, which are conducted when an employee files a complaint of unsafe conditions or when a serious accident occurs.

Occupational Safety and Health Act (OSHA) of 1970 *federal law setting and enforcing guidelines for protecting workers from unsafe conditions and potential health hazards in the workplace*

Spot inspections of plants in especially hazardous industries such as mining and chemicals are also made. Employers who fail to meet OSHA standards may be fined. A Miami-based company, Lead Enterprises Inc., was cited by OSHA as knowingly failing to protect employees from lead exposure despite knowing the potential hazards (brain damage, kidney disease, and reproductive system damage). The company, which produces various lead products, including fish tackles and lead diving weights, was cited for 32 safety and health violations after multiple inspections and fined more than $307,000 in penalties.[7] More recently, a massive explosion at a fertilizer plant in the town of West, Texas, in 2013 may have been partially caused by unsafe work practices. Moreover, preliminary evidence suggested that OSHA inspectors had also missed some warning signs of a potential disaster at the plant.

Other Legal Issues

In addition to these established areas of HR legal regulation, several emerging legal issues will likely become more important in the future. These include employee safety and health, various emerging areas of discrimination law, employee rights, and employment at will.

AIDS in the Workplace   Although AIDS is considered a disability under the Americans with Disabilities Act of 1990, the AIDS situation itself is severe enough that it warrants special attention. Employers cannot legally require an HIV test or

any other medical examination as a condition for making an offer of employment. Organizations must accommodate or make a good-faith effort to accommodate individuals with HIV, maintain the confidentiality of all medical records, and try to educate coworkers about AIDS.

Sexual Harassment *making unwelcome sexual advances in the workplace*

Sexual Harassment

Sexual harassment is defined by the EEOC as unwelcome sexual advances in the work environment. If the conduct is indeed unwelcome and occurs with sufficient frequency to create an abusive work environment, the employer is responsible for changing the environment by warning, reprimanding, or firing the harasser.[8] The courts have defined two types of sexual harassment:

Quid Pro Quo Harassment *form of sexual harassment in which sexual favors are requested in return for job-related benefits*

1   In cases of **quid pro quo harassment**, the harasser offers to exchange something of value for sexual favors. A male supervisor, for example, might tell or suggest to a female subordinate that he will recommend her for promotion or give her a raise in exchange for sexual favors.

Hostile Work Environment *form of sexual harassment deriving from off-color jokes, lewd comments, and so forth*

2   The creation of a **hostile work environment** is a subtler form of sexual harassment. A group of male employees who continually make off-color jokes and lewd comments and perhaps decorate the work environment with inappropriate photographs may create a hostile work environment for a female colleague, who may become uncomfortable working in that environment.

In recent years, the concept of harassment has been expanded to encompass unwelcome or inappropriate behaviors regarding ethnicity, religion, and age.

Employment at Will *principle, increasingly modified by legislation and judicial decision, that organizations should be able to retain or dismiss employees at their discretion*

Employment at Will

The concept of **employment at will** holds that both employer and employee have the mutual right to terminate an employment relationship at any time for any reason, with or without advance notice to the other. Over the last two decades, however, terminated employees have challenged the employment-at-will doctrine by filing lawsuits against former employers on the grounds of wrongful discharge.

In the last several years, such suits have put limits on employment-at-will provisions in certain circumstances. In the past, for example, organizations were guilty of firing employees who filed workers' compensation claims or took "excessive" time off to serve on jury duty. More recently, however, the courts have ruled that employees may not be fired for exercising rights protected by law.

Patriot Act *legislation that increased U.S. government's power to investigate and prosecute suspected terrorists*

The Patriot Act

In response to the terrorist attacks of September 11, 2001, the U.S. government passed legislation that increases its powers to investigate and prosecute suspected terrorists. This legislation, known as the **Patriot Act**, has several key implications for HRM. For instance, certain "restricted" individuals (including ex-convicts and aliens from countries deemed by the State Department to have "repeatedly provided support for acts of international terrorism") are ineligible to work with potentially dangerous biological agents. More controversial are sections granting government investigators access to previously confidential personal and financial records.

OBJECTIVE 3
Identify
the steps in staffing a company and discuss ways in which organizations recruit and select new employees.

Staffing the Organization

When managers have determined that new employees are needed and understand the legal context in which they operate, they must then turn their attention to recruiting and hiring the right mix of people. This involves two processes: (1) acquiring new employees from outside the company and (2) promoting current employees from within. Both external and internal staffing, however, start with effective *recruiting*.

Recruiting HR

Recruiting *process of attracting qualified persons to apply for jobs an organization is seeking to fill*

Recruiting is the process of attracting qualified persons to apply for the jobs that are open.

Internal Recruiting Internal recruiting means considering present employees as candidates for openings. Promotion from within can help build morale and keep high-quality employees from leaving. For higher-level positions, a skills inventory system may be used to identify internal candidates, or managers may be asked to recommend individuals to be considered.

Internal Recruiting *considering present employees as candidates for openings*

External Recruiting External recruiting involves attracting people outside the organization to apply for jobs. External recruiting methods include posting jobs on the company website or other job sites, such as Monster.com; holding campus interviews for potential college recruits; using employment agencies or executive search firms to scout out potential talent; seeking referrals by present employees; advertising in print publications; and hiring "walk-ins" (unsolicited applicants).

External Recruiting *attracting persons outside the organization to apply for jobs*

The organization must also keep in mind that recruiting decisions often go both ways—the organization is recruiting an employee, but the prospective employee is also selecting a job.[9] For instance, when unemployment is low (meaning there are fewer people seeking work), businesses may have to work harder to attract new employees. But when unemployment is higher (meaning there are more people looking for work), organizations may find it easier to recruit prospective employees without having to resort to expensive hiring incentives. But even if a firm can take its pick of the best potential employees, it still should put its best foot forward, treat all applicants with dignity, and strive for a good person–job fit. Hiring the wrong employee can cost the company about half of a low-skilled worker's annual wages or three to five times upper-level employees' annual wages. Therefore, hiring the "wrong" employee for $40,000 per year could cost the company at least $20,000. These costs stem from training, counseling, low productivity, termination, and recruiting and hiring a replacement.

One generally successful method for facilitating a good person–job fit is the so-called **realistic job preview (RJP)**. As the term suggests, the RJP involves providing the applicant with a real picture of what performing the job that the organization is trying to fill would be like.[10] For example, it would not make sense for a firm to tell an applicant that the job is exciting and challenging when in fact it is routine and straightforward, yet some managers do this to hire the best people. The likely outcome will be a dissatisfied employee who will quickly be looking for a better job. If the company is more realistic about a job, though, the person hired will be more likely to remain in the job for a longer period of time.

Realistic Job Preview (RJP) *providing the applicant with a real picture of what performing the job that the organization is trying to fill would be like*

Selecting HR

Once the recruiting process has attracted a pool of applicants, the next step is to select someone to hire. The intent of the selection process is to gather from applicants the information that will predict job success and then to hire the candidates likely to be most successful.

Application Forms The first step in selection is usually asking the candidate to fill out an application. An application form is an efficient method of gathering information about the applicant's previous work history, educational background, and other job-related demographic data. Application forms are seldom used for upper-level jobs; candidates for such positions usually provide the same information on their résumé. Most applications for larger firms are now prepared electronically and submitted at the firm's website.

Tests Employers sometimes ask candidates to take tests during the selection process. Tests of ability, skill, aptitude, or knowledge relevant to a particular job are usually the best predictors of job success, although tests of general intelligence or personality are occasionally useful as well. Some companies use a test of the "big five" personality dimensions discussed in Chapter 8 (or other personality measures) to predict success.

24 Hour Shifts?

Dock Strike in Hong Kong

Hong Kong Labor Relations

On average, dock workers in Hong Kong earn around US$2,300 per month. Many of them are outsourced, contract workers whose salaries have not increased in nearly a decade. This is against a backdrop of rising housing and living costs in Hong Kong. Most of the contract workers are indirectly employed by Li Ka-shing, thought to be the richest man in Asia.

The dock workers, seeking a pay increase of around 20 percent have been seen by many to be representative of some of the problems in labor relations in Hong Kong. There is extreme poverty rubbing shoulders with phenomenal growth and riches.

Under local laws, there is very little protection for the workers, but for Hong Kong International Terminals (HIT), owned by Hutchinson Whampoa, the strike is deeply embarrassing. The massive conglomerate, owned by Li, is active in a broad range of different business sectors from retail to telecoms and from property to port services. The issue for Hutchinson Whampoa was that to accede to the demands of the dock workers would set a precedent that could see other wage demands across their other operations. On the other hand, adopting a strong and uncompromising stance would be a public relations disaster.

Across the globe, corporations are under pressure to show that they are ethical and understanding employers. Even international brands like Apple have failed to convince consumers that complying with local labor laws is sufficient. Apple's share price took a fall when they were accused of being less than ethical in managing the working conditions of employees in Chinese factories where their products are manufactured. This is despite the fact that the workers in these factories were not directly employed by Apple.

Dock workers are amongst the worst paid employees in Hong Kong. The cost of living in Hong Kong has soared over the

leeyiutung/Fotolia

past decade, yet dock workers pay has only seen single digit percentage growth over the same period. Food prices alone are growing at a rate of at least 4 percent year-on-year in Hong Kong. The unique position of Hong Kong has produced a difficult set of circumstances. Whilst the economy is comparatively free to develop and expand, it relies on the value of the dollar. This is compared to the gradual increase in value of the Chinese Yuan. Given the fact that Hong Kong has to import some 90 percent of its food from the Chinese mainland, it is unsurprising that food prices are on the increase.

The economic difficulties have already been noted and commented upon by the Chinese Politburo Standing Committee. The key appears to be the lack of competition in Hong Kong which has allowed corporations such as Hutchinson to have such enormous power.

Lack of competition means higher prices for the consumer, but at the same time allows the dominant corporations to hold down wages. The fact that the Hong Kong dollar is pegged to

Interviews *Interviews* are a popular selection device, although they are actually often a poor predictor of job success. For example, biases inherent in the way people perceive and judge others on first meeting affect subsequent evaluations. Interview validity can be improved by training interviewers to be aware of potential biases and by tightening the structure of the interview. In a structured interview, questions are written in advance, and all interviewers follow the same question list with each candidate. Structured interviews tend to be used for jobs that are relatively routine, such as some administrative assistant positions, data entry jobs, and college admissions processing positions. For interviewing managerial or professional candidates, a somewhat less structured approach can be used. Although question areas and information-gathering objectives are still planned in advance, specific questions

the US dollar at such a poor rate (still set at the same rate as thirty years ago) has not helped.

After initially demanding 20 percent, the dock workers, after 40 days of strikes, accepted 9.8 percent. The situation has become critical, not only for the workers and Hutchinson, but for Hong Kong itself. Between 80–90,000 containers had been backed up at the docks. With Hong Kong being the third biggest container port in the region (after Shanghai and Singapore), the danger was that it would fall further behind its competitors. Some analysts even suggested that shippers might consider a permanent move away from Hong Kong if it appeared that the strikes would continue or flare up again in the future.

Both Hutchinson and the dock workers claimed victory in the dispute. Hutchinson pledged to ensure that the port operations were returned to normality as quickly as possible. The dock workers union was content that pay and conditions had been improved.

During the strike, the workers had set up a protest camp outside the headquarters of Li Ka-shing, the Cheung Kong Center in Hong Kong. One of the main points of contention was the fact that the outsourced workers were earning significantly less than HIT's own workers. It was the fact that HIT still retained some dock workers directly on their pay roll that allowed the port to stay partially operational during the strike.

As far as Hong Kong is concerned, Hutchinson's ownership of HIT is highly significant as they operate 16 of the 24 deep water berths in the port and this accounts for 70 percent of the shipping handling. Despite this, the strike cost Hutchinson an estimated US$100 million in revenue but, more importantly in the longer term, Shenzhen in China proved to be a viable alternative as a shipping hub.

Part of the problem in quickly resolving the dispute was the fact that the outsourced dock workers had to negotiate indirectly with Hutchinson. Clearly, agreements were in place between Hutchinson and the two main labor contractors, Global Stevedoring Service Co. and Everbest Port Services. Very quickly, the two companies expressed concern over the 20 percent pay increase demand by stating that they simply could not afford the increase.

Global Stevedoring Service Co. were even more blunt on the matter. They employed around 200 of the 450 workers that were on strike. Simply, they could not continue operations with around 75 percent of their employees on strike. They initially offered 7 percent, but this was rejected. It was a desperate situation for the company as their contract with HIT was due to expire at the end of June 2013. At that point, with the contract possibly terminated with HIT, there would be no jobs at all.

With the strike costing HIT an estimated US$645,000 per day, the onus was on them to seek a resolution, hence the compromise of 9.8 percent. Aside from the monetary losses, HIT also suffered a considerable blow to its corporate image. Analysts suggested that the negative coverage would harm its ability to gain a foothold in other ports overseas.

In the end, the dispute is generally seen as having a lose-lose outcome. On the one hand, the industrial action was successful to an extent and the general public were made more acutely aware of the issues facing contract workers in Hong Kong. On the other hand, it proved that unions in Hong Kong were not about to risk their own members' livelihoods for the sake of other workers. The Confederation of Trade Unions were critical of two dockers' unions whose members, working directly for HIT, continued to operate the ports at around 80 percent capacity throughout the course of the dispute.

As for the contractors working for Global Stevedoring Services Co., around 130 employees permanently lost their jobs when the company closed down at the end of April 2013. It remains to be seen whether other contractors will offer jobs to the former Global employees.[11]

vary with the candidates' backgrounds. Sometimes, companies are looking for especially creative employees and may try to learn more about the individual's creativity during an interview.

Other Techniques Organizations also use other selection techniques that vary with circumstances. Polygraph tests, once popular, are declining in popularity. On the other hand, organizations occasionally require applicants to take physical exams (being careful that their practices are consistent with the Americans with Disabilities Act). More organizations are using drug tests, especially in situations in which drug-related performance problems could create serious safety hazards. For example, potential employees who may be handling hazardous chemicals or medical waste or engaging in public transportation activities like driving busses are likely to be drug-tested. Some organizations also run credit checks on prospective employees. Reference checks with previous employers are also used, but they have been shown to have limited value because individuals are likely to only provide the names of references that will give them positive recommendations. Even worse, some applicants literally make up references.[12]

OBJECTIVE 4
Describe
the main components of a compensation and benefits system.

Compensation System *total package of rewards that organizations provide to individuals in return for their labor*

Compensation and Benefits

People who work for a business expect to be paid, and most workers today also expect certain benefits from their employers. Indeed, a major factor in retaining skilled workers is a company's **compensation system**, the total package of rewards that it offers employees in return for their labor. Finding the right combination of compensation elements is always complicated by the need to make employees feel valued, while holding down company costs.

Wages and Salaries

Wages and salaries are the dollar amounts paid to employees for their labor. **Wages** are paid for time worked. For example, if your job pays you $10 an hour, that is your wage. A **salary**, on the other hand, is paid for performing a job. A salaried executive earning $100,000 per year is paid to achieve results even if that means working 5 hours one day and 15 the next. Salaries are usually expressed as an amount paid per month or year.

In setting wage and salary levels, a company may start by looking at its competitors. Firms must also decide how their internal wage and salary levels will compare for different jobs. Although two employees may do exactly the same job, the employee with more experience may earn more.

The recession of 2008–2011 prompted some firms to reduce the wages and salaries they were paying to lower costs. For example, Hewlett-Packard reduced the salaries of all but its top performers by amounts ranging from 2.5 to 20 percent. CareerBuilder.com reduced all employee pay but also began giving all employees Friday afternoons off.

Incentive Programs

Studies have shown that beyond a certain point, more money will not produce better performance. Money motivates employees only if it is tied directly to performance. The most common method of establishing this link is the use of **incentive programs**, special pay programs designed to motivate high performance. Some programs are available to individuals, whereas others are distributed on a companywide basis.

A sales bonus is a typical incentive. Employees receive a **bonus**, special payments above their salaries, when they sell a certain number or certain dollar amount of goods for the year. Employees who fail to reach this goal earn no bonuses. **Merit salary systems** link pay raises to performance levels in nonsales jobs.

Executives commonly receive stock options as incentives. Halliburton CEO David Lesar, for example, can buy several thousand shares of company stock each year at a predetermined price. If his managerial talent leads to higher profits and stock prices, he can buy the stock at a price lower than the market value for which, in theory, he is largely responsible. He is then free to sell the stock at market price, keeping the profits for himself.

A newer incentive plan is called **pay for performance** (or **variable pay**). In essence, middle managers are rewarded for especially productive output with earnings that significantly exceed the cost of bonuses. The number of variable pay programs in the

United States has been growing consistently for the last decade, and most experts predict that they will continue to grow in popularity. Many firms say that variable pay is a better motivator than merit raises because the range between generous and mediocre merit raises is usually quite small.

Companywide Incentives Some incentive programs apply to all the employees in a firm. Under **profit-sharing plans**, for example, profits earned above a certain level are distributed to employees. Also, **gainsharing plans** distribute bonuses to employees when a company's costs are reduced through greater work efficiency. **Pay-for-knowledge plans** pay workers to learn new skills and to become proficient at different jobs.

Profit-Sharing Plan *incentive plan for distributing bonuses to employees when company profits rise above a certain level*

Gainsharing Plan *incentive plan that rewards groups for productivity improvements*

Pay-for-Knowledge Plan *incentive plan to encourage employees to learn new skills or become proficient at different jobs*

Benefits Programs

Benefits, compensation other than wages and salaries and other incentives offered by a firm to its workers, account for an increasing percentage of most compensation budgets. Most companies are required by law to pay tax for Social Security retirement benefits and provide **workers' compensation insurance**, insurance for compensating workers injured on the job. Most businesses also provide health, life, and disability insurance for their workers, as well as paid time off for vacations and holidays. Many also allow employees to use payroll deductions to buy stock at discounted prices. Counseling services for employees with alcohol, drug, or emotional problems are also becoming more common, as are on-site child-care centers. Some companies even provide reduced membership fees at gyms and health clubs, as well as insurance or other protection for identity theft.[13]

Benefits *compensation other than wages and salaries*

Workers' Compensation Insurance *legally required insurance for compensating workers injured on the job*

Retirement Plans Retirement plans (or pension plans) constitute another important—and sometimes controversial—benefit that is available to many employees. Most company-sponsored retirement plans are set up to pay pensions to workers when they retire. In some cases, the company contributes all the money to the pension fund. In others, contributions are made by both the company and employees. In recent years, some companies have run into problems because they have not set aside enough money to cover the retirement funds they have agreed to provide. Both FedEx and Goodyear, for instance, recently announced that they were freezing their pension programs to transition workers to riskier 401(k)s, in which payroll deductions are invested in stocks and other non-guaranteed funds.[14] This trend increased during the 2008–2011 recession. For example, 16 major U.S. employers stopped contributing to employee retirement accounts, and several more followed suit in 2010. Among these were Anheuser-Busch, Wells-Fargo, General Motors, AT&T, General Electric, and Saks.

Containing the Costs of Benefits As the range of benefits has increased, so has concern about containing the costs of these benefits. Many companies are experimenting with cost-cutting plans while still attracting and retaining valuable employees. One approach is the **cafeteria benefits plan**. A certain dollar amount of benefits per employee is set aside so that each employee can choose from a variety of alternatives.

cafeteria benefits plan *benefit plan that sets limits on benefits per employee, each of whom may choose from a variety of alternative benefits*

Another area of increasing concern is healthcare costs. Medical expenses have increased insurance premiums, which have increased the cost to employers of maintaining benefits plans. Many employers are looking for new ways to cut those costs. One increasingly popular approach is for organizations to create their own networks of healthcare providers. These providers agree to charge lower fees for services rendered to employees of member organizations. In return, they enjoy established relationships with large employers and, thus, more clients and patients. Insurers also charge less to cover the employees of network members because they make lower reimbursement payments.

entrepreneurship and new ventures

Whole Benefits?

Whole Foods Market (WFM) has 350 stores and 54,000 employees in North America and Great Britain, making it the leading natural and organic foods supermarket (and ninth-largest food and drug chain in the United States). Along the way, it's also gained a considerable reputation as a socially responsible company and a good place to work. WFM's motto is "Whole Foods, Whole People, Whole Planet," and its guiding "core value," according to co-CEO Walter Robb, is "customers first, then team members, balanced with what's good for other stakeholders....If I put our mission in simple terms," Robb continues, "it would be, No. 1, to change the way the world eats and, No. 2, to create a workplace based on love and respect."

WFM made *Fortune* magazine's first list of the "100 Best Companies to Work For" in 1998 and is one of 13 organizations to have made it every year since. Several writers have noted the company's growth (which means more jobs), salary-cap limits (the top earner gets no more than 19 times the average full-time salary), and generous health plan. However, the health plan has recently attracted a lot of attention for WFM—some of it bad. The structure of the company's healthcare program, which revolves around high deductibles and so-called *health savings accounts (HSAs)*, was first proposed in 2003. Under such a plan, an employee (a "team member," in WFM parlance) pays a deductible before his or her expenses are covered. Meanwhile, the employer funds a special account (an HSA) for each employee, who can spend the money to cover health-related expenditures. The previous WFM plan had covered 100 percent of all expenses, and when some employees complained about the proposed change, the company decided to put it to a vote. Nearly 90 percent of the workforce went to the polls, with 77 percent voting for the new plan. In 2006, employees voted to retain the plan, which now carries a deductible of around $1,300; HSAs may go as high as $1,800 (and accrue for future use). The company pays 100 percent of the premiums for eligible employees (about 89 percent of the workforce).

High-deductible plans save money for the employer (the higher the deductible, the lower the premium), and more importantly—at least according to founder and co-CEO John Mackey—they also make employees more responsible consumers. When the first $1,300 of their medical expenses comes out of their own pockets (or their own HSAs), he argues, people "start asking how much things cost. Or they get a bill and say, 'Wow, that's expensive.' They begin to ask questions. They may not want to go to the emergency room if they wake up with a hangnail in the middle of the night. They may schedule an appointment now."

But consumer advocates and HR specialists have attacked Mackey's policies. "High-deductible plans for low-wage workers," says Judy Dugan, research director of Consumer Watchdog,

Helen Sessions/Alamy

"are the next best thing to being uninsured: The upfront costs are so high that workers have to weigh getting health care against paying the rent (to the detriment of their health)." A former WFM executive points out, for example, that the firm's plan entails "astronomical deductibles and co-pays." The $1,300 deductible, he explains, "means that you, minimum-wage-earning worker, must pay $1,300 of your own money before you get any coverage applied for medical services. After that, for in-network visits, the rate is 20/80, up to a maximum of $4,600 out of pocket for the year. This means that if you get charged $10,000 for a special hospital test...you are still liable for...$2,000!"

As for the HSA, it has to cover all co-pays and all expenses not covered by the plan (such as mental health care). "There's way more going on here than 'health insurance,'" concludes the anonymous former exec. "...[The] system has massive hidden charges that routinely threaten and undermine the financial stability and, ultimately, [the] well-being of the employees."[15]

Developing the Workforce

OBJECTIVE 5
Describe
how managers develop the
workforce in their organization
through training and performance
appraisal.

After a company has hired new employees, it must acquaint them with the firm and their new jobs. Managers also take steps to train and develop employees and to further develop necessary job skills. In addition, every firm has some system for performance appraisal and feedback.

Training and Development

In HRM, **training** usually refers to teaching operational or technical employees how to do the job for which they were hired. **Development** refers to teaching managers and professionals the skills needed for both present and future jobs.[16] Most organizations provide regular training and development programs for managers and employees. For example, IBM spends more than $700 million annually on programs and has a vice-president in charge of employee education. U.S. businesses spend more than $50 billion annually on training and development programs away from the workplace (in 2010 the figure was $52.8 billion).[17] And this figure does not include wages and benefits paid to employees while they are participating in such programs.

Training *usually refers to teaching operational or technical employees how to do the job for which they were hired*

Development *usually refers to teaching managers and professionals the skills needed for both present and future jobs*

Assessing Training Needs The first step in developing a training plan is to determine what needs exist. For example, if employees do not know how to operate the machinery necessary to do their job, a training program on how to operate the machinery is clearly needed. On the other hand, when a group of office workers is performing poorly, training may not be the answer. The problem could be motivation, aging equipment, poor supervision, inefficient work design, or a deficiency of skills and knowledge. Only the last could be remedied by training. As training programs are being developed, the manager should set specific and measurable goals specifying what participants are to learn. Managers should also plan to evaluate the training program after employees complete it.

Common Training Methods Many different training and development methods are available. Selection of methods depends on many considerations, but perhaps the most important is training content. When the training content is factual material (such as company rules or explanations of how to fill out forms), assigned reading, programmed learning, and lecture methods work well. When the content is interpersonal relations or group decision making, however, firms must use a method that allows interpersonal contact, such as role-playing or case discussion groups. When employees must learn a physical skill, methods allowing practice and the actual use of tools and materials are needed, as in **on-the-job training** or **vestibule training**. (Vestibule training enables participants to focus on safety, learning, and feedback rather than on productivity.)

On-the-Job Training *training, sometimes informal, conducted while an employee is at work*

Vestibule Training *off-the-job training conducted in a simulated environment*

Web-based and other electronic media-based training are becoming popular. Such methods allow a mix of training content, are relatively easy to update and revise, let participants use a variable schedule, and lower travel costs.[18] On the other hand, they are limited in their capacity to simulate real activities and facilitate face-to-face interaction. Xerox, Massachusetts Mutual Life Insurance, and Ford have all reported tremendous success with these methods. In addition, most training programs actually rely on a mix of methods. Boeing, for example, sends managers to an intensive two-week training seminar involving tests, simulations, role-playing exercises, and flight simulation exercises.[19]

Finally, some larger businesses have started creating their own self-contained training facility, often called a *corporate university*. McDonald's was among the first to start this practice with its so-called Hamburger University in Illinois. All management trainees for the firm attend training programs there to learn exactly how long to grill a burger, how to maintain good customer service, and so on. The cult hamburger chain In-N-Out Burger also has a similar training venue it calls In-N-Out University. Other firms that use this approach include Shell Oil and General Electric.[20]

Evaluation of Training Training and development programs should always be evaluated. Typical evaluation approaches include measuring one or more relevant criteria (such as attitudes or performance) before and after the training, and determining whether the criteria changed. Evaluation measures collected at the end of training are easy to get, but actual performance measures collected when the trainee is on the job are more important. Trainees may say that they enjoyed the training and learned a lot, but the true test is whether their job performance improves after their training

Performance Appraisal

Performance Appraisal *evaluation of an employee's job performance to determine the degree to which the employee is performing effectively*

Once employees are trained and settled into their jobs, one of management's next concerns is performance appraisal.[21] **Performance appraisal** is a formal assessment of how well employees are doing their jobs. Employees' performance should be evaluated regularly for many reasons. One reason is that performance appraisal may be necessary for validating selection devices or assessing the impact of training programs. A second, administrative reason is to aid in making decisions about pay raises, promotions, and training. Still another reason is to provide feedback to employees to help them improve their present performance and plan their future careers.[22]

Because performance evaluations often help determine wages and promotions, they must be fair and nondiscriminatory. In the case of appraisals, managers use content validation to show that the appraisal system accurately measures performance on important job elements and does not measure traits or behavior that are irrelevant to job performance.

Common Appraisal Methods Two basic categories of appraisal methods commonly used in organizations are objective methods and judgmental methods. Objective measures of performance include actual output (number of units produced), scrap rate, dollar volume of sales, and number of claims processed. Objective performance measures may be contaminated by "opportunity bias" if some persons have a better chance to perform than others. For example, a sales representative selling snow blowers in Michigan has a greater opportunity than does a colleague selling the same product in Alabama. Fortunately, adjusting raw performance figures for the effect of opportunity bias and thereby arriving at figures that accurately represent each individual's performance is often possible.

Judgmental methods, including ranking and rating techniques, are the most common way to measure performance. Ranking compares employees directly with one another and orders them from best to worst. Ranking has a number of drawbacks. Ranking is difficult for large groups because the individuals in the middle of the distribution may be hard to distinguish from one another accurately. Comparisons of people in different work groups are also difficult. For example, an employee ranked third in a strong group may be more valuable than an employee ranked first in a weak group. Another criticism of ranking is that the manager must rank people on the basis of overall performance, even though each person likely has both strengths and weaknesses. Furthermore, rankings do not provide useful information for feedback. To be told that one is ranked third is not nearly as helpful as to be told that the quality of one's work is outstanding, its quantity is satisfactory, one's punctuality could use improvement, or one's paperwork is seriously deficient.

Rating differs from ranking in that it compares each employee with a fixed standard rather than with other employees. A rating scale provides the standard. Figure 10.2 gives examples of three graphic rating scales for a bank teller. Each consists of a performance dimension to be rated (punctuality, congeniality, and accuracy) followed by a scale on which to make the rating. In constructing graphic rating scales, performance dimensions that are relevant to job performance must be selected. In particular, they should focus on job behaviors and results rather than on personality traits or attitudes.

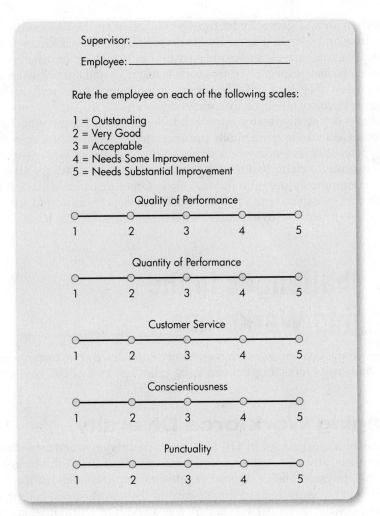

FIGURE 10.2 Sample Performance Evaluation Form

Errors in Performance Appraisal Errors or biases can occur in any kind of rating or ranking system.[23] One common problem is *recency error*, the tendency to base judgments on the subordinate's most recent performance because it is most easily recalled. Often a rating or ranking is intended to evaluate performance over an entire time period, such as six months or a year, so the recency error does introduce error into the judgment. Other errors include overuse of one part of the scale—being too lenient, being too severe, or giving everyone a rating of "average."

Halo error is allowing the assessment of an employee on one dimension to "spread" to ratings of that employee on other dimensions. For instance, if an employee is outstanding on quality of output, a rater might tend to give her or him higher marks than deserved on other dimensions. Errors can also occur because of race, sex, or age discrimination, intentionally or unintentionally. The best way to offset these errors is to ensure that a valid rating system is developed at the outset and then to train managers in how to use it.

One interesting innovation in performance appraisal used in some organizations today is called **360-degree feedback**, in which managers are evaluated by everyone around them—their boss, their peers, and their subordinates. Such a complete and thorough approach provides people with a far richer array of information about their performance than does a conventional appraisal given by just the boss. Of course, such a system also takes considerable time and must be handled so as not to breed fear and mistrust in the workplace.[24]

360-Degree Feedback *performance appraisal technique in which managers are evaluated by everyone around them—their boss, their peers, and their subordinates*

Performance Feedback The last step in most performance appraisal systems is giving feedback to subordinates about their performance. This is usually done in a private meeting between the person being evaluated and his or her boss.

The discussion should generally be focused on the facts: the assessed level of performance, how and why that assessment was made, and how it can be improved in the future. Feedback interviews are not easy to conduct. Many managers are uncomfortable with the task, especially if feedback is negative and subordinates are disappointed by what they hear. Properly training managers, however, can help them conduct more effective feedback interviews.[25]

Some firms use an aggressive approach to terminating people who do not meet expectations. General Electric actually implemented a system whereby each year the bottom 10 percent of its workforce is terminated and replaced with new employees. Company executives claim that this approach, although stressful for all employees, helps it to continuously upgrade its workforce. Other firms have started using this same approach. However, both Ford and Goodyear recently agreed to abandon similar approaches in response to age discrimination lawsuits.[26]

New Challenges in the Changing Workplace

OBJECTIVE 6

Discuss
workforce diversity, the management of knowledge workers, and the use of a contingent workforce as important changes in the contemporary workplace.

workforce diversity *the range of workers' attitudes, values, beliefs, and behaviors that differ by gender, race, age, ethnicity, physical ability, and other relevant characteristics*

In addition to the challenges we have already considered, HR managers face several new challenges reflecting the changing economic and social environments of business.

Managing Workforce Diversity

One extremely important set of HR challenges centers on **workforce diversity**, the range of workers' attitudes, values, beliefs, and behaviors that differ by gender, race, age, ethnicity, physical ability, and other relevant characteristics. In the past, organizations tended to work toward homogenizing their workforces, getting everyone to think and behave in similar ways. Partly as a result of affirmative action efforts, however, many U.S. organizations are now creating more diverse workforces than ever before.

Figure 10.3 projects the racial and ethnic composition of the U.S. workforce through 2050. The picture is clearly one of increasing diversity. The number of Caucasian Americans as a percentage of the total workforce is declining steadily, offset by increases in every other racial group. Most striking are the growing numbers of people of Hispanic origin (who may be members of any racial group). By 2050 the U.S. Department of Labor estimates that nearly a quarter of the workforce will be Hispanic.

Today, organizations are recognizing that diversity can be a competitive advantage. For example, by hiring the best people available from every single group rather than hiring from just one or a few groups, a firm can develop a higher-quality labor force. Similarly, a diverse workforce can bring a wider array of information to bear on problems and can provide insights on marketing products to a wider range of consumers.

Managing Knowledge Workers

Knowledge Workers *employees who are of value because of the knowledge they possess*

Traditionally, employees added value to organizations because of what they did or because of their experience. In the information age, however, employees who add value because of what they know are usually called **knowledge workers**. Knowledge workers, which include computer scientists, engineers, physical scientists, and game developers, typically require extensive and highly specialized training. Once they are on the job, retraining and training updates are critical to prevent their skills from becoming obsolete. It has been suggested, for example, that the half-life of a technical education in engineering is about three years.

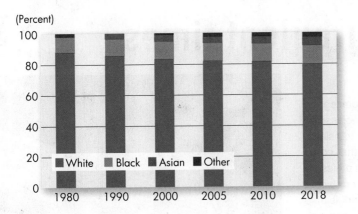

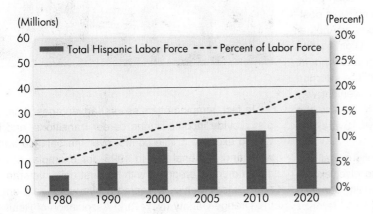

FIGURE 10.3 Distribution of the labor force by race 1990–2050
Source: http://www.dol.gov/asp/media/reports/workforce2007/ADW2007_
Full_Text.pdf (p. 38). U.S. Department of Labor, "America's Dynamic
Workforce," (August 2007), p. 38, at http://www.dol.gov/asp/media/reports/
workforce2007/ADW2007_Full_Text.pdf.

A firm's failure to update the skills of its knowledge workers will not only result in the loss of competitive advantage, it will also increase the likelihood that those workers will go to other firms that are more committed to updating their skills. Hence, HR managers must ensure that the proper training is prepared to enable knowledge workers to stay current while also making sure they are compensated at market rates.

A major part of this challenge is recruiting new knowledge workers on a regular basis. Given both the high demand for knowledge workers and their relative short supply, firms often resort to extreme measures to recruit the best-and-brightest. For example, Google, Facebook, and Zynga often compete head-to-head for programmers and software engineers. To help recruit knowledge workers, these firms offer such lavish perks as free massages, laundry services, gourmet meals and snacks, and premium coffee.[27]

Contingent and Temporary Workers

A final contemporary HR issue of note involves the growing use of contingent and temporary workers. Many employers use contingent and temporary workers to increase their flexibility and, in most cases, lower their costs.

Trends in Contingent and Temporary Employment A **contingent worker** is a person who works for an organization on something other than a permanent or full-time basis. Categories of contingent workers include independent contractors, on-call workers, temporary employees (usually hired through outside agencies), and contract and leased employees. Another category is part-time

contingent worker *employee hired on something other than a full-time basis to supplement an organization's permanent workforce*

managing in turbulent times

Temp or Perm?

A little more than 10 years ago New Yorker Diana Bloom logged on to Craigslist, an online network that posts free classified ads, and offered her services as a tutor, editor, and translator. She's been making a living on the short-term jobs that come her way from the website ever since. A former English professor who couldn't find secure long-term employment, Bloom works out of her home to take care of a young son. Temp work is also appealing, she says, because "I'm not very outgoing, and getting my foot in the door to companies would have been hard." Craigslist works in the other direction, too, with employers posting openings for jobs both permanent and temporary. Another New Yorker, Simone Sneed, scours the Craigslist "Gigs" section for jobs that last for perhaps a day, often for just a few hours. Whether as a backup singer or a grants writer, she's turned the strategy of patching together "gigs" into a convenient way to supplement the income from her full-time job. "I'll use the extra money to pay off my school loan," she says. "Every little bit helps."

In the current economic climate, unfortunately, overall job postings are down on Craigslist and everywhere else, except for short-term jobs, which usually include no health benefits, sick days, or paid vacations. If you're employed short term or part-time for economic reasons (probably because you got laid off), the Bureau of Labor Statistics (BLS) classifies you as "underemployed." Naturally, most people who are "underemployed" are, by definition, "overqualified." In fact, they often have years of professional experience but are willing to take jobs that don't call for their levels of training or experience.

Interestingly, for a lot of people, the adjustment to current labor-market conditions isn't necessarily as traumatic as you might think. A recent survey conducted by the temporary staffing agency Kelly Services found that as many as 26 percent of employed American adults regard themselves as "free agents" when it comes to the type of job that they're willing to take (up from 19 percent in 2006). Of all those polled, only 10 percent said that they're doing temporary work because they've been laid off from permanent jobs; 90 percent said that they're doing it because they like the variety and flexibility that temping afford them.

Mark Richardson/Alamy

In fact, temping offers several advantages. It can, for example, provide income during career transitions, and it's a good way to exercise a little control over the balance between your work and personal life. In 1995, for example, when she was seven months pregnant with her first child, veteran retail manager Stacey Schick accepted a two-week data entry job with the Orange County (New York) Association of Realtors. "I didn't know how to turn on a computer," she remembers, but "they needed bodies." Now the mother of two, Schick is still with the Association as its education coordinator. "I would never have considered it," she says, if a job in her field had come up, but the job she landed in has turned out to be a much better fit with her lifestyle: "It's afforded me the opportunity to have a family and be able to have time with them."

The path taken by Schick is called "temp-to-perm," and it offers employers several advantages as well. Companies that are hesitant to make commitments to untested employees can "try before they buy"; they get a chance to see employees in action before finalizing hiring decisions. Because there are no fees to pay when an employee goes from temp to perm, trying out temps is also cheaper than paying an agency outright to find a hire. The big savings, of course, come from benefits, which can amount to one-third of the total cost of compensating a permanent position.[28]

workers. In recent years there has been an explosion in the use of such workers by organizations. For instance, in 2010 about 12 percent of employed U.S. workers fell into one of these categories, up from 10 percent in 2008.

Managing Contingent and Temporary Workers One key to managing contingent workers effectively is careful planning and analysis. Rather than having to call in workers sporadically, and with no prior notice, organizations try to bring in specified numbers of workers for well-defined periods of time. For instance, most retailers hire temporary seasonal employees for the Christmas holiday shopping period. Based on their past experience, they generally know how many people they need to hire and when they need to hire them. Firms should also be able to document the labor-cost savings of using contingent workers.

A second key is recognizing what can and cannot be achieved by using contingent and temporary workers. For instance, these workers may lack the firm-specific knowledge to perform as effectively as a permanent employee would perform. They are also less committed to the organization and less likely to engage in organizational citizenship behaviors.

Finally, managers must make decisions about how to integrate contingent workers into the organization. These decisions may be as simple as whether to invite contingent workers to the holiday party, or they may be more complicated, such as whether to grant contingent workers access to such employee benefits as counseling services and child care.

Dealing with Organized Labor

A **labor union** is a group of individuals working together to achieve shared job-related goals, such as higher pay, shorter working hours, more job security, greater benefits, or better working conditions. **Labor relations** refers to the process of dealing with employees who are represented by a union.

Unionism Today

In the years immediately following World War II and continuing through the mid-1960s, most unions routinely won certification elections. In recent years, however, labor unions have been winning certification about half the time.[29] As a result, although millions of workers still belong to unions, union membership as a percentage of the total workforce has steadily declined. In 2007, only 12.1 percent of U.S. workers belonged to a labor union, down from 20.1 percent in 1983, when the U.S. Department of Labor first began compiling data.[30] As the recession of 2008–2011 began to increase fears about unemployment and wage cuts, union membership began to increase again, albeit only slightly. By 2010 it had dropped again, falling below prerecession levels. These trends are shown in Figure 10.4.

OBJECTIVE 7
Explain
why workers organize into labor unions and describe the collective bargaining process.

Labor Union *group of individuals working together to achieve shared job-related goals, such as higher pay, shorter working hours, more job security, greater benefits, or better working conditions*

Labor Relations *process of dealing with employees who are represented by a union*

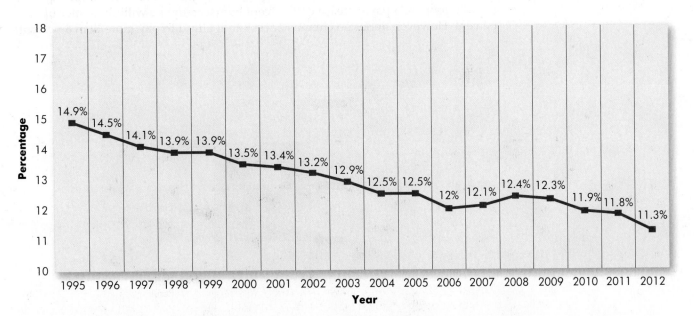

FIGURE 10.4 Percentage of Workers Who Belong to Unions: 1995–2010
Sources: U.S. Department of Labor, Bureau of Labor Statistics, www.aflcio.org/joinaunion/why/uniondifference/uniondiff11.cfm.

The Future of Unions Even though several of its members withdrew from the parent organization in 2005, the American Federation of Labor and Congress of Industrial Organizations (AFL-CIO), as well as independent major unions such as the Teamsters and the National Education Association (NEA), still play a major role in U.S. business. Unions in the traditional strongholds of goods-producing industries continue to wield considerable power as well. The United Auto Workers (UAW) was for decades one of the largest unions in the United States. But it, too, seems to be entering a period of decline. The traumas experienced by the U.S. auto industry in 2008–2009, for instance, required the UAW to make many major concessions to help Ford, DaimlerChrysler, and General Motors survive. In addition, auto plant closures will dramatically reduce the number of auto jobs in the years to come.

Another issue affecting the future of unionism is the geographic shift in the U.S. economy. For the most part, unionism in the United States started in the north and midwest regions and in cities such as Detroit, Pittsburgh, Cleveland, St. Louis, and Chicago. But over the past several decades there has been a pronounced shift as businesses have moved their operations to the south and southwest, areas that do not have a strong union heritage. For instance, Nucor Steel, profiled in Finding a Better Way, locates its facilities in smaller communities in the southern United States in part because it knows these workers are not prone to unionization.

Collective Bargaining

The power of unions comes from collective action, forcing management to listen to the demands of all workers rather than to just the few who speak out. **Collective bargaining** is the process by which labor and management negotiate conditions of employment for union-represented workers and draft a labor contract.

Collective Bargaining process by which labor and management negotiate conditions of employment for union-represented workers

Reaching Agreement on Contract Terms The collective bargaining process begins when the union is recognized as the exclusive negotiator for its members and union leaders meet with management representatives to agree on a contract. By law, both parties must sit down at the bargaining table and negotiate in good faith. Figure 10.5 shows what is called the "bargaining zone." For instance, in theory, employers want to pay as little as possible; they will generally pay more than the minimum, but there is also some upper limit beyond which they will not pay. Likewise, unions want the highest pay possible but expect to get less. But they too have a limit beyond which they will not go.

For example, suppose the bargaining issue is pay increases. The employer may initially propose a pay increase of 2 percent but (secretly) be willing to offer up to 6 percent. However, under no circumstances can it afford to pay more than 8 percent.

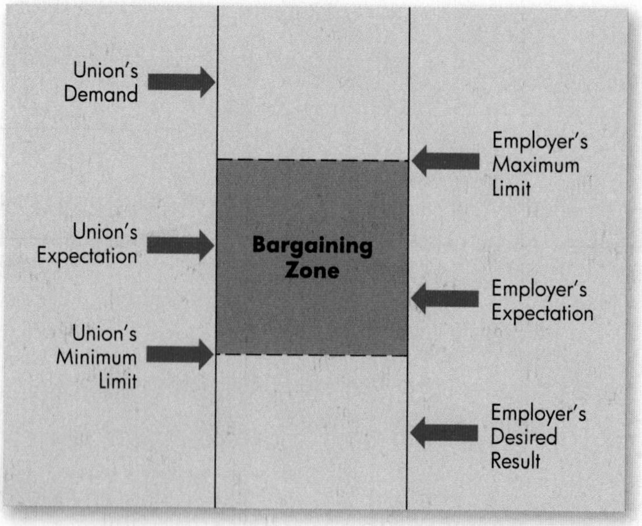

FIGURE 10.5 The Bargaining Zone

The union, meanwhile, may initially demand a 10 percent increase but (secretly) be willing to accept as little as 4 percent. Assuming each party negotiates in good faith and is willing to make concessions to the other, the real bargaining zone falls between the union minimum (4 percent) and the employer maximum (6 percent). The real outcome will then depend on such things as other items being negotiated and the skills of the respective negotiators.

Sometimes, this process goes quite smoothly. At other times, the two sides cannot agree. For instance, the preceding example should result in an agreement because the union minimum and the employer maximum provide a bargaining zone. But if the union demands no less than 8 percent and the employer is unwilling to give more than a 4 percent increase, there is no bargaining zone. Resolving the impasse depends in part on the nature of the contract issues, the willingness of each side to use certain tactics, such as strikes, and the prospects for mediation or arbitration.

Contract Issues The labor contract itself can address an array of different issues. Issues that are typically most important to union negotiators include *compensation*, *benefits*, and *job security*. Certain management rights, such as control over hiring policies and work assignments, are also negotiated in most bargaining agreements. Other possible issues might include such specific details as working hours, overtime policies, rest period arrangements, differential pay plans for shift employees, the use of temporary workers, grievance procedures, and allowable union activities (dues collection, union bulletin boards, and so forth).

COMPENSATION Compensation includes both current and future wages. One common tool for securing wage increases is a **cost-of-living adjustment (COLA)**. Most COLA clauses tie future raises to the *Consumer Price Index (CPI)*, a government statistic that reflects changes in consumer purchasing power. Almost half of all labor contracts today include COLA clauses.

Cost-of-Living Adjustment (COLA) *labor contract clause tying future raises to changes in consumer purchasing power*

A union might be uncomfortable with a long-term contract based solely on COLA wage increases. One solution is a **wage reopener clause**, which allows wage rates to be renegotiated at preset times during the life of the contract.

Wage Reopener Clause *clause allowing wage rates to be renegotiated during the life of a labor contract*

BENEFITS Employee benefits are also an important component in most labor contracts. Unions typically want employers to pay all or most of the costs of insurance for employees. Other benefits commonly addressed during negotiations include retirement benefits, paid holidays, and working conditions. Because of surging healthcare costs, employee health insurance premiums have become a major point of contention in recent years. For example, many employees have much larger co-pays today when they visit their doctor than was the case a few years ago. (A *co-pay* is the dollar amount a patient pays to the doctor; insurance then pays the remainder.)

JOB SECURITY Job security also remains an important agenda item in many bargaining sessions today. In some cases, a contract may dictate that if the workforce is reduced, seniority will be used to determine which employees keep their jobs. Unions are setting their sights on preserving jobs for workers in the United States in the face of business efforts to outsource production in some sectors to countries where labor costs are cheaper. For example, the AFL-CIO has been an outspoken opponent of efforts to normalize trade relations with China, fearing that more businesses might be tempted to move jobs there to take advantage of lower wage levels.

When Bargaining Fails An impasse occurs when, after a series of bargaining sessions, management and labor have failed to agree on a new contract or a contract to replace an agreement that is about to expire. Although it is generally agreed that both parties suffer when an impasse is reached and some action by one part against the other is taken, each side can use several tactics to support its cause until the impasse is resolved.

UNION TACTICS Historically, one of the most common union tactics has been the **strike**, which occurs when employees temporarily walk off the job and refuse to

Strike *labor action in which employees temporarily walk off the job and refuse to work*

work. The number of major strikes in the United States has steadily declined over the past few decades. From 1960 to 1980, for example, an average of 281 strikes occurred per year. In the 1980s there was an average of 83 major strikes per year; in the 1990s this figure fell to an average of 35 per year. Between 2000 and 2009 there was an average of 20 major strikes per year.[31] There were 19 major strikes in 2012.[32]

To support a strike, a union faced with an impasse has recourse to additional legal activities:

Picketing *labor action in which workers publicize their grievances at the entrance to an employer's facility*

Boycott *labor action in which workers refuse to buy the products of a targeted employer*

Work Slowdown *labor action in which workers perform jobs at a slower than normal pace*

- In **picketing**, workers march at the entrance to the employer's facility with signs explaining their reasons for striking.

- A **boycott** occurs when union members agree not to buy the products of a targeted employer. Workers may also urge consumers to boycott the firm's products.

- Another alternative to striking is a **work slowdown**. Instead of striking, workers perform their jobs at a much slower pace than normal. A variation is the *sickout*, during which large numbers of workers call in sick.

MANAGEMENT TACTICS   Like workers, management can respond forcefully to an impasse with the following:

Lockout *management tactic whereby workers are denied access to the employer's workplace*

- **Lockouts** occur when employers deny employees access to the workplace. Lockouts are illegal if they are used as offensive weapons to give management a bargaining advantage. However, they are legal if management has a legitimate business need (for instance, avoiding a buildup of perishable inventory). When the National Football League failed to reach a new contract agreement with its player's union in 2011, the league owners imposed a lockout until an agreement was reached. More recently, the Toronto Zoo locked out its employees in 2013 over a labor dispute, as did the St. Paul Chamber Orchestra.[33]

Strikebreaker *worker hired as a permanent or temporary replacement for a striking employee*

- A firm can also hire temporary or permanent replacements called **strikebreakers**. However, the law forbids the permanent replacement of workers who strike because of unfair practices. In some cases, an employer can obtain legal injunctions that either prohibit workers from striking or prohibit a union from interfering with its efforts to use replacement workers.

Mediation and Arbitration   Rather than wield these often unpleasant weapons against one another, labor and management can agree to call in a third party to help resolve the dispute:

Mediation *method of resolving a labor dispute in which a third party suggests, but does not impose, a settlement*

Arbitration *method of resolving a labor dispute in which both parties agree to submit to the judgment of a neutral party*

In **mediation**, the neutral third party (the mediator) can suggest, but cannot impose, a settlement on the other parties.

In **arbitration**, the neutral third party (the arbitrator) dictates a settlement between the two sides, which have agreed to submit to outside judgment. In some disputes, such as those between the government and public employees, arbitration is compulsory, or required by law.

Managing an organization's HR is both a complex and an important undertaking. Most businesses can buy the same equipment and use the same technology as their competitors. But differences in employee talent and motivation are not easily copied. Consequently, most well-managed companies today recognize the value provided by their employees and strive to ensure that the HR function is managed as efficiently and effectively as possible.

summary of learning objectives

OBJECTIVE 1

Define *human resource management* and explain how managers plan for their organization's human resource needs. (pp. 338–341)

Human resource management (HRM) is the set of organizational activities directed at attracting, developing, and maintaining an effective workforce. Human resources (HR) are critical for effective organizational functioning. HRM was once relegated to second-class status in many organizations, but its importance has grown dramatically in the last two decades. Its new importance stems from increased legal complexities, the recognition that HR are a valuable means for improving productivity, and the awareness today of the costs associated with poor HRM. *Human capital* reflects the organization's investment in attracting, retaining, and motivating an effective workforce. Hence, just as the phrase financial capital is an indicator of a firm's financial resources and reserves, so, too, does human capital serve as a tangible indicator of the value of the people who comprise an organization.

Job analysis is a systematic analysis of jobs within an organization resulting in two things: a *job description* and a *job specification*. A job description lists the duties and responsibilities of a job, whereas a job specification identifies the skills, abilities, and qualifications needed to perform the job. Managers must plan for future HR needs by assessing past trends, future plans, and general economic trends. Forecasting labor supply is really two tasks: (1) *forecasting internal supply* and (2) *forecasting external supply*. To analyze internal supply, HR managers often develop *employee information systems* (or skills inventories). The next step in HR planning is matching HR supply and demand.

OBJECTIVE 2

Discuss the legal context of human resource management and identify contemporary legal issues. (pp. 341–344)

A number of laws regulate various aspects of employee–employer relations, especially in the areas of equal employment opportunity, compensation and benefits, labor relations, and occupational safety and health. *Title VII of the Civil Rights Act of 1964* forbids discrimination in all areas of the employment relationship such as hiring, opportunities for advancement, compensation increases, lay-offs, and terminations against members of certain protected classes based on factors such as race, color, gender, religious beliefs, or national origin. In addition to enforcing rules against overt discrimination, the *Equal Employment Opportunity Commission (EEOC)* is also charged with evaluating employment requirements that have *adverse impact*. Several other laws have expanded the scope of anti-discrimination law. The *Age Discrimination in Employment Act*, passed in 1967, amended in 1978, and amended again in 1986, is an attempt to prevent organizations from discriminating against older workers. The Pregnancy Discrimination Act forbids discrimination against women who are pregnant. The *Americans with Disabilities Act* forbids discrimination on the basis of disabilities and requires employers to provide reasonable accommodations for disabled employees. The *Civil Rights Act of 1991* amended the original Civil Rights Act as well as other related laws by both making it easier to bring discrimination lawsuits (which partially explains the aforementioned backlog of cases) while simultaneously limiting the amount of punitive damages that can be awarded in those lawsuits.

Affirmative action was created through executive order and requires government contractors to make proactive attempts to recruit, hire, and promote employees from groups that are underrepresented in the organization

The *Fair Labor Standards Act*, passed in 1938 and amended frequently since then, sets a minimum wage and requires the payment of overtime rates for work in excess of 40 hours per week. The *Equal Pay Act of 1963* requires that men and women be paid the same amount for doing the same job. Employers who provide a pension plan for their employees are regulated by the *Employee Retirement Income Security Act (ERISA) of 1974*. The *Family and Medical Leave Act (FMLA) of 1993* requires employers to provide up to 12 weeks of unpaid leave for family and medical emergencies.

The *National Labor Relations Act* (also known as the Wagner Act), passed in 1935, sets up a procedure for employees to vote on whether to have a union. The *Labor-Management Relations Act* (also known as the Taft-Hartley Act) was passed in 1947 to limit union power. Taken together, these laws balance union and management power. Employees can be represented by a legally created and managed union, but the business can make nonemployee-related business decisions without interference.

The *Occupational Safety and Health Act (OSHA) of 1970* directly mandates the provision of safe working conditions. Under the Americans with Disabilities Act of 1990, AIDS is considered a disability and employers cannot require an HIV test or any other medical examination as a condition of employment. Sexual harassment, both quid pro quo harassment and hostile work environment, is forbidden under antidiscrimination law, as well.

In general, employees work under the legal concept of *employment at will*, which gives both the employee and the employer the right to terminate an employment relationship at any time. However, this concept has been tested in the courts and limited in scope by a variety of legislative provisions.

OBJECTIVE 3

Identify the steps in staffing a company and discuss ways in which organizations recruit and select new employees. (pp. 344–348)

Staffing an organization means recruiting and hiring the right mix of people. *Recruiting* is the process of attracting qualified persons to apply for open jobs, either from within the organization or from outside the organization. To help prospective employees understand the job, some employers offer a *realistic job preview (RJP)*.

The next step is the *selection process*, gathering information that will predict applicants' job success and then hiring candidates. Common selection techniques include application forms; tests of ability, aptitude, or knowledge; and interviews.

OBJECTIVE 4

Describe the main components of a compensation and benefits system. (pp. 348–350)

A company's compensation system is the financial rewards given by the organization to its employees in exchange for their work. *Wages* are the hourly compensation paid to operating employees. *Salary* refers to compensation paid for total contributions, as opposed to pay based on hours worked. A good compensation system can help attract qualified applicants, retain present employees, and stimulate high performance at a cost reasonable for one's industry and geographic area.

Companies may also try to link compensation to performance through *incentive programs*. Individual incentive programs include *bonuses, merit salary systems*, and *variable pay*. Companywide incentives include *profit-sharing, gainsharing*, and *pay-for-knowledge plans*.

Benefits are things of value other than wages that the organization provides to its workers. Most employers are required to pay into Social Security on behalf of employees and to maintain workers compensation insurance, protecting employees injured on the job. Many companies also provide health, life, and disability insurance. Other types of benefits include employee stock ownership plans, counseling services, on-site child care, and reduced fee memberships at gyms and health clubs. Many companies provide retirement plans for their employees, although many are funded entirely by employee contributions. Companies that offer *cafeteria benefit plans* set aside a certain dollar amount per employee for benefits, allowing the employee to select the benefits most important to their individual situation.

OBJECTIVE 5

Describe how managers develop the workforce in their organization through training and performance appraisal. (pp. 351–354)

In HRM, *training* usually refers to teaching operational or technical employees how to do the job for which they were hired. *Development* refers to teaching managers and professionals the skills needed for both present and future jobs. Most organizations provide regular training and development programs for managers and employees. The first step in developing a training plan is to determine what needs exist. Many different training and development methods are available—assigned reading, programmed learning, lecture, role-playing, case discussion groups, on-the-job training, vestibule training, web-based training, and other electronic media-based training. Training and development programs should always be evaluated for effectiveness.

Once employees are trained and settled into their jobs, one of management's next concerns is performance appraisal. *Performance appraisal* is a formal assessment of how well employees are doing their jobs. Because performance evaluations often help determine wages and promotions, they must be fair and nondiscriminatory. Two basic categories of appraisal methods commonly used in organizations are objective methods and judgmental methods. Objective measures of performance include actual output (number of units produced), scrap rate, dollar volume of sales, and number of claims processed. Judgmental methods, including ranking and rating techniques, are the most common way to measure performance. Ranking compares employees directly with one another and orders them from best to worst. Rating differs from ranking in that it compares each employee with a fixed standard rather than with other employees, with a rating scale providing the standard. Errors or biases can occur in any kind of rating or ranking system. One common problem is recency error—the tendency to base judgments on the subordinate's most recent performance because it is most easily recalled. Halo error is allowing the assessment of an employee on one dimension to "spread" to ratings of that employee on other dimensions. The last step in most performance appraisal systems is giving feedback to subordinates about their performance, usually done in a private meeting between the person being evaluated and his or her boss.

OBJECTIVE 6

Discuss workforce diversity, the management of knowledge workers, and the use of a contingent workforce as important changes in the contemporary workplace. (pp. 354–357)

Workforce diversity refers to the range of workers' attitudes, values, beliefs, and behaviors that differ by gender, race, age, ethnicity, physical ability, and other relevant characteristics. In the past, organizations tended to work toward homogenizing their workforces; however, today, many organizations are realizing that diversity can be a competitive advantage.

Employees who add value because of what they know are usually called *knowledge workers*, and managing them skillfully helps to determine which firms will be successful in the future. *Contingent workers*, including independent contractors, on-call workers, temporary employees, contract and leased employees, and part-time employees, work for organizations on something other than a permanent or full-time basis. Organizations must understand when it is appropriate to use contingent workers and how to integrate them into the organization.

OBJECTIVE 7

Explain why workers organize into labor unions and describe the collective bargaining process. (pp. 357–360)

Labor relations is the process of dealing with employees who are represented by a union. A *labor union* is a group of individuals working together to achieve shared job-related goals, such as higher pay, shorter working hours, more job security, greater benefits, or better working conditions. At one time, almost a third of the entire U.S. labor force belonged to a labor union, with the largest membership following World War II into the mid-1960s. Union membership fell from 20.1 percent of the workforce in 1983 to only 12.1 percent of the workforce in 2007.

The intent of *collective bargaining* is to agree on a labor contract between management and the union that is satisfactory to both parties. The contract contains agreements about such issues as wages, work hours, job security, promotion, layoffs, discipline, benefits, methods of allocating overtime, vacations, rest periods, and the grievance procedure. Sometimes, the process of collective bargaining goes quite smoothly and management and the union agree to the terms of a new contract. However, when bargaining fails, the union has the option to go on *strike*, *picket* the organization, organize a *boycott*, or implement a *work slowdown*. Management has options as well; they may *lockout* employees until an agreement has been reached or hire *strikebreakers*. Rather than wielding these weapons, labor and management can agree to call in a third party, either a *mediator* or *arbitrator*, to help resolve the dispute.

key terms

360-degree feedback (p. 353)
adverse impact (p. 342)
affirmative action (p. 342)
affirmative action plan (p. 342)
Age Discrimination in Employment Act (p. 342)
Americans with Disabilities Act (p. 342)
arbitration (p. 360)
benefits (p. 349)
bonus (p. 348)
boycott (p. 360)
cafeteria benefits plan (p. 349)
Civil Rights Act of 1991 (p. 342)
collective bargaining (p. 358)
compensation system (p. 348)
contingent worker (p. 355)
cost-of-living adjustment (COLA) (p. 359)
development (p. 351)
employee information system (skills inventory) (p. 340)
employment at will (p. 344)
Employment Retirement Income Security Act (ERISA) of 1974 (p. 342)
equal employment opportunity (p. 342)
Equal Employment Opportunity Commission (EEOC) (p. 342)
Equal Pay Act of 1963 (p. 342)

external recruiting (p. 345)
Fair Labor Standards Act (p. 342)
Family and Medical Leave Act (FMLA) of 1993 (p. 342)
gainsharing plan (p. 349)
hostile work environment (p. 344)
human capital (p. 339)
human resource management (HRM) (p. 338)
incentive program (p. 348)
internal recruiting (p. 345)
job analysis (p. 340)
job description (p. 340)
job specification (p. 340)
knowledge workers (p. 354)
labor relations (p. 357)
labor union (p. 357)
Labor-Management Relations Act (Taft-Hartley Act) (p. 343)
lockout (p. 360)
mediation (p. 360)
merit salary system (p. 348)
National Labor Relations Act (Wagner Act) (p. 343)
National Labor Relations Board (NLRB) (p. 343)

Occupational Safety and Health Act (OSHA) of 1970 (p. 343)
on-the-job training (p. 351)
Patriot Act (p. 344)
pay for performance (or variable pay) (p. 348)
pay-for-knowledge plan (p. 349)
performance appraisal (p. 352)
picketing (p. 360)
profit-sharing plan (p. 349)
quid pro quo harassment (p. 344)
realistic job preview (RJP) (p. 345)
recruiting (p. 344)
replacement chart (p. 340)
salary (p. 348)
sexual harassment (p. 344)
strike (p. 359)
strikebreaker (p. 360)
Title VII of the Civil Rights Act of 1964 (p. 341)
training (p. 351)
vestibule training (p. 351)
wage reopener clause (p. 359)
wages (p. 348)
work slowdown (p. 360)
workers' compensation insurance (p. 349)
workforce diversity (p. 354)

MyBizLab

Go to **pearsonglobaleditions.com/mybizlab** to complete the problems marked with this icon ✪.

questions & exercises

QUESTIONS FOR REVIEW

10-1. What are the advantages and disadvantages of internal and external recruiting? Under what circumstances is each more appropriate?

10-2. Why is the formal training of workers so important to most employers? Why don't employers simply let people learn about their jobs as they perform them?

✪ **10-3.** What different forms of compensation do firms typically use to attract and keep productive workers?

10-4. What is a knowledge worker? What strategies do companies use to retain knowledge workers?

QUESTIONS FOR ANALYSIS

✪ **10-5.** What are your views on drug testing in the workplace? What would you do if your employer asked you to submit to a drug test?

10-6. Workers at Ford, GM, and Chrysler are represented by the UAW. However, the UAW has been much less successful in its attempts to unionize U.S. workers employed at Toyota, Nissan, and Honda plants in the United States. Why do you think this is so?

10-7. What are the advantages and challenges of having a diverse workforce?

⭐ **10-8.** How much will benefit considerations affect your choice of an employer after graduation?

APPLICATION EXERCISES

10-9. Go online and search for at least three companies that are considered great places to work. Describe the compensation, benefits, and perks at each of these companies. Of the three, which is most appealing to you and why?

10-10. Interview the HR manager at a local company about their hiring processes. Describe how they recruit employees to apply for jobs, the steps in the selection process, and their orientation program for new employees.

building a business: continuing team exercise

Assignment

Meet with your team members to consider your new business venture and how it relates to the concepts of HRM discussed in this chapter. Develop specific responses to the following:

10-11. As your new venture grows, you will need to hire employees. How will you recruit people to apply for jobs within your organization?

10-12. Ideally, you will be able to select from many applicants for jobs within your company. How will you select the best employee from the pool of applicants?

10-13. How will employees be compensated in your company? How do you think that this compensation system will reflect your company's mission and goals?

10-14. What types of benefits will you offer to employees? Understanding the high cost of benefits, how have you selected these benefits?

10-15. Describe your system for performance appraisal and training. How will you reward good employees? When you have weak employees, how will you change their behavior?

building your business skills

STARTING FROM SCRATCH

Goal

To help you understand job analysis and the process of recruiting and selecting employees.

Background Information

You are an employee at growing home improvement contractor. The company has recently moved to a new office space, complete with a showroom highlighting some of the company's work. There are 15 employees working primarily in the office including the company president, the sales staff, and the accounting department. The company has decided that they need to hire a receptionist to greet prospective customers, as well as to assist in social networking and other marketing activities.

Method

Form a group of three to five "co-workers" from your office to form a hiring committee. The charge for your committee will be to complete the process of job analysis, creating a job description and job specification for the receptionist position. Because this is a completely new position, you are starting from scratch.

As a group, develop a job description that will clearly explain what the person is expected to do in this new position. Be as specific as possible. Once this is complete, your group must agree on a job specification—the qualifications that are required to be successful in the job.

FOLLOW-UP QUESTIONS

10-16. What was the most difficult part of developing a job description? Do you feel that you needed any additional information?

10-17. When developing the job specification, how did your group determine the education and experience necessary for the job?

10-18. Once your job specification is complete, you can advertise the position. Be specific about how you will recruit people to apply for this position.

10-19. Because this is an entry-level position, it is likely that you will receive a high number of applications. How will you screen the applications and decide who to interview? What knowledge, skills, or abilities will be most important in the person that you hire?

exercising your ethics

OPERATING TACTICALLY

The Situation

Assume that you work as a manager for a medium-sized, non-union company that is facing its most serious union-organizing campaign in years. Your boss, who is determined to keep the union out, has just given you a list of things to do to thwart the efforts of the organizers. For example, he has suggested each of the following tactics:

• Whenever you learn about a scheduled union meeting, you should schedule a "worker appreciation" event at the same time. He wants you to offer free pizza and to give cash prizes, which winners have to be present to receive.

- He wants you to look at the most recent performance evaluations of the key union organizers and to terminate the one with the lowest overall evaluation based on the "need to lower costs."
- He wants you to make an announcement that the firm is seriously considering such new benefits as on-site child care, flexible work schedules, telecommuting options, and exercise facilities. Although you know that the firm is indeed looking into these benefits, you also know that, ultimately, your boss will provide far less lavish benefits than he wants you to suggest.

The Dilemma

When you questioned the ethics—and even the legality—of these tactics, your boss responded by saying, "Look, all's fair in love and war, and this is war." He went on to explain that he was seriously concerned that a union victory might actually shut down the company's domestic operations altogether, forcing it to move all of its production capacities to lower-cost foreign plants. He concluded by saying that he was really looking out for the employees, even if he had to play hardball to help them. You easily see through his hypocrisy, but you also recognize some potential truth in his warning: If the union wins, jobs may actually be lost.

QUESTIONS TO ADDRESS

10-20. What are the ethical issues in this situation?

10-21. What are the basic arguments for and against extreme measures to fight unionization efforts?

10-22. What do you think most managers would do in this situation? What would you do?

team exercise

HANDLING THE LAYOFFS

The Situation

The CEO of a moderate-sized company is developing a plan for laying off some members of the company workforce. He wants each manager to rank his or her employees according to the order in which they should be laid off, from first to last.

The Dilemma

One manager has just asked for help. He is new to his position and has little experience to draw from. The members of the manager's team are as follows:

- Tony Jones: white male, 10 years with the company; average performer who reportedly drinks a lot after work
- Amanda Wiggens: white female; ambitious; 3 years with company; above-average performer; puts in extra time at work; is known to be abrasive when dealing with others
- Jorge Gonzalez: Latino, 20 years with the company; average performer; was laid off before but then called back when business picked up
- Dorothy Henderson: white female, 25 years with company, below-average performer, has filed five sexual harassment complaints in last 10 years
- Wanda Jackson: African American female, 8 years with company; outstanding performer; is rumored to be looking for another job

- Jerry Loudder: white male, single parent, 5 years with company; average performer
- Martha Strawser: white female, 6 years with company; excellent performer but spotty attendance, is putting husband through college

Team Activity

Assemble a group of four students. Your group has agreed to provide the manager with a suggested rank ordering of the manager's employees.

ACTION STEPS

10-23. Working individually, prepare this list, ranking the manager's employees according to the order in which they should be laid off, from first to last.

10-24. As a group, discuss the underlying legal and ethical issues in this situation.

10-25. Finally, develop a group recommendation about the order in which employees should be laid off.

10-26. Now that you have decided which employees to layoff, develop a set of recommendations about layoffs should be handled. Be sure to consider how to communicate your decision to the employees being laid off as well as those who remain.

cases

A Unique Partnership Drives Wegmans

Continued from page 338

Continued from page 338

At the beginning of this chapter you read about Wegmans and its approach to human resource management. Using the information presented in this chapter you should now be able to respond to these questions.

QUESTIONS FOR DISCUSSION

10-27. If you were an HR executive at Wegmans, would you focus more on *internal recruiting* or on *external recruiting*? Would your strategy for higher-level positions differ from your strategy for lower-level positions? How would current economic conditions influence your strategy?

10-28. As an HR executive at Wegmans, you need to hire a group of new employees as part of your management-trainee program—people who will be put on a track leading, ultimately, to positions as store managers. Briefly outline your program for developing these employees.

10-29. If you were an employee at Wegmans, how would you expect your annual performance appraisal to be conducted? Given the company's customer-relations strategy, which appraisal methods do you think would be most appropriate?

Food for Thought

If you've visited a grocery store recently, it's unlikely that you walked away thinking that this would be a great place to work. However, if you've visited Wegmans, a grocery store chain located mainly in the northeastern section of the United States, you might find something that would surprise you. Wegmans has been on *Fortune* magazine's "100 Best Companies to Work For" every year since the list began in 1998. One of the many things that makes Wegmans a great place to work is its attention to employee's needs. The company systematically analyzes the benefits most important to employees.

In a recent survey, the company found that three factors were most likely to influence someone to join the Wegmans team: flexible work schedules, company reputation, and health benefits. Surprisingly, the starting pay was ranked second to last out of 12 choices, indicating that wages and salaries are not as important as one might expect. The company also surveyed their current employees to find out the reasons that they stayed with the company. Health benefits and flexible work schedules topped the list, followed by job security.

Benefits offered at Wegmans are unusual, particularly for the grocery industry. Full-time employees are eligible for participation in the company's group health insurance, with Wegmans picking up 85 percent of the cost. Part-time employees working 24 hours a week or more are also eligible for individual coverage, a benefit almost unheard of in the industry. Other benefits include dental coverage, retirement and 401(k) plans, life insurance, and paid time off for vacation and sick days.

Wegmans soars above the industry standard by providing benefits such as adoption assistance and scholarships. Since 1984, the company has awarded more than $85 million in scholarships to employees. Wegmans' philosophy underlies these benefits, "We believe we can achieve our goals only if we fulfill the needs of our people." Scholarships of up to $1,500 per year are available for part-time employees and full-time employees may receive up to $2,200 per year. Cassie, a pharmacy intern at Wegmans, explains it this way, "I feel honored to be an employee for Wegmans, a company that exemplifies high standards and truly cares about their employees. They were supportive of my education and even provided me with a scholarship throughout pharmacy school. The knowledge that I have gained as an employee here is invaluable and I can't wait to begin my journey as a Wegmans' pharmacist."

QUESTIONS FOR DISCUSSION

10-30. Are you surprised that starting pay was less important to Wegmans' employees than flexible work schedules and health benefits? Why or why not?

10-31. Following Wegmans' lead, do you think that companies should consider lowering their wage rates and providing health benefits to full- and part-time employees?

10-32. Wegmans has invested quite heavily in their scholarship program. How do you think that this benefits the company?

10-33. What effect would benefits at Wegmans have on turnover at the company? How could this be a strategic advantage?

10-34. If you were developing a list of "100 Best Companies to Work For," what factors would weigh most heavily on your rankings and why?

crafting a business plan

PART 3: PEOPLE IN ORGANIZATIONS

Goal of the Exercise

At this point, your business has an identity and you've described the factors that will affect your business and how you will operate it. Part 3 of the business plan project asks you to think about your employees, the jobs they will be performing, and the ways in which you can lead and motivate them.

Exercise Background: Part 3 of the Business Plan

To complete this part of the plan, you need to refer back to the organizational chart that you created in Part 2. In this part of the business plan exercise, you'll take the different job titles you created in the organizational chart and give thought to the *skills* that employees will need to bring to the job *before* they begin. You'll also consider *training* you'll need to provide *after* they are hired, as well as how you'll compensate your employees. Part 3 of the business plan also asks you to consider how you'll lead your employees and keep them happy and motivated.

Your Assignment

STEP 1

Open the *Business Plan* file you began working on in Parts 1 and 2.

STEP 2

For the purposes of this assignment, you will answer the questions in "Part 3: People in Organizations:"

10-35. What do you see as the "corporate culture" of your business? What types of employee behaviors, such as organizational citizenship, will you expect?
Hint: Will your business demand a casual environment or a more professional environment? Refer to the discussion on employee behavior in Chapter 8 for information on organizational citizenship and other employee behaviors.

10-36. What is your philosophy on leadership? How will you manage your employees day to day?
Hint: Refer to the discussion on leadership in Chapter 9, to help you formulate your thoughts.

10-37. Looking back at your organizational chart in Part 2, briefly create a job description for each team member.
Hint: As you learned in this chapter, a job description lists the duties and responsibilities of a job; its working conditions; and the tools, materials, equipment, and information used to perform it. Imagine your business on a typical day. Who is working and what is each person's responsibilities?

10-38. Next, create a job specification for each job, listing the skills and other credentials and qualifications needed to perform the job effectively.
Hint: As you write your job specifications, consider what you would write if you were making an ad for the position. What would the new employee need to bring to the job to qualify for the position?

10-39. What sort of training, if any, will your employees need once they are hired? How will you provide this training?
Hint: Refer to the discussion of training in this chapter. Will you offer your employees on-the-job training? off-the-job training? vestibule training?

10-40. A major factor in retaining skilled workers is a company's compensation system—the total package of rewards that it offers employees in return for their labor. Part of this compensation system includes wages or salaries. What wages or salaries will you offer for each job? Why did you decide on that pay rate?
Hint: Refer to the discussion in this chapter for more information on forms of compensation. You may also want to check out sites such as www.salary.com, which includes a salary wizard you can use to determine how much people with different job titles are making in your area and across the United States.

10-41. As you learned in this chapter, incentive programs are special programs designed to motivate high performance. What incentives will you use to motivate your workforce?
Hint: Be creative and look beyond a simple answer, such as giving pay increases. Ask yourself, who are my employees and what is important to them? Refer to the discussion in this chapter for more information on the types of incentives you may want to consider.
Note: Once you have answered the questions, save your Word document. You'll be answering additional questions in later chapters.

MyBizLab

Go to **pearsonglobaleditions.com/mybizlab** *for the following Assisted-graded writing questions:*

10-42. In many organizations, there are experts who handled job analysis and recruiting. Explain why job analysis is important to an organization. Assume your organization needs to hire a new account auditor in a manufacturing firm. An account auditor is responsible for auditing accounts for the retailers who purchase in bulk from the manufacturer. Write a job description and job specifications for this position. If you were in charge of recruiting, where might you look to find someone to fulfill this position internally and externally?

10-43. In 2011, following the retirement of the NASA Space Shuttle Program, Boeing announced layoffs in the Space Exploration program. Boeing offered the 510 employees being laid off an option during the 60 period of advance notice. The first option was that the employee could stay until the day of termination, during which time Boeing would search for a job opening in another of their programs, but potentially in a different location. If the employee chose this option, there was potential that Boeing would not find them a position and they would still be terminated. The second option was the employee could forego Boeing's career transition services and search for a job in a different company. If the employee chose this option, Boeing would not attempt to relocate them. The employee had to inform Boeing in advance of their choice. Write an essay in which you answer the following questions: (a) Do you agree with this type of layoff? Why or why not? (b) What are the advantages and disadvantages of using this type of termination in mass layoffs? (c) What are alternatives that Boeing could have pursued? Source: http://www.dailytech.com/Boeing+Issues+Layoff+Notices+as+NASA+Retires+Space+Shuttle+Program/article21838.htm

10-44. Mybizlab Only—comprehensive writing assignment for this chapter.

end notes

1 *HR Magazine*, "Nothing Partial About These Benefits," vol. 48, No. 8 by Elayne Robertson Demby, August 1,2003, see http://www.shrm.org/Publications/hrmagazine/EditorialContent/Pages/0803demby.aspx:; "The Wegmans Way," by Matthew Boyle, January 24, 2005, *Fortune Magazine*. See: http://money.cnn.com/magazines/fortune/fortune_archive/2005/01/24/8234048/; Jon Springer, "Danny Wegman," *Supermarket News*, July 14, 2009, at http://supermarketnews.com, accessed on April 15, 2013; Michael A. Prospero, "Employee Innovator: Wegmans," *Fast Company*, October 2004, at www.fastcompany.com, accessed on April 15, 2011, see http://www.fastcompany.com/51347/employee-innovator-wegmans; Dan Mitchell, "Wegmans Price War Against Itself," *The Big Money*, November 2, 2009, at www.thebigmoney.com, accessed on April 15, 2013; "100 Best Companies to Work For," *Fortune*, 2011, at http://money.cnn.com, accessed on April 15, 2013; Business Civic Leadership Center, "Wegmans," *2009 Corporate Citizenship Awards* (U.S. Chamber of Commerce, 2009), at www.bclc.uschamber.com, accessed on April 15, 2013; "In 2010, Wegmans Announces Largest Group of Employee Scholarship Recipients Yet," press release, June 16, 2010, at www.wegmans.com, accessed on April 15, 2013; From: http://www.wholefoodsmarket.com/mission-values/core-values/declaration-interdependence.

2 Patrick Wright and Gary McMahan, "Strategic Human Resources Management: A Review of the Literature," *Journal of Management*, June 1992, pp. 280–319; see also Peter Cappelli, "Talent Management for the Twenty-First Century," *Harvard Business Review*, March 2008, pp. 74–84; and Edward E. Lawler III, "Making Human Capital a Source of Competitive Advantage," *Organizational Dynamics*, January–March 2009, pp. 1–7.

3 "From the Ashes, New Tech Start-Ups Can Bloom," *USA Today*, February 17, 2009, p. 1B.

4 Augustine Lado and Mary Wilson, "Human Resource Systems and Sustained Competitive Advantage: A Competency-Based Perspective," *Academy of Management Review*, 1994, Vol. 19, No. 4, pp. 699–727.

5 David Lepak and Scott Snell, "Examining the Human Resource Architecture: The Relationships among Human Capital, Employment, and Human Resource Configurations," *Journal of Management*, 2002, Vol. 28, No. 4, pp. 517–543. See also Wayne F. Cascio and Herman Aguinis, "Staffing Twenty-First Century Organizations," in James P. Walsh and Arthur P. Brief, *The Academy of Management Annals*, Vol. 2 (London: Routledge, 2008), pp. 133–166.

6 "Maryland First to OK "Wal-Mart Bill,'" *USA Today*, January 13, 2006, p. 1B.

7 "OSHA Claims Company Knowingly Overexposed Workers to Lead," *Advanced Safety and Health*, January 21, 2011, pp. 35–41.

8 "OSHA Claims Company Knowingly Overexposed Workers to Lead."

9 Robert Gatewood, Mary Gowan, and Gary Lautenschlager, "Corporate Image, Recruitment Image, and Initial Job Choice Decisions," *Academy of Management Journal*, 1993, Vol. 36, No. 2, pp. 414–427; see also Karen Holcombe Ehrhart and Jonathan Ziegert, "Why Are Individuals Attracted to Organizations?" *Journal of Management*, 2005, Vol. 31, No. 6, pp. 901–919; and Donald M. Truxillo and Talya N. Bauer, "Applicant Reactions to Organizations and Selection Systems," in Sheldon Zedeck (ed.), *Handbook of Industrial and Organizational Psychology*, Vol. 2: *Selecting and Developing Members for the Organization* (Washington, DC: American Psychological Association, 2010), pp. 379–398.

10 James A. Breaugh and Mary Starke, "Research on Employee Recruiting: So Many Studies, So Many Remaining Questions," *Journal of Management*, 2000, Vol. 26, No. 3, pp. 405–434.

11 *Hong Kong's raw capitalism under strain*, Craig Stephen http://www.marketwatch.com/story/hong-kongs-raw-capitalism-under-strain-2013-04-28;http://www.bbc.co.uk/news/business-22430016; http://www.clb.org.hk/en/content/dock-workers-two-shenzhen-ports-stage-strikes-higher-pay; http://www.scmp.com/news/hong-kong/article/1232519/strike-end-sees-all-involved-losers (all accessed 16/10/2013).

12 "Employee Relations Principles," NUCOR Corporation; "Pain, but No Layoffs at Nucor," *BusinessWeek*, March 26, 2009, at www.businessweek.com, accessed on March 25, 2011; Byrnes with Michael Arndt, "The Art of Motivation," *BusinessWeek*, May 1, 2006, at www.businessweek.com, accessed on March 26, 2011; "About Us," Nucor website, at www.nucor.com, accessed on April 2, 2011; "Nucor Reports Record Results for 2008," *Reuters*, January 27, 2009, at www.reuters.com, accessed on April 2, 2011; Kathy Mayer, "Nucor Steel: Pioneering Mill in Crawfordsville Celebrates 20 Years and 30 Million Tons," *AllBusiness*, September 1, 2008, at www.allbusiness.com, accessed on April 3, 2011.

13 "Some Employers Offer ID Theft Coverage," *USA Today*, September 12, 2005, p. 1B.

14 "FedEx, Goodyear Make Big Pension Plan Changes," *Workforce Management* (March 1, 2007), at http://www.workforce.com/section/00/article/24/77/95.html.

15 December 10, 2006, "Whole Foods' Second Banana on Being Green," from January/February 2007 by Bonnie Azab Powell (Boardmember.com), see https://cms.boardmember.com/Print.aspx?id=292; John Stossel et al.,

"Health Savings Accounts: Putting Patients in Control," *ABC News*, September 14, 2007, at http://abcnews. go.com, accessed on April 16, 2013, see http://abcnews. go.com/2020/Stossel/story?id=3602579&page=1; John Mackey, "The Whole Foods Alternative to ObamaCare," *Wall Street Journal*, August 11, 2009, at http://online.wsj. com, accessed on April 16, 2013; Judy Dugan, "Whole Foods' Crummy Insurance: What John Mackey Means by 'Choice,'" *Consumer Watchdog*, August 20, 2009, at www.consumerwatchdog.org, accessed on April 16, 2013, see http://www.consumerwatchdog.org/node/4187; Emily Friedman, "Health Care Stirs Up Whole Foods CEO John Mackey, Customers Boycott Organic Grocery Store," *ABC News*, August 14, 2009, at http://abcnews. go.com, accessed on April 16, 2013; Nick Paumgarten, "Food Fighter," *The New Yorker*, January 4, 2010, at www.newyorker.com, accessed on April 16, 2013; "Whole Foods CEO John Mackey Stepping Down as Chairman," *Huffington Post*, December 25, 2009, at www. huffingtonpost.com, accessed April 16, 2013.

[16] Kenneth B. Brown and Traci Sitzmann, "Training and Employee Development for Improved Performance," in Sheldon Zedeck (ed.), *Handbook of Industrial and Organizational Psychology*, Vol. 2: *Selecting and Developing Members for the Organization* (Washington, DC: American Psychological Association), pp. 469–504.

[17] "2010 Training Industry Report," *Training Magazine*, November 19, 2010, pp. 65–88.

[18] Renee DeRouin, Barbara Fritzsche, and Eduardo Salas, "E-Learning in Organizations," *Journal of Management*, 2005, Vol. 31, No. 6, pp. 920–940. See Fred Luthans, James B. Avey, and Jaime L. Patera, "Experimental Analysis of a Web-Based Training Intervention to Develop Positive Psychological Capital," *Academy of Management Learning & Education*, 2008, Vol. 7, No. 2, pp. 209–221 for a recent illustration.

[19] "'Boeing U': Flying by the Book," *USA Today*, October 6, 1997, pp. 1B, 2B. See also "Is Your Airline Pilot Ready for Surprises?" *Time*, October 14, 2002, p. 72.

[20] "The Secret Sauce at In-N-Out Burger," *BusinessWeek*, April 20, 2009, pp. 68–69; "Despite Cutbacks, Firms Invest in Developing Leaders," *Wall Street Journal*, February 9, 2009, p. B4.

[21] Jessica L. Wildman, Wendy L. Bedwell, Eduardo Salas, and Kimberly A. Smith-Jentsch, "Performance Measurement at Work: A Multilevel Perspective," in Sheldon Zedeck (ed.), *Handbook of Industrial and Organizational Psychology*, Vol. 1: *Building and Developing the Organization* (Washington, DC: American Psychological Association, 2010), pp. 303–341.

[22] See Paul Levy and Jane Williams, "The Social Context of Performance Appraisal: A Review and Framework for the Future," *Journal of Management*, 2004, Vol. 30, No. 6, pp. 881–905.

[23] See Michael Hammer, "The 7 Deadly Sins of Performance Measurement (and How to Avoid Them)," *MIT Sloan Management Review*, Spring 2007, pp. 19–30.

[24] See Angelo S. DeNisi and Avraham N. Kluger, "Feedback Effectiveness: Can 360-Degree Appraisals Be Improved?" *Academy of Management Executive*, 2000, Vol. 14, No. 1, pp. 129–139.

[25] Barry R. Nathan, Allan Mohrman, and John Milliman, "Interpersonal Relations as a Context for the Effects of Appraisal Interviews on Performance and Satisfaction: A Longitudinal Study," *Academy of Management Journal*, June 1991, pp. 352–369.

[26] "Goodyear to Stop Labeling 10% of Its Workers as Worst," *USA Today*, September 12, 2002, p. 1B.

[27] "Welcome to Silicon Valley: Perksville, USA," *USA Today*, July 5, 2012, p. 1A.

[28] "For Some, a Patchwork of Jobs Pays the Bills," *Boston.com*, March 27, 2009, at www.boston.com, accessed on April 15, 2013; Kristin Kridel, "Overqualified Applying for Temporary Work," *Spokesman.com*, March 4, 2009, at www.spokesman.com, accessed on April 15, 2013; Anne Fisher, "Be a Manager and a Temp?" *CNNMoney.com*, March 16, 2009, at www.cmfassociates.com, accessed on April 15, 2013; Sital Patel, "Skill Level of Temp Workers Rises amid Recession," *Fox Business*, February 27, 2009, at www.jobs-work-employment.com, accessed on April 15, 2013; U.S. Bureau of Labor Statistics (BLS); *The New York Times*, March 12, 2006, A Way to Try a Job on for Size Before Making a Commitment, By TANYA MOHN, see: http://www.nytimes.com/2006/03/12/jobs/12jmar.html?pagewanted=print; "Table 12. Private Industry, by Industry Group and Full-Time and Part-Time Status," news release, December 2010, at www.bls.gov, accessed on April 15, 2013.

[29] http://www.bls.gov/opub/cwc/cb20100628ar01p1.htm.

[30] U.S. Department of Labor, Bureau of Labor Statistics, at http://www.bls.gov/news.release/union2.nr0.htm, accessed on March 22, 2011.

[31] U.S. Department of Labor, Bureau of Labor Statistics, at http://www.bls.gov/news.release/pdf/wkstp.pdf, accessed on March 22, 2011.

[32] http://www.bls.gov/news.release/pdf/wkstp.pdf.

[33] http://www.thestar.com/news/gta/2013/04/09/zoo_lockout_could_threaten_panda_opening_union_says.html; http://www.twincities.com/allheadlines/ci_22978302/spco-lockout-appears-stalled.

[34] "Benefits." Wegmans.com. N.p., n.d. Web. 29 June 2013, wegmans.com.

[35] "Education." Wegmans.com. N.p., n.d. Web. 29 June 2013, wegmans.com.

[36] Walters, Candace. "Taking a Closer Look at Benefits: The Wegmans Way." *HR Works, Inc.* June 10, 2011 at. http://www.hrworks-inc.com/topics-in-hr/articles/3-benefits-administration-articles/350-taking-a-closer-look-at-benefits-the-wegmans-way, accessed on June 29, 2013.

[37] "Wegmans Food Markets." *CNNMoney*. Cable News Network, at http://money.cnn.com/magazines/fortune/bestcompanies/2011/snapshots/3.html, accessed on June 29, 2013.

Marketing Processes and Consumer Behavior

chapter 11

As consumers, we are the forces that drive marketing.

Those same marketing campaigns

push us in directions

without us even knowing it.

AFTER READING THIS CHAPTER, YOU SHOULD BE ABLE TO:

OBJECTIVE 1 **Explain** the concept of marketing and identify the five forces that constitute the external marketing environment.

OBJECTIVE 2 **Explain** the purpose of a marketing plan and identify its main components.

OBJECTIVE 3 **Explain** market segmentation and how it is used in target marketing.

OBJECTIVE 4 **Discuss** the purpose of marketing research, and compare the four marketing research methods.

OBJECTIVE 5 **Describe** the consumer buying process and the key factors that influence that processs.

OBJECTIVE 6 **Discuss** the four categories of organizational markets, and the characteristics of Business-to-Business (B2B) buying behavior

OBJECTIVE 7 **Discuss** the marketing mix as it applies to small business.

MyBizLab®

⭐ Improve Your Grade!

Visit **pearsonglobaleditions.com/mybizlab** for simulations, tutorials, and end-of-chapter problems.

simulations

videos

assisted-graded writing

Over 10 million students improved their results using the Pearson MyLabs.

Starbucks Brews a New
Marketing Mix

For lovers of upscale coffee products, Starbucks has long been the standout brand with a premium image as the "home of affordable luxury." With its well-established line of tasty lattes and Frappuccinos—some priced more than $4 and all presented by service-savvy baristas—Starbucks gained great popularity in the connoisseur coffee market. Seeking to tap the market's full potential, Chairman and CEO Howard Schultz spearheaded an ambitious expansion dream for 40,000 retail outlets globally, creating a massive network of stores dispensing Starbucks products, along with an infusion of Starbucks's "romance, warmth and theater," to millions of coffee gourmets. All of that changed, however, with the sting of the 2008 recession.

To stay afloat, Starbucks reconsidered all aspects of its marketing strategy, including downsizing the distribution network of retail stores, refashioning its line of products and prices, and promoting a repositioned Starbucks image. The new strategy, which presented Starbucks as being more affordable, reflected the company's tighter budget and realignment with the target market, as consumers adjusted to the realities of a down-turned economy as well. Instead of adding 2,500 locations annually, hundreds of the 17,000 locations were closed, including stores in areas such as Florida and California that saw widespread home foreclosures. Starbucks also planned fewer new store openings. The strategy also refocused Starbucks' products back onto what made Starbucks great—coffee—instead of side-tracking into movies and music. New entries in the product mix included a line of instant coffee (once shunned by Starbucks). In a competitive response to McDonald's and Dunkin' Donuts, Starbucks presented a line of recession-friendly value meals, including a choice of breakfast sandwich paired with a coffee product, at a reduced-price savings of as much as $1.20. To keep its customers and bolster sales, the company launched Starbucks Card Rewards, a customer loyalty promotion that got patrons free coffee refills and other extras, all to support the affordability image.[1]

Some observers at that time noted that the new approach—repositioning the brand to attract some cost-conscious customers—might also alienate others in the coffee connoisseur segment, but it was a marketing risk that Starbucks was willing to take.

Recently, even with more stable economic conditions, the reduced-price promotional measures continue to help bolster sales. Visitors to Daily Deals at LivingSocial.com, for example, were offered a $5 coupon that they would redeem

what's in it for me?

Adjusting its marketing strategy is an example of how a company can apply marketing basics in an innovative way to appeal to the forces of the external marketing environment. This chapter discusses these basics along with the marketing plan and components of the marketing mix, as well as target marketing and market segmentation. It also explores key factors that influence consumer and organizational buying processes. By grasping the marketing methods and ideas in this chapter, you will not only be better prepared as a marketing professional, but also as an informed consumer.

auremar/fotolia

for $10 of Starbucks products. In just one day some 1.5 million customers took the deal. Other customers at Starbucks stores took advantage of special receipts for morning purchases that earned them discounts on drinks purchased later that day.[2]

Even so, Starbucks insists on pushing forward to re-ensure the positioning of its brand as "the premier roaster and retailer of specialty coffee in the world." To support this marketing objective, and to increase the company's competitiveness, it is enlarging its distribution network, offering a new line of products, and moving into new target markets. In a reversal after closing 10 percent of U.S. stores during the recession, current plans call for opening 1,500 new stores in 2013–2017. With more than 11,000 U.S. stores and 18,000 stores worldwide in 2012, plans call for reaching 20,000 worldwide by 2014.[3]

Perhaps the most significant geographic region for worldwide expansion is China, not just because of its massive population, but also because of the emerging middle class, a major socioeconomic development in that country. China's strong economy brings with it a growing and prospering middle class, growing by 18 percent (250 million people) from 2000 to 2012. This economic segment is projected to more than double in size by 2020, bringing with it a massive purchasing power. Little wonder, then, that Starbucks' marketing strategy includes a segment of prospering China as a significant target market for the future.[4] (After studying the content in this chapter you should be able to answer a set of discussion questions found at the end of the chapter.)

OBJECTIVE 1
Explain
the concept of marketing and identify the five forces that constitute the external marketing environment.

What Is Marketing?

As consumers, we are influenced by the marketing activities of companies that want us to buy their products rather than those of their competitors. Being consumers makes us the essential ingredients in the marketing process. Every day, we express needs for such essentials as food, clothing, and shelter and wants for such nonessentials as entertainment and leisure activities. Our needs and wants are major forces that drive marketing.

What comes to mind when you think of marketing? Most of us think of marketing as advertisements for detergents and soft drinks. Marketing, however, encompasses a much wider range of activities. The American Marketing Association defines **marketing** as "activities, a set of institutions, and processes for creating, communicating, delivering, and exchanging offerings that have value for customers, clients, partners, and society at large ."[5] To see this definition in action we'll continue this chapter by looking at some marketing basics, including the ways marketers build relationships with customers. We'll then examine forces that constitute the external marketing environment, followed by marketing strategy, the marketing plan, the components of the marketing mix, and we'll discuss market segmentation and how it is used in target marketing. Next we'll examine marketing research, followed by a look at key factors that influence the buying processes of consumers and industrial buyers. Finally, we'll go beyond domestic borders to explore the international marketing mix and the marketing mix for small business.

Marketing *activities, a set of institutions, and processes for creating, communicating, delivering, and exchanging offerings that have value for customers, clients, partners, and society at large.*

Delivering Value

What attracts buyers to one product instead of another? Although our desires for the many goods and services may be unbounded, limited financial resources force most of us to be selective. Accordingly, customers buy products that offer the best value when it comes to meeting their needs and wants.

Value *relative comparison of a product's benefits versus its costs*

Value and Benefits   The **value** of a product compares its benefits with its costs. Benefits include not only the functions of the product, but also the emotional satisfaction associated with owning, experiencing, or possessing it. But every product has costs, including sales price, the expenditure of the buyer's time, and even the emotional costs of making a purchase decision. A satisfied customer perceives the benefits derived from the purchase to be greater than its costs. Thus, the simple but important ratio for value is derived as follows:

$$\text{Value} = \frac{\text{Benefits}}{\text{Costs}}$$

The marketing strategies of leading firms focus on increasing value for customers. Marketing resources are deployed to add benefits and decrease costs of products to provide greater value. To satisfy customers, a company may:

- Develop an entirely new product that performs better (provides greater performance benefits) than existing products;

- Keep a store open longer hours during a busy season (adding the benefit of greater shopping convenience);

- Offer price reductions (the benefit of lower costs);

- Offer information that explains how a product can be used in new ways (the benefit of new uses at no added cost).

Value and Utility To understand how marketing creates value for customers, we need to know the kind of benefits that buyers get from a firm's goods or services. As we discussed in Chapter 7, those benefits provide customers with **utility,** the ability of a product to satisfy a human want or need. Think about the competitive marketing efforts for Microsoft's Xbox series and those for Sony's competing PlayStation game consoles. In both companies, marketing strives to provide four kinds of utility in the following ways:

Utility *ability of a product to satisfy a human want or need*

- **Form utility.** Marketing has a voice in designing products with features that customers want. Microsoft's forthcoming Xbox 720 features a wide-angle projector for big-screen viewing, and Sony's new Playstation 4 (PS 4) touts a controller with six-axis sensor.

Form Utility *providing products with features that customers want*

- **Time utility**. Marketing creates a time utility by providing products *when* customers will want them. Both companies create Internet buzzes and rumors among gamers by hinting at upcoming release dates without specifics.

Time Utility *providing products when customers will want them*

- **Place utility.** Marketing creates a place utility by making products easily accessible; by making products available *where* customers will want them. Xbox 720 will be available at Microsoft's online store—microsoftstore.com; PS 4 will be accessible online at amazon.com and many brick-and-mortar retailers, including Best Buy and Target.

Place Utility *providing products where customers will want them*

- **Possession utility.** Marketing creates a possession utility by transferring product ownership to customers by setting selling prices, setting terms for customer credit payments, if needed, and providing ownership documents. Hints about prices from both companies have fueled rumors: Xbox 720 is assumed to have a $499 (approximate) price tag, or possibly a lower price (unspecified) for subscribing at a $10 monthly fee. Sony's advance notice for PS 4: "Affordable and less than PS 3."

Possession Utility *transferring product ownership to customers by setting selling prices, setting terms for customer credit payments, and providing ownership documents*

As you can imagine, marketing's responsibilities at Microsoft and Sony are extremely challenging in such a competitive arena, and the stakes are high. Because they determine product features, and the timing, place, and terms of sale that provide utility and add value for customers, marketers must understand customers' wants and needs. And in today's fast-moving industries those wants and needs must be determined quickly. Marketing's methods for creating utility are described in this and the following two chapters.

Goods, Services, and Ideas

The marketing of tangible goods is obvious in everyday life. It applies to two types of customers: those who buy consumer goods and those who buy industrial goods. In a department store, an employee may ask if you'd like to try a new cologne. A pharmaceutical company proclaims the virtues of its new cold medicine. Your local auto dealer offers an economy car at an economy price. These products are all **consumer goods,** tangible goods that you, the consumer, may buy for personal use. Firms that sell goods to consumers for personal consumption are engaged in consumer marketing, also known as business-to-consumer (B2C) marketing.

Consumer Goods *physical products purchased by consumers for personal use*

Marketing also applies to **industrial goods,** physical items used by companies to produce other products. Surgical instruments and bulldozers are industrial goods, as are components and raw materials such as integrated circuits, steel, coffee beans, and plastic. Firms that sell goods to other companies are engaged in industrial marketing, also known as business-to-business (B2B) marketing.

Industrial Goods *physical products purchased by companies to produce other products*

But marketing techniques are also applied to **services,** products with intangible (nonphysical) features, such as professional advice, timely information for decisions, or arrangements for a vacation. Service marketing, the application of marketing for services, continues to be a major growth area in the United States. Insurance companies, airlines, public accountants, and health clinics all engage in service marketing, both to individuals (consumer markets) and to other companies (industrial markets). Thus, the terms consumer marketing and industrial marketing include services as well as goods.

Services *products having nonphysical features, such as information, expertise, or an activity that can be purchased*

Finally, marketers also promote ideas, such as "inspirational values" as seen in "Encouragement, Pass It On," on YouTube and in the popular television commercials. Ads in theaters warn us against copyright infringement and piracy. Other marketing campaigns may stress the advantages of avoiding fast foods, texting while driving, or quitting smoking, or they may promote a political party or candidate.

Relationship Marketing and Customer Relationship Management

Although marketing often focuses on single transactions for products, services, or ideas, marketers also take a longer-term perspective. Thus, **relationship marketing** is a type of marketing that emphasizes building lasting relationships with customers and suppliers. Stronger relationships, including stronger economic and social ties, can result in greater long-term satisfaction, customer loyalty, and customer retention.[6] Starbucks's Card Rewards attracts return customers with free coffee refills and other extras. Similarly, commercial banks offer economic incentives to encourage longer lasting relationships. Longtime customers who purchase a certain number of the bank's products (for example, checking accounts, savings accounts, and loans) accumulate credits toward free or reduced-price products or services, such as free investment advice.

Relationship Marketing *marketing strategy that emphasizes building lasting relationships with customers and suppliers*

Like many other marketing areas, the ways that marketers go about building relationships with customers have changed dramatically. **Customer relationship management (CRM)** is an organized method that an enterprise uses to build better information connections with clients, so that managers can develop stronger enterprise-client relationships.

Customer Relationship Management (CRM) *organized methods that a firm uses to build better information connections with clients, so that stronger company-client relationships are developed*

The power of Internet communications coupled with the ability to gather and assemble information on customer preferences allows marketers to better predict what clients will want and buy. Viking River Cruises communicates with booked vacationers months in advance of departures, including e-mails with menus and food recipes from countries that vacationers will be visiting. Viking also encourages social networking among booked passengers to establish pre-voyage friendships, for faster face-to-face acquaintanceships once they board the riverboat.

Data Warehousing *the collection, storage, and retrieval of data in electronic files*

The compiling and storage of customers' data, known as **data warehousing,** provides the raw materials from which marketers can extract information that enables them to find new clients and identify their best customers. Marketers can then inform these priority clients about upcoming new products and postpurchase service reminders. **Data mining** automates the massive analysis of data by using computers to sift, sort, and search for previously undiscovered clues about what customers look at, react to, and how they might be influenced. Marketers use these tools to get a clearer picture of how knowing a client's preferences can satisfy those particular needs, thereby building closer, stronger relationships with customers.[7]

Toronto-based Fairmont Resort Hotels, for example, first used data mining to rebuild its customer-relations package by finding out what kinds of vacations their customers prefer and then placed ads where they were more likely to reach those customers. When data mining revealed the worldwide destinations of Fairmont customers, it helped determine Fairmont's decision to buy their customers' number-one preference, the Savoy in London.[8] Fairmont's enhanced CRM has attracted new guests and strengthened relationships and loyalty among existing clients, through Web-based promotions and incentives. Using profiles of guest information, Fairmont identifies target traveler segments and supplies travelers with personalized price discounts and special hotel services.[9] We'll discuss data warehousing and data mining in more detail in Chapter 14.

Data Mining *the application of electronic technologies for searching, sifting, and reorganizing pools of data to uncover useful information*

The Marketing Environment

Marketing plans and strategies are not determined unilaterally by any business—rather, they are strongly influenced by powerful outside forces. As you see in Figure 11.1, every marketing program must recognize the factors in a company's *external environment*, which is everything outside an organization's boundaries that might affect it. In this section we'll discuss how these external forces affect the marketing environment in particular.

Political-Legal Environment The **political-legal environment**, both global and domestic, have profound effects on marketing. For example, environmental legislation has determined the destinies of entire industries. The political push for alternative energy sources is creating new markets and products for emerging companies such as India's Suzlon Energy Limited (large wind turbines), wind-powered electric generators by Germany's Nordex AG, and wind farms and power plants by Spain's Gamesa Corporation. Marketing managers try to maintain favorable political and legal environments in several ways. To gain public support for products and activities, marketers use ad campaigns to raise public awareness

Political-Legal Environment *the relationship between business and government, usually in the form of government regulation of business*

FIGURE 11.1 The External Marketing Environment

of important issues. Companies contribute to political candidates and frequently support the activities of political action committees (PACs) maintained by their respective industries.

Sociocultural Environment

Sociocultural Environment *the customs, mores, values, and demographic characteristics of the society in which an organization functions*

The **sociocultural environment** also impacts marketing. Changing social values force companies to develop and promote new products, such as poultry and meat without antibiotics and growth hormones, for both individual consumers and industrial customers. Just a few years ago, organic foods were available only in specialty food stores such as Whole Foods. Today, in response to a growing demand for healthy foods, Target's Archer Farms product line brings affordable organic food to a much larger audience. New industrial products, too, reflect changing social values: A growing number of wellness programs are available to companies for improving employees' health. Quest Diagnostics, for example, a B2B company, supplies a "Blueprint for Wellness" service that assesses employee healthcare risks in client companies and recommends programs for reducing those risks. This and other trends reflect the values, beliefs, and ideas that shape society.

Technological Environment

Technological Environment *all the ways by which firms create value for their constituents*

The **technological environment** creates new goods and services. New products make existing products obsolete, and many products change our values and lifestyles. In turn, lifestyle changes often stimulate new products not directly related to the new technologies themselves. Mobile devices, the availability of a vast array of apps, and social media, for example, facilitate business communication just as prepackaged meals provide convenience for busy household cooks. Both kinds of products also free up time for recreation and leisure.

Economic Environment

Economic Environment *relevant conditions that exist in the economic system in which a company operates*

Because they determine spending patterns by consumers, businesses, and governments, the **economic environment** influences marketing plans for product offerings, pricing, and promotional strategies. Marketers are concerned with such economic variables as inflation, interest rates, and recession. Thus, they monitor the general business cycle to anticipate trends in consumer and business spending.

David R. Frazier/Alamy

Marketing strategies are strongly influenced by powerful outside forces. For example, new technologies create new products, such as the cell phone "gas station" shown here. These recharging stations enable customers to recharge their mobile devices just as they would refuel their cars. The screens at the stations also provide marketers with a new way to display ads to waiting customers.

managing in turbulent times

Feeling the Pressure for "Green"

Today's marketers are struggling with pressures from several outside forces: The political-legal, sociocultural, technological, and economic environments are all pushing for change. Industries ranging from automobiles to energy to housing are grappling with a common environmental theme: *green*. Public sentiment turned decidedly toward alternatives to gas-guzzling cars. Home buyers, too, want energy-efficient heating and cooling, such as geothermal heat, in their homes. Environmentalists are pushing for alternative energy sources, notably wind and solar power, to replace fossil fuels. Local utilities are offering incentives for construction using environmentally sensitive building designs to conserve energy. Purchases of tiny houses are growing. Solar-powered wells are replacing mechanical windmills on farms. In Washington, the Barack Obama administration and Congress continue their struggle to create more jobs and reduce the national debt while also meeting commitments for a cleaner environment using energy-saving technologies.

These outside pressures present challenges for all areas of marketing, from identifying the new target markets to designing new products for those markets and, in some cases, finding technologies to make those products. Success depends on coordinating the various marketing activities and making them compatible with one another. Marketers need to present a convincing rationale for a product's pricing and demonstrate how the product provides the benefits sought by the target markets. Distribution methods, how companies deliver products and after-services to customers, have to match up with promises in the promotional message so that, together, the marketing activities provide a persuasive package that delivers the desired value and benefits. Further, this integrated marketing strategy must be coordinated with financial management and production operations to provide timely customer satisfaction.

The marketing blueprint for Toyota's Prius automobile used an integrated marketing mix for meeting the challenge of *going green*. While developing the fuel-efficient hybrid technology, Toyota identified niche target markets of users in some 40 countries and determined a price range compatible with the company's performance reliability and quality reputation. Promotion in the U.S. market started two years before the car was released so customers could view and purchase a Prius. In one pre-launch promotion, Toyota teamed up with the Sierra

David Koscheck/Shutterstock

Club and lent the Prius to environmentally sensitive Hollywood superstars to provide exposure and allow car testing in the target market. The main ad campaign to general audiences emphasized that consumers can still have speed and comfort along with environmental friendliness. And pre-orders were delivered on time to buyers. As a result, the Prius became the most successful hybrid automobile in the United States and the rest of the world.[10]

The interconnected global economy has become an increasingly important concern for marketers worldwide. For example, in 2012, rising oil prices broke records on an almost daily basis. Fed up with gas prices, U.S. drivers drove less, decreasing the demand and prices for gasoline. When the global economy stagnated in 2008, the Canadian government demanded its automakers reduce production costs and auto prices to qualify for the government's bailout fund. More recently, the U.S. housing crisis has recovered somewhat from the recession, yet many former homeowners remain awash in debt they cannot afford to repay. As a result, money-strapped consumers have shifted to used cars (instead of new) and to down-sized, more modest housing. This product shift by consumers affects all areas of marketing—target markets, pricing, promotion, and distribution—for cars, fuel, and housing.[11]

Competitive Environment   In a **competitive environment,** marketers must convince buyers that they should purchase one company's products rather than another's. Because both consumers and commercial buyers have limited resources, every dollar spent on one product is no longer available for other purchases. Each marketing program, therefore, seeks to make its product the most attractive. Expressed in business terms, a failed program loses the buyer's dollar forever (or at least until it is time for the next purchase decision).

Competitive Environment *the competitive system in which businesses compete*

To promote products effectively, marketers must first understand which of three types of competition they face:

Substitute Product *product that is dissimilar from those of competitors, but that can fulfill the same need*

- **Substitute products** may not look alike or they may seem different from one another, but they can fulfill the same need. For example, your cholesterol level may be controlled with either of two competing products: a physical fitness program or a drug regimen. The fitness program and the drugs compete as substitute products.

Brand Competition *competitive marketing that appeals to consumer perceptions of benefits of products offered by particular companies*

- **Brand competition** occurs between similar products and is based on buyers' perceptions of the benefits of products offered by particular companies. For Internet searches, do you turn to the Google, Bing, or Yahoo? Brand competition is based on users' perceptions of the benefits offered by each product.

International Competition *competitive marketing of domestic products against foreign products*

- **International competition** matches the products of domestic marketers against those of foreign competitors. The intensity of international competition has been heightened by the formation of alliances, such as the European Union and the North American Free Trade Agreement (NAFTA). In 2009 the U.S. Air Force opened bidding to foreign manufacturers for three new planes to replace the existing Presidential Air Force One fleet (made by Boeing). If Europe's Airbus had won the contract it would have been the first time a U.S. president has flown in a non-U.S. made Air Force One.[12] Instead, however, Airbus withdrew from bidding, leaving Boeing the sole competitor. However, Airbus remains as a formidable competitor of Boeing in today's commercial aircraft industry.

Having identified the kind of competition, marketers can then develop a plan for attracting more customers.

OBJECTIVE 2
Explain
the purpose of a marketing plan and identify its main components

Developing the Marketing Plan

A marketing manager at a major home appliance manufacturing company explains the concept of *developing the marketing plan* by using the analogy of planning for a trip as follows:

- "First, you decide where you want to go and what you want to happen when you get there. Why take this trip and not others, instead?"
  [identify the *objective* or *goal* to be achieved]

- "At some stage you decide when the trip will happen and how you'll get to the destination."
  [*plan* for *when* it will happen, and for the *paths* (or *routes*) that will be taken to get there]

- "Every trip requires resources so you identify those resource requirements, and compare them against resources that are available."
  [*evaluate resource* requirements and availabilities]

- "If available resources are too expensive, then you adjust the trip so it becomes affordable."
  [*adjust plans* as needed to become *realistic* and *feasible*]

- "During and after the trip, you assess the successes (what went right) and the drawbacks (what went wrong) and remember them so you can make the next trip even better."
  [keep notes and data about what happened because *learning* from this experience increases the chances for *greater success on the next*]

Marketing Plan *detailed strategy for focusing marketing efforts on consumers' needs and wants*

As you will see, our discussion of the marketing plan contains many of the preceding elements. The **marketing plan** identifies the marketing objectives stating what marketing will accomplish in the future. It contains a strategy that identifies the specific activities and resources that will be used to meet the needs and desires of customers in the firm's chosen target markets, so as to accomplish the marketing objectives.

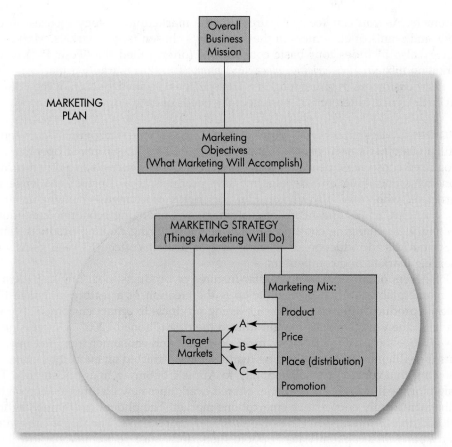

FIGURE 11.2 Components of the Marketing Plan

First and foremost, marketing plans are futuristic, showing what will be happening with marketing's upcoming activities. Every well-founded marketing plan, as shown in Figure 11.2, begins with objectives or goals setting the stage for everything that follows. **Marketing objectives**, the goals the marketing plan intends to accomplish, are the foundation that guides all of the detailed activities in the plan. The marketing objectives themselves, however, exist solely to support the company's overall business mission (at the top in Figure 11.2) and typically focus on maintaining or enhancing the organization's future competitive position in its chosen markets. Hypothetically, Starbucks' overall business mission could aim at being the world's leading retailer of specialty coffee. Two supporting marketing objectives, then, could be (1) a 5-percent increase in its worldwide market share by 2015, and (2) be the leading retailer (in dollar sales) of specialty coffee in China by 2018.

Marketing Objectives *the things marketing intends to accomplish in its marketing plan*

Marketing Strategy: Planning the Marketing Mix

The marketing team can develop a strategy once they have clarified the marketing objectives. Specifically, **marketing strategy** identifies the planned marketing programs, all the marketing activities that a business will use to achieve its marketing goals and when those activities will occur. If planned activities are not affordable, then marketers need to adjust the activities or goals until realistic plans emerge. Finally, because marketing planning is an ongoing process—not just a one-time endeavor—it can be improved through experience by learning from past triumphs and mistakes.

Marketing Strategy *all the marketing programs and activities that will be used to achieve the marketing goals*

Marketing managers are the people responsible for planning, organizing, leading, and controlling the organization's marketing resources toward supporting and accomplishing the organization's overall mission. To meet these responsibilities marketing managers, rely on mapping out a clear strategy for planning and implementing all the activities that result in the transfer of goods or services to

Marketing Manager *manager who plans and implements the marketing activities that result in the transfer of products from producer to consumer*

Marketing Mix *combination of product, pricing, promotion, and place (distribution) strategies used to market products*

Product *good, service, or idea that is marketed to fill consumers' needs and wants*

Product Differentiation *creation of a product feature or product image that differs enough from existing products to attract customers*

Pricing *process of determining the best price at which to sell a product*

Place (Distribution) *part of the marketing mix concerned with getting products from producers to consumers*

customers. As you can see in Figure 11.2, the marketing strategy focuses on the needs and wants of customers in the company's chosen target markets. Marketing strategy also includes four basic components (often called the "Four Ps") of the **marketing mix:** *product, pricing, place*, and *promotion*, that marketing managers use to satisfy customers in target markets. The specific activities for each of the Four Ps will be designed differently to best meet the needs of each target market.

Product Marketing begins with a **product,** a good, a service, or an idea designed to fill a customer's need or want. Starbucks's revised strategy in our opening case recognized consumers' needs for more affordable coffee products in a down-turned economy. Conceiving and developing new products is a constant challenge for marketers, who must always consider the factor of change—changing technology, changing wants and needs of customers, and changing economic conditions. Meeting these changing conditions often means changing existing products—such as Starbucks's introduction of its new line of instant coffee—to keep pace with emerging markets and competitors.

Producers often promote particular features of products to distinguish them in the marketplace. **Product differentiation** is the creation of a feature or image that makes a product differ enough from existing products to attract customers. For example, in the years since Apple introduced the first iPhone in 2007, a succession of newer models evolved with faster, more powerful, and consumer-friendlier innovations. The iPhone's industry-leading features have attracted an enormous customer following that contributes substantially to Apple's booming financial success. The design for the iPhone 5, for example, offered even more new features to keep on top in the increasingly competitive smartphone market. The phone was thinner, lighter, and had an aluminum back that avoids fingerprint streaks. The iSight camera offered a panorama capability, faster photo shots, and better performance in low light. With Apple's new iOS 6 software, the phone's Maps app received rave reviews for clarity and attractive navigation design.[13]

Meanwhile, Samsung surged onto the scene with its competitive Galaxy series, most recently the Galaxy S4, with equally attractive, distinct features. Compared with previous Galaxy models, the Galaxy S4 has a more powerful, removable battery, faster download and upload speeds, the popular Android operating system, and numerous additional features.[14]

So far, Samsung's smartphone features are attracting more customers, holding more than a 30 percent share of worldwide smartphone sales at the end of 2012, versus 19 percent for second-place Apple. In the U.S. market, however, Apple's 45 percent market share outpaced Samsung's nearly 27 percent for the last quarter of 2012.[15] We discuss product development more fully in Chapter 12.

Pricing The **pricing** of a product, selecting the best price at which to sell it, is often a balancing act. On the one hand, prices must support a variety of costs, such as operating, administrative, research costs, and marketing costs. On the other hand, prices can't be so high that customers turn to competitors. Successful pricing means finding a profitable middle ground between these two requirements. By offering a reduced price savings for its breakfast meals, Starbucks is promoting its affordability image.

Both low-and high-price strategies can be effective in different situations. Low prices, for example, generally lead to larger sales volumes. High prices usually limit market size but increase profits per unit. High prices may also attract customers by implying that a product is of high quality. We discuss pricing in more detail in Chapter 12.

Place (Distribution) In the marketing mix, **place** (or **distribution**) refers to *where* and *how* customers get access to the products they buy. When products are created, they must become available to customers at some *location* (*place*) such as a retail store, or on the Internet, or by direct delivery to the customer. *Distribution* is the set

Wenner Media Chair and CEO Jann Wenner (above) is hoping that his strategy for greater differentiation between his *Us Weekly* magazine and rival *People* will continue to pay off. *People* is news driven, reporting on ordinary people as well as celebrities, whereas *Us Weekly* features more coverage of celebrity sex and glitter.

of activities that moves products from producers to customers. Placing a product in the proper outlet, like a retail store, requires decisions about several activities, all of which are concerned with getting the product from the producer to the consumer. Decisions about warehousing and inventory control are distribution decisions, as are decisions about transportation options.

Firms must also make decisions about the *channels* through which they distribute products. Many manufacturers, for example, sell goods to other companies that, in turn, distribute them to retailers. Others sell directly to major retailers, such as Target and Sears. Still others sell directly to final consumers. We explain distribution decisions further in Chapter 13.

Promotion   The most visible component of the marketing mix is no doubt **promotion,** which is a set of techniques for communicating information about products. The most important promotional tools include advertising, personal selling, sales promotions, publicity/public relations, and direct or interactive marketing. Promotion decisions are discussed further in Chapter 13. Here we briefly describe four of the most important promotional tools.

Promotion *aspect of the marketing mix concerned with the most effective techniques for communicating information about products*

ADVERTISING **Advertising** is any form of paid nonpersonal communication used by an identified sponsor to persuade or inform potential buyers about a product. For example, financial advisory companies that provide investment and securities products reach their customer audience by advertising in *Fortune* magazine and on the *Bloomberg* television network.

Advertising *any form of paid nonpersonal communication used by an identified sponsor to persuade or inform potential buyers about a product*

PERSONAL SELLING Many products (such as insurance, custom-designed clothing, and real estate) are best promoted through **personal selling,** person-to-person sales. Industrial goods and services rely significantly on personal selling. When companies buy from other companies, purchasing agents and others who need technical and detailed information are often referred to the selling company's sales representatives.

Personal Selling *person-to person sales*

SALES PROMOTIONS Historically, relatively inexpensive items have often been marketed through **sales promotions,** which involve one-time direct inducements to buyers. Premiums (usually free gifts), coupons, and package inserts are all sales promotions meant to tempt consumers to buy products. More recently,

Sales Promotion *direct inducements such as premiums, coupons, and package inserts to tempt consumers to buy products*

American Eagle Outfitters (AEO) is a chain of more than 900 stores specializing in clothes, accessories, and personal care products designed to appeal to a demographic consisting of girls and guys ages 15 to 25. In 2006, the brand expanded its line with Aerie, a chain of standalone stores in the U.S. and Canada, and an online store, that sell girls' intimates, workout wear, and Aerie's Dormwear—a collection of leggings, hoodies, and fashionable sweats appropriate for lounging in the dorm or wearing to a morning class.

however, these promotions have expanded into B2B sales and to sales of larger items to consumers through Internet deals at sources such as Groupon.

Public Relations *communication efforts directed at building goodwill and favorable attitudes in the minds of the public toward the organization and its products*

PUBLIC RELATIONS **Public relations** includes all communication efforts directed at building goodwill. It seeks to build favorable attitudes in the minds of the public toward the organization and its products. The Ronald McDonald House Charities, and its association with McDonald's Corporation, is a well-known example of public relations.

Integrated Marketing Strategy *strategy that blends together the Four Ps of marketing to ensure their compatibility with one another and with the company's nonmarketing activities as well*

Blending It All Together: Integrated Strategy An **integrated marketing strategy** ensures that the Four Ps blend together so that they are compatible with one another and with the company's nonmarketing activities. As an example, Toyota has become the world's largest automaker. Its nearly 30-year auto superiority, even with its massive product recalls in 2008–2009, stems from a coherent marketing mix that is tightly integrated with its production strategy. Offering a relatively small number of different models, Toyota targets auto customers that want high quality, excellent performance reliability, and moderate prices (a good value for the price). With a smaller number of different models than U.S. automakers, fewer components and parts are needed, purchasing costs are lower, and less factory space is required for inventory and assembly in Toyota's lean production system. Lean production's assembly simplicity yields higher quality, the factory's cost savings led to lower product prices, and speedy production gives shorter delivery times in Toyota's distribution system. Taken together, this integrated strategy is completed when Toyota's advertising communicates its message of industry-high customer satisfaction.[16]

Marketing Strategy: Target Marketing and Market Segmentation

OBJECTIVE 3
Explain
market segmentation and how it is used in target marketing.

Target Market *the particular group of people or organizations on which a firm's marketing efforts are focused*

Market Segmentation *process of dividing a market into categories of customer types, or "segments" having similar wants and needs and who can be expected to show interest in the same products*

Marketers have long known that products cannot be all things to all people. The emergence of the marketing concept and the recognition of customers' needs and wants led marketers to think in terms of **target markets**—the particular groups of people or organizations on which a firm's marketing efforts are focused. Selecting target markets is usually the first step in the marketing strategy.

Target marketing requires **market segmentation**, dividing a market into categories of customer types or "segments" having similar wants and needs and who can be expected to show interest in the same products. Once they have identified segments, companies may adopt a variety of strategies. Some firms market products by targeting more than one segment. General Motors, for example, once offered automobiles with various features and at various price levels. GM's past strategy was to provide an automobile for nearly every segment of the market. The financial crisis, however, forced GM's changeover to fewer target markets and associated brands by closing Saturn, phasing out Pontiac, and selling or shutting down Hummer and Saab.

In contrast, some businesses have always focused on a narrower range of products, such as Ferrari's high-priced sports cars, aiming at just one segment. Note that segmentation is a strategy for analyzing consumers, not products. Once marketers identify a target segment, they can begin marketing products for that segment. The process of fixing, adapting, and communicating the nature of the product itself is called **product positioning.**

Product Positioning *process of fixing, adapting, and communicating the nature of a product*

Identifying Market Segments

By definition, members of a market segment must share some common traits that affect their purchasing decisions. In identifying consumer segments, researchers look at several different influences on consumer behavior. Five of the most important variables are discussed next.

Geographic Segmentation

Many buying decisions are affected by the places people call home. Urban residents don't need agricultural equipment, and sailboats sell better along the coasts than on the Great Plains. **Geographic variables** are the geographic units, from countries to neighborhoods, that researchers consider in a strategy of **geographic segmentation.** McDonald's restaurants in Germany, in contrast to those in the United States, offer beer on the menu. Pharmacies in Jackson Hole, Wyoming, sell firearms that are forbidden in Chicago. And, as our opening case discusses, Starbucks is targeting a larger geographic segment in China.

Geographic Variables *geographic units that may be considered in developing a segmentation strategy*

Geographic Segmentation *geographic units, from countries to neighborhoods, that may be considered in identifying different market segments in a segmentation strategy*

Demographic Segmentation

Demographic segmentation is a strategy used to separate consumers by demographic variables. **Demographic variables** describe populations by identifying traits, such as age, income, gender, ethnic background, marital status, race, religion, and social class, as detailed in Table 11.1. Depending on the marketer's purpose, a demographic segment can be a single classification (ages 20–34) or a combination of categories (ages 20–34, married without children, earning $25,000– $44,999 a year).

For example, Hot Topic started as a California-based chain specializing in clothes, accessories, and jewelry designed to appeal to the Generation Y and Millennials, a demographic consisting of U.S. consumers between born in the 1980s and 1990s. The theme was pop culture music because it was the biggest influence on the demographic's fashion tastes. More recently, Hot Topic has become a national retail chain for clothing, accessories, and entertainment products relating to today's pop culture.

Demographic Segmentation *a segmentation strategy that uses demographic characteristics to identify different market segments*

Demographic Variables *characteristics of populations that may be considered in developing a segmentation strategy*

Geo-Demographic Segmentation

As the name implies, **geo-demographic segmentation** is a combination strategy. **Geo-demographic variables** are a combination of geographic and demographic traits and is becoming the most common segmentation tool. An example would be Female Young Urban Professionals, well educated, 25- to 54-year-olds with high paying professional jobs living in the "downtown" zip codes of major cities. Chico's targets many women in this segment, offering stylish travel clothing well-suited to the needs of this subset in the larger population. Segmentation is more effective because the greater number of variables defines the market more precisely.

Geo-Demographic Segmentation *using a combination of geographic and demographic traits for identifying different market segments in a segmentation strategy*

Geo-Demographic Variables *combination of geographic and demographic traits used in developing a segmentation strategy*

table 11.1 Demographic Variables

Age	Under 5, 5–11, 12–19, 20–34, 35–49, 50–64, 65+
Education	Grade school or less, some high school, graduated high school, some college, college degree, advanced degree
Family Life Cycle	Young single, young married without children, young married with children, older married with children under 18, older married without children under 18, older single, other
Family Size	1, 2–3, 4–5, 6+
Income	Less than $15,000, $15,000–$24,999, $25,000–$50,000, $50,000–$100,000, $100,000–$200,000, more than $200,000
Nationality	African, American, Asian, British, Eastern European, French, German, Irish, Italian, Latin American, Middle Eastern, Scandinavian
Race	American Indian, Asian, African American, Caucasian
Religion	Buddhist, Catholic, Hindu, Jewish, Muslim, Protestant
Gender	Male, female

Psychographic Segmentation

Psychographic Segmentation *a segmentation strategy that uses psychographic characteristics to identify different market segments*

Psychographic Variables *consumer characteristics, such as lifestyles, opinions, interests, and attitudes, that may be considered in developing a segmentation strategy*

Markets can also be separated into a **psychographic segmentation** according to such **psychographic variables** as lifestyles, interests, personalities, and attitudes. For example, Burberry, "The Iconic British Luxury Brand" whose raincoats have been a symbol of British tradition since 1856, has repositioned itself as a global luxury brand, like Gucci and Louis Vuitton. The strategy calls for attracting a different type of customer—the top-of-the-line, fashion-conscious individual—who enjoys the prestige of shopping at stores like Neiman Marcus and Bergdorf Goodman. Psychographics are particularly important to marketers because, unlike demographics and geographics, they can be changed by marketing efforts. With the onset of global interdependence and open communications, marketing today is changing some traditional lifestyles and attitudes in nations around the globe. Polish companies, for example, have overcome consumer resistance by promoting the safety and desirability of using credit cards rather than depending on solely using cash.[17]

Behavioral Segmentation

Behavioral Segmentation *a segmentation strategy that uses behavioral variables to identify different market segments*

Behavioral Variables *behavioral patterns displayed by groups of consumers and that are used in developing a segmentation strategy*

Behavioral segmentation uses **behavioral variables** to market items, including such areas as heavy users (buy in bulk, the key to Sam's and Costco); situation buyers (Halloween is now the second-largest "holiday" in terms of spending); or specific purpose (All Free is a detergent for people who have skin reactions to additives in other detergents).

OBJECTIVE 4
Discuss
the purpose of marketing research, and compare the four marketing research methods.

Marketing Research *the study of what customers need and want and how best to meet those needs and wants*

Marketing Research

Marketing decisions are seldom perfect, yet the consequences of a firm's choices of marketing mix and segmentation strategy can be long lasting. Effective decisions must be customer focused and based on timely information about marketplace trends. **Marketing research**, the study of what customers need and want and how best to meet those needs and wants, is a powerful tool for gaining decision-making information.

The relationship of research to the overall marketing process is shown in Figure 11.3. Ultimately, its role is to increase competitiveness by clarifying the interactions among a firm's stakeholders (including customers), marketing variables, environmental factors, and marketing decisions. Researchers use several methods to obtain, interpret, and

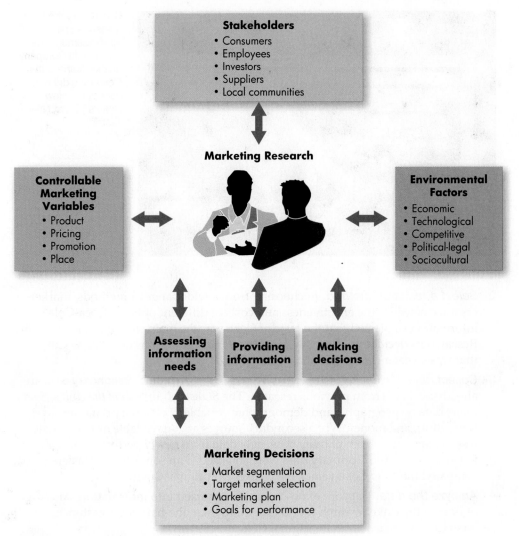

FIGURE 11.3 Market Research and the Marketing Process

apply information about customers. They determine the kinds of information needed for decisions on marketing strategy, goal setting, and target-market selection. In doing so, they may conduct studies on customer responses to proposed changes in the marketing mix. One researcher, for example, might study response to an experimental paint formula (new product). Another might explore the response to a price reduction (new price) on condominiums. Still a third might check responses to a proposed advertising campaign (new promotion). Marketers also try to learn whether customers will more likely purchase a product in a specialty shop or on the Internet (new place).

The importance of selling products in international markets has expanded the role of marketing research. For example, when a company decides to sell goods or services globally, it must decide whether to standardize products or to specialize by offering different versions for each market. Accordingly, market research's orientation has become increasingly globalized.

The Research Process

Market research can occur at almost any point in a product's life cycle. Typically, however, it's used in developing new or altered products. Following are the five steps in performing market research:

1 **Study the current situation.** What is the need and what is being done to meet it? In the mid-1980s Coca-Cola was alarmed by its declining market share. The company decided to undertake a now-famous market study to identify ways to recover its market position.

Contrary to the bold message in this 1980s advertisement, the Coca-Cola Company quickly learned that Coke fans did not accept the New Coke's "Great New Taste!")

2 *Select a research method.* In choosing from a wide range of methods, market-ers must consider the effectiveness and costs of different options. Coca-Cola's information suggested that the taste of Coke was the main source of the problem. Researchers decided to use taste tests for consumer opinions on a "New Coke" that was sweeter than original Coke.

Secondary Data *data that are already available from previous research*

3 *Collect data.* We distinguish here two types of research data. **Secondary data** are already available from previous research. The *Statistical Abstract of the United States* offers data on geographic and demographic variables. Secondary data can save time, effort, and money. When secondary sources are unavailable or inadequate, researchers must obtain **primary data**, new data from newly performed research. In Coca-Cola's study, primary data were collected from some 200,000 tasters who compared the New Coke versus the taste of the original Coke and Pepsi.

Primary Data *new data that are collected from newly performed research*

4 *Analyze the data.* Data are of no use until organized into information. Analysis of data in the Coke research found that more than one-half of the tasters rated New Coke to be tastier than original Coke and Pepsi.

5 *Prepare a report.* This report should sum up the study's methodology and findings. It should also identify solutions and, where appropriate, make recom-mendations on a course of action. Coca-Cola's resulting recommendation—to replace original Coke with the New Coke—was implemented. The decision was a costly disaster that eventually resulted in restoring original Coke under a new name—Classic Coke—and withdrawing of New Coke from the market. Research flaws had biased the results: (1) test tasters were not told that if New Coke was launched, then original Coke would no longer be available; and (2) consumers' long-standing attachment to the original Coke brand would be lost when the product was withdrawn from the market.[18]

This Coca-Cola example was a costly learning experience illustrating that even the most successful companies encounter occasional marketing mistakes. Although Coke's market research ultimately led them down the wrong path, many others, including Marriott Hotels and Resorts, Samsung Electronics, and Procter & Gamble personal care products, have conducted market research campaigns that led to increased market share and a better understanding of their markets.

Research Methods

The success of a research study often depends on the method a research team uses. Consider the following four basic methods of market research:

Observation *research method that obtains data by watching and recording consumer behavior*

1 **Observation** involves watching and recording consumer behavior. Today, infor-mation technology systems, including live camera feeds and computer record-ings, allow marketers to observe consumer preferences rapidly and with great

accuracy. Electronic scanners and data files at brick-and-mortar stores, along with data storage of television viewing, phone transactions, and website activity allow marketers to see each consumer's purchasing history, what products and brands that person prefers over a set period of time.

2   Sometimes, marketers must go a step further and ask questions. One way to get useful information is by taking **surveys**, a method of collecting data in which the researcher interacts with people to gather facts, attitudes, or opinions, either by mailing out or e-mailing questionnaires, by telephone calls, or by conducting face-to-face interviews. United Parcel Service (UPS) surveyed customers to find out how to improve service. Clients wanted more interaction with drivers because they can offer practical advice on shipping. As a result, UPS added extra drivers, proving them with more time with customers.

Survey *research method of collecting consumer data using questionnaires, telephone calls, and face-to-face interviews*

3   In a **focus group**, participants are gathered in one place, presented with an issue, and asked to discuss it. The researcher takes notes and makes video recordings but provides only a minimal amount of structure. This technique allows researchers to explore issues too complex for questionnaires and can produce creative solutions.

Focus Group *research method using a group of people from a larger population who are asked their attitudes, opinions, and beliefs about a product in an open discussion*

4   **Experimentation** compares the responses of the same or similar people under different circumstances. For example, a firm trying to decide whether to include walnuts in a new candy bar probably wouldn't learn much by asking people what they thought of the idea. But if it asked some people to try bars with nuts and some without, the responses could be helpful.

Experimentation *research method using a sample of potential consumers to obtain reactions to test versions of new products or variations of existing products*

Understanding Consumer Behavior

OBJECTIVE 5
Describe
the consumer buying process and the key factors that influence that process.

Although marketing managers can tell us what features people want in a new refrigerator, they cannot tell us why they buy particular refrigerators. What desire are consumers fulfilling? Is there a psychological or sociological explanation for why they purchase one product and not another? These questions and many others are addressed in the study of **consumer behavior,** the study of the decision process by which people buy and consume products.

Consumer Behavior *study of the decision process by which people buy and consume products*

Influences on Consumer Behavior

To understand consumer behavior, marketers draw heavily on such fields as psychology and sociology. The result is a focus on four major influences on consumer behavior: (1) *psychological*, (2) *personal*, (3) *social*, and (3) *cultural*. By identifying which influences are most active in certain circumstances, marketers try to explain consumer choices and predict future buying behavior.

Psychological influences include an individual's motivations, perceptions, ability to learn, and attitudes.

Personal influences include lifestyle, personality, and economic status.

Social influences include family, opinion leaders (people whose opinions are sought by others), and such reference groups as friends, coworkers, and professional associates.

Cultural influences include culture (the way of living that distinguishes one large group from another), subculture (smaller groups with shared values), and social class (the cultural ranking of groups according to such criteria as background, occupation, and income).

Psychological Influences *include an individual's motivations, perceptions, ability to learn, and attitudes that marketers use to study buying behavior*

Personal Influences *include lifestyle, personality, and economic status that marketers use to study buying behavior*

Social Influences *include family, opinion leaders (people whose opinions are sought by others), and such reference groups as friends, coworkers, and professional associates that marketers use to study buying behavior*

Cultural Influences *include culture, subculture, and social class influences that marketers use to study buying behavior*

Although these factors can have a strong impact on a consumer's choices, their effect on actual purchases is sometimes weak or negligible. Some consumers, for example, exhibit high **brand loyalty,** they regularly purchase products, such as McDonald's foods, because they are satisfied with their performance. Such people are less subject to influence and stick with preferred brands.[19] On the other hand,

Brand Loyalty *pattern of repeated consumer purchasing based on satisfaction with a product's performance*

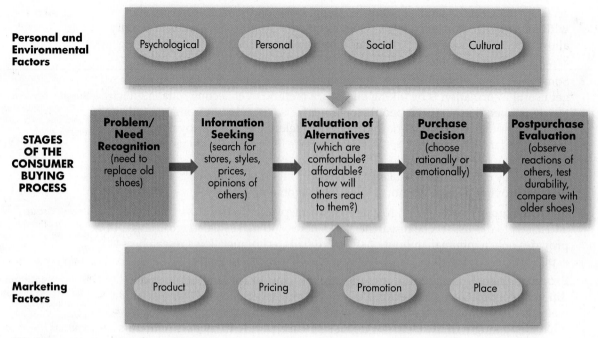

FIGURE 11.4 The Consumer Buying Process

the clothes you wear, the social network you choose, and the way you decorate your room, often reflect social and psychological influences on your consumer behavior.

The Consumer Buying Process

Students of consumer behavior have constructed various models to help show how consumers decide to buy products. Figure 11.4 presents one such model. At the core of this and similar models is an awareness of the many influences that lead to consumption. Ultimately, marketers use this information to develop marketing plans.

Problem or Need Recognition This process begins when the consumer recognizes a problem or need. Need recognition also occurs when you have a chance to change your buying habits. When you obtain your first job after graduation, your new income may let you buy things that were once too expensive for you. You may find that you need professional clothing, apartment furnishings, and a car. Bank of America and Citibank cater to such shifts in needs when they market credit cards to college students.

Information Seeking Having recognized a need, consumers often seek information. The search is not always extensive, but before making major purchases, most people seek information from personal sources, public sources, and experiences. Before buying joining a gym, you may read about your area gyms on yelp.com or you may visit several gyms in your neighborhood. From this information search, consumers develop an **evoked set** (or **consideration set**), which is the group of products they will consider buying.

Evoked Set (or consideration set) *group of products consumers will consider buying as a result of information search*

Evaluation of Alternatives If someone is in the market for skis, they probably have some idea of who makes skis and how they differ. By analyzing product attributes (price, prestige, quality) of the consideration set, consumers compare products before deciding which one best meets their needs.

Purchase Decision Ultimately, consumers make purchase decisions. "Buy" decisions are based on rational motives, emotional motives, or both. **Rational motives** involve the logical evaluation of product attributes: cost, quality, and

Rational Motives *reasons for purchasing a product that are based on a logical evaluation of product attributes*

finding a better way

The Truth about Your Online Customer Service

Online purchases are increasing as shoppers enjoy easy access to the vast array of products at their fingertips from the comfort of home. However, poor customer service can suddenly disappoint and anger customers, resulting in lost sales. So, how good are a company's online customer services, especially when compared to its online competitors? StellaService Inc. answered that question by providing a better way to measure online service, enabling it to become a market winner for online shoppers and retailers alike.

Following its startup in 2010, StellaService spent two years gathering data on customer satisfaction provided by thousands of online retailers including such giants as Amazon.com and LLBean.com. They measure satisfaction in four service areas—phone support, e-mail support, delivery, returns and refunds—for each retailer. Each area includes from 9 to as many as 25 different measurements. Phone support, for example, considers speed of answering the call and respondent's knowledge of the product, among its nine measurements. Delivery measurements include delivery time and product accuracy. By combining the various measurements, consumers can find summary scores for each of the four service areas. Results provide rankings of competitors, from top to bottom, showing where each retailer currently stands relative to competitors in each of the four areas of service. In the category of Sporting Goods, for example, Stella's monthly report might show Phone Support rankings among such firms as BassPro.com, Cabelas. com, DicksSportingGoods.com, etc., along with rankings on Delivery, E-mail Support, and Returns and Refunds. Rankings allow period-to-period tracking, revealing trends for improvements (or erosions) in each of the areas across time for each company.

With these measurements StellaServices hopes to better inform the consumer public on the range of customer service they can expect from online retailers. Knowing that success hinges on the validity and believability of their methods, Stella uses an independent third-party rating system; "secret shoppers" (trained employees) use strict and controlled measurement methods as they engage online retailers via e-mails, phone calls, and live chats to purchase, await deliveries, or make returns for refunds. As added assurance for validity Stella maintains a "Customer Service Measurement Process Audit" detailing its measurements, procedures for gathering and processing data, with specific steps to assure accuracy and validity. In 2012 KPMG, a Big Four auditing and CPA firm, stated in its Independent Auditing Report its opinion that StellaService's methodologies are complying with Stella's stated policies. This confirmation of validity should help in Stella's latest move, offering subscription services to retailers beginning in 2013. Subscribers, for the first time, can receive measured data showing their standing, along with competitors, on phone support, e-mail support, delivery, and returns and refunds. This service, for the first time, allows retailers to base decisions on objective and independent information about their online customer service.[20]

---

usefulness. **Emotional motives** involve nonobjective factors and include sociability, imitation of others, and aesthetics. For example, you might buy the same brand of jeans as your friends to feel accepted in a certain group, not because your friends happen to have the good sense to prefer durable, reasonably priced jeans.

Emotional Motives *reasons for purchasing a product that are based on nonobjective factors*

Postpurchase Evaluation Marketing does not stop with the sale of a product; what happens after the sale is also important. Marketers want consumers to be happy after buying products so that they are more likely to buy them again. Because consumers do not want to go through a complex decision process for every purchase, they often repurchase products they have used and liked. Not all consumers are satisfied with their purchases, of course. These buyers are not likely to purchase the same product(s) again and are much more apt to broadcast their experiences than are satisfied customers.

Organizational Marketing and Buying Behavior

OBJECTIVE 6
Discuss
the four categories of
organizational markets, and the
characteristics of B2B buying
behavior.

In the consumer market, buying and selling transactions are visible to the public. Equally important, though far less visible, are organizational (or commercial) markets. Marketing to organizations that buy goods and services used in creating and delivering consumer products or public services involves various kinds of markets and buying behaviors different from those in consumer markets.

Business Marketing

Business marketing involves organizational or commercial markets that fall into four B2B categories: (1) services companies, (2) industrial, (4) reseller, and (4) government and institutional markets. Taken together, the B2B markets do more than $25 trillion in business annually—more than two times the amount done in the U.S. consumer market.[21]

Services Companies Market *firms engaged in the business of providing services to the purchasing public*

Services Market   The **services companies market** encompasses the many firms that provide services to the purchasing public. Imagine, for example, the materials and supplies Disney World need to provide exceptional experiences for visitors. Similar needs exist to operate Continental Airlines, MTV, and the accounting firm Ernst & Young. Everything from veterinary clinics to hospitality services providers to healthcare centers and nursery schools buy resources needed to provide services to customers.

Industrial Market *organizational market consisting of firms that buy goods that are either converted into products or used during production*

Industrial Market   The **industrial market** includes businesses that buy goods to be converted into other products or that are used up during production. It includes farmers, manufacturers, and some retailers. For example, clock-making company Seth Thomas buys electronics, metal components, plastic, and glass from other companies to make clocks for the consumer market. The company also buys office supplies, tools, and factory equipment—items never seen by clock buyers—that are used during production.

Reseller Market *organizational market consisting of intermediaries that buy and resell finished goods*

Reseller Market   Before products reach consumers, they pass through a **reseller market** consisting of intermediaries, including wholesalers and retailers, that buy and resell finished goods. For example, as a leading distributor of parts and accessories for the pleasure boat market, Coast Distribution System, buys lights, steering wheels, and propellers and resells them to marinas and boat-repair shops.

Institutional Market *organizational market consisting of such nongovernmental buyers of goods and services as hospitals, churches, museums, and charitable organizations*

Government and Institutional Market   In addition to federal and state governments, there are some 89,000 local governments in the United States. State and local governments annually spend more than $3 trillion for durable goods, nondurables, services, and construction.[22] The **institutional market** consists of nongovernmental organizations, such as hospitals, churches, museums, and charities, that also use supplies and equipment as well as legal, accounting, and transportation services.

B2B Buying Behavior

In some respects, organizational buying behavior bears little resemblance to consumer buying practices. Differences include the buyers' purchasing skills and an emphasis on buyer-seller relationships.

Differences in Buyers   Unlike most consumers, organizational buyers purchase in large quantities and are professional, specialized, and well informed. Additional characteristics of B2B buyers include:

- Industrial buyers *buy in bulk or large quantities*. Because of this fact, and with so much money at stake, buyers are often experts about the products they buy. On a regular basis, B2B buyers study competing products and alternative suppliers by attending trade shows, by networking with others electronically, by reading trade literature, and by conducting technical discussions with sellers' representatives.

- As professionals, B2B buyers *are trained in methods for negotiating purchase terms.* Once buyer-seller agreements have been reached, they also arrange formal contracts.

- As a rule, industrial buyers *are company specialists in a line of items and are often experts about the products they buy.* As one of several buyers for a large bakery, for example, you may specialize in food ingredients. Another buyer may specialize in baking equipment, whereas a third may buy office equipment and supplies.

Differences in the Buyer-Seller Relationship Consumer-seller relationships are often impersonal, short-lived, one-time interactions. In contrast, B2B situations often *involve frequent and enduring buyer-seller relationships.* The development of a long-term relationship provides each party with access to the technical strengths of the other as well as the security of knowing what future business to expect. Thus, a buyer and a supplier may form a design team to create products to benefit both parties. Accordingly, industrial sellers emphasize personal selling by trained representatives who understand the needs of each customer.

Social Media and Marketing

Social networking as used by marketers today refers to communications that flow among people and organizations interacting through an online platform that facilitates building social relations among its users. **Social networking media** are the websites or access channels, such as Facebook, Twitter, LinkedIn, and YouTube, to which millions of consumers go for information and discussions before making their purchase decisions.

Social Networking *network of communications that flow among people and organizations interacting through an online platform*

Social Networking Media *websites or access channels, such as Facebook, Twitter, LinkedIn, and YouTube, to which consumers go for information and discussions*

Viral Marketing and Social Networking **Viral marketing** is a form marketing that relies on social networking and the Internet to spread information like a "virus" from person to person. The marketing purpose may be to increase brand awareness, to promote new product ideas, or to foster excitement for stimulating sales. Messages about new cars, sports events, and numerous other goods and services flow via networks among potential customers who pass the information on to others. Using various social network formats—games, contests, chat rooms, blogs, and bulletin boards—marketers encourage potential customers to try out products and tell other people about them. Marketers, including such giants as Bank of America, McDonald's, eBay, and Cisco, are using **corporate blogs** increasingly for public relations, branding, and otherwise spreading messages that stimulate chat about products to target markets.[23]

Viral Marketing *type of marketing that relies on the Internet to spread information like a "virus" from person to person about products and ideas*

Corporate Blogs *comments and opinions published on the Web by or for an organization to promote its activities*

Web-Driven Revenue with Social Networking Although many major consumer companies have their own Facebook page, small businesses, too, use social media channels to increase revenues by networking with customers in target markets. A2L Consulting, for example, offers services to law firms, such as jury consulting, pretrial services, courtroom technologies, and litigation graphics among other litigation services. The company uses multiple social networks, including Google+, YouTube, Pinterest, LinkedIn, and Twitter to increase Web-driven revenue. With 12,000 website visits each month in 2012 (up from 800 monthly in 2011), A2L's revenue results from Web traffic for 2012 were equally impressive—five times those for the year previously. Company representatives credited LinkedIn, from among the social-media networks used by A2L, as the most effective for connecting with this B2B target market.[24]

How effective can it be? Viral marketing and social networking can lead to consumer awareness faster and with wider reach than traditional media messages—and at a lower cost. Success of the movie *Avatar* is credited to 20th Century Fox's use of prerelease viral tactics for stimulating public awareness of the blockbuster movie. And A2L, the supplier of litigation services to law firms, credits social networking for increasing the firm's revenues. It works for two reasons. First, people rely on the Internet for information that they used to get from newspapers, magazines, and television. Equally important, however, is the interactive element; the customer becomes a participant in the process of spreading the word by forwarding information to and seeking information from other network users.

The continuing growth of social media is changing marketing practices of businesses, and consumer behavior, too. Facebook has become the Internet's most-used social media site, with more than one billion active users each month, and more than 650 million users each day. Although Facebook is the leader, Twitter is the faster growing network, ranking number two in size with more than 550 million registered users averaging nearly 60 million tweets each day. In 2012, alone, the number of users grew by 40 percent, ending the year with more than 20 percent of the world's monthly internet users visiting Twitter. These numbers reflect not only the huge size of the social media industry, but also the enormous population of participants that influence and persuade one another to explore new ideas and products, thus becoming both consumers and sellers. The industry's growth is attributed especially to (1) increasing numbers of mobile device users, (2) more participants in the older-than-55 demographic that are using Twitter, and (3) greater global reach to more potential users. As companies gain experience they are using social media in new ways. In addition to advertising promotions, Kellogg Company uses social media for consumer research and to get new product ideas. Procter & Gamble has learned that viral exposure on Facebook can generate more sales than TV advertising. eBay finds that its sellers and buyers use social media to guide other buyers and sellers to eBay's website. For students of marketing the social media trend has two clear implications: (1) As consumers using social media you will receive a growing number of tempting product exposures, and (2) As a user of social media who becomes familiar with its applications and technical operations, you will find a growing number of career opportunities in social media positions.[25]

The International Marketing Mix

Marketing internationally means mounting a strategy to support global business operations. Foreign customers differ from domestic buyers in language, customs, business practices, and consumer behavior. If they go global, marketers must reconsider each element of the marketing mix: product, pricing, place, and promotion.

International Products Some products can be sold abroad with virtually no changes. Coca-Cola and Marlboro are the same in Peoria, Illinois, and Paris, France. In other cases, U.S. firms have had to create products with built-in flexibility, like an electric shaver that is adaptable to either 120- or 230-volt outlets, so travelers can use it in both U.S. and European electrical outlets. Frequently, however, domestic products require a major redesign for buyers in foreign markets. To sell computers in Japan, for example, Apple had to develop a Japanese-language operating system.

International Pricing When pricing for international markets, marketers must consider the higher costs of transporting and selling products abroad. For example, because of the higher costs of buildings, rent, equipment, and imported meat, a McDonald's Big Mac that costs $4.20 in the United States has a price tag of $6.81 in Switzerland.

International Distribution In some industries, including consumer products and industrial equipment, delays in starting new international distribution networks can be costly, so companies with existing distribution systems often enjoy an advantage. Many companies have avoided time delays by buying existing businesses with already-established distribution and marketing networks. Procter & Gamble, for example, bought Revlon's Max Factor and Betrix cosmetics, both of which have

Indranil Kishor/Photoshot Holdings Ltd.

Before creating an international ad like this Chinese advertisement for Coca-Cola, it is crucial to research what disparities, such as meaning of words, traditions, and taboos, exist between different societies. For example, German manufacturers of backpacks label them as "body bags," not terribly enticing to the U.S. consumer. Can you guess why Gerber baby food is not sold in France? The French translation of Gerber is "to vomit"! Effective marketing does not just involve knowledge of culture abroad, but also requires a general sensitivity to social trends and language.

distribution and marketing networks in foreign markets. Many times, distribution methods used in the United States don't fit in international markets. For example, in Europe, Breathe Right Nasal Strips are identified as "medicinal" and must be sold in pharmacies.

International Promotion Occasionally, a good ad campaign is a good campaign just about anywhere. Quite often, however, U.S. promotional tactics do not succeed in other countries. Many Europeans believe that a product must be inherently shoddy if a company resorts to any advertising, particularly the U.S. hard-sell variety.

International marketers are ever more aware of cultural differences that can cause negative reactions to improperly advertised products. Some Europeans, for example, are offended by TV commercials that show weapons or violence. Meanwhile, cigarette commercials that are banned from U.S. television thrive in many Asian and European markets. Managers must carefully match product promotions to local customs and cultural values to successfully promote sales and avoid offending customers.

Because of the need to adjust the marketing mix, success in international markets is hard won. But whether a firm markets in domestic or international markets, the basic principles of marketing still apply; only their implementation changes.

Small Business and the Marketing Mix

OBJECTIVE 7
Discuss
the marketing mix as it applies to small business.

Many of today's largest firms were yesterday's small businesses. Behind the success of many small firms lies a skillful application of the marketing concept and an understanding of each element in the marketing mix.

entrepreneurship and new ventures

Social Networking for Jobs in Good Times and in Bad

If you're out of work, looking for a job, and wondering where to turn, help is as close as your iPad or iPod. Although troubled times continue to dampen demand for many products, others are getting a boost, such as service products like social networking sites. While popular entertainment sites, including Facebook, YouTube, and Twitter, began as cyber highways for recreational and friendship interactions, social networking today is used for much more than simply entertainment. In today's economy, there's a different kind of traffic—professional networking for career transition—among the list of cyber networking products for job-hunting assistance.

LinkedIn, started by five co-founders in the living room of Reid Hoffman in 2002, is an example of an interconnected network that now serves professionals in 200 countries and some 170 industries. Officially founded in 2003, this Mountain View, California, start-up had 4,500 members in the network after just one month. Today, profiles from more than 200 million members include executives from all *Fortune 500* companies. Users can post résumés, search companies, and find job openings. The LinkedIn jobs directory allows users choices for searching by industry, or by job function, geographic region, job title, or by company. However, the key attraction of the network is personal connections: one member knows other LinkedIn users, who link with still others, and so on as information flows to those looking for good candidates until they find a word-of-mouth prospect that looks good. The system is based on trusted relationships and connections, and it works; LinkedIn is the world's largest business network, and it connects a huge pool of talent that keeps on growing.

In addition to professionals looking for jobs, there are also business members, some searching for prospective employees,

Vika Sabo/Alamy

industry experts, potential clients, or new business opportunities. Others are interested in sharing the latest business developments within their networks of contacts. LinkedIn Groups, for example, consists of specialty network groups of businesses and professionals focused on particular industries, including Social Media Marketing, Finance and Accounting Professionals, or Business in Japan, to name just three of many. Group members may share industry-specific information on performance-enhancing practices, legal issues, current events, and even participate in determining new directions for their industry.

LinkedIn's further growth depends on the value it provides for meeting its members' needs for professional fulfillment. As the world's largest professional network on the Internet, LinkedIn's industry-leading innovations are yielding attractive financial results as well. Revenue leaped to $972 million for 2012, up from $522 the year before.[26]

Small-Business Products

Some new products and firms are doomed at the start because few customers want or need what they have to offer. Many fail to estimate realistic market potential, and some offer new products before they have clear pictures of their target segments. In contrast, a thorough understanding of what customers want has paid off for many small firms. Take, for example, the case of Little Earth Productions, Inc., a company that makes fashion accessories, such as handbags. Originally, the company merely considered how consumers would use its handbags. But after examining shopping habits, Little Earth Productions redesigned for better in-store display. Because stores can give handbags better visibility by hanging them instead of placing them on floors or low countertops, Little Earth Productions added small handles specifically for that purpose, resulting in increased sales.

Small-Business Pricing

Haphazard pricing can sink a firm with a good product. Small-business pricing errors usually result from a failure to estimate operating expenses accurately. The founder of Nomie Baby, makers of spill-proof removable car seat covers for infants, started by setting prices too low. Considering only manufacturing and materials costs, other costs—shipping, storage, designing—were mistakenly ignored and not covered by the original selling price. Thereafter, when startup prices were increased to cover all costs, sales fortunately did not diminish. Owners, for fear of pricing too high, often tend to under-price, resulting in financial crisis. Failing businesses have often been heard to say, "I didn't realize how much it costs to run the business!" Sometimes, however, firms discover their prices are too low, even when they cover all costs. Previously in the company's history, a computer error at Headsets.com posted cost-only prices rather than retail prices for the company's products on the internet. Surprisingly to the CEO, the erroneous low prices did not create a surge in sales. Instead, steady consumer response indicated that the firm's products were not as price-sensitive as originally believed, so the company raised original prices once, by 8 percent. Revenue rose as sales continued with little or no change from previous levels.[27] When small businesses set prices by carefully assessing costs and understanding their competitive market, many earn satisfactory profits.

Small-Business Distribution

The ability of many small businesses to attract and retain customers depends partly on the choice of location, especially for new service businesses.

In distribution as in other aspects of the marketing mix, however, smaller companies may have advantages over larger competitors. A smaller company may be able to address customers' needs more quickly and efficiently with an added personal touch. Everex Systems, Inc. of Fremont, California, designs and sells computers to wholesalers and dealers through a system that the company calls *zero response time*. Because Everex Systems is small and flexible, phone orders can be reviewed every two hours and factory assembly adjusted to match demand.

Small-Business Promotion

Successful small businesses plan for promotional expenses as part of start-up costs. Some hold down costs by using less expensive promotional methods, like publicity in local newspapers and online messaging. Other small businesses identify themselves and their products with associated groups, organizations, and events. Thus, a crafts gallery might join with a local art league to organize public showings of their combined products.

summary of learning objectives

OBJECTIVE 1

Explain the concept of marketing and identify the five forces that constitute the external marketing environment. (pp. 376–382)

Marketing is responsible for creating, communicating, and delivering value and satisfaction to customers. With limited financial resources, customers buy products that offer the best value, measured by the relationship between benefits and costs. Marketers must understand customers' wants and needs because they determine product features, and the timing, place, and terms of sale that provide utility and add value for customers. A product may be a tangible good, a service, or even an idea. Additionally, products may be classified as either consumer products or industrial products, when they are being marketed to businesses or nonprofit organizations. Although marketing often focuses on single transactions for products, services, or ideas, marketers also take a longer-term perspective by managing customer relationships to benefit the organization and its stakeholders. Customer *relationship marketing* emphasizes building lasting relationships with customers and suppliers. Stronger relationships, including stronger economic and social ties, can result in greater long-term satisfaction, customer loyalty, and customer retention.

Five outside factors comprise a company's external environment and influence its marketing programs: (1) the *political and legal environment* includes laws and regulations that may define or constrain business activities; (2) the *sociocultural environment* involves peoples' values, beliefs, and ideas that affect marketing decisions; (3) the *technological environment* includes new technologies that affect existing and new products; (4) the *economic environment* consists of conditions such as inflation, recession and interest rates that influence organizational and individual spending patterns; and (5) the *competitive environment* in which marketers must persuade buyers to purchase their products rather than their competitors'.

OBJECTIVE 2

Explain the purpose of a marketing plan and identify its main components. (pp. 382–386)

A *marketing plan* is a statement of all the future marketing activities and resources that will be used to meet the desires and needs of customers so that the firm's overall business mission will be accomplished. It begins with objectives or goals setting the stage for everything that follows. *Marketing objectives*—the things marketing intends to accomplish—are the foundation that guides all of the detailed activities in the marketing plan. The marketing objectives focus on maintaining or enhancing the organization's future competitive position in its chosen markets. A marketing strategy can be developed once the marketing objectives have been clarified. *Marketing strategy* identifies the planned marketing programs, including all the marketing activities that will be used for achieving the marketing goals, when those activities will occur, and the contents of its programs. If planned activities are not affordable—requiring more resources than are available—then activities, programs or goals are adjusted until realistic plans emerge.

Marketing strategy includes four basic components (often called the "Four Ps") of the *marketing mix*: product, pricing, place (distribution), and promotion, that marketing managers use to satisfy customers in target markets. The specific activities for each of the Four Ps are designed differently to best meet the needs of each target market. Marketing begins with a *product*, a good, service, or idea designed to fill a customer's need or want. Conceiving and developing new products is a constant challenge for marketers who must always consider changing technology, consumer wants and needs, and economic conditions. Producers often promote particular features of products to distinguish them in the marketplace. *Product differentiation* is the creation of a feature or image that makes a product differ enough from existing products to attract consumers. The *pricing* of a product is often a balancing act. Prices must be high enough to support a variety of operating, administrative, research, and marketing costs, but low enough that consumers don't turn to competitors. In the marketing mix, *place* (or distribution) refers to where and how consumers get access to the products they buy. The most visible component of the marketing mix is *promotion*, a set of techniques for communicating information about products. The most important promotional tools include advertising, personal selling, sales promotions, publicity/public relations, and direct or interactive marketing.

OBJECTIVE 3

Explain market segmentation and how it is used in target marketing. (pp. 386–388)

Marketers think in terms of *target markets*—particular groups of people or organizations on which a firm's marketing efforts are focused. Target marketing requires *market segmentation*—dividing a market into categories of customer types or "segments," such as age, geographic location, or level of income. Members of a market segment have similar wants and needs and share some common traits that influence purchasing decisions. Once they identify segments, companies adopt a variety of strategies for attracting customers in one or more of the chosen target segments. The following are five variables that are often used for segmentation: (1) *Geographic variables* are the geographical units that may be considered in developing a segmentation strategy. (2) *Demographic variables* describe populations by identifying such traits as age, income, gender, ethnic background, and marital status. (3) *Geo-demographic variables* combine demographic variables with geographic variables, such as an age category coupled with urban areas. (4) *Psychographic variables* include lifestyles, interests, and attitudes. (5) *Behavioral variables* include categories of behavioral patterns such as online consumers or large-volume buyers. Marketers search for segments showing promise for generating new sales if marketing efforts by other companies have overlooked or misjudged the segment's market potential. Such competitive weaknesses present marketing opportunities for other companies to enter into those segments. Desirable segments with market potential then become candidate target markets and, once chosen, they become part of the marketing strategy where its companion marketing mix is developed.

OBJECTIVE 4

Discuss the purpose of marketing research, and compare the four marketing research methods. (pp. 388–391)

Effective marketing decisions should be customer based and focused on timely information about trends in the marketplace. *Marketing research* is a tool for gaining such information; it is the study of what customers want and how best to meet those needs. Researchers use several methods to obtain, interpret, and apply information about customers. They determine the kinds of information needed for marketing strategy, goal setting, target-market selection, and developing new or altered products for specific market segments. Marketing research's orientation has become increasingly globalized because of the increasing importance of selling products internationally.

Research success depends on which of four basic research methods is used: (1) *Observation* means watching and recording consumer preferences and behavior. By using live camera feeds, computer tracking, and other electronic technologies marketers observe and record consumer preferences rapidly and with great accuracy. (2) The heart of any *survey* is a questionnaire on which participants record responses. Surveys can get responses to specific questions quickly and at relatively lower cost. (3) In a *focus group*, people are gathered in one place, presented with an issue or topic, and asked to discuss it. The researcher takes notes and makes video recordings, and encourages an open discussion by providing only a minimal amount of structure on the group's discussion. This technique allows researchers to explore issues too complex for questionnaires; it can produce creative ideas and solutions. (4) *Experimentation* compares the responses and behaviors of the same or similar people under different conditions that are of interest to the researcher. Experimentation can be relatively expensive because of costs of obtaining the experimental setting, securing participants, paying participants, plus payment to those who administer the experiment.

OBJECTIVE 5

Describe the consumer buying process and the key factors that influence that process. (pp. 391–393)

In the study of *consumer behavior*, marketers evaluate the decision process by which people buy and consume products. There are four major influences on consumer behavior. (1) *Psychological influences* include an individual's motivations, perceptions, ability to learn, and attitudes. (2) *Personal influences* include lifestyle, personality, and economic status. (3) *Social influences* include family, opinion leaders, and reference groups such as friends, coworkers, and professional associates. (4) *Cultural influences* include culture, subculture, and social class. At times, these influences have a significant impact on buying decisions, although consumers demonstrate high *brand loyalty* at times, regularly purchasing the same products.

Observers of consumer behavior have constructed various models to help marketer understand how consumers decide to purchase products. One model considers five influences that lead to consumption: (1) *Problem or need recognition*: The buying process begins when the consumer recognizes a problem or need. (2) *Information seeking*: Having recognized a need, consumers seek information. The information search leads to an evoked set (or consideration set)—a group of products they will consider buying. (3) *Evaluation of alternatives*: By analyzing product attributes (price, prestige, quality) of the consideration set, consumers compare products to decide which product best meets their needs. (4) *Purchase decision*: "Buy" decisions are based on rational motives, emotional motives, or both. *Rational motives* involve the logical evaluation of product attributes, such as cost, quality, and usefulness. *Emotional motives* involve nonobjective factors and include sociability, imitation of others, and aesthetics. (5) *Postpurchase evaluations*: Consumers continue to form opinions after their purchase. Marketers want consumers to be happy after the consumption of products so that they are more likely to buy them again.

OBJECTIVE 6

Discuss the four categories of organizational markets, and the characteristics of B2B buying behavior. (pp. 394–397)

The various organizational markets exhibit different buying behaviors from those in consumer markets. Business marketing involves organizational or commercial markets that fall into four B2B categories. (1) The *services companies market* encompasses the many firms that provide services to the purchasing public. Everything from pet care to hospitality services to health care and nursery schools, airlines, and more, buy resources needed to provide services to customers. (2) The *industrial market* consists of businesses that buy goods to be converted into other products or that are used during production. It includes farmers, manufacturers, and some retailers. (3) Before some products reach consumers, they pass through a *reseller market* consisting of intermediaries—wholesalers and retailers—that buy finished goods and resell them. (4) The *government and institutional market* includes federal, state, and local governments, and nongovernmental buyers—hospitals, churches, museums, and charities—that purchase goods and services needed for serving their clients. Taken together, these four organizational markets do more than two times the business annually than that of the U.S. consumer markets.

Unlike most consumers, organizational buyers purchase in large quantities and are professional, specialized, and well informed. As professionals, they are trained in methods for negotiating purchase terms. Once buyer-seller agreements have been reached, they also arrange formal contracts. In contrast with consumer-seller relationships that are often one-time interactions, B2B situations involve frequent and enduring buyer-seller relationships that provide each party, buyer and seller, with access to the technical strengths of the other. Thus, a buyer and a supplier may form a design team to create products to benefit both parties. Accordingly, industrial sellers emphasize personal selling by trained representatives who understand the needs of each customer.

OBJECTIVE 7

Discuss the marketing mix as it applies to small business.

(pp. 397–399)

Each element in the marketing mix can determine success or failure for any *small business*. Many *products* are failures because consumers don't need what they have to offer. A realistic market potential requires getting a clearer picture of what target segments want. Small-business *pricing* errors usually result from a failure to estimate startup costs and operating expenses accurately. In addition to facilities construction or rental costs, shipping, storage, wages, taxes, utilities, and materials costs, too, must be considered. By carefully assessing costs, and by learning what customers are willing to pay, prices can be set to earn satisfactory profits. Perhaps the most crucial aspect of *place*, or distribution, is location, especially for services businesses, because locational convenience determines the ability to attract customers. Although *promotion* can be expensive and is essential for small businesses, costs can be reduced by using less expensive promotional methods. Local newspaper articles, online messaging, and television programming cover business events, thus providing free public exposure.

key terms

advertising (p. 385)
behavioral segmentation (p. 388)
behavioral variables (p. 388)
brand competition (p. 382)
brand loyalty (p. 391)
competitive environment (p. 381)
consumer behavior (p. 391)
consumer goods (p. 378)
corporate blogs (p. 395)
cultural influences (p. 391)
customer relationship management (CRM) (p. 378)
data mining (p. 379)
data warehousing (p. 378)
demographic segmentation (p. 387)
demographic variables (p. 387)
economic environment (p. 380)
emotional motives (p. 393)
evoked set (or consideration set) (p. 392)
experimentation (p. 391)
focus group (p. 391)
form utility (p. 377)
geographic segmentation (p. 387)
geographic variables (p. 387)
geo-demographic segmentation (p. 387)

geo-demographic variables (p. 387)
industrial goods (p. 378)
industrial market (p. 394)
institutional market (p. 394)
integrated marketing strategy (p. 386)
international competition (p. 382)
market segmentation (p. 386)
marketing (p. 376)
marketing manager (p. 383)
marketing mix (p. 384)
marketing objectives (p. 383)
marketing plan (p. 382)
marketing research (p. 388)
marketing strategy (p. 383)
observation (p. 390)
personal influences (p. 391)
personal selling (p. 385)
place (distribution) (p. 384)
place utility (p. 377)
political-legal environment (p. 379)
possession utility (p. 377)
pricing (p. 384)
primary data (p. 390)
product (p. 384)
product differentiation (p. 384)

product positioning (p. 387)
promotion (p. 385)
psychographic segmentation (p. 388)
psychographic variables (p. 388)
psychological influences (p. 391)
public relations (p. 386)
rational motives (p. 392)
relationship marketing (p. 378)
reseller market (p. 394)
sales promotions (p. 385)
secondary data (p. 390)
services (p. 378)
services companies market (p. 394)
social influences (p. 391)
social networking (p. 395)
social networking media (p. 395)
sociocultural environment (p. 380)
substitute product (p. 382)
surveys (p. 391)
technological environment (p. 380)
time utility (p. 377)
target market (p. 386)
utility (p. 377)
value (p. 376)
viral marketing (p. 395)

MyBizLab

Go to **pearsonglobaleditions.com/mybizlab** to complete the problems marked with this icon ✪.

questions & exercises

QUESTIONS FOR REVIEW

11-1. What are the five forces in the external marketing environment?

11-2. How is the concept of the value package useful in marketing to consumers and industrial customers?

11-3. What is market segmentation and how is it used in target marketing?

⭐ **11-4.** How does the buying behavior of consumers differ from buyers in organizational markets?

QUESTIONS FOR ANALYSIS

11-5. Select an everyday product (personal fitness training, CDs, dog food, cell phones, or shoes, for example). Show how different versions of your product are aimed toward different market segments. Explain how the marketing mix differs for each segment.

⭐ **11-6.** Use the five-step model of rational decision making to describe the process of selecting a college. Does this model reflect the way that you made a decision about attending college? Why or why not?

11-7. Imagine being the marketing manager for a large U.S. hotel chain. How might the company have to adapt its marketing mix to move into foreign markets in South and Central America?

⭐ **11-8.** Choose an existing product that could benefit from viral marketing. Once you have identified the product, describe how you would use viral marketing to increase demand for the product.

APPLICATION EXERCISES

11-9. Identify a company with a product that interests you. Consider ways the company could use customer relationship management (CRM) to strengthen relationships with its target market. Specifically, explain your recommendations on how the company can use each of the four basic components of the marketing mix in its CRM efforts.

11-10. The U.S. Census collects an enormous amount of secondary data that is useful in marketing research. Go to the American Fact Finder home page at http://factfinder2.census.gov and collect data about people living in your zip code. Compare your zip code to your state as a whole in terms of factors such as age, race, household size, marital status, and educational attainment. Based on your data, what types of retail establishments would be specially appropriate to your area?

building a business: continuing team exercise

Assignment

Meet with your team members to consider your new business venture and how it relates to the marketing processes and consumer behavior topics in this chapter. Develop specific responses to the following:

11-11. Develop a "Statement of Marketing Objectives" for your company. Justify those marketing objectives by explaining how they contribute to the overall business mission of the company.

11-12. Identify the target market(s) for your business. Who are your customers? Describe the characteristics of customers in your target market(s).

11-13. Discuss how your team is going to identify the existing competitors in your chosen market. Based on the discussion, what are the key elements of your marketing plans that will give you a competitive edge over those competitors?

11-14. Consider, again, the customers in your target market(s). Are they individual consumers, or organizations, or a mix of both consumers and organizations? Describe in detail the buying process(es) you expect them to use for purchasing your product(s). Discuss whether the customer buying process should or should not be of concern for your company.

11-15. Develop a preliminary design of the marketing mix for your target market(s). Retain the design for carryover and refinement in the following marketing chapters.

building your business skills

DEALING WITH VARIABLES

Goal

To encourage you to analyze the ways in which various market segmentation variables affect business success.

Background Information

You and four partners are thinking of purchasing a heating and air conditioning (H/AC) dealership that specializes in residential applications priced between $2,000 and $40,000. You are

now in the process of deciding where that dealership should be located. You are considering four locations: Miami, Florida; Westport, Connecticut; Dallas, Texas; and Spokane, Washington.

Method

STEP 1

Working with your partnership group, examine some business information sources to learn how H/AC makers market residential products. Check for articles in the *Wall Street Journal, Business Week, Fortune,* and other business publication sources.

STEP 2

Continue your research by focusing on the specific marketing variables that define each prospective location. Check Census Bureau and Department of Labor data at your library and on the Internet and contact local chambers of commerce (by phone and via the Internet) to learn about the following factors for each location:

11-16. Geography

11-17. Demography (especially age, income, gender, family status, and social class)

11-18. Geo-demographic information

11-19. Psychographic factors (lifestyles, interests, and attitudes)

11-20. Behavioral patterns of consumers

STEP 3

As a group, determine which location holds the greatest promise as a dealership site. Base your decision on your analysis of market segment variables and their effects on H/AC sales.

FOLLOW-UP QUESTIONS

11-21. Which location did you choose? Describe the segmentation factors that influenced your decision.

11-22. Identify the two most important variables that you believe will affect the dealership's success. Why are these factors so important?

11-23. Which factors were least important? Why?

11-24. When equipment manufacturers advertise residential H/AC products, they often show them in different climate situations (winter, summer, or high-humidity conditions). Which market segments are these ads targeting? Describe these segments in terms of demographic and psychographic characteristics.

exercising your ethics

WEIGHING THE ODDS

The Situation

You are the quality control manager for a major dietary supplement company. Because your products are sold over the counter as nutritional supplements rather than as medications, you are not regulated by the Food and Drug Administration. Researchers have worked for years to develop a weight loss product that is safe and effective. Several years ago, researchers identified a naturally occurring compound that was effective in appetite suppression. Your company has done several years of testing and you have found that 85 percent of people using the supplement were able to lose at least 20 pounds in the first year of use. Additionally, those who continued to take the supplement were able to maintain their weight loss for an additional year. Company executives believe that this drug can bring billions of dollars in revenues in the first year of sales. Obesity has become an epidemic in the United States and much of the developed world and people who are obese are at a significantly greater risk of stroke, heart attack, and diabetes.

The Dilemma

You are reviewing the results of the clinical trials and are pleased to see that the product is effective. Just as you are ready to recommend that the company introduce the product to the market, you uncover some upsetting information. A small group of people who took the supplement during testing, actually less than 1 percent, developed a rare neurological disorder. It's not clear that the supplement is the cause of the disorder, but it was not observed in the control group that took a placebo. Because the risk is so small, the marketing manager is recommending that the company go ahead with introducing the supplement and monitor to see if consumers report a similar side effect. Commercialization of this product could make your company profitable and could potentially save thousands of lives by helping consumers lose weight, but you are unsure if this is the right thing to do.

QUESTIONS TO ADDRESS

11-25. How would you characterize the particular ethical issues in this situation?

11-26. From an ethical standpoint, what are the obligations of the quality control manager and the marketing manager regarding the introduction of the product in this situation?

11-27. If you were the quality control manager, how would you handle this matter?

team exercise

HOME AWAY FROM HOME

The Situation

Green Hills College is a rapidly growing private college located in the midwestern United States. Many of their students live on campus in dorms, but their growing enrollment has pushed a large percentage of the students off campus. A longtime resident of the community, Oliver Douglas, has decided to develop his farmland into student housing but is unsure exactly what type of housing is most appropriate.

The Dilemma

Although he's been a farmer most of his life, Oliver Douglas realizes that the best use of his property is to develop it into student housing. He has made contacts in the county zoning office and has been assured that they are willing to rezone his property for student housing, given the importance of the college to the local economy. Oliver has done his research and has realized that there are a lot of options. He can build dorm-style housing, apartments, townhouses, or even detached homes for students. Each has its pros and cons.

Team Activity

Assemble a group of four students and assign each group member to one of the following options for housing:

- Dorm-style housing
- Apartments
- Townhouses
- Detached homes

ACTION STEPS

11-28. As a group, describe the characteristics, wants, and needs of the target market.

11-29. In addition to students, who else will have an influence on housing decision?

11-30. Have each group member identify the pros and cons of the type of housing that they have been assigned.

11-31. Considering all the options, which housing option do you think makes most sense? Come to a group consensus and describe your reasoning.

11-32. Address each element of the marketing mix and describe how it will appeal to the target market.

cases

Starbucks Brews a New Marketing Mix

Continued from page 376

At the beginning of this chapter you read about Starbucks' marketing strategy—how it changed during the 2008 recession and, more recently, how it was changed again. Using the information presented in this chapter, you should now be able to answer the following questions.

QUESTIONS FOR DISCUSSION

11-33. What forces in the external environment are influencing the changes in Starbucks's marketing strategy? Explain.

11-34. How are the components of Starbucks's marketing mix being used for implementing the new marketing strategy?

11-35. Identify the main factors favoring success for Starbucks's crossover into the affordability market during the 2008 recession. What prominent factors at that time suggested major problems or even failure for this crossover attempt?

11-36. Applying this chapter's definition of product value to Starbucks's plans, what are the benefits in Starbucks's affordability offerings? What are the costs?

11-37. In what ways, if any, does the more recent Starbucks marketing strategy plan have any impact on the product value of its new and more-established luxury products? For the company's competitiveness?

Where Has All the Middle Gone?

Procter & Gamble (P&G), the iconic marketer of seemingly endless lines of household products since 1837, is confronted now with a puzzling marketing dilemma: "What's happening to the middle class in the United States? The number of mid-range shoppers is shrinking." With its lineup of popular brands such as Folgers, Clairol, Charmin, and Gillette, it is estimated that 98 percent of U.S. households are using at least one P&G product, a position that has grown largely by targeting middle-class consumers. Although its products are sold in more than 180 countries, U.S. consumers provide more than 35 percent of P&G sales and nearly 60 percent of annual profits.

The problem facing P&G is the shrinkage of middle-class purchasing power, a change that began with the 2008 recession and continues today in the nation's struggling economy. Many once well-off middle-class families are pinched with rising prices for gasoline, food, education, and health care but little or no wage increases. With a whopping 16 million people out of work or underemployed, along with millions of others wondering how and when they will be able financially to retire, middle-class families are reducing their household budgets. The nation's economic condition, as a result, has been dubbed by Citigroup as the "Consumer Hour Glass Theory." Advocates of the theory assert that purchasing power has shifted away from the once-massive middle and is concentrated now at the bottom and top. That's where consumer action is now, at the high-end market and the low-end market, and it will increase even more.[28]

Will middle-class shrinkage continue, or is it a passing blip that will recover in the near future? Based on P&G's research, Melanie Healey, group president for P&G's North America business, expects middle-class downsizing will be a continuing trend. Accordingly, P&G and other companies are rethinking their target markets. Aiming at the high-end segment in 2009, the company introduced its more expensive Olay Pro-X skincare product. Previously, P&G introduced Gains, the bargain-priced dish soap, which is aimed at the growing lower portion of the previous middle-class market following a dip in sales of the mid-priced Tide brand. Near the beginning of the recession, P&G's lower-priced Luvs diapers gained market share from the higher-priced Pampers brand. Following a path similar to that of P&G, H. J. Heinz has developed more food products for the lower-priced markets. Meanwhile, retailers focusing on lower-income consumers, such as Dollar General, are attracting customers from higher-priced Walmart and Target.[29]

Refocusing away from the mainstream middle onto high- and low-end consumers is a new marketing experience at P&G. They have increased market research on lower-income households, often using face-to-face interviews to gain in-depth understanding of these consumers. So far, the low-end and the high-end segments each are generally smaller than the former massive middle-class market, which means P&G is splitting its marketing efforts, rather than having just a single larger thrust. As one company official noted, historically they have been good at doing things on a larger scale, but now they are learning how to deal with smaller sales volumes for products in each of two segments. New product development is affected, too, because the high-end segment often involves fewer products with attractive extra features that will sell profitably at higher prices. P&G is betting that the Hourglass Theory has set the course for the company's future.

QUESTIONS FOR DISCUSSION

11-38. How would you best describe P&G's marketing strategy for the situation presented in this case? Explain why.

11-39. What elements of P&G's external marketing environment, if any, are influencing the company's marketing strategy? Explain your reasoning.

11-40. Why do you suppose P&G's marketing research includes face-to-face interviews for the situation described in this case? Would other forms of marketing research also be useful in this situation? Explain your reasoning.

11-41. Explain the roles of target marketing and market segmentation as they apply in this case.

11-42. In what ways are the components of P&G's marketing mix being affected by the situation described in this case? Give examples to illustrate.

MyBizLab

Go to **pearsonglobaleditions.com/mybizlab** *for the following Assisted-grading writing questions:*

11-43. Marketing in every business must consider the firm's external environment and the environmental forces (or "marketing environments") that effect marketing decisions, successes and failures. Recall and consider the major elements in the "marketing environment." Write an essay explaining how a firm's marketing strategy must consider each of those elements in the "marketing environment." In your discussion, give examples of how each element enters into the development of marketing strategy.

11-44. Consumer behavior includes many concepts and activities including "influences on consumer behavior" and "the consumer buying process." Suppose someone who is not familiar with these terms asks you what they mean. Write an essay that describes and gives examples of what marketers mean when they talk about "influences on consumer behavior." Continue the essay by describing "the consumer buying process" and how it is used by marketers. Are the two concepts, related to one another? Explain your answer.

11-45. Mybizlab Only—comprehensive writing assignment for this chapter.

end notes

1 Janet Adamy, "At Starbucks, a Tall Order for New Cuts, Store Closures," *Wall Street Journal*, January 29, 2009, pp. B1, B4; Associated Press, "Want Fries with That?" *Columbia Daily Tribune*, February 3, 2009, p. 6B; Rick Wartzman, "A Marketing Spill on Starbucks' Hands," *BusinessWeek*, February 20, 2009, at http://www.businessweek.com/managing/content/feb2009/ca20090220_819348.htm; Michael Arndt, "McDonald's Specialty Coffee Kick," May 14, 2008, at http://www.businessweek.com/bwdaily/dnflash/content/may2008/db20080514_138620.htm; Associated Press, "Starbucks to Sell Value-Meal Pairings for $3.95," *MSNBC.com*, February 9, 2009, at http://www.msnbc.msn.com/id/29099087.

2 Julie Jargon, "Coupons Boost Starbucks," *Wall Street Journal*, November 2, 2012, p. B6.

3 "Starbucks to Boost Footprint," *Columbia Daily Tribune*, December 5, 2012, p. 6B; Candice Choi, "Starbucks To Open 1,500 More Cafes In U.S. Over Next 5 Years," *Huffington Post*, December 5, 2012, at http://huffingtonpost.com/2012/12/05/starbucks-open-1500-cafes_n_2243965.html?view=print&comm_ref=false.

4 Laurie Burkitt and Bob Davis, "Chasing China's Shoppers," *Wall Street Journal*, June 15, 2012, pp. B1, B4.

5 American Marketing Association, "Definition of Marketing," at http://www.marketingpower.com/aboutama/pages/definitionofmarketing.aspx, accessed on March 18, 2013.

6 Philip Kotler and Gary Armstrong, *Principles of Marketing*, 12th ed. (Upper Saddle River, NJ: Prentice Hall, 2008), 7.

7 "CRM (customer relationship management)," *TechTarget.com*, at http://searchcrm.techtarget.com/definition/CRM, accessed on December 8, 2010 ; "Customer Relationship Management," *Wikipedia*, at http://en.wikipedia.org/wiki/Customer_relationship_management, accessed on December 8, 2010.

8 Poonam Khanna, "Hotel Chain Gets Personal with Customers," *Computing Canada*, April 8, 2005, p. 18.

9 "Fairmont Hotels & Resorts: Website Development and Enhanced CRM," *accenture*, at http://www.accenture.com/Global/Services/By_Industry/Travel/Client_Successes/FairmontCrm.htm, accessed on December 8, 2010.

[10] "Tiny House Purchases See Big Growth," *Columbia Daily Tribune*, December 4, 2010, p. 11; "Solar Wells Displace Windmills on Range," Columbia Daily Tribune, July 22, 2010, p. 8B; Shawn McCarthy and Greg Keenan, "Ottawa Demands Lower Auto Worker Costs," *The Globe and Mail*, January 19, 2009, at http://v1business.theglobeandmail.com/servlet/story/RTGAM.20090119.wrautos19/BNStory/Business; Gail Edmondson, Ian Rowley, Nandini Lakshman, David Welch, and Dexter Roberts, "The Race to Build Really Cheap Cars," *BusinessWeek*, April 23, 2007, at http://www.businessweek.com/magazine/content/07_17/b4031064.htm; McClatchy Newspapers (Las Vegas), "Downsizing to 'Right-Sizing,'" *Columbia Daily Tribune: Saturday Business*, January 31, 2009, p. 10; Jim Henry, "Prius Hybrid Aimed Small, Stood Tall," *Automotive News*, October 29, 2007, p. 150 (3 pages) at http://www.autonews.com/apps/pbcs.dll/article?AID=/20071029/ANA06/710290326/1078&Profile=1078#; Burrelles Luce, "Hitting the Right Note: Best Practices for Corporate Social Responsibility (CSR) Marketing," *E-Newsletter*, July 2007, at http://luceonline.us/newsletter/default_july07.php.

[11] Shawn McCarthy and Greg Keenan, "Ottawa Demands Lower Auto Worker Costs," *The Globe and Mail*, January 19, 2009, at http://v1business.theglobeandmail.com/servlet/story/RTGAM.20090119.wrautos19/BNStory/Business; McClatchy Newspapers, "Lemons into Lemonade," *Columbia Daily Tribune*, February 2, 2009, p. 7B.

[12] McClatchy Newspapers, "Airbus to Be Allowed to Bid to Replace Air Force One," *Columbia Daily Tribune*, January 25, 2009, p. 4D.

[13] Joanna Stern, "iPhone 5: The Best 5 New Features," *ABC News*, September 13, 2012, at http://abcnews.go.com/Technology/iphone-top-features/story?id=17228259#.

[14] Seth Barton, "Samsung Galaxy s4 Release Date, Price & Specs Unveiled," *Expert Reviews*, March 17, 2013, at http://www.expertreviews.co.uk/smartphones/1298554/samsung-galaxy-s4-release-date-price-specs-unveiled.

[15] Min-Jeong Lee and Yun-Hee Kim, "Samsung Bets Software Can Lift New Phone," *Wall Street Journal*, March 15, 2013, p. B4.

[16] Steve Schifferes, "The Triumph of Lean Production," *BBC News*, February 27, 2007, at http://news.bbc.co.uk/2/hi/business/6346315stm.

[17] "Financial Cards in Poland," Euromonitor International, (May 2008), at http://www.euromonitor.com/Consumer_Finance_in_Poland.

[18] Scott Smith, "Coca-Cola Lost Millions Because of This Market Research Mistake," Qualtrics (Qualtrics Blog), January 21, 2013, at http://www.qualtrics.com/blog/coca-cola-market-research/.

[19] "2008 Brand Keys Customer Loyalty Engagement Index," (March 18, 2008), at http://www.brandkeys.com/awards/cli08.cfm.

[20] "A World with Better Customer Service—Helping Consumers Find It, and Helping Businesses Achieve It," *StellaService*, at http://www.stellaservice.com/, accessed on March 25, 2013; Dana Mattioli, "Data Firm Attracts Funding," *Wall Street Journal*, February 28, 2013, p. B5; Don Davis, "StellaService Raises $15 Million and Starts Charging for its e-Retail Data," *Internet Retailer*, February 28,

2013, at http://www.internetretailer.com/2013/02/28/stellaservice-raises-15-million-and-starts-charging-data.

[21] "Lists and Structure of Governments," *United States Cencus Bureau, U.S. Department of Commerce*, at www.census.gov/govs/go, accessed on March 18, 2013.

[22] "Lists and Structure of Governments."

[23] Judy Strauss, Adel El-Ansary, and Raymond Frost, *E-Marketing*, 5th ed. (Upper Saddle River, NJ: Prentice Hall, 2007); "Ten Corporate Blogs Worth Reading," February 19, 2009, at http://www.blogtrepreneuer.com/2009/02/19/ten-corporate-blogs-worth-reading/.

[24] Emily Maltby and Shira Ovide, "Which Social Media Work?" *Wall Street Journal*, January 31, 2013, p. B8; "A2L Consulting Offers Its Complex Civil Litigation E-Book as a Free Download to Litigators and Litigation Support Professionals," *A2L Consulting*, January 15, 2013, at http://www.marketwire.com/press-release/a2l-consulting-offers-its-complex-civil-litigation-e-book-as-free-download-litigators-1745621.htm.

[25] Emil Protalinski, "Facebook Passes 1.11 Billion Monthly Active Users, 751 Million Mobile Users, and 665 Mission Daily Users," *TNW: The Next Web*, May 1, 2013, at http://thenextweb.com/facebook/2013/05/01/facebook-passes-1-11-billion-monthly-active-users-751-million-mobile-users-and-665-million-daily-users/; Jim Edwards, "Meet the 30 Biggest Social Media Advertisers of 2012 [Ranked]," *Business Insider*, September 27, 2012, at http://www.businessinsider.com/the-30-biggest-social-media-advertisers-of-2012-2012-9?op=1; T.J. McCue, "Twitter Ranked Fastest Growing Social media Platform in the World," *Forbes*, January 29, 2013, at http://www.forbes.com/sites/tjmccue/2013/01/29/twitter-ranked-fastest-growing-social-platform-in-the-world/.

[26] McClatchy Newspapers (Minneapolis), "Social Networking Sites Make Powerful Job-Hunting Tools," *Columbia Daily Tribune*, January 21, 2009, p. 7B; Press Release, "LinkedIn Launches New Tools to Boost HR Professionals' Efficiency as Responses to Job Postings Double in Challenging Economy," February 2, 2009, at http://press.linkedin.com/linkedin-new-hr-tools; *Linkedin.com*, accessed on March 3, 2013 at http://www.linkedin.com.

[27] Eilene Zimmerman, "Real-Life Lessons in the Delicate Art of Setting Prices," *New York Times*, April 20, 2011, at http://www.nytimes.com/2011/04/21/business/smallbusiness/21sbiz.html?pagewanted=all&_r=0.

[28] Roshni Bhatnagar, "Why Citi's Consumer Hourglass Theory Matters," *Northwestern Business Review*, January 3, 2012 at http://northwesternbusinessreview.org/why-citis-consumer-hourglass-theory-matters/.

[29] Ellen Byron, "As Middle Class Shrinks, P&G Aims High and Low," *Wall Street Journal*, September 12, 2011, pp. A1, A16; Aimee Groth, "The Consumer Hourglass Theory: This Is Why P&G, Saks, and Heinz Are Ignoring the Middle Class," *Business Insider*, September 24, 2011 at http://www.businessinsider.com/hourglass-consumer-theory-pg-citigroup-2011-9.

chapter 12 | Developing and Pricing Products

If you want to be number one, know what people

want and how much they want to pay.

Your company's success

depends on it.

AFTER READING THIS CHAPTER, YOU SHOULD BE ABLE TO:

OBJECTIVE 1   **Explain** the definition of a product as a value package and classify goods and services.

OBJECTIVE 2   **Describe** the new product development process.

OBJECTIVE 3   **Describe** the stages of the product life cycle (PLC) and methods for extending a product's life.

OBJECTIVE 4   **Identify** the various pricing objectives that govern pricing decisions, and describe the price-setting tools used in making these decisions.

OBJECTIVE 5   **Discuss** pricing strategies that can be used for different competitive situations and identify the pricing tactics that can be used for setting prices.

MyBizLab®

⭐ Improve Your Grade!

Visit **pearsonglobaleditions.com/mybizlab** for simulations, tutorials, and end-of-chapter problems.

simulations   videos   assisted-graded writing

Over 10 million students improved their results using the Pearson MyLabs.

iTunes
Is It

In 2012, iTunes continued to be the number-one music retailer in the United States, selling 29 percent of all music purchased by U.S. consumers. Since its beginning, Apple's giant storehouse of digital music has sold more than 25 billion songs, currently sells 15,000 songs per minute to more than 130 million customers, and holds more than 64 percent of the market share for global digital downloads. "Monkey Drums" (Goksel Vancin Remix) by Chase Buch was the 25 billionth download and was sold in Germany to Phillip Lüpke. He received a 10,000 Euro iTunes Gift Card as a remembrance of his milestone purchase.

Apple has perfected the art of creating a buzz by coupling iTunes's massive music library with stylish, must-have gadgets like the iPad, iPod, and iPhone. TV and online ads feature products showing off their groundbreaking functionality to the soundtracks of songs so infectious you can hardly resist shelling out $0.69 (for some songs), $0.99 (for most songs), or $1.29 (for the most popular songs) each at the iTunes music store. That three-tier (or "variable") pricing policy was part of former Apple CEO Steve Jobs's plan to keep a customer base of loyal purchasers from resorting to piracy. He criticized the "greedy" music industry for its push to raise digital download prices. But don't assume that Jobs was all generosity; his contentment with a relatively meager profit from the iTunes music store was more than made up for by the billions of dollars Apple rakes in each year from sales of its own iTunes-compatible MP3 players and smartphones.[1]

iTunes has also capitalized on the fastest method of product delivery—high-speed Internet—and the tech savvy of its target teen market. As a result of Apple's efforts, by 2012 only about one-third of U.S. teens purchased a CD, and brick-and-mortar retailers such as Walmart have reduced the amount of physical store space devoted to CDs.[2] As gadgets and software become increasingly affordable and user-friendly, teens aren't the only demographic flooding the market. Baby Boomers can tap into iTunes's increasing supply of classic music titles to replace their worn-out vinyl. iTunes shoppers of all ages, including older generations, can download books and informational podcasts through iTunes U, a distribution system which offers downloadable lectures, films, and other educational programs. (After studying the content in this chapter you should be able to answer a set of discussion questions found at the end of the chapter.)

what's in it for me?

Becoming the number-one retailer in any market takes a solid understanding of how to develop an attractive product and how best to set prices to achieve profit and market share objectives. This chapter describes what constitutes a good product, identifies important classifications of products, and discusses the activities involved in developing new products. We will also see that any product's marketing success depends on setting prices that appeal to each target audience. By understanding this chapter's methods for pricing you'll have a clearer picture of how to select pricing that is appropriate for meeting different business objectives, recognize and apply various price-setting tools, and revise pricing strategies and tactics as products move through their life cycles. You'll also be prepared to evaluate a company's product and pricing activities as they relate to its marketing programs and competitive potential.

Recent developments in the fast-moving music industry remind us that all products—including entertainment products—eventually change in response to new conditions in the surrounding environment. The iTunes pricing story follows the basic rules for developing new products in any industry: begin by identifying the changing demands of your target audience, develop new or revised products to meet those needs, and set prices to cover your costs. As you will see in this chapter, marketers can meet their goals only by making the right choices in both developing and pricing products.

As we saw in Chapter 11, managers are responsible for developing marketing plans and strategies for meeting customers' needs and wants. We saw that marketing strategy includes decisions on four components (the Four Ps) of the marketing mix: product, price, place, and promotion. In making their strategic decisions on iTunes, Apple faced a basic fact of business reality: it is virtually impossible to focus on one element of the marketing mix (such as product design) without encountering other marketing variables (such as product price). In this chapter, we'll look at two of the Four Ps. We'll start by looking at product development and how companies decide what products it will offer to its customers. Next, we'll look at the concept of *pricing* and the price-setting tools used in making pricing decisions. The next chapter will consider the remaining two elements in the marketing mix: place (distribution) and promotion.

OBJECTIVE 1

Explain

the definition of a product as a value package and classify goods and services.

What Is A Product?

In developing the marketing mix for any product, whether goods or services, marketers must consider what customers really want when they purchase products. Only then can these marketers plan strategies effectively. We begin this section where product strategy begins: by understanding that every product is a *value package* which provides benefits to satisfy the needs and wants of customers. Next, we describe the major *classifications of products*, both for consumers and organizations. Finally, we discuss the most important component in the offerings of any business: its *product mix*.

The Value Package

Whether it is a physical good, a service, or some combination of the two, customers get value from the various benefits, features, and rewards associated with a product. **Product features** are the qualities, tangible and intangible, that a company builds into its products, such as a 12-horsepower motor on a lawnmower. However, as we discussed previously, to attract buyers, features must also provide benefits; the lawnmower must also produce an attractive lawn. The owner's pleasure in knowing that the mower is nearby when needed is an intangible reward.

Product Features *tangible and intangible qualities that a company builds into its products*

Today's customer regards a product as a bundle of attributes, benefits, and features, which, taken together, marketers call the **value package**. Increasingly, buyers expect to receive products with greater value—with more benefits and features at reasonable costs—so firms must compete on the basis of enhanced value packages. Consider, for example, the possible attributes in a PC value package:

Value Package *a product is marketed as a bundle of value-adding attributes, including reasonable cost*

- Easy access to understandable prepurchase information

- Features, such as wireless capability

- Attractive color and design

- Useful software packages

- Attractive prices

- Fast, simple ordering via the Internet

- Secure credit card purchasing

- Assurance of speedy delivery
- Warranties
- Easy access to technical support

Although the computer includes physical *features*—processing devices and other hardware—many items in the value package are services or intangibles that, collectively, add value by providing *benefits* that increase the customer's satisfaction. Reliable data processing is certainly a benefit, but so too are speedy delivery and easy access to technical support. Today, more and more firms compete on the basis of enhanced value packages. Top-performing companies find that the addition of a simple new service often pleases customers far beyond the cost of providing it. Just making the purchase transaction faster and more convenient, for example, adds value by sparing customers long waits and cumbersome paperwork. Visitors to Walt Disney World are being greeted by members of the Disney cast using Apple's iPod touch to replace turnstiles and avoid waiting lines at entrances throughout the Central Florida park.

Classifying Goods and Services

We can classify products according to expected buyers, who fall into two groups: (1) buyers of consumer products and (2) buyers of organizational products. As we saw earlier in Chapter 11, the **consumer** and **industrial buying** processes differ significantly. Similarly, marketing products to consumers is vastly different from marketing products to companies and other organizations.

Consumer *person who purchases products for personal use*

Industrial Buyer *a company or other organization that buys products for use in producing other products (goods or services)*

Classifying Consumer Products Consumer products are commonly divided into three categories that reflect buyer behavior:

- **Convenience goods** (such as milk and newspapers) and **convenience services** (such as those offered by fast-food restaurants) are consumed rapidly and regularly. They are inexpensive and are purchased often and with little input of time and effort.

- **Shopping goods** (such as appliances and mobile devices) and **shopping services** (such as hotel or airline reservations) are more expensive and are purchased less often than convenience products. Consumers often compare brands, sometimes in different stores and via Internet searches. They may also evaluate alternatives in terms of style, performance, color, price, and other criteria.

- **Specialty goods** (such as wedding gowns) and **specialty services** (such as catering for wedding receptions or healthcare insurance) are extremely important and expensive purchases. Consumers usually decide on precisely what they want and will accept no substitutes. They often go from source to source, sometimes spending a great deal of money and time to get a specific product. These are outlined in Table 12.1.

Convenience Goods *inexpensive physical goods that are consumed rapidly and regularly*

Convenience Services *inexpensive services that are consumed rapidly and regularly*

Shopping Goods *moderately expensive, infrequently purchased physical goods*

Shopping Services *moderately expensive, infrequently purchased services*

Specialty Goods *expensive, rarely purchased physical goods*

Specialty Services *expensive, rarely purchased services*

Classifying Organizational Products Depending on how much they cost and how they will be used, industrial products can be divided into three categories. These are summarized in Table 12.2.

- **Production items** are goods or services that are used directly in the conversion (production) process, such as petroleum that is converted into gasoline, and passenger demand information that is converted into bus or train services. Most consumer products, including food, clothing, housing, and entertainment services are created from production items.

- **Expense items** are goods and services that are consumed within a year by organizations producing other goods or supplying other services. The term *expense items* stems from the tradition of accounting in which expenditures are classified as either (1) expense items or (2) capital items depending on how quickly they are

Production Items *goods or services that are used in the conversion (production) process to make other products*

Expense Items *industrial products purchased and consumed within a year by firms producing other products*

table 12.1 Categories of Consumer Products

Category	Description	Examples
Convenience goods and services	• Consumed rapidly and regularly • Inexpensive • Purchased often and with little input of time and effort	• Milk • Newspaper • Fast food
Shopping goods and services	• Purchased less often • More expensive • Consumers may shop around and compare products based on style, performance, color, price, and other criteria.	• Television set • Tires • Hotel reservation
Specialty goods and services	• Purchased infrequently • Expensive • Consumer decides on a precise product and will not accept substitutions and spends a good deal of time choosing the "perfect" item.	• Luxury jewelry • Wedding gown • Healthcare insurance

consumed. Thus, paper used in printers and building maintenance services are expense items if they are consumed within a year.

Capital Items *expensive, long-lasting, infrequently purchased industrial products, such as a building, or industrial services, such as a long-term agreement for data warehousing services*

- **Capital items** are longer-lasting (expensive and sometimes permanent) goods and services. They have expected lives of more than a year; they typically are expected to last several years. Buildings (offices, factories), fixed equipment (water towers, baking ovens), and accessory equipment (information systems, airplanes) are capital goods. Capital services are those for which long-term commitments are made, such as long-term insurance services, architectural services, and financial advisory services. Because capital items are expensive and long-lasting, they often involve decisions by high-level managers.

The Product Mix

Product Mix *the group of products that a firm makes available for sale*

The group of products that a company makes available for sale, whether consumer, industrial, or both, is its **product mix.** E*TRADE, for example, offers online financial investing and trading services, retirement planning, and educational resources. Black & Decker makes toasters, food blenders, electric drills, and a variety of other appliances and tools. 3M makes everything from Post-it Notes to optical systems and more than 1,000 tape products.

Many companies begin with a single product, such as simple coffee. Over time, they find that the initial product fails to suit every customer shopping for

table 12.2 Organizational Products

Category	Description	Examples
Production items	• Goods or services used directly in the production process	• Loads of tea processed into tea bags • Information processing for real-time production • Jet fuel used by airline services
Expense items	• Goods or services that are consumed within a year by firms producing other goods or supplying other services	• Oil and electricity for machines • Building maintenance • Legal services
Capital items	• Permanent (expensive and long-lasting) goods and services • Life expectancy of more than a year • Purchased infrequently so transactions often involve decisions by high-level managers	• Buildings (offices, factories) • Fixed equipment (water towers, baking ovens) • Accessory equipment (information systems, airplanes) • Financial advisory services

the product type. To meet market demand, they introduce similar products, such as flavored coffees and various roasts, designed to reach more customers. For example, Starbucks stores expanded the line of coffees by adding various Italian-style espresso beverages that include mochas, cappuccinos, lattes, and flavored blended crèmes, followed by lighter roasts. A group of products that are closely related because they function in a similar manner (e.g., flavored coffees) or are sold to the same customer group (e.g., stop-in coffee drinkers) who will use them in similar ways is a **product line**.

Companies may extend their horizons and identify opportunities outside existing product lines. The result, *multiple* (or *diversified*) *product lines*, is evident at ServiceMaster, which was among the first successful home services that offered mothproofing and carpet cleaning. The company then expanded its product line by adding other closely related services for homeowners: lawn care (TruGreen, ChemLawn), pest control (Terminix), and cleaning (Merry Maids). After years of serving *residential customers*, ServiceMaster added another product line of *business and industry services* including landscaping and janitorial services, education services (management of support services for schools and institutions, including physical facilities and financial and personnel resources), and healthcare services (management of support services—plant operations, asset management, laundry/linen supply—for long-term care facilities). Multiple product lines allow a company to grow rapidly and can help offset the consequences of slow sales in any one product line.

Product Line *group of products that are closely related because they function in a similar manner or are sold to the same customer group who will use them in similar ways*

Developing New Products

OBJECTIVE 2
Describe
the new product development process.

To expand or diversify product lines—in fact, just to survive—firms must develop and introduce streams of new products. Faced with competition and shifting customer preferences, no firm can count on a single successful product to carry it forever. Even products that have been popular for decades need constant renewal to keep up with changing technologies and consumer tastes.

Consider one of the best known brands in the United States, Levi's. Its riveted denim styles were once market leaders, but the company failed to keep pace with changing tastes, fell behind new products from competitors, and lost market share among 14- to 19-year-old males during the 1990s. Approaching the year 2000, at least one industry analyst felt forced to report that Levi's "hasn't had a successful new product in years." Things changed in 2003, on the 130th anniversary of the company's invention of jeans, when Levi's introduced the then-new Signature Brand of casual clothing to mass-channel shoppers, originally available in Walmart stores in the United States. The Signature Brand continues to have a popular following with convenient shopping access online at Google and websites of Walmart, Kmart, and Meijers. More recently, Levi's expanded to accommodate different body types and styles with Men's 501 Original Fit and 550 Relaxed Fit Jeans, and with women's 529 Curvy, Skinny, and Plus Size Jeans.

The New Product Development Process

For many years, the growing demand for improved health care has stimulated the development of new dietary supplements, heart medicines, and other pharmaceuticals, along with new equipment for diagnosing ailments, surgical procedures, and monitoring patient recovery. However, companies that develop and sell these products face a big problem. Developing new products costs well more than $100 million, sometimes even more than $1 billion, and can take as long as 8 to 10 years, or longer, to get a new product through the approval process at the U.S. Food and Drug Administration (FDA).

Testing, both for FDA approval and for marketing, can be the most time-consuming stage of development. For example, Merck & Co. is developing an experimental heart drug, called anacetrapib, to raise levels of good cholesterol, thereby reducing the risk

entrepreneurship and new ventures

This Business Is *App*solutely Booming

"Hamburger Buttons," "Swipe," "Edge gesture," and "Pull to Refresh" are just a few of the features provided by application (app) developers to make it easier to use your favorite apps. With an untold number of apps already available, a still-growing demand has created a genuine cottage industry. With product development underway at large firms such as Google and Apple, other smaller, home-based app developers, and high- and low-tech entrepreneurs are making successful careers in this booming industry. For example, 28-year-old Loren Brichter has quietly risen to a position of renown—"a high priest of app design"—among app developers. In 2007 he started his own apps-development company—Atebits. He is credited with creating user-friendly features that are now standard in many apps, such as the "cell swipe" that uncovers hidden buttons, sliding panels from the side of the screen, and in 2009 the "pull-to-refresh" feature, among others. With a degree in electrical engineering, Brichter started his career at Apple working on the iPhone technology in 2006. He later created the Tweetie app (including the "pull-to-refresh" feature), which along with Brichter's Atebits was purchased by Twitter in 2010. Since then, Twittie has been the official Twitter app on Apple devices. The selling price Brichter received for Atebits was reported to be in the "single millions." Most recently, Brichter has launched his new company—Atebits 2.0—to pursue making "fun and useful things, like an app that will be a game."

In contrast to Brichter's high-tech orientation, others with "non-tech" backgrounds also have become apps entrepreneurs. From his many travels, Mike Vichich, a 28-year-old business consultant, saw the possibilities for a new iPhone app to track credit-card rewards and to get the most value from his accumulated credit-card points. Although he understood the business side of the apps industry (Vichich has a business education), he had no technical background for understanding how to develop an app. He soon discovered several sources for getting started. For beginners, simple

Jean Whitehead

apps can be built using online tools, such as Appypie.com, Viziapps.com, and AppMakr by reading text and data into online templates. A more technical getting-started option is attending one of the intensive short-courses to learn computer coding for developing mobile apps. Another, more expensive, option is hiring a professional programmer or coding language specialist on contract, or as an employee. Vichich created his own three-month crash course, enough to learn the basics. He then recruited an app developer, found investors who provided $500,000 startup capital, and from there, Glyph, the iPhone app he envisioned, became available at the App Store in 2013. Early results include rave reviews for enabling adopters to get the most from their card rewards while also protecting their credit.

The successes of Brichter and Vichich, together, illustrate that visions for new products can stem from two different orientations, one technology-based, the other business-or user-based. Entrepreneurship occurs with the awareness that, by combining both orientations, innovative products will emerge for eager consumers.[3]

of heart attack. Merck & Co. conducted years of laboratory work and a lengthy test study, using 1,600 patients, and the results of that study then had to withstand further analysis. If successful, Merck could cash in on the growth of the cholesterol-lowering drug market, with industry estimates of peak sales potential ranging from $3 billion to $10 billion per year. However, getting that far through development requires an immense amount of time, patience, money, and risk of failure.[4]

Product development is a long and expensive process, and like Merck & Co., many firms have research and development (R&D) departments for exploring new product possibilities. Why do they devote so many resources to exploring product possibilities, rejecting many seemingly good ideas along the way? First, high *mortality rates* for new ideas mean that only a few new products reach the market. Second, for many companies, *speed to market* with a product is as important as care in developing it.

Product Mortality Rates

It is estimated that it takes 50 new product ideas to generate one product that finally reaches the market. Even then, only a few of these survivors become successful products. Many seemingly great ideas have failed as products. Creating a successful new product has become increasingly difficult—even for the most experienced marketers. Why? The number of new products hitting the market each year has increased dramatically; in some years as many as 180,000 new household, grocery, and drugstore items are introduced in the United States. In 2011, the U.S. consumer packaged goods industry alone launched 47,000 new products (foods, beverages, school supplies, and other nonfood products).[5] At any given time, however, the average North American supermarket carries a total of only 45,000 different items. Because of lack of space and customer demand, about 9 out of 10 new products will fail. Those with the best chances are innovative and deliver unique benefits. The single greatest factor in product failure is the lack of significant difference (i.e., the new product is very much like, or imitates, an existing product). Some prominent examples of this are Mr. Pibb (later, Pibb Xtra) versus Dr. Pepper, which although still on the market is a relatively minor competitor, and Burger King's Big King, their answer to the Big Mac.

The more rapidly a product moves from the laboratory to the marketplace, the more likely it is to survive. By introducing new products ahead of competitors, companies establish market leadership. They become entrenched in the market before being challenged by newer competitors. For example, sales of Apple's first iPad surged after its introduction in early 2010, and estimates are that more than 13 million units were sold by year end, for a 75-percent share of the world's tablet PC sales. While nearly every other company in the industry has tried to come out with competing products since 2011, iPad's fourth generation released at the end of 2012. With its early lead over competitors, iPad's visibility and popularity had made it a formidable market leader, holding a 54-percent share of market versus runner-up Android tablets' 43-percent share.[6] How important is **speed to market** (or *time compression*), a firm's success in responding rapidly to customer demand or market changes? One study reports that a product that is only three months late to market (three months behind the leader) loses 12 percent of its lifetime profit potential. After a six-month delay, it will lose 33 percent.

Speed To Market *strategy of introducing new products to respond quickly to customer or market changes*

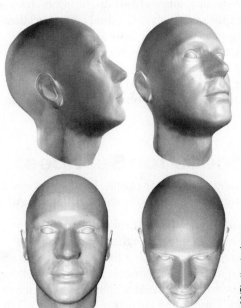

Designers used to create products, such as this head for a human-like toy, by sculpting models out of clay. Now they use "rapid prototyping," a technology that allows several employees to work simultaneously on 3D digital/visual "models" that can be e-mailed to clients for instant review. It now takes days, or just hours, instead of weeks to make an initial sculpture.

fixer00/Shutterstock

The Seven-Step Development Process

To increase their chances of developing a successful new product, many firms adopt some version of a seven-step process for developing physical goods (we will discuss the process for services next).

1 *Product ideas.* Product development begins with a search for ideas for new products. Ideas typically come from consumers, the sales force, R&D departments, suppliers, or engineering personnel. For the product development example discussed previously in this chapter, Merck & Co.'s research scientists by 2003 were convinced that a pill could be developed to prevent heart attacks.

2 *Screening.* This stage is designed to eliminate ideas that do not mesh with the firm's abilities or objectives. Representatives from marketing, engineering, operations, and finance provide input at this stage. Collaboration among Merck's scientific, marketing, and finance personnel concluded that the protein inhibitor called anacetrapib had reasonable prospects for commercial development.

3 *Concept testing.* Once ideas have been screened, companies use market research to get consumers' input about benefits and prices. Early test results for similar products by other companies indicated that Merck's product concept offered acceptable scientific chances for possible commercialization.

4 *Business analysis.* After gathering consumer opinions, marketers compare production costs and benefits to see whether the product meets minimum profitability goals. Merck's development team concluded that the product could become profitable, with a market potential of up to $10 billion, but revenues would be offset with projected high multiyear development costs.

5 *Prototype development.* Once the firm has determined the potential profitability of a product, engineering, R&D, or design groups produce a prototype. This can be extremely expensive, often requiring the use of three-dimensional computer models followed with expensive equipment to produce the first physical product. Initial development of Merck's anacetrapib required three to five years of laboratory-based chemical and biological science.

6 *Product testing and test marketing.* Applying lessons from the prototype, the company goes into limited production. It then tests the product to see if it meets performance requirements. If it does, it may be sold on a trial basis in limited areas to test consumer reaction. As of 2013, Merck had entered Phase III of continual testing that began in 2011, with some 20,000 patients, and is expected to be completed in 2017.

7 *Commercialization.* If test marketing proves positive, the company begins full-scale production and marketing. Because promotional and distribution channels must be established, this stage can be quite expensive. Gradual commercialization, with the firm providing the product to more and more areas over time, prevents undue strain on initial production capabilities. On the other hand, delays in commercialization give other firms the opportunity to bring out competing products. Merck's "go" or "no-go" for commercialization of anacetrapib depends on test results through 2017, and on the emergence of other new products that could upstage Merck's development efforts.

Variations in the Process for Services

The development of services involves many of the same stages. Basically, steps 2, 3, 4, 6, and 7 are the same. There are, however, important differences in steps 1 and 5:

1 *Service ideas.* The search for service ideas includes defining the *service value package*, identifying the tangible and intangible features that characterize the service, and stating service specifications. For example, a firm that wants to offer year-end cleaning services to office buildings might commit itself to the following specifications: The building interior will be cleaned with no interference in customer service by midnight, January 5, including carpets swept free of all dust and debris and washbowls and lavatory equipment polished.

The process design for this floor-cleaning service specifies who performs it, the equipment to be used, along with where and when the service will occur.

2 ***Service process design.*** Instead of prototype development, services require a three-part *service process design*. (1) *Process selection* identifies each step in the service, including sequence and timing. *Example (partial) process identification:* Office cleanings will be performed December 26–January 5, beginning at 8 P.M. through 5 A.M. Steps: (1) Furniture removal from office to hallway; (2) Dust, wash, and dry office walls and fixtures; (3) Power vacuum carpets; (4) Power wet-wash carpets; (5) Blow-dry carpets; (6) Return furniture to office; and (7) Final removal of cleaning equipment from client facility begins on January 5, to be completed by midnight. (2) *Worker requirements* states employee behaviors, skills, capabilities, and interactions with customers during the service encounter. *Example (partial) requirements:* One supervisor and 22 workers on 9-hour shifts (1 hour rest break) for 11 1/2 days. Crew supervisor (accessible 24/7) and two lead workers (during work hours) will interact with customer as needed. Workers will (1) be pre-briefed on furniture moving requirements, carpet characteristics, and safety requirements; (2) be skilled in operation of any and all cleaning equipment; and (3) respond courteously in encounters with client, referring questions to supervisor or lead workers. (3) *Facility requirements* designate all the equipment that supports service delivery. *Example equipment requirements (partial):* (1) 8 power-dolly transports for moving furniture; (2) 50 heavy covers for protecting furniture; (3) 10 industrial Class II power wet-washers for carpets; (4) 12 industrial-power carpet vacuums; (5) forty 5-gallon containers Get-it-All scrubbing/sanitizing cleanser; and (6) large-haul capacity truck to transport materials, supplies, and equipment to and from client facility.

Product Life Cycle

OBJECTIVE 3
Describe
the stages of the product life cycle (PLC) and methods for extending a product's life.

Product Life Cycle (PLC) *series of stages in a product's commercial life*

When a product reaches the market, it enters the **product life cycle (PLC)**, a series of stages through which it passes during its commercial life. Depending on the product's ability to attract and keep customers, its PLC may be a matter of months, years, or decades. Strong, mature products (such as Clorox bleach and H&R Block tax preparation) have had long productive lives.

Stages in the PLC

The life cycle for both goods and services is a natural process in which products are born, grow in stature, mature, and finally decline and die. Look at the two graphics in Figure 12.1. In Figure 12.1(a), the four phases of the PLC are applied to several products with which you are familiar:

Introduction. This stage begins when the product reaches the marketplace. Marketers focus on making potential customers aware of the product and its benefits. Extensive development, production, and sales costs erase all profits.

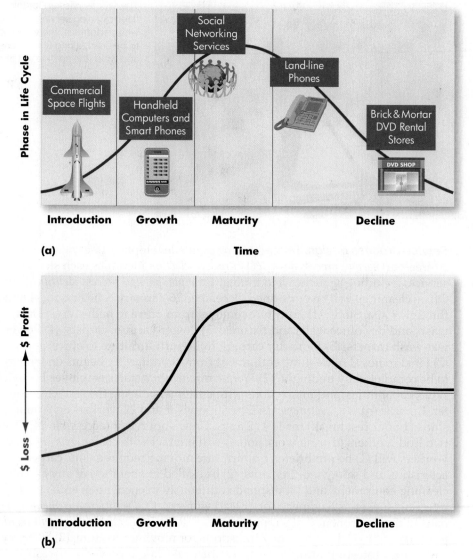

FIGURE 12.1 Products in the Life Cycle: (a) Phases and (b) Profit (or Loss)

Growth. If the new product attracts enough customers, sales start to climb rapidly. Marketers lower price slightly and continue promotional expenditures to increase sales. The product starts to show a profit as revenues surpass costs, and other firms move rapidly to introduce their own versions.

Maturity. This is typically the longest stage in the PLC for many products. Sales growth peaks then starts to slow. Although the product earns its highest profit level early in this stage, increased competition eventually forces price cutting, increasing the costs of advertising and promotional expenditures, and lower profits. Toward the end of the stage, sales start to fall.

Decline. Sales and profits continue to fall, as new products in the introduction stage take away sales. Firms end or reduce promotional support (ads and salespeople), but may let the product linger to provide some profits.

Figure 12.1(b) plots the relationship of the PLC to a product's typical profits (in black) or losses (in red). Although the early stages of the PLC often show financial losses, increased sales for successful products recover previous losses and continue to generate profits until the decline stage. Resulting from loss of profits, for example, Kodak quit marketing traditional film cameras in the United States in 2004. In 2012 the company announced it would stop making its newer line of digital cameras, too, because of declining profits. For many products, profitable life spans are short; that's why many firms, such as 3M (producer of Post-it Notes and thousands of other products) rely on innovation for constant replenishment of product lines.

Extending Product Life: An Alternative to New Products

Companies try to keep products in the maturity stage as long as they can. At year-end 2012, after 80 years in publication, *Newsweek* magazine mailed its final print issue. At the same time, *Newsweek's* life was extended by launching its new online-only version. Sales of TV sets, too, have been revitalized through the years by such feature changes as color, portability, stereo capability, enlarged flat-screen LCDs, home theater features, Internet streaming capabilities, and other newer features. In fact, companies can extend product life through a number of creative means. Foreign markets, for example, offer three approaches to longer life cycles:

1 In **product extension**, an existing product is marketed globally instead of just domestically. Coca-Cola, Kentucky Fried Chicken, and Levi's jeans are examples of many product extensions.

2 With **product adaptation**, the product is modified for greater appeal in different countries. In Germany, a McDonald's meal includes beer, and Ford puts the steering wheel on the right side for sales in Japan. Because it involves product changes, this approach is usually more costly than product extension.

3 **Reintroduction** means reviving, for new markets, products that are becoming obsolete in older ones. NCR, for instance, reintroduced manually operated cash registers in Latin America. Kodak boosted sales by reintroducing its cameras and film products in India. Kent & Curwen, a renowned English clothier founded in 1926, has only one store remaining in Britain but opened 95 stores in China.[7]

Product Extension *marketing an existing product globally instead of just domestically*

Product Adaptation *modifying an existing product for greater appeal in different countries*

Reintroduction *reviving obsolete or older products for new markets*

Identifying Products

As we noted previously, developing a product's features is only part of a marketer's job. Marketers must also identify products so that consumers recognize them. Two important tools for this task are *branding* and *packaging*.

Branding Products Coca-Cola is the best-known brand in the world. Some Coke executives claim that if all the company's other assets were obliterated, they could go to the bank and borrow $100 billion on the strength of the brand name alone. Indeed, Interbrand, the brand-ranking firm, says the Coke brand in 2012 was worth nearly $78 billion in terms of revenue generation from its ability to create demand for the product.

Jens Kalaene/picture alliance/ZB/Newscom

Branding *process of using symbols to communicate the qualities of a product made by a particular producer*

Industry observers regard brands as a company's most valuable asset.[8] **Branding** is a process of using names and symbols, like Coca-Cola, the Mercedes tri-star logo, or McDonald's golden arches, to communicate the qualities of a particular product made by a particular producer. Brands are designed to signal uniform quality; customers who try and like a product can return to it by remembering its name or its logo.

Several benefits result from successful branding, including brand loyalty and **brand awareness**, the brand name that first comes to mind when you consider a particular product category. What company, for example, comes to mind when you need to ship a document a long way on short notice? For many people, UPS has the necessary brand awareness.

Brand Awareness *extent to which a brand name comes to mind when a consumer considers a particular product category*

Table 12.3 shows the rankings of the top global brands based on estimates of each brand's dollar value. It reflects the earnings boost that each brand delivers—an index of a brand's power to increase sales and earnings, both present and future—and shows how much those future earnings are worth today. Only global brands, those with sales of at least 20 percent outside the home country, are included.

GAINING BRAND AWARENESS The expensive, sometimes fierce, struggle for brand recognition is perhaps nowhere more evident than in branding battles among dot-com firms. Collectively, the top Internet brands, Google (ranked 4th), Amazon.com (20th), and eBay (36th), spend billions a year, even though only Google, Amazon, and eBay have cracked the ranks of the top 50 global brands. Moreover, the mounting costs of establishing a brand identity mean that many more would-be e-businesses do and will probably fail.

With its growing importance in nearly every industry, marketers are finding more effective, less expensive ways to gain brand awareness. In addition to using viral marketing and social networking, recent successes have been found with *product placements*.

Product Placement *promotional tactic for brand exposure in which characters in television, film, music, magazines, or video games use a real product with its brand visible to viewers*

PRODUCT PLACEMENTS Although a commercial break usually means a trip to the kitchen, entertainment programming still gets our full attention. And that's when marketers are turning up the promotional juice with **product placement**, a promotional tactic for brand exposure in which characters in television, film, music, magazines, or video games use a real product with a brand visible to viewers.

Product placements are effective because the message is delivered in an attractive setting that holds the customer's interest. When used in successful films and TV shows, the brand's association with famous performers is an implied celebrity

table 12.3 World's 10 Most Valuable Brands

Rank	Brand	2012 Brand Value ($billions)
1	Coca-Cola	$77.8
2	Apple	$76.6
3	IBM	$75.5
4	Google	$69.7
5	Microsoft	$57.9
6	GE	$43.7
7	McDonald's	$40.1
8	Intel	$39.4
9	Samsung	$32.9
10	Toyota	$30.3

Sources: Adapted from Manish Modi, "Coca-Cola Retains Title as World's Most Valuable Brand," *Bloomberg*, October 2, 2012, at http://www.bloomberg.com/news/2012-10-03/coca-cola-retains-title-as-world-s-most-valuable-brand-table-.html; "Interbrand Releases 13th Annual Best Global Brands Report," *Interbrand*, at http://www.interbrand.com/en/best-global-brands/2012/downloads.aspx, accessed April 5, 2013.

endorsement. The idea is to legitimize the brand in the mind of the customer. In all, more than $5 billion is spent annually on product placements, especially in television, and major marketers are putting more into product placements instead of television advertisements. Reese's Pieces became an all-time placement success in Spielberg's blockbuster movie *E.T.* The then-new Mini Cooper brand was launched in the movie *The Italian Job.* In print placements, Hewlett-Packard computers appeared in the photo layouts in the IKEA catalog. Television placements are widespread, including Hyundai in *Leverage* and *Burn Notice,* and Junior Mints played a star role when one was dropped into a surgery incision on *Seinfeld.*

Product placements are especially effective for TV because digital video recorders (DVRs) remain popular. Viewers can use their DVRs to skip commercial breaks in recorded shows, but product placements within the programs are unavoidable.

Types of Brand Names   Just about every product has a brand name. Generally, different types of brand names—*national, licensed,* or *private*—increase buyers' awareness of the nature and quality of competing products. When customers are satisfied with a product, marketers try to build brand loyalty among the largest possible segment of repeat buyers.

NATIONAL BRANDS   **National brands** are produced by, widely distributed by, and carry the name of the manufacturer. These brands (for example, Direct TV, Progressive Insurance, Scotch tape and Scope mouthwash) are often widely recognized by customers because of national advertising campaigns, and they are, therefore, valuable assets. Because the costs of developing a national brand are high, some companies use a national brand on several related products. Procter & Gamble markets Ivory Shampoo, capitalizing on the name of its bar soap and dishwashing liquid. Although cost efficient, doing this can sometimes dilute the original brand's effectiveness. Coors Light Beer now outsells original Coors Beer.

National Brands brand-name product produced by, widely distributed by, and carrying the name of a manufacturer

LICENSED BRANDS   We have become used to companies (and even personalities) selling the rights to put their names on products. These are called **licensed brands.** For example, the popularity of auto racing is generating millions in revenues for the NASCAR brand, which licenses its name on car accessories, ladies and men's apparel, headsets, and countless other items with the names of popular drivers such as Martin, Johnson, Stewart, and Edwards. Harley-Davidson's famous logo, emblazoned on boots, eyewear, gloves, purses, lighters, and watches, brings the motorcycle maker more than $300 million annually. Along with brands such as Coors and Ferrari, licensing for character-based brands, such as Tinker Bell, Mickey Mouse, and other Disney characters, are equally lucrative. Marketers exploit brands because of their public appeal due to the image and status that customers hope to gain by associating with them.

Licensed Brands brand-name product for whose name the seller has purchased the right from an organization of individual

PRIVATE BRANDS   When a wholesaler or retailer develops a brand name and has a manufacturer put it on a product, the resulting name is a **private brand** (or **private label**). Sears, who carries such lines as Craftsman tools, Canyon River Blues denim clothing, and Kenmore appliances, is a well-known seller of private brands.

Private Brand (or Private Label) brand-name product that a wholesaler or retailer has commissioned from a manufacturer

Packaging Products   With a few exceptions, products need some form of **packaging** to reduce the risk of damage, breakage, or spoilage, and to increase the difficulty of stealing small products. A package also serves as an in-store advertisement that makes the product attractive, displays the brand name, and identifies features and benefits. Also, packaging features, such as no-drip bottles of Clorox bleach, add utility for consumers.

Packaging physical container in which a product is sold, advertised, or protected

Pricing process of determining what a company will receive in exchange for its products

Determining Prices

The second major component of the marketing mix is **pricing,** determining what the customer pays and the seller receives in exchange for a product. Setting prices involves understanding how they contribute to achieving the firm's sales objectives.

OBJECTIVE 4
Identify
the various pricing objectives that govern pricing decisions, and describe the price-setting tools used in making these decisions.

In this section, we first discuss the objectives that influence a firm's pricing decisions. Then we describe the major tools that companies use to meet those objectives.

Pricing to Meet Business Objectives

Pricing objectives are the goals that sellers hope to achieve in pricing products for sale. Some companies have *profit-maximizing pricing objectives*, others have *market share pricing objectives*, and still others are concerned with pricing for *e-business objectives*. Pricing decisions are also influenced by the need to compete in the marketplace, by social and ethical concerns, and even by corporate image. Most recently we've seen how prices of financial products, loans and other borrowing, are determined by the government's persuasion and its control of interest rates in times of crisis.

Profit-Maximizing Objectives The seller's pricing decision is critical for determining the firm's revenue, which is the result of the selling price times the number of units sold.

$$\text{Revenue} = \text{Selling price} \times \text{Units sold}$$

Companies that set prices to maximize profits want to set the selling price to sell the number of units that will generate the highest possible total profits. If a company sets prices too low, it will probably sell many units but may miss out on additional profits on each unit (and may even lose money on each exchange). If a company sets prices too high, it will make a large profit on each item but will sell fewer units. Again, the firm loses money, and it may also be left with excess inventory.

finding a better way

Fixed Prices in UAE

The UAE's Ministry of Economy published a list of 800 products with fixed-prices in July 2011. The ministry had reached an agreement with all of the major shopping outlets, with some 300 businesses complying with the requirements of the government.

The businesses agreed to ensure that the products on the list would have a stable price until the end of 2011. Amongst the products listed were mineral water, rice, sugar, cooking oil, flour, and dairy products.

Speaking at the time, Hashem Al Nuaimi, the Director of the Consumer Protection Division of the ministry, claimed that the initiative was designed to introduce transparency and stop unreasonable price increases. To enforce the agreement, inspectors would check the outlets. The outlets were also required to display price lists of the selected products. This included Carrefour and Lulu, both large hypermarket chains with around 80 percent market share between them.

The initiative cost US$55 million to implement and was the first such move by a country in the Middle East. The range of products was specifically chosen to ensure that it included around 50 percent of the regular purchases of the average consumer.

It was clear that the agreement worked, as in 2012 the initiative was rolled out to incorporate 1,650 basic commodities. The agreement now encompasses some 340 businesses. Larger hypermarkets are electronically linked to the ministry to ensure real-time, real-price checks. The prime reason for the price fixing was to ensure that the shopping basket for UAE consumers did

chrisdorney/Fotolia

not become over-inflated for Ramadan. Price inflation during this time had been common and was traditionally off-set by consumers hoarding food. During Ramadan, food consumption in the UAE rises by between 20-30 percent.

There were problems with some retailers and by the middle of 2012, the ministry had received over 4,000 complaints related to higher prices. Nevertheless, the message from the ministry was that there was no need to hoard as the initiative was designed to combat inflated pricing. Any monopolies or price manipulation would be punished by legal action or fines. There was no need for consumers to consider making unnecessarily large food purchases in expectation of price increases.[9]

In calculating profits, managers weigh sales revenues against costs for materials and labor, as well as capital resources (plant and equipment) and marketing costs (such as maintaining a large sales staff). To use these resources efficiently, many firms set prices to cover costs and achieve a targeted level of return for owners.

Market Share (Market Penetration) Objectives In the long run, a business must make a profit to survive. Because they are willing to accept minimal profits, even losses, to get buyers to try products, companies may initially set low prices for new products to establish **market share** (or **market penetration**), a company's percentage of the total industry sales for a specific product type. Even with established products, market share leadership may outweigh profit as a pricing objective. For brands such as Philadelphia Brand Cream Cheese and iTunes, dominating a market means that consumers are more likely to buy something they are familiar with. Market domination means continuous sales of more units and higher profits, even at lower unit prices.

Market Share (or Market Penetration) *company's percentage of the total industry sales for a specific product type*

Pricing for E-Business Objectives When pricing for Internet sales, marketers must consider different kinds of costs and different forms of consumer awareness. Many e-businesses reduce both costs and prices because of the Internet's unique marketing capabilities. Because the Web provides a more direct link between producer and customer, buyers often avoid the added costs of wholesalers and retailers.

Another factor is the ease of comparison shopping: Obviously, point-and-click shopping can be much more efficient than driving from store to store in search of the best price. Moreover, both consumers and business buyers can get lower prices by joining together on the Internet for greater purchasing power. Doctors and employees at Phoenix, Arizona's Arrowhead Health teamed with United Drugs Prescription Benefit Management to set up a new approach for buying generic and brand drugs at lower costs, thus saving money in the employees' prescription discount program. Two new tools include (1) websites that search for lower-price drug alternatives, and (2) a Web portal that serves as a gateway for listing nationwide average retail prices for drugs. The program enables employees and physicians to reduce prescription and benefits claims costs.[10]

Price-Setting Tools

Whatever a company's objectives, managers like to measure the potential impact before deciding on final prices. Two tools used for this purpose are *cost-oriented pricing* and *breakeven analysis*. Although each can be used alone, both are often used because they provide different kinds of information for determining prices that will allow the company to reach its objectives.

Cost-Oriented Pricing **Cost-oriented pricing** considers a firm's desire to make a profit and its need to cover operating costs.

Cost-Oriented Pricing *pricing that considers the firm's desire to make a profit and its need to cover operating costs*

$$\text{Selling price} = \text{Seller's costs} + \text{Profit}$$

A T-shirt store manager would price shirts by calculating the cost of making them available to shoppers. Thus, price would include the costs of store rent, employee wages, utilities, product displays, insurance, and the shirt manufacturer's price.

If the manufacturer's price is $8 per shirt and the store sells shirts for $8, the store won't make any profit. Nor will it make a profit if it sells shirts for $8.50 each, or even $10 or $11. To be profitable, the company must charge enough to cover product and other costs. Together, these factors determine the **markup**, the amount added to an item's purchase cost to sell it at a profit. In this case, a reasonable markup of $7 more than the purchase cost means a $15 selling price. The following equation calculates the markup percentage and determines what percent of every dollar of revenue is gross profit:

Markup *amount added to an item's purchase cost to sell it at a profit*

$$\text{Markup percentage} = \frac{\text{Markup}}{\text{Sales price}} \times 100\%$$

For our shirt retailer, the markup percentage is 46.7:

$$\text{Markup percentage} = \frac{\$7}{\$15} \times 100\% = 46.7\%$$

Out of every $1.00 taken in, $0.467 will be gross profit. Out of gross profit, the store must still pay rent, utilities, insurance, and all other costs.

For experienced price setters, an even simpler method uses a standard cost-of-goods percentage to determine the markup amount. Many retailers, for example, use 100 percent of cost-of-goods as the standard markup. If the manufacturer's price is $8 per shirt, the markup (100 percent) is also $8, so the selling price is $16.

Breakeven Analysis: Cost-Volume-Profit Relationships

> **Variable Cost** *cost that changes with the quantity of a product produced and sold*

> **Fixed Cost** *cost that is incurred regardless of the quantity of a product produced and sold*

> **Breakeven Analysis** *identifies the sales volume where total costs equal total revenues by assessing costs versus revenues at various sales volumes and showing, at any particular selling price, the amount of loss or profit for each volume of sales*

Using cost-oriented pricing, a firm will cover **variable costs**, costs that change with the number of units of a product produced and sold, such as raw materials, sales commissions, and shipping. Firms also need to pay **fixed costs**, costs, such as rent, insurance, and utilities, that must be paid *regardless of the number of units produced and sold*.

Costs, selling price, and the number of units sold determine how many units a company must sell before all costs, both variable and fixed, are covered, and it begins to make a profit. **Breakeven analyses** identifies the sales volume where total costs equal total revenues by assessing costs versus revenues for various sales volumes and showing, at any particular selling price, the amount of loss or profit for each volume of sales.

If you were the manager of a T-shirt store, how would you determine how many shirts you needed to sell to break even? We know that the *variable cost* of buying each shirt from the manufacturer is $8. This means that the store's annual variable costs depend on how many shirts are sold, the number of shirts sold times the $8 cost for each shirt. Say that *fixed costs* for keeping the store open for one year are $100,000 (no matter how many shirts are sold). At a selling price of $15 each, how many shirts must be sold *so that total revenues exactly cover both* fixed and variable costs? The answer is the **breakeven point**, which is 14,286 shirts:

> **Breakeven Point** *sales volume at which the seller's total revenue from sales equals total costs (variable and fixed) with neither profit nor loss*

$$\text{Breakeven point (in units)} = \frac{\text{Total Fixed Cost}}{\text{Price} - \text{Variable Cost}}$$

$$= \frac{\$100,000}{\$15 - \$8} = 14,286 \text{ shirts}$$

Look at Figure 12.2. If the store sells fewer than 14,286 shirts, it loses money for the year. If sales go higher than 14,286, profits grow by $7 for each additional shirt. If the store sells exactly 14,286 shirts, it will cover all its costs but earn zero profit.

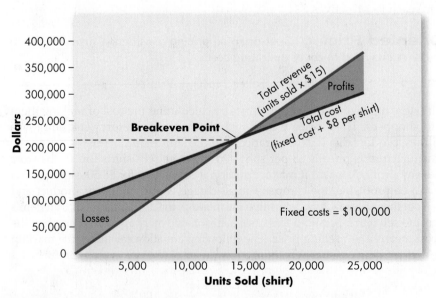

FIGURE 12.2 Breakeven Analysis

Using low-cost, direct-to-consumer selling and market share pricing, Dell profitably dominated the personal computer market, while its competitors—Apple, IBM, Compaq, and Hewlett-Packard—sold through retailers, adding extra costs that prevented them from matching Dell's low prices. Competitors have switched to direct-to-consumer sales, but Dell is strongly anchored as the industry's number-two PC seller (after HP).

Zero profitability at the breakeven point can also be seen by using the profit equation:

$$\text{Profit} = \frac{\text{Total}}{\text{Revenue}} - \left(\begin{array}{c}\text{Total} \\ \text{Fixed} \\ \text{Cost}\end{array} + \begin{array}{c}\text{Total} \\ \text{Variable} \\ \text{Cost}\end{array}\right)$$

$$= (14{,}286 \text{ shirts} \times \$15) - (\$100{,}000 \text{ Fixed Cost}$$
$$+ [14{,}286 \text{ shirts} \times \$8 \text{ Variable Cost}])$$

$$\$0 = (\$214{,}290) - (\$100{,}00 + \$114{,}288)$$

(rounded to the nearest whole shirt)

Pricing Strategies and Tactics

OBJECTIVE 5
Discuss
pricing strategies that can be used for different competitive situations and identify the pricing tactics that can be used for setting prices.

The pricing tools discussed in the previous section help managers set prices on specific goods. They do not, however, help them decide on pricing philosophies for diverse competitive situations. In this section, we discuss pricing *strategy* (pricing as a planning activity) and some basic pricing *tactics* (ways in which managers implement a firm's pricing strategies).

Pricing Strategies

Pricing is an extremely important element in the marketing mix, as well as a flexible marketing tool; it is certainly easier to change prices than to change products or distribution channels. This section will look at how pricing strategies can result in widely differing prices for similar products.

Pricing Existing Products   A firm has three options for pricing existing products:

1 Pricing above prevailing market prices for similar products to take advantage of the common assumption that higher price means higher quality
2 Pricing below market prices while offering a product of comparable quality to higher-priced competitors
3 Pricing at or near market prices

Godiva chocolates and Patek Phillipe watches price high by promoting prestige and quality images. In contrast, both Budget and Dollar car-rental companies promote themselves as low-priced alternatives to Hertz and Avis. Pricing below prevailing market price works if a firm offers a product of acceptable quality while keeping costs below those of higher-priced competitors.

Pricing New Products

Price Skimming setting an initially high price to cover new product costs and generate a profit

When introducing new products, companies must often choose between high prices or low prices. **Price skimming**, setting an initial high price to cover development and introduction costs and generate a large profit on each item sold, works only if marketers can convince customers that a new product is truly different from existing products and there is no foreseeable major competition on the horizon. Apple's introduction of the iPod is a good example. With no strong competitors entering the market for several years, Apple was able to maintain a high retail price with little discounting, even at Walmart. In contrast, **penetration pricing**, setting an initial low price to establish a new product in the market, seeks to create customer interest and stimulate trial purchases. Penetration strategy is the best strategy when introducing a product that has or expects to have competitors quickly. Gillette uses this strategy on nearly all of their new shaving systems to make sure the product receives a high early adoption rate.

Penetration Pricing setting an initially low price to establish a new product in the market

Startup firms often use one-price, fixed pricing for launching new products. Carbonite, Inc., started its online backup service in 2006 with its strategy of "one-flat-low price," no matter how much space you needed to back up your PC files.[11] Although its pricing strategy changed as the company grew, to date the company has backed up more than 300 billion computer files. The initial policy of Apple's iTunes was to use one low price per song, $0.99, to attract and build a customer base in the first five years. In 2009, with 75 million customers, the three-tier pricing, discussed in our opening story, was adopted to reflect differences in value among songs. Older or obscure tunes of lesser value are priced at $0.69, current hot songs are priced at $1.29, and still others sell for $0.99.

Fixed versus Dynamic Pricing for Online Business

The digital marketplace has introduced a highly variable pricing system as an alternative to conventional fixed pricing for both consumer and business-to-business (B2B) products. At present, fixed pricing is still the most common option for cybershoppers. E-tail giant Amazon.com has maintained this practice as its pricing strategy for its millions of retail items. In contrast, dynamic pricing, like eBay's auction bidding, uses flexibility between buyers and sellers in setting a price and uses the Web to instantly notify millions of buyers of product availability and price changes.

Another kind of dynamic pricing, the reverse auction, allows sellers to alter prices privately on an individual basis. At Priceline.com, for example, consumers set a price (below the published fixed price) they are willing to pay for airfare (or a rental car or a hotel room); then an airline can complete the sale by accepting the bid price. For B2B purchases, MediaBids.com uses reverse advertising auctions to sell ad space. A company will notify MediaBids that it is going to spend $1,000 for advertising. Publications then use their ad space as currency to place bids for the advertising dollars. The company can then accept the bid that offers the most ad exposure in the best publication.[12] Budget-conscious companies seeking legal advice are increasingly turning to reverse auctions for lower-cost contracts with law firms, as well. Competing law firms, bidding downward in online chat rooms, enter price bids to provide a client company's legal services. Law firms are concerned with reports that about 40 percent of the legal market is being decided in reverse auctions, and the auctions are cutting as much as 15 to 40 percent from traditional legal fees.[13]

Bundling

Bundling Strategy grouping several products together to be sold as a single unit at a reduced price, rather than individually

A **bundling strategy** groups several products together to be sold as a single unit, rather than individually. Suppose you have two insurance policies with different companies, one for life insurance and another for auto insurance. You may benefit from bundling, that is, by buying both policies as a "package" from just one company. First, your total premium payments may be reduced. In addition, you gain

managing in turbulent times

How Recessionary Times Became a Stimulus for Innovative Pricing and Promotion

The years from 2007 to 2012 were difficult years for consumers, employees, and companies. "We're not trying to make a profit; we just want to cover costs and keep our employees." This broadcast message illustrates how a construction company is using reduced pricing coupled with coordinated advertising promotions to stimulate demand in a slow economy. Unusual marketing conditions sometimes call for uncommon actions, including changes in pricing and promotions for attracting customers in different ways than usual. Some of these methods seem simple and straightforward, but others are downright creative and unique.

Price discounts and free shipping are among today's ordinary pricing attractions, but even those won't work without integrated promotions that get the cost-savings message to customers. Online B2B clothing wholesaler Apparelus.com and L. L. Bean highlight their free shipping in Internet marketing campaigns that can also include coupons and online chats, which stimulate buzz that informs customers about the cost savings.[14]

Although the 2008 recession was admittedly painful, it demonstrated that bad times can inspire historically innovative pricing and promotion methods. Auto dealers adopted newer, more radical tactics, with promotions that shifted costs, such as then-increasing gasoline prices, from customers to the dealers: "Buy a new car in 2009, and if gas prices exceed $2, we'll pay the gas bill." Gasoline prices at that time averaged $2.20 per gallon, and were projected to rise above $2.30. Even more extreme, as a safety net against rising job losses, in 2009 Ford and General Motors announced protection when customers bought a new vehicle and then lost their jobs. Ford offered to make monthly payments up to $700 for up to one year. GM covered payments up to $500 per month for up to nine months. Hyundai Motor Company allowed buyers to return a new car within a year because of the buyer's job loss and, in the event of a layoff, Hyundai would make payments for up to three months. Traces of those innovative promotions linger as recently as 2013, when electric car maker Tesla

Najiah Feanny/Corbis

offered to buy back the customer's car at a guaranteed price after three years. These offers were coordinated with advertising promotions—on radio, television, and the Internet—along with public relations and widespread publicity to boost sagging auto sales.[15]

Suppose you wanted to take a vacation during the recession, but your portfolio had gone south in the stock-market downfall? Elite Island Resorts may have had the answer you needed. In December 2008 and January 2009 you could have booked a deluxe Caribbean vacation by paying up to $5,000 per room with your then-depressed stock instead of credit cards. Elite Island promoted the unique "Roll Back Your Stock's Value" offer, accepting a list of some 100 stocks at their higher mid-2008 market values for payment. For example, Elite Island accepted American Express stock at its previous value of $40 per share although its value at the time had fallen to less than $22, and Goldman Sachs at $177 although its current value at the time was less than $72. By transferring the stock as payment, the resort was betting that the stock would eventually regain its value, and customers enjoyed the same price benefit as when their portfolio had been more valuable.[16]

The bottom-line results from these unique pricing/promotion methods are not publicly documented. However, the use of the creative tactics demonstrate that companies value marketing as a powerful force for meeting the challenges for survival in turbulent times.

---

the convenience of communicating with and making monthly payments to just one instead of two companies. The bundling company gains, too, with additional sales of two instead of just one product. CenturyLink, for example, offers a bundle of home phone, Internet, and DirectTV services that is priced below the combined individual prices for the three services.

Pricing Tactics

Regardless of its pricing strategy, a company may adopt one or more *pricing tactics*. Companies selling multiple items in a product category often use **price lining**, offering all items in certain categories at a limited number of prices. A department store,

Price Lining *setting a limited number of prices for certain categories of products*

Dynamic pricing, with online bidding screens on the wall, is a mainstream feature of this salesroom for the British Car Auctions (BCA) site in Brighouse, West Yorkshire, UK.

for example, might predetermine $175, $250, and $400 as the *price points* for men's suits, so all men's suits would be set at one of these three prices. Doing so allows the store to have a suit for all of the different customer segments it hopes to attract. Grocery stores use this strategy as well; for example, in canned goods they will carry a national brand, a store brand, and a generic brand.

Psychological pricing takes advantage of the fact that customers are not completely rational when making buying decisions. One type, **odd-even pricing**, is based on the theory that customers prefer prices that are not stated in even dollar amounts. Thus, customers regard prices of $1,000, $100, $50, and $10 as significantly higher than $999.95, $99.95, $49.95, and $9.95, respectively. Of course, the price set for a product is not always the price for which it sells. Sellers must often resort to price reductions, or **discounts**, to stimulate sales. Auto dealers, vacation resorts, airlines, and hotels offer discount prices to stimulate demand during off-peak seasons. Hyatt Hotels, like many others, offers commercial room discounts for frequent business users and for large-scale events such as conventions, trade shows, and special events. As you will see in this chapter's ending case, JCPenney created new problems when they stopped discounting in-store prices for retail customers.

International Pricing

When Procter & Gamble (P&G) reviewed its prospects for marketing products in new overseas markets, it encountered an unsettling fact. Because it typically priced products to cover hefty R&D costs, profitably priced items were out of reach for too many global consumers. The solution was, in effect, to reverse the process. Now P&G conducts research to find out what foreign buyers can afford and then develops products that those markets can buy. P&G penetrates markets with lower-priced items and encourages customers to trade up as they become able to afford higher-quality products.

Another strategy calls for increasing foreign market share by pricing products below cost. As a result, a given product is priced lower in a foreign market than in its own country. As we saw in Chapter 4, this practice is called *dumping*, which is illegal. In 2013 the Coalition of Gulf Shrimp Industries petitioned the U.S. International Trade Commission (ITC) to impose special tariffs on seven countries, China, Ecuador, India, Indonesia, Malaysia, Thailand, and Vietnam, accused of using government subsidies enabling unfair price reductions, or dumping, against the U.S. shrimp industry. If found to be true, international law allows the U.S. to impose penalties called "countervailing duties" on shrimp coming from those countries, as a remedy to balance prices.[17]

Psychological Pricing *pricing tactic that takes advantage of the fact that consumers do not always respond rationally to stated prices*

Odd-Even Pricing *psychological pricing tactic based on the premise that customers prefer prices not stated in even dollar amounts*

Discounts *price reduction offered as an incentive to purchase*

summary of learning objectives

OBJECTIVE 1

Explain the definition of a product as a value package and classify goods and services. (pp. 414–417)

Customers buy products to receive value that satisfies a want or a need. Thus, a successful product is a *value package*, a bundle of attributes that, taken together, provides the right features and offers the right benefits that satisfy customers' wants and needs. *Features* are the qualities, tangible and intangible, that are included with the product. To be satisfying, features must provide *benefits* that allow customers to achieve the end results they want. The value package has services and features that add value by providing benefits that increase the customer's satisfaction.

Products (both goods and services) can be classified according to expected buyers as either *consumer products* or *organizational products*. *Convenience products* are inexpensive consumer goods and services that are consumed rapidly and regularly. *Shopping products* are more expensive and are purchased less often than convenience products. *Specialty products* are extremely important and expensive goods and services. *Organizational products* are classified as either *production items, expense items*, or *capital items*. Production items are goods and services used directly in the production process. *Expense items* are goods or services consumed within a year to produce other products. *Capital items* are expensive and long-lasting goods and services that have expected lives of several years.

The group of products that a company makes available for sale is referred to as its *product mix*. Although many companies start with a single product, they tend to expand into product lines, a group of products that are closely related in function or target market. Companies may develop multiple product lines to serve different types of customers or to meet the needs of existing customers in new ways. Multiple product lines allow a company to grow and can help to offset the consequences of slow sales in any one product line.

OBJECTIVE 2

Describe the new product development process. (pp. 417–421)

To expand and diversity product lines, new products must be developed and introduced. Many firms have research and development (R&D) departments and services development teams for exploring new product possibilities by adopting a basic seven-step process: (1) *Product ideas*: searching for ideas for new products. (2) *Screening*: eliminating all product ideas that do not mesh with the firm's abilities or objectives. (3) *Concept testing*: using market research to get consumers' input about product benefits and prices. (4) *Business analysis*: comparing production costs and benefits to see whether a product meets minimum profitability goals. (5) *Prototype development*: producing a preliminary version of a product. (6) *Product testing and test marketing*: going into limited production, testing the product to see if it meets performance requirements, and, if so, selling it on a limited basis. (7) *Commercialization*: beginning full-scale production and marketing.

For the development of services there are two important differences in the seven-step model: (1) *Service ideas*: The search for service ideas includes defining the service value package identifying the tangible and intangible features that characterize the service, and stating service specifications. (2) *Service process design:* Instead of prototype development, services require a service process design that identifies each step in the service. It also identifies worker requirements—employee behaviors, skills, capabilities, and interactions with customers during the service encounter—and facility requirements.

OBJECTIVE 3

Describe the stages of the product life cycle (PLC) and methods for extending a product's life. (pp. 421–425)

The product life cycle (PLC) for a good or a service product is a series of four stages or phases characterizing the product's profit-producing life. (1) *Introduction*: This stage begins when the product reaches the marketplace. Marketers focus on consumers aware of the product and its benefits. Extensive development, production, and sales costs erase all profits. (2) *Growth*: Sales begin to climb and the product begins to show a profit, as marketers decrease prices slightly and continue promotional expenditures. Profits begin as revenues surpass costs. (3) *Maturity*: Typically the longest stage in the PLC, sales growth peaks, then starts to slow. The product's profits are highest early in this stage. As increased competition forces price-cutting, along with more advertising and promotional expenses, profits begin to diminish. (4) *Decline*: Sales and profits continue to fall as new products take away sales. Firms end or reduce promotional support (ads or salespeople are reduced), but modest support allows the product to linger with minimal profits. Eventually the product dies.

Three prominent methods are used for extending the lives of declining or even recently deceased products. (1) In *product extension*, an existing product is marketed globally instead of just domestically. A product that is in the maturity stage or even declining domestically may provide value to customers in other countries. (2) With *product adaptation*, the product is modified to contain changed features that appeal to new customers in different countries. (3) *Reintroduction* means reviving, for new markets, products that are becoming obsolete or have died in older ones.

Marketers must also identify products so that consumers recognize them. Branding is the process of using names and symbols to communicate the qualities of a particular product made by a particular producer. Branding can create brand awareness, in which buyers are aware of a brand, and brand loyalty, in which buyers demonstrate consistent buying behavior. Marketers can use product placement to increase brand awareness and brand loyalty. Product placement occurs when a brand is featured in television, film, magazines, or video games. There are three different kinds of brand names. *National brands* are produced by, widely distributed by, and carry the brand name of the manufacturer. When a company allows another company to use their brand name, that is a *licensed brand*. The final kind of brand name is a *private brand*, which is given to a product by the wholesaler or retailer rather than the manufacturer.

OBJECTIVE 4

Identify the various pricing objectives that govern pricing decisions, and describe the price-setting tools used in making these decisions. (pp. 425–429)

In pricing, managers decide what the company will get in exchange for its products. Pricing objectives refer to the goals that producers hope to attain as a result of pricing decisions. Two major pricing objectives are (1) *Pricing to maximize profits*: Set the price to sell the number of units that will generate the highest possible total profits. With prices set too low, the seller misses the chance to make additional profits on each of the many units sold. With prices set too high, a larger profit will be made on each unit, but fewer units will be sold. (2) *Market share objectives*: Pricing is used for establishing market share. The seller is willing to accept minimal profits, even losses, to get buyers to try products. They may use pricing to establish market share—a company's percentage of the total market sales for a specific product type.

Managers often prefer to measure the potential impact before deciding on final prices. For this purpose, two basic tools are used: (1) *Cost-oriented pricing* begins by determining total costs for making products available to buyers including wages, rent, materials, and insurance. Added to those costs is a *markup* for profit to arrive at a selling price. (2) *Breakeven analysis* is used to calculate the *breakeven point*: the number of sales units that must be sold for total revenue to equal total costs (which results in neither a profit nor a loss). To calculate the breakeven point, the company must identify all fixed and variable costs associated with the product. The formula for the breakeven point is the total fixed costs divided by the difference between the sales price and the unit variable cost.

OBJECTIVE 5

Discuss pricing strategies that can be used for different competitive situations and identify the pricing tactics that can be used for setting prices. (pp. 429–432)

Pricing for existing products can be set above, at, or below market prices for similar products. High pricing is often interpreted as meaning higher quality and prestige, and low pricing may attract greater sales volume by keeping costs below those of higher-priced competitors.

Pricing strategies for new products include *price skimming*—setting an initially high price to cover costs and generate a profit—may allow a firm to earn a large profit on each item sold; marketers must convince customers that a product is truly different from existing products. *Penetration pricing*—setting an initially low price to establish a new product in the market— seeks to generate customer interest and stimulate trial purchases. Strategies for e-businesses include dynamic versus fixed pricing. *Dynamic pricing* establishes individual prices by real-time interaction between the seller and each customer on the Internet. *Fixed pricing* is the traditional one-price-for-all arrangement.

Regardless of its pricing strategy, a company can then adopt any of three tactics for setting prices: (1) With *price lining*, any product category (such as lady's shoes) will be set at three or four price levels, and all shoes will be priced at one of those levels. (2) *Psychological pricing* acknowledges that customers are not completely rational when making buying decisions, as with *odd-even pricing* in which customers regard prices such as $10 as being significantly higher than $9.95. (3) *Discount pricing* uses price reductions to stimulate sales.

key terms

brand awareness (p. 424)
branding (p. 424)
breakeven analysis (p. 428)
breakeven point (p. 428)
bundling strategy (p. 430)
capital items (p. 416)
consumer (p. 415)
convenience goods (p. 415)
convenience services (p. 415)
cost-oriented pricing (p. 427)
discount (p. 432)
expense items (p. 415)
fixed cost (p. 428)
industrial buyer (p. 415)
licensed brand (p. 425)

market share (or market penetration) (p. 427)
markup (p. 427)
national brand (p. 425)
odd-even pricing (p. 432)
packaging (p. 425)
penetration pricing (p. 430)
price lining (p. 431)
price skimming (p. 430)
pricing (p. 425)
pricing objectives (p. 426)
private brand (private label) (p. 425)
product adaptation (p. 423)
product extension (p. 423)

product features (p. 414)
product life cycle (PLC) (p. 421)
product line (p. 417)
product mix (p. 416)
product placement (p. 424)
production items (p. 415)
psychological pricing (p. 432)
reintroduction (p. 423)
shopping goods (p. 415)
shopping services (p. 415)
specialty goods (p. 415)
specialty services (p. 415)
speed to market (p. 419)
value package (p. 414)
variable cost (p. 428)

MyBizLab

Go to **pearsonglobaleditions.com/mybizlab** to complete the problems marked with this icon ⭐.

questions & exercises

QUESTIONS FOR REVIEW

12-1. How does breakeven analysis help managers measure the potential impact of prices?

12-2. Discuss the goal of price skimming and penetration pricing.

12-3. What are the various classifications of consumer and industrial products? Give an example of a good and a service for each category other than those discussed in the text.

⭐ **12-4.** How is the concept of the value package useful in marketing to consumers and industrial customers?

QUESTIONS FOR ANALYSIS

12-5. Describe the four stages of the product life cycle and the marketing mix that is used in each. Provide at least one example of a product in each stage other than those provided in the text.

⭐ **12-6.** Some companies have very narrow product mixes, producing just one or two products, while others have many different products. What are the advantages of each approach?

12-7. Suppose that a small publisher selling to book distributors has fixed operating costs of $600,000 each year and variable costs of $3.00 per book. How many books must the firm sell to break even if the selling price is $6.00?

✪ **12-8.** Describe price skimming and penetration pricing. What types of new products would be best suited to price skimming? What types of products will be most successful with penetration pricing?

APPLICATION EXERCISES

12-9. For this exercise, select a car or truck that interests you and identify the target market. Once you've identified the target market, describe the features of the vehicle that appeal specifically to the target market.

12-10. Select a product and analyze pricing objectives for it. What information would you want if you were to adopt a profit-maximizing objective or a market share objective?

building a business: continuing team exercise

Assignment

Meet with your team members to consider your new business venture and how it relates to the product and pricing topics in this chapter. Develop specific responses to the following:

12-11. Consider the customers in your target market(s). Are they individual consumers, or are they organizations, or a combination of both? For each of your target markets, identify what customers will expect in the product features and in the value-package features.

12-12. Identify your business's product mix, including its product line(s), if any. How do you justify this product mix rather than others you might have chosen?

12-13. Will your product(s) require new product development, modifications of existing products, or are they fully developed and ready to go? How quickly do you anticipate your product(s) will be developed and ready for market? How long of a life span do you expect for your product(s)?

12-14. Consider various pricing objectives and strategies to use when your product(s) first goes to market. Which pricing objective(s) seems most appropriate for your entry into the market(s)? Identify the pricing strategy(s) that seem best-suited for your business. Explain.

12-15. Various pricing tactics, too, are available for planning your business. Describe the pricing tactics you expect to use on opening the business. Explain your choice(s). Might you resort to different pricing tactics as your product(s) move through various stages in the life cycle(s)? Explain your reasoning.

building your business skills

THE GREAT OUTDOORS

Goal

To understand the product and pricing strategy decisions made by marketers.

Background Information

You and your team have been hired as consultants by a manufacturer that has been making camping equipment for more than a century. Although their original target market was gold miners and loggers, they primarily sell to recreational campers. The company has a long history of quality, long-lasting products with few frills, including tents, sleeping bags, lanterns, and camp stoves.

Method

STEP 1

Working with your group, brainstorm ways that the company could make their products more appealing to recreational campers today. Be creative and think outside the box, how could the company make their tents, sleeping bags, lanterns, and camp stoves more exciting and desirable?

STEP 2

The company's marketing manager has suggested that the company branch out into other products for camping beyond the company's long established product line. Work with your group to develop a list of products that the company should consider selling. Don't filter your suggestions; try to develop a long and detailed list of options.

STEP 3

As a group, determine which new products as well as modifications to existing products hold the most promise and develop a recommendation that you present to your client.

FOLLOW-UP QUESTIONS

12-16. How do you think that the market for camping equipment has changed over the last 50 years? How did this influence your decision making?

12-17. As you developed your list of new products, which wants and needs of the target market were most important?

12-18. What pricing strategy should the company use for their existing products?

12-19. What pricing strategy should the company use for their new products? Is skimming or penetration more appropriate?

exercising your ethics

DRIVING A LEGITIMATE BARGAIN

The Situation

A firm's marketing methods are sometimes at odds with the consumer's buying process. This exercise illustrates how ethical issues can become entwined with personal selling activities, product pricing, and customer relations.

The Dilemma

In buying his first new car, Matt visited showrooms and websites for every make of SUV. After weeks of reading and test-driving, he settled on a well-known Japanese-made vehicle with a manufacturer's suggested retail price of $37,500 for the 2014 model. The price included accessories and options that Matt considered essential. Because he planned to own the car for at least five years, he was willing to wait for just the right package rather than accept a lesser-equipped car already on the lot. Negotiations with Gary, the sales representative, continued for two weeks. Finally, a sales contract was signed for $33,600, with delivery due no more than two or three months later if the vehicle had to be special-ordered from the factory and earlier if Gary found the exact car when he searched other dealers around the country. On April 30, to close the deal, Matt had to write a check for $1,000.

Matt received a call on June 14 from Angela, Gary's sales manager: "We cannot get your car before October," she reported, "so it will have to be a 2015 model. You will have to pay the 2015 price." Matt replied that the agreement called for a stated price and delivery deadline for 2014, pointing out that money had exchanged hands for the contract. When asked what the 2015 price would be, Angela responded that it had not yet been announced. Angrily, Matt replied that he would be foolish to agree now on some unknown future price. Moreover, he didn't like the way the dealership was treating him. He told Angela to send him back everything he had signed; the deal was off.

QUESTIONS TO ADDRESS

12-20. How would you characterize the particular ethical issues in this situation?

12-21. From an ethical standpoint, what are the obligations of the sales representative and the sales manager regarding the pricing of the product in this situation?

12-22. If you were responsible for maintaining good customer relations at the dealership, how would you handle this matter?

team exercise

The Situation

You are a member of a team of business students that have organized for the purpose of starting a small business selling iPhone5 cases from a mall kiosk. You have recently established a business relationship with an Indonesian manufacturer that can provide durable and attractive cases at a low cost.

The Dilemma

You have secured a kiosk at a local mall and believe that this is an excellent location for selling the iPhone 5 cases. However, you must decide on a pricing strategy for the phone cases. You have been provided with the following information:

- Your monthly expenses will be rent on the mall kiosk ($2,500) and hourly pay for your four employees. The kiosk will be open 300 hours per month and the hourly cost of an employee (including benefits) is $15/hour. In addition, you have hired a business manager who will handle ordering the inventory, maintaining the accounting records, and scheduling employees. The business manager's monthly salary is $6,000 per month.
- The Indonesian manufacturer of the phone cases has committed to delivering a variety of cases at a cost of $5 per case for the next year in return for a promise that you will order only from this supplier. There are no other vendors selling these cases within 100 miles and they are expected to be popular.

Team Activity

Assemble a group of four students and assign each group member to one of the following pricing philosophies:

- Because the future is uncertain, the primary objective of this business venture is to maximize profits.

- There is a considerable amount of competition in the market, so the business wishes to price at a level that will give them a large share of the market.
- The business wishes to establish a premium image for their phone cases.
- The business believes that repeat business is the key to success so they wish to use penetration pricing.

ACTION STEPS

12-23. Have each group member describe the pricing strategy that they think the business should use for phone cases based on their assigned philosophy. Be sure to list the benefits of each approach.

12-24. As a group, develop a consensus about the best pricing philosophy and a rationale for why you have selected this approach.

12-25. Using the information provided in the case, identify the fixed and variable costs.

12-26. Using the amounts calculated in Step 2, calculate the breakeven point at a sales price of $15, $20, $25, and $30. Based on these answers as well as your assessment about likely monthly sales, decide on the best price for the phone cases.

12-27. What other pricing tactics might you employ at the phone case kiosk to increase sales?

cases

iTunes Is It

Continued from page 414

Continued from page 414

At the beginning of this chapter you read about some features of the marketing practices for iTunes and the resulting changes in the purchasing habits of music lovers in the United States and around the world. Using the information presented in this chapter you should now be able to answer the following questions:

12-28. Consider the distribution channel for iTunes music products versus the channels used by brick-and-mortar retail music stores. What are the advantages and disadvantages of those channels for distributing these kinds of products?

12-29. What is (are) iTunes's target market(s)? What factors in the marketing environment, if any, are likely to change the pricing practices for iTunes products over the next few years?

12-30. How do you suppose Apple's pricing methods for iTunes products would change if competitors are able to overcome iTunes' commanding lead as the top music retailer?

12-31. In what ways might Apple benefit by jointly advertising its music products together with its digital-music-player products?

12-32. Would you advise iTunes to continue with the three-tier pricing system for music products or, instead, return to a one-price policy? Explain.

Singapore Retailers' Pricing Policy

To a great extent, the experience and pricing policies of Singaporean retailers is clear illustration that they face the same opportunities and threats as other retailers in far larger markets.

Focusing on the food retail market, it becomes clear that several retailers have opted to cater to specific segments of the market; this in turn determines their approach to pricing. On the other hand, there are retailers who have taken the decision to focus on price and to compete across several segments of the market.

Amongst the specialized retailers are those who actually face considerably less competition; they are located in relatively expensive neighborhoods. Cold Storage is a good example, they are the market leader for this segment which caters to the more affluent consumer and the Western expat. For the expat Japanese, Meidi-Ya flies in Japanese produce. Mustafa, focusing on South Asian consumers, is the specialist in Indian and Middle Eastern produce.

Many other companies seem to adopt a low-cost pricing strategy. Sheng Siong sources from China and Vietnam, they are focused on more general Singaporean consumer tastes. They tend to be located in high population areas where low price and convenience (and daily shopping) is demanded. As an alternative, the Shop n' Save chain maintains its low prices by only having a very limited range of stock items. It can concentrate on delivering these at highly competitive prices.

Singapore is well served by what is known as wet markets. These are essentially outdoor markets or independent retailers.

Many of them are specialists in one type of product (such as chicken, fruit, or vegetables). Not all of them compete purely on price, many focus on quality.

One major competitor to Cold Storage is the Fairprice chain. Whilst they may not always compare well in terms of quality with Cold Storage, they are often able to match their prices. They also have the pricing policy that guarantees that the price charged in one outlet will be exactly the same as those in their other outlets, regardless of the location. The problem for Fairprice is that moving into more expensive retail locations has driven up their costs, whilst their prices have remained competitive, which in turn makes them less profitable.

The global food retailer Carrefour left the Singaporean market in late 2012. Initially, they had tried to compete on price. They had also established their two hypermarkets in seemingly odd locations as far as consumers were concerned. Their outlets were in fashionable malls that were not traditionally associated with food shopping. Equally, the product range was focused on the expat communities rather than the typical Singaporean consumer.

As the competitive environment in Singapore begins to settle, the future of each of the chains could be remarkably different and not doomed to failure as Carrefour had discovered. Eventually, Sheng Siong will acquire better locations for their outlets and continue to compete on price, without sacrificing their product range. Fairprice are their closest competitor, but have the advantage of better locations.

Shop n' Save and Giant, owned by the same parent company, have made the decision to fully merge and trade under the Giant name. The former had been gradually losing market share to Sheng Siong, but this move is designed to reverse the trend.

Potential growth for all of the major players is possible as the wet market segment of the food trade gradually ages over the next decade or so. If successive generations decide not to continue the businesses in the face of greater competition, then there is another large segment of consumers that will need to be catered to in the future.[18]

QUESTIONS FOR DISCUSSION

12-33. How do you respond to the following question: Why would one food retailer's pricing and promotion strategy be expected to work well for a competing store chain?

12-34. Describe the characteristics you would expect to find in Giant's target market(s), as compared with those in Sheng Siong's target market(s)?

12-35. Explain how a company's target market is a relevant consideration for its pricing strategy.

12-36. Think about the product offerings for customers at your favored food store. Also, consider a competing store's customers and products. Do you expect that differences in the kinds of products of the two companies might result in differences in their pricing strategies? Explain.

12-37. Consider the *place* (distribution) where customers go to purchase general food products. Next, consider where customers go to purchase specialty food products. How do you suppose differences in the companies' distribution methods may result in differences in their pricing strategies?

MyBizLab

Go to **pearsonglobaleditions.com/mybizlab** *for the following Assisted-graded writing questions:*

12-38. Many business firms are continually developing new products (services or physical goods) to remain competitive. However, the process for product development is sometimes difficult, involving a number of obstacles and challenges that must be overcome. Write an essay identifying some major considerations for deciding if and when to engage in the "new product development" process. Give examples of the difficulties and challenges that may be encountered once the decision is made to develop a new product.

12-39. Companies always face various kinds of decisions for pricing their products in the marketplace. Pricing strategies for existing products, for example, are usually different than for pricing new products. (a) Compare and contrast pricing strategies for existing products versus pricing for new products. (b) Explain how "pricing to maximize profits" differs from "pricing to gain market share." (c) Pricing for products sold online is sometimes different than pricing for traditional face-to-face or in-store transactions. Explain how they may differ.

12-40. Mybizlab Only—comprehensive writing assignment for this chapter.

end notes

1 "iTunes Store Sets New Record with 25 Billion Songs Sold," *Apple.com* (press release), February 6, 2013, at http://www.apple.com/pr/library/2013/02/06iTunes-Store-Sets-New-Record-with-25-Billion-Songs-Sold.html; Hisham Dahud, "iTunes Dominates Music Sales, While Pandora's Footprint Soars," *Hypebot.com*, September 19, 2012, at http://www.hypebot.com/hypebot/2012/09/itunes-dominates-music-sales-while-pandoras-footprint-soars-study.html; Apple Inc., *Form 10-K* (October 27, 2010), at http://www.apple.com/investor/; Glenn Peoples, "iTunes Price Changes Hurt Some Rankings," *Billboard.biz*, April 10, 2009, at http://www.billboard.biz/bbbiz/content_display/industry/news/e3i7917210cb575a9b91b4543e3d671922a; Edward Christman, "UPDATE: First Half 2010 Sales Recap: Lady Antebellum, UMG Lead the Way," *Billboard.biz*, July 7, 2010, at http://www.billboard.biz/bbbiz/content_display/industry/news/e3ic639ed027f3e13c9f62b3cb6e00e1f0e.

2 Frederic Lardinois, "More Teens Now Listen To Music Through YouTube Than Any Other Source," *Techcrunch.com*, August 14, 2012, at http://techcrunch.com/2012/08/14/youtube-is-for-music/; Chris Maxcer, "iTunes Tops Music Vendor Charts," *E-Commerce Times* (April 4, 2008), at www.macnewsworld/story/62458.html; "Amazon Ties Walmart as Second-Ranked U.S. Music Retailer, Behind Industry-Leader iTunes," The *NBD Group* (press release), May 26, 2010, accessed at http://www.npd.com/press/releases/press_100526.html.

3 Emily Maltby and Angus Loten, "App Building, the Do-It-Yourself Way," *Wall Street Journal*, March 7, 2013, p. B4; Jessica E. Lessin, "High Priest of App Design, at Home in Philly," *Wall Street Journal*, March 18, 2013, pp. B1, B5; "Twitter's Loren Brichter Aims for Patent on Pull-to-Refresh," *MacNN News*, March 27, 2012, at http://www.macnn.com/articles/12/03/27/tech.already.used.in.many.third.party.titles/; Romain Dillet, "Tweetie Creator Loren Brichter's Next Act: Atebits 2.0 To 'Make Fun and Useful Things' [Like Games]," *TechCrunch*, October 15, 2012, at http://techcrunch.com/2012/10/15/tweetie-creator-loren-brichters-next-act-atebits-2-0-to-make-fun-and-useful-things-like-games/; "Twitter Acquires Atebits, Will Make Tweetie for iPad," *Electronista*, April 9, 2010, at http://www.electronista.com/articles/10/04/09/twitter.hand.picks.tweetie.for.apps/; Bryan M. Wolfe, "Glyph Users Can Maximize Their Card Rewards and Protect Their Credit," *AppAdvice*, February 13, 2013, at http://appadvice.com/appnn/2013/02/glyph-users-can-maximize-their-card-rewards-and-protect-their-credit.

4 Ron Winslow, "Cholesterol Drug Advances," *The Wall Street Journal*, November 18, 2010, pp. B1–2; "Anacetrapib for the Treatment of Dyslipidemia," *Issues in Emerging Health technologies: Canadian Agency for Drugs and Technologies in Health*, March 2013, at http://www.cadth.ca/media/pdf/EH0007-000Anacetrapib_e.pdf; John Carroll, "Anacetrapib," *FierceBiotech*, October 8, 2012, at http://www.fiercebiotech.com/special-reports/anacetrapib.

5 "New Products," *United States Department of Agriculture: Economic Research Service*, at http://www.ers.usda.gov/topics/food-markets-prices/processing-marketing/new-products.aspx#.UV2FtzemFcI, accessed on April 4, 2013; "Food Marketing System in the U.S.: New Product Introductions," *USDA Economic Research Service*, May 21, 2010, accessed at http://www.ers.usda.gov/Briefing/FoodMarketingSystem/new_product.htm.

6 "iPad," *Wikipedia*, accessed April 4, 2013, at http://en.wikipedia.org/wiki/IPad; Dan Graziano, "Android Is Nipping at Apple's Heels in the Tablet Market," *BGR*, December 5, 2012, at http://bgr.com/2012/12/05/tablet-market-share-2012/.

7 Kelvin Chan, "Tired Western Brands Find New Life in Asia," Yahoo! News, September 8, 2011, at http://news.yahoo.com/tired-western-brands-life-asia-070448945.html.

8 Manish Modi, "Coca-Cola Retains Title as World's most Valuable Brand," *Bloomberg*, October 2, 2012, at http://

www.bloomberg.com/news/2012-10-03/coca-cola-retains-title-as-world-s-most-valuable-brand-table-.html; "Interbrand Releases 13th Annual Best Global Brands Report," *Interbrand*, at http://www.interbrand.com/en/best-global-brands/2012/downloads.aspx, accessed on April 5, 2013.

[9] http://www.emirates247.com/news/emirates/fixed-price-list-for-products-in-uae-online-2011-07-16-1.407932; http://gulfnews.com/news/gulf/uae/government/uae-fixes-prices-of-1-650-consumer-products-this-year-1.1036661 (both accessed on October 16, 2013).

[10] "Local Arizona Healthcare Companies Join Forces to Create a Unique Prescription Benefit Program for," *HR.com*, February 3, 2009, at http://www.hr.com/SITEFORUM?&t=/Default/gateway&i=1116423256281&application=story&active=no&ParentID=1119278002800&StoryID=1233685483801&xref=http%3A//www.google.com/url%3Fsa%3Dt%26rct%3Dj%26q%3Dcompanies%2520join%2520forces%2520on%2520internet%2520to%2520reduce%2520drug%2520prices%26source%3Dweb%26cd%3D6%26sqi%3D2%26ved%3D0CFoQFjAF%26url%3Dhttp%253A%252F%252Fwww.hr.com%252Fhr%252Fcommunities%252F_local_arizona_healthcare_companies_join_forces_to_create_a_unique_prescription_benefit_program__eng.html%26ei%3DwRuFUYSeAbWv4APBz4GACA%26usg%3DAFQjCNHRtbBJU0H9GJtl-zttn4AV9eUi9w.

[11] "About Carbonite," at http://www.carbonite.com/en/about/company/our-story.

[12] "Reverse Auction," *Encyclopedia of Management. 2009. Encyclopedia.com.* (January 16, 2011), at http://www.encyclopedia.com/doc/1G2-3273100254.html; MediaBids.com, at http://www.mediabids.com/.

[13] Patrick G. Lee, "Pricing Tactic Spooks Lawyers," *Wall Street Journal*, August 2, 2011, p. B5.

[14] "Highlight Free Shipping Offers in Online Marketing Campaigns," *ClickThrough Search Engine Marketing Services*, February 16, 2009, at http://www.clickthrough-marketing.com/

highlight-free-shipping-offers-in-online-marketing-campaigns/19027764/; "Free Shipping Strategies Gain Retailers Loyal Customers," *ManageSmarter*, July 30, 2010, at http://www.salesandmarketing.com/article/free-shipping-strategies-gain-retailers-loyal-customers.

[15] "Ford, GM to Cover Car Payments if Buyer Loses Job," *Bloomberg News*, March 31, 2009, at http://www.chron.com/disp/story.mp/business/6351277.html; "Electric Car Maker Tesla Unveils Financing Program," *Yahoo! News*, April 2, 2013, at http://news.yahoo.com/electric-car-maker-tesla-unveils-221450404.html.

[16] "Use Those stocks to Pay for a Caribbean Vacation-at July 2008 Market Prices!," *Travel4People.com*, at http://www.travel4people.com/index.php?view=article&catid=1%3Anews1&id=314%3Ause-those-stocks-to-pay-for-a-caribbean-vacation-at-july-market-prices&tmpl=component&print=1&layout=default&page=&option=com_content&Itemid=49.

[17] "Hearing Set In US On Dumping Charges," *SeafoodSource.com*, January 4, 2013, at http://www.seafoodsource.com/newsarticledetail.aspx?id=19025.

[18] http://www.globalscorecard.net/live/download/Food_Retail_Formats_in_Asia_Understanding_Format_Success-Study.pdf; http://news.asiaone.com/News/AsiaOne+News/Singapore/Story/A1Story20101119-248126.html;

chapter 13 | Distributing and Promoting Products

Francis Vachon/Alamy

E-commerce brings consumers and businesses

together in ways

we could have never imagined.

By collecting purchase data,

retailers know what we want

before we do.

AFTER READING THIS CHAPTER, YOU SHOULD BE ABLE TO:

OBJECTIVE 1   **Explain** the meaning of *distribution mix* and identify the different channels of distribution.

OBJECTIVE 2   **Describe** the role of wholesalers and the functions performed by e-intermediaries.

OBJECTIVE 3   **Describe** the different types of retailing and explain how online retailers add value for consumers on the Internet.

OBJECTIVE 4   **Define** *physical distribution* and describe the major activities in the physical distribution process.

OBJECTIVE 5   **Identify** the objectives of promotion, the considerations in selecting a promotional mix, and discuss the various kinds of advertising promotions.

OBJECTIVE 6   **Outline** the tasks involved in personal selling and describe the various types of sales promotions.

MyBizLab®

✪ Improve Your Grade!

Visit **pearsonglobaleditions.com/mybizlab** for simulations, tutorials, and end-of-chapter problems.

Over 10 million students improved their results using the Pearson MyLabs.

With Its Worldly View, Netflix Wants an Entire Globe of Streamers

Who could have guessed that a tiny company that started offering online movie rentals delivered by mail in 1997 would emerge 16 years later as the world's leading Internet subscription service for watching movies and television shows? Perhaps not even Reed Hastings, co-founder and CEO of Netflix, could envision today's more than 33 million streaming members—more than 27 million in the United States, and 6 million in more than 40 other countries. And Hastings is betting that growth in both the domestic and international markets is a key to the company's future profitability.

Since introducing streaming in 2007, which allows members to instantly watch TV shows and movies on their PCs, Netflix has grown to hold a more than 30 percent share of the streaming market using a series of aggressive innovations that make viewing more convenient for customers. Collaboration with consumer electronics firms enabled delivery of streaming first on the Xbox 360 and Blu-ray disk players in 2008, followed with streaming on the PS3 and Internet-connected TVs in 2009. In 2010, the expansion of product delivery intensified when streaming became available on the Nintendo Wii, Apple iPad, iPhone, and iPod Touch, and other Internet-connected devices. For the price of $7.99 a month and with unlimited access to thousands of movies and TV episodes, the growing number of domestic streamers, nearly 6 million new subscribers in 2012, is the backbone of sorely needed new revenue for Netflix. Unlike other Internet-based companies that gain revenues from selling advertising space on their websites, Netflix relies on subscription revenues. The previous income base, before the onset of streaming, had been DVD rentals delivered by mail, but that base is declining more and more every year. By early 2013 DVD revenues had fallen more than 40 percent and DVD-by-mail subscribers had dropped from a previous high of nearly 25 million to just over 8 million, since 2011.

Although other countries offer promise for the future, the U.S. market is dominant because of its technological streaming capabilities, the availability of necessary media for viewing, and subscribers with the know-how and income to use it. Although online activity is especially popular among those in their teens and twenties, it is extending into other age groups as well. The Netflix list of children's movies and animation features is attracting younger viewers, and classic movies and TV episodes on sports, faith, and spirituality and musicals are gaining attention among the older-than-40 demographic.

what's in it for me?

To become the number-one retailer in any market takes a solid understanding of how best to distribute and promote products to customers. This chapter describes different types of wholesalers, retailers, and intermediaries, as well as how the online marketplace has changed the nature of how companies do business. By understanding this chapter's methods for distributing and promoting products, you'll have a clearer picture of how to sort out and identify the different kinds of people that are targeted by various companies, products, and advertising campaigns. As an informed consumer, you'll have a better self-understanding of being targeted with promotional exposures every day. You'll also be prepared to evaluate a company's distribution methods, advertising programs, and competitive potential.

As we saw in Chapter 12, marketing managers are concerned with deciding what products a company will offer to its customers and determining prices for those products. In this chapter, we'll look at the next two of the Four *P*s of the marketing mix. We'll start this chapter by looking at the concept of *place*, the *distribution mix*, and the different channels and methods of distribution. We'll then look at *promotion* and discuss the considerations in selecting a promotional mix. Finally, we'll discuss the tasks involved in personal selling and various types of sales promotions.

What are the next steps for Netflix? One is producing their own original programming and another is social media. With original programming, Netflix intends to build customer loyalty with content that fits more closely to streamers' viewing preferences, which is based on mounds of viewer streaming data. The company's first major production, *House of Cards*, a political drama series starring Kevin Spacey and Robin Wright, was both highly successful and expensive to produce. Before the series was produced, Netflix's data mining of viewers' streaming habits was encouraging; it had suggested the series would be a success, and it is, as witnessed by nine Emmy nominations in 2013. As just one example of providing viewer-pleasing convenience, Netflix made a surprise move by streaming all 13 first-season episodes together, so that viewers could see them at their own pace without having to wait a week or more between episodes.

As for social networking, CEO Hastings notes that social media is another key to building subscriber loyalty, so Netflix has launched a Facebook app for U.S. streamers who now can share with friends what they've been watching. Users can select "Friends' Favorites" or "Watched by Your Friends" on the Netflix home page. Each subscriber can tell the other what they watch and, as a result, both will end up watching more. Hopefully, more viewers will subscribe as word-of-mouth about Netflix circulates among friends.[1]

(After studying the content in this chapter you should be able to answer a set of discussion questions found at the end of the chapter.)

OBJECTIVE 1
Explain
the meaning of *distribution mix* and identify the different channels of distribution

Distribution Mix *combination of distribution channels by which a firm gets its products to end users*

The Distribution Mix

In addition to a good product mix and effective pricing, the success of any product also depends on its **distribution mix**, the combination of distribution channels by which a firm gets products to end users. In this section, we look at intermediaries and different kinds of distribution channels. Then we discuss some benefits consumers reap from services provided by intermediaries.

Intermediaries and Distribution Channels

Intermediary *individual or firm that helps to distribute a product*

Wholesaler *intermediary who sells products to other businesses for resale to final consumers*

Retailer *intermediary who sells products directly to consumers*

Distribution Channel *network of interdependent companies through which a product passes from producer to end user*

Direct Channel *distribution channel in which a product travels from producer to consumer without intermediaries*

Once called *middlemen*, **intermediaries** help to distribute goods, either by moving them or by providing information that stimulates their movement from sellers to customers. **Wholesalers** are intermediaries who sell products to other businesses for resale to final consumers. **Retailers** sell products directly to consumers.

Distribution of Goods and Services A **distribution channel** is the path a product follows from producer to end user. Figure 13.1 shows how four popular distribution channels can be identified according to the channel members involved in getting products to buyers.

CHANNEL 1: DIRECT DISTRIBUTION In a **direct channel,** the product travels from the producer to the consumer or organizational buyer without intermediaries. Avon, Dell, GEICO, and Tupperware, as well as many online companies, use this channel. Most business goods, especially those bought in large quantities, are sold directly by the manufacturer to the industrial buyer.

CHANNEL 2: RETAIL DISTRIBUTION In Channel 2, producers distribute consumer products through retailers. Goodyear, for example, maintains its own system of retail outlets. Levi's has its own outlets but also produces jeans for other

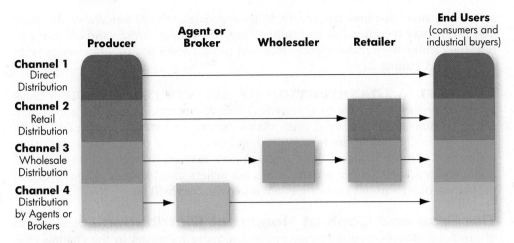

FIGURE 13.1 Channels of Distribution

retailers. Large outlets, such as Walmart, buy merchandise directly from producers, then resell to customers online and at Walmart retail stores. Consumers go online to buy popular products such as movie downloads and iTunes from online retailers. Many industrial buyers, such as businesses buying office supplies from Staples, rely on this channel.

CHANNEL 3: WHOLESALE DISTRIBUTION Once the most widely used method of nondirect distribution, Channel 2 requires a large and costly amount of floor space for storing and displaying merchandise at brick-and-mortar facilities. Wholesalers relieve the space problem by storing merchandise and

At this plant of an electrical components supplier, this employee assembles electrical systems according to a process that meets the requirements for their industrial customers. The finished assemblies are shipped from the plant to customers' facilities, illustrating a direct (producer to customer) channel of distribution.

Keith Dannemiller/ZUMAPRESS/Newscom

restocking store displays frequently. With approximately 90 percent of its space used to display merchandise and only 10 percent left for storage and office facilities, the combination convenience store and gas station's use of wholesalers is an example of Channel 3.

CHANNEL 4: DISTRIBUTION BY AGENTS OR BROKERS

Sales agents or brokers represent producers and receive commissions on the goods they sell to consumers or industrial users. **Sales agents,** including many online travel agents, generally deal in the related product lines of a few producers, such as tour companies, to meet the needs of many customers. **Brokers,** in such industries as real estate and stock exchanges, match numerous sellers and buyers as needed to sell properties, often without knowing in advance who they will be.

Sales Agent *independent intermediary who generally deals in the related product lines of a few producers and forms long-term relationships to represent those producers and meet the needs of many customers*

Broker *independent intermediary who matches numerous sellers and buyers as needed, often without knowing in advance who they will be*

The Pros and Cons of Nondirect Distribution

One downfall of nondirect distribution is higher prices; the more members in the channel, the more intermediaries making a profit by charging a markup or commission, and the higher the final price. Intermediaries, however, can provide *added value* by providing time-saving information and making the right quantities of products available where and when consumers need them. Figure 13.2 illustrates the problem of making chili without the benefit of a common intermediary, the supermarket. As a consumer, you would obviously spend a lot more time, money, and energy if you tried to gather all the ingredients from separate producers. In short, intermediaries exist because they provide necessary services that get products efficiently from producers to users.

Distribution Strategies

Selecting an appropriate distribution network is a strategic decision; it determines both the amount and cost of *market coverage* that a product gets, or how many of any kind of intermediary will be used. Generally, strategy depends on the type of product and the degree of market coverage that is most effective in getting it to the greatest number of customers. Marketers strive to make a product accessible in just enough locations to satisfy customers' needs. You can buy milk, for instance, in numerous retail outlets, but in many cities or regions there may be only one Rolls-Royce distributor. Three strategies, (1) *intensive,* (2) *exclusive,* and (3) *selective distribution,* provide different degrees of market coverage.

Intensive Distribution *strategy by which a product is distributed through as many channels as possible*

- **Intensive distribution** means distributing through as many channels and channel members as possible (both wholesalers and retailers). It is normally used for low-cost consumer goods with widespread appeal, such as candy and magazines. M&Ms candies enter the market through all suitable retail outlets—supermarkets, candy machines, drugstores, online, and so forth.

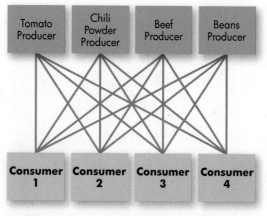 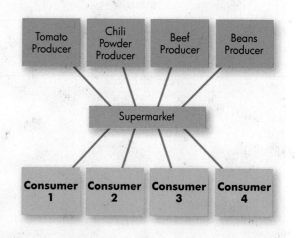

FIGURE 13.2 The Value-Adding Intermediary

- With **exclusive distribution,** a manufacturer grants the exclusive right to distribute or sell a product to a limited number of wholesalers or retailers, usually in a given geographic area. Such agreements are most common for high-cost prestige products. Rolex watches are sold only by "Official Rolex Jewelers."

- Using **selective distribution,** a producer selects only wholesalers and retailers that will give a product special attention in sales effort, display and promotion advantage, and so forth. Selective distribution is used most often for consumer products such as furniture and appliances. Frigidaire and Whirlpool use selective distribution for appliances to cement relationships with wholesalers who will market Frigidaire and Whirlpool over other brands.

Exclusive Distribution *strategy by which a manufacturer grants exclusive rights to distribute or sell a product to a limited number of wholesalers or retailers in a given geographic area*

Selective Distribution *strategy by which a company uses only wholesalers and retailers who give special attention in sales effort to specific products*

Channel Conflict and Channel Leadership

Manufacturers and services providers (such as Nike, LG Electronics, and Allied Insurance) may distribute through more than one channel, and many retailers (such as Walgreen's Pharmacies) are free to strike agreements with as many producers (like the makers of Tylenol, Advil, and Aleve) as capacity permits. In such cases *channel conflict* may arise. Conflicts are resolved through better coordination, and a key factor in coordinating the activities of organizations is *channel leadership*.

Channel Conflict

Channel conflict occurs when members of the channel disagree over roles or rewards. John Deere and State Farm Insurance would object to its dealers distributing tractors and insurance products of competing brands. Likewise, a manufacturer-owned outlet store runs the risk of alienating other retailers of its products when it discounts the company's products. Conflict may arise if one channel member has more power or is perceived as getting preferential treatment. Before Apple opened its retail stores, it distributed its products through many non-Apple retail stores. By opening its own retail outlets, channel conflict was created because the Apple stores substantially reduced sales at stores they formerly used to distribute and sell Apple products. Such conflicts, of course, can defeat the purpose of the system by disrupting the flow of goods.

Channel Conflict *conflict arising when the members of a distribution channel disagree over the roles they should play or the rewards they should receive*

Channel Leadership

Usually one channel member—the **channel captain** —can determine the roles and rewards of the others. Often the channel captain is a manufacturer or an originator of a service. Jewelry artisan Thomas Mann is in such demand that wholesalers and retailers wait years for the chance to distribute his Techno-Romantic creations. Mann selects channel members, sets prices, and determines product availability. In other industries, an influential wholesaler or a large retailer such as Walmart may be a channel captain because of large sales volume.

Channel Captain *channel member who is most powerful in determining the roles and rewards of other members*

Wholesaling

OBJECTIVE 2
Describe
the role of wholesalers and the functions performed by e-intermediaries.

The roles differ among the various intermediaries in distribution channels. Wholesalers provide a variety of services to buyers of products for resale or business use. In addition to storing and providing an assortment of products, some wholesalers offer delivery, credit, and product information. The range of services depends on the type of intermediary: *merchant wholesaler, agent/broker,* or *e-intermediary*.

Merchant Wholesalers

Most wholesalers are independent operations that sell various consumer or business goods produced by a variety of manufacturers. The largest group, **merchant wholesalers,** buys products from manufacturers and sells them to other businesses. They own the goods that they resell and usually provide storage and delivery.

Merchant Wholesalers *independent wholesaler who takes legal possession of goods produced by a variety of manufacturers and then resells them to other organizations*

Full-Service Merchant Wholesalers *merchant wholesaler that provides credit, marketing, and merchandising services in addition to traditional buying and selling services*

Limited-Function Merchant Wholesaler *merchant wholesaler that provides a limited range of services*

Drop Shippers *limited-function merchant wholesaler that receives customer orders, negotiates with producers, takes title to goods, and arranges for shipment to customers*

Full-service merchant wholesalers (about 80 percent of all merchant wholesalers) provide value-adding services, including credit, marketing advice, and merchandising services. **Limited-function merchant wholesalers** provide fewer services, sometimes merely storage. Customers are normally small operations that pay cash and pick up their own goods. **Drop shippers** don't even carry inventory or handle products; they take orders from customers, negotiate with producers to supply goods, take title to them, and arrange for shipment. Rack jobbers market consumer goods (mostly nonfood items) directly to retail stores, marking prices and setting up displays in a variety of stores. Procter & Gamble (P&G) uses rack jobbers to distribute products such as its Pamper diapers.

Agents and Brokers

Agents and brokers, including online e-agents, serve as independent sales representatives for many companies' products. They work on commission, usually about 4 to 5 percent of net sales. Unlike wholesalers, agents and brokers do not own their merchandise. Rather, they serve as sales and merchandising arms for producers or sellers who do not have their own sales forces.

The value of agents and brokers lies in their knowledge of markets and their merchandising expertise. They show sale items to potential buyers and, for retail stores, they provide such services as shelf and display merchandising and advertising layout. They remove open, torn, or dirty packages; arrange products neatly; and generally keep goods attractively displayed. Many supermarket products are handled through brokers.

The Advent of the E-Intermediary

e-Intermediary *Internet distribution channel member that assists in delivering products to customers or that collects information about various sellers to be presented to consumers, or they help deliver online products to buyers*

The ability of e-commerce to bring together millions of widely dispersed consumers and businesses has changed the types and roles of intermediaries. **E-intermediaries** are Internet-based channel members—wholesalers—who perform one or both of two functions: (1) they collect information about sellers and present it to consumers (such as kayak.com), or (2) they help deliver online products to buyers (such as Amazon.com).

Syndicated Selling *e-commerce practice whereby a website offers other websites commissions for referring customers*

Syndicated Sellers   **Syndicated selling** occurs when one website offers another a commission for referring customers. Expedia.com and Dollar Rent-A-Car illustrate syndicated selling perfectly. With millions of users each month, Expedia.com is a heavily visited travel-services website. Expedia has given Dollar Rent-A-Car a special banner on its Web page. When Expedia customers click on the banner for a car rental, they are transferred from the Expedia site to the Dollar site. Dollar pays Expedia a fee for each booking that comes through this channel. Although the Expedia intermediary increases the cost of Dollar's supply chain, it adds value for customers. Travelers avoid unnecessary cyberspace searches and are efficiently guided to a car-rental agency.

Shopping Agent (e-agent) *e-intermediary (middleman) in the Internet distribution channel that assists users in finding products and prices but does not take possession of products*

Shopping Agents   **Shopping agents (e-agents)** help online consumers by gathering and sorting information. Although they don't take possession of products, they know which websites and stores to visit, give accurate comparison prices, identify product features, and help consumers complete transactions by presenting information in a usable format—all in an instant. Hotwire.com is a well-known shopping agent for a variety of travel products. When you specify the product—hotels, flights, vacations, cars—Hotwire searches for vendors, does price comparisons, lists prices from low to high, and then transfers you to the websites of different e-stores.

Business-to-Business Brokers   E-commerce intermediaries provide online value-adding services for business customers. The pricing process between business-to-business (B2B) buyers and sellers of commodities and services can be outsourced, for example, to the online company MediaBids.com. As a pricing broker for advertising services, MediaBids links any large-volume buyer of advertising services with potential suppliers that bid to become the supplier for the industrial customer. Client companies (the buyers of advertising services), such as Biocentric Health Inc., Christian Science Monitor, and Simplicity Sofas, can pay a fixed annual subscription fee and receive networking into MediaBids' auction headquarters, where real-time bids come in from suppliers at remote locations. The website provides current information until the bidding ends with the low-price supplier. In brokering the auction transactions, MediaBids doesn't take possession of any products. As a broker, it brings together timely information and links businesses to one another.

Retailing

OBJECTIVE 3
Describe
the different types of retailing and explain how online retailers add value for consumers on the Internet.

There are more than 5 million brick-and-mortar retail establishments in the United States. Many consist only of owners and part-time help. Indeed, more than one-half of the nation's retailers account for less than 10 percent of all retail sales. Retailers also include huge operations, such as Walmart, the world's largest corporate employer, and Home Depot. Although there are large retailers in many other countries—Metro in Germany, Carrefour in France, and Aeon in Japan—most of the world's largest retailers are U.S. businesses.

Types of Brick-and-Mortar Retail Outlets

U.S. retail operations vary widely by type as well as size. They can be classified by their pricing strategies, location, range of services, or range of product lines. Choosing the right types of retail outlets is a crucial aspect of distribution strategy. This section describes U.S. retail stores by using three classifications: (1) *product-line retailers*, (2) *bargain retailers*, and (3) *convenience stores*.

Product-Line Retailers Retailers featuring broad product lines include **department stores**, which are organized into specialized departments: shoes, furniture, women's petite sizes, and so on. Stores are usually large, handle a wide range of goods, and offer a variety of services, such as credit plans and delivery. Similarly, **supermarkets** are divided into departments of related products: food products, household products, and so forth. They stress low prices, self-service, and wide selection.

In contrast, **specialty stores,** such as Lids, a retailer with more than 1,000 stores selling athletic fashion headwear, are small, serve specific market segments with full product lines in narrow product fields, and often feature knowledgeable sales personnel.

Department Store *large product-line retailer characterized by organization into specialized departments*

Supermarket *large product-line retailer offering a variety of food and food-related items in specialized departments*

Specialty Store *retail store carrying one product line or category of related products*

Bargain Retailers **Bargain retailers** carry wide ranges of products at low prices. **Discount houses** began by selling large numbers of items at substantial price reductions to cash-only customers. As name-brand items became more common, they offered better product assortments while still transacting cash-only sales in low-rent facilities. As they became firmly entrenched, they began moving to better locations, improving decor, selling better-quality merchandise at higher prices, and offering services such as credit plans and noncash sales.

Catalog showrooms mail catalogs to attract customers into showrooms to view display samples, place orders, and wait briefly while clerks retrieve orders from attached warehouses. **Factory outlets** are manufacturer-owned stores that avoid wholesalers and retailers by selling merchandise directly from factory to consumer. **Wholesale clubs,** such as Costco, offer large discounts on a wide range of brand-name merchandise to customers who pay annual membership fees.

Bargain Retailer *retailer carrying a wide range of products at bargain prices*

Discount House *bargain retailer that generates large sales volume by offering goods at substantial price reductions*

Catalog Showroom *bargain retailer in which customers place orders for catalog items to be picked up at on-premises warehouses*

Factory Outlet *bargain retailer owned by the manufacturer whose products it sells*

Wholesale Club *bargain retailer offering large discounts on brand-name merchandise to customers who have paid annual membership fees*

Convenience Stores **Convenience store** chains, such as 7-Eleven and Circle K stores, stress easily accessible locations, extended store hours, and speedy service. They differ from most bargain retailers in that they do not feature low prices.

Convenience Store *retail store offering easy accessibility, extended hours, and fast service*

finding a better way

Bye-Bye Cash Registers, Hello Tablets!

In the late 1800s a little-known saloon keeper in Ohio "found a better way" to prevent sales clerks from stealing from the cash drawer. Thus, the cash register began its long career among retailers. By as early as 1915 nearly 2 million of the machines had been sold to U.S. grocery stores, hotels, department stores and other retailers. Today, the cash register's future looks bleak as more and more stores are "finding a better way," using smartphones and tablets instead of the heavy, awkward, now-unattractive machines poised at the end of check-out lines. Mobile devices are on the rise because they are faster, simpler, more attractive, more flexible, and more convenient for shoppers and store owners. They also are far less expensive. An iPad that includes credit card readers costs $1,500 versus the register's $4,000 price tag. Urban Outfitters claims to have ordered its last register, planning instead to go entirely mobile at its chain of clothing stores, after a two-year trial run with iPod Touch devices that was well-received by Urban's customers. Similarly Nordstrom, the well-known department-store chain has been using iPod devices for two years, with plans to phase out registers nationwide by 2014.

In modernizing their stores, some are planning to ring up sales on iPods and iPads mounted on swivels stationed at counters. Others, including Walmart, are testing "Scan-and-Go" apps enabling customers to digitally "ring-up" items using their iPhone cameras to scan as they move through the store, instead of in line at checkout. A donut store in Portland, Oregon, hangs iPad registers on a track on the wall, allowing employees to slide iPads to customers for quick signing of their bills. JCPenney started using iPod Touch in 2012 at its 1,100 stores, with a goal

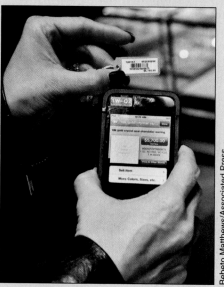

Bebeto Matthews/Associated Press

of all salespeople having one in hand, so the register will go to the customer instead of the customer going to the register. Other stores equip cashiers with mobile devices to approach customers waiting in line, where they scan purchases and tally sales totals to improve service by reducing waiting-in-line time.

Because payments technology continues to change, industry innovators are anticipating the emergence of even more "better ways." They foresee receipt printers disappearing, along with exchanges of cash that are no longer needed when the use of smartphones and other devices becomes more prominent for electronic payments. Retail shopping is expected, eventually, to involve no check-out, no cash, and no unwanted waiting, all for a better customer shopping experience.[2]

Nonstore Retailing

Some of the largest retailers sell all or most of their products without brick-and-mortar stores. Certain types of products, such as snack foods, pinball, jukeboxes, pool, and cigarettes, sell well from card and coin-operated machines. For all products, global annual sales through vending are projected to reach nearly $200 billion by 2015. Still, vending machine sales make up less than 1 percent of all U.S. retail sales.[3]

Nonstore retailing also includes **direct-response retailing,** in which firms contact customers directly to inform them about products and to receive sales orders. **Mail order (or catalog marketing**) is a popular form of direct-response retailing practiced by Crate & Barrel and Land's End. Less popular in recent years because of do-not-call registries, outbound **telemarketing** uses phone calls to sell directly to consumers. However, telemarketing also includes inbound toll-free calls from customers, a service which most catalog and other retail stores make available. Finally, more than 600 U.S. companies, including Mary Kay cosmetics, use **direct selling** to sell door to door or through home-selling parties. Avon Products, the world's largest direct seller, has more than 6 million door-to-door sales representatives in more than 100 countries.[4]

Direct-Response Retailing *form of nonstore retailing in which firms directly interact with customers to inform them of products and to receive sales orders*

Mail Order (catalog marketing) *form of nonstore retailing in which customers place orders for catalog merchandise received through the mail*

Telemarketing *form of nonstore retailing in which the telephone is used to sell directly to consumers*

Direct Selling *form of nonstore retailing typified by door-to-door sales*

Online Retailing

In 2012, global business-to-consumer (B2C) sales topped $1 trillion for the first time.[5] More than 85 percent of the world's online population—more than 1 billion consumers—have made purchases on the Internet. iTunes has outsold brick-and-mortar music retailers, and Amazon.com is the world's largest online retailer, selling nationally and internationally with annual sales of $48 billion.[6] **Online retailing** allows sellers to inform, sell to, and distribute to consumers via the web. Some of the largest U.S. "e-tailers" are shown in Table 13.1. In addition to large companies, millions of small businesses around the globe have their own websites.

Online Retailing *nonstore retailing in which information about the seller's products and services is connected to consumers' computers, allowing consumers to receive the information and purchase the products in the home*

Electronic Catalogs

E-catalogs use online displays of products to give millions of retail and business customers instant access to product information. The seller avoids mail distribution and printing costs, and once an online catalog is in place, there is little cost in maintaining and accessing it. About 90 percent of all catalogers are now on the Internet, with sales via websites accounting for more than 50 percent of all catalog sales.[7]

e-Catalog *nonstore retailing in which the Internet is used to display products*

Electronic Storefronts and Cybermalls

Each seller's website is an **electronic storefront** (or *virtual storefront*) from which shoppers collect information about products and buying opportunities, place orders, and pay for purchases. Producers of large product lines, such as Dell, dedicate storefronts to their own product lines. Other sites, such as Newegg.com, which offers computer and other electronics equipment, are category sellers whose storefronts feature products from many manufacturers.

Electronic Storefront *commercial website at which customers gather information about products and buying opportunities, place orders, and pay for purchases*

Search engines such as Yahoo! and Ask (Ask Jeeves) serve as **cybermalls**, collections of virtual storefronts representing diverse products and offering speed, convenience, 24-hour access, and efficient searching. After entering a cybermall, shoppers can navigate by choosing from a list of stores (L.L. Bean, Lids, or Macy's), product listings (sporting goods, ladies fashions, or mobile devices), or departments (apparel or bath/beauty).

Cybermall *collection of virtual storefronts (business websites) representing a variety of products and product lines on the Internet*

Interactive and Video Retailing

Today, retailers and B2C customers interact with multimedia sites using voice, graphics, animation, film clips, and access to live human advice. Many e-tailers provide real-time sales and customer service that allows customers to enter a live chat room with a service operator who can answer their specific product questions.

table 13.1 Leading Online Retailers in Selected Consumer Products Categories*

Consumer Product Category	Online Retailer
Mass Merchandise	Amazon.com
Office Supplies	Staples Inc.
Computers and Electronics	Apple Inc.
Video and Audio Entertainment	Netflix Inc.
Home Repair and Improvement	W.W. Grainger Inc.
Apparel and Accessories	L.L. Bean Inc.
Home Furnishings and Housewares	Williams-Sonoma Inc.
Toys	Toys "R" Us Inc.
Health and Beauty	Amway Global
Sporting Goods	Cabela's Inc.

*Adapted from "Top 500 Guide," Internet Retailer (2012), at www.internetretailer.com/top500/list/.

James Atoa/Photoshot Holdings Ltd.

Wolfgang Puck products are distributed regularly through QVC and HSN television networks. The chef's name-brand kitchen appliances and cookware are also marketed through such online outlets as eBay and Shopping.com, as well as the QVC and HSN websites.

Video Retailing *nonstore retailing to consumers via home television*

Video retailing, a long-established form of interactive marketing, lets viewers shop at home from channels on their TVs. QVC, for example, displays and demonstrates products and allows viewers to phone in or e-mail orders and is available on Facebook, YouTube, and Twitter. More recently, however, TV sets are available with Internet-ready capabilities, allowing online networking. A TV with built-in Wi-Fi or Ethernet becomes a platform for comfortable at-home online shopping with a large-screen visual display.

OBJECTIVE 4

Define

physical distribution and describe the major activities in the physical distribution process.

Physical Distribution *activities needed to move a product efficiently from manufacturer to consumer*

Physical Distribution

Physical distribution refers to the activities needed to move products from an intermediary or a manufacturer to customers and includes *warehousing* and *transportation operations.* Its purpose is to make goods available when and where customers want them, keep costs low, and provide services to satisfy customers. Because of its importance for customer satisfaction, some firms have adopted distribution as their marketing strategy of choice.

Consider, for example, the pioneering global distribution system of National Semiconductor, one of the world's largest microchip makers. Finished microchips were produced in plants around the world and shipped to hundreds of customers, such as IBM, Toshiba, and Hewlett-Packard, which also ran factories around the globe. Chips originally traveled 20,000 different routes on as many as 12 airlines and sat waiting at one location after another—on factory floors, at customs, in distributors' facilities, and in warehouses—before reaching customers. National streamlined the system by air-freighting chips worldwide from a single center in Singapore. Every activity—storage, sorting, and shipping—was centralized and run by FedEx. By outsourcing the activities, National's distribution costs were reduced, delivery times were cut by half, and sales increased. Acquired in 2011 by Texas Instruments (TI), National Semiconductor and its innovative global distribution system is TI's Silicone Valley Analog division that remains a world leader for producing high-performance analog components.

Warehousing Operations

Storing, or **warehousing,** is a major part of distribution management. In selecting a strategy, managers must keep in mind both the different characteristics and costs of warehousing operations. **Private warehouses** are owned by a single manufacturer, wholesaler, or retailer that deals in mass quantities and needs regular storage. Most are run by large firms that deal in mass quantities and need regular storage. JCPenney, for example, maintains its own warehouses to facilitate the movement of products to its retail stores.

Independently owned and operated **public warehouses,** which rent to companies only the space they need, are popular with firms needing storage only during peak periods and with manufacturers who need multiple storage locations to get products to multiple markets.

The digital age brings with it massive quantities of data that need to be safely stored, preserved, organized, and accessible to users. Many companies, to protect their valuable data resources, rely on remote off-site digital storage services such as *ZipCloud for Business* as a safety net. Home users, too, use daily online backup services, such as *Carbonite Backup* and *SOS Online Backup*, to protect against losing data when their computers crash. In the event of any physical catastrophe—floods, fires, earthquakes—at the client's facility, data can be restored online from the backup system.[8]

Warehousing *physical distribution operation concerned with the storage of goods*

Private Warehouse *warehouse owned by and providing storage for a single company*

Public Warehouse *independently owned and operated warehouse that stores goods for many firms*

Transportation Operations

Physically moving a product creates the highest cost many companies face. In addition to transportation methods, firms must also consider the nature of the product, the distance it must travel, the speed with which it must be received, and customer wants and needs.

Differences in cost among the major transportation modes—trucks, railroads, planes, digital transmission, water carriers, and pipelines—are usually most directly related to delivery speed.

With nearly 2 million drivers and a fleet of 8 million vehicles, trucks haul more than two-thirds of all tonnage carried by all modes of U.S. freight transportation. The advantages of trucks include flexibility for any-distance distribution, fast service, and dependability. Increasing truck traffic, however, is raising safety and courtesy concerns.

Joseph Sibilsky/Alamy

Specializing in long-haul shipping, U.S. Xpress Enterprises employs over 3,000 drivers to operate a fleet of 9,000 trucks and 26,000 trailers. Trucks have satellite capabilities, anti-collision radar, vehicle-detection sensors, computers for shifting through 10 speeds, and roomy cabs with sleepers, refrigerators, and microwaves.

Air is the fastest and most expensive mode of transportation for physical goods. Air-freight customers benefit from lower inventory costs by eliminating the need to store items that might deteriorate. Shipments of fresh fish, for example, can be picked up by restaurants each day, avoiding the risk of spoilage from packaging and storing.

For downloads of music, software, books, movies, and other digital products the transportation mode of choice, online transmission, is newer, faster, and less expensive than all other modes. It is also restricted to products that exist as digital bits that can be transmitted over communication channels.

Aside from digital transmission, water is the least expensive mode but, unfortunately, also the slowest. Networks of waterways—oceans, rivers, and lakes—let water carriers reach many areas throughout the world. Boats and barges are used mostly for moving bulky products (such as oil, grain, and gravel).

Railroads can economically transport high-volume, heavy, bulky items, such as cars, steel, and coal. However, their delivery routes are limited by fixed, immovable rail tracks.

Pipelines are slow and lack flexibility and adaptability, but for specialized products, such as liquids and gases, they provide economical and reliable delivery.

entrepreneurship and new ventures

Running in Two Speeds at Once: Paperless and Paper

One surprised invitee remembers the first time she received a *Paperless Post* invitation via e-mail. After clicking on the attractive virtual envelope there emerged a fancy upscale invitation, as if being pulled from the envelope. Her reaction included the word, "Genius!" Such responses are typical for this start-up's elegant paperless invitations. Started by sister-and-brother Alexa and James Hirschfeld in 2009, *Paperless Post* was focused on the online distribution channel, thus avoiding an industry-wide downslide in traditional postal deliveries for invitations. Aesthetically appealing hand-crafted, personalized card designs with digital stationery became a reality by using high-end digital technology with an emphasis on visual art, versus competitors' emphasis on efficiency. With more than 1.5 million customers, *Paperless Post* sold about 50 million digital e-cards in 2012 by e-mail or via social networks such as Google+ and Facebook at a price of about 20 cents each. Things changed, however, when half of the online customers requested paper versions for printed invitations, in addition to digital versions. Thus, began the journey into printed invitations of users' personalized digital invitations.

Customers indicated that online invitations work well for "ordinary" events, seasonal activities such as Mardi Gras, Kentucky Derby, or birthday parties, but special events, such as weddings, require elegant physical invitations printed on thick, high-quality paper. Would those customers be willing to buy products priced at 10 times digital prices, or more? With prices initially starting at $1.10 up to $2.50, the Hirschfelds launched the paper products line, positioning *Paperless Post* as a multiple distribution-channel firm—online, offline, and mobile. As a further enhancement for visual and tactile aesthetics the company teamed up with card maker Crane & Co,

Web Pix/Alamy

a longtime stationery and card maker, to create a deep line of paper cards available through the *Paper Post* website. By clicking on "paper cards" online users have access to Crane designs, as well as those by four other designers, offering choices of paper thicknesses, printing style in any of 14 colors, with an option to include photos, and a choice of five shapes. These enhanced capabilities are attracting customers willing to pay up to $6 for high-end, custom paper cards for special occasions. Developing these powerful customized capabilities became possible by raising some $12.3 million in startup funding. With more than 50 employees, the company has outgrown three offices in the New York area, and to date has sold more than 75 million cards.

For additional customer convenience iTunes offers the *Paperless Post* app for tracking the cards you've sent and collecting RSVPs. The app is touted as an event management tool for sending and receiving "the web's most beautiful cards."[9]

Distribution through Supply Chains as a Marketing Strategy

Instead of just offering advantages in product features, quality, price, and promotion, many firms have turned to supply chains that depend on distribution as a cornerstone of business strategy. This approach means assessing, improving, and integrating the entire stream of activities—upstream suppliers, wholesaling, warehousing, transportation, delivery, and follow-up services—involved in getting products to customers.

Since the 1960s, starting with Toyota in Japan, the industrial world has seen the rise of the just-in-time (JIT) inventory system, discussed in Chapter 7. Used for quality improvement and cost savings, it was primarily adopted by U.S. manufacturing firms coming by way of Ford Motor Company in the early 1980s. Along with JIT, the past 30 years have seen dramatic improvements in supply chain technology and management, and its adoption by the retail sector. In the 1980s, Walmart decided to build their own distribution system using the best practices of both JIT and supply chains instead of the industry practice of relying on outside freight haulers and wholesalers. Let's look at how this has enabled Walmart to dominate their competition and made them the leading retailer in the world:

Suppose you are shopping at Walmart and decide to pick up a *Mr. Coffee* 8-cup coffeemaker. When you check out, the scanner reads the bar code on the box and Walmart's inventory system is updated instantly, showing that a replacement coffeemaker is needed on the shelf; the replacement comes from "the back" of that store, where the remaining on-hand supply count is reduced in Walmart's computer system. Once the back-room supply dwindles to *its* automatic triggering number, Walmart's distribution warehouse receives a digital signal notifying that this store needs more *Mr. Coffee* 8-cup coffeemakers. At the same time, the computer system also notifies the manufacturer that Walmart's distribution warehouse needs a replenishment supply. The manufacturer's suppliers, too, are notified, and so on, continuing upstream with information that enables faster resupply coordination throughout the supply chain. Walmart's data mining system determines the reorder number for every product based on sales (daily, weekly, and even by time of the year). Because of Walmart's constant rapid restocking from upstream sources, its store shelves are resupplied without having to keep large inventories in its warehouses and retail stores, thus reducing inventory costs and providing lower prices.

Walmart's JIT system has allowed it to achieve as low as a 2-day turnaround from manufacturer to the store shelf, thus providing cost control and product availability. It maintains lower levels of inventory, meets customer demand, and keeps among the lowest prices in the retail industry. Another retailer that has been able to adopt this method on a similar scale and compete effectively with Walmart (but only in groceries) is the H-E-B Grocery Company's chain of stores in Texas. Its data mining software can evaluate what products are purchased when, and with what other products (so, for example, they know to have tamales available at Christmas with coupons for enchilada sauce), and use this information for forecasting upcoming demand.

The Importance of Promotion

Promotion refers to techniques for communicating information about products and is part of the *communication mix*, the total message any company sends to customers about its product. Promotional techniques, especially advertising, must communicate the uses, features, and benefits of products, and marketers use an array of tools for this purpose.

Promotional Objectives

The ultimate objective of any promotion is to increase sales. In addition, marketers may use promotion to *communicate information, position products, add value,* and *control sales volume.*

OBJECTIVE 5
Identify
the objectives of promotion, the considerations in selecting a promotional mix, and discuss the various kinds of advertising promotions.

Promotion *aspect of the marketing mix concerned with the most effective techniques for communicating information about and selling a product*

As we saw in Chapter 11, **positioning** is the process of establishing an easily identifiable product image in the minds of consumers by fixing, adapting, and communicating the nature of the product itself. First, a firm must identify which market segments are likely to purchase its product and how its product measures up against competitors. Then, it can focus on promotional choices for differentiating its product and positioning it in the minds of the target audience. As an example, when I say, "Ketchup," most people respond with…Heinz. "The Ultimate Driving machine" is…BMW. These ubiquitous associations are indicative of successful positioning.

Promotional mixes are often designed to communicate a product's *value-added benefits* to distinguish it from the competition. Mercedes automobiles and Ritz-Carlton Hotels, for example, promote their products as upscale goods and services featuring high quality, style, and performance, all at a higher price.

Promotional Strategies

Once its larger marketing objectives are clear, a firm must develop a promotional strategy to achieve them. Two prominent types of strategies are considered here:

- A **pull strategy** appeals directly to consumers who will demand the product from retailers. Pharmaceutical companies use *direct-to-consumer advertising* (DTC) to persuade consumers to aggressively request a product rather than to wait passively until the doctor suggests trying it. "Talk to your doctor about Allegra-D" is just one example of the vast number of television and online ads for prescription drugs, knee replacement systems, and other medical products. The resulting demand by end users stimulates demand for the product from wholesalers and producers.

- Using a **push strategy**, a firm markets its product to wholesalers and retailers who then persuade customers to buy it. Brunswick Corp., for instance, uses a push strategy to promote Bayliner pleasure boats, directing its promotions at dealers and persuading them to order more inventory. Dealers are then responsible for stimulating demand among boaters at outdoor shows and through other promotions in their market districts.

Many large firms combine pull and push strategies. General Mills, for example, advertises to create consumer demand (pull) for its breakfast cereals, including Lucky Charms, Cheerios, and Count Chocula. At the same time, it pushes wholesalers and retailers to stock them.

The Promotional Mix

Five of marketing's most powerful promotional tools are advertising, personal selling, sales promotions, direct or interactive marketing, and publicity and public relations. The best combination of these tools—the best **promotional mix**—depends on many factors. The most important is the target audience. As an example, two generations from now, 25 percent of the U.S. workforce will be Hispanic. With an estimated 52 million Hispanic Americans, the rise in Latinos' disposable income has made them a potent economic force, and marketers are scrambling to redesign and promote products to appeal to them. Spanish-language media is one obvious outlet; the audience for programming from Univision, the biggest Spanish-language media company in the United States, has ballooned by more than 50 percent since 2001 to become one of the top five TV networks in the United States.[10]

In establishing a promotional mix, marketers match promotional tools with the five stages in the buyer decision process:

1 When consumers first recognize the need to make a purchase, marketers use advertising and publicity, which can reach many people quickly, to make sure buyers are aware of their products.

2 As consumers search for information about available products, advertising and personal selling are important methods to educate them.

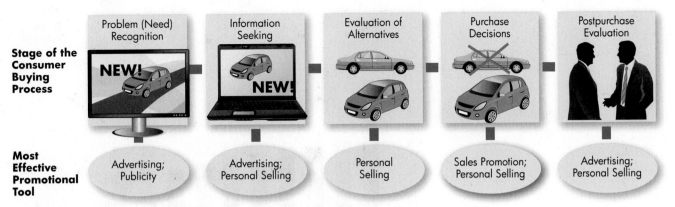

Stage of the Consumer Buying Process

| Problem (Need) Recognition | Information Seeking | Evaluation of Alternatives | Purchase Decisions | Postpurchase Evaluation |

Most Effective Promotional Tool

| Advertising; Publicity | Advertising; Personal Selling | Personal Selling | Sales Promotion; Personal Selling | Advertising; Personal Selling |

FIGURE 13.3 The Consumer Buying Process and the Promotional Mix
Source: Multi-Source

3 Personal selling can become vital as consumers compare competing products. Sales representatives can demonstrate product quality, features, benefits, and performance in comparison with competitors' products.

4 When buyers are ready to purchase products, sales promotion can give consumers an incentive to buy. Personal selling can help by bringing products to convenient purchase locations.

5 After making purchases, consumers evaluate products and note (and remember) their strengths and deficiencies. At this stage, advertising and personal selling can remind customers that they made wise purchases.

Figure 13.3 summarizes the effective promotional tools for each stage in the consumer buying process.

Advertising Promotions

Advertising is paid, nonpersonal communication by which an identified sponsor informs an audience about a product. In 2012, firms in the United States spent $140 billion on advertising—more than $15 billion by just 10 companies. The total of 2012 ad expenditures was well below the $280 billion spent in 2008, before the full effects of the recession.[11] Figure 13.4 shows U.S. advertising expenditures for the top-spending firms. Let's take a look at the different types of advertising media, noting some of the advantages and limitations of each.

Advertising Media Consumers tend to ignore the bulk of advertising messages that bombard them; they pay attention to what interests them. Moreover, the advertising process is dynamic, reflecting the changing interests and preferences of both customers and advertisers. A customer survey in 2008, for example, reports that mail ads are rated as most irritating and boring, and newspaper and magazine ads are least annoying. Yet, although newspaper ads are rated as more informative and useful than some other media, advertisers continue to shift away, using instead more online, cell phone, and PDA advertising because newsprint readership (the audience) is dwindling.[12]

Real-Time Ad Tracking Advertisers always want better information about who looks at ads and for how long. Which target audiences and demographics are more attracted to various ad contents? Accurate ad-watching behavior of shoppers in malls, theaters, and grocery stores is on the increase with assistance from high-tech real-time surveillance. As passing consumers watch ads on video screens, cameras watch the shoppers, and software analyzes the viewers' demographics and reactions to various ad contents and formats. The makers of the tracking system claim accuracy of up to 90 percent for determining gender, approximate age, and ethnicity. Once perfected, the system might measure your demographics, identify you with a target audience, then instantly change the presentation to a preferred product and visual format to attract and hold your attention.[13] Marketers must find out, then, who their customers are, which media they pay attention to, what

Advertising promotional tool consisting of paid, nonpersonal communication used by an identified sponsor to inform an audience about a product

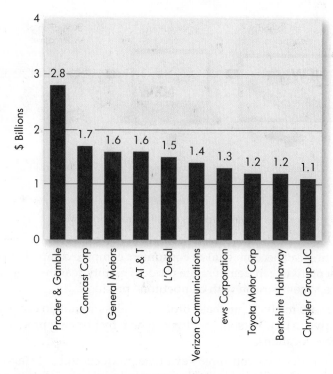

FIGURE 13.4 Top 10 U.S. National Advertisers
Adapted from "Kantar Media Reports U.S. Advertising
Expenditures Increased 3 Percent in 2012," *Kantar Media*,
March 11, 2013, at http://kantarmediana.com/intelligence/press/
us-advertising-expenditures-increased-3-percent-2012.

Advertising Media *variety of communication devices for carrying a seller's message to potential customers*

Media Mix *combination of advertising media chosen to carry a message about a product*

messages appeal to them, and how to get their attention. Thus, marketers use several different **advertising media,** specific communication devices for carrying a seller's message to potential customers. The combination of media through which a company advertises is called its **media mix.** Table 13.2 shows the relative sizes of media usage and their strengths and weaknesses.

OBJECTIVE 6
Outline

the tasks involved in personal selling and describe the various types of sales promotions.

Personal Selling *promotional tool in which a salesperson communicates one-on-one with potential customers*

Personal Selling

In the oldest and most expensive form of sales, **personal selling,** a salesperson communicates one-on-one with potential customers to identify their needs and align them with the product. Salespeople gain credibility by investing a lot of time getting acquainted with potential customers and answering their questions. This professional interaction is especially effective in relationship marketing. It gives the seller a clearer picture of the buyer's business and allows salespeople to provide buyers with value-adding services.

Personal Selling Situations

Salespeople must consider the ways in which personal sales activities are affected by the differences between consumer and industrial products:

Retail Selling *selling a consumer product for the buyer's personal or household use*

Industrial Selling *selling products to other businesses, either for the purpose of manufacturing or for resale*

- **Retail selling** is selling a consumer product for the buyer's personal or household use.

- **Industrial selling** is selling products to other businesses, either for the purpose of manufacturing or for resale.

Levi's, for instance, sells jeans to Gap Inc. (industrial selling). In turn, consumers purchase Levi's jeans at the Gap stores (retail selling).

table 13.2 Total U.S. Media Usage, Strengths, and Weaknesses

Advertising Medium	Percentage* of Advertising Outlays	Strengths	Weaknesses
Television	33%	Program demographics allow for customized ads Large audience	Most expensive
Internet	18%	Targeted audience Measurable success	Nuisance to consumers Easy to ignore
Direct mail	13%	Targeted audience Personal messages Predictable results	Easily discarded Environmentally irresponsible
Newspapers	13%	Broad coverage Ads can be changed daily	Quickly discarded Broad readership limits ability to target specific audience
Radio	10%	Inexpensive Large audience Variety of ready market segmentation	Easy to ignore Message quickly disappears
Magazines	10%	Often reread and shared Variety of ready market segmentation	Require advanced planning Little control over ad placement
Outdoor	3%	Inexpensive Difficult to ignore Repeat exposure	Presents limited information Little control over audience

A combination of additional unmeasured media such as yellow pages, catalogs, special events, sidewalk handouts, ads on transport vehicles, skywriting, movies, and door-to-door communications, are not included.

*Estimated. Based on the following sources: "U.S. Ad Spending Grew 6.5% in 2010 as Auto Surged and Pharma Hit a Low," *Advertising Age*, March 17, 2011, at http://adage.com/article/mediaworks/u-s-ad-spending-grew-6-5-2010-auto-rose-pharma-fell/149436/; "Online Ad spending Passes Print Advertising," *Sweet Spot Marketing*, January 17, 2011, at ; "U.S. Advertising Revenue, By Medium," *Business Insider*, October 27, 2009, at http://www.businessinsider.com/us-advertising-spending-by-medium-2009-10; "Ad Spending Continues 2009 Spiral, Forecasts Slightly Better for 2010," March 13, 2009, *Marketing Charts*, at http://www. marketing charts.com/television/ad-spending-continues-2009-spiral-forecasts-slightly-better-for-2010-8306/ jack-myers-media-business-report-projected-change-ad-spending-2009jpg/.

Each of these situations has distinct characteristics. In retail selling, the buyer usually comes to the seller, whereas the industrial salesperson typically calls on the prospective buyer. An industrial decision usually takes longer than a retail decision because it involves more money, decision makers, and weighing of alternatives. As we saw in Chapter 11, organizational buyers are professional purchasing agents accustomed to dealing with salespeople. Consumers in retail stores, in contrast, may actually be intimidated by salespeople.

Personal Selling Tasks

Salespeople must be adept at performing three basic tasks of personal selling. In **order processing**, a salesperson receives an order and sees to its handling and delivery. Route salespeople, who call on regular customers to check inventories, are often order processors. With the customer's consent, they may decide on the sizes of reorders, fill them directly from their trucks, and even stock shelves. In other situations, however, when potential customers are not aware that they need or want a product, **creative selling** involves providing information and demonstrating product

Order Processing *personal-selling task in which salespeople receive orders and see to their handling and delivery*

Creative Selling *personal-selling task in which salespeople try to persuade buyers to purchase products by providing information about their benefits*

managing in turbulent times

Direct Mail Marketing: Back from a "Slow Death"?

Recent years have witnessed consumers and marketers, alike, awaiting the final blow to what has been called "the slow demise" of direct-mail, or catalog, marketing. But don't expect that to happen any time soon. Amidst the nation's plodding economy, with nearly stagnate consumer spending, direct-mail marketing is growing, slowly but steadily, thank you. After contracting 1.6 percent annually for five years because of the recession, projections are calling for 1.4 percent yearly growth for 2013 through 2017.

One reason for the turnaround stems from reduced mailing costs offered by the United States Postal Service (USPS). To compete with lower-cost digital information channels, USPS wants to bulk up mail services, and catalog and other direct-mail activity is a major revenue source. For the decade ending in 2011, for example, direct mail as a percentage of all mail deliveries grew from 45 percent to 56 percent, whereas first-class deliveries fell from 100-plus billion pieces annually to just 69 billion pieces over the 10-year period.

A second, more compelling, driver of direct-mail's growth is the personalization made possible by more powerful data technologies coupled with massive amounts of data on individuals and families. Thousands of online sources accumulate information about every Internet user and household, from their purchasing transactions, social networking interactions, their choices of information sources and content, television viewing habits, and casual Internet surfing. The result is an explosion of data that enable businesses to target potential customers in specific ways. Add to this the analytic software that can search through mounds of data in mere microseconds, identifying individuals, households, and their locations that match ever-refined specifications for targeted potential customers. Instead of just demographics, data mining identifies potential qualitative characteristics, such as different lifestyle patterns and lifetime expectations of individuals.

S.D. Wilson/Alamy

An added stimulus for "smarter" direct-mail marketing is advancements in digital printing technology with greater flexibility and speed, enabling rapid runs of small-volume specialized advertising content. A toy company, for example, can create a catalog of upscale toys targeting households with 5-to-10-year olds living in upper-income neighborhoods, within a specific income range, with recent purchases of high-end toys. That same toy company can also design a campaign emphasizing lower-end toys targeted at lower-income families, living in specified areas with 1-to-5 year old children. Today's digital printers can quickly produce both catalogs with different graphics and printed content, from cover to back, and expedite mailings that begin to rival e-mails. Printing capabilities make it economically feasible to personalize catalog messages to dozens of smaller groupings of targeted customers, instead of just two or three groups. As a result, sharply targeted direct mail is becoming more economical by refocusing with messages tailored to detailed profiles of a limited number of recipients who are more likely to buy, rather than wasting mass mailings of a single message to everyone, including many who ignore it.[14]

Missionary Selling *personal-selling task in which salespeople promote their firms and products rather than try to close sales*

benefits to persuade buyers to complete a purchase. Creative selling is crucial for industrial products and high-priced consumer products, such as cars, for which buyers comparison shop. Finally, a salesperson may use **missionary selling** to promote a company and its products rather than simply to close a sale. Pharmaceutical companies often use this method to make doctors aware of the company and its products so they will recommend the company's products to others, or so the doctor will prescribe the products to patients. The sale of the product, then, is actually made at the pharmacy. In missionary selling, the goal may be to promote the company's long-term image as much as any given product. Another activity in missionary selling is after-sale technical assistance for complex products. IBM uses after-sale selling to ensure that industrial customers know how to use IBM equipment.

Depending on the product and company, sales jobs usually require individuals to perform all three tasks—order processing, creative selling, and missionary selling—to some degree.

The Personal Selling Process

Perhaps the most complex and challenging of these three sales tasks is creative selling. The creative salesperson is responsible for starting and following through on most of the steps in the personal selling process:

- *Prospecting and qualifying.* A salesperson must first have a potential customer, or prospect. **Prospecting** is the process of identifying potential customers. Salespeople find prospects through company personnel records, from social networking on sites such as LinkedIn, and customers, friends, and business associates. In **qualifying,** prospects must be assessed to determine whether they have the authority to buy and the ability to pay.

- *Approaching.* The *approach* refers to the first few minutes of a salesperson's contact with a qualified prospect. Because it affects the salesperson's credibility, the success of later stages depends on the prospect's first impression. A salesperson must, therefore, present a professional appearance and greet prospects in a manner that instills confidence.

- *Presenting and demonstrating.* Next, the salesperson makes a presentation, a full explanation of the product, its features, and its uses. Most important, the presentation links product benefits to the prospect's needs. A presentation may or may not include a demonstration.

- *Handling objections.* No matter what product is for sale, prospects will have some *objections*. At the very least, they may angle for discounts by objecting to price. Objections, however, not only indicate that the buyer is interested but also pinpoint the parts of the presentation that trouble the buyer.

- *Closing.* The most critical part of the selling process is the **closing,** in which the salesperson asks the prospect to buy the product. Successful salespeople recognize the signs that a customer is ready to buy. Prospects who start to figure out monthly payments are clearly indicating readiness to buy. Salespeople should then try to close the sale, either asking directly for the sale or implying a close indirectly. Questions such as "Could you take delivery Tuesday?" and "Why don't we start off with an initial order of 10 cases?" are implied closes. Indirect closes place the burden of rejecting the sale on the prospect, who may find it a little harder to say no.

- *Following up.* Follow-up is a key activity, especially in relationship marketing. For lasting relationships with buyers, good salespeople don't end the sales process with the closing. They want sales to be so successful that customers will buy

Prospecting *step in the personal selling process in which salespeople identify potential customers*

Qualifying *step in the personal selling process in which salespeople determine whether prospects have the authority to buy and ability to pay*

Closing *step in the personal selling process in which salespeople ask prospective customers to buy products*

bikeriderlondon/Shutterstock

from them again. Thus, they supply additional services, such as after-sale support that provides convenience and added value. Follow-ups include quick processing of customer orders, on-time delivery, speedy repair service, and timely answers to user questions.

Sales Promotions

Sales Promotion *short-term promotional activity designed to encourage consumer buying, industrial sales, or cooperation from distributors*

Sales promotions are short-term promotional activities designed to encourage consumer buying, industrial sales, or cooperation from distributors. They can increase the likelihood that buyers will try products, enhance product recognition, and increase purchase size and sales revenues.

Successful sales promotions provide potential customers with convenience and accessibility when the decision to buy occurs. If Harley-Davidson holds a one-week motorcycle promotion and you, an interested buyer, have no local dealer and no access to a demonstration ride, the promotion may be useless to you and you won't buy. In contrast, if Folgers offers a $1-off coupon that you can save and use later, the promotion is both convenient and accessible.

Coupon *sales-promotion technique in which a certificate is issued entitling the buyer to a reduced price*

Most consumers have taken part in a variety of sales promotions such as free *samples* (giveaways), which let customers try products without risk, and **coupon** promotions, which use certificates entitling buyers to discounts to encourage customers to try new products, lure them away from competitors, or induce them to repurchase (buy more of a product). Coupons are available from many sources, including newspapers, in mailings, and at check-out counters when shopping. Online coupon sites such as Coupons.com, CoolSavings.com, and Groupon provide access to printable cost-saving coupons and to some free coupons.

Premium *sales-promotion technique in which offers of free or reduced-price items are used to stimulate purchases*

Premiums are free or reduced-price items, such as pencils, coffee mugs, and six-month low-interest credit cards, given to consumers in return for buying a specified product. *Contests* can boost sales by rewarding high-producing distributors and sales representatives with vacation trips to Hawaii or Paris. Consumers, too, may win prizes by entering their cats in the Purina Cat Chow calendar contest, for example, by submitting entry blanks from the backs of cat-food packages.

Loyalty Programs *sales promotion technique in which frequent customers are rewarded for making repeat purchases*

Loyalty programs reward frequent buyers for making repeat purchases. Oceana Cruises and Tauck (the tour company) offer vacation specials with significant price reductions to loyal customers. Online and mail promotions, for example, may announce two-for-one prices on upcoming cruises, and reduced prices for upgrading to more luxurious accommodations. Tour specials may feature reduced airfares, along with free Internet access and shore excursions for repeat customers.

Point-of-Sale (POS) Display *sales-promotion technique in which product displays are located in certain areas to stimulate purchase or to provide information on a product*

To grab customers' attention in stores, companies use **point-of-sale (POS) displays** at the ends of aisles or near checkout counters to ease finding products and to eliminate competitors from consideration. In addition to physical goods, POS pedestals also provide services, namely information for consumers. Bank lobbies and physicians' waiting rooms, for example, have computer-interactive kiosks inviting clients to learn more about bank products and educational information about available treatments on consumer-friendly touch-screen displays. For B2B promotions, industries sponsor **trade shows** in which companies rent booths to display and demonstrate products to customers who have a special interest or who are ready to buy.

Trade Show *sales-promotion technique in which various members of an industry gather to display, demonstrate, and sell products*

Direct (or Interactive) Marketing

Direct (or Interactive) Marketing *one-on-one nonpersonal selling by nonstore retailers and B2B sellers using direct contact with prospective customers, especially via the Internet*

Direct (or interactive) marketing is one-on-one nonpersonal selling that tries to get consumers to make purchases away from retail stores and, instead, to purchase from home, at work, or by using a mobile device while traveling. This fast-growing selling method includes nonstore retailers (catalogs, telemarketing, home video shopping), direct mail, direct response advertising (such as infomercials and direct response magazine and newspaper ads), and most important, the Internet. When used by B2B businesses, direct marketing is primarily lead generation so a salesperson can close the sale where interest has been shown. In B2C businesses, it has primarily a selling goal. The advantage of direct marketing is that you can target the message to the individual and you can measure the results. For example, Amazon knows when you sign in who you are and what you have purchased in the past and makes recommendations based on your purchases. When you select a certain title or product, they can suggest other titles that other buyers of your selection have also purchased and in that way, increase the sale to you.

The Internet has enhanced traditional direct marketing methods, especially direct mail. By using *permission marketing*, a form of e-mail where the consumer gives a company permission to contact them, a list of customers' e-mails is compiled and they are regularly contacted with special offers and deals based on their past purchases. The e-mail is coming from a company the consumer has experience with and has agreed to receive their messages, and it contains a direct link to the company's website and the sale item. Companies such as Amazon, Dell, Gap, and Kate Spade are among those who have used this direct marketing method and technology successfully.

Publicity and Public Relations

Publicity is information about a company, a product, or an event transmitted by the general mass media to attract public attention. Although publicity is free, marketers have no control over the content media reporters and writers disseminate, and because it is presented in a news format, consumers often regard it as objective and credible. A classic publicity event occurred in 2005, for example: U.S. fast-food patrons were horrified when a customer said she found a human fingertip in a bowl of Wendy's chili. The publicity nightmare immediately bruised the food chain's reputation and cost about $15 million in lost sales in just six weeks.[15]

In contrast to publicity, **public relations** is company-influenced information that seeks either to build good relations with the public, by publicizing the company's charitable contributions, for example, or to deal with unfavorable events. In the Wendy's case, CEO Jack Schuessler's public relations response was decisive and focused: protect the brand and tell the truth. That meant there would be no payoff or settlement to keep it out of the news. Instead, Wendy's enlisted cooperation with the health department and police, did visual inspections, polygraphed employees, publicly announced a hotline for tips, and offered a reward for information, all leading to the conclusion that the reported episode was a hoax. Energetic public relations were an effective promotional tool for clearing the Wendy's name and preserving the company's reputation.[16]

Publicity *promotional tool in which information about a company, a product, or an event is transmitted by the general mass media to attract public attention*

Public Relations *company-influenced information directed at building goodwill with the public or dealing with unfavorable events*

summary of learning objectives

OBJECTIVE 1

Explain the meaning of *distribution mix* and identify the different channels of distribution. (pp. 446–449)

The success of any product depends on its distribution mix: The combination of distribution channels for getting products to end users—consumers and industrial buyers. *Intermediaries* help to distribute a producer's goods by moving them to customers: *Wholesalers* sell products to other businesses, which resell them to final users. *Retailers*, on the other hand, sell products directly to end users. In the simplest of four distribution channels—the *direct channel*—the producer sells directly to the consumer or organizational buyer without intermediaries. In *retail distribution*, producers distribute products through retailers who, in turn, distribute to the consumer or industrial customer. *Wholesale distribution* involves both a wholesaler and then a retailer before the product reaches the end user. In the last type of distribution channel, a sales agent or a broker sells to the consumer or to the industrial customer. A disadvantage of channels with more intermediaries is higher prices because each intermediary charges a markup or commission. However, intermediaries can provide added value by supplying time-saving information and ensuring that products arrive at the right time and place.

In addition to selecting the distribution channel, marketers must select a *market coverage strategy*. *Intensive distribution* means distributing through as many channels and channel members as possible, and *exclusive distribution* occurs when the manufacturer grants the exclusive right to distribute or sell a product to a limited number of wholesalers or retailers, usually for a specific geographic area. Finally, *selective distribution* is a midpoint between intensive and exclusive; it is a strategy in which the producer selects a limited number of wholesalers and retailers to sell their product.

OBJECTIVE 2

Describe the role of wholesalers and the functions performed by e-intermediaries. (pp. 449–451)

Wholesalers provide a variety of services—delivery, credit arrangements, and product information—to buyers of products for resale or business use. In buying and reselling products, wholesalers provide storage, marketing advice, and assist customers by marking prices and setting up displays. Most wholesalers are independent operations that sell goods produced by a variety of manufacturers. The largest group, *merchant wholesalers*, buys products from manufacturers and sells them to other businesses. They own the goods that they resell, store, and deliver. *Agents* and *brokers* work on commission and serve as independent sales representatives for many companies' products. Unlike wholesalers, agents and brokers do not own their merchandise. Rather, they serve as sales and merchandising arms for producers or sellers who do not have their own sales forces.

E-intermediaries are Internet-based channel members—wholesalers—who perform one or both of two functions: (1) they collect information about sellers and present it to consumers, or (2) they help deliver online products to buyers. One type of e-intermediary, the *syndicated seller*, is a website that receives commissions for referring online customers to other companies' websites. *Shopping agents* (*e-agents*) help online customers—both industrial customers and consumers—by gathering and sorting information, identifying websites to visit, providing comparison prices, and identifying product features.

OBJECTIVE 3

Describe the different types of retailing and explain how online retailers add value for consumers on the Internet. (pp. 451–454)

Retail stores can be organized into three classifications: product-line retailers, bargain retailers, and convenience stores. Product-line retailers include department stores, supermarkets, and specialty stores. *Department stores* have specialized departments for different products. These stores offer a variety of services, such as credit plans and delivery. Similarly, *supermarkets* are divided into departments, and they stress low prices, self-service, and wide selection. In contrast, *specialty stores* are small, offering a full product line in narrow product fields, with knowledgeable sales personnel.

Bargain retailers include discount houses, catalog showrooms, factory outlets, and wholesale clubs. *Catalog showrooms* allow customers to view display samples, place orders, and receive purchases from attached warehouses. *Discount houses* offer a wide variety of products at low prices. *Factory outlets* are manufacturer-owned stores that avoid intermediaries by selling merchandise directly from factory to consumer. *Wholesale clubs* offer large discounts on a wide range of merchandise to customers who pay annual membership fees.

Convenience stores stress easily accessible locations, extended store hours, and speedy service. However, they generally do not feature low prices on most products.

Nonstore retailing includes *direct-response* firms that contact customers to receive sales orders. *Mail order* (or *catalog marketing*) is one form of direct-response retailing, as is outbound *telemarketing* that uses phone calls to sell directly to consumers. Finally, *direct selling* uses door-to-door sales and home-selling parties.

Online retailing provides the convenience of shopping anywhere using the Internet and includes *e-catalogs, electronic storefronts, cybermalls,* and *interactive and video* retailing. *E-catalogs* use online displays of products and product information, thus avoiding mail distribution and printing costs. Each seller's website is an *electronic storefront* where shoppers collect information about products, place orders, and pay for purchases. *Cybermalls* are collections of virtual storefronts where shoppers can navigate from a list of stores or product listings. *Video retailing* lets viewers shop at home from channels on their TVs. For TVs with Internet-ready capabilities, users can relax comfortably at home while shopping online with a large-screen visual display.

OBJECTIVE 4

Define *physical distribution* and describe the major activities in the physical distribution process. (pp. 454–457)

Physical distribution refers to the activities needed to move products from an intermediary or a manufacturer to customers and includes *warehousing* and *transportation operations*. Its purpose is to make goods available when and where customers want them, keep costs low, and provide services to satisfy customers.

Physical distribution activities include providing customer services, warehousing, and transportation of products. Storing, or *warehousing*, includes *private warehouses*, owned by a single firm that deals in mass quantities and needs regular storage. Independently owned *public warehouses* rent to companies only the space they need, often for storage needs during peak periods. To store digital assets, many companies and home users rely on remote off-site digital storage services to protect against losing data. In the event of physical catastrophe— floods, fires, earthquakes—at the client's facility, data can be restored online from the backup system.

Transportation operations physically move products from suppliers to customers. Differences in cost among the major transportation modes, trucks, railroads, planes, water carriers (boats and barges), digital transmission, and pipelines, are usually most directly related to delivery speed. *Trucks* are the most-used carriers of all modes of U.S. freight transportation. The advantages of trucks include flexibility for any-distance distribution, fast service, and dependability. *Planes* are the fastest and most expensive mode of transportation for physical goods. *Online transmission* of products in digital form is faster and less expensive than all other modes. Aside from digital transmission, transporting by *water carriers* is the least expensive mode, but also the slowest. *Railroads* can economically transport high-volume, heavy, bulky items, such as cars, steel, and coal. However, delivery routes are limited by fixed, immovable rail tracks. *Pipelines* are slow and lack flexibility and adaptability, but for specialized products, like liquids and gases, they provide economical and reliable delivery.

OBJECTIVE 5

Identify the objectives of promotion, the considerations in selecting a promotional mix, and discuss the various kinds of advertising promotions. (pp. 457–460)

Promotion refers to techniques for communicating information about products and is part of the *communication mix*, the total message any company sends to customers about its products. Although the ultimate goal of any *promotion* is to increase sales, other goals include communicating information about the company and its products, positioning a product (establishing an identifiable image in the minds of consumers), adding value to distinguish a product from competing products, and controlling sales volume.

Once marketing objectives are clear, a firm must develop a promotional strategy to achieve them. A *pull strategy* appeals directly to consumers who will demand the product from retailers, whereas a *push strategy* occurs when a firm markets its products to wholesalers and retailers who then persuade customers to buy it. In deciding on the appropriate *promotional mix*—the best combination of promotional tools (e.g., advertising, personal selling, sales promotions, direct or interactive marketing, public relations)—marketers must consider the good or service being offered, characteristics of the target audience, the buyer's decision process, and the promotional mix budget. *Advertising* is paid, nonpersonal communication, by which an identified sponsor informs an audience about a product. To better understand how consumers respond to ads, marketers use *real-time ad tracking* to find out who their customers are, which media they pay attention to, what messages appeal to them, and how to get their attention. Marketers use several different *advertising media*—specific communication devices for carrying a seller's message to potential customers—each having its advantages and drawbacks. TV is the most-used and most expensive U.S. medium, with the largest audience. The Internet is the fastest-growing medium because it can target specific audiences and its ad success can be measured, but it is also easy to ignore. Outdoor advertising, one of the least-used of major media, is among the least expensive but is limited in the information it presents and exposure time is brief. Other often-used media include newspapers (broad readership), direct mail (for targeted audience), radio (low ad cost), and magazines (often shared and re-read). The combination of media through which a company advertises is called its *media mix*.

OBJECTIVE 6

Outline the tasks involved in personal selling and describe the various types of sales promotions. (pp. 460–465)

Personal selling is the oldest and most expensive form of promotion. Personal selling tasks include *order processing* (receiving an order and seeing to its handling and delivery), *creative selling* (providing information and demonstrating product benefits to persuade buyers), and *missionary selling* (activities that promote a company and its products). The first step in the personal selling process includes *prospecting* (identify potential customers) and *qualifying* (determining authority to buy and pay). The next step is *approaching* (initial moments of contact with prospect), followed by *presenting* and *demonstrating* (displaying and explaining the product and its use), *handling objections* (overcoming buyer problems), *closing* (asking the prospect to buy the product), and *following up* (supplying after-sales services).

Sales promotions are short-term promotional activities to encourage consumer buying, industrial sales, or cooperation from distributors. They can increase the likelihood that buyers will try products, enhance product recognition, and increase purchase size and sales revenues. Sales promotions include *point-of-sale (POS) displays* to attract consumer attention, help them find products in stores, offices, lobbies, and waiting rooms, and provide product information. *Loyalty programs* reward frequent buyers for past repeat purchases, by giving them reduced prices, upgraded products, or other special considerations. Other sales promotions give purchasing incentives, such as *samples* (customers can try products without having to buy them), *coupons* (a certificate for price reduction to encourage customers to try new products, lure them away from competitors, or induce them to buy more of a product, and *premiums* (free or reduced-price rewards for buying products). At *trade shows*, B2B sellers rent booths to display products to industrial customers. *Contests* intend to stimulate sales, with prizes to high-producing intermediaries and consumers who use the seller's products.

The final element of the promotional mix is publicity and public relations. *Publicity* is information about a company, product, or event transmitted by the general mass media to attract public attention. Although publicity is free, marketers have no control over the content media reports and writers disseminate, and because it is presented in a news format, consumers often regard it as objective and credible. In contrast to publicity, *public relations* is company-influenced information that seeks to build good relations with the public by publicizing the company's charitable contributions or to deal with unfavorable events.

key terms

advertising (p. 459)
advertising media (p. 460)
bargain retailer (p. 451)
broker (p. 448)
catalog showroom (p. 451)
channel captain (p. 449)
channel conflict (p. 449)
closing (p. 463)
convenience store (p. 451)
coupon (p. 464)
creative selling (p. 461)
cybermall (p. 453)
department store (p. 451)
direct (or interactive) marketing (p. 464)
direct channel (p. 446)
direct selling (p. 452)
direct-response retailing (p. 452)
discount house (p. 451)
distribution channel (p. 446)
distribution mix (p. 446)
drop shipper (p. 450)
e-catalog (p. 453)
e-intermediaries (p. 450)

electronic storefront (p. 453)
exclusive distribution (p. 449)
factory outlet (p. 451)
full-service merchant wholesaler (p. 450)
industrial selling (p. 460)
intensive distribution (p. 448)
intermediary (p. 446)
limited-function merchant wholesaler (p. 450)
loyalty program (p. 464)
mail order (catalog marketing) (p. 452)
media mix (p. 460)
merchant wholesaler (p. 449)
missionary selling (p. 462)
online retailing (p. 453)
order processing (p. 461)
personal selling (p. 460)
physical distribution (p. 454)
point-of-sale (POS) display (p. 464)
positioning (p. 458)
premium (p. 464)
private warehouse (p. 455)
promotion (p. 457)

promotional mix (p. 458)
prospecting (p. 463)
public relations (p. 465)
public warehouse (p. 455)
publicity (p. 465)
pull strategy (p. 458)
push strategy (p. 458)
qualifying (p. 463)
retail selling (p. 460)
retailer (p. 446)
sales agent (p. 448)
sales promotion (p. 464)
selective distribution (p. 449)
shopping agents (e-agents) (p. 450)
specialty store (p. 451)
supermarket (p. 451)
syndicated selling (p. 450)
telemarketing (p. 452)
trade show (p. 464)
video retailing (p. 454)
warehousing (p. 455)
wholesale club (p. 451)
wholesaler (p. 446)

MyBizLab

Go to **pearsonglobaleditions.com/mybizlab** to complete the problems marked with this icon ✪.

questions & exercises

QUESTIONS FOR REVIEW

13-1. Identify the channels of distribution. In what key ways do they differ from one another?

13-2. Describe the three levels of market coverage. When is each most appropriate?

13-3. Compare each of the major modes of transportation and identify at least one advantage of each.

✪ **13-4.** Select four advertising media and compare the advantages and disadvantages of each.

13-5. What are the steps in the personal selling process?

QUESTIONS FOR ANALYSIS

✪ **13-6.** Give examples of two products that typify the products sold to shoppers through each form of nonstore retailing. Explain why different products are best suited to each form of nonstore retailing.

13-7. Describe each major type of product line and bargain retailer and identify at least one example of each type.

✪ **13-8.** Choose two advertising campaigns: one that you think is effective and one that you think is ineffective. What makes one campaign better than the other?

APPLICATION EXERCISES

13-9. Identify a company that is a member in a supply chain. Explain how its presence in the chain affects the company's marketing decisions for pricing, promoting, and distributing its products.

13-10. Select a product and identify the media used in its promotion. On the whole, do you think the campaign is effective? Why or why not? If the campaign is not effective, what changes would you suggest to improve it?

building a business: continuing team exercise

Assignment

Meet with your team members to consider your new business venture and how it relates to the marketing issues relating to distributing and promoting products, as discussed in this chapter. Develop specific responses to the following:

13-11. Consider once again the target market(s) for your business. For that target market develop a "Statement of Promotional Objectives" for your company. What do you intend to accomplish with your chosen promotional objectives?

13-12. Considering your target market, discuss alternative promotional strategies that may be appropriate for your company. What are the pros and cons for each strategy you considered? Which strategy, at the present time, seems more favorable, and why?

13-13. Outline the elements for your promotional mix, including specific promotional tools to be included at the onset (opening) of your company. Rank order the relative importance of each tool in your promotional efforts. How might those rankings change, if at all, after your company is better established?

13-14. Develop a preliminary design of your company's start-up distribution mix, including the reasons for your choices on distribution channels and physical distribution. Explain why (how) your chosen distribution mix is appropriately matched to your target market.

13-15. Estimate the costs required to implement the distribution mix and promotional mix, if those mixes are to be ready-to-go when your company opens for business.

building your business skills

GREETING START-UP DECISIONS

Goal

To encourage you to analyze the potential usefulness of two promotional methods—personal selling and direct mail—for a start-up greeting card company.

Background Information

You are the marketing adviser for a local start-up company that makes and sells specialty greeting cards in a city of 400,000. Last year's sales totaled 14,000 cards, including personalized holiday cards, birthday cards, and special-events cards for individuals. Although revenues increased last year, you see a way of further boosting sales by expanding into card shops, grocery stores, and gift shops. You see two alternatives for entering these outlets:

Use direct mail to reach more individual customers for specialty cards.

Use personal selling to gain display space in retail stores.

Your challenge is to convince the owner of the start-up company which alternative is the more financially sound decision.

Method

STEP 1

Get together with four or five classmates to research the two kinds of product segments: personalized cards and retail store cards. Find out which of the two kinds of marketing promotions will be more effective for each of the two segments. What will be the reaction to each method by customers, retailers, and card-company owners?

STEP 2

Draft a proposal to the company owner. Leaving budget and production details to other staffers, list as many reasons as possible for adopting direct mail. Then, list as many reasons as possible for adopting personal selling. Defend each reason. Consider the following reasons in your argument:

- **Competitive environment.** Analyze the impact of other card suppliers that offer personalized cards and cards for sale in retail stores.
- **Expectations of target markets.** Who buys personalized cards and who buys ready-made cards from retail stores?
- **Overall cost of the promotional effort.** Which method, direct mail or personal selling, will be more costly?
- **Marketing effectiveness.** Which promotional method will result in greater consumer response?

FOLLOW-UP QUESTIONS

13-16. Why do you think some buyers want personalized cards? Why do some consumers want ready-made cards from retail stores?

13-17. Consider today's easy access to online sources of cards and to software for designing and making cards on home PCs. How does the availability of these resources affect your recommendation?

13-18. What was your most convincing argument for using direct mail? for using personal selling?

13-19. Can a start-up company compete in retail stores against industry giants, such as Hallmark and American Greetings?

exercising your ethics

THE CHAIN OF RESPONSIBILITY

The Situation

Because several stages are involved when distribution chains move products from supply sources to end consumers, the process offers ample opportunity for ethical issues to arise. This exercise encourages you to examine some of the ethical issues that can emerge during transactions among suppliers and customers.

The Dilemma

A customer bought an expensive wedding gift at a local store and asked that it be shipped to the bride in another state. Several weeks after the wedding, the customer contacted the bride, who had not confirmed receiving the gift. It hadn't arrived. Charging that the merchandise had not been delivered, the customer requested a refund from the retailer. The store manager uncovered the following facts:

- All shipments from the store are handled by a well-known national delivery firm.
- The delivery firm verified that the package had been delivered to the designated address two days after the sale.

- Normally, the delivery firm does not obtain recipient signatures; deliveries are made to the address of record, regardless of the name on the package.

The gift giver argued that even though the package had been delivered to the right address, it had not been delivered to the named recipient. It turns out that, unbeknownst to the gift giver, the bride had moved. It stood to reason, then, that the gift was in the hands of the new occupant at the bride's former address. The manager informed the gift giver that the store had fulfilled its obligation. The cause of the problem, she explained, was the incorrect address given by the customer. She refused to refund the customer's money and suggested that the customer might want to recover the gift by contacting the stranger who received it at the bride's old address.

QUESTIONS TO ADDRESS

13-20. What are the responsibilities of each party—the customer, the store, the delivery firm—in this situation?

13-21. From an ethical standpoint, in what ways is the store manager's action right? In what ways is it wrong?

13-22. If you were appointed to settle this matter, what actions would you take?

team exercise

A BIG PUSH FOR PUBLICITY

The Situation

A new theme park is opening just miles away from your college. It will feature lots of rides and roller coasters as well as a water park. There will be lots of food options, from fast food to fine dining, and something for everyone in the family. There are a few other theme parks within a 200-mile radius of your college, but this new park will be significantly closer than the competition.

The Dilemma

The developers of the theme part have been so impressed with your college that they have invited teams of students to develop proposals. Your group is one of several that have been charged with developing the promotional mix for the new theme park. You will present your proposal to the company and company executives will select the proposal that they think is most appropriate. Although this is, at the time, an activity for your class, it could turn into a full-time job with the company, so the stakes are high.

Team Activity

Assemble a group of four students and assign each group member to one of the following components of the promotional mix:

- Advertising
- Personal selling

- Sales promotion
- Publicity and public relations

ACTION STEPS

13-23. As a group, develop your promotional objectives. What are the initial objectives of your promotional campaign? Will these change over time?

13-24. Before discussing this as a group, and from the perspective of your assigned role, what specific promotional activities within your category would you recommend?

13-25. Together with your group, share ideas for promotion in each of the four categories.

13-26. As a group, select the promotional activities that will most effectively meet your promotional objectives. Develop a one- to two-page recommendation that you could present to the company's executives.

13-27. Do you think that the promotional mix will change over time? How might it be different in three years? Be sure to address this in your proposal.

cases

With Its Worldly View, Netflix Wants an Entire Globe of Streamers

Continued from page 446

At the beginning of this chapter you read about the Netflix growth in the online streaming market, including its innovative moves to create greater customer convenience during the period 2007–2013, and the phasing out of its DVD-by-mail offerings. Using the information presented in this chapter you should now be able to answer the following questions.

QUESTIONS FOR DISCUSSION

13-28. How would you describe the Netflix target market(s)? Explain your response.

13-29. Describe the distribution channel for moving products from sellers to buyers in this situation. What role do intermediaries play in this channel?

13-30. Describe the roles of physical distribution and warehousing in Netflix's current distribution mix. Do you anticipate any changes in these activities in the near future?

13-31. Suppose you are asked to characterize the Netflix promotional objectives, including positioning. How would you respond? Explain.

13-32. What do you suppose is the promotional mix used now by Netflix? How has that promotional mix changed since 2007? What changes do you expect in the promotional mix in the coming years? Explain.

Hollywood's New Marketing Campaign: Reviving Classic Movies

As film columnist Pete Hammond notes, "In Hollywood they say 'everything old is new again' and that has never been more true…" Consider, for example, the new 50th anniversary digital remake of the movie *The Great Escape* (1963) starring Steve McQueen, Disney's animated *Peter Pan* (1953), and Barbra Streisand with Omar Sharif in the romantic musical *Funny Girl* (1968), that along with hundreds of other classic films from Hollywood's past are finding renewed popularity. The revival of these so-called "catalog titles" is no accident; because disc sales of new movies have been on a 10-year decline, Hollywood studios have been on the hunt for new revenue sources. The result is an industrywide marketing campaign for reviving classic movies or, restated in marketing terms, it's an example of "product extension, or reintroduction of old brands." Although the campaign has not solved all of the industry's disc revenue woes, it is helping. Sales of new-release DVDs in 2012 were 50 percent below peak-year 2004's DVD sales, contrasted with the less drastic 23 percent decline for classic film discs. As sales of catalog titles continue to grow, they accounted for nearly 45 percent of the industry's 2012 film disc (DVD and Blu-ray) revenues. Overall, then, sales of catalog titles, rather than new releases, are providing an increasing share of total disc revenues.

A core demographic for the revival is older movie fans that remember and rewatch catalog titles, including many who want upgraded Blu-ray remakes of classic films such as the memorable *Rebel Without a Cause* (1955) with James Dean. These Blu-ray releases are especially important because they generate higher profit margins than standard DVDs. Younger viewers tend toward less-expensive rentals of current movies from Netflix and similar sources, and for digital formats, including online streaming and video on demand via cable and Internet. Growth in these less expensive options is a main reason for the industry's declining DVD sales. However, it is estimated that 80 percent of catalog-title disc purchases are made by price-conscious impulse shoppers, including younger viewers, at mass-market retail stores, such as Target and Walmart. Thus, two contrasting groups of buyers have emerged: (1) older viewers buying Blu-ray and other kinds of upgraded discs, and (2) buyers, both younger and older, seeking very low-priced DVDs. Accordingly, large retail stores are placing bins in the aisles packed with inexpensively-packaged DVDs priced as low as $5 for *Hook, Home Alone 2, Secondhand Lions*, and other catalog titles.

Along with Blu-ray upgrades, the marketing campaign includes increased retailer display space for classic films, eye-catching online marketing images, and newer packaging to entice the classic audience. Distributors are packaging thematic boxed sets of multiple disks, some with films starring a particular actor, such as Tom Hanks, others grouping together one type of films, such as famous musicals. Prominent firms Warner Bros. and the Paramount Pictures Library (Viacom Inc.), for example, are collaborating in combining related movies from different studios together in one package, including several John Travolta thrillers. Similarly, MGM in 2012 promoted *Bond 50: The Complete 22 Film Collection*, the 50th anniversary Blu-ray collection. These marketing efforts are having a visible public impact; Blu-ray disks of *Jaws*, and the *Bond 50 Collection* broke onto Rentrak Corp.'s Top-10 list of best sellers in 2012. The trend to revive classic films is moving internationally, too, with India's online retailers, Flipkart and Moviemart.com, experiencing an increased number of customers and more DVD sales of old and classic movies than new films. Domestically, reaching beyond DVDs and Blu-ray, Warner Bros. has launched a subscription streaming service for classic TV shows and movies. In addition to films and TV, the impact of the classic-movie trend appears to be stretching into seemingly unrelated industries; PureCostumes.com, purveyor of Halloween costumes, carries licensed costumes of such classic movies as *Breakfast at Tiffany's* and *Grease*. Who knows—perhaps the industry's marketing campaign, itself, may someday become known as a classic.[17]

QUESTIONS FOR DISCUSSION

13-33. Describe the advertising mix being used in Hollywood's new marketing campaign.

13-34. What are the main reasons for the new campaign? How do you recommend they measure results?

13-35. How might the marketing campaign benefit from a revised advertising mix? Explain your reasoning.

13-36. Identify the distribution channels that exist in the new marketing campaign. How might they become more effective?

13-37. Describe the target market(s) for the new marketing campaign. Are the advertising and distribution mixes well—suited to the target market(s)? Explain.

crafting a business plan

PART 4: PRINCIPLES OF MARKETING

Goal of the Exercise

So far, your business has an identity, you've described the factors that will affect your business, and you've examined your employees, the jobs they'll be performing, and the ways in which you can motivate them. Part 4 of the business plan project asks you to think about marketing's Four *Ps—product, price, place (distribution)*, and *promotion*—and how they apply to your business. You'll also examine how you might target your marketing toward a certain group of consumers.

Exercise Background: Part 4 of the Business Plan

In Part 1, you briefly described what your business will do. The first step in Part 4 of the plan is to more fully describe the product (good or service) you are planning to sell. Once you have a clear picture of the product, you'll need to describe how this product will "stand out" in the marketplace—that is, how will it differentiate itself from other products?

In Part 1, you also briefly described who your customers would be. The first step in Part 4 of the plan is to describe your ideal buyer, or target market, in more detail, listing their income level, educational level, lifestyle, age, and so forth. This part of the business plan project also asks you to discuss the price of your products, as well as where the buyer can find your product.

Finally, you'll examine how your business will get the attention and interest of the buyer through its *promotional mix*—advertising, personal selling, sales promotions, and publicity and public relations.

This part of the business plan encourages you to be creative. Have fun! Provide as many details as you possibly can, as this reflects an understanding of your product and your buyer. Marketing is all about finding a need and filling it. Does your product fill a need in the marketplace?

Your Assignment

STEP 1

Open the saved *Business Plan* file you began working on in Parts 1 to 3.

STEP 2

For the purposes of this assignment, you will answer the following questions in "Part 4: Principles of Marketing":

13-38. Describe your target market in terms of age, education level, income, and other demographic variables.
Hint: Refer to Chapter 11 for more information on the aspects of target marketing and market segmentation that you may want to consider. Be as detailed as possible about who you think your customers will be.

13-39. Describe the features and benefits of your product or service.
Hint: As you learned in Chapter 11, a product is a bundle of attributes—features and benefits. What features does your product have—what does it look like and what does it do? How will the product benefit the buyer?

13-40. How will you make your product stand out in the crowd?
Hint: There are many ways to stand out in the crowd, such as a unique product, outstanding service, or a great location. What makes your great idea special? Does it fill an unmet need in the marketplace? How will you differentiate your product to make sure that it succeeds?

13-41. What pricing strategy will you choose for your product, and what are the reasons for this strategy?
Hint: Refer to Chapter 12 for more information on pricing strategies and tactics. Because your business is new, so is the product. Therefore, you probably want to choose between price skimming and penetration pricing. Which will you choose, and why?

13-42. Where will customers find your product or service? (That is, what issues of the distribution mix should you consider?)
Hint: If your business does not sell its product directly to consumers, what types of retail stores will sell your product? If your product will be sold to another business, which channel of distribution will you use? Refer to this chapter for more information on aspects of distribution you may want to consider.

13-43. How will you advertise to your target market? Why have you chosen these forms of advertisement?
Hint: Marketers use several different advertising media—specific communication devices for carrying a seller's message to potential customers—each having its advantages and drawbacks. Refer to this chapter, for a discussion of the types of advertising media you may wish to consider here.

13-44. What other methods of promotion will you use, and why?
Hint: There's more to promotion than simple advertising. Other methods include personal selling, sales promotions, and publicity and public relations. Refer to the discussion of promotion in this chapter for ideas on how to promote your product that go beyond just advertising.
Note: Once you have answered the questions, save your Word document. You'll be answering additional questions in later chapters.

MyBizLab

Go to **pearsonglobaleditions.com/mybizlab** *for the following Assisted-graded writing questions:*

13-45. Consider distribution channels that exist for services products versus those for physical goods. Write an essay to describe some major differences you would expect in those channels. What are some similarities you would expect? Explain the reasons for the similarities and differences you expect. Use examples of services products and physical goods to illustrate and support your arguments.

13-46. Marketing promotions refer to methods for communicating information for various purposes about products, including the product's "value-added" benefits. Discuss in an essay why a firm promotes its product's "value-added" benefits. Then, use an example of promoting a service product to illustrate and support your argument. Finally, use another example for promoting a physical good to illustrate and support you argument.

13-47. Mybizlab Only—comprehensive writing assignment for this chapter.

end notes

[1] Sources: Darcy Travlos, "Netflix: Bull Case Trumps Bear Case For This Stock," *Forbes.com*, March 29, 2013, at www.forbes.com/sites/darcytravlos/2013/03/29/netflix-bull-case-trumps-bear-case-for-this-stock/2/; "Company Timeline: A Brief History of the Company That Revolutionized Watching of Movies and TV Shows," *Netflix*, at signup.netflix.com/MediaCenter/, accessed April 21, 2013; Julianne Pepitone, "Netflix Shares Surge On Surprise Profits," *CNNMoney*, January 24, 2013, at money.cnn.com/2013/01/23/technology/netflix-earnings/index.html; "Law Changed, Netflix Enables Facebook Sharing in the U.S." *AdAge.com*, March 13, 2013, at adage.com/article/media/netflix-finally-introduces-facebook-sharing-u-s/240322/; Lisa Bauman, Nina Deal, Peter Ishak, and Steven Johnson, "Netflix: Positioning and Marketing," *Memoirs of a Student*, at lisabauman.blogspot.com/2013/02/netflix-positioning-and-marketing, accessed April 21, 2013.

[2] Source: "No Sale: 'Cash Registers' Days Are Numbered, Retail Store Experts Say," Columbia Daily Tribune, March 22, 2013, p. 6B; Anne D'Innocenzio, "Cash Registers Disappearing at Retail Stores," *Ohio.com*, March 22, 2013, at www.ohio.com/business/cash-registers-disappearing-at-retail-stores-1.383688; Nick Wingfield, "With Tablets, Businesses Ring Up at More Fanciful Cash Registers," *New York Times*, April 21, 2013, at www.nytimes.com/2013/04/22/technology/with-tablets-businesses-ring-up-at-more-fanciful-cash-registers.html?pagewanted=all&_r=0.

[3] "Vending Machines: A Global Strategic Business Report," *CompaniesAndMarkets.com: Market Report*, September 1, 2010, at http://www.companiesandmarkets.com/Market-Report/vending-machines-a-global-strategic-business-report-companiesandmarkets.com.

[4] *AVON 2012 Annual Report*, at http://investor.avoncompany.com/phoenix.zhtml?c=90402&p=irol-reportsannual.

[5] "Ecommerce Sales Topped $1 Trillion for the First Time in 2012," *eMarketer*, February 5, 2013, at http://www.emarketer.com/Article/Ecommerce-Sales-Topped-1-Trillion-First-Time-2012/1009649.

[6] *YAHOO! FINANCE*, January 16, 2011, at http://finance.yahoo.com/q/is?annual&s=amzn.

[7] Bill Briggs, "E-commerce Overtook Catalog Sales for the First Time at L.L. Bean," *Internet Retailer*, March 17, 2010, at http://www.internetretailer.com/2010/03/17/e-commerce-overtook-catalog-sales-for-the-first-time-at-l-l-bea.

[8] Michael Muchmore, "The Best Online Backup Services," *PC Magazine*, October 28, 2010, at http://www.pcmag.com/article2/0,2817,2288745.asp.

[9] www.paperlesspost.com, accessed April 23, 2013; Angus Loten, "E-Card Founders Make Radical Shift," *Wall Street Journal*, October 18, 2012, p. B5; Ingrid Lunden, "Paperless Post Goes Retro And Launches Paper, A New Invitation Printing Business," *TechCrunch.com*, October 15, 2012, at http://techcrunch.com/2012/10/15/paperless-post-goes-retro-and-begins-paper-a-new-invitation-printing-business/; Teresa Novellino, "Why the Brother-Sister team at Paperless Post Went the Paper Route," *UPSTART Business Journal*, December 10, 2012, at http://upstart.bizjournals.com/entrepreneurs/hotshots/2012/12/10/why-paperless-post-went-the-paper-route.html?page=all.

[10] "Univision Communications and DIRECTV Sign Comprehensive Multi-Year Agreement," *DIRECTTV*, March 19, 2013, at http://news.directv.com/2013/03/19/univision-communications-and-directv-sign-comprehensive-multi-year-agreement/.

[11] "Kantar Media Reports U.S. Advertising Expenditures Increased 3 Percent in 2012," *Kantar Media*, March 11, 2013 at http://kantarmediana.com/intelligence/press/us-advertising-expenditures-increased-3-percent-2012; "100 Leading National Advertisers," *Docstoc*, accessed January 14, 2011, at http://www.docstoc.com/docs/8385834/100-Leading-National-Advertisers-US; "U.S. Advertising Revenue, By Medium," *Business Insider*, October 27, 2009, at http://www.businessinsider.com/us-advertising-spending-by-medium-2009-10.

[12] Nat Ives, "Consumers Are Bugged By Many Ads," *Advertising Age*, December 1, 2008, p. 6.

[13] "Ads Now Watching Shoppers," *Columbia Daily Tribune* (Associated Press), February 3, 2009, p. 7B.

[14] Joel Schectman, "A Smarter Way to Send Junk Mail," *Wall Street Journal*," January 1, 2013, p. B11; Brian Bradtke, "DRTV: Microtargeted TV," *Target Marketing*, February 2013, at http://www.targetmarketingmag.com/article/microtargeted-tv-addressable-television-emerging-direct-marketing-channel/1; Dianna Dilworth, "Direct Mail, Evolved," *Direct Marketing News*, March 1, 2013, at http://www.dmnews.com/direct-mail-evolved/article/280361/.

[15] Associated Press, "New Arrest in Wendy's Finger Case," *MSNBC.com* (May 19, 2005), at http://www.msnbc.msn.com/id/7844274.

[16] Ron Insana, "Wendy's Knew from Start Story Was a Hoax," *USA Today* (June 5, 2005), at http://www.usatoday.com/money/companies/management/2005-06-05-insana-wendys_x.htm.

[17] Ben Fritz, "Hollywood's New Star Has a Classic Look, *Wall Street Journal*, April 22, 2013, pp. B1, B4; U.N., Sushma, "Classic Movies Edge Out Blockbusters in Online Sales," *The Hindu Business Line*, July 6, 2012, at http://www.thehindubusinessline.com/industry-and-economy/info-tech/classic-movies-edge-out-blockbusters-in-online-sales/article3610282.ece, accessed on April 25, 2013; "Licensed Halloween Costume Sales Increase Significantly at PureCostumes.com Due to Hollywood Movie Box Office Hits Affecting Costume Trends," *PRWeb*, August 21, 2102, at http://www.prweb.com/releases/prwebPureCostumes/HollywoodMovies/prweb9822338.htm; Pete Hammond, "Hollywood's Proud Past Lives Again This Week With AFI, TCM Classic Film Festival and Danny Kaye Centennial," *Deadline Hollywood*, April 24, 2013, at http://www.deadline.com/2013/04/hollywoods-proud-past-lives-again-this-week-with-afi-tcm-classic-film-festival-and-danny-kaye-centennial/.

Higher Standards

Online Banking Alert

Change of Email Address

Your primary e-mail address for Bank of Am

Did You Know? You can change your address,
Online Banking and click on the "Customer Se

Because your reply will not be transmitted via secu
alert will not accept replies. If you would like to co
comments, please **sign in to Online Banking** and vi

er FDIC. **Equal Housing Lender** ⌂
poration. All rights reserved

Engineers alone do not design new products.

Customers, marketers, financiers, production

managers, and purchasing employees use

technology to collaborate

in ways that seemed impossible in the past.

AFTER READING THIS CHAPTER, YOU SHOULD BE ABLE TO:

OBJECTIVE 1   **Discuss** the impacts information technology is having on the business world.

OBJECTIVE 2   **Identify** the IT resources businesses have at their disposal and how these resources are used.

OBJECTIVE 3   **Describe** the role of information systems, the different types of information systems, and how businesses use such systems.

OBJECTIVE 4   **Identify** the threats and risks information technology poses on businesses.

OBJECTIVE 5   **Describe** the ways in which businesses protect themselves from the threats and risks information technology poses.

MyBizLab®

⭐ Improve Your Grade!

Visit **pearsonglobaleditions.com/mybizlab** for simulations, tutorials, and end-of-chapter problems.

simulations   **videos**   **assisted-graded**   **writing**

Over 10 million students improved their results using the Pearson MyLabs.

Online Pirates Feast on Economic Downturn

"Start a 'work-at-home' job as an 'international sales representative' or a 'shipping manager,' with excellent pay. Simply open a new bank account in your name, accept money transfers into the account, then forward the money to our customers at locations around the globe." For out-of-work computer users, this e-mail message can be quite appealing. In reality, the victim is tricked into becoming a "mule" in a money-laundering racket. The new "employee" provides anonymous racketeers a safe way to launder stolen or otherwise illegal money. As Internet money transfers arrive, the mule relays them (illegally) to a global network of recipient racketeers. With high unemployment, the volume of mule e-mails is growing; more job-seekers are taking the risk of being arrested.

Financial fears during economic slowdowns are a boon to scammers because businesses and consumers grasp at schemes that are ordinarily ignored. Fake websites, mobile devices, and Internet-based phones boast high-paying jobs, low-cost loans, and can't-miss lotteries. Text messages, saying victims' credit cards have been de-activated, lure bank customers into relaying account information. Internet-based phone users receive fake caller IDs of real hospitals, government agencies, banks, and other businesses in a now-popular form of telephone phishing that talks victims into reveal-ing personal information. Perhaps most impressive, cyber-thieves are using marketing techniques—most notably "targeting"—to reach specific audiences. Also known as "spear phishing," with targeting, scammers do research to identify wealthy indi-viduals, families, and professional money manag-ers. Victims receive friendly-sounding e-mails and social networking contacts containing contaminated attachments that, once opened, infect their comput-ers, exposing bank account and other identity infor-mation to scammers. Although computer security devices—spam filters, data encryption, firewalls, and anti-virus software—catch a vast number of intrusions, the threat remains.[1]

In one popular "work-at-home" scam, the unsus-pecting victim (the new online "employee") cashes checks sent from the "employer" in a foreign country and gets to keep 10 percent of the cash as a payment for service. The remaining 90 percent is sent via Western Union back to the employer. Because the checks are bogus, they bounce, and the victim must repay the full amounts to the bank. Alerting the public to another scam, SC Johnson,

what's in it for me?

Protecting against cyber-attacks is an extreme ex-ample of the way the Internet and related technol-ogies are reshaping the business landscape. But even the most traditional businesses must change with the times, whether those times are defined by paper and pencil, telephone and fax machine, or digital language translators and smartphones. Indeed, it may seem like the times are changing more rapidly with each passing year, and it is in this context that our discussion of the various kinds of information technol-ogy, their functions, and the benefits and risks associated with each as-sumes particular importance. By understanding the material in this chapter, you'll have a clearer picture of how tech-nology is used by and affects business, and how you can use it to your best advantage—as an employee, investor, manager, or as a business owner.

Andres Rodriguez/fotolia

the company that makes household products such as Raid, Windex, and Pledge furniture cleaner, warns of phony online job offers for work-at-home customer service jobs, falsely using the Johnson name. The scammers say the job pays trainees $20 an hour initially, advancing to $25 after training, but employees must first buy some training software—which, of course, they pay for but never receive.

Organizations, too, are victims of cyber invasions: Security consultants say that global cyber-attacks originating in China, and known as Night Dragon, have invaded computers of oil companies, stealing information on competitive bidding, financing, and operations practices. Some governments, to save money, are actively scamming others, using hackers to steal technology secrets for leading-edge military equipment, including defense systems of other countries. Organizations of all kinds are finding cyber security more difficult as more and more employees use their personal phones and computers for conducting business. Organizational information, then, is more widely dispersed and increasingly susceptible to intrusion via mobile-phone malware, virus-contaminated applications, and links containing spyware sent from text messages.[2]

(After studying the content in this chapter you should be able to answer a set of discussion questions found at the end of the chapter.)

Information Technology Impacts: A Driver of Changes for Business

OBJECTIVE 1
Discuss

the impacts information technology (IT) has had on the business world.

Information Technology (IT) *various appliances and devices for creating, storing, exchanging, and using information in diverse modes, including visual images, voice, multimedia, and business data*

The effect of **Information technology (IT)** on business has been immeasurable. In fact, IT, the various appliances and devices for creating, storing, exchanging, and using information in diverse modes, including visual images, voice, multimedia, and business data, has altered the structure of business organizations, radically changing the way employees and customers interact. We see ads all the time for the latest cell phones, iPads, laptops, PDAs, tablets, and smartphones, and most of us connect daily to the Internet. E-mail has become a staple in business, and even such traditionally "low-tech" businesses as nail salons and garbage collection companies are dependent on the Internet, computers, and networks. As consumers, we interact with databases of IT networks every time we withdraw money from an ATM, order food at McDonalds, or check on the status of a package at UPS.com. Technology and its effects are evident everywhere.

E-commerce *use of the Internet and other electronic means for retailing and business-to-business transactions*

E-commerce (short for *electronic commerce*), the use of the Internet and other electronic means for retailing and business-to-business transactions, has created new market relationships around the globe. In this section, we'll look at how businesses are using IT to bolster productivity, improve operations and processes, create new opportunities, and communicate and work in ways not possible before.

Creating Portable Offices: Providing Remote Access to Instant Information

IT appliances such as Samsung mobile phones and Apple iPhones, along with IBM wireless Internet access and PC-style office applications, save businesses time and travel expenses by enabling employees, customers, and suppliers to communicate from any location. IT's mobile messaging capabilities mean that a geographic separation between the workplace and headquarters is more common. Employees no longer work only at the office or the factory, nor are all of a company's operations performed at one place; employees take the office with them. When using such devices, off-site employees have continuous access to information, instead of being forced to be at a desk to access their files and the Internet. Client project folders, e-mail, and voice messaging are accessible from any location. Such benefits currently attract 80 million enthusiastic subscribers worldwide to BlackBerry® smartphones.[3]

Looking to the future, a possible next step for office portability is Google's "Project Glass." This is a head-mounted, Internet-connected information display that may someday be blended into peoples' everyday eyeglasses. Using Google's *Android* system, it will respond to voice commands for rapid visual access to the Internet's vast ocean of digital information, while on-the-move.[4]

Enabling Better Service by Coordinating Remote Deliveries

With access to the Internet, company activities may be geographically scattered but still remain coordinated through a networked system that provides better service for customers. Many businesses, for example, coordinate activities from one centralized location, but their deliveries flow from several remote locations, often at lower cost. When you order furniture—for example, a chair, a sofa, a table, and two lamps—from an Internet storefront, the chair may come from a warehouse in Philadelphia and the lamps from a manufacturer in California; the sofa and table may be shipped direct from different suppliers in North Carolina. Beginning with the customer's order, activities are coordinated through the company's network, as if the whole order were being processed at one place. This avoids the expensive in-between step of first shipping all the items to a central location.

Creating Leaner, More Efficient Organizations

Networks and technology are also leading to leaner companies with fewer employees and simpler structures. Because networks enable firms to maintain information linkages among both employees and customers, more work and customer satisfaction can be accomplished with fewer people. Bank customers connect into a 24-hour information system and monitor their accounts without employee assistance. Instructions that once were given to assembly workers by supervisors are now delivered to workstations electronically. IT communications provide better use of employee skills and greater efficiencies from physical resources. For example, truck drivers used to return to a shipping terminal to receive instructions from supervisors on reloading freight for the next delivery. Today, one dispatcher using IT has replaced several supervisors. Instructions to the fleet arrive on electronic screens in trucks on the road so drivers know in advance the next delivery schedule, and satellite navigation services, such as the XM NavTraffic, alert drivers of traffic incidents ahead so they can reroute to avoid delivery delays.[5]

Barack Obama's Blackberry uses an encrypted system for secure messaging with advisors and colleagues.

This Boeing aircraft was the result of collaboration among Boeing engineers, suppliers, and customers.

Antony Nettle/Alamy

Enabling Increased Collaboration

Collaboration among internal units and with outside firms is greater when firms use collaboration (collaborative) software and other IT communications devices, which we'll discuss later in this chapter. Companies are learning that complex problems can be better solved through IT-supported collaboration, either with formal teams or spontaneous interaction among people and departments. The design of new products, for example, was once an engineering responsibility. Now it is a shared activity using information from customers, along with people in marketing, finance, production, engineering, and purchasing who, collectively, determine the best design. For example, the design of Boeing's 787 Dreamliner aircraft is the result of collaboration, not just among engineers, but also from passengers (who wanted electric outlets to recharge personal electronic devices), cabin crews (who wanted more bathrooms and wider aisles), and air-traffic controllers (who wanted larger, safer air brakes). Although recent performance problems grounded the 787, solutions involved a worldwide network of technical collaboration among Boeing engineers, suppliers, customers, and NASA.[6]

Enabling Global Exchange

The global reach of IT enables business collaboration on a scale that was unheard of before. Consider Lockheed Martin's contract for designing and supplying thousands of Joint Strike Fighters in different versions for the United States, Britain, Italy, Denmark, Canada, and Norway. Lockheed can't do the job alone—over the project's 20-year life, more than 1,500 firms will supply everything from radar systems to engines to bolts. In just the start-up phase, Lockheed collaborated with Britain's BAE Systems along with more than 70 U.S. and 18 international subcontractors at some 190 locations, including an Australian manufacturer of aviation communications and a Turkish electronics supplier. In all, 40,000 remote computers are collaborating on the project using Lockheed's Internet-based system. Web collaboration on a massive scale is essential for coordinating design, testing, and construction while avoiding delays, holding down costs, and maintaining quality.[7]

Improving Management Processes

IT has also changed the nature of the management process. The activities and methods of today's manager differ significantly from those that were common just a few years ago. At one time, upper-level managers didn't concern themselves with all of the detailed information filtering upward from the workplace because it was expensive to gather, the collection and recording process was cumbersome, and information quickly became out of date. Workplace management was delegated to middle and first-line managers.

With electronic processing in digital databases, specialized software, and interactive networks, however, instantaneous information is accessible and useful to all levels of management. For example, consider *enterprise resource planning (ERP)*, which is an information system for organizing and managing a firm's activities across product lines, departments, and geographic locations. The ERP stores real-time information on work status and upcoming transactions and notifies employees when action is required if certain schedules are to be met. It coordinates internal operations with activities of outside suppliers and notifies customers of upcoming deliveries and billings. Consequently, more managers use it routinely for planning and controlling companywide operations. Today, a manager at Hershey Foods, for example, uses ERP to check on the current status of any customer order for Kisses or strawberry Twizzlers, inspect productivity statistics for each workstation, and analyze the delivery performance on any shipment. Managers can better coordinate companywide performance. They can identify departments that are working well together and those that are lagging behind schedule and creating bottlenecks.

Providing Flexibility for Customization

IT advances also create new manufacturing and service capabilities enabling businesses to offer customers greater variety, customizable options, and faster delivery cycles. Whether it's an iPhone app or a Rawlings baseball glove, today's design-it-yourself world is possible through fast, flexible manufacturing using IT networks. At Ponoko.com you can design and make just about anything, from electronics to furniture. Buyers and materials suppliers, meeting electronically, have rapidly generated thousands of product designs online. The designs can be altered to suit each buyer's tastes. Similarly, at San Francisco–based Timbuk2's website, you can "build your own" custom messenger bag at different price levels with your choice of size, fabric, color combination, accessories, liner material, strap, and even left- or right-hand access.[8] This principle of **mass customization** allows companies to produce in large volumes, and IT allows each item to feature the unique options the customer prefers. With IT, the old standardized assembly line has become quickly adaptable because workers have instantaneous access to assembly instructions for all the product options, and equipment can be changed quickly for each customer's order.

Mass Customization principle in which companies produce in large volumes, but each item features the unique options the customer prefers

As shown in Figure 14.1, flexible production and speedy delivery depend on an integrated network of information to coordinate all the activities among customers, manufacturers, suppliers, and shippers.

Service industries, too, including healthcare, banking, and recreation, are emphasizing greater flexibility for meeting customers' needs. Personalized pet care at HappyPetCare.net for example, relies on IT for scheduling customized activities—dog walking, pet boarding, pet sitting, house sitting, pet taxis, and other services. In tourism, at OceaniaCruises.com passengers have flexibility for selecting personalized onboard services for meals, recreation and entertainment activities, educational classes, and spa treatments. They also customize your air travel schedules along with personalized pre- and post-cruise land programs.

Providing New Business Opportunities

Not only is IT improving existing businesses, it is creating entirely new businesses where none existed before. For big businesses, this means developing new products, offering new services, and reaching new clients. Only a few years ago, today's multibillion-dollar behemoth known as Google was a fledgling search engine. That company boasts not just a search engine but hundreds of services including virtual maps, YouTube video, Twitter accounts and Facebook pages, instant messaging, Gmail (Google's e-mail service), and online voicemail and software services such as photo editing and document creation.

IT-based industries, including computer-backup and identity-theft protection, offer valuable services for individuals and business customers. Online backup protects against data loss resulting from hard-drive crashes, fire, flood, and other causes. Carbonite.com and Backblaze.com, for example, provide automatic continuous backup so clients can recover lost data quickly. For guarding against identity theft, firms such as LifeLock.com and IdentityGuard.com protect personal information that alerts clients to various information-theft risks and sends advice on steps for avoiding identity theft.

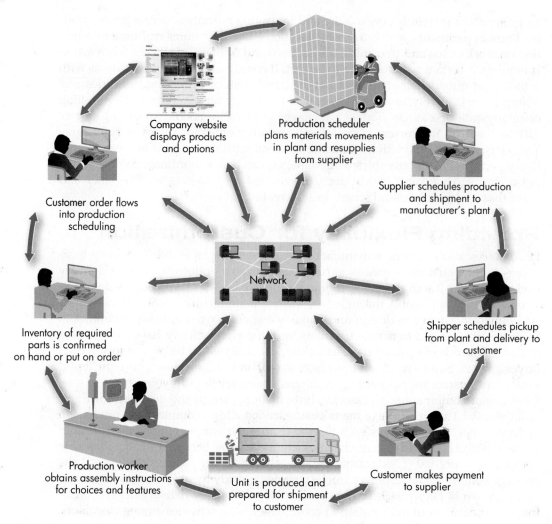

FIGURE 14.1 Networking for Mass Customization of a Physical Product

The IT landscape has also presented home-based businesses with new e-business opportunities. Consider Richard Smith. His love for stamp collecting began at age seven. Now, some 50 years after saving that first stamp, he's turned his hobby into a profitable eBay business. Each day begins at the PC in his home office, scanning eBay's listings for items available and items wanted by sellers and buyers around the world. With more than 6,000 sales transactions to date, Richard maintains a perfect customer rating and has earned more than $4,000 on each of several eBay transactions. Today, thousands of online marketplaces allow entrepreneurs to sell directly to consumers, bypassing conventional retail outlets, and enable business-to-business (B2B) selling and trading with access to a worldwide customer base. To assist start-up businesses, eBay's services network is a ready-made online business model, not just an auction market. Services range from credit financing to protection from fraud and misrepresentation, information security, international currency exchanges, and postsales management. These features enable users to complete sales transactions, deliver merchandise, and get new merchandise for future resale, all from the comfort of their own homes. Many eBay users, like Richard Smith, have carved profitable new careers with the help of these systems.

Improving the World and Our Lives

Can advancements in IT really make the world a better place? Developments in smartphones, social networking, home entertainment, automobile safety, and other applications have certainly brought enjoyment and convenience to the everyday lives of millions of people around the globe. Extending technology beyond previous

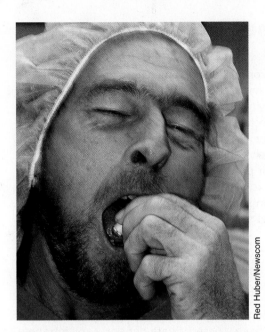

After this capsule is swallowed, the camera inside it can transmit almost 50,000 images during its eight-hour journey through the digestive tract.

Red Huber/Newscom

model cell phones and PCs, new technologies provide access to endless choices of *apps* (shorthand for *application software*), allowing each user to "build it your way," depending on what you want your device to do and how and where you'll be using it. Apps for computers and smartphones include *programs* for learning languages, music, work, games, traveling, art, and almost any other area of interest. Just two years after its opening, Apple's App Store had supplied more than 40 billion app downloads worldwide to users of Macs, iPhones, iPads, and iPod touches.

Social networking, a valuable service for individuals and organizations, is made possible by IT. The many forms of social media—blogs, chats, and networks such as LinkedIn, Twitter, and Facebook—are no longer just playthings for gossips and hobbyists. They're also active tools for getting a job. With the economic meltdown, millions of job seekers turned to online networking—tapping leads from friends, colleagues, and acquaintances—for contacts with companies that may be hiring. Peers and recruiters are networking using electronic discussion forums and bulletin boards at websites of professional associations and trade groups, technical schools, and alumni organizations. Some social sites provide occupation-specific career coaching and job tips: Scientists are connecting with Epernicus, top managers use Meet the Boss, and graduate students are connecting with Graduate Junction.[9]

Organizations, too, including hospitals and medical equipment companies are embracing IT advancements to provide better services. For example, when treating combat injuries, surgeons at Walter Reed Army Medical Center rely on high-tech imaging systems that convert two-dimensional photographs of their patients' anatomies into three-dimensional (3D) physical models for presurgical planning. These 3D mockups of shoulders, femurs, and facial bones give doctors the opportunity to see and feel the anatomy as it will be seen in the operating room, before they even use their scalpels. Meanwhile, pill-sized cameras that patients swallow are providing doctors with images of the insides of the human body, helping them to make better diagnoses for such ailments as ulcers and cancer.[10]

IT Building Blocks: Business Resources

OBJECTIVE 2
Identify
the IT resources businesses have at their disposal and how these resources are used.

Businesses today have a wide variety of IT resources at their disposal. In addition to the Internet and e-mail, these include communications technologies, networks, hardware devices, and software, as shown at technology media sites such as Techweb.com.

The Internet and Other Communication Resources

Internet *gigantic system of interconnected computer networks linked together by voice, electronic, and wireless technologies*

The **Internet** is a gigantic system of interconnected computer networks belonging to millions of collaborating organizations and agencies—government, business, academic, and public—linked together by voice, electronic, and wireless technologies.[12] Computers within the networks are connected by various communications protocols, or standardized coding systems, such as the **hypertext transfer protocol (HTTP)**, which is used for the **World Wide Web**, a branch of the Internet consisting of interlinked hypertext documents, or Web pages. Other protocols serve a variety of purposes such as sending and receiving e-mail. The World Wide Web and its protocols provide the common language that allows information sharing on the Internet. For thousands of businesses, the Internet has replaced the telephone, fax machine, and standard mail as the primary communications tool.

Hypertext Transfer Protocol (HTTP) *communications protocol used for the World Wide Web, in which related pieces of information on separate Web pages are connected using hyperlinks*

World Wide Web *branch of the Internet consisting of interlinked hypertext documents, or Web pages*

The Internet has spawned a number of other business communications technologies, including *intranets, extranets, electronic conferencing,* and *VSAT satellite communications.*

Intranet *organization's private network of internally linked websites accessible only to employees*

Intranets   Many companies have extended Internet technology by maintaining internal websites linked throughout the firm. These private networks, or **intranets**, are accessible only to employees and may contain confidential information on benefits programs, a learning library, production management tools, or product design resources. The Ford Motor Company's intranet is accessible to 200,000 people daily at workstations in Asia, Europe, and the United States. In addition to Ford employees, the intranet is accessible to Ford dealers and suppliers around the world. Sharing information on engineering, distribution, and marketing has reduced the lead time for getting new models into production and has shortened customer delivery times.[12]

Extranet *system that allows outsiders limited access to a firm's internal information network*

Extranets   **Extranets** allow outsiders limited access to a firm's internal information network. The most common application allows buyers to enter a system to see which products are available for sale and delivery, thus providing convenient product availability information. Industrial suppliers are often linked into customers' information networks so that they can see planned production schedules and

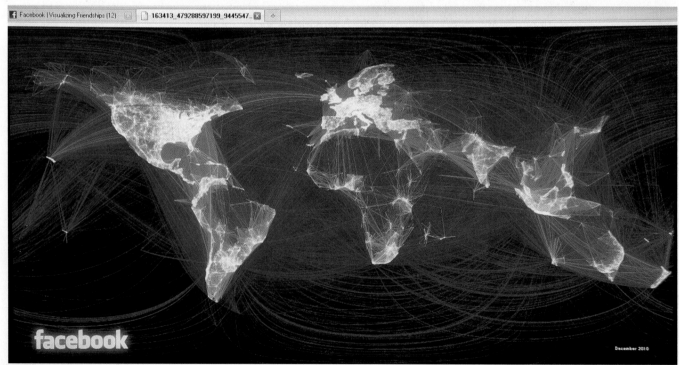

In this map of the Internet, from The Opte Project, each line represents a connection between computers or other network devices.

prepare supplies for customers' upcoming operations. The extranet at Chaparral Steel Company, for example, lets customers shop electronically through its storage yards and gives them electronic access to Chaparral's planned inventory of industrial steel products. Service industries, too, allow customers access to supplies of available services. For example, tour providers such as Tauck, Globus, and Viking River Cruises rely on major airlines such as Delta to provide flights for tour customers. Tour companies, by connecting into Delta's future flight schedules, reserve blocks of flight seats to accommodate tourists.

Electronic Conferencing **Electronic conferencing** allows groups of people to communicate simultaneously from various locations via e-mail, phone, or video, thereby eliminating travel time and providing immediate contact. One form, called *data conferencing*, allows people in remote locations to work simultaneously on one document. *Video conferencing* allows participants to see one another on video screens while the conference is in progress. For example, Lockheed Martin's Joint Strike Fighter project, discussed previously, uses Internet collaboration systems with both voice and video capabilities. Although separated by oceans, partners can communicate as if they were in the same room for redesigning components and production schedules. Electronic conferencing is attractive to many businesses because it eliminates travel and saves money.

Electronic Conferencing *IT that allows groups of people to communicate simultaneously from various locations via e-mail, phone, or video*

VSAT Satellite Communications Another Internet technology businesses use to communicate is **VSAT satellite communications.** VSAT (short for *very small aperture terminal*) systems have a transmitter-receiver (*transceiver*) that sits outdoors with a direct line of sight to a satellite. The hub, a ground-station computer at the company's headquarters, sends signals to and receives signals from the satellite, exchanging voice, video, and data transmissions. An advantage of VSAT is privacy. A company that operates its own VSAT system has total control over communications among its facilities, no matter their location, without dependence on other companies. A firm might use VSAT to exchange sales and inventory information, advertising messages, and visual presentations between headquarters and store managers at remote sites. For example, stores in Minneapolis, London, and Boston might communicate with headquarters in New York, sending and receiving information via a satellite, as shown in Figure 14.2.

VSAT Satellite communications *network of geographically dispersed transmitter-receivers (transceivers) that send signals to and receive signals from a satellite, exchanging voice, video, and data transmissions*

Networks: System Architecture

A **computer network** is a group of two or more computers linked together, either hardwired or wirelessly, to share data or resources, such as a printer. The most common type of network used in businesses is a **client-server network.** In client-server networks, *clients* are usually the laptop or desktop computers through which users make requests for information or resources. *Servers* are the computers that provide the services shared by users. In big organizations, servers are usually assigned a specific task. For example, in a local university or college network, an *application server* stores the word-processing, spreadsheet, and other programs used by all computers connected to the network. A *print server* controls the printers, stores printing requests from client computers, and routes jobs as the printers become available. An *e-mail server* handles all incoming and outgoing e-mail. With a client-server system, users can share resources and Internet connections—and avoid costly duplication.

Computer Network *group of two or more computers linked together by some form of cabling or by wireless technology to share data or resources, such as a printer*

Client-Server Network *common business network in which clients make requests for information or resources and servers provide the services*

Cloud computing modifies traditional networks by adding an externally located component—the "cloud"—that replaces the functions previously performed by application servers. With a cloud, information resources are retrieved via the Internet from a remote storage service, instead of relying on network-connected user-shared servers for storing data and software packages in client-server systems. Data and software resources are accessible through Internet-based devices, including laptops, desktops, tablets, mobile phones, and other devices with access to the Web. The cloud enhances user flexibility, especially for employees working remotely because users can access e-mails and data files from any online location, rather than from one particular location.

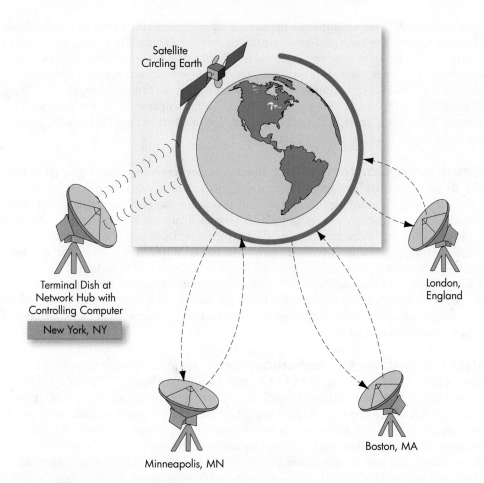

FIGURE 14.2 A VSAT Satellite Communication Network

Amazon's Simple Storage Service (S3), is an example of a *public* cloud that rents Internet storage space where users can store any amount of data and retrieve it at anytime from anywhere on the Web. S3 services have become cost savers for companies by eliminating the need for buying, installing, and maintaining in-house server computers, many of which have excessive unused storage capacity "just in case it's needed in the future." S3 allows you to store and manage your application data, search files online, upgrade software quickly, then download and share data. In contrast with public clouds, *private* cloud services such as JustCloud and ZipCloud provide an added layer of security by surrounding the user-company's storage with a firewall to ensure against intrusion. Private clouds provide added flexibility for creating customized data storage, automated data integration, and integrated software applications to better meet users' needs.

Networks can be classified according to geographic scope and means of connection (either wired or wireless).

Wide Area Networks (WANs)

Computers that are linked over long distances—statewide or even nationwide—through long-distance telephone wires, microwave signals, or satellite communications make up what are called **wide area networks (WANs).** Firms can lease lines from communications vendors or maintain private WANs. Walmart, for example, depends heavily on a private satellite network that links thousands of U.S. and international retail stores to its Bentonville, Arkansas, headquarters.

Local Area Networks (LANs)

In **local area networks (LANs)**, computers are linked in a smaller area such as an office or a building, using telephone wires, fiber-optic, or co-axial cables. For example, a LAN unites hundreds of operators who enter

Wide Area Network (WAN) *computers that are linked over long distances through telephone lines, microwave signals, or satellite communications*

Local Area Network (LAN) *computers that are linked in a small area, such as all of a firm's computers within a single building*

call-in orders at TV's Home Shopping Network facility. The arrangement requires only one computer system with one database and one software system.

Wireless Networks
Wireless networks use airborne electronic signals to link network computers and devices. Like wired networks, wireless networks can reach across long distances or exist within a single building or small area. For example, the BlackBerry® smartphones system shown in Figure 14.3 consists of devices that send and receive transmissions on the **wireless wide area networks (WWANs)** of more than 500 service providers—such as Cellular One (United States), T-Mobile (United Kingdom and United States), and Vodafone Italia (Italy)—in more than 90 countries throughout the world. The wireless format that the system relies on to control wireless messaging is supplied by BlackBerry Limited (formerly known as Research In Motion® [RIM®]), the company that makes the BlackBerry® smartphone, and is installed on the user-company's computer. A *firewall* provides privacy protection. We'll discuss firewalls in more detail later in the chapter.

Wireless Wide Area Network (WWAN) *network that uses airborne electronic signals instead of wires to link computers and electronic devices over long distances*

Wi-Fi
You've no doubt heard of "hotspots"—millions of locations worldwide, such as coffee shops, hotels, airports, and cities that provide wireless Internet connections for people on the go. Each hotspot, or **Wi-Fi** (a play on audio recording term *Hi-Fi*) access point, uses its own small network, called a **wireless local area network (wireless LAN or WLAN)**. Although wireless service is free at some hotspots, others charge a fee—a daily or hourly rate—for the convenience of Wi-Fi service.

Wi-Fi *technology using a wireless local area network*

Wireless Local Area Network (Wireless LAN or WLAN) *local area network with wireless access points for PC users*

The benefit of Wi-Fi is that its millions of users are not tethered to a wire for accessing the Internet. Employees can wait for a delayed plane in the airport and still be connected to the Internet through their wireless-enabled laptops or other devices. However, as with every technology, Wi-Fi has limitations, including a short range of distance. This means that your laptop's Internet connection can be severed if you move farther than about 300 feet from the hotspot. In addition, thick walls, construction beams, and

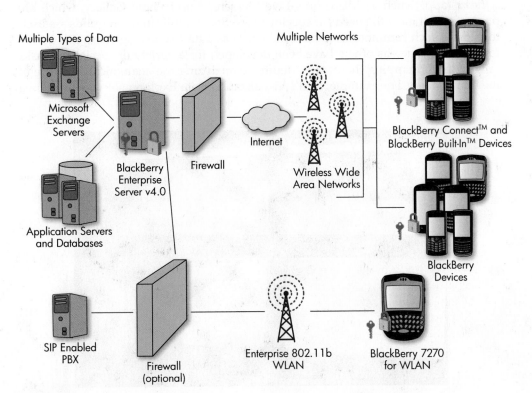

FIGURE 14.3 Core Components in BlackBerry Wireless Internet Architecture
Source: Image © 2013 Blackberry Limited. All Rights Reserved. Used with permission.

other obstacles can interfere with the signals sent out by the network. So, although a city may have hundreds of hotspots, your laptop must remain near one to stay connected. *WiMAX* (*Worldwide Interoperability for Microwave Access*), the next step in wireless advancements, improves this distance limitation with its wireless range of up to 30 miles.

Proposing a bolder approach for the future, the U.S. Federal Communications Commission in 2013 announced a proposed multiyear project for nationwide **"super Wi-Fi" networks** to be developed by the federal government. More powerful than today's networks, the super Wi-Fi would have further reach, stretching across major metropolitan areas and covering much of the rural countryside as well. Super Wi-Fi's stronger signals will flow more freely, without obstruction, through concrete walls, steel beams, forests and hills. The proposal would enable users to surf the Internet and make mobile phone calls without paying a monthly cell phone bill or Internet bill.[13]

Airlines, too, are expanding Wi-Fi service beyond just domestic flights by providing satellite-based Internet service on long-haul international flights. Japan Airlines offers Wi-Fi on routes between New York and Tokyo, in addition to flights between Tokyo and Los Angeles, Chicago, and Jakarta, Indonesia. Other airlines gearing up for Wi-Fi on long-haul flights include Air France, Delta, and United. Meanwhile, Qantas—the Australian airline—discontinued its trial program because of passenger disinterest in international Wi-Fi service.

Hardware and Software

Any computer network or system needs **hardware**, the physical components, such as keyboards, monitors, system units, and printers. In addition to the laptops and desktop computers, *handheld computers* and mobile devices are also used often in businesses. For example, Target employees roam the store aisles using handhelds to identify, count, and order items; track deliveries; and update backup stock at distribution centers to keep store shelves replenished with merchandise.

The other essential in any computer system is **software:** programs that tell the computer how to function. Software includes *system software*, such as Microsoft Windows 8 for PCs, which tells the computer's hardware how to interact with the software, what resources to use, and how to use them. It also includes *application software* (apps) such as Microsoft's Live Messenger and Photo Gallery, which are programs that meet the needs of specific users. Some application programs are used to address such common, long-standing needs as database management and inventory control, whereas others have been developed for a variety of specialized tasks ranging from mapping the oceans' depths to analyzing the anatomical structure of the human body. For example, IBM's Visualization Data Explorer software uses data

"Super Wi-Fi" Network *a powerful Wi-Fi network with extensive reach and strong signals that flow freely through physical objects such as walls*

Hardware *physical components of a computer network, such as keyboards, monitors, system units, and printers*

Software *programs that tell the computer how to function, what resources to use, how to use them, and application programs for specific activities*

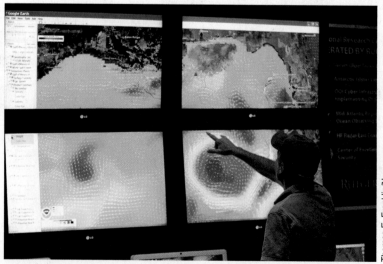

Thomas E. Franklin/Newscom

3-D computer modeling software gives engineers a better idea of where oil might be located.

from field samples to model the underground structure of an oil field. The imagery in the photo on the previous page, for example, provides engineers with better information on oil location and reduces the risk of their hitting less productive holes.

Finally *groupware*, software that connects group members for e-mail distribution, electronic meetings, message storing, appointments and schedules, and group writing, allows people to collaborate from their own desktop PCs, even if they're remotely located. It is especially useful when people work together regularly and rely heavily on information sharing. Groupware systems include IBM Lotus software and Novell GroupWise.

Information Systems: Harnessing the Competitive Power of IT

OBJECTIVE 3
Describe
the role of information systems, the different types of information systems, and how businesses use such systems.

Business today relies on information management in ways that no one could foresee a decade ago. Managers now treat IT as a basic organizational resource for conducting daily business. At major firms, every activity—designing services,

managing in turbulent times

When Cash Gets Scarce, Businesses Switch to Internet Bartering

For many companies, economic downturns involve tighter credit, a drop in sales revenues, and a shortage of cash for doing business. Without cash and credit, companies can't buy the materials, services, and supplies needed to produce products for customers, so business prospects grow even dimmer. Or do they? Enter an unexpected liberator—bartering. This ancient trade practice survives even today, but in an Internet-enhanced form with global reach and instantaneous access to a vast network of swap agreements. And best of all, it can be done without cash. For example, Firm A provides an advertising program for Firm B that, in return, has vacant building space needed by Firm A. Thus, the needs of both are met, and a cashless swap is born. As the recession deepened, the popularity of bartering grew. In 2010, BarterQuest.com had more than 50,000 monthly visitors from Australia, the United States, and elsewhere. Activity has tripled at U-Exchange.com, where its "Barter 101" gets you started, and you can swap as much as you like at no cost. Worldwide, the electronically based barter business has grown to a mega-billion-dollar industry.[14]

Whether it's B2B or business to consumer (B2C), online bartering is an efficient way around the economy's credit crunch because it enables companies and individuals to get goods and services without using cash. Restaurants, for example, can trade meals or catering for advertising or for cooking equipment. Bartering can also be a good way to move excessive inventory and get needed benefits in return. An unemployed electrician bartered with homeowners who needed electrical wiring; in

Shutterstock

return, the homeowners gave up unneeded furniture and laptops that the electrician later sold to make mortgage payments.

For avid swappers of services, websites such as PeopleTradingServices.com make it easy for small business owners to find barter matchups with hundreds of kinds of services, ranging from gardeners to songwriters to clergy. As a barter matchmaker, PeopleTradingServices.com posts members' profiles, lists services they trade, and provides a convenient way to contact member professionals online. Along with endless trading possibilities, the cash conservation can be a lifesaver for any cash-strapped small business during troubled times.[15]

Information system (IS) *system that uses IT resources to convert data into information and to collect, process, and transmit that information for use in decision making*

Data *raw facts and figures that, by themselves, may not have much meaning*

Information *meaningful, useful interpretation of data*

Information Systems Managers *managers who are responsible for the systems used for gathering, organizing, and distributing information*

ensuring product delivery and cash flow, and evaluating personnel—is linked to *information systems.* An **information system (IS)** uses IT resources that enable managers to take **data**, raw facts and figures that, by themselves, may not have much meaning, and turn those data into **information**, the meaningful, useful interpretation of data. Information systems also enable managers to collect, process, and transmit that information for use in decision making.

One company well-known for its strategic use of information systems is Walmart. The nerve center for company operations is a centralized IS in Bentonville, Arkansas. The IS drives costs down and raises efficiency because the same methods and systems are applied for all 10,000-plus stores in 27 countries. Data on the billions of sales transactions—time, date, and place—flow to Bentonville. The IS tracks millions of stock-keeping units (SKUs) weekly, enforces uniform reordering and delivery procedures on its more than 100,000 suppliers, including 20,000 in China, and regulates the flow of merchandise through its distribution centers and stores.

Beyond the firm's daily operations, information systems are also crucial in planning. Managers routinely use the IS to decide on products and markets for the next 5 to 10 years. The company's vast database enables marketing managers to analyze customer demographics for better marketing, and it is also used for financial planning, materials handling, and electronic funds transfers with suppliers and customers.

Walmart, like most businesses, regards its information as a private resource, an asset that's planned, developed, and protected. Therefore, it's not surprising that they have **information systems managers** who are responsible for the systems used for gathering, organizing, and distributing information, just as they have production, marketing, and finance managers. These managers use many of the IT resources we discussed previously—the Internet, communications technologies, networks, hardware, and software—to sift through information and apply it to their jobs.

Leveraging Information Resources: Data Warehousing and Data Mining

Almost everything you do leaves a trail of information about you. Your preferences in movie rentals, television viewing, Internet sites, and groceries; the destinations of your phone calls, your credit card charges, your financial status; personal information about age, gender, marital status, and even your health are just a few of the items about each of us that are stored in scattered databases. The behavior patterns of millions of users can be traced by analyzing files of information gathered over time from their Internet usage and in-store purchases.

Marc F. Henning/Alamy

Retailers such as Wal-Mart and Sam's Club rely on data warehousing and mining to keep shelves stocked with in-demand merchandise.

The collection, storage, and retrieval of such data in electronic files is called **data warehousing.** For managers, the data warehouse is a goldmine of information about their business. Indeed, Kroger Co., the Ohio-based grocery chain, collects data on customer shopping habits to find ways to gain greater customer loyalty. As part owner of a data-mining firm, Kroger accumulates information from its shopper cards, analyzes the data to uncover shopping patterns, and sends money-saving coupons to regular customers for the specific products they usually buy. Kroger's precision targeting pays off, especially in the recession economy. With a rate of coupon usage up to as much as 50 times the industry average, it's a money saver for Kroger customers and boosts the company's sales, too.[16]

Data Warehousing *the collection, storage, and retrieval of data in electronic files*

Data Mining After collecting information, managers use **data mining**, the application of electronic technologies for searching, sifting, and reorganizing pools of data to uncover useful information. Data mining helps managers plan for new products, set prices, and identify trends and shopping patterns. By analyzing what consumers actually do, businesses can determine what subsequent purchases they are likely to

Data Mining *the application of electronic technologies for searching, sifting, and reorganizing pools of data to uncover useful information*

entrepreneurship and new ventures

Speaking Loud and Clear: A New Voice Technology

IT users for years have sought a natural-sounding voice interface to enhance IT systems with vocal output, beyond traditional print or visual output. Vocal technologies, however, were less than effective, that is until 2005 when Matthew Aylett and Nick Wright formed CereProc (short for Cerebral Processing) in Edinburgh, Scotland.[17] From the outset, the firm has been dedicated to creating better synthetic voices with character and emotion that stimulates listeners with natural-sounding messages. Before CereProc, these lofty goals were prohibitive. Speech experts couldn't create text-to-voice software that sounds realistically conversational, varying tone-of-voice and providing various vocal inflections for different situations. Previous software couldn't adapt incoming text (from word processing or from text messages) into natural voice formats. To attack these challenges CereProc brought together a team of leading speech experts. It also partnered with leading universities and research programs in speech science technology and in developing new applications and markets for voice output.

The company's main product is CereVoice, an advanced text-to-voice technology available on mobile devices, PCs, servers, and headsets, and that has applications in most any company's products for better synthetic voices. Any computer's existing voice system can be replaced with more natural-sounding speech in a choice of accents, including Southern British English, Scottish, and American, that can be sampled with live voice demos at the firm's website.[18] Potential applications are endless—kitchen appliances, alarm systems, traffic controllers, automobile appliances, radio broadcasting, telephone messaging, and movies, to name a few. Although consumers may not see the CereVoice label, they will be hearing its various voices often in their everyday lives.

C.M. Wiggins/Newscom

CereProc's Voice Creation service can create a synthesized imitation of a person's voice, including its tones and inflections. That's how noted film critic, the late Roger Ebert, got his voice back, four years after losing the ability to speak following cancer-related surgery. CereProc's voice engineers used recordings of Ebert's voice from 40 years of past television broadcasts, capturing individual sounds and identifying various voice characteristics. With meticulous care, specialists then pieced them back together into software that mimics the Pulitzer-Prize winner's earlier voice. Ebert typed his comments into a computer that, in turn, converted the text into words that were spoken in his voice. This first-of-its-kind application made a memorable public appearance on the Oprah show, as Roger enthusiastically demonstrated his voice coming from the computer.[19] Beyond its technical success, this project vividly displays a compassionate side in CereProc's business.

make and then send them tailor-made ads. The *Washington Post*, for example, uses data-mining software to analyze census data and target households likely to respond to sales efforts.[20]

Information Linkages with Suppliers The top priority for Walmart's IS—improving in-stock reliability—requires integration of Walmart and suppliers' activities with store sales. That's why Procter & Gamble (P&G), Johnson & Johnson, and other suppliers connect into Walmart's information system to observe up-to-the-minute sales data on individual items, by store. They can use the system's computer-based tools—spreadsheets, sales forecasting, and weather information—to forecast sales demand and plan delivery schedules. Coordinated planning avoids excessive inventories, speeds up deliveries, and holds down costs throughout the supply chain while keeping shelves stocked for retail customers.

Types of Information Systems

Employees have a variety of responsibilities and decision-making needs, and a firm's IS may actually be a set of several systems that share information while serving different levels of the organization, different departments, or different operations. Because they work on different kinds of problems, managers and their employees have access to the specialized information systems that satisfy their different information needs.

In addition to different types of users, each business *function*—marketing, human resources, accounting, production, or finance—has special information needs, as do groups working on major projects. Each user group and department, therefore, may need a special IS.

Information Systems for Knowledge Workers
As we discussed in Chapter 10, *knowledge workers* are employees for whom information and knowledge are the raw materials of their work, such as engineers, scientists, and IT specialists who rely on IT to design new products or create new processes. These workers require **knowledge information systems**, which provide resources to create, store, use, and transmit new knowledge for useful applications—for instance, databases to organize and retrieve information, and computational power for data analysis.

Specialized support systems have also increased the productivity of knowledge workers. **Computer-aided design (CAD)** helps knowledge workers—and now ordinary people too, as we saw with consumers designing customized products at the

Knowledge Information System *information system that supports knowledge workers by providing resources to create, store, use, and transmit new knowledge for useful applications*

Computer-Aided Design (CAD) *IS with software that helps knowledge workers design products by simulating them and displaying them in three-dimensional graphics*

The 3-D computer model of this dinosaur is constructed from digital scans of fossilized tissue.

Mocart/Shutterstock

beginning of this chapter—design products ranging from cell phones to jewelry to auto parts by simulating them and displaying them in 3D graphics. In a more advanced version, known as *rapid prototyping,* the CAD system electronically transfers instructions to a computer-controlled machine that quickly builds a prototype—a physical model—of the newly designed product, such as a toy, an artificial limb for the disabled, or a solar panel. The older method—making handcrafted prototypes from wood, plastic, or clay—is replaced with faster, cheaper prototyping.

In archaeology, CAD is helping scientists uncover secrets hidden in fossils using 3D computer models of skeletons, organs, and tissues constructed with digital data from computed tomography (CT) scans of dinosaur fossils. From these models, scientists have learned, for example, that the giant apatosaurus's neck curved downward, instead of high in the air as once thought. By seeing how the animals' bones fit together with cartilage, ligaments, and vertebrae, scientists are discovering more about how these prehistoric creatures interacted with their environment.[21]

In a direct offshoot of computer-aided design, **computer-aided manufacturing (CAM)** uses computers to design and control the equipment needed in a manufacturing process. For example, CAM systems can produce digital instructions to control all the machines and robots on a production line say, as an example, in making jewelry boxes. CAM-guided machines cut the materials, move them through the stages of production, then assemble each stylish box without human physical involvement in production activities. CAD and CAM coupled together (CAD/CAM) is useful to engineers in a manufacturing environment for designing and testing new products and then designing the machines and tools to manufacture the new product.

Computer-Aided Manufacturing (CAM) *IS that uses computers to design and control equipment in a manufacturing process*

Information Systems for Managers

Each manager's information activities and IS needs vary according to his or her functional area (accounting or human resources and so forth) and management level. The following are some popular information systems used by managers for different purposes.

MANAGEMENT INFORMATION SYSTEMS

Management information systems (MIS) support managers by providing reports, schedules, plans, and budgets that can then be used for making both short- and long-term decisions. For example, at Walsworth Publishing Company, managers rely on detailed information—current customer orders, staffing schedules, employee attendance, production schedules, equipment status, and materials availability—for moment-to-moment decisions during the day. They require similar information to plan such mid-range activities as personnel training, materials movements, and cash flows. They also need to anticipate the status of the jobs and projects assigned to their departments. Many MIS—cash flow, sales, production scheduling, and shipping—are indispensable for helping managers complete these tasks.

Management Information System (MIS) *computer system that supports managers by providing information—reports, schedules, plans, and budgets—that can be used for making decisions*

For longer-range decisions involving business strategy, Walsworth managers need information to analyze trends in the publishing industry and overall company performance. They need both external and internal information, current and future, to compare current performance data to data from previous years and to analyze consumer trends and economic forecasts.

DECISION SUPPORT SYSTEMS

Managers who face a particular kind of decision repeatedly can get assistance from **decision support systems (DSS)**, interactive systems that create virtual business models and test them with different data to see how they respond. When faced with decisions on plant capacity, for example, Walsworth managers can use a capacity DSS. The manager inputs data on anticipated sales, working capital, and customer-delivery requirements. The data flow into the DSS processor, which then simulates the plant's performance under the proposed data conditions. A proposal to increase facility capacity by say, 10 percent could be simulated to find costs of operation, percent of customer order fulfillments, and other performance measures that would result with the expanded capacity. After experimenting with various data conditions, the DSS makes recommendations on the best levels of plant capacity—those that result in best performance—for each future time period.

Decision Support System (DSS) *interactive system that creates virtual business models for a particular kind of decision and tests them with different data to see how they respond*

OBJECTIVE 4
Identify
the threats and risks information
technology poses on businesses.

IT Risks and Threats

As with other technologies throughout history, IT continues to attract abusers set on doing mischief, with severity ranging from mere nuisance to outright destruction. Eager IT users everywhere are finding that even social networking and cell phones have a "dark side"—privacy invasion. Facebook postings of personal information about users have been intercepted and misused by intruders. Beacon, the former data-gathering service, caused a public uproar when it published peoples' online purchases publicly on their Facebook newsfeeds. And with cellular technology, some features of Bluetooth connections allow savvy intruders to read a victim's text messages, listen in on live conversations, and even view unwary users' photos.[22]

Businesses, too, are troubled with IT's dark side. Hackers break into computers, stealing personal information and company secrets, and launch attacks on other computers. Meanwhile, the ease of information sharing on the Internet has proven costly for companies who are having an increasingly difficult time protecting their intellectual property, and viruses that crash computers have cost companies many billions annually. In this section, we'll look at these and other IT risks. In the next section, we'll discuss ways in which businesses are protecting themselves from these risks.

Hackers

Breaking and entering no longer refers merely to physical intrusion. Today, it applies to IT intrusions as well. **Hackers** are cybercriminals who gain unauthorized access to a computer or network, either to steal information, money, or property or to tamper with data. Twitter reported that hackers may have intercepted information—names, passwords, e-mail addresses—of some 250,000 of the social media's users. With different motives than the Twitter intruders, Chinese-based hackers, including the Chinese government, are suspected of continuing cyber-attacks into the computer systems of several newspapers, including *The New York Times*, *The Washington Post*, and *The Wall Street Journal*. China-based intruders have been accused of a multiyear campaign to illegally gain corporate secrets and confidential information that can be used to frighten critics from writing unfavorable articles, accusations that the Chinese government has denied.[23]

Another common hacker activity is to launch *denial of service (DoS) attacks*. DoS attacks flood networks or websites with bogus requests for information and resources, thereby over-loading and shutting the networks or websites down, preventing legitimate users from accessing them.

Wireless mooching is a profitable industry for cybercriminals. In just five minutes, a *St. Petersburg Times* (Florida) reporter using a laptop found six unprotected wireless networks that were wide open to outside users.[24] Once inside an unsecured wireless network, hackers can use it to conduct illegal business, such as child pornography or money laundering. When police officers try to track down these criminals, they're long gone, leaving you, the network host, exposed to criminal prosecution.

As we saw in this chapter's opening case, hackers, such as the Night Dragon, often break into company networks to steal company or trade secrets. But it's not just hackers who are doing the stealing. Because the chances of getting caught seem slim, home users continue, illegally, to download unpaid-for movies, music, and other resources from file-swapping networks. A recent study shows that sound piracy costs the United States $12.5 billion and 71,060 jobs annually. However, these losses also showcase what can happen to businesses who fail to adapt to changes in technology. Until recent years, the recording industry was reluctant to embrace the Internet as a path for distribution, preferring to prosecute pirates rather than offer them legal online alternatives. On the other hand, Apple has benefitted immensely from its online (download) distribution models, enabling it to become the world's most popular music vendor.[25]

Hacker *cybercriminal who gains unauthorized access to a computer or network, either to steal information, money, or property or to tamper with data*

Identity Theft

Once inside a computer network, hackers are able to commit **identity theft**, the unauthorized stealing of personal information (such as Social Security number and address) to get loans, credit cards, or other monetary benefits by impersonating the victim. With up to 12 million victims each year, identity theft is among the fastest-growing crimes in the United States.

Clever crooks get information on unsuspecting victims by digging in trash, stealing mail, or using *phishing* or *pharming* schemes to lure Internet users to bogus websites. For instance, a cybercriminal might send a PayPal user an e-mail notifying him or her of a billing problem with his or her account. When the customer clicks on the PayPal Billing Center link, he or she is transferred to a spoofed (falsified) Web page, modeled after PayPal's. The customer then submits the requested information—credit card number, Social Security number, and PIN—into the hands of the thief. The accounts are soon empty.

Identity Theft *unauthorized use of personal information (such as Social Security number and address) to get loans, credit cards, or other monetary benefits by impersonating the victim*

Intellectual Property Theft

Nearly every company faces the dilemma of protecting product plans, new inventions, industrial processes, and other **intellectual property**, something produced by the intellect or mind that has commercial value. Its ownership and right to its use may be protected by patent, copyright, trademark, and other means.

Intellectual Property *something produced by the intellect or mind that has commercial value*

Computer Viruses, Worms, and Trojan Horses

Another IT risk facing businesses is rogue programmers who disrupt IT operations by contaminating and destroying software, hardware, or data files. Viruses, worms, and Trojan horses are three kinds of malicious programs that, once installed, can shut down any computer system. A *computer virus* exists in a file that attaches itself to a program and migrates from computer to computer as a shared program or as an e-mail attachment. It does not infect the system unless the user opens the contaminated file, and users typically are unaware they are spreading the virus by file sharing. It can, for example, quickly copy itself over and over again, using up all available memory and effectively shutting down the computer.

Worms are a particular kind of virus that travel from computer to computer within networked computer systems, without your needing to open any software to spread the contaminated file. In a matter of days, the notorious Blaster worm infected some 400,000 computer networks, destroying files and even allowing outsiders to take over computers remotely. The worm replicates itself rapidly, sending out thousands of copies to other computers in the network. Traveling through Internet connections and e-mail address books in the network's computers, it absorbs system memory and shuts down network servers, Web servers, and individual computers.

Unlike viruses, a *Trojan horse* does not replicate itself. Instead, it most often comes into the computer, at your request, masquerading as a harmless, legitimate software product or data file. Once installed, the damage begins. For instance, it may simply redesign desktop icons or, more maliciously, delete files and destroy information.

Spyware

As if forced intrusion isn't bad enough, Internet users unwittingly invite spies—masquerading as a friendly file available as a giveaway or shared among individual users on their PCs. This so-called **spyware** is downloaded by users that are lured by "free" software. Once installed, it crawls around to monitor the host's computer activities, gathering e-mail addresses, credit card numbers, passwords, and other inside information that it transmits back to someone outside the host system. Spyware

Spyware *program unknowingly downloaded by users that monitors their computer activities, gathering e-mail addresses, credit card numbers, and other information that it transmits to someone outside the host system*

authors assemble incoming stolen information to create their own "intellectual property" that they then sell to other parties to use for marketing and advertising purposes or for identity theft.[26]

Spam

Spam *junk e-mail sent to a mailing list or a newsgroup*

Spam, junk e-mail sent to a mailing list or a newsgroup (an online discussion group), is a greater nuisance than postal junk mail because the Internet is open to the public, e-mail costs are negligible, and massive mailing lists are accessible through file sharing or by theft. Spam operators send unwanted messages ranging from explicit pornography to hate mail to advertisements, and even destructive computer viruses. In addition to wasting users' time, spam also consumes a network's bandwidth, thereby reducing the amount of data that can be transmitted in a fixed amount of time for useful purposes. U.S. industry experts estimate spam's annual damage in lost time and productivity at between $20 and $50 billion in the U.S. alone.[27]

Although spammers sometimes gain significant incomes, they also risk anti-spanning prosecution that can be extremely costly. The judge in a lawsuit against Sanford Wallace, who proclaimed himself the "Spam King," issued a judgment for $711 million against Wallace, one of the largest fines ever in an anti-spamming case. He was accused of sending 27 million spam mailings to Facebook, using phishing to get passwords from thousands of Facebook users, then entering their accounts to post fraudulent information. He now faces criminal charges of electronic mail fraud, damage to protected computers, and criminal contempt.[28]

OBJECTIVE 5
Describe
the ways in which businesses protect themselves from the threats and risks IT poses.

IT Protection Measures

Security measures against intrusion and viruses are a constant challenge. Most systems guard against unauthorized access by requiring users to have protected passwords. Other measures include firewalls, special software, and encryption.

Preventing Unauthorized Access: Firewalls

Firewall *security system with special software or hardware devices designed to keep computers safe from hackers*

Firewalls are security systems with special software or hardware devices designed to keep computers safe from hackers. A firewall is located where two networks—for example, the Internet and a company's internal network—meet. It contains two components for filtering incoming data:

- The company's *security policy*—Access rules that identify every type of data that the company doesn't want to pass through the firewall.

- A *router*—A table of available routes or paths; a "traffic switch" that determines which route or path on the network to send each piece of data after it is tested against the security policy.

Only that information that meets the conditions of the user's security policy is routed through the firewall and permitted to flow between the two networks. Data that fail the access test are blocked and cannot flow between the two networks.

Preventing Identity Theft

Although foolproof prevention is impossible, steps can be taken to avoid being victimized. A visit to the Identity Theft Resource Center (http://www.idtheftcenter.

org) is a valuable first step to get information on everything from scam alerts to victim issues to legislation such as the Fair and Accurate Credit Transactions Act (FACTA). FACTA strengthens identity-theft protections by specifying how organizations must destroy information instead of dropping it in a dumpster. When a company disposes of documents that contain credit or Social Security information, they must be shredded, pulverized, or burned, and all electronic records (in computers and databases) must be permanently removed to keep them out of the hands of intruders.[29]

Preventing Infectious Intrusions: Anti-Virus Software

Combating viruses, worms, Trojan horses, and any other infectious software (collectively known as *malware*) has become a major industry for systems designers and software developers. Installation of any of hundreds of **anti-virus software** products protects systems by searching incoming e-mail and data files for "signatures" of known viruses and virus-like characteristics. Contaminated files are discarded or placed in quarantine for safekeeping.

Anti-Virus Software *product that protects systems by searching incoming e-mails and data files for "signatures" of known viruses and virus-like characteristics*

Many viruses take advantage of weaknesses in operating systems, such as Microsoft Windows, to spread and propagate. Network administrators must make sure that the computers on their systems are using the most up-to-date operating system that includes the latest security protection.

Protecting Electronic Communications: Encryption Software

Security for electronic communications is another concern for businesses. Unprotected e-mail can be intercepted, diverted to unintended computers, and opened, revealing the contents to intruders. Protective software is available to guard against those intrusions, adding a layer of security by encoding e-mails so that only intended recipients can open them. An **encryption system** works by scrambling an e-mail message so that it looks like garbled nonsense to anyone who doesn't possess the key.

Encryption System *software that assigns an e-mail message to a unique code number (digital fingerprint) for each computer so only that computer, not others, can open and read the message*

Avoiding Spam and Spyware

To help their employees avoid privacy invasion and to improve productivity, businesses often install anti-spyware and spam-filtering software on their systems. Although dozens of anti-spyware products provide protection—software such as Webroot Spy Sweeper and Microsoft Windows Defender—they can be continually updated to keep pace with new spyware techniques.

The federal CAN-SPAM Act of 2003 requires the Federal Trade Commission to shield the public from falsified header information, sexually explicit e-mails that are not so labeled, Internet spoofing (using trickery to make a message appear as if it came from a trusted source), and hijacking of computers through worms or Trojan horses. Although it cannot be prevented entirely, spam is abated by many Internet service providers (ISPs) that ban the spamming of ISP subscribers. In a now-classic punishment, an ISP in Iowa was awarded $1 billion in a lawsuit against 300 spammers that jammed the ISP system with an astounding 10 million e-mails a day. Anti-spam groups, too, promote the public's awareness of known spammers. The Spamhaus Project (http://www.spamhaus.org), for example, maintains a list of "The 10 Worst Spammers," career spammers that are responsible for most of the world's spam traffic.

finding a better way

The Pentagon's New Career Track: Cyberwarfare

KIM JAE-HWAN/AFP/Getty Images

The U.S. Air Force Weapons School, in graduating its first class of six cyber-trained airmen in 2012, has taken a significant plunge for full-scale entry onto the battlefield of cyberwarfare. Their battle stations are computer terminals. Their job is to find electronic intrusions, identify the intruders, take steps for defending and securing U.S. defense networks, and executing cyber-attacks as necessary to protect and advance U.S. technologies for cyberwarfare. Within the nation's military structure, the Air Force Weapons School resides within the U.S. Cyber Command that is responsible for computer warfare resources and capabilities across all branches of the military. Cyber Command also coordinates the military's capabilities and activities with resources at the National Security Agency. The Air Force program is part of the U.S. government's overall goal of ensuring a rapid offensive and defensive deployment capability that interfaces with other related programs, including those in the Central Intelligence Agency, Department of Homeland Security, and other intelligence agencies.

The nation's cyberwar activities have been on the increase since 2008. Among other actions, they include U.S. and Israeli use of the Stuxnet virus to cripple Iran's nuclear program in 2010, sending the nuclear facility's centrifuges out of control, thereby sabotaging Iran's weapons development without risking military or civilian casualties. In 2011 the United States developed plans for using cyberweapons against Libyan defense systems in advance of U.S. airstrikes. Although the stockpile of U.S. cyberweapons is a top secret, officials indicate weapons development is underway to cut off power supplies at specific target locations, along with capabilities for disabling enemy sea and air defenses. Along with these technical activities, however, the onset of the new cyberwarfare course also revolutionizes a whole way of thinking throughout the military that traditionally regarded electronics technologies as mainly communications tools. Now they are becoming recognized as strategic weaponry that holds hopes for conducting bloodless wars, and for protecting the nation's infrastructure from outside assaults on its air-traffic control system, electric power grids, communications systems, and water supplies, all of which could result in loss of human lives.

Cyber Command officials recognize that potential enemies—nations and individuals—can intrude for military and intelligence purposes into telephones, computer networks, and other communications technologies, so the United States must be prepared to counter and abate those intrusions, and respond offensively with an even greater cyberforce. To stop such intrusions, students at the Air Force Weapons School gained experience by (1) learning how a foe could launch a cyber-attack against a U.S. command center, (2) learning how to design and build a defense, (3) observing the success or failure of the proposed defense when an Air Force "aggressor team"—a tech-savvy Air Force "hacker"—tested to see if the defenses would hold up against intruders.

One hope is that the military's advanced cyberdefense techniques will find future uses in civilian applications for businesses and individuals. Cyber intrusions into U.S. businesses with high-value proprietary information—at petroleum refineries, facilities using advanced manufacturing technologies, and laboratories with secret developments in science and medicine—could benefit from the Air Force's "finding a better way" to defend against cyber attacks.[30]

Ethical Concerns in IT

It is apparent that IT developments and usage are progressing faster than society's appreciation for the potential consequences, including new ethical concerns. Along with IT's many benefits, its usage is creating previously unanticipated problems for which solutions are needed, yet they don't exist. Ease of access to computers, mobile devices, and the Internet, together with messaging capabilities and social networking, promote widespread public exposure about people's private lives, including

table 14.1 Areas for Ethical Concerns in Information Technology and Its Uses

- In a now-classic case of cyber-bullying, a 13-year-old girl hanged herself after being taunted by a hoax message on her MySpace page.
- Secret webcasts of other people's behavior have resulted in embarrassment and even death: A university student, leaving a final message on his Facebook page, jumped from a bridge to his death after other students covertly webcast his sexual activities with another student.
- IT is used increasingly for sending out cries for help. Many college students have posted public messages requesting physical and emotional support. Others, having read those messages, are unsure if they should respond, or not.
- Employers and employees struggle about the extent of personal use of the company's IT. Many employees admit they use social networking and personal e-mailing at work, but should they? Many company's say "no," adding that employees should know that the company has access to all e-mails sent, received, and stored on its IT system.
- States are forming database pools, sharing information to check on suspicious prescription drug activities. Data are gathered on purchases at pharmacies, physicians' prescriptions, and police records to identify drug abuse by individuals and companies within states, and are being shared across state lines.
- The Department of Homeland Security abandoned one of its major data-mining tools for combating terrorism after questions about its compliance with privacy rules. It was discovered that DHS had tested the data-mining program using information about real people, without ensuring the privacy of that information.
- To save money, IT users retrieve and share intellectual property—movies, articles, books, music, industrial information—with others, ignoring copyright, trademark, and patent protections. Written content is often taken from the Internet, inserted into the user's written work and is represented as the user's own original creation without citing its true source.
- Job seekers are being asked to answer unexpected questions by interviewers: "What is your Facebook username and password?" Some applicants are responding, "No, that's a terrible privacy invasion." Others are revealing the requested information to interviewers.

personal information about how they think and feel. Just how this information should be used, by whom, under what conditions, and with what restrictions, if any, are issues teeming with ethical considerations. Several real-life episodes with ethical implications are shown in Table 14.1. See if you can identify significant ethical issues among the episodes in the table.

summary of learning objectives

OBJECTIVE 1

Discuss the impacts information technology has had on the business world. (pp. 480–485)

The growth of IT—the various appliances and devices for creating, storing, exchanging, and using information in diverse modes, including visual images, voice, multimedia, and business data—has changed the very structure of business organizations. Its adoption provides new modes of communication, including portable offices using mobile messaging capabilities, resulting in the geographic separation of the workplace from headquarters for many employees. With access to the Internet, company activities may be geographically scattered but still remain coordinated through a networked system that provides better service for customers. Networks and technology are also leading to leaner companies with fewer employees and simpler structures. Because networks enable firms to maintain information linkages among employees and customers, more work and customer satisfaction can be accomplished with fewer people. It also contributes to greater flexibility in serving customers and enables closer coordination with suppliers. Company activities may be geographically scattered but remain coordinated through a network system that provides better service for customers. Many businesses coordinate activities from one centralized location, but their deliveries flow from several remote locations, often at lower cost. IT's global reach facilitates project collaboration with remote business partners and the formation of new market relationships around the globe. Just as electronic collaboration has changed the way employees interact with each other, IT networks have created new manufacturing flexibility for mass customization, and Internet access has brought new opportunities for small businesses.

OBJECTIVE 2

Identify the IT resources businesses have at their disposal and how these resources are used. (pp. 485–491)

The Internet and the World Wide Web serve computers with information and provide communication flows among networks around the world. For many businesses, the Internet has replaced the telephone, fax machine, and standard mail as the primary communications tool. To support internal communications, many companies maintain internal websites—*intranets*—accessible only to employees. Some firms give limited network access to outsiders via *extranets* allowing access to private information among businesses, customers, and suppliers for better planning and coordination of their activities. Electronic conferencing allows simultaneous communication globally among groups from various locations, saving travel time, time for information exchanges, and expenses. *VSAT satellite networks* provide private remote communications for voice, video, and data transmissions.

   Computer networks, including wide area networks and local area networks, enable the sharing of information, hardware, software, and other resources over wired or wireless connections. *Wi-Fi* provides wireless Internet connections through their laptops or other devices at "hotspots" or local access points. All computer networks or systems need hardware, the physical components such as keyboards, monitors, and printers. In addition, all systems require *software*, programs that tell the computer how to function. *Application software* includes programs to meet specific user needs, such as groupware with voice and video connections for remote collaboration.

OBJECTIVE 3

Describe the role of information systems, the different types of information systems, and how businesses use such systems. (pp. 491–495)

An *information system (IS)* uses IT resources that enable users to create, process, and transmit information for use in decision making. An IS often includes *data warehousing*, a vast collection, storage, and retrieval system, that provides the data resources needed for creating information. The IS also includes *data mining* capabilities, the application of technologies for searching, sifting, and reorganizing data, to uncover useful information for planning new products, setting prices, and identifying trends.

The IS is often a set of several systems that share information while serving different levels of an organization, different departments, or different operations. *Knowledge information systems* support knowledge workers—engineers, scientists, and other specialists—by providing resources to create, store, use, and transmit new knowledge they use for specialty applications. Knowledge systems include *computer-aided design (CAD)*, software systems that receive engineering data and convert them into three-dimensional displays, for rapid development of new products. *Computer-aided manufacturing (CAM)* uses computers to design and control the equipment needed in a manufacturing process. *Management information systems (MIS)* support managers by providing reports, schedules, plans, and budgets that can then be used for making decisions at all levels ranging from detailed daily activities to long-range business strategies. The many uses of information systems include experimenting with *decision support systems (DSS)*, interactive systems that create business models and test them with different data to see how the models respond under diverse business conditions, to test the effectiveness of potential decisions.

OBJECTIVE 4

Identify the threats and risks information technology poses on businesses. (pp. 496–498)

IT has attracted abusers that do mischief, with severity ranging from mere nuisance to outright destruction, costing companies millions. Everything from Facebook postings to Bluetooth usage to private computer systems are subject to break-ins and destruction. *Hackers* break into computers, stealing personal information and company secrets, tampering with data, and launching attacks on other computers. *Wireless moochers* use victims' networks for illegal activities, exposing the host to criminal prosecution. Once inside a computer network, hackers are able to commit *identity theft*, the unauthorized stealing of personal information to get loans, credit cards, or other monetary benefits by impersonating the victim. Even the ease of information sharing on the Internet poses a threat. It has proven costly for companies who are having a difficult time protecting their *intellectual property*, such as software products, movies, and music. Hackers break into company networks to steal anything of commercial value, including trade secrets, new inventions, and other valuable information that is protected by patent, copyright, or trademark. Another IT risk facing businesses is system shutdown and destruction of software, hardware, or data files by *viruses, worms*, and *Trojan horses* that can shut down a computer system, or otherwise disrupt IT operations by contaminating and destroying software, hardware, or data files. After invading a victim's computer, *spyware* gathers inside information and transmits it to outside spies. Masquerading as a friendly file available as a giveaway or shared among individual users on PCs and mobile devices, spyware is downloaded by unsuspecting users. Once installed, it monitors the host's electronic activities, gathers personal information, and transmits stolen information to an outside system. *Spam*, junk e-mail sent to a mailing list or news group, is costly in terms of lost time and productivity by overloading the network's capacity with massive mailings of unwanted messages.

OBJECTIVE 5

Describe the ways in which businesses protect themselves from the threats and risks IT poses. (pp. 498–501)

Most systems guard against unauthorized access by requiring users to have protected passwords. In addition, many firms rely on *firewalls*, security systems with special software or hardware devices that intercept would-be intruders, so that only messages that meet the conditions of the company's security policy are permitted to flow through the network. Firms can protect against identity theft by using assistance from advisory sources, such as the Identity Theft Resource Center, and by implementing the identity-theft protection provisions of the federal FACTA rule for maintaining and destroying personal information records. To combat infectious intrusions by viruses, worms, and Trojan horses, *anti-virus software* products search incoming e-mail and data files for "signatures" of known viruses and virus-like characteristics.

Contaminated files are discarded or placed in quarantine for safe keeping. Additional intrusion protection is available by installing *anti-spyware* and *spam filtering software*. *Encryption* adds security by encoding, scrambling messages so they look like garbled nonsense to anyone that doesn't possess they key, so that the message can be read only by intended recipients. The federal *CAN-SPAM Act* requires the Federal Trade Commission to shield the public from falsified header information, sexually explicit e-mails that are not so labeled, Internet spoofing (using trickery to make a message appear as if it came from a trusted source), and hijacking of computers through worms or Trojan horses. Although it cannot be prevented entirely, *spam* is abated by many Internet service providers (ISPs) that ban the spamming of ISP subscribers.

key terms

anti-virus software (p. 499)
client-server network (p. 487)
computer network (p. 487)
computer-aided design (CAD) (p. 494)
computer-aided manufacturing (CAM)
    (p. 495)
data (p. 492)
data mining (p. 493)
data warehousing (p. 493)
decision support system (DSS) (p. 495)
e-commerce (p. 480)
electronic conferencing (p. 487)
encryption system (p. 499)
extranet (p. 486)
firewall (p. 498)

hacker (p. 496)
hardware (p. 490)
hypertext transfer protocol (HTTP)
    (p. 486)
identity theft (p. 497)
information (p. 492)
information system (IS) (p. 492)
information systems managers (p. 492)
information technology (IT) (p. 480)
intellectual property (p. 497)
Internet (p. 486)
intranet (p. 486)
knowledge information system
    (p. 494)
local area network (LAN) (p. 488)

management information system (MIS)
    (p. 495)
mass customization (p. 483)
software (p. 490)
spam (p. 498)
spyware (p. 497)
"super Wi-Fi" network (p. 490)
VSAT satellite communications (p. 487)
wide area network (WAN) (p. 488)
Wi-Fi (p. 489)
wireless local area network (wireless
    LAN or WLAN) (p. 489)
wireless wide area network (WWAN)
    (p. 489)
World Wide Web (p. 486)

MyBizLab

Go to **pearsonglobaleditions.com/mybizlab** to complete the problems marked with this icon ✪.

questions & exercises

QUESTIONS FOR REVIEW

14-1. Why must a business manage information as a resource?
✪ **14-2.** How can electronic conferencing increase a company's productivity and efficiency?
14-3. What are the advantages and risks of cloud computing?
14-4. Why should companies be concerned about hackers?
14-5. What is the definition of *intellectual property*? List three examples of intellectual property.

QUESTIONS FOR ANALYSIS

14-6. Describe how a company might use data warehousing and data mining in its information system to better plan for new products.
✪ **14-7.** Aside from the examples in this chapter, describe one or more ways that IT presents new business opportunities for small businesses.
✪ **14-8.** Give three examples (other than those in this chapter) of how a company can become leaner and more efficient by adopting IT.

APPLICATION EXERCISES

14-9. Consider your daily activities—as a consumer, student, parent, friend, homeowner or renter, car driver, employee, etc.—and think about the ways that you are involved with IT systems. Make a list of your recent IT encounters and then recall instances in those encounters that you revealed personal information that could be used to steal your identity. Are some encounters on your list riskier than others? Why or why not?
14-10. After reading the first section of this chapter, consider how IT has changed the business of higher education. Identify at least three functions, services, or activities that would not have been available 25 years ago. How do you think that colleges and universities will change in the future because of advances in IT?

building a business: continuing team exercise

Assignment

Meet with your team members to consider your new business venture and how it relates to the information technology topics in this chapter. Develop specific responses to the following:

14-11. In what ways will your business be connected with IT? In what ways do you expect IT will enable collaboration among your employees? Identify examples of occasions where IT will be useful for providing remote access between employees, and remote access between employees and company data files.

14-12. In what ways will IT be used for collaboration with external stakeholders, such as customers, suppliers, and other constituents? What types of remote interactions do you expect, and what kinds of IT equipment and installations will be needed for those interactions? Discuss how your team is going to identify the IT equipment requirements at this stage of development of your business.

14-13. At what stage of your company's development will you begin planning for its information system(s), if any? Discuss the technical skills and information-management skills necessary for determining the kind(s) of information system(s) needed for your company's first two years of operation.

14-14. Based on your findings for Question 14-13, where will your company get the skills and resources for IS development and implementation? Have you included the anticipated costs for developing the information systems in your financial plan for year one, or will you do so? Explain why, or why not.

14-15. What measures, if any, will you take for protecting against intrusions into your company's IT system? What actions will be taken to prevent unauthorized access to information of customers, suppliers, and other external constituents? What security measures will be taken to protect non-IT information? Explain.

building your business skills

THE ART AND SCIENCE OF POINT-AND-CLICK RESEARCH

Goal

To learn how to use the Web to conduct research more effectively.

Background Information

In a survey of nearly 2,000 Web users, two-thirds said they used the Web to obtain work-related information. With billions of pages of information on the Web, the challenge for business users is: how best to find what they're seeking.

Method

You'll need a computer and access to the Web to complete this exercise.

STEP 1

Get together with three classmates and decide on a business-related research topic. Choose a topic that interests you—for example, "Business Implications of the War in Afghanistan," "Labor Disputes in Professional Sports," or "Marketing Music Lessons to Parents of Young Children."

STEP 2

Search the following sites for information on your topic (dividing sites among group members to speed the process):

- Dogpile (www.dogpile.com)
- Excite (www.excite.com)
- Google (www.google.com)
- Yahoo! (www.yahoo.com)

Take notes as you search so that you can explain your findings to other group members.

STEP 3

Working as a group, answer the following questions about your collective search:

> Which sites were the easiest to use?
>
> Which sites offered the most helpful results? What specific factors made these sites better than the others?
>
> Which sites offered the least helpful results? What were the problems?
>
> Why is it important to learn the special code words or symbols, called *operators*, that target a search? (Operators are words such as *AND*, *OR*, and *NOT* that narrow search queries. For example, using *AND* in a search tells most search engines to look only for sites in which all words appear in the results—American *AND* Management *AND* Association.)

FOLLOW-UP QUESTIONS

Research the differences between *search engines* and *subject directories*. Given your topic, would a search engine or a subject directory be more helpful for your research?

14-16. Why is it important to learn how to use a search site's Help function?

14-17. Look into some of the sites' Advanced Search pages. How do these pages affect your searches?

14-18. How has the Web changed the nature of business research?

exercising your ethics

TO READ OR NOT TO READ

The Situation

Companies are able to monitor the ways that their employees use the company e-mail system as well track a history of employee's Internet use while using company resources. This exercise illustrates how ethical issues may arise in tracking and using employee use of digital assets.

The Dilemma

You have recently been promoted to the position of a first-line manager at a local bio-technology company. This is a dream job and you are delighted to have been recognized for your hard work. As you are being oriented to your new job, the human resource (HR) manager explains that the company maintains logs of employee e-mails and tracks all Internet usage on company computers. You were surprised that you had not been informed about this when you were hired, but the HR director has assured you that this is completely legal. The company is concerned that employees may be wasting time on YouTube and other websites while at work, so they believe that there is a business purpose to this program. You will be expected to scan e-mail logs to make sure that employees are not sharing confidential information or trade secrets as well as monitor computer activities.

QUESTIONS TO ADDRESS

14-19. Given the factors in this situation, what, if any, ethical issues exist?

14-20. Do you think that the company is wise to monitor employees in this manner? Why or why not?

14-21. If you discovered that an employee was spending a lot of time on nonwork–related searches, how would you address the issue with the employee?

team exercise

THIS GAME IS GETTING SERIOUS

The Situation

Interactive games have become big-time entertainment for millions of enthusiasts playing side by side or among contestants anywhere on the Internet. Amidst the fun, questions can arise about the use of intellectual property and the ownership obligations of gamers. This exercise encourages you to examine some of the ethical issues that can surface in gaming.

The Dilemma

Tracy was enamored with a new adventure-and-strategy game from the moment she bought it. Her favorite character—Goddess Diaphanese—had accumulated overwhelming powers, thanks to Tracy's gaming skills and lots of trial and error, during two months of intense competition. Opponents were consistently overwhelmed by Diaphanese's mystical powers, and her ability to foresee the future, ward off attacks with invincible armor, and elevate her intellect to outsmart opponents in this virtual universe. Tracy's Diaphanese was, in effect, an invincible game character.

Another gamer wanted to buy Tracy's personal version of the game, but she decided instead to list it for sale on a popular Internet auction site. The bid price rose to more than 10 times the original game price when Tracy got an e-mail from the manufacturer objecting to her sale of the game, stating that both the game name and the character itself are intellectual properties of the firm. The message insisted that she withdraw the product from auction.

Tracy's response to the company stated that her game cartridge—including the unique version of the powerful Goddess Diaphanes—was not the same product she purchased months previously but, instead, was entirely different because months of thoughtful game playing. Accordingly, she was selling her creation—a one-of-a-kind, new product.

Team Activity

Assemble a group of four students and assign each group member to one of the following roles:

- Tracy
- auction winner buying Tracy's version of the game
- manufacturer of the game
- investor or owner of the company that manufactures the game

ACTION STEPS

14-22. Before hearing any of your group's comments, and from the perspective of your assigned role, write down the ethical issues, if any, that you see in this situation.

14-23. Before hearing any of your group's comments, what actions do you think your assigned role should have taken in this situation? Write down your recommended actions.

14-24. Gather your group together and reveal, in turn, each member's comments and recommendations.

14-25. Appoint someone to record main points of agreement and disagreement within the group. How do you explain the results? What accounts for any disagreement?

14-26. From an ethical standpoint, what does your group recommend Tracy do?

cases

Online Pirates Feast on Economic Downturn

Continued from page 480

At the beginning of this chapter you read about illicit activities of IT pirates and their methods for preying on victims, including both organizations and individuals around the globe. You saw that pirating aims to steal money and other resources by luring vulnerable potential victims with seemingly attractive offers of personal gain. Using the information presented in this chapter you should now be able to answer the following questions.

QUESTIONS FOR DISCUSSION

14-27. Think about recent spam e-mails you've seen on PCs, and scam messages received via cell phone or smartphone. What kinds of information were the intruders seeking?

14-28. Continuing with the preceding question, were you able to identify the e-mails and messages to be "scams" before opening them, or was it later after they were opened that you discovered their real contents?

14-29. In what ways might the "opened" message from a scammer be harmful to you? To your IT devices and systems?

14-30. What steps can you take (or have you taken) to protect against such intrusions? What costs would be involved for gaining that protection?

14-31. Consider the various it systems you use daily. What kinds of protective devices do they have to protect against invasion by cyber pirates?

Information Technology for Better Health Care

Going wireless to monitor a heart patient at home, a child's condition in an emergency department, an accident victim in an ambulance, and a patient's critical condition in a hospital room took a giant step forward after the Federal Communications Commission (FCC) authorized the use of Medical Body Area Network (MBAN) devices. MBAN is a wireless data system that transmits patients' conditions continuously so that changes can be detected quickly, and more serious problems detected before they fully develop. Small, lightweight low-power sensors—much like Band-Aids in appearance—are attached to the patient's body to monitor vital signs that are transmitted over short distances to nearby "receiver devices" that, in turn, relay data over longer distances to nurse stations, physicians' offices, and other staff locations for real-time noninvasive continuous observation. The FCC, which controls the allocation and use of U.S. wireless frequencies, has established a unique wireless spectrum giving MBAN devices a protected transmission frequency. Accordingly, the wireless medical devices do not have to use Wi-Fi networks, with their risks of interference from the devices of many other Wi-Fi users. MBAN's uncontaminated transmissions provide more information faster, enabling better health care at lower cost, than is possible with onsite continuous observation by nurses, healthcare technicians, and physicians.

Although wireless monitoring is noninvasive, an emerging surgical technique uses snake robots (snake-bots) that slither through patients' bodies while assisting in surgeries on hearts, prostates, and other body organs. Surgeons at New York Presbyterian Hospital, Columbia University Medical Center, and Cornell University Medical center, among other facilities, have been using robots as tools for years in thousands of surgeries. Snake-bots armed with miniature cameras, forceps, sensors, and scissors enable surgeons to see more and do more than previously possible. Instead of opening the chest cavity for heart surgery, a small incision provides an entry for the tiny snake that crawls to the location in need of repair. The surgeon, as if shrunken and placed inside the patient's heart, controls the snake's movements and activities while repairing the heart valve. The snake's small size is less damaging to the patient, enabling faster recovery than traditional surgery. Developers believe that, as the snakes become much smaller, the snake technology will eventually make intricate surgeries faster and easier, thus reducing costs.

Snake-bots are but one example of a broader class of robotic-assisted surgery. The Da Vinci Surgical System, for example, became the first robotic system approved by the U.S. Food and Drug Administration for use in a variety of surgical applications including vaginal and hysterectomy repair, prostate cancer, and mitral valve (heart) repair. The Da Vinci System is used in more than 45,000 operations each year at more than 800 hospitals in Europe and the Americas. The system's three components are: (1) a 3D vision system, (2) a surgeon's work station that translates hand movements into movements of surgical instruments, and (3) a patient-side station with robotic arms controlled by the surgeon. The robotic station's surgical actions are totally under the surgeon's control. Most intriguing, perhaps, is the surgeon does not need to be at the patient's surgical platform, so long as assisting professionals are nearby. This makes it possible for a surgeon in New York to remotely perform mitral valve repair on a patient in Germany or elsewhere.[31]

QUESTIONS FOR DISCUSSION

14-32. In what ways are the IT developments for health care presented in this case changing the activities, services, and organizational practices of hospitals and clinics? Explain your responses and give examples.

14-33. In what ways are healthcare customers being affected by the IT developments presented in this case? Are all of these affects positive, or might some be negative? Explain your response.

14-34. How would you describe the type of information system required for a robotic surgical system? What are the components you would expect to find in such an IS?

14-35. Suppose you are in charge of security for a hospital using the IT systems discussed in this case. Identify the kinds of IT risks and threats that should be expected. Beyond your own ideas, be sure to indicate other sources you would consult to help identify the risks and threats.

14-36. What protection measures can be taken to reduce the risks of intrusions and threats for the hospital's IT systems (for the systems discussed in this case)? Describe how you would determine the costs for implementing those protection measures.

MyBizLab

Go to **pearsonglobaleditions.com/mybizlab** *for the following Assisted-graded writing questions:*

14-37. Organizations of every kind, including governments, not-for-profits, and businesses, have experienced dramatic changes from the implementation and growth of information technology. (a) Describe ways that businesses have been improved by implementing IT. (b) Discuss how employees' activities have been changed with IT. In your discussion use examples to show how the changes have been beneficial. Show also some ways that IT presents new problems for organizations.

14-38. Some of the risks with IT include intrusions and abuses by outsiders, and the damages that can result from those activities. Organizations are continuously seeking ways to protect against those risks. (a) Why do companies try to protect against those risks? (b) Choose four major kinds of IT risks and explain the dangers they pose. (c) Identify and describe protection measures for guarding IT systems against cyber abuses.

14-39. Mybizlab Only—comprehensive writing assignment for this chapter.

end notes

1 M. P. McQueen, "Cyber-Scams on the Uptick in Downturn," *The Wall Street Journal*, January 29, 2009, pp. D1, D4; Joseph De Avila, "Beware of Facebook 'Friends' Who May Trash Your Laptop," *The Wall Street Journal*, January 29, 2009, pp. D1, D4; Byron Acohido and Jon Swartz, "Data Scams Have Kicked into High Gear as Markets Tumble," *USAToday*, January 28, 2009, at http://www.usatoday.com/tech/news/computersecurity/2009-01-28-hackers-data-scams_N.htm; Chris Wragge, "FBI Warns of High-Tech Cyber ID Theft," *wcbstv.com*, April 8, 2009, at http://wcbstv.com/local/cyber.criminals.fbi.2.980245.html; Jordan Robertson, "Bad Economy Helps Web Scammers Recruit 'Mules'," *ABC News*, December 9, 2008, at http://abcnews.go.com/print?id=6422327.

2 "Hackers in China Blamed for Cyber-Attacks," *Columbia Daily Tribune*, February 10, 2011, p. 5B, and at http://www.columbiatribune.com/news/2011/feb/10/hackers-in-china-blamed-for-cyber-attacks/?news; Mary Ann Milbourn, "Beware of Fake Job Offers," *The Orange County Register*, October 12, 2010, at http://economy.ocregister.com/2010/10/12/beware-of-fake-job-offers/42194/; Richard Eppstein, "Scammers Pop Up During Economic Downturns," *Toledo Biz Insider*, March 4, 2010, at http://www.toledoblade.com/article/20100304/BUSINESS11/100309863/-1/BUSINESS; Matt Warman, "Viruses on Smart-Phones: Security's New Frontier," *The Telegraph*, February 8, 2011, at http://www.telegraph.co.uk/technology/news/8311214/Viruses-on-smartphones-securitys-new-frontier.html.

3 Phil Goldstein, "RIM Unveils BlackBerry Z10 and Q10, but Pushes U.S. Launch to March," *FierceWireless*, January 30, 2013, at http://fiercewireless.com/story/rim-unveils-blackberry-z10-and-q10-pushes-us-launch-march/2013-01-30.

4 Joanna Stern, "Google's Project Glass is Ready, but for Developers' Eyes Only," January 16, 2013, at http://abcnews.go.com/blogs/technology/2013/01/googles-glass-is-ready-but-for-developers-eyes-only/.

5 See http://www.siriusxm.com/navtraffic/.

6 "Appropriator Asks NASA to Help Boeing Fix Dreamliner Problems," January 13, 2013, at http://fattah.house.gov/latest-news/appropriator-asks-nasa-to-help-boeing-fix-dreamliner-problems/.

7 "Lockheed Martin Aeronautics: Siemens' PLM Software," *Siemens*, at http://www.plm.automation.siemans.com/en_us/about-us/success/case_s, accessed on June 16, 2009.

8 Laura Northrup, "Timbuk2 Really, Really Wants You to Be Happy with Their Bags," *The Consumerist*, June 5, 2009, at http://www.consumerist.com/2009/06/timbuk2-really-really-wants-you-to-be-happy-with-their-bags.html.

9 David LaGesse, "How to Turn Social Networking into a Job Offer," *U.S. News & World Report*, May 11, 2009, at http://www.usnews.com/money/careers/articles/2009/05/11/how-to-turn-social-networking-into-a-job-offer.html.

10 3D Systems, "3D Systems Helps Walter Reed Army Medical Center Rebuild Lives," at http://www.3dsystems.com/appsolutions/casestudies/walter_reed.asp, accessed on June 15, 2009; Hannah Hickey, "Camera in a Pill Offers Cheaper, Easier Window on Your Insides," UWNews.org (January 24, 2008), at http://uwnews.org/article.asp?articleid=39292.

11 See http://www.internetworldstats.com/stats.htm.

12 "BAN AMRO Mortgage Group Offers One Fee to Ford Motor Company Employees," *Mortgage Mag*, February 14, 2005, at http://www.mortgagemag.com/n/502_003.htm; "An Intranet's Life Cycle," *morebusiness.com* (June 16, 1999), at http://www.morebusiness.com/getting_started/website/d928247851.brc; Sally Ahmed, "Ford Motor Company—Case Study," *Ezine Articles*, August 18, 2008, at http://ezinearticles.com/?Ford-Motor-Company---Case-Study&id=1420478.

13 "Companies Take Sides on Super Wi-Fi," *Columbia Daily Tribune*, February 4, 2013, p. 6B.

14 Emily Bazar, "Bartering Booms During Economic Tough Times," *USA Today*, February 25, 2009, at http://usatoday.

com/tech/webguide/internetlife/2009-02-25-barter_N. htm; Debbie Lombardi, "Bartering Can Boost Your Budget and Business," at http://www.bbubarter.com/news. aspx?NewsID=18, accessed on October 27, 2008; Donna Wright, "Hard Times Create Boom of Local Bartering," *BradentonHerald.com*, March 8, 2009, at http://www.bra-denton.com/874/v-print/story/1277848.html; "The Advantages of Business Bartering," *U-Exchange.com*, at http://www.u-exchange.com/advantages-business-bartering, accessed on February 24, 2011; Bob Meyer, "In-depth Look at U.S. Trade Exchange Industry's Size," *BarterNews*, April 24, 2012, at www.barternews.com.

[15] "What Do Bartering Websites Do?" at http://www.peo-pletradingservices.com, accessed on June 8, 2009; "BarterQuest, the Online Bartering Website, Is Out of Beta," *BarterQuest* (press release), January 16, 2010, at http://www.prlog.org/10535364-barterquest-the-online-bartering-website-is-out-of-beta.html.

[16] "Kroger Tailors Ads to Its Customers," *Columbia Daily Tribune*, January 12, 2009, 7B; Josh Pichler, "dunnhumby: Retailer's Secret Weapon," *Cincinnati.com*, January 31, 2013, at news.cincinnati.com/article/20130130/BIZ/301190100/dunnhumby-Retailers-secret-weapon?nclick_check=1.

[17] Glen Brizius, "CereProc: An Example of a Technology Finally Fulfilling Its Potential," *Associated Content in Technology*, March 16, 2010, at http://www.associatedcontent.com/article/2786052/cereproc_an_example_of_a_technology.html?cat=5.

[18] http://www.cereproc.com/en/products.

[19] Alyson Sheppard, "Giving Roger Ebert a New Voice: Q&A With CereProc," *Popular Mechanics*, March 8, 2010, at http://www.popularmechanics.com/science/health/prosthetics/rogerebertvoicetech; Hayley Millar, "New Voice for Film Critic," *BBC News*, March 3, 2010, at http://news.bbc.co.uk/2/hi/uk_news/scotland/edin-burgh_and_east/8547645.stm.

[20] "Data Mining Examples & Testimonials," at http://www.data-mining-software.com/data_mining_examples.htm, accessed February 24, 2011; Julia Angwin and Jennifer Valentino-DeVries, "New Tracking Frontier: Your License Plates," *Wall Street Journal*, September 29–30, 2012, pp. A1, A13; Anton Troianovski, "New Wi-Fi Pitch: Tracker," *Wall Street Journal*, June 19, 2012, p. B5.

[21] Jo Marchant, "Virtual Fossils Reveal How Ancient Creatures Lived," *NewScientist*, May 27, 2009, at http://www.new-scientist.com/article/mg20227103.500-virtual-fossils-reveal-how-ancient-creatures-lived.html.

[22] Matt Warman, "Viruses on Smartphones: Security's New Frontier," *The Telegraph*, February 8, 2011, at http://www.telegraph.co.uk/technology/news/8311214/Viruses-on-smartphones-securitys-new-frontier.html; Jacqui Cheng, "Canadian Group: Facebook 'A Minefield of Privacy Invasion'" May 30, 2008, at http://arstechnica.com/tech-policy/news/2008/05/canadian-group-files-complaint-over-facebook-privacy.ars; "Cell Phones a Much Bigger Privacy Risk Than Facebook," *Fox News*, February 20, 2009, at http://www.foxnews.com/printer_friendly_story/0,3566,497544,00.html.

[23] Siobhan Gorman, Devlin Barrett, and Danny Yadron, "China Hackers Hit U.S. Media," *Wall Street Journal*, February 1, 2013, pp. B1, B2; "Hackers Hit Twitter, Washington Post," *Columbia Daily Tribune*, February 4, 2013, p. 6B.

[24] Alex Leary, "Wi-Fi Cloaks a New Breed of Intruder," *St. Petersburg Times*, July 4, 2005, at http://www.sptimes.com/2005/07/04/State/Wi_Fi_cloaks_a_new_br.shtml.

[25] Donald Melanson, "Apple: 16 Billion iTunes Songs Downloaded, 300 Million iPods Sold," *Engadget*, October 4, 2011, at www.engadget.com/2011/10/04/apple-16-billion-itunes-songs-downloaded-300-million-ipods-sol/; Christopher Burgess and Richard Power, "How to Avoid Intellectual Property Theft," *CIO*, July 10, 2006, at http://www.cio.com/article/22837; "For Students Doing Reports," *RIAA*, at www.riaa.com/faq.php, accessed on February 4, 2013; Ben Sisario, "AC/DC Joins iTunes, as Spotify Emerges as Music's New Disrupter," *New York Times*, November 19, 2012, at mediadecoder.blogs.nytimes.com/2012/11/19/acdc-joins-itunes-as-spotify-emerges-as-musics-new-disrupter/.

[26] See http://www.webopedia.com/TERM/S/spyware.html.

[27] Donald A. Norman, "Got Spam?" *MAPI: Manufacturers Alliance for Productivity and Innovation*, October 24, 2012, at http://www.mapi.net/blog/2012/10/got-spam.

[28] "'Spam King' Faces Federal Fraud Charges," *Columbia Daily Tribune*, January 21, 2013, accessed at http://www.columbiatribune.com/wire/spam-king-faces-federal-fraud-charges/article_042ac575-7820-5bb4-bb17-3e425f2f24c0.html#.URE7hPKmFcI.

[29] Brad Carlson, "Organizations Face New Records-Destruction Rule," *Idaho Business Review*, July 25, 2005, at http://www.idahobusiness.net/archive.htm/2005/07/25/Organizations-face-new-recordsdestruction-rule.

[30] Julian E. Barnes, "Pentagon Digs In on Cyberwar Front," *Wall Street Journal*, July 6, 2012, p. A4; James Temple, "In Waging Cyber War, Battlefield Becomes Blurred," *SFGate*, June 10, 2012, at http://www.sfgate.com/technology/dotcommentary/article/In-waging-cyber-war-battlefield-becomes-blurred-3622760.php; "Commercial Cyberspying Offers Rich Payoff," *Columbia Daily Tribune*, February 20, 2013, p. 6B.

[31] Kate Linebaugh, "Medical Devices in Hospitals to Go Wireless," *Wall Street Journal*, May 24, 2012, p. B8; "Tiny Snake Robots Aid Surgery," *Columbia Daily Tribune*, May 30, 2012, p. A2; John Sandham, " "Robotic Assisted Surgery," *EBME Electrical and Biomedical Engineering*, December 2008, at http://www.ebme.co.uk/arts/robotic, accessed on May 11, 2013; iMedicalApps Team and Robert D. Primosch, "FCC Opens New Chapter in Wireless Medical Devices," *iMedicalApps*, June 6, 2012, at http://www.imedicalapps.com/2012/06/fcc-opens-chapter-wireless-medical-devices/.

chapter 15 | The Role of Accountants and Accounting Information

Johnny Lye/Shutterstock

"Crunching numbers" is not enough for today's

accountants. They need to

communicate,

think critically, and lead.

AFTER READING THIS CHAPTER, YOU SHOULD BE ABLE TO:

OBJECTIVE 1 **Explain** the role of accountants and distinguish between the kinds of work done by public accountants, private accountants, management accountants, and forensic accountants.

OBJECTIVE 2 **Explain** how the accounting equation is used.

OBJECTIVE 3 **Describe** the three basic financial statements and show how they reflect the activity and financial condition of a business.

OBJECTIVE 4 **Explain** the key standards and principles for reporting financial statements.

OBJECTIVE 5 **Describe** how computing financial ratios can help users get more information from financial statements to determine the financial strengths of a business.

OBJECTIVE 6 **Discuss** the role of ethics in accounting.

OBJECTIVE 7 **Describe** the purpose of the International Accounting Standards Board and explain why it exists.

MyBizLab®

✪ Improve Your Grade!

Visit **pearsonglobaleditions.com/mybizlab** for simulations, tutorials, and end-of-chapter problems.

simulations

videos

assisted-graded

writing

Over 10 million students improved their results using the Pearson MyLabs.

Frenkel's
Forensics

John Frenkel qualified as an accountant in 1978, and he has always been interested in forensic accounting. He established his company in 2001 and since 2006 has focused almost exclusively on forensic accountancy services.

A forensic accountant uses a combination of legal, investigative, and accounting skills in order to analyze often complex financial data. The services offered by the company spread across personal injury claims, business valuations, commercial disputes, fraud and tax investigations, computer forensics, and data analysis.

Some of the investigations illustrate the bizarre nature in which some individuals attempt to carry out frauds. In one such case, a business that had suffered from the flooding of their factory was claiming $8 million from their insurers for business interruption. They had already received $880,000 on account. The forensic accounting report revealed that the actual loss was only $640,000.

Tax investigations are often complex, particularly when dealing with overseas entertainers or sports personalities that visit the UK. It is the responsibility of the company that is making the payments to the non-UK resident to deduct tax and make payments to HM Revenue and Customs. The amount of tax that needs to be deducted is incredibly complex. In one case, the promoter of a U.S. rock band would have been required to have withheld $64,000 from a total of $320,000 that would have been payable to the band. This would represent twenty percent taxable income payable to revenue and customs. This did not take into account any other costs that the band would incur as a result of their tour. As a result, after forensic accounting, the tax liability was reduced to $45,000. In a similar case, an overseas Formula 1 driver who visited the UK to compete in the British Grand Prix was due to be paid $400,000 plus bonuses and image rights. Forensic accounting meant that HM Revenue and Customs were willing to reduce the tax demand of $160,000 (some 40 percent) to 6.9 percent or $27,500. Accounting scandals have seemed to peak during the difficult economic period, perhaps as a result of heavier financial pressures. This has meant a boom time for specialist forensic accountants, who are there to help prevent and detect attempts to cheat the system.

If income tax investigations are complex, then the question of frauds in value added tax in the UK is even more baffling. Value added tax is levied by the government on transactions carried out by businesses. The system effectively requires the company to collect VAT on the government's behalf from payments received from customers, set against VAT actually paid

what's in it for me?

For most of us, the words and ideas in accounting can seem like a foreign language, and the specialized terminology can be used to mask fraud and corruption. However, accounting terminology is a necessary tool that allows professionals in every industry to analyze growth, understand risk, and communicate detailed ideas about a firm's financial health. This chapter will cover the fundamental concepts of accounting and apply them to familiar business situations. By grasping the basic accounting vocabulary you—as an employee, taxpayer, or owner—will be able to participate when the conversation turns to the financial matters that constitute so great a part of a firm's daily operations.

by the company when they purchase products or services. The balance is then due to HM Revenue and Customs.

In one particular case, Frenkel investigated what is known as a carousel fraud. In effect, a series of parallel companies are set up, where the same goods are passed between them and the VAT paid is being reclaimed by each of the companies, but no VAT is being paid to HM Revenue and Customs. In this particular case, HM Revenue and Customs were trying to recover $24 million from a senior member of staff for one of the companies. The forensic accounting process involved looking at accounts going back six years. As a result of the findings, huge errors were uncovered, and the client's actual liabilities were $480,000.

In the UK, the Fraud Advisory Panel, a registered charity and a membership-based organization, was established in 1998 by an initiative launched by the Institute of Chartered Accountants in England and Wales. The panel has estimated that fraud in the UK currently costs $1,224 for every adult. In the first six months of 2011, $1.76 billion of fraud cases appeared in British courts. This was up by $974 million over the same period in 2010. Insurance fraud alone in the UK is estimated to have topped $3.19 billion per year. In effect, this adds $70 to each and every householder's annual insurance bill. It has also been estimated that some 2,500 fraudulent insurance claims were made every week in the UK in 2010.

According to PricewaterhouseCooper's Global Economic Crime Survey, published in November 2009, almost half of all UK businesses reported a fraud in the last twelve months. Accounting frauds and misappropriation were the most common. This means that, with fraud being so prevalent, the one guaranteed growth area in business will be forensic accounting.[1]

What Is Accounting, and Who Uses Accounting Information?

OBJECTIVE 1
Explain
the role of accountants and distinguish between the kinds of work done by public accountants, private accountants, management accountants, and forensic accountants.

Accounting (or accountancy)
comprehensive system for collecting, analyzing, and communicating financial information

Bookkeeping *recording of accounting transactions*

Accounting Information System (AIS) *organized procedure for identifying, measuring, recording, and retaining financial information for use in accounting statements and management reports*

Accounting (or accountancy) is a comprehensive system for collecting, analyzing, and communicating financial information to a firm's owners and employees, to the public, and to various regulatory agencies. To perform these functions, accountants keep records of taxes paid, income received, and expenses incurred, a process called **bookkeeping**, and they assess the effects of these transactions on business activities. By sorting and analyzing such transactions, accountants can determine how well a business is being managed and how financially strong it is.

Because businesses engage in thousands of transactions, ensuring consistent, dependable financial information is mandatory. This is the job of the **accounting information system (AIS)**, an organized procedure for identifying, measuring, recording, and retaining financial information so that it can be used in accounting statements and management reports. The system includes all of the people, reports, computers, procedures, and resources that are needed to compile financial transactions.[2]

Users of accounting information are numerous:

- *Business managers* use it to develop goals and plans, set budgets, and evaluate future prospects.

- *Employees and unions* use it to plan for and receive compensation and such benefits as health care, vacation time, and retirement pay.

- *Investors and creditors* use it to estimate returns to stockholders, determine growth prospects, and decide whether a firm is a good credit risk.

- *Tax authorities* use it to plan for tax inflows, determine the tax liabilities of individuals and businesses, and ensure that correct amounts are paid on time.

- *Government regulatory agencies* rely on it to fulfill their duties toward the public. The Securities and Exchange Commission (SEC), for example, requires firms to file financial disclosures so that potential investors have valid information about their financial status.

Who Are Accountants and What Do They Do?

The **controller**, or chief accounting officer, manages a firm's accounting activities by ensuring that the AIS provides the reports and statements needed for planning, decision making, and other management activities. This range of activities requires different types of accounting specialists. In this section, we begin by distinguishing between the two main fields of accounting: *financial* and *managerial*. Then, we discuss the different functions and activities of *certified public accountants*, *private accountants*, *management accountants*, and *forensic accountants*.

Controller *person who manages all of a firm's accounting activities (chief accounting officer)*

Financial versus Managerial Accounting

In any company, the two fields of accounting—financial and managerial—can be distinguished by the users they serve: those outside the company and those within.[3]

Financial Accounting A firm's **financial accounting** system is concerned with external information users: consumer groups, unions, stockholders, suppliers, creditors, and government agencies. It prepares reports such as income statements and balance sheets that focus on the activities of the company as a whole rather than on individual departments or divisions.[4]

Financial Accounting *field of accounting concerned with external users of a company's financial information*

Managerial Accounting **Managerial (management) accounting** serves internal users. Managers at all levels need information to make departmental decisions, monitor projects, and plan future activities. Other employees also need accounting information. Engineers must know certain costs, for example, before making product or operations improvements, purchasing agents use information on materials costs to negotiate terms with suppliers, and to set performance goals, salespeople need past sales data for each geographic region and for each of its products.

Managerial (Management) Accounting *field of accounting that serves internal users of a company's financial information*

Certified Public Accountants

Public accountants offer accounting services to the public and are distinguished by their independence from the clients they serve. That is to say, they typically work for an accounting firm providing services for outside client firms in which the public accountant has no vested interest, thus avoiding any potential biases in conducting their professional services. Among public accountants, **certified public accountants (CPAs)** are licensed by a state after passing an exam prepared by the American Institute of Certified Public Accountants (AICPA). Preparation for certification begins with majoring in a college program studying the theory, practices, and legal aspects of accounting. In addition to the CPA exam, certification in most states requires some practice, varying up to two years, in a private company or government entity under the direction of a CPA. Once certified, the CPA can perform services beyond those allowed by non-CPAs.[5] Whereas some CPAs work as individual practitioners, many form or join existing partnerships or professional corporations.

Certified Public Accountant (CPA) *accountant licensed by the state and offering services to the public*

Sometimes, companies ignore GAAP and accountants fail to disclose violations. Richard Causey (right) was Chief Account Executive at now-bankrupt Enron, and was responsible for the firm's public accounting statements. Pleading guilty to securities fraud, he was sentenced to seven years in prison and forfeited $1.25 million.

Ron Sachs/Newscom

The "Big Four" Public Accounting Firms

Although thousands of CPA companies of various sizes, ranging from small local operations to large multinationals, are active in the United States, about one-half of their total revenues go to the four biggest CPA firms (listed with their headquarters):

Deloitte Touche Tohmatsu (U.S.)

Ernst & Young (United Kingdom)

PricewaterhouseCoopers, PwC (United Kingdom)

KPMG (Netherlands)

In addition to prominence in the United States, international operations are important for all four of these companies. They have experienced especially rapid growth in recent years for CPA services in Asia and Latin America. Each of the Big Four firms has more than 150,000 employees worldwide[6]

CPA Services

Virtually all CPA firms, whether large or small, provide auditing, tax, and management services. Larger firms such as Deloitte Touche Tohmatsu and Ernst & Young earn much of their revenue from auditing services, though consulting (management advisory) services constitute a major growth area. Smaller firms earn most of their income from tax and management services.

Audit *systematic examination of a company's accounting system to determine whether its financial reports reliably represent its operations*

Generally Accepted Accounting Principles (GAAP) *accounting guidelines that govern the content and form of financial reports*

AUDITING

An **audit** examines a company's AIS to determine whether financial reports reliably represent its operations.[7] Organizations must provide audit reports when applying for loans, selling stock, or when going through a major restructuring. Independent auditors who do not work for the company must ensure that clients' accounting systems follow **generally accepted accounting principles (GAAP)**, which are formulated by the Financial Accounting Standards Board (FASB) of the AICPA and govern the content and form of financial reports.[8] The auditing of a firm's financial statements is one of the services that can be performed only by a CPA. The SEC is the U.S. government agency that legally enforces accounting and auditing rules and procedures. Ultimately, the CPA performing the audit will certify whether the client's reports comply with GAAP.

TAX SERVICES **Tax services** include assistance not only with tax-return preparation but also with tax planning. A CPA's advice can help a business structure (or restructure) operations and investments and perhaps save millions of dollars in taxes. Staying abreast of tax-law changes is no simple matter. Some critics charge that the changing of tax regulations has become a full-time vocation among some state and federal legislators who add increasingly complicated laws and technical corrections on taxation each year.

Tax Services *assistance provided by CPAs for tax preparation and tax planning*

MANAGEMENT ADVISORY SERVICES As consultants, accounting firms provide **management advisory services** ranging from personal financial planning to planning corporate mergers. Other services include production scheduling, information systems studies, AIS design, and even executive recruitment. The staffs of the largest CPA firms sometimes include engineers, architects, mathematicians, and psychologists, all of whom are available for consulting.

Management Advisory Services *assistance provided by CPA firms in areas such as financial planning, information systems design, and other areas of concern for client firms*

Noncertified Public Accountants Many accountants don't take the CPA exam; others work in the field while getting ready for it or while meeting requirements for state certification. Many small businesses, individuals, and even larger firms rely on these non-CPAs for income-tax preparation, payroll accounting, and financial-planning services so long as they abide by local and state laws. Non-CPAs often put together financial statements that are used in the firm for internal purposes, based on information provided by management. These statements may include a notification that auditing methods were not used in their preparation.

The CPA Vision Project The continuing talent shortage in accounting, spanning years 2006–2012, has led the profession to rethink its culture and life-style.[9] With grassroots participation from CPAs, educators, and industry leaders, the AICPA, through its CPA Vision Project, is redefining the role of the accountant for today's world economy. The Vision Project identifies a unique combination of skills, technology, and knowledge, called **core competencies for accounting**, that will be necessary for the future CPA. The AICPA summarizes the project's core purpose as follows: "CPAs…Making sense of a changing and complex world."[10] As Table 15.1 shows, those skills, which include communication, critical thinking, and leadership, go far beyond the ability to "crunch numbers." They include certain communications skills, along with skills in critical thinking and leadership. Indeed,

Core Competencies For Accounting *the combination of skills, technology, and knowledge that will be necessary for the future CPA*

table 15.1 Emerging Competencies for Success in Accounting

Skills in Strategic Thinking and Critical Problem Solving	The accountant can combine data with reasoning and professional knowledge to recognize and help solve critical problems for better strategic action.
Communications, Interpersonal Skills, and Effective Leadership	The accountant can communicate effectively in various business situations using meaningful communications skills that provide interpersonal effectiveness and leadership.
Dedication to Meeting Customer Needs	The accountant surpasses the competition in understanding each client's unique needs, in meeting those needs, and in visualizing the client's future needs.
Ability to Integrate Diverse Information	The accountant can combine financial and other kinds of information to gain new meaning that provides clients with useful insights and understanding for solving problems.
Proficiency with Information Technology	The accountant can use information technology (IT) in performing services for clients and can identify IT applications that the client can adopt for added value to the business.

Source: Based on "The CPA Vision Project and Beyond," *The American Institute of Certified Public Accountants,* at http://www.aicpa.org/RESEARCH/CPAHORIZONS2025/CPAVISIONPROJECT/Pages/CPAVisionProject.aspx, accessed on February 11, 2013.

the CPA Vision Project foresees CPAs who combine specialty skills with a broad-based orientation to communicate more effectively with people in a wide range of business activities.

Private Accountants and Management Accountants

Private Accountant *salaried accountant hired by a business to carry out its day-to-day financial activities*

To ensure integrity in reporting, CPAs are always independent of the firms they audit. However, many businesses also hire their own salaried employees, **private accountants**, to perform day-to-day activities.

Private accountants perform numerous jobs. An internal auditor at ConocoPhillips, for example, might fly to the North Sea to confirm the accuracy of oil-flow meters on offshore petroleum drilling platforms. A supervisor responsible for $2 billion in monthly payouts to vendors and employees may never leave the executive suite, with duties such as hiring and training, assigning projects, and evaluating performance of accounting personnel. Large businesses employ specialized accountants in such areas as budgeting, financial planning, internal auditing, payroll, and taxation. In small businesses, a single person may handle all accounting tasks.

Management Accountant *private accountant who provides financial services to support managers in various business activities within a firm*

Certified Management Accountant (CMA) *professional designation awarded by the Institute of Management Accountants (IMA) in recognition of management accounting qualifications*

Although private accountants may be either CPAs or non-CPAs, most are **management accountants** who provide services to support managers in various activities (marketing, production, engineering, and so forth). Many hold the **certified management accountant (CMA)** designation, awarded by the Institute of Management Accountants (IMA), recognizing qualifications of professionals who have passed IMA's experience and examination requirements. With more than 65,000 worldwide members, IMA is dedicated to supporting accounting professionals to create quality internal controls and financial practices in their companies.

Forensic Accountants

Forensic Accounting *the practice of accounting for legal purposes*

One of the fastest-growing areas in accounting is **forensic accounting**, the use of accounting for legal purposes.[11] Sometimes known as "the private eyes of the corporate culture," forensic accountants must be good detectives. They look behind the corporate façade instead of accepting financial records at face value. In combining investigative skills with accounting, auditing, and the instincts of a bloodhound, they assist in the investigation of business and financial issues that may have application to a court of law. Forensic accountants may be called on by law enforcement agencies, insurance companies, law firms, private individuals, and business firms for both investigative accounting and litigation support in crimes against companies, crimes by companies, and civil disagreements. They may conduct criminal investigations of Internet scams and misuse of government funds. Civil cases often require investigating and quantifying claims of personal injury loss as a result of negligence and analyzing financial issues in matrimonial disputes. Forensic accountants also assist business firms in tracing and recovering lost assets from employee business fraud or theft.

Investigative Accounting Law enforcement officials may ask a forensic accountant to investigate a trail of financial transactions behind a suspected crime, as in a money-laundering scheme or an investment swindle. The forensic accountant, being familiar with the legal concepts and procedures of the case, would then identify and analyze pertinent financial evidence—documents, bank accounts, phone calls, computer records, and people—and present accounting conclusions and their legal implications. They also develop reports, exhibits, and documents to communicate their findings.

Litigation Support Forensic accountants assist in the application of accounting evidence for judicial proceedings by preparing and preserving evidence for these proceedings. They also assist by presenting visual aids to support trial evidence, by testifying as expert witnesses, and, especially, in determining economic damages in any case before the court. A divorce attorney, for example, may suspect that assets are being understated and request financial analysis by a forensic accountant. A movie producer may need help in determining damages for breach of contract by an actress who quits before the film is completed.

CERTIFIED FRAUD EXAMINERS One specific area within forensic accounting, the **Certified Fraud Examiner (CFE)** designation, is administered by the ACFE. The CFE's activities focus specifically on fraud-related issues, such as fraud detection, evaluating accounting systems for weaknesses and fraud risks, investigating white-collar crime on behalf of law enforcement agencies, evaluating internal organizational controls for fraud prevention, and expert witnessing. Many CFEs, like Al Vondra from our opening story, find employment in corporations seeking to prevent fraud from within. The CFE examination covers four areas:

Certified Fraud Examiner (CFE) *professional designation administered by the ACFE in recognition of qualifications for a specialty area within forensic accounting*

1 *Fraud prevention and deterrence* Includes why people commit fraud, theories of fraud prevention, and professional code of ethics

2 *Financial transactions* Examines types of fraudulent financial transactions incurred in accounting records

3 *Fraud investigation* Pertains to tracing illicit transactions, evaluating deception, and interviewing and taking statements

4 *Legal elements of fraud* Includes rules of evidence, criminal and civil law, and rights of the accused and accuser

Eligibility to take the exam includes both educational and experience requirements. Although a minimum of a bachelor's degree is required, it does not have to be in accounting or any other specific field of study. Candidates without a bachelor's degree, but with fraud-related professional experience, may substitute two years of experience for each year of academic study. Experience requirements for certification include at least two years in any of several fraud-related areas, such as auditing, criminology, fraud investigation, or law.

Federal Restrictions on CPA Services and Financial Reporting: Sarbox

The financial wrongdoings associated with firms such as ImClone Systems, Tyco, WorldCom, Enron, Arthur Andersen, and others have not gone unnoticed in legislative circles. Federal regulations, in particular the **Sarbanes-Oxley Act of 2002 (Sarbox or SOX)**, have been enacted to restore and maintain public trust in corporate accounting practices.

Sarbanes-Oxley Act Of 2002 (Sarbox Or Sox) *enactment of federal regulations to restore public trust in accounting practices by imposing new requirements on financial activities in publicly traded corporations*

Sarbox restricts the kinds of nonaudit services that CPAs can provide. Under the Sarbox law, for example, a CPA firm can help design a client's financial information system, but not if it also does the client's auditing. Hypothetically, an unscrupulous accounting firm's audit might intentionally overlook a client's false financial statements if, in return, the client rewards the accounting firm with a contract for lucrative nonaccounting services, such as management consulting. This was a core allegation in the Enron-Arthur Andersen scandal. Author Andersen, one of the world's largest accounting firms, filed audits that failed to disclose Enron's shaky financial condition that eventually led to the massive energy company's bankruptcy and to Anderson's dissolution. Andersen's auditor gained more money from consulting at Enron than it got for auditing.[12] By prohibiting auditing and nonauditing services to the same client, Sarbox encourages audits that are independent and unbiased.

Sarbox imposes new requirements on virtually every financial activity in publicly traded corporations, as well as severe criminal penalties for persons committing or concealing fraud or destroying financial records. CFOs and CEOs, for example, have to pledge that the company's finances are correct and must vouch for the methods and internal controls used to get those numbers. Companies have to provide a

table 15.2 Selected Provisions of the Sarbanes-Oxley Act[13]

- Creates a national Accounting Oversight Board that, among other activities, must establish the ethics standards used by CPA firms in preparing audits.
- Requires that auditors retain audit working papers for specified periods of time.
- Requires auditor rotation by prohibiting the same person from being the lead auditor for more than 5 consecutive years.
- Requires that the CEO and CFO certify that the company's financial statements are true, fair, and accurate.
- Prohibits corporations from extending personal loans to executives and directors.
- Requires that the audited company disclose whether it has adopted a code of ethics for its senior financial officers.
- Requires that the SEC regularly review each corporation's financial statements.
- Prevents employers from retaliating against research analysts who write negative reports.
- Imposes criminal penalties on auditors and clients for falsifying, destroying, altering, or concealing records (10 years in prison).
- Imposes a fine or imprisonment (up to 25 years) on any person who defrauds shareholders.
- Increases penalties for mail and wire fraud from 5 to 20 years in prison.
- Establishes criminal liability for failure of corporate officers to certify financial reports.

Source: Multi-Source

system that is safe for all employees to anonymously report unethical accounting practices and illegal activities without fear of retaliation. Table 15.2 provides brief descriptions of several of Sarbox's many provisions.

OBJECTIVE 2

Explain

how the accounting equation is used.

Accounting Equation *Assets = Liabilities + Owners' Equity; used by accountants to balance data for the firm's financial transactions at various points in the year*

The Accounting Equation

All accountants rely on record keeping to enter and track transactions. Underlying all record-keeping procedures is the most basic tool of accounting, the **accounting equation**:

$$\text{Assets} = \text{Liabilities} + \text{Owners' Equity}$$

After each financial transaction (e.g., payments to suppliers, sales to customers, wages to employees), the accounting equation must be in balance. If it isn't, then an accounting error has occurred. To better understand the importance of this equation, we must understand the terms *assets*, *liabilities*, and *owners' equity*.

The inventory at this auto dealership is among the company's assets: The cars constitute an economic resource because the firm will benefit financially as it sells them.

Alex Segre/Alamy

Assets and Liabilities

An **asset** is any economic resource that is expected to benefit a firm or an individual who owns it. Assets for accounting purposes include land, buildings, equipment, inventories, and payments due the company (accounts receivable). Google, the Internet search and information provider, for example, held assets amounting to $93.798 billion at year end 2012.[14]

A **liability** is a debt that a firm owes to an outside party. The total of Google's liabilities—all the debt owed to others—was $22.083 billion at the end of 2012.

Asset *any economic resource expected to benefit a firm or an individual who owns it*

Liability *debt owed by a firm to an outside organization or individual*

Owners' Equity

You may have heard of the *equity* that a homeowner has in a house, the amount of money that could be made (or lost) by selling the house and paying off the mortgage. Similarly, **owners' equity** is the amount of money that owners would receive if they sold all of a company's assets and paid all of its liabilities. Google's financial reports for 2012 declared shareholders' equity of $71.715 billion. For the Google example, we see that the accounting equation is in balance, as it should be.

Owners' equity *amount of money that owners would receive if they sold all of a firm's assets and paid all of its liabilities*

$$\text{Assets} = \text{Liabilities} + \text{Owners' Equity}$$
$$\$93.798 = \$22.083 + \$71.715 \text{ billion}$$

We can rewrite the equation to highlight how owners' equity relates to assets and liabilities.

$$\text{Assets} - \text{Liabilities} = \text{Owners' Equity}$$

Another term for this is *net worth*: the difference between what a firm owns (assets) minus what it owes (liabilities) is its net worth, or owners' equity. If a company's assets exceed its liabilities, owners' equity is *positive*. At Google, owners' equity is $71.715 billion (= $93.798 − $22.083). If the company goes out of business, the owners will receive some cash (a gain) after selling assets and paying off liabilities. If liabilities outweigh assets, owners' equity is *negative*; assets are insufficient to pay off all debts, and the firm is bankrupt. If the company goes out of business, the owners will get no cash, and some creditors won't be paid.

Owners' equity is meaningful for both investors and lenders. Before lending money to owners, for example, lenders want to know the amount of owners' equity in a business. A larger owners' equity indicates greater security for lenders. Owners' equity consists of two sources of capital:

1 The amount that the owners originally invested

2 Profits (also owned by the owners) earned by and reinvested in the company

When a company operates profitably, its assets increase faster than its liabilities. Owners' equity, therefore, will increase if profits are retained in the business instead of paid out as dividends to stockholders. Owners' equity also increases if owners invest more of their own money to increase assets. However, owners' equity can shrink if the company operates at a loss or if owners withdraw assets.

Financial Statements

As noted previously, accountants summarize the results of a firm's transactions and issue reports to help managers make informed decisions. Among the most important reports are **financial statements**, which fall into three broad categories: *balance sheets, income statements,* and *statements of cash flows.* Together, these reports indicate the firm's financial health and what affected it. In this section, we discuss these three financial statements as well as the function of the budget as an internal financial statement.

OBJECTIVE 3
Describe
the three basic financial statements and show how they reflect the activity and financial condition of a business.

Financial Statement *any of several types of reports summarizing a company's financial status to stakeholders and to aid in managerial decision making*

Balance Sheets

Balance Sheet *financial statement that supplies detailed information about a firm's assets, liabilities, and owners' equity*

Balance sheets supply detailed information about the accounting equation items: *assets, liabilities,* and *owners' equity.* Because they also show a firm's financial condition at one point in time, they are sometimes called *statements of financial position.* Figure 15.1 is a simplified presentation of the balance sheet for Google, Inc.

Assets From an accounting standpoint, most companies have three types of assets: *current, fixed,* and *intangible.*

Current Asset *asset that can or will be converted into cash within a year*

Liquidity *ease with which an asset can be converted into cash*

CURRENT ASSETS **Current assets** include cash and assets that can be converted into cash within a year. The act of converting something into cash is called *liquidating.* Assets are normally listed in order of **liquidity**, the ease of converting them into cash. Debts, for example, are usually paid in cash. A company that needs but cannot generate cash—a company that's not "liquid"—may be forced to sell assets at reduced prices or even to go out of business.

By definition, cash is completely liquid. *Marketable securities* purchased as short-term investments are slightly less liquid but can be sold quickly. These include stocks or bonds of other companies, government securities, and money market certificates. Many companies hold other nonliquid assets such as *merchandise inventory,* the cost of merchandise that's been acquired for sale to customers and is still on hand. Google has no merchandise inventory because it sells services rather than physical goods.

Fixed Asset *asset with long-term use or value, such as land, buildings, and equipment*

Depreciation *accounting method for distributing the cost of an asset over its useful life*

FIXED ASSETS **Fixed assets** (such as land, buildings, and equipment) have long-term use or value, but as buildings and equipment wear out or become obsolete, their value decreases. Accountants use **depreciation** to spread the cost of an asset over the years of its useful life. To reflect decreasing value, accountants calculate an asset's useful life in years, divide its worth by that many years, and subtract the resulting amount each year. Every year, therefore, the remaining value (or net value) decreases on the books. In Figure 15.1, Google shows fixed assets of $15.334 billion after depreciation.

Google, Inc.
Summary of Balance Sheet (condensed)
as of December 31, 2012
(in millions)

Assets		Liabilities and Shareholders' Equity	
Current assets:		Current liabilities:	
Cash	$14,778	Accounts payable	$10,893
Marketable securities	33,310	Other	3,444
Other	12,366	**Total current liabilities**	**$14,337**
Total current assets	**$60,454**		
		Long-term liabilities:	
Fixed assets:		All long-term debts	$2,988
Property and equipment, net	$11,854	Other	4,758
Other	3,480	**Total long-term liabilities**	**$7,746**
Total fixed assets	**$15,334**		
		Total liabilities	**$22,083**
Intangible assets:			
Intangible assets	$7,473	Shareholders' equity:	
Goodwill	10,537	Paid-in capital	$23,373
Total intangible assets	**$18,010**	Retained earnings	48,342
		Total shareholders' equity	**$71,715**
Total assets	**$93,798**	**Total liabilities and shareholders' equity**	**$93,798**

Google's balance sheet for year ended December 31, 2012. The balance sheet shows clearly that the firm's total assets are equal to its total liabilities and owners' equity.

FIGURE 15.1 Google's Balance Sheet
Source: Modified from "Google Inc. Consolidated Balance Sheets," *United States Securities Exchange Commission,* at http://www.sec.gov/Archives/edgar/data/1288776/000119312513028362/d452134d10k.htm#tx452134_23, accessed on February 9, 2013.

INTANGIBLE ASSETS Although their worth is hard to set, **intangible assets** have monetary value in the form of expected benefits, which may include fees paid by others for obtaining rights or privileges—including patents, trademarks, copyrights, and franchises—to your products. **Goodwill** is the amount paid for an existing business beyond the value of its other assets. A purchased firm, for example, may have a particularly good reputation or location. Google declares both intangible assets and goodwill in its balance sheet.

Intangible Asset *nonphysical asset, such as a patent or trademark, that has economic value in the form of expected benefit*

Goodwill *amount paid for an existing business above the value of its other assets*

Liabilities   Like assets, liabilities are often separated into different categories. **Current liabilities** are debts that must be paid within one year. These include **accounts payable (payables)**, unpaid bills to suppliers for materials as well as wages and taxes that must be paid in the coming year. Google has current liabilities of $14.337 billion. **Long-term liabilities** are debts that are not due for at least a year. These normally represent borrowed funds on which the company must pay interest. The long-term liabilities of Google are $7.746 billion.

Current Liability *debt that must be paid within one year*

Accounts Payable (Payables) *current liability consisting of bills owed to suppliers, plus wages and taxes due within the coming year*

Long-Term Liability *debt that is not due for at least one year*

Owners' Equity   The final section of the balance sheet in Figure 15.1 shows owners' equity (shareholders' equity) broken down into *paid-in capital* and *retained earnings*. When Google was first formed, it sold a small amount of common stock that provided its first *paid-in capital*. **Paid-in capital** is money invested by owners. Google's paid-in capital had grown to $23.373 billion by year end 2012, and includes proceeds from Google's initial public offering of stock in 2004 that created additional funds that were needed for expansion.

Paid-In Capital *money that is invested in a company by its owners*

Retained earnings are net profits kept by a firm rather than paid out as dividend payments to stockholders. They accumulate when profits, which can be distributed to shareholders, are kept instead for the company's use. At the close of 2012, Google had retained earnings of $48.342 billion. The total of stockholders' equity—paid-in capital plus retained earnings—had grown to $71.715 billion.

Retained Earnings *earnings retained by a firm for its use rather than paid out as dividends*

The balance sheet for any company, then, is a barometer for its financial condition at one point in time. By comparing the current balance sheet with those of previous years, creditors and owners can better interpret the firm's financial progress and future prospects in terms of changes in its assets, liabilities, and owners' equity.

Income Statements

The **income statement** is sometimes called a **profit-and-loss statement** because its description of revenues and expenses results in a figure showing the firm's annual profit or loss. In other words,

Income Statement (Profit-and-Loss Statement) *financial statement listing a firm's annual revenues and expenses so that a bottom line shows annual profit or loss*

$$\text{Profit (or Loss)} = \text{Revenues} - \text{Expenses}$$

Popularly known as the *bottom line*, profit or loss is probably the most important figure in any business enterprise. Figure 15.2 shows the 2012 income statement for Google, whose bottom line was $10.737 billion. The income statement is divided into four major categories: (1) *revenues*, (2) *cost of revenues*, (3) *operating expenses*, and (4) *net income*. Unlike a balance sheet, which shows the financial condition at a specific *point in time*, an income statement shows the financial results that occurred during a *period of time*, such as a month, quarter, or year.

Revenues   When a law firm receives $250 for preparing a will or a supermarket collects $65 from a grocery shopper, both are receiving **revenues**, the funds that flow into a business from the sale of goods or services. In 2012, Google reported revenues of $50.175 (rounded) billion from the sale of advertising and Web-search services to Google Network members, such as AOL.

Revenues *funds that flow into a business from the sale of goods or services*

Cost of Revenues (Cost of Goods Sold)   In the Google income statement, the **cost of revenues** section shows the costs of obtaining the revenues from other companies during the year. These are fees Google must pay its network

Cost of Revenues *costs that a company incurs to obtain revenues from other companies*

Google, Inc.
Summary of Income Statement (condensed)
as of December 31, 2012
(in millions)

Revenues (gross sales)		**$50,175**
Cost of revenues	20,634	
Gross profit		**$29,541**
Operating expenses:		
Research Development	6,793	
Selling, Administrative and General	9,988	
Total operating expenses		**$16,781**
Operating income (before taxes)		12,760
Income taxes*		2,023
Net income		**$10,737**

*approximated

Google's income statement for year ended December 31, 2012. The final entry on the income statement, the bottom line, reports the firm's profit or loss.

FIGURE 15.2 Google's Income Statement
Source: Modified from "Google Inc. Consolidated Statements of Income," *U.S. Securities Exchange Commission*, at http://www.sec.gov/Archives/edgar/data/1288776/000119312513028362/d452134d10k.htm#tx452134_23, accessed on February 9, 2013.

members—revenue sharing from advertising income—and also include expenses arising from the operation of Google's data centers, including labor, energy, and costs of processing customer transactions. The cost of revenues for Google in 2012 was $20.634 billion.

Although cost of revenues is a relevant income statement category for service providers such as Google, goods producers do not use it. Instead, income statements for manufacturing firms such as Procter & Gamble use the corresponding category, **cost of goods sold**, which are the costs of obtaining materials to make physical products sold during the year.

Cost of Goods Sold *costs of obtaining materials for making the products sold by a firm during the year*

GROSS PROFIT Managers are often interested in **gross profit**, a preliminary, quick-to-calculate profit figure that considers just two pieces of data—revenues and cost of revenues (the direct costs of getting those revenues)—from the income statement. To calculate gross profit, subtract cost of revenues from revenues obtained by selling the firm's products.

Gross Profit *preliminary, quick-to-calculate profit figure calculated from the firm's revenues minus its cost of revenues (the direct costs of getting the revenues)*

OPERATING EXPENSES In addition to costs directly related to generating revenues, every company has general expenses ranging from erasers to the CEO's salary. Like cost of revenues and cost of goods sold, **operating expenses** are resources that must flow out of a company if it is to earn revenues. As shown in Figure 15.2, Google had operating expenses of $16.781 billion.

Research development expenses result from exploring new services and technologies for providing them to customers. *Selling expenses* result from activities related to selling goods or services, such as sales-force salaries and advertising expenses. *Administrative and general expenses*, such as management salaries and maintenance costs, are related to the general management of the company.

Operating Expenses *costs, other than the cost of revenues, incurred in producing a good or service*

Operating and Net Income Operating income compares the gross profit from operations against operating expenses. This calculation for Google ($29.541 billion − $16.781 billion) reveals an operating income, or income before taxes, of $12.760 billion. Subtracting income taxes from operating income ($12.760 billion − $2.023 billion) reveals **net income** (**net profit** or **net earnings**). Google's net income for the year was $10.737 billion.

Operating Income *gross profit minus operating expenses*

Net Income (Net Profit or Net Earnings) *gross profit minus operating expenses and income taxes*

The step-by-step information in an income statement shows how a company obtained its net income for the period, making it easier for shareholders and other stakeholders to evaluate the firm's financial health.

Statements of Cash Flows

Some companies prepare only balance sheets and income statements. However, the SEC requires all firms whose stock is publicly traded to issue a third report, the **statement of cash flows**, which describes yearly cash receipts and cash payments. Because it provides the most detail about how the company generates and uses cash, some investors and creditors consider it one of the most important statements of all. It shows the effects on cash of three aspects of a business: *operating activities, investing activities,* and *financing activities.* Google's (simplified) 2012 statement of cash flows is reproduced in Figure 15.3.

Statement of Cash Flows *financial statement describing a firm's yearly cash receipts and cash payments*

- **Cash Flows from Operations.** This first section of the statement concerns main operating activities: cash transactions involved in buying and selling goods and services. For the Google example, it reveals how much of the year's cash balance results from the firm's main line of business, sales of advertising and Web-search services. Operating activities at Google contributed net cash inflows amounting to $16.619 billion in 2012.

- **Cash Flows from Investing.** The second section reports net cash used in or provided by investing. It includes cash receipts and payments from buying and selling stocks, bonds, property, equipment, and other productive assets. These sources of cash are not the company's main line of business. Purchases of property, equipment, and investments made by Google, for example, consumed $48.281 billion of net cash. A cash outflow is shown in parentheses.

- **Cash Flows from Financing.** The third section reports net cash from all financing activities. It includes cash inflows from borrowing or issuing stock, as well as outflows for payment of dividends and repayment of borrowed money. Google's financing activities provided a net cash inflow of $1.229 billion.

Google, Inc.
Summary of Statement of Cash Flows (condensed)
as of December 31, 2012
Increase (Decrease) in Cash
(in millions)

Net cash provided by operating activities		**$16,619.**
Cash from investments:		
Purchases of property, equipment, and investments	(48,281.)	
Cash inflows from investment activities	35,225.	
Net cash used in investing activities		**(13,056.)**
Cash flows from financing activities:		
Repayment of debt	(14,781.)	
Borrowings	16,109.	
Other	(99.)	
Net cash provided by financing activities		**1,229.**
Net increase in cash		4,792.
Cash at beginning of year		9,983.
Cash at end of year		**$14,775.**

Google's statement of cash flows for year ended December 31, 2012. The final entry shows year-end cash position resulting from operating activities, investing activities, and financing activities.

FIGURE 15.3 Google's Statement of Cash Flows
Source: Modified from "Google Inc. Consolidated Statements of Cash Flows," *United States Securities Exchange Commission*, at http://www.sec.gov/Archives/edgar/data/1288776/000119312513028362/d452134d10k.htm#tx452134_23, accessed on February 9, 2013.

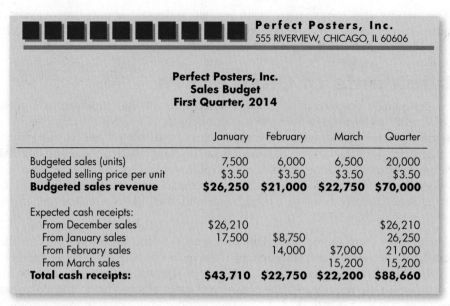

FIGURE 15.4 Perfect Posters' Sales Budget

- The overall change in cash from these three sources is $4.792 billion for the year. The amount is added to the beginning cash (year-end cash from the 2011 balance sheet) to arrive at 2012's ending cash position of $14.775 billion. When creditors and stockholders know how a firm obtained and used funds during the course of a year, it's easier for them to interpret year-to-year changes in the balance sheet and income statement.

The Budget: An Internal Financial Statement

Budget *detailed statement of estimated receipts and expenditures for a future period of time*

For planning, controlling, and decision making, the most important internal financial statement is the **budget**, a detailed report on estimated receipts and expenditures for a future period of time. Although that period is usually one year, some companies also prepare three- or five-year budgets, especially when considering major capital expenditures. The budget differs from the other statements we have discussed in that budgets are not shared outside the company; hence the "internal financial statement" title.

Although the accounting staff coordinates the budget process, it needs input from many areas regarding proposed activities and required resources. Figure 15.4 is a sales budget for a hypothetical wholesaler, Perfect Posters. In preparing next year's budget, accounting must obtain from the sales group projections for units to be sold and expected expenses for the coming year. Then, accounting draws up the final budget and, throughout the year, compares the budget to actual expenditures and revenues. Discrepancies signal potential problems and spur action to improve financial performance.

<table>
<tr><td>**OBJECTIVE 4**
Explain
the key standards and principles
for reporting financial statements.</td><td>## Reporting Standards and Practices</td></tr>
</table>

Accountants follow standard reporting practices and principles when they prepare external reports. The common language dictated by standard practices and spelled out in GAAP is designed to give external users confidence in the accuracy and meaning of financial information. GAAP cover a range of issues, such as when to recognize revenues from operations and how to make full public disclosure of financial information. Without such standards, users of financial statements wouldn't be able to compare information from different companies, and would misunderstand—or be led to misconstrue—a company's true financial status. Forensic accountants, such as Al Vondra from the opening case watch for deviations from GAAP as indicators of possible fraudulent practices.

Revenue Recognition and Activity Timing

The reporting of revenue inflows, and the timing of other transactions, must abide by accounting principles that govern financial statements. **Revenue recognition**, for example, is the formal recording and reporting of revenues at the appropriate time. Although a firm earns revenues continuously as it makes sales, earnings are not reported until the *earnings cycle* is completed. This cycle is complete under two conditions:

Revenue Recognition formal recording and reporting of revenues at the appropriate time

1 The sale is complete and the product delivered.
2 The sale price has been collected or is collectible (accounts receivable).

The end of the earnings cycle determines the timing for revenue recognition in a firm's financial statements. Suppose a toy company in January signs a sales contract to supply $1,000 of toys to a retail store with delivery scheduled in February. Although the sale is completed in January, the $1,000 revenue should not then be recognized (not be reported in the firm's financial statements) because the toys have not been delivered and the sale price is not yet collectible, so the earnings cycle is incomplete. Revenues are recorded in the accounting period—February—in which the product is delivered and collectible (or collected). This practice ensures that the statement gives a fair comparison of what was gained (revenues) in return for the resources that were given up (cost of materials, labor, and other production and delivery expenses) for the transaction.

Full Disclosure

To help users better understand the numbers in a firm's financial statements, GAAP requires that financial statements also include management's interpretations and explanations of those numbers. The idea of requiring input from the manager is known as the **full disclosure** principle. Because they know about events inside the company, managers prepare additional information to explain certain events or transactions or to disclose the circumstances behind certain results. For example, previous annual reports and financial statements filed by Borders, the well-known bookseller, had discussed the competitive and economic risks facing the company before it eventually filed for bankruptcy in 2011. The disclosures noted that consumer spending trends were shifting to Internet retailers and eBooks, and away from in-store purchasing, thus posing risks for Borders' cash flows and overall financial condition. Management's discussion noted there could be no assurance that Borders would muster adequate financial resources to remain competitive and, indeed, it soon happened. On filing for bankruptcy, Borders' liabilities of $1.29 billion had surpassed its assets of $1.28 billion. This one-time book-industry giant closed its last U.S. store in September 2011.[15]

Full Disclosure guideline that financial statements should not include just numbers but should also furnish management's interpretations and explanations of those numbers

Analyzing Financial Statements

OBJECTIVE 5
Describe
how computing financial ratios can help users get more information from financial statements to determine the financial strengths of a business.

Financial statements present a lot of information, but how can it be used? How, for example, can statements help investors decide what stock to buy or help lenders decide whether to extend credit? Answers to such questions for various stakeholders—employees, managers, unions, suppliers, the government, customers—can be answered as follows: Statements provide data, which can, in turn, reveal trends and be

managing in turbulent times

The "Fairness" Dilemma: What's an Asset's Real Value?

Think of a personal possession, such as a car or a diamond. What is its monetary worth, or value? Is it the amount you paid, or what you could get by selling it today, or what you would expect if you sell two years from now? Businesses face similar questions when valuing assets on the balance sheet. Consider the Boston home buyer who paid $475,000 in 2006 when a bank generously valued the property at more than $525,000, allowing the new homeowner to borrow the full amount of the purchase price. The bank's asset (the mortgage loan) was valued at $475,000 and the borrower's property was valued at $525,000. Today, the borrower has vacated the house, unable to make payments. The bank holds the repossessed the property; it is unsellable at a $360,000 asking price. In the event of future economic recovery, the bank expects that the property will be worth at least $500,000. So, what should be the asset value on the balance sheet—$475,000 or $360,000 or $500,000? Borrowers, too, are grappling with such questions in the weak real estate market. In 2012, some 15 million U.S. home mortgage loans were "underwater": the amounts owed were greater than the market values of those homes.[16]

The core problem is market shutdown: In a recession, there is no functioning market that sets a "fair market price" for many assets. With no buyers, once-valuable properties and financial investments have become "toxic assets": They are unsellable, often having no current market value. Difficulty worsens when market shutdown runs headlong into an accounting rule known as "mark-to-market," resulting in potential business closures.[17]

Mark-to-market—or "fair value accounting"—requires that assets be priced on balance sheets at current market value. Doing so, however, forces a major write-down for toxic assets at companies facing inactive markets for housing, cars, and financial securities, and it forces accounting losses that may cause "bleeding" companies to fold. Advocates for relaxing mark-to-market argue that presently distressed assets will become more

Maxx-Studio/Shutterstock

valuable later, as the economy recovers, so currently depressed values are not at all "fair" indicators of their worth. Instead, they say, mark-to-market exaggerates the scale of their losses in an economic downturn.[18]

Relief for some troubled firms came in early 2009, with unusual action by the U.S. Financial Accounting Standards Board (FASB), an independent organization that sets accounting guidelines. FASB relaxed mark-to-market accounting for financial institutions. Banks now have more flexibility for valuing toxic assets, using estimates from their internal computer models instead of reporting assets at currently distressed market prices. Opponents to the change, however, warn that relaxed rules could let banks hide the true, low value of assets and deceive investors at a time when trust in financial reporting is most needed.[19]

---

applied to create various *ratios* (comparative numbers). We can then use these trends and ratios to evaluate a firm's financial health, its progress, and its prospects for the future.

Ratios are normally grouped into three major classifications:

Solvency Ratio *financial ratio, either short or long term, for estimating the borrower's ability to repay debt*

Profitability Ratio *financial ratio for measuring a firm's potential earnings*

Activity Ratio *financial ratio for evaluating management's efficiency in using a firm's assets*

1 **Solvency ratios** for estimating short-term and long-term risk

2 **Profitability ratios** for measuring potential earnings

3 **Activity ratios** for evaluating management's use of assets

Depending on the decisions to be made, a user may apply none, some, or all of these ratios.

Solvency Ratios: Borrower's Ability to Repay Debt

What are the chances that a borrower will be able to repay a loan and the interest due? This question is first and foremost in the minds of bank lending officers, managers of pension funds and other investors, suppliers, and the borrowing company's own financial managers. Solvency ratios provide measures of a firm's ability to meet its debt obligations.

The Current Ratio and Short-Term Solvency Short-term solvency ratios measure a company's liquidity and its ability to pay immediate debts. The most commonly used of these is the **current ratio**, or "banker's ratio." This ratio measures a firm's ability to generate cash to meet current obligations through the normal, orderly process of selling inventories and collecting revenues from customers. It is calculated by dividing current assets by current liabilities. The higher a firm's current ratio, the lower the risk to investors.

Short-Term Solvency Ratio *financial ratio for measuring a company's ability to pay immediate debts*

Current Ratio *financial ratio for measuring a company's ability to pay current debts out of current assets*

As a rule, a current ratio is satisfactory at 2:1 or higher—that is, if current assets more than double current liabilities. A smaller ratio may indicate that a firm will have trouble paying its bills.

How does Google measure up? Look again at the balance sheet in Figure 15.1. Judging from current assets and current liabilities at the end of 2012, we see that

$$\frac{\text{Current assets}}{\text{Current liabilities}} = \frac{\$60.454 \text{ billion}}{\$14.337 \text{ billion}} = 4.2$$

The industry average for companies that provide business services is 1.4. Google's current ratio of 4.2 indicates the firm is a good short-run credit risk.

Long-Term Solvency Stakeholders are also concerned about long-term solvency. Has the company been overextended by borrowing so much that it will be unable to repay debts in future years? A firm that can't meet its long-term debt obligations is in danger of collapse or takeover, a risk that makes creditors and investors quite cautious. To evaluate a company's risk of running into this problem, creditors turn to the balance sheet to see the extent to which a firm is financed through borrowed money. Long-term solvency is calculated by dividing **debt** (total liabilities) by owners' equity. The lower a firm's debt, the lower the risk to investors and creditors. Companies with more debt may find themselves owing so much that they lack the income needed to meet interest payments or to repay borrowed money.

Debt *company's total liabilities*

Sometimes, high debt can be not only acceptable but also desirable. Borrowing funds gives a firm **leverage**, the ability to make otherwise unaffordable investments. In *leveraged buyouts*, firms have willingly taken on sometimes huge debts to buy out other companies. If owning the purchased company generates profits above the cost of borrowing the purchase price, leveraging often makes sense. Unfortunately, many buyouts have caused problems because profits fell short of expected levels or because rising interest rates increased payments on the buyer's debt.

Leverage *ability to finance an investment through borrowed funds*

Profitability Ratios: Earnings Power for Owners

It's important to know whether a company is solvent in both the long and the short term, but risk alone is not an adequate basis for investment decisions. Investors also want some indication of the returns they can expect. Evidence of earnings power is available from profitability ratios, such as *earnings per share*.

Defined as net income divided by the number of shares of common stock outstanding, **earnings per share** determines the size of the dividend that a firm can pay shareholders. As an indicator of a company's wealth potential, investors use this ratio to decide whether to buy or sell the firm's stock. As the ratio goes up, stock value increases because investors know that the firm can better afford to pay dividends. Naturally, stock loses market value if financial statements report a decline

Earnings Per Share *profitability ratio measuring the net profit that the company earns for each share of outstanding stock*

entrepreneurship and new ventures

How Will Twitter Turn Tweets into Treasure?

Widely accepted accounting measurements provide useful information about established firms but are a bit foggier with start-ups. Consider the continuing questions from the investment community about Twitter's ambiguous financial status. With several firms interested in buying Twitter, how can they know its market value, variously estimated to have risen from $4.5 billion in 2011 up to $11 billion in 2013, without solid financial data? The real numbers are confidential in closely held Twitter. As to its profitability, Twitter reports, "we spend more money than we make." Since Twitter was launched in 2006, its total losses have not been reported publicly. When (and how) will losses blossom into profitability? As stated by cofounder and former CEO Evan Williams, "We will make money, and I can't say exactly how because…we can't predict how the businesses we're in will work." And until they know *how*, they don't know *when* profits will occur.[20]

Twitter's balance sheet is another source of ambiguity. The accounting equation requires a fixed relationship among three items: Assets = Liabilities + Owners' Equity. Twitter insiders have a clear accounting of its outstanding liabilities. Paid-in capital (a part of shareholders' equity) is known, too: It includes the cofounders' personal investments plus a series of venture capital infusions, bringing the suspected total to well more than $1 billion.[21]

Questions also arise for valuing assets. For example, Twitter acquired the assets of *Values of n* to get needed technology and intellectual property into its operations. Exactly how Twitter will use them is unknown, so how should they be valued? Twitter's greatest asset is a massive loyal customer base with a

Pixellover RM 1/Alamy

phenomenal growth rate—200 million users per month and up to 400 million Tweets daily—and its enormous advertising potential. Celebrities, media, politicians, including Pope Benedict and First Lady Michelle Obama are Tweeters. Organizations such as Papa Johns, Starbucks, JetBlue, The Home Depot, and Toyota USA are using Twitter for sales and marketing promotions. Although Twitter's advertising revenues are increasing, many believe that much of its advertising potential has not yet materialized. Should this untapped advertising potential be recognized as an intangible asset? At what value? While the company's market, customer base, and products are rapidly emerging, how should its many assets—tangible and intangible—be valued? On what basis can those valuations be justified? Clearly, these issues at Twitter are less well settled than at well-established firms.[22]

---

in earnings per share. For Google, we can use the net income total from the income statement in Figure 15.2, together with the number of outstanding shares of stock, to calculate earnings per share as follows:

$$\frac{\text{Net income}}{\text{Number of common shares outstanding}} = \frac{\$10{,}737.0 \text{ million}}{332.3 \text{ million shares of stock}} = \frac{\$32.31}{\text{per share}}$$

This means that Google had net earnings of $32.31 (rounded) for each share of stock during 2012. In contrast, Time Warner's recent earnings were $3.09 per share, and Microsoft earned $1.82.

Activity Ratios: How Efficiently Is the Firm Using Its Resources?

The efficiency with which a firm uses resources is linked to profitability. As a potential investor, you want to know which company gets more mileage from its resources. Information obtained from financial statements can be used for *activity ratios* to measure this efficiency. For example, two firms use the same amount of resources or assets to perform a particular activity. If Firm A generates greater profits or sales, it has used its resources more efficiently and so enjoys a better activity

finding a better way

Ageing Asia

According to the global policy forum, the Organization for Economic Co-operation and Development (OECD), Asia's ageing will be at its most rapid in the period 2010–2030. Given the fact that pension planning is a long-term process, Asia needs to act very quickly to avoid the problems that have beset the United States and Europe in their attempts to fund the elderly.

Malaysia is one of six countries in Asia that has a defined contribution (DC) scheme. The scheme is known as the Employees Provident Fund or KWSP. This is publicly managed and the benefits are reliant upon the amount that the individual has contributed (along with the returns earned on the investment of that contribution). Malaysia, with a nominal retirement age of 55 for both genders, incorporates the expectation that pensioners will collect their pensions for a period of around 25 years (although the average is between 19–24 years). Malaysian pensioners are also paid a lump sum when they retire.

A survey conducted by the international banking corporation HSBC in the summer of 2012 investigated the current fears and concerns of Malaysians regarding retirement and pensions. The net result of the survey was the unsurprising news that not many Malaysians were actually saving for retirement at all.

Over 40 percent claimed that they were not adequately prepared for retirement and a further 10 percent claimed that had made no preparations for retirement. Nearly a third of all respondents (from the 1,000 questioned) had never saved for retirement; this included nearly 20 percent in the 55–64 age group.

The United Nations estimate that by 2050, 20 percent of all Malaysians would be over 65 years. HSBC calculated that given the respondents hoped to live a further 17 years

wirojsid/Fotolia

after retirement, they would only have sufficient funds to last 12 years. When asked as to the level of income they would need in order to live a comfortable retirement life, the expectation of respondents stated that they would need just over 80 percent of their working income. Their retirement income would therefore have to be just in excess of US$24,000.

The reasons behind this lack of planning are universal issues. Day to day expenses are too high, property purchases were seen as an investment and there was an expectation of support from children, having invested in their education.

For Malaysian accountants and financial advisors there are rays of hope. Whilst much retirement planning in Malaysia could be described as "informal", those that did seek professional help were far more likely to save. Some 60 percent of those who had consulted a professional had a retirement plan in place and over two-thirds had actually saved more for their retirement than had been originally planned.[23]

---

ratio. It may apply to any important activity, such as advertising, sales, or inventory management. Consider the activity of using the firm's resources to increase sales. As an example, suppose from its income statements we find that Google increases its annual sales revenues and does it without increasing its operating costs. Its sales activity has become more efficient. Investors like to see these year-to-year increases in efficiencies because it means the company is getting "more bang for the buck"—revenues are increasing faster than costs.

Bringing Ethics into the Accounting Equation

OBJECTIVE 6
Discuss
the role of ethics in accounting.

The purpose of ethics in accounting is to maintain public confidence in business institutions, financial markets, and the products and services of the accounting profession. Without ethics, all of accounting's tools and methods would be meaningless because their usefulness depends, ultimately, on veracity in their application.

Why Accounting Ethics?

In addition to the business world's many favorable opportunities and outcomes, there are also instances of misconduct. Amid public reports of unscrupulous activity, ethics remains an area in which one person who is willing to "do the right thing" can make a difference—and people do, every day. The role of ethics in the groundbreaking scandal from a decade ago remains a classic example: Refusing to turn a blind eye to unethical accounting around her at Enron, the now-failed giant energy corporation, Lynn Brewer tried to alert people inside about misstatements of the company's assets. When that failed, she, along with colleagues Sherron Watkins and Margaret Ceconi, talked with the U.S. Committee on Energy and Commerce to voice concerns about Enron's condition. To Brewer, maintaining personal and professional integrity was an overriding concern, and she acted accordingly.

Code of Professional Conduct
code of ethics for CPAs as maintained and enforced by the AICPA

AICPA's Code of Professional Conduct The **code of professional conduct** for public accountants in the United States is maintained and enforced by the AICPA. The institute identifies six ethics-related areas—listed in Table 15.3—with which accountants must comply to maintain certification. Comprehensive details for compliance in each area are spelled out in the AICPA Code of Professional Conduct. The IMA maintains a similar code to provide ethical guidelines for the management accounting profession.

In reading the AICPA's code, you can see that it forbids misrepresentation and fraud in financial statements. Deception certainly violates the call for exercising moral judgments (in "Responsibilities"), is contrary to the public interest (by deceiving investors) and does not honor the public trust (in "The Public Interest"). Misleading statements destroy the public's confidence in the accounting profession and in business in general. Although the code prohibits such abuses, its success depends, ultimately, on its acceptance and use by the professionals it governs.

table 15.3 Highlights from the Code of Ethics for CPAs

By voluntarily accepting Certified Public Accountant membership, the accountant also accepts self-enforced obligations, listed here, beyond written regulations and laws.	
Responsibilities as a Professional	The CPA should exercise their duties with a high level of morality and in a manner that is sensitive to bringing credit to their profession.
Serving the Public Interest	The CPA should demonstrate commitment to the profession by respecting and maintaining the public trust and serving the public honorably.
Maintaining Integrity	The CPA should perform all professional activities with highest regards for integrity, including sincerity and honesty, so as to promote the public's confidence in the profession.
Being Objective and Independent	The CPA should avoid conflicts of interest, and the appearance of conflicts of interest, in performing their professional responsibilities. They should be independent from clients when certifying to the public that the client's statements are true and genuine.
Maintaining Technical and Ethical Standards through Due Care	The CPA should exercise "due care," through professional improvement, abiding by ethical standards, updating personal competence through continuing accounting education, and improving the quality of services.
Professional Conduct in Providing Services	The CPA in public practice should abide by the meaning and intent of the Code of Professional Conduct when deciding on the kinds of services and the range of actions to be supplied competently and diligently for clients.

Source: Based on "Code of Professional Conduct," *AICPA*, at www.aicpa.org/Research/Standards/CodeofConduct/Pages/sec50.aspx, accessed on February 17, 2013.

table 15.4 Examples of Unethical and Illegal Accounting Actions[24]

Corporation	Accounting Violation
AOL Time Warner	America Online (AOL) inflated ad revenues to keep stock prices high before and after merging with Time Warner.
Freddie Mac	This U.S. government corporation fraudulently misstated $5 billion in earnings.
HCA, Columbia/HCA	Healthcare association and hospital defrauded Medicare, Medicaid, and TRICARE through false cost claims and unlawful billings (paid $1.7 billion in civil penalties, damages, criminal fines, and penalties).
Tyco	CEO Dennis Kozlowski illegally used company funds to buy expensive art for personal possession (he received an 8- to 25-year prison sentence).
Waste Management	Overstated income in financial statements (false and misleading reports) by improperly calculating depreciation and salvage value for equipment.
WorldCom	Hid $3.8 billion in expenses to show an inflated (false) profit instead of loss in an annual income statement.

Violations of Accounting Ethics and GAAP Unethical and illegal accounting violations have dominated the popular press in recent years. Some of the more notorious cases, listed in Table 15.4, violated the public's trust, ruined retirement plans for thousands of employees, and caused shutdowns and lost jobs. As you read each case, you should be able to see how its violation relates to the presentation of balance sheets and income statements in this chapter. In each case, adversity would have been prevented if employees had followed the code of professional conduct. In each case, nearly all of the code's six ethics-related areas were violated and "professionals" willingly participated in unethical behavior. Such unscrupulous behavior was the impetus for Sarbox.

Internationalizing Accounting

OBJECTIVE 7
Describe
the purpose of the International Accounting Standards Board and explain why it exists.

Accounting in its earliest forms is known to have existed more than 7,000 years ago in Mesopotamia and Egypt for recording trade transactions and keeping track of resources. With the passage of time each country or region's accounting practices were refined to meet its needs in commerce while also accommodating local cultural traditions and developments in its laws. Although unique practices served each region well, they later posed problems as international business became prominent. By the late twentieth century it was apparent that the upsurge in multinational organizations and the global economy demanded more uniformity among accounting practices. The development of "universal" procedures would allow governments and investors in, say, China, Brazil, and Italy to read, interpret, and compare financial statements from all those countries, whereas such comparisons even today are difficult if not sometimes impossible.

International Accounting Standards Board

Established in 2001 and housed at London, England, the **International Accounting Standards Board (IASB)** is an independent, nonprofit organization responsible for developing a set of global accounting standards and for gaining the support and cooperation of the world's various accounting organizations to implement those standards.

International Accounting Standards Board (IASB) *organization responsible for developing a set of global accounting standards and for gaining implementation of those standards*

finding a better way

Accounting Practices for the Small Business

This chapter's accounting fundamentals apply to all businesses, large and small alike. However, some additional considerations are relevant for small firms, especially for new start-ups. Most new firms are started by entrepreneurs who are not accountants, many of whom know little about accounting. Fortunately, experienced help is available from firms specializing in small-business accounting to guide start-ups on "things to avoid" and "things to do" while getting acquainted with accounting-related tasks.[25]

S.E.A. Photo/Alamy

Five Things for the Start-up Owner to Do

- Do as many of the accounting and bookkeeping chores yourself, as time allows, rather than delegating them to others. Firsthand experience is the best way to improve your knowledge of accounting for your business.

- Get acquainted with a small-business accounting firm that is accessible for answering questions and providing guidance with special accounting needs in your industry.

- Focus your initial efforts on learning the most basic reporting practices—balance sheets, income statements, statements of cash flows—so that you understand what information each report contains, how to interpret that information, and you can explain to others the purposes of the reports.

- Always keep your personal records and transactions separated from the records and transactions of the business. Intermingling of personal and business data creates serious tax problems and raises questions of credibility about your firm's financial condition.

- Establish internal procedures to ensure that all of the firm's bills are paid, all income is received, and all financial transactions are accounted for. Knowing the true financial status of the business depends on controlling and verifying all its transactions.

Five Things for the Start-up Owner to *Not* Do

- Do not use the money you have set aside for taxes, including payroll and sales taxes, for other purposes.

Governments set tax due dates and tax rates and are unforgiving when those requirements are not met. Chances increase for not meeting your obligations when set-asides are used for other purposes.

- Do not rely on verbal agreements. They should be treated as a source of disagreement. Memories can be short, so instead of verbal agreements with suppliers, employees, lenders, local officials, and others, put everything in writing.

- Do not overestimate how much money you will be earning, especially early on. For planning purposes, be conservative in estimating future incomes and expenses. Avoid overestimating future incomes from sales, and avoid underestimating outflows for payments on rent, supplies, salaries, and other expenses.

- Do not allow anyone else to write checks on behalf of the business. Many start-ups become shut-downs when the bank account is suddenly emptied by a trusted employee who can no longer be located.

- Don't be remiss in billing. Before paying any bill, be sure to have evidence that the amount billed to you by the supplier matches the purchase order that was sent to that supplier. It is not unusual to be over- or undersupplied, without corresponding offsets in payments due.

IASB's 15 board members from various countries are full-time accounting experts with technical and international business experience.[26] Because the board cannot command sovereign nations to accept its recommended standards, its commitment to gaining cooperation around the world is a continuing task. Yet, international acceptance is essential for success. Accordingly, the board's task is a long-term process that requires working with various countries to design proposed standards. As an example, for any IASB proposal to be accepted in the United States, it must first be approved by the U.S.-based FASB and by the U.S. SEC. However, IASB's efforts extend beyond the United States, to all nations. The expected timeline reaches beyond 2015 for convergence of the many local GAAP into one global set of practices.

Why One Set of Global Practices?

Although more than 100 countries have adopted IASB's accounting practices, nearly 40 others, including China, Canada, and the United States, continue to use their national GAAP.[27] U.S.-based global companies such as Google, Caterpillar, and Microsoft may prepare different financial reports using local accounting practices for each country in which they conduct business. They also report the company's overall performance in a set of consolidated statements that combines the financial results of all its global affiliates, using U.S. GAAP. Using different accounting standards, however, can result in vastly different pictures of a firm's financial health. Income statements, balance sheets, and statements of cash flows using local GAAPs versus IASB practices, for example, may contain conflicting information with inconsistencies leading to confusion and misunderstandings among investors and other constituents. To emphasize this point, Sir David Tweedie, Chairman of the IASB, notes that a company using IASB standards can report balance sheet figures that are twice the size of those using U.S. GAAP accounting standards.[28] Which of the reports tells how well the company is doing? Such inconsistencies in reporting are unacceptable in a global economy and, accordingly, protection against them is a goal of IASB.

Example Areas Targeted for Aligning U.S. GAAP and IASB
Among the many differences between the practices of U.S. GAAP and IASB—some reports identify more than 400 such discrepancies—the following examples illustrate some discrepancies and proposals for convergence toward universal standards in financial reporting.

- *In valuing assets* (reported on the balance sheet), U.S. GAAP allows an asset to be written down if for some reason its value decreases. However, the value cannot later be rewritten up, even if it its actual value has increased. IASB standards, in contrast, do allow such write-ups reflecting increased market value, so the reported value of a company's assets can be quite different, depending on the chosen accounting system.[29]

- *In revenue recognition*, when revenues from customers should be recognized (reported), and in what amounts on the income statement, the U.S. GAAP and IASB procedures differ from each other. A current joint proposal, if approved, would remove existing inconsistencies and provide a single standard that recognizes revenue at the time the goods and services are transferred to the customer, and in the amounts that are expected to be received (or are received) from the customer.[30]

- *In devaluing of financial assets*, such as writing down bad loans in the financial crisis, both U.S. GAAP and IASB currently use the same procedure: After a loss occurs (but not until after the fact) the loan's value can be written down in the firm's financial statements, reflecting its lower value. Both groups, however, believe an "expected loss model" that recognizes (and reports) likely loan losses *ahead of time* will provide more timely information for investors and financial planners. A joint proposal for such a procedure has been presented.[31]

- *In fair value disclosure* the FASB and IASB jointly propose new standards for improving the comparability of fair value disclosures in financial statements. Unlike dissimilar disclosure practices among many local GAAP, both groups want the reported "fair value" for an asset, a liability, and an item in shareholders' equity to have the same meaning under both FASB and IASB procedures. The disclosure should identify the techniques and inputs used to measure fair value so that users can more clearly assess and compare financial statements.[32]

Timetable for Implementation The U.S. SEC has targeted 2015 as the earliest date that U.S. companies will be required to use IASB procedures for financial reporting. To meet the 2015 target, however, IASB must first demonstrate that its standards are developed adequately for use in the U.S. financial reporting system. Doing so would include assuring that investors have developed an understanding of and education in using IASB standards. Accounting education, too, must be updated to prepare U.S. accounting students for IASB, as well as updating practitioners in CPA firms. In 2011, the AICPA began a gradual process of introducing international standards in the CPA examinations. Most of the exam's new questions addressed some of the areas of difference between U.S. GAAP and International Financial Reporting Standards. Finally, the SEC must make a decision to phase in IASB all at once or, instead, to sequence its adoption beginning with a limited number of companies before final phase-in. The SEC's final report was delayed most recently until 2013, at the earliest. So, the U.S. wait continues while the challenges of switching to IFRS are resolved.[33]

summary of learning objectives

OBJECTIVE 1

Explain the role of accountants and distinguish between the kinds of work done by public accountants, private accountants, management accountants, and forensic accountants. (pp. 514–520)

The role of accountants is to maintain a comprehensive system for collecting, analyzing, and communicating financial information for use by external constituents and within firms for planning, controlling, and decision making. It measures business performance and translates the results into information for management decisions. The users of accounting information include business managers, employees and unions, investors and creditors, tax authorities, and government regulatory agencies.

The *controller*, or chief accounting officer, manages a firm's accounting activities by ensuring that the *accounting information system* provides the reports and statements needed for planning, decision making, and other management activities. Accounting activities may be either financial or managerial. *Financial accounting* is concerned with external users of information, such as consumer groups, unions, stockholders, and government agencies and focuses on the entity as a whole. *Managerial accounting*'s focus is internal users, such as managers, engineers, purchasing agents, and salespeople. Managerial accounting focuses on the detailed information needed to make decisions within the organization.

Public accountants offer accounting services to individuals and businesses outside their organization and are distinguished by their independence from the clients they serve. *Certified public accountants (CPAs)* are licensed professionals who provide auditing, tax, and management advisory services for other firms and individuals. Only CPAs can audit a firm's financial statements, and CPAs are always independent of the firms they audit. Many businesses hire their own salaried employees—*private accountants*—to perform internal accounting activities, such as internal auditing, taxation, cost analysis, and budgeting. Among private accountants, *certified management accountants* have passed the profession's experience and examination requirements for proficiency to provide internal accounting services that support managers in various activities (such as marketing, production, and engineering). *Forensic accountants* use accounting for legal purposes by providing investigative and litigation support in crimes against companies, crimes by companies, and civil cases.

OBJECTIVE 2

Explain how the accounting equation is used. (pp. 520–521)

Accountants use the following equation to balance the data pertaining to financial transactions:

$$\text{Assets} - \text{Liabilities} = \text{Owners' Equity}$$

After each financial transaction (e.g., payments to suppliers, sales to customers, wages to employees), the accounting equation must be in balance. If it isn't, then an accounting error has occurred. An *asset* is any economic resource that is expected to benefit a firm or an individual who owns it. Assets include land, buildings, equipment, inventory, and payments due the company (accounts receivable). A liability is a debt that the firm owes to an outside party. Owners' equity consists of capital from two sources: (1) The amount that the owners originally invested; and (2) Profits (also owned by the owners) earned by and reinvested in the company. Owners' equity is meaningful for both investors and lenders. Before lending money to owners, lenders want to know the amount of owners' equity in a business. A larger owners' equity indicates greater security for lenders. As shown from the accounting equation, if assets exceed liabilities, owners' equity is positive; if the firm goes out of business, owners will receive some cash (a gain) after selling assets and paying off liabilities. If liabilities outweigh assets, owners' equity is negative; assets aren't enough to pay off debts. If the company goes under, owners will get no cash and some creditors won't be paid, thus losing their remaining investments in the company.

OBJECTIVE 3

Describe the three basic financial statements and show how they reflect the activity and financial condition of a business. (pp. 521–526)

Accounting summarizes the results of a firm's transactions and issues reports—including *financial statements*—to help managers and other stakeholders make informed decisions. The *balance sheet* (sometimes called the *statement of financial position*) supplies detailed information about the accounting equation items—assets, liabilities, and owners' equity—that together are a barometer of the firm's financial condition at a point in time. By comparing the current balance sheet with those of previous years, creditors and owners can better interpret the firm's financial progress and future prospects in terms of changes in assets, liabilities, and owners' equity.

The *income statement* (sometimes called a *profit-and-loss statement*) describes revenues and expenses to show a firm's annual profit or loss during a period of time, such as a year. The information in an income statement shows how a company obtained its net income for the accounting period, making it easier for shareholders and other stakeholders to evaluate the firm's financial health.

A publicly traded firm must issue a *statement of cash flows*, which describes its yearly cash receipts (inflows) and payments (outflows). It shows the effects on cash during the year from three kinds of business activities: (a) cash flows from operations, (b) cash flows from investing, and (c) cash flows from financing. The statement of cash flows then reports the overall change in the company's cash position at the end of the accounting period. When creditors and stockholders know how a firm obtained and used funds during the course of a year, it's easier for them to interpret year-to-year changes in the balance sheet and income statement.

For planning, controlling, and decision making, the most important internal financial statement is the *budget*, a detailed report on estimated receipts and expenditures for a future period of time. Budgets are internal documents and not usually shared outside the company.

OBJECTIVE 4

Explain the key standards and principles for reporting financial statements. (pp. 526–527)

Accountants follow standard reporting practices and principles when they prepare financial statements. The common language dictated by standard practices and spelled out in generally accepted accounting principles (GAAP) is designed to give external users confidence in the accuracy and meaning of financial information. Without these standards, users wouldn't be able to compare information from different companies, and they might misunderstand—or be led to misconstrue—a company's true financial status.

Two of the most important standard reporting practices and principles are revenue recognition and full disclosure. *Revenue recognition* refers to the rules associated with the recording and reporting of revenues in financial statements. All firms earn revenues continuously as they make sales, but earnings are not reported until the earnings cycle is completed. This cycle is complete under two conditions: (a) The sale is complete and the product delivered; (b) the sale price has been collected or is collectible (accounts receivable). This practice assures interested parties that the statement gives a fair comparison of what was gained (revenues) for the resources that were given up (cost of materials, labor, and other expenses) for the transaction.

Full disclosure recognizes that a firm's managers have inside knowledge—beyond just the numbers reported in its financial statements—that can explain certain events, transactions, or otherwise disclose the circumstances behind certain results. Full disclosure means that financial statements include management interpretations and explanations to help external users understand the financial information contained in statements.

OBJECTIVE 5

Describe how computing financial ratios can help users get more information from financial statements to determine the financial strengths of a business. (pp. 527–531)

Financial statements contain data that can be used in *ratios* (comparative numbers) to analyze the financial health of a company in terms of solvency, profitability, and efficiency in performing activities. Ratios can help creditors, investors, and managers assess a firm's current status and check its progress by comparing current with past statements. *Solvency ratios* use balance sheet data to measure the firm's ability to meet (repay) its debts. The most commonly used solvency ratio is known as the current ratio. The *current ratio* measures the ability to meet current (short-term) liabilities out of current assets. It is calculated by dividing current assets by current liabilities. The higher a firm's current ratio, the lower the risk to investors. A smaller ratio may indicate that a firm will have trouble paying its bills. Stakeholders are also concerned about long-term solvency. *Long-term solvency ratios* compare the firm's total liabilities (including long-term debt) against the owners' equity. High indebtedness (a high ratio) can be risky because it requires payment of interest and repayment of borrowed funds that may not be available.

Profitability ratios, such as earnings per share, measure current and potential earnings. Investors are interested in this ratio because it indicates the firm's earnings power and the returns they can expect from their investments. *Activity ratios* reflect management's use of assets by measuring the efficiency with which a firm uses its resources for a particular activity, such as sales, advertising, or inventory management. Sales efficiency, for example, can be measured from income statement data for annual sales revenues as compared with sales expenses. Sales efficiency has increased if the year-to-year growth in sales revenues is larger than the growth in sales expenses.

OBJECTIVE 6

Discuss the role of ethics in accounting. (pp. 531–533)

The purpose of ethics in accounting is to maintain public confidence in business institutions, financial markets, and the products and services of the accounting profession. Without ethics, all of accounting's tools and methods would be meaningless because their usefulness depends, ultimately, on truthfulness in their application. Accordingly, professional accounting associations such as the AICPA and IMA enforce codes of professional conduct that include ethics-related areas, such as the accountant's responsibilities, the public interest, integrity, and due care. The codes prohibit, among other areas, misrepresentation and fraud in financial statements because misleading statements destroy the public's confidence in the accounting profession and in business in general. Although the code prohibits such abuses, its success depends ultimately on its acceptance and use by the professionals it governs.

OBJECTIVE 7

Describe the purpose of the International Accounting Standards Board and explain why it exists. (pp. 533–536)

The International Accounting Standards Board (IASB) is an independent, nonprofit organization established for the purpose of developing a set of global accounting standards and for gaining the support and cooperation of the world's various accounting organizations to implement those standards. It exists because the upsurge in multinational organizations and the global economy demands more uniformity among accounting practices, so that accounting reports become more understandable across nations and regions. Because the board cannot command sovereign nations to accept its recommended standards, its commitment to gaining cooperation around the world is a continuing task that requires working with various countries to design proposed international standards. Although more than 100 countries have adopted IASB's accounting practices, nearly 40 others, including China, Canada, and the United

States, continue to use their national accounting standards that are often not comparable and can result in vastly different pictures of a firm's financial health. The development of "universal" procedures would allow governments and investors everywhere to read, interpret, and compare financial statements from every country, whereas such comparisons even today are difficult if not sometimes impossible. Different accounting standards, such as how assets are valued and how revenues should be recognized, can result in vastly different pictures of a firm's financial health. Income statements, balance sheets, and statements of cash flows using U.S GAAP versus IASB practices may contain conflicting information with inconsistencies leading to confusion and misunderstandings among investors and other constituents. The U.S. SEC has targeted 2015 as the earliest date that U.S. companies will be required to use IASB procedures for financial reporting. To meet the 2015 target, however, IASB must first demonstrate that its standards are developed adequately for use in the U.S. financial reporting system.

key terms

accounting (or accountancy) (p. 514)
accounting equation (p. 520)
accounting information system (AIS) (p. 514)
accounts payable (payables) (p. 523)
activity ratio (p. 528)
asset (p. 521)
audit (p. 516)
balance sheet (p. 522)
bookkeeping (p. 514)
budget (p. 526)
Certified Fraud Examiner (CFE) (p. 519)
certified management accountant (CMA) (p. 518)
certified public accountant (CPA) (p. 518)
code of professional conduct (p. 532)
controller (p. 515)
core competencies for accounting (p. 517)
cost of goods sold (p. 524)
cost of revenues (p. 523)
current asset (p. 522)
current liability (p. 523)

current ratio (p. 529)
debt (p. 529)
depreciation (p. 522)
earnings per share (p. 529)
financial accounting (p. 515)
financial statement (p. 521)
fixed asset (p. 522)
forensic accounting (p. 518)
full disclosure (p. 527)
generally accepted accounting principles (GAAP) (p. 516)
goodwill (p. 523)
gross profit (p. 524)
income statement (profit-and-loss statement) (p. 523)
intangible asset (p. 523)
International Accounting Standards Board (IASB) (p. 533)
leverage (p. 529)
liability (p. 521)
liquidity (p. 522)
long-term liability (p. 523)

management accountant (p. 518)
management advisory services (p. 517)
managerial (management) accounting (p. 515)
net income (net profit, net earnings) (p. 524)
operating expenses (p. 524)
operating income (p. 524)
owners' equity (p. 521)
paid-in capital (p. 523)
private accountant (p. 518)
profitability ratio (p. 528)
retained earnings (p. 523)
revenue recognition (p. 527)
revenues (p. 523)
Sarbanes-Oxley Act of 2002 (SARBOX or SOX) (p. 519)
short-term solvency ratio (p. 529)
solvency ratio (p. 528)
statement of cash flows (p. 525)
tax services (p. 517)

MyBizLab

Go to **pearsonglobaleditions.com/mybizlab** to complete the problems marked with this icon ✪.

questions & exercises

QUESTIONS FOR REVIEW

✪ **15-1.** Who are the users of accounting information and for what purposes do they use it?

15-2. Identify the three types of services performed by CPAs.

15-3. Explain the ways in which financial accounting differs from managerial (management) accounting.

15-4. Discuss the activities and services performed by forensic accountants.

15-5. What are the three basic financial statements, and what major information does each contain?

QUESTIONS FOR ANALYSIS

✪ **15-6.** If you were planning to invest in a company, which of the three types of financial statements would you most want to see? Why?

⭐ **15-7.** Use the accounting equation to determine your net worth. Identify your assets and liabilities. With this information, how would you increase your net worth in the future?

15-8. Consider possible reasons why it is taking so long for IASB's accounting standards to become fully adopted for use in the United States. Using the Internet as your source for information, identify five or more barriers that have deterred implementation of the standards, and explain how (or why) each has (or is) causing implementation delays.

APPLICATION EXERCISES

15-9. Interview an accountant at a local business, nonprofit organization, or government entity. How does the firm use budgets? How does budgeting help managers plan business activities? How does budgeting help them control activities? Give examples.

15-10. Interview the manager of a local retailer, wholesale business, or manufacturing firm about the role of ethics in that company's accounting practices. Is ethics in accounting an important issue to the manager? If the firm has its own private accountants, what measures are taken for ensuring ethical practices internally? What steps, if any, does the company take to maintain ethical relationships in its dealings with CPA firms?

building a business: continuing team exercise

Assignment:

Meet with your team members to consider your new business venture and how it relates to the accounting topics in this chapter. Develop specific responses to the following:

15-11. Develop an outline for the kinds of accounting resources your firm needs for the first year of company operations. Identify plans for obtaining those resources.

15-12. Accountants, to perform their work, require data and information to be used in the various tasks they provide. Develop a list of the kinds of data and information that will be needed by the accountant(s) to provide accounting services for your business. Who will create the necessary data and information?

15-13. Based on the development of your business to date, create a preliminary or pro-forma income statement for your firm's first-year of operation. Be sure it includes listings of relevant terms from the accounting equation. See if you can estimate anticipated data for each element in the income statement.

15-14. Based on the development of your business to date, create a preliminary or pro-forma balance sheet for your firm's first-year of operation. Be sure it includes listings of relevant terms from the accounting equation. See if you can estimate anticipated data for each element in the balance sheet.

15-15. Consider the sources for start-up funds you will need to finance your business. What financial ratios (ratio analysis), if any, are likely to be of interest to lending institutions, personal investors (including yourselves), or other providers of funds. Explain why ratio analysis will be of interest to them, or why it will not be of interest.

building your business skills

PUTTING THE BUZZ IN BILLING

Goal

To encourage you to think about the advantages and disadvantages of using an online system for handling accounts receivable and accounts payable electronically.

Method

STEP 1

As the chief financial officer of a Midwestern utility company, you are analyzing the feasibility of switching to a totally electronic bill-paying system. You decide to discuss the ramifications of the choice with three associates (choose three classmates to take on these roles). Your discussion requires that you research existing electronic payment systems. Specifically, using online and library research, you must find out as much as you can about the electronic bill-paying systems developed by Visa, Intuit, IBM, and the Checkfree Corporation.

STEP 2

After you have researched this information, brainstorm the advantages and disadvantages of switching to an electronic system.

FOLLOW-UP QUESTIONS

15-16. What cost savings are inherent in the electronic system for both your company and its customers? In your answer, consider such costs as handling, postage, and paper.

15-17. What consequences would your decision to adopt an electronic system have on others with whom you do business, including manufacturers of electronic processing equipment, the U.S. Postal Service, and banks?

15-18. Switching to an electronic system would mean a large capital expense for new computers and software. How could analyzing the company's income statement help you justify this expense?

15-19. How are consumers likely to respond to paying bills electronically? Are you likely to get a different response from individuals than you get from business customers?

exercising your ethics

GIVE AND TAKE WITH ACCOUNTING CLIENTS

The Situation

CPAs provide valuable services for their clients, both businesses and individuals. Although it's important to make clients happy, accountants have additional considerations when preparing financial statements and tax returns.

The Dilemma

Aaron Ault is the owner of a small contracting business. In late January 2014, he delivered original expense and income records so that his CPA, Katrina Belinski, could prepare 2013 financial statements and tax returns for Ault's small business firm. Several weeks later, Katrina delivered the completed financial statements and tax return to Ault. Aaron was pleased with the financial statements but realized that he was going to owe a lot of money in taxes. His business is just recovering from tough times during the recession and he can't afford to pay such a large tax bill. One particularly large job was completed at the end of the year, and Ault has decided that he'd like to record this during the current year. This would result in a much lower taxable income for 2013. However, Ault is disappointed with Belinski and tells him that she's not able to make this change and he's threatening to take his business elsewhere. Belinski is torn because Ault has been a long-time client and she doesn't want to lose his business.

QUESTIONS TO ADDRESS

15-20. What are the ethical issues in this situation?

15-21. What are the basic arguments for and against Aaron Ault's position in this situation? for and against Katrina Belinski's position?

15-22. What do you think that Ault and Belinski should do in this situation?

team exercise

CONFIDENTIALLY YOURS

The Situation

Accountants are often entrusted with private, sensitive information that should be used confidentially. In this exercise, you're encouraged to think about ethical considerations that might arise when an accountant's career choices come up against a professional obligation to maintain confidentiality.

The Dilemma

Assume that you're the head accountant in Turbatron, a large electronics firm that makes components for other manufacturing firms. Your responsibilities include preparing Turbatron's financial statements that are then audited for financial reporting to shareholders. In addition, you regularly prepare confidential budgets for internal use by managers responsible for planning departmental activities, including future investments in new assets. You've also worked with auditors and CPA consultants who assess financial problems and suggest solutions.

Now let's suppose that you're approached by another company, Electroblast, one of the electronics industry's most successful firms, and offered a higher-level position. If you accept, your new job will include developing Electroblast's financial plans and serving on the strategic planning committee. Thus, you'd be involved not only in developing strategy but also in evaluating the competition, perhaps even using your knowledge of Turbatron's competitive strengths and weaknesses. Your contractual commitments with Turbatron do not bar you from employment with other electronics firms.

Team Activity

Assemble a group of four to five students and assign each group member to one of the following roles:

- Head accountant (leaving Turbatron)
- General manager of Turbatron
- Shareholder of Turbatron
- Customer of Turbatron
- General manager of Electroblast (if your team has five members)

ACTION STEPS

15-23. Before hearing any of your group's comments on this situation, and from the perspective of your assigned role, are any ethical issues confronting the head accountant in this situation? If so, write them down.

15-24. Return to your group and reveal ethical issues identified by each member. Were the issues the same among all roles or did differences in roles result in different issues?

15-25. Among the ethical issues that were identified, decide as a group which one is most important for the head accountant. Which is most important for Turbatron?

15-26. What does your group finally recommend be done to resolve the most important ethical issue(s)?

15-27. What steps do you think Turbatron might take in advance of such a situation to avoid any difficulties it now faces?

cases

Frenkel's Forensics

Continued from page 514

Continued from page 514

At the beginning of this chapter you read about CFEs and their role in fighting various kinds of fraudulent accounting practices, especially during troubled economic times. It also discussed examples of fraud by the public at large, along with the resulting financial losses to U.S. businesses. Using the information presented in this chapter you should now be able to answer the following questions.

QUESTIONS FOR DISCUSSION

15-28. What factors do you think are most important in protecting your business against fraud?

15-29. Suppose you are hoping for a career as a forensic accountant. How do recent trends in fraud provide new opportunities for such a career?

15-30. An external auditor may suspect some irregularities in a client firm's accounting practices. In what ways might a forensic accountant be of assistance?

15-31. Consider the antifraud training for a company's employees. Which topics should be included in that training?

15-32. What ethical issues, if any, are involved in the decision to investigate a suspected case of fraud in a business's accounting activities?

Future Directions for the Modern Accountant

Lessons from the global recession along with evolving information technologies are among the prominent forces shaping the future for accounting professionals. However, the accountant's knowledge of business aided by analytical and technical skills, although essential, are not sufficient capabilities for meeting current and future market demands in this changing profession. The traditional accountant's role was centered on analyzing historical financial data, creating financial statements, and providing interpretations of financial data and documents to facilitate business decisions. The expectations for the modern CPAs, increasingly, call for the more intimate role of leadership in demonstrating financial implications for many additional facets of the business including its overall operations, strategy, data management, human resources, and technical resources. The accountant, in this increasingly invasive participation with client firms, uses additional competencies beyond those of the traditional financial accounting expert. In consultative roles, accountants are being asked for guidance on broad issues including business development, evaluating strategic opportunities, assessments of risks and threats, and strategies for using massive databases to identify promising directions for developing new products, improving customer service, and evaluating new lines of business to gain competitive advantage. Beyond just technical expertise, these kinds of participation require thorough knowledge of the client's business and the markets in which they operate.

The following trends have emerged and are contributing to the additional roles of the modern accountant:

- *Fewer restrictions from physical and geographic boundaries* With increasing globalization many foreign-based firms are interacting with firms based elsewhere around the world. Coupled with modern technology, accountants and clients in other countries are working together remotely. An accountant based at a company office, or at an office-in-the-home, in Omaha, Nebraska, can provide services to a client located in Singapore.
- *Social media have changed relationships and the way business is conducted* Modern accountants establish professional relationships through active participation through social media. No longer do CPAs rely on face-to-face interactions at occasional professional meetings. Social media such as LinkedIn provide platforms for at-your-fingertips remote interactions allowing exchanges of information, professional advice, and temporary collaborations among accountants to serve clients in need of particular skill sets. New business opportunities arise, too, when accountants use a social networking presence to establish their business reputations.
- *Effectiveness as a communicator is a must for the accountant* Communication skills are vital in the modern accountant's role in advising clients on global business trends and strategic perspectives. The accountant's thorough knowledge, to be leveraged into meaningful advice, must be communicated to clients on time, clearly and convincingly, both verbally and in writing. Effectiveness can be critical in a variety of communications contexts, ranging from formal presentations, to ad hoc interactive group meetings, to one-to-one informal conversations, either face to face or remotely.
- *Project management in the accountant's expanded role* Serving as project manager is becoming commonplace for accountants because they provide guidance on the client's strategy, overall operations, and business development. These broad-based issues typically involve large-scale teams of specialists requiring long-term participation in activities such as financial forecasting, product and process engineering, financial interpretations, cost estimation, and huCman resources analysis. Success depends on the project manager's ability to decompose the project into manageable tasks, gain acceptance of task assignments, encourage timely reporting by task groups, and merge the project's many steps into coherent conclusions.

It is evident, then, that tomorrow's accountants need to be prepared with more than just traditional skills. They need to know the nature of the client's business and its competitive environment. That same accountant has to understand how to assist that client in gaining greater competitive advantage.[34]

QUESTIONS FOR DISCUSSION

15-33. In what ways, if any, does the discussion in this case apply to management accountants rather than to CPAs? Explain your response.

15-34. In what ways, if any, does the discussion in this case apply to forensic accountants rather than to CPAs? Explain your response.

15-35. Consider the restrictions on CPA services by provisions of the Sarbanes-Oxley Act (Sarbox). In what ways, if any, does this case's description of the modern accountant's activities conflict with Sarbox? Explain your response.

15-36. This chapter presents several methods for financial statement analysis. Considering the activities of the modern accountant (as described in this case), might the modern accountant use the chapter's methods of financial statement analysis? Explain why, or why not.

15-37. Ethics has a long-standing role in the accounting profession. Will the emerging role of the modern accountant bring with it a greater emphasis on ethics (as compared with traditional accounting)? Explain.

crafting a business plan

PART 5: MANAGING INFORMATION

Goal of the Exercise

This part of the business plan asks you to think about your business in terms of *information technology needs* and *costs*.

Exercise Background: Part 5 of the Business Plan

In Chapter 13 we discussed the major impact that IT—computers, the Internet, software, and so on—has had on businesses today. This part of the business plan asks you to assess how you will use technology to improve your business. Will you, for example, use a database to keep track of your customers? How will you protect your business from hackers and other IT security risks?

This part of the business plan also asks you to consider the costs of doing business, such as salaries, rent, and utilities. You'll also be asked to complete the following financial statements:

- *Balance Sheet* The balance sheet is a foundation for financial reporting. This report identifies the valued items of the business (its *assets*) as well as the debts that it owes (its *liabilities*). This information gives the owner and potential investors a "snapshot" into the health of the business.
- *Income Statement (or Profit-and-Loss Statement)* This is the focus of the financial plan. This document will show you what it takes to be profitable and successful as a business owner for your first year.

Your Assignment

STEP 1

Open the saved *Business Plan* file you began working on in Parts 1 to 4.

STEP 2

For the purposes of this assignment, you will answer the following questions in "Part 5: Managing Information":

15-38. What kinds of IT resources will your business require?
Hint: Think about the employees in your business and what they will need to do their jobs. What computer hardware and software will they need? Will your business need a network and an Internet connection? What type of network? Refer to Chapter 14 for a discussion on IT resources you may want to consider.

15-39. How will you use IT to keep track of your customers and potential customers?

Hint: Many businesses—even small businesses—use databases to keep track of their customers. Will your business require a database? What about other information systems? Refer to Chapter 14 for more information on these topics.

15-40. What are the *costs* of doing business? Equipment, supplies, salaries, rent, utilities, and insurance are just some of these expenses. Estimate what it will cost to do business for one year.
Hint: The *Business Plan Student Template* provides a table for you to insert the costs associated with doing business. Note that these are just estimates—just try your best to include accurate costs for the expenses you think will be a part of doing business.

15-41. How much will you charge for your product? How many products do you believe that you can sell in one year (or how many customers do you think your business can attract)? Multiply the price that you will charge by the number of products that you hope to sell or the amount you hope each customer will spend. This will give you an estimate of your *revenues* for one year.
Hint: You will use the amounts you calculate in the costs and revenues questions in this part of the plan in the accounting statements in the next part, so be as realistic as you can.

15-42. Create a balance sheet and an income statement (profit-and-loss statement) for your business.
Hint: You will have two options for creating these reports. The first option is to use the Microsoft Word versions that are found within the *Business Plan Student Template* itself. The second option is to use the specific Microsoft Excel templates created for each statement, which are found on the book's companion website at www.pearsonhighered.com/ebert. These Excel files are handy to use because they already have the worksheet calculations preset—all you have to do is "plug in" the numbers and the calculations will be performed automatically for you. If you make adjustments to the different values in the Excel worksheets, you'll automatically see how changes to expenses, for example, can improve the "bottom line."
Note: Once you have answered the questions, save your Word document. You'll be answering additional questions in later chapters.

MyBizLab

Go to **pearsonglobaleditions.com/mybizlab** for the following Assisted-graded writing questions:

15-43. The stakeholders of every business—employees, managers, owners, governments, the public—want information about the firm's financial health. Accordingly, companies maintain three basic financial statements reflecting that firm's activity and financial condition. (a) What are those three statements and the information they contain? (b) Be sure to discuss the kinds of accounting specialists that participate, and those that may not participate, in preparing those statements.

15-44. Generally accepted accounting principles (GAAP) are followed by accountants for preparing a company's external financial reports. Write an essay explaining where those accounting principles (GAAP) come from and the reasons why they exist. (a) Be sure in your discussion to tell who enforces GAAP. (b) Also, include discussion of GAAP's "full disclosure" requirement. (c) Finally, discuss whether or not any of the GAAP practices apply to recording transactions in the firm's financial statements.

15-45. Mybizlab Only—comprehensive writing assignment for this chapter.

end notes

[1] Fraud Advisory Panel, www.fraudadvisorypanel.org; Action Fraud, www.actionfraud.org.uk; Frenkels, www.frenkels.com; Global Economic Crime Survey (United Kingdom Report), PricewaterhouseCooper, 2009.

[2] See Marshall B. Romney and Paul John Steinbart, *Accounting Information Systems*, 11th ed. (Upper Saddle River, NJ: Prentice Hall, 2009), Chapter 1.

[3] See Anthony A. Atkinson, Robert S. Kaplan, Ella Mae Matsumura, and S. Mark Young, *Management Accounting*, 5th ed. (Upper Saddle River, NJ: Prentice Hall, 2007), Chapter 1.

[4] See Walter T. Harrison and Charles T. Horngren, *Financial Accounting and Financial Tips*, 7th ed. (Upper Saddle River, NJ: Prentice Hall, 2007), Chapter 1.

[5] "Public Accounting Tips," *LifeTips.com*, at http://accountingjobs.lifetips.com/cat/64430/public-accounting/index.html, accessed on September 13, 2010; "Business Glossary," *AllBusiness.com*, at http://www.allbusiness. com/glossaries/review/4954577-1.html, accessed on March 20, 2011.

[6] Michael Cohn, "Big Four Firms Saw Big Revenue Increase in 2012," *accountingTODAY for the WebCPA*," January 10, 2013, at http://www.accountingtoday.com/news/Big-Four-Firms-Saw-Big-Revenue-Increase-2012-65309-1.html.

[7] See Alvin A. Arens, Randal J. Elder, and Mark S. Beasley, *Auditing and Assurance Services: An Integrated Approach*, 13th ed. (Upper Saddle River, NJ: Prentice Hall, 2010), Chapter 1.

[8] See Meg Pollard, Sherry T. Mills, and Walter T. Harrison, *Financial and Managerial Accounting* Ch. 1–14 (Upper Saddle River, NJ: Prentice Hall, 2008), Chapter 1.

[9] "2012 Talent Shortage Survey," *ManpowerGroup*, at http://www.manpowergroup.us/campaigns/talent-shortage-2012/, accessed February 11, 2013.

[10] "The CPA Vision Project and Beyond," *The American Institute of Certified Public Accountants*, at http://www.aicpa.org/RESEARCH/CPAHORIZONS2025/CPAVISIONPROJECT/Pages/CPAVisionProject.aspx, accessed on February 11, 2013.

[11] D. Larry Crumbley, Lester E. Heitger, and G. Stevenson Smith, *Forensic and Investigative Accounting*, 5th ed. (Chicago: CCH, 2011), Chapter 1.

[12] Michael Rapoport, "Eyebrows Go Up as Auditors Branch Out," Wall Street Journal, December 7, 2012, pages C1, C2.

[13] "Executive Summary of the Sarbanes-Oxley Act of 2002 P.L. 107–204," Conference of State Bank Supervisors, at http://www.csbs.org/legislative/leg-updates/Documents/ExecSummary-SarbanesOxley-2002.pdf; "Sarbanes-Oxley Executive Summary," *Securities Law Update* (Orrick, Herrington & Sutcliffe LLP), August 2002, at http://www.orrick.com/fileupload/144.pdf.

[14] "Consolidated Balance Sheets," *United States Securities Exchange Commission*, at http://www.sec.gov/Archives/edgar/data/1288776/000119312513028362/d452134d10k.htm#tx452134_23, accessed on February 9, 2013.

[15] "Borders Files for Bankruptcy, to Close 200 Stores," *Reuters*, February 16, 2011 at http://www.reuters.com/article/2011/02/17/us-borders-idUSTRE71F2P220110217.

[16] Iain MacWhirter, "Mortgage Madness Will End in Inflation, Inflation, Inflation OPINION," *The Sunday Herald*, September 16, 2007, at http://findarticles.com/p/articles/mi_qn4156/is_20070916/ai_n20503579/; Les Christie, "Half of Mortgage Borrowers Under 40 Are Underwater," *CNNMoney*, August 23, 2012, at http://money.cnn.com/2012/08/23/real_estate/underwater-mortgage-borrowers/index.html.

[17] Louis R. Woodhill, "One Way to Deal With Toxic Assets," *Real Clear Markets*, January 23, 2009, at http://www.realclearmarkets.com/articles/2009/01/one_way_to_deal_with_toxic_ass.html; Patrick F. Gannon, "Demystifying Mark-To-Market," *Forbes.com*, April 21, 2009, at http://www.forbes.com/2009/04/21/mark-to-market-personal-finance-guru-insights-accounting-standards.html.

[18] Steven L. Henning, "Controlling the Real-World Risks of Mark-to-Market Valuation," *WebCPA*, June 1, 2009, at http://www.webcpa.com/ato_issues/2009_9/-50466-1.html?pg=3; John Berlau, "The Mark-to-Market Relief Rally," *OpenMarket.org*, April 2, 2009, at http://www.openmarket.org/2009/04/02/the-mark-to-market-relief-rally/.

[19] http://www.oecd.org/els/soc/41941763.pdf; http://www.thestar.com.my/Business/Business-News/2013/08/09/Malaysians-not-saving-enough-for-retirement-says-HSBC.aspx (both accessed 16/10/2013).

[20] Rafe Needleman, "Twitter CEO: The Revenue's Coming Soon, But I Won't Tell You How," *CNet.com*, December 2, 2008 at http://news.cnet.com/8301-17939_109-10112037-2.html; Chris Snyder, "Twitter Could 'Go for Years' without Earning a Dime, Investor Says," *Epicenter: The Business of Tech*, February 13, 2009, at http://www.wired.com/epicenter/2009/02/twitter-still-l/;

"JPMorgan Twitter Deal Is Said to Value Startup at $4.5 Billion," *MoneyNews.com*, March 1, 2011, at http://www.moneynews.com/FinanceNews/JPMorgan-Twitter-Deal-Value/2011/03/01/id/387853; Kelly Clay, "Twitter Possibly Worth More Than $10 Billion," *Forbes*, July 27, 2012, at http://www.forbes.com/sites/kellyclay/2012/07/27/twitter-possibly-worth-more-than-10-billion/; Katherine Rushton, "Twitter Worth 11 Billion, Likely to Float in 2014," *THE TELEGRAPH*, January 3, 2013, at http://www.telegraph.co.uk/finance/newsbysector/mediatechnologyandtelecoms/digital-media/9778773/Twitter-worth-11bn-likely-to-float-in-2014.html.

[21] Peter Delevett, "Twitter Lands $800 Million Venture Capital Deal, Breaking Record," *MercuryNews.com*, August 2, 2011, at http://www.mercurynews.com/wiretap/ci_18596988.

[22] Hugo Sumner, "Twitter in 2012—the Record Breaking Year," *BUSINESS2COMMUNITY*, January 22, 2013, at http://www.business2community.com/twitter/twitter-in-2012-the-record-breaking-year-0384141; Kate Kaye, "Tracking 'Promoted Trends': Twitter Draws Diverse Advertisers," *ClickZ*, March 2, 2011, at http://www.clickz.com/clickz/news/2030238/tracking-promoted-trends-twitter-draws-diverse-advertisers; "What Is Twitter Worth? Twitter Is Valued at Over $4 Billion Dollars," *Wealthvest*, January 26, 2011, at http://www.wealthvest.com/blog/tag/twitter-stock-symbol/.

[23] http://www.oecd.org/els/soc/41941763.pdf; http://www.thestar.com.my/Business/Business-News/2013/08/09/Malaysians-not-saving-enough-for-retirement-says-HSBC.aspx (both accessed 16/10/2013).

[24] Ciel S. Cantoria, Edited by Linda Richter, "Unraveling the Details of 10 High-Profile Accounting Scandals," *BRIGHT HUB*, December 30, 2010, at http://www.brighthub.com/office/finance/articles/101200.aspx; "The Biggest Accounting Scandals of All Time (PHOTOS)," *Huffington Post*, May 17, 2010 at http://www.huffingtonpost.com/2010/03/17/biggest-accounting-scanda_n_502181.html#s74418&title=Madoff_Scandal_; "The Corporate Scandal Sheet," *Citizen Works* (August 2004), at http://www.citizenworks.org/enron/corp-scandal.php; "Largest Health Care Fraud Case in U.S. History Settled," *Department of Justice* (June 26, 2003), at http://www.usdoj.gov/opa/pr/2003/June/03_civ_386.htm; "Kozlowski Is Found Guilty," *TheStreet.com*, June 17, 2005, at http://www.thestreet.com/story/10228619/1/kozlowski-is-found-guilty.html.

[25] "10 Do's and Don'ts on Small Business Accounting Practice," *BassFishingGuide*, , at http://bassfishingguide.hubpages.com/hub/10-Dos-And-Donts-On-Small-Business-Accounting-Practice, accessed on May 30, 2013.

[26] "IASB and FASB Propose a New Joint Standard for Revenue Recognition," *Financial Accounting Standards Board*, June 24, 2010, at http://www.fasb.org/cs/ContentServer?c=FASBContent_C&pagename=FASB%2FFASBContent_C%2FNewsPage&cid=1176156953088.

[27] "IFRS Overview," *NYSSCPA.ORG*, at http://www.nysscpa.org/ifrs/overview.htm, accessed on March 10, 2011.

28 "IASB and FASB Propose to Align Balance Sheet Netting Requirements Differences in IFRS and US GAAP Offsetting Requirements to be Eliminated," *FASB: Financial Accounting Standards Board*," (news release) January 28, 2011, at http://www.fasb.org/cs/Content Server?c=FASBContent_C&pagename=FASB/ FASBContent_C/NewsPage&cid=1176158186333.

29 John Briginshaw, "What Will the International Financial Reporting Standards (IFRS) Mean to Businesses and Investors?" *Graziadio Business Review*, 2008, Volume 11 Issue 4, at http://gbr.pepperdine.edu/2010/08/what-will-the-international-financial-reporting-standards-ifrs-mean-to-businesses-and-investors/.

30 "IASB and FASB Propose a New Joint Standard for Revenue Recognition," *Financial Accounting Standards Board*, June 24, 2010, at http://www.fasb.org/cs/ContentServer?c=F ASBContent_C&pagename=FASB%2FFASBContent_C% 2FNewsPage&cid=1176156953088.

31 "IASB and FASB Propose Common Solution for Impairment Accounting," *FASB: Financial Accounting Standards Board*," (news release) January 31, 2011, at http://www.fasb.org/cs/ContentServer?c=FASB Content_C&pagename=FASB/FASBContent_C/ NewsPage&cid=1176158192211.

32 "FASB, IASB Propose Changes in Fair Value Standards," *Insurance Networking News*, June 29, 2010, at http:// www.insurancenetworking.com/news/insur-ance_fair_value_standards_accounting_IASB_FASB_ GAAP_IFRS-25136-1.html; "Measurement Uncertainty Analysis Disclosure for Fair Value Measurements," *International Accounting Standards Board*, June 2010, at http://www.iasb.org/NR/rdonlyres/07855A41-D0A9-4197-ADF9-15A1088E466A/0/ EDMeasurementUncertaintyAnalysis0610.pdf.

33 Alexandra Defelice and Matthew G. Lamoreaux, "No IFRS Requirement Until 2015 or Later Under New SEC Timeline," *Journal of Accountancy*, February 24, 2010, at http://www.journalofaccountancy.com/ Web/20102656.htm; Michael Rapoport, "Delay Seen (Again) for New Rules on Accounting," *Wall Street Journal*, July 6, 2012, pp. C1, C2; Michael Rapoport, "Accounting Panel Expresses 'Regret' Over U.S. Stance," *Wall Street Journal*, July 16, 2012, p. C5; Shane Gastecki, "CPA Candidates Are Confronted by Significant Changes to Exam," *accountingWEB*, June 14, 2011, at http://www.accountingweb.com/topic/ education-careers/cpa-candidates-are-confronted-significant-changes-exam, accessed on February 18, 2013.

34 Iwona Tokc-Wilde, "#AAYP 2013: Modern Accountants—People Who Think Differently," *AccountancyAge*, May 1, 2013, at http://www.accountancyage.com/aa/ feature/2265153/-aayp-2013-modern-accountants-people-who-think-differently; "Intuit 2020 Report Depicts Future of the Accounting Profession: A New Mindset and Model Required to Thrive in a Connected World," *Intuit Inc.*, February 2, 2011, at http://about. intuit.com/about_intuit/press_room/press_release/ articles/2011/Intuit2020ReportDepictsFuture.html; Rich Walker, "Intuit 2020 Report Depicts Future of the Accounting Profession," *Intuit Accountants News Central*, February 2, 2011, at https://blog.accountants. intuit.com/intuit-news/intuit%C2%AE-2020-report-depicts-future-of-the-accounting-profession/; "Accountants—the Old and the New," *CA Saga*, August 15, 2012, at http://contractaccountants.word-press.com/2012/08/15/accountants-the-old-and-the-new/; "The Many Hats of a Modern Accountant," *Jobs. net*, May 14, 2013, at http://www.jobs.net/Article/ CB-6-Talent-Network-Finance-Ins-The-Many-Hats-of-a-Modern-Accountant/.

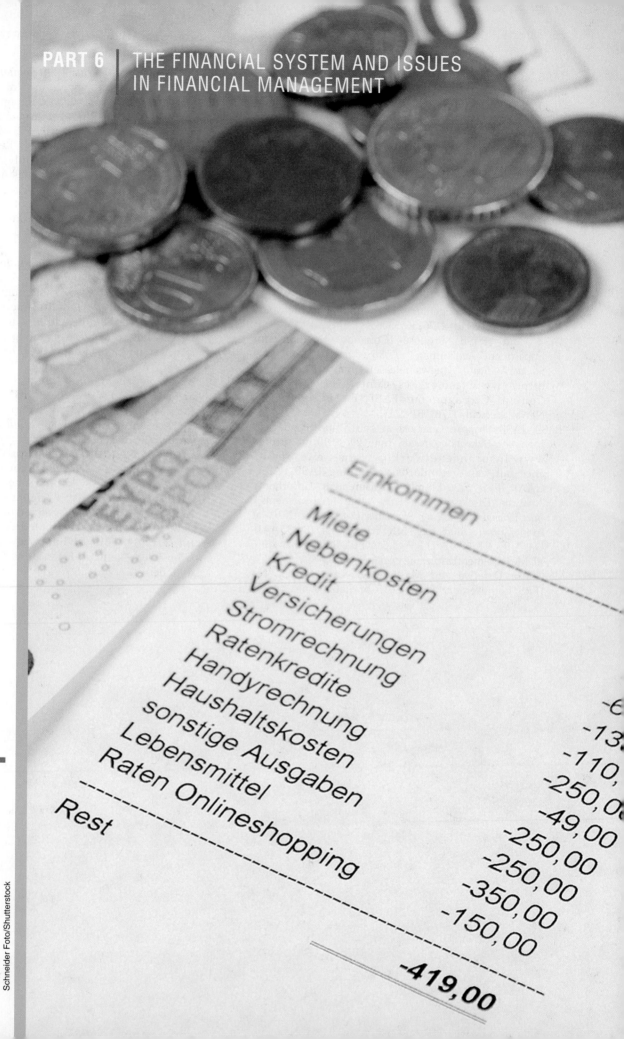

chapter 16

Understanding Money and the Role of Banking

Schneider Foto/Shutterstock

Einkommen

Miete
Nebenkosten
Kredit
Versicherungen
Stromrechnung
Ratenkredite
Handyrechnung
Haushaltskosten
sonstige Ausgaben
Lebensmittel
Raten Onlineshopping

Rest

-6
-13,
-110,
-250,0
-49,00
-250,00
-250,00
-350,00
-150,00

-419,00

Making money is more than just dollars and sense.

Technology and a flat world

complicate matters;

businesses need to ask

where their money comes from,

who is using it,

and why.

AFTER READING THIS CHAPTER, YOU SHOULD BE ABLE TO:

OBJECTIVE 1 **Define** *money* and identify the different forms that it takes in the nation's money supply.

OBJECTIVE 2 **Describe** the different kinds of financial institutions that compose the U.S. financial system and explain the services they offer.

OBJECTIVE 3 **Explain** how financial institutions create money and describe the means by which they are regulated.

OBJECTIVE 4 **Discuss** the functions of the Federal Reserve System and describe the tools that it uses to control the money supply.

OBJECTIVE 5 **Identify** three important ways in which the money and banking system is changing.

OBJECTIVE 6 **Discuss** some of the institutions and activities in international banking and finance.

MyBizLab®

⭐ Improve Your Grade!

Visit **pearsonglobaleditions.com/mybizlab** for simulations, tutorials, and end-of-chapter problems.

simulations **videos** **assisted-graded writing**

Over 10 million students improved their results using the Pearson MyLabs.

A Tale of Two Worlds
in Banking

Once upon a time, in an economic climate far, far away, banking was a steady, quiet, money-making industry regarded by some as, well, rather mundane or even boring. Nothing is further removed from the turbulent and controversial world of banking today.

Banking's external environments—especially economic, global, and political-legal—are significantly demanding and challenging, starting with the largest national banking systems, and continuing on down to the smallest community banks. Following the global economic meltdown of 2008, the U.S. Federal Reserve Bank and European Central Bank, for example, have taken ambitious steps to staunch the damage at thousands of banks in their jurisdictions. Individual banks, both large and small, are redefining the products they offer, changing sources of revenue to compete and survive, and otherwise addressing obligations to the communities they serve.

Governments are relying on banks as instruments of national policy for economic stability, using diverse responses for different conditions. We see, for example, while central banks in China and India are raising key interest rates, those in the euro zone and the United States are holding rates at near-historic lows because remedies for stagnant economies differ from cures for those that are booming. Countries with severe downturns, high unemployment, and increasing national debt—the United States, Portugal, Greece, Ireland, and Spain among others—use low interest rates and financial bailouts to stimulate borrowing and create jobs. Meanwhile, banks in China and India are increasing lending rates to make borrowing more expensive for businesses and consumers. The goal is to slow down rapid economic expansion and reduce fears of runaway inflation. At the same time, Japan's economy—broken by a terrible earthquake and tsunami—needs lower interest rates for easier borrowing to rebuild the devastated economy.[1]

Countries with massive debt face double-trouble for recovery. The first obstacle is difficulty borrowing outside money for economic recovery, although some have received emergency financing from the International Monetary Fund. Second, when national debt increases, the value of its currency falls on foreign exchange markets, its money then buys less than before, so each of its citizens suffers lower real wealth.[2]

Meanwhile, many U.S. banks have good reason to remain cautious during the slow economic recovery. The failure of Crescent Bank and Trust in Jasper, Georgia, has cost the Federal Deposit Insurance Corporation (FDIC) more than $240 million and that's

Sergey Nivens/fotolia

what's in it for me?

Dealing in matters of money is vastly more complicated than counting the cash and coins in your pocket, especially when technology and globalization come into play. At its core are questions about where money comes from, how national economies depend on it, and the public's trust in its value. This chapter will give you a solid understanding of the different forms of money and how its supply is created and controlled by different kinds of financial institutions and government regulations.

just one example among the 157 U.S. bank failures in 2010, after another 140 closures in 2009, followed by another 143 closures through 2012, which is the highest since 1992.[3] The nation's remaining 5,900 lenders, too, remain shaken by the housing market collapse. As uncollectable loans continue because of out-of-work borrowers, banks are left with unsellable foreclosed properties.

To regain profits, larger banks are charging for formerly "free" services. Bank of America, for example, charges additional monthly fees for an account if you want to get paper statements or want to bank with a teller. "Free checking" is dwindling away as banks again begin charging a fee for each check. Smaller banks, in contrast, hope to keep those traditionally free services as a strategy for attracting customers for survival.[4]

Adding fuel to the revenue fire is the Federal Reserve Board's new limit on debit-card fees that banks and credit card companies charge merchants when customers pay with debit cards. Stores previously paid usage fees between 1 and 2 percent of each sale, totaling some $16 billion from 38 billion debit card transactions annually. The new rule limits the fee to 24 cents per transaction, thus reducing bank/card company revenues down to $10 billion. The issue for banks then becomes one of finding new revenue sources to make up for the $6 billion revenue loss.[5]

Taking lessons from the continuing global financial crisis, and seeking greater economic stability, regulators worldwide are proposing broader rules to provide future global stability in banking. Regulators from more than 20 nations have proposed the "Basel (Switzerland) III Requirements" to be adopted by 2019. They call for banks to keep larger cushions of cash on hand to guard against future losses, with tighter rules on loans to businesses and consumers.[6]

OBJECTIVE 1
Define
money and identify the different forms that it takes in the nation's money supply.

What Is Money?

When someone asks you how much money you have, do you count the dollar bills and coins in your pockets? Do you include your checking and savings accounts? What about stocks and bonds? Do you count your car? Taken together, the value of all these combined is your personal wealth. Not all of it, however, is "money." This section considers more precisely what *money* is and does.

The Characteristics of Money

Modern money generally takes the form of stamped metal or printed paper issued by governments. Theoretically, however, just about anything *portable*, *divisible*, *durable*, and *stable* can serve as **money**. To appreciate these qualities, imagine using something that lacks them—for example, a 1,000-pound cow used as a unit of exchange in ancient agrarian economies.

Money *object that is portable, divisible, durable, and stable, and that serves as a medium of exchange, a store of value, and a measure of worth*

- *Portability.* Try lugging 1,000 pounds of cow from shop to shop. In contrast, modern currency is light and easy to handle.

- *Divisibility.* How would you divide your cow if you wanted to buy a hat, a book, and a radio from three different stores? Is a pound of head worth as much as a pound of leg? Modern currency is easily divisible into smaller parts with fixed values—for example, a dollar for 10 dimes.

- *Durability.* Your cow will lose value every day (and eventually die). Modern currency, however, neither dies nor spoils, and if it wears out, it can be replaced. It is also hard to counterfeit—certainly harder than cattle breeding.

- *Stability.* If cows were in short supply, you might be able to make quite a deal for yourself. In the middle of an abundant cow year, however, the market would be flooded with cows, so their value would fall. The value of our paper money also fluctuates, but it is considerably more stable and predictable.

Cattle are not portable, divisible, durable, or stable, making them an unsuitable medium of exchange in the modern monetized economy.

Photos.com/Jupiterimages

The Functions of Money

Imagine a successful cow rancher who needs a new fence. In a *barter economy*, one in which goods are exchanged directly for one another, he or she would have to find someone who is willing to exchange a fence for a cow (or parts of it). If no fence maker wants a cow, the rancher must find someone else—for example, a wagon maker—who does want a cow. Then, the rancher must hope that the fence maker will trade for a new wagon. In a money economy, the rancher would sell his or her cow, receive money, and exchange the money for such goods as a new fence.

Money serves three functions:

1 *It is a medium of exchange.* Like the rancher "trading" money for a new fence, money is used to buy and sell things. Without money, we would be bogged down in a system of barter.

2 *It is a store of value.* Pity the rancher whose cow gets sick on Monday and who wants to buy some clothes on the following Saturday, by which time the cow may have died and lost its value. In the form of currency, however, money can be used for future purchases and "stores" value.

3 *It is a measure of worth.* Money lets us measure the relative values of goods and services. It acts as a measure of worth because all products can be valued and accounted for in terms of money. For example, the concepts of $1,000 worth of clothes or $500 in labor costs have universal meaning.

We see, then, that money adds convenience and simplicity to our everyday lives, for consumers and businesses alike. Employees, consumers, and businesses use money as the measure of worth for determining wages and for buying and selling products—everything from ice cream to housing rentals. Consumers with cash can make purchases wherever they go because businesses everywhere accept money as a medium for exchange. And because money is stable, businesses and individuals save their money, trusting that its value will be available for future use.

M-1: The Spendable Money Supply

For money to serve its basic functions, both buyers and sellers must agree on its value, which depends in part on its *supply*—how much money is in circulation. When the money supply is high, the value of money drops. When it is low, that value increases.

Instead of using a modern monetary system, traders like Muhammed Essa in Quetta, Pakistan, transfer funds through handshakes and code words. The ancient system is called *hawala*, which means "trust" in Arabic. The worldwide *hawala* system, though illegal in most countries, moves billions of dollars past regulators annually and is alleged to be the system of choice for terrorists because it leaves no paper trail.

Unfortunately, there is no single agreed-on measure of the supply of money. The oldest and most basic measure, **M-1,** counts only the most liquid, or spendable, forms of money—cash, checks, and checking accounts.

- Paper money and metal coins are **currency (cash)** issued by the government and widely used for small exchanges. Law requires creditors to accept it in payment of debts.

- A **check** is essentially an order instructing a bank to pay a given sum to a payee. Checks are usually, but not always, accepted because they are valuable only to specified payees and can be exchanged for cash.

- **Checking accounts,** or **demand deposits,** are money because their funds may be withdrawn at any time on demand.

These are all noninterest-bearing or low-interest–bearing forms of money. As of January 2013, M-1 in the United States totaled $2.52 trillion.[7]

M-2: M-1 Plus the Convertible Money Supply

M-2, a second measure of the money supply, is often used for economic planning by businesses and government agencies. **M-2** includes everything in M-1 plus other forms of money that are not quite as liquid, for example, short-term investments that are easily converted to spendable forms, including *time deposits, money market mutual funds*, and *savings accounts*. Totaling $10.45 trillion in January 2013, M-2 accounts for most of the nation's money supply.[8] It measures the store of monetary value available for financial transactions by individuals and small businesses. As this overall level increases, more money is available for consumer purchases and business investments. When the supply is tightened, less money is available; financial transactions, spending, and business activity slow down.

Unlike demand deposits, **time deposits,** such as certificates of deposit (CDs), have a fixed term, are intended to be held to maturity, cannot be transferred by check, and

M-1 *measure of the money supply that includes only the most liquid (spendable) forms of money*

Currency (Cash) *government-issued paper money and metal coins*

Check *demand deposit order instructing a bank to pay a given sum to a specified payee*

Checking Account (Demand Deposit) *bank account funds, owned by the depositor, that may be withdrawn at any time by check or cash*

M-2 *measure of the money supply that includes all the components of M-1 plus the forms of money that can be easily converted into spendable forms*

Time Deposit *bank funds that have a fixed term of time to maturity and cannot be withdrawn earlier or transferred by check*

pay higher interest rates than checking accounts. Time deposits in M-2 include only accounts of less than $100,000 that can be redeemed on demand, with penalties for early withdrawal.

With **money market mutual funds,** investment companies buy a collection of short-term, low-risk financial securities. Ownership of and profits (or losses) from the sale of these securities are shared among the fund's investors.

Figure 16.1 shows how M-1 and M-2 have grown since 1979. For many years, M-1 was the traditional measure of liquid money. Because it was closely related to gross domestic product, it served as a reliable predictor of the nation's real money supply.

Money Market Mutual Fund *fund of short-term, low-risk financial securities purchased with the pooled assets of investor-owners*

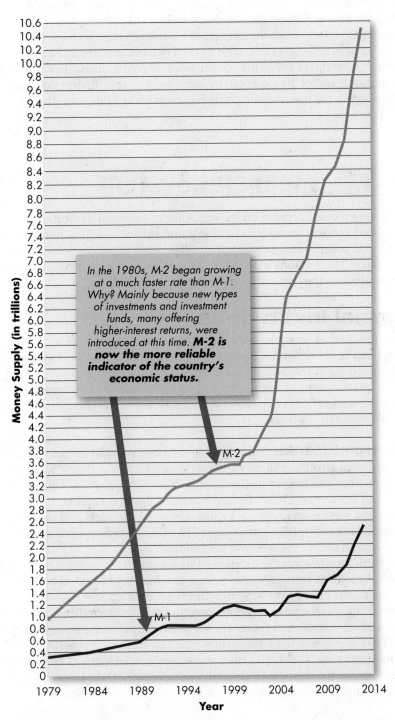

FIGURE 16.1 Money Supply Growth
Source: "Money Stock Measures," *Federal Reserve*, at www.federalreserve.gov/releases/h6/current/, accessed on May 19, 2013.

This situation changed in the early 1980s, with the introduction of new types of investments and the easier transfer of money among investment funds to gain higher interest returns. As a result, M-2 today is regarded as a more reliable measure than M-1.

Credit Cards and Debit Cards: Plastic Money?

The use of credit and debit cards has become so widespread that many people refer to them as "plastic money." Credit cards, however, are not money and, accordingly, are not included in M-1 or M-2 when measuring the nation's money supply. Why? Because spending with a credit card creates a debt, but does not move money until later when the debt is paid by cash or check. Debit card transactions, in contrast, transfer money immediately from the consumer's bank account, so they affect the money supply the same way as spending with a check or cash, and are included in M-1.

Although consumers enjoy the convenience of credit cards, they also are finding that irresponsible use of the cards can be hazardous to your financial health. A discussion on managing the use of credit cards is presented in Appendix III: Managing Your Personal Finances.

OBJECTIVE 2
Describe
the different kinds of financial institutions that compose the U.S. financial system and explain the services they offer.

The U.S. Financial System

Many forms of money depend on the existence of financial institutions that provide money-related services to both individuals and businesses. Just how important are these financial institutions, how do they work, and what are some of the services that they offer? The sections that follow explain their role as creators of money and discuss the services they offer in the U.S. banking system.

Financial Institutions

The main function of financial institutions is to ease the flow of money from users with surpluses to those with deficits by attracting funds into checking and savings accounts. Incoming funds will be loaned to individuals and businesses and perhaps invested in government securities. U.S. consumers have access to more than 90,000 U.S. branches and offices of *commercial banks*, *savings institutions*, *credit unions*, and various *nondeposit institutions*.

Commercial Bank *company that accepts deposits that it uses to make loans, earn profits, pay interest to depositors, and pay dividends to owners*

Commercial Banks Federally insured **commercial banks** accept deposits, make loans, earn profits, and pay interest and dividends. Some 5,900 commercial banks range from the largest institutions in New York, such as Citigroup, Bank of America, and JPMorgan Chase, to tiny banks dotting the rural landscape. Bank liabilities, or holdings owed to others, include checking accounts and savings accounts. U.S. banks hold assets totaling more than $12 trillion, consisting of a wide variety of loans to individuals, businesses, and governments.[9]

Prime Rate *interest rate available to a bank's most creditworthy customers*

Every bank receives a major portion of its income from interest paid on loans by borrowers. As long as terms and conditions are clearly revealed to borrowers, banks may set their own interest rates, within limits set by each state. Traditionally, banks only offered the lowest rate, or **prime rate,** to their most creditworthy commercial customers. Most commercial loans are set at markups over prime, like prime + 1, which means 1 percent over the prime rate. To remain competitive with lower-interest foreign banks, U.S. banks offer some commercial loans at rates below prime. Figure 16.2 shows the changes in the prime rate since 2000. Lower rates in 2008–2013 encouraged banks to continue lending in the economic downturn.

Savings Institutions Savings institutions include mutual savings banks and savings and loan associations. They are also called *thrift institutions* because they were established decades ago to promote the idea of savings among the general population.

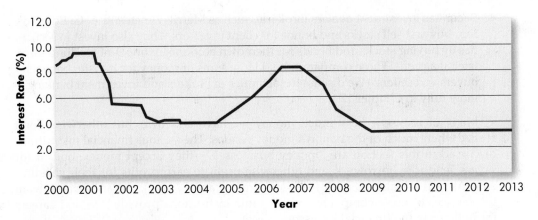

FIGURE 16.2 The Prime Rate
Source: "Prime Interest Rate History," at http://www.fedprimerate.com/wall_street_journal_prime_rate_history.htm, accessed on June 20, 2013.

Savings and Loan Associations
Like commercial banks, **savings and loan associations (S&Ls)** accept deposits, make loans, and are owned by investors. Most S&Ls were created to encourage savings habits and provide financing for homes; they did not offer check services. Today they have ventured into a variety of other loans and services.

Savings and Loan Association (S&L) *financial institution accepting deposits and making loans primarily for home mortgages*

Mutual Savings Banks
In a **mutual savings bank,** all depositors are considered owners of the bank. All profits are divided proportionately among depositors, who receive dividends. About 600 U.S. mutual savings banks attract most of their funds in the form of savings deposits, and funds are loaned out in the form of mortgages.

Mutual Savings Bank *financial institution whose depositors are owners sharing in its profits*

Credit Unions
A **credit union** is a nonprofit, cooperative financial institution owned and run by its members. Its purpose is to promote *thrift*, careful management of one's money or resources, and to provide members with a safe place to save and borrow at reasonable rates. Members pool their funds to make loans to one another. Each credit union decides whom it will serve, such as a group of employees, people in a particular community, or members of an association. Many universities and the U.S. Navy, for examples, have credit unions, among the nation's 7,400 credit unions.

Credit Union *nonprofit, cooperative financial institution owned and run by its members, usually employees of a particular organization*

Nondeposit Institutions
A variety of other organizations takes in money, provides interest or other services, and makes loans. Unlike commercial banks, these *nondeposit institutions* use inflowing funds for purposes other than earning interest for depositors. Four of the most important are (1) *pension funds*, (2) *insurance companies*, (3) *finance companies*, and (4) *securities investment dealers*.

1. A **pension fund** is a pool of funds that is managed to provide retirement income for its members. *Public pension funds* in the United States include Social Security and the more than $3 trillion in retirement programs for state and local government employees. *Private pension funds*, operated by employers, unions, and other private groups, cover about 36 million people and have total assets of $20 trillion, up from $13 trillion during the 2008 recession.[10]

Pension Fund *nondeposit pool of funds managed to provide retirement income for its members*

2. **Insurance companies** accumulate money from premiums charged for coverage. They invest these funds in stocks, real estate, and other assets. Earnings pay for insured losses, such as death benefits, automobile damage, and healthcare expenses.

Insurance Company *nondeposit institution that invests funds collected as premiums charged for insurance coverage*

3. **Finance companies** specialize in making loans to businesses and consumers. HFC Beneficial, for example, offers mortgage refinancing and personal loans. *Commercial finance companies* lend to businesses needing capital or long-term funds. *Consumer finance companies* devote most of their resources to providing small noncommercial loans to individuals.

Finance Company *nondeposit institution that specializes in making loans to businesses and consumers*

Securities Investment Dealer (Broker) *financial institution that buys and sells stocks and bonds both for investors and for its own accounts*

4   **Securities investment dealers (brokers),** such as Merrill Lynch and A. G. Edwards Inc., buy and sell stocks and bonds for client investors. They also invest in securities by buying stocks and bonds for their own accounts in hopes of reselling them later at a profit. These companies hold large sums of money for transfer between buyers and sellers. (We discuss the activities of brokers and investment banking more fully in Chapter 17.)

Many of us know how much money we have and owe, but otherwise don't realize where much of the nation's money resides. The various financial institutions discussed in this section are "money businesses"—they accept money, hold it for savers, lend it to borrowers, and otherwise use it to earn profits for their constituents. As individuals, many of us at one time or another seek out and benefit from the services of these companies. These same institutions provide jobs and careers for millions in the financial industry.

The Growth of Financial Services

The finance business today is highly competitive. No longer is it enough for commercial banks to accept deposits and make loans. Most, for example, also offer bank-issued credit and debit cards, safe-deposit boxes, ATMs, electronic money transfer, online banking, and foreign currency exchange. In addition, many offer pension, trust, international, and brokerage services and financial advice.

Individual Retirement Account (IRA) *tax-deferred pension fund that wage earners set up to supplement retirement funds*

Trust Services *management by a bank of an estate, investments, or other assets on behalf of an individual*

Pension and Trust Services   Individual retirement accounts (IRAs) are tax-deferred pension funds that wage earners and their spouses can set up to supplement other retirement funds. Advantages and drawbacks to various kinds of IRAs—*traditional, Roth,* and *education*—are discussed in Appendix III.

Many commercial banks offer **trust services,** the management of funds left in the bank's trust. In return for a fee, the trust department will perform such tasks as making your monthly bill payments and managing your investment portfolio. Trust departments also manage the estates of deceased persons.

International Services   Suppose a U.S. company wants to buy a product from a Chinese supplier. For a fee, it can use one or more of three services offered by its bank:

Letter of Credit *bank promise, issued for a buyer, to pay a designated firm a certain amount of money if specified conditions are met*

Banker's Acceptance *bank promise, issued for a buyer, to pay a designated firm a specified amount at a future date*

1   *Currency Exchange:* It can exchange U.S. dollars for Chinese yuan to pay the supplier.

2   *Letters of Credit:* It can pay its bank to issue a **letter of credit,** a promise by the bank to pay the Chinese firm a certain amount if specified conditions are met.

3   *Banker's Acceptances:* It can pay its bank to draw up a **banker's acceptance,** which promises that the bank will pay some specified amount at a future date.

A banker's acceptance requires payment by a particular date. Letters of credit are payable only after certain conditions are met. The Chinese supplier, for example, may not be paid until shipping documents prove that the merchandise has been shipped from China.

Financial Advice and Brokerage Services   Many banks, both large and small, help their customers manage their money. Depending on the customer's situation, the bank, in its role as financial advisor, may recommend different investment opportunities. The recommended mix might include CDs, mutual funds, stocks, and bonds. Many banks also serve as securities intermediaries, using their own stockbrokers to buy and sell securities and their own facilities to hold them.

Electronic Funds Transfer (EFT) *communication of fund-transfer information over wire, cable, or microwave*

Electronic Funds Transfer   Electronic funds transfer (EFT) provides for payments and collections by transferring financial information electronically. PayPal offers online payments and money transfers among businesses and individuals,

managing in turbulent times

Getting Serious with Credit Standards

While banks were trying to avoid drowning in bad loans, borrowers and lenders alike were questioning how the banks got into the 2008-onward financial mess. Many observers today continue to blame subprime mortgage lending. Unlike prime mortgages, subprime loans are made to high-risk borrowers, those with bad credit histories, excessive debt, inadequate income, or other indicators that they will not repay the lender. In return for riskier loans, borrowers pay higher interest rates. As the housing market tumbled, delinquencies skyrocketed on millions of subprime loans. Whereas about 6 percent of mortgage loans were uncollectable from 2000 to 2005, thereafter delinquencies increased, nearing 30 percent by 2008, and on into 2010. Lenders extended too much credit to weak borrowers.[11]

Jupiter Images

Reports indicate that the subprime crisis can be traced to overly relaxed credit standards. One study found that many loan applications listed fraudulent information. Some borrowers, taking advantage of lax lending practices to live beyond their means, lied about their income and assets to secure loans. Other misinformation is attributed to mortgage brokers eager to get otherwise unqualified borrowers approved for loans. Some lenders went so far as to have a relative pose as a borrower's fake employer and falsify W-2 forms to gain approval. These problems were compounded further by those within the banking and finance system who knew that rampant fraud was occurring but looked the other way, as long as profits kept rolling in.[12]

Stuck with uncollectable loans, unsellable foreclosed properties, and big financial losses, the industry tightened credit standards and lending practices. Federal bank examiners insisted that loan officers use greater caution and judgment to identify creditworthy borrowers and avoid weak loans. Lenders switched to independent real estate appraisers, who have no direct contact with loan officers, to get accurate rather than inflated property appraisals. Along with requiring bigger down payments, lenders today are requiring higher minimum credit scores. Lenders are also reducing limits on credit card balances. With a dire lesson learned, it appears that tighter standards are having a positive affect; at the end of 2012 the delinquency rate had fallen to 5.5 percent (the percentage of mortgage borrowers 60 or more days past due). When 2013 interest rates dipped to an all-time low, many would-be borrowers were frustrated by lenders' continuing intentions to use tight credit standards for the foreseeable future.[13]

---

nationally and internationally, in various currencies, requiring only that recipients have an e-mail address. Consumers using debit cards and mobile devices instead of writing personal checks enjoy EFT's convenience and speed at the checkout. In addition, EFT systems provide automatic payroll deposit, ATM transactions, bill payment, and automatic funds transfer. Such systems can help a businessperson close an important business deal by transferring money from San Francisco to Miami within a few seconds. The U.S. Treasury reports that it costs $1.03 to issue a check payment, but only $0.105 to issue an EFT payment. The U.S. Social Security system expects savings of more than $1 billion during the next decade by phasing out paper check payments in 2013, and instead using paperless payments for federal benefits.[14]

Automated teller machines (ATMs) allow customers to withdraw money, make deposits, transfer funds between accounts, and access information on their accounts. About 445,000 machines are located in U.S. bank buildings and other locations.[15] Increasingly, ATMs have become multilingual global fixtures. As Figure 16.3 shows, among the world's more than 2 million ATMs, most are located outside the United States, and many U.S. banks offer international ATM services.[16] China is expected to become the world's largest ATM market by 2015.

Automated Teller Machine (ATM)
electronic machine that allows bank customers to conduct account-related activities 24 hours a day, 7 days a week

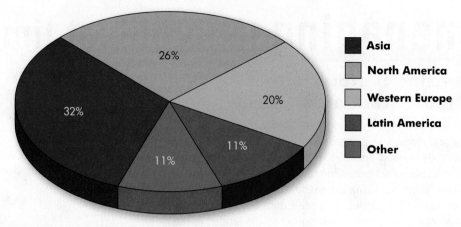

FIGURE 16.3 Global Dispersion of ATMs

Financial Institutions Create Money and Are Regulated

OBJECTIVE 3
Explain
how financial institutions create money and describe the means by which they are regulated.

When individuals make decisions about spending and saving money, they often don't realize they are taking a financial risk. Getting more value for your money requires an awareness of how the value of your money, including savings, changes—and it does change. As the value of money goes down, your purchasing power goes down. Conversely, purchasing power goes up as the value of your money increases. By predicting changes in value you can time your spending and savings decisions to get the most for your money. Predictions of future values become possible by (1) understanding how money is created—the topic of this section—and by (2) understanding how the Federal Reserve controls the supply of money—the topic in a following section.

Financial institutions provide a special service to the economy: they create money. They don't print bills and mint coins, but by taking in deposits and making loans, they expand the money supply.

As Figure 16.4 shows, the money supply expands because banks are allowed to loan out most (although not all) of the money they take in from deposits. If you deposit $100 in your bank and banks are allowed to loan out 90 percent of all their

Deposit	Money Held in Reserve by Bank	Money to Lend	Total Supply
$100.00	$10.00	$90.00	**$190.00**
90.00	9.00	81.00	**271.00**
81.00	8.10	72.90	**343.90**
72.90	7.29	65.61	**409.51**
65.61	6.56	59.05	**468.56**

FIGURE 16.4 How Banks Create Money

deposits, then your bank will hold $10 in reserve and loan $90 of your money to borrowers. (You still have $100 on deposit.) Meanwhile, a borrower—or the people paid by the borrower—will deposit the $90 loan money in a bank (or banks). The bank will then have another $81 (90 percent of $90) available for new loans. The banks, therefore, have turned your original $100 into $271 ($100 + $90 + $81). The chain continues, with borrowings from one bank becoming deposits in the next.

Regulation of the Banking System

Because commercial banks are essential to the creation of money, the government regulates them to ensure a sound and competitive financial system. Federal and state agencies regulate banks to ensure that the failure of some will not cause the public to lose faith in the banking system itself.

The **Federal Deposit Insurance Corporation (FDIC)** supervises banks and insures deposits in banks and thrift institutions. The FDIC is a government agency, created by President Franklin D. Roosevelt to restore public confidence in banks during the Depression era. More than 99 percent of the nation's commercial banks and savings institutions pay fees for membership in the FDIC. In return, the FDIC guarantees the safety of all accounts—checking, savings, and CDs—of every account owner up to the maximum of $250,000. If a bank collapses, the FDIC promises to pay each depositor for losses up to $250,000 per account. A person with more money can establish accounts in more than one bank to protect sums in excess of $250,000. (A handful of the nation's 5,900 commercial banks are insured by states rather than by the FDIC.) To ensure against multiple bank failures, the FDIC maintains the right to examine the activities and accounts of all member banks.

What happens with banks that fail, such as the nearly 300 U.S. banks that failed in 2009 and 2010? The FDIC becomes responsible for disposing of failed banks. One option is to sell them to other banks that are then responsible for the liabilities of the failed banks. Alternatively, the FDIC can seize the assets of the failed banks and undertake two activities: (1) Pay insurance to depositors and (2) dispose of the banks' assets and settle their debts, all at the lowest cost to the FDIC's insurance deposit fund. The resulting net gain (or loss) is put into (or paid from) the insurance deposit fund. As the recession of 2008 deepened, this fund had dwindled to $13 billion in 2009, down from $45 billion in 2008, before recovering to $33 billion in 2012. With more bank closures expected, the FDIC was raising assessments against member banks to restore the fund's reserves.[17]

Federal Deposit Insurance Corporation (FDIC) *federal agency that guarantees the safety of deposits up to $250,000 in the financial institutions that it insures*

Devout Muslims can't pay or receive interest—a fact that tends to complicate banking operations. Because money has to work in order to earn a return, institutions like the Shamil Bank in Bahrain invest deposits directly in such ventures as real estate and pay back profit shares rather than interest.

The Federal Reserve System

Perched atop the U.S. financial system and regulating many aspects of its operation is the **Federal Reserve System (the Fed),** the nation's central bank, established by Congress in 1913. This section describes the structure of the Fed, its functions, and the tools it uses to control the nation's money supply.

The Structure of the Fed

The Fed consists of a board of governors, a group of reserve banks, and member banks. As originally established by the Federal Reserve Act of 1913, the system consisted of 12 relatively autonomous banks and a seven-member committee whose powers were limited to coordinating the activities of those banks. By the 1930s, however, both the structure and function of the Fed had changed dramatically.

The Board of Governors
The Fed's board of governors consists of seven members appointed by the U.S. President for overlapping terms of 14 years. The chair of the board serves on major economic advisory committees and works actively with the administration to formulate economic policy. The board plays a large role in controlling the money supply. It alone determines the reserve requirements, within statutory limits, for depository institutions. It also works with other members of the Fed to set discount rates and handle the Fed's sale and purchase of government securities.

Reserve Banks
The Fed consists of 12 districts, as shown in Figure 16.5. Each Federal Reserve Bank holds reserve deposits from and sets the discount rate for commercial banks in its geographic region. Reserve banks also play a major role in the nation's check-clearing process.

Open Market Committee
The Federal Open Market Committee is responsible for formulating the Fed's monetary policies to promote economic stability and growth by managing the nation's money supply. Its members include the Board of Governors, the president of the Federal Reserve Bank of New York, and the presidents of four other Reserve Banks, who serve on a rotating basis.

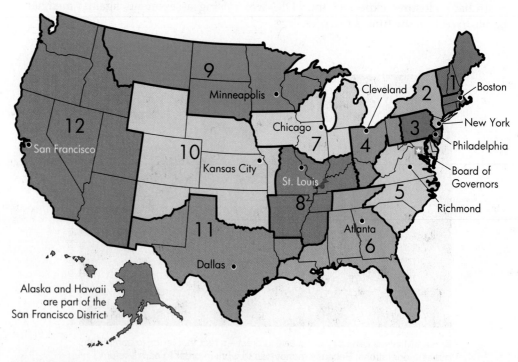

FIGURE 16.5 The Twelve Federal Reserve Districts
Source: http://www.federalreserve.gov/otherfrb.htm, accessed on July 30, 2013.

Member Banks All nationally chartered commercial banks and some state-chartered banks are members of the Fed. The accounts of all member bank depositors are automatically covered by the FDIC.

Other Depository Institutions Although many state-chartered banks, credit unions, and S&Ls do not belong to the Fed, they are subject to its regulations, pay deposit insurance premiums, and are covered by the FDIC or the National Credit Union Administration (NCUA), an independent federal agency that supervises and insures federal credit unions.

The Functions of the Fed

In addition to chartering national banks, the Fed serves as the federal government's bank and the "bankers' bank," regulating a number of banking activities. Most importantly, it controls the money supply.

The Government's Bank The Fed produces the nation's paper currency and decides how many bills to produce and destroy. It also lends money to the government by buying bonds issued by the Treasury Department to help finance the national deficit.

The Bankers' Bank Individual banks that need money can borrow from the Fed and pay interest on the loans. In addition, the Fed provides storage for commercial banks, which are required to keep funds on reserve at a Federal Reserve Bank.

Check Clearing The Fed also clears checks for commercial banks to ensure that cash is deducted from the check writer's bank account and deposited into the check receiver's account. With electronic payments, however, the number of paper checks processed is falling, with fewer than 7 billion cleared by the Fed in 2012, down from a peak of 60 billion in 2000. Consumers prefer the convenience of debit and credit cards and electronic transactions such as direct deposits and online payments. Even with paper checks, however, the clearing is faster because banks now send the Fed electronic images for presentment, payment, and record keeping (instead of shipping the checks). As a result, the Fed now has just one full-service check-processing site, instead of the 45 locations needed as recently as 2003.[18]

Controlling the Money Supply The Fed is responsible for the conduct of U.S. **monetary policy,** the management of the nation's economic growth by managing the money supply and interest rates. By controlling these two factors, the Fed influences the ability and willingness of banks throughout the country to loan money.

Monetary Policy *management of the nation's economic growth by managing the money supply and interest rates*

As defined in Chapter 1, *inflation* is a period of widespread price increases throughout an economic system. It occurs if the money supply grows too large. Demand for goods and services increases, and the prices of everything rise. To reduce China's inflationary conditions in 2010–2011, and again in 2013, banking officials decreased the money supply, hoping to slow that nation's economic growth. In contrast, *deflation* occurs when the supply of goods outpaces the supply of money, so demand for goods and services falls. Decreasing prices lead businesses to cut output, and also leads to rises in unemployment. The Fed, with its goal of economic stability, uses the money supply to avoid extreme inflation or deflation. Because commercial banks are the main creators of money, much of the Fed's management of the money supply takes the form of regulating the supply of money through commercial banks.

The Tools of the Fed

According to the Fed's original charter, its primary duties were to supervise banking and to manage the nation's currency. The duties of the Fed have evolved to include an emphasis on the broad economic goals as discussed in Chapter 1, especially growth and stability. The Fed's role in controlling the nation's money supply stems from its role in setting policies to help reach these goals. To control the money supply, the Fed uses *reserve requirements*, *interest rate controls*, and *open-market operations*.

Reserve Requirement *percentage of its deposits that a bank must hold in cash or on deposit with the Fed*

Reserve Requirements

The **reserve requirement** is the percentage of its deposits that a bank must hold, in cash or on deposit, with a Federal Reserve Bank. High requirements mean that banks have less money to lend and the money supply is reduced. Conversely, low requirements permit the supply to expand. Because the Fed sets requirements for all depository institutions, it can adjust them to make changes to the overall supply of money in the economy. The Fed's reserve requirements for 2013 depend on the sizes of depositors' accounts. The smallest accounts are exempt (0-percent reserve), for account transactions more than $12.4 million the reserve is 3 percent, and the rate is 10 percent for account transactions greater than $79.5 million.

Discount Rate *interest rate at which member banks can borrow money from the Fed*

Interest Rate Controls

As the bankers' bank, the Fed loans money to banks. The interest rate on these loans is known as the **discount rate.** If the Fed wants to reduce the money supply, it increases the discount rate, making it more expensive for banks to borrow money and less attractive for them to loan it. Conversely, low rates encourage borrowing and lending and expand the money supply.

Federal Funds Rate (Key Rate) *interest rate at which commercial banks lend reserves to each other, usually overnight*

More familiar to consumers, the **federal funds rate (or key rate)** reflects the rate at which commercial banks lend reserves overnight to each other. Although the Fed can't actually control this rate, which is determined by the supply and demand of bank reserves, it can control the supply of those reserves to create the desired rate. By instructing its bond traders to buy fewer government bonds, the supply of reserves was decreased, resulting in a series of key rate increases—from a then-historic low of 1 percent in 2004 up to 5.25 percent in 2006—to slow a booming U.S. economy. The Fed then reversed its policy as the economy lost momentum, cutting the target rate gradually down to 0.25 percent in 2008 (to boost the economy during the recession), followed by 0.00–0.25 percent in 2009, and then continuing at 0.00–0.25 percent into 2013, to encourage the economic recovery.[19]

Open-Market Operations *the Fed's sale and purchase of securities in the open market*

Open-Market Operations

Open-market operations refer to the Fed's sale and purchase of securities (usually U.S. Treasury notes and short-term bonds) in the open market, as directed by the Fed's Open-Market Committee. Open-market operations are particularly effective because they act quickly and predictably on the money supply. The Fed buys government securities from a commercial dealer, whose bank account is credited for the transaction, thus giving that bank more money to lend, so this transaction expands the money supply.

The opposite happens when the Fed sells securities. Selling treasury securities to investors allows the U.S. government to raise money and contract the money supply. These securities may include Treasury bills (T-bills), T-notes, and T-bonds with maturity dates ranging from short-term (a few weeks) to long-term (up to 30 years). Treasury securities are highly liquid because they are actively traded on national securities markets, and traditionally have been considered a risk-free investment because they are backed by the U.S. government.

OBJECTIVE 5
Identify
three important ways in which the money and banking system is changing.

The Changing Money and Banking System

The U.S. money and banking systems continue to change today. Government emergency intervention aims to stabilize a troubled financial system. Enforcement of antiterrorism regulations deters criminal misuse of the financial system. And with the expansion of banking services, electronic technologies affect how you obtain money and how much interest you pay for it.

finding a better way

In Search of a Much-Needed Economic "Fix," the Fed Finds a Better Way

Economic fear gripped the United States with the collapse of the housing market, one of the backbones of the nation's economic health. While housing prices were rising rapidly in the years between 2000 and 2005, many citizens saw home ownership as a profitable investment. "If I buy now and hold on, after a few years I'll sell and make enough money to do the things I've always wanted," became a common theme. The buying binge was underway. By 2007 it became clear that real estate was overpriced, market demand suddenly evaporated, and property owners found themselves holding unsellable houses, unless they sold at a substantial loss. Even worse, commercial banks and other lenders found themselves holding trillions of dollars in mortgages that borrowers were unable to repay. Financial institutions also owned "mortgage-backed securities," asset-backed investments secured by a collection of mortgages, that became nearly worthless when the housing boom collapsed. The onset of recession led to passage of economic stimulus packages in 2008 and 2009 to offset the slowing economy and stop the rising unemployment that reached 10 percent, the highest in decades.

The Federal Reserve System's open market operations in late 2008 were the most aggressive buying of long-term treasury bonds in history—$300 billion—to fight the recession with lower interest rates. When interest rates reached all-time lows beginning in 2009, the United States economy still remained sluggish. Nearly 10 percent of the workforce remained unemployed. Banks and other lending institutions, stung by delinquent borrowers and barely profitable interest returns, were reluctant to grant loans to businesses and individuals. The Fed, already setting federal funds rates of 0.00–0.25 percent, and unable to lower interest rates further by using open market operations, sought to "find a better way."

An unconventional monetary policy—*quantitative easing (QE)*—was set into motion to inject more money directly into the economy, rather than indirectly by decreasing interest rates. With QE, the central bank creates new money by simply crediting its own bank account via a mere electronic transaction. Only a central bank, such as the Fed, can make such a transaction

rSnapshotPhotos/Shutterstock

because the Fed's money is accepted as legitimate payment by everyone. Spending this new money results in cheaper borrowing, which, in turn, encourages greater spending, stimulates greater demand, and ultimately defeats the recession. With QE, unlike open-market operations, the Fed buys any of a commercial bank's various assets—corporate bonds, properties, and securities—rather than buying just government bonds owned by banks. With more money in hand, banks tend to make more loans to businesses and individuals, thus stimulating economic growth.

In 2009 the Fed started buying $600 billion in mortgage-backed securities held by banks and continued by buying bank debt and bank-owned Treasury notes. The Fed's purchases from banks had reached more than $2 trillion through 2010, had grown to more than $3 trillion through early 2013. These actions are credited with stimulating the gradual economic recovery, with unemployment down to a still-robust 7.5 percent and an improved housing market by early 2013. One risk of QE is the possible need for higher future taxes to cover the Fed if it loses money on the purchases it makes from banks. Although some claim the Fed's actions are essential for economic recovery, critics fear QE may create so much money and spending that it destroys the value of the nation's currency and creates spiraling inflation. Even with these risks, the Fed's use of QE, to date, seems to be a "better way" for easing into recovery for the nation's economic health.[20]

Government Intervention for Stabilizing the U.S. Financial System

The financial world was shaken with the 2008 collapse of Lehman Brothers, the leading U.S. investment bank. Lehman's bankruptcy was soon followed by the threat of another giant's demise, as Bear Stearns teetered and then was bought by JPMorgan Chase. But JPMorgan Chase's purchase of Bear Stearns became possible only when the Federal Reserve stepped forward with $26 billion to guarantee potential losses on Bear Stearns's assets. With a goal of stabilizing the fractured financial system, the government continues its unprecedented infusion of funding for U.S. financial institutions.

Government Emergency Investment   By mid-2009, the Fed's investments reached nearly $300 billion, mostly in lending programs to commercial banks. Banks used the loans to get rid of bad mortgages and other hard-to-sell assets, thereby gaining cash for lending to bank customers. Another source of funds, the Troubled Asset Relief Program (TARP), a temporary program under the U.S. Treasury, was included in the government's bailout efforts. TARP support included $15 billion to auto-financing companies at risk of failure and $235 billion in direct investments to some 600 banks to encourage lending. Other government sources provided more than $130 billion to rescue Freddie Mac and Fannie Mae, two government-sponsored enterprises on the verge of financial failure. Freddie Mac and Fannie Mae (also known as FM2) buy home mortgages from the original lenders—for example, from banks—and hold them or resell them. In 2008, FM2 held 80 percent of U.S. home mortgages, many of which turned bad in the collapsed housing market, and many more that continue to default today. FM2 still held some $5 trillion in mortgage assets as of 2013. As a result, critics are questioning whether the government should be involved in the mortgage loan business.[21]

Assurances of Repayment   In return for its investments, the government imposes various kinds of assurances. The Fed's loans to banks, for example, are secured by the banks' assets. That is, the Fed holds some of the banks' assets, such as commercial loans, residential mortgages, and asset-backed securities as collateral until the banks repay the Fed. In return for TARP funds, the U.S. Treasury holds preferred stock (dividend-paying ownership shares) of the banks. The Treasury also holds *warrants*, which give the right to buy shares of the banks' stock in the future at a preset price. In addition to creating the government's precedent-setting part ownership, TARP also imposes stricter executive compensation requirements. In the bailout of FM2, both firms were taken over by the Federal Housing Finance Agency (FHFA) because the failure of either would severely damage global financial markets along with the U.S. economy. FHFA took full control over the two firms' assets and operations.[22]

Anticrime and Antiterrorism Regulations

Enforcement of antiterrorism regulations deters criminal misuse of the financial system. Under provisions of the *Bank Secrecy Act (BSA)*, the U.S. Department of the Treasury imposed a $24 million fine on the New York branch of a Jordan-based Arab Bank for failing to implement required monitoring and record-keeping methods to deter funding of crimes. The enforcement of BSA regulations includes tracking and reporting on suspicious transactions, such as a sudden increase in wire transfers or cash transactions exceeding $10,000, to cut off funding of criminal and terrorist activities.[23]

Banks are subject to prosecution when they fail to maintain systems for identifying and reporting suspicious activities that indicate possible drug transactions and money laundering. In violation of the BSA, a Miami, Florida, bank agreed to pay a $55 million penalty to the U.S. government following charges that it did not operate an effective anti-money laundering program. A Puerto Rico bank was assessed a $21 million penalty for not filing suspicious activity reports when repeated cash deposits were made into one account, often in paper bags in small denominations, totaling $20 million. A California bank was cited for not maintaining an effective anti-money laundering program when proceeds from cocaine sales were transferred from Mexico for deposit into accounts at the bank. The U.S. Treasury Department, recognizing the rising popularity of virtual currencies and possibilities of their use in money laundering, announced in 2013 that the federal banking rules also apply to firms that issue exchange money that exists only online and is not issued by any government. This means that online currencies, such as *Bitcoin*, must undertake bookkeeping requirements of the BSA, including reporting of financial transactions exceeding $10,000.[24]

The *USA PATRIOT Act*, passed in 2001 and designed to reduce terrorism risks, requires banks to better know the customer's true identity by obtaining and verifying their name, address, date of birth, and Social Security (or tax identification) number. They must also implement a *customer identification program (CIP)* to verify identities, keep records of customer activities, and compare identities of new customers with government terrorist lists. Enforcement resides with examiners from the Department of the Treasury.

The Impact of Electronic Technologies

Banks are among the most enthusiastic adopters of technology to improve efficiency and customer service. Customers of JPMorgan Chase include more than 13 million mobile users, and at Bank of America more than 100,000 checks each day are deposited remotely by mobile devices.[25] In addition to EFT systems and mobile devices, banks offer access via telephone, TV, and Internet banking, which allow customers to make around-the-clock transactions. Each business day, trillions of dollars exist in and among banks and other financial institutions in purely electronic form. Each day, the Fed's Fedwire funds transfer system, the world's largest electronic payments system, processes about $5 trillion in transactions for nearly 10,000 financial institutions.

Automated Clearing House (ACH) Network ACH is an electronic funds transfer system that provides interbank clearing of electronic payments for the nation's financial institutions. The ACH network allows businesses, government, and consumers to choose an electronic-over-paper alternative for payments (instead of written checks); the system is green, safe, and efficient.

ACH payments include:

- Internet-initiated debit and credit payments by businesses and consumers

- Business-to-business (B2B) electronic payments

- Direct deposit of payroll, Social Security benefits, and tax refunds

- Federal, state, and local tax payments

- E-checks

- Direct payment of consumer bills: mortgages, loans, utility bills, and insurance premiums

- E-commerce payments

In 2011, the ACH system processed some 20 billion payments that were initiated or received by customers at more than 15,000 U.S. businesses and financial institutions. Those payments totaled more than $33 trillion. With the federal government's use of ACH, each direct deposit that replaces a check saves $0.925. With each one billion of direct deposits, the federal savings is nearly $1 trillion.

The ACH system is governed by NACHA, the Electronic Payments Association, which administers and enforces the association's strict *NACHA Operating Rules* for sound risk management practices. Although NACHA was formed within the American Bankers Association, it later became an independent not-for-profit association that launched the Accredited ACH Professional program and established the system's operating rules.[26]

Check 21: Making the Paper Check Go Away The *Check Clearing for the 21st Century Act (Check 21)*, which became federal law in 2004, allows a receiving bank to make an electronic image of a paper check and electronically send the image to the paying bank for instant payment instead of waiting days for the paper check to wind its way back to the sender. More banks are adopting check image processing (Check 21) and benefitting from its speed and cost efficiency: less paper handling, reduced reliance on physical transportation, faster collection times, and elimination of expensive float. Today, almost 99 percent of the items processed by the Fed are images instead of in paper form. The days of writing a check, mailing it, and having several days to put money in the account to cover it are numbered, as a result of faster check clearing.[27]

Blink Credit Card "Blink" technology uses a computer chip that sends radio-frequency signals in place of the magnetic strips that have been embedded in credit cards for the past 30 years. The "contactless" payment system lets consumers wave the card in front of a merchant's terminal at a gas pump or in a department store without waiting to swipe and sign. Radio-frequency identification, although new to credit cards, is familiar on toll roads with electronic passes that allow drivers to avoid waiting in line to pay.

entrepreneurship and new ventures

Cultivating a Social Side for Community Banking

While the U.S. banking system struggles out of a once-distressed economy, smaller community banks are confronted with vigorous challenges from larger banks that stretch across state lines, competing for local consumers and commercial customers. State-chartered Fidelity Bank, serving Central Massachusetts, is an example. With headquarters in Leominster (population 41,000) and full-service facilities in five nearby towns, Fidelity's primary competitive advantage is its commitment to long-term community relationships developed since being established in 1888.

Unlike many smaller banks across the nation, Fidelity experienced a relatively successful year, remaining financially sound through the challenging 2009 economic environment. Continuing its success, Fidelity assisted a record number of homeowners refinance their mortgages in 2012, saving them millions of dollars a year, while helping many others purchase new homes. New commercial and business loan production, too, increased by 77 percent. The bank expanded in 2012 by acquiring depositors from People's United Bank in Leominster. The bank's commercial lending operation has gained recognition by the Small Business Administration for offering new business loan products, with faster and more effective approval processes. By streamlining its services, customers are using mobile banking—"like carrying a branch bank in your pocket"—for "anywhere/anytime" access to their accounts, and text messaging provides quick information on account balances.[28]

Fidelity's newest initiative is a social media program for strengthening customer and community relationships. It aims for broader exposure of the bank's brand through a visible and widespread presence in the social media. The focal resource is a publicly accessible blog, available at Fidelity's website, designed to encourage communications among customers,

Paul Rapson/Alamy

bank employees, and the local communities at large. Its content is then broadcast outward in digital space via connectivity with social media including Twitter, YouTube, LinkedIn, and Facebook. Aided by social media specialists—Digital Brand Expressions—Fidelity's upgraded media reach involves increasing the bank's listings in major search engines, expanding keyword links from other websites, and using podcasts for competitive advantage. The program enables monitoring of how Fidelity is being talked about in the social media, frequencies of messages, and then taking steps to guide employees toward more effective communicating with constituents. Measurements of frequencies for social network mentions and types of message content can then be compared to changes in product acceptance—savings, loans, investments, and insurance—among consumers and business customers. The results will enable the bank to determine the success of its social media program in terms of profitability and customer satisfaction. The program also helps fulfill Fidelity's mission, which is "Like smart friends, we care deeply about your well-being and use our hearts and our heads to help you get where you want to be."[29]

Debit Cards Unlike credit cards, **debit cards** do not increase the funds at an individual's disposal but allow users only to transfer money between accounts to make retail purchases. Debit cards are used more than credit cards as payment for U.S. consumer transactions. However, the risk of financial loss is greater for debit cards. Federal law limits the credit card user's liability to $50 for stolen or fraudulent use. Protection against debit card losses can be higher—ranging up to $500—depending on how quickly the lost card is reported.[30]

Many stores use **point-of-sale (POS) terminals** to communicate relevant purchase information with a customer's bank. A customer inserts a card, and the bank automatically transfers funds from the customer's account to the store's account.

Smart Cards A **smart card** has an embedded computer chip that can be programmed with "electronic money." Also known as *electronic purses* or *stored-value cards*, smart cards have existed for more than a decade. They are most popular in gas-pump payments, followed by prepaid phone service, ATMs, self-operated checkouts, vending machines, and automated banking services.[31]

Debit Card plastic card that allows an individual to transfer money between accounts

Point-of-Sale (POS) Terminal electronic device that transfers funds from the customer's bank account to pay for retail purchases

Smart Card credit-card-sized plastic card with an embedded computer chip that can be programmed with electronic money

International Banking and Finance

Electronic technologies permit nearly instantaneous financial transactions around the globe. These business exchanges—the prices asked and paid—are affected by *values of the currencies* among the various nations involved in the transactions. Once agreements are reached, the *international payments process* that moves money between buyers and sellers on different continents is not subject to any worldwide policy system beyond loosely structured agreements among countries.

OBJECTIVE 6
Discuss
some of the institutions and activities in international banking and finance.

Citizens of the Republic of Belarus, along with visitors from other countries, rely on information about current exchange rates between the Belarusian ruble (Br) and currencies of other countries. The BelarusBank is a local provider of currency exchange services.

Tatyana Zenkovich/Photoshot Holdings Ltd.

Currency Values and Exchange Rates

Euros, pesos, yuans, dollars, and yen; money comes in all sizes and stripes. With today's global activities, travelers, shoppers, investors, and businesses often rely on banks to convert their dollars into other currencies. When it comes to choosing one currency over others, the best choice changes from day to day. Why? Because every currency's value changes, reflecting global supply and demand—what traders are willing to pay—for one currency relative to others. One index for the value of the U.S. dollar, for example, is the average of its foreign exchange values against the currencies of a large group of major U.S. trading partners. The resulting **exchange rate,** the value of one currency compared to the value of another, reveals how much of one currency must be exchanged for another. At any one time, then, some currencies are "strong"—selling at a higher price and worth more—whereas others are "weak." Rates of exchange among currencies are published daily in financial media around the world, and at online foreign currency exchange (forex) markets.[32]

Exchange Rate *the value of one currency compared to the value of another*

Strong Currency or Weak: Which Is Better?
Most people would prefer a "strong" currency, right? Well, not so fast. It depends on how it will be used. Using money for international activities, such as taking a vacation, is one of those "good news–bad news" situations.

Consider the value of the euro versus the U.S. dollar, as exchange rates fluctuated for those currencies during the years since 2002. As a citizen in one of the 17 euro-area countries—for example, France—suppose you were going to take a vacation to the United States in 2002 but, instead, you chose to delay that vacation until 2011. Now, compare your vacation costs if you had gone in 2002 versus 2011, based on currency exchange rates at those times. Each euro in 2011 paid for about $1.45 of the trip (based on currency exchange rates at that time). However, each euro would have covered only $0.87 in 2002 (based on prevailing exchange rates). That's the good news: The stronger euro in 2011 means more purchasing power against the weaker dollar for French vacationers. It's bad news, though, for French innkeepers because Americans could go elsewhere to avoid expensive European travel that requires $1.45 to pay for each euro of vacation cost, up from only $0.83 to pay per euro nine years previously. Simply put, that $0.83 cup of coffee at a French sidewalk café in 2002 now (in 2011) costs $1.45. In this example of the U.S. dollar to euro, the American's vacation purchasing power has declined as the dollar has weakened against the euro.

The stronger euro proved to be a stumbling block for Europe's economy, especially for industries that export to non-euro countries with weaker currencies. Prices (in U.S. dollars) had to be increased, for example, on German-made Mercedes and BMW auto exports to the United States to cover the higher euro-based manufacturing costs, causing weaker U.S. demand and sales. Although the weaker dollar hurt many European firms that export products to the United States, others gained by increasing their U.S. investments. When DaimlerChrysler, for example, produces Mercedes M-class autos in Alabama, it pays in weaker dollars for manufacturing them, exports cars to Europe, and sells in euros for windfall profits. On balance, however, many euro-based firms have faced sagging sales, with slower revenue growth the result of a strong euro.

Bank Policies Influence Currency Values
In managing the money supply and interest rates, the Fed strongly influences the dollar's strength against other currencies. The European Central Bank (ECB) has the same role in the euro zone. The raising of interest rates tends to increase an economic system's currency value, whereas lowering the rate has the opposite effect. Europe's economic recovery is slower than desired when the euro is strong because euro-zone companies are less competitive against global counterparts. Even so, the ECB had refused to weaken the euro by cutting interest rates, even while the 17-nation euro region was well into the global recession. With lower rates, the supply of euros would increase, and the price of euros would fall, stimulating Europe's economy. But the

ECB fears it would also stimulate too much inflation. ECB finally cut interest rates to a record low 0.5 percent in 2013 as the euro region remained in recession. The rate cut was followed by a decrease of 1 percent in the value of the euro on world currency markets.[33]

In contrast, the U.S. Federal Reserve continues with low interest rate policies to stimulate the ailing economy and in doing so contributes to a relatively weak dollar. The weaker dollar makes U.S. goods cheaper and more attractive on the world's markets, thus maintaining or even increasing U.S. export sales. At the same time, the weaker dollar makes foreign imports more expensive, so U.S. consumers can afford fewer imported products, many of which are available only from foreign manufacturers. Some must-have commodities, too, such as petroleum, are priced worldwide in U.S. dollars, so as the dollar's value falls, the price of oil increases because it takes more of those weaker U.S. dollars to buy each barrel.[34] We see, then, some of the ways that banking and banking policies significantly influence currency values.

Why care, then, about currency exchange rates? Currencies matter greatly to companies when they buy, sell, and invest with other companies around the globe. Individuals, too, have similar concerns as when farmers buy grain from Brazil and tractors made in Japan or India, sometimes at higher prices and other times at lower prices, depending on currency exchange rates of the countries involved. Those exchange rates can be the difference between making a living and losing money during any year. Prices for consumer products, such as electronics by Samsung and autos made in Sweden or Germany, depend on currency exchange rates, too. As an investor looking toward retirement, you may buy an individual retirement account (IRA) in the T. Rowe Price European Stock Fund, or alternatively invest in any of the many other global opportunities for accumulating wealth to meet future needs and dreams. In all of these endeavors the success or disappointments in your decisions—if and when to buy and to not buy—will be influenced by changes in currency exchange rates. Likewise, as a potential entrepreneur your business success will be determined, in part, by changes in currency exchange rates.

The International Payments Process

Financial settlements between buyers and sellers in different countries are simplified through services provided by banks. For example, payments from U.S. buyers start at a local bank that converts them from dollars into the seller's currency, such as into euros to be sent to a seller in Greece. At the same time, payments and currency conversions from separate transactions also are flowing between Greek businesses and U.S. sellers in the other direction.

If trade between the two countries is in balance—if money inflows and outflows are equal for both countries—then *money does not actually have to flow between the two countries.* If inflows and outflows are not in balance at the U.S. bank (or at the Greek bank), then a flow of money—either to Greece or to the United States—is made to cover the difference.

International Bank Structure

There is no worldwide banking system comparable, in terms of policy making and regulatory power, to the system of any industrialized nation. Worldwide banking stability relies on a loose structure of agreements among individual countries or groups of countries.

Two United Nations agencies, the *World Bank* and the *International Monetary Fund*, help to finance international trade. Unlike true banks, the **World Bank** (technically, the International Bank for Reconstruction and Development) provides only a limited scope of services. For instance, it funds national improvements by making loans to build roads, schools, power plants, and hospitals. The resulting improvements eventually enable borrowing countries to increase productive capacity and international trade.

World Bank *UN agency that provides a limited scope of financial services, such as funding improvements in underdeveloped countries*

International Monetary Fund (IMF)
UN agency consisting of about 150 nations that have combined resources to promote stable exchange rates, provide temporary short-term loans, and serve other purposes

Another U.N. agency, the **International Monetary Fund (IMF),** is a group of some 150 nations that have combined resources for the following purposes:

- To promote the stability of exchange rates

- To provide temporary, short-term loans to member countries

- To encourage members to cooperate on international monetary issues

- To encourage development of a system for international payments

The IMF makes loans to nations suffering from temporary negative trade balances. By making it possible for these countries to continue buying products from other countries, the IMF facilitates international trade. However, some nations have declined IMF funds rather than accept the economic changes that the IMF demands. For example, some developing countries reject the IMF's requirement that they cut back social programs and spending in order to bring inflation under control.

summary of learning objectives

OBJECTIVE 1

Define *money* and identify the different forms that it takes in the nation's money supply. (pp. 552–556)

Modern money takes the form of stamped metal or printed paper issued by governments. However, any item that's *portable, divisible, durable,* and *stable* satisfies the basic characteristics of money. Money also serves as a *medium of exchange* (it is generally accepted as payment for buying and selling things), a *store of value* (it can be saved and used for future purchases), and a *measure of worth* (it acts as a measure of worth because all products can be valued in terms of money).

A nation's money supply is usually measured in two ways. *M-1,* the spendable money supply, includes the most liquid (or spendable) forms of money: currency (cash), checks, and checking accounts (demand deposits). *M-2* includes M-1 plus other forms of money that are not quite as liquid but are converted easily to spendable forms: time deposits, money market funds, and savings accounts. M-2 is often used for economic planning by businesses and government agencies because it accounts for most of the nation's money supply. M-2 measures the store of monetary value available for consumer purchases and business investments.

OBJECTIVE 2

Describe the different kinds of financial institutions that compose the U.S. financial system and explain the services they offer. (pp. 556–560)

Federally insured commercial banks offer checking accounts and accept deposits that they use to make loans and earn profits for shareholders. Every bank receives a major portion of its income from interest paid on loans by borrowers. As long as terms and conditions are clearly revealed to borrowers, banks may set their own interest rates, within limits set by each state. Traditionally, banks only offered the lowest rate, or *prime rate,* to their most creditworthy commercial customers.

Banks also offer (1) pension services such as IRAs or other pension options, and trust services in which the bank manages funds on behalf of and in accordance with the wishes of the client that entrusts funds to the bank; (2) international services, including currency exchanges, letters of credit, and banker's acceptances; (3) financial advice by recommending various investment opportunities, and brokerage services in which the bank's stockbrokers can buy and sell securities and hold them in the bank for the client; (4) *electronic funds transfer (EFT),* payments and collections by transferring financial information electronically; and (5) ATMs for conveniently accessible financial transactions.

Savings institutions, also called thrift institutions, include mutual savings banks and savings and loan associations. *Savings and loan associations (S&Ls)* are owned by shareholders. Most S&Ls were created to encourage savings habits and provide financing for homes. Today, S&Ls accept deposits and make loans and offer many of the same services as commercial banks. In *mutual savings banks,* all depositors are owners of the bank, and all profits are divided among them. *Credit unions* are nonprofit cooperative financial institutions, owned and run by their members who pool their funds to make loans to one another at reasonable rates. Other organizations called *nondeposit institutions*—pension funds, insurance companies, finance companies, and securities investment dealers—take in money, provide interest or other services, and make loans.

OBJECTIVE 3

Explain how financial institutions create money and describe the means by which they are regulated. (pp. 560–561)

The nation's money supply—the amount of money in circulation—expands because banks and other financial institutions can loan out most of the money they take in from deposits. The loans create additional deposits as follows: Out of a deposit of $100, the bank may hold

$10 in reserve and loan 90 percent—$90—to borrowers. There will still be the original $100 on deposit, and borrowers (of the $90) will also deposit the $90 loans in their banks. Now, the borrowers' banks have $81 of new deposits available for new loans (90 percent of $90). Banks, therefore, have turned the original $100 deposit into $271 ($100 + $90 + $81) of deposits. The chain continues, with borrowings from one bank becoming deposits in the next.

The government regulates all nationally charted commercial banks and most state chartered banks to ensure a sound financial system. Federal and state agencies regulate banks to ensure that the failure of some will not cause the public to lose faith in the banking system. The *Federal Deposit Insurance Corporation (FDIC)* insures deposits and guarantees the safety of all deposits up to $250,000 per account in each bank. To ensure against failures, the FDIC examines the activities and accounts of all member banks and thrift institutions. The FDIC becomes responsible for disposing of failed banks by selling them to other banks or by seizing the assets of failed banks and then (1) paying insurance to depositors and (2) disposing of the failed bank's assets and settling their debts.

OBJECTIVE 4

Discuss the functions of the Federal Reserve System and describe the tools that it uses to control the money supply. (pp. 562–564)

The *Federal Reserve System (the Fed)* is the nation's central bank that regulates many aspects of the United States financial system. Although some state-chartered banks, credit unions, and S&Ls do not belong to the Fed, they are subject to its regulations and pay deposit insurance premiums. The Fed consists of a board of governors, a group of reserve banks, and member banks. The Fed's board of governors consists of seven members appointed by the U.S. President for overlapping terms of 14 years. The Fed consists of 12 districts, each with a Federal Reserve Bank. The Fed's Open Market Committee is responsible for formulating the monetary policies to promote economic stability and growth by managing the nation's money supply and interest rates. As the government's bank, the Fed produces currency and lends money to the government by buying bonds issued by the Treasury Department to help finance the national debt. As the bankers' bank, it lends money to member banks, provides storage for funds that commercial banks are required to keep on reserve at a Federal Reserve Bank, and clears checks for commercial banks.

The Fed is responsible for the conduct of U.S. *monetary policy*, the management of the nation's economic growth by managing the money supply and interest rates. Among its tools for controlling the money supply, the Fed specifies *reserve requirements* (the percentage of its deposits that a commercial bank must hold), it sets the *discount rate* at which the Fed lends money to banks, and it conducts *open-market operations* to buy and sell securities in the open market. When the Fed buys securities from a commercial dealer, the dealer's bank account is immediately credited, so that bank has more money to lend and thus the money supply expands and interest rates fall. The opposite happens when the Fed sells securities to investors. Money in the buyer's bank account is reduced, reducing the money supply and increasing interest rates.

OBJECTIVE 5

Identify three important ways in which the money and banking system is changing. (pp. 564–569)

The U.S. money and banking systems continue to change today. Government emergency intervention aims to stabilize a troubled financial system. Enforcement of antiterrorism regulations deters criminal misuse of the financial system. The Federal Reserve took unprecedented investment actions to stabilize the U.S. financial system following the collapse of major banks in 2008. Commercial banks received massive loans to cover bad mortgages and other toxic assets and to encourage lending to stimulate the sagging economy. The Troubled Asset Relief Program (TARP), a temporary program under the U.S. Treasury, was included in the government's bailout effort, providing billions of dollars to auto-financing companies at risk of failure and billions more to over 600 banks to encourage lending. Other government sources provided funds to rescue Freddie Mac and Fannie Mae who held vast numbers of defaulted mortgages in the collapsed housing market.

Anticrime and antiterrorism regulations have been enacted to detect and abate use of the financial system for illegal purposes. The Bank Secrecy Act requires financial institutions to deter funding of crimes by tracking and reporting suspicious transactions. The USA PATRIOT Act requires banks to implement a customer identification program to verify identities and compare them with government lists of terrorists.

Banks have adopted new technologies to improve efficiency and customer service. ACH is an electronic funds transfer system that provides interbank clearing of electronic payments for the nation's financial institutions. The ACH network allows businesses, government, and consumers to choose an electronic-over-paper alternative for payments (instead of written checks). In addition to EFT systems and mobile devices, banks offer access through telephone, TV, and Internet banking. *Electronic check clearing* speeds up the check-clearing process, and the "blink" credit card speeds up consumer checkout by replacing magnetic strip cards with contactless cards. *Debit card*s allow the transfer of money from the cardholder's account directly to others' accounts.

OBJECTIVE 6

Discuss some of the institutions and activities in international banking and finance. (pp. 569–572)

Changes in currency values and exchange rates reflect global supply and demand—what traders are willing to pay for various currencies. The resulting exchange rate—the value of one currency compared to the value of another—reveals how much of one currency must be exchanged for another. At any one time, then, some currencies are "strong"—selling at a higher price and worth more—whereas others are "weak." In managing the money supply and interest rates, the Fed strongly influences the dollar's strength against other currencies. The European Central Bank (ECB) has the same role in the euro zone. The raising of interest rates tends to increase an economic system's currency value, whereas lowering the rate has the opposite effect.

Country-to-country transactions rely on an international payments process that moves money between buyers and sellers in different nations. If trade between two countries is in balance—if money inflows and outflows are equal for both countries—money does not have to flow between the two countries. If inflows and outflows are not in balance, then a flow of money between them is made to cover the difference.

Because there is no worldwide banking system, global banking stability relies on agreements among countries. Two United Nations agencies help to finance international trade: (1) The *World Bank* funds loans for national improvements so borrowers can increase productive capacity and international trade. (2) The *International Monetary Fund* makes loans to nations suffering from temporary negative trade balances and to provide economic and monetary stability for the borrowing country.

key terms

automated teller machine (ATM) (p. 559)
banker's acceptance (p. 558)
check (p. 554)
checking account (demand deposit) (p. 554)
commercial bank (p. 556)
credit union (p. 557)
currency (cash) (p. 554)
debit card (p. 569)
discount rate (p. 564)

electronic funds transfer (EFT) (p. 558)
exchange rate (p. 570)
Federal Deposit Insurance Corporation (FDIC) (p. 561)
federal funds rate (key rate) (p. 564)
Federal Reserve System (the Fed) (p. 562)
finance company (p. 557)
individual retirement account (IRA) (p. 558)
insurance company (p. 557)

International Monetary Fund (IMF) (p. 572)
letter of credit (p. 558)
M-1 (p. 554)
M-2 (p. 554)
monetary policy (p. 563)
money (p. 552)
money market mutual fund (p. 555)
mutual savings bank (p. 557)
open-market operations (p. 564)

pension fund (p. 557)
point-of-sale (POS) terminal (p. 569)
prime rate (p. 556)
reserve requirement (p. 564)

savings and loan association
  (S&L) (p. 557)
securities investment dealer (broker)
  (p. 558)

smart card (p. 569)
time deposit (p. 554)
trust services (p. 558)
World Bank (p. 571)

MyBizLab

Go to **pearsonglobaleditions.com/mybizlab** to complete the problems marked with this icon ✪.

questions & exercises

QUESTIONS FOR REVIEW

✪ **16-1.** Explain the four characteristics of money.

16-2. What are the components of M-1 and M-2?

16-3. Explain the roles of commercial banks, savings and loan associations, credit unions, and nondeposit institutions in the U.S. financial system.

16-4. Describe the structure of the Federal Reserve System.

QUESTIONS FOR ANALYSIS

✪ **16-5.** Do you think credit cards should be counted in the money supply? Why or why not? Support your argument by using the definition of *money*.

✪ **16-6.** Should commercial banks be regulated, or should market forces be allowed to determine the kinds of loans and the interest rates for loans and savings deposits? Why?

16-7. Customers who deposit their money in online-only checking and savings accounts can often get higher interest rates than at brick-and-mortar banks. Why do you think that online banks can offer these rates? What might be some drawbacks to online-only banking?

16-8. Start with a $1,000 deposit and assume a reserve requirement of 15 percent. Now trace the amount of money created by the banking system after five lending cycles.

APPLICATION EXERCISES

16-9. The Federal Reserve Bank maintains historical and current data on exchange rates. If you used $5,000 to purchase Chinese yuan five years from today, how many yuan would you have received? What would those yuan be worth today? (Use the data on the Fed site to calculate these values and explain your calculations.)

16-10. Interview the manager of a local commercial bank. Identify the ways in which the bank has implemented requirements of the Bank Secrecy Act and the USA PATRIOT Act. What costs has the bank incurred to implement the federal requirements?

building a business: continuing team exercise

Assignment

Meet with your team members to consider your new business venture and how it relates to the money and banking topics in this chapter. Develop specific responses to the following:

16-11. In what ways is (will be) your firm connected with banks and other financial institutions? In what ways, if any, are such institutions important to your business?

16-12. Sales of the product(s) your business offers to customers will depend, in part, on their ability to pay for those products. In what ways, if any, will customers rely on financial institutions for such purchases? Will your company assist customers in connecting with financial institutions to finance their purchases?

16-13. Consider the ways that currency exchange rates will affect your company. Consider also how those rates will affect your customers and their willingness to buy your product(s). Discuss how your team will adjust pricing of your product(s) when the U.S. dollar is strong and when the dollar is weak versus other currencies.

16-14. In what ways will your plans and methods for marketing change, if at all, when the currency values of the U.S. dollar change significantly? Explain.

16-15. Discuss how your team will determine if, and in what ways, your company must comply with the Bank Secrecy Act and the USA Patriot Act in conducting your company's business. Will these acts be a serious concern for your firm? Discuss why, or why not.

building your business skills

FOUR ECONOMISTS IN A ROOM

Goal

To encourage you to understand the economic factors considered by the Fed in determining current interest rates.

Background Information

One of the Fed's most important tools in setting monetary policy is the adjustment of the interest rates it charges member banks to borrow money. To determine interest rate policy, the Fed analyzes current economic conditions from its 12 districts. Its findings are published eight times a year in a report commonly known as the "Beige Book."

Method

STEP 1

Working with three other students, access the Fed's website at www.federalreserve.gov/. Look for the heading "A-Z Index," and then in the index click on the subheading "Beige Book." When you reach that page, read the summary of the current report.

STEP 2

Working with group members, study each of the major summary sections:

- Consumer spending
- Manufacturing
- Construction and real estate
- Banking and finance
- Nonfinancial services
- Labor market, wages, and pricing
- Agriculture and natural resources

Working with team members, discuss ways in which you think key information contained in the summary might affect the Fed's decision to raise, lower, or maintain interest rates.

STEP 3

Using an online search engine, find articles published in *Barron's*, the highly respected financial publication. Look for articles published immediately following the appearance of the most recent "Beige Book." Search for articles analyzing the report. Discuss with group members what the articles say about current economic conditions and interest rates.

STEP 4

Based on your research and analysis, what factors do you think the Fed will take into account to control inflation? Working with group members, explain your answer in writing.

STEP 5

Working with group members, research what the Fed chairperson says about interest rates. Do the chairperson's reasons for raising, lowering, or maintaining rates agree with your group's analysis?

FOLLOW-UP QUESTIONS

16-16. What are the most important factors in the Fed's interest rate decision?

16-17. Consider the old joke about economists that goes like this: When there are four economists in a room analyzing current economic conditions, there are at least eight different opinions. Based on your research and analysis, why do you think economists have such varying opinions?

exercising your ethics

TELLING THE ETHICAL FROM THE STRICTLY LEGAL

The Situation

When upgrading services for convenience to customers, commercial banks are concerned about setting prices that cover all costs so that, ultimately, they make a profit. This exercise challenges you to evaluate one banking service—ATM transactions—to determine if any ethical issues also should be considered in a bank's pricing decisions.

The Dilemma

A regional commercial bank in the western United States has more than 300 ATMs serving the nearly 400,000 checking and savings accounts of its customers. Customers are not charged a fee for their 30 million ATM transactions each year, as long as they use their bank's ATMs. In fact, the company realizes that it is less expensive for customers to use the ATM compared to a deposit or withdrawal transaction processed by a teller in the bank or at a drive through window. There are costs associated with maintaining the ATM and the bank charges noncustomers a $3 ATM fee. The bank's officers are reexamining their policies on ATM surcharges because of public protests against other banks with similar surcharges in Santa Monica, New York City, and Chicago. Iowa has gone even further, becoming the first state to pass legislation that bans national banks from charging ATM fees for noncustomers. To date, the courts have ruled that the access fees are legal, but some organizations—such as the U.S. Public Interest Research Group (PIRG)—continue to fight publicly against them.

In considering its current policies, our western bank's vice president for community relations is concerned about more than mere legalities. She wants to ensure that her company is "being a good citizen and doing the right thing." Any decision on ATM fees will ultimately affect the bank's customers, its image in the community and industry, and its profitability for its owners.

QUESTIONS TO ADDRESS

16-18. From the standpoint of a commercial bank, can you find any economic justification for ATM access fees?

16-19. Based on the scenario described for our bank, do you find any ethical issues in this situation? Or do you find the main issues legal and economic rather than ethical?

16-20. As an officer for this bank, how would you handle this situation?

team exercise

VIRTUAL BANKING: AN IDEA WHOSE TIME HAS COME?

The Situation

Key Savings and Loan is a multibranch bank located in the Midwest. The company's headquarters is in Indiana and they have more than 35 branches scattered across Illinois, Indiana, Michigan, and Ohio, an area that has, unfortunately, become known as the "Rust Belt." The company has been well managed and profitable for decades, but they are finding it difficult to add new customers or replace ones that leave.

The Dilemma

A member of the bank's board of directors has recommended that the bank consider closing its branch operations and operate as a virtual bank. Their existing customers could maintain their accounts and would have 24-hour access online. Mobile deposit technology will allow customers to deposit checks from their homes and offices. Customers will continue to be able to withdraw cash through ATMs, either those owned by the bank or through the national network. Other banking services would be available online, as well, such as car loans and mortgages. Closing the branches will save the company millions of dollars, but they have employees and customers to consider.

Team Activity

Assemble a group of four students and assign each group member to one of the following roles:

- Bill Decker (bank customer)
- Gloria Liu (bank employee)
- Carolyn Kleen (vice president, financial security)
- Karl Marcks (bank stockholder, investor)

ACTION STEPS

16-21. Before hearing any of your group's comments on this situation, and from the perspective of your assigned role, what are the advantages and disadvantages of becoming a virtual bank?

16-22. Join your group and share the advantages and disadvantages of becoming a virtual bank.

16-23. Do you think that going virtual would attract new customers? What types of customers would be most interested in virtual banking?

16-24. What are the potential risks of virtual banking for both the bank and the customer? How can each protect themselves?

16-25. What new services might Key Savings and Loan be able to offer if they go virtual?

cases

A Tale of Two Worlds in Banking

Continued from page 552

At the beginning of this chapter you read about some features of banking systems, banking activities, and the role of banks in determining the economic well-being of various nations and regions of the world. Using the information presented in this chapter you should be able to answer the following questions:

16-26. Under what economic conditions might you expect the Fed to raise interest rates? To lower them? Explain.

16-27. With continuing high unemployment, increasing numbers of home buyers are unable to meet home mortgage payments, forcing banks to either foreclose on these properties, or find other ways to handle non-payments on loans. What action would you propose instead of foreclosure? Identify the consequences you would expect from that action.

16-28. Suppose you are a businessperson planning to build a new facility in either the United States or the euro zone. How might your choice of where and when to build be influenced by monetary policies of the European Central Bank and the Fed?

16-29. Why do economically stressed countries with massive debt have difficulty borrowing outside money needed for economic recovery? Explain.

16-30. If banks are required to keep larger cushions of cash on hand rather than loaning out that money (as proposed in the Basel III Requirements), in what ways will the U.S. economy be affected?

Global Trading Partner Resets Its Economic Compass

Although Japan may be a small nation, with a population of just 127 million people and relatively limited natural resources, it remains one of the world's economic powers. In the current era of global interdependence there is no better example of continuing economic relationships—in terms of both trade and capital flows—than that between Japan and the United States. The two countries share some significant economic similarities: Both are strong industrialized economies that enjoy high standards of living, and both countries experienced slow growth and recession from the 2008 global financial crisis. At the same time there are significant differences: The U.S. population of 316 million people is about 2-1/2 times that of Japan's population; Japan has the world's third-largest gross domestic product (GDP) of more than $5 trillion, placing it behind the United States ($15 trillion) and China, and ahead of Germany, France, and Brazil; people in the United States tend to spend more and save less, whereas the Japanese population has a long-standing devotion to saving, resulting at times in a deflationary economy; and Japan, unlike the United States, has experienced slow economic growth throughout the past two decades.

As recently as 1989 Japan was the largest source of U.S. imports, but that status has been gradually changing. In 2011 Japan was the fourth-largest supplier (behind Canada, Mexico, and China) of goods imported to the United States—electrical machinery, vehicles, organic chemicals, optic and medical instruments, and agricultural products—amounting to $129 billion. As a trading partner, Japan was the U.S.'s fourth-largest goods export market—including medical instruments, cereals, aircraft, and machinery—amounting to $66 billion and nearly 5 percent of all U.S. exports in 2011. The resulting U.S. trade deficit with Japan was $63 billion.

Its decreasing role in trade with the United States is attributed, among other factors, to Japan's problems with deflation and the relatively high value of its currency—the yen. Deflationary pressures since the early 1990s stem from the Japanese penchant for saving, rather than spending, together with the Bank of Japan's long-standing monetary policy that limits the supply of money. With limited availability of credit and personal spending, prices have tended downward (the opposite of inflation) and purchases were delayed in anticipation of even lower future prices. Along with diminished profits, employment and incomes suffered, as did the economic expectations of the Japanese people. Meanwhile, the yen's high value—fluctuating at various times between 100 and 150 yen per U.S. dollar—gradually deterred other countries from purchasing Japan's products, resulting in years of sluggish, and even recessionary, economic performance.

After years of economic sluggishness, Japan took a dramatic step in a new direction with the election of new Prime Minister Shinzo Abe in December 2012. The Bank of Japan quickly launched a new antideflation program using a more aggressive monetary policy in which the boosting of consumer confidence is a key component for overcoming the deflationary mind-set. The new policy will double the amount of yen held by individuals during the next two years, seeking to increase spending and raise Japan's annual inflation rate to 2 percent. The central bank is injecting the equivalent of $630 billion in Japan's economy in 2013, a massive amount relative to the size of Japan's economy, using methods similar to those of the U.S. Federal Reserve's "quantitative easing." The bank's monetary easing is intended to boost the economy, drive interest rates down to near zero, weaken the yen, and promote Japan's entrepreneurship and competition. Soon after these announcements, the yen dropped on international currency exchanges, falling quickly to 88 yen per U.S. dollar, before returning back from its losses to nearly 100 yen. This relatively weak yen offers promise for increasing the demand for Japanese products abroad.

Although supporters cite the upside of Shinzo Abe's policies (now called "Abenomics"), others are a bit more cautious in noting some downside risks as well. Critics fear that by weakening of the yen, new tensions will arise with other countries that may have to reduce prices of their products to compete against Japan in global markets. It could also mean that imports to Japan from other countries will fall because Japanese consumers will have less purchasing power with a weaker yen.[35]

QUESTIONS FOR DISCUSSION

16-31. Describe the actions Japan's central bank is taking to overcome deflation. How will each of those actions contribute to achieving the goal of eliminating deflation?

16-32. The Bank of Japan will inject the equivalent of $630 billion into Japan's economy in 2013. In what ways (how) will those funds enter the economy? That is, explain what specific actions the bank could use to get those funds into the economy.

16-33. Consider the ways that Japan's economy would likely be affected by having a strong yen versus a weak yen. Compare and discuss the positive implications and the negative implications for both a strong and a weak yen.

16-34. How will Japan's new monetary policies have an impact on the U.S. economy? Identify and discuss the ways those policies will be felt in the United States.

16-35. Consider Japan's trading status as the fourth-largest source of U.S. imports, and the fourth-largest market for U.S. goods exports. Would you expect that status to change soon relative to other U.S. trading partners such as Canada, China, Germany and others? Explain.

MyBizLab

Go to **pearsonglobaleditions.com/mybizlab** *for the following Assisted-graded writing questions:*

16-36. Modern money has been described as coins and printed bills that are portable, divisible, durable, and stable. (a) Explain the meaning of each of those four characteristics and tell why they are important features of money. (b) Discuss the importance of the money supply and the role it plays in the national economy. In your discussion be sure to distinguish between two measures—M-1 and M-2—of the supply of money.

16-37. Think about various kinds of financial institutions in the U.S. financial system. (a) Using any three of those institutions, discuss similarities and differences in the services they offer, and the roles they play in the financial system. (b) Explain how financial institutions create money. Give an example.

16-38. Mybizlab Only—comprehensive writing assignment for this chapter.

end notes

1 "Why Did the ECB Raise Interest rates?" http://www.ibtimes.com/articles/131734/20110407/why-ecb-raise-interest-rates.htm; "Central Bank Raises Interest Rates Again," http://www.bendbulletin.com/article/20110406/NEWS0107/104060346/; "China Raises key Interest Rates By Quarter Percentage...," http://www.startribune.com/business/119239139.html; "India Raises Interest Rates for Eighth Time...," http://www.bloomberg.com/news/2011-03-17/india-raises-interest-rates-for-eighth-time-in-a-year-to-reduce-inflation.html; Patricia Kowsmann and Charles Forelle, "Portugal Pleads for Rescue," *The Wall Street Journal*, April 7, 2011, p. A1; "EU/IMF Bailout for Ireland....," *International Business Times*, http://hken.ibtimes.com/articles/84575/20101122/ireland-bailout.htm; Michael Winfrey, "Past EU/IMF Bailouts Show Risks, Pluses for Greece," *Reuters*, May 4, 2010, http://www.reuters.com/article/2010/05/04/us-greece-bailouts-analysis-idUSTRE6434XY20100504.

2 Steve Schifferes, "'$10 Trillion' Credit Crunch Cost," *BBC News*, July 31, 2009, http://news.bbc.co.uk/2/hi/8177814.stm; Kimberly Amadeo, "Value of the U.S. Dollar," January 10, 2011, at http://useconomy.about.com/od/tradepolicy/p/Dollar_Value.htm.

3 "Bank Failures in Brief," *FDIC*, at www.fdic.gov/bank/historical/bank/, accessed on May 23, 2013.

4 Associated Press, "Shrinking Profits Kill Bank Freebie," *Columbia Daily Tribune*, October 20, 2010, p. 5B.

5 Sandra Block and Hadley Malcolm, "Battle over Debit Swipe Fees Goes On," *USAToday.com*, May 10, 2012, at http://usatoday30.usatoday.com/money/perfi/credit/story/2012-05-10/credit-debit-card-swipe-fees-retailers-banks/54889030/1; Associated Press, "Bankers, Merchants Feud over Fees," *Columbia Daily Tribune*, March 14, 2011, p. 7B.

6 David Enrich and Damian Paletta, "Global Bank Pact Advances," *The Wall Street Journal*, June 4, 2010, pp. A1, A14; Associated Press, "Bankers Outline New Global Rules," *Columbia Daily Tribune*, September 13, 2010, p. 6B.

7 "Money Stock Measures," *Federal Reserve*, at www.federalreserve.gov/releases/h6/current/, accessed on May 19, 2013.

8 Ibid.

9 "Economic Research," *Federal Reserve Bank of St. Louis*, at research.stlouisfed.org/fred2/series/USNUM, accessed on May 19, 2013; "Assets and Liabilities of Commercial Banks in the United States," *Board of Governors of the Federal Reserve System*, May 17, 2013, at http://www.federalreserve.gov/releases/h8/current/.

10 Kevin Olsen, "100 Largest U.S. Public Pension Funds' Assets Still Short of 2007 Peak," *Pensions&Investments*, March 28, 2013, at http://www.pionline.com/article/20130328/DAILYREG/130329880; "Pension Fund Assets Hit Record USD 20.1 Trillion in 2011 But Investment Performance Weakens," *Pension Markets in Focus*, September 2012, at http://www.oecd.org/daf/fin/private-pensions/PensionMarketsInFocus2012.pdf.

11 Shane M. Sherland, "The Past, Present, and Future of Subprime Mortgages," *Finance and Economics Discussion Series, Divisions of Research and Statistics and Monetary Affairs: Federal Reserve Board* (Washington, DC; November 2008); Michael Gerrity, "MBA Reports Mortgage Loan Delinquencies, Foreclosure Starts Decrease in Q2," *World Property Channel*, August 26, 2010, at http://www.worldpropertychannel.com/us-markets/residential-real-estate-1/real-estate-news-mortgage-bankers-association-national-delinquency-survey-delinquency-rate-for-mortgage-loans-foreclosure-actions-bank-foreclosures-loan-default-rates-3077.php.

12 Richard Bitner, "Confessions of a Subprime Lender," *Newsweek* (March 12, 2008), at http://www.newsweek.com/id/121512/page/1; Tyler Cowen, "So We Thought. But Then Again..." *New York Times*, January 13, 2008, at http://www.nytimes.com/2008/01/13/business/13view.html?_r=2&scp=1&sq=Tyler+Cowen&oref=login&oref=slogin; Robert H. Frank, "Don't Blame All Borrowers," *Washington Post* (April 27, 2008), at http://www.washingtonpost.com/wp-dyn/content/article/2008/04/25/AR2008042502783.html.

13 Bert Ely, "Don't Push Banks to Make Bad Loans," *Wall Street Journal*, February 2, 2009, p. A17; Jeannine Aversa, "Banks Aren't Budging on Tight Lending Standards," *HuffingtonPost.com*, February 2, 2009, at http://www.huffingtonpost.com/2009/02/02/banks-arent-budging-on-ti_n_163325.html; Jeremy M. Simon, "Lending Standards Keep Tightening, Fed Says," *CreditCards.com*, May 4, 2009, at http://www.creditcards.com/credit-card-news/2009-q1-senior-loan-officers-survey-lending-standards-tighten-1276.php; Danny King, "Banks Tighten Mortgage Standards for FHA-Insured Loans," *DailyFinance*, November 17, 2010, at http://www.dailyfinance.com/story/credit/banks-tighten-mortgage-standards-for-fha-insured-loans-fico-score/19722792/; Rex Nutting, "Most Banks Tighten Credit Standards Further, Fed Says," *Market Watch*, May 4, 2009, at http://www.marketwatch.com/story/most-banks-tighten-credit-standards-further; "TransUnion: National Mortgage Loan Delinquency Rate Continues Downward Track in Third Quarter," *Yahoo! Finance*, November 13, 2012, at http://finance.yahoo.com/news/transunion-national-mortgage-loan-delinquency-110000585.html.

14 "Electronic Funds Transfer," *Financial Management Service*, at http://fms.treas.gov/eft/index.html, accessed April 20, 2011; "Government to Phase Out Checks in March 2013," *Columbia Daily Tribune*, December 21, 2011, at http://www.columbiatribune.com/news/2010/dec/21/government-to-phase-out-checks-in-march-2013/.

15 "Cashing Out: ATM Manufacturing in the US Industry Market Research Report Now Available from IBISWorld," *IBISWorld*, April 16, 2013, at http://www.prweb.com/releases/2012/4/prweb9402825.htm, accessed on May 19, 2013; "China to Become World's Largest ATM Market by 2015," *SmartCards Trends*, September 30, 2010, at http://www.smartcardstrends.com/det_atc.php?idu=12793&main=ea272859892ed0adacb020e361fae6e0; Frederick Lowe, "China Expected to Become the World's Top ATM Market," *ATM Marketplace*, September 30, 2010, at http://www.atmmarketplace.com/article_print/176973/

China-expected-to-become-the-world-s-top-ATM-market; "Global ATM Market to Pass 2.5 Million by 2013," *the-infoshop.com* (press release), September 10, 2008, at http://www.the-infoshop.com/press/rbr71603_en.shtml.

16 Ibid.

17 Brian W. Smith and Melissa R. Hall, "Troubled Banks and Failed Banks: Opportunities for Investment," *Pratt's Journal of Bankruptcy Law* at http://www.lw.com/upload/pubContent/_pdf/pub2296_1.pdf, accessed on April 20, 2010; Ralph F. MacDonald III, Christopher M. Kelly, Brett P. Barragate, Kevyn D. Orr, and James C. Olson, "United States: Bank Failures in 2008 and a Look Ahead to 2009," *Jones Day*, January 28, 2009, at http://www.mondaq.com/article.asp?articleid=72796; "2008–2011 bank Failures in the United States," *Wikipedia*, at http://www.wikipedia.org/wiki/2008_United_States_bank_failures, accessed on April 20 2011; Rob Williams, "How Secure Is the FDIC Deposit Insurance Fund?" *Charles Schwab*, September 16, 2009, at http://www.schwab.com/public/schwab/research_strategies/market_insight/investing_strategies/other_choices/how_secure_is_the_fdic_deposit_insurance_fund.html.

18 "Ask Dr. Econ: Is the Fed Still in the Business of Processing Checks?" *Federal Reserve Bank of San Francisco*, 1st Quarter, 2012, at http://www.frbsf.org/education/activities/drecon/2012/Dr-Econ-q1.html, accessed on May 21, 2013; Katy Jacob, Daniel Littman, Richard D. Porter, and Wade Rousse, "Two Cheers for the Monetary Control Act," *Chicago Fed Letter (June 2010, Number 275): The Federal Reserve Bank of Chicago*, at http://www.chicagofed.org/digital_assets/publications/chicago_fed_letter/2010/cfljune2010_275.pdf; Paul W. Bauer and Geoffrey R. Gerdes, "The Check Is Dead! Long Live the Check! A Check 21 Update," *Federal Reserve Bank of Cleveland*, September 21, 2009, at http://www.clevelandfed.org/research/commentary/2009/0609.cfm; Jim Savage, "Federal Reserve Banks Complete Check Processing Infrastructure Changes," *Board of Governors of the Federal Reserve System*, March 2, 2010, at http://www.federalreserve.gov/newsevents/press/other/20100302a.htm.

19 "Open Market Operations," *Board of Governors of the Federal Reserve System*, February 6, 2013, at http://www.federalreserve.gov/monetarypolicy/openmarket.htm#2006.

20 Jon Hilsenrath, "Fed Maps Exit From Stimulus," *Wall Street Journal*, May 11–12, 2013, pp. A1, A2; "Quantitative Easing," *Financial Times Lexicon*, at http://lexicon.ft.com/Term?term=quantitative-easing, accessed on May 21, 2013; "Labor Force Statistics from the Current Population Survey," *United States Bureau of Labor Statistics*, at www.bls.gov/cps/ accessed on May 22, 2013; Nick Timiraos, "Housing Prices Are on a Tear, Thanks to the Fed," *Wall Street Journal*, April 8, 2013, p. A2; Jon Hilsenrath and Liz Rappaport, "Fed Inches Toward Plan to Purchase U.S. Bonds," *Wall Street Journal*, January 29, 2009, p. A4; Neil Irwin, "Fed to Pump $1.2 Trillion into Markets," *The Washington Post*, March 19, 2009, at http://www.washingtonpost.com/wp-dyn/content/article/2009/03/18/AR2009031802283.html; Rita Nazareth, "Most U.S. Stocks Rise on Durable Goods, Pare Gains on Fed," *Bloomberg.com*, June 24, 2009, at http://www.bloomberg.com/apps/news?pid-20670001&sid=a_dIjb; Jon Hilsenrath, "Fed to Keep Lid on Bond Buys," *Wall Street Journal*, June 12, 2009, at http://www.online.wsj.com/article/SB124477575898508951.html; Jon Hilsenrath, "Fed Treads Into a Once-Taboo Realm," *Wall Street Journal*," November 5, 2010, p. A6.

21 David Goldman, "CNNMoney.com's Bailout Tracker," *CNNMoney.com*, at http://money.cnn.com/news/storysupplement/economy/bailouttracker/, accessed on April 21, 2011; John Griffith, "7 Things You Need to Know About Fannie Mae and Freddie Mac," *Center for American Progress*, September 6, 2012, http://www.americanprogress.org/issues/housing/report/2012/09/06/36736/7-things-you-need-to-know-about-fannie-mae-and-freddie-mac/.

22 Michael R. Crittenden, "Regulators See Risk in U.S. Bank Stakes," *Wall Street Journal*, April 24, 2009, at http://online.wsj.com/article/SB124051525463449225.html; Rebecca Christie, "Treasury May Keep U.S. Bank Stakes After Buyback (Update 3)," *Bloomberg.com*, April 17, 2009, at http://www.bloomberg.com/apps/news?pid=newsarchive&sid=a9F3N8vvrHgY; David Goldman, "CNNMoney.com's Bailout Tracker," *CNNMoney.com*, April 21, 2011, at http://money.cnn.com/news/story-supplement/economy/bailouttracker/; Mark Jickling, "Fannie Mae and Freddie Mac in Conservatorship," *CRS Report for* Congress, September 15, 2008, at http://fpc.state.gov/documents/organization/110097.pdf.

23 "U.S. Authorities Fine Arab Bank," *Al Bawaba* (August 18, 2005), p. 1; Paul R. Osborne, "BSA/AML Compliance Provides Opportunity to Improve Security and Enhance Customer Experience," *ABA Bank Compliance*, July/August 2005, p. 4.

24 Jason Webb, "American Express Bank Forfeits $55 Million for Bank Secrecy Act Violations," *Associated Content*, August 7, 2007, at http://www.associatedcontent.com/article/339208/american_express_bank_forfeits_55_million.html?cat=17; "Banco Popular de Puerto Rico Enters into Deferred Prosecution Agreement with U.S. Department of Justice," *U.S. Department of Justice*, January 16, 2006, at http://www.usdoj.gov/opa/pr/2003/January/03_crm_024.htm; Union Bank of California Enters into Deferred Prosecution Agreement and Forfeits $21.6 Million to Resolve Bank Secrecy Act Violations," *U.S. Department of Justice*, September 17, 2007, at http://www.usdoj.gov/opa/pr/2007/September/07_crm_726.html; Jeffrey Sparshott, "Web Money Gets Laundering Rules," *Wall Street Journal*, March 23, 2013, pp. C1, C2.

25 Robin Sidel, "Banks Make Smartphone Connection," *Wall Street Journal*, February 12, 2013, pp. C1, C2.

26 "ACH Payment Volume Exceeds 20.2 Billion for 2011," *NACHA*, April 12, 2012, at https://www.nacha.org/node/1130; "Supporting the Nation's Payment System," *The Federal Reserve Bank of Philadelphia*, April 22, 2011, at http://www.philadelphiafed.org/about-the-fed/who-we-are/payment-system.cfm; "Intro to the ACH Network," *NACHA: The Electronic Payments Association*, at http://nacha.org/c/intro2ach.cfm, accessed on April 22, 2011; "NACHA Reports 18.76 Billion ACH Payments in 2009," *NSF Check Processing*, April 7, 2010, at http://www.nsfcheckprocessing.com/achnetwork.htm.

[27] Katy Jacob, Daniel Littman, Richard D. Porter, and Wade Rousse, "Two Cheers for the Monetary Control Act," *Chicago Fed Letter (June 2010, Number 275): The Federal Reserve Bank of Chicago*, at http://www.chicagofed.org/digital_assets/publications/chicago_fed_letter/2010/cfljune2010_275.pdf; Paul W. Bauer and Geoffrey R. Gerdes, "The Check Is Dead! Long Live the Check! A Check 21 Update," *Federal Reserve Bank of Cleveland*, September 21, 2009, at http://www.clevelandfed.org/research/commentary/2009/0609.cfm; Jim Savage, "Federal Reserve Banks Complete Check Processing Infrastructure Changes," *Board of Governors of the Federal Reserve System*, March 2, 2010, at http://www.federalreserve.gov/newsevents/press/other/20100302a.htm.

[28] "Annual Report 2012," *Fidelity Bank*, at www.fidelitybankonline.com/home/fiFiles/static/documents/AnnualReport2012.pdf, accessed on May 22, 2013; "The New Normal: Annual Report 2009," *Fidelity Bank*, at http://www.fidelitybankonline.com/home/fiFiles/static/documents/AnnualReport2009.pdf, accessed on April 13, 2011; "Fidelity Bank launches Innovative Social Media Program," *Citi biz list*, February 15, 2011, at http://boston.citybizlist.com/7/2011/2/15/Fidelity-Bank-Launches-Innovative-Social-Media-Program-.aspx.

[29] "Digital Brand Expressions," at https://www.digitalbrand-expressions.com, accessed on April 12, 2011.

[30] Martin Kaste, "Consumers Opt for Debit Over Credit Cards," *NPR*, June 28, 2009, at http://www.npr.org/templates/story/story.php?storyId=105974724.

[31] "About Smart Cards: Introduction: Primer," *Smart Card Alliance*, accessed April 22, 2011 at http://www.smartcardalliance.org/pages/smart-cards-intro-primer.

[32] "Summary Measures of the Foreign Exchange Value of the Dollar," *Federal Reserve Statistical Release H:10*, accessed April 23, 2011 at http://www.federalreserve.gov/releases/H10/Summary/.

[33] Jana Randow and Jeff Black, "ECB Cuts Interest Rates to Record Low as Recession Lingers," *Bloomberg.com*, May 2, 2013, at http://www.bloomberg.com/news/2013-05-02/ecb-cuts-key-interest-rate-to-record-low-as-recession-lingers.html.

[34] Kimberly Amadeo, "Value of the U.S. Dollar," *About.com*, at http://useconomy.about.com/od/tradepolicy/p/Dollar_Value.htm, accessed on April 23, 2011.

[35] "U.S.-Japan Economic Harmonization Initiative," *Office of the United States Trade Representative*, at http://www.ustr.gov/countries-regions/japan-korea-apec/japan, accessed on May 25, 2013; William H. Cooper, "U.S.-Japan Economic Relations: Significance, Prospects, and Policy Options," *Congressional Research Service*, February 20, 2013, at fpc.state.gov/documents/organization/206128.pdf; Takashi Mochizuki and Matthew Walter, "Yen Resumes Its Fall Against the Dollar," *Wall Street Journal*, January 18, 2013, p. C4; Michael Casey, "Japan's Biggest Export? Deflation," *Market Watch*, May 8, 2013, at http://www.marketwatch.com/story/japans-biggest-export-deflation-2013-05-08; "Japanese Yen," *Wikipedia*, at en.wikipedia.org/wiki/Japanese_yen, accessed on May 22, 2013; David Jolly, "Japan's Moves to Weaken the Yen Have a Global Effect," *New York Times*, April 8, 2013, at http://www.nytimes.com/2013/04/09/business/global/yen-slides-close-to-level-of-100-to-the-dollar.html?_r=0; Martin Fackler, "Japan's New Optimism Has Name: Abenomics," *New York Times*, May 20, 2013, at http://www.nytimes.com/2013/05/21/world/asia/hope-in-japan-that-abenomics-may-be-turning-things-around.html?pagewanted=all.

Corbis

Are you lucky enough to make it

in the business world?

What if luck

has nothing to do with it?

How many wealth-seekers actually

find what they want,

and what are their secrets?

AFTER READING THIS CHAPTER, YOU SHOULD BE ABLE TO:

OBJECTIVE 1   **Explain** the concept of the time value of money and the principle of compound growth, and discuss the characteristics of common stock.

OBJECTIVE 2   **Identify** reasons for investing and the investment opportunities offered by mutual funds and exchange-traded funds.

OBJECTIVE 3   **Describe** the role of securities markets and identify the major stock exchanges and stock markets.

OBJECTIVE 4   **Describe** the risk–return relationship and discuss the use of diversification and asset allocation for investments.

OBJECTIVE 5   **Describe** the various ways that firms raise capital and identify the pros and cons of each method.

OBJECTIVE 6   **Identify** the reasons a company might make an initial public offering of its stock, explain how stock value is determined, and discuss the significance of market capitalization.

OBJECTIVE 7   **Explain** how securities markets are regulated.

MyBizLab®

✪ Improve Your Grade!

Visit **pearsonglobaleditions.com/mybizlab** for simulations, tutorials, and end-of-chapter problems.

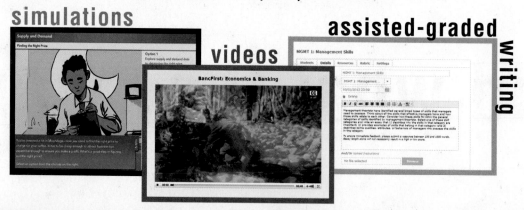

Over 10 million students improved their results using the Pearson MyLabs.

Investing in
Green

Traders are accustomed to using financial markets for investing in just about everything, ranging from pig bellies to movie production, in hopes of gaining a profit. New financial markets for commodities known as carbon credits, however, are driven, not just by profit motive, but by a sense of social responsibility. The economic incentives of emissions trading (ET) bring together both environmental polluters and green investors in an effort to both turn a profit and save the planet.

In 2009, the U.S. Congress proposed a version of ET called Cap and Trade. Regulators in various countries are setting limits on the amounts of industrial pollutants companies can release. A leading example, the European Union's (EU's) Emissions Trading Scheme (ETS), was started by the European Commission in 2005 to meet carbon reductions in accordance with the Kyoto Protocol on Climate Change. The ETS annually sets a cap for the total amount of carbon dioxide (CO_2) emissions allowed for each EU member state and company. The state totals and the EU total cannot exceed the caps.

Companies are issued a permit containing a number of "credits" (or "allowances") representing the right to emit a certain amount of CO_2. Any company producing below its CO_2 cap can sell its surplus allowances to other, more pollution-prone companies that need more credits to keep operating. That's where trading comes into play; it's like a stock exchange that quickly matches up buyers and sellers of emissions credits.

With ET, environmentally oriented companies sell unneeded emissions allowances and gain a financial return on past investments for reducing pollution. Such companies view environmental cleanup not as an expense but as a responsible investment. Other companies, finding it cheaper to avoid such investments, are facing higher costs as they bid for others' unused carbon credits. The trading scheme is adding a new financial incentive for cleaner industries that reduce carbon emissions and other greenhouse gases.[1]

While the EU gains experience with carbon trading, skeptics are raising critical questions. Some EU companies are believed to be reporting false measurements; by initially exaggerating the firm's emissions, they receive an inflated number of allowances and gain bonus profits by selling the excess allowances. They can also inflate reported emissions reductions and sell the extra allowances for profit.[2] Critics also cite the unpredictability of allowance prices on

what's in it for me?

ET is just one of countless activities drawing investors of every kind to the world's financial markets. Businesses from all over the world, representing every industry, converge there each day, seeking funds that can be used to finance their endeavors and pay off their debts. Individual investors gather as well, in person or—more often—online, looking to make their money "work" for them by profitably trading commodities, stocks, and bonds. This chapter will help you understand the various ways this is possible, whether your goals are short or long term, whether you are motivated by the desire for profit or security, or simply because you enjoy the challenges inherent in the successful raising and investing of capital.

the trading markets; costs for emitting a ton of carbon dioxide vary from below 10 euro to more than 30 euro. Analysts insist that, until they trade near 100 euro, prices won't encourage serious investments for reducing CO_2 emissions.[3]

Amidst an unfavorable political climate, industry objections, and a suspicious EU experience, 2010 legislation to cap U.S. carbon emissions came to an abrupt halt in the Senate. Cap and Trade would have increased costs to businesses and consumers at a time of economic sluggishness, high unemployment, and burgeoning national debt. It would have included a market for trading U.S. emissions allowances.

If the legislation *had* become law, the Chicago Climate Exchange (CCX), with voluntary trading launched in 2003, provided a ready-made market for the new emissions credits; 450 major organizations were CCX members, committed to meeting annual CO_2 reduction targets. Members had already received allowances based on measured emissions levels. Thereafter, by exceeding scheduled targets, surplus reductions became unused allowances that could be sold, or banked for later use. Firms failing to meet targets had to purchase allowances on the CCX market.[4] CCX became inactive at year end 2010. Although supporters hope for cap-and-trade enactment in the second term of the Barack Obama administration, it remains at a standstill in 2013.

Although the EU experience remains controversial and the U.S. cap-and-trade program has stalled, others are going forward. China, for example, is planning to curb inflated greenhouse gas emissions from its expanding manufacturing industries. Striving for a 45-percent reduction of carbon discharges by 2020, climate officials are getting advice from EU leaders for developing China's centralized emissions trading program.[5]

OBJECTIVE 1
Explain
the concept of the time value of money and the principle of compound growth, and discuss the characteristics of common stock.

Maximizing Capital Growth

Wise investments are the key to growing your money, especially if you are seeking to accumulate capital to start your own business or simply as a cushion for a sound financial future. In searching for investment opportunities, a number of concepts come into play for evaluating alternative investments and sorting out the good from the bad.

The Time Value of Money and Compound Growth

The most-proven "road to wealth" lies in a strategy of saving and investing over a period of years. Only rarely does a "one-in-a-million" opportunity provide a quick fortune. Although the popular "I want it all, and I want it now!" mentality sounds good, it becomes a reality for few wealth-seekers.

Time Value of Money *principle that invested money grows, over time, by earning interest or some other form of return*

Compound Growth *compounding of interest over time—with each additional time period, interest returns accumulate and earn more interest*

The **time value of money,** perhaps the single most important concept in business finance, recognizes the basic fact that, when it's invested over time, money grows by earning interest or yielding some other form of return. Time value stems from the principle of **compound growth,** the cumulative growth from interest paid to the investor over given time periods. With each additional time period, an investment grows as interest payments accumulate and earn more interest, thus multiplying the earning capacity of the investment.

The Rule of 72 We can better appreciate the concept of the "time value of money" with a practical example: How long does it take to double an investment? A handy rule of thumb is called the "Rule of 72." You can find the number of years needed to double your money by dividing the annual interest rate (in percent) into 72. If, for example, you reinvest annually at 8 percent, you'll double your money in about 9 years:

$$\frac{72}{8} = 9 \text{ years to double the money}$$

By the same reasoning, if you reinvest annually at 4 percent, your money will double in about 18 years.

The Rule of 72 can also calculate how much interest you must get if you want to double your money in a given number of years: Simply divide 72 by the desired number of years. If you want to double your money in 10 years, you need to get 7.2 percent:

$$\frac{72}{10} = 7.2 \text{ percent interest needed to double the money}$$

The lesson for the investor is clear: seek *higher* interest rates because money will double more frequently.

Making Better Use of Your Time Value What if you invested $10,000 at 7 percent interest for one year? You would earn $700 on your $10,000 investment. If you reinvested the principal amount plus the interest you earned during the first year, and reinvested interest annually for another four years, you'd end up with $14,025. Now, if you were planning for retirement and reinvested that money at the same interest rate for another 25 years, you could retire with $76,122—almost eight times the amount you started with!

Figure 17.1 illustrates how the returns from an initial investment of $10,000 accumulate substantially over longer periods of time. Notice that the gains for the last 10 years are much greater than for the first 10 years, illustrating the power of compound growth. Each year, the interest rate is applied to a larger sum. Notice also the larger gains from higher interest rates. Even a seemingly small increase in interest rates, from 7 to 8 percent, results in much larger accumulations.

As you can see from Figure 17.1, the best way to take advantage of the time value of money is to obtain a high rate of return on your investment. However, various kinds of investments offer opportunities for fulfilling different financial objectives, such as aggressive growth, financial safety, and others, which we discuss later.

Common Stock Investments

History has shown that one way to achieve a high rate of return, compared with many other ways, is to invest in the stock market. Consider the average rate of return on the U.S. stock market, as of the beginning of 2012. The 100-year average (1912–2012) was

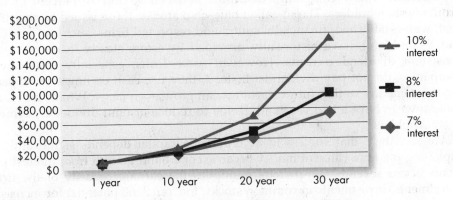

FIGURE 17.1 Amount to Which an Initial $10,000 Investment Grows

Stock *portion of ownership of a corporation*

more than 9 percent annually, and the most recent 25-year average return was more than 12 percent.[6] A **stock** is a portion of the ownership of a corporation. The company's total ownership is divided into small parts called *shares* that can be bought and sold to determine how much of the company (how many shares of stock) is owned by each shareholder. This widespread ownership has become possible because of the availability of different types of stocks and because markets have been established that enable individuals to conveniently buy and sell them.

Common Stock *most basic form of ownership, including voting rights on major issues, in a company*

Although several types of stock exist, common stock is the most prominent. A share of **common stock** is the most basic form of ownership in a company. Individuals and other companies purchase a firm's common stock in the hope that it will increase in value and provide dividend income; in addition, each common share has a vote on major issues that are brought before the shareholders.

Stock values are usually expressed in two different ways: as (1) *market value* and (2) *book value*.

Market Value *current price of a share of stock in the stock market*

1   A stock's real value is its **market value,** the current price of a share in the stock market. Market value reflects the amount that buyers are willing to pay for a share of the company's stock.

Book Value *value of a common stock expressed as the firm's owners' equity divided by the number of common shares*

2   The **book value** for a share of common stock is determined as the firm's owners' equity (from the balance sheet) divided by the number of common shares owned by all shareholders. Book value is used as a comparison indicator because the market value for successful companies is usually greater than its book value. Thus, when market price falls to near book value, some profit-seeking investors buy the stock on the principle that it is underpriced and will increase in the future.

Investment Traits of Common Stock

Common stocks are among the riskiest of all investments. Uncertainties about the stock market itself can quickly change a given stock's value. Furthermore, when companies have unprofitable years, or when economic conditions go sour, they often cannot pay dividends and potential investors become wary of future stock values, so share price drops. U.S. stocks, for example, lost more than half their value in the recession years 2008 and early 2009. On the up side, however, common stocks offer high growth potential; when a company's performance brightens, because of public acceptance of a hot new product, for example, share price can sharply increase. Historically, stock values generally rise with the passage of time. By mid-2013, U.S. common stocks had recovered their lost values, and many had moved on to new record levels.

Dividend *payment to shareholders, on a per-share basis, out of the company's earnings*

Dividends

A **dividend** is a payment to shareholders, on a per-share basis, from the company's earnings. Dividend payments are optional and variable; the corporation's board of directors decides whether and when a dividend will be paid, as well as the amount that is best for the future of the company and its shareholders. Many companies distribute between 30 and 70 percent of their profits to shareholders. The so-called **blue-chip stocks,** those issued by the strongest, well-established, financially sound and respected firms, such as Coca-Cola and ExxonMobil, have historically provided investors steady income through consistent dividend payouts. However, some firms, especially fast-growing companies, do not pay dividends. Instead, they use cash earnings for expanding the company so that future earnings can grow even faster. What's more, any company can have a bad year and decide to reduce or omit dividend payments to stockholders.

Blue-Chip Stock *common stock issued by a well-established and respected company with a sound financial history and a stable pattern of dividend payouts*

We see, then, that success in accumulating capital depends significantly on exploiting the time value of money because compound growth from interest payments across several time periods multiplies the earning capacity of the firm's investments. Investments in common stocks, too, offer the potential for increasing capital growth, but only if the stock provides dividend income and its market value increases.

Investing to Fulfill Financial Objectives

Mutual funds and exchange-traded funds are popular alternatives to stocks because they offer attractive investment opportunities for various financial objectives and often do not require large sums of money for entry. In addition, the simple and easy transaction process makes them accessible to the public.

Mutual funds are created by companies such as T. Rowe Price and Vanguard that pool cash investments from individuals and organizations to purchase bundles of stocks, bonds, and other securities. The bundles are expected to appreciate in market value and otherwise produce income for the mutual fund and its investors. Thus, investors, as part owners, expect to receive financial gains as the fund's assets become increasingly valuable. If you invest $1,000 in a mutual fund with assets worth $100,000, you own 1 percent of that fund. Investors in **no-load funds** are not charged sales commissions when they buy into or sell out of funds. Investors in **load funds** generally pay commissions of 2 percent to 8 percent.

Reasons for Investing

It's relatively easy to open a mutual fund account online or by phone. There are numerous funds that meet any chosen financial objective. The funds vary in their investment goals; different funds are designed to appeal to the different motives and goals of investors. Three of the most common objectives are (1) financial stability, (2) conservative growth, and (3) aggressive growth.

- *Stability and Safety.* Funds stressing safety seek only modest growth with little fluctuation in principal value regardless of economic conditions. They include *money market mutual funds* and other funds that preserve the fund holders' capital and reliably pay current income. Typical assets of these funds include lower-risk U.S. corporate bonds, U.S. government bonds, and other similarly safe short-term securities that provide stable income from interest and dividends.

- *Conservative Capital Growth.* Mutual funds that stress preservation of capital and current income but also seek some capital appreciation are called *balanced funds.* Typically, these funds hold a mixture of long-term municipal bonds, corporate bonds, and common stocks with good dividend-paying records for steady income. The common stocks offer potential for market appreciation (higher market value), though there is always the risk of price declines if the general stock market falls.

- *Aggressive Growth.* *Aggressive growth funds* seek maximum long-term capital growth. They sacrifice current income and safety by investing in stocks of new (and even troubled) companies, firms developing new products and technologies, and other higher-risk securities. They are designed for investors who can accept the risk of loss inherent in common stock investing with severe price fluctuations but also the potential for superior returns over time.

Most Mutual Funds Don't Match the Market

Many, but not all, mutual funds are managed by "experts" who select the fund's stocks and other securities that provide the fund's income. Unfortunately, some estimates indicate that up to 80 percent of these managed funds do not perform as well as the average return of the overall stock market as a result of costly management expenses and underperforming stocks.[7] This underperformance disadvantage has resulted in the emergence of passively managed funds, in which the fund manager invests by using a fixed, predetermined strategy that replaces judgmental choices for

OBJECTIVE 2
Identify

reasons for investing and the investment opportunities offered by mutual funds and exchange-traded funds.

Mutual Fund *company that pools cash investments from individuals and organizations to purchase a portfolio of stocks, bonds, and other securities*

No-Load Fund *mutual fund in which investors pay no commissions when they buy in or sell out*

Load Fund *mutual fund in which investors are charged sales commissions when they buy in or sell out*

buying and selling its stock holdings. Those choices are predefined by the strategy, not by the fund manager. The most widespread use of passively managed funds is with index mutual funds, which seek to mimic the holdings and performance of a particular market index. As an example, the widely watched S&P 500 market index, which is discussed later, consists of 500 specific common stocks. Any mutual fund company can establish its own index fund by purchasing shares of those same 500 companies, thus matching the market performance of the S&P 500. The selection of which stocks to purchase in an index fund is relatively automatic—it holds many of the same stocks as the market it tracks—and requires little human input, thus reducing management expenses.

Exchange-Traded Funds

Exchange-Traded Fund (ETF)
bundle of stocks or bonds that are in an index that tracks the overall movement of a market but unlike a mutual fund can be traded like a stock

As with an index mutual fund, an **exchange-traded fund (ETF)** is a bundle of stocks (or bonds) that are in an index that tracks the overall movement of a market. Unlike a mutual fund, however, an ETF can be traded like a stock. Each share of an ETF rises and falls as market prices change continuously for the market being tracked.

ETFs offer three areas of advantage over mutual funds. First, they can be traded throughout the day like a stock, they have low operating expenses, and they do not require high initial investments. Because they are traded on stock exchanges (hence, "exchange traded"), ETFs can be bought and sold—priced continuously—any time throughout the day. This *intraday trading* means you can time your transaction during the day to buy or sell when (or if) the market reaches a desired price. Mutual fund shares, in contrast, are priced once daily, at the end of the day. Thus, when you buy or sell during the day, you don't find out the share price until after the day has ended.

Second, whereas many mutual funds pass the costs of expensive active management onto shareholders, an ETF is bound by a rule that specifies what stocks will be purchased and when; once the rule is established, little or no active human decisions are involved. The *lower annual operating expenses* mean that, for the buy-and-hold investor, annual fees for ETFs are as low as 0.04 percent of assets; annual fees for mutual funds average 1.4 percent.[8]

Finally, unlike mutual funds, ETFs require no minimum investment, meaning they offer *ease of entry* for investors getting started without much money.[9] On the other hand, because ETFs must be bought and sold through a broker, they require payment of a brokerage commission (transaction fees). Traders who buy and sell frequently can end up paying more in transactions fees, even surpassing a mutual fund's high management expenses.[10]

We see, then, because firms have different financial objectives for investing, they often consider other alternatives, in addition to common stocks, such as mutual funds with varying degrees of safety and stability, funds that seek conservative capital growth, and riskier aggressive growth funds. ETFs are available to those firms that have the time to track moment-to-moment stock market movements for intraday trading. By allowing low minimum investments, ETFs offer ease of entry in addition to low annual operating expenses.

OBJECTIVE 3
Describe
the role of securities markets and identify the major stock exchanges and stock markets.

Securities *stocks, bonds, and mutual funds representing secured, or asset-based, claims by investors against issuers*

Securities Markets *markets in which stocks and bonds are sold*

The Business of Trading Securities

Stocks, bonds, and mutual funds are known as **securities** because they represent *secured*, or financially valuable claims on the part of investors. The markets in which stocks and bonds are sold are called **securities markets.** By facilitating the buying and selling of securities, the securities markets provide the capital that companies rely on for survival. Mutual funds, on the other hand, are not bought and sold on securities markets but are managed by financial professionals in the investment companies that create, buy, and sell the funds.

Primary and Secondary Securities Markets

In **primary securities markets,** new stocks and bonds are bought and sold by firms and governments. Sometimes, new securities are sold to single buyers or small groups of buyers. These *private placements* are desirable because they allow issuers to keep their plans confidential.

Most new stocks and some bonds are sold on the wider public market. To bring a new security to market, the issuing firm must get approval from the U.S. **Securities and Exchange Commission (SEC),** the government agency that regulates U.S. securities markets. The firm also relied, traditionally, on the services of an **investment bank,** a financial institution that specialized in issuing and reselling new securities. All that changed, however, in the financial collapse of 2008, when the fall of Lehman Brothers became the largest bankruptcy in U.S. history, Bear Stearns was purchased by JPMorgan Chase, and the two remaining large U.S. investment banks—Morgan Stanley and Goldman Sachs—were allowed to become bank holding companies (much like a commercial bank).[11] Although the companies' structures have changed, they still provide three important investment banking services:

1 Advise companies on the timing and financial terms of new issues.

2 *Underwrite*—buy and assume liability for—new securities, thus providing the issuing firms with 100 percent of the money (less commission). The inability to resell the securities is a risk that the banks must bear.

3 Create distribution networks for moving new securities through groups of other banks and brokers into the hands of individual investors.

New securities, however, represent only a small portion of traded securities. *Existing* stocks and bonds are sold in the much larger **secondary securities market,** which is handled by such familiar bodies as the New York Stock Exchange and by online trading with electronic communication networks.

> **Primary Securities Market** *market in which new stocks and bonds are bought and sold by firms and governments*

> **Securities and Exchange Commission (SEC)** *government agency that regulates U.S. securities markets*

> **Investment Bank** *financial institution that specializes in issuing and reselling new securities*

> **Secondary Securities Market** *market in which existing (not new) stocks and bonds are sold to the public*

Stock Exchanges

Most of the buying and selling of stocks, historically, has been handled by organized *stock exchanges*. A **stock exchange** is an organization of individuals coordinated to provide an institutional auction setting in which stocks can be bought and sold.

> **Stock Exchange** *an organization of individuals to provide an institutional auction setting in which stocks can be bought and sold*

Founded in 1792 and located at the corner of Wall and Broad Streets in New York City, the New York Stock Exchange sees billions of shares change hands each day.

Peter Foley/Newscom

The Trading Floor Each exchange regulates the places and times at which trading may occur. The most important difference between traditional exchanges and the electronic market is the geographic location of the trading activity. Brokers at an exchange trade face-to-face on the *trading floor* (also referred to as an *outcry market*). The electronic market, on the other hand, conducts trades electronically among thousands of dealers in remote locations around the world.

Trading floors today are equipped with vast arrays of electronic communications equipment for displaying buy and sell orders or confirming completed trades. A variety of news services furnish up-to-the-minute information about world events and business developments. Any change in these factors, then, may be swiftly reflected in share prices.

The Major Stock Exchanges Among the stock exchanges that operate on trading floors in the United States, the New York Stock Exchange is the largest. Today it faces stiff competition from both the electronic market in the United States and large foreign exchanges, such as those in London and Tokyo.

THE NEW YORK STOCK EXCHANGE For many people, "the stock market" means the *New York Stock Exchange (NYSE)*. Founded in 1792, the NYSE is the model for exchanges worldwide. The merger with Euronext in 2007 formed NYSE Euronext, bringing together marketplaces across Europe and the United States, representing one-third of stock trading worldwide. Only firms meeting certain minimum requirements—earning power, total value of outstanding stock, and number of shareholders—are eligible for listing on the NYSE.[12]

Today's NYSE is a *hybrid market* that uses both floor and electronic trading. When a client places an order through a brokerage house or online, it is transmitted to a broker on the NYSE floor. Floor brokers who want to trade that stock meet together to agree on a trading price based on supply and demand, and the order is executed. Alternatively, buyers can use the NYSE's Direct+ service to automatically execute trades electronically.

GLOBAL STOCK EXCHANGES As recently as 1980, the U.S. market accounted for more than half the value of the world market in traded stocks. Market activities, however, have shifted as the value of shares listed on foreign exchanges continues to grow. Table 17.1 identifies several stock exchanges, among hundreds of exchanges around the world, and the annual dollar volume of shares traded at each exchange. While new exchanges are emerging in Vietnam, Laos, and Rwanda, earlier

table 17.1 Selected Global Stock Exchanges and Markets

Country/Region	Stock Exchange	Total Value of Trades, Year Ended 31 December 2011 (billions of U.S. dollars)
Australia	Australian Securities Exchange	1,197
Brazil	Sao Paulo (BM&F)Stock Exchange	931
Canada	Toronto Stock Exchange	1,542
China	Shanghai Stock Exchange	3,658
Hong Kong	Hong Kong Stock Exchange	1,447
Japan	Tokyo Stock Exchange	3,972
United Kingdom	London Stock Exchange	2,871
United States/Europe	NYSE/Euronext	20,161

Source: "List of Stock Exchanges," based on www.world-stock-exchanges.net/top10.html, accessed on June 4, 2013.

startups are flourishing in cities from Shanghai to Warsaw, and others are merging or partnering in different regions. NYSE Euronext, for example, gained a valuable presence in the Middle East by joining with Qatar Exchange, which enabled Qatar to become a stronger international exchange.[13]

THE NASDAQ MARKET The **National Association of Securities Dealers Automated Quotation (NASDAQ) System,** the world's oldest electronic stock market, was established in 1971. Whereas buy and sell orders to the NYSE are gathered on the trading floor, NASDAQ orders are gathered and executed on a computer network connecting 500,000 terminals worldwide. Currently, NASDAQ is working with officials in an increasing number of countries in replacing the trading floors of traditional exchanges with electronic networks like NASDAQ's.

The stocks of some 3,400 companies, both emerging and well known, are traded by NASDAQ. Examples include Marvell, Apple, Microsoft, Intel, and Staples. Although the volume of shares traded surpasses that of the NYSE, the total market value of NASDAQ's U.S. stocks is less than that of the NYSE.

International Consolidation and Cross-Border Ownership

A wave of technological advances, along with regulatory and competitive factors, has propelled the consolidation of stock exchanges and the changeover from physical to electronic trading floors across international borders. Electronic communication networks have opened the door to around-the-clock and around-the-globe trading. Every major European stock exchange had gone electronic by the close of the twentieth century, and by 2010 the United States had caught up. Stock exchanges that didn't have enough savvy with electronic technologies to stay competitive have merged or partnered with those having more advanced trading systems. The intensified competition among stock exchanges has brought speedier transactions and lower transaction fees for investors.

Nonexchange Trading: Electronic Communication Networks

In 1998, the SEC authorized the creation of **electronic communication networks (ECNs),** electronic trading systems that bring buyers and sellers together outside traditional stock exchanges by automatically matching buy and sell orders at specified prices. ECNs gained rapid popularity because the trading procedures are fast and efficient, often lowering transaction costs per share to mere pennies. They also allow after-hours trading (after traditional markets have closed for the day) and protect traders' anonymity.[14]

ECNs must register with the SEC as broker-dealers. The ECN then provides service to subscribers, that is, other broker-dealers and institutional investors. Subscribers can view all orders at any time on the system's website to see information on what trades have taken place and at what times. Individual investors must open an account with a subscriber (a broker-dealer) before they can send buy or sell orders to the ECN system.

Individual Investor Trading

While more than half of all U.S. citizens have some form of ownership in stocks, bonds, or mutual funds, more than half of the adults have holdings worth $5,000 or more.[15] Many of these investors are novices who seek the advice of experienced professionals, or brokers. Investors who are well informed and experienced, however, often prefer to invest independently without outside guidance.

Stock Brokers Some of the people on the trading floor are employed by the stock exchange. Others are trading stocks for themselves. Many, however, are **stock brokers** who earn commissions by executing buy and sell orders for outside customers. Although they match buyers with sellers, brokers do not own the securities. They earn commissions from the individuals and organizations for whom they place orders.

National Association of Securities Dealers Automated Quotation (NASDAQ) System world's oldest electronic stock market consisting of dealers who buy and sell securities over a network of electronic communications

Electronic Communication Network (ECN) electronic trading system that brings buyers and sellers together outside traditional stock exchanges

stock broker individual or organization that receives and executes buy and sell orders on behalf of outside customers in return for commissions

Discount Brokers As with many other products, brokerage assistance can be purchased at either discount or at full-service prices. Discount brokers, such as E*TRADE and Scottrade, offer well-informed individual investors who know what they want to buy or sell a fast, low-cost way to participate in the market. Buying 200 shares of a $20 stock in 2013 cost the investor a service fee of $7 at Scottrade, and $7.99 to $9.99 at E*Trade. Price differences are obvious even among the discount brokers, but the highest discount price is well below the price of a full-service broker. Sales personnel receive fees or salaries, not commissions. Unlike many full-service brokers, many discount brokers do not offer in-depth investment advice or person-to-person sales consultations. They do, however, offer automated online services, such as stock research, industry analysis, and screening for specific types of stocks.

Full-Service Brokers Despite the growth in online investing, full-service brokers remain an important resource, both for new, uninformed investors and for experienced investors who don't have time to keep up with all the latest developments. Full-service brokers, such as Merrill Lynch Wealth Management, offer clients consulting advice in personal financial planning, estate planning, and tax strategies, along with a wider range of investment products. In addition to delivering and interpreting information, financial advisors can point clients toward investments that might otherwise be lost in an avalanche of online financial data.

Online Investing The popularity of online trading stems from convenient access to the Internet, fast, no-nonsense transactions, and the opportunity for self-directed investors to manage their own investments while paying low fees for trading.

Online investors buy into and sell out of the stocks of thousands of companies daily. Consequently, keeping track of who owns what at any given time has become a monumental burden. Relief has come from **book-entry ownership.** Historically, shares of stock have been issued as physical paper certificates; now they are simply recorded in the companies' books, thereby eliminating the costs of storing, exchanging, and replacing certificates.

Book-Entry Ownership *procedure that holds investors' shares in book-entry form, rather than issuing a physical paper certificate of ownership*

Tracking the Market Using Stock Indexes

For decades investors have used stock indexes to measure market performance and to predict future movements of stock markets. Although not indicative of the status of individual securities, **market indexes** provide useful summaries of overall price trends, both in specific industries and in the stock market as a whole. Market indexes, for example, reveal *bull* and *bear market* trends. **Bull markets** are periods of rising stock prices, generally lasting 12 months or longer; investors are motivated to buy, confident they will realize capital gains. Periods of falling stock prices, usually 20 percent off peak prices, are called **bear markets;** investors are motivated to sell, anticipating further falling prices.

As Figure 17.2 shows, the past three decades have been characterized primarily by bull markets, including the longest in history, from 1981 to the beginning of 2000. In contrast, the period 2000 to 2003 was characterized by a bear market. The period 2007–2009 was the second-worst bear market of all time, exceeded only by that of 1929–1932.[16] The data that characterize such periods are drawn from four leading market indexes: the Dow Jones, Standard & Poor's, NASDAQ Composite, and the Russell 2000 (not shown in Figure 17.2).

Market Index *statistical indicator designed to measure the performance of a large group of stocks or track the price changes of a stock market*

Bull Market *period of rising stock prices, lasting 12 months or longer, featuring investor confidence for future gains and motivation to buy*

Bear Market *period of falling stock prices marked by negative investor sentiments with motivation to sell ahead of anticipated losses*

The Dow The **Dow Jones Industrial Average (DJIA)** is the oldest and most widely cited U.S. market index. It measures the performance of the industrial sector of the U.S. stock markets by focusing on just 30 blue-chip, large-cap companies as reflectors of the economic health of the many similar U.S. firms. The Dow is an

Dow Jones Industrial Average (DJIA) *oldest and most widely cited market index based on the prices of 30 blue-chip, large-cap industrial firms on the NYSE*

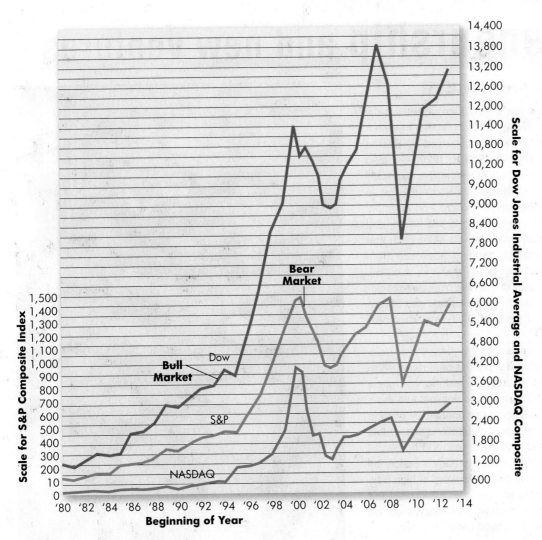

FIGURE 17.2 Bull and Bear Markets
Source: Yahoo! Finance, at http://finance.yahoo.com.

average of the stock prices for these 30 large firms, and traders and investors use it as a traditional barometer of the market's overall movement. Because it includes only 30 of the thousands of companies on the market, the Dow is only an approximation of the overall market's price movements.

Over the decades, the Dow has been revised and updated to reflect the changing composition of U.S. companies and industries. Recent modifications occurred in 2008–2009, when three companies were added—Kraft Foods, insurance giant Travelers Companies, and technology titan Cisco Systems—replacing insurance company American International Group, banker Citigroup, and auto icon General Motors. Replacing the three outgoing firms, all facing substantial financial and restructuring upheavals, the new additions better represent today's food- and technology-based economy and the prominence of the financials industry.[17]

The S&P 500 Because it considers very few firms, the Dow is a limited gauge of the overall U.S. stock market. The **S&P 500**, the Standard and Poor's Composite Index, is a broader report, considered by many to be the best single indicator of the U.S. equities market. It consists of 500 large-cap stocks, including companies from various sectors—such as information technology, energy, industrials, financials, health care, consumer staples, and telecommunications—for a balanced representation of the overall large-cap equities market.

S&P 500 *market index of U.S. equities based on the performance of 500 large-cap stocks representing various sectors of the overall equities market*

entrepreneurship and new ventures

An Entrepreneurship of Evil

Bernard Madoff's scheme was not a new idea; it dates back to 1899, when a New Yorker, William Miller, cheated investors out of $1 million. Miller's method was popularized by Boston businessman Charles Ponzi, who, in 1919 to 1920, swindled millions of dollars from unsuspecting investors; he expected to net a 50-percent profit in 90 days. Madoff's contribution to Ponzi-scheme history is the enormity of its size and duration: It reached more than $50 billion, perhaps up to $65 billion, and lasted at least 10 years. So convincing was his sales pitch that the minimum investment, reportedly ranging anywhere from $100,000 to $1 million, was paid willingly by a star-studded list, including the Wilpon family (owner of the New York Jets), actor Kevin Bacon, Baseball Hall of Famer Sandy Koufax, and Steven Spielberg, along with a host of banks, universities, churches, and charities.

Ponzi-scheme victims fit a certain pattern. Many are unsophisticated investors, do not rely on a professional representative, believe that unusually high returns are realistic, and place unfounded faith in personal relationships and tips that lure them into making bad decisions. Ponzi connivers operate by offering abnormally large returns, deflecting prying questions and doubts with personal reassurances and high dividends, and bolstering the scheme's allure by paying high returns to early investors by using new money raised from new clients. As word of high payoffs spreads, more new investors are attracted; otherwise, the scheme falls apart, and the investments disappear. Without an ever-growing pool of new clients, the payoff money runs dry.

Madoff's scheme collapsed when nervous investors, worried about the economic downturn in 2008, asked to withdraw their money. As new money ran dry, the fraud was soon exposed; a federal judge, calling the scheme especially evil, ordered that Bernard Madoff Investment Securities LLC be liquidated, and sentenced Madoff to a 150-year prison term. Meanwhile, victims have filed more than 15,000 claims against the fraud. Investor claims may be eligible for up to $500,000 each from the Securities Investment Protection Corporation (SIPC), a private

Steven Hirsch/Newscom

fund authorized by Congress to protect securities investors. Some of the massive losses, but certainly not all, may be recovered from the liquidated company's assets. About $11 billion of lost funds had been recovered as of 2012. Meanwhile, the end question from Madoff's evil remains unanswered: What percentage of losses will eventually be recovered?[18]

NASDAQ Composite Index *market index that includes all NASDAQ-listed companies, both domestic and foreign, with a high proportion of technology companies and small-cap stocks*

The NASDAQ Composite　Because it considers more stocks, some Wall Street observers regard the **NASDAQ Composite Index** as one of the most useful of all market indexes. Unlike the Dow and the S&P 500, all NASDAQ-listed companies, not just a selected few, are included in the index for a total of approximately 3,400 firms, mostly in the United States but in other countries as well. However, it includes a high proportion of technology companies, including small-company stocks, and a smaller representation of other sectors—financial, consumer products, and industrials.

Russell 2000 Index *specialty index that uses 2,000 stocks to measure the performance of the smallest U.S. companies*

The Russell 2000　Investors in the U.S. small-cap market are interested in the **Russell 2000 Index,** a specialty index that measures the performance of the smallest U.S. companies based on market capitalization. As the most quoted index focusing on the small-cap portion of the U.S. economy, its stocks represent a range of sectors such as financials, consumer discretionary, health care, technology, materials, and utilities.

Index-Matching ETFs Countless other specialty indexes exist for specific industries, countries, and economic sectors to meet investors' diverse needs. Additionally, many ETFs are available to investors for duplicating (or nearly duplicating) the market performance of popular stock-market indexes. For example, one ETF, Standard & Poor's Depository Receipts (SPDRS, known as *Spiders*), owns a portfolio of stocks that matches the composition of the S&P 500 index. Similarly the Fidelity® NASDAQ Composite Index® Tracking Stock holds a portfolio of equities for tracking the NASDAQ Composite Index.

We have seen that the securities markets, the markets in which stocks and bonds are bought and sold, provide the capital that companies rely on for survival. These markets also provide investment opportunities by which companies trade securities to increase the firm's wealth. Firms issuing new securities raise capital with the assistance of investment banking services. Existing securities are traded throughout the day in the secondary securities market (where buyers and sellers make transactions at the major stock exchanges) and through ECNs. For trading securities, many individuals and companies rely on the services of securities brokers, and other self-directed traders use online trading to self-manage their investments. Investors often use stock indexes to measure market performance and to predict future market movements of stock markets. Market indexes reveal bull and bear markets, revealing the risks and opportunities for gaining and losing wealth that are inherent in securities investments.

The Risk–Return Relationship

OBJECTIVE 4
Describe
the risk–return relationship and discuss the use of diversification and asset allocation for investments.

Individual investors have different motivations and personal preferences for safety versus risk. That is why, for example, some individuals and firms invest in stocks whereas others invest only in bonds. Although all investors anticipate receiving future cash flows, some cash flows are more certain than others. Investors generally expect to receive higher returns for higher uncertainty. They do not generally expect large returns for secure, stable investments such as government-insured bonds. The investment's time commitment, too, contains an element of risk. While short-term investments are generally considered to be less risky, longer-term investments are subject to future uncertainties in the economy and financial markets. As of mid-2013, the average rate of return on a 1-year U.S. Treasury bill was 0.13 percent, versus 1.02 percent on a 5-year bill, and 2.10 percent on a 10-year bill. Each type of investment, then, has a **risk–return (risk–reward) relationship**: safer investments tend to offer lower returns, riskier investments tend to offer higher returns (rewards).

Figure 17.3 shows the general risk–return relationship for various financial instruments, along with the types of investors they attract. Thus, conservative investors, who have a low tolerance for risk, will opt for no-risk U.S. Treasury Bills (fully insured by the U.S. government), or even intermediate-term high-grade corporate bonds that rate low in terms of risk on future returns, but also low on the size of expected returns. The reverse is true of aggressive investors who prefer the higher risks and potential returns from long-term junk bonds and common stocks.[19]

Risk–Return (Risk–Reward) Relationship *principle that safer investments tend to offer lower returns whereas riskier investments tend to offer higher returns (rewards)*

Investment Dividends (or Interest), Appreciation, and Total Return

In evaluating potential investments, investors look at returns from dividends (or from interest), returns from price appreciation, and total return.

Dividends The rate of return from dividends paid to shareholders is commonly referred to as the **current dividend yield** (or, in the case of interest from a loan, the **current interest yield**) and is calculated by dividing the yearly dollar amount of dividend income by the investment's current market value. In 2013, for example, each share of AT&T stock was receiving annual dividends payments of $1.80. If, on a

Current Dividend Yield and Current Interest Yield *yearly dollar amount of income divided by the investment's current market value, expressed as a percentage*

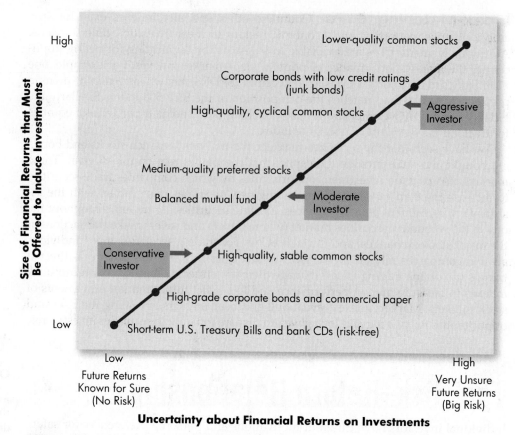

FIGURE 17.3 Potential Financial Returns Rise with Riskier Investments.
Source: Multi-Source.

particular day, the share price was $35.67, the current yield would be 5.05 percent or ($1.80/$35.67 × 100). This dividend can then be compared against current yields from other investments. Larger dividend yields, of course, are preferred to smaller returns.

Price Appreciation
Another source of returns depends on whether the investment is increasing or decreasing in dollar value. **Price appreciation** is an increase in the dollar value of an investment. Suppose, for example, you purchased a share of AT&T stock for $35.67, then sold it one year later for $37.45. The price appreciation is $1.78 or ($37.45 − 35.67). This profit, realized from the increased market value of an investment, is known as a **capital gain.**

Total Return
The sum of an investment's current dividend (interest) yield and capital gain is referred to as its total return. Total return cannot be accurately evaluated until it's compared to the investment that was required to get that return. Total return as a percentage of investment is calculated as follows:

Total return (%) = (Current dividend payment + Capital gain)/
Original investment × 100.

To complete our AT&T example, the total return as a percentage of our one-year investment would be 10.04 percent or [($1.80 + $1.78)/$35.67 × 100]. Note that larger total returns are preferred to smaller ones.

Fantasy Stock Markets
Enthusiasts of baseball, football, and hockey aren't the only fans energized by fantasy games. Fantasy stock markets are all the rage for learning how securities markets work, for trying your hand at various investment strategies, and earning

Price Appreciation *increase in the dollar value of an investment at two points in time (the amount by which the price of a security increases)*

Capital Gain *profit realized from the increased value of an investment*

a fantasy fortune (or going broke!). Internet-based games, including free ones such as *Wall Street Survivor* and *How the Market Works*, provide an investment experience that is educational, challenging, and entertaining. Starting with an initial sum in virtual cash with which to manage their own fantasy portfolio of real companies, participants must live with real market results. It's a learn-by-doing experience—using Web-based symbol lookups to enter stock ticker symbols, searching various information sources for research on companies of interest, making buy and sell decisions, and then discovering the financial results as real market prices change for the portfolio holdings. Many students and business practitioners are finding these "games" to be a valuable resource for learning the "how to" of online investing.

Managing Risk with Diversification and Asset Allocation

Investors seldom take an extreme approach—total risk or total risk avoidance—in selecting their investments. Extreme positions attract extreme results; instead, most investors select a mixed portfolio of investments—some riskier and some more conservative—that, collectively, provides the overall level of risk and financial returns that feels comfortable. After determining the desired *risk–return* balance, they then achieve it in two ways: through (1) *diversification* and (2) *asset allocation*.

Diversification **Diversification** means buying several different kinds of investments rather than just one. For example, diversification as applied to common stocks means that you invest in stocks of several different companies, companies in different industries, and companies in various countries. The risk of loss is reduced by spreading the total investment across different kinds of stocks because although any one stock may tumble, the chances are less that all of them will fall at the same time. More diversification is gained when assets are spread across a variety of investment alternatives—stocks, bonds, mutual funds, precious metals, real estate, and so on. Employees who did not have diversified investments and, instead, had all their retirement funds invested in their firm's stock can lose everything if their company goes bankrupt or invests poorly. The collapse of Enron Corporation in 2001, one of the 10 largest U.S. firms, was a financial disaster for its thousands of employees because Enron's retirement program was invested solely in Enron common stock. The stock price dropped from near $90 per share to nearly $5, effectively wiping out employees' retirement savings. Putting all their eggs in one basket was an extremely risky position, as they sorrowfully learned. When their firm's stock took a free fall as a result of a market collapse and scandal, the retirement funds disappeared.

Diversification *purchase of several different kinds of investments rather than just one*

Asset Allocation **Asset allocation** is the proportion (the relative amounts) of funds invested in (or allocated to) each of the investment alternatives. You may decide for example, to allocate 50 percent of your funds to common stocks, 25 percent to a money market mutual fund, and 25 percent to a U.S. Treasury bond mutual fund. Ten years later, with more concern for financial safety, you may decide on a less risky asset allocation of 20 percent, 40 percent, and 40 percent in the same investment categories, respectively. In this example, the portfolio has been changed from moderate-risk to lower-risk investments for the purpose of preserving the investor's accumulated capital. The asset allocation was changed accordingly.

Asset Allocation *relative amount of funds invested in (or allocated to) each of several investment alternatives*

Performance Differences for Different Portfolios Once an investor has chosen an investment objective with an acceptable risk level, he or she can put the tools of diversification and asset allocation to use in their investor's *portfolio*. A **portfolio** is the combined holdings of all the financial investments—stocks, bonds, mutual funds, real estate—of any company or individual.

Just like investors, investment funds have different investment objectives—ranging from aggressive growth/high risk to stable income/low volatility—and their holdings are diversified accordingly among hundreds of company stocks, corporate bonds, or government bonds that provide the desired orientation. The money in a diversified

Portfolio *combined holdings of all the financial investments of any company or individual*

Finding a Better Way

Mass Communications with IT Puts Stock Trading within Easy Reach

Trading stocks as recently as just a decade ago could have been a somewhat cumbersome chore, delayed by time lags before the general public could access trade information, such as market trends, daily high and low prices for each stock, and current trading prices. Moment-to-moment information was available only by calling a stockbroker or by visiting a brokerage where New York Stock Exchange (NYSE) data were visible to visitors for each transaction flowing on an overhead screen. Many investors relied on newspaper reports summarizing the most recent day's market transactions before deciding if the time was right to buy or sell stocks.

Today's trading environment is a new and different world. Instead of reading the *Wall Street Journal* to see what happened yesterday, mass communications with television and online networks provide current market information accessible nearly anywhere—at home, while traveling, at work—keeping investors apprised of the status of their investments and the markets. Financial television networks, such as CNBC, MSNBC, Bloomberg Television, and Fox Business, display transactions and market conditions as they occur at NYSE and NASDAQ exchanges, along with continuous reports on the Dow, S&P 500, and NASDAQ indexes. Investors and traders seeking financial opportunities abroad have access to developments in global financial markets including those in China, Australia, Europe, and elsewhere, including information on currency exchange rates.

With access to the Web, investors seeking market information on specific stocks can visit any of the online sources, such as *Yahoo! Finance*, *Bloomberg.com*, *money.msn.com*, and *marketwatch.com*, for market quotes and financial information, including historical trade data, at any time. Going beyond mere information gathering, Web trading has become a popular tool for investors. Logging on through your favorite Web browser, you can place trades—buying and selling stocks, bonds, and commodities—by establishing an account with one of the many online brokers. With mobile access, Web traders using a broker such as *TradeStation* can check prices, place trades, create charts, manage their account balances, and get access to market research and education resources, along with portfolio analysis and reports. Users can keep track of trading opportunities 24/7 from anywhere using a

incamerastock/Alamy

smartphone, tablet, or mobile device. Many Web brokers, both large and small, are luring customers with offerings of new stock-trading apps, including free ones, such as *iSwim*, *Bloomberg*, *Yahoo! stocks*, and *DailyFinance*. With the growing availability of investment-related applications for mobile devices, some Web-trading firms report that mobile apps account for more than 15 percent of their customer activity.

Online access has increased the popularity of day trading. As contrasted with investing, in which a buyer intends to hold the stock (or other financial instrument) into the future before selling for a long-term profit, a stock trader intends to hold a stock for only a brief period of time before selling to capture a short-term profit. Day trading is an even more specialized form of trading because the buying and selling is accomplished within one day, without holding the stock overnight. Day traders rely on speedy transactions to profit from the difference between buying and selling prices during the day, sometimes holding a stock for only a few seconds or minutes before selling. Unlike the previous era, when only financial companies had access to stock exchanges and market information, today's technology puts trading within easy reach of individual investors.[20]

portfolio is allocated in different proportions among a variety of funds; if all goes according to plan, most of these funds will meet their desired investment objectives and the overall portfolio will increase in value.

A risk–return relationship is inherent in every business investment. Whereas safer investments tend to offer lower returns, riskier investments tend to offer higher returns (rewards). Different types of investments vary along the risk–reward continuum, and most firms strive for a mixture of investments that, overall, provide that firm's desired risk–return posture. Each investment's total financial return is the sum of its capital gain and dividend (interest) yield. After determining the desired risk–return balance, investors use two methods for achieving it: (1) diversification, and (2) asset allocation. Diversification means buying several different kinds of investments rather than just one. Asset allocation is the proportion of funds invested in each of the investment alternatives. Diversification and asset allocation, together, are essential to protect against the uncertainties (risks) inherent in any single investment.

Financing the Business Firm

OBJECTIVE 5
Describe
the various ways that firms raise capital and identify the pros and cons of each method.

If you invest wisely, you may earn enough money to start your own firm; but that's only the first step in the complicated process of financing a business. Every company needs cash to function. Although a business owner's savings may be enough to get a firm up and running, businesses depend on sales revenues to survive. When current sales revenues are insufficient to pay for expenses, firms tap into various other sources of funds, typically starting with the owners' savings (as discussed in Chapter 15, owners contribute funds, or paid-in capital, from their own pockets). If a firm needs more money, they can turn to borrowing from banks, soliciting cash from private outside investors, or selling bonds to the public.

Secured Loans for Equipment

Money to purchase new equipment often comes in the form of loans from commercial banks. In a **secured loan (asset-backed loan)** the borrower guarantees repayment of the loan by pledging the asset as **collateral** to the lender. Suppose a local trucking company gets a $320,000 bank loan to purchase eight dump trucks. The borrower pledges the trucks and the company's office building as collateral to the bank. That is, if the borrower defaults, or fails to repay the loan, the bank can take possession of the borrower's pledged assets and sell them to recover the outstanding debt. However, as we learned in the 2008 recession, assets from loans defaulted by businesses and home buyers may have little or no value.

Secured Loan (Asset-Backed Loan) *loan to finance an asset, backed by the borrower pledging the asset as collateral to the lender*

Collateral *asset pledged for the fulfillment of repaying a loan*

The amount of money that is loaned and must be repaid is the **loan principal.** However, borrowers also pay the lender an additional fee, **interest,** for the use of the borrowed funds. The amount of interest owed depends on an **annual percentage rate (APR)** that is agreed on between the lender and borrower. The interest amount is found by multiplying the APR by the loan principal.

Loan Principal *amount of money that is loaned and must be repaid*

Interest *fee paid to a lender for the use of borrowed funds; like a rental fee*

Annual Percentage Rate (APR) *one-year rate that is charged for borrowing, expressed as a percentage of the borrowed principal*

Working Capital and Unsecured Loans from Banks

Firms need more than just fixed assets for daily operations; they need current, liquid assets available to meet short-term operating expenses such as employee wages and marketing expenses. The firm's ability to meet these expenses is measured by its working capital:

Working capital = Current assets − Current liabilities

Positive working capital means the firm's current assets are large enough to pay off current liabilities (see Chapter 15). Negative working capital means the firm's current liabilities are greater than current assets, so it may need to borrow money from a commercial bank. With an **unsecured loan,** the borrower does not have to put up collateral. In many cases, however, the bank requires the borrower to maintain a *compensating balance,* the borrower must keep a portion of the loan amount on deposit with the bank in a non–interest-bearing account.

Unsecured Loan *loan for which collateral is not required*

Firms with bad credit scores typically cannot get unsecured loans. Because access to such loans requires a good credit history, many firms establish a relationship with a commercial bank and, over time, build a good credit record by repaying loan principal and interest on time.

In extreme conditions, however, even a good credit history may not be enough. During the deepening recession, the cash shortages at most banks prevented loans of nearly any kind to business customers, thereby slowing down the economy even more. Even after vast injections of cash from TARP and other government sources, banks lagged far behind in supplying loans to meet working-capital needs of cash-strapped business borrowers.

Small business entrepreneurs, especially, often underestimate the value of establishing bank credit as a source of funds. Some banks offer financial analysis, cash flow planning, and suggestions based on experiences with other local firms. Some provide loans to small businesses in bad times and work to keep them going. Obtaining credit, therefore, begins with finding a bank that can—and will—support a small firm's financial needs. Once a line of credit is obtained, the small business can seek more liberal credit policies from other businesses. Sometimes, for instance, suppliers give customers longer credit periods—say, 45 or 60 days rather than 30 days—to make payments. Liberal trade credit terms with their suppliers let firms increase short-term funds and avoid additional borrowing from banks.

Obtaining longer-term loans is more difficult for new businesses than for established companies. With unproven repayment ability, start-up firms can expect to pay higher interest rates than older firms. If a new enterprise displays evidence of sound financial planning, however, the U.S. Small Business Administration (SBA, see Chapter 3), may support a guaranteed loan. The presentation of a business plan demonstrates to any lender that the borrower is a good credit risk. The business plan is a document that tells potential lenders why the money is needed, the amount, how the money will be used to improve the company, and when it will be paid back.

Planning for *cash flow requirements* is especially valuable for meeting the small business's financial needs. It also demonstrates to lenders the borrower's prudent use of financial resources. The firm's success or failure may hinge on anticipating those times when either cash will be short or excess cash can be expected. Consider how the owner would compare the expected cash inflows, cash outflows, and net cash position (inflows minus outflows) month by month for Slippery Fish Bait Supply Co., a highly seasonal business. Bait stores (Slippery's customers) buy heavily from Slippery during the spring and summer months. Revenues outpace expenses, leaving surplus funds that can be invested. During the fall and winter, however, expenses exceed revenues. Slippery must borrow funds to keep going until revenues pick up again in spring. Comparing predicted cash inflows from sales with outflows for expenses will show the firm's expected monthly cash-flow position. Such information can be invaluable for the small-business manager. By anticipating shortfalls, managers can seek funds in advance and minimize their costs. By anticipating excess cash, a manager can plan to put the funds to work in short-term, interest-earning investments.

Angel Investors and Venture Capital

Angel Investors *outside investors who provide new capital for firms in return for a share of equity ownership*

Once a business has been successfully launched it needs additional capital for growth. Outside individuals who provide such capital are called **angel investors.** It is estimated that more than 5 million angel investors are supplying funds for U.S. business startups. Peter Thiel supplied an initial $500,000 angel investment in Facebook's early years. In return for their investment, angel investors typically expect a sizable piece of ownership in the company (up to 50 percent of its equity). They may also want a formal say in how the company is run. If the firm is bought by a larger company or if it sells its stock in a public offering, the angel may receive additional payments.

Venture Capital *private funds from wealthy individuals seeking investment opportunities in new growth companies*

Angel investors help many firms grow rapidly by providing what is known as **venture capital,** private funds from wealthy individuals or companies (see Chapter 3) that seek investment opportunities in new growth companies. In most cases, the growth firm turns to venture capital sources because they have not yet built enough credit history to get a loan from commercial banks or other lending institutions.

Sale of Corporate Bonds

Corporations can raise capital by issuing bonds. A **corporate bond** is a formal pledge (an IOU) obligating the issuer to pay interest periodically and repay the principal at maturity (a preset future date) to the lender. The federal government also issues bonds to finance projects and meet obligations, as do state and local governments (called *municipal bonds*) for financing the building of schools, roads, and sewage disposal systems.

Characteristics of Corporate Bonds The bondholder (the lender) has no claim to ownership of the company and does not receive dividends. However, interest payments and repayment of principal are financial obligations; payments to bondholders have priority over dividend payments to stockholders in cases of financial distress.

Each new bond issue has specific terms and conditions spelled out in a **bond indenture,** a legal document identifying the borrower's obligations and the financial returns to lenders. One of the most important details is the **maturity date** (or **due date**), when the firm must repay the bond's **face value** (also called **par value,** or the amount purchased) to the lender.

Corporate bonds have been traditionally issued to fund outstanding debts and major projects for various lengths of time. Short-term bonds mature in less than 5 years after they are issued. Bonds with 5- to 10-year lives are considered intermediate term, and anything longer than 10 years is considered long term. Longer-term corporate bonds are somewhat riskier than shorter-term bonds because they are exposed to greater unforeseen economic conditions that may lead to default.

Default and Bondholders' Claim A bond is said to be in **default** if the borrower fails to make payment when due to lenders. Bondholders may then file a **bondholders' claim,** a request for court enforcement of the bond's terms of payment. When a financially distressed company cannot pay bondholders, it may seek relief by filing for **bankruptcy,** the court-granted permission not to pay some or all debts. After a restructured General Motors emerged from bankruptcy in 2009, the holders of the old General Motors Corporation's $24 billion in bonds wondered how much payment, if any, they would recover from the financially strapped company. In the 2011 settlement, investors holding bonds in the old GM received stock shares in the new GM that provided a recovery rate of about 40 percent on the dollar of the original bond investment.[21]

Risk Ratings To aid investors in making purchase decisions, several services measure the default risk of bonds. Table 17.2, for example, shows the rating systems of two well-known services, Moody's and Standard & Poor's. The highest (safest) grades are AAA and Aaa, and the lowest are C and D, representing speculative and highly risky bonds. Low-grade bonds are usually called *junk bonds*. Negative ratings do not necessarily keep issues from being successful. Rather, they raise the interest rates that issuers must offer to attract lenders.

Flawed Ratings Misread Recession Risks The financial meltdown of 2008 has raised questions about whether any good purpose is being served by credit-rating agencies. Among many other investors, California Public Employees

Corporate Bond *formal pledge obligating the issuer (the company) to pay interest periodically and repay the principal at maturity*

Bond Indenture *legal document containing complete details of a bond issue*

Maturity Date (Due Date) *future date when repayment of a bond is due from the bond issuer (borrower)*

Face Value (Par Value) *amount of money that the bond buyer (lender) lent the issuer and that the lender will receive on repayment*

Default *failure of a borrower to make payment when due to a lender*

Bondholders' Claim *request for court enforcement of a bond's terms of payment*

Bankruptcy *court-granted permission for a company to not pay some or all debts*

table 17.2 Bond Rating Systems

Rating System	High Grades	Medium Grades (Investment Grades)	Speculative	Poor Grades
Moody's	Aaa, Aa	A, Baa	Ba, B	Caa to C
Standard & Poor's	AAA, AA	A, BBB	BB, B	CCC to D

Retirement Fund (Calpers), the nation's largest public pension fund, has filed a suit against the three top agencies—Moody's, Standard & Poor's, and Fitch—charging losses caused by "wildly inaccurate and unreasonably high" credit ratings. Calpers officials relied on ratings for investments that turned sour—many failing altogether. Skepticism of agencies' ratings has soared following the collapse of highly rated giants such as Lehman Brothers, Goldman Sachs, and Citigroup, along with high ratings on billions of dollars of mortgage-backed securities that eventually became toxic. Recent lawsuits, including those by the states of Ohio and Connecticut, accuse credit rating agencies of reckless assessments that misled investors.[22]

Managing in Turbulent Times

Weakening South African Housing Market?

South African house prices increased at a rate of 253.7 percent in the period 2000 to 2007. With the global financial crisis in 2008, this growth period ended. In response, the South African Reserve Bank cut interest rates a dozen times to help stimulate a recovery. By the time South Africa hosted the FIFA World Cup in 2010, house prices were again increasing. Since then, there has been a marked slowdown.

It is generally recognized that there are four major factors that have contributed to the buoyancy of the South African housing market in the past decade. In the first place, a financially stable black middle class has emerged post-Apartheid. Average GDP growth has helped fuel their disposable income, and government policy has encouraged investment in property. The second factor is that during Apartheid, a huge amount of capital was exported. Government policy was to require that capital to return to South Africa by 2004. Much of this capital has subsequently been invested in property. Thirdly, South Africa has enjoyed a period of political stability; this has led to the currency being stronger, the housing market catching up with the rest of the economy, and a general sense of confidence to invest. The final factor was the introduction of the Financial Sector Charter in 2003, which underpinned the system of providing mortgages to low-income South Africans. In 2003, the total value of mortgages in South Africa stood at $43.1 million; four years later this had reached $110.8 million.

Jeff_Rivard/Fotolia

Other key changes are that overseas nationals can now own property in South Africa. However, there are two factors that seem to be having a negative impact on the housing market. The first is the National Credit Act, which aims to ensure that borrowers are not overextended. In effect, it restricts the funds that people can borrow through the requirement that lenders assess the creditworthiness of each borrower. The second factor is a response to global conditions. Interest rates then gradually rose in South Africa as part of an attempt to control inflation. This in turn has lead to a slowing of the number of mortgages approved, but it is still an upward trend, rising at around 20 percent per year.[23]

Mortgage-backed securities (MBS) became a trillion-dollar investment industry during the pre-2007 housing market boom. Financial institutions bundled home mortgages into packages and resold them as securities to eager investors who trusted in the securities' risk ratings given by Moody's, Standard & Poor's, and Fitch. Each MBS is a group of mortgages bundled together to form a debt obligation (a bond) that entitles the holder (the investor) to the cash that flows in from the mortgages. Unknown to investors, some $3 trillion of MBSs contained subprime mortgages—high-risk loans to applicants with bad credit, low income, and low down payments—most of which had received high ratings (AAA) by credit-rating agencies. Misled by flawed risk assessments, investors were left with little or nothing when the highly rated securities turned toxic, causing the collapse of the housing and financial markets.[24]

Mortgage-Backed Security (MBS) *mortgages pooled together to form a debt obligation—a bond—that entitles the holder (investor) to cash that flows in from the bundled mortgages*

Becoming a Public Corporation

Initial public offerings (IPOs), the first sale of a company's stock to the general public, are a major source of funds that fuel continued growth for many firms and introduce numerous considerations inherent in running a public company. In one of the biggest IPOs in history, Facebook's public offering of common stock in 2012, with an opening price of $38 per share, raised more than $100 billion. In this section, we discuss many of the issues public companies face, such as potential loss of control, fluctuating share prices, how businesses use market capitalization, and how they choose capital sources.

OBJECTIVE 6
Identify
the reasons a company might make an initial public offering of its stock, explain how stock value is determined, and discuss the significance of market capitalization.

Initial Public Offering (IPO) *first sale of a company's stock to the general public*

In early 2011 Google shares were trading at $586 per share.

Leah Overstreet/Newscom

Going Public Means Selling off Part of the Company

Private owners lose some control of the company when shares are sold to the public. Common shareholders usually have voting rights in corporate governance, so they elect the board of directors and vote on major issues put forth at the company's annual shareholders' meeting. Anyone owning a large proportion of the company's shares gains a powerful position in determining who runs the corporation and how.

Corporate Raider *investor conducting a type of hostile corporate takeover against the wishes of the company*

At an extreme, a **corporate raider,** an investor conducting a type of hostile (unwanted) takeover, buys shares on the open market, attempting to seize control of the company and its assets. The raider then sells off those assets at a profit, resulting in the company's disappearance.

A company is ripe for raiding when its stock price falls so shares can be cheaply bought, although its assets still have high value.

Stock Valuation

What determines a stock's value after it is offered to the general public? Investors' assessments of the company's management record in past ventures, expectations for competing in the industry, and belief in the public's acceptance of the company's products are among many factors that affect a stock's value, which in turn affect the value of the business. In addition, different investors measure value differently, and their measurements may change according to circumstance. Because of the uncertainties involved in stock prices, investment professionals believe day-to-day prices to be a generally poor indicator of any stock's real value. Instead, a long-run perspective considers the company's financial health, past history of results and future forecasts, its record for managerial performance, and overall prospects for competing successfully in the coming years. Accordingly, any stock's value today looks beyond the current price and is based on expectations of the financial returns it will provide to shareholders during the long run.

Why Shares Are Different Prices
In June 2013 the price of Google Inc. was about $880 per share on the NYSE, GE shares traded at about $24, Delta Airlines shares were priced at about $18, and Berkshire Hathaway shares traded for $172,900.[25]

Why such differences? One reason is supply and demand for each company's shares; another is because some corporations want the shares to sell within a particular price range, say between $20 and $80, believing it will attract a larger pool of investors. If the price gets too high, many investors can't afford to buy shares. A company can restore shares to the desired lower range by a **stock split,** a stock dividend paid in additional shares to shareholders. Here's how it works. Suppose company X has 100,000 common shares outstanding that are trading at $100 per share, but the company wants it priced in the $20 to $80 range. X can declare a 2-for-1 stock split, meaning the company gives shareholders one additional share for each share they own. Now X has 200,000 shares outstanding but its financial performance has not changed, so the stock price immediately falls to $50 per share. Every shareholder's investment value, however, is unchanged: they previously owned one share at $100, and now they own two shares at $50 each.

Stock Split *stock dividend paid in additional shares to shareholders, thus increasing the number of outstanding shares*

Comparing Prices of Different Stocks
Consider a trading day in early June, 2013 when PepsiCo's share price was $81.04, and Coca-Cola was $40.74 per share. Does the price difference mean that PepsiCo is a better company than Coca-Cola because its shares are more expensive? Or does it mean that Coke shares are a better value because they can be bought at a lower price than PepsiCo's? In fact, neither of these two reasons is correct. Share prices alone do not provide enough information to determine which is the better investment. Table 17.3 can help us make a better comparison with further information.

First, earnings per share (EPS) are greater for PepsiCo ($3.90 versus $1.91 per share). Although you pay more to own a PepsiCo share, earnings per dollar of

table 17.3 Financial Comparison: Coca-Cola and PepsiCo

	Coca-Cola	PepsiCo
Recent price	$40.74	$81.04
EPS	$1.91	$3.90
Dividend yield	2.75%	2.80%

Source: Yahoo!Finance, June 5, 2013 at http://finance.yahoo.com/q?s=PEP&ql=1; Yahoo!Finance, June 5, 2013 at http://finance.yahoo.com/q?s=KO&ql=0.

investment are slightly higher than for Coke ($3.90 earnings/$81.04 investment = $0.048 Pepsi; versus $1.91 earnings/$40.74 investment = $0.047 Coke): PepsiCo's earnings were about 4.8 cents for each dollar of its share price, whereas Coca-Cola earned almost the same at 4.7 cents. Both companies generated about the same earnings power for each dollar of shareholder investment.

Now consider annual dividends paid to shareholders. The dividend yield from Coca-Cola was 2.75 percent. That is, the dividend payment amounted to a 2.75 percent return on the shareholder's $40.74 investment, or $1.12 = ($40.74 × 2.75%). PepsiCo's dividend payment was about $2.27 or ($81.03 × 2.80%), representing a slightly larger return (yield) on shareholder investment than Coca-Cola (2.80% versus 2.75%).

Based on this limited information, it's not clear which of the two companies is the better investment. A more complete evaluation would compare historical performance consistency over a period of several years, along with indicators of each firm's prospects for the future.

Market Capitalization

A widely used measure of corporate size and value is known as **market capitalization (market cap),** the total dollar value of all the company's outstanding shares, calculated as the current stock price multiplied by the number of shares outstanding. As indicated in Table 17.4, the investment industry categorizes firms according to size of capitalization.

Market Capitalization (Market Cap) *total dollar value of all the company's outstanding shares*

Investors typically regard larger market caps as less risky, and firms with small market caps (small-cap firms) as being particularly risky investments. As of June 2013, Apple, Inc.'s market capitalization of $415 billion was the largest among U.S. companies, followed closely by Exxon-Mobil at $406 billion.

Choosing Equity versus Debt Capital

Firms can meet their capital needs through two sources: (1) *debt financing* (from outside the firm) or (2) *equity financing* (putting the owners' capital to work).

Pros and Cons for Debt Financing Long-term borrowing from sources outside the company, **debt financing,** via loans or the sale of corporate bonds is a major component in most U.S. firms' financial planning.

Debt Financing *long-term borrowing from sources outside a company*

table 17.4 Corporation Sizes Based on Capitalization

Capitalization Category	Range of Capitalization
Micro-Cap	below $250 million
Small-Cap	$250 million–$2 billion
Mid-Cap	$2 billion–$10 billion
Large-Cap	over $10 billion

In mid-2011 China's CNOOC Ltd. share price was $17.98, and there were 44.67 billion common shares outstanding. Its market cap was over $800 billion, making the oil-and-gas producer the largest company in the world.

Frederic J. Brown/Newscom

LONG-TERM LOANS Long-term loans are attractive for several reasons:

- Because the number of parties involved is limited, loans can often be arranged quickly.

- The firm need not make public disclosure of its business plans or the purpose for which it is acquiring the loan. (In contrast, the issuance of corporate bonds requires such disclosure.)

Long-term loans also have some disadvantages. Borrowers, for example, may have trouble finding lenders to supply large sums. Long-term borrowers may also face restrictions as conditions of the loan. For example, they may have to pledge long-term assets as collateral or agree to take on no more debt until the loan is paid.

CORPORATE BONDS Bonds are attractive when firms need large amounts for long periods of time. The issuing company gains access to large numbers of lenders through nationwide bond markets. On the other hand, bonds entail high administrative and selling costs. They may also require stiff interest payments, especially if the issuing company has a poor credit rating. Bonds also impose binding obligations on the firm, in many cases for up to 30 years, to pay bondholders a stipulated sum of annual or semiannual interest, even in times of financial distress. If the company fails to make a bond payment, it goes into default. A classic example is WorldCom, which filed for bankruptcy in 2002 when it was the nation's number-two long-distance phone company. With $102 billion in assets, WorldCom's bankruptcy at the time was the largest in U.S. history. Even with those massive assets, however, the firm was crushed by its $41 billion debt, $24 billion of which was in bonds. Facing prospects that the firm would default on upcoming interest payments, many of its creditors began withholding additional money unless loans were secured with WorldCom assets. With more than 1,000 creditors—including Citibank, JPMorgan Chase, and Credit Suisse First Boston—the firm was allowed to operate while in bankruptcy. In 2003, WorldCom changed its name to MCI, before emerging from bankruptcy status in 2004.

Pros and Cons for Equity Financing Although debt financing often has strong appeal, **equity financing,** looking inside the company for long-term funding, is sometimes preferable. Equity financing includes either issuing common stock or retaining the firm's earnings.

Equity Financing *using the owners' funds from inside the company as the source for long-term funding*

THE EXPENSE OF COMMON STOCK The use of equity financing by means of common stock can be expensive because paying dividends is more expensive than paying bond interest. Interest paid to bondholders is a business expense and therefore a tax deduction for the firm. Payments of cash dividends to shareholders are not tax deductible.

RETAINED EARNINGS AS A SOURCE OF CAPITAL As presented in Chapter 15, *retained earnings* are net profits retained for the firm's use rather than paid out in dividends to stockholders. If a company uses retained earnings as capital, it will not have to borrow money and pay interest. If a firm has a history of reaping profits by reinvesting retained earnings, it may be attractive to some investors. Retained earnings, however, mean smaller dividends for shareholders. This practice may decrease the demand for—and the price of—the company's stock.

We have seen, then, that becoming a public corporation means selling off part of the ownership through an initial public offering. Several factors determine the stock's value after that stock is available to the general public. The day-to-day price is a weak indicator of the stock's value, whereas prospects for the firm's future financial health, the performance record of its management, and prospects for competing in the future are considerations that determine the stock's value. Market capitalization, the current stock price multiplied by the number of shares outstanding, is a widely used measure of company size and overall value. A public corporation's continued growth is accompanied by the need for more capital that can be met through two sources: debt financing or equity financing. Borrowing via long-term loans and the issuance of corporate bonds can provide a large supply of funds but also imposes binding obligations on the firm. Likewise, funds can be raised by issuing additional common stock or by increasing retained earnings, but doing so means smaller dividends for shareholders. These practices may decrease the demand for—and the price of—the company's stock.

Regulating Securities Markets

OBJECTIVE 7
Explain
how securities markets are regulated.

The U.S. government, along with various state agencies, plays a key role in monitoring and regulating the securities industry. Businesses cannot exist in the United States without the public's trust, and the public's willingness to participate in business ownership and everyday transactions with companies. Regulation of the U.S. securities markets plays a vital role in maintaining the public's trust in fair and open business ownership.

The Securities and Exchange Commission

The U.S. SEC is the regulation and enforcement agency that oversees the markets' activities, including the ways securities are issued. The SEC was created in 1934 to prevent the kinds of abuses that led to the stock market crash of 1929. The SEC regulates the public offering of new securities by requiring that all companies file prospectuses before proposed offerings commence. To protect investors from fraudulent issues, a **prospectus** contains pertinent information about both the offered security and the issuing company. False statements are subject to criminal penalties.

The SEC also enforces laws against **insider trading,** the use of special knowledge about a firm for profit or gain. It is illegal, for example, for an employee of a firm to tell others about an anticipated event that may affect the value of that firm's stock, such as an acquisition or a merger, before news of that event is made public. Those in possession of such insider knowledge would have an unfair advantage over other investors.

Prospectus *registration statement filed with the SEC, containing information for prospective investors about a security to be offered and the issuing company*

Insider Trading *illegal practice of using special knowledge about a firm for profit or gain*

54-year old Raj Rajaratnam was sentenced to 11 years in federal prison after being convicted for insider trading.

Steve Hirsch/Newscom

Regulations against Insider Trading

In March 2011 the U.S. Attorney began criminal trial in New York against Raj Rajaratnam, founder of Galleon Group, on charges that the billionaire fund manager profited from illegal stock tips with a network of financial insiders. Reports indicate the accused gained profits of up to $60 million by using illicit information, confidential company information not available to the public, revealing that stock prices of various companies would be increasing or falling. In conjunction with his arrest in 2009, charges were leveled against 26 others in the case—executives and securities traders—19 of whom pleaded guilty. In May 2011, Rajaratnam was convicted on 14 charges and faced possible maximum prison sentences totaling up to 205 years. He was finally sentenced to serve 11 years in prison, the longest ever for an insider-trading violation. In addition to the criminal trial, he faces additional civil charges brought by the SEC. As a U.S. Attorney stated some years previously, "Insider trading is a crime. Corporate executives are prohibited from enriching themselves while the public remains in the dark about the true financial condition of their companies."[26]

The SEC offers a reward to any person who provides information leading to a civil penalty for illegal insider trading. The courts can render such a penalty of up to three times the illegal profit that was gained, and the reward can, at most, be 10 percent of that penalty.

Along with the SEC's enforcement efforts, the stock exchanges and securities firms have adopted self-regulation by participating with the Financial Industry Regulatory Authority (FINRA) in detecting and stopping insider action, and violations of other industry regulations. Established in 2003, FINRA's mission is to protect U.S. investors by overseeing the nation's brokerage firms and securities representatives. The major U.S. stock markets are under contract that allows FINRA to regulate those markets by writing rules, examining securities firms, enforcing the rules, and enforcing federal securities laws as well.

summary of learning objectives

OBJECTIVE 1

Explain the concept of the time value of money and the principle of compound growth, and discuss the characteristics of common stock. (pp. 588–590)

The time value of money, perhaps the single most important concept in business finance, recognizes the basic fact that, when it's invested over time, money grows by earning interest or yielding some other form of return. Time value stems from the principle of *compound growth*—the cumulative growth from interest paid to the investor over given time periods. With each additional time period, the investment grows as interest payments accumulate and earn more interest, thus multiplying the earning capacity of the investment.

The "Rule of 72" is a practical example that illustrates the concept of the time value of money. The rule shows the number of years required for an initial investment to double in value, depending on the interest rate received in return for the investment. The rule demonstrates that higher rates of return (interest) result in fewer years required to double the original investment.

A share of *common stock* is the most basic form of ownership in a company. Individuals and organizations purchase a firm's common stock in the hope that it will increase in value and provide dividend income. Each common share has a vote on major issues that are brought before the shareholders. A stock's real value is its *market value*—the current price of a share in the stock market—reflecting the amount buyers are willing to pay for a share of the company's stock. Common stocks are among the riskiest of all investments because uncertainties about the stock market can quickly change the stock's value. *Blue-chip stocks* are issued by the strongest and most well-established, financially sound, and respected firms. They have historically provided investors steady income through consistent dividend payouts.

OBJECTIVE 2

Identify reasons for investing and the investment opportunities offered by mutual funds and exchange-traded funds. (pp. 591–592)

Mutual funds are attractive investments because different funds are designed to appeal to different financial motives and goals of investors. Three of the most common alternative objectives for investing in mutual funds are stability and safety, conservative capital growth, and aggressive growth. Funds stressing stability and safety seek only modest growth while preserving the fund holders' capital and reliably paying modest current income. Conservative capital growth funds stress preservation of capital and current income but also seek some capital appreciation. Aggressive growth funds seek maximum long-term capital growth.

Unfortunately, many mutual funds do not perform as well as the average return of the overall stock market as a result of costly management expense and underperforming stocks. Index mutual funds, however, closely match the performance of a particular market. An exchange-traded fund (ETF), as with an index mutual fund, is a bundle of stocks (or bonds) that are an index that tracks the overall movement of a market. However, ETFs offer three areas of advantage over mutual funds: They can be traded throughout the day like a stock (whereas a mutual fund cannot be traded like a stock), they have low operating expenses, and they require low initial investments resulting in ease of entry for investors getting started without much money. Because they are traded on stock exchanges (hence, "exchange traded"), ETFs can be bought and sold—priced continuously—any time throughout the day. Mutual fund shares, in contrast, are priced once daily, at the end of the day.

OBJECTIVE 3

Describe the role of securities markets and identify the major stock exchanges and stock markets. (pp. 592–599)

The markets in which stocks and bonds are sold are called *securities markets*. By facilitating the buying and selling of securities, the securities markets provide the capital that companies rely on for survival. In *primary securities markets*, new stocks and bonds are bought and sold by firms and governments. Sometimes, new securities are sold to single buyers or small groups of buyers. These private placements are desirable because they allow issuers to keep their business plans confidential. Firms issuing new securities must get approval from the SEC. Issuing firms also usually rely on investment banking services to issue and resell new securities. Investment banks provide several important services. (1) They advise companies on the timing and financial terms of the new issue. (2) The investment bank buys and assumes liability for the new securities, a process referred to *underwriting*. (3) Investment banks create distribution networks for moving new securities through groups of other financial institutions into the hands of individual investors. In contrast with new securities issues, *existing* stocks and bonds are sold in the much larger *secondary securities market*, consisting largely of *stock exchanges*. A stock exchange is an organization of individuals coordinated to provide an institutional auction setting in which stocks can be bought and sold. Major stock exchanges include the New York Stock Exchange, the NASDAQ market in the United States, NYSE Euronext, along with various other foreign exchanges such as the London Stock Exchange and the Tokyo Exchange, and by online trading with other stock exchanges around the globe.

In 1998, the SEC authorized the creation of *electronic communication networks (ECNs)*, electronic trading systems that bring buyers and sellers together outside traditional stock exchanges by automatically matching buy and sell orders at specified prices. ECNs gained rapid popularity because the trading procedures are fast and efficient, often lowering transaction costs per share to mere pennies. They also allow after-hours trading (after traditional markets have closed for the day) and protect traders' anonymity.

Stock brokers are financial services professionals who earn commissions by executing buy and sell orders for outside customers. As with many other products, brokerage assistance can be purchased at either discount or at full-service prices. Discount brokers, such as E*TRADE and Scottrade, offer well-informed individual investors who know what they want to buy or sell a fast, low-cost way to participate in the market. Full-service brokers, such as Merrill Lynch Wealth Management, offer clients consulting advice in personal financial planning, estate planning, and tax strategies, along with a wider range of investment products.

Although not indicative of the status of individual securities, *market indexes*, such as the Dow Jones Industrial Average and S&P 500, provide useful summaries of overall price trends, both in specific industries and in the stock market as a whole. Market indexes, for example, reveal *bull* and *bear market* trends. *Bull markets* are periods of rising stock prices, generally lasting 12 months or longer; investors are motivated to buy, confident they will realize capital gains. Periods of falling stock prices, usually 20 percent off peak prices, are called *bear markets*; investors are motivated to sell, anticipating further falling prices.

OBJECTIVE 4

Describe the risk–return relationship and discuss the use of diversification and asset allocation for investments. (pp. 599–603)

Individual investors have different motivations and personal preferences for safety versus risk. While all investors anticipate receiving future cash flows, some cash flows are more certain than other riskier returns. Investors generally expect to receive higher financial returns for investments having higher uncertainty. They do not expect large returns from secure, stable investments. Each type of investment, then, has a risk–return (risk–reward) relationship. The risk–return relationship is the principle that investors expect to receive higher returns for riskier investments and lower returns for safer investments. Conservative investors who have a low tolerance for risk will seek safer investments with low expected returns. The reverse is true for aggressive investors who prefer taking higher risks with the potential for higher returns.

When evaluating potential investments, investors look at returns from dividends or interest, returns from price appreciation, and total return. The rate of return from dividends paid to shareholders is commonly referred to as the *current dividend* yield. In the case of interest from a loan, the term *interest yield* is used. *Price appreciation* is an increase in the value of an investment over time. *Total* return is the sum of the investment's dividend or interest yields and the *capital gain* from price appreciation.

Diversification and asset allocation are tools for helping investors achieve the desired risk–return balance for an investment portfolio. *Diversification* means buying several different kinds of investments—stocks of different companies, securities of companies in different industries, investments in different countries, combinations of stocks/bonds/real estate/precious metals—to reduce the risk of loss if the value of any one investment should fall. *Asset allocation* is the proportion of overall money invested in each of various investment alternatives so that the overall risks for the portfolio are low, moderate, or high, depending on the investor's objectives and preferences.

OBJECTIVE 5

Describe the various ways that firms raise capital and identify the pros and cons of each method. (pp. 603–607)

Every company needs cash to function. Firms often begin with the owner's personal savings. As more money is needed it is obtained from sales revenues, borrowing from banks, cash from private investors, by issuing bonds, or selling stock. Money to purchase new equipment often comes in the form of loans from commercial banks. In a *secured loan (asset-backed loan)* the borrower guarantees repayment of the loan by pledging the asset as *collateral* to the lender. The amount of money that is loaned and must be repaid is the *loan principal*. However, borrowers also pay the lender an additional fee, *interest*, for the use of the borrowed funds. The amount of interest owed depends on an *annual percentage rate (APR)* that is agreed on between the lender and borrower. The interest amount is found by multiplying the APR by the loan principal. With an *unsecured loan*, the borrower does not have to put up collateral. In many cases, however, the bank requires the borrower to maintain a *compensating balance*, the borrower must keep a portion of the loan amount on deposit with the bank in a non-interest–bearing account.

Once a business has been successfully launched it needs additional capital for growth. Outside individuals who provide such capital are called *angel investors*. Angel investors help many firms grow rapidly by providing what is known as *venture capital*, private funds from wealthy individuals or companies that seek investment opportunities in new growth companies. In most cases, the growth firm turns to venture capital sources because they have not yet built enough credit history to get a loan from commercial banks or other lending institutions.

Corporations can raise capital by issuing bonds. A *corporate bond* is a formal pledge (an IOU) obligating the issuer to pay interest periodically and repay the principal at maturity (a preset future date) to the lender. The federal government also issues bonds to finance projects and meet obligations, as do state and local governments (called *municipal bonds*) for financing the building of schools, roads, and sewage disposal systems.

OBJECTIVE 6

Identify the reasons a company might make an initial public offering of its stock, explain how stock value is determined, and discuss the significance of market capitalization. (pp. 607–611)

The initial public offering (IPO)—the first sale of a company's stock to the general public—is a major source of funds for fueling the growth of many firms. IPOs reach far more potential investors, thereby providing access to a larger pool of funds than is available from the owner's personal funds and other private sources. A stock's real value is its market value—the current price of a share in the stock market. Market value reflects the amount that buyers are willing to pay for a share of the company's stock at any given time. However, the valuing of any stock today looks beyond the current price and is based on expectations of the financial returns it will provide to shareholders during the long run. A long-run perspective considers the company's financial health, past history of results and future forecasts, its record for managerial performance, and overall prospects for competing successfully in the coming years. Although supply and demand is a major determiner of a stock's price, another factor is a company's desire that its shares sell within a particular price range, believing it will attract a larger pool of investors. If the stock's market price gets too high, many investors cannot afford to buy shares. A company can restore shares to the desired lower price range by using a stock split in which the company gives shareholders an additional stock holding for each share they own. The market price per share falls immediately after the split, but with a larger number of shares every shareholder's investment value is unchanged.

Market capitalization, the total market value of all the company's outstanding shares, is a widely used measure of corporate size and value. Investors leaning toward risk avoidance typically regard larger market-cap firms as less risky, and firms with small market-caps (small-cap firms) as being particularly risky investments. Thus, the persistent demand for large-cap stocks tends to sustain or increase their market values.

Although debt financing often has strong appeal, *equity financing*, looking inside the company for long-term funding, is sometimes preferable. Equity financing includes either issuing common stock or retaining the firm's earnings. The use of equity financing by means of common stock can be expensive because paying dividends is more expensive than paying bond interest. Interest paid to bondholders is a business expense and therefore a tax deduction for the firm. Payments of cash dividends to shareholders are not tax deductible. *Retained earnings* are net profits retained for the firm's use rather than paid out in dividends to stockholders. If a company uses retained earnings as capital, it will not have to borrow money and pay interest. If a firm has a history of reaping profits by reinvesting retained earnings, it may be attractive to some investors. Retained earnings, however, mean smaller dividends for shareholders. This practice may decrease the demand for—and the price of—the company's stock.

OBJECTIVE 7

Explain how securities markets are regulated. (pp. 611–612)

The U.S. government, along with various state agencies, plays a key role in monitoring and regulating the securities industry. The U.S. Securities and Exchange Commission (SEC) is the regulation and enforcement agency that oversees the markets' activities. The SEC regulates the public offering of new securities by requiring companies to file *prospectuses* before proposed offerings commence. To protect investors from fraudulent securities issues, the prospectus contains information about the offered security and the issuing company. False statements are subject to criminal penalties.

The SEC also enforces laws against *insider trading*—the use of special knowledge about a firm for profit or gain. An example of illegal insider trading includes an employee of a firm telling others about an anticipated event that may affect the value of that firm's stock, such as an acquisition or a merger, before news of that event is made public. Those in possession of such insider knowledge would have an unfair advantage over other investors. The SEC offers a reward to any person who provides information leading to a civil penalty for illegal insider trading.

Along with the SEC's enforcement, the stock exchanges and securities firms have adopted self-regulation by participating with the Financial Industry Regulatory Authority (FINRA) in detecting and stopping violations of industry regulations. FINRA's mission is to protect U.S. investors by overseeing the nation's brokerage firms and securities representatives. FINRA regulates the U.S. stock markets by writing rules, examining securities firms, enforcing the rules, and enforcing federal securities laws.

key terms

angel investors (p. 604)
annual percentage rate (APR) (p. 603)
asset allocation (p. 601)
bankruptcy (p. 605)
bear market (p. 596)
blue-chip stock (p. 590)
bond indenture (p. 605)
bondholders' claim (p. 605)
book value (p. 590)
book-entry ownership (p. 596)

bull market (p. 596)
capital gain (p. 600)
collateral (p. 603)
common stock (p. 590)
compound growth (p. 588)
corporate bond (p. 605)
corporate raider (p. 608)
current dividend yield and current
    interest yield (p. 599)
debt financing (p. 609)

default (p. 605)
diversification (p. 601)
dividend (p. 590)
Dow Jones Industrial Average (DJIA)
    (p. 596)
electronic communication network
    (ECN) (p. 595)
equity financing (p. 611)
exchange-traded fund (ETF) (p. 592)
face value (par value) (p. 605)

initial public offering (IPO) (p. 607)
insider trading (p. 611)
interest (p. 603)
investment bank (p. 593)
load fund (p. 591)
loan principal (p. 603)
market capitalization (market cap) (p. 609)
market index (p. 596)
market value (p. 590)
maturity date (due date) (p. 605)
mortgage-backed security (MBS) (p. 607)
mutual fund (p. 591)
NASDAQ Composite Index (p. 598)

National Association of Securities
    Dealers Automated Quotation
    (NASDAQ) system (p. 595)
no-load fund (p. 591)
portfolio (p. 601)
price appreciation (p. 600)
primary securities market (p. 593)
prospectus (p. 611)
risk–return (risk–reward) relationship
    (p. 599)
Russell 2000 Index (p. 598)
S&P 500 (p. 597)
secondary securities market (p. 593)

secured loan (asset-backed loan)
    (p. 603)
securities (p. 592)
Securities and Exchange Commission
    (SEC) (p. 593)
securities markets (p. 592)
stock (p. 590)
stock broker (p. 595)
stock exchange (p. 593)
stock split (p. 608)
time value of money (p. 588)
unsecured loan (p. 603)
venture capital (p. 604)

MyBizLab

Go to **pearsonglobaleditions.com/mybizlab** to complete the problems marked with this icon ⊛.

questions & exercises

QUESTIONS FOR REVIEW

17-1. Explain the concept of the *time value of money*.

17-2. What do mutual funds and exchange-traded funds offer, and how do they work?

⊛ **17-3.** What is a corporate bond? Why would a company use bonds as a source of financing?

17-4. How does the market value of a stock differ from the book value of a stock?

17-5. How do firms meet their needs through debt financing and equity financing?

QUESTIONS FOR ANALYSIS

17-6. After researching several stocks online, you notice that they have continually fluctuated in price. What might be the reason for this? Is a higher-priced stock a better investment than a lower-priced stock? What factors would you consider in purchasing stocks?

⊛ **17-7.** Which type of fund do you think you would invest in, a mutual fund or an exchange-traded fund? What is the difference, and why would you favor one over the other?

⊛ **17-8.** Suppose that you are a business owner and you need new equipment and immediate funds to meet short-term operating expenses. From what sources could you gain the capital you need, and what are some of the characteristics of these sources?

APPLICATION EXERCISES

17-9. Go to http://www.sec.gov to research how a new security is approved by the Securities and Exchange Commission. What is the process involved and how long would it take? Next, contact a financial institution such as Merrill Lynch and request information about their procedures for issuing or reselling new securities. Share this information with your classmates.

17-10. There have been a number of high profile cases in recent years concerning insider trading. Use an online search to find a case involving insider trading. Who was accused of insider trading and what was their relationship to the company? Were they convicted of insider trading, and, if so, what was the penalty? Finally, how could the person accused of insider trading avoided these charges?

building a business: continuing team exercise

Assignment

Meet with your team members to consider your new business venture and how it relates to the finance topics in this chapter. Develop specific responses to the following:

17-11. What role will debt financing play in your business' financial plan? What types of debt financing will you use? Why?

17-12. As your business grows, will you consider bringing in angel investors or venture capital? Why or why not?

17-13. Would you consider selling stock to the general public? What advantages would a public sale of stock bring? Are there any downsides to this decision?

17-14. If you decide to sell stock through an initial public offering, what factors will be most important in the valuation of your stock?

17-15. How will the financing of your business change over time?

building your business skills

MARKET UPS AND DOWNS

Goal

To encourage you to understand the forces that affect fluctuations in stock prices.

Background Information

Investing in stocks requires an understanding of the various factors that affect stock prices. These factors may be intrinsic to the company itself or part of the external environment.

- Internal factors relate to the company itself, such as an announcement of poor or favorable earnings, earnings that are more or less than expected, major layoffs, labor problems, new products, management issues, and mergers.
- External factors relate to world or national events, such as wars, recessions, weather conditions that affect sales, the Fed's adjustment of interest rates, and employment figures that are higher or lower than expected.

By analyzing these factors, you will often learn a lot about why a stock did well or why it did poorly. Being aware of these influences will help you anticipate future stock movements.

Method

STEP 1

Working alone, choose a common stock that has experienced considerable price fluctuations in the past few years. Here are several examples (but there are many others): IBM, JPMorgan Chase, AT&T, Amazon.com, United Health Care, and Apple. Find the symbol for the stock (for example, JPMorgan Chase is JPM) and the exchange on which it is traded (JPM is traded on the NYSE).

STEP 2

Use online searches to find a source that provides a historical picture of daily stock closings. Find your stock, and study its trading pattern.

STEP 3

Find four or five days over a period of several months or even a year when there have been major price fluctuations in the stock. Then research what happened on that day that might have contributed to the fluctuation.

STEP 4

Write a short analysis that links changes in stock price to internal and external factors. As you analyze the data, be aware that it is sometimes difficult to know why a stock price fluctuates.

STEP 5

Get together with three other students who studied different stocks. As a group, discuss your findings, looking for fluctuation patterns.

FOLLOW-UP QUESTIONS

17-16. Do you see any similarities in the movement of the various stocks during the same period? For example, did the stocks move up or down at about the same time? If so, do you think the stocks were affected by the same factors? Explain your thinking.

17-17. Based on your analysis, did internal or external factors have the greater impact on stock price? Which factors had the more long-lasting effect? Which factors had the shorter effect?

17-18. Why do you think it is so hard to predict changes in stock price on a day-to-day basis?

exercising your ethics

ARE YOU ENDOWED WITH GOOD JUDGMENT?

The Situation

Every organization faces decisions about whether to make conservative or risky investments. Let's assume that you have been asked to evaluate the advantages and drawbacks of conservative versus risky investments, including all relevant ethical considerations, by Youth Dreams Charities (YDC), a local organization that assists low-income families in gaining access to educational opportunities. YDC is a not-for-profit firm that employs a full-time professional manager to run daily operations. Overall, governance and policy making reside with a board of directors—10 part-time, community-minded volunteers who are entrusted with carrying out YDC's mission.

For the current year, 23 students receive tuition totaling $92,000 paid by YDC. Tuition comes from annual fund-raising activities (a white-tie dance and a seafood carnival) and from financial returns from YDC's $2.1 million endowment. The endowment has been amassed from charitable donations during the past 12 years, and this year it has yielded some $84,000 for tuitions. The board's goal is to increase the endowment to $4 million in five years to provide $200,000 in tuition annually.

The Dilemma

Based on the finance committee's suggestions, the board is considering a change in YDC's investment policies. The current, rather conservative, approach invests the endowment in low-risk instruments that have consistently yielded a 5-percent annual return. This practice has allowed the endowment to grow modestly (at about 1 percent per year). The remaining investment proceeds (4 percent) flow out for tuition. The proposed plan would invest one-half of the endowment in conservative instruments and the other half in blue-chip stocks. Finance committee members believe that—with market growth—the endowment has a good chance of reaching the $4 million goal within five years. Although some board members like the prospects of faster growth, others think the proposal is too risky. What happens if, instead of increasing, the stock market collapses and the endowment shrinks? What will happen to YDC's programs then?

QUESTIONS TO ADDRESS

17-19. Why might a conservative versus risky choice be different at a not-for-profit organization than at a for-profit organization?

17-20. What are the main ethical issues in this situation?

17-21. What action should the board take?

team exercise

PLAYING THE MARKET

The Situation

The world of finance is fast paced and uncertain. Those with an eye for investments, and a little luck, can make a fortune. However, there are as many losers as winners and no one enters this game thinking that they will end up with less money.

The Dilemma

Your group has been asked to advise a Rose Richmont, a client who has $500,000 to invest in a tax-sheltered account, such as an IRA. As such, you will not be considering taxes on capital gains or interest, but simply the total return on the investment. Rose is 45 years of age and is interested in seeing a large return. To retain her as a client, you would like to select a portfolio that would show an immediate profit. You have one day to select the investments for Richmont's portfolio. You may invest in stocks, bonds, mutual funds, and money market funds. One month from today, you will meet with your client to report on how her portfolio is performing. You are hoping to report a significant increase in her $500,000 investment so that you can retain her as a client.

Team Activity

Assemble a group of four to five students and assign each member the task of selecting three to four good investment options for Rose Richmont.

ACTION STEPS

17-22. Individually, research investment options for Richmont's portfolio. Be sure collect data on past returns as well as reasons that you believe that the investment will perform well in the future.

17-23. Return to your group and share your investment recommendations.

17-24. After considering all the recommendations, develop a diversified portfolio for Richmont. You may wish to use an online site such as Yahoo! finance to determine the number of bonds or shares of stocks that you can purchase. Identify the specific investments and the amounts allocated to each investment.

17-25. One month from today, measure the value of Rose's portfolio. Has the portfolio increased or decreased in value? How will you explain the performance of the portfolio to your client?

cases

Investing in Green

Continued from page 588

At the beginning of this chapter you read about some features of the proposed ET program for controlling carbon emissions into the environment. The proposal included establishment of a U.S. ET market—a so-called "stock exchange"—where buyers and sellers could exchange carbon credits (or allowances). Using the information presented in this chapter you should be able to answer the following questions:

17-26. If the proposed 2010 legislation had become law (or if it does become law), do you believe it would have been (or will be) desirable for the U.S. cap-and-trade market to become part of a global (multinational) ET market? Explain why, or why not.

17-27. Should future U.S. ET markets be regulated? If yes, in what ways and by what regulatory agency? If no, identify possible risks that may result.

17-28. Suppose you are CEO of a firm whose activities are known to release CO_2 emissions. What factors would you consider in evaluating your possible opposition to

mandatory emissions reductions? What factors would you consider in evaluating your support of mandatory cap-and-trade?

17-29. Suppose you are a potential investor in several companies in various industries. In what ways would your investment decisions be influenced by enactment of mandatory cap-and-trade legislation?

17-30. Consider a voluntary emissions reduction program that includes allowances trading, such as the Chicago Climate Exchange system, as an alternative to mandatory cap-and-trade. Can a voluntary program succeed in the United States? Explain why, or why not.

Time to Gogo?

If you've flown lately, you may be familiar with the in-flight internet service Gogo. The company's roots go back to 1991, when the company, then called Aircell, developed technology for in-flight phone services. In 2006, the company made a major change in strategy when it secured a 10-year license through the Federal Communications Commission for in-flight Internet services. Industry leaders including Virgin, America, Delta, United, and Frontier have been offering Gogo in-flight services since 2008.

The company uses a network of cell towers to provide Internet access to passengers on more than 1,900 planes. Southwest is the only major airline in the United States not aligned with Gogo, having signed an agreement with a competitor, Row 44.[27]

Over the years, the company has grown through attention to innovation, as well as debt and equity financing. However, the enormous technology costs associated with expanding their network has resulted in losses each year. As of March 31, 2013, the company had $419 million dollars in assets, but $264 million in debt financing. The company's common and preferred stock was held by company executives and a number of venture capital firms.[28]

Gogo realizes that international expansion is critical to their long-term plan. Though they can achieve greater saturation of the domestic market by having their equipment installed on more planes, international expansion is the key to turning a profit. The company has begun this effort, signing an agreement with Delta to install their equipment on all 170 planes in their international fleet.

Gogo had originally planned to offer its stock to the public in December 2011. However, an extremely sluggish economy and disappointing results for other 2011 IPOs convinced Gogo to wait. In June 2011, Gogo's IPO resulted in the sale of 11 million shares at $17 each.[29] As a result, the company raised $187 million to fund their international expansion. The IPO was underwritten by Wall Street heavy hitters such as Morgan Stanley, JPMorgan, and UBS.[30] However, the price of the stock fell quickly over the following month, down to just more than $12 within weeks of the IPO. Should Gogo successfully penetrate the international market, investors in Gogo stock could see a huge return on investment. However, there's certainly considerable uncertainty about the future and only time will tell if this risky investment will pay off.

QUESTIONS FOR DISCUSSION

17-31. Given the risk, what would motivate an investor to purchase stock in Gogo?

17-32. Why would Gogo sell stock rather than taking on additional debt financing? Do you think that this was a good decision?

17-33. What role did underwriters, such as Morgan Stanley, JPMorgan, and UBS, play in the IPO?

17-34. Use a Web source, such as Yahoo! Finance or www.nasdaq.com to obtain the current price of Gogo stock. What has happened to the price of the stock over the last 6 months?

17-35. Using the data provided from the web source in the previous step, is Gogo a small or large cap stock? How would this affect the risk associated with this investment?

crafting a business plan

PART 6: FINANCIAL ISSUES

Goal of the Exercise

In this final part of the business plan project, you'll consider how you'll finance your business as well as create an executive summary for your plan.

Exercise Background: Part 6 of the Business Plan

In the previous part of the business plan, you discussed the costs of doing business, as well as how much revenue that you expect to earn in one year. It's now time to think about how to finance the business. To get a "great idea" off the ground requires money. But how will you get these funds?

You'll then conclude this project by creating an *executive summary*. The purpose of the executive summary is to give the reader a quick snapshot into your proposed business. Although this exercise comes at the end of the project, once you're done writing it, you'll end up placing the executive summary at the *beginning* of your completed business plan.

Your Assignment

STEP 1

Open the saved *Business Plan* file you began working on in Parts 1 to 5.

STEP 2

For the purposes of this assignment, you will answer the following questions, shown in "Part 6: Financial Issues:"

17-36. How much money will you need to get your business started?
Hint: Refer back to Part 5 of the plan, where you analyzed the costs involved in running your business.

Approximately how much will you need to get your business started?

17-37. How will you finance your business? For example, will you seek out a bank loan? Borrow from friends? Sell stocks or bonds initially or as your business grows?
Hint: Refer to Chapter 16 for information on securities, such as stocks and bonds. Refer also to Appendix I: Financial Risk and Risk Management and Chapter 3 for more information on sources of short-term and long-term funds.

17-38. Now, create an executive summary for your business plan. The executive summary should be brief—no more than two pages long—and should cover the following points:

- The name of your business
- Where your business will be located
- The mission of your business
- The product or service you are selling
- Who your ideal customers are
- How your product or business will stand out in the crowd
- Who the owners of the business are and what experience they have
- An overview of the future prospects for your business and industry

Hint: At this point, you've already answered all of these questions, so what you need to do here is put the ideas together into a "snapshot" format. The executive summary is really a sales pitch—it's the investor's first impression of your idea. Therefore, as with all parts of the plan, write in a clear and professional way.

Congratulations on completing the business plan project!

MyBizLab

Go to **pearsonglobaleditions.com/mybizlab** *for the following Assisted-graded writing questions:*

17-39. Suppose you are managing the securities investments for the firm where you work. Several employees have heard hallway conversations about something called a "risk-return relationship" that sounds important, but are unsure what it means. (a) Write an essay that explains the risk-return relationship and its importance. (b) Discuss the meanings of *diversification* and *asset allocation*. Be sure to explain how they relate to managing investment risk.

17-40. Common stocks are widely traded on several stock exchanges that allow the public to buy and sell as market prices fluctuate moment-to-moment and day-to-day. The market value of a firm's stock quickly becomes public knowledge because regulations govern trading to ensure the fairness of information about publicly-traded stocks. (a) Recall that *market capitalization* is one measure of corporate size and value. Define market capitalization and show in an example how it is calculated. (b) What is a *prospectus* and what information does it contain? (c) What is meant by "insider trading" and what is the U.S. federal agency that regulates against it?

17-41. Mybizlab Only—comprehensive writing assignment for this chapter.

end notes

1 John Carey, "House Passes Carbon Cap-and-Trade Bill," *Bloomberg Businessweek*, June 26, 2009, at http://www.businessweek.com/blogs/money_politics/archives/2009/06/house_passes_ca.html.

2 Nathaniel Gronewold, "3. Markets: Europe's Carbon Emissions Trading—Growing Pains or Wholesale Theft?" *E&E Publishing LLC*, January 31, 2011, at http://www.eenews.net/public/climatewire/2011/01/31/3.

3 Martin Livermore, "Cap and Trade Doesn't Work," *Wall Street Journal*, June 25, 2009, at http://online.wsj.com/article/SB124587942001349765.html.

4 Marianne Lavelle, "A U.S. Cap-and-Trade Experiment To End," *National Geographic News*, November 3, 2010, at http://news.nationalgeographic.com/news/news/energy/2010/11/101103-chicago-climate-exchange-cap-and-trade-election/; "US Senate Drops Bill to Cap Carbon Emissions," *GuardianNews*, July 23, 2010, at http://www.guardian.co.uk/environment/2010/jul/23/us-senate-climate-change-bill; Gerard Wynn and Pete Harrison, "U.S. Cap and Trade Plans Risk European Mistakes," *Reuters*, May 15, 2009, at http://www.reuters.com/article/2009/05/15/us-carbon-usa-analysis-idUSTRE54E4EZ20090515; Nathanial Gronewold, "Chicago Climate Exchange Closes Nation's First Cap-And-Trade System but Keeps Eye to the Future," *New York Times*, January 3, 2011, at http://www.nytimes.com/cwire/2011/01/03/03climatewire-chicago-climate-exchange-closes-but-keeps-ey-78598.html.

5 "EU Advises China on Cap and Trade," *Carbon Positive*, November 8, 2010, at http://www.carbonpositive.net/viewarticle.aspx?articleID=2170.

6 Craig Whitfield, "What Returns Should We Expect from the Stock Market?" *Whitfield & Company*, January 3, 2012, at http://www.whitfieldco.com/blog/?p=39.

7 "Advantages and Disadvantages of Mutual Funds," *The Motley Fool*, at http://www.fool.com, accessed on February 11, 2008; "Who Pays for Cap and Trade?" *Wall Street Journal*, March 9, 2009, at http://online.wsj.com/article/SB123655590609066021.html.

8 "Why Exchange-Traded Funds?" *Yahoo! Finance Exchange-Traded Funds Center*, at http://finance.yahoo.com/etf/education/02, accessed on January 16 2008; Andrea Coombes, "Calculating the Costs of an ETF," *Wall Street Journal*, October 23, 2012, at http://online.wsj.com/article/SB10000872396390444024204578044293008576204.html.

9 Andrew Bary, "Embracing ETFs," *Barron's*, November 15, 2010, pp. 29–34.

10 Ibid.

11 "U.S. Investment Banking Era Ends," *UPI.com*, September 22, 2008, at http://www.upi.com/Business_News/2008/09/22/US-Investment-banking-era-ends/UPI-96221222086983/.

12 New York Stock Exchange, at http://www.nyse.com, accessed on June 4, 2013.

13 "The State of Qatar Launches 'Qatar Exchange' as it Signs Today Formal Terms of Strategic Partnership with NYSE Euronext," *NYSE News Release*, June 19, 2009, at http://www.nyse.com/press/1245406656784.html.

14 "Electronic Communication Network (ECN)," *Investing-Answers*, accessed on June 4, 2013 at http://www.investinganswers.com/financial-dictionary/stock-market/electronic-communication-network-ecn-757.

15 "Just 25% Recognize That Most Americans Are Investors," *Rasmussen Reports*, February 11, 2011, at http://www.rasmussenreports.com/public_content/business/general_business/february_2011/just_25_recognize_that_most_americans_are_investors.

16 Steven E. Norwitz, ed., "A Bear Market of Historic Proportions," *T. Rowe Price Report*, Spring 2009, p. 1.

17 "Dow Jones to Change Composition of the Dow Jones Industrial Average," *Dow Jones (Press Release)*, June 1,

2009, at http://www.djindexes.com/mdsidx/html/pressrelease/press-release-archive.html#20090601.

[18] Rahul Sharma, "Second Circuit Rules that SIPA Customer Protections Are for Customers Only," *Weil: The Bankruptcy Blog*, March 25, 2013, at http://business-finance-restructuring.weil.com/sipa-proceedings/second-circuit-rules-that-sipa-customer-protections-are-for-customers-only/; Alex Altman, "A Brief History of: Ponzi Schemes," *Time*, January 8, 2009, at http://www.time.com/time/magazine/article/0,9171,1870510,00.html; "How Much Did Madoff Scheme Cost?" *CNNMoney.com*, January 5, 2009, at http://money.cnn.com/2009/01/02/news/companies/madoff/index.htm; "The Man Who Figured Out Madoff's Scheme," *CBS News*, June 14, 2009, at http://www.cbsnews.com/stories/2009/02/27/60minutes/main4833667.shtml; Associated Press, "Investors Named in Madoff List," *Columbia Daily Tribune*, February 5, 2009, p. 7B; Diana B. Henriques, "Claims Over 15,400 in Fraud by Madoff," *New York Times*, July 9, 2009, at http://www.nytimes.com/2009/07/10/business/10madoff.html?ref=nyregion.

[19] Carl Beidelman, *The Handbook of International Investing* (Chicago, 1987), p. 133.

[20] Theresa W. Carey, "Cut the Cord," *Barrons.com*, March 12, 2012, at http://online.barrons.com/article/SB50001424052748704759704577267660673833538.html#articleTabs_article%3D0; "Stock Market: Why is Stock Market Data Delayed by 20 Minutes (NYSE, NASDAQ) to the General Public?," *QUORA*, August 25, 2010, at http://www.quora.com/Stock-Market/Why-is-stock-market-data-delayed-by-20-minutes-NYSE-NASDAQ-to-the-general-public; "Online Trading Software," *TradeStation*, at http://www.tradestation.com/, accessed on June 7, 2013; "Where Can I Find Information About Pre-and After-Hours Trading on the NYSE and the Nasdaq?," *INVESTOPEDIA*, February 26, 2009, at http://www.investopedia.com/ask/answers/06/preaftermarket.asp; Adam Milton, "What is Day Trading?," *About.com*, at http://daytrading.about.com/od/daytradingbasics/a/WhatIsDayTradin.htm, accessed on June 8, 2013.

[21] David Welch, "Old GM Bondholders Getting Shares in New General Motors May Depress Price," *Bloomberg.com*, April 6, 2011, at http://www.bloomberg.com/news/2011-04-06/old-gm-bondholders-getting-shares-in-new-general-motors-may-depress-price.html.

[22] Ajay Kumar, "Can We Trust Moody's, Fitch, Standard & Poor?" *CommodityOnline*, at http://www.commodityonline.com/printnews.php?news_id=15888, accessed on July 22, 2009; David Evans and Caroline Salas, "Flawed Credit Ratings Reap Profits as Regulators Fail (Update 1)," *Bloomberg.com*, April 29, 2009, at http://www.bloomberg.com/apps/news?pid=20670001&sid=au4oIx.judz4; Leslie Wayne, "Calpers Sues over Ratings of Securities," *New York Times*, July 15, 2009, at http://www.nytimes.com/2009/07/15/business/15calpers.html; David Segal, "Ohio Sues Rating Firms for Losses in Funds," *New York Times*, November 20, 2009, at http://www.nytimes.com/2009/11/21/business/21ratings.html; Lynn Hume, "Connecticut AG Sues All Three Rating Agencies, *The Bond Buyer*, July 31, 2008, at http://www.bondbuyer.com/issues/117_145/-292250-1.html.

[23] Global Property Guide, http://www.globalpropertyguide.com/Africa/South-Africa/Price-History, http://www.globalpropertyguide.com/Africa/South-Africa/Price-History-Archive/South-Africa-House-price-rises-slowing-1210.

[24] "Mortgage-Backed Securities," *U.S. Securities and Exchange Commission*, June 25, 2007, at http://www.sec.gov/answers/mortgagesecurities.htm; "Mortgage-Backed Security," *riskglossary.com*, at http://www.riskglossary.com/link/mortgage_backed_security.htm, accessed on July 24, 2009.

[25] *Yahoo! Finance*, June 9, 2013 at http://finance.yahoo.com/.

[26] Reuters, "Rajaratnam Insider Trading Trial Begins," March 9, 2011, *Huffington Post*, at http://www.huffingtonpost.com/2011/03/09/rajaratnam-trial_n_833326.html; U.S. Department of Justice, "Joseph P. Nacchio Indicted by Federal Grand Jury: Former Chief Executive Officer of Qwest Communications Charged with Insider Trading, Selling Over $100 Million Stock," (December 20, 2005), at http://lawprofessors.typepad.com/whitecollarcrime_blog/files/nacchio_indictment.pdf.

[27] Koenig, David. "IPO Shares of Flight Web Service Gogo Fall." *USA Today*. June 22, 2013, http://www.usatoday.com/story/money/business/2013/06/22/gogo-nasdaq-airlines-wifi/2448083/, accessed on July 16, 2013.

[28] "GOGO: Summary for Gogo Inc.—Yahoo! Finance." *Yahoo! Finance* July 16, 2013.

[29] Matherson, Nathaniel. "A Few Recent IPO Misses May Offer Value, or Not." *The Motley Fool*. July 9, 2013, at http://beta.fool.com/natematherson/2013/07/09/poor-performing-ipo-draft/39274/ accessed on July 16, 2013.

[30] "Gogo—This Recent Public Offering Is Not Going Yet." *Seeking Alpha*. June 28, 2013, http://seekingalpha.com/article/1526942-gogo-this-recent-public-offering-is-not-going-yet, accessed on July 16, 2013.

appendix I

Risk Management

In this appendix, we describe other types of risks that businesses face and analyze some of the ways in which they typically manage them.

Coping with Risk

Businesses constantly face two basic types of **risk**—uncertainty about future events. **Speculative risks,** such as financial investments, involve the possibility of gain or loss. **Pure risks** involve only the possibility of loss or no loss. Designing and distributing a new product, for example, is a speculative risk—the product may fail, or it may succeed and earn high profits. In contrast, the chance of a warehouse fire is a pure risk.

For a company to survive and prosper, it must manage both types of risk in a cost-effective manner. We can define the process of **risk management** as conserving the firm's earning power and assets by reducing the threat of losses as a result of uncontrollable events. In every company, each manager must be alert for risks to the firm and their impact on profits.

The risk-management process usually involves five steps:

Step 1: Identify Risks and Potential Losses
Managers analyze a firm's risks to identify potential losses.

Step 2: Measure the Frequency and Severity of Losses and Their Impact
To measure the frequency and severity of losses, managers must consider both history and current activities. How often can the firm expect the loss to occur? What is the likely size of the loss in dollars?

Step 3: Evaluate Alternatives and Choose the Techniques that Will Best Handle the Losses
Having identified and measured potential losses, managers are in a better position to decide how to handle them. They generally have four choices:

- A firm opts for **risk avoidance** by declining to enter or by ceasing to participate in a risky activity.

- When avoidance is not practical or desirable, firms can practice **risk control**—the use of loss-prevention techniques to minimize the frequency or severity of losses.

- When losses cannot be avoided or controlled, firms must cope with the consequences. When such losses are manageable and predictable, the firm may decide to cover them out of company funds. The firm is said to assume or retain the financial consequences of the loss; hence, the practice is known as **risk retention.**

- When the potential for large risks cannot be avoided or controlled, managers often opt for **risk transfer** to another firm—namely, an insurance company—to protect itself.

Risk *uncertainty about future events*

Speculative Risk *risk involving the possibility of gain or loss*

Pure Risk *risk involving only the possibility of loss or no loss*

Risk Management *process of conserving the firm's earning power and assets by reducing the threat of losses as a result of uncontrollable events*

Risk Avoidance *practice of avoiding risk by declining or ceasing to participate in an activity*

Risk Control *practice of minimizing the frequency or severity of losses from risky activities*

Risk Retention *practice of covering a firm's losses with its own funds*

Risk Transfer *practice of transferring a firm's risk to another firm*

Step 4: Implement the Risk-Management Program

The means of implementing risk-management decisions depend on both the technique chosen and the activity being managed.

- Risk avoidance for certain activities can be implemented by purchasing those activities from outside providers.

- Risk control might be implemented by training employees and designing new work methods and equipment for on-the-job safety.

- For situations in which risk retention is preferred, reserve funds can be set aside from revenues.

- When risk transfer is needed, implementation means selecting an insurance company and buying the appropriate policies.

Step 5: Monitor Results

New types of risks emerge with changes in customers, facilities, employees, and products. Insurance regulations change, and new types of insurance become available. Consequently, managers must continuously monitor a company's risks, re-evaluate the methods used for handling them, and revise them as necessary.

Insurance as Risk Management

To deal with some risks, both businesses and individuals may choose to purchase insurance. Insurance is purchased by paying **insurance premiums**—payments to an insurance company to buy a policy and keep it active. In return, the insurance company issues an **insurance policy**—a formal agreement to pay the policyholder a specified amount in the event of certain losses. In some cases, the insured party must also pay a **deductible,** an agreed-on amount of the loss that the insured must absorb before reimbursement is made. Buyers find insurance appealing because they are protected against large, potentially devastating losses in return for a relatively small sum of money.

With insurance, individuals and businesses share risks by contributing to a fund from which those who suffer losses are paid. Insurance companies are willing to accept these risks because they make profits by taking in more premiums than they pay out to cover policyholders' losses. Although many policyholders are paying for protection against the same type of loss, by no means will all of them suffer such a loss.

Insurance Premium *fee paid to an insurance company by a policyholder for insurance coverage*

Insurance Policy *formal agreement to pay the policyholder a specified amount in the event of certain losses*

Deductible *amount of the loss that the insured must absorb before reimbursement is made*

Insurable versus Uninsurable Risks

Like every business, insurance companies must avoid certain risks. Insurers divide potential sources of loss into *insurable risks* and *uninsurable risks.* They issue policies only for insurable risks. Although there are some exceptions, an insurable risk must meet the following four criteria:

1 *Predictability:* The insurer must be able to use statistical tools to forecast the likelihood of a loss. This forecast also helps insurers determine premiums charged to policyholders.

2 *Casualty:* A loss must result from an *accident*, not from an intentional act by the policyholder. To avoid paying in cases of fraud, insurers may refuse to cover losses when they cannot determine whether policyholders' actions contributed to them.

3 *Unconnectedness:* Potential losses must be random and must occur independently of other losses. No insurer can afford to write insurance when a large percentage of those who are exposed to a particular kind of loss are likely to suffer such a loss. By carefully choosing the risks that it will insure, an insurance company can reduce its chances of a large loss or insolvency.

4 *Verifiability:* Insured losses must be verifiable as to cause, time, place, and amount.

Special Forms of Insurance for Business

Businesses have special insurable concerns—*liability, property, business interruption, key person insurance,* and *business continuation agreements.*

LIABILITY INSURANCE Liability means responsibility for damages in case of accidental or deliberate harm to individuals or property. **Liability insurance** covers losses resulting from damage to people or property when the insured party is judged liable.

A business is liable for any injury to an employee when the injury arises from activities related to the occupation. When workers are permanently or temporarily disabled by job-related accidents or disease, employers are required by law to provide **workers' compensation coverage** for medical expenses, loss of wages, and rehabilitation services.

PROPERTY INSURANCE A firm purchases **property insurance** to cover injuries to itself resulting from physical damage to or loss of real estate or personal property. Property losses may result from fire, lightning, wind, hail, explosion, theft, vandalism, or other destructive forces.

BUSINESS INTERRUPTION INSURANCE In some cases, loss to property is minimal in comparison to loss of income. If a firm is forced to close down for an extended time, it will not be able to generate income. During this time, however, certain expenses—such as taxes, insurance premiums, and salaries for key personnel—may continue. To cover such losses, a firm may buy **business interruption insurance.**

KEY PERSON INSURANCE Many businesses choose to protect themselves against loss of the talents and skills of key employees, as well as the recruitment costs to find a replacement and training expenses once a replacement is hired. **Key person insurance** is designed to offset both lost income and additional expenses.

BUSINESS CONTINUATION AGREEMENTS Who takes control of a business when a partner or associate dies? Surviving partners are often faced with the possibility of having to accept an inexperienced heir as a management partner. This contingency can be handled in **business continuation agreements,** whereby owners make plans to buy the ownership interest of a deceased associate from his or her heirs. The value of the ownership interest is determined when the agreement is made. Special policies can also provide survivors with the funds needed to make the purchase.

Liability Insurance *insurance covering losses resulting from damage to people or property when the insured party is judged liable*

Workers' Compensation Coverage *coverage provided by a firm to employees for medical expenses, loss of wages, and rehabilitation costs resulting from job-related injuries or disease*

Property Insurance *insurance covering losses resulting from physical damage to or loss of the insured's real estate or personal property*

Business Interruption Insurance *insurance covering income lost during times when a company is unable to conduct business*

Key Person Insurance *special form of business insurance designed to offset expenses entailed by the loss of key employees*

Business Continuation Agreement *special form of business insurance whereby owners arrange to buy the interests of deceased associates from their heirs*

appendix II

The Legal Context of Business

In this appendix, we describe the basic tenets of U.S. law and show how these principles work through the court system. We'll also survey a few major areas of business-related law.

The U.S. Legal and Judicial Systems

Laws are the codified rules of behavior enforced by a society. In the United States, laws fall into three broad categories according to their origins: *common*, *statutory*, and *regulatory*.

Laws *codified rules of behavior enforced by a society*

Types of Law

Law in the United States originated primarily with English common law. U.S. law includes the U.S. Constitution, state constitutions, federal and state statutes, municipal ordinances, administrative agency rules and regulations, executive orders, and court decisions.

Common Law Court decisions follow *precedents*, or the decisions of previous cases. Following precedent lends stability to the law by basing judicial decisions on cases anchored in similar facts. This principle is the keystone of **common law**—the body of decisions handed down by courts ruling on individual cases.

Common Law *body of decisions handed down by courts ruling on individual cases*

Statutory Law Laws created by constitutions or by federal, state, or local legislative acts constitute **statutory law.** Under the U.S. Constitution, federal statutes take precedence over state and local statutes.

Statutory Law *law created by constitution(s) or by federal, state, or local legislative acts*

Regulatory Law Statutory law and common law have long histories. Relatively new is **regulatory (or administrative) law**—law made by the authority of administrative agencies.

Regulatory (Administrative) Law *law made by the authority of administrative agencies*

Although Congress retains control over the scope of agency action, regulations have the force of statutory law once passed. Government regulatory agencies act as a secondary judicial system, determining whether regulations have been violated and then imposing penalties. Much agency activity consists of setting standards for safety or quality and monitoring the compliance of businesses.

Congress has created many new agencies in response to pressure to address social issues. In some cases, agencies were established in response to public concern about corporate behavior. The activities of these agencies have sometimes forced U.S. firms to consider the public interest almost as routinely as they consider their own financial performance.

Keeping an Eye on Business Today a host of agencies regulate U.S. business practices, including:

- Equal Employment Opportunity Commission (EEOC)

- Environmental Protection Agency (EPA)

- Food and Drug Administration (FDA)
- Federal Trade Commission (FTC)
- Occupational Safety and Health Administration (OSHA)

Trends in Deregulation and Regulation Although government regulation has benefited U.S. business in many ways, it is not without its drawbacks. Businesspeople complain—with some justification—that government regulations require too much costly paperwork. Many people in both business and government support broader **deregulation**—the elimination of rules that restrict business activity. Deregulation, they argue, is a primary incentive to innovation; deregulated industries are forced to innovate to survive in fiercely competitive industries. Those firms that are already conditioned to compete by being more creative will outperform firms that have been protected by regulatory climates in their home countries.

Deregulation *elimination of rules that restrict business activity*

However, it appears likely that there will be a trend back toward more regulation in the United States, at least for the near future For one thing, many critics blame the financial crisis and economic recession of 2008 on the uncontrolled actions of major U.S. banks and have been calling for more regulation to help prevent a future recurrence of the same mistakes. Indeed, during the Obama administration business regulation has increased substantially.

The U.S. Judicial System

Much of the responsibility for law enforcement falls to the courts. Litigation is a significant part of contemporary life, and we have given our courts a voice in a wide range of issues, some touching personal concerns, some ruling on matters of public policy that affect all our lives.

The Court System There are three levels in the U.S. judicial system—*federal*, *state*, and *local*. Federal courts hear cases on questions of constitutional law, disputes relating to maritime laws, and violations of federal statutes. They also rule on regulatory actions and on such issues as bankruptcy, postal law, and copyright or patent violation. Both the federal and most state systems embody a three-tiered system of *trial*, *appellate*, and *supreme courts*.

Trial Court *general court that hears cases not specifically assigned to another court*

TRIAL COURTS At the lowest level of the federal court system are the **trial courts,** the general courts that hear cases not specifically assigned to another court. Every state has at least one federal trial court, called a *district court*.

Trial courts also include special courts and administrative agencies. Special courts hear specific types of cases, such as cases involving tax evasion, fraud, international disputes, or claims against the U.S. government. Within their areas of jurisdiction, administrative agencies also make judgments much like those of courts.

Courts in each state deal with the same issues as their federal counterparts. However, they may rule only in areas governed by state law. For example, a state special court would hear a case involving state income tax laws. Local courts in each state system also hear cases on municipal ordinances, local traffic violations, and similar issues.

APPELLATE COURTS A losing party may disagree with a trial court ruling. If that party can show grounds for review, the case may go before a federal or state **appellate court.** These courts consider questions of law, such as possible errors of legal interpretation made by lower courts. They do not examine questions of fact.

Appellate Court *court that reviews case records of trials whose findings have been appealed*

SUPREME COURTS Cases still not resolved at the appellate level can be appealed to the appropriate state supreme courts or to the U.S. Supreme Court. If it believes that an appeal is warranted or that the outcome will set an important precedent, the U.S. Supreme Court also hears cases appealed from state supreme courts.

Business Law

Most legal issues confronted by businesses fall into one of six basic areas: *contract, tort, property, agency, commercial,* or *bankruptcy law*. These areas cover a wide range of business activity.

Contract Law

A **contract** is any agreement between two or more parties that is enforceable in court. As such, it must meet six conditions. If all these conditions are met, one party can seek legal recourse from another if the other party breaches, or violates, the terms of the agreement.

1 *Agreement.* Agreement is the serious, definite, and communicated offer and acceptance of the same terms.

2 *Consent.* A contract is not enforceable if any of the parties has been affected by an honest mistake, fraud, or pressure.

3 *Capacity.* To give real consent, both parties must demonstrate legal **capacity** (competence). A person under legal age (usually 18 or 21) cannot enter into a binding contract.

4 *Consideration.* An agreement is binding only if it exchanges **considerations**— items of value. Note that items of value do not necessarily entail money. Contracts need not be rational, nor must they provide the best possible bargain for both sides. They need only include legally sufficient consideration. The terms are met if both parties receive what the contract details.

5 *Legality.* A contract must be for a lawful purpose and must comply with federal, state, and local laws and regulations.

6 *Proper form.* A contract may be written, oral, or implied from conduct. It must be written, however, if it involves the sale of land or goods worth more than $500. It must be written if the agreement requires more than a year to fulfill. All changes to written contracts must also be in writing.

Breach of Contract Contract law offers a variety of remedies designed to protect the reasonable expectations of the parties and, in some cases, to compensate them for actions taken to enforce the agreement. As the injured party to a breached contract, any of the following actions might occur:

- You might cancel the contract and refuse to live up to your part of the bargain.

- You might sue for damages up to the amount that you lost as a result of the breach.

- If money cannot repay the damage you suffered, you might demand specific performance, or require the other party to fulfill the original contract.

Tort Law

Tort law applies to most business relationships *not* governed by contracts. A **tort** is a *civil*—that is, noncriminal—injury to people, property, or reputation for which compensation must be paid. Trespass, fraud, defamation, invasion of privacy, and even assault can be torts, as can interference with contractual relations and wrongful use of trade secrets. There are three classifications of torts: *intentional, negligence,* and *product liability*.

Intentional Torts **Intentional torts** result from the deliberate actions of another person or organization. To remedy torts, courts will usually impose **compensatory damages**—payments intended to redress an injury actually suffered. They may also impose **punitive damages**—fines that exceed actual losses suffered by plaintiffs and are intended to punish defendants.

Contract *agreement between two or more parties enforceable in court*

Capacity *competence required of individuals entering into a binding contract*

Consideration *item of value exchanged between parties to create a valid contract*

Tort *civil injury to people, property, or reputation for which compensation must be paid*

Intentional Tort *tort resulting from the deliberate actions of a party*

Compensatory Damages *monetary payments intended to redress injury actually suffered because of a tort*

Punitive Damages *fines imposed over and above any actual losses suffered by a plaintiff*

Negligence *conduct that falls below legal standards for protecting others against unreasonable risk*

Negligence Torts   Most suits involve charges of **negligence**—conduct that falls below legal standards for protecting others against unreasonable risk.

Product Liability *tort in which a company is responsible for injuries caused by its products*

Product Liability Torts   In cases of **product liability,** a company may be held responsible for injuries caused by its products.

Strict Product Liability *principle that liability can result not from a producer's negligence but from a defect in the product itself*

Strict Product Liability   Since the early 1960s, businesses have faced a number of legal actions based on the relatively new principle of **strict product liability**—the principle that liability can result not from a producer's negligence but from a defect in the product itself. An injured party need only show the following:

1   The product was defective.
2   The defect was the cause of injury.
3   The defect caused the product to be unreasonably dangerous.

Because plaintiffs need not demonstrate negligence or fault, these suits have a good chance of success.

Property Law

Property *anything of value to which a person or business has sole right of ownership*

Property is anything of value to which a person or business has sole right of ownership. Legally speaking, the right of ownership is itself property.

Within this broad general definition, we can divide property into four categories:

Tangible Real Property *land and anything attached to it*

1   **Tangible real property** is land and anything attached to it.

Tangible Personal Property *any movable item that can be owned, bought, sold, or leased*

2   **Tangible personal property** is any movable item that can be owned, bought, sold, or leased.

Intangible Personal Property *property that cannot be seen but that exists by virtue of written documentation*

3   **Intangible personal property** cannot be seen but exists by virtue of written documentation.

Intellectual Property *property created through a person's creative activities*

4   **Intellectual property** is created through a person's creative activities.

Protection of Intellectual Rights   The U.S. Constitution grants protection to intellectual property by means of copyrights, trademarks, and patents. Copyrights and patents apply to the tangible expressions of an idea, not to the ideas themselves.

Copyright *exclusive ownership right belonging to the creator of a book, article, design, illustration, photo, film, or musical work*

Copyrights   Copyrights give creators exclusive ownership rights to their intellectual property. Copyrights extend to creators for their entire lives and to their estates for 70 years thereafter.

Trademark *exclusive legal right to use a brand name or symbol*

Trademarks   Because the development of products is expensive, companies must prevent other firms from using their brand names. Often, they must act to keep competitors from seducing consumers with similar or substitute products. A producer can apply to the U.S. government for a **trademark**—the exclusive legal right to use a brand name.

Trademarks are granted for 20 years and may be renewed indefinitely if a firm continues to protect its brand name. If a firm allows the brand name to lapse into common usage, it may lose protection. Common usage takes effect when a company fails to use the ® symbol to indicate that its brand name is a registered trademark. It also takes effect if a company seeks no action against those who fail to acknowledge its trademark.

Patent *exclusive legal right to use and license a manufactured item or substance, manufacturing process, or object design*

Patents   Patents provide legal monopolies for the use and licensing of manufactured items, manufacturing processes, substances, and designs for objects. A patentable invention must be *novel, useful,* and *nonobvious.* Patents are valid for 20 years, with the term running from the date on which the application was *filed,* not the date on which the patent itself was *issued.*

Restrictions on Property Rights Property rights are not always absolute. For example, rights may be compromised under the following circumstances:

- Utility companies typically have rights called *easements*, such as the right to run wire over private property or to lay cable or pipe under it.

- Under the principle of **eminent domain,** the government may, on paying owners fair prices, claim private land to expand roads or erect public buildings.

Eminent Domain *principle that the government may claim private land for public use by buying it at a fair price*

Agency Law

The transfer of property often involves agents. An **agent** is a person who acts for and in the name of another party, called the **principal.** Courts have ruled that both a firm's employees and its outside contractors may be regarded as its agents.

Agent *individual or organization acting for and in the name of another party*

Principal *individual or organization authorizing an agent to act on its behalf*

Authority of Agents Agents have the authority to bind principals to agreements. They receive that authority, however, from the principals themselves; they cannot create their own authority. An agent's authority to bind a principal can be **express, implied,** or **apparent.**

Express Authority *agent's authority, derived from written agreement, to bind a principal to a certain course of action*

Implied Authority *agent's authority, derived from business custom, to bind a principal to a certain course of action*

Responsibilities of Principals Principals have several responsibilities to their agents. They owe agents reasonable compensation, must reimburse them for related business expenses, and should inform them of risks associated with their business activities. Principals are liable for actions performed by agents *within the scope of their employment.* If agents make untrue claims about products or services, the principal is liable for making amends. Employers are similarly responsible for the actions of employees. Firms are often liable in tort suits because the courts treat employees as agents. Businesses are also increasingly being held accountable for *criminal* acts by employees. Court findings have argued that firms are expected to be aware of workers' negative propensities, to check their employees' backgrounds, and to train and supervise employees properly.

Apparent Authority *agent's authority, based on the principal's compliance, to bind a principal to a certain course of action*

Commercial Law

Managers must be well acquainted with the most general laws affecting commerce. Specifically, they need to be familiar with the provisions of the **Uniform Commercial Code (UCC),** which describes the rights of buyers and sellers in transactions. One key area of coverage by the UCC, contracts, was discussed previously. Another key area is warranties.

A **warranty** is a seller's promise to stand by its products or services if a problem occurs after the sale. Warranties may be express or implied. The seller specifically states the terms of an **express warranty,** whereas an **implied warranty** is dictated by law. Implied warranties embody the principle that a product should (1) fulfill the promises made by advertisements and (2) serve the purpose for which it was manufactured and sold. It is important to note, however, that warranties, unlike most contracts, are easily limited, waived, or disclaimed. Consequently, they are the source of tort action more often, as dissatisfied customers seek redress from producers.

Uniform Commercial Code (UCC) *body of standardized laws governing the rights of buyers and sellers in transactions*

Warranty *seller's promise to stand by its products or services if a problem occurs after the sale*

Express Warranty *warranty whose terms are specifically stated by the seller*

Implied Warranty *warranty, dictated by law, based on the principle that products should fulfill advertised promises and serve the purposes for which they are manufactured and sold*

Bankruptcy Law

Both organizations and individuals can seek debt relief by filing for bankruptcy—the court-granted permission not to pay some or all incurred debts. Many individuals and businesses file for bankruptcy each year, and their numbers continue to increase. Three main factors account for the increase in bankruptcy filings:

1 The increased availability of credit
2 The "fresh-start" provisions in current bankruptcy laws
3 The growing acceptance of bankruptcy as a financial tactic

Involuntary Bankruptcy *bankruptcy proceedings initiated by the creditors of an indebted individual or organization*

Voluntary Bankruptcy *bankruptcy proceedings initiated by an indebted individual or organization*

In some cases, creditors force an individual or firm into **involuntary bankruptcy** and press the courts to award them payment of at least part of what they are owed. Far more often, however, a person or business chooses to file for court protection against creditors. In general, individuals and firms whose debts exceed total assets by at least $1,000 may file for **voluntary bankruptcy.**

Business Bankruptcy   One of three plans resolves a business bankruptcy:

1   Under a *liquidation plan*, the business ceases to exist. Its assets are sold and the proceeds are used to pay creditors.

2   Under a *repayment plan*, the bankrupt company simply works out a new payment schedule to meet its obligations. The time frame is usually extended, and payments are collected and distributed by a court-appointed trustee.

3   *Reorganization* is the most complex form of business bankruptcy. The company must explain the sources of its financial difficulties and propose a new plan for remaining in business. Reorganization may include a new slate of managers and a new financial strategy. A judge may also reduce the firm's debts to ensure its survival.

Legislation passed since 1994 restricts how long a company can protect itself in bankruptcy while continuing to do business. Critics have charged that many firms have succeeded in operating for many months under bankruptcy protection. During that time, they were able to cut costs and prices, not only competing with an unfair advantage, but also dragging down overall industry profits. The new laws place time limits on various steps in the filing process. The intended effect is to speed the process and prevent assets from being lost to legal fees.

The International Framework of Business Law

International Law *general set of cooperative agreements and guidelines established by countries to govern the actions of individuals, businesses, and nations*

Laws vary from country to country, and many businesses today have international markets, suppliers, and competitors. Managers need a basic understanding of the international framework of business law that affects the ways in which they can do business. Issues, such as pollution across borders, are matters of **international law—** the general set of cooperative agreements and guidelines established by countries to govern the actions of individuals, businesses, and nations themselves.

International law has several sources. One source is custom and tradition. Among countries that have been trading with one another for centuries, many customs and traditions governing exchanges have gradually evolved into practice. Although some trading practices still follow ancient unwritten agreements, there has been a clear trend in more recent times to approach international trade within a more formal legal framework. Key features of that framework include a variety of formal trade agreements.

Another important source of international law is the formal trade treaties that nations negotiate with one another. Governing entities such as the World Trade Organization and the European Union, for instance, also provide legal frameworks within which participating nations agree to abide.

Managing Your Personal Finances

Dealing with personal finances is a lifelong job involving a crucial choice between two options:

1 Committing to the rational management of your personal finances by controlling them, helping them grow, and therefore enjoying greater personal satisfaction and financial stability.

2 Letting the financial chips fall where they may and hoping for the best (which seldom happens) and therefore inviting frustration, disappointment, and financial distress.

Personal finance management requires consideration of cash management, financial planning and control, investment alternatives, and risk. Let's start by looking at one key factor in success: the personal financial plan. We'll then discuss the steps in the planning process and show how you can make better decisions to manage your personal finances.

Building Your Financial Plan

Financial planning is the process of looking at your current financial condition, identifying your goals, and anticipating steps toward meeting those goals. Because your goals and finances will change as you get older, your plan should always allow for revision. Figure AIII.1 summarizes a step-by-step approach to personal financial planning.

Financial Planning *process of looking at one's current financial condition, identifying one's goals, and anticipating requirements for meeting those goals*

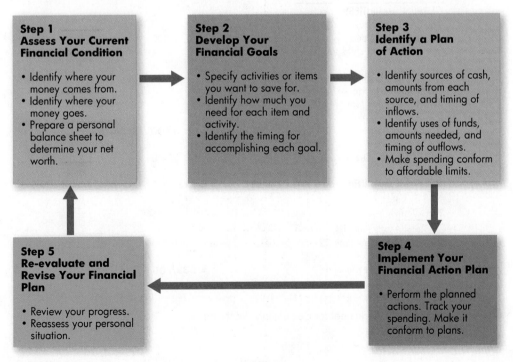

Step 1
Assess Your Current Financial Condition

- Identify where your money comes from.
- Identify where your money goes.
- Prepare a personal balance sheet to determine your net worth.

Step 2
Develop Your Financial Goals

- Specify activities or items you want to save for.
- Identify how much you need for each item and activity.
- Identify the timing for accomplishing each goal.

Step 3
Identify a Plan of Action

- Identify sources of cash, amounts from each source, and timing of inflows.
- Identify uses of funds, amounts needed, and timing of outflows.
- Make spending conform to affordable limits.

Step 4
Implement Your Financial Action Plan

- Perform the planned actions. Track your spending. Make it conform to plans.

Step 5
Re-evaluate and Revise Your Financial Plan

- Review your progress.
- Reassess your personal situation.

FIGURE AIII.1 Developing a Personal Financial Plan

Assessing Your Current Financial Condition

Personal Net Worth *value of one's total assets minus one's total liabilities (debts)*

The first step in developing a personal financial plan is assessing your current financial position. Your **personal net worth** is the value of all your assets minus all your liabilities (debts) *at the present time.* The worksheet in Figure AIII.2 provides some sample calculations for developing your own personal "balance sheet." Because assets and liabilities change over time, updating your balance sheet not only allows you to monitor changes but also provides more accurate information for realistic budgeting and planning.

Assets: What You Own		Example Numbers	Your Numbers
LIQUID ASSETS:			
1. Cash	$	300	____
2. Savings	+	3,700	____
3. Checking	+	1,200	____
INVESTMENTS:			
4. IRAs	+	12,400	____
5. Securities	+	500	____
6. Retirement Plan	+	—	____
7. Real Estate (other than primary residence)	+	—	____
HOUSEHOLD:			
8. Cars (market value)	+	18,000	____
9. House (market value)	+	—	____
10. Furniture	+	3,400	____
11. Personal Property	+	6,600	____
12. Other assets		—	____
13. Total Assets (add lines 1–12)	=	**$46,100**	____
Liabilities (Dept): What You Owe			
CURRENT LIABILITIES:			
14. Credit-card balance	$	1,300	____
15. Unpaid bills due	+	1,800	____
16. Alimony and child support	+	—	____
LONG-TERM LIABILITIES:			
17. Home mortgage	+	—	____
18. Home equity loan	+	—	____
19. Car loan	+	4,100	____
20. Student loan	+	3,600	____
21. Other liabilities	+	2,400	____
22. Total Liabilities (add lines 14–21)	=	**$13,200**	____
Net Worth			
23. Total Assets (line 13)		$ 46,100	____
24. Less: Total Debt (line 22)	–	13,200	____
25. Results: Net Worth	=	**$32,900**	____

FIGURE AIII.2 Worksheet for Calculating Net Worth

Develop Your Financial Goals

Step 2 involves setting three different types of future goals: *immediate* (within one year), *intermediate* (within five years), and *long-term* (more than five years). The worksheet in Figure AIII.3 will help you establish these goals. By thinking about your finances in three different time frames, you'll be better able to set measurable goals and completion times, or to set priorities for rationing your resources if, at some point, you're not able to pursue all your goals.

Because step 3 (identifying a plan of action) and step 4 (implementing your plan) will affect your assets and liabilities, your balance sheet will change over time. As a result, step 5 (re-evaluating and revising your plan) needs periodic updating.

Name the Goal	Financial Requirement (Amount) for This Goal	Time Frame for Accomplishing Goal	Importance (1= Highest, 5 = Lowest)
Immediate Goals:			
Live in a better apartment			
Establish an emergency cash fund			
Pay off credit-card debt			
Other			
Intermediate Goals:			
Obtain adequate health, life, disability, liability, property insurance			
Save for wedding			
Save to buy new car			
Establish regular savings program (5% of gross income)			
Save for college for self			
Pay off major outstanding debt			
Make major purchase			
Save for home remodeling			
Save for down payment on a home			
Other			
Long-Term Goals:			
Pay off home mortgage			
Save for college for children			
Save for vacation home			
Increase personal net worth to $___ in ___ years.			
Achieve retirement nest egg of $ __ in ___ years.			
Accumulate fund for travel in retirement			
Save for long-term care needs			
Other			

FIGURE AIII.3 Worksheet for Setting Financial Goals

Making Better Use of the Time Value of Money

As discussed in Chapter 17, the value of time with any investment stems from the principle of compound growth, the compounding of interest received over several time periods. With each additional time period, interest receipts accumulate and earn even more interest, thus, multiplying the earning capacity of the investment. Whenever you make everyday purchases, you're giving up interest that you could have earned with the same money if you'd invested it instead. From a financial standpoint, "idle" or uninvested money, which could be put to work earning more money, is a wasted resource.

Planning for the Golden Years

The sooner you start saving, the greater your financial power will be—you will have taken advantage of the time value of money for a longer period of time. Consider coworkers Ellen and Barbara, who are both planning to retire in 25 years, as can be seen in Figure AIII.4.

Over that period, each can expect a 10 percent annual return on investment (the U.S. stock market averaged more than 10 percent for the 75 years before the 2008 recession). Their savings strategies, however, are different: Barbara begins saving immediately, whereas Ellen plans to start later but invest larger sums. Barbara will invest $2,000 annually for each of the next 5 years (years 1 through 5), for a total investment of $10,000. Ellen, meanwhile, wants to live a little larger by spending rather than saving for the next 10 years. Then, for years 11 through 20, she'll start saving $2,000 annually, for a total investment of $20,000. They will both allow annual

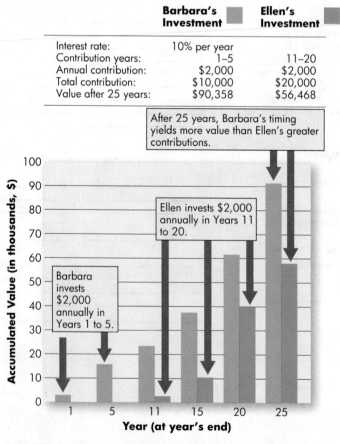

	Barbara's Investment	Ellen's Investment
Interest rate:	10% per year	
Contribution years:	1–5	11–20
Annual contribution:	$2,000	$2,000
Total contribution:	$10,000	$20,000
Value after 25 years:	$90,358	$56,468

After 25 years, Barbara's timing yields more value than Ellen's greater contributions.

Ellen invests $2,000 annually in Years 11 to 20.

Barbara invests $2,000 annually in Years 1 to 5.

FIGURE AIII.4 Compounding Money over Time

n	1%	2%	4%	6%	8%	10%
1	1.010	1.020	1.040	1.060	1.080	1.100
2	1.020	1.040	1.082	1.124	1.166	1.210
3	1.030	1.061	1.125	1.191	1.260	1.331
4	1.041	1.082	1.170	1.262	1.360	1.464
5	1.051	1.104	1.217	1.338	1.469	1.611
6	1.062	1.126	1.265	1.419	1.587	1.772
7	1.072	1.149	1.316	1.504	1.714	1.949
8	1.083	1.172	1.369	1.594	1.851	2.144
9	1.094	1.195	1.423	1.689	1.999	2.358
10	1.105	1.219	1.480	1.791	2.159	2.594
15	1.161	1.346	1.801	2.397	3.172	4.177
20	1.220	1.486	2.191	3.207	4.661	6.727
25	1.282	1.641	2.666	4.292	6.848	10.834
30	1.348	1.811	3.243	5.743	10.062	17.449

Note: n = number of time periods; % = various interest rates

FIGURE AIII.5 Timetable for Growing $1.00

returns to accumulate until they retire in year 25. Ellen expects to have a larger retirement fund than Barbara because she has contributed twice as much, but she is in for a surprise. Barbara's retirement wealth will be much larger—$90,364 versus Ellen's $56,468—even though she invested only half as much. Barbara's advantage lies in the length of her savings program. Her money is invested longer—over a period of 21 to 25 years—with interest compounding over that range of time. Ellen's earnings are compounded over a shorter period—6 to 15 years. Granted, Ellen may have had more fun in years 1 to 10, but Barbara's retirement prospects look brighter.

Time Value as a Financial-Planning Tool

A good financial plan takes into account future needs, the sources of funds for meeting those needs, and the time needed to develop those funds. When you begin your financial plan, you can use various time-based tables to take into account the time value of money. Figure AIII.5 shows how much a $1.00 investment will grow over different lengths of time and at different interest rates.

A timetable like this can determine the factor at which your money will multiply over a given period of time and at a given interest rate. It can also help you determine how long and at what interest rate you will need to invest to meet your financial goals. For example, if you wanted to double your money in less than 10 years, you would have to find an interest rate of return of at least 8 percent. The catch is that to obtain a high interest rate, you will have to make riskier investments, such as buying stocks. Because higher interest rates carry greater risks, it is unwise to "put all your eggs in one basket." A sound financial plan will include more conservative investments, such as a bank savings account, to mitigate the risks of more speculative investments.

Conserving Money by Controlling It

A major pitfall in any financial plan is the temptation to spend too much, especially when credit is so easy to get. Because many credit-card issuers target college students and recent graduates with tempting offers appealing to the desire for financial independence, it is important that you arm yourself with a solid understanding of the financial costs entailed by credit cards. The same lessons apply equally to other loans, such as home mortgages, cars, and student financial aid.

Credit Cards: Keys to Satisfaction or Financial Handcuffs?

Although some credit cards don't charge annual fees, all of them charge interest on unpaid (outstanding) balances. Figure AIII.6 reprints part of a page from Bankrate. com's credit-card calculator at www.bankrate.com/brm/calc/MinPayment.asp. Using the table as a guide, suppose you owe $5,000 for credit-card purchases, and your card company requires a minimum monthly payment (minimum payment due [MPD]) of 5 percent of the unpaid balance. The interest rate is 18 percent APR (annual percentage rate) on the outstanding balance.

If you pay only the monthly minimum, it will take you 115 months—more than 9 1/2 years—to pay off your credit-card debt. During this time you will pay $2,096.70 in interest, almost half again the principal balance! Repayment takes so long because you are making only the MPD, which decreases with each monthly payment.

Save Your Money: Lower Interest Rates and Faster Payments

Figure AIII.6 confirms two principles for saving money that you can apply when borrowing from any source, not just credit cards: Look for lower interest rates and make faster repayments.

Seeking Lower Interest Rates Look again at Figure AIII.6 and compare the cost of borrowing $5,000 at 18 percent with the cost of borrowing it at 9 percent. If you assume the same 5-percent minimum monthly payment, a 9-percent APR will save you $1232.14 in interest during the repayment period—a nearly 59 percent savings.

Making Faster Payments Because money has a time value, lenders charge borrowers according to the length of time for which they borrow it. In general, longer lending periods increase the cost, and shorter periods are cheaper. Using Figure AIII.6, compare the costs of the 5-percent MPD with the faster 10-percent MPD. The faster schedule cuts the repayment period from 115 to 55 months and, at 18 percent APR, reduces interest costs by $1,222.84.

Combining both faster repayment and the lower interest rate cuts your total interest cost to $450.30—a savings of $1,695.07 over the amount you'd pay if you made slower repayments at the higher rate.

Declining Asset Value: A Borrower's Regret Financially speaking, nothing's more disappointing than buying an expensive item and then discovering that it's not worth what you paid. For example, if you buy a $5,000 used car with a credit card at 18 percent APR and make only the MPD, as in the preceding example, you'll end up spending a total of $7,407.50 over 9 1/2 years. By that time, however,

| Balance = $5,000 | MPD 3% | | MPD 5% | | MPD 10% | |
APR	Months	Costs	Months	Costs	Months	Costs
6%	144	$5,965.56	92	$5,544.58	50	$5,260.74
9%	158	$6,607.24	96	$5,864.56	51	$5,401.63
12%	175	$7,407.50	102	$6,224.26	53	$5,550.32
18%	226	$9,798.89	115	$7,096.70	55	$5,873.86
21%	266	$11,704.63	123	$7,632.92	57	$6,050.28

Note: APR, annual percentage rate; MPD, minimum payment due

FIGURE AIII.6 Paying off Credit-Card Debt

the car you bought will be worth less than $1,000. Some of this loss in asset value can be avoided through realistic planning and spending—by knowing and staying within your financial means.

Financial Commitments of Home Ownership

Deciding whether to rent or buy a home involves a variety of considerations, including life stage, family needs, career, financial situation, and preferred lifestyle. If you decide to buy, you have to ask yourself what you can afford, and that requires asking yourself questions about your personal financial condition and your capacity for borrowing. Figure AIII.7 summarizes the key considerations in deciding whether to rent or buy.

How Much House Can You Afford?

Buying a home is the biggest investment in most people's lives. Unfortunately, many make the mistake of buying a house that they can't afford, resulting in unnecessary stress and even devastating financial loss. This happened on a massive scale in the housing downfall that began in 2007 and has not fully recovered. The seeds for destruction sprouted during the years 2000–2007 when millions of optimistic home buyers borrowed beyond their means by getting larger loans than they could afford. With the rising demand for home ownership, housing prices became inflated and borrowers responded by seeking unrealistically larger loans. They expected market prices would continue to rise indefinitely, thereby providing a profitable investment. Borrowers were aided by lenders using loose credit standards, unlike the time-proven standards that will be presented here, leading to unrealistic repayment requirements. By 2007 the housing market was oversold and the U.S. economy entered a severe recession. With rising unemployment, borrowers were unable to meet monthly payments, especially when interest rates (and thus payments) on loans increased; housing vacancies increased and property values plummeted. Borrowers lost their homes and the equity they had built up in them. Economists predict that the collapsing housing market will continue into 2014.

In addition to loan payments, the typical demands of ownership, time and other resources for maintaining and improving a home, tend to cut into the money left over for recreation, eating out, taking vacations, and so on. You can reduce the financial pressure by calculating in advance a realistic price range—one that not only lets you buy a house but also lets you live a reasonably pleasant life once you're in it.

Most people need a loan to buy a house, apartment, or condominium. A **mortgage loan** is secured by the property—the home—being purchased. Because the size of a loan depends on the cost of the property, both borrowers and lenders want to know whether the buyer can afford the house he or she wants. To determine how much you can afford, one time-tested (though somewhat conservative) rule recommends

Mortgage Loan *loan secured by property (the home) being purchased*

Renting	Buying
• No down payment to get started	• Must make payments for mortgage, property taxes, and insurance
• Flexibility to leave	• Equity builds up over time
• No obligation for upkeep or improvements	• More privacy
• No groundskeeping	• Value of property may increase
• Easy cash-flow planning (a single monthly payment)	• Lower income taxes: mortgage-interest and property tax payments reduce taxable income
• May provide access to recreation and social facilities	• Financial gains from selling house can be exempt from taxes
• Rental conditions may be changed by owner	• Greater control over use of property and improvements
• Timing for repairs controlled by owner	• The home can become a source of cash by refinancing with another mortgage loan or a home-equity loan

FIGURE AIII.7 To Buy or Not to Buy

Interest Rate (%)	Length of Loan				
	3 Years	5 Years	10 Years	20 Years	30 Years
5.0	$299.71	$188.71	$106.07	$66.00	$53.68
6.0	304.22	193.33	111.02	71.64	59.96
6.5	306.49	195.66	113.55	74.56	63.21
7.0	308.77	198.01	116.11	77.53	66.53
8.0	313.36	202.76	121.33	83.65	73.38
9.0	318.00	207.58	126.68	89.98	80.47
10.0	322.67	212.47	132.16	96.51	87.76
11.0	327.39	217.42	137.76	103.22	95.24
12.0	332.14	222.44	143.48	110.11	102.86

FIGURE AIII.8 Monthly Payments on a $10,000 Loan

keeping the price below 2 1/2 times your annual income. If your income is $48,000, look for a house priced below $120,000.

Any such calculation, however, will give you just a rough estimate of what you can afford. You should also consider how much money you have for a down payment and how much you can borrow. Lending institutions want to determine a buyer's borrowing capacity, the borrower's ability to meet the *recurring costs* of buying and owning.

PITI Every month, the homeowner must pay **p**rincipal (pay back some of the borrowed money), along with **i**nterest, **t**axes, and homeowner's **i**nsurance, or PITI, for short. As Figure AIII.8 shows, the size of principal and interest payments depends on (1) the mortgage amount, (2) the length of the mortgage loan, and (3) the interest rate.

In evaluating loan applications, lenders use PITI calculations to estimate the buyer's ability to meet monthly payments. To determine how much someone is likely to lend you, calculate 28 percent of your gross monthly income (that is, before taxes and other deductions). If your PITI costs don't exceed that figure, your loan application probably will receive favorable consideration. With a monthly gross income of $4,000, for example, your PITI costs shouldn't exceed $1,120 (28 percent of $4,000). Additional calculations show a house price of $162,382 is the most this borrower can afford. Figure AIII.9 gives a sample calculation, and you should be able to make step-by-step computations by plugging your own numbers into the worksheet.

Other Debt In evaluating financial capacity, lenders also look at any additional outstanding debt, such as loans and credit-card bills. They will generally accept indebtedness (including PITI) up to 36 percent of gross income. Because PITI itself can be up to 28 percent, you might be allowed as little as 8 percent in other long-term debt. With your $4,000 monthly gross income, your total debt should be less than $1,440 ($1,120 for PITI and $320 for other debt). If your total debt exceeds $1,440, you may have to settle for a smaller loan than the one you calculated with the PITI method. Websites such as http://mortgages.interest.com provide mortgage calculators for testing interest rates, lengths of loans, and other personal financial information.

Cashing Out from Tax Avoidance (Legally)

Personal expenditures always require cash outflows; some also reduce your tax bill and save you some cash. Individual retirement accounts (IRAs) and some education savings accounts have this effect. (Before you commit any money to these instruments or activities, check with an expert on tax regulations; they change from time to time.)

ASSUMPTIONS:

30-year mortgage
Closing costs (fees for property, survey, credit report, title search,
    title insurance, attorney, interest advance, loan origination) = $5,000
Funds available for closing costs and down payment = $25,000
Interest rate on mortgage = 6½% per year
Estimated real estate taxes = $200 per month
Estimated homeowner's insurance = $20 month

Example Numbers   Your Numbers

1. Monthly income, gross (before taxes or deductions)........$4,000
2. Apply PITI ratio (0.28 x amount on line 1) to determine
    borrower's payment capacity:
    0.28 x $4,000 = ...$1,120
3. Determine mortgage payment (principal and interest)
    by subtracting taxes and insurance from
    PITI (line 2)..–$ 220
4. Result: Maximum mortgage payment
    (principal and interest)................................. $900

5. Using Table Figure AIII.11, find the monthly mortgage payment
    on a $10,000 loan at 6½% interest for
    30 years.. $63.21
6. Since each $10,000 loan requires a $63.21 monthly payment,
    how many $10,000 loans can the borrower afford
    with the $900 payment capacity? The answer is
    determined as follows:
        $900.00/$63.21 =
        14.2382 loans of $10,000 each

7. Result: Maximum allowable mortgage loan [calculated
    as follows]:
        14.2382 loans (from line 6 above)
        x $10,000 per loan] = ...**$142,382**

8. Result: Maximum house price borrower can afford
    using PITI (amount of house that can be bought with
    available funds):

    From loan...........................$142,382
    From down payment............$ 25,000
    Less closing cost.................–$ 5,000
               ....**$162,382**

FIGURE AIII.9 Worksheet for PITI Calculations

The IRA Tax Break

With a **traditional individual retirement account (IRA)**, you can make an annual tax-deductible savings deposit of up to $5,000, depending on your income level. IRAs are long-term investments, intended to provide income after age 59 1/2. For distant future savings, an IRA boasts immediate cash advantages over a typical savings account because it reduces your current taxable income by the amount of your contribution.

Here's how it works: You're a qualified employee with a federal income tax rate of 20 percent in year 2009. If you contribute $4,000 to an IRA, you avoid $800 in income taxes (0.20 × $4,000 = $800). Your untaxed contributions and their accumulated earnings will be taxed later when you withdraw money from your IRA. The tax break is based on the assumption that, after you retire, you're likely to have less total income and will have to pay less tax on the money withdrawn as income from your IRA.

Traditional Individual Retirement Account (IRA) *provision allowing individual tax-deferred retirement savings*

Assumptions: Initial contribution and earnings average 10 percent growth annually. Initial contribution and earnings remain invested for 40 years. Income tax rate is 30 percent.	Traditional IRA	Roth IRA
Initial cash contribution to IRA	$3,000	$3,000
Income tax paid initially: $4,285 income x 30% tax rate = $1,285 tax	0	1,285
Total initial cash outlay	**$3,000**	**$4,285**
Accumulated earnings (40 years)	$132,774	$132,774
Initial contribution	+ 3,000	+ 3,000
Total available for distribution after 40 years	= $135,774	= $135,774
Income tax at time of distribution	− $40,732	0
After-tax distribution (cash)	**= $95,042**	**= $135,774**

FIGURE AIII.10 Cash Flows: Roth IRA versus Traditional IRA

IRA Risks If you underestimate your future cash requirements and have to withdraw money before you reach 59 1/2, you'll probably get hit with a 10-percent penalty. You can, however, make penalty-free withdrawals under certain circumstances: buying a first home, paying college expenses, and paying large medical bills.

The unpredictability of future income tax rates also poses a financial risk. If tax rates increase substantially, future IRA withdrawals may be taxed at higher rates, which may offset your original tax savings.

Roth IRA *provision allowing individual retirement savings with tax-free accumulated earnings*

Roth IRA versus Traditional IRA The **Roth IRA** is the reverse of the traditional IRA in that contributions are not tax deductible, withdrawals on initial contribution are not penalized, and withdrawals on accumulated earnings after the age of 59 1/2 are not taxed.

Figure AIII.10 shows the significant advantage of this last feature. Accumulated earnings typically far outweigh the initial contribution, so although you pay an extra $1,285 in front-end taxes, you get $40,732 in additional cash at retirement—and even more if income-tax rates have increased.

IRAs and Education Depending on your income level, you can contribute up to $2,000 annually to a Coverdell Education Savings Account (also known as an *Education IRA*) for each child under age 18. As with the Roth IRA, your initial contribution is not tax deductible, your earnings are tax-free, and you pay no tax on withdrawals to pay for qualified education expenses. However, the Education IRA requires that you use the money by the time your child reaches age 30. Funds that you withdraw but don't use for stipulated education expense are subject to taxation plus a 10-percent penalty.

Protecting Your Net Worth

With careful attention, thoughtful saving and spending, and skillful financial planning (and a little luck), you can build up your net worth over time. Every financial plan should also consider steps for preserving it. One approach involves the risk–return relationship discussed in Chapter 17. Do you prefer to protect your current assets, or are you willing to risk them in return for greater financial growth? At various life stages and levels of wealth, you should adjust your asset portfolio to conform to your risk and return preferences: conservative, moderate, or aggressive.

Why Buy Life Insurance?

You can think of life insurance as a tool for financial preservation. As explained in Appendix 1, a life insurance policy is a promise to pay beneficiaries after the death of the insured party who paid the insurance company premiums during his or her lifetime.

What Does Life Insurance Do?

Upon the death of the policyholder, life insurance replaces income on which someone else is dependent. The amount of insurance you need depends on how many other people rely on your income. For example, while insurance makes sense for a married parent who is a family's sole source of income, a single college student with no financial dependents needs little or no insurance.

How Much Should I Buy?

The more insurance you buy, the more it's going to cost you. To estimate the amount of coverage you need, begin by adding up all your annual expenses—rent, food, clothing, transportation, schooling, debts to be paid—that you pay for the dependents who'd survive you. Then multiply the total by the number of years that you want the insurance to cover them. Typically, this sum will amount to several times—even 10 to 20 times—your current annual income.

Why Consider Term Insurance?

Term insurance pays a predetermined benefit when death occurs during the stipulated policy term. If the insured outlives the term, the policy loses its value and simply ceases. Term-life premiums are significantly lower than premiums for whole-life insurance.

Unlike term life, *whole-life insurance*, also known as *cash-value insurance*, remains in force as long as premiums are paid. In addition to paying a death benefit, whole life accumulates cash value over time—a form of savings. Paid-in money can be withdrawn; however, whole-life savings earn less interest than most alternative forms of investment.

How Much Does It Cost?

The cost of insurance depends on how much you buy, your life expectancy, and other statistical risk factors. To get the best match between your policy and your personal situation, you should evaluate the terms and conditions of a variety of policies. You can get convenient comparisons on websites such as www.intelliquote.com.

appendix IV

Unions and Labor Management

This appendix is an expansion of material covered in the last section of Chapter 10. After reading it you should better understand how and why workers organize into labor unions, how unions and businesses relate to each other, and how the collective bargaining process works.

Why Do Workers Unionize?

A **labor union** is a group of individuals working together to achieve shared job-related goals, such as higher pay, shorter working hours, more job security, greater benefits, or better working conditions.[1] **Labor relations** is the process of dealing with employees who are represented by a union.

Labor unions grew in popularity in the United States in the nineteenth and early twentieth centuries. The labor movement was born with the Industrial Revolution, which also gave birth to a factory-based production system that carried with it enormous economic benefits. Job specialization and mass production allowed businesses to create ever greater quantities of goods at ever lower costs.

But there was also a dark side to this era. Workers became more dependent on their factory jobs. Eager for greater profits, some owners treated their workers like other raw materials, as resources to be deployed with little or no regard for the individual worker's well-being. Many businesses forced employees to work long hours—60-hour weeks were common, and some workers were routinely forced to work 12 to 16 hours a day. With no minimum-wage laws or other controls, pay was also minimal and safety standards virtually nonexistent. Workers enjoyed no job security and received few benefits. Many companies, especially textile mills, employed large numbers of children at poverty wages. If people complained, nothing prevented employers from firing and replacing them at will.

Unions appeared and ultimately prospered because they constituted a solution to the worker's most serious problem; they forced management to listen to the complaints of all their workers rather than to just the few who were brave (or foolish) enough to speak out. The power of unions, then, comes from collective action. **Collective bargaining** is the process by which union leaders and managers negotiate common terms and conditions of employment for the workers represented by unions. Although collective bargaining does not often occur in small businesses, many midsize and larger businesses must engage in the process.

> **Labor Union** *a group of individuals working together to achieve shared job-related goals, such as higher pay, shorter working hours, more job security, greater benefits, or better working conditions*

> **Labor Relations** *the process of dealing with employees who are represented by a union*

> **Collective Bargaining** *the process by which union leaders and managers negotiate common terms and conditions of employment for the workers represented by unions*

The Evolution of Unionism in the United States

As we discuss the growth—and the more recent decline—of the unionism in this section, it is important to remember that the influence of labor unions goes far beyond their membership. For example, many nonunion members have benefited from the improved working conditions won by unions. Union gains often set standards for entire industries, and some organizations make workplace improvements just to keep unions out.

Early Unions

Labor unions grew up with the United States. The earliest formal organizations of U.S. workers appeared during the Revolutionary War. These early organizations were craft unions; each limited itself to representing workers whose common interest was a specific skilled job, and each sought to promote the economic welfare of the skilled craftspeople who made up its membership.

For example, the Federal Society of Journeymen Cordwainers, formed in Philadelphia in 1794, worked to better the pay and working conditions of shoemakers. The Cordwainers was also one of the first unions to encounter legal roadblocks to collective action. When the union struck for higher wages in 1806, the court ruled in favor of employers, who claimed that unions were illegal "combinations" conspiring to restrain trade. The court's ruling applied the *common law conspiracy doctrine*, the principle that the public interest was harmed when two or more people conspired to do something jointly. Unions continued to organize, but for the next four decades, they found it extremely difficult to take action in the face of the conspiracy doctrine.

A milestone in the history of U.S. labor occurred with the formation of the Knights of Labor in 1869. Like previous unions, the Knights began as a craft union. Soon, however, the organization set larger goals for itself. In a drive to organize any workers who were interested in its representation, the Knights expanded to encompass workers in numerous fields (noteworthy exceptions were lawyers, bankers, and bartenders). The Knights was also the first union that actively sought women and blacks as members, and one of the few unions that has ever focused on political lobbying rather than collective bargaining as a means of reaching its goals.

The Knights championed such traditional union issues as better working conditions, campaigning especially for the eight-hour day, and the abolition of child labor. At the same time, the union also hoped to achieve a broad range of social goals. Chief among these were such liberal, or reformist, objectives as worker ownership of factories and free public land for those who wished to farm.

These same goals also attracted to the labor movement a variety of radicals and other political reformers, many of whom came in the waves of European immigrants who had begun arriving a few decades previously. Their activities were directed against what they saw as the oppressive nature of the industrial capitalist system, and their tactics did not necessarily reflect the typical strategies of the labor unions. Spurred by a severe depression in 1873, for example, a series of violent labor actions characterized labor-management relations from the mid-to-late 1870s. Demonstrators and locked-out strikers blockaded factories, battled strikebreakers in the streets of major cities, and exchanged fire with municipal police, state militia, and armed private agents. Assassinations and bombings led to the trial and execution of anarchists and labor agitators.

However, much of the violence in this period came in direct response to the extraordinary pressures of the depression. Most U.S. laborers were conservative by nature and sought the stability of organizations such as the Knights of Labor. Under the leadership of Terence V. Powderly, the Knights grew to include roughly 700,000 members by the mid-1880s. The union was never successful, however, at increasing the number of skilled workers among its members. In addition, it was weakened by internal disagreements about social goals and outside charges of union violence. By the turn of the century, the Knights had disbanded.

The Emergence of the Major Unions

With its focus on the social welfare of unskilled workers, the Knights of Labor tended to forget that its economic strength lay with its skilled craft workers. As a result of this oversight, many of these workers soon began to look for organizations that would better represent their interests, namely, unions whose primary concern was to improve wages, hours, and working conditions.

The American Federation of Labor

Many workers disenchanted with the social agenda of the Knights of Labor found a home in the **American Federation of Labor (AFL).** Made up of craft unions, the AFL was formed in 1886 by Samuel Gompers and other veteran organizers. Unlike the Knights of Labor, the AFL stressed no broad, idealistic legislative or political program. Gompers himself saw the labor union as an integral component, not the inherent enemy, of the capitalist system: "As we get a 25-cents-a-day wage increase," he argued, the process "brings us nearer the time when a greater degree of social justice and fair dealing will obtain among men." The enduring importance of the AFL lies in the fact that it established a solid organizational basis for collective bargaining, economic action, and a pragmatic approach to union-management relations.

American Federation of Labor (AFL) an association of craft unions formed in 1886 by Samuel Gompers and others; the AFL had no political or social agenda but simply sought to improve working conditions and pay for its members

The AFL grew rapidly in the early decades of the twentieth century, and by the end of World War I, membership had reached more than 5 million. The 1920s proved difficult for the AFL because increased employer resistance to unions contributed to a steady decline in membership. By 1929, membership had dropped to 3.4 million.

The Great Depression of the 1930s witnessed further membership decline. By 1933, membership stood at just 2.9 million. In the same year, however, newly elected President Franklin D. Roosevelt introduced the nation to the New Deal, a far-reaching program aimed at stimulating the U.S. economy and creating jobs. The New Deal inspired an era of recovery for organized labor. Moreover, as we will see later in this appendix, the New Deal Congress passed a series of laws that made it easier for workers to organize.

The Congress of Industrial Organizations

By the mid-1930s, the advent of mass production had significantly increased the demand for semi-skilled workers in the automobile, steel, and mining industries. The AFL, while continuing to grow throughout the 1930s, remained open only to skilled craftspeople. In fact, most AFL leaders opposed **industrial unionism,** the organizing of employees by industry rather than by skill or occupation. When a 1935 convention of AFL unions confirmed this stance, dissident leaders, including John F. Lewis of the United Mine Workers, objected bitterly. Ultimately, the AFL expelled 32 national unions, which in 1938 banded together to form the **Congress of Industrial Organizations (CIO).**

Industrial Unionism the organizing of employees by industry rather than by skill or occupation

Congress of Industrial Organizations (CIO) an association of industrial unions formed in 1938 after being expelled from the American Federation of Labor (AFL)

Soon, the CIO had organized the auto, steel, mining, meatpacking, paper, textile, and electrical industries. By the early 1940s, CIO unions claimed close to 5 million of the slightly more than 10 million unionized U.S. workers. Not surprisingly, the AFL soon abandoned rigid craft unionism and began to charter industrial unions.

The AFL-CIO

Union membership continued to increase during World War II, reaching more than 14 million by the end of the war. However, a series of postwar strikes led Congress to curtail the power of unions. Partly in response to this change, and partly in response to growing conflicts within their ranks, leaders of the AFL and the CIO began merger negotiations. These meetings culminated in the 1955 formation of the AFL-CIO, with a total membership of 15 million. At the same time, organized labor reached its membership zenith, claiming almost 35 percent of the nonfarm workforce.

Today, in addition to lobbying for pro-union issues, the AFL-CIO settles jurisdictional disputes between unions. Remember, however, that the AFL-CIO is not a union itself. Rather, it is a federation of 86 individual unions with about 13 million individual members who belong to various trade or industrial departments (such as building trades, maritime trades, and public employees). The United Food and Commercial Workers is a union, as are the International Brotherhood of Teamsters and the National Education Association.

Unionism Today

While understanding the historical context of labor unions is important, so too is appreciating the role of unionism today, especially trends in union membership, union-management relations, and bargaining perspectives. We discuss these topics in the sections that follow.

Trends in Union Membership

Since the mid-1950s, U.S. labor unions have experienced increasing difficulties in attracting new members. Although millions of workers still belong to labor unions, union membership *as a percentage of the total workforce* has continued to decline at a steady rate. In 1977, for example, more than 26 percent of U.S. wage and salary employees belonged to labor unions. Today, that figure is about 14 percent. Figure AIV.1(a) traces the decades-long decline in union membership. Moreover, if public employees are excluded from consideration, then only around 11 percent of all private industry wage and salary employees currently belong to labor unions. Figure AIV.1(b) illustrates the different trends in membership for public employees versus private nonfarm employees.

Furthermore, just as union membership has continued to decline, so has the percentage of successful union-organizing campaigns. In the years immediately following World War II and continuing through the mid-1960s, most unions routinely won certification elections. In recent years, however, labor unions have been winning certification fewer than 50 percent of the time in which workers are called on to vote. By the same token, of course, unions still do win. Meat cutters at a Florida Walmart store recently voted to unionize, the first-ever successful organizing campaign against the retailing giant. "You'll see a lot more attention to Wal-Mart now," exulted one AFL-CIO official. "It's not like Wal-Mart stands out as some unattainable goal."[2]

From most indications, then, the power and significance of U.S. labor unions, although still quite formidable, are also measurably lower than they were just a few decades ago. A number of factors help to explain the decline in union membership.

Composition of the Workforce Traditionally, union members have been predominantly white males in blue-collar jobs. But as most of us know, today's workforce is increasingly composed of women and ethnic minorities. Because these

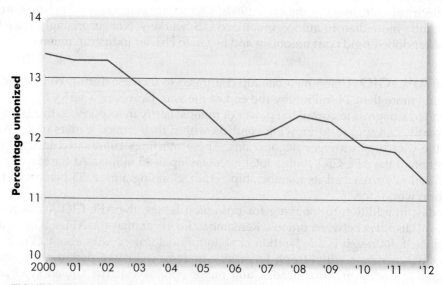

FIGURE AIV.1 (A) Trends in Union Membership
Source: www.bls.gov

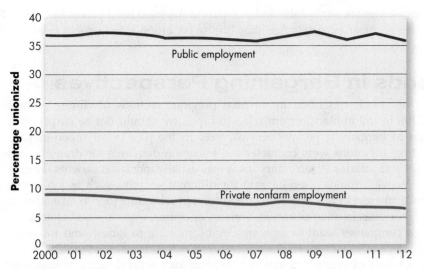

FIGURE AIV.1 (B) Trends in Union Membership
Source: www.bls.gov

groups have much weaker traditions of union affiliation, their members are less likely to join unions when they enter the workforce. In a related trend, much of the workforce has shifted toward geographic areas in the South and toward occupations in the service sector that have traditionally been less heavily unionized.

Anti-Unionization Activities A second reason is more aggressive anti-unionization activity on the part of employers. Although the National Labor Relations Act and other laws specify strict management practices with regard to labor unions, companies are still free to pursue certain strategies intended to eliminate or minimize unionization. Both Motorola and Procter & Gamble, for example, now offer no-layoff guarantees for most of their employees and have created a formal grievance system for all workers. These arrangements were once available only through unions. But because these and other firms offer them independent of any union contract, employees have two fewer reasons for unionizing.

Some companies have also worked to create much more employee-friendly work environments and to treat all employees with respect and dignity. One goal of this approach is to minimize the attractiveness of labor unions for employees. Many Japanese manufacturers who have set up shop in the United States have successfully avoided unionization efforts by the United Auto Workers (UAW) by providing job security, higher wages, and a work environment in which employees are allowed to participate and be actively involved in plant management.

Trends in Union-Management Relations

The gradual decline in unionization in the United States has been accompanied by some significant trends in union-management relations. In some sectors of the economy, perhaps most notably the automobile and steel industries, labor unions still remain quite strong. In these areas, unions have large memberships and considerable power in negotiating with management. The UAW, for example, is still one of the strongest unions in the United States.

In most sectors, however, unions are clearly in a weakened position, and as a result, many have taken much more conciliatory stances in their relations with management. This situation contrasts sharply with the more adversarial relationship that once dominated labor relations in this country. Increasingly, for instance, unions recognize that they don't have as much power as they once held and that it is in their own best interests, as well as in those of the workers that they represent, to work with management instead of working against it. Ironically, then, union-management relations are in many ways better today than they have been in many years. Admittedly, the improvement is attributable in large part to the weakened power of unions. Even so, however, most experts agree that improved union-management relations have benefited both sides.

Trends in Bargaining Perspectives

Given the trends described in the two previous sections (declining membership and shifts in union-management relationships), we should not be surprised to find changes in bargaining perspectives as well. In the past, most union-management bargaining situations were characterized by union demands for dramatic increases in wages and salaries. A secondary issue was usually increased benefits for members. Now, however, unions often bargain for different benefits, such as job security. Of particular interest in this area is the trend toward relocating jobs to take advantage of lower labor costs in other countries. Unions, of course, want to restrict job movement, whereas companies want to save money by moving facilities—and jobs—to other countries.

As a result of organizational downsizing and several years of relatively low inflation in this country, many unions today find themselves, rather than striving for wage increases, fighting against wage cuts. Similarly, as organizations are more likely to seek lower health care and other benefits, a common goal of union strategy is preserving what's already been won. Unions also place greater emphasis on improved job security. A trend that has become especially important in recent years is toward improved pension programs for employees.

Unions have also begun increasingly to set their sights on preserving jobs for workers in the United States in the face of business efforts to relocate production in some sectors to countries where labor costs are lower. For example, the AFL-CIO has been an outspoken opponent of efforts to normalize trade relations with China, fearing that more businesses might be tempted to move jobs there. General Electric has been targeted for union protests recently because of its strategy to move many of its own jobs—and those of key suppliers—to Mexico.[3]

The Future of Unions

Despite declining membership and some loss of power, labor unions remain a major factor in the U.S. business world. The 86 labor organizations in the AFL-CIO, as well as independent major unions (such as the Teamsters and the National Education Association), still play a major role in U.S. business. Moreover, some unions still wield considerable power, especially in the traditional strongholds of goods-producing industries. Labor and management in some industries, notably airlines and steel, are beginning to favor contracts that establish formal mechanisms for greater worker input into management decisions. Inland Steel, for instance, recently granted its major union the right to name a member to the board of directors. Union officers can also attend executive meetings.

The big question still remains: will unions dwindle in power and perhaps disappear, or can they evolve, survive to face new challenges, and play a new role in U.S. business? They will probably evolve to take on new roles and responsibilities. More and more unions are asking for—and often getting—voices in management. In 1980, for example, as a part of the Chrysler bailout, UAW president Douglas Fraser became the first labor official appointed to the board of directors of a major corporation. Several other companies have since followed suit.

By the same token, unions are increasingly aware that they must cooperate with employers if both are to survive. Critics of unions contend that excessive wage rates won through years of strikes and hard-nosed negotiation are partly to blame for the demise of large employers such as Eastern Airlines. Others argue that excessively tight work rules limit the productivity of businesses in many industries. More often, however, unions are working with organizations to create effective partnerships in which managers and workers share the same goals: profitability, growth, and effectiveness with equitable rewards for everyone.

Contemporary Union Structure

Just as each organization has its own unique structure, each union creates a structure that best serves its own needs. As Figure AIV.2 shows, a general structure characterizes most national and international unions. A major function of unions is to provide service and support to both members and local affiliates. Most of these services are carried out by the types of specialized departments shown in Figure AIV.2. In other unions, departments serve specific employment groups. The Machinists' Union—the International Association of Machinists and Aerospace Workers—has departments for automotive, railroad, and airline workers.

Locals

At the same time, most national unions are composed of **local unions (locals),** which are organized at the level of a single company, plant, or small defined geographic region. The functions of these locals vary, depending not only on governance arrangements but also on bargaining patterns in particular industries. Some local unions bargain directly with management regarding wages, hours, and other terms of employment. Many local unions are also active in disciplining members for violations of contract standards and in pressing management to consider worker complaints. Local unions also serve as grassroots bases for union political activities, registering voters and getting them out to vote on election day.

Each department or unit represented at the local level elects a **shop steward,** a regular employee who acts as a liaison between union members and supervisors. For example, if workers have a grievance, they take it to the steward, who tries to resolve the problem with the supervisor. If the local is large, the union might hire a full-time **business agent** (or **business representative**) to play the same role.

Within a given union, the main governing bodies are the national union (or international union when members come from more than one country) and its officers. Among their other duties, national and international unions charter local affiliates and establish general standards of conduct and procedures for local operations. For example, they set dues assessments, arrange for the election of local officers, sanction strikes, and provide guidance in the collective bargaining process. Many

Local Unions (locals) *organized at the level of a single company, plant, or small geographic region*

Shop Steward *a regular employee who acts as a liaison between union members and supervisors*

Business Agent or Business Representative *a full-time employee hired to act as a liaison between union members and supervisors if a local union is large*

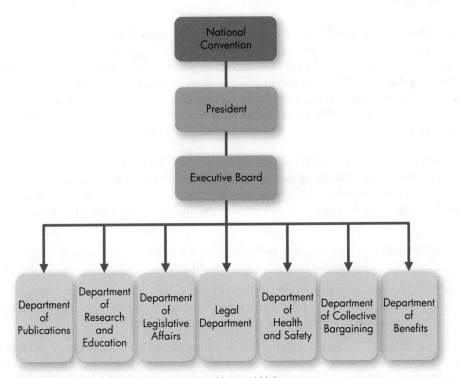

FIGURE AIV.2 Organization of a Large National Union

national unions also engage in a variety of political activities, such as lobbying. They may also help coordinate organizing efforts and establish education programs.

Given the magnitude of their efforts, it is little wonder that unions often take on many of the same characteristics as the companies for which their members work. For example, almost all large unions have full-time administrators, formal organizational structures (see Figure AIV.2), goals and strategic plans, and so forth. James P. Hoffa, current president of the International Brotherhood of Teamsters, earns an annual salary of $300,000 and oversees a large full-time staff.[4] Because of their size, power, and importance, Congress has passed numerous laws to govern union activities. It is to these laws that we now turn our attention.

Laws Governing Labor-Management Relations

Like almost every other aspect of labor-management relations today, the process of unionizing workers is governed by numerous laws, administrative interpretations, and judicial decisions. In fact, the growth and decline of unionism in the United States can be traced by following the history of labor laws.

For the first 150 years of U.S. independence, workers were judged to have little legal right to organize. Indeed, interpretation of the 1890 Sherman Antitrust Act classified labor unions as monopolies, thus making them illegal. During the first 30 years of the twentieth century, however, social activism and turmoil in the labor force changed the landscape of U.S. labor relations.

The Major Labor Laws

Five major federal laws, all enacted between 1932 and 1959, laid the groundwork for all the rules, regulations, and judicial decisions governing union activity in the United States. A number of more recent laws have dealt with specific groups and specific issues.

Norris-LaGuardia Act During the 1930s, labor leaders finally persuaded lawmakers that the legal environment discriminated against the collective efforts of workers to improve working conditions. Legislators responded with the **Norris-LaGuardia Act** in 1932. This act imposed severe limitations on the ability of the courts to issue injunctions prohibiting certain union activities, including strikes. Norris-LaGuardia also outlawed **yellow-dog contracts,** requirements that workers state that they did not belong to and would not join a union.

National Labor Relations (Wagner) Act In 1935 Congress passed the **National Labor Relations Act** (also called the **Wagner Act**), which is the cornerstone of contemporary labor relations law. This act put labor unions on a more equal footing with management in terms of the rights of employees to organize and bargain:

- It gave most workers the right to form unions, bargain collectively, and engage in group activities (such as strikes) to reach their goals.

- It forced employers to bargain with duly elected union leaders and prohibited employer practices that unjustly restrict employees' rights (e.g., discriminating against union members in hiring, promoting, and firing).

The Wagner Act also established the **National Labor Relations Board (NLRB)** to administer its provisions. Today, the NLRB administers virtually all labor law in this country. For example, it determines the appropriate unit for conducting bargaining at any workplace. The NLRB also oversees most of the elections held by employees

Norris-LaGuardia Act *act that imposed severe limitations on the ability of the courts to issue injunctions prohibiting certain union activities, including strikes*

Yellow-Dog Contracts *requirements that workers state that they did not belong to and would not join a union*

National Labor Relations Act or Wagner Act *act that put labor unions on a more equal footing with management in terms of the rights of employees to organize and bargain*

National Labor Relations Board (NLRB) *established by the Wagner Act to administer its provisions*

to determine whether they will be represented by particular unions. It decides who is eligible to vote and who will be covered by bargaining agreements once they have been reached.

Fair Labor Standards Act Enacted in 1938, the **Fair Labor Standards Act** addressed issues of minimum wages and maximum work hours:

- It set a minimum wage (originally $.25 an hour) to be paid to workers. The minimum wage has been increased many times since 1938 and now stands at $7.25 per hour.

- It set a maximum number of hours for the workweek, initially 44 hours per week, later 40 hours.

- It mandated time-and-a-half pay for those who worked beyond the legally stipulated number of hours.

- It outlawed child labor.

Fair Labor Standards Act addressed issues of minimum wages and maximum work hours

Taft-Hartley Act Supported by the Norris-LaGuardia, Wagner, and Fair Labor Standards Acts, organized labor eventually grew into a powerful political and economic force. But a series of disruptive strikes in the immediate post–World War II years turned public opinion against unions. Inconvenienced by strikes and the resulting shortages of goods and services, the public became openly critical of unions and pressured the government to take action. Congress responded by passing the Labor-Management Relations Act (more commonly known as the Taft-Hartley Act) in 1947.

UNFAIR AND ILLEGAL UNION PRACTICES The Taft-Hartley Act defined certain union practices as unfair and illegal. For example, it prohibited such practices as featherbedding (requiring extra workers solely to provide more jobs) and refusing to bargain in good faith. It also generally forbade the **closed shop,** a workplace in which only workers already belonging to a union may be hired by an employer. Instead, Taft-Hartley promoted open shops by allowing states to enact **right-to-work laws.** Such laws prohibit both union shops and agency shops, thus making it illegal to require union membership as a condition of employment. A **union shop** requires employees to join a union within a specified period after being hired. An **agency shop** requires employees to pay union fees even if they choose not to join. To date, 21 states have enacted right-to-work laws. As you can see from Figure AIV.3, most of those states are in the South and West.

Closed Shop a workplace in which only workers already belonging to a union may be hired by an employer

Right-To-Work Laws such laws prohibit both union shops and agency shops, thus making it illegal to require union membership as a condition of employment

Union Shop requires employees to join a union within a specified period after being hired

Agency Shop requires employees to pay union fees even if they choose not to join

INJUNCTIONS AND COOLING-OFF PERIODS Passed in the wake of crippling strikes in the steel industry, the Taft-Hartley act also established procedures for resolving any strike deemed to pose a national emergency. Initially, the concept of national emergency was broadly interpreted. For example, virtually any large company could claim that a strike was doing irreparable harm to its financial base and that the nation's economy would be harmed if workers were not forced back to their jobs.

Today, however, the courts use a more precise definition of national emergency. For example, a strike must affect a whole industry or most of it. Similarly, the use of Taft-Hartley is more restrictive. Now the president may request an injunction requiring that workers restrain from striking for 60 days. During this cooling-off period, labor and management must try to resolve their differences.

ENFORCED RESOLUTION If differences are not resolved during the cooling-off period, the injunction may be extended for another 20 days. During this period, employees must vote, in a secret ballot election, on whether to accept or reject the employer's latest offer. If they accept the offer, the threat of strike is ended and the contract signed. If they do not accept the offer, the president reports to Congress and the workers may either be forced back to work under threat of criminal action or fired and replaced by nonunion employees. Presidential intervention has been invoked only 35 times since Taft-Hartley was passed.

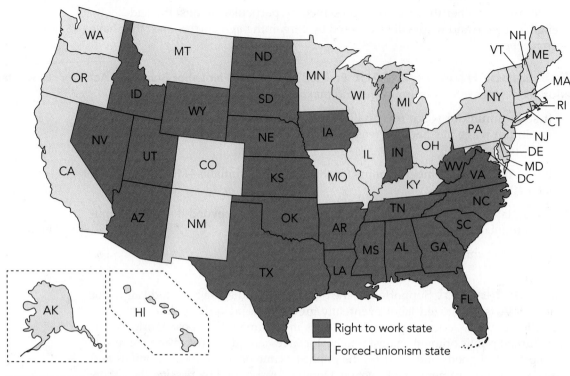

FIGURE AIV.3 Right-to-Work States

Landrum-Griffin Act The National Labor Relations Act was further amended by the **Landrum-Griffin Act** in 1959. Officially titled the **Labor-Management Reporting and Disclosure Act,** this law resulted from congressional hearings that revealed unethical, illegal, and undemocratic union practices. The act thus imposed regulations on internal union procedures:

- It required the election of national union leaders at least once every five years.

- It gave union members the right to participate in various union affairs.

- It required unions to file annual financial disclosure statements with the Department of Labor.

How Unions Are Organized and Certified

Many of the laws described previously address the issue of union certification. Figure AIV.4 illustrates a simplified version of this process. First, there must be some interest among workers in having a union. Sometimes this interest comes from dissatisfied employees; sometimes it is stirred by professional organizers sent by unions themselves. For example, the United Auto Workers has for years dispatched organizers to promote interest among workers at the Honda plant in Marysville, Ohio. To date, they have had no success in Marysville or in Smyrna, Tennessee, where Nissan built its major U.S. plant. The process unfolds as follows:

1 *Defining the bargaining unit*. Interested organizers start by asking the NLRB to define the **bargaining unit**, the group of employees who will be represented by the union. For instance, a bargaining unit might be all nonmanagement employees in an organization or all electrical workers at a certain plant.

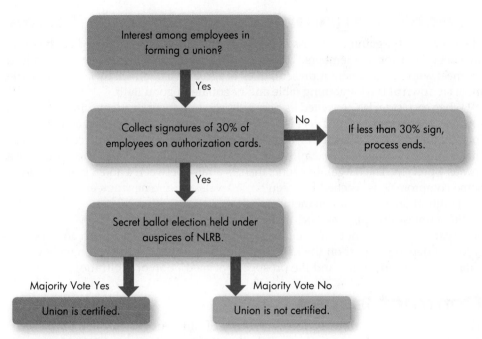

FIGURE AIV.4 Certifying a Labor Union

2 *Gaining authorization.* Organizers must then get 30 percent of the eligible workers within the bargaining unit to sign authorization cards requesting a certification election. If less than 30 percent of the workers want an election, the process ends.

3 *Conducting an election.* If the required number of signatures is obtained, the organizers petition the NLRB to conduct the election. The NLRB then holds a secret ballot election. If a simple majority of those voting approves the certification, the union becomes the official bargaining agent of eligible employees. If a majority fails to approve certification, the process ends and an election cannot be called again for at least one year.

Unions are not necessarily permanent fixtures in a workplace, and if conditions warrant, a union may be *decertified.* For example, workers may become disenchanted with a union and may even feel that they are being hurt by its presence. They may believe that management is trying to be cooperative while the union is refusing to negotiate in good faith.

Decertification requires two conditions:

1 The union must have served the unit as its official bargaining agent for at least one year.

2 There must be no labor contract currently in effect.

If these conditions are met, employees or their representatives can solicit signatures on decertification cards. If 30 percent of the employees in the unit sign, the NLRB conducts a decertification election. If a majority of those voting favor decertification, the union is removed as the unit's official bargaining agent. Following decertification, a new election cannot be requested for at least one year.

Collective Bargaining

When a union has been legally certified, it assumes the role of official bargaining agent for the workers whom it represents. Collective bargaining is an ongoing process involving both the drafting and the administering of the terms of a labor contract.

Reaching Agreement on Contract Terms

The collective bargaining process begins when the union is recognized as the exclusive negotiator for its members. The bargaining cycle itself begins when union leaders meet with management representatives to agree on a contract. By law, both parties must sit down at the bargaining table and negotiate in good faith.

When each side has presented its demands, sessions focus on identifying the *bargaining zone*. The process is shown in Figure AIV.5. For example, although an employer may initially offer no pay raise, it may expect to grant a raise of up to 6 percent. Likewise, the union may initially *demand* a 10-percent pay raise while *expecting* to accept a raise as low as 4 percent. The bargaining zone, then, is a raise between 4 and 6 percent. Ideally, some compromise is reached between these levels and the new agreement submitted for a ratification vote by union membership.

Sometimes, this process goes quite smoothly. At other times, however, the two sides cannot—or will not—agree. The speed and ease with which such an impasse is resolved depend in part on the nature of the contract issues, the willingness of each side to use certain tactics, and the prospects for mediation or arbitration.

Contract Issues

The labor contract itself can address an array of different issues. Most of these concern demands that unions make on behalf of their members. In this section we will survey the categories of issues that are typically most important to union negotiators: *compensation*, *benefits*, and *job security*. Although few issues covered in a labor contract are company sponsored, we will also describe the kinds of *management rights* that are negotiated in most bargaining agreements.

First, note that bargaining items generally fall into two categories:

- *Mandatory items* are matters over which both parties must negotiate if either wants to. This category includes wages, working hours, and benefits.

- *Permissive items* may be negotiated if both parties agree. A union demand for veto power over the promotion of managerial personnel would be a permissive bargaining item.

Illegal items may not be brought to the table by either party. A management demand for a nonstrike clause would be an illegal item.

Compensation The most common issue is compensation. One aspect of compensation is current wages. Obviously, unions generally want their employees to earn higher wages and try to convince management to raise hourly wages for all or some employees.

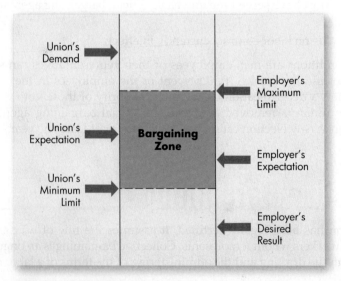

FIGURE AIV.5 The Bargaining Zone

Of equal concern to unions is future compensation, wage rates to be paid during subsequent years of the contract. One common tool for securing wage increases is a **cost-of-living adjustment (COLA).** Most COLA clauses tie future raises to the *consumer price index*, a government statistic that reflects changes in consumer purchasing power. The premise is that as the CPI increases by a specified amount during a given period of time, wages will automatically be increased. Almost half of all labor contracts today include COLA clauses.

Wage reopener clauses are now included in almost 10 percent of all labor contracts. Such a clause allows wage rates to be negotiated at preset times during the life of the contract. For example, a union might be uncomfortable with a long-term contract based solely on COLA wage increases. A long-term agreement might be more acceptable, however, if management agrees to renegotiate wages every two years.

Benefits   Employee benefits are also an important component in most labor contracts. Unions typically want employers to pay all or most of the costs of insurance for employees. Other benefits commonly addressed during negotiations include retirement benefits, paid holidays, and working conditions.

Job Security   Nevertheless, the UAW's top priority in its most recent negotiations with U.S. automakers has been job security, an increasingly important agenda item in many bargaining sessions today. In some cases, demands for job security entail the promise that a company not move to another location. In others, the contract may dictate that if the workforce is reduced, seniority will be used to determine which employees lose their jobs.

Other Union Issues   Other possible issues might include such things as working hours, overtime policies, rest period arrangements, differential pay plans for shift employees, the use of temporary workers, grievance procedures, and allowable union activities (dues collection, union bulletin boards, and so forth).

Management Rights   Management wants as much control as possible over hiring policies, work assignments, and so forth. Unions, meanwhile, often try to limit management rights by specifying hiring, assignment, and other policies. At a DaimlerChrysler plant in Detroit, for example, the contract stipulates that three workers are needed to change fuses in robots, a machinist to open the robot, an electrician to change the fuse, and a supervisor to oversee the process. As in this case, contracts often bar workers in one job category from performing work that falls in the domain of another. Unions try to secure jobs by defining as many different categories as possible (the DaimlerChrysler plant has more than 100). Of course, management resists the practice, which limits flexibility and makes it difficult to reassign workers.

When Bargaining Fails

An impasse occurs when, after a series of bargaining sessions, management and labor have failed to agree on a new contract or a contract to replace an agreement that is about to expire. Although it is generally agreed that both parties suffer when an impasse is reached and action is taken, each side can use several tactics to support its cause until the impasse is resolved.

Union Tactics   When their demands are not met, unions may bring a variety of tactics to the bargaining table. Chief among these is the strike, which may be supported by *pickets*, *boycotts*, or *both*.

THE STRIKE   A **strike** occurs when employees temporarily walk off the job and refuse to work. Most strikes in the United States are **economic strikes,** triggered by stalemates over mandatory bargaining items, including such noneconomic issues as working hours. For example, the Teamsters union struck United Parcel Service (UPS) a few years ago over several noneconomic issues. Specifically, the union wanted the firm to transform many of its temporary and part-time jobs into permanent and full-time

Cost-of-Living Adjustment (COLA) *labor contract clause tying future raises to changes in consumer purchasing power*

Wage Reopener Clauses *allow wage rates to be negotiated at preset times during the life of the contract*

strike *occur when employees temporarily walk off the job and refuse to work*

economic strikes *strikes triggered by stalemates over mandatory bargaining items, including such noneconomic issues as working hours*

jobs. Strikers returned to work only when UPS agreed to create 10,000 new jobs. More recently, the same union struck Union Pacific Corp. in Lockheed-Martin plant in Fort Worth, Texas, staged a two-week strike. Reflected the president of the union local: "I think our people gained a lot of respect for taking a stand. We had a good strike."

Still, there are far fewer strikes today than there were in previous years. For example, there were 222 strikes in the United States in 1960 involving a total of 896,000 workers. In 1970, 2,468,000 workers took part in 381 strikes. But in 1990 there were only 44 strikes involving 185,000 workers. Since 1990, the largest number of major strikes in one year was 45 in 1994. There were only 19 major strikes in 2012.[5]

Not all strikes are legal. **Sympathy strikes** (also called **secondary strikes**), which occur when one union strikes in sympathy with action initiated by another, may violate the sympathetic union's contract. **Wildcat strikes**, strikes unauthorized by the union that occur during the life of a contract, deprive strikers of their status as employees and thus of the protection of the national labor law.

OTHER LABOR ACTIONS To support a strike, a union faced with an impasse has recourse to additional legal activities:

- In **picketing**, workers march at the entrance to the employer's facility with signs explaining their reasons for striking.

- A **boycott** occurs when union members agree not to buy the products of a targeted employer. Workers may also urge consumers to boycott the firm's products.

- Another alternative to striking is a work **slowdown**. Instead of striking, workers perform their jobs at a much slower pace than normal. A variation is the sickout, during which large numbers of workers call in sick. Pilots at American Airlines engaged in a massive "sickout" a few years ago, causing the airline to cancel thousands of flights before a judge ordered them back into the cockpit.[6]

Management Tactics
Like workers, management can respond forcefully to an impasse:

Lockouts *occur when employers deny employees access to the workplace*

- **Lockouts** occur when employers deny employees access to the workplace. Lockouts are illegal if they are used as offensive weapons to give management a bargaining advantage. However, they are legal if management has a legitimate business need (for instance, avoiding a buildup of perishable inventory). Although rare today, ABC once locked out its off-camera employees because they staged an unannounced one-day strike during a critical broadcasting period.[7] Likewise, NFL players were locked out during contract negotiations in 2011 and the referees were locked out during contract negotiations in 2012.

Strikebreakers *temporary or permanent replacements*

A firm can also hire temporary or permanent replacements called **strikebreakers.** (The NFL employed temporary referees during the 2012 lockout.) However, the law forbids the permanent replacement of workers who strike because of unfair practices. In some cases, an employer can also obtain legal injunctions that either prohibit workers from striking or prohibit a union from interfering with its efforts to use replacement workers.

Mediation and Arbitration
Rather than wield these often unpleasant weapons against one another, labor and management can agree to call in a third party to help resolve the dispute:

Mediation *a neutral third party (the mediator) can advise, but cannot impose a settlement on the other parties*

- In **mediation,** the neutral third party (the mediator) can advise, but cannot impose a settlement on the other parties.

Voluntary Arbitration *a neutral third party (the arbitrator) dictates a settlement between the two sides, who have agreed to submit to outside judgment*

- In **voluntary arbitration,** the neutral third party (the arbitrator) dictates a settlement between the two sides, who have agreed to submit to outside judgment.

Compulsory Arbitration *used to settle disputes between the government and public employees such as firefighters and police officers*

- In some cases, arbitration is legally required to settle bargaining disputes. **Compulsory arbitration** is used to settle disputes between the government and public employees such as firefighters and police officers.

Administering a Labor Agreement

Once a labor agreement has been reached, its details are written into the form of a contract legally enforceable in the courts. Labor contracts almost always have precise agreements as to how the agreement will be enforced. In some cases, of course, enforcement is quite clear. If the two sides agree that the company will increase wages by 2 percent per year over the next three years according to a pre-scribed schedule, then there is little opportunity for disagreement. Wage increases can be mathematically calculated and union members will see the effects in their paychecks. But other provisions may be much more prone to misinterpretation and different perceptions.

Suppose, for example, that a labor contract specifies the process for allocating overtime assignments. Such strategies are often complex, and the employer may have to take into account a variety of factors, such as seniority, previous overtime allocations, the hours or days in which the overtime work is needed, and so forth. Now suppose that a factory supervisor is trying to follow the labor contract and of-fers overtime to a certain employee. This employee, however, indicates that before accepting, it may be necessary to check with his wife to learn more about other obli-gations and commitments. The supervisor, however, may feel the pressure of a dead-line and award the overtime opportunity to a second employee. If the first employee objects to this course of action, the he may file a complaint with the union.

When such differences of opinions arise, the union member takes the complaint to the shop steward. The shop steward may advise the employee that the supervisor handled things properly, but there are other appeal mechanisms, and the employee, even if refuted by the shop steward, still has channels for appeal.

Of course, if the shop steward agrees with the employee, the shop steward may follow prescribed methods for pursuing the complaint. The prescribed methods might include talking with the supervisor to get the other side of the story and then provide for lines of appeal on up the hierarchy of both the union and the company. In some cases, mediation or arbitration may be called into play, as may other efforts to resolve the dispute. The overtime, for example, may be reassigned to the first employee. Or the overtime may remain with the second employee while the first employee is also paid.

Let's return for a moment to the agreement reached by the Teamsters and United Parcel Service that we described previously. In early 2000, the union became con-cerned that UPS was not moving quickly enough to create the new jobs to which it had agreed two years earlier. The union submitted its complaint to arbitration and won. UPS was given a specific timetable for adding the new jobs as agreed.[8]

end notes

[1] David Lipsky and Clifford Donn, *Collective Bargaining in American Industry* (Lexington, MA: Lexington Books, 1981).

[2] David Koenig, "Labor Unions Say Recent Victories Signal a Comeback," Associated Press news release published in *The Bryan-College Station Eagle*, June 11, 2000, pp. E1, E6.

[3] Aaron Bernstein, "Welch's March to the South," *Business Week*, December 6, 1999, pp. 74, 78.

[4] Paula Dwyer, "Hoffa at Halftime," *Business Week*, June 26, 2000, pp. 156–160.

[5] http://www.bls.gov/news.release/pdf/wkstp.pdf.

[6] Stephanie Amour, "Will Fine Divide or Solidify Pilots?" *USA Today*, February 15, 1999, p. 1B.

[7] Stephanie Amour, "ABC Locks Out Striking Employees," *USA Today*, November 3, 1998, p. B1.

[8] Dwyer, "Hoffa at Halftime," pp. 156–160.

glossary

A

Absenteeism when an employee does not show up for work.

Absolute Advantage the ability to produce something more efficiently than any other country can.

Accommodative Stance approach to social responsibility by which a company, if specifically asked to do so, exceeds legal minimums in its commitments to groups and individuals in its social environment.

Accountability obligation employees have to their manager for the successful completion of an assigned task.

Accounting (or accountancy) comprehensive system for collecting, analyzing, and communicating financial information.

Accounting Information System (AIS) organized procedure for identifying, measuring, recording, and retaining financial information for use in accounting statements and management reports.

Accounting Equation Assets = Liabilities + Owner's Equity; used by accountants to balance data for the firms financial transactions at various points in the year.

Accounts Payable (Payables) current liability consisting of bills owed to suppliers, plus wages and taxes due within the coming year.

Acquisition the purchase of one company by another.

Activity Ratio financial ratio for evaluating management's efficiency in using a firm's assets.

Adverse Impact when minorities and women meet or pass the requirement for a job at a rate less than 80 percent of the rate of majority group members.

Advertising any form of paid nonpersonal communication used by an identified sponsor to persuade or inform potential buyers about a product.

Advertising promotional tool consisting of paid, nonpersonal communication used by an identified sponsor to inform an audience about a product.

Advertising Media variety of communication devices for carrying a seller's message to potential customers.

Affect a person's feelings toward something.

Affirmative Action intentionally seeking and hiring employees from groups that are underrepresented in the organization.

Affirmative Action Plan written statement of how the organization intends to actively recruit, hire, and develop members of relevant protected classes.

Age Discrimination in Employment Act outlaws discrimination against people older than 40 years.

Agency Shop requires employees to pay union fees even if they choose not to join.

Agent individual or organization acting for and in the name of another party.

Aggregate Output the total quantity of goods and services produced by an economic system during a given period.

American Federation of Labor (AFL) an association of craft unions formed in 1886 by Samuel Gompers and others; the AFL had no political or social agenda but simply sought to improve working conditions and pay for its members.

Americans With Disabilities Act forbids discrimination on the basis of disabilities and requires employers to provide reasonable accommodations for disabled employees.

Angel Investors outside investors who provide new capital for firms in return for a share of equity ownership.

Annual Percentage Rate (APR) one-year rate that is charged for borrowing, expressed as a percentage of the borrowed principal.

Anti-Virus Software product that protects systems by searching incoming e-mails and data files for "signatures" of known viruses and virus-like characteristics.

Apparent Authority agent's authority, based on the principal's compliance, to bind a principal to a certain course of action.

Appellate Court court that reviews case records of trials whose findings have been appealed.

Arbitration method of resolving a labor dispute in which both parties agree to submit to the judgment of a neutral party.

Assembly Line Layout a same-steps layout in which a product moves step by step through a plant on conveyor belts or other equipment until it is completed.

Asset any economic resource expected to benefit a firm or an individual who owns it.

Asset Allocation relative amount of funds invested in (or allocated to) each of several investment alternatives.

Association of Southeast Asian Nations (ASEAN) organization for economic, political, social, and cultural cooperation among Southeast Asian nations.

Attitudes a person's beliefs and feelings about specific ideas, situations, or people.

Audit systematic examination of a company's accounting system to determine whether its financial reports reliably represent its operations.

Authoritarianism the extent to which a person believes that power and status differences are appropriate within hierarchical social systems, such as organizations.

Authority power to make the decisions necessary to complete a task.

Automated Teller Machine (ATM) electronic machine that allows bank customers to conduct account-related activities 24 hours a day, 7 days a week.

B

Balance of Trade the economic value of all the products that a country exports minus the economic value of all the products it imports.

Balance of Payments flow of all money into or out of a country.

Balance Sheet financial statement that supplies detailed information about a firm's assets, liabilities, and owner's equity.

Banker's Acceptance bank promise, issued for a buyer, to pay a designated firm a specified amount at a future date.

Bankruptcy court-granted permission for a company to not pay some or all debts.

Bargain Retailer retailer carrying a wide range of products at bargain prices.

Bear Market period of falling stock prices marked by negative investor sentiments with motivation to sell ahead of anticipated losses.

Behavioral Approach to Leadership focused on determining what behaviors are employed by leaders.

Behavioral Segmentation a segmentation strategy that uses behavioral variables to identify different market segments.

Behavioral Variables behavioral patterns displayed by groups of consumers and that are used in developing a segmentation strategy.

Benefits compensation other than wages and salaries.

"Big Five" personality traits five fundamental personality traits especially relevant to organizations.

Blue-Chip Stock common stock issued by a well-established and respected company with a sound financial history and a stable pattern of dividend payouts.

Board of Directors governing body of a corporation that reports to its shareholders and delegates power to run its day-to-day operations while remaining responsible for sustaining its assets.

Bond Indenture legal document containing complete details of a bond issue.

Bondholder's Claim request for court enforcement of a bond's terms of payment.

Bonus individual performance incentive in the form of a special payment made over and above the employee's salary.

Book Value value of a common stock expressed as the firm's owners equity divided by the number of common shares.

Book-Entry Ownership procedure that holds investor's shares in book-entry form, rather than issuing a physical paper certificate of ownership.

Bookkeeping recording of accounting transactions.

Boycott labor action in which workers refuse to buy the products of a targeted employer.

Branch Office foreign office set up by an international or multinational firm.

Brand Competition competitive marketing that appeals to consumer perceptions of benefits of products offered by particular companies.

Brand Loyalty pattern of repeated consumer purchasing based on satisfaction with a product's performance.

Brand Awareness extent to which a brand name comes to mind when a consumer considers a particular product category.

Branding process of using symbols to communicate the qualities of a product made by a particular producer.

Breakeven Analysis identifies the sales volume where total costs equal total revenues by assessing costs versus revenues at various sales volumes and showing, at any particular selling price, the amount of loss or profit for each volume of sales.

Breakeven Point sales volume at which the seller's total revenue from sales equals total costs (variable and fixed) with neither profit nor loss.

Broker independent intermediary who matches numerous sellers and buyers as needed, often without knowing in advance who they will be.

Budget detailed statement of estimated receipts and expenditures for a future period of time.

Bull Market period of rising stock prices, lasting 12 months or longer, featuring investor confidence for future gains and motivation to buy.

Bundling Strategy grouping several products together to be sold as a single unit at a reduced price, rather than individually.

Business Interruption Insurance insurance covering income lost during times when a company is unable to conduct business.

Business Continuation Agreement special form of business insurance whereby owners arrange to buy the interests of deceased associates from their heirs.

Business Agent or Business Representative a full-time employee hired to act as a liaison between union members and supervisors if a local union is large.

Business organization that provides goods or services to earn profits.

Business Cycle short-term pattern of economic expansions and contractions.

Business Ethics ethical or unethical behaviors by employees in the context of their jobs.

Business Plan document in which the entrepreneur summarizes his or her business strategy for the proposed new venture and how that strategy will be implemented.

Business Practice Law law or regulation governing business practices in given countries.

Business (or Competitive) Strategy strategy, at the business-unit or product-line level, focusing on improving a firm's competitive position.

Business Process Reengineering rethinking and radical redesign of business processes to improve performance, quality, and productivity.

C

Cafeteria Benefits Plan benefit plan that sets limits on benefits per employee, each of whom may choose from a variety of alternative benefits.

Capacity competence required of individuals entering into a binding contract.

Capacity amount of a product that a company can produce under normal conditions.

Capital funds needed to create and operate a business enterprise.

Capital Items expensive, long-lasting, infrequently purchased industrial products, such as a building, or industrial services, such as a long-term agreement for data warehousing services.

Capital Gain profit realized from the increased value of an investment.

Capitalism system that sanctions the private ownership of the factors of production and encourages entrepreneurship by offering profits as an incentive.

Cartel association of producers whose purpose is to control supply and prices.

Catalog Showroom bargain retailer in which customers place orders for catalog items to be picked up at on-premises warehouses.

Centralized Organization organization in which most decision-making authority is held by upper-level management.

Certified Public Accountant (CPA) accountant licensed by the state and offering services to the public.

Certified Management Accountant (CMA) professional designation awarded by the Institute of Management Accountants (IMA) in recognition of management accounting qualifications.

Certified Fraud Examiner (CFE) professional designation administered by the ACFE in recognition of qualifications for a specialty area within forensic accounting.

Chain of Command reporting relationships within a company.

Channel Conflict conflict arising when the members of a distribution channel disagree over the roles they should play or the rewards they should receive.

Channel Captain channel member who is most powerful in determining the roles and rewards of other members.

Charismatic Leadership type of influence based on the leaders personal charisma.

Check demand deposit order instructing a bank to pay a given sum to a specified payee.

Checking Account (Demand Deposit) bank account funds, owned by the depositor, that may be withdrawn at any time by check or cash.

Chief Executive Officer (CEO) top manager who is responsible for the overall performance of a corporation.

Civil Rights Act of 1991 amended the original Civil Rights Act.

Classical Theory of Motivation theory holding that workers are motivated solely by money.

Client-Server Network common business network in which clients make requests for information or resources and servers provide the services.

Closed Shop a workplace in which only workers already belonging to a union may be hired by an employer.

Closely Held (or Private) Corporation corporation whose stock is held by only a few people and is not available for sale to the general public.

Closing step in the personal selling process in which salespeople ask prospective customers to buy products.

Coalition an informal alliance of individuals or groups formed to achieve a common goal.

Code of Professional Conduct code of ethics for CPAs as maintained and enforced by the AICPA.

Coercive Power the power to force compliance by means of psychological, emotional, or physical threat.

Cognition the knowledge a person presumes to have about something.

Cognitive Dissonance when two sets of cognitions or perceptions are contradictory or incongruent.

Collateral asset pledged for the fulfillment of repaying a loan.

Collective Bargaining the process by which union leaders and managers negotiate common terms and conditions of employment for the workers represented by unions.

Collective Bargaining process by which labor and management negotiate conditions of employment for union-represented workers.

Collusion illegal agreement between two or more companies to commit a wrongful act.

Commercial Bank company that accepts deposits that it uses to make loans, earn profits, pay interest to depositors, and pay dividends to owners.

Committee and Team Authority authority granted to committees or teams involved in a firm's daily operations.

Common Law body of decisions handed down by courts ruling on individual cases.

Common Stock most basic form of ownership, including voting rights on major issues, in a company.

Communism political system in which the government owns and operates all factors of production.

Comparative Advantage the ability to produce some products more efficiently than others.

Compensation System total package of rewards that organizations provide to individuals in return for their labor.

Compensatory Damages monetary payments intended to redress injury actually suffered because of a tort.

Competition vying among businesses for the same resources or customers.

Competitive Product Analysis process by which a company analyzes a competitor's products to identify desirable improvements.

Competitive Environment the competitive system in which businesses compete.

Compound Growth compounding of interest over time with each additional time period, interest returns accumulate and earn more interest.

Compulsory Arbitration used to settle disputes between the government and public employees such as firefighters and police officers.

Computer Network group of two or more computers linked together by some form of cabling or by wireless technology to share data or resources, such as a printer.

Computer-Aided Design (CAD) IS with software that helps knowledge workers design products by simulating them and displaying them in three-dimensional graphics.

Computer-Aided Manufacturing (CAM) IS that uses computers to design and control equipment in a manufacturing process.

Conceptual Skills abilities to think in the abstract, diagnose and analyze different situations, and see beyond the present situation.

Congress of Industrial Organizations (CIO) an association of industrial unions formed in 1938 after being expelled from the American Federation of Labor (AFL).

Consideration item of value exchanged between parties to create a valid contract.

Consistency dimension of quality that refers to sameness of product quality from unit to unit.

Consumer Price Index (CPI) a measure of the prices of typical products purchased by consumers living in urban areas.

Consumer Goods physical products purchased by consumers for personal use.

Consumer Behavior study of the decision process by which people buy and consume products.

Consumer person who purchases products for personal use.

Consumerism form of social activism dedicated to protecting the rights of consumers in their dealings with businesses.

Contingency Planning identifying aspects of a business or its environment that might entail changes in strategy.

Contingent Worker employee hired on something other than a full-time basis to supplement an organization's permanent workforce.

Contract agreement between two or more parties enforceable in court.

Controller person who manages all of a firm's accounting activities (chief accounting officer).

Controlling management process of monitoring an organization's performance to ensure that it is meeting its goals.

Convenience Goods inexpensive physical goods that are consumed rapidly and regularly.

Convenience Services inexpensive services that are consumed rapidly and regularly.

Convenience Store retail store offering easy accessibility, extended hours, and fast service.

Cooperative form of ownership in which a group of sole proprietorships or partnerships agree to work together for common benefits.

Copyright exclusive ownership right belonging to the creator of a book, article, design, illustration, photo, film, or musical work.

Core Competencies for Accounting the combination of skills, technology, and knowledge that will be necessary for the future CPA.

Corporate Social Audit systematic analysis of a firm's success in using funds earmarked for meeting its social responsibility goals.

Corporate Governance roles of shareholders, directors, and other managers in corporate decision making and accountability.

Corporate Strategy strategy for determining the firm's overall attitude toward growth and the way it will manage its businesses or product lines.

Corporate Culture the shared experiences, stories, beliefs, and norms that characterize an organization.

Corporate Blogs comments and opinions published on the Web by or for an organization to promote its activities.

Corporate Bond formal pledge obligating the issuer (the company) to pay interest periodically and repay the principal at maturity.

Corporate Raider investor conducting a type of hostile corporate takeover against the wishes of the company.

Corporation business that is legally considered an entity separate from its owners and is liable for its own debts; owners liability extends to the limits of their investments.

Cost-of-Living Adjustment (COLA) labor contract clause tying future raises to changes in consumer purchasing power.

Cost-Oriented Pricing pricing that considers the firm's desire to make a profit and its need to cover operating costs.

Cost of Revenues costs that a company incurs to obtain revenues from other companies.

Cost of Goods Sold costs of obtaining materials for making the products sold by a firm during the year.

Counterproductive Behaviors behaviors that detract from organizational performance.

Coupon sales-promotion technique in which a certificate is issued entitling the buyer to a reduced price.

Creative Selling personal-selling task in which salespeople try to persuade buyers to purchase products by providing information about their benefits.

Credit Union nonprofit, cooperative financial institution owned and run by its members, usually employees of a particular organization.

Crisis Management organization's methods for dealing with emergencies.

Cultural Influences include culture, subculture, and social class influences that marketers use to study buying behavior.

Currency (Cash) government-issued paper money and metal coins.

Current Asset asset that can or will be converted into cash within a year.

Current Liability debt that must be paid within one year.

Current Ratio financial ratio for measuring a company's ability to pay current debts out of current assets.

Current Dividend Yield and Current Interest Yield yearly dollar amount of income divided by the investment's current market value, expressed as a percentage.

Customer Departmentalization dividing an organization to offer products and meet needs for identifiable customer groups.

Customer Relationship Management (CRM) organized methods that a firm uses to build better information connections with clients, so that stronger company-client relationships are developed.

Cybermall collection of virtual storefronts (business websites) representing a variety of products and product lines on the Internet.

D

Data Warehousing the collection, storage, and retrieval of data in electronic files.

Data Mining the application of electronic technologies for searching, sifting, and reorganizing pools of data to uncover useful information.

Data raw facts and figures that, by themselves, may not have much meaning.

Debit Card plastic card that allows an individual to transfer money between accounts.

Debt company's total liabilities.

Debt Financing long-term borrowing from sources outside a company.

Decentralized Organization organization in which a great deal of decision-making authority is delegated to levels of management at points below the top.

Decision-Making Skills skills in defining problems and selecting the best courses of action.

Decision Tree Approach approach to leadership that provides decision rules for deciding how much participation to allow.

Decision Making choosing one alternative from among several options.

Decision-Making Process recognizing and defining the nature of a decision situation, identifying alternatives, choosing the "best" alternative, and putting it into practice.

Decision Support System (DSS) interactive system that creates virtual business models for a particular kind of decision and tests them with different data to see how they respond.

Decisional Roles a category of managerial roles including entrepreneur, disturbance handler, resource allocator, and negotiator.

Deductible amount of the loss that the insured must absorb before reimbursement is made.

Default failure of a borrower to make payment when due to a lender.

Defensive Stance approach to social responsibility by which a company meets only minimum legal requirements in its commitments to groups and individuals in its social environment.

Delegation process through which a manager allocates work to subordinates.

Demand the willingness and ability of buyers to purchase a good or service.

Demand and Supply Schedule assessment of the relationships among different levels of demand and supply at different price levels.

Demand Curve graph showing how many units of a product will be demanded (bought) at different prices.

Demographic Segmentation a segmentation strategy that uses demographic characteristics to identify different market segments.

Demographic Variables characteristics of populations that may be considered in developing a segmentation strategy.

Department Store large product-line retailer characterized by organization into specialized departments.

Departmentalization process of grouping jobs into logical units.

Depreciation accounting method for distributing the cost of an asset over its useful life.

Depression a prolonged and deep recession.

Deregulation elimination of rules that restrict business activity.

Detailed Schedule schedule showing daily work assignments with start and stop times for assigned jobs.

Development usually refers to teaching managers and professionals the skills needed for both present and future jobs.

Direct Channel distribution channel in which a product travels from producer to consumer without intermediaries.

Direct-Response Retailing form of nonstore retailing in which firms directly interact with customers to inform them of products and to receive sales orders.

Direct Selling form of nonstore retailing typified by door-to-door sales.

Direct (or interactive) marketing one-on-one nonpersonal selling by nonstore retailers and B2B sellers using direct contact with prospective customers, especially via the Internet.

Discount House bargain retailer that generates large sales volume by offering goods at substantial price reductions.

Discount Rate interest rate at which member banks can borrow money from the Fed.

Discounts price reduction offered as an incentive to purchase.

Distribution Mix combination of distribution channels by which a firm gets its products to end users.

Distribution Channel network of interdependent companies through which a product passes from producer to end user.

Diversification purchase of several different kinds of investments rather than just one.

Divestiture strategy whereby a firm sells one or more of its business units.

Dividend payment to shareholders, on a per-share basis, out of the company's earnings.

Division department that resembles a separate business in that it produces and markets its own products.

Divisional Structure organizational structure in which corporate divisions operate as autonomous businesses under the larger corporate umbrella.

Domestic Business Environment the environment in which a firm conducts its operations and derives its revenues.

Double Taxation situation in which taxes may be payable both by a corporation on its profits and by shareholders on dividend incomes.

Dow Jones Industrial Average (DJIA) oldest and most widely cited market index based on the prices of 30 blue-chip, large-cap industrial firms on the NYSE.

Drop Shippers limited-function merchant wholesaler that receives customer orders, negotiates with producers, takes title to goods, and arranges for shipment to customers.

Dumping practice of selling a product abroad for less than the cost of production.

E

e-Intermediary Internet distribution channel member that assists in delivering products to customers or that collects information about various sellers to be presented to consumers.

e-Catalog nonstore retailing in which the Internet is used to display products.

e-Commerce use of the Internet and other electronic means for retailing and business-to-business transactions.

Earnings Per Share profitability ratio measuring the net profit that the company earns for each share of outstanding stock.

Economic Strikes strikes triggered by stalemates over mandatory bargaining items, including such noneconomic issues as working hours.

Economic Environment relevant conditions that exist in the economic system in which a company operates.

Economic System a nation's system for allocating its resources among its citizens.

Economic Indicator a statistic that helps assess the performance of an economy.

Economic Environment relevant conditions that exist in the economic system in which a company operates.

Electronic Storefront commercial website at which customers gather information about products and buying opportunities, place orders, and pay for purchases.

Electronic Conferencing IT that allows groups of people to communicate simultaneously from various locations via e-mail, phone, or video.

Electronic Funds Transfer (EFT) communication of fund-transfer information over wire, cable, or microwave.

Electronic Communication Network (ECN) electronic trading system that brings buyers and sellers together outside traditional stock exchanges.

Embargo government order banning exportation or importation of a particular product or all products from a particular country.

Eminent Domain principle that the government may claim private land for public use by buying it at a fair price.

Emotional Intelligence (Emotional Quotient, Eq) the extent to which people are self-aware, can manage their emotions, can motivate themselves, express empathy for others, and possess social skills.

Emotional Motives reasons for purchasing a product that are based on nonobjective factors.

Employee Stock Ownership Plan (ESOP) arrangement in which a corporation holds its own stock in trust for its employees, who gradually receive ownership of the stock and control its voting rights.

Employee Behavior the pattern of actions by the members of an organization that directly or indirectly influences the organizations effectiveness.

Employee-Focused Leader Behavior leader behavior focusing on satisfaction, motivation, and well-being of employees.

Employee Information System (Skills Inventory) computerized system containing information on each employee's education, skills, work experiences, and career aspirations.

Employee Retirement Income Security Act (ERISA) of 1974 ensures the financial security of pension funds by regulating how they can be invested.

Employment at Will principle, increasingly modified by legislation and judicial decision, that organizations should be able to retain or dismiss employees at their discretion.

Encryption System software that assigns an e-mail message to a unique code number (digital fingerprint) for each computer so only that computer, not others, can open and read the message.

Entrepreneur individual who accepts the risks and opportunities involved in creating and operating a new business venture.

Entrepreneur business person who accepts both the risks and the opportunities involved in creating and operating a new business venture.

Entrepreneurship the process of seeking business opportunities under conditions of risk.

Environmental Analysis process of scanning the business environment for threats and opportunities.

Equal Employment Opportunity Commission (EEOC) federal agency enforcing several discrimination-related laws.

Equal Employment Opportunity legally mandated nondiscrimination in employment on the basis of race, creed, sex, or national origin.

Equal Pay Act of 1963 requires that men and women be paid the same amount for doing the same job.

Equity Theory theory of motivation holding that people evaluate their treatment by the organization relative to the treatment of others.

Equity Financing using the owner's funds from inside the company as the source for long-term funding.

Escalation of Commitment condition in which a decision maker becomes so committed to a course of action that she or he stays with it even when it appears to have been wrong.

Established Market one in which many firms compete according to relatively well-defined criteria.

Ethical Behavior behavior conforming to generally accepted social norms concerning beneficial and harmful actions.

Ethical Compliance the extent to which the members of the organization follow basic ethical (and legal) standards of behavior.

Ethical Leadership leader behaviors that reflect high ethical standards.

Ethics beliefs about what is right and wrong or good and bad in actions that affect others.

Euro a common currency shared among most of the members of the EU (excluding Denmark, Sweden, and the United Kingdom).

European Union (EU) agreement among major European nations to eliminate or make uniform most trade barriers affecting group members.

Evoked Set (or Consideration Set) group of products consumers will consider buying as a result of information search.

Exchange Rate rate at which the currency of one nation can be exchanged for the currency of another nation.

Exchange Rate the value of one currency compared to the value of another.

Exchange-Traded Fund (ETF) bundle of stocks or bonds that are in an index that tracks the overall movement of a market, but unlike a mutual fund can be traded like a stock.

Exclusive Distribution strategy by which a manufacturer grants exclusive rights to distribute or sell a product to a limited number of wholesalers or retailers in a given geographic area.

Expectancy Theory theory of motivation holding that people are motivated to work toward rewards that they want and that they believe they have a reasonable chance of obtaining.

Expense Items industrial products purchased and consumed within a year by firms producing other products.

Experimentation research method using a sample of potential consumers to obtain reactions to test versions of new products or variations of existing products.

Expert Power power derived from information or expertise.

Export product made or grown domestically but shipped and sold abroad.

Exporter firm that distributes and sells products to one or more foreign countries.

Express Authority agent's authority, derived from written agreement, to bind a principal to a certain course of action.

Express Warranty warranty whose terms are specifically stated by the seller.

External Environment everything outside an organization's boundaries that might affect it.

External Recruiting attracting persons outside the organization to apply for jobs.

Extranet system that allows outsiders limited access to a firm's internal information network.

F

Face Value (Par Value) amount of money that the bond buyer (lender) lent the issuer and that the lender will receive on repayment.

Factors of Production resources used in the production of goods and services labor, capital, entrepreneurs, physical resources, and information resources.

Factory Outlet bargain retailer owned by the manufacturer whose products it sells.

Fair Labor Standards Act addressed issues of minimum wages and maximum work hours.

Fair Labor Standards Act sets a minimum wage and requires the payment of overtime rates for work in excess of 40 hours per week.

Family and Medical Leave Act (FMLA) of 1993 requires employers to provide up to 12 weeks of unpaid leave for family and medical emergencies.

Federal Deposit Insurance Corporation (FDIC) federal agency that guarantees the safety of deposits up to $250,000 in the financial institutions that it insures.

Federal Reserve System (The Fed) central bank of the United States, which acts as the government's bank, serves member commercial banks, and controls the nation's money supply.

Federal Funds Rate (Key Rate) interest rate at which commercial banks lend reserves to each other, usually overnight.

Finance Company nondeposit institution that specializes in making loans to businesses and consumers.

Financial Planning process of looking at one's current financial condition, identifying ones goals, and anticipating requirements for meeting those goals.

Financial Accounting field of accounting concerned with external users of a company's financial information.

Financial Statement any of several types of reports summarizing a company's financial status to stakeholders and to aid in managerial decision making.

Firewall security system with special software or hardware devices designed to keep computers safe from hackers.

First-Mover Advantage any advantage that comes to a firm because it exploits an opportunity before any other firm does.

First-Line Manager manager responsible for supervising the work of employees.

Fiscal Policies policies used by a government regarding how it collects and spends revenue.

Fixed-Position Layout labor, equipment, materials, and other resources are brought to the geographic location where all production work is done.

Fixed Cost cost that is incurred regardless of the quantity of a product produced and sold.

Fixed Asset asset with long-term use or value, such as land, buildings, and equipment.

Flat Organizational Structure characteristic of decentralized companies with relatively few layers of management.

Flextime Programs method of increasing job satisfaction by allowing workers to adjust work schedules on a daily or weekly basis.

Focus Group research method using a group of people from a larger population who are asked their attitudes, opinions, and beliefs about a product in an open discussion.

Follow-Up operations control activity for ensuring that production decisions are being implemented.

Foreign Direct Investment (FDI) arrangement in which a firm buys or establishes tangible assets in another country.

Forensic Accounting the practice of accounting for legal purposes.

Form Utility providing products with features that customers want.

Franchise arrangement in which a buyer (franchisee) purchases the right to sell the good or service of the seller (franchiser).

Full-Service Merchant Wholesalers merchant wholesaler that provides credit, marketing, and merchandising services in addition to traditional buying and selling services.

Full Disclosure guideline that financial statements should not include just numbers but should also furnish management's interpretations and explanations of those numbers.

Functional Strategy strategy by which managers in specific areas decide how best to achieve corporate goals through productivity.

Functional Departmentalization dividing an organization according to groups' functions or activities.

Functional Structure organization structure in which authority is determined by the relationships between group functions and activities.

G

Gainsharing Plan incentive plan that rewards groups for productivity improvements.

Gantt Chart production schedule that breaks down large projects into steps to be performed and specifies the time required to perform each step.

GDP Per Capita gross domestic product divided by total population.

General Partnership business with two or more owners who share in both the operation of the firm and the financial responsibility for its debts.

General (or Active) Partner partner who actively manages a firm and who has unlimited liability for its debts.

General Agreement on Tariffs and Trade (GATT) international trade agreement to encourage the multilateral reduction or elimination of trade barriers.

Generally Accepted Accounting Principles (GAAP) accounting guidelines that govern the content and form of financial reports.

Geo-Demographic Segmentation using a combination of geographic and demographic traits for identifying different market segments in a segmentation strategy.

Geo-Demographic Variables combination of geographic and demographic traits used in developing a segmentation strategy.

Geographic Departmentalization dividing an organization according to the areas of the country or the world served by a business.

Geographic Variables geographic units that may be considered in developing a segmentation strategy.

Geographic Segmentation geographic units, from countries to neighborhoods, that may be considered in identifying different market segments in a segmentation strategy.

Global Business Environment the international forces that affect a business.

Globalization process by which the world economy is becoming a single interdependent system.

Goal Orientation the manner in which people are motivated to work toward different kinds of goals.

Goal objective that a business hopes and plans to achieve.

Goods Operations (Goods Production) activities producing tangible products, such as radios, newspapers, buses, and textbooks.

Goodwill amount paid for an existing business above the value of its other assets.

Grapevine informal communication network that runs through an organization.

Gross Domestic Product (GDP) total value of all goods and services produced within a given period by a national economy through domestic factors of production.

Gross National Product (GNP) total value of all goods and services produced by a national economy within a given period regardless of where the factors of production are located.

Gross Profit preliminary, quick-to-calculate profit figure calculated from the firms revenues minus its cost of revenues (the direct costs of getting the revenues).

H

Hacker cybercriminal who gains unauthorized access to a computer or network, either to steal information, money, or property or to tamper with data.

Hardware physical components of a computer network, such as keyboards, monitors, system units, and printers.

Hawthorne Effect tendency for productivity to increase when workers believe they are receiving special attention from management.

Hierarchy of Human Needs Model theory of motivation describing five levels of human needs and arguing that basic needs must be fulfilled before people work to satisfy higher-level needs.

High-Contact System level of customer contact in which the customer is part of the system during service delivery.

Hostile Work Environment form of sexual harassment deriving from off-color jokes, lewd comments, and so forth.

Human Relations Skills skills in understanding and getting along with people.

Human Resource Management (HRM) set of organizational activities directed at attracting, developing, and maintaining an effective workforce.

Human Capital reflects the organizations investment in attracting, retaining, and motivating an effective workforce.

Hypertext Transfer Protocol (HTTP) communications protocol used for the World Wide Web, in which related pieces of information on separate Web pages are connected using hyperlinks.

I

Identity Theft unauthorized use of personal information (such as Social Security number and address) to get loans, credit cards, or other monetary benefits by impersonating the victim.

Implied Authority agents authority, derived from business custom, to bind a principal to a certain course of action.

Implied Warranty warranty, dictated by law, based on the principle that products should fulfill advertised promises and serve the purposes for which they are manufactured and sold.

Import product made or grown abroad but sold domestically.

Importer firm that buys products in foreign markets and then imports them for resale in its home country.

Incentive Program special compensation program designed to motivate high performance.

Income Statement (Profit-and-Loss Statement) financial statement listing a firm's annual revenues and expenses so that a bottom line shows annual profit or loss.

Independent Agent foreign individual or organization that agrees to represent an exporters interests.

Individual Differences personal attributes that vary from one person to another.

Individual Retirement Account (IRA) tax-deferred pension fund that wage earners set up to supplement retirement funds.

Industrial Unionism the organizing of employees by industry rather than by skill or occupation.

Industrial Goods physical products purchased by companies to produce other products.

Industrial Market organizational market consisting of firms that buy goods that are either converted into products or used during production.

Industrial Buyer a company or other organization that buys products for use in producing other products (goods or services).

Industrial Selling selling products to other businesses, either for the purpose of manufacturing or for resale.

Inflation occurs when widespread price increases occur throughout an economic system.

Informal Organization network, unrelated to the firm's formal authority structure, of everyday social interactions among company employees.

Information Resources data and other information used by businesses.

Information Technology (IT) various appliances and devices for creating, storing, exchanging, and using information in diverse modes, including visual images, voice, multimedia, and business data.

Information system (IS) system that uses IT resources to convert data into information and to collect, process, and transmit that information for use in decision making.

Information meaningful, useful interpretation of data.

Information Systems Managers managers who are responsible for the systems used for gathering, organizing, and distributing information.

Initial Public Offering (IPO) first sale of a company's stock to the general public.

Insider Trading illegal practice of using special knowledge about a firm for profit or gain.

Insider Trading illegal practice of using special knowledge about a firm for profit or gain.

Institutional Investor large investor, such as a mutual fund or a pension fund, that purchases large blocks of corporate stock.

Institutional Market organizational market consisting of such nongovernmental buyers of goods and services as hospitals, churches, museums, and charitable organizations.

Insurance Premium fee paid to an insurance company by a policyholder for insurance coverage.

Insurance Policy formal agreement to pay the policyholder a specified amount in the event of certain losses.

Insurance Company nondeposit institution that invests funds collected as premiums charged for insurance coverage.

Intangible Personal Property property that cannot be seen but that exists by virtue of written documentation.

Intangible Asset nonphysical asset, such as a patent or trademark, that has economic value in the form of expected benefit.

Integrated Marketing Strategy strategy that blends together the Four Ps of marketing to ensure their compatibility with one another and with the company's nonmarketing activities as well.

Intellectual Property property created through a person's creative activities.

Intellectual Property something produced by the intellect or mind that has commercial value.

Intensive Distribution strategy by which a product is distributed through as many channels as possible.

Intention part of an attitude that guides a person's behavior.

Intentional Tort tort resulting from the deliberate actions of a party.

Interest fee paid to a lender for the use of borrowed funds; like a rental fee.

Intermediary individual or firm that helps to distribute a product.

Intermediate Goal goal set for a period of one to five years into the future.

Internal Recruiting considering present employees as candidates for openings.

International Law general set of cooperative agreements and guidelines established by countries to govern the actions of individuals, businesses, and nations.

International Firm firm that conducts a significant portion of its business in foreign countries.

International Organizational Structures approaches to organizational structure developed in response to the need to manufacture, purchase, and sell in global markets.

International Competition competitive marketing of domestic products against foreign products.

International Accounting Standards Board (IASB) organization responsible for developing a set of global accounting standards and for gaining implementation of those standards.

International Monetary Fund (IMF) UN agency consisting of about 150 nations that have combined resources to promote stable exchange rates, provide temporary short-term loans, and serve other purposes.

Internet gigantic system of interconnected computer networks linked together by voice, electronic, and wireless technologies.

Intranet organization's private network of internally linked websites accessible only to employees.

Intrapreneuring process of creating and maintaining the innovation and flexibility of a small-business environment within the confines of a large organization.

Intuition an innate belief about something, often without conscious consideration.

Inventory Control process of receiving, storing, handling, and counting of all raw materials, partly finished goods, and finished goods.

Investment Bank financial institution that specializes in issuing and reselling new securities.

Involuntary Bankruptcy bankruptcy proceedings initiated by the creditors of an indebted individual or organization.

ISO 9000 program certifying that a factory, laboratory, or office has met the quality management standards set by the International Organization for Standardization.

ISO 14000 certification program attesting to the fact that a factory, laboratory, or office has improved its environmental performance.

J

Job Specialization the process of identifying the specific jobs that need to be done and designating the people who will perform them.

Job Satisfaction degree of enjoyment that people derive from performing their jobs.

Job Enrichment method of increasing job satisfaction by adding one or more motivating factors to job activities.

Job Redesign method of increasing job satisfaction by designing a more satisfactory fit between workers and their jobs.

Job Analysis systematic analysis of jobs within an organization.

Job Description description of the duties and responsibilities of a job, its working conditions, and the tools, materials, equipment, and information used to perform it.

Job Specification description of the skills, abilities, and other credentials and qualifications required by a job.

Joint Venture strategic alliance in which the collaboration involves joint ownership of the new venture.

Just-in-Time (Jit) Production type of lean production system that brings together all materials at the precise time they are required at each production stage.

K

Key Person Insurance special form of business insurance designed to offset expenses entailed by the loss of key employees.

Knowledge Workers employees who are of value because of the knowledge they possess.

Knowledge Information System information system that supports knowledge workers by providing resources to create, store, use, and transmit new knowledge for useful applications.

L

Labor Union a group of individuals working together to achieve shared job-related goals, such as higher pay, shorter working hours, more job security, greater benefits, or better working conditions.

Labor Relations the process of dealing with employees who are represented by a union.

Labor (Human Resources) physical and mental capabilities of people as they contribute to economic production.

Labor-Management Relations Act (also known as the *Taft-Hartley Act*) passed to limit union power.

Labor Union group of individuals working together to achieve shared job-related goals, such as higher pay, shorter working hours, more job security, greater benefits, or better working conditions.

Labor Relations process of dealing with employees who are represented by a union.

Landrum-Griffin Act or Labor-Management Reporting and Disclosure Act amendment to the National Labor Relations Act that imposed regulations on internal union procedures.

Law of Demand principle that buyers will purchase (demand) more of a product as its price drops and less as its price increases.

Law of Supply principle that producers will offer (supply) more of a product for sale as its price rises and less as its price drops.

Laws codified rules of behavior enforced by a society.

Leader Member Exchange (lmx) Model approach to leadership that stresses the importance of variable relationships between supervisors and each of their subordinates.

Leadership the processes and behaviors used by someone, such as a manager, to motivate, inspire, and influence the behaviors of others.

Leadership Substitutes individual, task, and organizational characteristics that tend to outweigh the need for a leader to initiate or direct employee performance.

Leadership Neutralizers factors that may render leader behaviors ineffective.

Leading management process of guiding and motivating employees to meet an organization's objectives.

Lean Production System production system designed for smooth production flows that avoid inefficiencies, eliminate unnecessary inventories, and continuously improve production processes.

Legal Compliance the extent to which the organization conforms to local, state, federal, and international laws.

Legitimate Power power granted through the organizational hierarchy.

Letter of Credit bank promise, issued for a buyer, to pay a designated firm a certain amount of money if specified conditions are met.

Leverage ability to finance an investment through borrowed funds.

Liability Insurance insurance covering losses resulting from damage to people or property when the insured party is judged liable.

Liability debt owed by a firm to an outside organization or individual.

Licensed Brands brand-name product for whose name the seller has purchased the right from an organization of individual.

Licensing Arrangement arrangement in which firms choose foreign individuals or organizations to manufacture or market their products in another country.

Limited Partnership type of partnership consisting of limited partners and a general (or managing) partner.

Limited Partner partner who does not share in a firm's management and is liable for its debts only to the limits of said partner's investment.

Limited Liability legal principle holding investors liable for a firm's debts only to the limits of their personal investments in it.

Limited Liability Corporation (LLC) hybrid of a publicly held corporation and a partnership in which owners are taxed as partners but enjoy the benefits of limited liability.

Limited-Function Merchant Wholesaler merchant wholesaler that provides a limited range of services.

Line Authority organizational structure in which authority flows in a direct chain of command from the top of the company to the bottom.

Line Department department directly linked to the production and sales of a specific product.

Liquidity ease with which an asset can be converted into cash.

Load Fund mutual fund in which investors are charged sales commissions when they buy in or sell out.

Loan Principal amount of money that is loaned and must be repaid.

Lobbying the use of persons or groups to formally represent an organization or group of organizations before political bodies.

Local Unions (locals) organized at the level of a single company, plant, or small geographic region.

Local Content Law law requiring that products sold in a particular country be at least partly made there.

Local Area Network (LAN) computers that are linked in a small area, such as all of a firm's computers within a single building.

Lockout management tactic whereby workers are denied access to the employer's workplace.

Lockouts occur when employers deny employees access to the workplace.

Locus of Control the extent to which people believe that their behavior has a real effect on what happens to them.

Long-Term Goal goal set for an extended time, typically five years or more into the future.

Long-Term Liability debt that is not due for at least one year.

Low-Contact System level of customer contact in which the customer need not be part of the system to receive the service.

Loyalty Programs sales promotion technique in which frequent customers are rewarded for making repeat purchases.

M

M-1 measure of the money supply that includes only the most liquid (spendable) forms of money.

M-2 measure of the money supply that includes all the components of M-1 plus the forms of money that can be easily converted into spendable forms.

Machiavellianism used to describe behavior directed at gaining power and controlling the behavior of others.

Mail Order (catalog marketing) form of nonstore retailing in which customers place orders for catalog merchandise received through the mail.

Make-To-Order Operations activities for one-of-a-kind or custom-made production.

Make-To-Stock Operations activities for producing standardized products for mass consumption.

Management process of planning, organizing, leading, and controlling an organization's resources to achieve its goals.

Management By Objectives (MBO) set of procedures involving both managers and subordinates in setting goals and evaluating progress.

Management Information System (MIS) computer system that supports managers by providing information reports, schedules, plans, and budgets that can be used for making decisions.

Management Advisory Services assistance provided by CPA firms in areas such as financial planning, information systems design, and other areas of concern for client firms.

Management Accountant private accountant who provides financial services to support managers in various business activities within a firm.

Managerial Ethics standards of behavior that guide individual managers in their work.

Managerial (Management) Accounting field of accounting that serves internal users of a company's financial information.

Market Economy economy in which individuals control production and allocation decisions through supply and demand.

Market mechanism for exchange between buyers and sellers of a particular good or service.

Market Price (Equilibrium Price) profit-maximizing price at which the quantity of goods demanded and the quantity of goods supplied are equal.

Market Segmentation process of dividing a market into categories of customer types, or "segments" having similar wants and needs and who can be expected to show interest in the same products.

Market Share (or Market Penetration) company's percentage of the total industry sales for a specific product type.

Market Value current price of a share of stock in the stock market.

Market Index statistical indicator designed to measure the performance of a large group of stocks or track the price changes of a stock market.

Market Capitalization (Market Cap) total dollar value of all the company's outstanding shares.

Marketing activities, a set of institutions, and processes for creating, communicating, delivering, and exchanging offerings that have value for customers, clients, partners, and society at large.

Marketing Plan detailed strategy for focusing marketing efforts on consumer's needs and wants.

Marketing Objectives the things marketing intends to accomplish in its marketing plan.

Marketing Strategy all the marketing programs and activities that will be used to achieve the marketing goals.

Marketing Manager manager who plans and implements the marketing activities that result in the transfer of products from producer to consumer.

Marketing Mix combination of product, pricing, promotion, and place (distribution) strategies used to market products.

Marketing Research the study of what customers need and want and how best to meet those needs and wants.

Markup amount added to an items purchase cost to sell it at a profit.

Mass Customization principle in which companies produce in large volumes, but each item features the unique options the customer prefers.

Master Limited Partnership form of ownership that sells shares to investors who receive profits and that pays taxes on income from profits.

Master Operations Schedule schedule showing which products will be produced, and when, in upcoming time periods.

Materials Management process of planning, organizing, and controlling the flow of materials from sources of supply through distribution of finished goods.

Matrix Structure organizational structure created by superimposing one form of structure onto another.

Maturity Date (Due Date) future date when repayment of a bond is due from the bond issuer (borrower).

Media Mix combination of advertising media chosen to carry a message about a product.

Mediation a neutral third party (the mediator) can advise, but cannot impose a settlement on the other parties.

Mediation method of resolving a labor dispute in which a third party suggests, but does not impose, a settlement.

Merchant Wholesalers independent wholesaler who takes legal possession of goods produced by a variety of manufacturers and then resells them to other organizations.

Merger the union of two corporations to form a new corporation.

Merit Salary System individual incentive linking compensation to performance in nonsales jobs.

Middle Manager manager responsible for implementing the strategies and working toward the goals set by top managers.

Mission Statement organization's statement of how it will achieve its purpose in the environment in which it conducts its business.

Missionary Selling personal-selling task in which salespeople promote their firms and products rather than try to close sales.

Mixed Market Economy economic system featuring characteristics of both planned and market economies.

Monetary Policies policies used by a government to control the size of its money supply.

Monetary Policy management of the nation's economic growth by managing the money supply and interest rates.

Money object that is portable, divisible, durable, and stable, and that serves as a medium of exchange, a store of value, and a measure of worth.

Money Market Mutual Fund fund of short-term, low-risk financial securities purchased with the pooled assets of investor-owners.

Monopolistic Competition market or industry characterized by numerous buyers and relatively numerous sellers trying to differentiate their products from those of competitors.

Monopoly market or industry in which there is only one producer that can therefore set the prices of its products.

Mortgage Loan loan secured by property (the home) being purchased.

Mortgage-Backed Security (MBS) mortgages pooled together to form a debt obligation—a bond—that entitles the holder (investor) to cash that flows in from the bundled mortgages.

Motivation the set of forces that cause people to behave in certain ways.

Multinational (or Transnational) Corporation form of corporation spanning national boundaries.

Multinational Firm firm that designs, produces, and markets products in many nations.

Mutual Savings Bank financial institution whose depositors are owners sharing in its profits.

Mutual Fund company that pools cash investments from individuals and organizations to purchase a portfolio of stocks, bonds, and other securities.

Myers-Briggs Type Indicator (MBTI) a popular questionnaire that some organizations use to assess personality types.

N

NASDAQ Composite Index market index that includes all NASDAQ-listed companies, both domestic and foreign, with a high proportion of technology companies and small-cap stocks.

National Labor Relations Act or Wagner Act act that put labor unions on a more equal footing with management in terms of the rights of employees to organize and bargain.

National Labor Relations Board (NLRB) established by the Wagner Act to administer its provisions.

National Debt the amount of money the government owes its creditors.

National Competitive Advantage international competitive advantage stemming from a combination of factor conditions, demand conditions, related and supporting industries, and firm strategies, structures, and rivalries.

National Labor Relations Act (also known as the *Wagner Act*) sets up a procedure for employees to vote on whether to have a union.

National Labor Relations Board (NLRB) established by the Wagner Act to enforce its provisions.

National Brands brand-name product produced by, widely distributed by, and carrying the name of a manufacturer.

National Association of Securities Dealers Automated Quotation (NASDAQ) System world's oldest electronic stock market consisting of dealers who buy and sell securities over a network of electronic communications.

Natural Monopoly industry in which one company can most efficiently supply all needed goods or services.

Need for Achievement an individual's desire to accomplish a goal or task as effectively as possible.

Need for Affiliation an individual's desire for human companionship.

Need for Power the desire to control one's environment, including financial, material, informational, and human resources.

Negligence conduct that falls below legal standards for protecting others against unreasonable risk.

Net Income (Net Profit or Net Earnings) gross profit minus operating expenses and income taxes.

Niche a segment of a market that is not currently being exploited.

No-Load Fund mutual fund in which investors pay no commissions when they buy in or sell out.

Nominal GDP GDP measured in current dollars or with all components valued at current prices.

Nonprogrammed Decision decision that is relatively unstructured and that occurs with low frequency.

Norris-LaGuardia Act act that imposed severe limitations on the ability of the courts to issue injunctions prohibiting certain union activities, including strikes.

North American Free Trade Agreement (NAFTA) agreement to gradually eliminate tariffs and other trade barriers among the United States, Canada, and Mexico.

O

Observation research method that obtains data by watching and recording consumer behavior.

Obstructionist Stance approach to social responsibility that involves doing as little as possible and may involve attempts to deny or cover up violations.

Occupational Safety and Health Act (OSHA) of 1970 federal law setting and enforcing guidelines for protecting workers from unsafe conditions and potential health hazards in the workplace.

Odd-Even Pricing psychological pricing tactic based on the premise that customers prefer prices not stated in even dollar amounts.

Officers top management team of a corporation.

Offshoring the practice of outsourcing to foreign countries.

Oligopoly market or industry characterized by a handful of (generally large) sellers with the power to influence the prices of their products.

On-the-Job Training training, sometimes informal, conducted while an employee is at work.

Online Retailing nonstore retailing in which information about the sellers products and services is connected to consumers computers, allowing consumers to receive the information and purchase the products in the home.

Open-Market Operations the Fed's sale and purchase of securities in the open market.

Operating Expenses costs, other than the cost of revenues, incurred in producing a good or service.

Operating Income gross profit minus operating expenses.

Operational Plan plan setting short-term targets for daily, weekly, or monthly performance.

Operations (Production) activities involved in making products, goods, and services for customers.

Operations (Production) Management systematic direction and control of the activities that transform resources into finished products that create value for and provide benefits to customers.

Operations (Production) Managers managers responsible for ensuring that operations activities create value and provide benefits to customers.

Operations Process set of methods and technologies used to produce a good or a service.

Operations Capability (Production Capability) special ability that production does especially well to outperform the competition.

Operations Control process of monitoring production performance by comparing results with plans and taking corrective action when needed.

Order Processing personal-selling task in which salespeople receive orders and see to their handling and delivery.

Organization Chart diagram depicting a company's structure and showing employees where they fit into its operations.

Organizational Stakeholders those groups, individuals, and organizations that are directly affected by the practices of an organization and who therefore have a stake in its performance.

Organizational Analysis process of analyzing a firm's strengths and weaknesses.

Organizational Structure specification of the jobs to be done within an organization and the ways in which they relate to one another.

Organizational Citizenship positive behaviors that do not directly contribute to the bottom line.

Organizational Commitment an individual's identification with the organization and its mission.

Organizing management process of determining how best to arrange an organization's resources and activities into a coherent structure.

Outsourcing the practice of paying suppliers and distributors to perform certain business processes or to provide needed materials or services.

Outsourcing replacing internal processes by paying suppliers and distributors to perform business processes or to provide needed materials or services.

Owner's equity amount of money that owners would receive if they sold all of a firm's assets and paid all of its liabilities.

P

Packaging physical container in which a product is sold, advertised, or protected.

Paid-In Capital money that is invested in a company by its owners.

Participative Management and Empowerment method of increasing job satisfaction by giving employees a voice in the management of their jobs and the company.

Patent exclusive legal right to use and license a manufactured item or substance, manufacturing process, or object design.

Path Goal Theory theory of leadership that is a direct extension of the expectancy theory of motivation.

Patriot Act legislation that increased U.S. government's power to investigate and prosecute suspected terrorists.

Pay for Performance (Variable Pay) individual incentive that rewards a manager for especially productive output.

Pay-for-Knowledge Plan incentive plan to encourage employees to learn new skills or become proficient at different jobs.

Penetration Pricing setting an initially low price to establish a new product in the market.

Pension Fund nondeposit pool of funds managed to provide retirement income for its members.

Perfect Competition market or industry characterized by numerous small firms producing an identical product.

Performance dimension of quality that refers to how well a product does what it is supposed to do.

Performance Behaviors the total set of work-related behaviors that the organization expects employees to display.

Performance Appraisal evaluation of an employee's job performance to determine the degree to which the employee is performing effectively.

Person-Job Fit the extent to which a person's contributions and the organization's inducements match one another.

Personal Net Worth value of one's total assets minus one's total liabilities (debts).

Personal Selling person-to person sales.

Personal Influences include lifestyle, personality, and economic status that marketers use to study buying behavior.

Personal Selling promotional tool in which a salesperson communicates one-on-one with potential customers.

Personality the relatively stable set of psychological attributes that distinguish one person from another.

PERT Chart production schedule specifying the sequence of activities, time requirements, and critical paths for performing the steps in a project.

Philanthropic Giving the awarding of funds or gifts to charities or other worthy causes.

Physical Resources tangible items that organizations use in the conduct of their businesses.

Physical Distribution activities needed to move a product efficiently from manufacturer to consumer.

Picketing labor action in which workers publicize their grievances at the entrance to an employer's facility.

Place Utility providing products where customers will want them.

Place (Distribution) part of the marketing mix concerned with getting products from producers to consumers.

Planned Economy economy that relies on a centralized government to control all or most factors of production and to make all or most production and allocation decisions.

Planning management process of determining what an organization needs to do and how best to get it done.

Point-of-Sale (POS) Display sales-promotion technique in which product displays are located in certain areas to stimulate purchase or to provide information on a product.

Point-of-Sale (POS) Terminal electronic device that transfers funds from the customer's bank account to pay for retail purchases.

Political-Legal Environment the relationship between business and government.

Political Action Committees (PACs) special organizations created to solicit money and then distribute it to political candidates.

Political-Legal Environment the relationship between business and government, usually in the form of government regulation of business.

Portfolio combined holdings of all the financial investments of any company or individual.

Positioning process of establishing an identifiable product image in the minds of consumers.

Positive Reinforcement reward that follows desired behaviors.

Possession Utility transferring product ownership to customers by setting selling prices, setting terms for customer credit payments, and providing ownership documents.

Power Orientation the beliefs that people in a culture hold about the appropriateness of power and authority differences in hierarchies such as business organizations.

Power the ability to affect the behavior of others.

Premium sales-promotion technique in which offers of free or reduced-price items are used to stimulate purchases.

Price Skimming setting an initially high price to cover new product costs and generate a profit.

Price Lining setting a limited number of prices for certain categories of products.

Price Appreciation increase in the dollar value of an investment at two points in time (the amount by which the price of a security increases).

Pricing Objectives the goals that sellers hope to achieve in pricing products for sale.

Pricing process of determining the best price at which to sell a product.

Pricing process of determining what a company will receive in exchange for its products.

Primary Data new data that are collected from newly performed research.

Primary Securities Market market in which new stocks and bonds are bought and sold by firms and governments.

Prime Rate interest rate available to a banks most creditworthy customers.

Principal individual or organization authorizing an agent to act on its behalf.

Private Enterprise economic system that allows individuals to pursue their own interests without undue governmental restriction.

Private Brand (or Private Label) brand-name product that a wholesaler or retailer has commissioned from a manufacturer.

Private Warehouse warehouse owned by and providing storage for a single company.

Private Accountant salaried accountant hired by a business to carry out its day-to-day financial activities.

Privatization process of converting government enterprises into privately owned companies.

Proactive Stance approach to social responsibility by which a company actively seeks opportunities to contribute to the well-being of groups and individuals in its social environment.

Process Departmentalization dividing an organization according to production processes used to create a good or service.

Process Layout (Custom-Product Layout) physical arrangement of production activities that groups equipment and people according to function.

Product Liability tort in which a company is responsible for injuries caused by its products.

Product Departmentalization dividing an organization according to specific products or services being created.

Product Layout (Same-Steps Layout) physical arrangement of production steps designed to make one type of product in a fixed sequence of activities according to its production requirements.

Product good, service, or idea that is marketed to fill consumers needs and wants.

Product Differentiation creation of a product feature or product image that differs enough from existing products to attract customers.

Product Positioning process of fixing, adapting, and communicating the nature of a product.

Product Features tangible and intangible qualities that a company builds into its products.

Product Mix the group of products that a firm makes available for sale.

Product Line group of products that are closely related because they function in a similar manner or are sold to the same customer group who will use them in similar ways.

Product Life Cycle (PLC) series of stages in a product's commercial life.

Product Extension marketing an existing product globally instead of just domestically.

Product Adaptation modifying an existing product for greater appeal in different countries.

Product Placement promotional tactic for brand exposure in which characters in television, film, music, magazines, or video games use a real product with its brand visible to viewers.

Production Items goods or services that are used in the conversion (production) process to make other products.

Productivity a measure of economic growth that compares how much a system produces with the resources needed to produce it.

Productivity the amount of output produced compared with the amount of resources used to produce that output.

Professional Corporation form of ownership allowing professionals to take advantage of corporate benefits while granting them limited business liability and unlimited professional liability.

Profit Center separate company unit responsible for its own costs and profits.

Profit-Sharing Plan incentive plan for distributing bonuses to employees when company profits rise above a certain level.

Profitability Ratio financial ratio for measuring a firm's potential earnings.

Profits difference between a business's revenues and its expenses.

Programmed Decision decision that is relatively structured or recurs with some frequency (or both).

Promotion aspect of the marketing mix concerned with the most effective techniques for communicating information about products.

Promotion aspect of the marketing mix concerned with the most effective techniques for communicating information about and selling a product.

Promotional Mix combination of tools used to promote a product.

Property Insurance insurance covering losses resulting from physical damage to or loss of the insured's real estate or personal property.

Property anything of value to which a person or business has sole right of ownership.

Prospecting step in the personal selling process in which salespeople identify potential customers.

Prospectus registration statement filed with the SEC, containing information for prospective investors about a security to be offered and the issuing company.

Protectionism practice of protecting domestic business against foreign competition.

Psychographic Segmentation a segmentation strategy that uses psychographic characteristics to identify different market segments.

Psychographic Variables consumer characteristics, such as lifestyles, opinions, interests, and attitudes, that may be considered in developing a segmentation strategy.

Psychological Contract set of expectations held by an employee concerning what he or she will contribute to an organization (referred to as *contributions*) and what the organization will in return provide the employee (referred to as *inducements*).

Psychological Influences include an individual's motivations, perceptions, ability to learn, and attitudes that marketers use to study buying behavior.

Psychological Pricing pricing tactic that takes advantage of the fact that consumers do not always respond rationally to stated prices.

Public Relations communication efforts directed at building goodwill and favorable attitudes in the minds of the public toward the organization and its products.

Public Warehouse independently owned and operated warehouse that stores goods for many firms.

Public Relations company-influenced information directed at building goodwill with the public or dealing with unfavorable events.

Publicity promotional tool in which information about a company, a product, or an event is transmitted by the general mass media to attract public attention.

Publicly Held (or Public) Corporation corporation whose stock is widely held and available for sale to the general public.

Pull Strategy promotional strategy designed to appeal directly to consumers who will demand a product from retailers.

Punishment unpleasant consequences of an undesirable behavior.

Punitive Damages fines imposed over and above any actual losses suffered by a plaintiff.

Purchasing Power Parity the principle that exchange rates are set so that the prices of similar products in different countries are about the same.

Purchasing acquisition of the materials and services that a firm needs to produce its products.

Pure Risk risk involving only the possibility of loss or no loss.

Push Strategy promotional strategy designed to encourage wholesalers or retailers to market products to consumers.

Q

Qualifying step in the personal selling process in which salespeople determine whether prospects have the authority to buy and ability to pay.

Quality combination of "characteristics of a product or service that bear on its ability to satisfy stated or implied needs".

Quality Control action of ensuring that operations produce products that meet specific quality standards.

Quality Improvement Team total quality management tool in which collaborative groups of employees from various work areas work together to improve quality by solving common shared production problems.

Quality Ownership principle of total quality management that holds that quality belongs to each person who creates it while performing a job.

Quid Pro Quo Harassment form of sexual harassment in which sexual favors are requested in return for job-related benefits.

Quota restriction on the number of products of a certain type that can be imported into a country.

R

Rational Motives reasons for purchasing a product that are based on a logical evaluation of product attributes.

Real GDP GDP adjusted to account for changes in currency values and price changes.

Realistic Job Preview (RJP) providing the applicant with a real picture of what performing the job that the organization is trying to fill would be like.

Recession a period during which aggregate output, as measured by GDP, declines.

Recruiting process of attracting qualified persons to apply for jobs an organization is seeking to fill.

Referent Power power based on identification, imitation, loyalty, or charisma.

Regulation the establishment of laws and rules that dictate what organizations can and cannot do.

Regulatory (Administrative) Law law made by the authority of administrative agencies.

Reintroduction reviving obsolete or older products for new markets.

Relationship Marketing marketing strategy that emphasizes building lasting relationships with customers and suppliers.

Replacement Chart list of each management position, who occupies it, how long that person will likely stay in the job, and who is qualified as a replacement.

Reseller Market organizational market consisting of intermediaries that buy and resell finished goods.

Reserve Requirement percentage of its deposits that a bank must hold in cash or on deposit with the Fed.

Responsibility duty to perform an assigned task.

Retail Selling selling a consumer product for the buyers personal or household use.

Retailer intermediary who sells products directly to consumers.

Retained Earnings earnings retained by a firm for its use rather than paid out as dividends.

Revenue Recognition formal recording and reporting of revenues at the appropriate time.

Revenues funds that flow into a business from the sale of goods or services.

Reward Power the power to give or withhold rewards.

Right-To-Work Laws such laws prohibit both union shops and agency shops, thus making it illegal to require union membership as a condition of employment.

Risk uncertainty about future events.

Risk Management process of conserving the firm's earning power and assets by reducing the threat of losses as a result of uncontrollable events.

Risk Avoidance practice of avoiding risk by declining or ceasing to participate in an activity.

Risk Control practice of minimizing the frequency or severity of losses from risky activities.

Risk Retention practice of covering a firm's losses with its own funds.

Risk Transfer practice of transferring a firm's risk to another firm.

Risk Propensity the degree to which a person is willing to take chances and make risky decisions.

Risk Propensity extent to which a decision maker is willing to gamble when making a decision.

Risk Return (Risk Reward) Relationship principle that safer investments tend to offer lower returns whereas riskier investments tend to offer higher returns (rewards).

Roth IRA provision allowing individual retirement savings with tax-free accumulated earnings.

Russell 2000 Index specialty index that uses 2,000 stocks to measure the performance of the smallest U.S. companies.

S

S Corporation hybrid of a closely held corporation and a partnership, organized and operated like a corporation but treated as a partnership for tax purposes.

S&P 500 market index of U.S. equities based on the performance of 500 large-cap stocks representing various sectors of the overall equities market.

Salary compensation in the form of money paid for discharging the responsibilities of a job.

Sales Promotion direct inducements such as premiums, coupons, and package inserts to tempt consumers to buy products.

Sales Agent independent intermediary who generally deals in the related product lines of a few producers and forms long-term relationships to represent those producers and meet the needs of many customers.

Sales Promotion short-term promotional activity designed to encourage consumer buying, industrial sales, or cooperation from distributors.

Sarbanes-Oxley Act of 2002 (Sarbox or Sox) enactment of federal regulations to restore public trust in accounting practices by imposing new requirements on financial activities in publicly traded corporations.

Savings and Loan Association (S&L) financial institution accepting deposits and making loans primarily for home mortgages.

Secondary Data data that are already available from previous research.

Secondary Securities Market market in which existing (not new) stocks and bonds are sold to the public.

Secured Loan (Asset-Backed Loan) loan to finance an asset, backed by the borrower pledging the asset as collateral to the lender.

Securities Investment Dealer (Broker) financial institution that buys and sells stocks and bonds both for investors and for its own accounts.

Securities stocks, bonds, and mutual funds representing secured, or asset-based, claims by investors against issuers.

Securities Markets markets in which stocks and bonds are sold.

Securities and Exchange Commission (SEC) government agency that regulates U.S. securities markets.

Selective Distribution strategy by which a company uses only wholesalers and retailers who give special attention in sales effort to specific products.

Self-Efficacy a person's belief about his or her capabilities to perform a task.

Self-Esteem the extent to which a person believes that he or she is a worthwhile and deserving individual.

Service Operations (Service Production) activities producing intangible and tangible products, such as entertainment, transportation, and education.

Services products having nonphysical features, such as information, expertise, or an activity that can be purchased.

Services Companies Market firms engaged in the business of providing services to the purchasing public.

Sexual Harassment making unwelcome sexual advances in the workplace.

Shop Steward a regular employee who acts as a liaison between union members and supervisors.

Shopping Goods moderately expensive, infrequently purchased physical goods.

Shopping Services moderately expensive, infrequently purchased services.

Shopping Agent (e-agent) e-intermediary (middleman) in the Internet distribution channel that assists users in finding products and prices but does not take possession of products.

Short-Term Goal goal set for the near future.

Short-Term Solvency Ratio financial ratio for measuring a company's ability to pay immediate debts.

Shortage situation in which quantity demanded exceeds quantity supplied.

Situational Approach to Leadership assumes that appropriate leader behavior varies from one situation to another.

Small Business Administration (SBA) government agency charged with assisting small businesses.

Small Business independently owned business that has relatively little influence in its market.

Small Business Investment Company (SBIC) government regulated investment company that borrows money from the SBA to invest in or lend to a small business.

Small Business Development Center (SBDC) SBA program designed to consolidate information from various disciplines and make it available to small businesses.

Smart Card credit-card-sized plastic card with an embedded computer chip that can be programmed with electronic money.

Social Responsibility the attempt of a business to balance its commitments to groups and individuals in its environment, including customers, other businesses, employees, investors, and local communities.

Social Orientation a person's beliefs about the relative importance of the individual versus groups to which that person belongs.

Social Learning learning that occurs when people observe the behaviors of others, recognize their consequences, and alter their own behavior as a result.

Social Influences include family, opinion leaders (people whose opinions are sought by others), and such reference groups as friends, co-workers, and professional associates that marketers use to study buying behavior.

Social Networking network of communications that flow among people and organizations interacting through an online platform.

Social Networking Media websites or access channels, such as Facebook, Twitter, LinkedIn, and YouTube, to which consumers go for information and discussions.

Socialism planned economic system in which the government owns and operates only selected major sources of production.

Sociocultural Environment the customs, mores, values, and demographic characteristics of the society in which an organization functions.

Software programs that tell the computer how to function, what resources to use, how to use them, and application programs for specific activities.

Sole Proprietorship business owned and usually operated by one person who is responsible for all of its debts.

Solvency Ratio financial ratio, either short or long term, for estimating the borrower's ability to repay debt.

Spam junk e-mail sent to a mailing list or a newsgroup.

Span of Control number of people supervised by one manager.

Specialty Goods expensive, rarely purchased physical goods.

Specialty Services expensive, rarely purchased services.

Specialty Store retail store carrying one product line or category of related products.

Speculative Risk risk involving the possibility of gain or loss.

Speed to Market strategy of introducing new products to respond quickly to customer or market changes.

Spin Off strategy of setting up one or more corporate units as new, independent corporations.

Spyware program unknowingly downloaded by users that monitors their computer activities, gathering e-mail addresses, credit card numbers, and other information that it transmits to someone outside the host system.

Stability condition in which the amount of money available in an economic system and the quantity of goods and services produced in it are growing at about the same rate.

Stabilization Policy government economic policy intended to smooth out fluctuations in output and unemployment and to stabilize prices.

Staff Authority authority based on expertise that usually involves counseling and advising line managers.

Staff Members advisers and counselors who help line departments in making decisions but who do not have the authority to make final decisions.

Staff Schedule assigned working times in upcoming days for each employee on each work shift.

Standard of Living the total quantity and quality of goods and services people can purchase with the currency used in their economic system.

State of Certainty when the decision maker knows with reasonable certainty what the alternatives are and what conditions are associated with each alternative.

State of Risk when the availability of each alternative and its potential payoffs and costs are all associated with probability estimates.

State of Uncertainty when the decision maker does not know all the alternatives, the risks associated with each, or the likely consequences of each alternative.

Statement of Cash Flows financial statement describing a firm's yearly cash receipts and cash payments.

Statutory Law law created by constitution(s) or by federal, state, or local legislative acts.

Stock Broker individual or organization that receives and executes buy and sell orders on behalf of outside customers in return for commissions.

Stock portion of ownership of a corporation.

Stock Exchange an organization of individuals to provide an institutional auction setting in which stocks can be bought and sold.

Stock Split stock dividend paid in additional shares to shareholders, thus increasing the number of outstanding shares.

Stockholder (or Shareholder) owner of shares of stock in a corporation.

Strategic Alliance strategy in which two or more organizations collaborate on a project for mutual gain.

Strategic Alliance arrangement (also called *joint venture*) in which a company finds a foreign partner to contribute approximately half of the resources needed to establish and operate a new business in the partner's country.

Strategic Management process of helping an organization maintain an effective alignment with its environment.

Strategic Goal goal derived directly from a firm's mission statement.

Strategic Plan plan reflecting decisions about resource allocations, company priorities, and steps needed to meet strategic goals.

Strategic Leadership leader's ability to understand the complexities of both the organization and its environment and to lead change in the organization so as to enhance its competitiveness.

Strategy broad set of organizational plans for implementing the decisions made for achieving organizational goals.

Strategy Formulation creation of a broad program for defining and meeting an organization's goals.

Strict Product Liability principle that liability can result not from a producer's negligence but from a defect in the product itself.

Strike labor action in which employees temporarily walk off the job and refuse to work.

Strikebreaker worker hired as a permanent or temporary replacement for a striking employee.

Subsidy government payment to help a domestic business compete with foreign firms.

Substitute Product product that is dissimilar from those of competitors, but that can fulfill the same need.

Supermarket large product-line retailer offering a variety of food and food-related items in specialized departments.

Supplier Selection process of finding and choosing suppliers from whom to buy.

Supply Chain (Value Chain) flow of information, materials, and services that starts with raw-materials suppliers and continues adding value through other stages in the network of firms until the product reaches the end customer.

Supply the willingness and ability of producers to offer a good or service for sale.

Supply Curve graph showing how many units of a product will be supplied (offered for sale) at different prices.

Supply Chain Management (SCM) principle of looking at the supply chain as a whole to improve the overall flow through the system.

Surplus situation in which quantity supplied exceeds quantity demanded.

Survey research method of collecting consumer data using questionnaires, telephone calls, and face-to-face interviews.

"Super Wi-Fi" Network a powerful Wi-Fi network with extensive reach and strong signals that flow freely through physical objects such as walls.

SWOT Analysis identification and analysis of organizational strengths and weaknesses and environmental opportunities and threats as part of strategy formulation.

Syndicated Selling e-commerce practice whereby a website offers other websites commissions for referring customers.

T

Tactical Plan generally short-term plan concerned with implementing specific aspects of a company's strategic plans.

Tall Organizational Structure characteristic of centralized companies with multiple layers of management.

Tangible Real Property land and anything attached to it.

Tangible Personal Property any movable item that can be owned, bought, sold, or leased.

Target Market the particular group of people or organizations on which a firm's marketing efforts are focused.

Tariff tax levied on imported products.

Task-Focused Leader Behavior leader behavior focusing on how tasks should be performed to meet certain goals and to achieve certain performance standards.

Tax Services assistance provided by CPAs for tax preparation and tax planning.

Technical Skills skills needed to perform specialized tasks.

Technological Environment all the ways by which firms create value for their constituents.

Telecommuting form of flextime that allows people to perform some or all of a job away from standard office settings.

Telemarketing form of nonstore retailing in which the telephone is used to sell directly to consumers.

Tender Offer offer to buy shares made by a prospective buyer directly to a target corporation's shareholders, who then make individual decisions about whether to sell.

Theory X theory of motivation holding that people are naturally lazy and uncooperative.

Theory Y theory of motivation holding that people are naturally energetic, growth-oriented, self-motivated, and interested in being productive.

360-Degree Feedback performance appraisal technique in which managers are evaluated by everyone around them—their boss, their peers, and their subordinates.

Time Orientation the extent to which members of a culture adopt a long-term versus a short-term outlook on work, life, and other elements of society.

Time Management Skills skills associated with the productive use of time.

Time Utility providing products when customers will want them.

Time Deposit bank funds that have a fixed term of time to maturity and cannot be withdrawn earlier or transferred by check.

Time Value of Money principle that invested money grows, over time, by earning interest or some other form of return.

Title VII of the Civil Rights Act of 1964 forbids discrimination in all areas of the employment relationship.

Top Manager manager responsible for a firm's overall performance and effectiveness.

Tort civil injury to people, property, or reputation for which compensation must be paid.

Total Quality Management (TQM) all activities involved in getting high-quality goods and services into the marketplace.

Trade Deficit situation in which a country's imports exceed its exports, creating a negative balance of trade.

Trade Surplus situation in which a country's exports exceed its imports, creating a positive balance of trade.

Trade Show sales-promotion technique in which various members of an industry gather to display, demonstrate, and sell products.

Trademark exclusive legal right to use a brand name or symbol.

Traditional Individual Retirement Account (IRA) provision allowing individual tax-deferred retirement savings.

Training usually refers to teaching operational or technical employees how to do the job for which they were hired.

Trait Approach to Leadership focused on identifying the essential traits that distinguished leaders.

Transactional Leadership comparable to management, it involves routine, regimented activities.

Transformational Leadership the set of abilities that allows a leader to recognize the need for change, to create a vision to guide that change, and to execute the change effectively.

Transportation activities in transporting resources to the producer and finished goods to customers.

Trial Court general court that hears cases not specifically assigned to another court.

Trust Services management by a bank of an estate, investments, or other assets on behalf of an individual.

Turnover annual percentage of an organization's workforce that leaves and must be replaced.

Two-Factor Theory theory of motivation holding that job satisfaction depends on two factors, hygiene and motivation.

U

Uncertainty Orientation the feeling individuals have regarding uncertain and ambiguous situations.

Unemployment the level of joblessness among people actively seeking work in an economic system.

Unethical Behavior behavior that does not conform to generally accepted social norms concerning beneficial and harmful actions.

Uniform Commercial Code (UCC) body of standardized laws governing the rights of buyers and sellers in transactions.

Union Shop requires employees to join a union within a specified period after being hired.

Unlimited Liability legal principle holding owners responsible for paying off all debts of a business.

Unsecured Loan loan for which collateral is not required.

Utility product's ability to satisfy a human want or need.

V

Value-Added Analysis process of evaluating all work activities, materials flows, and paperwork to determine the value that they add for customers.

Value relative comparison of a product's benefits versus its costs.

Value Package a product is marketed as a bundle of value-adding attributes, including reasonable cost.

Variable Cost cost that changes with the quantity of a product produced and sold.

Venture Capital Company group of small investors who invest money in companies with rapid growth potential.

Venture Capital private funds from wealthy individuals seeking investment opportunities in new growth companies.

Vestibule Training off-the-job training conducted in a simulated environment.

Video Retailing nonstore retailing to consumers via home television.

Viral Marketing type of marketing that relies on the Internet to spread information like a "virus" from person to person about products and ideas.

Virtual Leadership leadership in settings where leaders and followers interact electronically rather than in face-to-face settings.

Voluntary Bankruptcy bankruptcy proceedings initiated by an indebted individual or organization.

Voluntary Arbitration a neutral third party (the arbitrator) dictates a settlement between the two sides, who have agreed to submit to outside judgment.

VSAT Satellite communications network of geographically dispersed transmitter-receivers (transceivers) that send signals to and receive signals from a satellite, exchanging voice, video, and data transmissions.

W

Wage Reopener Clauses allow wage rates to be negotiated at preset times during the life of the contract.

Wages compensation in the form of money paid for time worked.

Warehousing storage of incoming materials for production and finished goods for distribution to customers.

Warranty seller's promise to stand by its products or services if a problem occurs after the sale.

Whistle-Blower employee who detects and tries to put an end to a company's unethical, illegal, or socially irresponsible actions by publicizing them.

Wholesale Club bargain retailer offering large discounts on brand-name merchandise to customers who have paid annual membership fees.

Wholesaler intermediary who sells products to other businesses for resale to final consumers.

Wi-Fi technology using a wireless local area network.

Wide Area Network (WAN) computers that are linked over long distances through telephone lines, microwave signals, or satellite communications.

Wireless Wide Area Network (WWAN) network that uses airborne electronic signals instead of wires to link computers and electronic devices over long distances.

Wireless Local Area Network (Wireless LAN or WLAN) local area network with wireless access points for PC users.

Work Team groups of operating employees who are empowered to plan and organize their own work and to perform that work with a minimum of supervision.

Work Sharing (Job Sharing) method of increasing job satisfaction by allowing two or more people to share a single full-time job.

Work Slowdown labor action in which workers perform jobs at a slower than normal pace.

Workers Compensation Coverage coverage provided by a firm to employees for medical expenses, loss of wages, and rehabilitation costs resulting from job-related injuries or disease.

Workers Compensation Insurance legally required insurance for compensating workers injured on the job.

Workforce Diversity the range of workers attitudes, values, beliefs, and behaviors that differ by gender, race, age, ethnicity, physical ability, and other relevant characteristics.

World Trade Organization (WTO) organization through which member nations negotiate trading agreements and resolve disputes about trade policies and practices.

World Wide Web branch of the Internet consisting of inter-linked hypertext documents, or Web pages.

World Bank UN agency that provides a limited scope of financial services, such as funding improvements in underdeveloped countries.

Y

Yellow-Dog Contracts requirements that workers state that they did not belong to and would not join a union.

index

A

ABB Asea Brown Boveri, 137
Abbott Fund, 82f
Abercrombie & Fitch (A&F), 45
Absenteeism, 274
Absolute advantage, 144
ABS Visual Staff Scheduler® PRO (VSS Pro) software, 248
Accountability, 73, 211
Accountancy. *See* Accounting
Accountants. *See also* Accounting; specific types of
   reporting standards and practices for, 526–527
   role of, 515–520
   vision project of, 517–518
Accounting. *See also* Accountants; Financial statements
   core competencies for, 517, 517t
   defined, 514
   equation for, 520–521
   ethics, 531–533
   fair value, 528
   financial, 515
   information for, users of, 514–515
   internationalizing, 533–536
   investivative, 518
   managerial, 515
Accounting information system (AIS), 514
Accounting supervisor, 175
Accounts, 350, 554. *See also* specific types of
Accounts payable, 523
Achievement, need for, 285
Achievement-oriented leader behavior, 311
Acquired needs theory, 285
Acquisition, 121
Active partners, 116
Activity ratios, 530–531
Activity timing, 527
Adam Hat Company, 291
Adidas, 323
Administrative expenses, 524
ADT Ltd., 65
Advanced Development Programs (ADP), 220
Adverse impact, 342
Advertising, 385, 459–460, 460f
   to customers, ethics of, 78
   direct-to-consumer, 458
   media for, 459–460, 461t

morally objectionable, 78
   real-time ad tracking and, 459–460
Advil, 449
Aeon, 451
Aéropostale, 33
Affect, defined, 279
Affiliation, need for, 285
Affirmative action plan, 342
Age Discrimination in Employment Act, 341t, 342
A.G. Edwards Inc., 558
Agents
   distribution by, 448
   e-, 450
   economic, 67
   independent, 148
   primary, 67
   sales, 448
   shopping, 450
   wholesaling, 450
Aggregate output, 47–50, 49
Aggression in workplace, 275
Aggressive goal behavior, 152
Aggressive growth funds, 591
Agreeableness, 275
AIDS, 343–344
AIG, 317
Air Arabia, 186
Airbus, 45, 319, 321–323, 382
Air France, 490
Air pollution, 74–75
Alcoa, 85
A2L Consulting, 395
Aldi, 105
Aleve, 449
Ali, Adel, 186
Al-Jaidah, 305–306
Aller Aqua, 253
Alliances
   global, 138–139
   strategic, 120, 149
Allied Insurance, 449
Allocation of assets, 601
Al Nuaimi, Hashem, 426
Alternative workplaces, 292–293
Amazon, 102, 111, 203, 286, 315, 393, 424, 430, 453, 465, 488
American Airlines, 76, 121
American Bankers Association, 567
American Express, 72, 173, 180, 181, 182, 431

American Federation of Labor and Congress of Industrial Organizations (AFL-CIO), 358, 359
American Institute of Certified Public Accountants (AICPA), 515, 516, 532–533t
American International Group, 597
American Marketing Association, 376
American Red Cross, 66, 203
American Society for Quality, 244
Americans with Disabilities Act, 341t, 342–343
Andersen, Arthur, 72, 312, 519
Android, 481
Angel investors, 604
Anheuser-Busch, 74, 349
Annual percentage rate (APR), 603
Anticrime regulations, 566–567
Antiterrorism regulations, 566–567
Anti-virus software, 499
AOL, 110, 523
Apparelus.com, 431
Apple, Inc., 32, 46, 78, 100, 104, 135, 171, 175, 255, 346, 384, 396, 413–414, 415, 418, 419, 429, 445, 449, 485, 496, 595, 609
Application forms, 345
Application server, 487
Application software, 485, 490
Appraisal of performance, 352–354, 353f
Approach, defined, 463
Aquafina, 184
Arbitration, 360
Archer Farms, 380
Arrested Development, 100
Arrowhead Health, 427
Ash, Mary Kay, 111, 312
Ask (Ask Jeeves), 453
Assembly line layout, 243–244
Assets, 522–523
   accounting equation, 521
   allocation of, 601
   current, 522
   defined, 521
   devaluing, 535
   fixed, 522
   intangible, 523
   loans backed by, 603
   toxic, 528
   valuing, 535
Association of Certified Fraud Examiners (ACFE), 513–514

Association of Southeast Asian Nations (ASEAN), 138, 139f
Atebits, 418
AT&T, 349, 599–600
Attitudes at work, 278–280
Audi, 184
Audit/auditing, 87, 516
Authoritarianism, 278
Authority, 211
  of centralized organizations, 208–209
  committee, 212–213
  of decentralized organizations, 209–210
  distributing, 208–211
  forms of, 212–213
  line, 212, 212f
  span of control and, 211
  staff, 212, 212f
  team, 212–213
Automated Clearing House (ACH) Network, 567
Automated teller machines (ATMs), 559, 560f
Avatar, 395
Avon Products, 446, 452
Aylett, Matthew, 493

B

Baby Boomers, 413
Backblaze.com, 483
Bacon, Kevin, 598
Balanced funds, 591
Balance of payments, 142–143
Balance of trade, 50, 50f, 140–142, 141–142f
Balance sheets, 522–523, 522f
Banana Republic, 45
Bank Andara, 41
Banker's acceptance, 558
Banker's bank, 563
Banking system, 564–569
  anticrime regulations for, 566–567
  antiterrorism regulations for, 566–567
  electronic technologies in, 567–569
  international, 569–572
  money, regulation of, 560–561, 560f
Bank of America, 71, 82f, 392, 395, 552, 556, 567
Bankruptcy, 605
Banks
  banker's, 563
  commercial, 556
  currency values, policies influencing, 570–571
  government's, 563
  investment, 593
  member, 563
  mutual savings, 557
  reserve, 562, 562f
  unsecured loans from, 603–604
Bank Secrecy Act (BSA), 566
Bargaining zone, 358
Bargain retailers, 451
Barter economy, 553

BarterQuest.com, 491
"Basel (Switzerland) III Requirements," 552
BassPro.com, 393
Bath & Body Works, 121
Bay Area Rapid Transit (BART) system, 237–238
Bayliner, 458
Beacon, 496
Bear market, 596, 597f
Bear Stearns, 565–566, 593
Behaviors
  aggressive goal, 152
  buying, 394–395
  consumer, 391–393
  counterproductive, 272, 274–275
  decision making, aspects of, 323–324
  defined, 272
  directive leader, 311
  of employees, 150–152, 151f, 272–275
  ethical, 65–68
  of leaders, 309, 311
  leadership, approaches to, 309
  modification of, 289
  motivation for, goals for, 289
  organizational citizenship and, 273
  participative leader, 311
  passive goal, 152
  performance and, 272–273
  segmentation of, 388
  supportive leader, 311
  task-focused leader, 309
  unethical, 66
  variables of, 388
Belgian Law of Well-being (2007), 274
Benedict, Pope, 530
Benefits, 349
  legal issues with, 342–343
  value-added, 458
Bergdorf Goodman, 388
Berkshire Hathaway, 608
Bernard Madoff Investment Securities LLC, 598
Berytech, 180
Best Buy, 135
Bethlehem Steel, 104
Betrix, 396
Better Business Bureau, 81
Better survival rates, 112
Bezos, Jeff, 315
Bich, Marcel, 107
"Big five" personality traits, 275–276
Bigfoot Entertainment, 286
"Big four" public accounting firms, 516
Big Mac index, 49, 49f
Bing, 382
Biocentric Health Inc., 451
Bitcoin, 567
BlackBerry, 255, 480, 489
Black & Decker, 417
Blink credit card, 568
Blockbuster, 99–100, 107
Blogs, corporate, 395

Bloomberg, 385, 602
Bloomberg Television, 602
Bloom, Diana, 356
Blue Bell, 185
Blue-chip stocks, 590
Blumenthal, Neil, 107
BMW, 458
Board of directors, 120
Board of governors, 562
Boeing, 45, 70, 75, 108, 317, 319, 321–322, 382, 482
Bonaparte, Napoleon, 308
Bondholder's claim, 605
Bonds, 50
  corporate, 605–607, 605t, 610
  indenture of, 605
  municipal, 605
Bonus, 348
Book-entry ownership, 596
Bookkeeping, 514
Boots and Coots, 121
Borders, 527
Borrower's ability to repay debt, 529
Boycott, 360
Branch offices, 149
Branding, defined, 422. *See also* Brands
Brands
  awareness of, 423–424
  competition with, 382
  licensed, 425
  loyalty to, 391–392
  names for, types of, 424–425
  national, 425
  private, 425
Break-even analysis, 427–429, 428f
Break-even point, 428
Breathe Right Nasal Strips, 397
Brewer, Lynn, 532
Brichter, Loren, 418
Brick-and-mortar retail outlets, 451
Brin, Sergey, 167, 169
Bristol-Myers Squibb Foundation, Inc., 82f
British Airways, 78
British Petroleum (BP), 82f, 86, 145
Brokerage services, 558
Brokers, 448, 450–451, 558, 596
Brooks, Carl, 316
Broyhill, 104
Brunswick Corp., 458
Buch, Chase, 413
Budget, 526, 526f
Budwig, Darin, 183
Building Solutions, 183
Bull market, 596, 597f
Bullying, 274
Bundling strategy, 430–431
Burberry, 388
Bureau of Labor Statistics (BLS), 356
Burger King, 419
Burn Notice, 425
Business. *See also* International business; Small business
  benefits of, 33

concept of, 32–33
cycle of, 36, 47
defined, 32
domestic, 33, 34f
ethics of, 65–70
external environments of, 33–36
global, 33, 34, 34f
launching a, 99–100
laws for practicing, 154
plan for, 108
process reengineering for, 256
services for, 417
strategy of, 182, 238–240
Business managers, 514
Business marketing, 394
Business-to-business (B2B) marketing, 378, 394–395
Business-to-business brokers, 450–451
ButterflEYE, 180
Buyers, 394–395
Buying
behavior when, 394–395
of existing business, 109
process for, 392–393, 392f
Buyouts, 529

C

Cabelas, 393
Cabot Cheese, 117
Cafeteria benefits plan, 349
California Public Employees Retirement Fund (Calpers), 605–606
Calvin Klein, 78
Candy industry, 63–64
CAN-SPAM Act, 499
Canyon River Blues, 425
Capacity, 240–241
Cap and Trade, 587–588
Capital, 37. See also Stocks
conservative growth of, 591
gaining, 600
human, 339
insufficient, 113
maximizing growth of, 588–590, 589f
paid-in, 523
retained earnings as source of, 611
venture, 604
working, 603–604
Capitalism, defined, 39
Capital items, 416
Caputo, Sara, 271
Carbonite Backup, 455, 483
Carbon offsets, 77t
Carey, Dennis, 313
Caring, 68
Carnival, 187
Carrefour, 426, 451
Cartels, 154
Casabella, 137
Case, Steve, 110
Cash, 554. See also Money

Cash flows, 525–526, 525f, 604
Catalog marketing, 452
Catalog showrooms, 451
Caterpillar (CAT), 82, 174, 255–256, 535
Ceconi, Margaret, 532
Cellular One, 489
Central Intelligence Agency, 72, 500
Centralized organizations, 208–209
CenturyLink, 431
CereProc, 493
Certainty, state of, 319
Certificates of deposit (CDs), 554
Certified Development Company (530) program, 111
Certified Fraud Examiner (CFE), 519
Certified management accountant (CMA), 518
Certified public accountants (CPAs), 515–518
auditing by, 516
defined, 515
federal restrictions on, 519–520
financial reporting by, 519–520
services offered by, 516–517
Chain of command, 203
Chambers, John, 111
Channel captain, 449
Channel conflict, 449
Chaparral Steel Company, 487
Charismatic leadership, 312
Charities, 66
Chase Bank Credit Card Services, 146
Check, 554
Check clearing, 563
Check Clearing for the 21st Century Act (Check 21), 567–568
Checking accounts, 554
Che Guevara, 133
ChemLawn, 417
Chenault, Kenneth, 180, 182
Chettero, Nicole, 64
Chevrolet, 150, 171
Chicago Climate Exchange (CCX), 588
Chief executive officer (CEO), 173
Chief financial officer (CFO), 173, 175
Chief information officer (CIO), 175
Children's Online Privacy Protection Act, 76
Chinese Petroleum, 137
Chinese Politburo Standing Committee, 347
Chinook helicopter plant, 75
Chiquita, 154
Chrysler, 40, 148
Circle K, 451
Circuit City, 33, 51, 148, 178
Cisco Systems, 111, 395, 597
Citibank, 392, 610
Citi Foundation, 82f
Citigroup, 72, 556, 597, 606
Civil Rights Act of 1991, 341t, 342
Clark Equipment, 212
Classical theory of motivation, 282

Clayton Act, 46
Clean Harbors, 113
Client relationships, 292
Clorox bleach, 421, 425
Closely held corporations, 118, 119t
Closing, defined, 463
Cloud computing, 487
CNBC, 602
Cnooc Ltd., 305
Coaches, 315. See also Leaders
Coalition, 323
Coalition of Gulf Shrimp Industries, 432
Coast Distribution System, 394
Coblin, James M., 347
Coca-Cola, 82f, 147, 175, 182, 188, 389–390, 396, 423, 608–609
Code of professional conduct, 532–533t
Codes of ethics, 65, 69–70, 532t
Coercive power, 307–308
Cognition, 279
Cognitive dissonance, 279
Collaboration, 482
Collateral, 603
Collective bargaining, 358–360, 358f. See also Contracts
Collectivism, 151, 315
Collette Vacations, 250
Collusion, 77
Commercial banks, 556
Commercial finance companies, 557
Commitment, 79, 280, 323–324
Common stocks, 590, 611
Communication
corporate culture and, 188–189
electronic, 499
resources for, 486–487
VSAT satellite, 487, 488f
Communication mix, 457
Communism, 39
Companies
finance, 557
insurance, 557
minority enterprise small business investment, 110
non-loss/non-dividend, 41
practices within, 68–70
small business investment, 110
venture capital, 110
Company-wide incentive programs, 349
Comparative advantage, 144–145
Compensating balance, 603
Compensation, 342–343, 348–349
Competence of managers, 113
Competition
brand, 382
defined, 44
degrees of, 41, 44–46, 45t
international, 382
in market economy, 44–46
monopolistic, 44–46, 45t
oligopoly and, 44, 45–46, 45t
perfect, 44–45, 45t
Competitive advantage, 144–145

Competitive environment, 381–382
Competitive product analysis, 254
Competitive strategy, 182
Compound growth, 588
Computer-aided design (CAD), 494–495
Computer-aided manufacturing (CAM), 495
Computer-based scheduling operations, 247–248
Computer numerically controlled (CNC), 206
Computers
  handheld, 490
  spam on, 498
  spyware on, 497–498
  Trojan Horses on, 497
  viruses on, 497
  virus on, 497
  worms on, 497
Conceptual management skills, 177–178
Conferencing, 487
Conscientiousness, 275
Consideration set, 392
Consistency, defined, 245
Construction industry, 103
Consumer Bill of Rights, 76, 77f
Consumer finance companies, 557
Consumerism, 76
Consumer price index (CPI), 51, 359
Consumer Reports, 337
Consumers
  behaviors of, 391–393
  buying process for, 392–393, 392f
  choices of, 32–33
  defined, 415
  goods for, 378
Consumer Watchdog, 350
Contagion, 74
Container Store, 72, 313
Contemporary Landscape Services, 203
Contemporary social consciousness, 73–74
Contemporary theory of motivation, 287–288
Contests, 464
Continental Airlines, 121, 180, 189, 394
Contingency planning, 187
Contingent workers, 355–357
Contracts, 358–360
  psychological, 280–281
Control/controlling
  of air pollution, 74
  defined, 170
  interest rate, 564
  inventory, 250
  locus of, 277
  management, functions of, 170–171, 170f
  operations, 249–251
  quality, 251
  span of, 211
Controller, 175, 515
Control systems, weak, 113
Convenience goods, 415

Convenience services, 415
Convenience stores, 451
Convertible money supply, 554–556, 555f
CoolSavings.com, 464
Cooperatives, 114, 115t, 117
Coors, 425
Co-pay, 359
Cornell University, 338
Corporate blogs, 395
Corporate bonds, 605–607, 605t, 610
Corporate culture, 188–189
Corporate entities. *See* Corporations
Corporate officers, 120
Corporate raider, 608
Corporate strategy, 182
Corporate university, 351
Corporations, 117–121, 117f. *See also* specific types of
  culture within, 181, 188
  defined, 118
  foundations of, 81, 82t
  governance in, 120
  managing, 120
  multinational, 119, 119t
  ownership of, special issues in, 120–121
  scandals within, 72
  social audit of, 87
  types of, 118–119, 119t
Costco, 451
Cost-of-living adjustment (COLA), 359
Cost-oriented pricing, 427–428
Costs, 427–429
  of benefits, containing, 349
  fixed, 428
  of goods sold, 523–524
  of poor total quality management, 252–254
  of revenues, 523–524
  variable, 428
Counterproductive behaviors, 272, 274–275
Countervailing duties, 432
Coupons, 463–464
Coupons.com, 464
Courtyard by Marriott, 245
Craftsman, 425
Craigslist, 356
Crane & Co, 456
Crate & Barrel, 452
Creative selling, 461–462
Credit cards, 556, 568
Creditor nation, 50
Creditors, 515
Credit Suisse First Boston, 72, 610
Credit union, 557
Crescent Bank and Trust, 551
Crisis management, 187
Cross-border ownership, 595
Cross-cultural leadership, 315–316
Crossovers from big business, 111
Cultural beliefs, 150
Cultural environment, 149–152

Culture
  concept of, 315
  corporate, 33, 181, 188–189
  influences on, 391
  national, 150–152, 151f
  organizational, 86
Currency, 554. *See also* Money
  exchanging, 558
  values of, 570–571
Current assets, 522
Current dividend yield, 599
Current interest yield, 599
Current liabilities, 523
Current ratio, 529
Customer identification program (CIP), 567
Customer relationship management (CRM), 378
Customers
  advertising to, ethics of, 78
  contact with, 237–238
  departmentalization of, 207
  ethics of advertising to, 78
  external, 255
  identifying, 255
  interacting with, 236
  internal, 255
  needs of, adapting to, 146
  operations process, presence in, 236
  residential, 417
  rights of, 76
  social responsibility towards, 74, 76–78
  stakeholder model of responsibility for, 71–72
  unfair pricing to, 77–78
Customer service, improving, 245
Custom-product layout, 243
Cybermalls, 453
Cycle of business, 36, 47
Cyclical unemployment, 52

D

Daewoo, 137
Daimler, 73, 83, 358, 570
Data
  analyzing, 390
  collecting, 390
  conferencing, 487
  defined, 492
  mining, 379, 493–494
  secondary, 390
  warehousing, 378–379, 492–493
Day After Tomorrow, The, 74
Day trading, 602
Debit cards, 556, 569
Debt
  borrower's ability to repay, 529
  defined, 529
  financing, 609
  financing for, 609–610
  national, 50
Debtor nation, 50

Decentralized organizations, 209–210
Decisional roles, 176–177, 176t
Decision support systems (DSS), 495
Decision tree approach, 311
Decisions/decision making, 318–324
    alternatives to, 321–322
    behavioral aspects of, 323–324
    commitment to, 323–324
    conditions for, 318–320
    defined, 318
    delegation process for, 211, 211t
    hierarchy of, 208–213 (See also Authority)
    intuition and, 323
    management skills for, 178
    nature of, 318–320
    nonprogrammed, 318
    political forces in, 323
    process for, 318
    programmed, 318
    purchase, 392–393
    rational, 320–323, 321f
    risk propensity and, 324
    situations for, recognizing and
        defining, 320–321
    types of, 318
Deep Gold, 286
Default, 605
defined contribution, 531
Deflation, 51, 563
Delegation process, 211, 211t
DELiA*s, 33
Dell Inc., 42, 71, 100, 102, 105, 109, 146,
        149, 185, 257, 446, 453, 465
Dell, Michael, 100, 102, 105–106
Deloitte Touche Tohmatsu, 516
Delta Airlines, 204, 487, 490, 608
Demand and supply. *See also* Demands;
        Suppliers/supplies
    curves of, 42
    forecasting, 340
    laws of, 42–44
    in market economy, 41–44, 43f
    matching, 340–341
    schedule for, 42
    shortages and, 42–44
    surpluses and, 42–44
Demand deposits, 554
Demands, 32–33. *See also* Demand and
        supply
    defined, 42
    international, 146
    law of, 42
    for services, 113
Demographic segmentation/variables, 387
Demonstration, 463
Denial of service (DoS) attacks, 496
Departmentalization, 206–208, 208f
Department stores, 451
Dependability, 238
Depository institutions, 563
Deposits, 554–555
Depreciation, 522
Depressions, 51–52

Designs
    computer-aided, 494–495
    service process, 421
Detailed scheduling operations, 247
Deterring fraud, 519
Devaluing assets, 535
Developing countries, 136
Development, 351–354
Diamond Foods, 73
DicksSportingGoods.com, 393
Digital Brand Expressions, 568
Direct channel, 446
Direct distribution, 446
Direct influence, regulation through, 83
Directive leader behavior, 311
Direct marketing, 464–465
Direct regulation, 83
Direct-response retailing, 452
Direct selling, 452
Direct-to-consumer (DTC)
        advertising, 458
DirectTV, 46, 425, 431
Disclosure, 527, 535
Discount brokers, 596
Discount houses, 451
Discounts, 430, 564
Dish Network, 308
Disney Magic, 187
Disney, Roy, 205
Disney, Walt, 170, 186–187, 205
Disney World, 187, 394
Disseminator, 176
Distribution, 399. *See also* Personal sell-
        ing; Promotions; Retailing/retail-
        ers; Wholesaling; specific types of
    by agents, 448
    of authority, 208–211
    by brokers, 448
    channels of, 446–449, 447–448f
    of goods, 446–448
    intensive, 448
    international, 396–397
    physical, 454–457
    for products, 384–385
    of services, 446–448
    strategies for, 384–385, 448–449
    through supply chains, 457
Distribution mix, 446
District sales managers, 175
Disturbance handler, 176
Diversification, 182, 601
Diversity in workplace, 354
Divestitures, 120–121
Dividends, 120, 590
    current yield for, 599
    defined, 590
Divisibility of money, 552
Divisional organizational structure,
        213–214, 214f
Division controller, 175
Division manager, 173
Divisions, 213
Dr. Pepper, 419

Dole, 154
Dollar Rent-A-Car, 450
Domestic business, 33, 34f
Donald, Jim, 313
Double Click, 168
Double taxation, 118
Dower, Deborah, 242
Dow Jones Industrial Average (DJIA),
        596–597
Dreamworks, 219
Drop shippers, 450
Dugan, Judy, 350
Duke Energy, 187
Dumping, 154, 432
Duncan, David, 72
Dunkin' Donuts, 109, 375
Duplicate facilities, 46
DuPont, 75
Durability of money, 552
Dutt, James, 307–308
Dynamic pricing, 430

E

E-agents, 450
Early behavioral theory of motivation,
        282–287
    Herzberg's two-factor theory, 284–285
    human resources models, 283
    Maslow's hierarchy of human needs
        model, 283–284
    needs, other important, 285–286
Earnings
    cycle of, 527
    net, 524–525
    retained, 523, 611
Earnings per share (EPS), 529–530, 608–609
Ease of entry, 592
EasyJet, 232
eBay, 102, 106, 111, 395, 396, 424, 430, 484
Ebert, Roger, 493
Economic agents, 67
Economic environment, 380
Economic stability, 51–52
Economic systems, 37–40. *See also*
        Economy
Economist, The, 231
Economy. *See also* Market economy
    barter, 553
    external environments in, 33, 34f, 36
    growth of, 47
    indicators within, 46–52
    international trade, differences in, 152
    market, 39–40
    planned, 38–39
    U.S., 52
Edmunds, Gladys, 113
Edmunds Travel Consultants, 113
Education for becoming managers,
        171–172
Education individual retirement
        accounts, 558
Edwards, Carl, 425

E-intermediaries, 450–451
Electrolux, 74
Electronic Arts, 211
Electronic catalogs, 453
Electronic commerce (e-commerce), 111,
    112f, 480
Electronic communication networks
    (ECNs), 595
Electronic communications, 499
Electronic conferencing, 487
Electronic funds transfer (EFT),
    558–559, 599
Electronic Payments Association, 567
Electronic purses, 569
Electronic storefronts, 453
Electronic technologies, 567–569
Eli Lilly and Company, 72, 82f
Elite Island Resorts, 431
E-mail, 178, 498
E-mail server, 487
Embargo, 133–134, 153
Emirates Airlines, 186, 202
Emissions trading (ET), 587
Emissions Trading Scheme (ETS), 587
Emotional intelligence, 277
Emotionality, 275–276
Emotional motives, 392–393
Emotional quotient (EQ), 277
Emotions, managing, 277
Empathy, 277
Employee-focused leader behavior, 309
Employee information systems, 340
Employee Retirement Income Security
    Act (ERISA) of 1974, 341t, 342
Employees, 78–79. *See also* Motivation;
    individual differences
    behaviors of, 150–152, 151f, 272–275
    ethical behaviors towards, 65–66
    jobs for, matching of, 280–282
    social commitments to, 79
    social responsibility towards, 74, 78–79
    stakeholder model of responsibility
        for, 71, 72
Employee stock ownership plans
    (ESOP), 120
Employment at will, 344
Empowerment, 291
Encryption software/system, 499
Engagement, 272
Engardio, Pete, 209
Enrichment programs for jobs, 291–292
Enron-Arthur Andersen scandal, 519
Enron Corporation, 66, 69, 72, 178, 312,
    317, 519, 601
Enterprise, 33, 41
Enterprise resource planning (ERP),
    482–483
Entertainment-driven corporations, 46
Entrepreneurs, 37, 105, 176, 604
Entrepreneurship, 105–106
Environment
    air pollution in, 74–75
    analysis of, 184

competitive, 381–382
economic, 380
external, 33–36, 34f, 379
hostile work, 344
internal, 33
land pollution in, 76
marketing, 379–382, 379f
political-legal, 379
social responsibility towards, 74–76
technological, 380
water pollution in, 75
workplace, challenges in changing,
    354–357
Environmental management system, 255
E-partnering, 182
Epernicus, 485
Equal employment opportunity,
    341–342, 341t
Equal Employment Opportunity
    Commission (EEOC), 83,
    342, 344
Equal Pay Act of 1963, 341t, 342
Equilibrium price, 42
Equipment, secured loans for, 603
Equity
    defined, 521
    financing, 611
    negative, 521
    owners', 521, 523
    positive, 521
    sweat, 115
    theory of, 287–288
Ergen, Charlie, 308
Ernst & Young, 394, 516
Established market, 107
E.T., 425
Ethical behaviors, 65–68
Ethical compliance, 85
Ethical judgments, 68, 69f
Ethical leadership, 317
Ethical norms, 68
Ethics
    accounting, 531–533
    ambiguities of, 65
    business, 65–70
    codes of, 65, 69–70
    customers, of advertising to, 78
    defined, 66
    employees, commitments to, 79
    individual, 65, 81
    information technology, concerns in,
        500–501, 501t
    instituting programs for, 69, 70
    laws of, 65
    managerial, 65–67
    real world, 65
    workplace, 64–70
Etihad Airways, 186
E*TRADE, 416, 596
Euro, 143
Europe, 136–137
European Central Bank (ECB), 551,
    570–571

European Union (EU), 138, 139f
European Union Regulation 261/2004,
    231
Everbest Port Services, 347
Everex Systems, Inc., 399
Evoked set, 392
Exchange
    currency, 558
    global, 482
    medium of, 553
    rates of, 143, 570–571
    stock, 593–595
Exchange-traded fund (ETF), 592
Exclusive distribution, 449
Executive Leadership Council, 316
Executive Order 11246, 341t
Executive Succession System (ESS), 340
Existing products, 429–430
Expectancy theory, 287
Expedia.com, 450
Expense items, 415–416
Expenses, 524, 592
Experience for becoming manager, 172–173
Experimentation, 391
Expert power, 308
Exporters, 147
Exports, 135, 141f
Extended Stay Hotels, 313
Extension of products, 423
External customers, 255
External environments, 33–36, 34f, 379
External recruiting, 345
External supply, 340
Extranets, 486–487
Extraversion, 276
Extroverts, 276
ExxonMobil, 70, 73, 82f, 147, 609

F

Facebook, 102, 104, 106, 114, 355,
    395–396, 398, 446, 454, 456, 485,
    496, 498, 568, 604, 607
Face value, 605
Factory outlets, 451
Fair and Accurate Credit Transactions
    Act (FACTA), 499
Fair Labor Standards Act, 341t, 342
Fair market price, 528
Fairmont Resort Hotels, 379
Fair trade, 63–64
"Fair Trade Certified," 64
Fair Trade-certified products, 64
Fairtrade Labeling Organizations (FLO),
    63–64
"Fairtrade Minimum Price," 63
Fair value accounting, 528
Fair value disclosure, 535
False Claims Act, 79, 86
Family and Medical Leave Act (FMLA)
    of 1993, 341t, 342
Fannie Mae, 566
Fantastic Sam's, 109

Fantasy stock markets, 600–601
Favors, 84
Federal Deposit Insurance Corporation (FDIC), 551, 561
Federal Express (FedEx), 42, 72, 84, 144, 215, 235, 238, 239–240, 243, 349, 454
Federal funds rate, 564
Federal Housing Finance Agency (FHFA), 566
Federal Open Market Committee, 562, 564
Federal Reserve Act of 1913, 562
Federal Reserve Bank, 562–564
Federal Reserve Board, 552
Federal Reserve System (the Fed), 52, 560, 562–565
   defined, 562
   functions of, 563
   structure of, 562–563
   tools of, 563–564
Federal restrictions, 519–520
Federal Trade Commission (FTC), 76, 83, 499
FedExpac, 84
Feedback, 353–354
Female Young Urban Professionals, 387
Ferrari, 387, 425
Ferriola, John J., 347
Fidelity Bank, 568
Fidelity® NASDAQ Composite Index® Tracking Stock, 599
Figurehead, 175
Finance companies, 557
Finances/financing, 603–607. *See also* Corporate bonds
   angel investors for, 604
   capital for, 603–604
   cash flows from, 525–526
   debt, 609–610
   equity, 611
   international, 569–572
   investors, management for, 79–80
   loans for, 603–604
   misrepresentation of, 80
   small business, 110–111
Financial accounting, 515
Financial advice, 558
Financial firms, 103
Financial Industry Regulatory Authority (FINRA), 612
Financial institutions, 556–558
Financial managers, 175
Financial planning, 108
Financial reporting, 519–520
Financial safety, 591
Financial Sector Charter (2003), 606
Financial stability, 591
Financial statements, 521–526
   analysis of, 527–531
   balance sheets on, 522–523, 522f
   budget on, 526, 526f
   defined, 521
   income statements on, 523–525, 524f

   internal, 526
   statement of cash flows on, 525–526, 525f
Financial system, U.S., 556–559
Financial transactions, 519
Fiorina, Carly, 218
Firewalls, 498
First-line managers, 174, 174t
First-mover advantages, 107–108
Fiscal policies, 52
Fitch, 606, 607
Fixed assets, 522
Fixed costs, 428
Fixed exchange rate, 143
Fixed position, 243–244
Fixed pricing, 430
Flaster, Michael, 183
Flat organizational structure, 210–211, 210f
Flexibility
   for customization, 483, 484f
   strategies for, 238
Flextime programs, 292–293
Floating exchange rate, 143
Florida Citrus Growers, 117
FlyDubai, 186
Focus groups, 391
Followers, leadership through eyes of, 311–312
Follow-up, 249, 463
Ford Motor Company, 74, 77f, 102, 120, 137, 147, 149, 169, 170, 174, 204, 214, 318, 351, 354, 358, 457, 486
Foreign Corrupt Practices Act, 83
Foreign direct investment (FDI), 149
Forensic accountants, 513–514, 518–519
Forensic accounting, 513–514, 518
Fortune, 72, 338, 385
Fox Business, 602
Franchise, 109
Franchisee, 109
Franchiser, 109
Franchising, 109
Fraud, 519
Fraud Advisory Panel, 514
Freddie Mac, 566
Freedom of choice, 44
Free market, 133
Free software, 497
Frenkel, John, 513–514
Frigidaire, 449
Frito-Lay, 173, 174
FTD, 146
Full disclosure, 527
Full-service brokers, 596
Full-service merchant wholesalers, 450
Functional departmentalization, 207
Functional organizational structure, 213, 213f
Functional strategy, 182–183
Funds
   aggressive growth, 591
   balanced, 591

   exchange-traded, 592
   load, 591
   mutual, 554–555, 591
   no-load, 591
   pension, 557
   private pension, 557
   public pension, 557

G
Gainsharing, 349
Gainsharing plans, 349
Galleon Group, 612
Gallup poll, 99
Gamesa Corporation, 379
GameStop, 74
Gantt graphical method, 248, 248f
Gap Inc., 45, 460, 465
Gasoline prices, 31–32
Gates, Bill, 111
GEICO, 446
Gender, leadership and, 315
General Agreement on Tariffs and Trade (GATT), 138
General Electric (GE), 77f, 82f, 181, 185, 216, 233, 291, 349, 351, 354, 608
General expenses, 524
Generally accepted accounting principles (GAAP), 516, 533, 535
General Mills, 173, 458
General Motors (GM), 40, 47, 51, 74, 75, 117–118, 120, 137, 150, 349, 358, 387, 431, 597, 605
General partners/partnerships, 115–116
Generation Y, 387
Geo-demographic segmentation/variables, 387
Geographic clusters, 136–138
Geographic departmentalization, 207–208
Geographic segmentation/variables, 387
Ghosn, Carlos, 316
Ghriskey, Timothy M., 215
Gilboa, Dave, 107
Gillette, 430
Gleissner, Michael, 286
Global alliances, 138–139
Global business, 33, 34, 34f
Global corporations, 105
Global economy, 134–139. *See also* International business
   alliances in, 138–139
   cultural environment in, 149–152
   international trade in, 140–145, 140t
   major world marketplaces in, 136–138
   trade agreements in, 138–139
Global exchange, 482
Global Fraud Studies, 514
Globalization, 134, 148
Global management skills, 179
Global opportunities, 112
Global Stevedoring Service Co., 347
Global stock exchanges, 594–595, 594t
Global supply chains, 257

Globus, 487
Gmail, 483
Goals
achieving, 169
corporate culture and setting, 181
defined, 179
of entrepreneurship, 105–106
intermediate, 181
long-term, 181
orientation of, 152
setting, 108, 180–181
short-term, 181
strategic, 184
types of, 181
Go Compare, 232
Godiva, 245
Goetzmann, Gordon, 72
Going green challenge, 381
Goldman Sachs, 431, 593, 606
Goods. *See also* Services
consumer, 378
convenience, 415
distribution of, 446–448
industrial, 378
manufacturing operations for, 235–236
marketing of, 378
operations and, 232–234, 233–234f
physical, 250
production of, 237
as products, 415–416
shopping, 415
specialty, 415
Goodwill, 523
Goodyear, 104, 349, 354, 446
Google, Inc., 32, 111, 167–169, 183, 188,
203, 355, 382, 417, 418, 424, 481,
483, 521–525, 529, 530–531, 535, 608
Gordon, Gil, 293
Government market, 394
Governments
banks of, 563
emergency investment by, 566
intervention by, 565–566
markets for, 394
organizations, influences on, 83–84
regulatory agencies of, 515
social responsibility and, 82–84
Graduate Junction, 485
Grapevine, 219
Graziado School of Business and
Management, 272
Green marketing, 76, 77t
Grocery Dash, 241
Gross, Bill, 306
Gross domestic product (GDP), 47–49,
48f, 48t, 233–234, 234f
Gross national product (GNP), 47
Gross profit, 524
Groupon, 464
Groupware, 491
Grubman, Jack, 72
Grupo Gigante, 154
Gucci, 388

H

Hackers, 496
Halliburton Corporation, 121, 149, 340, 348
Halo error, 353
Hamburger University, 351
Handheld computers, 490
HappyPetCare.net, 483
Harassment, 275, 344
Hardware, 490–491
Harford, Tim, 64
Harley-Davidson, 425, 463
Hastings, Reed, 99–100, 107, 445–446
Hawthorne Works of Western
Electric, 282
Hawthrone effect, 282
Hayhow, Jack, 313
Health, legal issues with, 343
Health savings accounts (HSAs), 350
H-E-B Grocery Company, 457
Hedlund, Marc, 320
Heinz, 458
Henderson, Jill, 280–281
Hershey Foods, 147, 483
Hertz, 149
Herzberg, Frederick, 284
Herzberg's two-factor theory, 284–285
Hewlett-Packard, 70, 73, 176, 188, 204,
218, 425, 454
HFC Beneficial, 557
Hierarchy of human needs model,
283–284
High-contact systems, 237–238
High-income countries, 136
Hirschfeld, Alexa and James, 456
Hitler, Adolf, 308, 312
Hobeika, Hind, 180
Hoffman, Reid, 398
Hofstede, Geert, 151
Home Depot, 135, 451, 530
Home Shopping Network, 489
Homeshoring, 209
Honda, 145
Hong Kong International Terminals
(HIT), 346, 347
Hoskins, Nick, 134
Hostile work environment, 344
Hot Topic, 387
Hotwire.com, 450
House of Cards, The, 100, 446
How the Market Works, 601
The HP Way, 70
H&R Block, 421
Hui Lu, 286
Human capital, 339
Human resource management (HRM).
See also Human resources (HR)
of benefits, 349
of compensation, 348–349
defined, 338
foundations of, 338–341
job analysis and, 340
legal context of, 341–344
of organized labor, 357–360

skills for, 177
strategic importance of, 338–339
workforce development and, 351–354
of workplace environment, 354–356
Human resource managers, 174
Human resources (HR). *See also* Human
resource management (HRM)
demand and supply for, 340–341
models of, 283
planning for, 339–341, 339f
recruiting, 344–345
selecting, 345–348
staffing of, 344–348
Hummer, 387
Hurricane Katrina, 65, 78
Hurricane Rita, 78
Hurricane Sandy, 187, 218
Hutchinson Whampoa, 346, 347
Hyatt Hotels, 432
Hybrid market, 594
Hygiene factors, 284
Hypertext transfer protocol (HTTP), 486
Hyundai Motor Company, 137, 425, 431

I

IBM, 81, 111, 117, 147, 351, 454, 462,
490–491
Ideas, marketing of, 378
IdentityGuard.com, 483
Identity theft, 497–499
Identity Theft Resource Center, 498–499
IKEA, 425
Illinois Tool Works Foundation, 82f
ImClone, 80
Imperial Oil, 150
Imperial Tobacco, 134
Importers, 147
Imports, 134, 141f
Incentive programs, 348–349
Income
net, 524–525
operating, 524–525
statements of, 523–525, 524f
Incompetence of managers, 113
Incorporation, 117–118
Independent agents, 148
Index
Big Mac, 49, 49f
market, 596
stock, 596–599, 597f
Index-matching ETFs, 599
Indirect influence, 83
Indirect regulation, 83
Individual differences, 275–280
attitudes at work, 278–280
defined, 275
personality at work, 275–278
Individual ethics, 65, 81
Individual investor trading, 595–596
Individualism, 151, 315
Individual retirement accounts (IRAs),
558, 571

Individual value/valuation, 65
Inducements, 280–281
Industrial buying, 415
Industrial goods, 378
Industrial market, 394
Industrial selling, 460
Industry services, 417
Inexperience of managers, 113
Infectious intrusions, 499
Inflation, 51, 426, 563
Influences, 83, 391–392
Informal groups, 218–219
Informal organizational structure, 218–220
Information
    for accounting, users of, 514–515
    defined, 492
    instant, remote access to, 480–481
    inventories of, 250–251
    management of, 250
    resources for, 37–38, 492–494
    seeking, 392
    suppliers, linkages with, 494
Informational roles, 176, 176t
Information managers, 175
Information system (IS), 340, 492, 514
    knowledge, 494–495
    for managers, 492, 495
    types of, 494–496
Information systems managers, 492
Information technology (IT)
    building blocks of, 485–491
    for collaboration, increasing of, 482
    communication resources for, 486–487
    customization, flexibility for, 483, 484f
    defined, 480
    for efficient organizations, 481
    ethical concerns in, 500–501, 501t
    for global exchange, 482
    hardware, 490–491
    impacts of, 480–485
    for improving everyday lives, 484–485
    information resources and,
        leveraging, 492–494
    information systems as, 494–496
    Internet as, 486–487
    for management processes, 482–483
    networks, use of, 487–490
    for new business opportunities, 483–484
    portable offices, use of, 480–481
    power of, 491–495
    protection measures for, 498–501
    remote deliveries using, 481
    risks and threats to, 496–498
    software and, 490–491
Initial public offerings (IPOs), 121, 167,
    607–611
    debt financing, pros and cons of,
        609–610
    defined, 607
    equity financing, pros and cons of, 611
    market capitalization and, 609, 609t
    selling parts of company and, 608
    stock valuation and, 608–609

In-N-Out Burger, 351
Innovation, 101, 102
Insider trading, 79–80, 611–612
Inspirational value/valuation, 378
Instabeat, 180
Instant information, remote access to,
    480–481
Institute of Management Accountants
    (IMA), 518
Institutional investors, 121
Institutional market, 394
Institutional ownership, 120, 121
Insufficient capital, 113
Insurance companies, 557
Insurance films, 103
Intangibility, 236
Intangible assets, 523
Intangible services, 236
Intel, 82f, 595
Intellectual property, 497
Intellectual property theft, 497
Intensive distribution, 448
Intention, 279
Interactive marketing, 464–465
Interactive retailing, 453
Interbrand, 423
Interest, 599–600
    conflict of, 66
    current yield of, 599
    defined, 603
    primary agents of, 67
    rates of, controls, 564
Intermediaries, 446–448, 448f
Intermediate goals, 181
Internal customers, 255
Internal environment, 33
Internal financial statements, 526
Internal recruiting, 345
Internal Revenue Service (IRS), 116
Internal supply, 340
International Academy of Film and
    Television (IAFT), 286
International accounting, 533–536
International Accounting Standards
    Board (IASB), 533–535
International Bank for Reconstruction
    and Development, 571
International banking, 569–572
International business
    expansion of, 144, 145–146, 146f
    levels of international involvement in,
        147–148
    management of, 145–149
    organizational structure of, 148–149
International communities, 73
International competition, 382
International consolidation, 595
International demand, gauging, 146
International distribution, 396–397
International finance, 569–572
International Financial Reporting
    Standards, 536
International firms, 147

International marketing mix, 396–397
International Monetary Fund (IMF), 551,
    571–572
International organizational structure,
    215–216, 217f
International Organization for
    Standardization (ISO), 255
International pricing, 396, 432
International products, 396
International promotion, 397
International services, 558
International trade, 140–145, 140t
    balance of payments and, 142–143
    balance of trade and, 140–142, 141–142f
    barriers to, 152–153
    competitive advantage in, 144–145
    economic differences in, 152
    exchange rates in, 143
    legal differences in, 153–154
    political differences in, 153–154
Internet, 486–487
Internet service providers (ISPs), 499
Interpersonal roles, 175–176, 176t
Interviews, 346–347
Intimate Brands, 121
Intraday trading, 592
Intranets, 486
Intrapreneuring, 219–220
Introverts, 276
Intuition, 323
Inventor, 220
Inventory
    controlling, 250
    of information, 250–251
    just-in-time system for, 457
    merchandise, 522
    of skills, 340
Investigative accounting, 518
Investing/investments
    cash flows from, 525
    foreign direct, 149
    online, 596
    stock, 589–590
Investment banks, 593
Investment dividends, 599–600. *See also*
    Interest
Investors, 515
    angel, 604
    improper financial management for,
        79–80
    institutional, 121
    social responsibility towards, 74, 79–80
    stakeholder model of responsibility
        of, 71, 72–73
ISO 9000, 255
ISO 14000, 255
Italian Job, The, 425

J

Jackson, Phil, 312
Jazeera Airways, 186
J.C. Penney, 188, 432, 452, 455

J. Crew, 45
Jeffries, Michael, 202
JetBlue, 46, 530
Jobs
 analysis of, 340
 commitment to, 280
 creation of, 101–102
 description of, 340
 for employees, matching of, 280–282
 enrichment programs for, 291–292
 redesign programs for, 292
 rotation of, 291
 satisfaction of, 280
 security of, 359
 specialization in, 204–205
 specification of, 340
Job-sharing programs, 292
Job shops, 243
Jobs, Steve, 312, 413
John Deere, 289, 449
John Hancock Insurance, 293
Johnson, Jimmy, 425
Johnson & Johnson, 70, 71, 82f, 86, 214, 494
Johnson, Kelly, 220
Joint Strike Fighters, 482, 487
Joint ventures, 120, 149
JPMorgan Chase, 73, 82f, 556, 565, 567, 593, 610
Judgmental methods, 352
Judgments, ethical, 68, 69f
Jung, Andrea, 315
Jung, Carl, 276
Junior Mints, 425
Junk e-mail, 498
JustCloud, 488
Justice, 68
Just-in-time (JIT) inventory system, 457

K

Kahneman, Daniel, 290
Ka-shing, Li, 346–347
Kate Spade, 465
Katzeff, Paul, 133–134
Kelleher, Herb, 170, 173
Kellogg Company, 396
Kelly Services, 356
Kenmore, 425
Kennedy, John F., 76
Kent, Carol, 337
Kent & Curwen, 423
Kentucky Fried Chicken, 423
Keny-Guyer, Neal, 41
Kerns, Charles, 272
Key rate, 564
Kias, 241
King, Martin Luther Jr., 312
Kinko's Copy Centers, 243
Kjerulf, Alexander, 271–272
Kmart, 32, 417
Knight, Jason, 320
Knowledge information systems, 494

Knowledge workers, 354, 494–495
Kodak, 32, 51, 422, 423
Korean Air Lines, 78
Korn Ferry International, 313
Koufax, Sandy, 598
KPMG, 393, 516
Kraft Foods, 45, 207, 597
Kroc, Ray, 109
Kroger Co., 493
Kyoto Protocol on Climate Change, 587

L

Labor, 37
 organized, 357–360
 productivity and, 252
Labor-Management Relations Act, 341t, 343
Labor relations, 202, 343, 357
Labor union, 357. See also Unions
Land pollution, 76
Lands' End, 71, 452
Language, 150
Larson, Paul, 272
Late fees, 99–100
Launching a business, 99–100
Lauren, Ralph, 153
Laws
 business practice, 154
 of demand and supply, 42–44
 of ethics, 65
 local content, 154
 of supply, 42
Layout, 242–244
Leader–member exchange (LMX) model, 311
Leaders
 behaviors of, 309, 311
 as coaches, 315
 group, 174
 role of, 175
Leading/leadership. See also Decisions/ decision making
 behavioral approaches to, 309
 charismatic, 312
 cross-cultural, 315–316
 defined, 169, 306
 in distribution, 449
 early approaches to, 308–309
 emerging issues in, 317
 ethical, 317
 followers, through eyes of, 311–312
 gender and, 315
 management and, 169–170, 306–307, 306f, 318–324
 nature of, 306–308, 314–316
 neutralizers of, 314, 314t
 organization, 86
 path-goal theory of, 309–310
 power and, 307–308
 situational approaches to, 310–311, 310f
 special issues in, 313–314
 strategic, 317

substitutes for, 313–314, 314t
 trait approaches to, 308
 transactional, 312
 transformational, 311–312
 virtual, 317
Lean production systems, 250
Learning organizational structure, 217–218
Legal compliance, 85
Legal issues
 employees, commitments to, 79
 human resource management, context of, 341–344
 international trade, differences in, 153–154
Legitimate power, 307
Lehman Brothers, 565, 606
Lenova, 204
Lesar, David, 348
Letter of credit, 558
Leverage, 529
Leverage, 425
Leveraged buyouts, 529
Levi Strauss, 291, 417, 423, 446–447, 460
LG Electronics, 449
Liabilities, 523
 accounting equation for, 521
 current, 523
 defined, 521
 limited, 118
 long-term, 523
 unlimited, 115
Liaison role of managers, 175
Licensed brands, 425
Licensing agreements/arrangements, 149
Lids, 451, 453
LifeLock.com, 483
Limited-function merchant wholesalers, 450
Limited liabilities, 118
Limited liability corporations (LLC), 119, 119t
Limited partners/partnerships, 116
Limited, The, 121
Lincoln, Abraham, 308
Line authority, 212, 212f
Line departments, 212
Line managers, 212
Linens-N-Things, 33
LinkedIn, 395, 398, 463, 485, 568
Lion's Club, 81
Liquidating, 522
Liquidity, 522
Liszt, Franz, 206
Litigation support of forensic accountants, 518–519
Little Earth Productions, Inc., 398
Little League baseball, 73
LivingSocial.com, 375
L.L. Bean, 71, 393, 431, 453
Load funds, 591
Loans
 asset-backed, 603
 long-term, 609–610

principal of, 603
secured, 603
special purpose, 110
unsecured, 603–604
Lobbying, 84
Local area networks (LANs), 488–489
Local communities, 71, 73
Local content laws, 154
Location, operations planning for, 241–242
Lockheed Martin, 86, 220, 482, 487
Lockouts, 360
Locus of control, 277
Logan Aluminum, 246–247
Lombardi, Vince, 312
Long-term goals, 181
Long-term liabilities, 523
Long-term loans, 609–610
Long-term solvency ratios, 529
Louis Vuitton, 154, 388
Low-contact systems, 237
Lower annual operating expenses, 592
Lower-middle-income countries, 136
Low-income countries, 136
Loyalty programs, 464
Loyalty to brand, 391
Lucasfilm Foundation, 82f
Lufthansa, 77–78
Lulu, 426
Lüpke, Phillip, 413

M

Machiavellianism, 278
Machiavelli, Niccolo, 278
Mackey, John, 350
Macy's, 453
Madoff, Bernard, 67, 79, 598
Magee, David, 86
Mail order, 452
Majestic Crest theater, 286
Major League Baseball, 289
Major stock exchanges, 594–595
Make-to-order operations, 237
Make-to-order shops, 243
Make-to-stock operations, 237
Management. *See also* Human resource management (HRM); Managers; Strategic management; Total quality management (TQM)
    areas of, 174–175
    art of, 171
    contingency planning and, 187
    corporate culture and, 188–189
    of corporations, 120
    crisis, 187
    customer relationship, 378
    defined, 168
    of emotions, 277
    functions of, 168–171
    of information, 250
    of international business, 145–149
    leadership and, 306–307, 306f, 318–324

levels of, 173–174, 174t
materials, 249–251
participative, 291
planning, functions of, 169
process of, 168–173, 482–483
of production, 234–235
quality, 252–254
roles in, 175–177, 176t
science of, 171
scientific, 171, 282
skills in, 177–179
supply chain, 256–257
time, 178
of U.S. economy, 52
Management accountants, 518
Management accounting, 515
Management advisory services, 517
Management by objectives (MBO), 289
Management information systems (MIS), 495
Managerial accounting, 515
Managerial ethics, 65–67
Managers. *See also* Management; specific types of
    becoming, 171–173
    competence of, 113
    defined, 167
    e-mail for, 178
    incompetence of, 113
    inexperience of, 113
    information system for, 492, 495
    liaison role of, 175
    marketing by, 174–175, 383–384
    meetings for, 178
    paperwork for, 178
    telephone calls for, 178
    types of, 173–175
Mango, 201, 202
Mann, Thomas, 449
Manufacturing, 104, 137
    computer-aided, 495
    of goods, 235–236
    industry for, 103
    of services, 235–236
Marketable securities, 522
Market cap, 609
Market coverage, 448
Market economy, 39. *See also* Economy
    competition in, 44–46
    defined, 39
    demand and supply in, 41–44, 43f
    mixed, 39–40
    private enterprise in, 44–46
    pure, 39
Market indexes, 596
Marketing. *See also* Markets; specific types of
    business-to-business, 394–395
    business-to-consumer, 377
    consumer behavior and, 391–393
    defined, 376
    environment of, 379–382, 379f
    of goods, 378

of ideas, 378
interactive, 464–465
by managers, 174–175, 383–384
objectives of, 383
organizational, 394–397
permission, 465
plan for, 382–386, 383f
products in, 420
relationship, 378–379
research on, 388–391
of services, 378
small business, 397–399
strategies for, 383–388
value in, 376–377
vice-president for, 175
viral, 395
Marketing managers, 175
Marketing mix, 383–386
Market penetration objectives, 427
Markets. *See also* Marketing; specific types of
    capitalization of, 609, 609t
    defined, 39
    economics of systems of, 41–46
    free, 133
    outcry, 594
    price in, 42
    reseller, 394
    segmentation of, 387–388, 388t
    services companies, 394
    speed to, 419
    value/valuation of, 590
Market share objectives, 427
Marketwatch.com, 602
Markopolos, Harry, 86
Markup, 427–428
Marlboro, 396
Marriott Hotels and Resorts, 390
Martha Stewart Living Omnimedia, 215
Martha Stewart scandal, 80
Martin, Mark, 425
Marvel, 137, 595
Marx, Karl, 39
Mary Kay, 452
Maslow, Abraham, 283–284
Maslow's hierarchy of human needs model, 283–284
Massachusetts Mutual Life Insurance, 351
Mass customization, 483
MasterCard, 182
Master operations scheduling, 246–247, 246–247f
Materials management, 249–251
Matrix organizational structure, 214–215, 216f
Maturity date, 605
Matz, Jack, 105
Maxwell House, 207
Maytag, 257
Mazda, 120
McClelland, 285

McDonald's Corporation, 46, 81, 109, 135, 144, 146, 149, 172, 208, 209, 242, 351, 375, 386, 387, 391, 395, 396, 423, 480
McGregor, Douglas, 283
MCI, 610
McKim, Alan, 113
McLaughlin, Edward, 338
McNamara, Anne, 76
McNamara, Stephen, 232
Media, 395–396, 459–460, 461t
MediaBids.com, 430, 450–451
Media mix, 460
Mediation, 360
Medicare, 86
Medium of exchange, 553
Meetings for managers, 178
Meet the Boss, 485
Meijers, 417
Mellinger, Doug, 112
Member banks, 563
Menendez, Robert, 316
Mercedes, 424, 458, 570
Merchandise inventory, 522
Merchants of Green Coffee, 133
Merchant wholesaler/wholesaling, 449–450
Merck & Co., 76, 82f, 175, 417–420
Merck Pharmaceuticals, 273
Mercy Corps, 41
Mergers, 121, 201, 202
Mergers and acquisitions (M&As), 120, 121
Merit salary systems, 348
Merkel, Angela, 315
Merrill Lynch, 280–281, 558, 596
Merry Maids, 417
MetLife Foundation, 82f
Metro, 451
Metropolitan Life, 72, 293
Mexico, 137
Mickey Mouse, 425
Microcredit, 41
Microfinance, 41
Microfinance institutions (MFI), 41
Microloans, 41, 110
Microsoft, 72, 109, 114, 135, 149, 176, 215, 292, 338–339, 377, 490, 499, 530, 535, 595
Middle managers, 173, 174t
Middlemen, 446. *See also* Intermediaries
Midnight Movie, 286
Millennia's, 387
Miller, William, 598
Mini Cooper, 425
Mining data, 379, 493–494
Minorities, opportunities for, 111–112
Minority enterprise small business investment companies (MESBICs), 110
Mint.com, 320
Missionary selling, 462

Mission statements, 181, 203
Mr. Coffee, 457
Mr. Pibb, 419
Mitsubishi, 85
Mixed market economy, 39–40
Modified work schedules, 292–293
M-1 money, 553–556, 555f
Monetary policies, 52, 563
Money. *See also* Banking system; Federal Reserve System (the Fed); U.S. financial system
  banking system, regulation of, 560–561, 560f
  characteristics of, 552
  defined, 552
  functions of, 553
  international banking, 569–572
  international finance, 569–572
  M-1, 553–554
  M-2, 554–556
  plastic, 556
  portability of, 552
  stability of, 552
  supply of, 563
  time value of, 588–589
Money market mutual funds, 554, 555
Money.msn.com, 602
Monitor, 176
Monopolistic competition, 44–46, 45t
Monopoly, 46
Monsanto, 175
Montgomery Ward, 178
Moody's, 605, 606, 607
Morale, 280
Moral harassment, 274
Morally objectionable advertising, 78
Morgan Stanley, 593
Morial, Marc H., 316
Mortality rates for new products, 419
Mortgage-backed securities (MBS), 565, 607
Moser, Robert, 137
Motivation
  behaviors, goals for, 289
  classical theory of, 282
  contemporary theory of, 287–288
  defined, 282
  early behavioral theory of, 282–287
  punishment for, 290
  strategies and techniques for enhancing, 289–293
Motorola, 215, 254–255
MSNBC, 602
MSN Money, 239–240
MTV, 394
M-2 money, 554–556, 555f
Mulally, Alan, 169–170
Multinational corporations, 119, 119t
Multinational firms, 147–148, 147t
Municipal bonds, 605
Murdoch, Rupert, 312
Muret, Thierry, 245
Museum of Modern Art, 168

Mutual funds, 554–555, 591–592
Mutual savings bank, 557
Myers-Briggs Type Indicator (MBTI), 276–277
Myrddin Group, 272
MySpace, 114

N

NACHA, 567
NASA, 214, 482
NASCAR, 425
NASDAQ Composite Index, 596, 598–599
National Association of Securities Dealers Automated Quotation (NASDAQ) System, 595, 602
National brands, 425
National competitive advantage, 145
National Credit Act, 606
National Credit Union Administration (NCUA), 563
National culture, 150–152, 151f
National debt, 50
National Education Association (NEA), 358
National Federation of Independent Business, 110
National Football League, 289, 360
National Labor Relations Act, 341t, 343
National Labor Relations Board (NLRB), 83, 343
National Rifle Association (NRA), 84
National Security Agency, 500
National Semiconductor, 107, 454
National teachers' retirement system (TIAA CREF), 121
National Urban League, 316
NationsBank, 175
Nationwide Insurance Foundation, 82f
Natural monopoly, 46
Naval Oceanographic Office Major Shared Resource Center, 86
NCR, 423
Needs
  for achievement, 285
  for affiliation, 285
  of customers, adapting to, 146
  other important, 285–286
  for power, 285–286
  for recognition, 392
Negative equity, 521
Neglect, 113
Neiman Marcus, 388
Nescafé Café con Leche, 133
Nestlé, 137, 145, 147
Net earnings, 524–525
Netflix, 99–100, 104, 107, 113, 445–446
Net income, 524–525
Net profit, 524–525
Networks/networking, 487–490
  electronic communication, 595
  local area, 488–489
  social, 395–396

"super Wi-Fi," 490
wide area, 488
Wi-Fi, 489–490
wireless, 489, 489f
wireless local area, 489
wireless wide area, 489
Net worth, 521
New business. *See* Small business
Newegg.com, 453
Newington, Tim, 72
New products
developing, 417–421
mortality rates for, 419
pricing of, 430
product life cycle extension as
alternative to, 423
News Corp., 312
Newsweek, 78, 423
New ventures. *See* Small business
New York Stock Exchange (NYSE), 83,
116, 593–594, 602, 608
New York Times, The, 117, 496
New York Yankees, 323
Niche, 107
Niches in established markets, 107
Night Dragon, 480, 496
Nike, 175, 323, 449
Nikon, 181
Nintendo, 445
Nippon Steel, 137
No-load funds, 591
Nomie Baby, 399
Nominal gross domestic product, 49
Noncertified public accountants, 517
Noncorporate business ownership,
114–117, 115t
Nondeposit institutions, 557–558
Nondirect distribution, 448
Non-loss/non-dividend company, 41
Nonprogrammed decisions, 318
Nonstore retailing, 452
Nooyi, Indra, 173, 180, 315
Nordex AG, 379
Nordstrom, 74, 452
North America, 136
North American Free Trade Agreement
(NAFTA), 75, 138, 382
Novartis Patient Assistance Foundation,
Inc., 82f
Novell, 491
Nucor Steel, 358
NYSE Euronext, 595

O

Obama, Barack, 35, 40, 52, 84, 311,
381, 588
Obama, Michelle, 530
Objections, defined, 463
Observation, 390–391
Occupational Safety and Health Act
(OSHA) of 1970, 341t, 343
Oceana Cruises, 464, 483

Ocean Spray, 117
Odd-even pricing, 432
Office manager, 174
Officers, 120
chief executive, 120, 173
chief financial, 173, 175
chief information, 175
corporate, 120
defined, 120
Offshoring, 146, 209
Oil prices, 31–32
Oligopoly, 44, 45–46, 45t
Omaha Steaks, 85
Oman Air, 186
Omniva Policy Systems, 72
O'Neil, Lorraine Brennan, 319–320
Online customer service, 393
Online investing, 596
Online retailing, 453–454, 453t
On-the-job training, 351
Open market committee, 562
Open-market operations, 564
Openness, 276
Operating expenses, 524
Operating income, 524–525
Operations. *See also* Operations planning;
Productions; specific types of
business strategy as driver of,
238–240
capability of, 238
cash flows from, 525
controlling, 249–251
defined, 232–233
goods and, 232–234, 233–234f
management of, 234–235
plans for, 169, 185
processes for, 236–238
process of, 236
scheduling for, 246–249
service, 232, 233–234, 233–234f
transportation, 454, 455–456
value through, creating, 234–238, 235f
vice-presidents for, 174
Operations managers, 173–174, 235
Operations planning, 240–246, 240f
capacity for, 240–241
for layout, 242–244
for location, 241–242
methods of, 245–246
quality of, 244–245
Opportunities, 33, 483–484
Opportunity bias, 352
Oprah, 493
Opus Training and ReallyEasyHR, 313
Orange County (New York) Association
of Realtors, 356
Order processing, 461
Organic fair trade, 64
Organic products, 64
Organizational analysis, 185
Organizational charts, 169, 203, 203f
Organizational citizenship, 272–273
Organizational commitment, 280

Organizational culture, 86
Organizational grapevine, 219–219
Organizational marketing, 394–397
business-to-business buying behavior
and, 394–395
international marketing mix and,
396–397
social media and, 395–396
Organizational products, 415–416, 416t
Organizational structure, 202–204
building blocks of, 204–208
decision-making hierarchy and,
208–213
defined, 202
departmentalization and, 206–208
determinants of, 203–204
divisional, 213–214, 214f
flat, 210–211, 210f
forms of, 213–218
functional, 213, 213f
informal, 218–220
international, 215–216, 217f
of international business, 148–149
job specialization and, 204–205
learning, 217–218
matrix, 214–215, 216f
organizational charts and, 203, 203f
tall, 210–211, 210f
team, 217
for twenty-first century, 216–218
virtual, 217, 217f
Organization leadership, 86
Organization for Economic Cooperation and Development
(OECD), 531
Organization of Petroleum Exporting
Countries (OPEC), 154
Organizations. *See also* specific types of
core principles of, 69–70, 70f
ethical behaviors towards, 66–67
government influences of/on, 83–84
information technology, more efficient for, 481
mission of, 203
strategy of, 203
Organized labor, 357–360
collective bargaining and, 358–360, 358f
unionism and, 357–358, 357f
Organizing, defined, 169
Oscar Mayer, 207
Outcry market, 594
Outsourcing, 146, 209, 257
Overqualified, defined, 356
Overstringing, 206
Owners' equity, 521, 523
Ownership
book-entry, 596
of corporations, special issues in,
120–121
institutional, 120–121
noncorporate business, 114–117, 115t
of quality, 254
stock, 120

P

Pacific Asia, 137–138
Packaging, 77t, 425
Page, Larry, 167–169
Paid-in capital, 523
Pampers, 450
Panera Bread, 74
Papa Johns, 530
Paperless Post, 456
Paperwork for managers, 178
Paradise Laundry, 242
Paris Roissy Charles de Gaulle
        Airport, 144
Parma, 154
Participative leader behavior, 311
Participative management, 291
Partners/partnerships, 114, 115–116,
        115t
    active, 116
    advantages of, 115–116
    disadvantages of, 116
    general, 115–116
    limited, 116
    silent, 115
Par value, 605
Passive goal behavior, 152
Path-goal theory, 309–310
Patriot Act, 344
Paul, John II, 312
Payables, 523
Pay-for-knowledge plans, 349
Pay for performance, 348–349
Payments
    balance of, 142–143
    process for, 571
    variable, 348–349
PayPal, 114, 497, 558
PCMC, 209
Peanut Corporation of America, 81
Penetration pricing, 430
Pension fund, 557
Pension services, 558
Penske Truck Leasing, 209
People's United Bank, 568
People-Trading Services.com,
        491
Pepperdine University, 272
PepsiCo, 75, 173, 180, 182, 185, 188, 390,
        608–609
Per capita gross domestic product,
        48, 48f
Perfect competition, 44–45, 45t
Perfect Posters, 526
Performance
    appraisal of, 352–354, 353f
    behaviors and, 273
    defined, 245
    pay for, 348–349
    portfolios, differences for different,
        601–603
Performance behaviors, 272. *See also*
        Employees
Permanent work, 355, 356

Permission marketing, 465
Pernod-Ricard, 134
Personal contacts, 84
Personal influences, 391
Personality, 275–278
    "big five" traits of, 275–276
    defined, 275
    emotional intelligence and, 277
    Myers-Briggs framework for, 276–277
    other types of, 277–278
Personal selling, 385, 460–465
    defined, 460
    direct marketing for, 464
    process for, 463
    publicity and, 465
    public relations and, 465
    situations for, 460–461
    tasks for, 461–462
Person-job fit, 282
Peugeot Citroens, 241
Pharming, 497
Philadelphia Brand Cream Cheese, 427
Philanthropic giving, 85
Phishing, 497
Physical distribution, 454–457
Physical goods, 250
Physical resources, 37
Picketing, 360
Pilon Café Cubano, 133
Pinterest, 395
Pizza Hut, 149
Place/placement, 384–385, 593
Planned economy, 38–39
Plans/planning, 339–341, 339f
    for business, 108
    cafeteria benefits, 349
    contingency, 187
    defined, 169
    enterprise resource, 482–483
    financial, 108
    gainsharing, 349
    hierarchy of, 182f, 185
    management, functions of, 169
    marketing, 382–386, 383f
    operations, 169, 185, 240–246, 240f
    pay-for-knowledge, 349
    profit-sharing, 349
    retirement, 349
    strategic, 185
    tactical, 169, 185
Plant manager, 173, 174
Plastic money, 556
Pledge, 480
PNC Foundation, 82f
Poilâne, Lionel, 144
Point-of-sale (POS) displays/terminals,
        464, 569
Political action committees (PACs),
        84, 380
Political-legal environment, 33, 34f, 35, 379
Politics, 153–154, 323
Ponoko.com, 483
Pontiac, 387

Ponzi, Charles, 598
Porsche, 184
Portability of money, 552
Portable offices, 480–481
Portfolios, 601–603
Positioning, defined, 458
Positive equity, 521
Post, 207
Postini, 168
Postpurchase evaluation, 393
Power
    coercive, 307–308
    defined, 307
    expert, 308
    leadership and, 307–308
    legitimate, 307
    need for, 285–286
    orientation of, 151–152
    referent, 308
    reward, 307
    tolerance to, 152
Pregnancy Discrimination Act,
        341t, 342
Premiums, 464
Presentation, 463
President, 120, 173
Presidential Air Force One, 382
Priceline.com, 430
Prices/pricing, 384, 399
    appreciation of, 600
    concept of, 414
    cost-oriented, 427–428
    to customers, 77–78
    defined, 425
    determining, 425–429
    dynamic, 429–430
    equilibrium, 42
    fair market, 528
    fixed, 429–430
    gasoline, 31–32
    gouging of, 78
    international, 396, 432
    lining of, 431
    market, 42
    to meet business objectives, 426–427
    of new products, 430
    objectives of, 426–427
    odd-even, 432
    oil, 31–32
    penetration, 430
    points for, 432
    psychological, 432
    of shares, 608
    skimming, 430
    of stocks, 608–609, 609t
    strategies for, 384, 429–430
    tactics for, 431–432
    tools for setting, 427–428
PricewaterhouseCoopers, 513
Primary agents, 67
Primary securities market, 593
Prime rate, 556, 557f
Prince, The (Machiavelli), 278

Principles of Scientific Management, The (Taylor), 282
Print server, 487
Private accountants, 518
Private brands, 425
Private cloud, 488
Private corporations, 118
Private enterprise, 41, 44–46
Private label, 425
Private pension fund, 557
Private placements, 593
Private property rights, 44
Private warehouses, 455
Privatization, 40
Problem recognition, 392
Process, 243, 243f
  departmentalization of, 207
  flows of, 245, 246f
  of identification, 421
  of selection, 421
Procter & Gamble (P&G), 173, 390, 396, 425, 432, 450, 494
Production items, 415
Production managers, 235
Production. *See also* Operations
  capability of, 238
  defined, 232
  factors of, 37–38
  of goods, 232, 237
  just-in-time, 250
  management of, 234–235
  operations for, 238–240
  processes of, 77t
  quality and, connection between, 252
  of service, 232
Production supervisors, 174
Productivity, 49–50, 252
Product-line retailers, 451
Product mix, 416–417
Products, 243–244, 244f, 398. *See also* Gross domestic product (GDP); New products; Prices/pricing
  adaptation of, 423
  branding of, 423–424, 424t
  business analysis of, 420
  champion, 220
  classifications of, 414
  commercialization of, 420
  competitive analysis of, 254
  concept testing of, 420
  consumer, 415, 416t
  defined, 384
  demand for, 113
  departmentalization of, 207
  differentiation between, 384
  existing, 429
  extension of, 423
  Fair Trade-certified, 64
  features of, 414
  goods as, 415–416
  gross national, 47
  ideas for, 420
  identifying, 423–424

international, 396
life cycle of, 421–425, 422f
lines of, 417
modification of, 77t
organic, 64
organizational, 415–416, 416t
packaging, 425
place for, 384–385
placement of, 424–425
positioning of, 387
prototype development of, 420
screening, 420
services as, 415–416
strategies for, 384
substitute, 382
testing, 420
value package for, 414–415
Professional conduct, code of, 532–533t
Professional corporations, 119, 119t
Profitability ratios, 528–530
Profit center, 206
Profits, 427–429
  concept of, 32–33
  defined, 32
  lure of, 44
  net, 524–525
  objectives for maximizing, 426–427
Profit-sharing plans, 349
Program Evaluation and Review Technique (PERT), 248–249, 249f
Programmed decisions, 318
Progressive Insurance, 425
Project manager, 174
Project scheduling, 248–249
Promotional mix, 458–459, 459f
Promotions, 399
  advertising of, 459–460, 460f
  defined, 385, 457
  importance of, 457–460
  international, 397
  objectives of, 457–458
  sales, 463
  strategies for, 385–386, 458
Property, 44, 497
Proprietorships, 114–115, 115t
Prospecting, 463
Prospectus, 611
Protectionism, 153–154
PRT Group, 112
Prudential, 175
Psychographic segmentation/variables, 388
Psychological contracts, 280–281
Psychological influences, 391
Psychological pricing, 432
Public accounting firms, "big four," 516
Public cloud, 488
Public corporations, 118, 119
Publicity, 465
Publicly held corporations, 119, 119t
Public pension fund, 557
Public relations, 386, 465
Public relations managers, 175

Public warehouses, 455
Pull strategy, 458
Punishment, 289–290
Purchase decision, 392–393
Purchasing, 250
Purchasing power parity, 49
Pure market/planned economy, 39
Purina Cat Chow, 464
Push strategy, 458

Q

Qantas Airways, 202
Qatar Airways, 186
Qatar Exchange, 595
Qatar Petroleum International, 305–306
Qualifying, 463
Quality
  building, 251
  controlling, 251
  defined, 244–245
  improvement of, 251–256
  of intangible services, 236
  managing, 252–254
  of operations planning, 244–245
  ownership of, 254
  production and, connection between, 252
  as strategy, 238
Quality circles, 254
Quality improvement teams, 254–255
Quantitative easing (QE), 565
Quest Diagnostics, 380
Quick footed business, 253
Quid pro quo harassment, 344
Quotas, 153
QVC, 454

R

Racial harassment, 275
Radiant Organizing, 271
Radio Shack de México, 154
Raid, 480
Rajaratnam, Raj, 612
Raju, Ramalinga, 513
Ralph Lauren, 45
Ramada, 109
Rampart Investments, 86
Randolph, Marc, 99
Rapid prototyping, 495
Rates
  annual percentage, 603
  better survival, 112
  discount, 564
  of exchange, 143, 570–571
  federal funds, 564
  of interest, controls, 564
  key, 564
  prime, 556, 557f
Rational decision making, 320–323, 321f
Rational motives, 392–393
Ratios, 528–531

Rawlings, 483
Real gross domestic product, 48–49
Real growth rate, 47–48
Realistic job preview (RJP), 345
Real-time ad tracking, 459–460
Real world ethics, 65
Recency error, 353
Recession risks, 605–607
Recessions, 51–52
Recruiting, 344–345
Recycling, 76
Redesign programs for jobs, 292
Reebok, 323
Reengineering, 256–257
Reese's Pieces, 425
Referent power, 308
Regional marketing managers, 175
Regulations
    anticrime, 566–567
    antiterrorism, 566–567
    defined, 83
    direct, 83
    indirect, 83
    for securities market, 611–612
    through direct influence, 83
    zoning, 253
Reinforcement, 289–290
Reintroduction, 423
Related diversification, 182
Relationship marketing, 378–379
Relationships
    client, 292
    risk-return, 599–603, 600f
    risk–reward, 599
    seller, 395
Reliant Energy, 187
RE/Max, 109
Remote deliveries, 481
Repayment, assurances of, 566
Replacement charts, 340
Reporting
    financial, 519–520
    relationships, 203
    standards and practices for
        accountants, 526–527
Research and development
    expenses, 524
Research and development managers, 175
Research In Motion®, 489
Reseller market, 394
Reserve banks, 562, 562f
Reserve requirements, 564
Residential customers, 417
Resources
    activity ratios, efficient use of, 530–531
    for communication, 486–487
    information, 37–38, 492–494
    physical, 37
Responsibility. *See also* Social
        responsibility
    defined, 211
    stakeholder model of, 71–73
    for total quality management, 254

Restructuring, 201, 202
Retail distribution, 446–447
Retailing industry, 103
Retailing/retailers, 451–454
    bargain, 451
    brick-and-mortar retail outlets,
        types of, 451
    defined, 446
    direct-response, 452
    interactive, 453
    nonstore, 452
    online, 453–454, 453t
    video, 453–454
Retail selling, 460
Retained earnings, 523, 611
Retirement plans, 349
Revenues, 523–524
    recognition of, 527, 535
    web-driven, 395–396
Revised Uniform Limited Partnership
        Act, 116
Revlon, 396
Reward power, 307
Riceland, 117
Rights, 68
Risk propensity, 278, 324
Risk-return relationship, 599–603, 600f
    asset allocation and, 601
    diversification and, 601
    fantasy stock markets and, 600–601
    investment dividends and, 599–600
    performance and, 601–603
    price appreciation and, 600
    total return and, 600
Risk–reward relationship, 599
Risks, state of, 319
Ritz-Carlton Hotels, 458
Rive, Lyndon, 183
Rive, Peter, 183
Robb, Walter, 350
Robinson, Jr., Charles W., 86
Rockefeller, John D., 73
Rolex, 449
Ronald McDonald House Charities,
        81, 386
Roosevelt, Franklin D., 561
Roth individual retirement accounts, 558
Router, 498
Rubbermaid, 219
"Rule of 98," 588–589
Russell 2000 Index, 596, 598
Ryanair, 231–232

S

Saab, 387
Sabotage, 275
SA Express, 201, 202
Safety, 343, 591
Sahaab, 186
St. Luke's Hospital of Kansas City,
        251–252, 254
St. Paul Chamber Orchestra, 360

St. Petersburg Times, 496
Saks, 349
Salaries, 348
Sales
    of corporate bonds, 605–607
    forecasting, 108
    promotion and, 385, 464
Sales agents, 448
Salvation Army, 66
Same-steps layout, 243–244
Samsung, 137, 384, 390
Sanofi-aventis Patient Assistance
        Foundation, 82f
Sarbanes-Oxley Act of 2002 (Sarbox or
        SOX), 80, 519–520, 520t
Saturn, 387
Satyam Computer Services Ltd., 513
Save-a-Lot, 238
Savings accounts, 554
Savings and loan associations
        (S&Ls), 557
Savings institutions, 556
Savoy in London, 379
Scania, 184
Schedules/scheduling, 42, 246–249
Schick, Stacey, 356
Schuessler, Jack, 465
Schultz, Howard, 37, 106, 181, 317, 375
Science Applications International
        Corporation, 86
Scientific management, 171, 282
SC Johnson, 77f, 480
Scope, 425
S corporations, 119, 119t
Scotch tape, 425
Scottrade, 596
Sears, 74, 206, 425
Secondary data, 390
Secondary securities market, 593
Secured loans, 603
Securities. *See also* Securities market
    defined, 592
    marketable, 522
    mortgage-backed, 565, 607
    policies on, 498
Securities and Exchange Commission
        (SEC), 79, 83, 86, 515, 593, 611
Securities investment dealers, 558
Securities Investment Protection
        Corporation (SIPC), 598
Securities market. *See also* Trade/trading
    defined, 592
    primary, 593
    regulating, 611–612
    risk-return relationship in, 599–603, 600f
    secondary, 593
    stock exchanges and, 593–595
    stock indexes for tracking, 596–599, 597f
Segmentation, 387–388
Seinfeld, 425
Selection, process of, 421
Selective distribution, 449
Self-awareness, 277

Self-efficacy, 277–278
Self-esteem, 278
Self-motivation, 277
Seller relationships, 395
Selling
    creative, 461–462
    direct, 452
    expenses of, 524
    industrial, 460
    missionary, 462
    parts of company, 608
    personal, 385, 460–465
    retail, 460
Sensing, Keith, 286
Servers, 487
Service Corps of Retired Executives
        (SCORE), 111
ServiceMaster, 417
Service operations, 233–234, 233–234f
Service process design, 421
Services. *See also* Goods
    brokerage, 558
    business, 417
    certified public accountants, offered
        by, 516–517
    convenience, 415
    customer, 245
    defined, 378
    demand for, 113
    denial of, 496
    developing new, 420–421
    distribution of, 446–448
    ideas for, 420
    industry, 417
    intangible, 236
    management advisory, 517
    manufacturing operations for, 235–236
    marketing of, 378
    producing, 232, 237, 250–251
    as products, 415–416
    shopping, 415
    specialty, 415
    for taxes, 517
    trust, 558
Services companies market, 394
Services industry, 103
Service value package, 420
Seth Thomas, 394
7(a) loans programs, 110
7 Eleven, 109, 451
Sexual harassment, 275, 344
Shareholders, 120. *See also* Stockholders
Shares, 120. *See also* Stocks
    earnings per, 529, 608–609
    pricing of, 608
Shell Oil, 81, 172, 173, 203, 218, 293, 351
Sherman Antitrust Act, 46
Sherritt International, 134
Shinohara, Yoshiko, 106
Shopping agents, 450
Shopping goods/services, 415
Shortage, 42–44
Short-term goals, 181

Short-term solvency ratios, 529
Sickout, 360
Siemens AG, 83
Silent partner, 115
Singapore Airlines, 319
Singleton, Tommie, 513
Situational theories, 309
Skills inventories, 340
Skoda, 184
Slippery Fish Bait Supply Co., 604
Slumdog Millionaire, 146
Small business, 100–104
    business plan for, 108
    defined, 100
    distinctive competencies in, 106–108
    entrepreneurs for, 604
    failure of, 113
    financing, 110–111
    importance of, 101–102, 101f
    information technology for, 483–484
    marketing in, 397–399
    operating a, 106–111
    popular areas of, 102–104, 103f
    social responsibility and, 81–82
    starting a, 106–111
    success of, 113
    trends of, 111–112
Small Business Administration (SBA),
        100, 110–111
Small Business Development Center
        (SBDC), 111
Small business investment companies
        (SBICs), 110
Smart cards, 569
Smisek, Jeffrey, 180, 310
Smith, Fred, 215
SmithKline lab, 86
Smith, Richard, 484
Sneed, Simone, 356
Social audit, 87
Social business enterprise (SBE), 41
Social commitments, 79
Social influences, 391
Socialism, 39–40
Social learning, 289
Social media, 395–396
Social networking, 395–396, 398
Social orientation, 151
Social responsibility, 71–74
    accommodative stance to, 81
    approaches to, 80–81, 80f
    areas of, 74–80
    contemporary social consciousness
        and, 73–74
    towards customers, 74, 76–78
    defensive stance to, 81
    defined, 71
    towards employees, 74, 78–79
    towards environment, 74–76
    evaluating, 86–87
    government and, 82–84
    implementing programs for, 80–82
    towards investors, 74, 79–80

    managing, 84–87
    obstructionist stance to, 80–81
    proactive stance to, 81
    small business and, 81–82
    stakeholder model of, 71–73
Social skills, 277
Société Bic, 107
Sociocultural external environments,
        33, 34f, 35–36
Socio-Economic Council of Flanders, 274
Software, 490–491
    anti-virus, 499
    application, 485, 490
    defined, 490
    encryption, 499
    free, 497
SolarCity, 183
Sole proprietorships, 114–115, 115t
Sollers, 149
Solomon, Lawrence, 64
Solvency ratios, 528–529
Sony, 78, 85, 377
So, Peter, 148
SOS Online Backup, 455
South African Airways (SAA), 201–202
South African Reserve Bank, 606
Southwest Airlines, 109, 173, 203
Souza Cruz, 134
S&P 526, 592, 597
Spacey, Kevin, 446
Spam, 498–499
Spamhaus Project, 499
Span of control, 211
Special purpose loans, 110
Specialty goods, 415
Specialty services, 415
Specialty stores, 451
Speed to market, 419
Spendable money supply, 553–554
Spielberg, Steven, 425, 598
Spin offs, 120–121
Spoing!, 271
Spokesperson, 176
Sponsor, 220
Spyware, 497–499
Sreekanti, Kumar, 72
Stability
    economic, 51–52
    financial, 591
    of money, 552
Stabilization policies, 52
Staff/staffing, 344–348
    authority of, 212, 212f
    members of, 212
    scheduling of, 247–248
Stakeholders
    corporate, 71, 71f
    model of responsibility for, 71–73
    organizational, 71
Standard of living, 47–50
Standard & Poor's, 596–597, 605, 606, 607
Standard & Poor's Depository Receipts
        (SPDRS), 599

Stanford University, 167
Staples, 447, 595
Starbucks, 37–38, 46, 72, 77f, 100, 109, 135, 171, 180–181, 185, 203, 313, 317, 318, 375–376, 378, 383–384, 417, 530
Star of Science, 180
Star Wars, 318
Start-ups. *See* Small business
State Farm Insurance, 449
Statement of cash flows, 525–526, 525f
Statements
    financial, 521–526
    income, 523–525, 524f
    mission, 181, 203
State of certainty, 319
State of risk, 319
State of uncertainty, 319–320
Statistical Abstract of the United States, 390
Steamboat Willy, 205
Steinway, Heinrich Jr., 206
Steinway & Sons, 206
StellaService Inc., 393
Stennis Space Center, 86
Stewart, Martha, 80
Stewart, Tony, 425
Stock brokers, 595
Stock exchanges, 593–595
Stockholders, 120
Stock indexes, 596–599, 597f
Stock-keeping units (SKUs), 492
Stocks, 120
    blue-chip, 590
    common, 590, 611
    defined, 590
    investing in, 589–590
    ownership of, 120
    pricing of, 608–609, 609t
    splitting, 608
    valuation of, 608–609
Stored-value cards, 569
Storing, defined, 455
Strategic alliances, 120, 149
Strategic goals, 184
Strategic leadership, 317
Strategic management, 179–185
    defined, 179
    formulating, 183–185, 184f
    goal setting and, 180–181
    plans for, hierarchy of, 182f, 185
    types of, 182–183
Strategic plans, 185
Strategies. *See also* specific types of
    business, 182, 182f
    competitive, 182, 182f
    corporate, 182, 182f
    defined, 179
    for distribution, 448–449
    formulating, 184, 184f
    functional, 182–183, 182f
    hierarchy of, 182, 182f
    for marketing, 383–388
    for supply chains, 256–257

Strike, 359–360
Strikebreakers, 360
Structure, 201. *See* Organizational structure
Studebaker, 178
Stuxnet virus, 500
Subchapter S corporations, 119, 119t
Subsidies, 153
Substitute leadership, 313–314, 314t
Substitute products, 382
Subway, 109
Sun, The, 312
Supermarkets, 451
Supervisors, 174–175
"Super Wi-Fi" networks, 490
Suppliers/supplies
    defined, 42, 553
    external, 340
    information, linkages with, 494
    internal, 340
    law of, 42
    money, 553–556, 555f, 563
    selection of, 250
    stakeholder model of responsibility for, 71, 73
Supply chain management (SCM), 257
Supply chains, 256–257, 256f, 457
Supportive leader behavior, 311
Surplus, 42–44, 140
Surveys, 391
Sustainability, 77t
Suzlon Energy Limited, 379
Suzuki, 137
Sweat equity, 115
SWOT analysis, 184–185
Symbols, 150
Syndicated sellers, 450

T

Taco Bell, 242
Tactical plans, 169, 185
Taft-Hartley Act, 341t, 343
Tall organizational structure, 210–211, 210f
Tandy Corporation, 154
Target Corporation, 45, 73, 74, 85, 380, 490
Target market, 386
Tariffs, 153
Task-focused leader behavior, 309
Teams
    authority of, 212–213
    quality improvement, 254–255
    structures of, 217, 291
    work, 213
Teamsters, 358
Technical management skills, 177
Technological environments, 33, 34–35, 34f, 380

Technological management skills, 179
Techweb.com, 485
Telebook, 286
Telecommuniting, 293
Telemarketing, 452
Telephone calls, 178
Temporary workers, 355–357
Tempstaff, 106
Tender offer, 118
10 Minute Manicure, 319
Terminix, 417
Tesla, 431
Tests/testing, 345, 420
Texas Instruments (TI), 70, 174, 203, 454
Thanksgiving Coffee Co., 133–134
Theft, 275, 497–499
Theory X, 283
Theory Y, 283
Thiel, Peter, 114, 604
360-degree feedback, 353
3M Company, 176, 219, 238, 416, 423
3 Needles, 286
Thrift institutions, 556
Timbuk2, 483
Time
    compression of, 419
    deposits of, 554–555
    management of, 178
    orientation of, 152
    value of, 588–589
    zero response, 399
Times, 312
Time Warner, 530
Tindell, Kip, 313
Tinker Bell, 425
Title VII of the Civil Rights Act of 1964, 341, 341t
T-Mobile, 489
TNT Post Group N.V., 40
Tootsie Roll Industries, 254
Top managers, 173, 174t
Toronto Zoo, 360
Toshiba, 137, 254, 454
Total quality management (TQM)
    costs of poor, 252–254
    defined, 252
    quality improvement and, 251–256
    responsibility for, 254
    tools for, 254–256
Total return, 600
Toxic assets, 528
Toxic waste disposal, 76
Toyota, 75, 102, 145, 238, 239, 252–253, 381, 386, 457, 530
TradeStation, 602
Trade/trading, 592–599
    agreements for, 138–139
    balance of, 50f, 140–142, 141–142f
    day, 602
    deficit of, 50, 140, 142, 142f
    emissions, 587